2014
PowerBoat Guide

Standard Edition

Ed McKnew & Mark Parker

American Marine Publishing, Inc.

Table of Contents

Table of Contents

Table of Contents

About The Prices

Retail high-low values are provided for most models built since 1995. The prices quoted in this book reflect the market conditions we expect to prevail for the 2014 model year. Needless to say, assigning vaules in today's uncertain boating market is a difficult undertaking but there are some constants when it comes to resale values. For example, boats from high-end manufacturers are consistent leaders when it comes to retained value. Trawlers and motor yachts — especially those from quality builders — typically retain roughly 50% of their original purchase price after five years of ownership. Very high-end trawlers may retain 60–70% of their original value after five years, especially those that are well equipped and maintained to high standards.

The prices in this book are provided as rough estimates only. Do not take them too literally.

Ed McKnew

Ed McKnew began his career in the boating industry in 1979 when he purchased a small brokerage operation in Traverse City, Michigan. Moving to Texas in 1980, Ed continued to sell boats in Clear Lake until 1987 when he and partner Mark Parker published the first edition of the PowerBoat Guide. Ed has spent the past two decades serving as editor of the PowerBoat Guide while living in both Florida and northern Michigan. He has a bachelors degree in Business from Oakland University in Rochester, MI.

Mark Parker

Mark Parker has been a yacht broker since 1982, first in Texas and, starting in 1990, in South Florida. Mark started his boating career as a mate, then a captain and managed to complete an education along the way with a BA in Marketing. Mark and Ed started writing the first PowerBoat Guide in 1987 and have worked together ever since to keep the publication up to date. Now closing in on three decades of full time yacht brokerage service, Mark spends his spare time in the Bahamas and touring on his motorcycle.

For the most part, the contents of this book are straightforward and easily understood. Before launching into the pages, however, please review the following few paragraphs.

Pricing Information

Boat prices are compiled from 1995, the base year for our calculations. Prices are not provided for models built before 1995 or for those models whose resale activity is insufficient to determine a reliable price range.

The *Retail High* is the average selling price of a clean, well-equipped and well-maintained boat with low-to-moderate engine hours. Boats with an exceptional equipment list, outstanding maintenance, or those with unusually low hours will usually sell at a figure higher than the published Retail High.

The *Retail Low* is the average selling price of a boat with below-average maintenance, poor equipment, high-time engines, or excessive wear. High-time boats in poor condition will generally sell for less than the published Retail Low.

The prices presented in this book reflect our best estimates of boat values for the model year 2014. They are intended for general use only and are not meant to represent precise market values.

Factory Specifications

The specifications listed for each model are self-explanatory although the following factors are noted:

Clearance refers to bridge clearance, or the height above the waterline to the highest point on the boat. Note that this is often a highly ambiguous piece of information since the manufacturer may or may not include such things as an arch, hardtop, or mast. Use this figure with caution.

Weight is a factory-provided specification that may or may not be accurate. Manufacturers differ in the way they compute this figure. For the most part, it refers to a dry boat with no gear.

Marine Surveyor Directory

ABYC .... American Boat & Yacht Council
IAMI .... International Assoc. of Marine Investigators
NAMS .... National Association of Marine Surveyors
NFPA .... National Fire Prevention Association
SAMS .... Society of Accredited Marine Surveyors
SNAME .... Society of Naval Architects & Marine Engineers

ALABAMA

James Dinges
AYS Marine
100 Ayreswood Dr.
Dothan, AL 36303
334-479-0570 Cell: 256-603-1076
jdinges@hiwaay.net
SAMS, ABYC

Christopher Collier
C.E. Collier & Assoc., Inc.
PO Box 643
Coden, AL 36523-0643
251-873-4382 Cell: 251-610-1546
CEmarine1@aol.com
ABYC, NAMS, NFPA

Gary Swearengin AMS
GDS Marine Services, LLC
1001 Riverchase Rd. SE
Huntsville AL 35803-2327
256-881-2589 Cell: 256-682-1745
www.gdssco.com
Survey@gdssco.com
ABYC, SAMS, NFPA

Joseph "Tommy" Backe Jr.
Honor Marine Services
4108 Indian Hills Rd.
Decatur, AL 35603
256-566-4732
jtbacke@aol.com
SAMS, ABYC

Dennis Heine
Nautical Services, Inc
767 Wedgewood Dr.
Gulf Shores, AL 36542
251-979-5006
www.nauticalservicesinc.com
nsi@mchsi.com
SAMS, ABYC, NFPA

D.J. Smith
Port City Marine Services Inc.
13051 Kipling Trace
Theodore, AL 36582
251-661-5426 Cell: 251-421-5426
www.portcitymarineservices.com
masurveyor@aol.com
ABYC, SAMS, NAMI

Richard Schiehl
Schiehl & Associates LLC
6650 River Pl
Gulf Shores, AL 36542-2518
251-979-5912 Cell: 251-9795912
www.alabamamarinesurveyor.com/
rschiehl@gulftel.com
ABYC, NAMS

ALASKA

Rick Martin
Marine Surveyors of SE Alaska
PO Box 2124
Wrangell, AK 99929
907-874-4548
rick@marinesurveyorsofsoutheastalaska.com
NAMS

James Steffen
Norcoast Marine Surveyors, Inc.
PO Box 936
Sitka, AK 99835-0936
907-747-5394 Cell: 907-738-6394
www.marinesurveyor.com/norcoast
1norcoast@gmail.com
ABYC, SAMS, NAMI, NFPA

Ronald Long
Ronald E. Long Marine Surveys
PO Box 2464
Seward, AK 99664
907-224-7068 Cell: 907-362-1107
longmarinesurvey@hotmail.com
ABYC, SNAME

ARIZONA

James Avery
Arizona Marine Surveyors LLC
17615 N 134th Ave
Sun City West, AZ 85375
Cell: 623-363-4290
www.marinesurvey.org
averyjamesr@gmail.com
ABYC, SAMS

Gary Goldstein
Gary's Marine Surveys
1830 E Broadway Blvd #124-402
Tucson, AZ 85719
866-356-1236 Cell: 520-370-7187
www.garysmarinesurveys.com/
gary@garysmarinesurveys.com
SAMS, ABYC, NFPA

ARKANSAS

John Linck
Linck Marine Surveying
600 Pine Forest Dr. Suite 4D
Maumelle, AR 72113
501-231-9350 Cell: 501-231-9350
www.Marinesurveyor.com/Linck
JELMarine@aol.com
ABYC, SAMS

CALIFORNIA

Clark Barthol
Clark Barthol Marine Surveyors
27 Buccaneer St
Marina del Rey, CA 90292-5103
310-823-3350 Cell: 310-612-1955
cbarms@aol.com
ABYC, NAMS, NFPA

Ron Grant
Grant Marine Surveys
31091 Paseo Valencia
San Juan Capistrano, CA 92675
949-240-8353
vaimalu9@gmail.com

Odus Hayes
Marine Services
PO Box 1122
Sausalito, CA 94966-1122
415-461-8425 Cell: 415-860-0295
ohayesurvey@aol.com
SAMS, ABYC

Brendan J. Schmidt
Marine Surveyor
9 Virginia Ct.
Walnut Creek, CA 94596
925-934-5744
bschmidtcms@yahoo.com
NAMS, ABYC

F.Lee Frain Jr.
Maritime Consultant, Inc.
PO Box 3457
Newport Beach, CA 92659
949-675-2881
MaritimeConsultant@att.net
ABYC, NAMS

Richard L. Avant Jr. SA
Port San Luis Marine Survey
1755 Hi Mountain Rd.
Arroyo Grande, CA 93420
805-489-2177 Cell: 805 709-2975
http: //pslmarinesurvey.com/
Richard@pslmarinesurvey.com
SAMS, ABYC

Peggy Feakes
R.J. Whitfield & Associates
835 Yerba Buena Ave
Stockton, CA 95210
209-956-8488 Cell: 209-406-9679
www.rjwsurvey.com
peggy@rjwsurvey.com
SAMS

Randell B. Sharpe
Sharpe Surveying & Consulting
242 Inverness Ct
Alameda, CA 94502-6421
510-337-0706 Cell: 510-337-0706
www.sharpesurveying.com
rsharpe@sharpesurveying.com
ABYC, SAMS, SNAME, NFPA

Gary Beck, AMS
Yachtsman Marine LLC
5318 E. 2nd St. #415
Long Beach, CA 90803
562-234-3585 Cell: 562-234-3585
www.vesselsurveyor.com
yachtsmanmarine@aol.com
ABYC, SAMS, NFPA

Rick Gorman
Pacific Marine Surveyors
6475 E.- Pacific Coast Hwy #222
Long Beach, CA 90803
714-746-7380 Cell: 714-746-7380
www.pacificmarinesurveyors.com
boatchecker@gmail.com
ABYC, SAMS, NFPA

COLORADO

James Beck
Columbine Marine Service
PO Box 3545
Breckenridge, CO 80424-3545
970-453-0350 Cell: 970-393-2425
svptarmigan@earthlink.net
ABYC, SAMS

CONNECTICUT

Chris Nebel AMS
Advanced Marine Surveyors
51 W. Lake Ave
Guilford, CT 06437
203-623-0301 Cell: 203-623-0301
ww.advancedmarinesurveyors.com
captainchris@thatboatguy.com
SAMS, ABYC, NFPA

Phillip Gaudreau
Allpoint Marine Services LLC
11 Pettipaug Rd.
Haddam Neck, CT 06424
860-638-7667 Cell: 860-638-7667
pgaudreau41@comcast.net
ABYC, SAMS

Barnaby Blatch
Atlantic Marine Survey
5 Elizabeth Court
Mystic, CT 06355-3111
860-536-4354Cell: 860-460-0060
www.marinesurveyor.com/atlantic
bblatch0@gmail.com
AYBC, SAMS, NAMS

James Curry
James M. Curry Yacht Surveys
5 Pleasant Hill Lane
Clinton, CT 06413-2535
860-669-3119 Cell: 860-834-1600
jcurry01@snet.net
ABYC, SAMS, NAMI

Capt. John B. Wenz
JB Wenz, Marine Survey & Consulting
PO Box 15
Essex, CT 06426
860-578-3982 Cell: 845-527-6107
www.ctyachtsurvey.com
john@ctyachtsurvey.com
SAMS, ABYC, NFPA

Adrian Johnson
Johnson Marine Services
PO Box 271
West Mystic, CT 06388-0271
860-572-8866 Cell: 860-235-2990
www.johnsonmarineservices.com
aj@johnsonmarineservices.com,
ABYC, SAMS

Jan Muntz
Muntz Marine Surveyors
60 6th St. #3101
Stamford, CT 06905
914-763-6359 Cell: 914-525-5939
www.muntzmarinesurveyors.com
muntzmarine@optonline.net
ABYC, SAMS

William Robbins
New England Marine Survey LLC
302 Plains Rd.
Haddam, CT 06438
860-227-4071
www.newenglandmarinesurvey.com
billrobbins@newenglandmarinesurvey.com
SAMS

DELAWARE

Joyce Nolen
Nolen's Marine Surveying
26355 Pin Tail Rd.
Millsboro, DE 19966
Cell: 443-350-3447
www.captnolen.com
nms@captnolen.com
ABYC, SAMS, NFPA

FLORIDA

Arlen Leiner
AAC Marine Group, Inc.
11201 SW 12th St.
Ft. Lauderdale, FL 33315
727-647-7112 Cell: 954-895-2628
www.aacmarinesurveyor.com
captaleiner@gmail.com
ABYC, SAMS, SNAME

Capt. Ronald W. Morgan
Accredited Marine Consultants, Inc.
313 Lake Circle # 113
West Palm Beach, FL 33408-5227
561-845-1953 Cell: 561-845-1953
www.AccMarCon.com
Capt_RWMorgan@Bellsouth.net
SAMS

Gary Frankovich
Accurate Marine Surveys Inc.
10455 Docksider Dr. W.
Jacksonville, FL 32257-6375
Cell: 904-377-0475
www.marinesurveyor.com/accurate
frankovich@marinesurveyor.com
SAMS, ABYC

Dewey Acker
Acker Marine Survey Co.
801 73rd St., Ocean
Marathon, FL 33050-5101
305-743-2397 Cell: 305-664-6327
www.ackermarinesurvey.com
ackermarinesurveys@att.net
SAMS

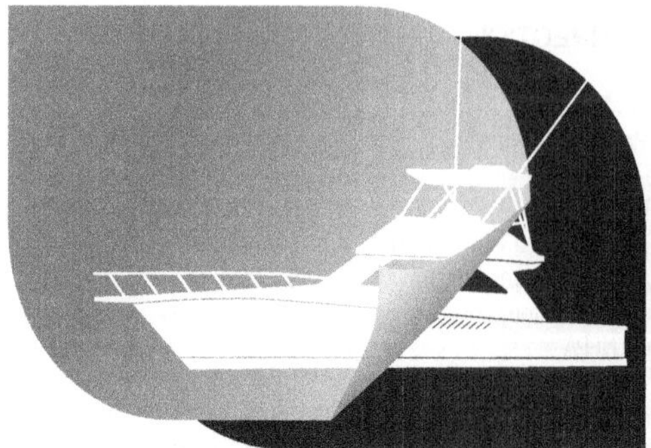

FLORIDA NAUTICAL SURVEYORS

For Clients

We have led the surveying industry with the technical knowledge gained over 41 years by Malcolm Elliott that included college time, commercial ships, boat building and marine engineering.

Our team of experienced surveyors can carry out all services expected of them to the highest of standards and we provide detailed reports within 24 hours.

For Banks & Brokers

We provide condition & valuation surveys for any boat in their inventory or collateral and have a reputation that the leading banks and credit companies turn to for an honest valuation carried out with the highest integrity.

With our experience and knowledge we are seen as an asset by many brokers who recommend us to assist the clients in walking them through the whole process & we have many letters thanking us from both brokers and the clients.

Celebrating 21 Years of Surveying in South Florida

Experience, over 41 years in the marine business from cadet engineer to chief engineer, from boat builder to boat owner and to the last 21 years as a leading yacht surveyor used by the largest yacht brokerage company in the world for their trade's, used by the largest banks in these troubled times but most importantly requested by more private clients than anybody else.

Of over 150 Viking 61 convertibles built our team have inspected over 93 of them, we have inspected many new builds and consulted with the builders on changes and improvements.

In one recent month we inspected 11 yachts between 108 & 177 feet plus 17 other yachts from 30 to 90 feet.

Clients, brokers, bankers and attorneys all call us for advise, experience and our trusted name.

Malcolm Elliott, the founder of Florida Nautical Surveyors and his team of experienced surveyors would like to thank you all for the last 21 years of business and we look forward to serving you in the future.

Services

All survey services +

- Audio Gauging
- Thermal Imaging
- Moisture Testing
- Paint Thickness Testing
- Vibration Analysis
- Digital Video Boro-scoping

2727 NE 32ND STREET, FORT LAUDERDALE, FLORIDA 33306
PHONE 954-801-2140 EMAIL FNSURVEYS@AOL.COM

www.FLORIDANAUTICALSURVEYORS.com

John Allinson II
Allinson Associates, Inc.
222 University Blvd N. #2
Jacksonville, FL 32211-7534
904-721-2177 Cell: 904-721-2177
www.allinson.com
jna2@allinson.com
SAMS, ABYC, SNAME, NFPA

Johnny Smith
Anchor Marine Services, LLC
2720 Semoran Drive
Pensacola, FL 32503
850-982-5079 Cell: 850-982-5079
www.anchormarineonline.com
marine.surveys@yahoo.com
ABYC, SAMS

Richard D. Flynn
Apollo Marine Surveying & Consulting LLC
235 Apollo Beach Blvd #144
Apollo Beach, FL 33572
813-645-8284 Cell: 941-730-3190
www.apollomarinesurvey.com
rick@apollomarinesurvey.com
SAMS, ABYC, NAMI

Glenn Reagan
Aqua Marine Surveying & Services
5818 SW 88th Pl.
Ocala, FL 34476-6103
352-598-6750
www.aquamarinesurveying.weebly.com
aquamarinesurveying@embarqmail.com
ABYC, SAMS, AMS

James Purvis
Aqua Marine Surveyors LLC
1619 Myrtlewood Ln
Niceville, FL 32578
850-225-4659 Cell: 850-225-4659
www.aquamarinesurveyors.weebly.com
am_surveyors@me.com
SAMS, ABYC

Patrick Guckian
Aquarius Marine Systems
160 SE Duxbury Ave
Port St Lucie, FL 34983-2604
772-871-0364
www.aquariusmarinesytems.com
aquariusmarinesy@bellsouth.net
ABYC, SNAME, SAMS

Stephen D. Danzig
Atlantic Marine Surveys, LLC
3948 3rd St. S. #145
Jacksonville Beach, FL 32250
904-273-6523 Cell: 904-588-2123
www.atlanticmarinesurveys.com
Steve@AtlanticMarineSurveys.com
SAMS

Brian Galley
Brian Galley & Assoc
9423 S. Ocean Dr. #77
Jenson Beach, FL 34957
772-692-1893 Cell: 772-932-4034
www.mariensurveyor.com/galley
bgsurveyor@yahoo.com
SAMS

Capt. Ric Corley
Captain Tom Corley & Son Marine Surveyors
1701 Grant Ave
Panama City, FL 32401-1140
850-784-9939 Cell: 850-527-5287
www.captcorleyandson.com
yatesadams@me.com
ABYC, NAMS, SAMS, IAMI

Charles Graf
CG Marine Surveying & Consulting
119 S. Riverwalk Dr. #6
Palm Coast, FL 32137
386-283-0506
cgmarine@cfl.rr.com
SAMS

Ted Crosby
Crosby Marine Services
7081 SW 20th St.
Plantation, FL 33317
954-583-9969
cmscms1@att.net
NAMS

Michael Schneider
Custom Offshore Systems
15719 121st Ter N.
Jupiter, FL 33478
561-313-5593
customoffshoresystems@gmail.com
SAMS

Capt Kevin Duchak
Duchak Maritime LLC
317 NW 36th Ave
Deerfield Beach, FL 33442
508-641-0749 Cell: 508-641-0749
duchakmaritime@msn.com
ABYC, NFPA

Dylan Bailey
Dylan Bailey Yacht Surveying
171 Twine St.
St. Augustine, FL 32084
904-537-1104
dbyachtservices&gmail.com
dbyachtsurvey.com
SAMS, ABYC

Vivian & Ed Rowe
Ed Rowe & Associates
9116 86th Pl.
Vero Beach, FL 32967
772-589-7463 Cell: 954-328-5780
eroweassoc@comcast.net
ABYC, SAMS

Malcolm Elliott
Florida Nautical Surveyors
2727 NE 32nd St
Ft. Lauderdale, FL 33306-1507
954-630-2141 Cell: 954-801-2140
www.floridanauticalsurveyors.com
fnsurveys@aol.com

Rolland Freeman
Freeman & Company, Marine Survey
588 Bayview Dr.
Long Boat Key, FL 34228
941-383-2952 Cell: 941-705-8800
freemanmarinesvy@aol.com
SAMS

Ned Hickel
Gale Force Surveys
1521 Alton Road #545
Miami Beach, FL 33139-8713
305-799-6080 Cell: 305-799-6080
www.galeforcesurveys.com
info@galeforcesurveys.com
SAMS

Bill Gladding
Gladding Marine Surveying
1738 Pickwick Pl
Fleming Island, FL 32003-7286
904-945-0511 Cell: 904-945-0511
gladdings@msn.com
bill@gladdingmarinesurvey.com
SAMS, ABYC

Lou Gonzalez, AMS
Global International Marine Surveyors
10773 NW 58th St. #530
Miami, FL 33178
305-718-9742 Cell: 305-986-2563
Globalmarsurvey@aol.com
SAMS

Robert R. Garay
Global Yacht & Ship Surveyors
6805 SW 89th Ct
Miami, FL 33173-2429
305-270-1553 Cell: 305-986-3362
marinesurveys@gmail.com
SAMS

John Roche
Governors Landing Associates LLC
5811 Atlantic Blvd #12
Jacksonville, FL 32207
904-657-0007 Cell: 904-657-0007
www.LandingMarineSurvey.com/
roche@landingmarinesurvey.com
SAMS, ABYC

Van D. Kline, AMS
Gulf Coast Marine Survey, Inc.
12635 115th St North
Largo, FL 33778-1809
727-588-0546 Cell: 727-278-8162
www.gulfcoastmarinesurvey.com
vankline@yahoo.com
ABYC, SAMS

Arthur A. Whiting
Harden Marine Associates, Inc.
202 S. 22nd St. Ste 203
Tampa, FL 33605-6396
813-248-3505 Cell: 813-600-0981
awhiting3@aol.com
ABYC, SAMS, SNAME

David Huffman
Huffman Marine Surveyors
16219 W River Rd
Inglis, FL 34449
954-205-3153 Cell: 954-205-3153
www.huffmarinesurveyors.com
dwhuffman@earthlink.net
ABYC, NAMS

Darryl Ogden
Hurricane Pass Marine Services Inc
PO Box 1297
Panama City, FL 32402-1297
877-243-5262 Cell: 877-243-5262
www.hurricanepassmarine.com/
survey@hurricanepassmarine.com
ABYC

Steven Berlin
Independent Marine Surveyors
17080 Safety St Unit 105
Ft. Myers, FL 33908
239-466-4544 Cell: 239-940-3175
www.indmsi.com
indmarine@embarqmail.com
SAMS

Matthew W. Jones
Jones Marine Surveyors Inc.
6131 SW 20th St.
Plantation, FL 33317-5226
954-791-6224
www.JonesMarine.com.
Sylvia@JonesMarine.com
ABYC, NFPA

Thomas Nolan
Latitude Marine
PO Box 249
Deerfield Beach, FL 33443-0249
954-421-0502
www.boatinspect.com
latitudemarine@comcast.net
ABYC, SAMS

Richard Learned
Learned Associates, Marine Surveyor
702 NW Sunset Dr.
Stuart,FL 34994-7613
772-692-7740
www.learnedmarinesurvey.com
rflearned@learnedmarinesurvey.com

Marc Slakoff
Marc Slakoff & Associates
757 SE 17th St. #432
Ft. Lauderdale, FL 33316
954-525-7930
www.yachtsurveyors.com
marc.slakoff@yachtsurveyors.com
SAMS

Daniel Mattos
Marine Engine Surveyor, Inc.
3450 Metro Pkwy Unit 5
Ft. Myers, FL 33916-7504
239-461-0366
drmamse@earthlink.net
SAMS

Stanley Konz
Maritime Surveying LLC
348 Pearl Ave
Sarasota, FL 34243-1522
941-351-6163 Cell: 941-737-3495
www.boatquotes.com
skonz1@tampabay.rr.com
ABYC, SAMS, SNAME

Kurt Merolla, CMS
Merolla Yacht & Boat Marine Surveyors, Inc.
2500 NE 48th Lane #504
Ft. Lauderdale, FL 33308
954-772-8090 Cell: 954-401-5399
www.YachtSurveyor.org
YotSurveyR@aol.com
ABYC, NAMS, SNAME

Noel Miley, AMS
Miley Marine Surveying & Consulting, Inc.
1021 Twin Lakes Rd,
Longwood, FL 32750-4537
877-897-4180 Cell: 407-443-7052
www.floridamarinesurveyors.us
boatpkr@aol.com
ABYC, SAMS

R.Joel Sparrow
Milligan & Sparrow, Inc.
2901 S Bayshore Dr. 11D
Coconut Grove, FL 33133-6016
305-274-4133
sparrowmarine@bellsouth.net
SAMS

Capt. Sadu R. Frehm
MSB Marine Surveyors Bureau
4660 122nd Dr. North
West Palm Beach, FL 33411
561-795-9516 Cell: 561-676-4069
www.msbmarinesurveyors.com
sadufrehm@gmail.com
SAMS, NAMI, ABYC

Jonathan Howe
Nautical Services Group, Inc
2442 Marathon Lane
Ft. Lauderdale, FL 33312
954-584-5819Cell: 954-557-7563
www.marinesurveyor.com/nsg
nautserv@aol.com
ABYC, SAMS, NFPA

Edward R. Cozzi
Performance Marine Surveyors, Inc.
290 W Palmetto Park Rd. #314
Boca Raton, FL 33432
Cell: 954-895-4633
www.performancemarinesurveyors.com
msurveyorcoz@gmail.com

Scott Grabner
Power & Sail Marine Surveyors, Inc.
PO Box 10685
Daytona Beach, FL 32120
386-631-2528 Cell: 386-631-2528
www.powerandsailmarinesurveyors.com
pwrsail@msn.com
SAMS

Mark Rhodes
Rhodes Marine Surveyors & Consultants
1646 SE Ballantrae Blvd
Port St. Lucie, FL 34952-5605
772-398-0860 Cell: 954-646-3760
marmarklhp@aol.com
ABYC, SAMS

Gerry Schmitt
Schmitt Marine
PO Box 4539
Ft. Pierce, FL 34949-4539
561-971-6562
gschm4287@aol.com
SAMS

Scott Carlson
Scott Carlson Marine Surveyor
660 NE 119th St.
Miami, FL 33161
305-891-0445 Cell: 786-295-0573
scsail4@aol.com
ABYC, SAMS

Mark Wallace
Sea Worthy Marine Surveys
1124 Ricardo Place NE
St. Petersburg, FL 33702-1466
727-577-8125 Cell: 727-433-0935
Capt.mjw@verizon.net
SAMS

Paul Squire
Simex International LLC
1380 SW 25th Ave
Ft. Lauderdale, FL 33312
954-610-7995 Cell: 954-854-8181
www.simexmarinesurveyor.com
simex@comcast.net
SNAME, ABYC, NFPA, ACSM, RINA

Steve Snider
Snider Marine Surveyors
328 N. Ocean Blvd Ste 502
Pompano Beach, FL 33062-5142
954-942-4803 Cell: 954-444-9136
www.florida-boatsurvey.com
powerboatsurvey@msn.com
SAMS

T.J. Day
South East Fire & Marine Associates, Inc.
1749 SW 4th Street
Ft. Lauderdale, FL 33312-7539
954-527-1981
Cell: 954-536-1981
sefmarine@aol.com
ABYC, SAMS, NFPA

Stephen J. Klaity
South Florida Marine Surveyors
2000 NW 37th Ave
Coconut Creek, FL 33066-3010
954-975-5149 Cell: 954-270-8005
www.southfloridamarinesurveyors.net
soflmarinesurveyors@msn.com
ABYC, SAMS, NFPA

John Banister
Suenos Azules Marine Surveying & Consulting
4521 PGA Blvd #461
Palm Beach Gardens, FL 33418
561-255-4139Cell: 561-255-4139
www.SuenosAzules.com
suenos.azules@yahoo.com
SAMS, ABYC, NFPA, IAMI

Richard F. Davis
The Marine Specialists
10001 Gulf Blvd.
Treasure Island, FL 33706
727-631-5646 Cell: 727-631-5646
www.themarinespecialists.com/
marspec@verizon.net
SAMS

Gordon Wright
Wright Way Marine Surveys
1017 Lewis Cove Road
Delray Beach, FL 33483-6512
561-927-0087 Cell: 561-702-1027
gordonw95@gmail.com
ABYC, SAMS

David C. Robertson
Yacht Surveying & Consulting
3415 North A1A
Ft. Pierce, FL 34949
772-342-5833
couragelll@msn.com
ABYC, SAMS

GEORGIA

Charles Bullock
American Marine Surveyors
3446 M Winder Hwy Ste PMB 326
Flowery Branch, GA 30542-3087
770-967-1883
amsur@mindspring.com
SNAME, NAMI, NFPA, ABYC

William Collier
Collier Marine Enterprises
4385 Pool Rd
Winston, GA 30187
Cell: 404-312-0445
colliermarineenterprises.com
collier_marine_1900@yahoo.com
SAMS, ABYC

Thomas Eve
Eve Marine Surveyors
31 Richmond Dr.
Savannah, GA 31406
912-355-5911
www.marinesurveyors.com/ems/
evesurvey@aol.com
SAMS, ABYC, IAMI, NFPA

ILLINOIS

Rick Lenschow
Certified Marine Surveyors
716 Edward St
Sycamore. IL 60178-2011
866-627-7878 Cell: 866-627-7878
www.cmsurveyors.com
rick@cmsurveyors.com
ABYC, SAMS, NAMI, NFPA

Jerome Starczowski
Davis & Company
PO Box 359
Lisle, IL 60532
800-223-8816x109
jstarczowski@daviscoltd.com
ABYC, SAMS

John Walsh
Marine Services Corp
14001 Cottage Grove Ave
Dolton, IL 60419
708-841-5660
lc@marineservicescorp.com
ABYC

John Russell
Marine Specialists
PO Box 322
Winthrop Harbor, IL 60096
847-731-1400
www.facebook.com/marinespecialists
expertinboats@aol.com
ABYC, NFPA, NAMI

INDIANA

Timothy Dry
Captain Timothy Dry LLC
2715 Floral Trail
Long Beach, IN 46360
219-872-2286 Cell: 219-871-9052
timdry@earthlink.net
SAMS, ABYC

Lloyd Kittredge
Lake Effect Surveying
801 Ivy St.
Chesterton, IN 46304-3227
219-926-5186 Cell: 219-877-7982
kittsurvey@frontier.com
ABYC, SAMS

KENTUCKY

Greg Weeter
Riverlands Marine Surveyors & Consultants
935 Riverside Dr.
Louisville, KY 40207-1036
502-897-9900 Cell: 502-640-9900
www.riverlandsmarine.com
greg@riverlandsmarine.com
ABYC, SAMS, NAMS

LOUISIANA

J. Kevin Martin
Arthur H. Terry & Co LLC
700 Mariners Plaza Ste 704
Mandeville, LA 70448-4799
985-727-4495 Cell: 985-707-3776
www.yachtsurveying.com
kevin@yachtsurveying.com
SAMS, ABYC

Hjalmar Breit
Breit Marine Surveying
23747 Hwy 40
Bush, LA 70431
504-283-2929Cell: 504-559-3075
hbreitiii@aol.com
NAMS, ABYC

Kristoffer Diel
Maritime Enterprises & Research, Intl.
PO Box 53946
Lafayette, LA 70505
504-236-8151 Cell: 504-236-8151
www.marinesurveyor.com/diel
yachtsurveys@msn.com
SAMS, NAMS, ABYC, SNAME

Charlie Hazouri
Offshore Marine Inspections
500 Mandeville St Unit 10
New Orleans, LA 70117
Cell: 504-450-8044
www.offshorenola.com
offshorenola@me.com
NAMS, ABYC

Curtley L. Boudreaux
Southeast LA. Marine Surveying
PO Box 321
Lockport, LA 70374-0321
504-532-6703 Cell: 985-532-3549
boud6057@bellsouth.net
SAMS, SNAME, NAMI

MAINE

Robert Lynch
Atlantic Maritime Services
81 Spring St.
Brunswick, ME 04011
207-650-2714 Cell: 207-650-2714
bob2dboat@gmail.com

Earle Brown
Brown's Marine Services
62 Heather Hill Rd.
Lincolnville, ME 4849
207-681-2958
earle@brownsmarineservices.com
ABYC

Geordie King
King Marine Surveyors LLC
26 Thunder Rock Rd.
Eliot, ME 03903
207-703-0569 Cell: 207-337-8706
kinggeordie@comcast.net
ABYC, SAMS

John Marples
Marples Marine
295 Bayview Rd.
Penobscot, ME 04476
207-326-8096 Cell: 207-326-8096
marplesmarine@gmail.com
ABYC, NAMS

MARYLAND

Arthur Johnson
Art Johnson Marine Surveys
441 N Walnut St
Rising Sun, MD 21911-1605
410-658-3994 Cell: 443-553-3228
SAMS

Alan Gaidelis
Bayside Marine Surveying, Inc.
6903 Harewood Park Drive
Middle River, MD 21220
410-335-3955
www.baysidemarinesurveying.com
Yachtinspector@aol.com
ABYC, SAMS

Bill Weyant
East Coast Marine Consulting Inc.
PO Box 27
Havre de Grace, MD 21078
410-322-6701 Cell: 410-322-6701
www.eastcoastmarineconsulting.com
ECMarineConsulting@comcast.net
ABYC, SAMS, NFPA

Fredric S. Wise III
Fred Wise Yacht Survey LLC
14154 Gregg Neck Rd
Galena, MD 21635-1307
410-648-5052 Cell: 410-708-4788
wiseyacht@gmail.com
SAMS, ABYC

William Woodside A.M.S.
G-B Marine Services Inc
117 Congressional Dr.
Stevensville, MD 21666-3325
410-643-0951 Cell: 410-980-3241
www.marylandmarinesurveyors.com
gbmarineservices@yahoo.com
SAMS, ABYC

Richard Levy
Independent Marine Survey, LLC
5715 Ross Neck Road
Cambridge, MD 21613
410-221-1108
labradog@dmv.com
ABYC, SAMS

John McDevitt
Marine Safety and Fire Protection
PO Box 99
Grasonville, MD 21638
610-220-5619
jmcdevittcaptain@aol.com
SAMS

Jack Hornor
Marine Survey & Design Co.
PO Box 463
Neavitt, MD 21652
www.msdco.com
jack@msdco.com
ABYC, NAMS, SNAME

Derek Rhymes
Marine Surveyor
PO Box 6188
Annapolis, MD 21401
410-268-4404 Cell: 866-608-4404
www.allboatsurveys.com
derek@allboatsurveys.com
ABYC, NAMS, SAMS

Catherine McLaughlin
Marine Surveyor
5839 Clam Cove
Rock Hall, MD 21661
410-348-51188
mclaughlin@baybroadband.net
NAMS, SAMS

Frank Pettolina
Pettolina Marine Surveying & Consulting
9800 Mooringview Lane #14
Ocean City, MD 21842-9387
410-251-0575
surveyfp@yahoo.com
ABYC, SAMS

Harry Seemans
Quaker Neck Marine Surveying
PO Box 69
Bozman, MD 21612-0069
410-745-5452 Cell: 410-829-3007
www.quakerneck.com
seemans@atlanticbb.net
ABYC, SAMS

Curtis Sarratt
Sarratt Marine Surveyeys
1414 Catlyn Pl
Annapolis, MD 21401
410-279-3546 Cell: 410-279-3546
SarrattSurveys@msn.com
SAMS, ABYC

Lon Acheson
SurvTech Inc.
895 Gallant Fox Lane
Davidsonville, MD 21035-0372
Cell: 301-318-1089
www.survtech.us
survtech@comcast.net
ABYC, SAMS

Jon Sheller
Sheller Engineering Associates
309 Highview Rd
Tracys Landing, MD 20779-9720
410-867-7919 Cell: 410-349-7016
jons2011@aol.com
SAMS, ABYC

MASSACHUSETTS

Thomas Hill
Atlantic & Pacific Marine Consultants
27 Ferry St
Gloucester, MA 01930-4834
978-283-7006
tom@apmc1.net
SAMS, ABYC

Robert Bevans
Bevans Marine Services
243 Valley Rd.
Plymouth, MA 02360
781-718-3313
bobbevans48@gmail.com

Edwin Boice
Edwin C. Boice Inc.
PO Box 898
East Dennis, MA 02641-0898
508-385-2683 Cell: 617-797-3033
edwinboice@hotmail.com
SAMS, NAMS

Robert Gallagher
Gallagher Marine Surveyors
6 Fosters Point
Beverly, MA 01915
978-807-2163; Cell: 978-807-2163
www.gallaghermarinesurveyors.com
captbgallagher@comcast.net
ABYC, SAMS

George Gallup AMS
Gallup Yacht Surveying
13 Sherman Terrace
Lynn, MA 01902-2743
781-598-5465 Cell: 781-598-5465
www.GallupYachtSurveying.com/
George@GallupYachtSurveying.com
ABYC, SAMS, NFPA

Patrick Goodrow
High Tech Marine Surveys
85 Humphrey St.
Marblehead, MA 01945
781-290-6782
www.hightechmarinesurveys.com
goodrow@gmail.com
ABYC, SAMS

Joseph Lombardi
Ocean Technical Services, LLC
9 Butternut Lane
Gloucester, MA 01930
508-958-1299 Cell: 508-958-1299
www.oceantechserv.com
joe@oceantechserv.com
ABYC, SAMS, SNAME

Timothy Pitts
Ocean Way Tech, Inc.
PO Box 158
East Falmouth, MA 02536-0158
508-564-8680 Cell: 508-564-8680
www.oceanwaytech.com
tpitts@capecod.net
SAMS

Peter Spang
Turnstone Marine Survey
PO Box 201
Marstons Mills, MA 02648-0201
508-737-5052
www.turnstonemarinesurvey.com
surveyor@turnstonemarinesurvey.com
ABYC, SAMS

MICHIGAN

Melvin Surdel
A-1 Marine Surveying
PO Box 80
Douglas, MI 49406
708-259-6436 Cell: 813-205-8711
www.A1marinesurveying.com
ssn578688@aol.com
ABYC, SNAME

Angel Zeno
A&A Marine Surveying, LLC
715 Glenwood Dr.
Elk Rapids, MI 49629
616-826-9121 Cell: 616-826-9121
www.aamarinesurvey.com
Angelzeno@aamarinesurvey.com
SAMS, ABYC

Les Salliotte
Downriver Marine Surveyors
2304 18th St
Wyandotte, MI 48192-4140
734-516-1176 Cell: 734-516-1176
www.downrivermarinesurveyors.com
lessalliotte@aol.com
ABYC, SAMS, BOATUS, NFPA

Dennis Parsons
Interstate Marine Survey
PO Box 277
Port Austin, MI 48467
989-738-7131 Cell: 248-761-2636
www.interstatemarinesurvey.com
ims.boat@yahoo.com
ABYC, SAMS

Bob Ptak
Lakeshore Professional Marine Surveys
LLC2172 84th St
Newaygo, MI 49337
616-340-1931 Cell: 616-340-1931
www.promarinesurveys.com
bobptak@promarinesurveys.com
ABYC, SAMS

Marc Nugent
Manitou Boatworks
1124 Willow St.
Traverse City, MI 49684
231-649-6776
www.boatworks.us
mboatworks@yahoo.com
ABYC, SAMS, SNAME

Thomas VanDerMaas
Marine Surveyor
408 Notre Dame St
Grosse Pointe, MI 48230-1548
313-910-9290
tom_vandermaas@hotmail.com
SAMS, ABYC

Jack Morman
Morman Marine Surveyors
37790 Lakeshore Dr.
Harrison Township, MI 48045-5713
586-469-3898 Cell: 586-764-4898
www.mormanmarinesurveyors.com
mormanmarinesurveyors@gmail.com
SAMS, ABYC, NFPA

John M. Dionne
South Arm International, Inc.
PO Box 861
East Jordan, MI 49727-0861
231-536-7343
southarm@att.net
SAMS, ABYC

MINNESOTA

Randy Jensen
Jno. B. Lee Company
PO Box 1E
Minnetonka, MN 55345-0905
952-470-5991
www.marinesurveyor.com/lee/
jnoblee@aol.com
ABYC, SAMS

MISSISSIPPI

Jim Twiggs
Accurate Marine Surveyors
2071 Carolwood Dr.
Biloxi, MS 39532
228-388-4070
captjim@marinesurveyor.ms
ABYC, SAMS

MISSOURI

Michael Hunter
Hunter Consulting & Survey
PO Box 14761
Springfield, MO 65814
417-929-0005 Cell: 417-929-0005
www.huntersurveying.com
michael@huntersurveying.com
ABYC, SAMS, NAMS

Roy L. Smith
R.L. Smith & Assoc. LLC
PO Box 562
Festus, MO 63028
314-566-9134
www.rlsmithsurvey.com
roy@rlsmithsurvey.com
NAMS, SAMS, ABYC

NEVADA

Steven D. Jones SA
Bluewater Marine Survey
104 Forest Lane
Boulder City, NV 89005
702-324-1884 Cell: 702-324-1884
bluewatermarinesurvey@embarqmail.com
SAMS, ABYC

James Lang
Northstar Marine Survey
3215 S. Tenaya Way
Las Vegas, NV 89117
702-274-7770 Cell: 702-274-7780
jlsearay@aol.com
SAMS, ABYC

NEW HAMPSHIRE

David Condino
Outer Island Marine Services
PO Box 4731
Portsmouth, NH 03802-4731
508-954-5760 Cell: 508-954-5760
Capt_Condino@verizon.net
SAMS, SNAME, NFPA

NEW JERSEY

Alan Ritter
ARC Marine Survey
PO Box 476
Rio Grande, NJ 08424
609-827-6142
arcmarinesurvey@yahoo.com
SAMS, ABYC

Philip Topps
Bay Shore Marine Services, LLC
20 Davids Lane
Little Egg Harbor, NJ 08087
609-812-1535 Cell: 201-390-4964
www.marinesurveyor.com/BayShore
SouthernCross6@verizon.net
SAMS, ABYC

John Klose, AMS
Bayview Assoc.
PO Box 368
Barnegat Light, NJ 08006
609-494-4924
jkboats@gmail.com
ABYC, SAMS, SNAME

Bob Duane
Bob Duane Marine Services, Inc
819 Donna Drive
Point Pleasant, NJ 08742-4503
732-295-5951 Cell: 732-300-5705
bobduane@comcast.net
ABYC, SAMS

Bob Johnson
Bob Johnson Marine Services
307 Hall Ave
Point Pleasant, NJ 08742
732-714-8730 Cell: 732-814-0735
www.boatsurveyor.us
bobjsurveyor@comcast.net
SAMS

Blair Bugher
Bugher Marine Services
7 Harrison Ln
Princeton Junction, NJ 08550-1623
609-275-2600Cell: 609-558-9932
www.bughermarine.com
blair@bughermarine.com
SAMS, SNAME, ABYC

Ronald Rybicki
Captain Ron's Marine Surveys LLC
102 Walchest Dr.
Toms River, NJ 08753
718-702-7998
www.captainronsmarinesurveys.com
captronsmarine@gmail.com
SAMS, ABYC

Jeff McDaniel
Case-McDaniel Marine Group
17 Avenue D
Atlantic Highlands, NJ 07716
732-291-7400 Cell: 732-768-0990
jeff@casemac.com
ABYC, SAMS

Peter Downham Sr.
Downham Marine Services LLC
300 Monmouth Ave
Marmora, NJ 08223-1324
609-705-6808 Cell: 609-705-6808
dms542@comcast.net
SAMS, ABYC

Dave Christopher
Pro 44 Marine Group
550 N. Lakeshore Dr.
Brick, NJ 08723
732-552-6555 Cell: 732-552-6555
www.pro44marinegroup.com
dave@pro44marinegroup.com
SAMS, ABYC

Reinier Van Der Herp
RV Marine Surveying
126 Station Dr.
Forked River, NJ 08731
609-693-9005 Cell: 609-618-8511
www.rvmarinesurveying.com
rvmarinesurveying@gmail.com
SAMS, NAMS, ABYC, IAMI

Kenneth Bruno
SeaTech Marine Services
26 Kansas Road
Little Egg Harbor, NJ 08087-1037
800-367-8388
brunostms@aol.com
SAMS

John F. Spencer
Spencer Marine Surveys, LLC
104 Longman St
Toms River, NJ 08753-2439
732-255-4700 Cell: 732-267-6979
spencermarine@comcast.net
ABYC, SAMS

William E. Hymans
The Boat Doc Marine Surveys, LLC
4 Brewster Ct.
Pennington, NJ 08534-1817
609-730-1200 Cell: : 609-213-1882
www.theboatdocmarinesurveys.com
billhymans@aol.com
SAMS

NEW YORK

Ronald Alcus
Alcus Marine Technical Services, Inc.
PO Box 700
Moriches, NY 11955-0700
631-874-1000
alcusmt@aol.com
ABYC, SAMS

Shawn G. Bartnett
Bartnett Marine Services, Inc.
52 Ontario St.
Honeoye Falls, NY 14472-1120
585-624-1380
bartmarser@aol.com
ABYC, NAMS, SNAME, NAMI, NFPA

James R. Smith
Captains Boating Services LLC
1941 Fix Rd.
Grand Island, NY 14072
716-773-7374 Cell: 716-830-3429
jrs1202@yahoo.com
SAMS, ABYC

William J. Falkenheimer
Coast Marine Services
23 Pine Hill Park
Valatie, NY 12184
518-449-3391 Cell: 518-265-3605
www.coastmarineservices.com
capten1@msn.com
ABYC, SAMS, SNAME, IAMI, NFPA

Joseph Oldak
Farragut Marine Service Company
192 Farragut Cir
New Rochelle, NY 10801-5739
914-589-0104 Cell: 914-589-0104
www.FarragutMarine.com
marinesurveyor@farragutmarine.com
SAMS, ABYC

Paul Pellegrino
Island-Wide Maritime Services
PO Box 937
Nesconset,NY 11767-0937
Cell: 516-729-6832
pmp409@optonline.net
ABYC, SAMS

Anthony Macchia
Mac Marine Surveys
3230 Tierney Place
Bronx, NY 10465-4024
718-597-4416 Cell: 917-572-0933
amac710@verizon.net
ACMS

Stephen Maddock
Maddock Marine Services
PO Box 796
Hampton Bays, NY 11946-0701
516-728-7970
boatsurvey@aol.com
NAMS

Anthony L. Fazio
Marine Surveyor
PO Box 81
East Northport, NY 11731-0081
516-429-7365 Cell: 516-429-7365
fazioams@optonline.net
ABYC, SAMS

Charlie Gruetzner
Oceanis Marine Services, Inc.
1124 Main St.
Peekskill, NY 10566
914-737-0253 Cell: 945-216-0497
www.oceanismarine.com
charlie@oceanismarine.com
SAMS, SNAME, ABYC

Wayne E. Robinson, AMS
Robinson Marine Services, Inc.
838 Dumar Dr
Elbridge, NY 13060-9749
315-689-6854 Cell: 315-246-3253
wer1441@aol.com
ABYC, SAMS

Scott Schiffman
Scott J. Schiffman and Assoc.
1204 Ave U Ste 1160
Brooklyn, NY 11229
718-377-6764
ABYC, USSA, MMS, NFPA

Roy Scott
Scott Marine Surveyors and Consultants
174 Minrol St.
Port Jefferson Station, NY 11716
631-696-1010 Cell: 631-697-1013
www.royscottmarine.com
roy@royscottmarine.com
SAMS, ABYC

Anthony Peel
Shipshape Surveying
30 Manor Lane
Copiague, NY 11726-5204
631-608-3127 Cell: 631-926-2993
makopeel@yahoo.com
SAMS, ABYC

Al Prisco C.M.S.
Small Craft & Yacht Services
67 Palmer Trail
Carmel, NY 10512
845-228-1071 Cell: 914-645-3525
www.marinesurveyorny.com
boatsurvey@yahoo.com
ABYC, SNAME, NFPA

Anthony Somma
Somma Marine Surveying
81 Belfast Ave
Staten Island, NY 10306-2103
718-351-7497 Cell: 347-210-0379
www.tonysomma.com
asomma@aol.com
ABYC, SAMS

Peter Luciano
Stay New Yacht Service
50 Davinport Ave #2F
New Rochelle, NY 10805-3660
914-260-6092 Cell: 914-260-6092
sloopquest@aol.com
ABYC, SAMS

NORTH CAROLINA

T.Fred Wright
Carolina/Atlantic Marine Services
PO Box 77053
Charlotte, NC
28271-7000
704-708-5709 Cell: 704-953-9486
www.marinesurveyor.com/cams/
tfredwright@aol.com
ABYC, SAMS, NAMS

John Day
Day Yacht Services, Inc
2707 Homes Dr.
Morehead City, NC 28557
252-241-7287 Cell: 252-241-7287
www.dayyachtservices.com
sday@ec.rr.com

Bob Eldridge
R.J. Eldridge Marine Surveying
PO Box 15558
Wilmington, NC 28408-5558
910-232-8356 Cell: 910-232-8356
rjesurveys@gmail.com
SAMS, ABYC

Todd Reynolds
YachtWise, LLC
206 Causeway Dr. #74
Wrightsville Beach, NC 28480-0074
910-431-2608 Cell: 910-431-2608
yachtwise@ec.rr.com
SAMS, ABYC

OHIO

Fritz Everson
Everson Boat Works LLC
160 Sunset Dr.
Sandusky, OH 44870
419-626-3321
www.eversonboatworks.com
fritzeverson@yahoo.com
SAMS

Mark Mastrangelo
Marine Surveyor
PO Box 62
Gypsum, OH 43433
419-502-6099
mamastra@msn.com
NAMS

OKLAHOMA

Thomas Benton
Marine Damage Consultants
PO Box 627
Ketchum, OK 74349-0627
918-782-1001 Cell: 918-782-1001
www.marinedamageconsultants.com
benton@marinedamageconsultants.com
ABYC, SAMS, NAMS

James McDougal
Marine Specialty Inspections LLC
PO Box 470925
Tulsa, OK 74114
918-836-3263 Cell: 918-836-3263
msisurveyor@cox.net
SAMS, ABYC

Harold Cantrell
Tri-State Marine Surveyors
410 Lakeland Drive
Eufaula, OK 74432
918-689-7897 Cell: 918-689-0097
hrcantrell@sbcglobal.net
ABYC, NAMS, NAMI

PENNSYLVANIA

William Mullin, AMS
Boatcheck Marine Surveyors
1051 Bolton Ct
Bensalem, PA 19020
215-327-9219 Cell: 215-327-9219
www.boatcheck.net
wmullin@boatcheck.net
SAMS, ABYC

Edward Fry
Fry Associates, Inc.
228 Berkeley Rd.
Devon, PA 19333
433-875-4600 Cell: 954-494-1557
www.frycoyachts.com
edfry@frycoyachts.com
ABYC, SNAME

Charles Miller
North Coast Marine Services
1903 W 8th St #169
Erie, PA 16505-4936
814-835-8233 Cell: 814-833-9098
ncms@neohio.twcbc.com
SAMS

Robert Stefanowicz
Susquehanna Marine Surveys
1404 Montfort Dr.
Harrisburg, PA 17110-3015
717-233-4989 Cell: 717-497-8974
www.americanyachtsurveyors.com
smsurveys@msn.com
SAMS, ABYC

Charles Ulrick
Ulrick Marine Surveying
528 Sugar Tree Rd.
Holland, PA 18966-1835
215-416-9349 Cell: 215-416-9349
www.yachtexam.com
yachtexam@gmail.com
ABYC, SAMS, NFPA

PUERTO RICO

Joseph Barlia
American Marine Surveyor Inc.
PO Box 587
Ceiba, PR 00735
787-397-8028 Cell: 787-948-3932
www.americanmarinesurveyor.com
americanmarinesurveyor@gmail.com
ABYC, SAMS, SNAME

Carlos Suarez
Carlos Suarez & Associates
PO Box 141737
Arecibo, PR 00614-1737
787-879-1048 Cell: 787-635-7030
suarez.307@hotmail.com
ABYC, SAMS

Ciro Malatrasi
Marine Surveyor & Consultant
El Batey Street, 1#6
Fajardo, PR 00738
787-504-4066
ciromsurveys@yahoo.com
SAMS, ABYC

RHODE ISLAND

Stephen Mainella
Atlantic Marine Surveyors
81 County Rd
Barrington, RI 02806-4506
401-245-2087
atlanticmarinesurveyors@gmail.com
SAMS

Dwight Escalera
Executive Marine Services
64 Deer Trail Rd.
Wakefield, RI 02879
401-369-0487
www.execmarine.com
dwight@executivemarine.com
SAMS, ABYC, NFPA

Whitney E. "Ned" Jones
Jones Maritime Services
PO Box 52
Newport, RI 02840
401-588-1742 Cell: 401-588-1742
www.jones-maritime.com/
ned@jones-maritime.com
SAMS, ABYC

Dennis Layfield
Marine Safety Consultants, Inc.
42 Jacqueline Way
Tiverton, RI 02878-2783
401-816-5540 Cell: 401-499-3948
dennis70@cox.net
NAMS

SOUTH CAROLINA

Neil K. Haynes
Blue Water Surveys, Inc.
1739 Maybank Hwy #T
Charleston, SC 29412-2103
843-559-2857
www.boatsurveyor.com
nhaynes@boatsurveyor.com

David P. Hill
Carolina Yacht Services, Inc.
24 Nuffield Rd.
Charleston, SC 29407
843-571-5808 Cell: 843-607-3834
uphilldph@knology.net
ABYC, SAMS, NFPA

Richard Newsome
Dana C. McLendon
PO Box 481
Isle of Palms, SC 29451-0481
843-886-3852 Cell: 843-813-5210
dcmsurvey@bellsouth.net
ABYC, SAMS

Louis M. Harrison
Harrison Marine
3520 Johan Blvd
Johns Island, SC 29455-8917
843-559-3383 Cell: 843-729-6490
harrisonimc@aol.com
ABYC, SAMS

Peter Stevenson, AMS
Marine Surveys, Inc.
226 Sitton Rd.
Easley, SC 29642
864-855-0504 Cell: 864-444-3297
www.marinesurveysinc.com
pete@marinesurveysinc.com
SAMS, ABYC

TENNESSEE

Gary Wright
American Marine Specialists
2425 N. Shore Acres Rd
Soddy Daisy, TN 37379-7949
423-451-0128 Cell: 423-400-0001
www.marinesurveyor-sams.com
gr.wright@epbfi.com
SAMS, ABYC

Carl Ecklund
Captain's Marine
140 Cunningham Dr.
Athens, TN 37303
866-515-1115 Cell: 423-453-8608
ecklundcs@cs.com
SAMS

Gale Chapman
Gale C Marine, Inc.
PO Box 110664
Nashville, TN 37222-0664
615-943-4789 Cell: 615-430-6902
www.galecmarine.com
gcmarine@comcast.net
NAMS

C. Stanley Johnson
Riverport Marine Surveying, Inc.
286 Stonewall St
Memphis TN 38112-5143
901-278-2161 Cell: 901-485-2072
www.riverportms.com
riverportms@aol.com
ABYC, SAMS, NAMS, IAMI

John Chilton
Southwind Marine Services
998 Thompson Rd
Pegram, TN 37143-2402
615-646-0491 Cell: 615-419-6462
www.southwindmarineservices.com
jchil10223@aol.com
SAMS, ABYC

James R. Tipton
Tipton Marine Surveys
530 Donna Dr.
Lenoir City, TN 37771
865-406-3029 Cell: 865-406-3029
www.tiptonmarinesurveys.com
jtipton178@gmail.com
SAMS, ABYC

TEXAS

Kurtis Samples
Anchor Marine Consultants
7324 Gaston Ave #124-169
Dallas, TX 75214
214-796-4305 Cell: 214-796-4305
kkboat@airmail.net
SAMS

Bobby Brown
Blue Water Surveyors
9434 Zyle Rd.
Austin, TX 78737
214-522-3505 Cell: 214-704-7750
www.bluewatersurveyors.com
bluwater@airmail.net
SAMS

Joseph Curry
Capt. Curry Marine Surveyor
13231 Vista Del Mundo
San Antonio, TX 78216-2245
210-492-7142 Cell: 210-492-7142
www.curryboatpoking.com
captcurry@yahoo.com
ABYC, SAMS, NAMI

Louis Stahlberg
LHS Marine Services
PO Box 1587
League City, TX 77574-1587
281-639-3014 Cell: 281-639-3014
www.lhsmarine.com/
lstahlberg@comcast.net
ABYC, NAMS

Clinton Evans
Nautilus Marine Services, Inc.
PO Box 8343
Corpus Christi, TX 78468
361-850-3317 Cell: 361-850-3317
www.marinesurveyor.com/nautilus
cesurveyor@aol.com
SAMS, ABYC

Casey Auten
Professional Marine Surveys
11180 Morrow Bay Lane
Frisco, TX 75035
972-556-2829 Cell: 580-490-1660
www.professionalmarinesuveyors.com
autlake@gmail.com
ABYC, SAMS

Donald Neese
Subuacuatica Marine Surveys
416 Blanco St.
San Marcos, TX 78666
512-353-7622 Cell: 512-757-5723
www.subacuaticasurveys.com
neese.don@gmail.com
SAMS, ABYC

James G. Merritt
Tangent Development Co.
1715 Harliquin Run
Austin, TX 78758-6121
512-837-9170 Cell: 512-731-5708
survrjim@austin.rr.com
ABYC, SAMS, SNAME

VIRGINIA

Richard Milner, AMS
Dynamic Marine Surveys
8172 Shore Drive #101
Norfolk, VA 23518
Cell: 757-418-4008
www.dynamicmarineinc.com/
rmilner@dynamicmarineinc.com
SAMS, ABYC, NFPA

Capt. G. Emory Shover
Eastern Marine Services, LLC
6505 Palisades Dr.
Centreville, VA 20121-3811
540-220-4346 Cell: 540-220-4346
www.easternmarineservices.com
easternmarineservices@gmail.com
SAMS, ABYC

William H. "Bill" Coker, III
Entre Nous Marine Services
400 Crockett Rd.
Seaford, VA 23696
757-833-5900 Cell: 757-871-2085
surveyenms@msn.com
ABYC, SAMS

R.Earl Joyner, CMI
Lighthouse Marine Surveying
1722 Back Creek Rd.
Seaford, VA 23696
866-860-5672 Cell: 757-870-1111
www.marinesurveying.com
earl@marinesurveying.com
ABYC, IAMI, NFPA

VERMONT

George Little
Tamarack Marine Surveys
82 Turquoise Dr
Colchester, VT 05446-6597
802-864-5214 Cell: 802-233-5214
www.tamarackmarinesurveys.com
grayluders@yahoo.com
SAMS, ABYC

WASHINGTON

Stephen Berg
Berg Marine Surveys
1004 Commercial Ave #354
Anacortes, WA 98221-4117
360-301-6879 Cell: 360-301-6879
www.bergmarinesurveys.com
steve@bergmarinesurveys.com
SAMS, ABYC

Thomas Laing, Jr.
Commercial Marine Service, Inc.
PO Box 33836
Seattle, WA 98133-0836
425-742-7424 Cell: 206-660-4654
www.cmservice.us
tommy@cmservice.us
NAMS, SNAME

Charles W. Solarek
CWS Maritime Services
12407 17th Ave SE
Everett,WA 98208
206-225-3045
www.surveyorsforhire.com
cws@surveyorsforhire.com
SAMS, ABYC

Jane Christen
Michel & Christen Marine Damage Surveyors
501 E Bayview Dr
Shelton, WA 98584-7300
800-794-0089
mcms@marinelosssurveyors.com
ABYC, SAMS, SNAME

David Wilson
Wilson & Associates Marine Surveyors, LLC
9621 241st Pl SW
Edmonds, WA 98020-6511
206-396-6284 Cell: 206-396-6284
www.marinesurveyor.com/wilson
wilson@marinesurveyor.com
SAMS, ABYC

WASHINGTON DC

Guy R. Nolan
Cascade Corporation
1000 Water St SW
Washington, DC 20024-2425
571-344-1239 Cell: 571-344-1239
cascadegrn@starpower.net
ABYC, SAMS, SNAME, NFPA

WISCONSIN

Chris Kelly, AMS, CMI
BoatDamage.com, LLC
7528 Pershing Blvd B-135
Kenosha, WI 53142-4316
800-299-3197 Cell: 800-299-3197
www.boatdamage.com
email@boatdamage.com
AYBC, SAMS, SNAME

Capt. Scott D. Schoeler
C3 Marine Services LLC
PO Box 081425
Milton, WI 53408
218-343-6794 Cell: 218-343-6794
www.c3marine.com
SDSchoeler@C3Marine.com
ABYC, SAMS, NFPA

Richard E. Lawrence
Lawrence Marine Service Inc.
9746 Sheridan Rd
Pleasant Prairie, WI 53158-5403
262-694-5609 Cell: 262-945-0217
lawrencemarineserviceinc.com
lawrencemarine@wi.rr.com
ABYC

Jim Ledenbach
Superior Marine Survey
PO Box 745
Ashland, WI 54806
715-292-1311
superiorsurveyor@yahoo.com
SAMS

US VIRGIN ISLANDS

Stephen Bajor
International Marine Surveyors
6263 Estate Nazareth
St. Thomas, USVI 00802
800-524-8292
www.bajoryachts.com/
bajor00802@gmail.com
ABYC, SAMS

CANADA

Timothy McGivney &
Trevor Sallmon
Aegis Marine Surveyors
4051 Prospect Rd.
N. Vancouver, BC V7N3L6
CANADA
604-983-2050 Cell: 604-250-5601
tjmcgivney@shaw.ca
ABYC, NAMS

Chris Small
Chris Small Marine Surveyors
800-15355 24th Ave Ste 183
White Rock, BC V4A2H9
CANADA
604-681-8825 Cell: 604-538-5509
marinesurveyors@telus.net
NAMS

Kenneth W. Rorison
Kenneth R. Rorison Marine Surveyors
11416 Sycamore Pl
Sidney, BC V8L5L2
CANADA
250-655-3425 Cell: 250-812-3351
krorison@shaw.ca
NAMS, ABYC, SNAME

Adam Bishop
Bishop Marine Service Ltd
207 Clemence St.
Whitby, ON L1N1E7
CANADA
adambishop79@yahoo.ca
SAMS

Gerry Montpellier
G.R. Montpellier Appraisals
18 Sauve St. RR #3
Sudbury, ON P0M1L0
CANADA
705-855-9363
motorsport.north@sympatico.ca

Barry Goodyear
Ra Kon Marine Surveyors & Appraisers
1826 St. John's Rd.
Innisfil, ON L9S1T4
CANADA
705-431-9485Cell: 905-853-8100
www.rakon.ca
bgoodyear@rakon.ca
ABYC, NFPA

Greg Piper
Sandpiper Marine Services
19 Lakeview Ave
Port Dover, ON N0A1N8
CANADA
519-583-2686
www.sandpipermarine.com
greg@sandpipecom

CAYMAN ISLANDS

Michael Pickthorne
Alpha Marine Surveyors
24 Warwick Dr.
George Town, Grand Cayman KY1-1103
345-949-9210 Cell: 345-916-1765
www.a1marinecayman.com
a1marine@candw.ky
ABYC, NAMS

Yacht Broker & Dealer Directory

ALABAMA

Bill Thompson Yacht Sales
PO Box 201
Orange Beach, AL 36561
www.billthompsonyachts.com
Sales@billthompsonyachtsales.com

Marine Group Emerald Coast
27075 Marina Rd.
Orange Beach, AL 36561
251-981-9200/850-380-3993
www.marinegroupec.com
jdavis@marinegroupec.com
Brokerage Sales, New Boat Sales

CALIFORNIA

Adair Yachts
16832 P.C.H. PO Box 980
Sunset Beach, CA 90742
562-592-6220
www.adairyachts.com
Adairyachts@gmail.com
Brokerage Sales, Service Yard

Ardell Yacht & Ship Brokers
2101 W. Coast Hwy
Newport Beach, CA 92663-4712
949-642-5735
www.ardell.com
yachts-ca@ardell.com
Brokerage Sales

Big Bay Yachts
2700 Dickens St.
San Diego, CA 92106
619-222-1124
www.bigbayyachts.com
scott@bigbayyachts.com
New Boat Sales, Brokerage Sales

CFB Marine Group
1880 Harbor Island Dr. #F
San Diego,CA 92101
619-291-9300
www.cfbmarine.com
bruce@cfbmarine.com
Brokerage

Charlotte Schmidt Yacht Sales
1101 Spinnaker Dr.
Ventura, CA 93001
805-290-6386
www.yachtworld.com/charlotteschmidt
terry.channel.islands@gmail.com
New Boat Sales, Brokerage Sales

Chuck Hovey Yachts
717 Lido Park Drive
Newport Beach, CA 92663-4461
949-675-8092
www.chuckhoveyyachts.com
info@chuckhoveyyachts.com
New Boat Sales, Brokerage Sales

Delta Yacht Sales
11285 Crocker Grove Lane
Gold River, CA 95670
916-798-8667
www.deltayachtsales.net
deltayachtsales@aol.com

Denison Yacht Sales
13555 Fiji Way
Marina del Rey, CA 90292
310-821-5883
www.denisonyachtsales.com
nereus@denisonyachtsales.com
New Boat Sales, Brokerage Sales

Dick Simon Yachts, Inc.
34571 Golden Lantern
Dana Point, CA 92629-3040
949-493-2011
www.dicksimonyachts.com
dick@dicksimonyachts.com
Brokerage Sales

Fraser Yachts
4990 N. Harbor Dr. Ste #200
San Diego, CA 92106
619-225-0588
www.fraseryachts.com

Hampton Yacht Group
2751 W. Coast Hwy #200
Newport Beach, CA 92663
949-870-2239
www.HYGofCalifornia.com
bill@yachtkings.com
New Boat Sales, Brokerage Sales

Kusler Yachts
2617 San Marcos Ave
San Diego, CA 92104
619-952-0860
www.kusleryachts.com

Lucky's Land & Sea
2440 Starmount Way
El Dorado Hills, CA 95762
916-878-1692
www.luckyslandandsea.com
yachtdude@hotmail.com
New Boat Sales, Brokerage Sales

Mariners Group
19521 Pompano Lane #108
Huntington Beach, CA 92648-2840
www.marineryachtsales.com
art@marineryachtsales.com
Brokerage

Newport Coast Yachts
Shoreline Marina
Newport Beach, CA 90802
888-4-1-YACHT
www.newportcoastyachts.com
CMe4yachts@aol.com
Brokerage Sales, New Boat Sales

Oceanic Yacht Sales
308 Harbor Dr
Sausalito, CA 94949
415-599-5506
www.oceanicyachts.com
Rick@oceanicyachts.com
New Boat Sales, Brokerage

Real Yacht Sales
4349 Vassar St.
Ventura, CA 93003-1946
805-216-2391
www.yachtworld.com/realyachts
realyachts@msn.com

Richard Boland Yacht Sales
1070 Marina Village Pkwy Ste 107
Alameda, CA 94501-1031
510-521-6213
www.richardbolandyachts.com
rbys@aol.com

San Diego Yachts
1199 Pacific Hwy Unit 1104
San Diego, CA 92101-8418
619-232-1660
www.yachtsus.com
levitetz@hotmail.com
Brokerage Sales

Scott B. Jones International
670 Lido Park Dr.
Newport Beach, CA 92663
949-637-3100
www.scottbjones.com
sjonesintl@aol.com
New Boat Sales, Brokerage Sales

South Mountain Yachts
10 Corniche Dr.
Monarch Beach, CA 92629
949-842-2344
www.SouthMountainYachts.com
lou@SmyYachts.com
Brokerage Sales

Stan Miller Yachts
2540 Shelter Island Dr. Ste A
San Diego, CA 92106
619-224-1510
www.stanmiller.com
nikki@stanmiller.com

Vaught's Yacht Sales
5866 E Naples Plaza
Long Beach, CA 90803-5008
562-438-8669
www.vysyachts.com

West Coast Yachts
2600 Newport Blvd Ste 122
Newport Beach, CA 92663-3745
949-673-2060
www.westcoastmarine.com

Yorath Yachts
16400 Pacific Coast Hwy #107
Huntington Beach, CA 92649-1852
714-840-2373
www.yorathyachts.com

CONNECTICUT

Maritime Boat Sales
3 Essex Square
Essex, CT 06426
www.maritimeboatsales.net
sean@maritimeboatsales.net

Offshore Marine Services, Ltd.
350 Chestnut St.
Cheshire, CT 06410-2029
888-YACHT-01
www.OffshoreYachtSales.com
Brokers@OffshoreYachtSales.com
Brokerage Sales

Robert Christopher Yacht Sales
425 Fairfield Ave
Stamford, CT 06902-7656
203-356-0400
www.robertchristopheryacht.com

FLORIDA

4Yacht, Inc.
757 SE 17th St #317
Ft. Lauderdale, FL 33316
954-650-5203
chadsyachts@gmail.com
Brokerage Sales

Admiral Yacht Sales Inc.
3024 Harbor Dr.
St. Augustine, FL 32084
904-237-2598
www.yachtworld.com/admiralyacht
mark@admiralyachtsales.net
New Boat Sales, Brokerage Sales,
Service Yard

AFC Yacht and Ship Brokers, Inc.
2921 NE 48th St.
Lighthouse Point, FL 33064
954-788-8840
www.afcyacht.webs.com
afcyacht@msn.com
Brokerage Sales

Ardell Yacht & Ship Brokers
1550 SE 17th St
Ft. Lauderdale, FL 33316-1700
954-993-4195
www.ardell.com
brian@ardell.com
New Boat Sales, Brokerage Sales

Atlantic Yacht & Ship
850 NE 3rd St #213
Dania, FL 33004
954-921-1500
www.atlanticyachtandship.com
info@ayssales.com
Brokerage Sales

Borden & Associates Yacht Sales
301 W. Atlantic Ave Ste O-5
Delray Beach, FL 33444
561-296-0500
www.bordenyachts.com
info@bordenyachts.com

Camper & Nicholson
450 Royal Palm Way #100
Palm Beach, FL 33480-4139
561-655-2121
www.camperandnicholsons.com
palmbeach@camperandnicholsons.com
New Boat Sales, Brokerage Sales

Cape Yacht Management
5828 Cape Harbour Dr. #206
Cape Coral, FL 33914-8621
239-542-8838
www.yachtworld.com/capeyachtmanagement/
peterreycroft@comcast.net

Crown International Yacht Sales
1751 Mound St. Ste 204
Sarasota, FL 34236
941-552-6713
www.crownyachtsales.com
barry@crownyachtsales.com
Brokerage Sales

Curtis Stokes & Assoc.
1323 SE 17th St. #168
Ft. Lauderdale, FL 33316
954-684-0218
www.curtisstokes.net
curtis@curtisstokes.net,

Denison Yacht Sales
401 SW 1st Ave
Ft. Lauderdale, FL 33301
954-763-3971
www.DenisonYachtSales.com
bob@denisonyachtsales.com
New Boat Sales, Brokerage Sales

Diversified Yacht Services
751 Fishermans Wharf
Ft. Myers Beach, FL 33931
239-209-7790
www.DYSinc.com

Edwards Yacht Sales
510 Brookside Dr.
Clearwater, FL 33764
727-507-8222
www.EdwardsYachtSales.com
yachts@edwardsyachtsales.com
Brokerage Sales

Export Yacht Sales
2116 Ave B
Riviera Beach, FL 33404
561-842-0020
www.exportyachtsales.com

FCM Yacht Sales/Florida Coast Marine
The Palm Beaches, FL
561-756-2628
www.fcmyachts.com
dkennedy@fcmyachts.com
Brokerage

Ferretti Group
110 N. Dixie Hwy
Stuart, FL 34994
772-600-4922
www.ferrettigroupamerica.com

Fillingham Yacht Sales
105 15th Ave SE
St. Petersburg, FL 33701
727-460-5687
www.fillinghamyachts.com
captbob@fillinghamyachts.com
Brokerage, Service Yard

Florida Coast Marine
2010 Harbortown Dr Ste #0
Ft. Pierce, FL 34946
772-489-0110
www.fcmyachts.com
info@fcmyachts.com
Brokerage, Service Yard,

Florida Yachts International
2550 S Bayshore Dr Ste 2
Miami, FL 33133-4743
305-854-6020
www.floridayachtsinternational.com

Galati Yacht Sales
126 Harbor Blvd
Destin, FL 32541-7344
850-654-1575
www.galatiyachts.com
info@galatiyachts.com
Brokerage Sales

Grand Slam Yacht Sales Inc.
3482 Lakeshore Blvd
Jacksonville, FL 32210
904-652-8401
www.GrandSlamYachtSales.com
jboothyacht@yahoo.com
New Boat Sales, Brokerage Sales,
Service Yard

Gulf Coast Boat & Yacht Sales
777 Walkerbilt Rd. #8
Naples, FL 34110
727-251-4056
www.gulfcoastboatsales.com
noblegreek0@gmail.com
Brokerage

Gulf Coast Yacht Sales, Inc.
101 16th Ave S. Ste 1
St. Petersburg, FL 33701
727-822-5516
www.gcyachts.com
info@gcyachts.com
New Boat Sales, Brokerage Sales,
Service Yard

Mark Parker
HMY Yacht Sales
2401 PGA Blvd Ste 100
Palm Beach Gardens, FL 33410
www.hmy.com
mparker@HMY.com

Holmes & Owen Yacht Sales
3423 Lakeshore Blvd
Jacksonville, FL 32210
904-387-5432
www.hoyachtsales.com
barton@hoyachtsales.com
Brokerage Sales, New Boat Sales

InterMarine Boats
320 N. Federal Hwy
Ft. Lauderdale, FL 33004
561-747-0005
www.intermarineboats.com

Island Yacht Sales
1100 Main St
Ft. Myers Beach, FL 33931-2235
239-765-6060
www.islandyachtsales.net
joe@isyachtsales.com
Brokerage Sales

JDR's Island Yacht Sales
1555 SE 14th Ct
Deerfield Beach, FL 33441-7331
954-520-2222
www.yachtworld.com/islandyacht
repojay@bellsouth.net
Brokerage Sales

Keith Yacht Sales
2099 Ardley Ct.
N. Palm Beach, FL 33408
561-234-9888
www.keithyachtsales.com
keithyachtsales@comcast.net

Luke Brown Yachts
1500 Cordova Rd. #200
Ft. Lauderdale, FL 33316-2190
954-525-6617
www.lukebrown.com
sales@lukebrown.com
New Boat Sales, Brokerage Sales

Marcali Yachts
1401 Lee St Ste B
Ft. Meyers, FL 33901
239-275-3600
www.marcaliyacht.com
marc@marcaliyacht.com
Brokerage Sales

Mare Blue Yacht Brokerage
1525 SW 13 Ave
Miami, FL 33145
305-354-9600
www.mareblue.com
brokerage@mareblue.com

Marina One Yacht Sales
580 N Federal Hwy
Deerfield Beach, FL 33441-2224
954-421-2500
www.marinaone.com

MarineMax
18167 US Hwy 19 North #300
Clearwater, FL 33764-3510
727-536-2628
www.marinemax.com

MarineMax
8053 Laurel Ridge Ct
Delray Beach, FL 33446
www.marinemax.com

MarineMax
1485 S. Tamiami Trail
Venice, FL 34285
941-485-3388
www.marinemax.com
taylor.macpherson@marinemax.com
Brokerage Sales

Marlow Marine Sales, Inc.
4204 13th Street Ct W
Palmetto, FL 34221-5705
941-729-3370
www.marlowmarine.com
sales@marlowmarine.com
New Boat Sales, Brokerage Sales,
Service Yard

Massey Yacht Sales
10131 Cherry Hills Ave
Bradenton, FL 34202
www.masseyyacht.com
yachtsales@masseyyacht.com

Naples Yacht Brokerage
PO Box 882
Naples, FL 34102
239-434-8338
www.naplesyachtbrokerage.com
naplesyb@earthlink.net

Nio Yacht Group
13205 Gulf Blvd #C
Madeira Beach, FL 33708-2630
727-639-2862
www.NioGroupInc.com
niogroup@aol.com
Brokerage Sales

Palm Beach Power Boats
105 S. Narcissus Ave Ste 712
West Palm Beach, FL 33401
561-514-0855
www.palmbeachpowerboats.com
rob@pbpbi.com
Brokerage Sales

Paradigm Yacht Sales
5828 Cape Harbour Dr. #101
Cape Coral, FL 33914
239-541-2004
www.paradigmyachts.com
yachtsales@paradigmyachts.com
Brokerage Sales

Peter Kehoe & Assoc.
101 N. Riverside Dr. #123
Pompano Beach, FL 33062-5051
954-767-9880
www.peterkehoe.com
peterkehoe@peterkehoe.com

Pier One Yacht Sales
1200 W. Retta Esplanade #43
Punta Gorda, FL 33950
941-286-8055
www.pieroneyachtsales.com

POP Yachts International
6384 Tower Lane Ste A
Sarasota, FL 34240
941-894-3215
www.PopYachts.com
scott@popyachts.com
Brokerage Sales

Punta Gorda Yacht Brokers
520 King St.
Punta Gorda, FL 33950-3600
941-575-6765
www.puntagordayachtbrokers.com

Rejoyce Yacht Sales
3060 NE 46th St
Ft. Lauderdale, FL 33308
www.royalcoachman.com

Ross Yacht Sales LLC
500 Main St.
Dunedin, FL 34698
727-210-1800
www.rossyachtsales.com
sales@rossyachtsales.com
New Boat Sales, Brokerage Sales

Sarasota Yacht & Ship
1306 Main St.
Sarasota, FL 34236-5614
941-365-9095
www.sarasotayacht.com
info@sarasotayacht.com
New Boat Sales, Brokerage, Service Yard

Southwest Florida Yachts
3444 Marinatown Lane #10
N. Ft. Myers, FL 33903
239-656-1339
www.swfyachts.com

Ben Wofford
The Marine Group
2401 PGA Blvd Ste 164
Palm Beach Gardens, FL 33410
561-762-4382
www.marinegroup.com
bwofford@marinegroup.com
Brokerage Sales

United West Florida Yachts
4880 37th St S
St. Petersburg, FL 33711-4530
727-460-0228
www.westfloridayachts.com
roger@wflyachts.com
Brokerage Sales, Service Yard

United Yacht Sales
200 Biscayne Blvd Way #4107
Miami, FL 33131-4011
305-984-5179
www.yachtworldtoday.com
jbeird@unitedyacht.com
New Boat Sales, Brokerage Sales

United Yacht Sales
956 Scenic Gulf Dr. Villa #106
Miramar Beach, FL 32550
850-499-7013
www.unitedyacht.com
atroyer@unitedyacht.com

United Yacht Sales
620 NW Dixie Hwy Ste 101
Stuart, FL 34994
888-922-4814
www.uystc.com
ccooke@unitedyacht.com
New Boat Sales, Brokerage Sales

Westport
2957 State Rd. 84
Ft. Lauderdale, FL 33312-7702
954-316-6364
www.westportyachts.com
info@westportyachtsales.com
New Boat Sales, Brokerage Sales,
Service Yard

Woods & Associates Yacht Brokerage
2301 SE 17th St.
Ft. Lauderdale, FL 33316
954-764-4880
www.woodsyachts.com
rpw@woodsyachts.com

World Class Yacht Sales Inc.
1673 Oak Park Ct.
Tarpon Springs, FL 34689
727-945-7500
www.world-yachts.com
worldyachts@wcyachtsales.com
Brokerage Sales

Worldwide Yacht Sales, Inc.
3501 Del Prado Blvd
Cape Coral, FL 33904
239-841-2865
www.worldwideyachts.net
bill@worldwideyachts.net
scott@worldwideyachts.net
New Boat Sales, Brokerage Sales,
Service Yard

Yacht Brokers, LLC
645 S Beach St.
Daytona Beach, FL 32114-5007
386-253-6266
www.DaytonaYachts.com
Joe@DaytonaYachts.com
Brokerage Sales

Yacht Sales Consultants, Inc.
4561 SW Long Bay Dr.
Palm City, FL 34990-8810
772-463-2645
www.yscinc.com
matt@yscinc.com
Brokerage Sales

ILLINOIS

Elite Yachts
14001 Cottage Grove
Dolton, IL 60419
708-841-5660
www.eliteyachtbrokerage.com
bw@eliteyachtschicago.com
New Boat Sales, Brokerage Sales,
Service Yard

Spring Brook Marina
623 W. River Dr.
Seneca, IL 61360
815-357-8666
www.springbrookmarina.com
sales@springbrookmarina.com
New Boat Sales, Brokerage, Service Yard

Windy City Yacht Brokerage LLC
523 Rosebud Dr. S.
Lombard, IL 60148
312-440-9500
www.windycityyachts.com
jeff@windycityyachts.com
Brokerage Sales

KENTUCKY

Green Turtle Bay Yacht Sales
239 Jetty Drive
Grand Rivers, KY 42045
866-383-7085, 800-498-0428
www.greenturtlebayyachtsales.com
bhuffman@greenturtlebay.com
yachtsales@greenturtlebay.com
Brokerage Sales, Service Yard

Marine Sales and Service
2929 River Rd.
Louisville, KY 40206
502-897-1881
www.mssboats.com
doug@mssboats.com
New Boat Sales, Brokerage Sales,
Service Yard

Paradigm Yacht Sales
PO Box 1043
Louisville, KY 40059
502-292-0444
www.paradigmyachts.com
george@paradigmyachts.com
Brokerage Sales

Paradigm Yacht Sales
8208 Montero Dr.
Prospect, KY 40059
www.paradigmyachts.com
dick@paradigmyachts.com

LOUISIANA

Whelton Marine LLC
700 Mariner's Plaza Dr. #704B
Mandeville, LA 70448
888-258-2897
www.wheltonmarine.com
gtwhelton@yahoo.com
Brokerage Sales

MARYLAND

CFL Marine
114 Carroll Island Rd.
Baltimore, MD 21220-2208
410-627-0948
www.yachtworld.com/cfl
cbboats@msn.com

Coastline Yacht Sales
2501 Boston St.
Baltimore, MD 21224
443-257-8973
www.CoastlineYachtSales.net
treyschaefer@msn.com
Brokerage Sales

Giordano & Dour Yacht Sales Inc.
PO Box 428
North East, MD 21901-0428
410-287-5030
www.yachtworld.com/gdys
theboatguy@msn.com
Brokerage Sales

Integrity Yacht Sales
389 Deale Rd. Ste C
Tracys Landing, MD 20779
301-261-5775
www.integrityyachtsales.com
vicki@integrityyachtsales.com
Brokerage Sales

Jonathan Foster Yacht Sales
2818 Solomons Island Rd.
Edgewater, MD 21037
410-224-4944
www.jfboats.com
jnpfoster@aol.com
Brokerage Sales

Knot 10 Yacht Sales
3028 Kent Narrows Way S.
Grasonville, MD 21638
410-827-9090
www.knot10.com

Martin Bird & Associates
326 First St. #35
Annapolis, MD
21403-2682
410-268-1086
www.martinbird.com
chetpawlowicz@martinbird.com

McDaniel Yacht Basin, Inc.
PO Box E
North East, MD 21901-0286
410-287-8121
www.mcdanielyacht.com
yachtoffice@mcdanielyacht.com
New Boat Sales, Brokerage Sales,
Service Yard

Mears Point Yacht Sales
428 Kent Narrows Way North
Grasonville, MD 21638-1022
www.mearspointyachtsales.com
mike@mearspoint.com
Brokerage Sales

Sassafras Harbor Marina
PO Box 68
Georgetown, MD 21930
888-221-5022
www.sassafrasharbormarina.com
shmys@baybroadband.net
New Boat Sales, Brokerage Sales,
Service Yard

Sundance Boat Sales
2010 Knollview Dr.
Pasadena, MD 21122
410-439-9900
www.yachtworld.com/sundanceboat
sundanceboat@aol.com
New Boat Sales, Brokerage Sales

Yachtfinders Annapolis, LLC
98 Shipwright St.
Annapolis, MD 21401
410-353-5524
www.yachtworld.com/yachtfindersan-
napolis/
NickC@YachtFindersAnnapolis.com
Brokerage Sales

MASSACHUSETTS

Allen Harbor Marine Service, Inc.
335 Lower County Road
Harwich Port, MA 02646-0445
508-430-6008
www.allenharbor.com
info@allenharbor.com
New Boat Sales, Brokerage Sales,
Service Yard

Boston Yacht Sales
145 Falmouth Heights Rd.
Falmouth, MA 02540-3565
508-495-4078
www.bostonyacht.com
info@bostonyacht.com

Boston Yacht Sales
275 River St.
North Weymouth, MA 02191-2238
781-331-2400
www.bostonyacht.com
keeponfishin@aol.com

Certified Sales
19 Uxbridge Rd.
Mendon, MA 01756
508-478-0200
www.certifiedsales.com
brian@certifiedsales.com

Niemiec Marine Inc.
173 Popes Island
New Bedford, MA 02740-7252
508-997-7390
www.niemiecmarine.com
bniemiec@niemiecmarine.com

Oyster Harbors Marine
122 Bridge St
Osterville, MA 02655-2303
508-428-2017
www.oysterharborsmarine.com
amy@oysterharborsmarine.com
New Boat Sales, Brokerage Sales,
Service Yard

Slip's Capeway Marine
747 Hill St.
Raynham, MA 02767-1020
508-822-6948
www.slipscapewaymarine.com
jackpills@aol.com

South Shore Dry Dock Marine
612 Plain St
Marshfield, MA 02050-2740
781-834-9790
www.southshoredrydock.com
ssdrydock@aol.com

MICHIGAN

Anchorage Yacht Sales
1815 Ottawa Beach Rd.
Holland, MI 49424
616-399-6304
www.aysboats.com
boats@aysboats.com

Bay Breeze Yacht Sales
12935 W. Bayshore Dr. #125
Traverse City, MI 49684
866-941-5884
www.baybreezeyachtsales.com
jay@baybreezeyachtsales.com
New Boat Sales, Brokerage Sales

Bergmann Marine
05953 Loeb Rd
Charlevoix, MI 49720-9562
231-547-3957
www.bergmannmarine.com
bergmann@freeway.net
Brokerage Sales, Service Yard

Denison Yacht Sales
2150 South Shore Dr.
Holland, MI 49423
616-218-7183
www.denisonyachtsales.com/2013/05/fred-schmitt-michigan-yacht-broker/
Fred@DenisonYachtSales.com
New Boat Sales, Brokerage Sales

Gregory Boat Company
9666 E Jefferson
Detroit, MI 48214-2993
313-823-1900
www.gregoryboat.com
gary@gregoryboat.com

McMachen Boating Center
30200 N River Rd
Harrison Twp, MI 48045-1879
586-469-0223
www.mcmachenboatingcenter.com
mcmachenboatingcenter@comcast.net
New Boats, Brokerage, Service Yard

Michigan Boat Brokers, Inc.
16885 Lake Rd.
Spring Lake, MI 49456-1227
616-318-2024
www.yachtworld.com/miboats
ronolin@comcast.net
Brokerage Sales

North Shore Marina
18275 Berwyck St.
Spring Lake, MI 49456
616-842-1488
www.northshoremarina.com
sales@NorthShoreMarina.com

Pier 1000 Marina
1000 Riverview Drive
Benton Harbor, MI 49022-5028
616-927-4471
www.pier1000.com
chillout@pier1000.com

Reed Yacht Sales
17819 Oakwood Dr.
Spring Lake, MI 49456
616-842-8899
www.toledobeachwest.com
brentreed@reedyachtsales.com

South River Yacht Sales
30099 S. River Rd.
Harrison Township, MI 48045
586-783-6600x10
www.cashforyourboatnow.com
andy@southrivermarine.com

Starboard Yachts Inc.
1111 Ottawa Beach Rd.
Holland, MI 49424
616-796-0505
www.starboardyachts.com
erob@starboardyachts.com
New Boat Sales, Brokerage Sales

SuperBrokers of Traverse City
13310 SW Bay Shore Dr.
Traverse City, MI 49684
231-922-3002
www.superbrokers.com
superbro@superbrokers.com
Brokerage Sales

Temptation Yacht Sales, Inc.
49 Macomb Place #14
Mt. Clemens, MI 48043
586-463-8060
www.temptationyachtsales.com
paul@temptationyachtsales.com
Brokerage Sales

Walstrom Marine
801 Front St.
Bay Harbor, MI 49770
231-439-2741
www.walstrom.com

Walstrom Marine
501 E. Bay St.
Harbor Springs, MI 49740-1607
231-526-2141
www.walstrom.com
boats@walstrom.com
New Boat Sales, Brokerage Sales, Service Yard

MINNESOTA

Lighthouse Yacht Sales
16052 32nd St. S.
Afton, MN 55126
651-217-2193
www.lighthouseyachtsalesmn.com
dave@lighthouseyachtsalesmn.com
Brokerage Sales

Midwest Yacht Sales
6413 St. Croix Trail N.
Stillwater, MN 55082
651-49-2000
www.yachtworld.com/midwestyacht/

MISSOURI

Lake Services Boat Brokerage
51 Anemone Ct.
Lake Ozark, MO 65049
573-216-1599
www.yachtworld.com/lakeservices/
lakeservices@charter.net

Ozark Yacht Brokers, Inc.
PO Box 40
Lake Ozark, MO 65049-0040
573-365-8100
www.ozarkyachts.com
capjay@ozarkyachts.com

Safe Harbor Yacht Sales
2021 Westview Ave
Kirkwood, MO 63122
636-250-3500
www.safeharboryachts.com

NORTH CAROLINA

Bluewater Yacht Sales
10 Marina St, Pierhouse A5
Wrightsville Beach, NC 28480-1727
910-256-6643
www.bluewateryachtsales.com
JRiggs@BluewaterYachtSales.com

Marina Management Services
208 Arendell St.
Morehead City, NC 28557
252-726-6862
www.moreheadcityyachtbasin.com
littman@moreheadcityyachtbasin.com

United Yacht Sales of the Carolinas
2002 Eastwood Rd #106
Wilmington, NC 28403
800-526-2836
www.unitedyacht.com
service@unitedyacht.com
New Boat Sales, Brokerage Sales

NEW HAMPSHIRE

Northeast Yachts
185 Wentworth Rd.
Portsmouth, NH 03801-5624
603-433-3222
www.neyachts.com
skipper@neyachts.com
New Boat Sales, Brokerage Sales

NEW JERSEY

Prestige Yacht Sales
217 Riverside Dr.
Brick, NJ 08724
732-202-0200
www.prestigeyachtsales.com
prestyacht@aol.com
Brokerage Sales

South Jersey Yacht Sales at Canyon Club Marina
900 Ocean Dr.
Cape May, NJ 08204
609-884-1600
www.southjerseyyachtsales.com
LPiergross@SouthJerseyYachtSales.com
New Boat Sales, Brokerage Sales, Service Yard

NEW YORK

City Island Yacht Sales
673 City Island Ave
City Island, NY 10464
718-885-2300
www.cityislandyacht.com

Coeymans Landing Marina
PO Box 769
Coeymans, NY 12045
518-756-6111
www.coeymanslandingmarina.com
captnc7@aol.com

Lighthouse Marina
PO Box 1250
Aquebogue, NY 11931
631-722-3400
www.lighthousemarina.com
sales@lighthousemarina.com

Long Island Marine Group
81 Fort Salonga Rd
Northport, NY 11768-2889
631-261-5464
www.yachtworld.com/limg
longislandmarine@aol.com

MarineMax
155 W. Shore Rd.
Huntington, NY 11743
631-424-2710
www.marinemax.com

Oakdale Service Inc.
520 Shore Dr.
Oakdale, NY 11769-2030
631-589-1087
www.oakdaleyacht.com
tom@oakdaleyacht.com

Signature Yacht Sales
3773 Savage Rd
Geneva, NY 14456-9105
315-729-3595
www.signatureyachtsales.com
sys14456@gmail.com
Brokerage Sales

Smith Boys Marine
280 Michigan St
North Tonawanda, NY 14120-6845
716-695-3472
www.smithboys.com
rsmith@smithboys.com
New Boat Sales, Brokerage Sales, Service Yard

OHIO

Catawba Island Marina
4422 Barnum Rd.
Port Clinton, OH 43452
419-797-4414
www.cicclub.com
marina@cicclub.com

Freeman Eckley
5260 Liberty Ave
Vermilion, OH 44089-1308
440-967-0260
www.freeman-eckley.com

Lake & Bay Yacht Sales
510 Stone St.
Marblehead, OH 43440-0237
419-798-8511
www.yachtworld.com/lakeandbay
lakeandbay@roadrunner.com
New Boat Sales, Brokerage Sales

South Shore Marine
1611 Sawmill Parkay
Huron, OH 44839-2247
419-433-5798
www.SouthShoreMarine.com
tom@southshoremarine.com
New Boat Sales, Brokerage Sales, Service Yard

OKLAHOMA

Ugly John's Custom Boats
32550 Thunder Bay Rd.
Afton, OK 74331
918-782-4414
www.uglyjohns.com
phil@uglyjohns.com

PUERTO RICO

CFR Yacht Sales, Inc.
PO Box 16816
San Juan, PR 00908-0816
787-722-7088
www.cfryachts.com
carlosluis@cfryachtsales.com

RHODE ISLAND

Rice International
427 Congden Hill Rd.
Saunderstown, RI 02874-2100
401-294-6400
www.riceinternational.com
jeff@riceinternational.com
Brokerage Sales

SOUTH CAROLINA

Charleston Harbor Yacht Sales
24 Patriots Point Rd.
Mt. Pleasant, SC 29464
843-425-6888
www.charlestonharboryachtsales.com
john@charlestonharboryachtsales.com
Brokerage Sales

Myrtle Beach Yacht Sales
15 Chapin Cr.
Myrtle Beach, SC 29572
843-455-6807
www.MyrtleBeachYachtSales.com
MyrtleBeachYachtSales@gmail.com
Brokerage Sales

TENNESSEE

Captain's Choice
PO Box 351
Pickwick Dam, TN 38365
662-279-0303
www.captainschoiceofpickwick@com
captainschoiceofpickwick@gmail.com
Brokerage Sales

TEXAS

American Yacht Sales
3304 N Wyoming Ave
Dickinson, TX 77539-3011
281-334-6531
www.americanyachtsales.com
sales@americanyachtsales.com
Brokerage Sales

Cedar Mills Yacht Sales
500 Harbour View Rd.
Gordonville, TX 76245
903-523-4574
www.cedarmills.com
rick@cedarmills.com
New Boat Sales

Eriksen Marine
5975 Hiline Rd
Austin, TX 78734-1150
512-266-3493
www.eriksenmarine.com
mike@eriksenmarine.com
Brokerage Sales, Service Yard

Fox Yacht Sales
203 W. Cotter
Port Aransas, TX 78373
361-749-4870
www.foxyachtsales.com
foxyachtsales@centurytel.net
Brokerage Sales

Galati Yacht Sales
7819 Broadway St. #100
Galveston, TX 77554-9103
281-474-1470
www.galatiyachts.com
lsmith@galatiyachts.com

Grandpappy Point Marina
132 Grandpappy Dr
Denison, TX 75020-2638
903-465-6330
www.grandpappy.com
jcottingame@grandpappy.com,
Brokerage Sales, Service Yard

Jay Bettis & Company
2509 Nasa Rd 1
Seabrook, TX 77586-3452
281-326-3333
www.jb-yachts.com
info@jb-yachts.com
New Boat Sales, Brokerage Sales

Little Yacht Sales/Texas Power Yachts
500 Mariners Dr. Pier 4, 6/7
Kemah, TX 77565
281-334-6500
www.LittleYachtSales.com
info@LittleYachtSales.com
New Boat Sales, Brokerage Sales

Texas Sportfishing Yacht Sales
2102 Marina Bay Dr.
Kemah, TX 77565
281-535-2628
www.texassportfishingyachtsales.com
txyachts@quikus.com
New Boat Sales, Brokerage Sales

VIRGINIA

North Point Yacht Sales
319 Court St.
Portsmouth, VA 23704
410-280-2038
www.NorthPointYachtSales.com
peter@NorthPointYachtSales.com

Sea D.A. Yacht Sales & Brokerage
2100 Marina Shores Dr.
Virginia Beach, VA 23451
757-963-5210
www.seadayachts.com
seadayachts@live.com
Brokerage Sales

WASHINGTON

Anchor Yacht Brokers
2415 T Ave Ste 112
Anacortes, WA 98221
360-299-0545
www.anchoryachtbrokers.com
captaingalen@yahoo.com
Brokerage Sales

Breakwater Marina Yacht Sales
5603 N Waterfront Dr.
Tacoma, WA 98407-6536
253-752-6663
www.breakwatermarina.com
michael@breakwatermarina.com
Brokerage Sales

Crow's Nest Yacht Sales
809 Fairview Pl. N #150
Seattle, WA 98109-4452
206-625-1580
www.crowsnestyachts.com
reception@crowsnestyachts.com
Brokerage Sales, New Boat Sales

Elliott Bay Yacht Sales
2601 W Marina Place Ste D
Seattle, WA 98199-4331
206-285-9563
www.elliottbayyachtsales.com
paul@elliottbayyachtsales.com
Brokerage Sales

NW Explorations
2623 S Harbor Loop Dr.
Bellingham, WA 98225-2000
360-676-1248
www.nwexplorations.com
sales@nwexplorations.com
Brokerage Sales, Service Yard

West Yachts
1019 Q Ave Ste D
Anacortes, WA 98221-4100
360-299-2526
www.west-yachts.com
info@west-yachts.com
New Boat Sales, Brokerage

WISCONSIN

Emerald Yacht-Ship Group
3107 Six Mile Rd. #3
Racine, WI 53402
262-681-0600
www.emeraldyachtship.com
sales@emeraldyachtship.com
Brokerage Sales

Skipper Buds
5381 Westport Rd.
Madison, WI 53704
608-246-2628
www.skipperbuds.com

CANADA

Calibre Yacht Sales
415 West Esplanade
N. Vancouver, BC V7M1A6
CANADA
604-929-0651
www.calibreyachts.com
richard@calibreyachts.com

Custom Yacht Sales Ltd.
1955 Swartz Bay Rd.
Sidney, BC V8L3X9
CANADA
250-656-8771
www.customyachtsales.com

Bridge Yachts Ltd.
49 Harbour St. Box 1329
Port Dover, ON N0A1N0
CANADA
519-583-3199
www.bridgeyachts.com
bridge@bridgeyachts.com
New Boat Sales, Brokerage Sales,
Service Yard

Simcoe Yacht Sales
Unit 26 1111 Wilson Rd. North
Oshawa, ON L1G8C2
CANADA
905-576-8288
www.SimcoeYachts.com
info@simcoeyachts.com
Brokerage Sales

Westwind Yacht Sales
67 Juneau Rd.
Victoria Harbour, ON L0K2A0
CANADA
705-528-9979
www.WestwindYachtsCanada.com
westwind@csolve.net
Brokerage

Broker/Dealer Directory

2014

PowerBoat Guide

Standard Edition

Albemarle

Quick View

- The Albemarle 24 Express was the first model introduced by the company in 1978.
- By the late 1980s Albemarle was offering a full line of deep-V fishing boats.
- Albemarle's smaller boats are well known for their jackshaft power options, an inboard/outboard installation that places the engine in the center of the boat.
- Albemarle was acquired by the Brunswick Corporation in 2005 where it became part of the Hatteras Group.
- In January, 2009 Brunswick sold Albemarle to Scott McLaughlin, a North Carolina investor with experience in the boat business.
- An Albemarle owners group can be found at www.albemarleboatowners.com.

Albemarle Boats • Edenton, NC • www.albemarleboats.com

Albemarle 262 Center Console

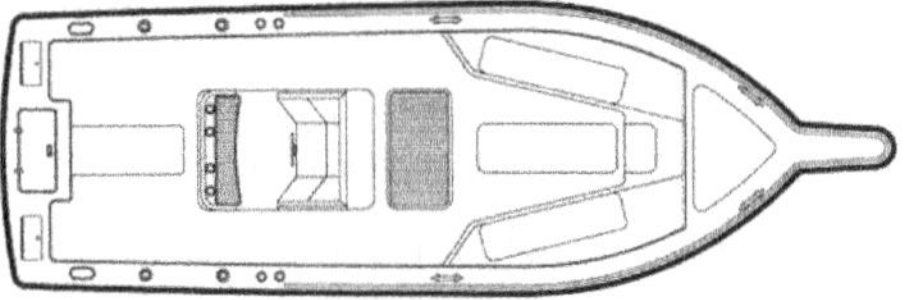

The Albemarle 262 is a well-built offshore fisherman whose practical layout and quality construction will appeal to experienced anglers who know what they want in a trailerable center console. Introduced as a sterndrive model with power supplied via a 6-foot jackshaft from an amidships-mounted engine, the 262 is a relatively heavy boat for her size and she performs well in rough seas. Standard features included an in-transom circulating live well, built-in tackle locker, dry storage forward, removable fish box and transom-mounted bait boxes at the corners. Although an outboard version was available, the center-mounted engine location of the jackshaft model improves the boat's overall handling characteristics and makes for a more stable fishing platform. Either way, there's a large standup compartment in the console useful for storage or the installation of a marine head. A popular model during her production years, the Albemarle 262 will cruise at 23–24 knots with the standard 310hp Volvo Duoprop jackshaft (around 33 knots top), while the outboard version—the Albemarle 260—will deliver a cruising speed of around 36 knots with a pair of 225hp bracket-mounted Mercs.

See Page 667 For Price Data

Length w/Pulpit	28'0"	Weight, I/B	6,800#
Hull Length	25'10"	Fuel	172 gals.
Beam	8'6"	Water	14 gals.
Draft	3'0"	Hull Type	Deep-V
Weight, O/B	6,250#	Deadrise Aft	24°

Albemarle 265/268 XF

1993–Current

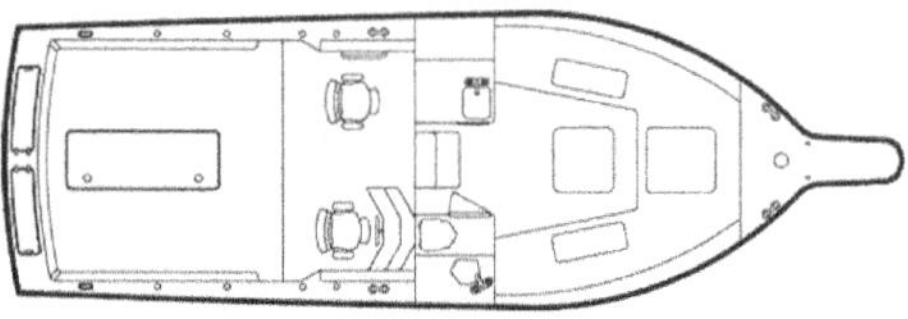

This popular jackshaft-powered express has long ranked among the best in her class by experienced anglers. Indeed, she combines the company's traditionally bulletproof construction and uncluttered layout with a deep-V hull capable of handling a nasty offshore chop. After many years of production as the 265 Express, Albemarle designers decided to rework the hull in 2003, reducing transom deadrise from 24 degrees to 21 degrees in an effort to introduce greater low-speed stability to her slender 8-foot, 6-inch hull. Now called the 268 Express, the center engine location (under the bridge deck) keeps the cockpit free of the engine box common to most sterndrive boats. There are many impressive features in this boat, beginning with a deep, well-equipped cockpit and including an efficient helm layout and one of the best-appointed cabins—with full galley, teak woodwork, and a standup head compartment—to be found in a 26-footer. No lightweight, the 265/268 Express is known for her good headsea performance. Those powered with a 320hp Volvo gas engine will cruise in the mid 20s (30+ knots top). A late-model 268 with a single 285hp Volvo diesel runs a few knots slower.

See Page 667 For Price Data

Length w/Pulpit	28'0"	Weight, I/B	7,500#
Hull Length	25'10"	Fuel	172 gals.
Beam	8'6"	Water	14 gals.
Draft	2'10"	Hull Type	Deep-V
Weight, O/B	6,950#	Deadrise, 265/268	24°/21°

Albemarle 27/280 Express

1984–2007

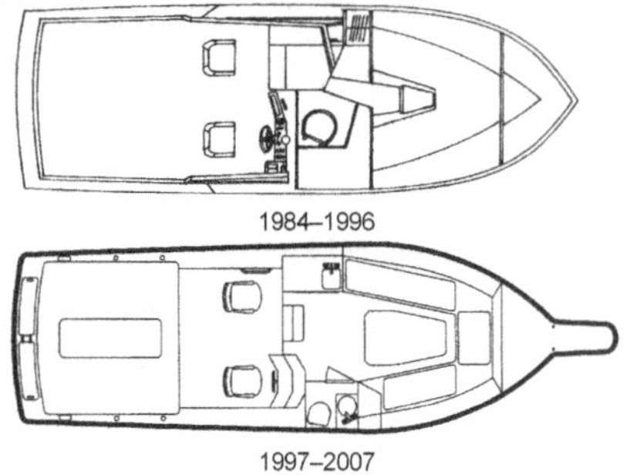
1984–1996

1997–2007

One of the few boats under 30 feet able to handle a full tower, the Albemarle 280 series began life back in 1984 as the sterndrive-powered Albemarle 27. Jackshaft power became available in 1986, and in 1996 a major facelift—including a redesigned floorplan and a slightly raised deckhouse for improved cabin headroom—prompted Albemarle to reintroduce her as the 280/282/285 Express Fisherman. (The 280 model has twin inboards; the 282 has single jackshaft power; and the 285 has twin jackshaft sterndrives.) No lightweight, anglers have long appreciated the spacious and well-arranged cockpit of the 27/280 with its generous rod storage and topnotch fishing amenities. Below, the accommodations are spacious for a boat this size with V-berth forward, compact galley, and a standup head with shower. The interior is finished with quality hardware and fabrics throughout and accented with teak trim. Several engine choices were offered over the years including inboards as well as Albemarle's signature jackshaft power installations. Twin 280hp Volvo inboards cruise at 23–24 knots, and jackshaft models with twin 270hp Volvos cruise at 28–29 knots. A very popular model.

See Page 667 For Price Data

Length w/Pulpit	29'1"	Fuel, Twin I/B	260 gals.
Hull Length	27'1"	Fuel, Single JS	172 gals.
Beam	9'6"	Water	14 gals.
Draft	3'0"	Hull Type	Deep-V
Weight	9,500#	Deadrise Aft	24°

Albemarle 290 XF

The Albemarle 290XF was introduced in 2008 as a replacement for the company's very successful 280XF. With her bold styling (note the flared bow and hullside "gills") and wide 10'9" beam, the 290XF is roomier than her predecessor and prop pockets built into her solid fiberglass, deep-V hull allow her to operate in fairly skinny water. Her raised bridge deck layout consists of a roomy (about 60-square-foot) cockpit with two insulated fish boxes, one 49-gallon in the cockpit sole, and one 43-gallon box in the transom. A 21-gallon livewell is located at the port forward corner of the cockpit where it's close to the tackle/bait prep station. Like most modern express boats, the entire bridge deck lifts on hydraulic rams for engine access. The boat's belowdecks layout—nicely finished with teak joinery and a teak-and-holly sole—includes a compact galley with microwave, a large stand-up head with shower, and V-berths forward with backrests that can be deployed to form upper single bunks. The side decks on this boat are wide and the windshield is tall—positive features both. With a pair of Yanmar 315hp diesels, the 290XF will cruise at 25–26 knots (about 30 knots top).

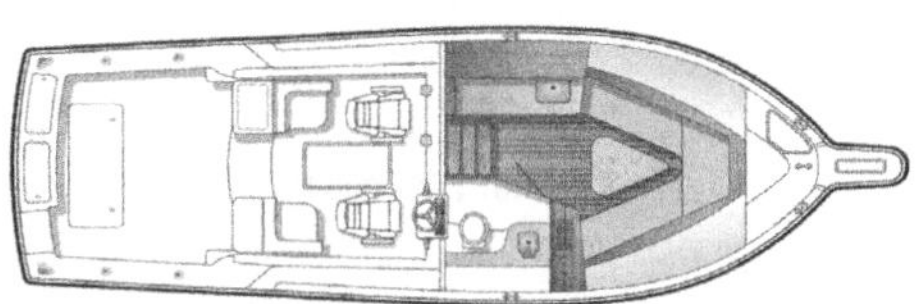

See Page 667 For Price Data

Length w/Pulpit	30'6"	Fuel	265 gals.
Hull Length	28'6"	Water	28 gals.
Beam	10'9"	Clearance	8'2"
Draft	2'8"	Hull Type	Deep-V
Weight	12,500#	Deadrise Aft	21°

Albemarle 30 Express; 305 Express; 310XF

The Albemarle 310XF (called the 30 Express in 1995–96; 305 Express in 1997–2003) is a tournament-level sportfisherman with the eye appeal of a custom boat. She's heavily built on a solid fiberglass hull with a flared bow and a wide 11-foot beam. (Indeed, at over 15,000 pounds the 310 is built like a tank compared with most other 30-foot fishing boats.) Albemarles have long been known for their comfortable ride and good handling qualities, but the 310's huge cockpit—one of the largest to be found in a boat this size—comes as a surprise. Here, an angler will find such fish-friendly amenities as split tackle centers, generous livewell capacity, removable fish boxes, transom door, and lots of storage. The center-mounted helm position, with its excellent visibility, is definitely one of the boat's best features. For service access, the entire bridge deck can be hydraulically raised to get at the engines. Note that both the cabin and bridge deck layouts were updated in 2004 when the fuel capacity was also bumped up. A good performer, twin 350hp Cat diesels cruise the Albemarle 310 in the high 20s and reach a top speed of about 30 knots.

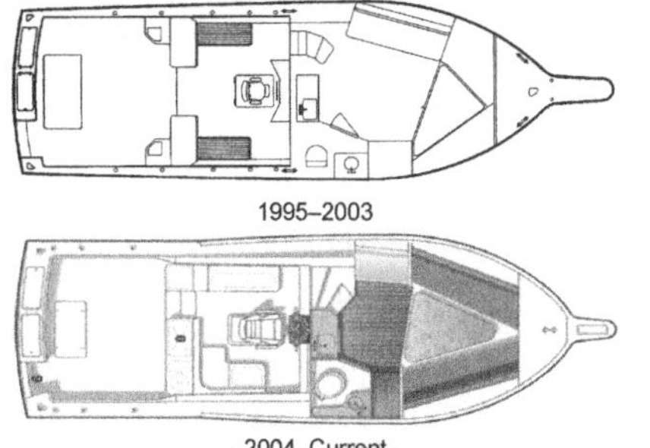

See Page 667 For Price Data

Length w/Pulpit	32'2"	Fuel	300/325 gals.
Hull Length	30'6"	Water	30 gals.
Beam	11'0"	Waste	15 gals.
Draft	2'10"	Hull Type	Deep-V
Weight	15,500#	Deadrise Aft	18°

Albemarle 320 Express

Sharing the same solid fiberglass deep-V hull as the original 32 Flybridge, the Albemarle 320 Express is a heavily built offshore sportfisherman with a handsome profile and plenty of built-in fishing amenities. Albemarle has a history of building no-nonsense fishing boats, and the 320 Express is a very substantial platform indeed. Aside from her good looks and rugged construction, she's loaded with practical features that anglers will find most appealing including a split bait and tackle rigging station, livewell and abundant storage. The raised helm provides excellent visibility and the side decks are wide enough to allow safe passage forward. The below decks accommodations are limited but tastefully finished with berths for four, a full galley, and an enclosed standup head. For engine access, the entire bridge deck can be hydraulically raised at the flip of a switch. Note that in 1999 the deck, cockpit and helm were redesigned, a transom door became standard, the interior was rearranged and the fuel tank was relocated under the cockpit. A good-running boat, 350hp Cat diesels cruise the 320 Express at a quick 27–28 knots and reach a top speed in excess of 30 knots.

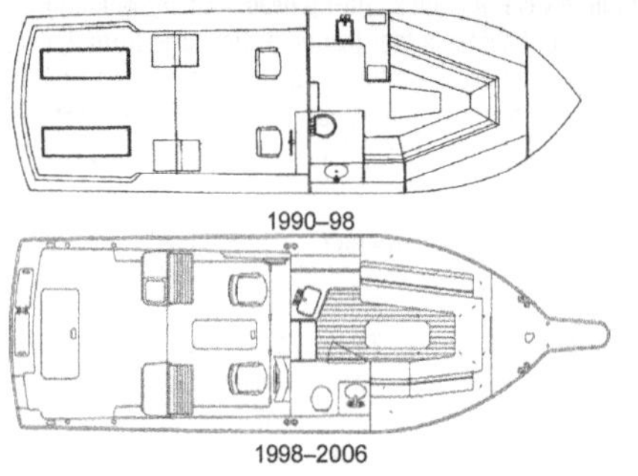

1990–98

1998–2006

See Page 667 For Price Data

Length w/Pulpit	34'9"	Fuel	300 gals.
Hull Length	32'2"	Water	30 gals.
Beam	11'0"	Waste	NA
Draft	3'0"	Hull Type	Deep-V
Weight	17,000#	Deadrise Aft	18°

Albemarle 325 Convertible

One of the smallest flybridge boats built in recent years, the Albemarle 325 is a top-quality convertible sportfisherman with a spacious cockpit and a comfortable, first-class interior. Hull construction is solid fiberglass, and her moderate beam and flared bow combine to produce a hull that is fast and comfortable in a variety of sea conditions. Although she's only 32 feet in length, there's a real salon in the 325 with room for a sofa and chairs. A double berth is fitted in the stateroom of early models although V-berths soon became standard. Attractively decorated and featuring plenty of teak joinery and trim, this is a comfortable if not expansive interior. To address some complaints about a harsh ride, a major redesign occurred in 1999 when the engines were moved forward 10 inches, a single fuel tank replaced the original three-tank configuration, and the trim tabs were recessed into the hull. Cabin headroom was also increased in 1999, and a transom door and lift-out fish box were added in the cockpit. Early models with 330hp Volvo gas engines cruise at 22 knots (30+ knots top). Later models with twin 350hp 3116 Cat diesels cruise in the mid 20s (around 30 knots top).

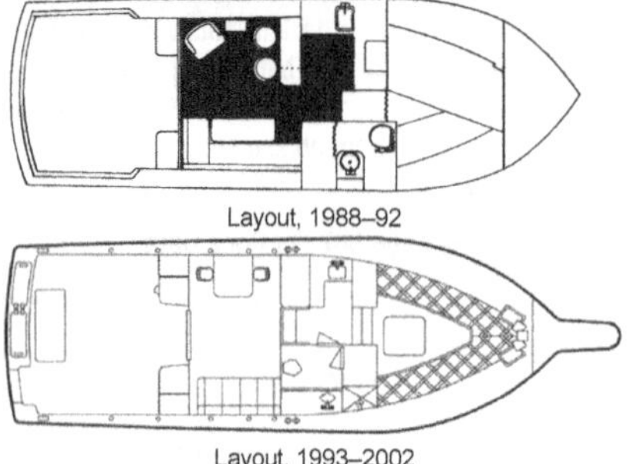

Layout, 1988–92

Layout, 1993–2002

See Page 667 For Price Data

Length w/Pulpit	34'9"	Fuel	300 gals.
Hull Length	32'2"	Water	30 gals.
Beam	11'0"	Waste	25 gals.
Draft	3'0"	Hull Type	Deep-V
Weight	18,000#	Deadrise Aft	18°

Albemarle 410 XF

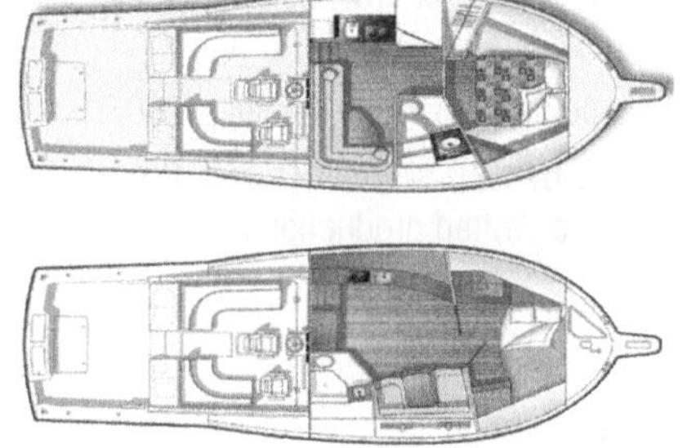

Largest express boat in the Albemarle fleet, the 410 XF is a quality fishing machine from a company known for building some of the better fishing boats on the market. The styling is classic; the construction is solid; and the seakeeping qualities of the 410 are excellent. She's built on a modified-V hull with a solid fiberglass bottom, cored hullsides, and a relatively wide beam. The interior is arranged with a single stateroom forward (with a privacy door) and a plush U-shaped dinette to starboard, opposite a compact galley. The grain-matched teak joinery is impressive, and there's a fold-down rod storage locker above the settee. Unlike some express fishing boats this size, the helm of the 410 is on the centerline, which makes for the best possible visibility. The lounge seating aft of the helm will easily seat six, the cockpit is big and well arranged, and the entire bridge deck lifts on hydraulic rams for access to the engineroom. A transom door is standard as are a bait-prep station with sink and tackle storage, livewell, transom fish box, and fresh- and raw-water washdowns. Cat 710hp diesels cruise the Albemarle 410 at a fast 30 knots (about 35 knots top).

See Page 667 For Price Data

Length w/Pulpit	43'6"	Fuel	600 gals.
Hull Length	41'0"	Water	100 gals.
Beam	15'9"	Waste	25 gals.
Draft	4'0"	Hull Type	Modified-V
Weight	32,000#	Deadrise Aft	15°

Albin

Quick View

- Albin Marine was the sucessor to Albin Motor, originally founded in Sweden in 1899 as a marine diesel engine and boat manufacturer.
- Albin initially built only sailboats. Their first powerboat design, the Albin 25 Double Cabin, was introduced in 1969.
- During most of the 1980s Albin was one of the leading importers and distributors of Taiwan-built trawlers.
- By the late 1980s Albin began producing a series of Downeast cruising and fishing boats at their facilities in Portsmouth, RI.
- Following several years of declining sales, Albin went out of business in the fall of 2007.
- The molds to several Albin models were purchased by C&C Marine (Bristol, RI) in 2009 with the intention of producing future Albins on a limited production basis.
- An Albin owners group can be found at nowhere.

No longer in business.

Albin 27 Family Cruiser

1983–95

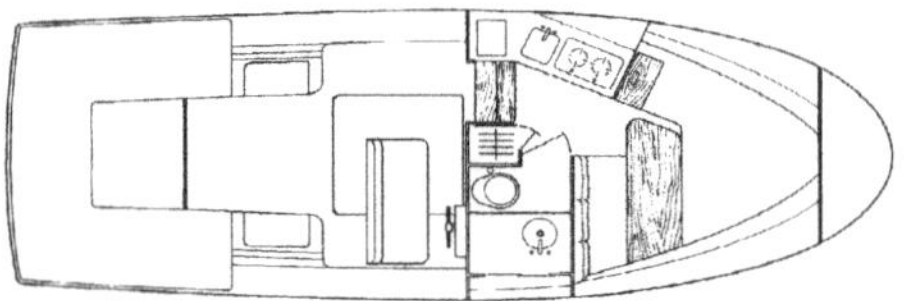

The Albin 27 Family Cruiser is a descendant of the Swedish-built Albin 25 Cruiser, one of the best-selling small craft ever produced. The 27 was an extremely popular model for Albin thanks to her fuel-efficient operation, affordable price, and sturdy, solid fiberglass construction. A full-length keel provides sure-footed tracking when the seas pick up, and a shallow draft makes the 27 ideal for cruising the Intercoastal or inland lake regions. While her twin-cabin accommodations are necessarily basic (she is, after all, only a 27-footer), they are nonetheless adequate for the cruising couple or an undemanding small family. The forward cabin features a good-sized double berth, full galley, dinette, hanging locker, and a surprising amount of storage. Perhaps the best feature of the Albin 27 is her center-cockpit layout with its inboard seating and protected helm. Built in the U.S., Albin 27s require relatively little maintenance and they handle a chop quite well for a small boat. Several small diesel engines were available over the years, all of which consume only 2–3 gph at a cruising speed of 10–12 knots. Note that a bow thruster and additional fuel were standard in later models.

See Page 667 For Price Data

Length Overall	26'9"	Fuel	72 gals.
Length WL	24'4"	Water	40 gals.
Beam	9'8"	Waste	25 gals.
Draft	2'6"	Hull Type	Semi-Disp.
Weight	6,500#	Deadrise Aft	NA

Albin 27 Sport Cruiser

The Albin 27 Sport Cruiser—a redesigned version of the company's very popular 27 Family Cruiser—combines the utility of a large, open cockpit with the security of a semi-enclosed helm and the economy of a single diesel engine. This is a boat that will appeal to fishermen, divers, and cruisers who place a premium on simplicity and economy. Hull construction is solid fiberglass, and a full-length keel provides sure-footed tracking as well as grounding protection for the running gear. The most compelling feature of the 27 Sport Cruiser is her huge cockpit where several anglers can enjoy fishing without rubbing elbows. Helm visibility is excellent in all directions, and the center windshield panel opens to provide fresh air on a hot day. Below, the Sport Cruiser's compact cabin includes a double berth forward, galley with sink and stove, hanging locker, and an enclosed head with shower. Twin hatches in the cockpit sole provide excellent engine access. Drawing just 2 feet, 6 inches of draft, the Sport Cruiser is ideal for exploring shallow inland waters. Several 6-cylinder diesel engines were offered over the years, any of which burn about 2 gallons per hour at 10–12 knots. Neat boat.

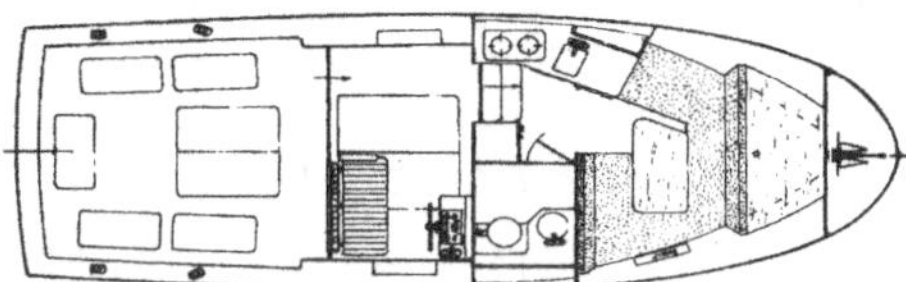

See Page 667 For Price Data

Length Overall	26'9"	Fuel	100 gals.
Length WL	24'4"	Water	40 gals.
Beam	9'8"	Waste	25 gals.
Draft	2'6"	Hull Type	Semi-Disp.
Weight	6,750#	Deadrise Aft	NA

Albin 28 TE

The Albin 28 Tournament Express is a sturdy fishboat/family cruiser with a practical deck layout, a skeg-protected rudder and cabin accommodations for four. The 28 is a rather traditional-looking boat with a hint of Downeast styling, and her foam-cored hull boasts a prop-protecting skeg for increased tracking and stability. While the centerline engine box dominates the cockpit (standard power is a single V-drive inboard), there's still enough working space for a couple of undemanding anglers. A hardtop (optional) with sliding side windows provides weather protection for the helm, and a drop curtain or optional bulkhead door encloses it completely. Belowdecks, the compact interior is accented with mica cabinets, teak trim, and a classy teak-and-holly sole. A wide quarter berth extends beneath the bridge deck, and a bow thruster was standard. Note that for 2003 a Flush Deck option moved the engine forward, under the wheelhouse, narrowing the quarter berth but opening up the cockpit. Among several engine choices, a single 300hp Yanmar (or Cummins) diesel will cruise at 18 knots with a top speed of 22–23 knots.

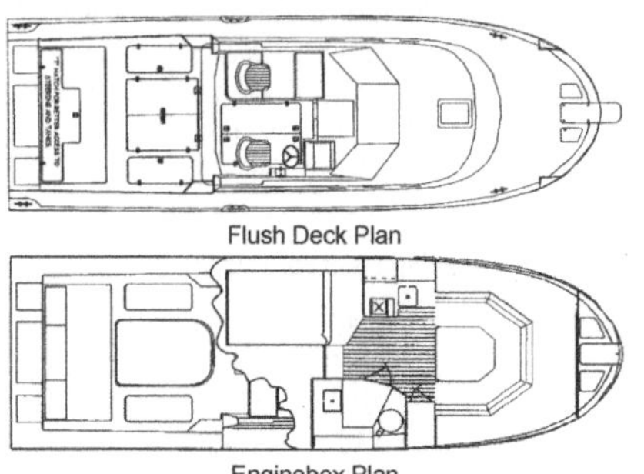
Flush Deck Plan

Enginebox Plan

See Page 667 For Price Data

Length	29'11"	Fuel	132 gals.
Beam	10'0"	Water	36 gals.
Draft	3'2"	Waste	20 gals.
Weight	7,500#	Hull Type	Modified-V
Clearance	7'9"	Deadrise Aft	16°

Albin 30 Family Cruiser

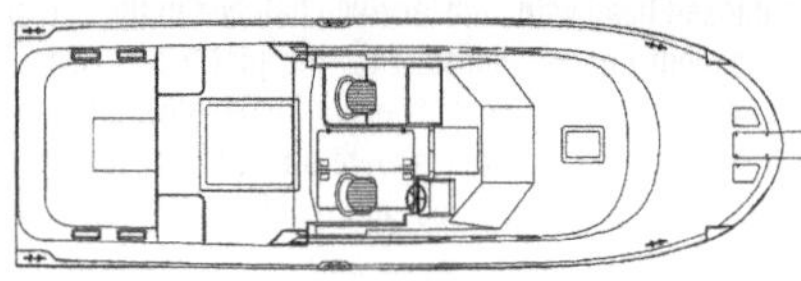

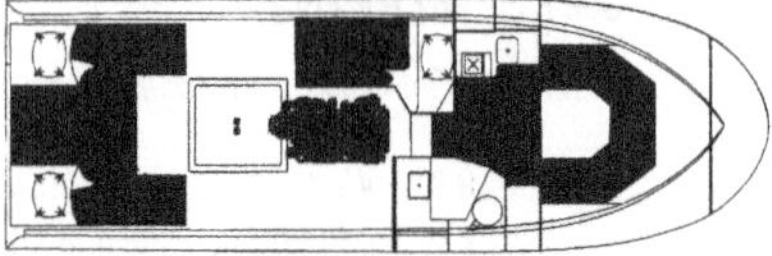

Introduced in 2004, the Albin 30 Family Cruiser is the successor to the company's popular 27 Family Cruiser manufactured from 1983–95. This is an ideal small cruiser for the family whose priorities include economical operation, easy handling, and—perhaps most important of all—an affordable price. The hull of the Albin 30 is solid fiberglass, and a skeg-mounted rudder provides protection for the running gear in the event of grounding. Her split-plan layout offers sleeping accommodations for five adults in two separate cabins. The galley and head are in the forward cabin where a convertible U-shaped dinette and portside quarter berth will sleep three, and twin single berths in the aft cabin can be converted into a queen bed. The cockpit is deep enough to keep youngsters safe and secure, and visibility from the semi-enclosed helm is excellent. A hatch between the helm and companion seats provides good access to the engine. Additional features include an in-floor cockpit storage well, wide side decks, ten opening ports, and a bow pulpit. A single 300hp Perkins diesel will cruise the Family Cruiser at an economical 16–17 knots and reach a top speed of around 22 knots.

See Page 668 For Price Data

Length Overall	31'5"	Fuel	126 gals.
Length WL	26'8"	Water	26 gals.
Beam	10'0"	Waste	18 gals.
Draft	3'2"	Hull Type	Modified-V
Weight	9,800#	Deadrise Aft	19°

Albin 31 TE

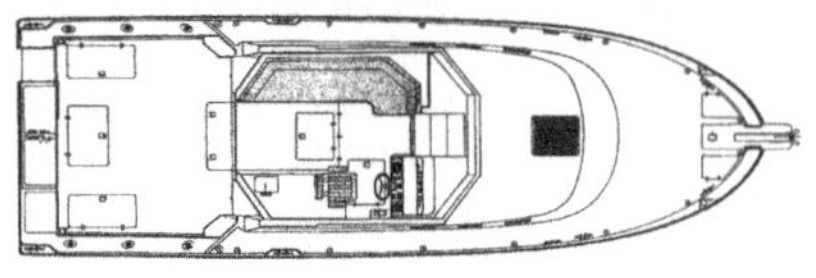

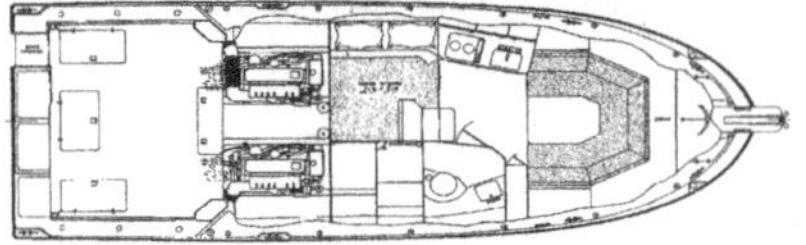

Based on the smaller Albin 28 Tournament Express, the Albin 31 TE is a distinctive Downeast-style fisherman whose spacious interior allows her to double as a capable family cruiser. She's built on a modified-V hull with a fairly wide beam for a 31-footer, and the single-engine version comes with a bow thruster and skeg-protected prop. In her standard mode, the Albin 31 has a three-sided pilothouse enclosure with the bridge deck open to the cockpit, although a pair of optional doors can make the wheelhouse a fully enclosed cabin. The cockpit comes with a transom baitwell and fish box, and a transom door is standard along with in-deck storage and rod holders. The interior sleeps four with an athwartship double berth aft of the galley and a convertible dinette/double berth forward. There's a separate stall shower in the head—a big plus on any small boat with cruising aspirations. Additional features include easy access to the engines, wide side decks, an opening windshield, transom shower, and raw-water washdown. Among several engine options, a single 370hp Cummins diesel will cruise at 16 knots, and twin 315hp Yanmar diesels cruise at 22–24 knots. Over 200 were built.

See Page 668 For Price Data

Length w/Pulpit	33'0"	Fuel	300 gals.
Hull Length	31'8"	Water	73 gals.
Beam	12'4"	Waste	40 gals.
Draft	3'10"	Hull Type	Modified-V
Weight	14,000#	Deadrise Aft	14°

Albin 32+2 Command Bridge

1989–2003

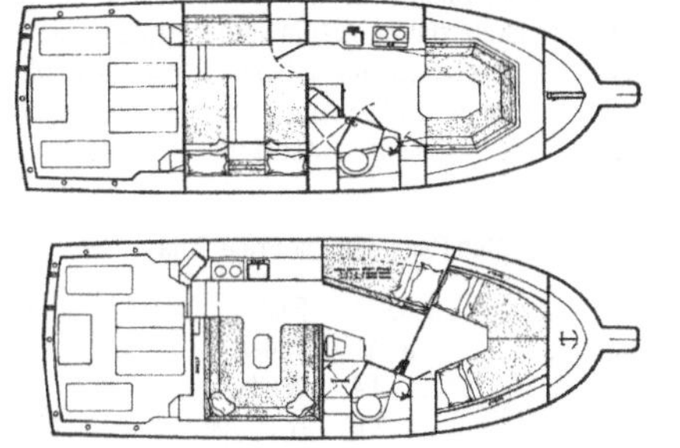

The Albin 32+2 Command Bridge (called the 32 Sportfisher until 1997) represented a departure from Albin's trawler-boat heritage when she was introduced back in 1989—an attempt to crack the sportfishing market with a practical and fuel-efficient trunk cabin express cruiser. She's built on a seakindly modified-V hull with a full-length, prop-protecting keel and moderate transom deadrise. Originally offered with a convertible dinette forward and a private stateroom aft, a tri-cabin layout was available since 1995. (Note that the deckhouse and flybridge were also updated in 1995.) Cabin headroom is excellent thanks to the step-up command bridge, there's a stall shower in the head, and the galley (in the original floorplan) has been called a model of efficiency. Twin hatches in the cockpit sole provide good access to the engine and V-drive unit. Additional features include wide side decks, a transom door, an integral swim platform (since 1997), and teak interior trim. Among several single- and twin-engine installations, a single 300hp Cummins (or Cat) diesel will cruise the Albin 32+2 Command Bridge around 18 knots (23–24 knots top) with a 700+ mile range. A bow thruster was standard in later models.

See Page 668 For Price Data

Length Overall	36'9"	Fuel	260 gals.
Hull Length	34'11"	Water	117 gals.
Beam	12'2"	Waste	20 gals.
Draft	3'10"	Hull Type	Modified-V
Weight	15,000#	Deadrise Aft	13°

Albin 35 Command Bridge

2004–07

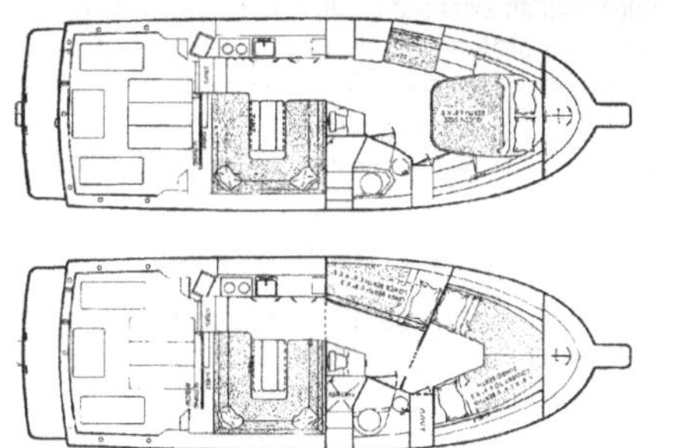

A stretched version of popular Albin 32+2 (1989–2003), the large cockpit and roomy interior of the Albin 35 Command Bridge—combined with her efficient single-diesel propulsion—offers something different in the world of sportfishing boats. Like her predecessor, the 35 CB is an unusual looking boat with a low-profile bridgedeck barely chest-high above the cockpit. The upside of this design is easy helm access, especially important for singlehandling (no more 7-foot ladder to climb up and down as required on a typical flybridge boat). Another plus are the very wide sidedecks, a safety feature seldom found on modern boats. Two single-level floorplans were offered in the 35 Command Bridge: The more popular single-stateroom plan has a queen berth forward and a stall shower in the head, while a so-called "tri-cabin" layout has V-berths forward and a guest stateroom with over/under single berths. The teak and holly cabin sole is a nice touch. Cockpit features include two in-deck fish boxes, transom livewell, wet bar with sink, and transom door. A full-length keep protects the running gear. Cruise at 16 knots (low 20s top) with a single 370hp Yanmar diesel.

See Page 668 For Price Data

Length w/Pulpit	36'9"	Fuel	260 gals.
Beam	12'4"	Water	115 gals.
Draft	3'10"	Waste	20 gals.
Weight	18,000#	Hull Type	Modified-V
Clearance	8'10"	Deadrise Aft	13°

Albin 35 TE

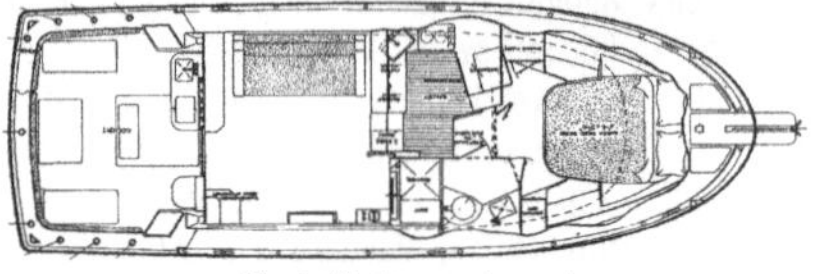
Single Stateroom Layout

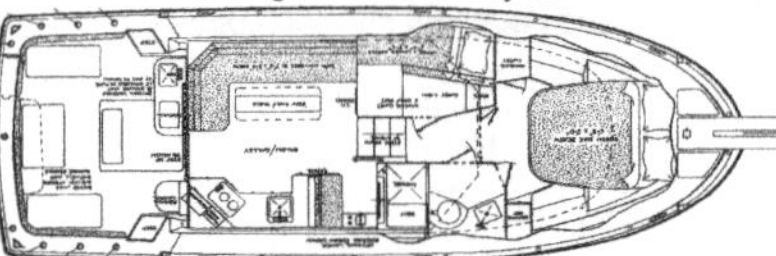
Two Stateroom Floorplan

The Albin 35 Tournament Express is a hardtop version of the Albin 35 Convertible. She's a moderately priced family cruiser/weekend fisherman with roomy accommodations and a cockpit that's large enough to meet the needs of weekend anglers. Built on a fully cored hull with moderate beam, a flared bow and a shallow keel, the solid, workmanlike construction of the Tournament Express is noteworthy. Buyers had a choice of interior layouts. The standard version has a single-stateroom with the galley down, and the alternate floorplan moves the galley into the salon and adds a second stateroom on the lower level. Either way, the interior of the Albin 35 is bright and cheery and the wraparound cabin windows provide excellent helm visibility in all directions. Additional features include wide side decks, six opening cabin ports and opening salon windows, transom door, integral bow pulpit, and a separate stall shower in both floorplans. Among several single- and twin-screw engine options, a pair of 370hp Cummins diesels cruise the 35 Tournament Express at an economical 24 knots and reach a top speed of just under 30 knots.

See Page 668 For Price Data

Length w/Pulpit	36'11"	Fuel	370 gals.
Hull Length	34'11"	Water	160 gals.
Beam	12'4"	Waste	27 gals.
Draft	3'0"	Hull Type	Modified-V
Weight	18,000#	Deadrise Aft	13°

Albin 36 Express Trawler

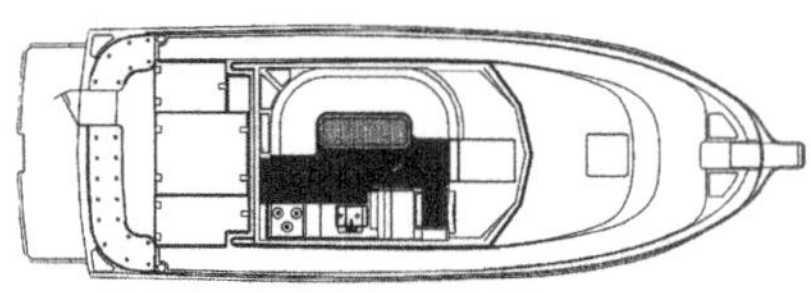

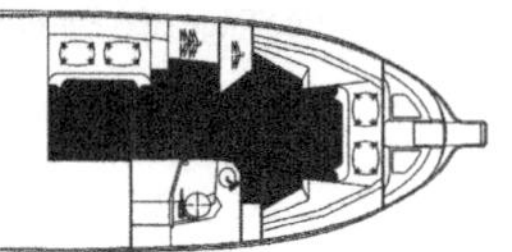

The Albin 36 Express Trawler—a 33-footer with a three-foot swim platform—is a sturdy, well-built sedan cruiser whose stylish, reverse-slanted front windshield is certainly her most distinguishing feature. Her trawler-style appearance is a bit deceiving; she actually rides on a planing hull with a shallow, full-length keel which allows her to reach cruising speeds far in excess of conventional trawlers with their slower semi-displacement hulls. Belowdecks, the two-stateroom interior of the Albin 36 is arranged with V-berths forward and a midcabin to port with an athwartship double berth extending under the salon floor. To make this second stateroom possible, the engines are aft in the Albin 36, under the cockpit sole, where V-drives are used to deliver the power. A lower helm was standard. Additional features include a spacious flybridge with an extended hardtop and fold-down radar mast, an integral swim platform with handrails, side exhausts, and a transom door. Among several engine options, a single 420hp Cat diesel will cruise at 12–13 knots, and pair of 270hp Cummins diesels cruise at 16–17 knots and reach a top speed of around 20 knots.

See Page 668 For Price Data

Length w/Pulpit	37'5"	Clearance	11'10"
Hull Length	36'0"	Fuel	380 gals.
Beam	12'9"	Water	120 gals.
Draft	3'3"	Hull Type	Modified-V
Weight	18,000#	Deadrise Aft	12°

Albin 40 North Sea Cutter

2005–07

Introduced in 2005, the 40 North Sea Cutter was the first of a series of Albin boats built in Mainland China. She's a "performance trawler," meaning that while she has a trawler-like appearance on the outside, she rides on a traditional modified-V hull capable of very untrawler-like speeds. Trawler purists don't have much good to say about the breed, but performance trawlers are popular these days since not everyone wants to be limited to sailboat cruising speeds. In any event, the 40 is a practical and very solid boat. Her floorplan is uniquely arranged with owner's stateroom forward rather than aft. The small aft cabin, with its cockpit access door and convertible U-shaped dinette, can be used as a den/office or second stateroom. The owner's stateroom is surprisingly spacious and includes divided head/shower compartments. With the galley to starboard in the salon, seating space is limited to the L-shaped dinette. One of the more appealing features on the Albin 40 is her large cockpit—an excellent jumping-off point for swimming and diving. On the downside, the aft cabintop dimensions are modest. Yanmar 370hp diesels cruise at 20 knots (mid 20s top).

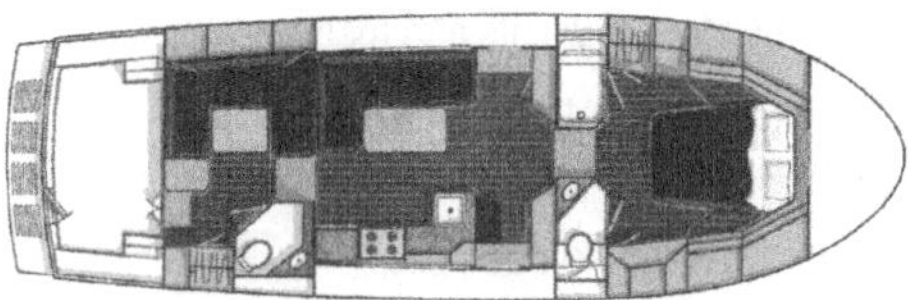

See Page 668 For Price Data

Length	39'6"	Fuel	500 gals.
Beam	13'0"	Water	200 gals.
Draft	4'0"	Waste	40 gals.
Weight	25,000#	Hull Type	Modified-V
Clearance	NA	Deadrise Aft	NA

Albin 45 Command Bridge

2003–07

Rugged construction, a practical interior, and a conservative, low-profile appearance are the hallmarks of the Albin 45 Command Bridge, a boat equally well suited to the demands of hardcore anglers and active family cruisers. Like many Albin designs, the 45 rides on a modified-V hull with generous beam and a shallow keel for directional stability. The two-stateroom, two-head interior of the Command Bridge includes a huge master stateroom forward with a king-size berth, two hanging lockers, and a built-in vanity. The guest stateroom can be configured as an office or utility area (a washer/dryer was optional), and both heads share a common shower stall. Compared with many 45-footers, the main salon is rather small, dominated by a large U-shaped sofa, full-size galley area, and varnished cherry woodwork. The cockpit, with over 100 square feet of fishing space, came standard with a transom door, sink, and shower. The helm is on the centerline on the raised bridge deck. Additional features include a teak-and-holly cabin sole, wide walkarounds, bow pulpit, and an integrated swim platform. With many diesel options to choose from, cruising speeds will run in the low to mid 20s.

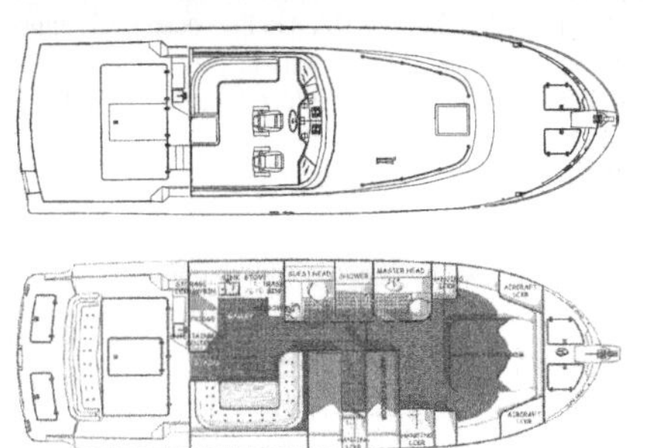

See Page 668 For Price Data

Length w/Pulpit	48'2"	Fuel, Std.	600 gals.
Hull Length	44'4"	Fuel, Opt.	800 gals.
Beam	16'0"	Water	200 gals.
Draft	3'11"	Hull Type	Modified-V
Weight	36,000#	Deadrise Aft	14°

Azimut

Quick View

- Azimut, Italy's largest boat manufacturer, was founded in 1969 when university student Paolo Vitelli began chartering sailing boats.
- The company soon became a of distributer several European yacht brands, and in 1974 Vitelli began producing his own line of Italian-built yachts.
- In 1985 Azimut acquired custom megayacht builder Benetti.
- In 1993 the company's new generation of full-production motor cruisers was introduced, many of which were imported into the American market.
- From the late nineties onwards, with the acquisition of new boatyards at Fano, Italy, the restructuring of the Benetti boatyards at Viareggio and the construction of a new site at Avigliana, Azimut became one of the leading European builders of yachts and megayachts.
- An alliance with Sea Ray in 1998 brought the full Azimut line to North America, providing Azimut owners with Sea Ray's extensive dealer network and product support.
- Azimuts are currently distributed in the US by select MarineMax dealers.

Azimut Yachts • Turin, Italy • www.azimutyachts.com

Azimut 39 Flybridge

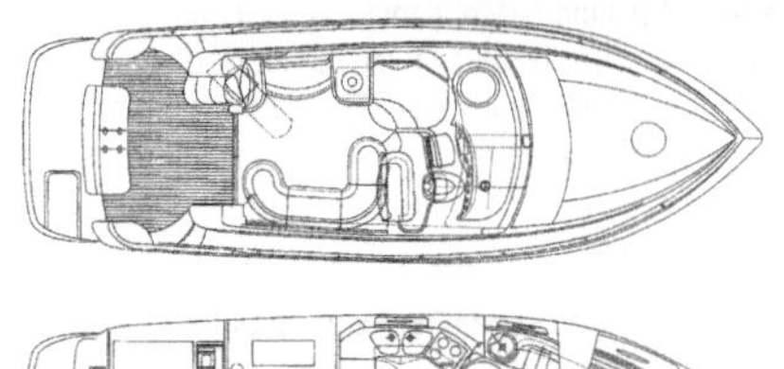

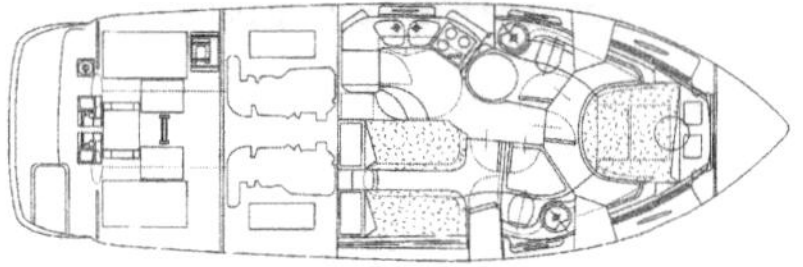

Solid construction, superb performance and distinctive design are the hallmarks of the Azimut 39, one of the more popular Azimut models of recent years. The styling is dramatic—note the two elliptical windows beneath the main salon window and the extended flybridge overhang—and her two-stateroom, galley-down layout is an impressive display of Italian workmanship and design. Like all Azimut yachts, the interior is a high-end blend of lacquered cherry woodwork, quality hardware and designer fabrics throughout. Visibility from the lower helm is excellent in all directions in spite of the teardrop windows. Molded steps in the cockpit lead up to the small flybridge where low side railings make one feel very insecure when standing. Additional features include a teak cockpit sole, power side windows, a low-profile radar arch, underwater exhausts, and built-in bench seating in the cockpit. Like most European boats, the engineroom is a tight fit and access to the motors is exceedingly difficult. A good performer with standard 355hp Cat 3126 diesels, the Azimut 39 will cruise comfortably in the mid 20s and reach a top speed of close to 30 knots.

See Page 668 For Price Data

Length	39'10"	Water	132 gals.
Beam	13'3"	Clearance	12'0"
Draft	3'7"	Headroom	6'4"
Weight	22,000#	Hull Type	Modified-V
Fuel	264 gals.	Deadrise Aft	14.6°

Azimut 42 Flybridge

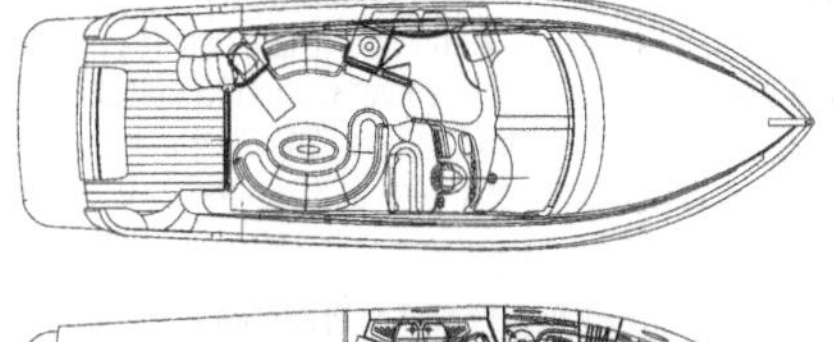

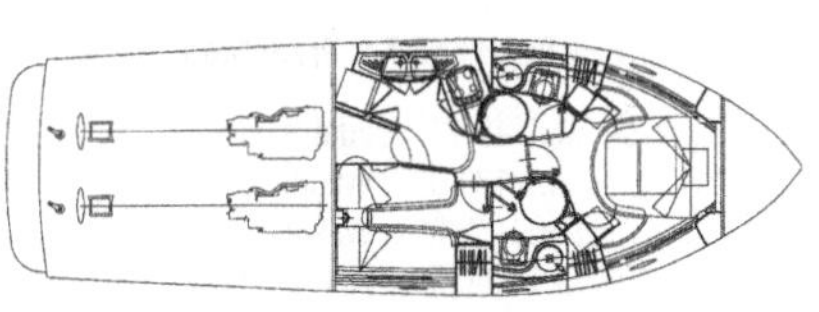

The Azimut 42 is Italian styling at its best in a midsize performance yacht. Inside and out, the quality built into all Azimut yachts is simply undeniable. Introduced in 1999, the 42 is built on a fully cored deep-V hull with moderate beam and prop pockets to reduce draft. The interior, with its sculpted overhead lining, is unusually bright and open thanks to the vast amount of window space in the salon. High-gloss cherry woodwork is liberally applied throughout, and faux leather ceilings complement the designer fabrics and wall coverings. Visibility from the elevated lower helm is very good (but there's no chart flat). Beautiful as she is, there are a couple of downsides to the Azimut 42 seen in many European yachts. For one thing, the ultra-low side rails on the flybridge make this a very insecure place to be when the weather gets rough. And secondly, the engineroom—accessed from the cockpit lazarette—is just too tight. Standard features include wide side decks, molded flybridge steps, a spacious aft deck with twin transom doors, a swim platform, and a large foredeck sun pad. An excellent performer with 390hp Cats, the Azimut 42 will cruise in the high 20s and reach a top speed of 32–33 knots.

See Page 668 For Price Data

Length	43'4"	Fuel	317 gals.
Beam	13'6"	Water	132 gals.
Draft	3'5"	Headroom	6'4"
Weight	24,000#	Hull Type	Deep-V
Clearance	14'6"	Deadrise Aft	17°

Azimut 43 Flybridge

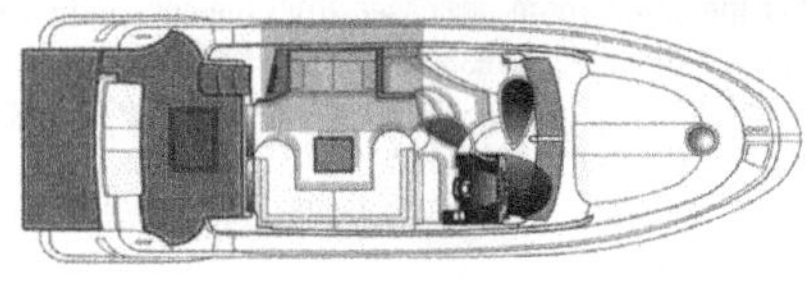

Sleek and powerful, the 43 Flybridge took Azimut styling to the next level when she was introduced in 2007. This is a relatively small yacht by European standards but there's nothing small about the impression she makes to anyone who steps aboard. With her luxury-class accommodations and spacious flybridge, this is a yacht meant for cruising in the fast lane. A lavish main salon dominates the galley-down interior of the 43 whose tiered windows offer truly panoramic outside views. Headroom at the lower helm position is tight, but most 43s sold into the American market will likely be operated from the flybridge so that's probably not a serious issue. Both staterooms are roomy and comfortable, and both heads are fitted with separate stall showers. Note the big opening port over the galley counter—nice touch. For a 43-footer, the flybridge is huge with wraparound lounge seating fit for a small crowd. Additional features include an extended teak bathing platform, cockpit table with chairs, bow thruster, and a huge foredeck sun pad. On the downside, the engineroom is a seriously tight fit. Cummins 480hp diesels cruise the Azimut 43 at a respectable 24–26 knots (about 30 knots top).

See Page 668 For Price Data

Length	42'4"	Fuel	290 gals.
Beam	13'10"	Water	132 gals.
Draft	4'2"	Waste	40 gals.
Weight	30,000#	Hull Type	Deep-V
Clearance	NA	Deadrise Aft	21°

Azimut 43S

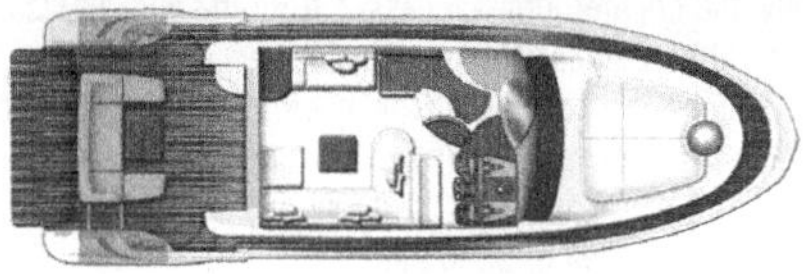

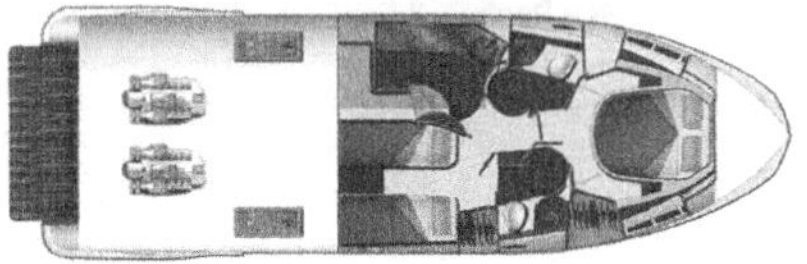

The stunning Azimut 43S is notable not just for her leading-edge styling or acclaimed interior, but also because she was the first Azimut model to incorporate pod drives as standard equipment. That alone gave her a performance (and economy) edge on most competitive sportyachts of her day—an advantage that proved short-lived, however, as pod drives are rapidly taking over the market these days. Azimuts have always been noted for their designer interiors so it's no surprise that the accommodations aboard the 43S are both lavish and tasteful. Tiered windows and a huge power sunroof bathe the salon in copious natural lighting. Both staterooms are roomy and comfortable (note the hullside windows in the guest cabin), and both heads are fitted with separate stall showers. Note the big opening port over the galley counter. Additional features include a U-shaped cockpit lounge, hydraulic swim platform, and a big foredeck sun pad. Triple hatches provide good (but not great) engine access. Volvo 370hp IPS diesels—small for a boat this size—cruise efficiently at 24–25 knots. Later models with Volvo 435hp IPS drives cruise at 30 knots.

See Page 668 For Price Data

Length	43'10"	Fuel	290 gals.
Beam	13'10"	Water	132 gals.
Draft	3'9"	Waste	35 gals.
Weight	28,000#	Hull Type	Modified-V
Clearance	16'2"	Deadrise Aft	14°

Azimut 46 Flybridge

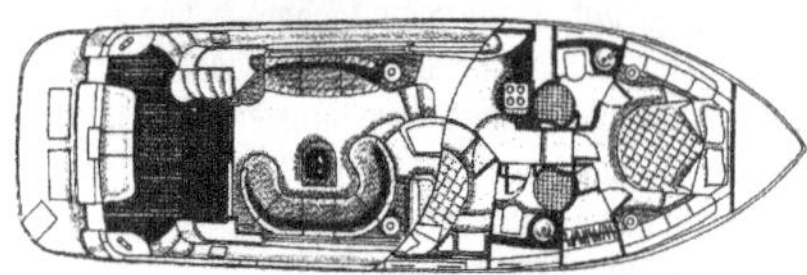
2-Stateroom Interior

3-Stateroom Interior

With its elliptical, electrically operated windows, recessed salon skylights and futuristic profile, the Azimut 46 remains as stylish today as she was at her introduction in 1997. Like her predecessors in the Azimut fleet, the 46 is built on a fully cored deep-V hull with propeller tunnels to reduce draft. Her two-stateroom floorplan is notable for its comfort and meticulous workmanship. The salon is an ultra-stylish entertaining area surrounded by vast amounts of window space and beautiful high-gloss cherry woodwork. Typical of European yachts, the galley is set below the salon level where it's hidden from view. The forward stateroom is particularly appealing with its walk-in wardrobe and opening windows (rather than portlights). A pair of sliding glass doors open to the cockpit where molded steps ascend to the spacious, low-profile flybridge. Note that the engineroom, accessed from the cockpit lazarette, is a tight fit. Additional features include circular flybridge settees*f*, a huge swim platform, anchor-wash system, and bow thruster. Twin 435hp Cat diesels cruise in the low 20s (27–28 knots top). Optional 455hp Cats will run a knot or two faster. A hugely popular yacht, over 350 were sold.

See Page 668 For Price Data

Length	49'0"	Fuel	449 gals.
Beam	14'4"	Water	132 gals.
Draft	3'4"	Headroom	6'5"
Weight	27,000#	Hull Type	Deep-V
Clearance	NA	Deadrise Aft	18°

Azimut 50 Flybridge

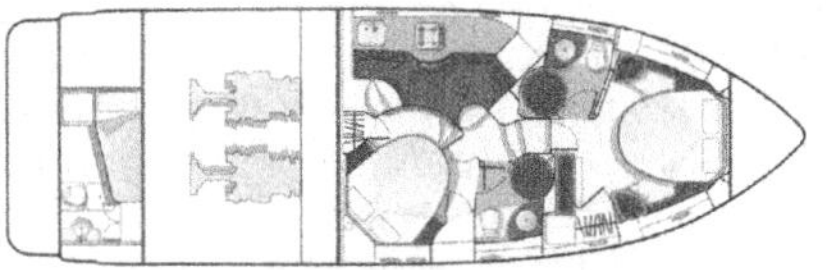
Two Staterooms

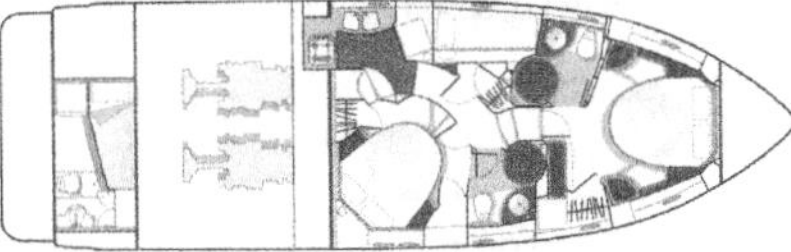
Three Staterooms

Introduced in 2004, the Azimut 50 is a high-style Italian cruising yacht (note the distinctive shark-fin windows) from a company that always seems to get it right. The 50 is a very polished and sophisticated yacht with sweeping lines, posh interior accommodations, and a comfortable ride. Her lavish two-stateroom interior—most 50-foot flybridge yachts have three—is arranged with facing sofas in the main cabin, an amidships master stateroom with diagonal queen bed, two full heads, and a spacious forward stateroom with an island berth. The galley size depends on the layout: it's very spacious in the two-stateroom configuration, but small when the third stateroom is added. While visibility from the lower helm is okay, the seating ergonomics are poor. Notably, Azimut's satin-finished cherry joinery is more subdued than the flashy high-gloss woodwork found in most late-model yachts. Additional features include a large cockpit lazarette, extended swim platform, spacious engine compartment, and a large flybridge with wraparound lounge seating aft of the helm. MAN 660hp—or Cat 715hp—diesels cruise in the mid-to-high 20s and reach a top speed of just over 30 knots.

See Page 668 For Price Data

Length	52'6"	Headroom	6'6"
Beam	14'11"	Fuel	581 gals.
Draft	3'11"	Water	132 gals.
Weight	46,000#	Hull Type	Modified-V
Clearance	18'5"	Deadrise Aft	13°

Azimut 54/58 Flybridge

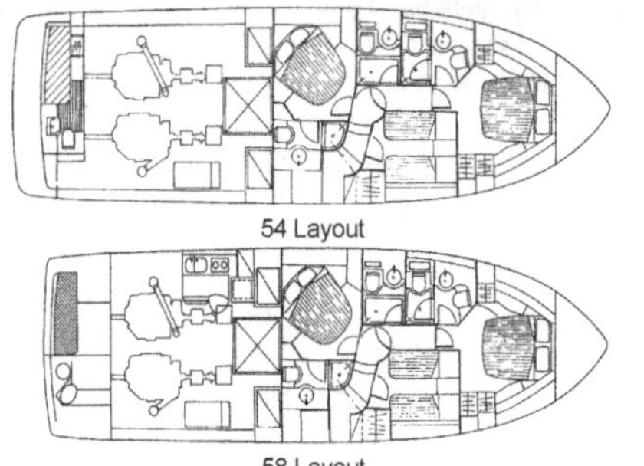
54 Layout

58 Layout

The Azimut 58 is an extended-platform version of the original Azimut 54 (1993–97). A good-selling model (over 150 were delivered during her production years), she's built on a deep-V hull with moderate beam and propeller pockets to reduce shaft angles and draft. While several floorplan options were offered, the "America" version has the galley, settee, and wet bar abaft the open main helm position and three staterooms and heads forward. (Note the fourth stateroom/crew quarters aft, beneath the cockpit, with a single berth and toilet.) The interior appointments are lavish with high-gloss lacquered woodwork, plush furnishings, and beautiful detailing on display throughout. An appealing feature of this yacht is her large aft deck with its teak sole and twin walk-throughs to the swim platform. The flybridge is very spacious with twin sun pads, a wet bar, and seating for a small crowd. At just under 50,000 pounds, the 58 is a relatively light boat for her size. She'll cruise at 23 knots with a pair of 600hp V-drive Cats (about 27 knots top), and optional 765hp MTUs cruise at a fast 28 knots and reach a top speed of 32–33 knots.

See Page 668 For Price Data

Length, 54	54'7"	Weight, 58	48,500#
Length, 58	57'8"	Fuel	688 gals.
Beam	15'1"	Water	238 gals.
Draft	4'1"	Hull Type	Deep-V
Weight, 54	44,092#	Deadrise Aft	18°

Azimut 55 Flybridge

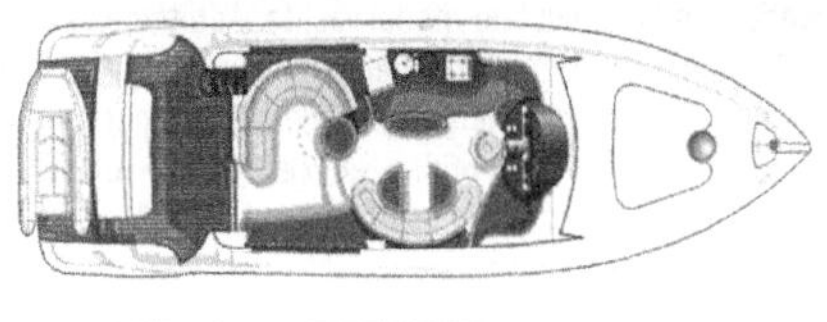

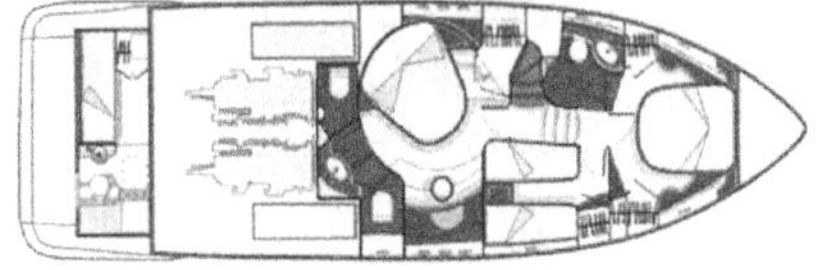

The Azimut 55 incorporates a styling scheme that sets her apart from previous Azimut designs. Gone are the elliptical cabin windows of previous years, replaced in the 55 by a pair of distinctive fin-shaped salon windows. Azimut designers also added three new vertical glass panels in the hullsides, a subtle innovation that introduces natural lighting into the master stateroom. Built on a good-running deep-V hull with prop pockets, the three-stateroom, two-head floorplan of the Azimut 55 is arranged with both the galley and dinette forward, on the pilothouse level. The inboard serving counter in the galley is a nice touch, and there's a bidet in the aft head compartment. What other aft-cockpit 55-footer offers the delights of a full-beam owner's cabin? (Note that the pilothouse offers neither direct bridge access nor a deck door.) The cockpit, shaded by the bridge overhang, has a teak sole and provides access to both the engineroom and aft crew quarters. Additional features include an extended swim platform, a well-arranged flybridge with dinghy storage aft, and power side windows at the lower helm. Twin 660hp (or 710hp) Cats cruise the Azimut 55 in the mid 20s and reach a top speed of around 30 knots.

See Page 668 For Price Data

Length	57'5"	Fuel	665 gals.
Beam	15'7"	Water	169 gals.
Draft	4'0"	Headroom	6'5"
Weight	44,600#	Hull Type	Deep-V
Clearance	16'2"	Deadrise Aft	16.6°

Azimut 62 Flybridge

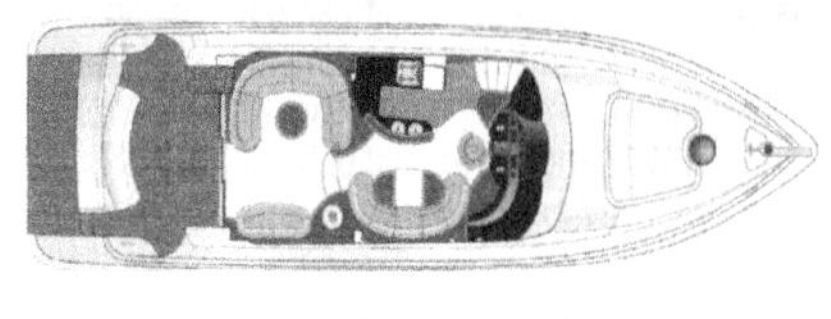

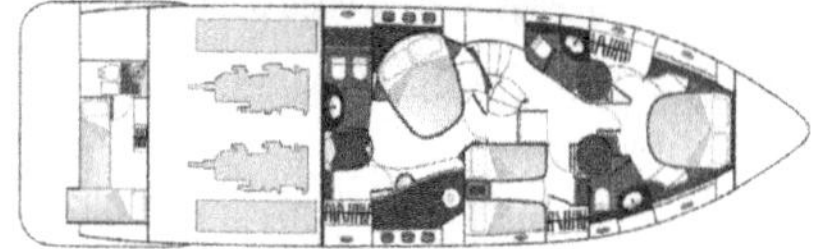

The Azimut 62 replaced the very popular 54/58 of which over 150 were built in eight years. Azimut has always enjoyed a reputation for innovative design; with the 62, the company produced a visually appealing yacht with practical accommodations and exceptional build quality. An expansive, fully integrated salon/dinette/helm area with posh furnishings and high-gloss cherry joinery dominates her opulent three-stateroom interior. The owner's suite is amidships, and all three heads contain a shower enclosure. Crew quarters astern are optional, and side visibility from the lower helm is restricted because of the thick mullions on the outboard windshield edges. The cockpit is simply and logically arranged—a transom gate to starboard opens to the swim platform, and a hatch in the floor leads down to a surprisingly spacious engineroom. Topside, the flybridge has an aft sundeck, barbecue, wet bar, sun pad, and an L-shaped settee. Additional features include decent side decks, a taller-than-average radar arch, foredeck sun pad, and a cockpit boarding platform. Twin 900hp MAN diesels cruise the Azimut 62 in the mid 20s and reach 30+ knots wide open.

See Page 668 For Price Data

Length	65'1"	Fuel	898 gals.
Beam	16'5"	Water	265 gals.
Draft	4'6"	Max Headroom	6'10"
Weight	60,400#	Hull Type	Deep-V
Clearance	19'9"	Deadrise Aft	17°

Azimut 62S

Introduced in 2006 to enthusiastic industry reviews, the Azimut 62S is a world-class sportyacht whose sleek Italian styling is matched by her lavish accommodations and thoughtful amenities. She may not be the largest yacht in the marina but few can match her for flat-out sex appeal. Built on a deep-V hull with distinctive square-shaped portholes and tiered side windows, the main deck layout includes a big salon with a power sunroof above. Offered with two or three staterooms, the two-stateroom floorplan replaces the second guest cabin with a versatile lower salon/lounge with self-contained galley. Both layouts feature a truly opulent amidships owner's suite with six hull windows on either side. Note that the island berth in the forward VIP cabin splits apart into V-berths—an innovative touch indeed. There's also a small crew cabin aft, next to the transom garage. Sliding glass doors open from the salon to the aft deck with its centerline sun pad, wet bar and grill. The garage can hold an inflatable or RIB. Finally, there's a cut out in the forward sun pad for your wine and champagne. A good open-water performer, Cat 1,015hp C-18 V-drive diesels cruise at 28 knots (low 30s wide open).

Two Staterooms

Three Staterooms

See Page 668 For Price Data

Length	62'6"	Fuel	713 gals.
Beam	16'1"	Water	238 gals.
Draft	5'0"	Waste	100 gals.
Weight	56,800#	Hull Type	Deep-V
Clearance	NA	Deadrise Aft	19°

Azimut 68 Plus

Beautifully styled and impeccably detailed, the Azimut 68 Plus achieves an impressive balance of advanced engineering, luxurious accommodations and superb open-water performance. Indeed, the palatial interior of the 68 Plus is nothing short of spectacular in its execution. The salon, with its lacquered cherry woodwork, sweeping curves, and plush furnishings is overwhelming in both size and comfort. The full-beam master stateroom—with unique vertical hull windows—is like a hotel suite, and each of the three guest cabins has a private head. (Note that the largest head is down a few steps from the salon where it doubles as a day head.) On deck, the cockpit has plenty of lounging space and a bridge overhang provides protection from the weather. Additional features include sliding deck doors, raised bulwarks, a huge foredeck sun pad and a big anchor locker with a chainwash. Like most Italian yachts, the engineroom and crew quarters are small and both helms of the 68 suffer from limited visibility. Built on a modified-V hull with propeller tunnels, twin 1,150 MTUs cruise the Azimut 68 Plus at 26–28 knots and reach a top speed of 30+ knots.

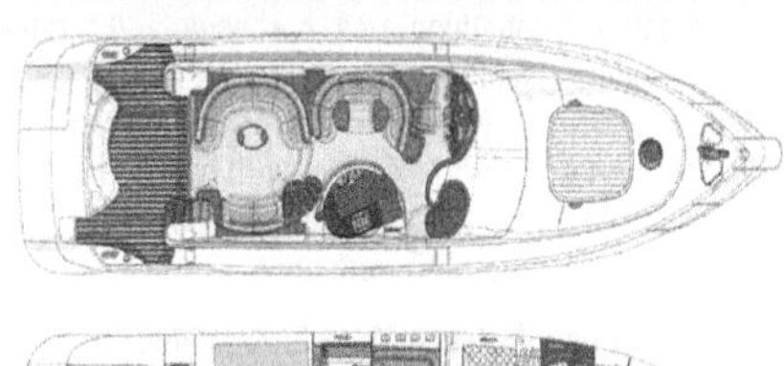

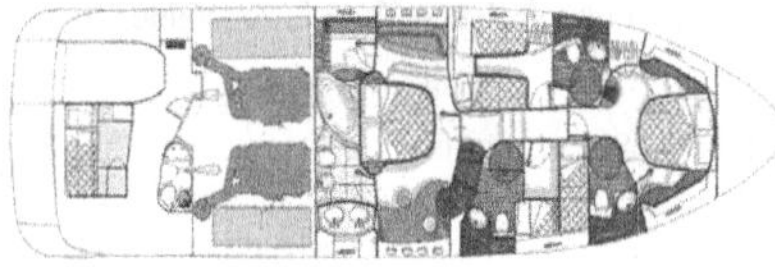

Not Enough Resale Data to Set Values

Length Overall	70'10"	Fuel	1,268 gals.
Beam	17'8"	Water	317 gals.
Draft	5'5"	Waste	66 gals.
Weight	80,000#	Hull Type	Modified-V
Clearance	23'6"	Deadrise Aft	16°

Azimut 68S

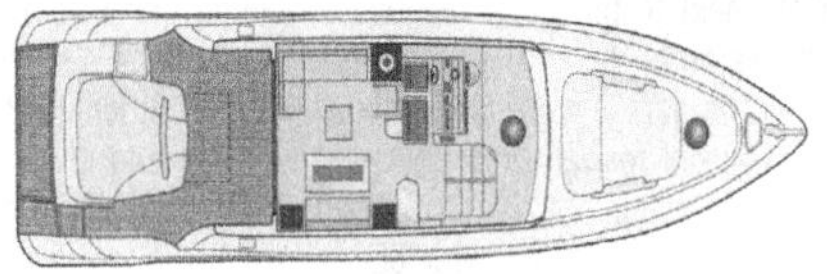

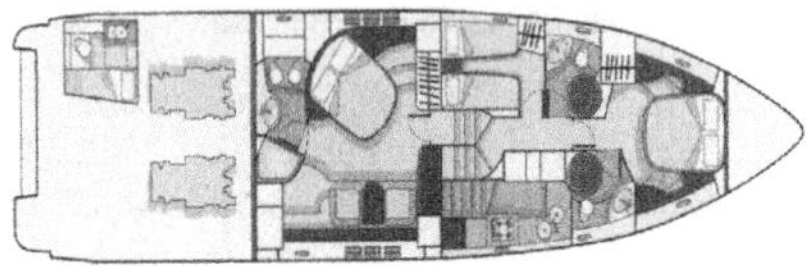

Azimut pushed the styling envelope in a big way in 2005 with the introduction of the 68S. She was, as one writer called her, a "strikingly different 68-footer," the company's first new express in 20 years. Built on a modified-V hull with distinctive square-shaped portholes and tiered side windows, the main deck layout features a spacious, single-level salon with a deluxe entertainment center and an enormous sunroof above. There are three staterooms on the lower level including a full-beam amidships master with king bed and port lights on either side. Next forward to port is the guest cabin with twin berths and a full bathroom which doubles as a day head. The VIP is furthest forward with an island queen berth and private head and shower. There's also a small crew cabin aft, next to the transom garage. Sliding glass doors open from the salon to the aft deck with its huge centerline sun pad, wet bar and grill. You can board from a hydraulic passerelle or from port and starboard boarding gates in the transom. The compact engineroom is accessed through an aft deck hatch. Note the teak hydraulic lift/swim platform. MTU 1,360hp V-drive diesels cruise at a fast 30 knots (33–35 knots top).

See Page 668 For Price Data

Length	68'0"	Fuel	845 gals.
Beam	17'1"	Water	251 gals.
Draft	5'2"	Waste	88 gals.
Weight	72,500#	Hull Type	Modified-V
Clearance	NA	Deadrise Aft	15°

Azimut 70 SeaJet

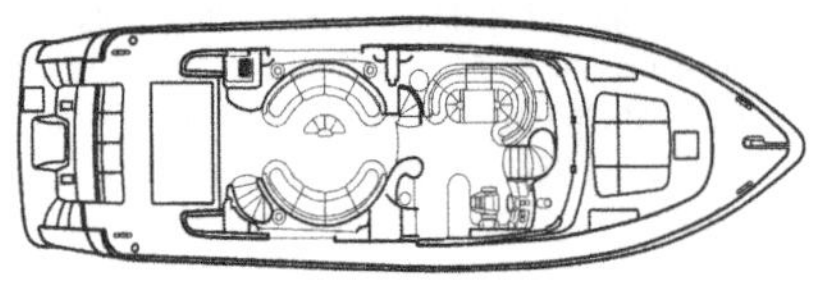

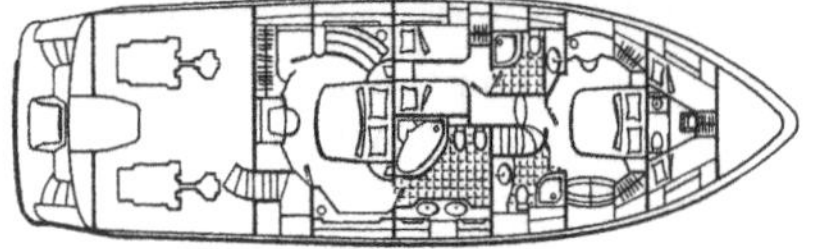

Those who are drawn to the rakish styling and flowing curves of Italian-built yachts will find much to admire in the Azimut 70 SeaJet. With her aggressive profile, sweptback windshield, and distinctive elliptical side windows, the SeaJet seemed years ahead of her U.S counterparts in the luxury motor yacht market. Built on a high-performance deep-V hull with prop pockets, the Azimut 70's engineroom is aft—an unusual configuration in a yacht this size—where V-drives are used to deliver the power. The SeaJet's gorgeous three-stateroom, galley-up interior is a rich blend of lacquered cherry woodwork, designer fabrics, and custom-crafted hardware throughout. The extended flybridge shelters the aft deck where a table seats eight, and a transom garage (with a winch) houses a PWC. The flybridge is loaded with amenities including a big curved settee, sunbathing area, barbecue, and a retractable dinghy davit. Standard features include a deck access door at the lower helm, a well-arranged engineroom, crew quarters forward, and a bow thruster. A superb performer with twin V-drive 1,150hp MTUs, the SeaJet will cruise at a steady 24 knots (28–29 knots top). A popular model, about 40 were built.

Not Enough Resale Data to Set Values

Length Overall	70'0"	Clearance	20'2"
Length WL	67'6"	Fuel	1,190 gals.
Beam	18'3"	Water	398 gals.
Draft	5'6"	Hull Type	Deep-V
Weight	108,000#	Deadrise Aft	18°

Azimut 78 Ultra

1994–98

A striking yacht with her aggressive profile and classic Italian lines, the Azimut 78 Ultra is a finely crafted production motor yacht whose lively performance comes as a surprise considering her size and displacement. The dominant feature of the 78 Ultra are her elliptical cabin windows, a styling feature incorporated into several other Azimut models during the late 1990s. Too, the flybridge is wider than usual thanks to an extension of the deck surface out over the side decks. Several floorplans were offered for the 78 Ultra including an "American" version with four staterooms (not counting the forward crew quarters). The galley is completely separated from the salon and wheelhouse. There's a formal dining area in the spacious salon, and wide side decks lead to the foredeck sunning area. Additional features include a rich cherrywood interior, a large aft deck with an eight-place dining table, teak decks, a storage garage, and inside access to the flybridge. Built to ABS standards, the Azimut 78 Ultra will cruise at 23 knots with twin 1,150hp MTUs, and she'll reach a top speed of 26–27 knots. Over 45 of these yachts were built during her production run.

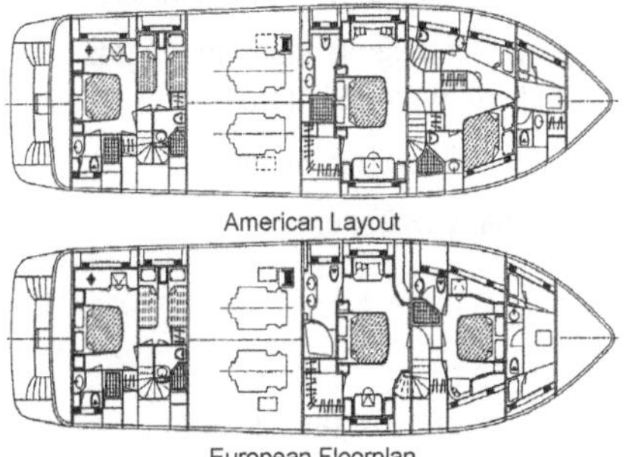

American Layout

European Floorplan

Not Enough Resale Data to Set Values

Length	78'0"	Fuel	1,546 gals.
Beam	19'5"	Water	412 gals.
Draft	5'8"	Headroom	6'6"
Weight	125,400#	Hull Type	Deep-V
Clearance	NA	Deadrise Aft	18°

Azimut 80 Carat

2001–06

Beautiful styling, elegant accommodations, and outstanding performance define the Azimut 80, a high-end luxury yacht whose "dorsal fin" windows and vertical hull ports are notably distinctive design elements. The main deck opens into a spacious and impeccably styled salon with facing settees, high-gloss cherrywood joinery and luxurious furnishings. A formal dining area is forward, opposite the narrow galley, and there are four staterooms and heads on the lower level including a full-beam master. Note that twin garages in the transom of the Azimut 80 have pushed the crew quarters forward of the engineroom, which explains why the staterooms seem rather compact for a yacht this size. The engineroom, reached from either the crew quarters or the swim platform, is unusually spacious, and V-drives allow the motors to be set well aft in the hull. The flybridge is a wide-open entertainment platform with a wet bar, barbecue, seating for ten and space for a tender. Additional features include a protected aft deck, galley access to the crew quarters, a huge foredeck sun pad, and teak decks. Twin 1,300hp MTU diesels cruise the Azimut 80 at 23 knots (25–26 knots top), and 1,500 MTUs cruise a knot or two faster.

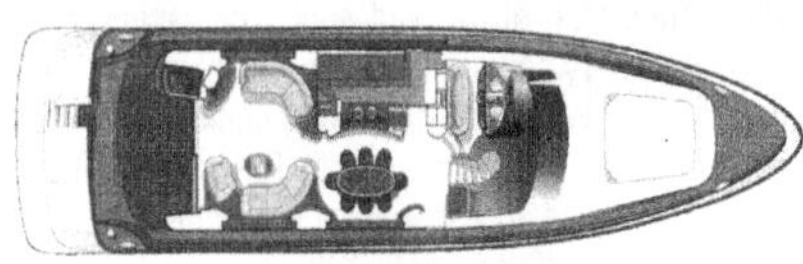

Deckhouse Layout

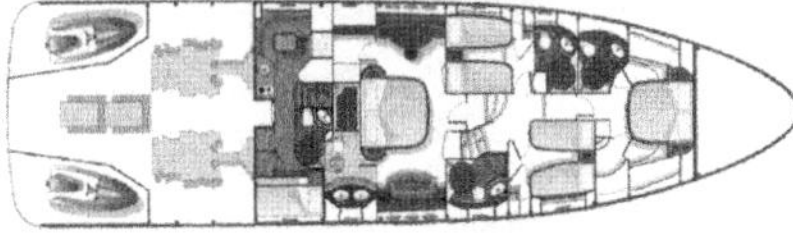

Lower Level Floorplan

Not Enough Resale Data to Set Values

Length	78'8"	Fuel	1,584 gals.
Beam	19'0"	Water	396 gals.
Draft	5'11"	Headroom	6'6"
Weight	114,000#	Hull Type	Modified-V
Clearance	NA	Deadrise Aft	13°

Back Cove

Quick View

- Founded in 2003, Back Cove Yachts is a sister company to Maine-based Sabre Yachts.
- Back Coves were originally marketed as an alternative to Sabre's premium series of Downeast performance trawlers and cruisers.
- The company's first model, the Back Cove 29, enjoyed considerable market success thanks to her classic Downeast styling, economical operation, and versatile layout.
- Current Black Cove models are offered in hardtop and express versions in lengths from 30 to 37 feet. The company delivered its 500th boat in the fall of 2012.
- Back Coves are built in a 240,000-square-foot facility in Rockland, Maine.
- A Back Cove blog for owners can be found at the company website.

Back Cove Yachts • Rockland, ME • www.backcoveyachts.com

Back Cove 26

Building on the success of the Back Cove 29 (2004–09), the Back Cove 26 is a scaled-down version of 29, but with a pipe-supported hardtop (optional) rather than the 29's integrated hardtop. Like all Back Cove models, the 26 combines classic Downeast styling with sophisticated construction and many quality features. "Simplicity" is a word often used to described the 26; the layout is nothing unusual, but her wide 9-foot, 4-inch beam results in considerably more cockpit and cabin space than one expects to find in a 26-foot boat. Port and starboard molded steps in the cockpit lead to the side and fore deck, and the large (and high) windshield has opening side panels for ventilation. Below, the forward dinette converts to sleep two comfortably. Aft of the dinette on the starboard side is a full head with shower, and on the port side is a small galley with refrigerator, stove, and sink. The cabin, an appealing blend of cherry joinery and premium hardware, sports a handsome teak-and-holly sole. Wide side decks and cockpit jump seats are a plus, and a bow thruster was standard. The entire helm deck lifts on gas struts for engine access. Cruise efficiently at 22 knots (mid 20s top) with a single 260hp Yanmar diesel.

See Page 668 For Price Data

Length	26'6"	Water	30 gals.
Beam	9'4"	Waste	30 gals.
Draft	2'6"	Headroom	5'7"
Weight	8,500#	Hull Type	Modified-V
Fuel	100 gals.	Deadrise Aft	14°

Back Cove 29

2004–09

The Back Cove 29 is notable in that she was the first of what soon became a series of Back Cove models produced in recent years by Sabre Yachts. With her Downeast lines and single-diesel power, the Back Cove 29 combined beauty and simplicity at a price competitive with similar Downeast boats her size from other manufacturers. Built on a modified-V with Divinycell coring and a prop pocket to reduce the shaft angle, her modest 2-foot, 6-inch draft allows the 29 to operate in unusually shallow water. At the semi-enclosed helm, sliding side windows and an opening center windshield section provide ventilation on hot days. Storage boxes are beneath both helm chairs, and an L-lounge to port on the bridge deck seats three. Note that a center hatch in the bridge deck sole lifts for engine access. Below, the Back Cove's well-appointed cabin is accented with cherry cabinets, ash ceiling strips, and a teak-and-holly sole. The galley is to port, head to starboard, and the V-berth is forward—practical accommodations indeed for two adults. Wide side decks are a plus, and so are the sturdy bow rails. A bow thruster was standard. Cruise efficiently at 20 knots (26–27 knots top) with a single Yanmar 315hp diesel inboard.

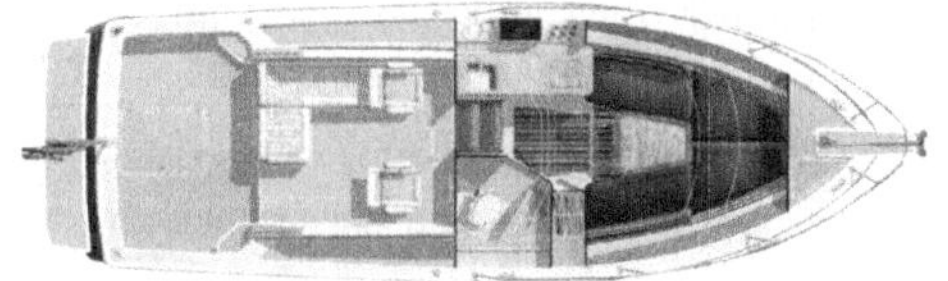

See Page 668 For Price Data

Length	29'5"	Fuel	150 gals.
Beam	10'5"	Water	30 gals.
Draft	2'6"	Waste	30 gals.
Weight	10,000#	Hull Type	Modified-V
Clearance	8'4"	Deadrise Aft	16°

Back Cove 33/34

2007–Current

The Back Cove 33 (called the Back Cove 34 since 2012) is a practical and stylish Downeast cruiser whose single-diesel efficiency, versatile layout, and leading-edge construction make her one of the more appealing boats in her class. Like all Back Cove models to date, the 33 rides on a vacuum-bagged, PVC-cored hull with a reverse transom and a shallow prop pocket. The layout is as simple as it is elegant; a large bench seat in the cockpit and raised dinette on the semi-enclosed bridge deck provide seating for family and friends. Note that the in-line galley is positioned behind the helm, opposite the dinette, rather than in the cabin. The entire bridge deck lifts on hydraulic rams for engine access. Belowdecks is a large and comfortable V-berth forward, convertible L-settee with a inlaid teak table to port, and a large head with separate stall shower to starboard. (Note that a queen berth forward is standard in the 34 model.) The cabin is finished with varnished cherry joinery, premium hardware, and an elegant teak and holly sole. Wide side decks are a plus, and a Stidd helm chair and bow/stern thrusters are standard. Cruise at 20 knots with 435hp Cummins—or 440hp Yanmar—diesel (mid 20s top).

Back Cove 33

Back Cove 34

See Page 668 For Price Data

Length	34'4"	Fuel	185 gals.
Beam	12'0"	Water	80 gals.
Draft	3'1"	Waste	40 gals.
Weight	16,000#	Hull Type	Modified-V
Clearance	NA	Deadrise Aft	14°

Bayliner

Quick View

- Bayliner was a tiny Arlington, WA, builder of runabouts when purchased by Orin Edson in 1965.
- Under Edson's leadership the company established the assembly-line production methods that enabled Bayliner to offer its products at prices other manufacturers were unable to match.
- By the mid 1980s Bayliner had grown to become the largest builder of recreational pleasure boats in America.
- Bayliner was purchased in 1986 by industry-giant Brunswick Corporation.
- Bayliner products have always been known for affordable pricing although quality-control standards were the subject of controversy in past years.
- With several plants producing some 3,000 boats annually, Bayliner in the year 2000 was by far the largest builder of production boats in the world.
- In 2002 Bayliner's larger cruising yachts were spun off to create Meridian Yachts—a decision that may have been related to the company's ongoing reputation for marginal quality.
- A Bayliner Owner's Club can be found at baylinerownersclub.org/forum.

Bayliner Boats • www.bayliner.com

Bayliner 275 SB Cruiser

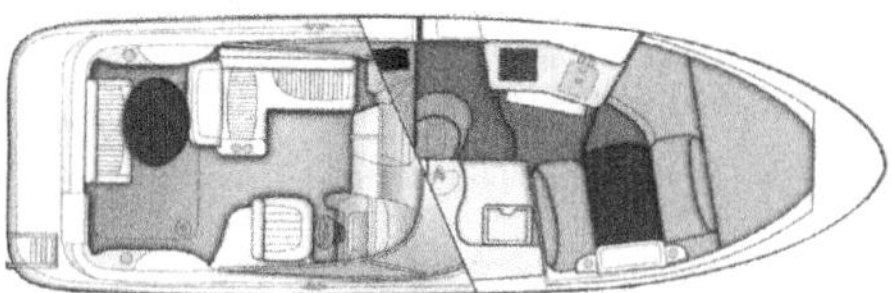

This affordable family cruiser combines sporty styling with the spaciousness of a broad, 9-foot, 5-inch beam and the economy of a single, small-block engine. There's a lot to like about this boat—while Bayliners are still priced at the lower end of the market they're no longer the cheap, poorly finished Bayliners of old. The chief attribute of the 275 is space, and plenty of it. Indeed, her cockpit and interior dimensions are larger by far than many of her 27-foot competitors. The midcabin layout is a model of space efficiency with the dinette cleverly integrated into the forward double berth. The galley is as big as you'll find in a boat this size with generous storage and enough counter space to actually be useful. A curtain offers a bit of privacy for those in the aft berth, and the standup head includes a marine toilet as well as a shower. Topside, the roomy cockpit of the 275 can seat six passengers without being crowded. Standard features include a transom shower, carry-on cooler, transom live well, and a removable cockpit table. Like most trailerable cruisers, the Bayliner 275's modest fuel capacity limits her range. Expect a top speed of close to 30 knots with a single 250hp MerCruiser engine.

See Page 668 For Price Data

Length	26'7"	Fuel	77 gals.
Beam	9'5"	Water	31 gals.
Draft, Up	1'9"	Waste	20 gals.
Draft, Down	3'2"	Hull Type	Modified-V
Weight	6,485#	Deadrise Aft	15°

Bayliner 2855 Ciera Sunbridge

1994–99

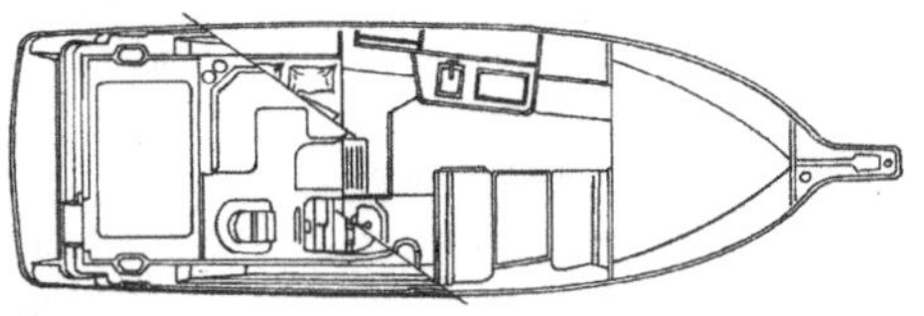

Last in a series of successful Bayliner 2855 Ciera Sunbridge models, this version is actually a makeover of the previous 2855 Ciera Sunbridge (1991–93) with improved styling, a revised interior (bigger galley), and increased storage space. The hull is basically the same as the earlier 2855 with an extra inch of beam (according to the factory specs), and slightly more deadrise at the transom. While she's definitely on the light side compared with similar boats her size, the 2855 rides quite well in a chop thanks to her deep-V hull design. The midcabin floorplan is arranged in the traditional manner with double berths fore and aft, compact galley, and a booth-style dinette that converts to sleep two. Privacy curtains separate both sleeping areas, and headroom is adequate throughout most of the cabin. Topside, a big U-shaped lounge (with a removable table) is opposite the helm. Lacking side decks, a windshield walk-through provides access to the foredeck. Additional features include a slide-out jump seat behind the companion lounge, a transom door, a sport arch, and colorful hull graphics. A light boat with modest fuel capacity, a single 300hp sterndrive will cruise at 20 knots (30+ wide open).

See Page 668 For Price Data

Length w/Pulpit	30'3"	Clearance	8'6"
Beam	9'7"	Fuel	109 gals.
Draft, Up	1'8"	Water	33 gals.
Draft, Down	3'4"	Hull Type	Deep-V
Weight	6,510#	Deadrise Aft	22°

Bayliner 2855 Ciera SB; 285 SB Cruiser

2000–12

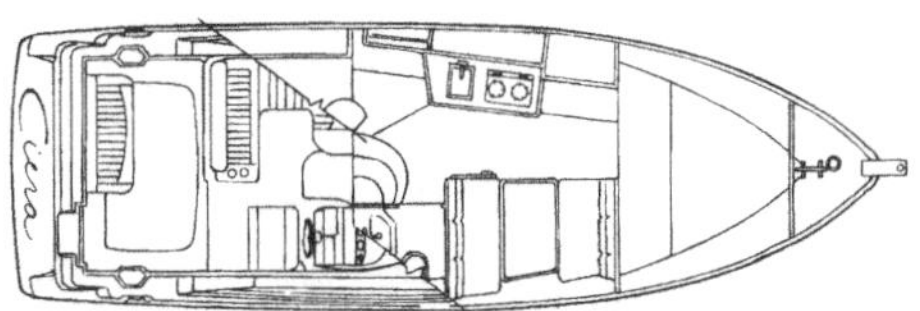

The Bayliner 285 (called the 2855 Ciera Sunbridge in 2000–02) is similar to previous 28-foot Bayliner express boats in her contemporary styling, roomy accommodations, and a very affordable price. Built on a solid fiberglass deep-V hull with a relatively wide beam, the midcabin floorplan of the 255 is arranged with a V-berth forward with privacy curtain and the owner's stateroom aft with a solid privacy door and plenty of storage. The dinette will seat four comfortably, and three overhead deck hatches provide ventilation and additional lighting. A full galley, standup head, and generous storage round out the interior. In the cockpit, Bayliner introduced a unique L-shaped lounge seat in the 285 that converts into a sun pad or an aft-facing bench seat. A fold-down bench seat is installed at the transom, and a transom door opens to an extended swim platform. Lacking side decks, an opening panel in the windshield provides access to the foredeck. Among several engine options, a single 300hp MerCruiser sterndrive will cruise the Bayliner 285 at 20 knots and reach a top speed of just over 30 knots.

See Page 668 For Price Data

Length	28'7"	Fuel	89 gals.
Beam	9'11"	Water	28 gals.
Draft, Up	2'1"	Waste	30 gals.
Draft, Down	3'5"	Hull Type	Modified-V
Weight	8,056#	Deadrise Aft	17°

Bayliner 2859 Super Classic; 2859 Ciera Express

1993–2002

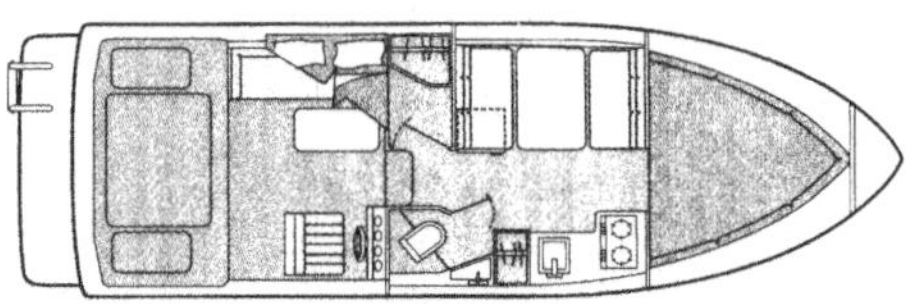

Originally called the 2859 Super Classic (1993–95), the Bayliner 2859 Ciera Cruiser is a conservatively styled hardtop cruiser whose modest price and practical layout had great appeal to budget-minded buyers. The layout of this boat is similar to most hardtop models her size with the helm and sofa on the bridge deck and the dinette, galley and V-berth on the lower level. What sets the 2859 apart from the norm is her amidships berth (located beneath the bridge deck), an arrangement that brings the total sleeping capacity to six. A privacy curtain separates the forward berth from the salon, and there's a handheld shower in the head compartment. While the cockpit of the 2859 Express is fairly small, it's still large enough for a couple of light-tackle anglers or a couple of folding deck chairs. Additional features include a well-equipped galley with plenty of storage, a swim platform and boarding ladder, and a transom door. Among several sterndrive engine options offered over the years, a single 310hp MerCruiser will cruise at an economical 22 knots and reach a top speed of around 30 knots. Note the modest fuel capacity.

See Page 668 For Price Data

Length	27'9"	Fuel	102 gals.
Beam	9'9"	Water	36 gals.
Draft, Up	1'7"	Waste	30 gals.
Draft, Down	3'0"	Hull Type	Modified-V
Weight	7,597#	Deadrise Aft	15°

Bayliner 288 Classic Cruiser

1996–2005

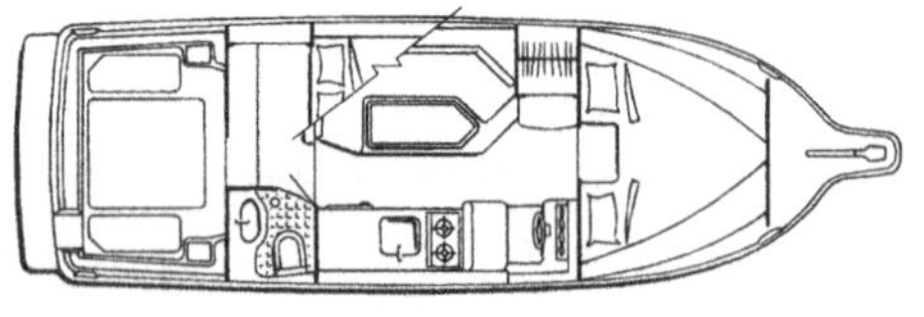

Called the 2858 Ciera Command Bridge from 1996–2002, the popular Bayliner 288 Classic Cruiser has the distinction of being one of the smaller flybridge cruisers built in recent years. The reason there are so few under-30-foot flybridge boats on the market is easily understood: the added weight of two or three adults on the flybridge of any small boat increases rolling and detracts from overall stability. With her wide beam and small bridge, however, the 288 Classic offsets this problem to a large extent. For a 28-footer, the accommodations are impressive. The layout includes a private midcabin berth below the raised salon settee, a V-berth forward, an enclosed head and shower aft, and a full galley in the salon. A lower helm is standard, and large cabin windows and excellent headroom add considerably to the sense of space. Like all Bayliners, the detailing and joinery leave a lot to be desired but the low price will certainly appeal to budget-minded boaters. Note that the fuel tank is small and the side decks are narrow. A single 310hp MerCruiser sterndrive engine provides a cruising speed of around 22 knots and a top speed of 32–33 knots.

See Page 669 For Price Data

Length w/Pulpit	30'7"	Fuel	113 gals.
Beam	10'0"	Water	34 gals.
Draft, Up	1'8"	Waste	26 gals.
Draft, Down	3'2"	Hull Type	Modified-V
Weight	6,100#	Deadrise Aft	18°

Bayliner 300/315 SB Cruiser

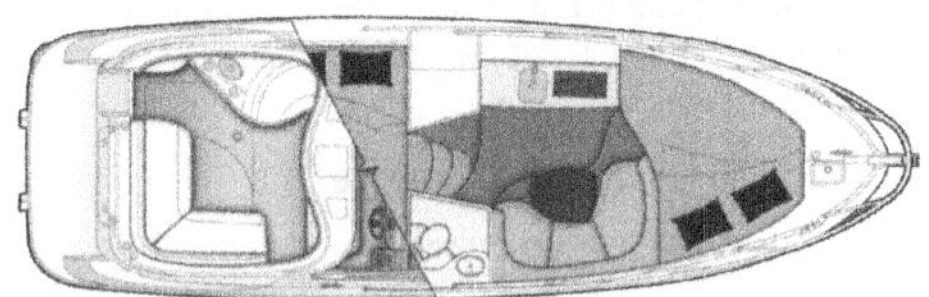

With her sleek lines and affordable price, this versatile express (called the Bayliner 300 SB Cruiser in 2008; 315 SB Cruiser since 2009) targets entry-level boaters with an eye for value. The market for family cruisers in this size range is extremely competitive. No surprise, then, that Bayliner designers strove to include a host of features into this boat to set her apart from the pack. Perhaps her most notable attribute is a surprisingly roomy interior, a feat made possible by carrying the beam well forward in the hull. While it's not uncommon to see a 30-footer sleep six, it's often at the expense of galley and seating space. Not so on the 315, especially when the dinette table is removed and stowed. Overall, the accommodations are comfortable if not spacious, which is more than can be said of many cruisers her size. Note that the midcabin berth has a fixed door rather than a curtain—definitely a plus. Topside, the helm is well arranged with tiered gauges and dash space for flush-mounting two small video displays. The overhead arch has a bimini with boot, and standard camper canvass converts to cockpit into a sleeping area when the weather is warm. Twin 260hp MerCruiser I/Os cruise at 25 knots (mid 30s top).

See Page 668 For Price Data

Length	30'6"	Fuel	120 gals.
Beam	10'0"	Water	33 gals.
Draft, Up	2'1"	Waste	30 gals.
Draft, Down	3'4"	Hull Type	Modified-V
Weight	9,098#	Deadrise Aft	18°

Bayliner 3055 SB Cruiser; 305 SB Cruiser

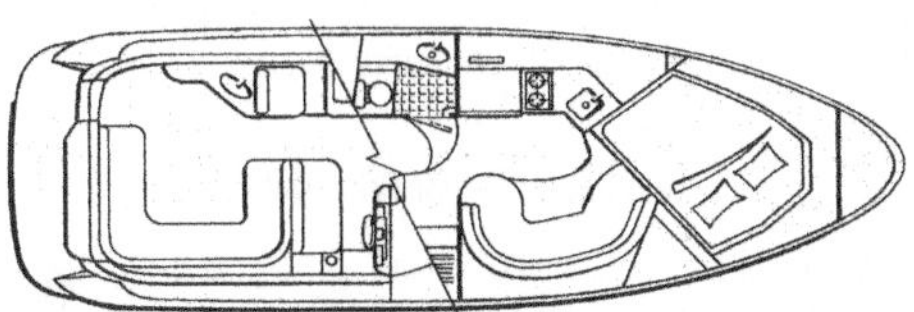

The affordably priced Bayliner 305 (called the 3055 Ciera Sunbridge from 1999–2002) is an entry-level family cruiser with several very attractive features. With a wide 11-foot beam, the 305 is a roomy boat both inside and out, and while the mediocre finish reflects her low price, there is still much to admire from the standpoint of comfort and practicality. Headroom—well over 6 feet—is excellent in this boat, and the generous beam results in a surprisingly expansive cabin layout. The midcabin floorplan is arranged in the conventional manner with double berths fore and aft, an enclosed head to port, adequate storage, and a well-equipped galley. In the cockpit, a U-shaped lounge features a removable table and converts to a sun pad. A wet bar/entertainment center is to port, and a transom door opens to the integral swim platform with its retractable swim ladder and built-in shower. Lacking side decks, a walk-through windshield provides access to the bow. A pair of 220hp MerCruisers sterndrives cruise in the low 20s (about 30 knots top), and later models with a pair of 300hp Mercs cruise in the high 20s and top out at over 40 knots.

See Page 5669 For Price Data

Length Overall	31'6"	Fuel	148 gals.
Beam	11'0"	Water	35 gals.
Draft, Up	1'9"	Waste	30 gals.
Draft, Down	2'9"	Hull Type	Modified-V
Weight	11,857#	Deadrise Aft	17°

Bayliner 325 SB Cruiser

2005–07

During her production years the Bayliner 325 was one of the best boating values in her class, combining a spacious cockpit and cabin with sporty styling and good open-water performance. The main cabin is big and open with a settee that wraps around the bow section creating seating for eight. The galley, on the starboard side, is equipped with a dual-voltage fridge, two-burner electric stove, microwave, and a porthole so the chef can see the water while preparing a meal. Behind the stairs is a large double berth with dressing seat, hanging locker and—for real privacy—a door rather than the ubiquitous draw curtain. The head is conveniently located close to the stairs, and features an electric toilet and hot shower. One of the standout features in this deep cabin is the tremendous amount of natural light that floods into the saloon through the side portholes and deck hatches. Topside, there are twin seats at the helm, a curved seat on the opposite side for the navigator, and a large, L-shape lounge aft. Additional features include a walk-through windshield, extended swim platform, tilt steering, and windlass. Cruise at 26–28 knots (around 40 top) with twin 320hp MerCruiser I/Os.

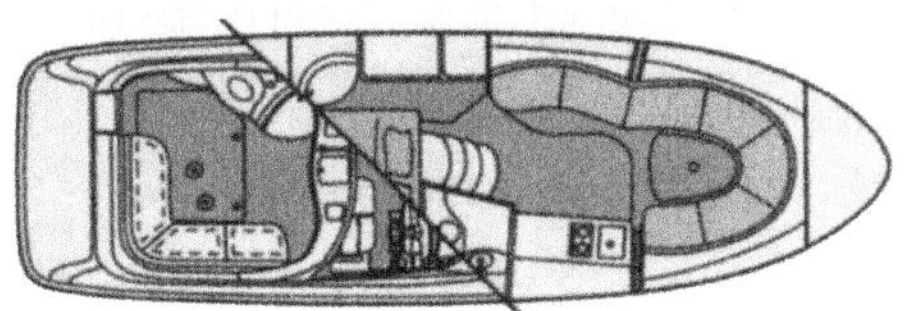

See Page 669 For Price Data

Length	35'0"	Fuel	175 gals.
Beam	11'6"	Water	31 gals.
Draft, Up	1'9"	Waste	30 gals.
Draft, Down	3'4"	Hull Type	Modified-V
Weight	11,319#	Deadrise Aft	18°

Bayliner 3255 Avanti Sunbridge

1995–99

Introduced in 1995 and remaining in production for the next four years, the Bayliner 3255 Avanti Sunbridge is a conservative family express whose major attractions were an affordable price and generous cabin accommodations. Built on a lightweight, solid fiberglass hull with a relatively wide beam and moderate transom deadrise, the reverse arch of the 3255 is her most prominent styling feature. The midcabin floorplan is arranged in the conventional manner with double berths fore and aft and a full galley, enclosed head and shower, convertible dinette, and a good-size hanging locker in the salon. (Note that an accordion pocket door separates the forward stateroom from the salon.) On deck, a U-shaped settee (with a removable table) is opposite the helm in the bi-level cockpit. The side decks are narrow and getting around the arch to access the side decks isn't easy. Additional features include a cockpit wet bar, transom door, integral bow pulpit, swim platform, and a foredeck sun pad. Optional 310hp MerCruiser sterndrives cruise the Bayliner 3255 Avanti Sunbridge at 19–20 knots and deliver top speeds of around 32 knots.

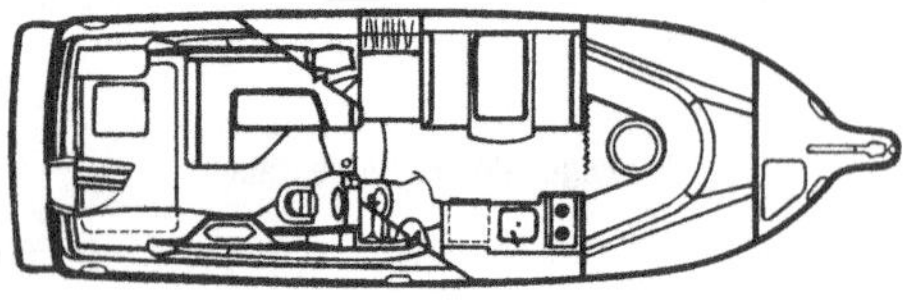

See Page 669 For Price Data

Length w/Pulpit	35'0"	Fuel	180 gals.
Hull Length	32'11"	Water	35 gals.
Beam	11'0"	Waste	30 gals.
Draft	3'0"	Hull Type	Modified-V
Weight	11,000#	Deadrise Aft	16°

Bayliner 3258 Command Bridge

1995–2000

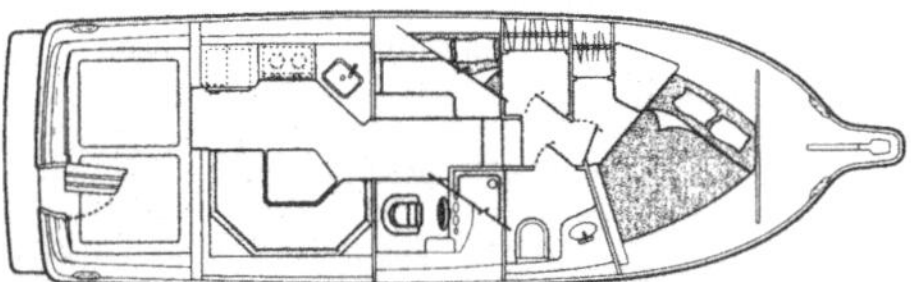

With her rakish lines and aggressive profile, the 3258 Command Bridge was an attractive choice for late 1990s Bayliner buyers looking for a spacious flybridge sedan at an affordable price. Like all Bayliner models of her era, she was built on a lightweight, solid fiberglass hull with moderate beam and transom deadrise. The cabin window treatment is very eurostyle—easily her most distinctive feature—and the small cockpit virtually guarantees an exceptionally roomy interior layout. The 3258's salon is split into two distinct areas. The forward section is a step up from the salon sole with a small settee opposite the helm. In the aft section of the salon, a U-shaped dinette faces the in-line galley with its generous counter space. The entrance to the aft cabin is forward, beneath the windshield, and the head (which has a separate stall shower) is under the lower helm console. Given the expansive interior dimensions, it's no surprise that the cockpit of the 3258 is small. Note too that the side decks are practically nonexistent. A radar arch, bow pulpit, and a transom door were standard. Twin 250hp MerCruiser I/Os cruise at 20–22 knots (high 20s top), and 310hp Mercs cruise at 25 knots (mid 30s top).

See Page 669 For Price Data

Length w/Platform	35'2"	Weight	10,230#
Hull Length	32'11"	Fuel	180 gals.
Beam	11'0"	Water	52 gals.
Draft, Up	2'0"	Hull Type	Modified-V
Draft, Down	3'3"	Deadrise Aft	17°

Bayliner 3270 Explorer; 3270/3288 Motor Yacht

1981–95

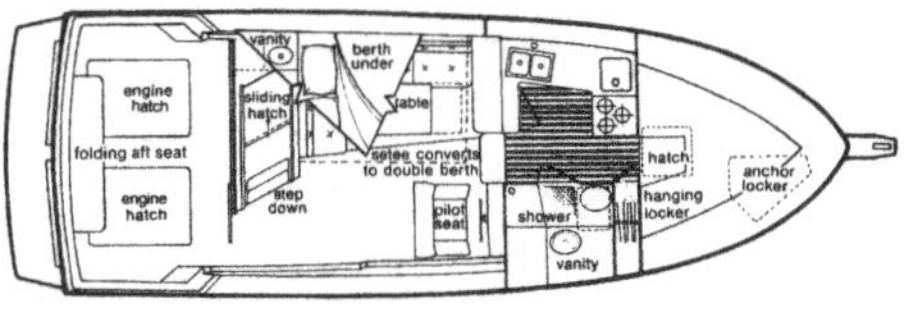

A popular model for many years and the all-time best-selling boat in her class, the Bayliner 3288 Motor Yacht was introduced back in 1981 as the 3270 Explorer. She became the Bayliner 3270 Motor Yacht in 1985, and evolved into the 3288 Motor Yacht in 1989. First marketed (in an era of escalating fuel prices) as an efficient family cruiser, the original flybridge was updated and a radar arch became standard in 1985. The midcabin floorplan of the 3270/3288 remained essentially unchanged over the years aside from minor cosmetic updates. A lower helm was standard, the salon is quite spacious with big wraparound cabin windows, and the private aft cabin extends beneath the elevated dinette in the salon. The cockpit is fitted with teak handrails, and the side decks are wide enough for easy access to the bow. The 3288's lightweight hull results in an extremely fuel-efficient package. The engine compartment, accessed via two cockpit hatches, is a tight fit. Early models with 110hp Hino diesels cruise at 12 knots, and later models with 150hp turbo Hinos cruise at 16–17 knots. A pair of 5.7-liter gas inboards cruise at 16–18 knots. Over 3,000 are said to have been sold.

See Page 669 For Price Data

Length Overall	32'1"	Fuel	200 gals.
Beam	11'6"	Water	65 gals.
Draft	2'11"	Waste	23 gals.
Weight	12,500#	Hull Type	Modified-V
Clearance	13'10"	Deadrise Aft	12°

Bayliner 3388 Motor Yacht

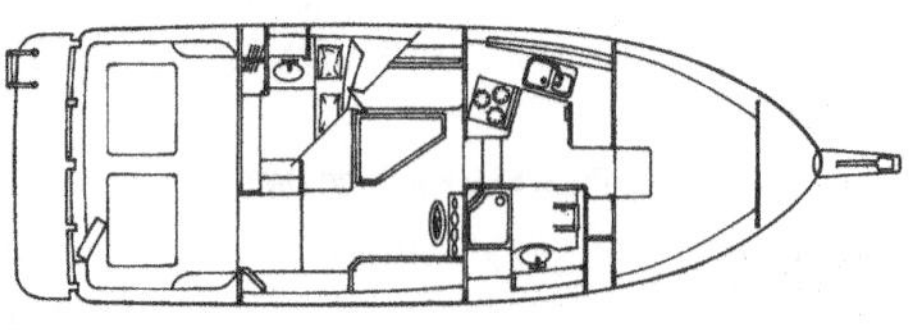

The Bayliner 3388 Motor Yacht was one of the most affordable twin-diesel family cruisers available during her production years. She's basically an updated version of the popular Bayliner 3288 MY (1981–95) with a fresh profile and several hull refinements. The midcabin interior of the 3388 is similar to her predecessor with the galley down and amidships guest cabin located beneath the elevated dinette. A lower helm was standard, and there's a separate stall shower in the head compartment. An accordion door provides privacy for the forward stateroom. If there's a downside to the 3388 it has to be the unusual salon arrangement; the staircase leading down to the midcabin, just inside the salon door, causes the dinette to be moved so far forward that it's hard to get between it and the lower helm chair. Consequently, the salon is far less spacious than one might expect in a 33-footer. Additional features include a low-profile sport arch, prop pockets, swim platform, and bow pulpit. Note that the cabin and flybridge are a single mold that, according to Bayliner, reduced problems with window leakage. Standard 260hp gas inboards cruise the Bayliner 3388 at 15–16 knots (mid 20s top).

See Page 669 For Price Data

Length	32'11"	Fuel	200 gals.
Beam	11'6"	Water	90 gals.
Draft	2'8"	Waste	30 gals.
Weight	15,500#	Hull Type	Modified-V
Clearance	13'6"	Deadrise Aft	6°

Bayliner 3488 Avanti Command Bridge

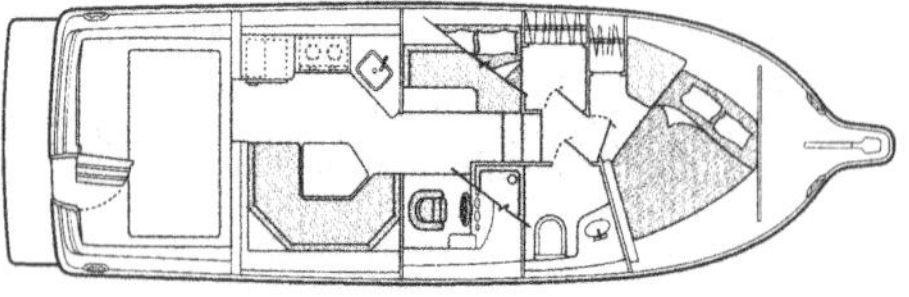

Produced for several years in the late 1990s, the Bayliner 3488 Avanti Command Bridge is a handsome and very spacious flybridge cruiser whose affordable price made her an appealing choice for many budget-minded buyers. Bayliner's production-line manufacturing process has always allowed the company to deliver a lot of boat for the money, and this was particularly true of the 3488—a design that undercut the competition by thousands of dollars. Built on a solid fiberglass modified-V hull, the Avanti's midcabin interior is arranged with two staterooms, one forward and the other tucked below the elevated settee opposite the lower helm. There's a separate stall shower in the head (a convenience not always found in a 34-footer), and the L-shaped galley in the salon provides plenty of counter space and storage. The Avanti's cockpit is large enough for a couple of deck chairs, and the flybridge has the helm forward with wraparound guest seating. Additional features include a molded bow pulpit, radar arch, and a swim platform. Standard 310hp MerCruiser gas inboards (with V-drives) will cruise the 3488 Avanti at 18 knots and reach a top speed of close to 30 knots.

See Page 669 For Price Data

Length Overall	36'7"	Fuel	180 gals.
Hull Length	34'4"	Water	52 gals.
Beam	11'0"	Waste	52 gals.
Draft	3'5"	Hull Type	Modified-V
Weight	12,549#	Deadrise Aft	17°

Bayliner 3488 Command Bridge

2001–02

The 3488 Command Bridge was the first boat built using Bayliner's modular production system, a process of assembling prebuilt modules—the engineroom, forward stateroom, and salon modules, etc.—into the hull. This construction process reduced production costs and, according to the Bayliner, provided a more precise fit with improved structural integrity. Built on a solid fiberglass hull with very modest deadrise and an integral swim platform, the 3488's conservative styling and practical midcabin floorplan make for an altogether pleasant and practical family cruiser. Both staterooms are fitted with double berths; a lower helm is optional; and a spacious galley with plenty of counter and storage space is to starboard in the salon. On deck, a flybridge overhang shades the small cockpit from the sun. Molded steps lead up to the flybridge, which is large for a 34-footer. Additional features include a stall shower in the head, a teak-and-holly galley sole, and a transom door. Standard 260hp MerCruiser gas inboards cruise at 14 knots (about 20 knots top), and optional 250hp Cummins diesels cruise at 18 knots and reach a top speed of 22–23 knots.

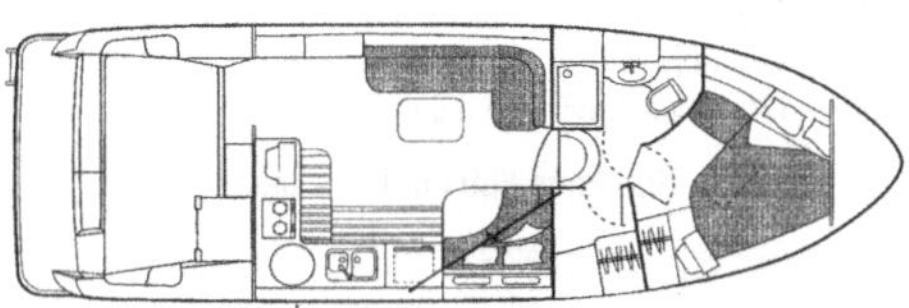

See Page 669 For Price Data

Length	35'0"	Fuel	224 gals.
Beam	11'8"	Water	92 gals.
Draft	3'2"	Waste	30 gals.
Weight	17,000#	Hull Type	Modified-V
Clearance, Arch	13'6"	Deadrise Aft	7.5°

Bayliner 3587 Motor Yacht

1995–99

At first appearance, the Bayliner 3587 Motor Yacht appears to be a relatively straightforward 35-foot aft-cabin design with little to differentiate her from other small motor yachts. Looks can be deceiving—the 3587 provides three staterooms where her competitors offer only two. The third stateroom is located beneath the (elevated) dinette, and while it's not really a full-size cabin, there is a roomy double berth and partial standing headroom along with a privacy door and a large hanging locker. To accomplish this innovative floorplan, Bayliner engineers moved the galley up into the salon and employed a rather awkward combination of three doors forward leading to the two staterooms and the head. If the salon dimensions are limited, the owner's aft cabin is surprisingly roomy and includes an island berth, head, vanity, and shower. Additional features include a lower helm, a bigger-than-average aft deck and relatively wide side decks. The engineroom is a tight fit. Standard 7.4-liter gas inboards cruise the 3587 MY at 18–19 knots and reach a top speed of about 28 knots. Note that the Bayliner 4087 Cockpit MY introduced in 1997 is the same boat with a cockpit extension.

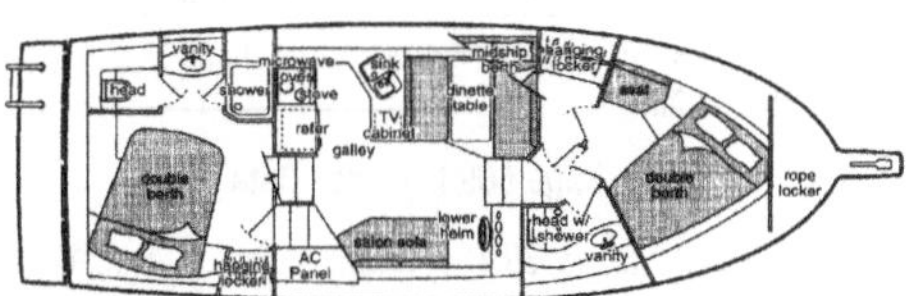

See Page 669 For Price Data

Length Overall	37'3"	Fuel	220 gals.
Hull Length	34'8"	Water	77 gals.
Beam	13'1"	Waste	68 gals.
Draft	3'9"	Hull Type	Modified-V
Weight	22,000#	Deadrise Aft	10°

Bayliner 3788 Motor Yacht

Aside from her modern, contemporary lines and long list of standard equipment, the most notable feature about the Bayliner 3788 Motor Yacht was her extremely affordable price. Indeed, she was one of the least expensive family cruisers of her size and type available during her production years. She was constructed on a lightweight, solid fiberglass hull with low transom deadrise and a wide beam. Her two-stateroom, galley-up floorplan is efficiently arranged with a queen berth in the forward stateroom and a double berth in the small second cabin that extends below the standard lower helm. A bathtub is fitted in the head compartment, and the engineroom (accessed via two gas-assist salon hatches) provides good service access to the motors. Outside, the cockpit is small but the side decks are wide and safe. On the downside, the flybridge ladder is quite steep. Because of her shallow transom deadrise and wide beam, the 3788 can be a hard ride when the seas pick up. Standard 7.4-liter gas inboards cruise at 19 knots (about 30 knots top), and twin 250hp Cummins diesels cruise the 3788 MY at 19–20 knots with a top speed of about 24 knots. Note that an updated Bayliner 3788 model came out in 2001.

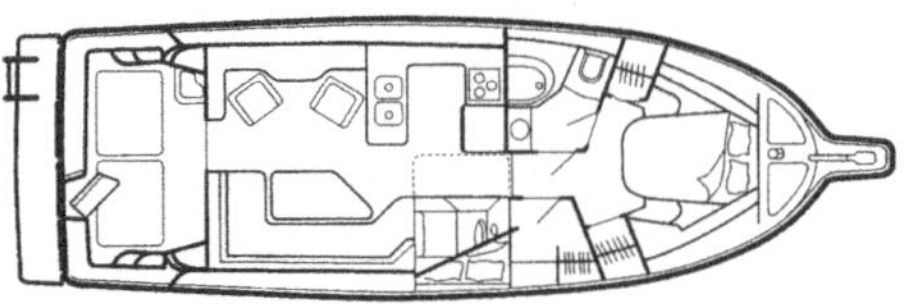

See Page 669 For Price Data

Length	38'6"	Water	100 gals.
Beam	13'4"	Waste	30 gals.
Draft	2'11"	Headroom	6'5"
Weight	20,000#	Hull Type	Modified-V
Fuel	250 gals.	Deadrise Aft	10°

Bayliner 3788 Motor Yacht

The Bayliner 3788 Motor Yacht is an updated version of the original 3788 Motor Yacht (1996–99) with a fresh appearance and a new two-stateroom interior. Built on a conventional modified-V hull with a relatively flat 10 degrees of transom deadrise, the 3788 is a good-looking boat with more than a hint of European styling. Large cabin windows make the salon seem open and spacious, and the dinette (or optional lower helm station) is elevated to provide headroom for the mid-stateroom beneath. The galley is up, and the master stateroom has a walkaround center berth. Hatches in the salon sole provide access to the engine compartment. Topside, the flybridge accommodates five adults, and a long overhang shades the cockpit. Molded steps (instead of a ladder) make reaching the flybridge easy and safe. Additional features include a swim platform, transom door, opening side windows, foredeck sun pad and a tub/shower in the head. Standard 310hp MerCruiser gas inboards cruise at 17–18 knots. Optional 330hp Cummins diesels cruise the 3788 at 20 knots and reach a top speed of around 25 knots. Note that a revised version of this boat was introduced in 2003 as the Meridian 381 Sedan.

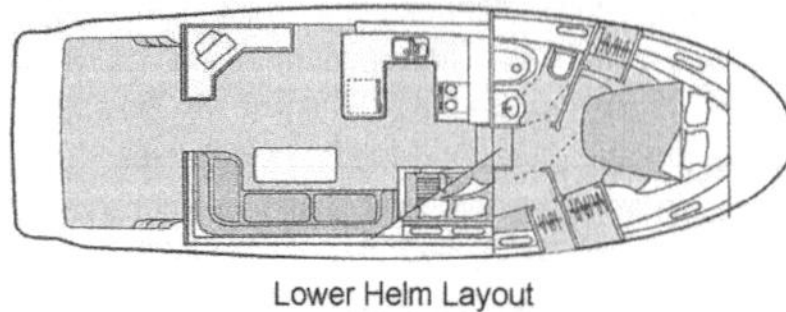
Lower Helm Layout

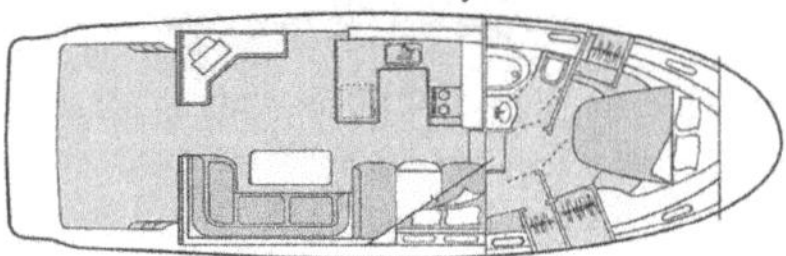
Dinette Layout

See Page 669 For Price Data

Length	39'4"	Water	125 gals.
Beam	13'7"	Waste	36 gals.
Draft	3'4"	Headroom	6'5"
Weight	22,274#	Hull Type	Modified-V
Fuel	300 gals.	Deadrise Aft	7.5°

Bayliner 3870/3888 Motor Yacht

1983–94

A good-selling boat for Bayliner during her decade-long production run, the 3888 Motor Yacht (called the 3780 MY from 1983–89) has long been recognized as a good value for those seeking a comfortable diesel cruiser at an affordable price. Built on a low-deadrise modified-V hull, the key feature of the 3870/3888 was her innovative midcabin floorplan with a double berth that extends under the salon sole. A lower helm was standard in the salon, and there's a surprisingly large master stateroom forward. Note that there are two heads in this layout, one with a tub/shower stall. On deck, the cockpit is large enough for a couple of deck chairs, and there's seating for three on the flybridge. Early models were powered with twin 135hp Mitsubishi 6-cylinder diesels, but these engines were dropped in 1986 in favor of U.S. Marine 175hp diesels—an update that boosted the cruising speed from 14 to 16 knots. Later models with twin 210hp Hino diesels cruise at 17–18 knots. Fuel consumption at cruising speed is about a mile per gallon, which makes the 3888 MY an extremely fuel-efficient boat. About a thousand were built during her production years, a truly remarkable figure for a boat this size.

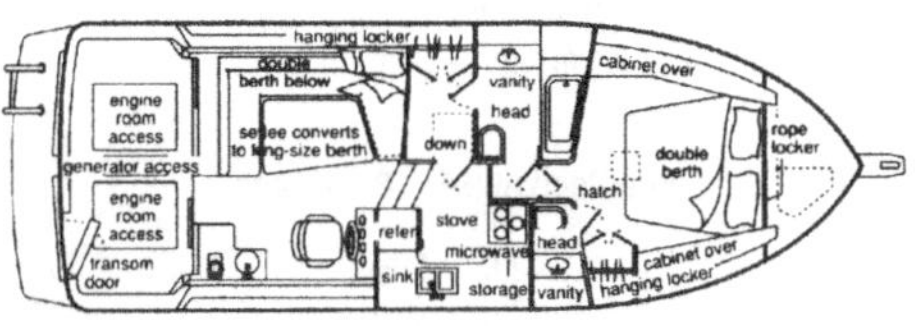

Prices Not Provided for Pre-1995 Models

Length	38'2"	Fuel	304 gals.
Beam	13'5"	Water	80 gals.
Draft	3'2"	Waste	40 gals.
Weight	17,500#	Hull Type	Modified-V
Clearance	14'10"	Deadrise Aft	6°

Bayliner 3988 Motor Yacht

1995–2002

A stylish boat in her day with a rakish bridge and canted windows, the Bayliner 3988 is a value-priced family cruiser with roomy accommodations and a long list of standard equipment. She's built on a shallow-deadrise modified-V hull with moderate beam and prop pockets to reduce shaft angles. Inside, the two-stateroom, two-head floorplan is arranged with an island bed forward and a double berth in the small second stateroom that extends below the elevated dinette in the salon. The master head is fitted with a bathtub that provides sitting headroom only since it's located beneath the lower helm station. Large salon windows make the interior seem spacious and completely wide open. Additional features include a stylish integral swim platform with shower and transom door, port and starboard cockpit steps, wide side decks, and a comfortable flybridge with seating for six. Most 3988s were delivered with twin Hino or Cummins diesels ranging from 200 to 330 horsepower. Among them, twin 250hp Cummins diesels cruise at 20 knots (about 24 knots top), and later models with the 330hp Cummins engines cruise at 24 knots and reach 27–28 knots top.

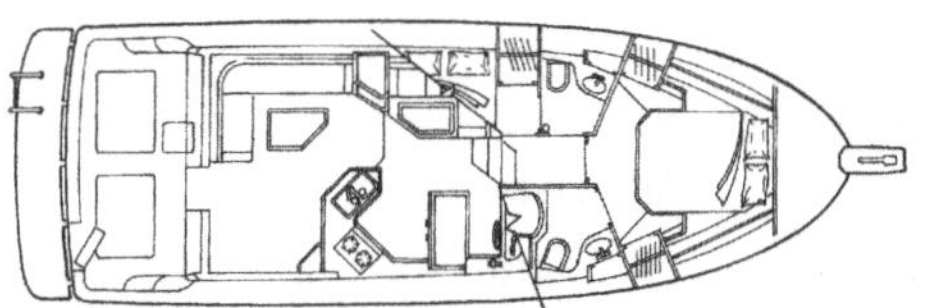

See Page 669 For Price Data

Length w/Pulpit	46'3"	Fuel	298 gals.
Hull Length	39'0"	Water	100 gals.
Beam	14'1"	Waste	36 gals.
Draft	3'3"	Hull Type	Modified-V
Weight	21,000#	Deadrise Aft	10°

Bayliner 4085 Avanti Sunbridge

1997-99

Bayliner built a loyal following among entry-level boaters over the years with their series well-designed family cruisers at super-competitive prices. The 4085 Avanti was a good example of Bayliner's market prowess—what brokers like to call a lot of boat for the money. Built on a solid fiberglass modified-V hull with a relatively wide beam, her midcabin floorplan is arranged with double berths in both staterooms and a convertible U-shaped lounge and full galley in the salon. Note that each stateroom has a privacy door (rather than curtains), and the head is fitted with a separate stall shower. The amidships lounge/stateroom has a small sofa and partial standing headroom at the entrance. On deck, there's a double-wide seat at the helm followed by a large circular settee aft (with a removable table) and a full wet bar to port. The Avanti's deep swim platform can store a personal watercraft. Additional features include a gas-assist engineroom hatch, side-dumping exhausts and a reverse arch. Standard 310hp V-drive MerCruiser inboards cruise at a modest 15–16 knots (about 25 knots top), and optional 315hp Cummins diesels cruise around 25–26 knots.

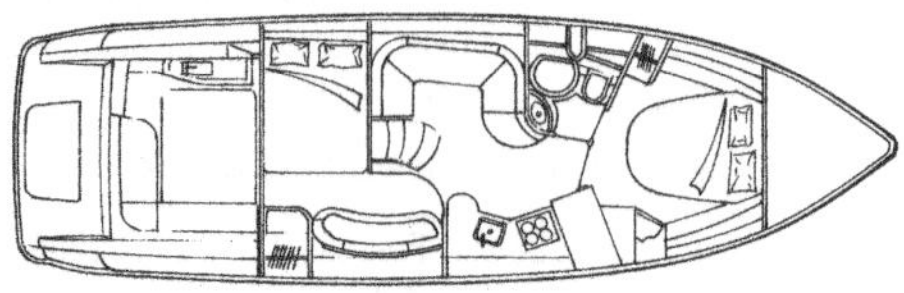

See Page 669 For Price Data

Length	42'0"	Fuel	330 gals.
Beam	13'5"	Water	77 gals.
Draft	3'5"	Waste	45 gals.
Weight	22,100#	Hull Type	Modified-V
Clearance, Arch	12'11"	Deadrise Aft	16°

Bayliner 4087 Cockpit MY

1997–2001

A popular model, the Bayliner 4087 is a cockpit version of the company's 3587 Motor Yacht. From the outside, she appears to be a relatively straightforward cockpit motor yacht with little to differentiate her from other boats of her type. Looks can be deceiving—the 4087 provides three staterooms where her competitors offer only two. The third stateroom is located beneath the (elevated) dinette, and while it's not really a full-size cabin, there is a roomy double berth and partial standing headroom along with a privacy door and a large hanging locker. To accomplish this innovative floorplan, Bayliner engineers moved the galley into the salon and employed a rather awkward combination of three doors forward leading to the two staterooms and the head. If the salon dimensions are limited, the owner's aft cabin is surprisingly roomy and includes an island berth, head, vanity, and shower. Additional features include a lower helm, a bigger-than-average aft deck and relatively wide side decks. The engineroom is small. Standard 310hp gas inboards cruise the 4087 Cockpit MY at 18–19 knots and reach a top speed of 27–28 knots top. Optional Cummins 270hp diesels cruise at 20–21 knots.

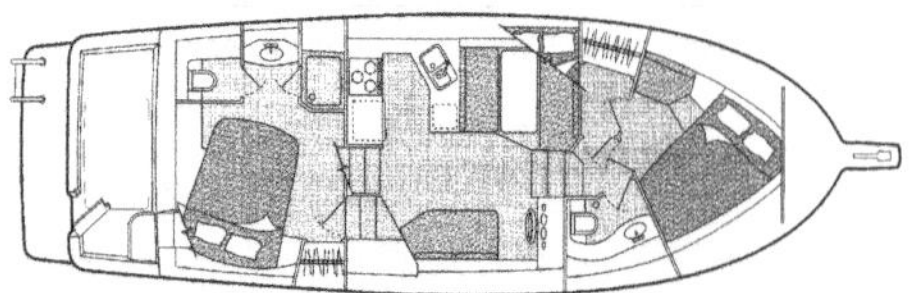

See Page 669 For Price Data

Length Overall	41'5"	Water	77 gals.
Beam	13'1"	Waste	68 gals.
Draft	3'9"	Clearance	15'5"
Weight	24,000#	Hull Type	Modified-V
Fuel	220 gals.	Deadrise Aft	10°

Bayliner 4587 Cockpit MY

The Bayliner 4587 Cockpit MY is a cockpit version of Bayliner's 4387 Aft Cabin MY. The prop pockets used on the 4387 were eliminated in the 4587 and a spray rail was added at the chine for a drier ride, but in most other respects the two boats are very similar. Produced for only two years during the mid-1990s, the 4587 MY might best be described as a plain, uninspiring boat with mediocre styling and unimpressive finish. The two-stateroom floorplan is arranged with the galley and dinette down, and large wraparound salon windows provide excellent outside visibility from the lower helm. Both staterooms have double berths, but only the aft head compartment has a separate stall shower. This isn't a high-end interior with plush carpets and expensive furnishings, but it is spacious and designed to appeal to budget-minded buyers. The aft deck is quite spacious (although the hardtop looks cheap), and the cockpit came with a transom door and lazarette storage. Note that engine access is tight, and for a boat this size the fuel capacity is very limited. Standard 250hp Hino diesels cruise at an efficient 18–19 knots and reach a top speed of around 26 knots. Optional 310hp Hino diesels are a knot or two faster.

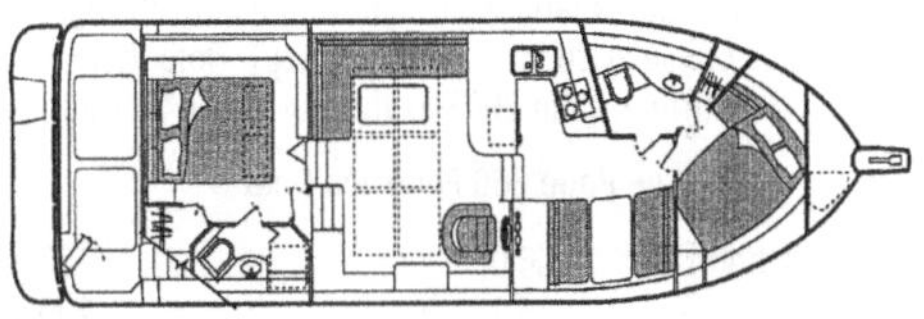

See Page 669 For Price Data

Length	45'1"	Fuel	300 gals.
Beam	14'3"	Water	100 gals.
Draft	3'0"	Waste	50 gals.
Weight	22,000#	Hull Type	Modified-V
Clearance	14'0"	Deadrise Aft	14°

Bayliner 4788 Pilothouse MY

The Bayliner 4788 Pilothouse MY is a slightly restyled and lengthened version of the very popular 4550/4588 Pilothouse MY that Bayliner produced from 1984–93. Aside from the additional two feet of hull length, Bayliner designers reversed the radar arch on the 4788 and softened the flybridge profile for a sleeker and more modern appearance. Inside, the superb pilothouse floorplan of the original 4588 was continued in the newer model with few changes. The L-shaped lounge was moved to starboard in the salon, and the increased hull length of the 4788 can be seen in the enlarged galley and salon dimensions. Two of the three staterooms are fitted with double berths, and the third cabin—which opens to the master stateroom—has a settee with hinged upper and lower berths. Visibility from the raised pilothouse is excellent. The cockpit is sheltered from the sun by a bridge overhang, and the side decks are wide enough for safe and secure foredeck passage. On the downside, the engineroom is a tight fit. Early models with 315hp Hino diesels cruise at an efficient 18 knots, and later models with 370hp Cummins diesels cruise at 20–21 knots.

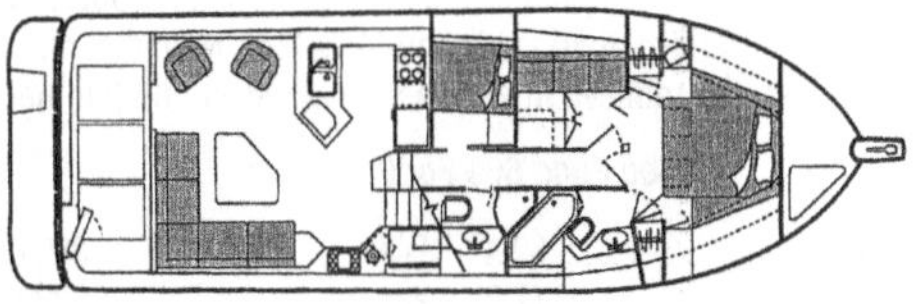

See Page 669 For Price Data

Length w/Pulpit	54'0"	Fuel	444 gals.
Hull Length	47'4"	Water	200 gals.
Beam	15'1"	Waste	48 gals.
Draft	3'4"	Hull Type	Modified-V
Weight	29,990#	Deadrise Aft	6°

Bayliner 5288 Pilothouse

1999–2002

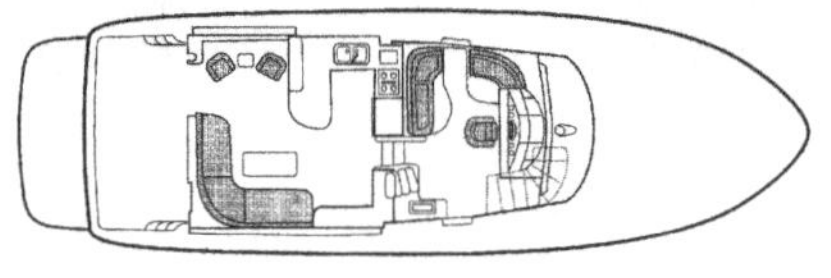

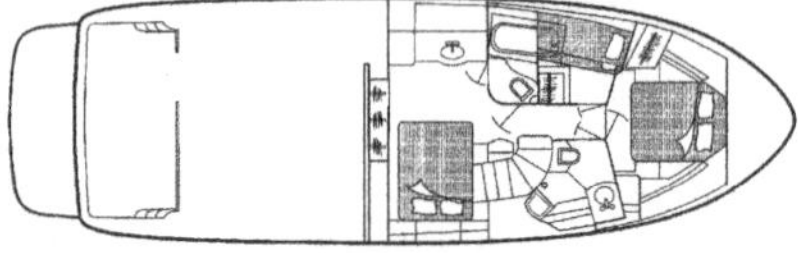

The Bayliner 5288 is a well-styled pilothouse motor yacht whose principal attributes were her luxury-class accommodations and a very competitive price. Like most of Bayliner's larger yachts, the 5288 was constructed on a fully cored, low-deadrise hull with a relatively wide beam. One of the big reasons for the popularity of pilothouse designs in recent years is their all-season cruising capability. Perched in the elevated wheelhouse with near 360-degree visibility, the helmsman of the 5288 can run day or night, regardless of the weather, in air-conditioned or heated comfort. There are three staterooms in the 5288, two with double berths and over/under bunks in the small portside guest cabin. While the salon isn't particularly spacious for a 52-footer, it does include a comfortable L-shaped dinette and a breakfast bar. In the cockpit, the molded flybridge steps swing up for access to a spacious engineroom. Additional features include reasonably wide, well-secured side decks, underwater exhausts, sidedeck courtesy lights, a tub/shower in the owner's head, and a large flybridge with dinghy storage. MAN 600hp diesels cruise at 20 knots (mid 20s top). Note that she was restyled and reintroduced in 2003 as the Meridian 540 Pilothouse.

See Page 669 For Price Data

Length w/Platform	56'0"	Fuel	700 gals.
Beam	16'3"	Water	200 gals.
Draft	4'10"	Waste	73 gals.
Weight	47,560#	Hull Type	Modified-V
Clearance	21'3"	Deadrise Aft	12°

Bayliner 5788 Motor Yacht

1997–2002

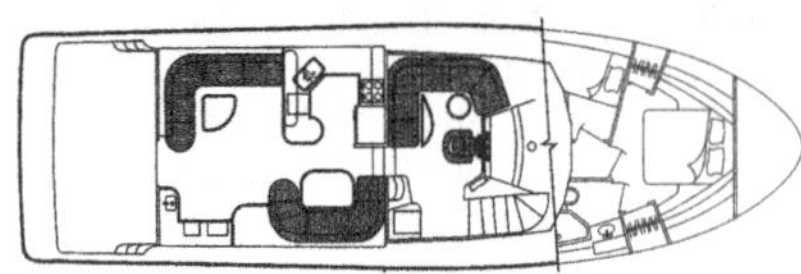

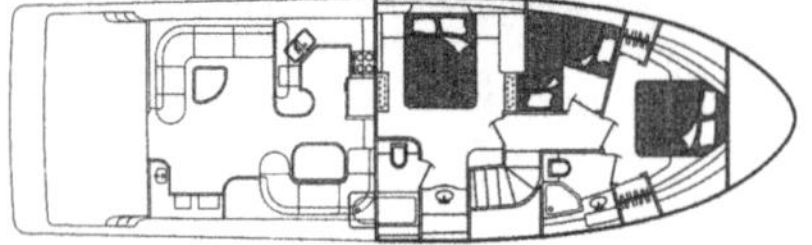

The Bayliner 5788, with its flowing lines and distinctive pilothouse styling, was the flagship of the Bayliner fleet during her production years. By any standard, her most attractive feature was an extremely low price compared with other yachts her size from other manufacturers. Built on a lightweight, fully cored hull, the wide beam of the 5788 results in a spacious interior with three staterooms and two full heads, one with a tub. The floorplan is typical of most pilothouse yachts with the galley forward in the salon and the full-beam owner's stateroom located beneath the pilothouse. The separate dinette of the 5788 is notable—most pilothouse floorplans delete this convenience for lack of salon space. Visibility from the raised pilothouse is very good. Bayliner used an abundance of traditional teak woodwork throughout the interior of the 5788, and while the decor isn't glitzy, the overall impression is one of space and comfort. In the small cockpit, the flybridge steps lift up for access to a spacious engineroom. It should be said that the finish of the 5788 is better than earlier Bayliner models. MAN 610hp diesels cruise at 20 knots (mid 20s top). Note that she was restyled and reintroduced in 2003 as the Meridian 580 Pilothouse.

See Page 669 For Price Data

Length	59'4"	Fuel	800 gals.
Beam	17'2"	Water	222 gals.
Draft	4'11"	Waste	76 gals.
Weight	49,000#	Hull Type	Modified-V
Clearance, Arch	19'7"	Deadrise Aft	10°

Bertram

Quick View

- Bertram began building boats in 1961 with the introduction of the world-famous Bertram 31, a classic fishing boat design with a then-radical deep-V hull. (Note that the first fiberglass Bertram *hull* was a racing boat, the Bertram 31 Glass Moppie.)
- During the 1970s and 1980s, Bertram experienced an era of steady growth while diversifying its lineup to include several motoryacht designs as well as sportfishing boats.
- Early on, Bertram focused its marketing on the company's Hunt-designed deep-V hulls.
- Bertram and Hatteras were arch-rivals in the 1980s, with Hatteras eventually winning out thanks to a more diverse model selection and better interiors.
- Financial difficulties—owing to a poor U.S. economy and Bertram's concentration on sportfishing boats only—forced a shutdown of the firm in 1993.
- In 1998 Bertram Yacht was purchased by the Ferretti Group, an Italian yachting conglomerate.
- After 50 years of operation in Miami, Bertram relocated in 2012 to Merritt Island, FL.

Bertram Yachts • www.bertram.com

Bertram 30 Moppie

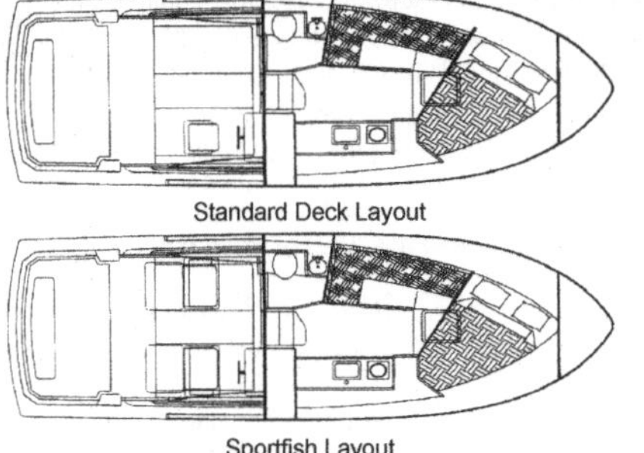
Standard Deck Layout

Sportfish Layout

A versatile boat designed to accommodate the needs of weekend cruisers as well as hard-core anglers, the Bertram 30 Moppie is a well-styled inboard express whose upscale price reflected her quality construction and superior engineering. Built on a beamy, solid fiberglass deep-V hull, the Moppie's clean lines exude sex appeal even without the integral swim platform and molded bow pulpit common to most modern express boats. Three deck plans made her adaptable to fishing, cruising, or daytime activities. The standard layout has only a helm seat on the bridgedeck; the Sport Cruiser features a large L-shaped settee opposite the helm; and the Sportfish version comes with a companion seat, bait-prep center, washdowns and rod holders. The interior is the same for all three versions with a double berth forward, a small galley, convertible dinette, and a standup head with shower. Access to the motors, below the bridgedeck, is very good, and a transom door was standard. Twin 310hp gas engines cruise the Moppie at 22 knots and reach 30+ knots top. Optional 300hp Cummins (or Cat) diesels cruise at 27 knots (31 top), and 340hp Cats cruise about 29–30 knots and reach 33 knots wide open.

See Page 669 For Price Data

Length	30'6"	Fuel	275 gals.
Beam	11'3"	Water	30 gals.
Draft	3'1"	Cockpit	64 sq. ft.
Weight	13,200#	Hull Type	Deep-V
Clearance	7'3"	Deadrise Aft	18.5°

Bertram 36 Convertible

Lasting only two years in production, the Bertram 36 combines the offshore capabilities of a deep-V hull with an interior designed for comfortable family-style cruising. She's built on a relatively beamy hull for her length with reverse chines, a solid fiberglass bottom, and cored hullsides. Most convertibles this size are designed with a single-stateroom, galley-down floorplan that allows for a more spacious and open salon. The Bertram 36, however, comes with a two-stateroom, galley-up teak interior. The result is a fairly compact salon, but what really makes this an unusual layout is the addition of a unique "half dinette" aft of the galley, an arrangement dictated by the engine boxes that extend into the cabin. With nearly 100 square feet of space, the cockpit is among the largest to be found in a 36-footer. Both engine boxes are cushioned and the consoles above them contain a tackle center and an optional freezer or livewell. There's also an in-sole fish box, a transom fish box, and a transom door. Topside, the helm console of the Bertram 36 is huge with plenty of room for flush-mounting an array of electronics. Engine access is excellent. Twin 450hp Cummins diesels deliver a cruising speed of 25 knots (28–30 knots top).

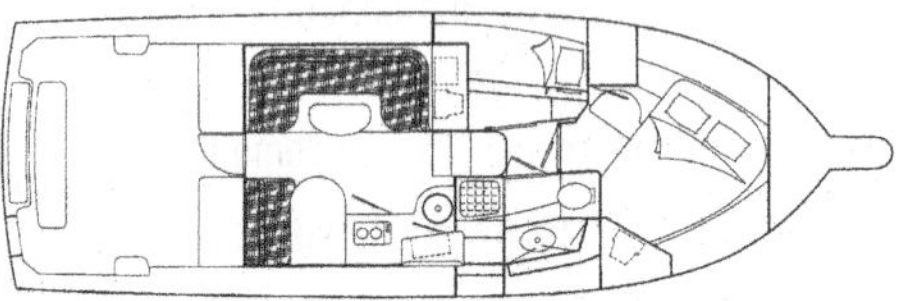

See Page 669 For Price Data

Length	35'10"	Fuel	400 gals.
Beam	13'0"	Water	75 gals.
Draft	3'10"	Cockpit	97 sq. ft.
Weight	22,500#	Hull Type	Deep-V
Clearance	11'9"	Deadrise Aft	17.5°

Bertram 36 Moppie

The Bertram 36 Moppie is an upscale express whose classic good looks and rugged construction will appeal to anglers seeking a premium open sportfisherman or a capable weekend cruiser. Heavily built on a solid fiberglass deep-V hull with a relatively wide beam, the Moppie could be configured with different cockpit layouts for fishing or cruising (see floorplans below). Bertram engineers did an excellent job in designing a wide-open and comfortable cabin layout. There's a separate stall shower in the head (a real plus), the sofa converts to upper and lower berths, the galley is fitted with stove, microwave and refrigerator, and the forward queen berth can be separated from the salon with a privacy curtain. Outside, the entire bridge deck can be raised on hydraulic rams for engine access. Additional features include a cockpit transom door, maple interior woodwork, and a bow pulpit. Among several engine options, twin 420hp Cummins diesels cruise the 36 Moppie at 26 knots and deliver a top speed in the neighborhood of 30 knots. Note that the Moppie was dropped from the lineup in 1998 but reintroduced with a slightly revised interior the following year.

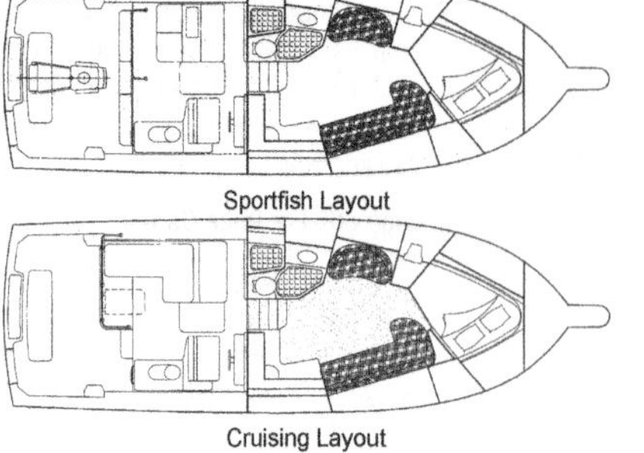
Sportfish Layout

Cruising Layout

See Page 669 For Price Data

Length	35'10"	Fuel	400 gals.
Beam	13'0"	Water	75 gals.
Draft	3'8"	Waste	30 gals.
Weight	18,700#	Hull Type	Deep-V
Clearance	8'0"	Deadrise Aft	17.5°

Bertram 390 Convertible

The Bertram 390 Convertible combined the classic elements of a Bertram sportfishing machine with the curvaceous, Ferretti-inspired styling common to all of Bertram's more recent product introductions. While her sleek styling was a departure from earlier, more conservative Bertram models, the deep-V hull of the 390 is pure Bertram—a stretched version of the company's popular 37 Convertible hull with a stepped sheer, moderate beam, and a large fishing cockpit. The high-gloss cherry (or teak) interior of the 390 features a particularly comfortable salon with a dinette forward, a notable feature in a boat this size. The galley is on the midlevel between the salon and staterooms, and the guest cabin is fitted with side-by-side berths rather than the over/under bunks so often found in guest staterooms. Topside, the helm is on the centerline and the console has plenty of space for electronics. Additional features include cockpit access to the engineroom (where a single fuel tank forward of the engines consumes a lot of space), overhead rod storage in the salon, and wide side decks. A quality yacht, twin 480hp Volvo V-drive diesels cruise the Bertram 390 Convertible at 24–25 knots and reach a top speed of about 30 knots.

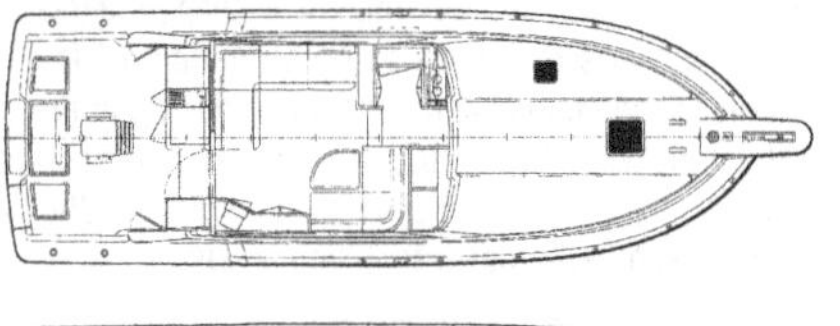

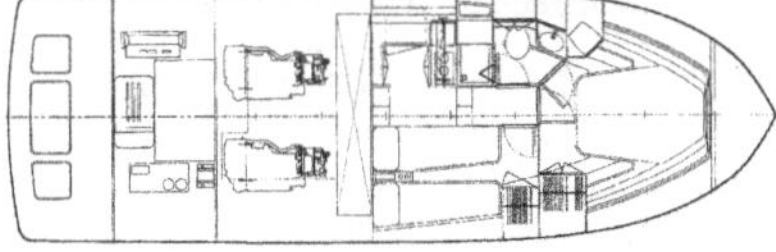

See Page 669 For Price Data

Length w/Pulpit	41'8"	Fuel	459 gals.
Hull Length	39'0"	Water	106 gals.
Beam	13'4"	Waste	37 gals.
Draft	4'0"	Hull Type	Deep-V
Weight	34,398#	Deadrise Aft	18°

Bertram 43 Convertible

A good-selling boat for Bertram, the 43 Convertible is still highly regarded with experienced anglers for her rugged construction, rakish good looks and superb open-water performance. She was built on a deep-V hull with cored hullsides and a solid fiberglass bottom, and with nearly 15 feet of beam, the 43 is a spacious boat inside. Several floorplans were offered during her production years with the two-stateroom, galley-up configurations being the most popular. Regardless of the layout, however, the 43's interiors were extremely well finished with modern decors, quality hardware, and high-end furnishings. The cockpit—reinforced for a fighting chair—came with a transom door and direct engineroom access. Note that in 1994 the genset was moved from under the cockpit into to the engineroom, and the cabin windows were slightly restyled. Additional features include side-dumping exhausts, good service access to the engines, molded tackle centers, and a wrap-around flybridge helm console. Twin 535hp 6V92s cruise at 23–24 knots with a top speed of 28 knots. Optional 655hp MTUs (available in 1995–96) will cruise at 26 knots and hit 30+ knots top.

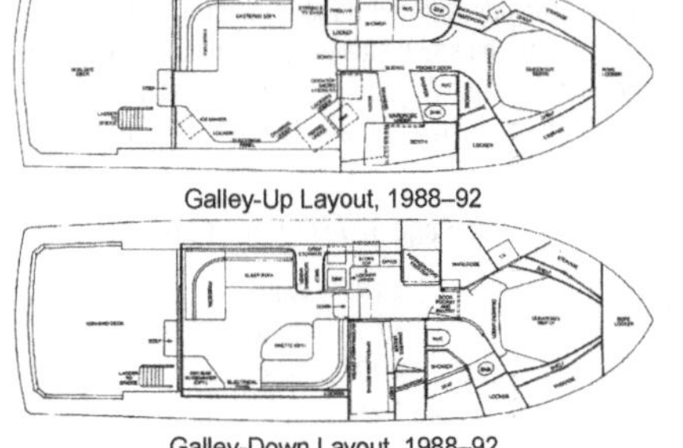

Galley-Up Layout, 1988–92

Galley-Down Layout, 1988–92

See Page 670 For Price Data

Length	43'4"	Fuel	546 gals.
Beam	14'11"	Water	160 gals.
Draft	4'4"	Cockpit	120 sq. ft.
Weight	41,890#	Hull Type	Deep-V
Clearance	13'5"	Deadrise Aft	17°

Bertram 450 Convertible

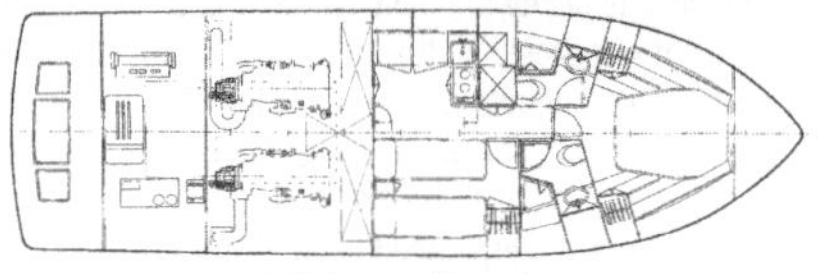
2-Stateroom Floorplan

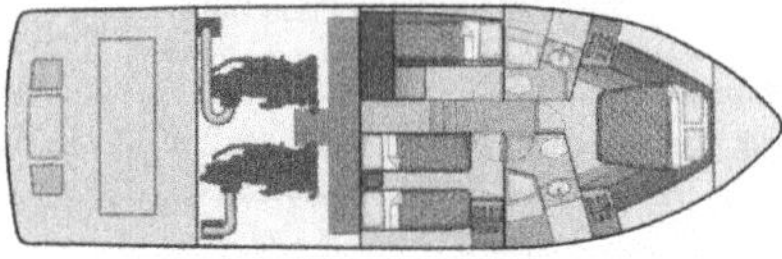
3-Stateroom Floorplan

Introduced in 1998 following the Ferretti Group's acquisition of Bertram Yachts, the 450 Convertible reflects the Italian styling influences common to all late-model Bertram products. Like her predecessors, the 450 is built on Bertram's signature deep-V hull with a stepped sheer and low cockpit freeboard. The Ferretti influence is clearly evident in the 450's standard two-stateroom interior with its high-gloss woodwork and posh decor. The galley, with its unobtrusive under-counter refrigeration, is on the middle level in this layout, and side-by-side single berths—rather than over/under bunks—are found in the guest cabin. (Note that an optional three-stateroom, galley-up floorplan became available in 2005.) While the salon dimensions are indeed expansive in the 450, the cockpit is slightly smaller than competitive sportfishing yachts in this class. On the spacious flybridge, a U-shaped settee forward of the helm converts to a huge sun pad. Additional features include overhead rod storage and an elevated dinette in the salon, a washer/dryer locker in the forward passageway, and a compact but well-arranged engineroom. Cruise at 26 knots with 660hp Cats (30 knots top); 28 knots (32 top) with 800hp MANs.

See Page 670 For Price Data

Length w/Pulpit	48'3"	Clearance	13'5"
Hull Length	45'3"	Fuel	618 gals.
Beam	14'11"	Water	159 gals.
Draft	4'4"	Hull Type	Deep-V
Weight	46,305#	Deadrise Aft	18°

Bertram 46 Convertible

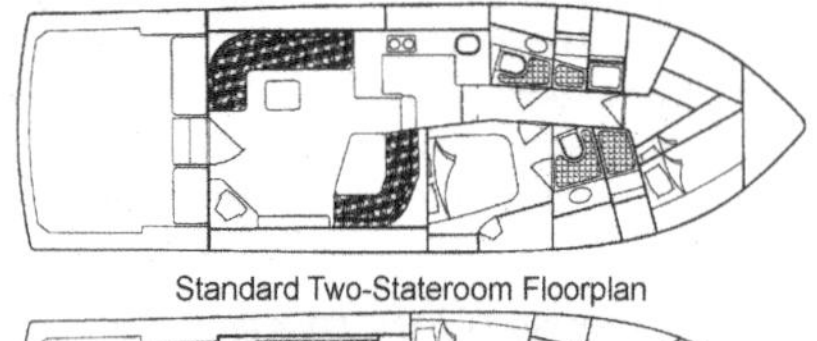
Standard Two-Stateroom Floorplan

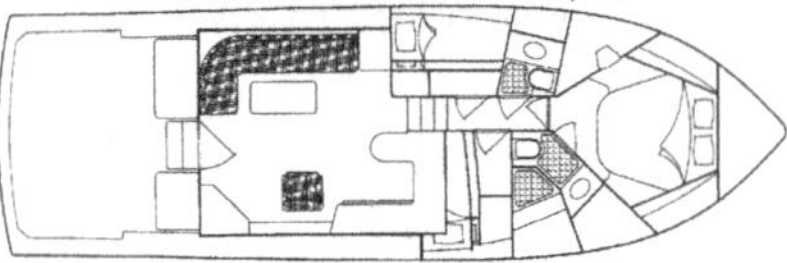
Optional Three-Stateroom Floorplan

Few production boats attained the classic status enjoyed by the original Bertram 46 Convertible (1971–87), a legendary tournament machine with superb all-weather handling characteristics. This more recent Bertram 46 was a completely redesigned boat with a more contemporary profile, a vastly upgraded interior, and faster cruising speeds. (Note the long foredeck; the house sits well aft giving the boat a very rakish appearance.) Her deep-V hull is drier and considerably more stable at trolling speeds than the original 46 thanks to widened chine flats. The standard two-stateroom floorplan of the 46 is arranged with a mid-level galley two steps down from the salon. The owner's stateroom is amidships (where it should be), and both head compartments are fitted with separate stall showers. Note that in the optional three-stateroom arrangement, the owner's stateroom is forward and the galley is forward in the salon. Topside, the flybridge is huge. On the downside, the engineroom is on the small side—very unusual in a Bertram product until recent years. A good performer, standard 8V92 diesels cruise the Bertram 46 at a fast 26–27 knots (about 31 knots top).

See Page 670 For Price Data

Length	46'3"	Water	175 gals.
Beam	15'1"	Cockpit	120 sq. ft.
Draft	4'10"	Clearance	13'5"
Weight	46,100#	Hull Type	Deep-V
Fuel	800 gals.	Deadrise Aft	17.5°

Bertram 46 Moppie

1993–96

Introduced in 1993, the Bertram 46 Moppie was built on a stretched version of the proven Bertram 43 Convertible hull with cored hullsides, a wide beam, and a relatively steep 17 degrees of transom deadrise. This was one of the bigger express cruisers produced in the early 1990s, and like previous Moppies the 46 was aimed at the market for both serious anglers and upscale cruisers alike. Offered with several interior layouts, the single-stateroom floorplan (with two heads—very unusual) appealed more to the sportfish market while the two-stateroom layout is more suited for cruising activities. Either way, there's seating on the bridge deck for a small crowd, and the sportfish version came with molded tackle centers in the cockpit. Until 1995, the Moppie had reversed engines with V-drive-like shaft couplers; thereafter, the engine installations were straight inboards. Also in 1995, the genset was moved from under the cockpit into the more protected environment of the engineroom. A good-running boat and a comfortable ride in a chop, a pair of 735hp 8V92s cruise the Bertram 46 Moppie at a fast 28–29 knots and reach top speeds in the neighborhood of 32 knots.

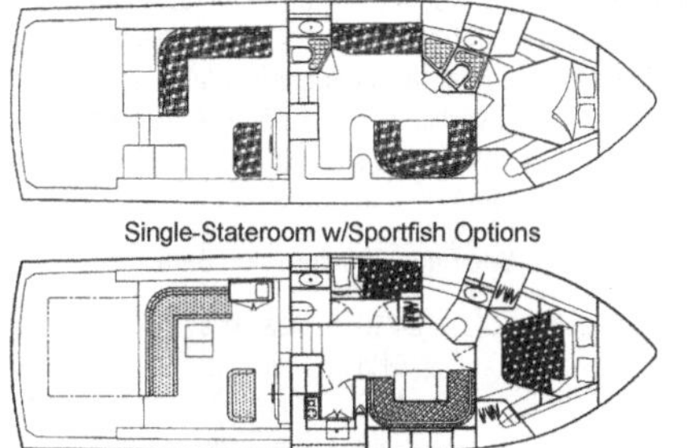
Single-Stateroom w/Sportfish Options

Two-Stateroom w/Cruising Options

See Page 670 For Price Data

Length	46'0"	Fuel	650 gals.
Beam	14'11"	Water	135 gals.
Draft	4'8"	Cockpit	106 sq. ft.
Weight	42,000#	Hull Type	Deep-V
Clearance	9'1"	Deadrise Aft	17°

Bertram 50 Convertible

1987–97

A beautifully styled boat whose muscular profile will probably never be dated, the Bertram 50 Convertible is considered by many to represent the state of the art in production 50-foot sportfishermen. Built on a rugged deep-V hull with cored hullsides and a relatively wide beam, her superb seakeeping and handling qualities are almost legendary. Initially offered in a three-stateroom layout with the galley up, a spacious two-stateroom, galley-down interior with an enormous salon became available in 1988. She received a complete update in 1994 including two new floorplans and a revised deckhouse profile with new windows and stripes. A transom door and tackle center were standard in the cockpit, and a wraparound helm console (also updated for '94) eliminates the need for an overhead electronics box. A good performer, 735hp 8V92 diesels cruise at 24 knots (27 knots top) with a range of over 400 miles. Twin 820hp MAN diesels, introduced in 1989, provide cruising speeds of 26–27 knots (31 knots top) and—beginning in 1994—optional 900hp 12V71s cruise at a fast 29 knots. A good-selling boat during her decade-long production run, resale values remain strong in all markets.

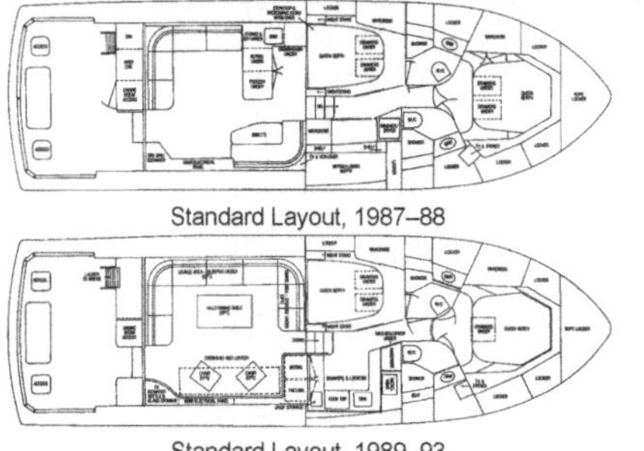
Standard Layout, 1987–88

Standard Layout, 1989–93

See Page 670 For Price Data

Length	50'0"	Fuel	1,046 gals.
Beam	16'2"	Water	175 gals.
Draft	5'0"	Waste	60 gals.
Weight	56,531#	Hull Type	Deep-V
Clearance	15'9"	Deadrise Aft	17°

Bertram 510 Convertible

2000–10

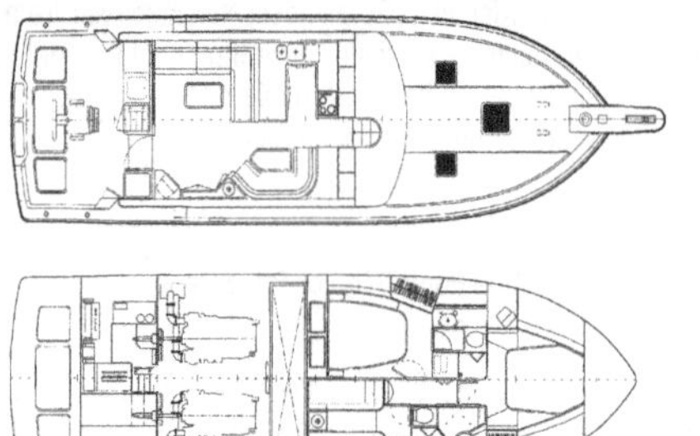

Introduced in 2000, the Bertram 510 Convertible reflects the Italian styling influences common to all late-model Bertrams introduced after the company's 1998 acquisition by Ferretti Yachts. With her elliptical windows and sweeping curves, the 510 was a clear departure from the classic Bertram look. Retained, however, is the time-tested Bertram deep-V hull, a large fishing cockpit, and the rugged construction long associated with the Bertram nameplate. (Note that the 510 is built on a stretched version of the company's 50 Convertible hull.) The three-stateroom interior of the 510 is an impressive display of practical design and quality workmanship. The galley and dinette are forward in the salon, and the cherry wood joinery is finished to a rich and lustrous glow. Topside, the centerline helm is located well aft on the bridge to permit the inclusion of a U-shaped settee/dinette forward. Additional features include a separate control room aft of the engineroom for the generator and washer/dryer, a centerline fuel tank, and a rod storage locker in the salon overhead. Twin 1,050hp MAN diesels cruise the 510 at a fast 30 knots (33–34 knots top), and 1,300 MANs will top out at nearly 40 knots.

See Page 670 For Price Data

Length w/Pulpit	54'10"	Clearance	15'6"
Hull Length	51'5"	Fuel	1,040 gals.
Beam	16'2"	Water	185 gals.
Draft	5'0"	Hull Type	Deep-V
Weight	65,489#	Deadrise Aft	18°

Bertram 54 Convertible

1995–2003

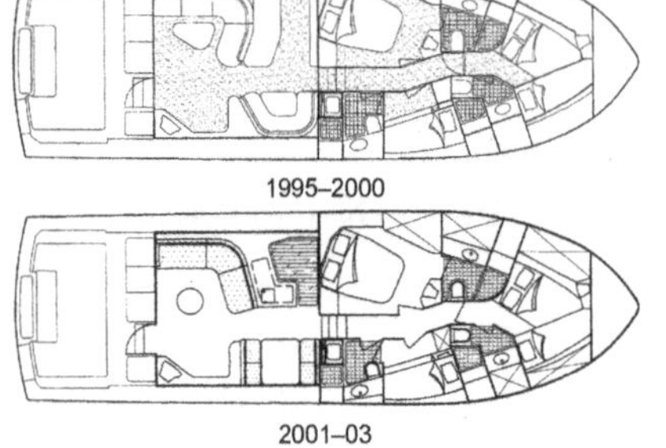
1995–2000

2001–03

Bertram introduced the first 54 Convertible in 1981 and went on to sell 177 of them before concluding production in 1992. By any standard, she was a classic boat with all of the assets one associates with a true tournament sportfishing yacht. When the company decided to introduce a new 54 Convertible in 1995, Bertram's engineers retained the proven deep-V hull of the original 54 that was, of course, the foundation of her legendary success. The most notable change of the new 54 is her muscular, more aggressive appearance. The deckhouse is now further aft on the deck, a cockpit overhang became part of the flybridge (eliminating the need for a canvas shade), and the flybridge windscreen of the original 54 was eliminated. The three-stateroom interior (updated in 2001) is an impressive display of elegant design and superb workmanship. The galley and dinette are forward in the salon, and the cherrywood paneling is finished to a beautiful high gloss. Note that a single fuel tank in the engineroom replaced the saddle tanks found in the original Bertram 54. A superb open-water performer, a pair of 1,100hp 12V-92 Detroits (or 1,250hp Cats) will cruise at 29 knots and reach a top speed of 32–33 knots.

See Page 670 For Price Data

Length	54'0"	Fuel	1,453 gals.
Beam	16'11"	Water	250 gals.
Draft	5'2"	Cockpit	144 sq. ft.
Weight	75,400#	Hull Type	Deep-V
Clearance	16'8"	Deadrise Aft	17°

Bertram 570 Convertible

2002–08

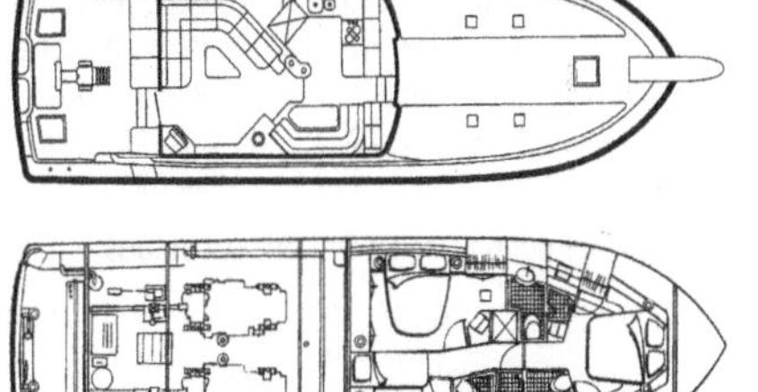

Exceptional seakeeping abilities, superior engineering, and quality construction have always characterized Bertram products, but it has only been since 1998, when the Ferretti Group purchased the company, that Bertram styling really came of age. Built on a stretched version of the legendary Bertram 54 hull with cored hullsides and a solid fiberglass bottom, the three-stateroom, three-head floorplan of the 570 is arranged with the galley and dinette forward on the deckhouse level, a step up from the salon. The master suite is amidships, and each head has a separate stall shower. The accommodations are plush with well-crafted joinery, premium appliances, and designer fabrics. In the cockpit, an oversized transom door (with gate) is standard along with a full tackle center with sink, freezer, and livewell. The expansive engineroom—always a Bertram specialty—is expertly laid out with good access to all systems. Additional features include an integral bow pulpit, an overhead salon rod locker, washer/dryer, and a huge flybridge with U-shaped lounge seating forward of the helm. A fast ride with 1,300 MAN diesels, the Bertram 570 cruises at 30 knots and reaches a top speed of 33–34 knots.

See Page 670 For Price Data

Length w/Pulpit	60'6"	Fuel	1,585 gals.
Hull Length	57'0"	Water	250 gals.
Beam	16'11"	Clearance	15'4"
Draft	5'3"	Hull Type	Deep-V
Weight	84,452#	Deadrise Aft	17°

Bertram 60 Convertible

1990–2005

Standard Floorplan, 1990–94

1999–2005

A good-selling model, the Bertram 60 projects the muscular styling common to all late-model Bertram designs. Notably, she's built on a stretched and reworked version of the Bertram 54 hull—one of the best open-water boats in the business. An extensive selection of three- and four-stateroom floorplans was offered in this boat over the years and two of the more popular arrangements are shown below. In later years, the interior decor reflected the European styling influences of the Ferretti Group, the Italian conglomerate that purchased Bertram in 1998. The cockpit comes complete with an oversized transom door, molded tackle center, and direct engineroom access, and the wraparound flybridge helm console is one of the best to be found in any big convertible. A few of her more notable features include a well-arranged engineroom, a huge flybridge with U-shaped lounge seating forward, wide side decks, and—since 1997—side exhausts. No lightweight, twin 1,400hp 16V92 diesels cruise the Bertram 60 at an honest 31 knots and reach 34–35 knots wide open. More recent models with 1,400hp Cat 3412 diesels cruise at a fast 32 knots (mid 30s top). A closed-bridge model was introduced in late 1995.

See Page 670 For Price Data

Length	60'0"	Fuel	1,630 gals.
Beam	16'11"	Water	250 gals.
Draft	5'6"	Cockpit	148 sq. ft.
Weight	93,500#	Hull Type	Modified-V
Clearance	16'8"	Deadrise Aft	17°

Bertram 630 Convertible

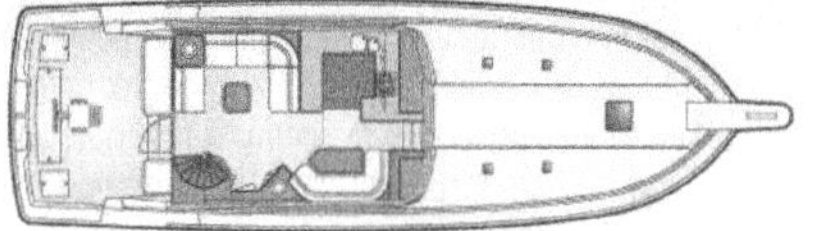

3 Staterooms

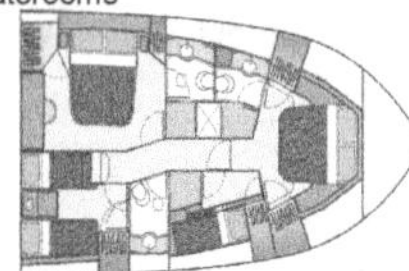

4 Staterooms

Classic convertible styling, 40-knot speed, and the only stairway bridge access in her class characterize the 630 Convertible, Bertram's replacement for the hugely popular Bertram 60 Convertible built from 1990 through 2005. To boost her top-end speed, Bertram engineers gave the 630 less transom deadrise than her deep-V predecessor in addition to adding a pair of long prop pockets to reduce the shaft angles. The bottom is solid fiberglass, and a long keel provides excellent directional stability. Available with three or four staterooms, the high-gloss cherry interior includes the latest in luxury appointments as well as the same high level of fit and finish one expects in a Bertram yacht. From the cockpit, the circular bridge access stairway is easier to navigate than a traditional bridge ladder. (Note that on the closed bridge model, the stairwell is inside the salon.) Topside, the 630's state-of-the-art flybridge is large enough to accommodate a small crowd. Additional features include a removable aft salon window, power-actuated helm console, two 25-kw gensets, central vacuum system, and a bow pulpit. A pair of MTU 2,000hp engines cruise the Bertram 630 at 35 knots and reach an honest 40 knots wide open.

Not Enough Resale Data to Set Values

Length w/Pulpit	66'9"	Fuel	1,849 gals.
Beam	18'1"	Water	251 gals.
Draft	5'3"	Waste	100 gals.
Weight	95,609#	Hull Type	Modified-V
Clearance	NA	Deadrise Aft	16°

Bertram 670 Convertible

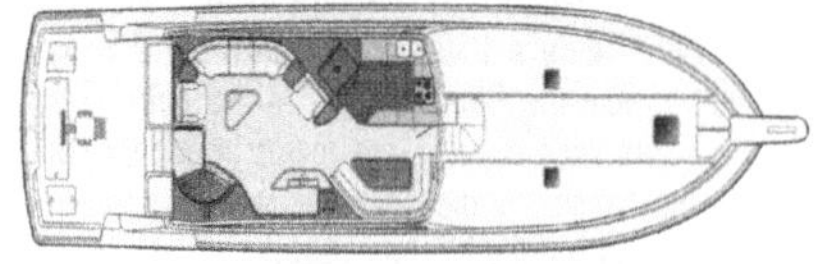

The 670 Convertible is one of the "new-breed" Bertrams developed following the 1998 purchase of the company by the Ferretti Group. She shares the same flowing lines seen in other recent Bertram models with the house well aft on the deck, a stepped sheer, and low cockpit freeboard. The hull is of course a deep-V (in keeping with the Bertram tradition), however the 670's prop pockets are a Bertram first. The Ferretti influence is most evident belowdecks where the standard four-stateroom, four-head interior is a lavish display of European elegance. The salon, which is open to the galley and dinette, is a blend of high-gloss cherry woodwork, expensive furnishings and impressive detailing. The cockpit is fitted out with the requisite fishing amenities—bait-prep center, freezer, transom door, etc. A spiral staircase to the right of the salon door (redesigned in 2004) leads up to the huge flybridge with its U-shaped lounge, grill, and a concealed electronics console in the dash. Additional standard features include a bow thruster, frameless cabin windows, and trolling valves. Twin 2000hp 16-cylinder MTU diesels cruise the Bertram 670 at 32 knots (35+ knots wide open). Note that an enclosed flybridge was optional.

Not Enough Resale Data to Set Values

Length w/Pulpit	71'6"	Fuel	2,008 gals.
Hull Length	67'5"	Water	264 gals.
Beam	18'8"	Clearance	16'8"
Draft	6'0"	Hull Type	Deep-V
Weight	105,840#	Deadrise Aft	18°

Black Watch

Quick View

- Black Watch was one of several manufacturers owned by The Ted Hood Companies, a Rhode Island-based builder of custom and semicustom yachts.
- Beginning with a 30-footer introduced in 1986, Black Watch offered a series of high-quality sportfishing models, all priced at the upper end of the market.
- Black Watch boats were built on Hunt-designed, fully cored hulls.
- Popular boats for several years, the last Black Watch boats were produced in the late 1990s.
- The company was subsequently sold to investors who relocated to Australia where an attempt was made to continue production.

No longer in business.

Black Watch 26 Express

1988–97

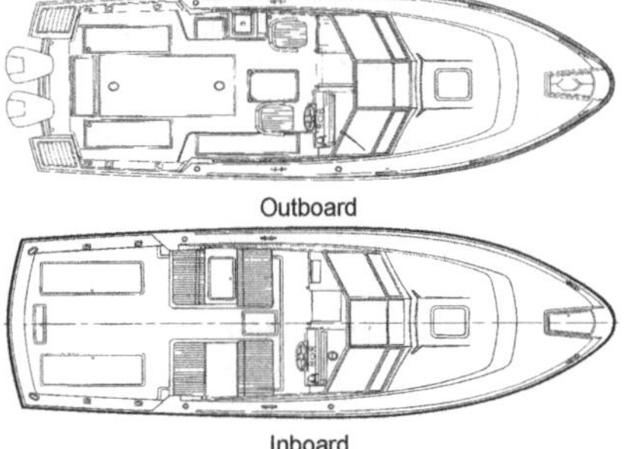

Outboard

Inboard

The Black Watch 26 is a roomy, heavily-built express designed for the kind of offshore work that keeps most boats her size tied up at the docks in bad weather. She's built on a fully cored deep-V hull with a mega-wide 9-foot, 8-inch beam. Available with inboard or outboard power (inboard models are fitted with engine boxes), the Black Watch 26 provides anglers with a big fishing cockpit with two in-deck fish boxes and—in the outboard version—a nifty 7-foot starboard rod locker. A 30-gallon livewell was standard, and there's space at the helm console for flush-mounting a full array of electronic add-ons. Belowdecks, the accommodations include over/under V-berths, a small galley area, and an enclosed head compartment with shower—not bad for a small fishing boat. The side decks are wide enough for safe access to the bow, and sight-lines from the helm are excellent. Several engine options were available during her production run. Those powered with twin 200hp outboards cruise in the mid 20s and reach a top speed of about 40 knots. Inboard models (available after 1990) with 240hp gas engines cruise at 25 knots and deliver a top speed in the neighborhood of 35 knots.

See Page 670 For Price Data

Length	26'1"	Fuel	200/240 gals.
Beam	9'8"	Water	25 gals.
Draft	2'6"	Max HP, OB	450
Weight, Outbd.	4,800#	Hull Type	Deep-V
Weight, Inbd.	8,300#	Deadrise Aft	19°

Black Watch 30 Flybridge

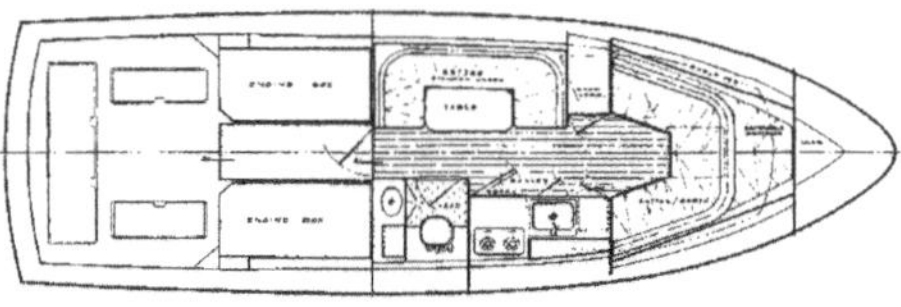

A popular model for Black Watch during the early 1990s, the 30 Flybridge is a Hunt-designed deep-V cruiser whose solid construction and versatile design made her a class standout. Slightly top-heavy in appearance (thanks to an oversize flybridge), she's built on a fully cored hull with a wide 10'11" beam. At just 12,000 pounds, the 30 is a relatively light boat for her size. Below, the surprisingly roomy interior of the Black Watch 30—with a stand-up head, convertible dinette, and adult-sized V-berths—is more than suitable for a few days away from home. The teak-and-holly cabin sole is a nice touch, and convenient storage cabinets and drawers are found throughout. The large 80-square foot cockpit of the Black Watch 30 came standard with an athwartships storage locker/fish box, and clever roll-back motor boxes provide good access to the engines. Additional features include large cabin windows, sturdy bow railings, anchor locker, and a molded bow pulpit. On the downside, the side decks are seriously narrow. Standard gas engines cruise in the low 20s (30+ knots top), and optional 300hp Cummins diesels cruise at an economical 25–26 knots.

Not Enough Resale Data to Set Values

Length	30'1"	Fuel	270 gals.
Beam	10'11"	Water	40 gals.
Draft	3'0"	Cockpit	80 sq. ft.
Weight	12,000#	Hull Type	Deep-V
Clearance	9'6"	Deadrise Aft	18°

Black Watch 30 Sportfisherman

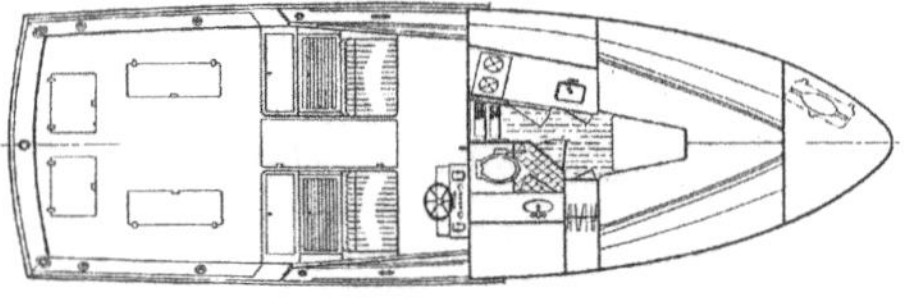

Introduced in 1986, the Black Watch 30 was well received among serious anglers for her extraordinary handling abilities, handsome profile, and high-tech construction. Her balsa-cored deep-V hull earned an early reputation for good handling and seakeeping characteristics, and with nearly 11 feet of beam she's a stable platform at trolling speeds. The deck layout of the 30 SF is dedicated to serious fishing activities, and her large unobstructed cockpit is set low to the water. A transom door is offset to starboard, and a pair of removable fish boxes are built into the cockpit sole. Engine boxes provide excellent access to the engines while serving as convenient seats from which to watch the baits. Inside, the cabin accommodations are fairly basic with berths for four (the backrests of the convertible dinette swing up to create single berths), an enclosed head with shower, storage lockers, and a small galley area. Visibility from the well-arranged helm is excellent in all directions. A good performer, twin 350hp gas engines cruise around 24 knots (34 knots top), and optional 300hp Cummins (or Cat) diesels cruise economically at a fast 28 knots and reach 31–32 knots wide open.

See Page 670 For Price Data

Length	30'1"	Fuel	240 gals.
Beam	10'11"	Water	50 gals.
Draft	2'10"	Waste	20 gals.
Weight	9,000#	Hull Type	Deep-V
Clearance	7'0"	Deadrise Aft	18°

Blackfin

Quick View

- Blackfin began operations in 1973 producing a 24-foot deep-V center console.
- Blackfin turned out a succession of popular, tournament-level fishing boats over the years earning the company a reputation as a quality South Florida builder.
- The company went through several owners and reorganizations during their history, and in 1997 Blackfin filed for bankruptcy for the final time.
- Saltshaker Boats purchased some of the Blackfin molds from bankruptcy and briefly re-introduced the Blackfin 29 Combi and 29 Flybridge models.
- A Blackfin owner's group can be found at www.blackfinowners.com.

No longer in business.

Blackfin 27 Sportsman

1995–98

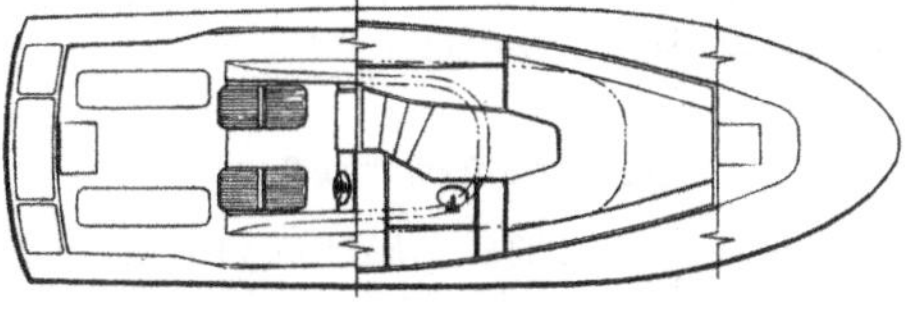

A distinctive and notably innovative design, the curved helm of the Blackfin 27 Sportsman projects the distinctive appearance of a South Florida custom-built boat. A superb rough-water performer, she's heavily constructed on a solid fiberglass deep-V hull, and her 10-foot beam is relatively wide compared with many other 27-footers. While the cabin can't be called spacious, it's large enough to offer the basics including a V-berth, a compact galley, storage lockers, and a marine head. The spacious bi-level cockpit comes standard with two large in-deck fish boxes, a 35-gallon livewell, and a centerline transom fish box. There's plenty of space in the helm console for an array of flush-mounted electronic add-ons. Originally introduced as an outboard-powered model, Blackfin began offering inboard power in 1996. Twin 250hp Yamaha outboards cruise a tower-equipped 27 Sportsman at 26 knots (approximately 38 knots top), and a pair of Yanmar 230hp diesels cruise at a brisk 26–27 knots and reach a top speed in the neighborhood of 33 knots. Note that since 2001, an updated outboard-powered version of the 27 Sportsman—the Salt Shaker 300 Walkaround—has been built on a limited production basis.

See Page 670 For Price Data

Length	27'9"	Weight, Diesel	10,980#
Beam	10'0"	Fuel	240 gals.
Draft, Outboard	1'11"	Water	30 gals.
Draft, Inboard	2'10"	Hull Type	Deep-V
Weight, Gas	9,850#	Deadrise Aft	24°

Blackfin 29 Combi

1983–98

An awesome rough-water boat in spite of her small size, the Blackfin 29 Combi was heavily built on a solid fiberglass deep-V hull with a relatively wide beam with plenty of flare at the bow. A low center of gravity—especially on the inboard—makes her a stable trolling platform, at least until a tower is added. Below, the Combi's compact cabin includes a convertible dinette/V-berth forward, a mini-galley, and a standup head with shower. The cockpit can handle a small chair and engine access is excellent. A popular boat for many years, she was updated in 1995 as the Blackfin 29-2 Combi with a restyled bridge deck, curved windshield, integral bow pulpit, and a new helm console with more space for electronic add-ons. The original 29 Combi has engine boxes; in the 29-2 model the boxes were redesigned to form aft-facing lounge seats. Standard 320hp gas engines cruise the 29 Combi at 23–24 knots, and optional 230hp Volvo diesels cruise at 25 knots. Those with Cummins 315hp diesels cruise at 28–29 knots and reach a top speed in the neighborhood of 32 knots. Note that an updated version of this model—called the 301 Open—was produced in later years by Salt Shaker Marine.

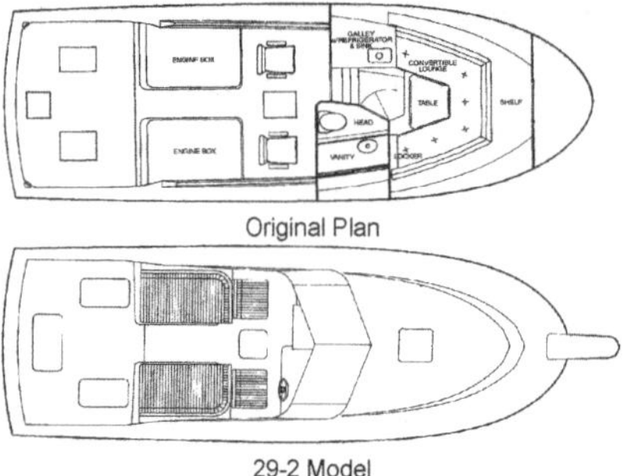
Original Plan

29-2 Model

See Page 670 For Price Data

Length w/Pulpit	32'6"	Fuel	250 gals.
Beam	10'6"	Water	30 gals.
Draft	2'10"	Waste	20 gals.
Weight, Dsl.	12,120#	Hull Type	Deep-V
Weight, Gas	10,025#	Deadrise Aft	22°

Blackfin 29 Flybridge

1986–99

You can count the number of production 29-foot flybridge sportfishing boats on one hand; most under-30-foot fishing boats are express designs. An exception to the rule, the 29 Flybridge was an extremely popular boat for Blackfin. Heavily built and expensive to buy, she's a superb fishing boat with a clean, unobstructed cockpit and an easy-to-reach flybridge with seating for four. The fact that she has a comfortable interior only adds to her appeal. Finished with teak trim, the upscale accommodations allow her to serve as a very capable family cruiser. Raised engine boxes forward of the cockpit provide excellent access to the motors and double as bait-watching seats. Note that the flybridge was revised in 1995 with lounge seating installed forward of the newly redesigned helm console, and in 1999 the floorplan was updated. Twin 320hp Crusaders cruise the Blackfin 29 at 22 knots (about 30 knots top). Optional 230hp Volvos cruise at 24 knots (27–28 top), and those with 315hp Cummins diesels cruise at 26 knots and reach 30 knots wide open. Note that a revised version of the Blackfin 29 was produced in later years by Salt Shaker Maine.

1986–98

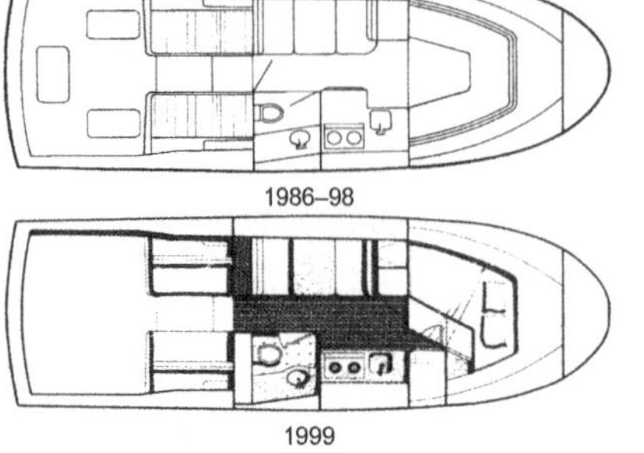
1999

See Page 670 For Price Data

Length w/Pulpit	32'6"	Weight, Diesel	13,604#
Hull Length	29'4"	Fuel	250/263 gals.
Beam	10'6"	Water	50 gals.
Draft	2'6"	Hull Type	Deep-V
Weight, Gas	11,109#	Deadrise Aft	22°

Blackfin 31 Combi

If the Blackfin 31 Combi has a different look than previous Combi models, it's because she's a remake of the earlier North Coast 31 (1988–90), a highly regarded deep-V fisherman from Massachusetts. In developing the 31 Combi, Blackfin engineers replaced the original North Coast floorplan with a new dinette layout that is more open and suitable for family cruising. Lounge seating was also added opposite the helm. The result is a family-friendly offshore fisherman with civilized, almost up-scale, cruising accommodations—a rarity in a serious fishboat. In 1995 Blackfin revised the layout with a larger head compartment, a portside dinette, and a convertible dinette forward. Additional features of the 31 Combi include unusually wide side decks, hydraulically operated engineroom hatch, a well-designed helm console, cockpit storage boxes, and a transom door. An excellent sea boat with a notably sharp entry, standard 320hp gas engines cruise the 31 Combi at 20–21 knots and reach about 30 knots top. Optional 300hp Cat diesels cruise at 25–26 knots and reach a top speed of approximately 30 knots.

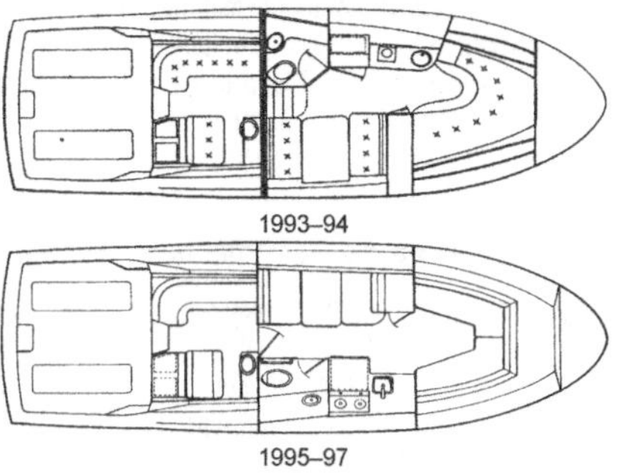
1993–94

1995–97

See Page 670 For Price Data

Length w/Pulpit	33'10"	Weight, Diesel	15,500#
Hull Length	30'8"	Fuel	300 gals.
Beam	11'10"	Water	70 gals.
Draft	2'11"	Hull Type	Deep-V
Weight, Gas	13,300#	Deadrise Aft	21°

Blackfin 33 Combi

A good-looking boat, the Blackfin 33 Combi is about as good as it gets in a midsize express fisherman. She was built on a solid fiberglass deep-V hull (borrowed from the Blackfin 33 Flybridge) with considerably more transom deadrise than other production boats. Her profile is low, the beam is wide, and the ride is superb. An expensive boat to begin with, her well-appointed interior will come as a surprise to those expecting the plain-Jane cabin accommodations common to most thoroughbred fishing machines. Indeed, the light ash woodwork, off-white cabinets, Avonite countertops and halogen lighting present a warm and inviting appearance. (Note that the interior was updated in 1996 and 1998.) The Combi's bi-level cockpit is ideally arranged with lounge seating opposite the helm and a big fishing platform aft. The entire bridge deck can be raised hydraulically for access to the engines, and the side decks are notably wide and well secured. Additional features include a huge in-deck fish box in the cockpit, transom door and gate, and a big L-shaped settee opposite the helm. A great open-water ride, optional 375hp Cats cruise the 33 Combi at a fast 27 knots and reach 31–32 knots top.

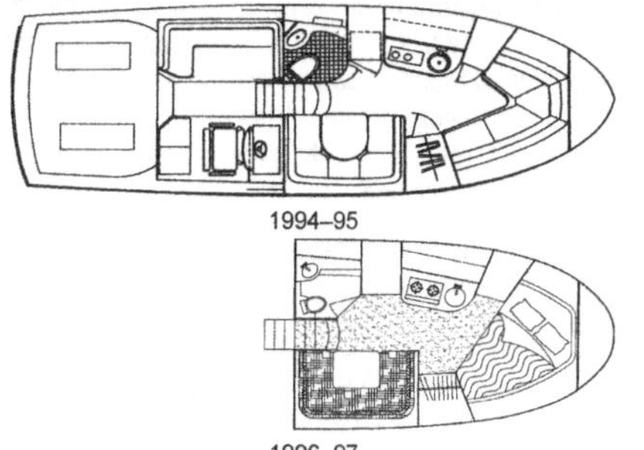
1994–95

1996–97

See Page 670 For Price Data

Length	32'11"	Fuel	340 gals.
Beam	12'0"	Water	80 gals.
Draft	2'11"	Waste	12 gals.
Weight	19,132#	Hull Type	Deep-V
Clearance	NA	Deadrise Aft	22°

Blackfin 33 Convertible

1990–99

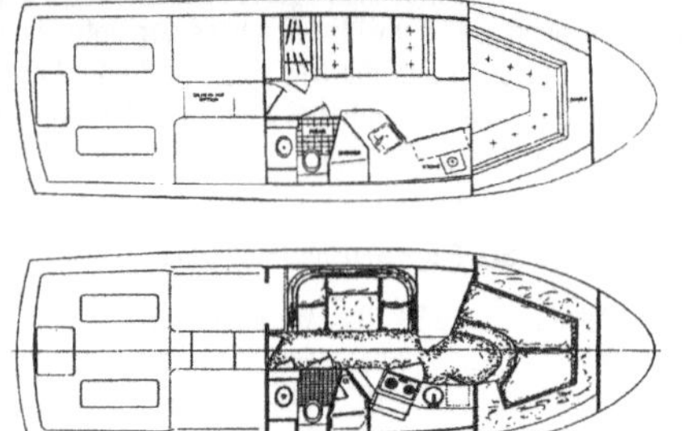

Replacing the classic Blackfin 32 Sportfisherman in 1990, the Blackfin 33 Convertible is a better-handling boat in just about every respect than her predecessor—no small feat considering the popularity of the 32. Blackfin never used any coring materials in their hulls so there's nothing high-tech here in the way of construction. Indeed, the 33 is a straightforward deep-V design with plenty of beam, a well-flared bow, and very low freeboard. Several floorplans were offered over the years, all sleeping four and having a separate stall shower in the head. Topside, the flybridge is big for a 33-footer with bench seating forward of the helm and a large console for flush-mounting electronics. Anyone who ever fished a Blackfin 32 will appreciate the 33's enlarged cockpit and standard transom door. Engine boxes are retained in the newer model and service access is excellent. Additional features include two in-deck fish boxes, cockpit washdowns, a bow pulpit, and plenty of rod storage. Not inexpensive, twin 320hp gas engines cruise around 22 knots (about 32 knots top), and a pair of 320hp or 375hp Cat diesels cruise at 24 and 27 knots respectively and reach top speeds in the low 30s.

See Page 670 For Price Data

Length w/Pulpit	36'0"	Weight, Diesel	20,169#
Hull Length	32'11"	Fuel	340 gals.
Beam	12'0"	Water	80 gals.
Draft	2'11"	Hull Type	Deep-V
Weight, Gas	17,645#	Deadrise Aft	22°

Blackfin 36/38 Combi

1986–98

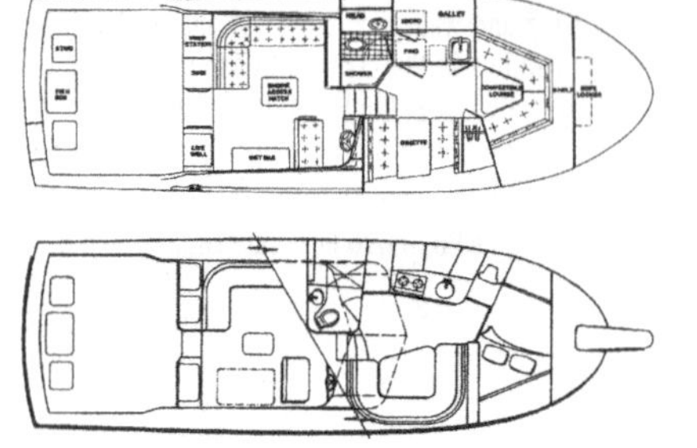

A solid, no-nonsense offshore fisherman, the Blackfin 38 Combi is a stretched version of the original 36 Combi introduced back in 1986. (She became the 38 Combi in 1988 when the cockpit was lengthened by two feet.) An expensive boat in her day, the Combi rides on a solid fiberglass deep-V hull with a well-flared bow and a wide 14-foot, 5-inch beam. The bi-level cockpit layout is excellent. An L-shaped lounge seat is opposite the helm, and the livewell and tackle center divide the bridge deck from the huge aft cockpit. Belowdecks, the off-white interior of the Combi was updated several times over the years and all can be described as well-appointed and more upscale than one might expect in a serious fishing boat. With most of the Combi's length devoted to cockpit space, the cabin dimensions are modest for a 38-footer but still adequate for comfortable weekend cruising. Notable features include a doublewide helm seat, a spacious engine compartment, a transom door and gate, wide side decks, and generous interior storage. A great sea boat, 485hp 6-71s cruise at 27 knots (30 top), and 550hp 6V92s (or 600hp Volvos) cruise around 29–30 knots and reach 33 knots wide open.

See Page 670 For Price Data

Length	38'3"	Fuel	514 gals.
Beam	14'5"	Water	100 gals.
Draft	3'9"	Waste	25 gals.
Weight	34,170#	Hull Type	Deep-V
Clearance	8'9"	Deadrise Aft	18°

Blackfin 36/38 Convertible

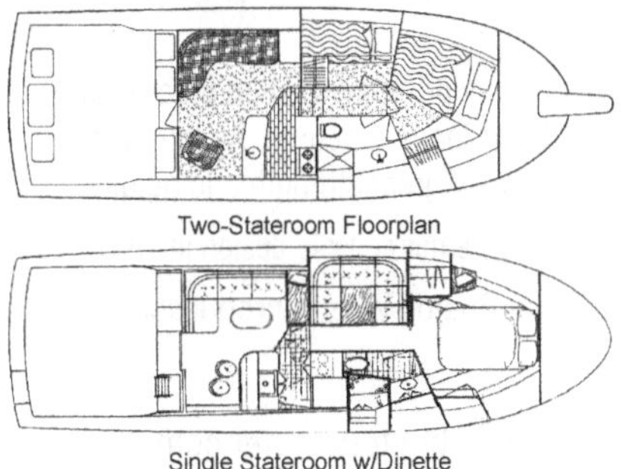
Two-Stateroom Floorplan

Single Stateroom w/Dinette

A handsome yacht whose sky-high price humbled all but the most affluent buyers of her era, the Blackfin 38 Convertible is a stretched version of the original Blackfin 36 Convertible introduced back in 1986. (She became a 38-footer in 1988 when the cockpit was lengthened by two feet.) From her rakish profile to her superb seeking characteristics, the Blackfin 38 set a very high standard for under-40-foot flybridge fishing boats. The cockpit is huge, and her well-planned flybridge provides excellent helm visibility and plenty of guest seating. Several single- and twin-stateroom floorplans were offered over the years (two of which are featured here) with most owners choosing a galley-up, two-stateroom configuration or a single-stateroom/dinette layout. Where the early interiors were finished with teak, later models were trimmed with light oak woodwork. A good performer, twin 375hp Cats cruise the 36 Convertible at 20 knots (about 25 knots top). For the 38 Convertible, a pair of 425hp Cats cruise at 23 knots (26 top); 485hp Detroit 6-71 diesels cruise at 25 knots (28 knots wide open); and 550hp 6V92s will produce an honest 27-knot cruise (about 30 knots top).

See Page 670 For Price Data

Length w/o Pulpit	38'3"	Fuel	514 gals.
Beam	14'5"	Water	135 gals.
Draft	4'0"	Waste	40 gals.
Weight	35,970#	Hull Type	Deep-V
Clearance	13'0"	Deadrise Aft	18°

Boston Whaler

Quick View

- Boston Whaler was founded in Braintree, MA, in 1958 by Richard Fisher.
- Whaler's first model, a foam-cored 13-footer with a unique squared-off bow, was an instant success and thousands were sold over the years.
- The company gained national notoriety in 1961 when Fisher appeared in a Life Magazine photo showing him sitting in his revolutionary boat as it was being sawed in half.
- In 1996, Brunswick Corporation purchased Boston Whaler. Combined with Sea Ray, it founded what would become the Brunswick Boat Group, now the largest manufacturer of pleasure boats in the world.
- Famed for its unsinkable hull, Boston Whaler's unique "Unibond" construction process is comprised of two fiberglass skins between which a liquid foam is poured. As the foam expands and hardens, it forms a single, sandwich-like hull of great strength and rigidity.
- Boston Whaler is generally credited with introducing the first center console design in 1961.
- Originally manufactured in Massachusetts, the current Boston Whaler production facility is located in Edgewater, Florida.

Boston Whaler Boats • Edgewater, FL • www.bostonwhaler.com

Boston Whaler 26 Outrage

1998—2002

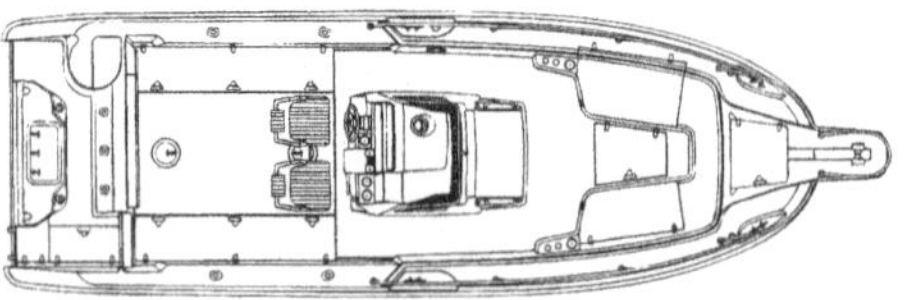

The Boston Whaler 260 Outrage (called the 26 Outrage from 1998–2001) is a good-looking center console with a well-arranged deck layout and plenty of fishing amenities. Like all Whalers, the Outrage is unsinkable thanks to her Unibond foam-core construction, and her deep-V hull is designed with wide, reverse chines for increased lift and stability. This is a well-built boat with excellent hardware and a better-than-average level of finish. Enclosed rod storage racks, a 30-gallon abovedeck livewell, electronics box, bait-prep station, and big in-deck fish boxes are features that qualify the 260 Outrage a serious offshore fishing boat. A leaning post is standard, and a foldaway stern seat provides additional guest seating for family and friends. A marine head can be installed in the large console compartment. Additional features include a raw-water washdown, walk-through transom, recessed trim tabs, anchor locker and a bow pulpit. A good performer with a dry ride, twin 225hp Mercury outboards cruise the Boston Whaler 260 Outrage at a fast 30 knots and deliver a top speed in excess of 40 knots.

See Page 670 For Price Data

Length w/Pulpit	27'10"	Fuel	200 gals.
Beam	8'6"	Water	20 gals.
Hull Draft	1'3"	Max HP	500
Weight	4,350#	Hull Type	Deep-V
Clearance, T-Top	8'4"	Deadrise Aft	20°

Boston Whaler 27 Offshore

1991–98

An unconventional design, the Boston Whaler 27 Offshore is a walkaround fisherman whose combined hardtop/semi-enclosed helm configuration was unique in her day. Like all Whalers, her foam-filled deep-V hull is unsinkable, and her broad, well-flared bow prevent stuffing in big head seas. A dedicated fishing boat, the Offshore came standard with two big in-deck fish boxes, a two-sink bait-prep station with cutting boards and tackle drawers, livewell, built-in rod holders and rod racks throughout. The fold-down splashwell door at the transom is notable; when folded in it allows anglers to stand well above the outboards in order to easily walk a fish around the props. The hardtop and windshield provide good weather protection, and an overhead electronics console was also standard. The Offshore's cuddy, with its V-berth, head, and storage is larger than one might expect in a 27-footer thanks to her generous 10-foot beam. Additional features include a molded pulpit, cockpit bolsters, opening ports for cabin ventilation, wide side decks, and bow seating for three. A rock-solid ride in a chop and a good all-around performer, twin 225 outboards cruise easily at 26 knots and reach 40+ knots top.

Floorplan Not Available

See Page 670 For Price Data

Length	26'7"	Fuel	243 gals.
Beam	10'0"	Water	30 gals.
Draft	1'9"	Max HP	500
Weight	5,800#	Hull Type	Modified-V
Clearance	NA	Deadrise Aft	20°

Boston Whaler 270 Outrage

2003–08

Like all Boston Whaler models, the 270 Outrage is a well engineered, heavily built boat whose exemplary finish and expensive price place her in the upper ranks of production fishing boats. The 270 is also a particularly handsome design, although with her drooping aft sheer she doesn't look like any previous Boston Whaler model. Console head compartments are pretty much standard these days in a center console boat this size, however, the 270 Outrage went a step further by adding the convenience of a sink and shower in addition to the marine head. A leaning post (with a removable backrest) is standard; a hideaway bench seat folds into the transom; and there are a total of eleven rod holders placed around the cockpit including three at the transom. Additional fishing amenities include lockable rod storage lockers, a 400-quart, in-deck fish box at the bow, 23-gallon livewell, transom door, cockpit bolsters, and lockable console storage. (For this much money, a good sound system might also have been standard.) An 8-foot, 6-inch beam makes the 270 Outrage one of the larger trailerable center consoles available. Twin 225hp Mercury outboards will deliver a top speed of around 45 knots.

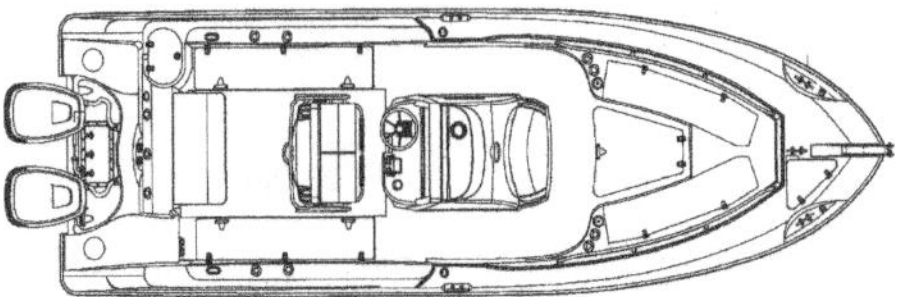

See Page 670 For Price Data

Length	27'0"	Fuel	200 gals.
Beam	8'6"	Water	20 gals.
Hull Draft	1'8"	Max HP	450
Dry Weight	5,160#	Hull Type	Deep-V
Clearance, Top	8'9"	Deadrise Aft	22°

Boston Whaler 275 Conquest

The Boston Whaler 275 Conquest was one of the biggest and most expensive 27-footers on the market when she was introduced in 2002. She's heavily built on a deep-V hull and, like all Whaler models, the inner hull is filled with closed-cell foam making her unsinkable even if swamped. While the Conquest is primarily a fishing boat, her spacious interior and generous cockpit seating also make her a capable weekend cruiser. A foldaway transom seat (which makes switching from cruising to fishing a breeze), two large in-deck fish boxes, a transom door and a circular livewell are standard in the cockpit, and a comfortable settee/lounge is opposite the helm. The cabin is arranged with a convertible V-berth/dinette forward, an enclosed head (with sitting headroom), a compact galley, and a compact midcabin berth more useful for storage than sleeping. Additional features include an integrated transom, bow pulpit, wide side decks, plenty of rod storage (inside and out), and tackle storage. An upmarket and altogether impressive package, twin 200hp outboards deliver a cruising speed of 24–25 knots and a top speed of close to 40 knots.

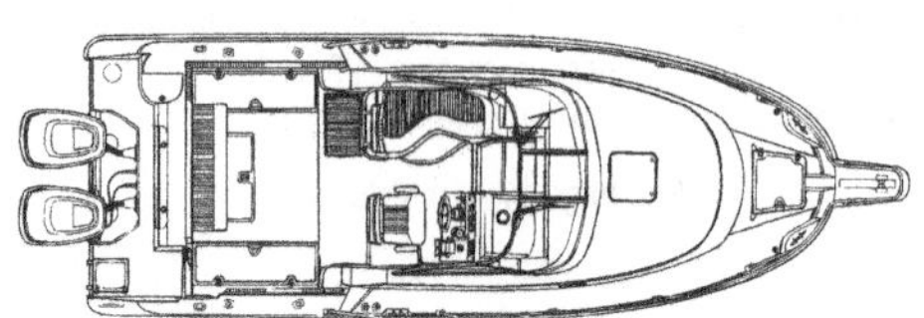

See Page 670 For Price Data

Length w/Pulpit	28'8"	Fuel	192 gals.
Beam	9'7"	Water	30 gals.
Hull Draft	1'6"	Max HP	500
Dry Weight	6,200#	Hull Type	Deep-V
Clearance w/Hardtop	8'9"	Deadrise Aft	20°

Boston Whaler 28 Conquest; 295 Conquest

The Boston Whaler 295 Conquest (called the 28 Conquest from 1999–2001) combines the fishability of a well-designed offshore express with the cruising comforts of a midcabin interior in an attractive and well-built package. Like all Whalers, the Conquest is unsinkable thanks to her Unibond foam-core construction. This is an expensive boat with handsome lines and above-average finish throughout. Anglers will find the Conquest's large cockpit fully equipped with a 30-gallon abovedeck livewell, under-gunwale rod racks, coaming bolsters, two in-deck fish boxes, rod holders and built-in tackle drawers. An aft-facing seat behind the helm and a full-width stern seat that folds into the transom provide additional seating. Belowdecks, the Conquest's cabin is functional and well arranged with a convertible dinette/V-berth forward, a mid-berth beneath the companionway steps, a teak-and-holly sole, a compact galley, and an enclosed standup head compartment. A transom door, swim platform, bow pulpit, and swim ladder were standard. Twin 225hp outboards will deliver a cruising speed of 25 knots and top speed in the neighborhood of 38 knots.

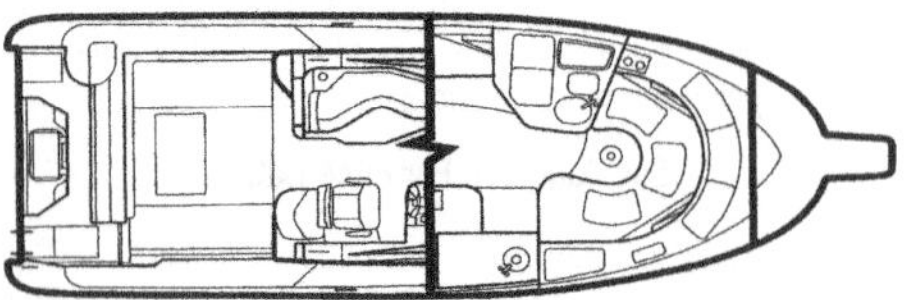

See Page 670 For Price Data

Length w/Pulpit	30'8"	Fuel	296 gals.
Hull Length	28'5"	Water	40 gals.
Beam	10'4"	Max HP	500
Hull Draft	1'8"	Hull Type	Deep-V
Dry Weight	8,500#	Deadrise Aft	20°

Boston Whaler 28 Outrage; 290 Outrage

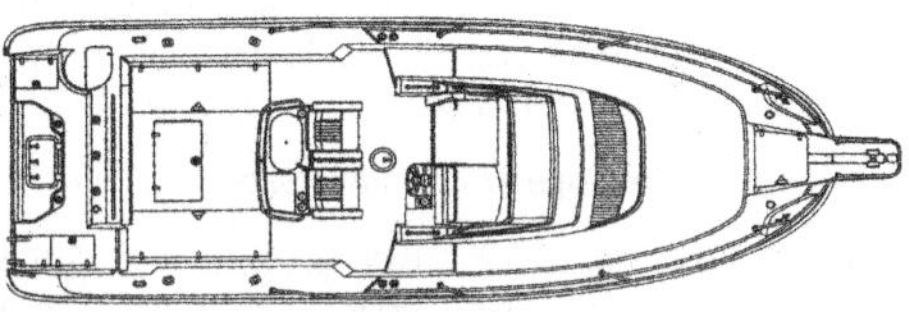

Historically, all of Boston Whaler's Outrage models have been center consoles. The 290 Outrage, however (called the 28 Outrage from 1999–2001), might easily be viewed as a walkaround since she features a surprisingly spacious cuddy with cruising-style accommodations. She's built on an easy-riding deep-V hull with a relatively wide beam, and like all Boston Whalers her foam-filled hull construction insures that she'll be unsinkable even when fully swamped. There's a lot of fishing space in the 290's cockpit thanks to her generous beam, and wide walkways provide easy passage to the bow with its bench seat, anchor locker, and bow pulpit. At the helm, adjustable padded seats double as leaning-post bolsters. Fishing amenities include a 30-gallon abovedeck recirculating livewell, two in-deck fish boxes, nine flush-mounted rod holders, bait-prep station with two sinks, tackle drawers, fresh- and raw-water washdowns, and a transom door. There's an enclosed head in the cabin, and a filler converts the twin berths into a large double berth. An expensive boat with a high level of finish, twin 225hp Mercury outboards cruise the Boston Whaler 290 Outrage at 25 knots with a top speed of around 40 knots.

See Page 670 For Price Data

Length w/Pulpit	30'8"	Fuel	296 gals.
Beam	10'4"	Water	40 gals.
Draft, Up	1'8"	Max HP	500
Draft, Down	3'0"	Hull Type	Deep-V
Weight	7,000#	Deadrise Aft	20°

Boston Whaler 280 Outrage

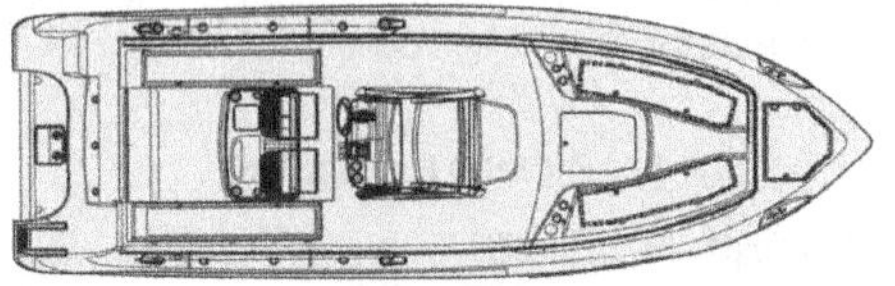

For decades, Boston Whaler has ranked among the best builders of deep-V center consoles in the business. And since quality never comes cheap, Whalers are always among the most expensive boats to buy. Introduced in 2009, the 280 Outrage is a hardcore center console meant for serious fishing as well as comfortable coastal cruising. With her three-sided, tempered glass windshield, electric forward vent window, and integrated T-top (with floodlights and life jacket storage) the 280 offers something different from previous Whaler designs. Highlights include a foldaway transom seat, aft-facing amidships seats, lockable rod storage, 40-gallon livewell with clear-top window, two macerated fish boxes, full-length cockpit bolsters, and over 20 rod holders. Note the through-stem anchor system and recessed windlass. The console compartment includes a VacuFlush toilet. Built on a new Whaler hull with generous freeboard and a relatively wide 9'4" beam, the 280 Outrage has more transom deadrise than any previous Whaler model. As with all Boston Whalers, her foam-filled hull is unsinkable. Twin 300hp Verado four-stroke outboards top out at close to 50 knots.

See Page 670 For Price Data

Length	27'7"	Fuel	200 gals.
Beam	9'4"	Water	28 gals.
Hull Draft	1'8"	Max HP	600
Dry Weight	6,100#	Hull Type	Deep-V
Clearance w/Hardtop	8'10"	Deadrise Aft	23°

Boston Whaler 285 Conquest

2006–2010

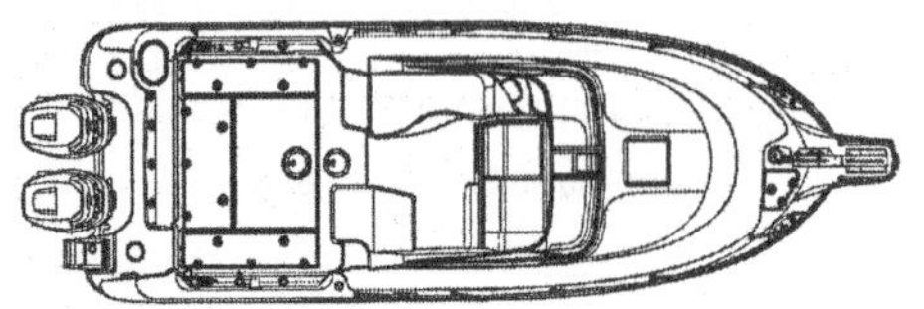

Introduced in 2006, the 285 Conquest is a roomy day boat whose serious fishing amenities and comfortable cabin will appeal to family anglers who enjoy an occasional overnight or weekend trip. Constructed with Boston Whaler's patented Unibond system, the 285 is, like her sisterships, unsinkable—always a comforting thought. Her raised sheerline gives her a muscular look to match Whaler's reputation for building rugged and seakindly boats. The cockpit is large and uncluttered with insulated fish boxes in the sole, a 20-gallon livewell in the port corner, a folding bench seat on the centerline, and a transom door to starboard. The bulkhead under the aft-facing seat holds a tackle center. On the raised helm deck, a curved seat for two opposite the helm converts to a full-length lounge. There's space in the dash for mounting two big-screen video displays. An optional sunshade cranks out to cover the whole cockpit. The 285's well-appointed interior features an enclosed head with shower, convertible dinette (with a removable dining table), galley pod, and a transverse double berth beneath the helm deck. About 40 knots max with 225 Mercs. Replaced in 2011 with all-new 285 Conquest model.

See Page 670 For Price Data

Length	30'2"	Fuel	207 gals.
Beam	9'8"	Water	30 gals.
Draft, Drives Up	1'8"	Max HP	450
Draft, Drives Down	3'2"	Hull Type	Deep-V
Hull Weight	6,200#	Deadrise Aft	20°

Boston Whaler 305 Conquest

2004–Current

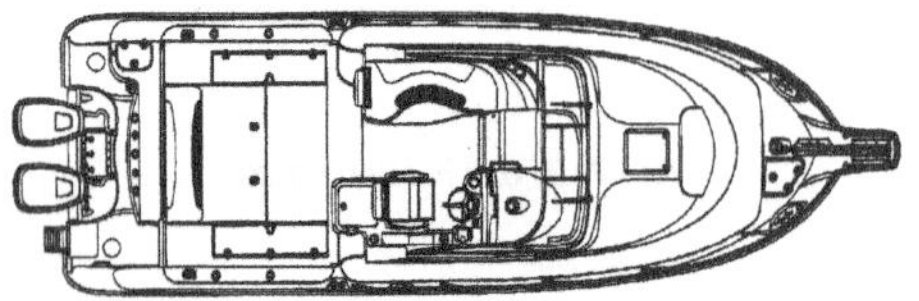

The unsinkable legend that is Boston Whaler continues with the 305 Conquest, a heavily built 30-foot express designed for serious anglers with a yen for quality. The 305 is a refinement of the popular 295 Conquest (1999–2003) with a larger cockpit, an updated interior, and a redesigned helm and transom. The Conquest's list of fishing features begins with plenty of rod storage (under the gunwales and inside the cabin) and includes a 24-gallon transom livewell, cockpit rigging station, two insulated in-deck fish boxes with pump-outs, and an enormous hatch in the sole that provides unprecedented access to the bilge. Visibility from the 305's raised bridge deck is excellent, and a comfortable lounge seat across from the helm seats two guests. Below, the Conquest sleeps four adults—two in the forward V-berth and two more in the midcabin double berth. Cherrywood cabinets and faux granite counters highlight the galley. Additional features include a bow pulpit, wide side decks, and a hideaway bench seat that pulls out from the transom. Note that a hardtop is standard. No lightweight, twin 225hp Mercury outboards will deliver a top speed of 32–33 knots.

See Page 670 For Price Data

Length w/Pulpit	32'1"	Fuel	300 gals.
Hull Length	30'1"	Water	40 gals.
Beam	10'7"	Max HP	600
Hull Draft	1'8"	Hull Type	Deep-V
Dry Weight	8,500#	Deadrise Aft	20°

Boston Whaler 320 Outrage

Boston Whaler's largest center console in 2003, the 320 Outrage is built to compete with the big boys in the offshore center-console market. Like all Whaler products, the 320 is a very high-quality boat with unsinkable construction, a superb deck layout, and excellent range. Built on a slender deep-V hull with a small keel pad for increased lift, the 320 is a good headsea boat and an excellent open-water performer. Fishing activities center around the custom bait-prep center behind the helm seats with its 45-gallon livewell, sink, cutting board, and raw-water washdown. There are three in-deck fish boxes (two 80-gallon boxes aft and a 100-gallon box forward), and both the helm and companion seat bolsters flip up so you can sit or stand, tucked in by padded armrests. In the dash, a large electronics flat conceals twin 10-inch displays. A sturdy fiberglass hardtop is standard equipment on the 320 Outrage that also boasts its own anchoring system including a standard windlass. Additional features include a foldaway rear seat, console head/storage compartment with marine toilet, foldaway console rod rack, and a transom shower. Twin 250hp Mercury outboards deliver in excess of 40 knots.

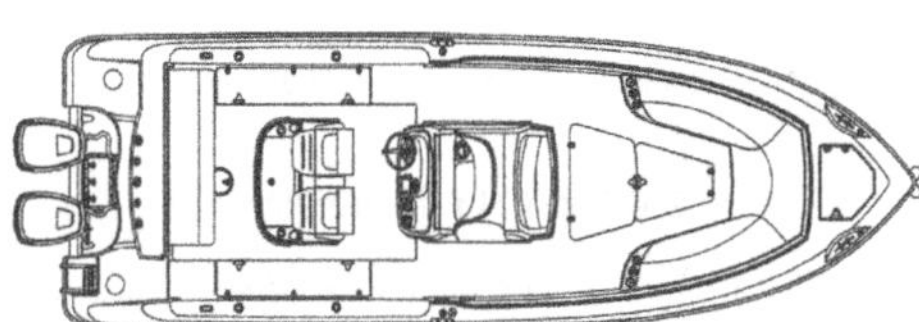

See Page 670 For Price Data

Length	32'2"	Fuel	300 gals.
Beam	10'2"	Water	40 gals.
Hull Draft	1'10"	Max HP	600
Dry Weight	8,500#	Hull Type	Deep-V
Clearance, Top	9'11"	Deadrise Aft	23°

Boston Whaler 320 Outrage Cuddy

The 320 Outrage Cuddy is unlike any previous Boston Whaler design. Where many boats claim to be versatile, the 320 gives real meaning to the term by combining the amenities of a serious fishing boat with the comforts of a well-equipped cabin. From the helm station aft, the Outrage Cuddy is identical to the 320 Outrage Center Console introduced a few years earlier. A foldaway bench seat spans the transom, and insulated fish boxes are located in either side of the cockpit sole. At the helm, a deluxe leaning post includes an aerated 45-gallon livewell, bait prep station, sink, and tackle boxes. An L-shaped lounge forward of the console has storage underneath, and there's another storage locker under a hatch in the sole. Behind the L-lounge, the refreshment center has a top-loading refrigerator/freezer and storage. Across from the lounge are nonskid stairs leading up to the foredeck. The 320's well-appointed cuddy features teak flooring, overhead rod racks, and a U-shaped seating area that converts to a V-berth large enough for two adults. Note that the fiberglass hardtop extends forward to cover the bow cockpit area as well as the console. Over 40 knots top with twin 250hp Mercs.

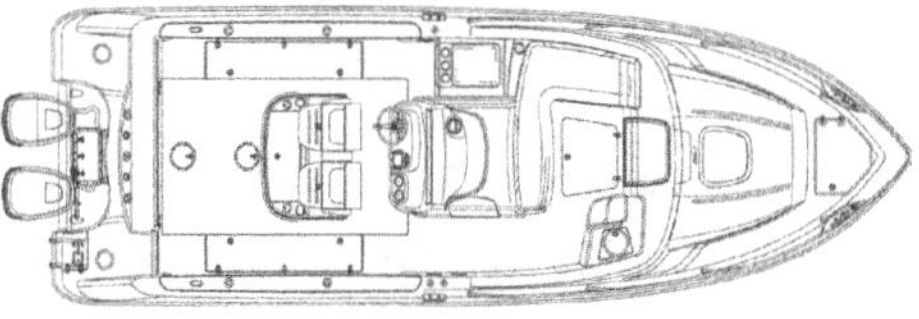

See Page 670 For Price Data

Length	32'2"	Fuel	300 gals.
Beam	10'2"	Water	40 gals.
Hull Draft	1'10"	Max HP	600
Dry Weight	9,000#	Hull Type	Deep-V
Clearance, Top	9'10"	Deadrise Aft	23°

Boston Whaler 34 Defiance

1999–2002

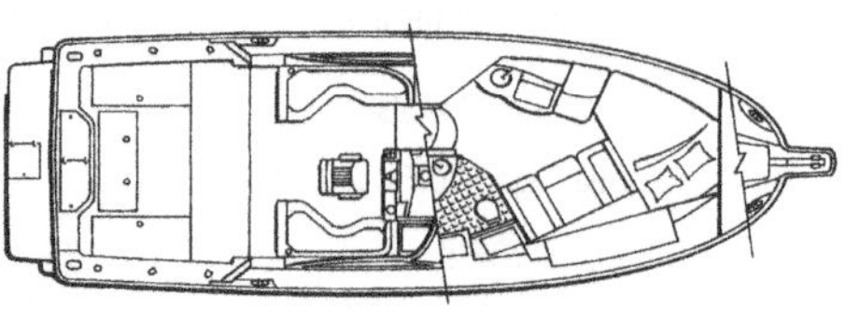

The Boston Whaler 34 Defiance (called the 350 Defiance in 2002) is a premium express fisherman with a number of innovative features to go with her upscale price. The Defiance is built on a deep-V hull with generous beam and wide, spray-deflecting chines. Like other Whalers, foam flotation between the inner and outer hulls makes her unsinkable. In the cockpit, aft-facing seats at the corners conceal a cooler to port and a freezer to starboard, and the transom door slides into the transom—very slick. A livewell is built into the transom, and a full bait-prep station is forward, next to the cockpit freezer. For engine access, the entire bridge deck slides aft on rollers (rather than lifting from the back on hydraulic rams), which makes getting at the motors very easy, even while running. The exhaust is expelled beneath the hull while the boat is on plane and above the waterline at slow speeds. Additional features include a spacious, well-finished interior, a centerline helm with flanking settees, and a power windshield vent. Twin 340hp Cat diesels cruise at 24 knots (27–28 knots top), and optional 420hp Yanmars cruise at 26 knots and reach a top speed of about 30 knots.

See Page 671 For Price Data

Length w/Pulpit	37'6"	Clearance, Top	8'2"
Hull Length	34'6"	Fuel	384 gals.
Beam	13'3"	Water	72 gals.
Draft	2'11"	Hull Type	Deep-V
Weight	19,000#	Deadrise Aft	20°

Boston Whaler 345 Conquest

2007–Current

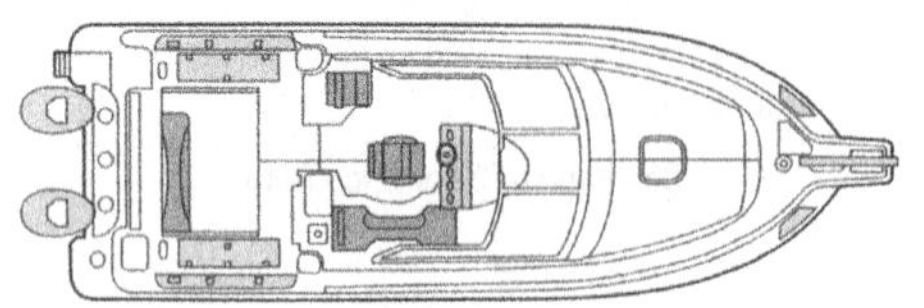

Introduced in 2007, the 345 Conquest is a distinctive pilothouse express whose integrated windshield/hardtop offers protection from sun, wind and spray. Like all Whalers, the 345 is built to fish. Her large cockpit comes equipped with two in-deck macerated fish boxes, a 40-gallon transom livewell, bait-prep center with sink and cutting board, and a very sturdy fold-down rear bench seat. There's also a refrigerator/freezer in the cockpit, and a hot/cold shower is standard. A hatch in the cockpit sole provides easy access to the boat's mechanical systems. Below decks, the Conquest is clearly meant for long-range comfort. A centerline island berth is forward, and U-shaped seating under the helm deck quickly converts to another double. The entire cabin is trimmed in teak and the counters are granite; overall, the boat can sleep five people. Note that the helm is centered in the 345, putting the captain in the best piloting (and social) position possible. The center windshield pane opens outward to provide breeze at the helm. A huge hatch provides access to tanks, pumps, etc., and a generator and AC are standard. Triple 250hp Mercury Verados deliver 40+ knots wide open.

See Page 671 For Price Data

Length w/Pulpit	35'11"	Fuel	421 gals.
Beam	11'8"	Water	64 gals.
Hull Draft	1'10"	Max HP	900
Hull Weight	14,200#	Hull Type	Modified-V
Weight w/Engines	20,000#	Deadrise Aft	15°

Boston Whaler 370 Outrage

2010–Current

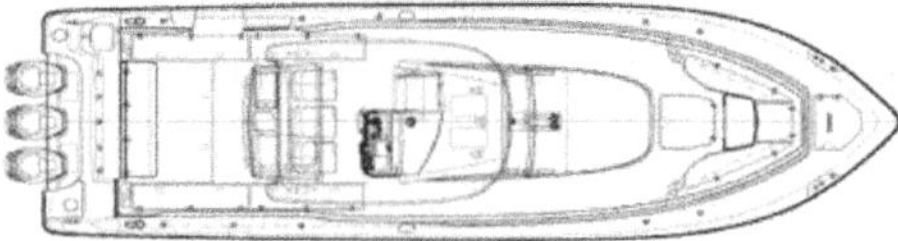

The largest Whaler built to date, the 370 Outrage is arguably the most sophisticated, tricked-out, and expensive center console on the market. Exceptional as both an offshore fishing boat and entertaining platform for family and friends, the 370 combines space and luxury in an unsinkable package loaded with innovative features. Fishing amenities include a 24-gallon livewell in the aft port corner, five in-deck fish boxes, and a deluxe leaning post/bait prep center with 55-gallon main livewell. A passenger seat flips out of the aft bulkhead, and a large hullside dive door allows boarding from a floating dock. There are three independent helm seats, all with flip-down armrests and bolsters. Note the integrated hardtop/windshield with retractable sunshade. A horseshoe-shaped lounge (with a huge storage locker under) is forward, and the anchor mounts through the stem that eliminates the need for a bow roller. Below, the 370's full-height cabin has berths for two. Additional features include lockable console front storage, pump room with diesel genset, bow thruster, and cockpit galley with refrigerator/freezer and grill. Triple 300hp Verado outboards cruise the 370 Outrage at 30 knots (40+ top).

See Page 671 For Price Data

Length	37'6"	Fuel	425 gals.
Beam	11'6"	Water	60 gals.
Draft, Up	2'0"	Max HP	900
Draft, Down	3'4"	Hull Type	Modified-V
Dry Weight	13,500#	Deadrise Aft	15°

Cabo

Quick View

- The Cabo Yachts story began in 1988 when Henry Mohrschladt and Michael Howarth sold their sailboat company, Pacific Seacraft Corp., and set out to build a premium sportfishing boat.
- Based in Adelanto, CA, Cabo's fheir first production model, the Cabo 35 Flybridge, was introduced in 1991 to enthusiastic reviews.
- Cabo went on the establish itself as one of the premier builders of high-end sportfishing boats—a remarkable feat in an industry dominated by East Coast manufacturers.
- Cabo was acquired by industry-giant Brunswick Corporation in 1996.
- In 2010 Brunswick consolidated production of its Hatteras and Cabo brands at the Hatteras facility in New Bern, N.C., closing the California plant where Cabo yachts were produced.
- With production at a record low, parent-company Brunswick announced early in 2013 its decision to exit the sport fishing industry and seek a buyer for Cabo Yachts.

Cabo Yachts • New Bern, NC • www.caboyachts.com

Cabo 31 Express

1995–2004

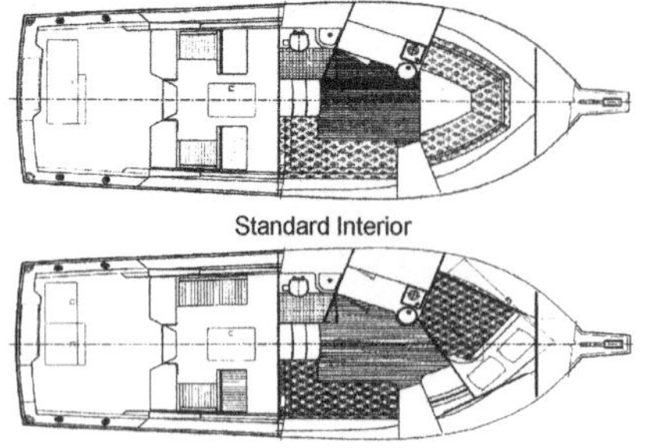

Standard Interior

Offset Double Berth

The Cabo 31 Express is a premium offshore fisherman whose precise handling, exceptional performance and superb engineering set her apart from just about every other boat in her class. She's heavily built on an easy-riding deep-V hull with a relatively wide beam, a sharp entry, and balsa coring in the hullsides. While the Cabo 31 is obviously designed for serious anglers, the upscale cabin accommodations are surprisingly spacious for a boat of this type with berths for four adults, a complete galley area, decent storage, and an enclosed, standup head with shower. Cockpit amenities include a bait-prep center, transom fish box, rod storage, fresh and saltwater washdowns, and a transom door with gate. The entire bridge deck can be raised hydraulically for access to the motors. Among several diesel engine options (gas engines are standard), twin 350hp Cat 3116 diesels cruise the Cabo 31 at 26–27 knots and reach a top speed of about 30 knots. The larger 420hp Cat (or Yanmar) diesels cruise at an honest 29–30 knots (about 35 knots top). Note the generous 350-gallon fuel capacity. An expensive boat with a loyal following, in 2002 the hull chines were retooled for a drier ride.

See Page 671 For Price Data

Length w/Pulpit	33'2"	Fuel	350 gals.
Hull Length	31'0"	Water	50 gals.
Beam	12'5"	Headroom	6'5"
Draft	3'2"	Hull Type	Modified-V
Weight	15,000#	Deadrise Aft	17.5°

Cabo 32 Express

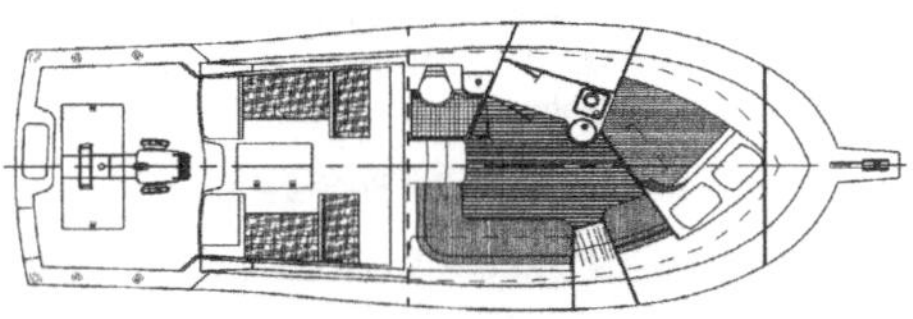

Experienced boaters and marine industry pros alike agree that Cabo builds a great fishing boat. Starting with the Cabo 35 Flybridge in 1992, the company introduced a series of high-end fishing machines designed for serious, hardcore anglers. The 32 Express—smallest model in the Cabo fleet—is a fast-action battlewagon with the premium amenities and features found in Cabo's larger boats. There's much to admire about the 32; she's one of the best-looking express boats her size to be found, and Cabo's obsessive attention to detail is on display in every nook and cranny. But it's the super-wide 13'3" beam that really sets the Cabo 32 apart from the competition. Indeed, she has a bigger cockpit, wider bridge deck, and more spacious interior than any boat in her class. A bait prep center, 45-gallon transom livewell, coaming pads, and large-capacity fish box are standard in the cockpit. The entire bridge deck sole lifts on hydraulic rams for engine access. Below decks, the Cabo's upscale (and surprisingly spacious) interior features a double berth forward, convertible dinette, and full service galley—comfortable accommodations for four. No lightweight, she'll cruise at 28 knots with 480 Yanmar diesels (30+ wide open).

See Page 671 For Price Data

Length w/Pulpit	35'0"	Fuel	350 gals.
Hull Length	32'10"	Water	50 gals.
Beam	13'3"	Waste	12 gals.
Draft	2'8"	Hull Type	Modified-V
Weight	19,100#	Deadrise Aft	17.5°

Cabo 35 Express

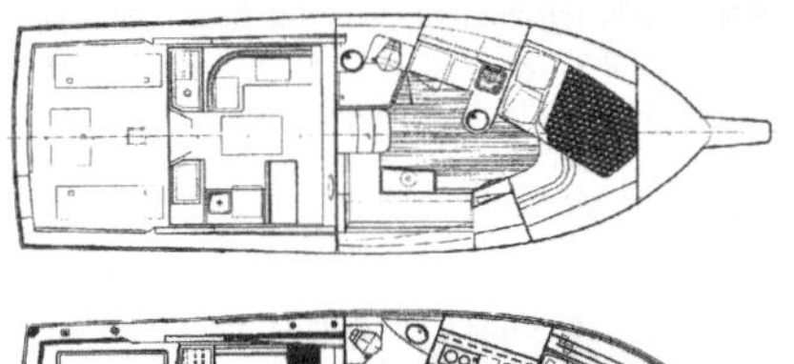

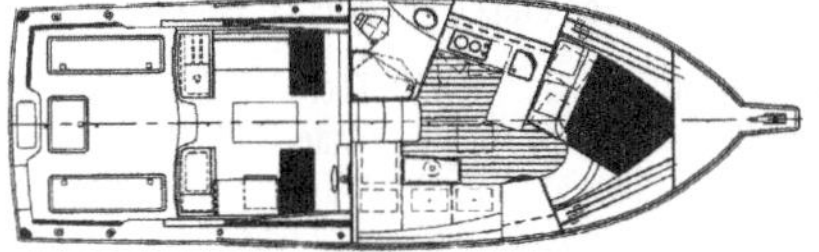

Introduced in 1993, the Cabo 35 Express is a top-level sportfishing machine whose impeccable detailing, superior engineering, and rugged construction made her one of the post popular boats in her class. Constructed on a modified-V hull with a relatively wide beam and a shallow keel, the hull was updated in 2000 with a finer entry to provide a softer ride and improved head-sea performance. While a centerline double berth was offered in early models, more recent interiors were offered with a traditional V-berth or an offset double berth forward. Cabin headroom is excellent and the decor is very upscale for a fishing boat. The cockpit is big for a 35-footer and comes standard with a bait-prep center, transom door, two in-deck storage boxes, cockpit coaming, washdowns and plenty of rod storage. An L-shaped settee is opposite the helm (a companion seat is optional), and the entire bridge deck lifts hydraulically for access to the motors. In 2002 the deck tooling was updated and side vents were added to the windshield. A good performer, those with 375hp Cats cruise in the mid 20s (about 30 knots top). Later models with 461hp Cats cruise at 28 knots and top out in the low 30s.

See Page 671 For Price Data

Length w/Pulpit	37'6"	Fuel	400 gals.
Hull Length	34'6"	Water	100 gals.
Beam	13'0"	Waste	16 gals.
Draft	2'10"	Hull Type	Modified-V
Weight	20,000#	Deadrise Aft	16°

Cabo 35 Flybridge

1992–2008

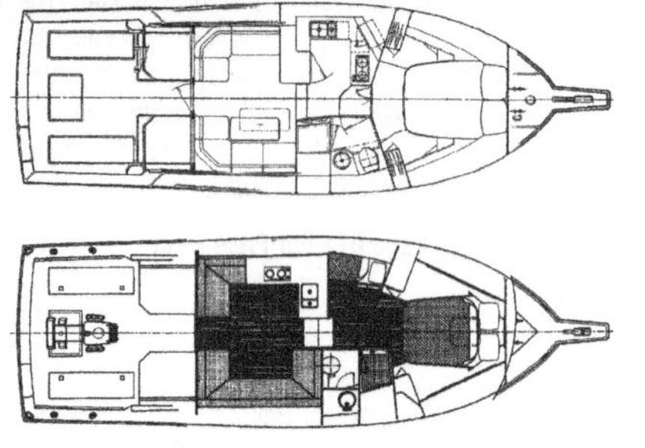

Cabo's first boat, the Cabo 35 Flybridge ranks among the most popular boats of her type built in recent years. Where many small flybridge boats have a tall profile, Cabo kept the height of the 35 low by placing the motors in cockpit engine boxes (rather than under the salon sole), which both lowers her profile and makes for a more comfortable ride. Built on a modified-V hull, early models were often criticized for their poor head-sea performance. Those issues were successfully resolved in 2000 when the hull was re-designed with a finer entry and widened chines. Considering her oversized cockpit, the Cabo's interior is surprisingly spacious. The galley-up layout includes an 8-foot settee with hidden rod storage in the salon and an island berth in the stateroom, while the galley-down floorplan has a stall shower in the head. Additional features include two in-deck fish boxes, transom door and gate, good cabin headroom, single-lever helm controls, and wide side decks with sturdy rails. A sought-after boat on the used market, those with 375hp 3208 Cats cruise in the mid 20s (about 30 knots top), and later models with 450hp 3116 Cats cruise at 28 knots with a top speed of just over 30 knots.

See Page 671 For Price Data

Length w/Pulpit	37'6"	Fuel	400 gals.
Hull Length	34'6"	Water	100 gals.
Beam	13'0"	Waste	16 gals.
Draft	2'6"	Hull Type	Modified-V
Weight	20,000#	Deadrise Aft	16°

Cabo 38 Express

2008–10

Since 1991, Cabo Yachts has been manufacturing advanced sportfishing boats that have earned the company a worldwide reputation for leading-edge quality and performance. Designed by Michael Peters Yacht Design, the 38 is an entirely new hull from the ground up. With her 15'1" beam, she's got more cockpit and cabin space than anything in her class. Tournament anglers will find themselves at home in the wide cockpit with its big 48-gallon transom livewell, outward-opening transom door, insulated fish boxes, and a molded bait-prep/tackle station with freezer and cutting board. The entire helm deck—which is huge for a 38-foot boat—can be raised hydraulically to provide good access to the Cabo's gelcoated engineroom. Below decks, the spacious (and very understated) cabin sleeps four and includes a fully equipped galley with microwave and under-counter refrigeration, stand-up head with separate stall shower, and more storage and counter space that most crews will ever use. Designed for hard-core anglers who know what they want, the Cabo 38 Express cruise at a solid 30 knots with 715hp Cat—or 800hp MAN—diesels (mid to high 30s top).

See Page 671 For Price Data

Length w/Pulpit	40'8"	Fuel	500 gals.
Hull Length	38'0"	Water	95 gals.
Beam	15'1"	Waste	35 gals.
Draft	3'8"	Hull Type	Modified-V
Weight	26,000#	Deadrise Aft	17°

Cabo 40 Express

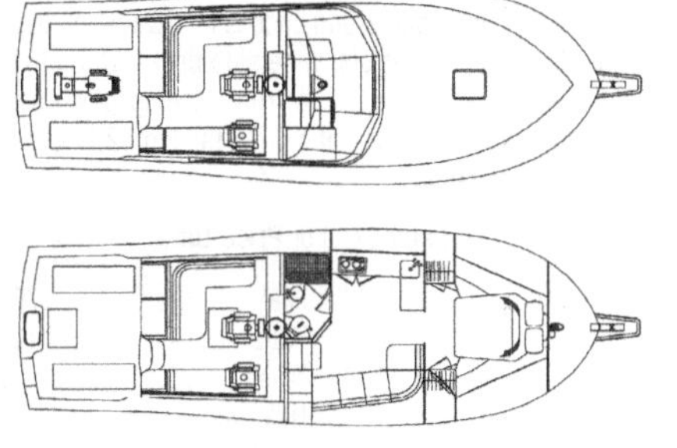

Among the best in her class, the Cabo 40 is a hardcore fishing machine from a company whose reputation for quality and performance is second to none. Built on a modified-V hull with deep propeller pockets and a well-flared bow, the Cabo 40 is a strikingly handsome boat whose muscular profile reflects her superb open-water performance. The 40's big 90-square-foot cockpit features a pair of in-deck fish boxes, a 45-gallon transom livewell, freezer, and a beefy transom door with top gate. The helm—a real piece of work—is on the centerline on the raised bridge deck where an L-shaped settee to port will accommodate several guests. Belowdecks, the 40's generous 15-foot, 9-inch beam is on full display in the wide-open salon with its warm teak joinery and plush furnishings. The starboard settee seats six and converts to upper/lower berths, and the large master stateroom is fitted with an island double berth and two hanging lockers. Additional features include single-lever controls, tremendous rod storage, hydraulic bridge deck lift, and 10KW generator. Cruise at 28–30 knots with 715hp Cats; low to mid 30s with 800hp MANs. Zeus pod drives became available in 2010.

See Page 671 For Price Data

Length w/Pulpit	42'10"	Headroom	6'3"
Beam	15'9"	Fuel	550 gals.
Draft	3'5"	Water	95 gals.
Weight	28,000#	Hull Type	Modified-V
Clearance	14'2"	Deadrise Aft	16.5°

Cabo 40 Flybridge

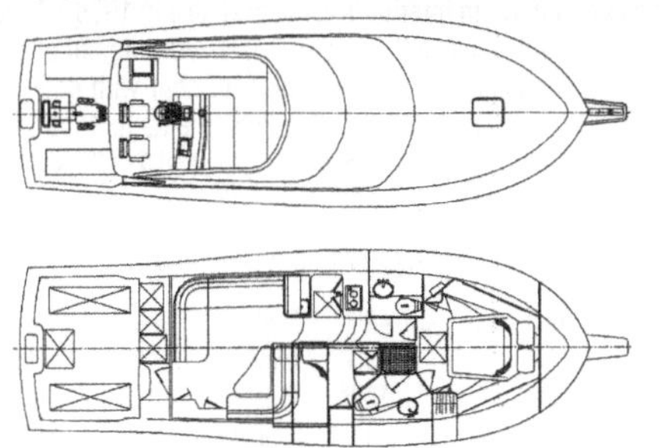

In the world of midsize sportfishing boats, the Cabo 40 Flybridge gets top billing for her world-class engineering, luxury-class amenities, and cutting-edge performance. Built on the same modified-V hull (with prop pockets) used in the production of the Cabo 40 Express, the interior of the 40 Flybridge will please anglers who journey to the canyons for a few days of fishing as well as families pursuing an extended vacation. The standard two-stateroom layout has the galley down and an L-shaped dinette to starboard in the salon—a surprisingly spacious arrangement expertly finished with Corian counters, quality fabrics, and traditional teak woodwork. The roomy cockpit comes equipped with all the usual features including tackle storage, large-capacity livewell, bait freezer, and two large in-deck fish boxes. Topside, the center helm console (with single-lever electronic controls) offers excellent sightlines in all directions. Note the near-standing headroom in the engineroom. Additional features include recessed trim tabs, bow pulpit, and a huge belowdeck storage locker under the galley sole. Cruise at 28–30 knots with 715hp Cats; low to mid 30s with 800hp MANs.

See Page 671 For Price Data

Length w/Pulpit	42'10"	Fuel	550 gals.
Hull Length	40'2"	Water	95 gals.
Beam	15'9"	Waste	22 gals.
Draft	3'5"	Hull Type	Modified-V
Weight	32,000#	Deadrise Aft	16.5°

Cabo 43 Flybridge

With her rakish profile, meticulous detailing and remarkable performance, the Cabo 43 Flybridge more than justified her sky-high price with affluent anglers. Indeed, this is a beautifully styled sportfisherman with a near-perfect balance of form and function. She's built on a constant-deadrise deep-V hull with no lifting strakes—unusual in a modern hull and similar to the original deep-V hulls pioneered by Bertram in the 1960s. Belowdecks, her two-stateroom, two-head layout is arranged with the galley down and the master stateroom amidships. An L-shaped dinette is opposite the sofa in the salon, and the head is fitted with a separate stall shower. These are very upscale accommodations with quality fabrics and plenty of varnished teak joinery and trim. Because the cockpit is so large, the salon dimensions are admittedly modest—a compromise most anglers are quick to concede. Additional features include cockpit engineroom access, a transom door with gate, single-lever helm controls, wide side decks, Corian countertops, and an integral bow pulpit. A truly exciting performer, twin 800hp MAN diesels cruise the Cabo 43 in the high 20s and reach a top speed of 34–35 knots.

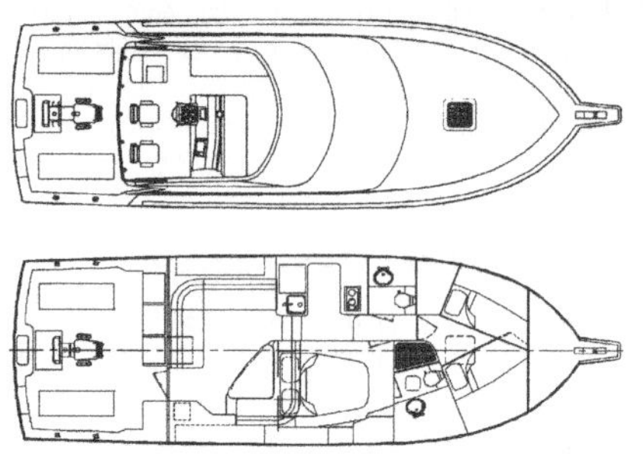

See Page 671 For Price Data

Length w/Pulpit	46'0"	Fuel	700 gals.
Hull Length	43'2"	Water	100 gals.
Beam	15'1"	Waste	28 gals.
Draft	4'4"	Hull Type	Deep-V
Weight	33,500#	Deadrise Aft	18.5°

Cabo 45 Express

One of the largest express fishermen available, the premium price of the Cabo 45 is enough to bring all but the most affluent anglers to their knees. She's constructed on a beamy good-riding modified-V hull with cored hullsides, a deep forefoot, and a well-flared bow. Aside from her rakish profile, perhaps the most distinctive feature of the Cabo 45 is her huge bridge deck with its centerline helm, integral electronics console, and expansive lounge seating. The fully equipped cockpit comes with a transom livewell (with a window), a beautifully designed tackle center, and two huge in-deck fish boxes. The engineroom, beneath the bridge deck, is massive with excellent service access to the motors. The standard single-stateroom interior of the Cabo 45 is meticulously finished, and the spacious salon provides seating for a small crowd. (Note that a two-stateroom interior became available in 1999.) Additional features include enclosed storage for over 20 rods, an electrically controlled windshield vent, and a transom door with gate. Among several diesel options, 660hp Cats cruise the Cabo 45 at 25 knots (about 30 knots top), and 800hp Cats cruise at 28–29 knots. Over 100 have been built.

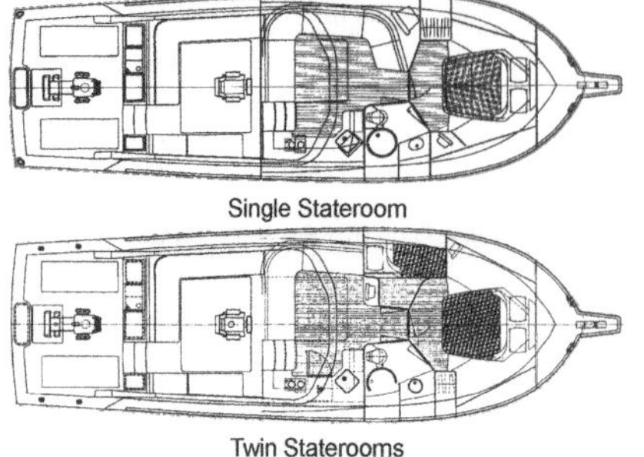
Single Stateroom

Twin Staterooms

See Page 671 For Price Data

Length w/Pulpit	48'1"	Fuel	800 gals.
Hull Length	45'1"	Water	100 gals.
Beam	15'8"	Waste	40 gals.
Draft	4'0"	Hull Type	Modified-V
Weight	33,000#	Deadrise Aft	11.5°

Cabo 47/48 Flybridge

2000–08

The Cabo 48 (called the Cabo 47 until 2003) is a premium, high-quality flybridge convertible whose uncompromising design and quality construction place her in the leading ranks of mid-range sportfishing boats. Cabos have an enviable reputation for fit and finish and the 48 is a showcase of Cabo's engineering excellence. Built on a modified-V hull with cored hullsides and a well-flared bow, the cockpit is huge—largest of any sportfishing boat in this class—and comes with a full array of fishing amenities including an excellent bait-prep center, in-deck fish boxes and a lighted 50-gallon transom livewell. The original galley-up, two-stateroom floorplan was arranged with the master stateroom forward, twin berths in the guest cabin, and separate stall showers in both heads. In 2003, a new three-stateroom floorplan relocated the master suite to port with the main guest cabin forward and a small guest stateroom to starboard. (Note that the 48, with its three-stateroom floorplan, has a slightly smaller cockpit than the original 47 model.) An excellent open-water performer, 800hp MANs cruise the Cabo 48 at 28 knots (32–33 knots top), and optional 1,150hp MANs will reach a top speed of over 30 knots.

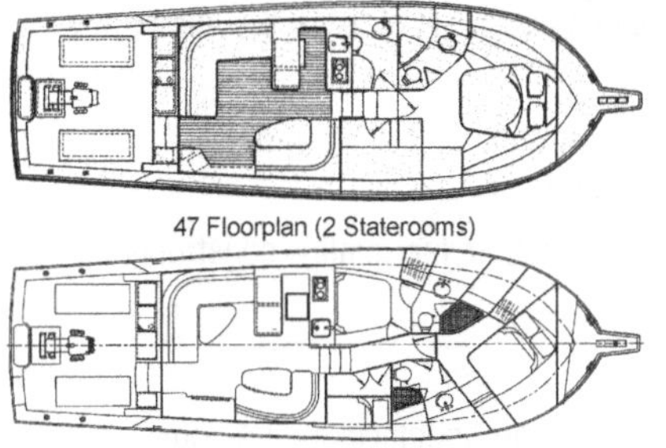
47 Floorplan (2 Staterooms)

48 Floorplan (3 Staterooms)

See Page 671 For Price Data

Length w/Pulpit	50'7"	Clearance	16'0"
Hull Length	47'7"	Fuel	900 gals.
Beam	15'8"	Water	100 gals.
Draft	4'0"	Hull Type	Modified-V
Weight	45,000#	Deadrise Aft	11.5°

Cabo 52 Express

2006–Current

Fast, powerful, and far-ranging, the Cabo 52 took express-boat size and muscle to the next level when she was introduced in 2006. (Not to be outdone, Viking unveiled their own 52-foot express the following year, the Viking 52 Open.) If bigger is really better, the Cabo 52 should easily satisfy the needs of the most demanding offshore angler. Built on a modified-V hull with a solid fiberglass bottom, the oversized cockpit and enormous bridgedeck of the 52 are made possible by the boat's broad 17'9" beam. Standard fishing amenities include a bait-rigging station with freezer, 75-gallon transom livewell, two large in-deck fish boxes, and tackle storage drawers. Forward, a centerline helm position provides the captain with a clear 360-degree view of the action. The cavernous twin-stateroom interior of the Cabo 52 boasts a spacious main salon with U-shaped leather sofa to port, overhead rod storage, and a full-service galley opposite with Sub-Zero refrigerator/freezer, garbage disposal, and Corian counters. Note the day head aft of the galley. Additional features include Stidd helm chairs (3), teak-and-holly cabin sole, and a huge walk-in engineroom. MAN 1,550hp engines cruise at 33–35 knots (about 40 knots top).

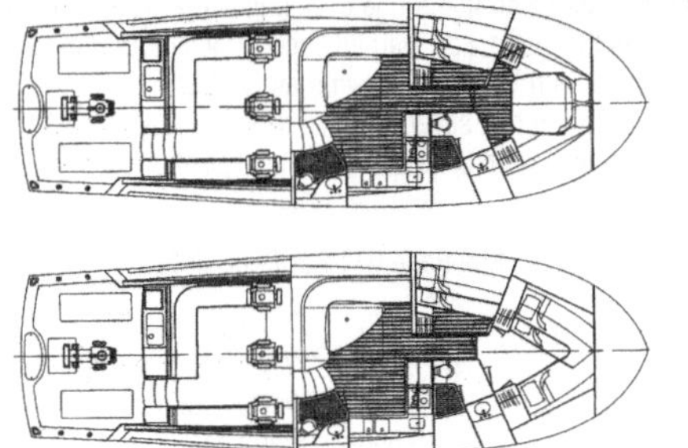

Not Enough Resale Data to Set Values

Length w/Pulpit	54'11"	Fuel	1,400 gals.
Hull Length	52'1"	Water	200 gals.
Beam	17'9"	Headroom	6'8"
Draft	4'11"	Hull Type	Modified-V
Weight	55,950#	Deadrise Aft	16°

Carolina Classic

Quick View

- Carolina Classic Boats was founded in 1992 by Mac Privott, still the company's owner.
- The first Carolina Classics—the Classic 25 and Classic 28—made their debut to a receptive market in 1994.
- Teaming up with his brother, Privott saw the company grow rapidly during the 1990s.
- By the time the Carolina Classic 35 was introduced in the fall of 1998 the company was building close to 100 boats a year.
- Noted for their bold Carolina styling, all Carolina Classic boats ride on deep-V hulls and are noted for their excellent seakeeping qualities.
- Carolina Classic boats enjoy a solid industry reputation for quality construction, strong owner loyalty, and excellent resale values.

Carolina Classic Boats • Edenton, NC • www.carolinaclassicboats.com

Carolina Classic 25

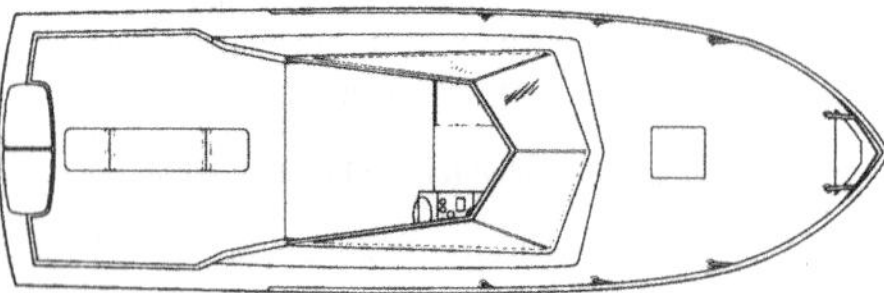

The Carolina Classic 25 is a no-frills sportfishermen whose clean lines, jackshaft drive system, and efficient layout will appeal to offshore anglers looking for a heavily built trailerable boat with long-range capability. The engine is amidships, set deep in the hull where the weight adds to the hull's low center of gravity and is connected to the outdrive by a jackshaft which runs under the cockpit sole. This means no engine box taking up valuable cockpit space—no small factor in a boat this size—and it also allows for the installation of a livewell at the transom. (The central location of the engine also makes for a good-handling boat in rough water.) On the downside, there's no in-deck fishbox although the livewell can be used for that purpose when required. The Classic's bi-level cockpit comes with fresh and saltwater washdowns and four rodholders. A centerline hatch on the bridge deck lifts hydraulically for complete access to the motor. For overnight accommodations, the small cuddy is fitted with V-berths, a swing-away electric head, and secure rod storage. Among several gas or diesel engine options, a single 7.4-liter Volvo gas engine delivers a top speed of about 40 knots.

See Page 671 For Price Data

Length	25'2"	Fuel	165 gals.
Beam	8'6"	Water	23 gals.
Draft	2'6"	Waste	18 gals.
Weight	8,500#	Hull Type	Deep-V
Clearance	NA	Deadrise Aft	24°

Carolina Classic 28

1994–Current

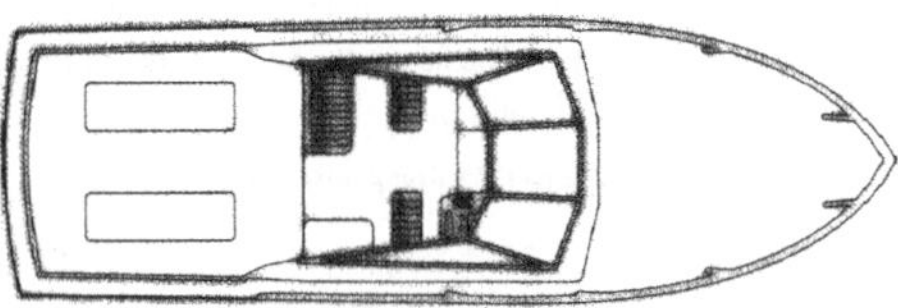

A recreation of the popular Albemarle 280, the Carolina Classic 28 evolved when former Albemarle employee Mac Privet started Carolina Classic in 1992. Construction is solid fiberglass, and her wide 10-foot, 6-inch beam results in a very roomy cockpit. In spite of the fact that she's a dedicated fishboat, the 28 has a surprisingly complete cabin below with a big V-berth, standup head with shower, compact galley, air-conditioning, and teak-framed joinery. The engines are very accessible—the entire bridge deck can be raised on a pair of hydraulic rams at the push of a button. The cockpit has plenty of room for a mounted chair and includes a pair of in-deck fish boxes, rod holders, transom livewell, tackle center with sink, and fresh- and saltwater washdowns. Additional features include side-dumping exhausts, wide side decks, high gunwales, and a well-arranged helm with room for flush-mounted electronics. Among several engines offered over the years, twin 300hp Volvo gas engines (with jackshafts) will cruise at 25–26 knots (40+ knots top). Twin 250hp inboard Cummins diesels—a popular option—cruise at 25 knots (30+ top), and 330hp Cummins cruise at 30 knots (mid 30s top).

See Page 671 For Price Data

Length	28'5"	Fuel, Diesel	220 gals.
Beam	10'6"	Water	55 gals.
Draft	2'6"	Waste	15 gals.
Weight	15,000#	Hull Type	Deep-V
Fuel, Gas	260 gals.	Deadrise Aft	24°

Carolina Classic 32

2004–Current

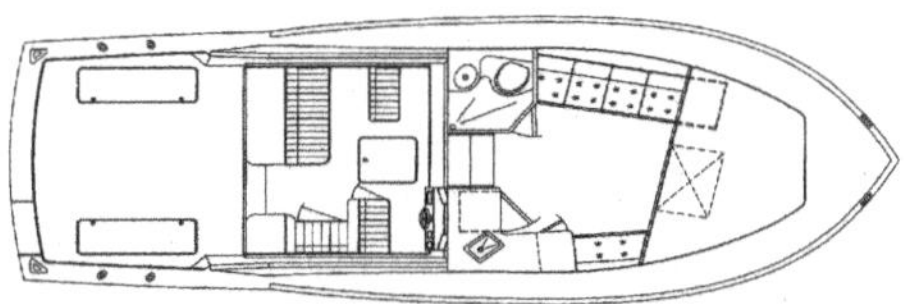

The Carolina Classic 32 incorporates the top-of-the-line features that serious anglers demand in a quality offshore fishing machine. With her signature flared bow, 13-foot beam and 80-square-foot cockpit, this is a boat that inspires confidence and pride of ownership. The Classic's roomy cockpit features twin 50-gallon fish boxes, tackle and rigging station, secure rod storage, transom door, and a bait station with freshwater sink, icebox, and tackle storage. The helmdeck—with comfortable seating for six—rises electrically for full access to the large engine compartment. Belowdecks is a nicely finished cabin with everything required for a night or two away from home. Air-conditioning, a Corian galley counter, and a teak-and-holly sole are standard, and a 7-foot bunk and athwartships double berth provide the sleeping accommodations. (Note that ledges over the forward berth permit custom rod holders.) Additional features include recessed trim tabs, fresh- and saltwater washdowns, generator, and a huge 355-gallon fuel capacity. No lightweight, twin 440hp Yanmar diesels cruise the Carolina Classic in the high 20s and reach a top speed of 32–33 knots.

See Page 671 For Price Data

Length	32'0"	Fuel	355 gals.
Beam	13'0"	Water	50 gals.
Draft	3'6"	Cockpit	80 sq. ft.
Weight	26,000#	Hull Type	Deep-V
Clearance	NA	Deadrise Aft	20°

Carolina Classic 35

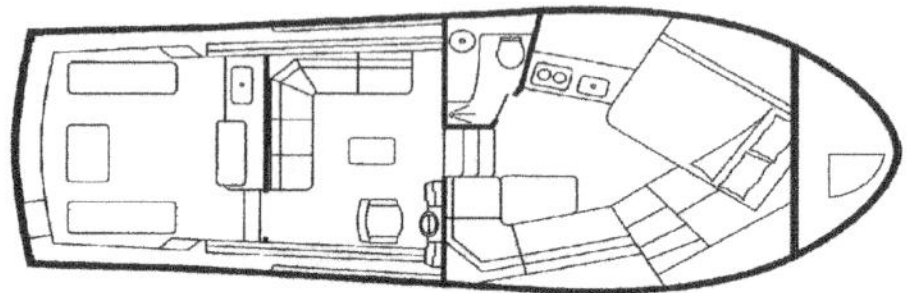

The Carolina Classic 35 is a heavily built express whose solid construction, excellent deck layout and upscale interior will appeal to experienced anglers who can afford a top-shelf offshore fishboat. Built on a solid fiberglass deep-V hull with a wide 13-foot, 6-inch beam and a well-flared bow, the large cockpit of the Classic 35 is set up for serious fishing with twin in-deck fish boxes, a wide transom door, and a built-in tackle center with sink, freezer, cutting board and storage. The cockpit is flawless with high sides and toe kick space all around. The bridge deck—which rises up on hydraulic rams for engine access—has a comfortable L-shaped lounge opposite the helm for four or five guests. Below, you'll find cabin amenities such as a standup shower, a fully appointed galley including sink, stove and microwave, and a spacious double berth and settee—upscale accommodations indeed for a dedicated fishing boat. Additional features include a spacious engine compartment, wide side decks, and a very well arranged helm console. A terrific rough-water performer, a pair of 480hp Cummins (or Volvo) diesels cruise the Carolina Classic 35 in the mid 20s and reach a top speed in excess of 30 knots.

See Page 671 For Price Data

Length	34'9"	Fuel	400 gals.
Beam	13'6"	Water	55 gals.
Draft	3'6"	Waste	35 gals.
Weight	25,000#	Hull Type	Deep-V
Clearance	NA	Deadrise Aft	18°

Carver

Quick View

- Carver began in the boatbuilding business in the late 1950s with a line of small wood runabouts built in Pulaski, WI.
- Carver gradually offered larger and larger boats, making the move from wood to fiberglass in the late 1960s and early 1970s.
- By the mid 1970s the company was well into fiberglass construction with a full line of inboard and sterndrive boats marketed primarily in the Great Lakes market.
- By the 1980s Carver had grown to be a major builder of affordable family cruisers, sport boats, and motor yachts with a nationwide network of dealers
- In 1991, Carver was acquired by Genmar Holdings, Inc.
- In 2004 Carver started Marquis Yachts, a series of Italian-designed motoryachts built in Pulaski, Wisconsin.
- In 2009 Carver, as part of the Genmar Corp., declared chapter XI bankruptcy.
- Now a subsidiary by J&D Acquisitions, Carver Yachts is recognized as a leader in the manufacture of upscale motoryachts and family cruisers.

Carver Yachts • Pulaski, WI • www.carveryachts.com

Carver 26 Command Bridge; 280 Sedan

1991–98

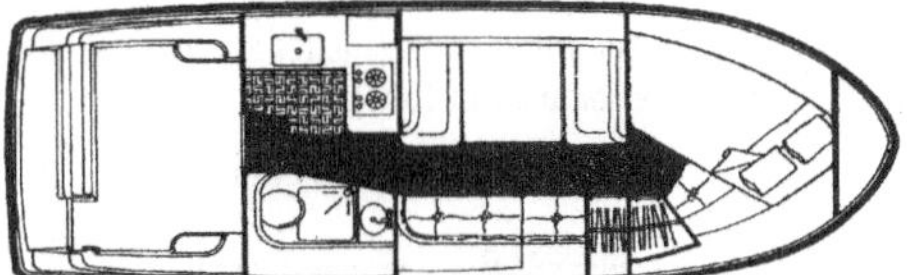

Although she was best known as the 280 Sedan, this model was originally introduced in 1991 as the Carver 26 Command Bridge, a good-looking small inland cruiser with clean-cut lines and a sporty profile. (She became the 280 Sedan in 1993 when Carver began including swim platforms in their length measurements, and in 1998 Carver called her the 280 Voyager.) Now out of production, the 280 was one of the smallest flybridge cruisers then (or since) available on the market. She's a beamy boat for her length and the house is placed well forward on the deck in order to maximize interior space. The cabin is bright and well arranged with wraparound windows, good headroom throughout, and plenty of seating. A lower helm was a popular option. Fortunately, Carver designers left some room in the floorplan for a fair-size cockpit that has enough room for a couple of deck chairs. Topside, the compact flybridge will seat two passengers aft of the helm. A relatively heavy boat for her size, single or twin sterndrives engine options were offered. Twin MerCruiser (or Volvo) V-6 sterndrives cruise the Carver 280 Sedan/Voyager at a respectable 18–20 knots and reach 30+ wide open.

See Page 672 For Price Data

Length w/Pulpit	29'11"	Fuel	112 gals.
Hull Length	27'9"	Water	45 gals.
Beam	9'6"	Waste	20 gals.
Draft	2'4"	Hull Type	Modified-V
Weight	9,778#	Deadrise Aft	15°

Carver 280 Mid-Cabin Express

The 280 Mid-Cabin Express began life in 1988 when she was introduced as the Carver 25 Montego, an affordable midcabin cruiser with modern lines and—for a 25-footer—surprisingly spacious accommodations. Built on a solid fiberglass deep-V hull with a wide beam and an integral swim platform, Carver redesigned this boat for 1993, dropping the Montego designation and reintroducing her as the 280 Mid-Cabin Express. The hull remained the same, but the 280 has a redesigned deckhouse, a more stylish curved windshield, and a new, much improved cabin layout with the head aft—rather than in the middle of the cabin as before—and a starboardside dinette. The level of finish is a bit disappointing. Where the original 25 Montego slept four, the 280 Express can sleep six. The cockpit didn't change much during her production years: a cutout in the transom leads to the swim platform, and a bench seat and table were standard. Available with single or twin sterndrives, a 280 Express fitted with a single 300hp Volvo Duoprop gas engine will cruise at 23 knots and reach 33–34 knots top. Twin engines were optional. Note that she was called the 528 Montego in 1991 and 1992.

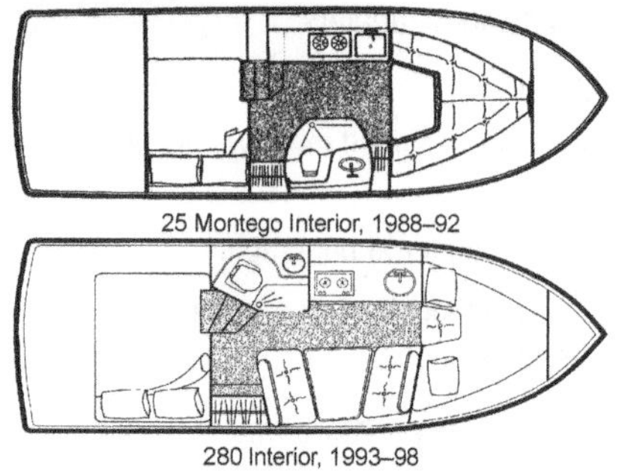
25 Montego Interior, 1988–92

280 Interior, 1993–98

See Page 672 For Price Data

Length	29'10"	Fuel	100 gals.
Beam	9'6"	Water	25 gals.
Draft	3'3"	Waste	18 gals.
Weight	5,900#	Hull Type	Modified-V
Clearance	NA	Deadrise Aft	19°

Carver 310 Mid-Cabin Express

Carver designers applied some unusual styling features to the 310 Mid-Cabin and the result is a hull and deck mold with more dips and curves than most anything else on the market. Hull construction is solid fiberglass, and a wide beam and relatively high freeboard combine to provide a very roomy interior. Two floorplans were available in the 310. The standard layout had a spacious salon with an extra-large L-shaped lounge aft that converts to private sleeping quarters with privacy curtain. The alternate floorplan offered a midcabin stateroom at the expense of a smaller salon. Outside, the cockpit has a doublewide helm seat with a wet bar opposite. The wraparound seating aft of the helm converts to a sun lounge. Additional features include a foredeck sun pad, walk-through windshield, side exhausts, and radar arch. Available with V-drive or sterndrive power, optional 5.8-liter Volvo I/Os cruise at 25 knots (about 42 knots top), and 5.7-liter Crusader (or Mer-Cruiser) inboards cruise at 24 knots (about 34–35 knots top). This model, with some changes, became the Trojan 320 Express in 1998. (Note that Carver produced Trojans for a few years following their purchase of the company in 1993).

Standard Floorplan

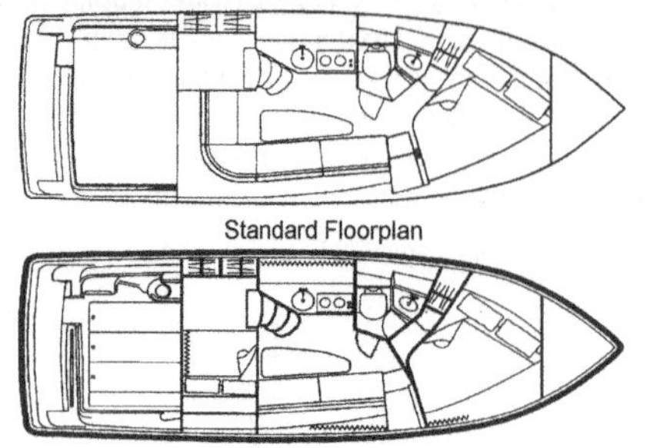
Alternate Floorplan

See Page 672 For Price Data

Length	31'3"	Fuel	180 gals.
Beam	10'10"	Water	56 gals.
Draft	2'8"	Waste	28 gals.
Weight	11,400#	Hull Type	Modified-V
Clearance, Arch	10'11"	Deadrise Aft	12°

Carver 310 Santego

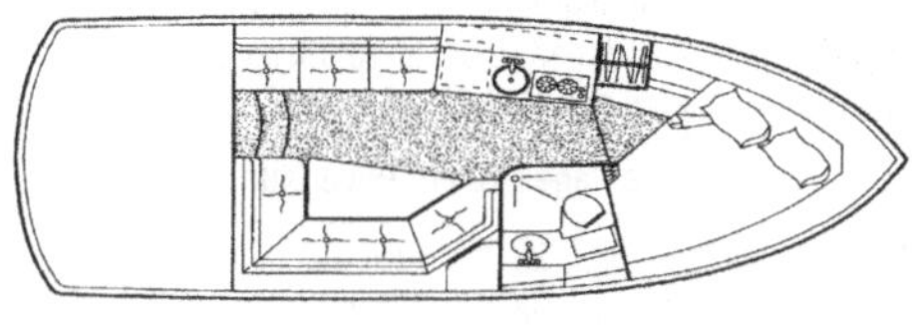

Entry-level buyers seeking a maxi-volume family cruiser with the amenities of a small apartment will find much to like in the 310 Santego. Introduced in 1994, she was built on a beamy modified-V hull with an integral swim platform, a bow pulpit, and relatively high freeboard. Note the absence of side decks; the Santego's full-width cabin is extended to the hullsides resulting in a notably spacious and wide-open interior. Stepping below from the small cockpit, the floorplan is arranged on a single level with the owner's stateroom forward and lounge seating on both sides of the salon. The starboard dinette converts to a double berth, and the portside lounge converts to an upper and lower bunk and includes a privacy curtain. Additional features include a doublewide helm seat with guest seating forward, good engine access, cockpit shower, transom door, and swim platform with storage lockers. Available with V-drive inboard or sterndrive power, twin 4.3-liter Volvo I/Os cruise the 310 Santego at 18 knots (about 30 knots top), and 5.7-liter inboards cruise at 22 knots and reach 30 knots top. Note that the fuel capacity was increased in 1997 to 164 gallons.

See Page 672 For Price Data

Length w/Pulpit	33'5"	Clearance	9'10"
Hull Length	31'3"	Fuel	130/164 gals.
Beam	11'0"	Water	66 gals.
Draft	2'9"	Waste	30 gals.
Weight	12,500#	Hull Type	Modified-V

Carver 320 Voyager

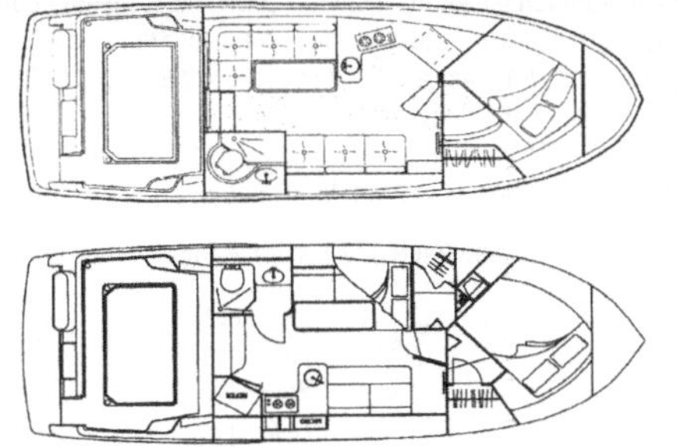

Introduced in 1994, the Carver 320 Voyager was marketed as an inexpensive, entry-level family cruiser with a stylish profile and generous cabin accommodations. She was built on a solid fiberglass hull with a wide beam and a moderate 16 degrees of deadrise at the transom. The Voyager, which is a very roomy boat below, was originally offered with or without a lower helm; without the helm, there was room for a stall shower in the head. Either way, the stateroom has an offset double berth (and a privacy door), and the dinette and salon sofa convert into double berths. In 1996, Carver introduced a completely new two-stateroom floorplan with the head and galley aft in the salon and a mini-cabin beneath the elevated dinette. Outside, the integral swim platform features a built-in fender rack and a hideaway boarding ladder. Access to the engines and V-drives is via hatches in the cockpit sole. The oversize flybridge of the 320 Voyager has the helm forward and guest seating for five. The side decks are narrow and foredeck access is heel-to-toe. Standard 350-cid Crusader gas engines cruise at 17 knots and deliver a top speed of 27–28 knots.

See Page 672 For Price Data

Length	35'0"	Fuel	188 gals.
Beam	11'10"	Water	56 gals.
Draft	2'11"	Waste	20 gals.
Weight	15,200#	Hull Type	Modified-V
Clearance	NA	Deadrise Aft	16°

Carver 325/326 Aft Cabin

1995–2001

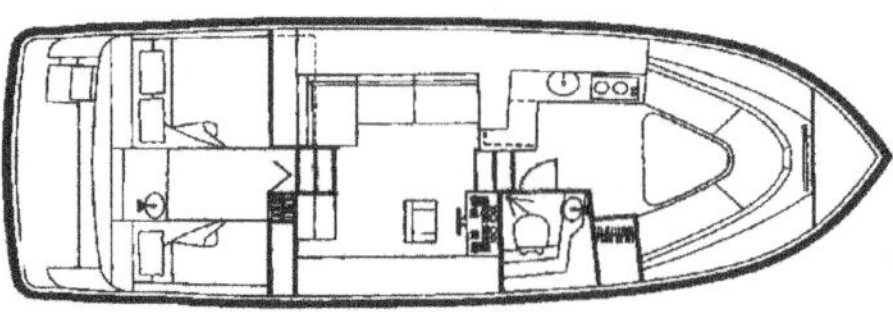

Introduced in 1991 as the Carver 28 Aft Cabin, this boat went through several name changes in subsequent years. From 1993–94 she was called the 300 Aft Cabin. In 1995—when an integral swim platform was added to the hull—she became the 325 Aft Cabin; and finally, in 1999 she became the 326 Aft Cabin. (The 325/326 model is pictured above.) For many, it's difficult to see the appeal of such a small double-cabin design. There's no way to avoid a cramped interior, and the top-heavy profile of any small flybridge boat is bound to be ungainly. That said, the 325/326 Aft Cabin was built on a very beamy hull to get as much interior volume below as possible. A lower helm is standard, and wraparound cabin windows make the salon seem larger than it actually is. Lacking its own head, the aft cabin is thoughtfully fitted with a sink and vanity. (Note that the double berth in the aft cabin extends slightly below the salon sole.) Outside, the small aft deck barely has enough room for a couple of deck chairs, and there's seating for three on the small flybridge. Upgrades in 1997 included an aft deck hardtop and a radar arch. Standard 300hp gas engines cruise at 17 knots with a top speed of 25–26 knots.

See Page 672 For Price Data

Length w/Pulpit	35'0"	Fuel	162 gals.
Hull Length	32'2"	Water	51 gals.
Beam	11'11"	Waste	20 gals.
Draft	2'11"	Hull Type	Modified-V
Weight	15,100#	Deadrise Aft	16°

Carver 32 Mariner; 330 Mariner

1985–96

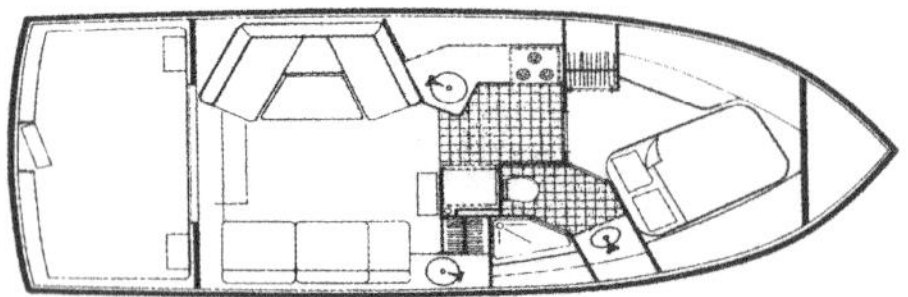

The Carver 32 Mariner (called the 330 Mariner from 1994–96) was introduced in 1985 as a downsized version of the larger 36 Mariner, a very popular model for Carver. While it's true that the 32 Mariner has drawn a lot of abuse over the years for her ungainly appearance, over 650 of these boats were sold during a decade-long production run, which says a lot about Carver's ability to please the public. The great appeal of the 32 Mariner is the enormous single-level, step-down interior that successfully uses every possible square inch of space available in the hull. The result is a truly social boat with an apartment-size salon featuring facing settees. (Natural lighting is poor, however, because the cabin windows are so tiny.) A ladder in the salon provides convenient inside access to the flybridge, which is another huge entertainment center in itself. Additional features include a centerline transom door, bow pulpit, swim platform, and a foredeck sun pad. Standard 270hp gas engines (with V-drives) are located beneath the cockpit. A thirsty and decidedly hard-riding boat in a chop, the Carver 32 Mariner burns around 20 gallons per hour at a modest cruising speed of 16 knots. The top speed is around 25–26 knots.

See Page 672 For Price Data

Length w/Pulpit	35'5"	Clearance	10'10"
Hull Length	32'3"	Fuel	192 gals.
Beam	12'4"	Water	92 gals.
Draft	2'9"	Hull Type	Modified-V
Weight	12,000#	Deadrise Aft	6°

Carver 33/35/36 Super Sport

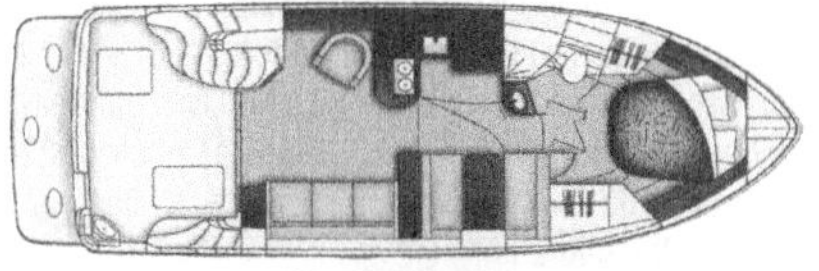
Standard Interior

Mid-Cabin Interior

Carver introduced this sporty cruiser (called the 33 Super Sport in 2005–06; 35 SS in 2007; 36 SS in 2008) in an effort to recapture some of the entry-level boaters the company had forfeited in previous years with their move into the big-boat market. She was the smallest model in the Carver fleet, and while not inexpensive, the 33 did offer the features boaters were looking for in a small flybridge cruiser. Chief among her attributes is a spacious and exceedingly comfortable interior. The large, full-beam salon maximizes interior volume and a convertible dinette, nicely equipped galley (with upright refrigerator and Corian counter), and a separate stall shower in the head make this a very livable boat for the cruising family. In the cockpit, molded sidedeck steps and molded bridge steps make getting around the Super Sport easy. A transom door opens to an extended swim platform deep enough to carry a dinghy. Additional features include a large engineroom (reached via a hatch in the salon sole), generous cabin storage, radar arch, and good helm visibility both fore and aft. On the downside, the Super Sport's modified-V hull isn't too fond of a chop. Crusader 320hp gas engines cruise at 18 knots (26–28 knots top.)

See Page 672 For Price Data

Length	37'3"	Fuel	311 gals.
Beam	13'1"	Water	78 gals.
Draft	3'1"	Waste	37 gals.
Weight	21,753#	Hull Type	Modified-V
Clearance	14'8"	Deadrise Aft	11.5°

Carver 350 Mariner

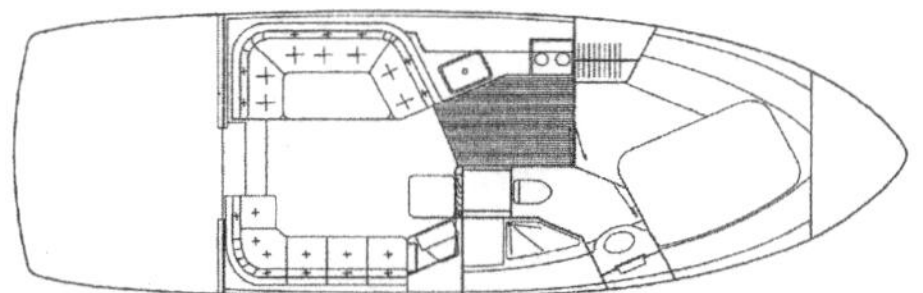

Introduced in 1997, the Carver 350 Mariner is aimed at first-time buyers whose desire for interior volume overwhelms any concerns they might have for aesthetics. Indeed, the Mariner is a truly unattractive boat with a full-bodied profile that might best be described as bloated. That said, the Mariner is notable for her expansive single-level interior as well as her roomy flybridge with its lounge seating for several guests. Instead of conventional side decks, wide walkways sweep up from the deck to the bridge, a design that makes it easy to get around the boat. Below, the Mariner's full-beam salon, accessed through a double sliding door or directly from the bridge via a hatch and ladder, is remarkable for its size and comfort. A sofa and convertible dinette will seat eight, and the full galley offers all the comforts of home. The master stateroom has an angled double berth and direct access to the head, which has a separate shower stall. The engine compartment, which is under the cockpit sole, is a tight fit. Note that the foredeck bench seat converts into a sun pad. No racehorse, twin 320hp V-drive gas engines cruise at 14–15 knots and reach a top speed of around 20 knots.

See Page 672 For Price Data

Length	36'7"	Fuel	246 gals.
Beam	12'9"	Water	75 gals.
Draft	3'1"	Waste	20 gals.
Weight	18,800#	Headroom	6'3"
Clearance, Arch	14'2"	Hull Type	Modified-V

Carver 355/356 Motor Yacht

The Carver 356 Motor Yacht (called the 355 MY during 1995–98) is an updated version of the Carver 33/350 Motor Yacht built from 1991 through 1994. An integral swim platform was added to the new model while the floorplan was revised and the fuel tankage was increased for better range. Like all Carvers of her era, the 355/356 was built on a solid fiberglass hull with modest transom deadrise and a shallow keel for stability. Key to her enduring popularity was an expansive, wide-open interior with the cruising amenities of a much larger boat. A dinette is forward in the salon, and there's plenty of storage in the galley, which includes a full-size refrigerator. Notably, the double berth in the forward stateroom of the 356 is comfortable enough for two adults—an improvement from the small forward berth of the earlier 33/350 model. On the small aft deck, a transom gate opens to a set of molded steps leading down to the swim platform. A hardtop, radar arch, and bow pulpit were standard and a lower helm station was optional. Among several engine options offered over the years, a pair of 320hp gas inboards cruise the Carver 355/356 MY at 17–18 knots and reach a top speed in the mid 20s.

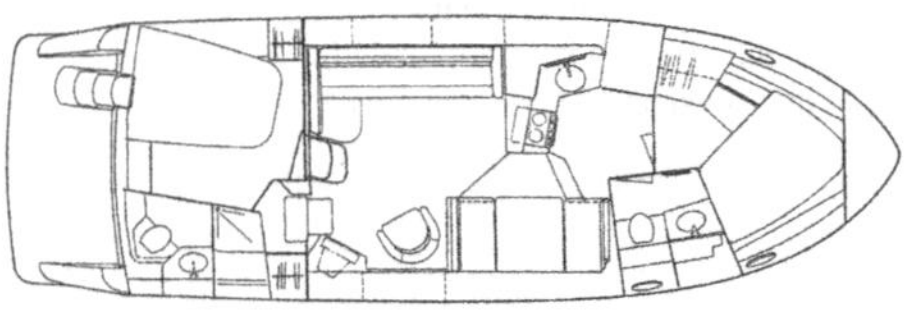

See Page 672 For Price Data

Length w/Pulpit	41'2"	Fuel	318 gals.
Beam	13'3"	Water	70 gals.
Draft	3'3"	Waste	36 gals.
Weight	23,400#	Hull Type	Modified-V
Clearance, Arch	17'6"	Deadrise Aft	11°

Carver 36 Mariner

An updated version of Carver's original 36 Mariner built back in the 1980s, the new 36 Mariner combines the spacious single-level interior of her predecessor with contemporary styling and a surprisingly good turn of speed. By any standard, this is a big 36-footer with the ability to entertain a small crowd without being crowded. The Mariner's full-beam salon features a posh Ultraleather lounge and dinette, high-gloss cherry woodwork and a full entertainment center with TV and stereo CD. The extra-large head includes a separate stall shower, and the galley has plenty of storage and counter space. Topside, flanking stairways lead from the cockpit to the enormous bridge where port and starboard lounges and an aft bench seat can seat up to ten guests. Twin transom lockers house fenders and lines, keeping the small cockpit clear of miscellaneous clutter. Air conditioning, generator, flybridge wet bar, swim ladder and transom shower were all standard. A wide beam and very modest transom deadrise make the Mariner a notably stable boat, but she's a stiff ride when the seas pick up. Crusader 375hp V-drive inboards (gas) will cruise at 20 knots (26–27 knots wide open). She's no beauty, that's for sure.

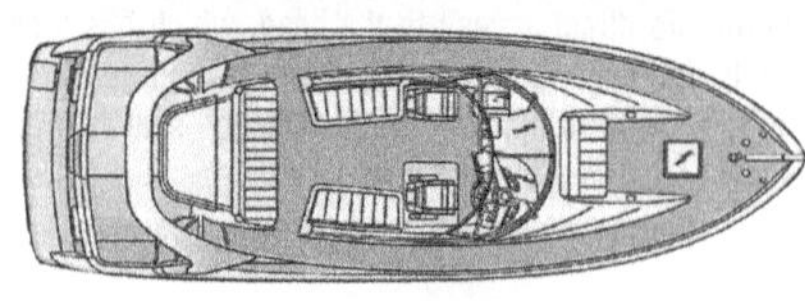

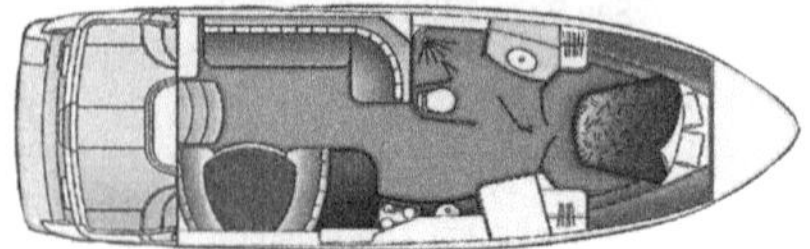

See Page 672 For Price Data

Length	36'7"	Fuel	250 gals.
Beam	12'9"	Water	75 gals.
Draft	37"	Waste	31 gals.
Weight	19,500#	Hull Type	Modified-V
Clearance, Arch	14'2"	Deadrise Aft	4°

Carver 36 Motor Yacht

The Carver 366 Motor Yacht (called the 346 MY in 2002) has about as much on-board living space as you're likely to find on a 36-foot, aft-cabin yacht. True, she's not the prettiest boat on the water, and her raised side decks give the impression of excess freeboard, but the vast interior of the 366 is not to be denied. Built on a beamy modified-V hull with cored hullsides and a solid fiberglass bottom, the impression of space in the full-width salon is enhanced by tiered cabin windows and earth-tone decor. The original 346 floorplan featured a wide-open salon with the galley down and stall showers in both heads. The 366 layout introduced in 2003 has a dinette across from the mid-level galley—a major improvement—with only a single stall shower aft. (Note that storage space in the compact aft stateroom is at a premium.) Outside, there's room on the aft deck for a few pieces of deck furniture, and the flybridge is arranged with a wet bar, an L-shaped lounge, and seating for three at the helm. A central vacuum system, transom and bow washdowns, and a swim platform were standard. A stiff ride in a chop, twin 385hp gas inboards cruise at 17–18 knots (mid 20s top), and 310hp Volvo diesels cruise in the low 20s.

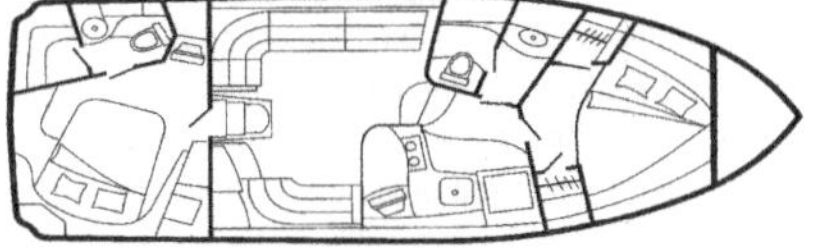
346 Interior (2002 Only)

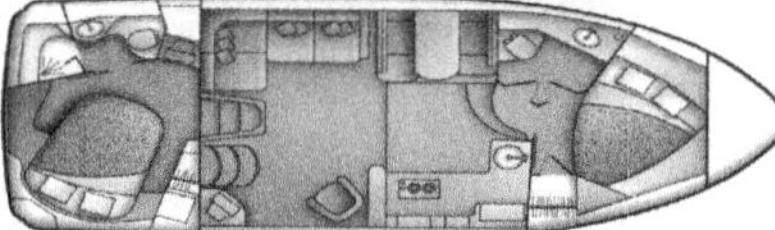
Standard Layout

See Page 672 For Price Data

Length	36'11"	Fuel	250 gals.
Beam	13'2"	Water	70 gals.
Draft	2'4"	Waste	36 gals.
Weight	21,800#	Hull Type	Modified-V
Headroom	6'6"	Deadrise Aft	16°

Carver 360 Sport Sedan

The mission of the Carver 360 Sport Sedan—or 36 Sport Sedan as she's often called—was to pack as much living space as possible into a compact yacht. In that regard, she achieves her purpose, albeit at the expense of aesthetics. Sporting a full-size cockpit and a huge swim platform, the 360 Sport Sedan is a versatile cruising yacht whose expansive two-stateroom interior is her most appealing feature. The main cabin is arranged with a unique raised dinette/lounge forward with Ultraleather seating, and all bulkheads, counters, drawers and furniture are high-gloss cherrywood. A curved staircase below the dinette leads down to the aft guest stateroom with convertible twin berths, and the forward stateroom with an island berth. The hardwood floor in the galley area is a nice touch, and the tiered windows admit plenty of natural lighting into the salon. Getting around the Sport Sedan is easy: in each forward corner of the cockpit, a five-step stairway leads to the raised side decks while an additional staircase takes you to the bridge. Topside, the helm is on the centerline flanked by companion seats. The engineroom is a tight fit. Twin 320hp gas inboards cruise at 18 knots (low 20s top).

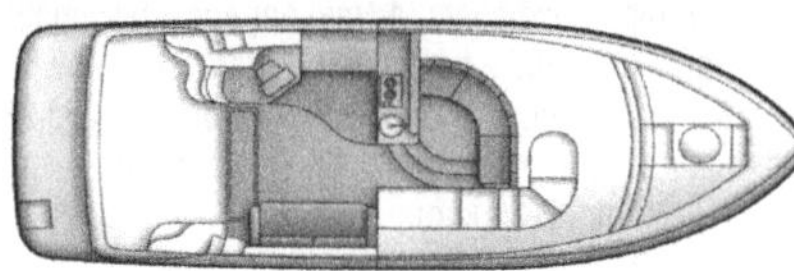
Main Deck Plan

Lower Level Plan

See Page 672 For Price Data

Length	37'8"	Fuel	280 gals.
Beam	13'2"	Water	75 gals.
Draft	2'7"	Waste	25 gals.
Weight	24,746#	Hull Type	Modified-V
Clearance, Arch	14'6"	Deadrise Aft	14°

Carver 36 Aft Cabin; 370 Aft Cabin

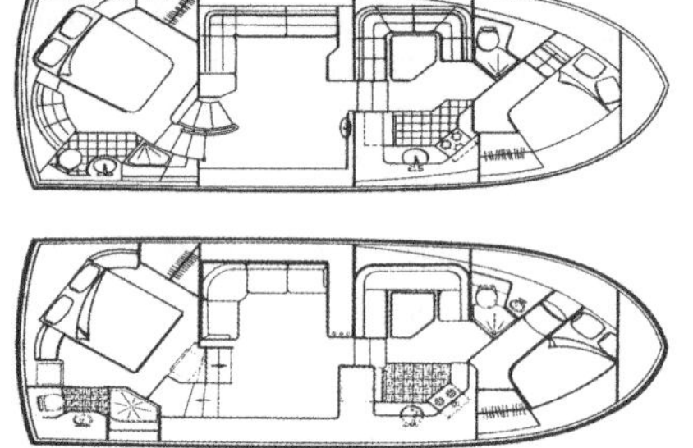

The Carver 370 Aft Cabin (called the 36 Aft Cabin from 1990–92) is a beamy double-cabin family cruiser with a surprisingly spacious interior and a somewhat boxy profile. This is a much more open boat than Carver's earlier 36 Aft Cabin model (1982–89) thanks primarily to a wider beam and greater freeboard. Notably, she's built on a fairly deep-deadrise modified-V hull which accounts for her soft and comfortable ride in choppy seas. Like all of Carver's recent motor yacht designs, the hullsides are cored with balsa and the bottom is solid fiberglass. Inside, Carver engineers managed to pack double berths into both staterooms as well as provide two head compartments, a big U-shaped dinette, and reasonably spacious main salon dimensions—not bad for just a 36-foot hull. A lower helm station was a popular option. The aft deck is quite spacious compared with those of similar models in this size range, and the centerline helm console on the flybridge allows plenty of guest seating. No racehorse, standard 7.4-liter inboard gas engines cruise the Carver 370 in the neighborhood of 15–16 knots and deliver a top speed of about 24 knots.

See Page 672 For Price Data

Length w/Pulpit	41'3"	Clearance	15'0"
Hull Length	38'2"	Fuel	240 gals.
Beam	13'10"	Water	80 gals.
Draft	3'1"	Hull Type	Modified-V
Weight	18,500#	Deadrise Aft	19°

Carver 370/374 Voyager

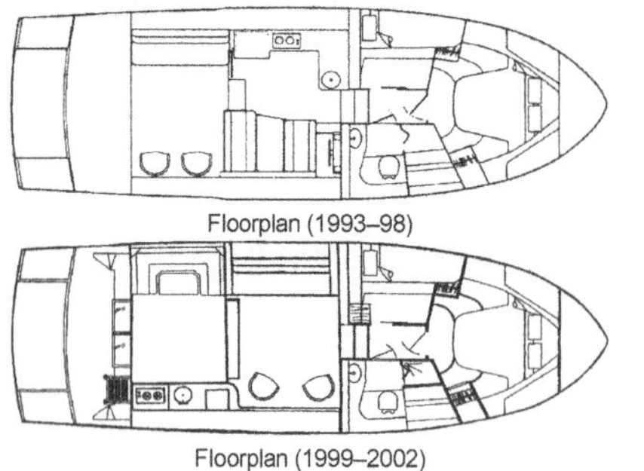
Floorplan (1993–98)

Floorplan (1999–2002)

A popular boat, the Carver 374 Voyager (called the 370 Voyager until 2000 when she received an exterior face-lift) will appeal to those who appreciate the built-in versatility of a raised pilothouse layout. Until 1999, the Voyager's two-stateroom floorplan was arranged with both galley and dinette on the bridge deck level leaving the salon as a wide-open entertaining area. In 1999 the layout was revised with the galley and dinette moved aft, into the salon, and the bridge deck became the salon. Each of these floorplans has its advantages although the original layout is more commonplace in a pilothouse design. Either way, the Voyager is a big boat inside, and one has the impression of being on a larger boat. The cockpit is large enough for a couple of deck chairs, and there's seating for six on the flybridge. Additional features of the 370/374 Voyager include side-dumping exhausts, a transom door, reasonably wide side decks, radar arch and a bow pulpit. Among several engine options, twin 310hp gas engines cruise at 16 knots (around 25 knots top), and a pair of 330hp Cummins diesels cruise at 24 knots and reach a top speed of 28–29 knots.

See Page 672 For Price Data

Length w/Pulpit	40'1"	Fuel	297 gals.
Hull Length	37'1"	Water	83 gals.
Beam	13'3"	Waste	35 gals.
Draft	3'8"	Hull Type	Modified-V
Weight	21,350#	Deadrise Aft	11°

Carver 34/638/380 Santego

Introduced as the 34 Santego in 1989, Carver's marketing gurus confused everyone by calling her the 638 Santego in 1992 before finally settling on the 380 Santego designation in 1993. This was a popular boat in the Carver fleet for many years thanks to her spacious condo-style interior and a very competitive pricing structure. The Santego's expansive salon—with facing wraparound settees and twin dinettes—create the kind of party-time accommodations seldom encountered in a boat this size. A pair of full-height sliding glass cockpit doors provides an abundance of exterior lighting, and the wide-open expanse of a single-level floorplan has to be seen. There's seating for a crowd on the huge flybridge where concealed steps in the windshield fold out to provide a walkway to the foredeck. Hatches in the cockpit sole provide good access to the motors and V-drives, and there's built-in lounge seating in the small cockpit. On the downside, Carver never replaced the Santego's bolt-on swim platform with a more stylish integral platform. A surprisingly good-riding boat in a chop, standard big-block gas engines cruise at 18 knots and reach 26–27 knots top.

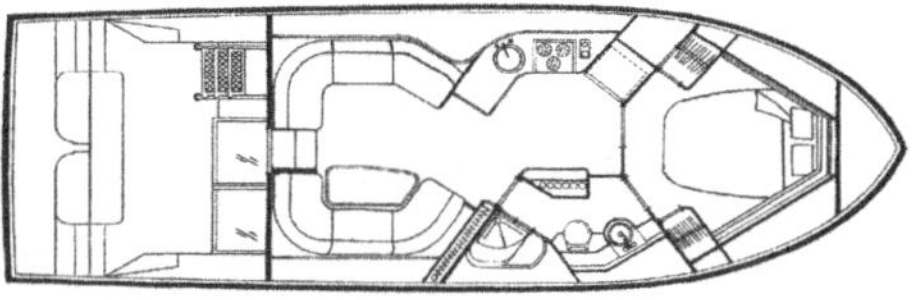

See Page 672 For Price Data

Length w/Pulpit	41'8"	Fuel	216 gals.
Beam	13'2"	Water	90 gals.
Draft	3'4"	Waste	37 gals.
Weight	19,300#	Hull Type	Modified-V
Clearance	NA	Deadrise Aft	19°

Carver 38 Super Sport

Notable for her rakish styling and spacious accommodations, the Carver 38 Super Sport offers American buyers an affordable alternative to midsize European flybridge yachts. Like most Carver products, the 38 manages to offer most of the features buyers are looking for in a boat of this type. Foremost among her attributes is an exceedingly comfortable interior. The large, full-beam salon maximizes interior volume, and a convertible dinette, wide-open galley (with wood plank flooring and Corian counter), and two double staterooms make this a very livable boat for the cruising family. In the sizable cockpit, molded sidedeck steps and molded bridge steps make getting around the Super Sport easy. A transom door opens to an extended swim platform deep enough to carry a dinghy. Additional features include a large engineroom (reached via a hatch in the salon sole), generous cabin storage, radar arch, and a flybridge wet bar. An optional sport package adds rod holders, a transom livewell, and a pair of in-deck fish boxes. On the downside, the Super Sport's low-deadrise hull isn't too fond of a chop. MerCruiser 375hp gas engines cruise at 20 knots (high 20s top).

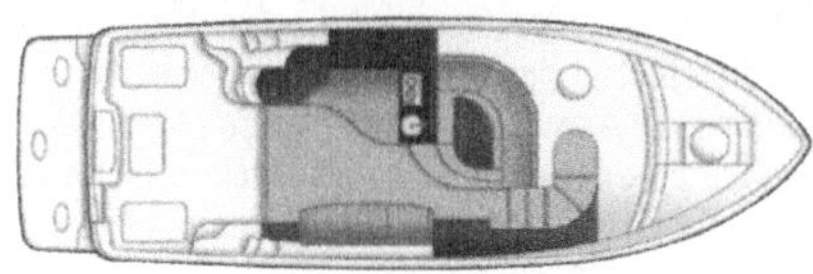

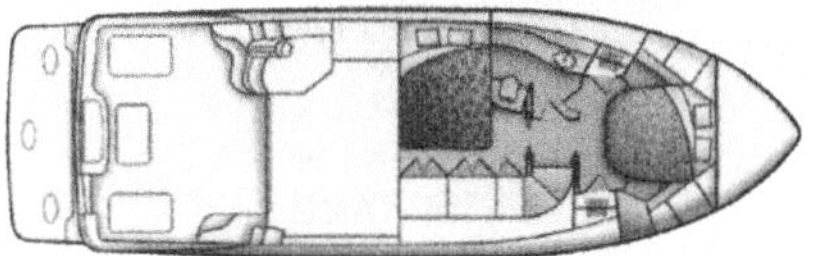

See Page 672 For Price Data

Length	39'11"	Fuel	334 gals.
Beam	13'5"	Water	86 gals.
Draft	2'4"	Waste	45 gals.
Weight	25,000#	Hull Type	Modified-V
Clearance	14'1"	Deadrise Aft	14°

Carver 38 Aft Cabin; 390 Aft Cabin

1987–95

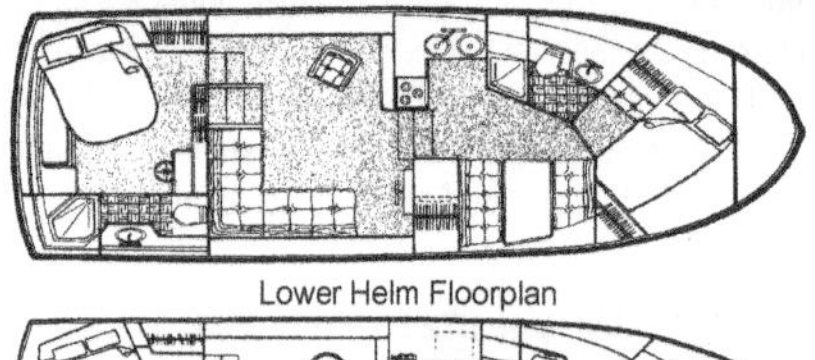

Lower Helm Floorplan

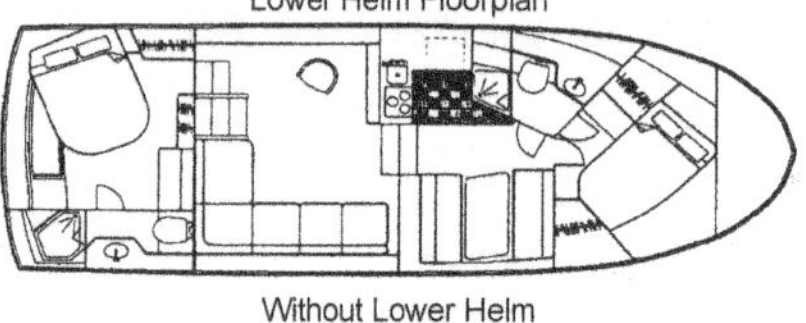

Without Lower Helm

A popular model during her production years, the Carver 390 Aft Cabin (called the 38 Aft Cabin from 1987–92) is a traditionally styled double-cabin cruiser whose truly expansive accommodations come as a genuine surprise in a boat this size. Like most Carver models of her era, she was built on low-deadrise modified-V hull with a wide beam and relatively high freeboard. For the first few years Carver offered a choice of interior plans, one with a V-berth forward and the other—which became standard in 1993—with an angled double berth forward. Both heads came with separate stall showers, and a full-size dinette is opposite the galley two steps down from the salon level. (Note that a lower helm was a popular option.) This is a lot to pack into a 38-foot hull, and it comes as no surprise that the salon and staterooms are quite small. The aft deck is also limited in size with room for a couple of deck chairs and not much more. With her relatively heavy displacement, the 390 is a handful for gas engines to push. Standard big-block Crusaders cruise at a modest 14–15 knots with a top speed of just over 20 knots. Optional 375hp Cat (or 370hp Cummins) diesels cruise at 20 knots (mid 20s top).

See Page 672 For Price Data

Length	42'6"	Fuel	280 gals.
Beam	14'0"	Water	91 gals.
Draft	3'4"	Waste	75 gals.
Weight	22,750#	Hull Type	Modified-V
Clearance	NA	Deadrise Aft	12°

Carver 396 Motor Yacht; 39/40 Motor Yacht

2000–07

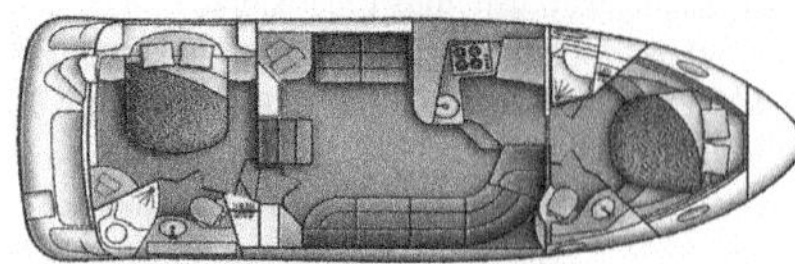

Standard Floorplan

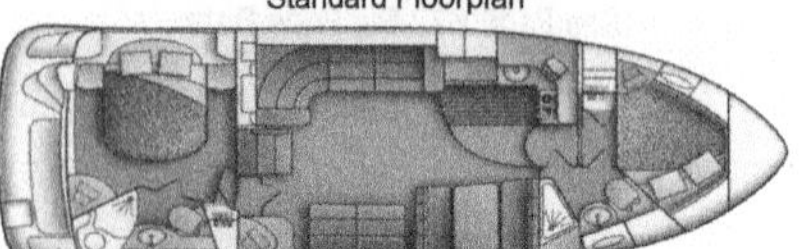

Dinette Floorplan

A bold departure from Carver's past history of conservative styling, the 396 Motor Yacht (called the 39 MY in 2005–6; 40 MY in 2007) is a scaled-down version of Carver's equally controversial 506 MY (also introduced in 2000) with the same tiered elliptical cabin windows, too-high freeboard, and overdone Euro styling. Belowdecks, however, the 396 is a stunning display of interior volume unmatched in a boat this size. The salon—easily the most impressive aspect of the boat—is immense with a panoramic outside view and about seven feet of headroom. The full-beam salon configuration is made possible by raising the side decks to eye level, which is why the boat appears to have so much freeboard. Both staterooms have walkaround double berths (note the athwartships berth in the master suite), and heads have separate stall showers. Note that in 2003 a dinette floorplan became available. Wing doors and a hardtop protect the aft deck from the elements; a molded stairway leads to the swim platform, and there's seating for a small crowd on the flybridge Twin 370hp gas engines cruise at 14–15 knots (around 24 knots top), and 370hp Cummins diesels cruise at 18 knots (22–23 knots top).

See Page 672 For Price Data

Length	40'7"	Fuel	330 gals.
Beam	13'11"	Water	90 gals.
Draft	3'6"	Waste	72 gals.
Weight	29,500#	Hull Type	Modified-V
Clearance	18'0"	Deadrise Aft	16°

Carver 390/400/404 Cockpit MY

1993–2003

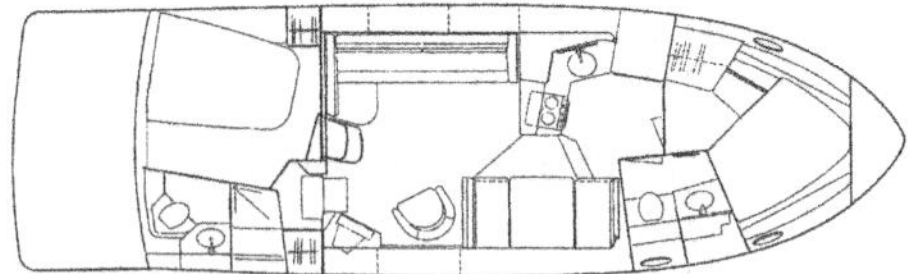

The Carver 404 Cockpit Motor Yacht (called the 390 Cockpit MY in 1993–95; 400 CMY in 1996–98; 404 CMY in 1999–2003) is a cockpit version of Carver's popular 355/356 Motor Yacht. Aside from the versatility that cockpits offer—they make great diving or fishing platforms, and boarding is a lot less hassle—the extra waterline length usually adds a knot or two to the speed while improving the boat's overall profile. Like her smaller sistership, the interior is surprisingly complete and includes two heads, a roomy galley, full dinette, and double berths in both staterooms. The staterooms are small as is the engineroom, and storage space is at a premium (especially in the aft cabin), but the layout certainly delivers on its promise of big-boat accommodations. A lower helm was a popular option, and the salon is open and surprisingly spacious. Additional features include attractive light oak interior woodwork, relatively wide side decks, and a well-arranged flybridge with plenty of guest seating. Standard gas engines cruise at 17 knots (about 25 knots top), and optional 315hp Cummins diesels cruise easily at 20 knots (mid 20s wide open).

See Page 672 For Price Data

Length	43'5"	Fuel	318 gals.
Beam	13'3"	Water	70 gals.
Draft	3'3"	Waste	36 gals.
Weight	24,300#	Hull Type	Modified-V
Clearance	NA	Deadrise Aft	11°

Carver 405/406 Aft Cabin MY

1997–2002

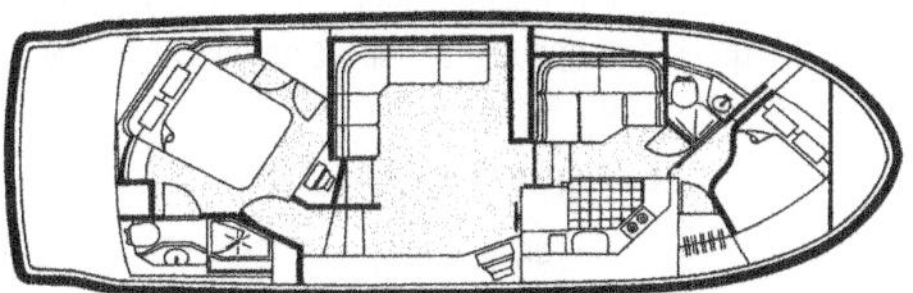

The Carver 406 is, like most Carvers built in the 1990s, a conservative, heavily built double-cabin cruiser whose principal characteristics were a spacious floorplan and an affordable price. She was introduced in 1997 as the 405 Aft Cabin, becoming the 406 Aft Cabin in 1999 when the cabin windows were slightly redesigned. A cockpit version of the Carver 370 Aft Cabin (1990–96), she rides on a deep-deadrise hull—unusual in a late-model Carver motor yacht. Hull construction is solid fiberglass, and with nearly 14 feet of beam the 406 is a seriously spacious boat inside. Her efficient two-stateroom interior is arranged with the galley and dinette down from the salon. Angled double berths are found in each stateroom, and the only stall shower is aft. Light maple woodwork and big wraparound deckhouse windows make the salon seem larger than the actual dimensions suggest. The aft deck is large enough for entertaining a few friends, and the walkaround helm console on the flybridge provides plenty of topside seating. A hardtop and radar arch were popular options. Standard gas inboards cruise at a leisurely 16 knots, and optional 330hp Cummins diesels cruise at 20–21 knots.

See Page 672 For Price Data

Length	42'3"	Fuel	342 gals.
Beam	13'10"	Water	70 gals.
Draft	3'3"	Waste	64 Gals.
Weight	27,900#	Hull Type	Modified-V
Clearance, Arch	17'2"	Deadrise Aft	20°

Carver 41 Cockpit MY

2005–07

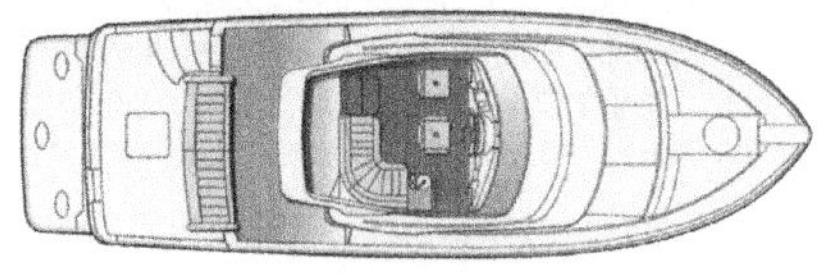

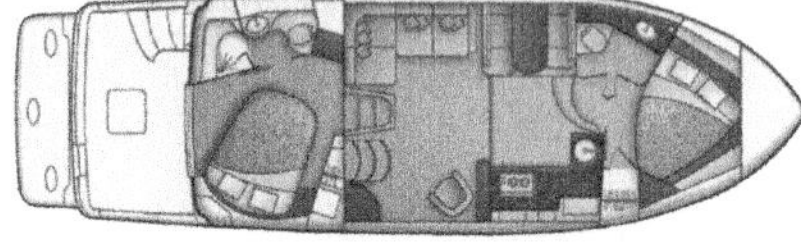

Sweeping lines, comfortable accommodations, and solid construction characterize the Carver 41 Cockpit MY, a well-conceived cruising yacht with an impressive array of standard features. Carver was nearly alone in building a boat of this type and size during her production years—indeed, cockpit motor yachts are a vanishing breed these days. Among several appealing attributes, the full-beam salon of the 41 Cockpit MY is notable for its excellent natural lighting and easy-on-the-eye decor. Angled double berths in both staterooms make the most of available space, and the L-shaped galley includes recessed coffee maker and under-counter refrigeration. A particularly useful feature is the sliding door in the master stateroom that opens directly into the cockpit. On the aft deck, a standard hardtop and wing doors provide protection from the elements. Perhaps the best feature of the Carver 41 is her large cockpit, the place to be when you're ready to slow down and enjoy the water. On the downside, the side decks are narrow and there's no stall shower in the forward head. A good performer with 370hp Volvo diesels, she'll cruise efficiently in the mid 20s and hit a top speed of 26–27 knots.

See Page 672 For Price Data

Length	42'11"	Fuel	360 gals.
Beam	13'5"	Water	70 gals.
Draft	2'7"	Waste	50 gals.
Weight	26,000#	Hull Type	Modified-V
Clearance	15'1"	Deadrise Aft	15°

Carver 410 Sport Sedan

2002–03

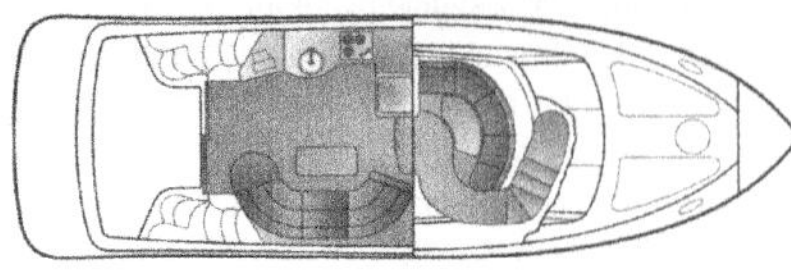

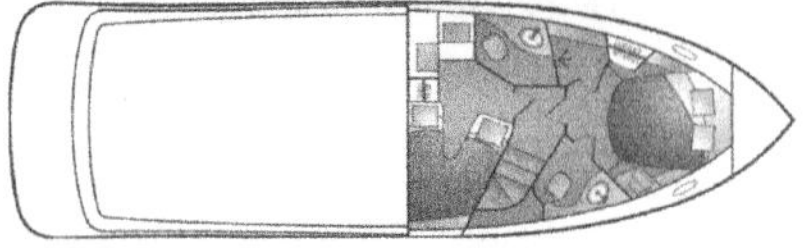

Introduced in 2002, the Carver 410 Sport Sedan was aimed at buyers more focused on expansive cabin accommodations than exterior beauty. The interior is larger than most 40-foot sedans, especially in the salon, and while the high-sided styling may have its detractors the 410 manages to deliver the features most cruisers are looking for at an affordable price. Built on a modified-V hull with generous beam and cored hullsides, the wide-open spaces in the Sport Sedan's salon are the result of raising the side decks to near-flybridge level. A curved settee is to starboard in the salon, the galley is just opposite, and an aft-facing dinette is forward. (A lower helm was optional.) There are two staterooms and two heads on the lower level, and a hatch in the salon sole provides access to the engineroom. In the cockpit, molded steps to port lead around the house to the bow, and starboard-side steps lead up to the flybridge with its wet bar, circular lounge, and three helm chairs. Additional features include an integral swim platform, transom door, radar arch, and an entertainment center. Volvo 375hp gas engines cruise at 15 knots, and optional 370hp Volvo diesels cruise at 18 knots (24–25 knots top).

See Page 673 For Price Data

Length	46'4"	Fuel	400 gals.
Beam	13'11"	Water	95 gals.
Draft	2'8"	Waste	75 gals.
Weight	31,625#	Hull Type	Modified-V
Clearance, Arch	19'2"	Deadrise Aft	13°

Carver 42 Mariner

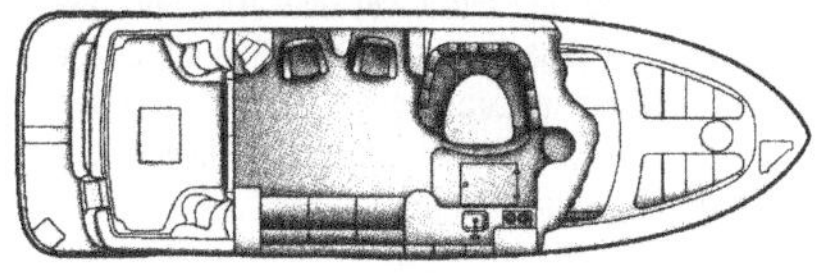

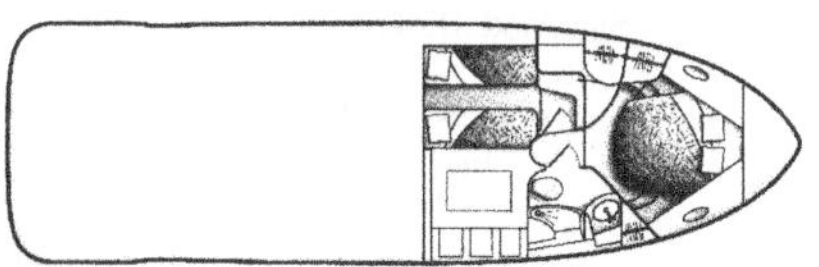

Introduced in 2004, the Carver 42 Mariner gets high marks for delivering the comfort and entertainment potential buyers demand in a modern cruising yacht. Indeed, her raised-walk deck design and expansive floorplan make the 42 Mariner one of the roomiest boats in her class. The highlight of the interior is a cavernous, full-beam salon with high-gloss cherry cabinetry, Ultraleather seating, and large step-down galley with under-counter refrigerator/freezer. (Note the big storage locker under the galley sole.) Both staterooms share a single head compartment, and a filler piece quickly converts the twin single berths in the guest cabin into a comfortable double. Flanking stairways lead from the cockpit up to the Mariner's spacious flybridge where three skipper's chairs face the helm and a circular aft lounge seats several guests. In the cockpit, a bridge overhang provides some shelter from sun and rain. Additional features include a flybridge wet bar, radar arch, foredeck sun pads, cockpit lazarette, satellite radio system, and an extended swim platform. Optional 370hp Volvo diesels cruise the Carver 42 at 20 knots and reach a top speed of 24–25 knots.

See Page 673 For Price Data

Length	44'5"	Fuel	400 gals.
Beam	13'11"	Water	95 gals.
Draft	32"	Waste	35 gals.
Weight	31,280#	Hull Type	Modified-V
Clearance, Arch	19'2"	Deadrise Aft	17°

Carver 42/43 Super Sport

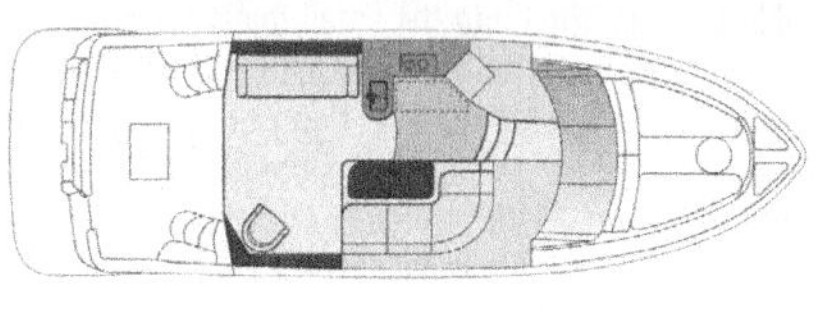

With her bold styling, spacious accommodations and evolutionary IPS pod drives, the 43 Super Sport (called the 42 SS in 2006–07) took Carver design and comfort to the next level. Her full-beam interior is made possible by raising the side decks to nearly flybridge level, a design element borrowed from Silverton's popular "SideWalk" deck layouts introduced a few years back. The result is an interior whose dimensions are easily among the largest in her class. The combined salon/galley/dinette of the Super Sport, with its cherry joinery and Ultraleather seating, offers room for nonstop entertaining. (The original circular dining table was replaced in 2007 with a more practical L-shaped design.) Both staterooms have walkaround queen berths—unusual in a boat this size. A large utility room beneath galley sole provides abundant pantry storage or space for a washer/dryer. The party-time flybridge is enormous (for a 43-footer, that is), and the wide cockpit (with storage lockers) includes a transom door for easy boarding. Several of these boats have been sold with hydraulic swim platforms. A true liveaboard cruiser, Volvo 370hp diesels with IPS drives and joystick controls cruise at 24 knots (about 28 knots top).

See Page 673 For Price Data

Length	43'7"	Fuel	400 gals.
Beam	13'11"	Water	90 gals.
Draft	3'10"	Waste	50 gals.
Weight	33,650#	Hull Type	Modified-V
Clearance, Arch	19'7"	Deadrise Aft	NA

Carver 430 Cockpit MY

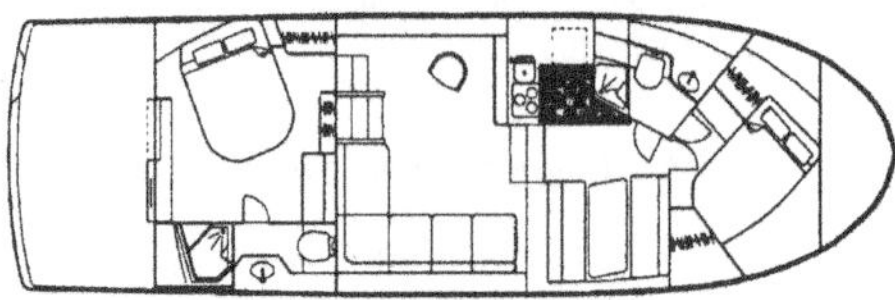

The 430 Cockpit MY is basically a Carver 390 MY (1987–95) with a stretched hull. The extra length of the cockpit gives the 430 a much-improved profile over the 390's stocky motor yacht appearance, and the extra hull length also adds a knot or two in speed. Carver packed a lot of living space into the interior of the 430 with double berths in both staterooms, a full dinette, a roomy salon area, and stall showers in both heads. (A lower helm station was optional.) A sliding door in the master stateroom leads directly out to the cockpit—a practical and extremely useful convenience. The foredeck can be fitted with sun pads, and wide side decks make getting around the deckhouse easy and safe. While the cockpit dimensions aren't notably spacious, a transom door and swim platform were standard, and there's enough room in the cockpit for some diving gear or even a wet bike. The poor performance with standard 454-cid gas engines (14–15 knots cruise) is to be expected; gas engines just don't get it in a boat this size although they're hardly a rarity. Optional 375hp Cat diesels cruise in the neighborhood of 21 knots and reach a top speed of 24–25 knots.

See Page 673 For Price Data

Length	47'10"	Fuel	390 gals.
Beam	14'0"	Water	91 gals.
Draft	3'4"	Waste	75 gals.
Weight	28,700#	Hull Type	Modified-V
Clearance	15'4"	Deadrise Aft	11°

Carver 43/47 Motor Yacht

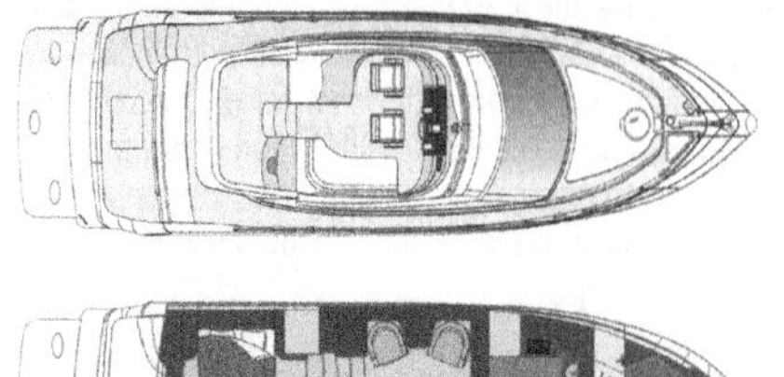

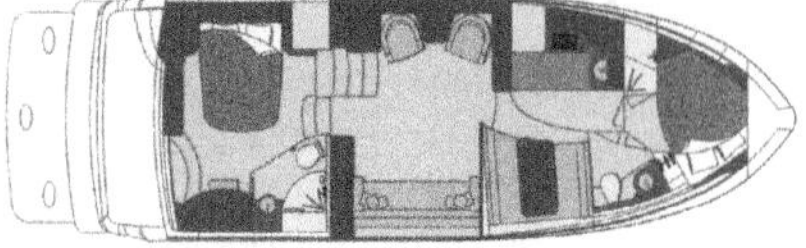

A versatile yacht with a high-sided profile, the Carver 43 Motor Yacht (called the Carver 47 MY in 2008–09) combines the spacious interior common to all late-model Carver yachts with the added practicality of a small cockpit for swimming, diving, or just watching the world go by. The 43's side decks are raised to eye level to permit the inclusion of a full-beam salon, a design style used by several motoryacht builders in recent years to maximize interior volume. In this case, it works—the salon of the 43/47, with nearly seven feet of headroom, is enormous for a boat this size. Bathed in natural lighting and finished with high-gloss cherry joinery, the galley-down floorplan features a wide-open salon with leather settee and two barrel chairs, booth-style dinette, and full-service galley with hardwood floor and Corian countertop. An offset double berth is fitted into the small guest stateroom forward, and a queen berth is in the aft stateroom with its en-suite head, vanity, and private cockpit access. Wing doors, an aft deck wet bar, and bow thruster were standard. Note that the extended swim platform can support a PWC. No racehorse, Yanmar 370hp diesels cruise the Carver 43/47 at a sedate 16–18 knots.

See Page 673 For Price Data

Length w/Platform	49'2"	Fuel, Diesel	580 gals.
Beam	14'2"	Water	90 gals.
Draft	3'6"	Waste	75 gals.
Weight	35,811#	Hull Type	Modified-V
Fuel, Gas	400 gals.	Deadrise Aft	NA

Carver 440/445 Aft Cabin

Introduced in 1993 as the 440 Aft Cabin, Carver engineers updated this conservatively styled motor yacht in 1997 with a new integral boarding platform and, in the process, re-branded her as the 445 Aft Cabin. She's a big boat on the inside, and her unusually spacious salon is among the larger to be found in a boat this size. Built on a solid fiberglass hull with a relatively wide beam and a shallow keel, her two-stateroom, galley-down floorplan is arranged with double berths fore and aft and separate stall showers in both heads. A full-size dinette is opposite the galley, and a choice of teak or maple interior woodwork was available. A lower helm was optional. The aft deck is on the small side (thanks to the huge salon dimensions), although the flybridge is large enough to entertain a small group of friends. Additional features include excellent interior headroom, fairly wide side decks, a foredeck sun pad, and—on the 445 model—staircase-style molded boarding steps built into the integral swim platform. Offered with several gas or diesel engine options, twin 330hp Cummins diesels cruise at 17–18 knots (about 22 knots top).

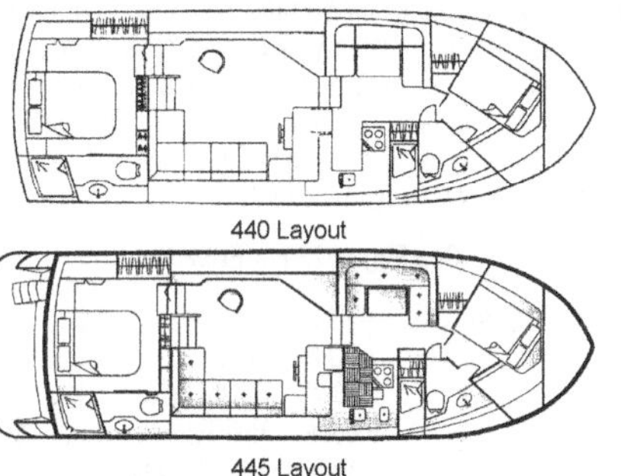
440 Layout

445 Layout

See Page 673 For Price Data

Length	47'8"	Fuel	476 gals.
Beam	15'0"	Water	165 gals.
Draft	4'3"	Waste	80 gals.
Weight	32,000#	Hull Type	Modified-V
Clearance, Arch	18'9"	Deadrise Aft	14°

Carver 444 Cockpit MY

The Carver 444 is a cockpit version of Carver's popular 396 Motor Yacht with the same interior, a little more fuel, and the added versatility of a 60-square-foot cockpit. She's also a somewhat better looking boat than the ungainly 396, at least in our opinion. On the inside the 444 is a stunning display of interior volume unmatched in a boat this size. The salon—easily the most impressive aspect of the boat—is immense with a panoramic outside view and almost seven feet of headroom. The full-beam salon was created by raising the side decks to eye level, which is why the boat appears to have so much freeboard. The two-stateroom, galley-down floorplan is arranged with double berths and separate stall showers fore and aft. Note that hanging locker space is sparse. Topside, wing doors and a hardtop protect the aft deck, and there's plenty of flybridge seating. The cockpit is a great swimming and diving platform while also providing an easy place to board. Interestingly, the extra waterline length of the 444 Cockpit MY gives her a little more speed than the 396 MY. She'll cruise at 20 knots with optional 370hp Cummins diesels and reach a top speed of about 24 knots.

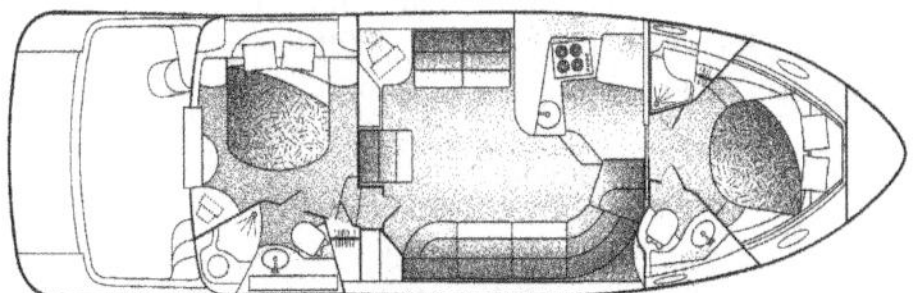

See Page 673 For Price Data

Length	46'6"	Fuel	404 gals.
Beam	13'11"	Water	90 gals.
Draft	3'6"	Waste	72 gals.
Weight	33,860#	Hull Type	Modified-V
Clearance, Arch	18'0"	Deadrise Aft	16°

Carver 450 Voyager

1999–2004

A handsome yacht with an elegant profile, the 450 Voyager is a downsized version of Carver's popular 530 Voyager introduced the previous year. Built on a modified-V hull with propeller pockets and a moderate 15 degrees of transom deadrise, the floorplan of the 450 Voyager is quite innovative. Because the galley is located in the isle way opposite the elevated lower helm (and not in the deckhouse as with most pilothouse designs), the salon is huge. There are two staterooms and two full heads below, and visibility from the lower helm—with its curved Ultraleather lounge—is superb. Facing settees and a built-in entertainment center dominate the salon with its oversized wraparound cabin windows. On deck, a flybridge extension partially shelters the cockpit where the engineroom is accessed via the lazarette. On the downside, the side decks are narrow and galley storage is limited. Additional features include cherry interior joinery, a deck access door at the lower helm (a great convenience), a big swim platform, and an extremely well arranged flybridge. A good performer with optional 450hp Cummins diesels, the 450 Voyager will cruise at 19–20 knots and reach a top speed of around 23 knots.

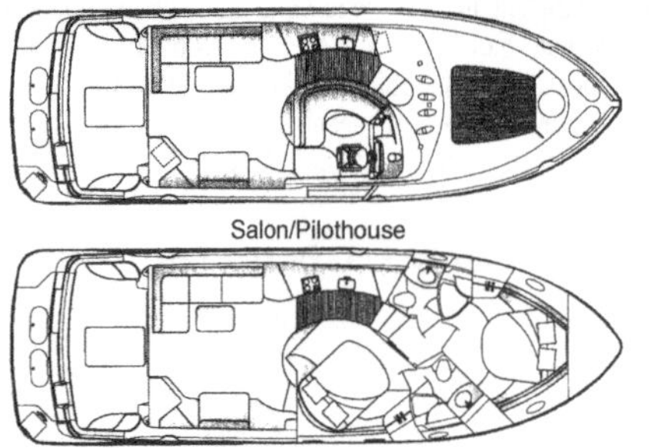
Salon/Pilothouse

Salon/Lower Level

See Page 673 For Price Data

Length w/Platform	46'11"	Fuel	560 gals.
Beam	14'11"	Water	150 gals.
Draft	3'7"	Waste	80 gals.
Weight	39,600#	Hull Type	Modified-V
Clearance	16'8"	Deadrise Aft	15°

Carver 455/456 Aft Cabin MY

1996–2000

The Carver 456 Aft Cabin (called the 455 Aft Cabin until 1999 when Carver engineers revised the cabin windows) was one of the roomier aft-cabin designs her size on the market during the late 1990s. As such, she appealed to a cross section of cruising families looking for as much boat as possible for the money. Like most of Carver's motor yacht models, she rides on a modified-V hull with a relatively wide beam, cored hullsides, and a shallow keel. The original three-stateroom layout is quite unusual—the galley is aft in the salon (rather than forward of the salon where it usually is), which allows for an enormous forward stateroom. There, a folding bulkhead conceals a small guest cabin: leave the bulkhead open and the space becomes part of the forward stateroom. Note that a second floorplan option with a dinette table (rather than the U-shaped dinette settee) in the salon became available in 1998. Additional features include a tub/shower in the forward head, a good-sized engineroom, wide side decks, staircase-style boarding steps and side exhausts. Twin 315hp Cummins diesels cruise the 455/456 Aft Cabin at 16 knots (about 20 knots top), and 340hp Cats deliver an 18-knot cruising speed (low 20s top).

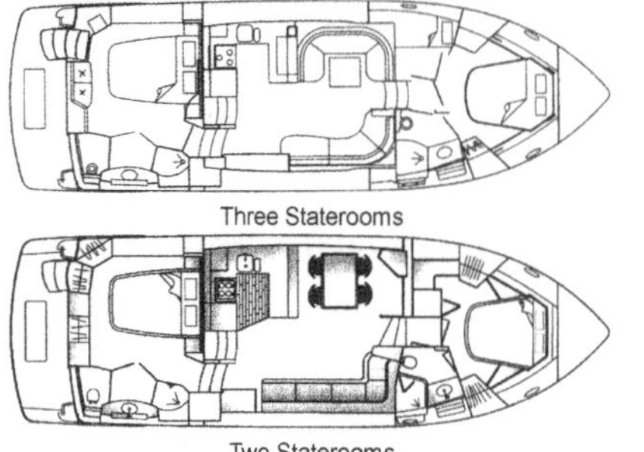
Three Staterooms

Two Staterooms

See Page 673 For Price Data

Length	45'9"	Fuel	464 gals.
Beam	15'4"	Water	132 gals.
Draft	4'7"	Waste	80 gals.
Weight	35,000#	Hull Type	Modified-V
Clearance	18'9"	Deadrise Aft	14°

Carver 460 Voyager; 46 Voyager

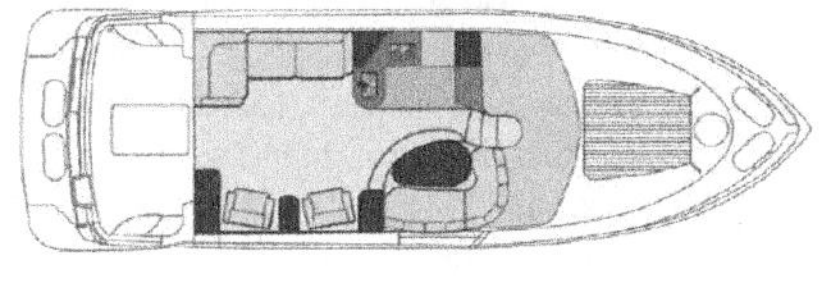

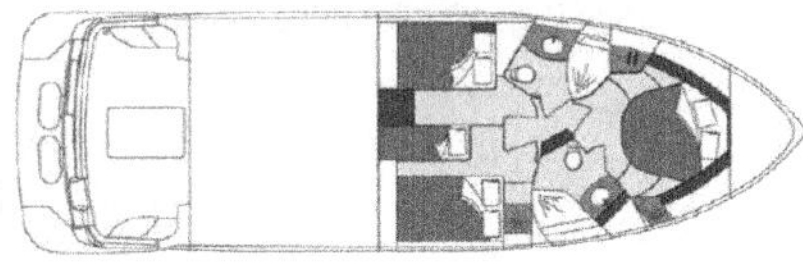

The 46 Voyager (called the 460 Voyager in 2004–06) is a revised version of Carver's popular 450 Voyager built from 1999 to 2003. With the 46, Carver designers replaced the 450's inventive two-stateroom, lower-helm interior with a three-stateroom, two-head layout with no lower helm. The result is an exceedingly capable cruising yacht with the sleeping accommodations of a larger boat. The salon, with its rich cherrywood joinery and deluxe entertainment center, is dominated by a vast Ultraleather settee with twin extending leg rests. Forward, a home-size galley with separate freezer and Corian counters is opposite the raised dinette (with its spectacular outside view). A washer/dryer is located in the port guest cabin, and to starboard is the VIP stateroom with a single and double, with the option of using an insert to create a huge sleeping area. Sliding glass doors open to a fairly small cockpit with an engineroom access hatch. Topside, the bridge deck includes a wet bar with icemaker, starboard seating lounge, dinette, and two forward helm chairs. Note that the 46 Voyager's fuel capacity is the largest in her class. Cummins 480hp diesels cruise at 19–20 knots (low 20s top).

See Page 673 For Price Data

Length w/Platform	46'11"	Fuel	560 gals.
Beam	14'11"	Water	150 gals.
Draft	3'7"	Waste	80 gals.
Weight	39,600#	Hull Type	Modified-V
Clearance	16'8"	Deadrise Aft	15°

Carver 466 Motor Yacht

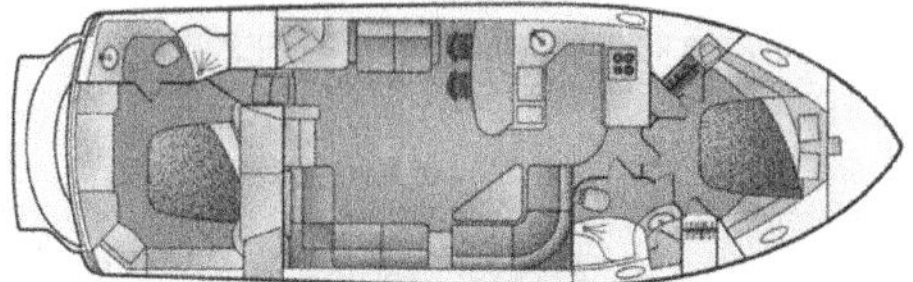

With her spacious accommodations and extensive inventory of upscale amenities, the 466 Motor Yacht took Carver's concept of cruising comfort to the next level when she was introduced in 2001. There's an astonishing amount of living space in the 466; by elevating the side decks to eye level, Carver designers were able to give this yacht an enormous full-width salon whose dimensions rival your average 55-footer. Like all Carvers, the 466 rides on a solid fiberglass hull with a wide beam and moderate transom deadrise. Her two-and-a-half-stateroom floorplan (a tiny mid-berth is under the salon settee) is arranged with the mid-level galley separated from the salon by a serving counter. The full-beam salon—trimmed with varnished cherry woodwork—is huge with seating for a small crowd and a dinette area forward. The fore and aft staterooms are fitted with queen berths (note that the berth in the master suite faces aft), and each head has a separate stall shower. Additional features include an aft-deck hardtop, wing doors, and a large flybridge with seating for eight. No beauty when it comes to styling elegance, twin 480hp Volvo diesels cruise the 466 MY at 20 knots (low 20s top).

See Page 673 For Price Data

Length	46'11"	Fuel	480 gals.
Beam	14'11"	Water	130 gals.
Draft	3'7"	Waste	80 gals.
Weight	37,000#	Hull Type	Modified-V
Clearance	19'5"	Deadrise Aft	14°

Carver 500/504 Cockpit MY

1996–2000

The 504 Cockpit MY is basically a cockpit version of Carver's 455/456 Aft Cabin (1996–2000) with additional fuel and water capacity and, of course, the added versatility and convenience of a cockpit. (Note that she was called the 500 Cockpit MY from 1996–98.) She rides on a conventional modified-V hull with a relatively wide beam, cored hullsides, and a shallow keel for directional stability. Along with a practical and comfortable two- or three-stateroom interior, the 504 Cockpit MY has an excellent deck layout. Molded steps lead down to the functional cockpit with a walk-through transom door, an oversized integral swim platform, and direct access to the master stateroom—a convenient feature lacking in most cockpit yachts. Topside, the flybridge is comfortably arranged and provides plenty of seating around the helm console. Additional features include a tub/shower in the forward head compartment, a good-sized engineroom, wide side decks, and side exhausts. Among several engine choices (the standard gas engines were hardly up to the demands of a yacht this size), optional 420hp Cummins diesels cruise at 20 knots (about 24 knots top).

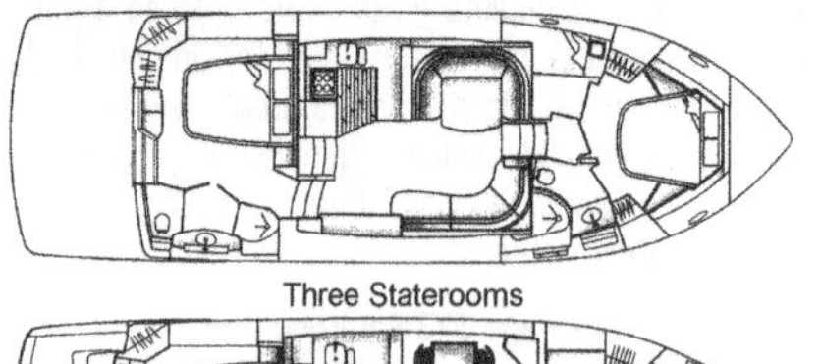
Three Staterooms

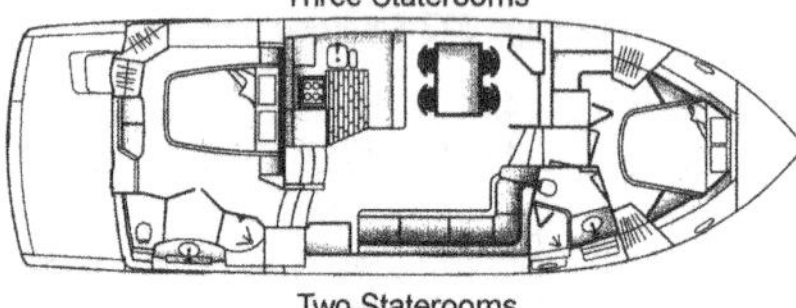
Two Staterooms

See Page 673 For Price Data

Length	49'7"	Fuel	688 gals.
Beam	15'4"	Water	200/350 gals.
Draft	4'7"	Waste	80 gals.
Weight	43,100#	Hull Type	Modified-V
Clearance, Arch	18'9"	Deadrise Aft	14°

Carver 506 Motor Yacht

2000–04

A truly distinctive yacht, the Carver 506 Motor Yacht is proof positive that a cavernous, condo-like interior is more important to some buyers than outside appearances. The styling is similar to Carver's equally controversial 396 Motor Yacht, also introduced in the year 2000, with the same elliptical tiered cabin windows and bulked-up, top-heavy appearance. On the inside, however, the 506 is a stunning display of interior volume unmatched in a boat this size. The enormous full-width salon—focal point of the boat with nearly 7 feet of headroom—is made possible by raising the side decks to eye level, which is why the boat seems to have so much freeboard. The three-stateroom, galley-down floorplan features a formal dining area across from the galley, three heads and salon seating for a small crowd. Topside, wing doors and aft-deck enclosure panels were standard; a molded stairway leads to the swim platform, and the flybridge hardtop has a retractable sunroof above the helm. A capable performer but a stiff ride in a chop, twin 450hp Cummins diesels cruise the Carver 506 MY at 17 knots and reach a top speed in the neighborhood of 21–22 knots.

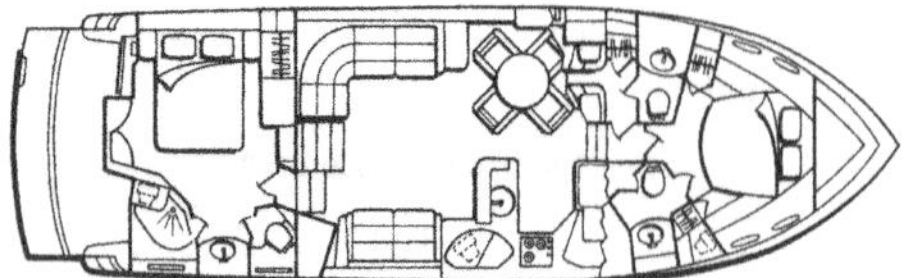

See Page 673 For Price Data

Length	51'7"	Fuel	510 gals.
Beam	15'4"	Water	158 gals.
Draft	4'6"	Waste	95 gals.
Weight	47,900#	Hull Type	Modified-V
Clearance	20'1"	Deadrise Aft	13°

Carver 52 Voyager

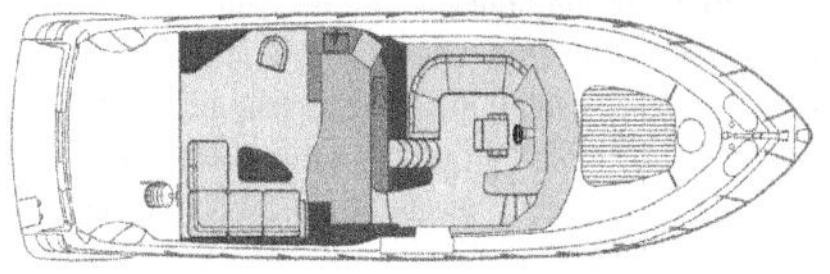

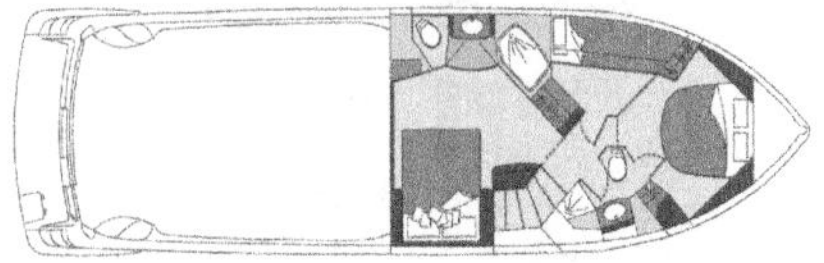

Introduced in 2007, the Carver 52 Voyager is a well-built pilothouse yacht who's conservative lines and leisurely performance will probably not serve as a template for next-generation yacht designers. She is spacious and luxurious, however, although the combined salon/galley layout differs from most pilothouse yachts where the galley is forward, close to the dinette. The result is an especially open salon with large windows providing panoramic views of the outdoors. The pilothouse door is a plus—not all motoryachts this size have one—but rear visibility from the lower helm is compromised by raised galley cabinets. There are three staterooms and two heads below, including a full-beam master with vertical hullside ports and a tub/shower in the private head. Both the master suite and the VIP stateroom are equipped with queen-sized berths, and space for a washer/dryer is found in the master stateroom. Topside, the Voyager's vast flybridge offers lounge seating for a small crowd. Bow and stern thrusters are standard. Built on a modified-V hull with cored hullsides and a solid fiberglass bottom, Volvo 575hp diesels cruise the 52 Voyager at a respectable 20–22 knots (mid 20s top).

Not Enough Resale Data to Set Values

Length	53'9"	Fuel	800 gals.
Beam	15'4"	Water	200 gals.
Draft	4'9"	Waste	100 gals.
Weight	48,500#	Hull Type	Modified-V
Clearance, Arch	19'0"	Deadrise Aft	13°

Carver 530 Voyager Pilothouse

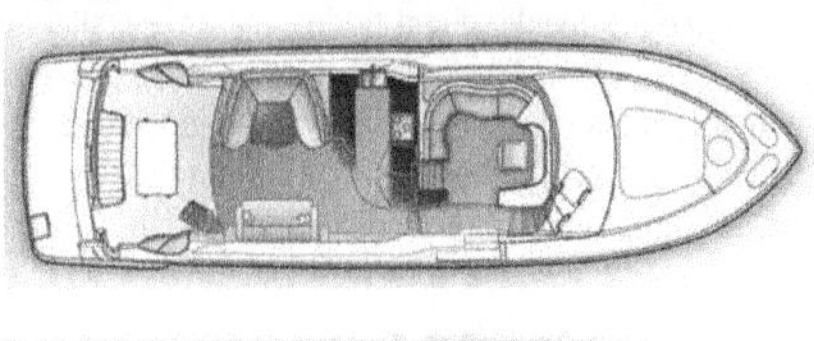

Introduced in 1998, the Carver 530 was a striking departure from the conservative (some might say boring) designs of earlier Carver models. Pilothouse yachts have become increasingly popular in recent years thanks to their sleek profiles and all-weather cruising capabilities. Judging from her sales success it's evident that the Carver 530 came along at the right time. Built on a low-deadrise, modified-V hull with a deep forefoot and shallow keel, the 530's three-stateroom cherrywood interior is arranged with the galley in the salon in typical pilothouse fashion. The full-beam owner's stateroom is amidships, and the salon has close to seven feet of headroom. Forward, the dinette/pilothouse has a wraparound helm with a tilt-back swivel seat, direct bridge access, excellent visibility, and joystick steering. Additional features include cockpit access to the engineroom, a spacious flybridge with an L-shaped settee and davit, sea chests (to reduce through-hull openings), and side exhausts. Among several engine options, twin 450hp Cummins diesels cruise the Voyager at 17 knots (about 20 knots top), and optional 675hp Volvo diesels cruise at 20 knots and reach a top speed of 22–23 knots.

See Page 673 For Price Data

Length w/Platform	53'9"	Fuel	800 gals.
Beam	15'4"	Water	200 gals.
Draft	4'9"	Waste	100 gals.
Weight	48,500	Hull Type	Modified-V
Clearance, Arch	19'0"	Deadrise Aft	13°

Carver 564 Cockpit MY

2002–06

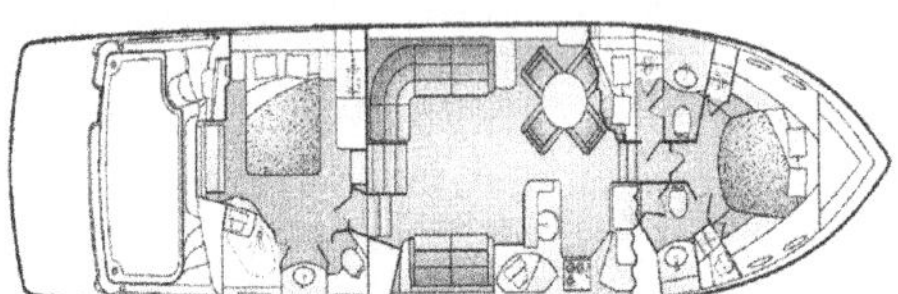

The Carver 564 is a cockpit version of the company's 506 Motor Yacht. The 564 carries some additional fuel; other than that—and the cockpit—the two boats are the same. Like her sistership, the 564 may not be everyone's idea of beauty, but on the inside she's an impressive display of interior volume unmatched in a yacht this size. The salon—easily the most impressive aspect of the boat—is immense with a panoramic view and about 7 feet of headroom. The full-width salon of the 564 is made possible by raising the side decks to eye level, which is why the boat seems to have so much freeboard. The three-stateroom, mid-galley floorplan features a dedicated dining area across from the galley, three heads, and seating in the salon for a small crowd. Note that the master stateroom has direct cockpit access. Cherry woodwork and joinery are found throughout the interior, and Corian counters are used in the galley. Topside, wing doors and an aft-deck hardtop are standard, and the flybridge hardtop has a retractable sunroof above the helm. Twin 450hp Cummins diesels cruise the 564 CMY at 18 knots (21–22 knots top), and 675hp Volvo diesels cruise at 22 knots (mid 20s top).

See Page673 For Price Data

Length	59'2"	Fuel	646 gals.
Beam	15'4"	Water	158 gals.
Draft	4'6"	Waste	95 gals.
Weight	54,167#	Hull Type	Modified-V
Clearance, Arch	20'11"	Deadrise Aft	13°

Carver 570 Voyager PH; 56 Voyager Sedan

2001–09

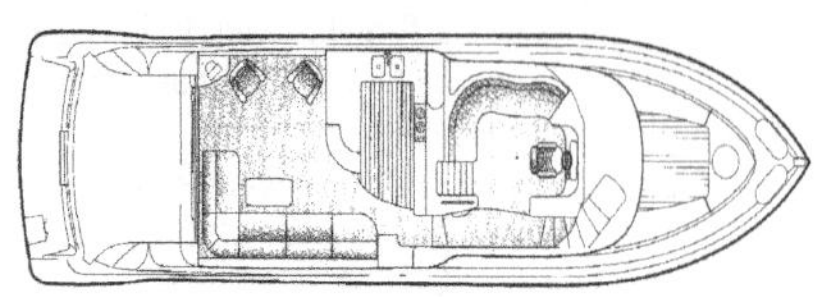

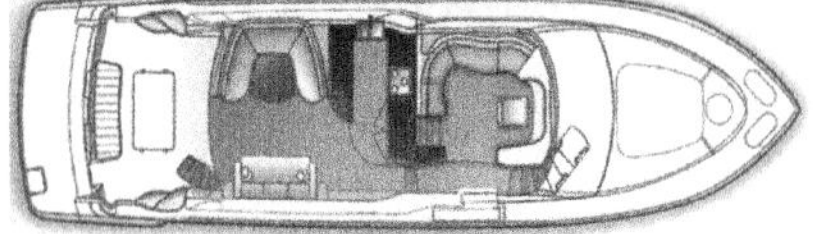

The Carver 570 Voyager (called the 570 Voyager PH in 2001–04; 57 Voyager PH in 2005–06; 56 Voyager Sedan 2007–09) is a stretched version of the company's 530 Voyager model with an extended salon and an enlarged galley. The 570—at one time the largest boat in the Carver fleet—is a strikingly handsome yacht with a sleek pilothouse profile and spacious interior accommodations. Built on a modified-V hull with moderate deadrise, the 15-foot, 4-inch beam of the Voyager is quite narrow for a boat of this length. Inside, her three-stateroom cherrywood interior is arranged with the galley in the salon as it is in many raised pilothouse boats. The full-beam owner's stateroom is amidships, and the salon has close to 7 feet of headroom. Forward, the pilothouse has a wraparound helm console with a tilt-back swivel seat, a big L-shaped settee for guests, direct bridge access, excellent visibility, and joystick steering. Additional features include cockpit access to the engineroom, a spacious bridge with a hidden davit, and sea chests (to reduce through-hull openings). Cummins 450hp diesels cruise at 17 knots, and optional 635 Cummins diesels cruise in the low 20s.

See Page 673 For Price Data

Length	59'2"	Fuel	800 gals.
Beam	15'4"	Water	200 gals.
Draft	4'9"	Waste	100 gals.
Weight	52,500#	Hull Type	Modified-V
Clearance, Arch	19'0"	Deadrise Aft	13°

Century

Quick View

- The first Century fishing boat made its debut in 1933 when the fledgling company introduced an all-mahogany skiff with two bench seats and an outboard bracket.
- In 1953 the company began building boats dedicated to skiing, fishing and pleasure cruising.
- By the mid-1980s Century was concentrating on the growing family cruiser market, offering a series of models up to 30 feet in length.
- In 1987, the company was purchased by Glasstream, and by the early 1990s the company fleet had expanded to include a 36-foot express cruiser.
- The boating recession of the early 1990s took its toll on Century, however, and by 1993 the company was struggling.
- Yamaha purchased Century in 1995 as part of a plan to grow market share for its outboard motors in the offshore category. Sales peaked in 2007 at more than 1,000 boats annually.
- With wholesale and retail sales in sharp decline, Yamaha discontinued production of Century Boats in December, 2009.

No longer in business.

Century 2600 Center Console

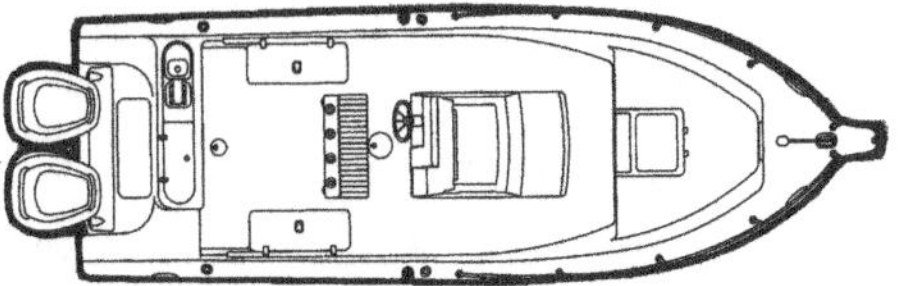

Quick and agile, the Century 2600 Center Console (note that an earlier, less popular, 2600 Center Console was built by Century during 1996–2001) is a trailerable, high-performance fishboat whose chief attributes are a space-efficient deck layout and—during her production years, at least—a very competitive price. With a hull weight of 4,200 pounds, the 2600 a relatively light boat for her size which contributes greatly to both speed and economy. Like most modern center consoles, the 2600 has an enclosed head compartment under the console (fitted with a portable head and an opening port), and the helm area is fitted with a leaning post (with a backrest), ice chest, and electronics box with lockable doors. A 42-gallon baitwell is built into the transom, and a pair of macerated fish boxes are found in the cockpit sole. Additional features include a pressurized water system with two showers, transom sink with cutting board, an integrated dive platform, tilt-out tackle trays, transom door, and cockpit bolsters. The twin fuel fills are a convenient touch. A good open-water performer, twin 225 Yamaha outboards reach a top speed of 45+ knots.

See Page 673 For Price Data

Length	26'4"	Fuel	200 gals.
Beam	8'6"	Water	20 gals.
Hull Draft	1'3"	Max HP	450
Dry Weight	5,800#	Hull Type	Deep-V
Clearance, T-Top	8'10"	Deadrise Aft	20°

Century 2600 Walkaround

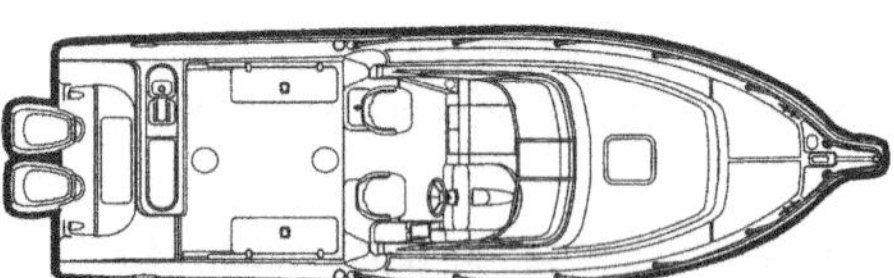

The Century 2600 Walkaround (note that Century built an earlier 2600 Walkaround with a wider 8'9" beam in 1996–2001) is a capable and good-looking trailerable fishing boat with an array of standard features that anglers and cruisers will appreciate. Walkaround boats are nearly always a design compromise—their purpose is to meet the demands of both anglers and weekend cruisers. In the case of the Century 2600, these goals are well met indeed. The cockpit —which is surprisingly uncluttered considering her modest beam—boasts a transom bait-prep station (with sink, cutting board and large 42-gallon aerated livewell), 4-tray tackle box forward, twin insulated fish boxes in the sole, and locking rod storage cabinets under each gunwale. The compact cabin provides an adult-size V-berth, removable table, enclosed head with shower, and small galley with sink and icebox. Note the two opening ports for ventilation. On the downside, the walkways around the cabin are a bit narrow. Running on a solid fiberglass deep-V hull, the Century 2600 Walkaround will cruise at 30 knots with a pair of 200hp Yamaha outboards (40–42 knots top).

See Page 673 For Price Data

Length w/Pulpit	26'4"	Fuel	150 gals.
Beam	8'6"	Water	20 gals.
Hull Draft	18"	WaterMax HP	450
Dry Weight	5,800#	Hull Type	Deep-V
Load Capacity	3,000#	Deadrise Aft	20°

Century 2900/2901 Center Console

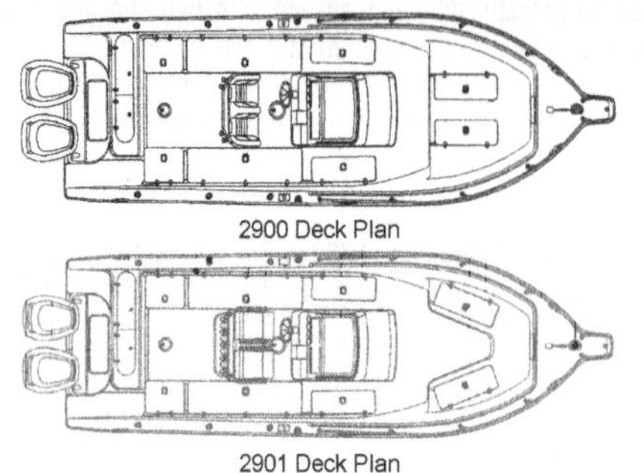

2900 Deck Plan

2901 Deck Plan

A scaled-down version of the 3100 Center Console, the Century 2900 (called the 2901 Center Console in 2007–08) is a well-built offshore fisherman with a roomy cockpit and a couple of innovative storage features. She rides on smooth-running deep-V hull, and a wide 9'6" beam makes the 2900 a stable fishing platform at trolling speeds. The console has plenty of dry space above the wheel for flush-mounting electronics and, while most modern center console designs these days have an in-console head, in the Century 2900 this roomy compartment sports a small bunk forward along with a sink and a portable head under the bunk—a unique setup. Storage space abounds: two in-deck fish boxes aft and two smaller boxes flanking the console, in-deck battery boxes, tilt-out tackle trays in the hullsides and another pair of insulated storage boxes under the casting platform. Additional features include a lighted transom livewell, transom sink, raw-water washdown, bow pulpit, and transom door. Range, with a generous 300 gallons of fuel capacity, is excellent. A good performer with twin 250hp Yamaha outboards, The 2900/2901 Center Console will cruise at 30 knots and reach a top speed of 40+ knots.

See Page 673 For Price Data

Length	29'4"	Water	22 gals.
Beam	9'6"	Waste	7 gals.
Hull Draft	1'10"	Max HP	600
Hull Weight	7,000#	Hull Type	Deep-V
Fuel	300 gals.	Deadrise Aft	23°

Century 3000 Center Console

The Century 3000 was the first big center console produced by Century and, like her competitors from Pursuit, Marlin, Jupiter, Intrepid, Ocean Master, etc., she's a big center console with the kind of exciting performance that serious anglers will appreciate. While the beam of the Century is just under the 10-foot trailerable max (with a permit, that is), she's wide enough to provide a big-boat fishing platform and comfortable enough to handle seas with ease. Built on a rugged deep-V hull with cored hullsides, she's a relatively light boat for her size. The layout provides plenty of fishing space for four anglers, and there's a head and even a sleeping berth hidden inside the console. Storage space abounds including two large in-deck fish boxes and two inwale storage lockers. A circulating livewell and bait-prep center are built into the transom, and there's another insole fish box at the transom. Additional features include a well-arranged helm console, leaning post, washdown, and lounge seating forward. A good-running boat with plenty of eye appeal, twin 250hp Yamahas cruise at 30 knots and reach a top speed of over 40 knots depending on the load.

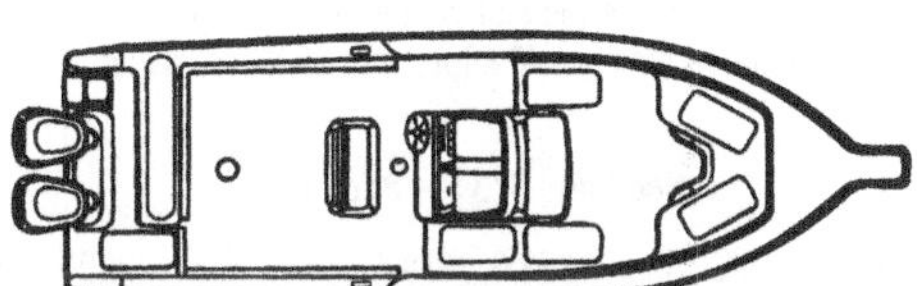

See Page 673 For Price Data

Length w/Pulpit	30'11"	Fuel	270 gals.
Hull Length	29'2"	Water	20 gals.
Beam	9'8"	Max HP	500
Draft	2'11"	Hull Type	Deep-V
Dry Weight	5,500#	Deadrise Aft	20°

Century 3000 Sport Cabin

A versatile boat, the Century 3000 Sport Cabin combines a (reasonably) fishable cockpit with the cabin amenities of a small family cruiser. Built on a solid fiberglass deep-V hull with moderate beam and wide chines, the Sport Cabin's unusual deck layout is arranged with the helm well aft on the bridgedeck in order to provide built-in lounge seating for passengers between the console and the cabin. While this configuration eats up some valuable space in the cockpit, the additional seating makes the Sport Cabin a true dual-purpose boat with open-air accommodations for a small crowd. Two large in-deck fish boxes and a transom livewell are standard in the cockpit, and fiberglass boxes under the pedestal seats house a fish box and (to port) tackle drawers. A small fishing area forward of the house is accessed by wide walkaround side decks. Below, the cabin contains a dinette/V-berth forward, small galley with sink and refrigerator, enclosed head, and midcabin double berth aft. Additional features include a wet bar, transom door, cockpit bolsters, raw-water washdown, and lockable rod storage. Twin 250hp Yamaha outboards deliver a top speed of 40+ knots.

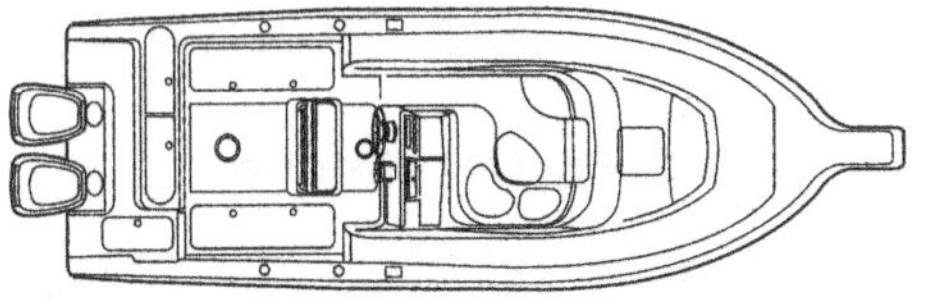

See Page 673 For Price Data

Length w/Pulpit	30'11"	Fuel	270 gals.
Hull Length	29'2"	Water	20 gals.
Beam	9'10"	Max HP	500
Draft	2'11"	Hull Type	Deep-V
Dry Weight	6,800#	Deadrise Aft	20°

Century 3100/3200 Center Console

1999–2009

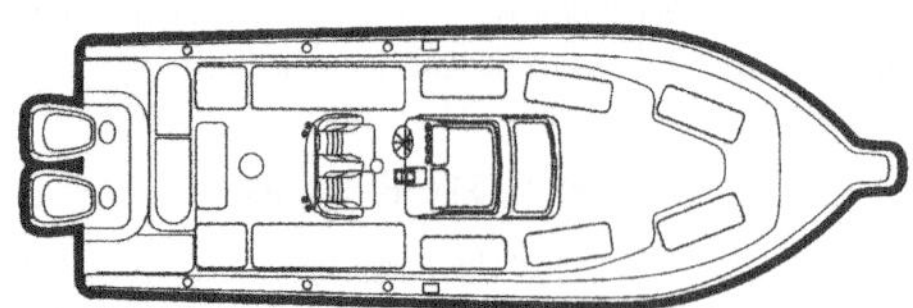

The Century 3200 Center Console (called the 3100 until 2001) is a solid, well-built offshore fisherman with a roomy cockpit and a couple of innovative storage features. She's constructed on a solid fiberglass deep-V hull, and a wide beam makes this a stable fishing platform at trolling speeds. The large console has twin lockable acrylic hatches for flush-mounting electronics and, while most modern center console designs these days have an in-console head, in the Century 3200 this roomy compartment sports a small bunk forward along with a sink, shower, and a portable head under the bunk—a unique setup. Storage is exceptional; there are two macerated in-deck fish boxes aft and four smaller boxes forward, flanking the console, two in-deck battery boxes, tilt-out tackle trays in the hull sides and another pair of insulated storage boxes under the casting platform. Additional features include a huge transom livewell, a tall windshield, transom sink, raw-water washdown, hydraulic tilt steering, cockpit lighting, bow pulpit, transom door and trim tabs. This was the biggest center console ever built by Century. Top speed of close to 40 knots with 250hp Yamahas.

See Page 673 For Price Data

Length w/Pulpit	32'6"	Fuel	300 gals.
Beam	10'6"	Water	30 gals.
Draft, Up	1'8"	Max HP	700
Dry Weight	8,500#	Hull Type	Deep-V
Clearance, Top	9'6"	Deadrise Aft	23°

Century 3100/3200 Walkaround

2000–07

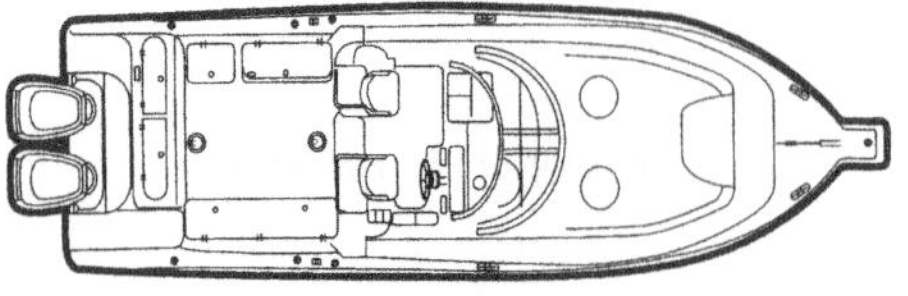

The Century 3200 Walkaround (called the 3100 Walkaround in her first year of production) is a rugged, well-conceived express that many industry pros consider a lot of boat for the money. Built on an aggressive deep-V hull with generous beam and an integrated transom, the 3100/3200 is a versatile boat. As a fisherman, she offers an uncluttered cockpit with two in-deck (macerated) fish boxes, transom sink with cutting board and washdowns, ice chest, and transom door. The rear seat conceals a very large aerated livewell. Cockpit jump seats are standard, and a lockable electronics cabinet is built into the helm console. The side decks, while not broad, are wide enough to get around easily. Note the nifty lift-out tackle box, port/starboard fuel fills, and bow seating. Below decks, the cruise-equipped interior boasts a well-appointed galley with stove, refrigerator and microwave, large V-berth/dinette forward, enclosed head with shower, and adult-size midberth aft. Cabin headroom is very good, and opening ports and two deck hatches provide plenty of ventilation. A 4kw diesel generator (with 10-gallon fuel tank) was optional. Twin 250hp Yamaha outboards top out at close to 40 knots.

See Page 673 For Price Data

Length w/Pulpit	32'6"	Water	30 gals.
Beam	10'6"	Waste	8 gals.
Draft, Engines Down	3'4"	Max HP	600
Dry Weight	9,400#	Hull Type	Deep-V
Fuel	300 gals.	Deadrise Aft	23°

Chaparral

Quick View

- Chaparral Boats (originally Fiberglass Fabricators) was founded in 1965 by William "Buck" Pegg in Ft. Lauderdale, Florida. The company's bellwether boat at the time was the 15-foot tri-hull with a sticker price of $675.
- Originally based in Ft. Lauderdale, Chaparral relocated in 1976 when the Larsen boat manufacturing facility in Nashville, GA, became available due to Larsen's bankruptcy.
- In 1986 Chaparral Boats was purchased by RPC Energy Services of Atlanta, Georgia.
- By 2000, Chaparral had grown to become the forth-largest independent sportboat builder in the United Staes.
- Chaparral currently builds a wide range of bow riders, performance boats, deck boats, and family fishing boats.
- Now into its fifth decade, Chaparrals are distributed worldwide through a network of domestic and international dealers.

Chaparral Boats • Nashville, GA • www.chapparalboats.com

Chaparral 260 Signature

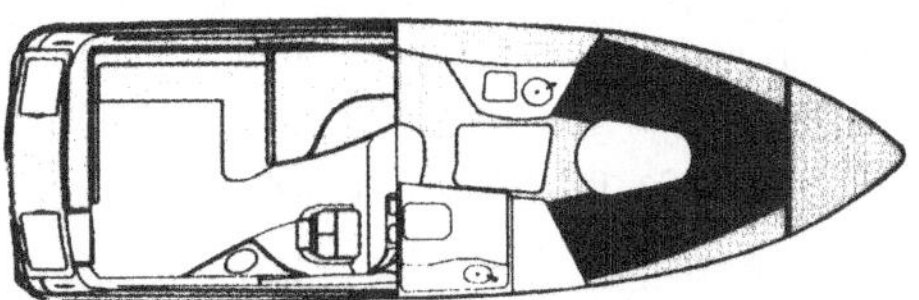

The Chaparral Signature 260 (note that she was introduced in 1996 as the Signature 25) is a classy family weekender whose quality construction and good overall performance make her a standout among trailerable cruisers her size. She rides on a balsa-cored modified-V hull, and Chaparral claims that her "Extended V-Plane" bottom design translates into quicker planing and a softer ride. The Signature 260 is indeed a good-handling boat and visibility from the raised helm is excellent. Below decks, the midcabin floorplan provides overnight accommodations for four adults in a cabin that boasts a full 6 feet of headroom. Considering the size of the cockpit, the interior of the Signature 25/260 is quite generous and includes an enclosed head compartment as well as a small galley and adequate storage. A curved settee is opposite the stylish woodgrain helm, and—lacking side decks—a walk-thru windshield provides access to the foredeck. A wet bar and hideaway aft lounge are standard in the cockpit. A very good-running boat, a single 7.4-liter MerCruiser I/O will cruise the Signature 260 at a respectable 23 knots while delivering a top speed in the neighborhood of 38 knots.

See Page 673 For Price Data

Length	25'7"	Clearance	7'2"
Beam	8'6"	Fuel	82 gals.
Draft, Up	1'5"	Water	25 gals.
Draft, Down	2'9"	Hull Type	Deep-V
Weight	5,977#	Deadrise Aft	20°

Chaparral 260 SSi

There's no shortage of quality 26-foot bowriders on the water these days. With new models introduced almost every year, big trailerable bowriders are an especially competitive segment of the runabout market. Introduced in 2001, the Chaparral 260 SSi is functional, well styled, and well equipped for a fun day on the water. She's built on a solid fiberglass deep-V hull with an aggressive 22 degrees of transom deadrise, enough to smooth out some fairly rough water. The cockpit design of the 260 SSi—wraparound lounge seating aft, swivel helm and companion seats, wet bar with sink and ice chest, etc.—is similar to most bowriders her size; the SSi's smooth finish is often the only difference. A lockable head/change compartment with sink and opening port is built into the portside helm console. The wood-grained instrument panel and mahogany steering wheel are nice touches. A transom shower, bow ice chest, in-floor storage, and removable cocktail table were standard; an extended swim platform was optional. A good performer for her size, a single 320hp Volvo DuoProp I/O delivers a cruising speed in the mid 30s (45 mph top).

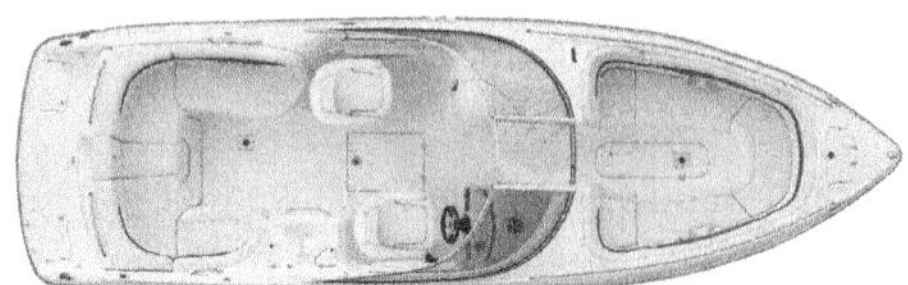

See Page 673 For Price Data

Length	25'6"	Clearance	5'8"
Beam	8'6"	Fuel	79 gals.
Draft, Up	22"	Water	15 gals.
Draft, Down	35"	Hull Type	Deep-V
Weight	5,200#	Deadrise Aft	22°

Chaparral 265 SSi

The Chaparral 265 SSi is a cuddy version of the company's 260 SSi bowrider produced from 2001–06. If anything, the 265 was a more popular model than the open-bow 260, although both were good sellers for Chaparral during their production years. Like her sibling, the 265 is functional, well styled, and well equipped. She's built on a solid fiberglass deep-V hull with an aggressive 22 degrees of transom deadrise, enough to smooth out some fairly rough water. The cockpit design—wraparound lounge seating aft, swivel helm and companion seats, wet bar with sink and ice chest, etc.—is similar to most cuddy runabouts her size; the SSi's smooth finish is often the only significant difference. Below, the well-appointed cabin features a wraparound leather settee forward, compact galley with sink and refrigerator, and quality vinyl overheads and wall coverings. A transom shower, beverage holders, in-floor storage, and removable cocktail table were standard; a sport arch and extended swim platform were optional. A good performer for her size, a single 320hp Volvo DuoProp I/O delivers a cruising speed in the mid 30s (45 mph top).

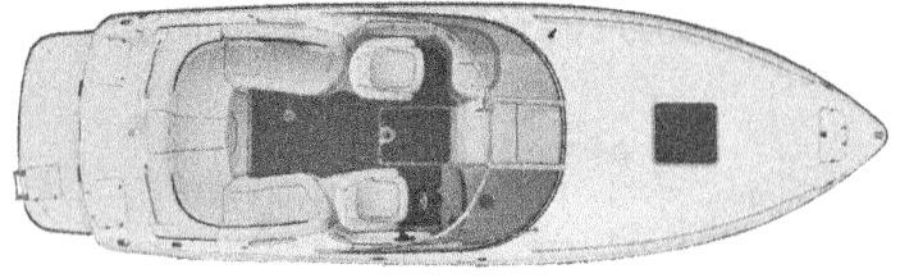

See Page674 For Price Data

Length Overall	27'9"	Clearance	5'8"
Beam	8'6"	Fuel	79 gals.
Draft, Up	22"	Water	15 gals.
Draft, Down	35"	Hull Type	Deep-V
Weight	5,234#	Deadrise Aft	22°

Chaparral 26/27/270 Signature

Called the Signature 26 when she was introduced in 1992 and the Signature 27 from 1993 to 1999, Chaparral renamed this model the Signature 270 for the year 2000. This was the second of three Chaparral products to carry the Signature 27 model designation; the original Signature 27 (1988–1991) was trailerable with a narrower beam. Featuring good-quality materials and solid construction, the 27/270 was priced slightly above the average for sportcruisers her size. An elevated foredeck provides marginal headroom below at the expense of a somewhat top-heavy exterior appearance. The cabin layout is arranged with a circular dinette/V-berth forward, a compact galley and head, and a snug midcabin stateroom aft. Outside, an L-shaped lounge is opposite the helm, and a hideaway bench seat is fitted at the transom. With no windshield opening and narrow side decks, foredeck access is difficult. Additional features include an integral bow pulpit, anchor locker, transom door, and a removable cockpit table. Among several single and twin sterndrive engine options, a single 300hp MerCruiser sterndrive will cruise at 25 knots and reach a top speed of 34–35 knots.

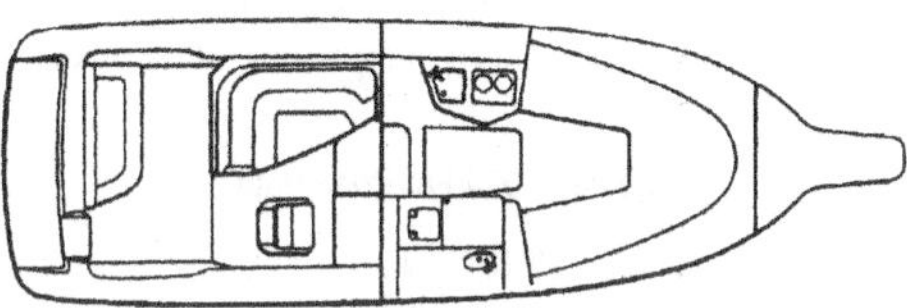

See Page 674 For Price Data

Length w/Pulpit	28'5"	Fuel	105 gals.
Beam	9'0"	Water	25 gals.
Draft, Drive Up	2'1"	Waste	25 gals.
Draft, Drive Down	2'9"	Hull Type	Modified-V
Weight	6,249#	Deadrise Aft	20°

Chaparral 270 Signature

Twenty-seven feet is the practical size limit for trailerable express cruisers. Beyond that, and the boat would be too heavy for most family tow vehicles. If the attraction of a trailerable boat this size is versatility—you can literally take it anywhere—the downside is living space. The maximum beam for a (legally) trailerable boat is 8'6", and on a 27-footer that translates into a small cockpit and a claustrophobic interior. That said, the 270 Signature ranks among the better boats in this market segment thanks to her sharp styling, space-efficient layout, and better-than-average finish. With 6'2" of cabin headroom and berths for four, the 270's interior is a match for competitive models from Sea Ray and Regal. A galley trash bin is a thoughtful touch as are the forward mirrored bulkhead and the soft-touch vinyl headliner. The cockpit features a reversible double helm seat, sun lounge, wet bar with sink and ice chest, removable table, and a two-person transom seat with storage under. The transom locker can stow two fenders and a hose, and there's space at the dash for a small video display. A single 375hp MerCruiser I/O delivers a top speed in the range of 35–40 knots.

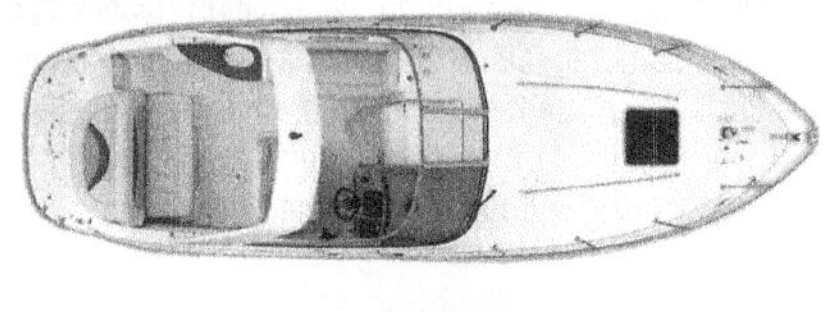

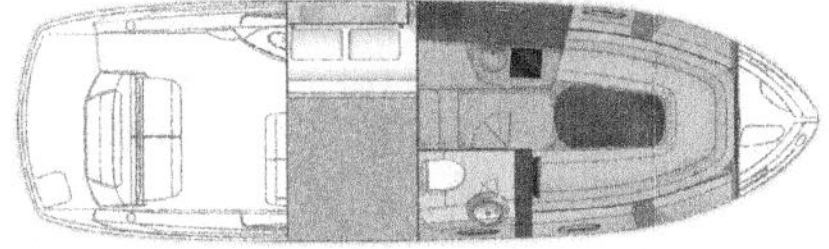

See Page 674 For Price Data

Length	28'11"	Fuel	87 gals.
Beam	8'6"	Water	29 gals.
Draft, Up	1'5"	Waste	28 gals.
Draft, Down	2'9"	Hull Type	Modified-V
Weight	7,450#	Deadrise Aft	18°

Chaparral 275 SSi

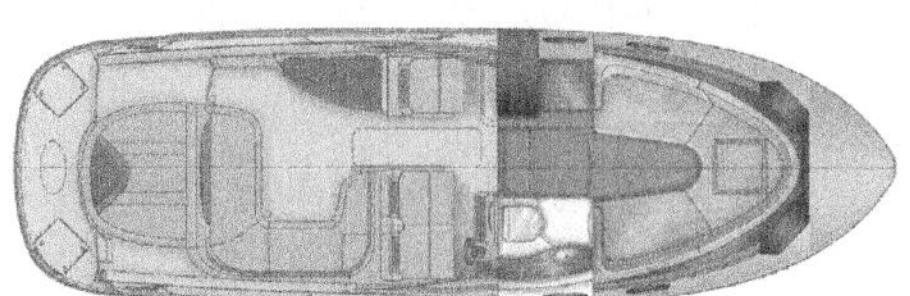

Designed for daytime fun in the sun, the well-appointed cabin and large, party-time cockpit of the Chaparral 275 SSi combine to make this one of the more attractive runabouts her size on the water. For many boaters, 27 feet is the perfect length for a sportboat: roomy enough for as many as 10, and small enough to trailer—with a heavy-duty tow vehicle and overwide permit, that is. Built on a smooth-running deep-V hull, the 275's U-shaped cockpit seating has a clever three-position back seat that easily converts to a sun pad or aft-facing chaise lounge. At the helm, a double-wide bolster seat includes individual flip up bases. Fore and aft boarding ladders (with top-rung grab handles) make boarding easy from deep water or a sandy beach. Below, the 275's cozy cabin comfortably sleeps two and includes a compact galley with refrigerator and microwave, and an enclosed head with VacuFlush toilet and sink. A transom shower, power engine hatch, and pop-up cleats are standard; a fold-down arch and thru-hull exhaust system were popular options. Not inexpensive, a single 280hp Volvo Duuprop tops out at close to 40 knots.

See Page 674 For Price Data

Length	28'10"	Fuel	105 gals.
Beam	9'0"	Water	13.5 gals.
Draft, Up	1'10"	Waste	3.5 gals.
Draft, Down	3'0"	Hull Type	Deep-V
Weight	7,300#	Deadrise Aft	22°

Chaparral 270/280 Signature

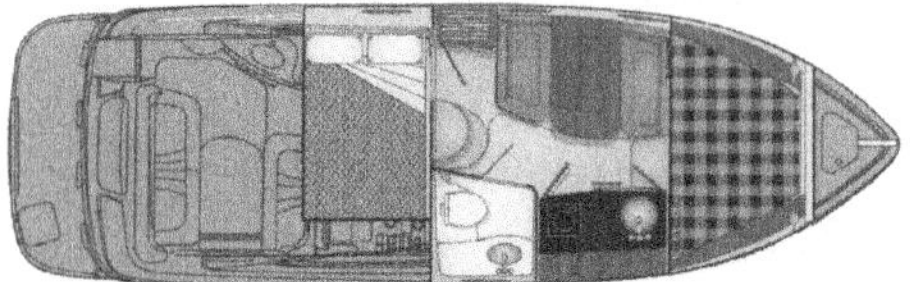

Introduced in 2003 as the 270 Signature (and called the 280 Signature in 2006–09), this stylish pocket cruiser made good on Chaparral's claim of quality construction and roomy accommodations. Unlike most other 27-footers with trailerable 8-foot, 6-inch beams, the 270/280's wide 9-foot, 6-inch beam insures a more livable interior as well as a larger cockpit. A handsome boat on the outside, the interior of the Signature 270 sleeps six: two in the forward V-berth, two in the aft cabin, and two more when the dinette is converted. The galley is a little light on storage and counter space; the head, on the other hand, is surprisingly roomy. Privacy curtains separate the sleeping areas from the main cabin, and the upscale decor is a blend of cherry joinery, designer fabrics, and vinyl wall coverings. In the cockpit, the helm has a tilt wheel and dual flip-up seating. Lacking side decks, a walk-through windshield provides access to the foredeck. Additional features include a transom storage locker, cockpit entertainment center, radar arch, and a well-designed engineroom with a push-button lift. Among several engine options, twin 225hp Volvo I/Os will top out at close to 40 knots.

See Page 674 For Price Data

Length w/Platform	29'3"	Fuel	100 gals.
Beam	9'6"	Water	29 gals.
Draft, Up	1'5"	Waste	28 gals.
Draft, Down	2'9"	Hull Type	Modified-V
Weight	9,100#	Deadrise Aft	20°

Chaparral 280 SSi

1999–2006

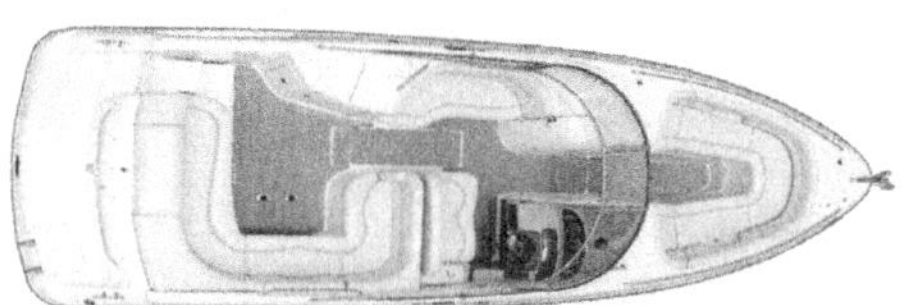

The Chaparral 280 SSi was among the most popular big bowriders available following her introduction in 1999 thanks to an enviable blend of smart styling, first-rate construction and excellent performance. Built on a deep-V hull, the 280's versatile cockpit layout—with its comfortable seating and luxury appointments—is one of her most compelling features. The galley is fitted with a sink, pressure water and refrigerator, and the enclosed head compartment comes complete with a sink, storage bin and opening port for ventilation. A walk-through transom provides easy access to the swim platform, and the helm is thoughtfully designed with additional electronics in mind. Forward, the bow seating area is arranged with hinged seat storage, gunwale drink holders and a spacious in-floor ski locker. Flush-mount bi-fold doors separate the cockpit from the bow to reduce the effects of wind while driving at higher speeds. Recessed trim tabs are standard, and a radar arch and extended swim platform have been popular options. A good performer, twin 300hp Volvo sterndrive engines cruise the 280 SSi at 30 knots and reach a top speed in excess of 50 knots.

See Page 674 For Price Data

Length w/Platform	29'6"	Fuel	143 gals.
Hull Length	27'6"	Water	30 gals.
Beam	9'3"	Waste	9.5 gals.
Draft	2'11"	Hull Type	Deep-V
Weight	6,800#	Deadrise Aft	22°

Chaparral 2835 SS; 285 SSi

1999–2006

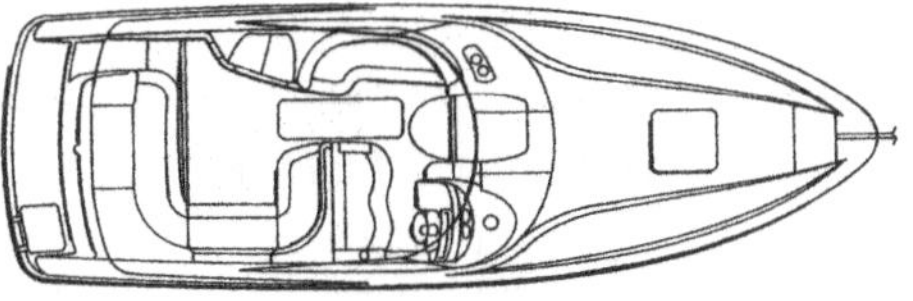

Big day boats with spacious cockpits and modest cabins have become increasing popular in recent years with owners who place a greater emphasis on open-air fun than interior comforts. (Indeed, in most boats of this type the interiors see very little use.) Built on a soft-riding deep-V hull, the 285 SSi (called the 2835 SS in 1999) is a well-built sportboat whose combination of solid performance and quality construction have made her a very popular model for Chaparral. The large, divided cockpit is fitted with a U-shaped lounge opposite the helm, fore and aft facing lounges, a removable cocktail table that converts the lounges into a sun pad, wet bar with sink, and a walk-through transom. An electric lift mechanism raises the aft section of the U-shaped lounge and makes access to the engine compartment easy. Cabin amenities include a dinette/double berth, mini-galley, four opening ports, and a private head compartment with a pull-up shower and vacuum-flush toilet. Additional features include an eye-catching burlwood dash panel and side exhausts. A good performer, twin 300hp Volvo sterndrive engines cruise the 285 SSi at 30 knots and reach a top speed in excess of 50 knots.

See Page 674 For Price Data

Length w/Platform	29'6"	Fuel	143 gals.
Hull Length	27'6"	Water	30 gals.
Beam	9'3"	Waste	9.5 gals.
Draft	2'11"	Hull Type	Deep-V
Weight	7,200#	Deadrise Aft	22°

Chaparral 28/29 Signature

For many boaters, this popular Chaparral model (called the Signature 28 in 1991–92; 29 Signature in 1993–2000) struck the right mix of quality construction and upscale accommodations. She was considered a very stylish boat when she was introduced back in 1991, and a generous 9'9" beam results in a spacious and notably versatile interior. The layout is a little different from most midcabin designs: a V-berth area is all the way forward followed by an aft-facing wraparound dinette that spans the full width of the interior. A high/low table converts the dinette into a double berth, while the aft cabin is separated from the main salon with a privacy door rather than just a curtain. The cockpit is arranged in two sections: a three-person bench seat stows away in the transom, and a large U-shaped settee is forward, opposite the helm. On the downside, the side decks are quite narrow. As many as six people can be seated comfortably in the cockpit, and visibility from the helm is excellent. A bow pulpit, radar arch, and cockpit wet bar were all standard. Twin 190hp MerCruiser sterndrives cruise the Signature 28/29 in the mid 20s and reach a top speed of around 35 knots.

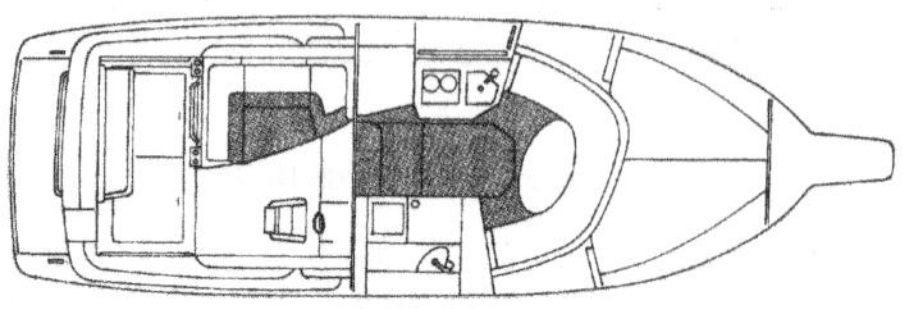

See Page 674 For Price Data

Length w/Pulpit	31'11"	Weight	8,200#
Hull Length	29'3"	Fuel	121 gals.
Beam	9'9"	Water	30 gals.
Draft, Up	1'11"	Hull Type	Modified-V
Draft, Down	2'9"	Deadrise Aft	20°

Chaparral 280/290 Signature

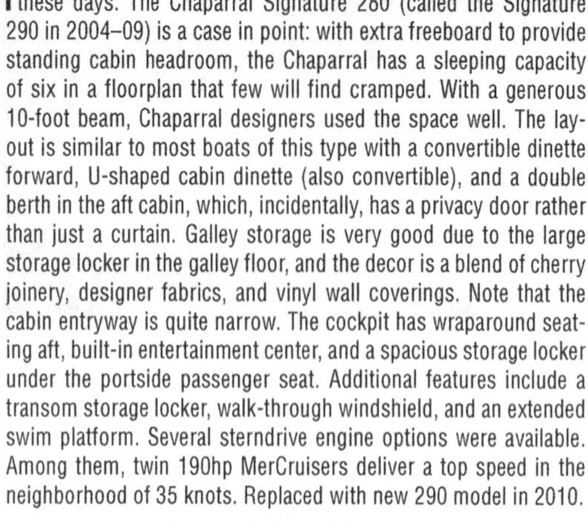

It's surprising what manufacturers can put into a 28-foot boat these days. The Chaparral Signature 280 (called the Signature 290 in 2004–09) is a case in point: with extra freeboard to provide standing cabin headroom, the Chaparral has a sleeping capacity of six in a floorplan that few will find cramped. With a generous 10-foot beam, Chaparral designers used the space well. The layout is similar to most boats of this type with a convertible dinette forward, U-shaped cabin dinette (also convertible), and a double berth in the aft cabin, which, incidentally, has a privacy door rather than just a curtain. Galley storage is very good due to the large storage locker in the galley floor, and the decor is a blend of cherry joinery, designer fabrics, and vinyl wall coverings. Note that the cabin entryway is quite narrow. The cockpit has wraparound seating aft, built-in entertainment center, and a spacious storage locker under the portside passenger seat. Additional features include a transom storage locker, walk-through windshield, and an extended swim platform. Several sterndrive engine options were available. Among them, twin 190hp MerCruisers deliver a top speed in the neighborhood of 35 knots. Replaced with new 290 model in 2010.

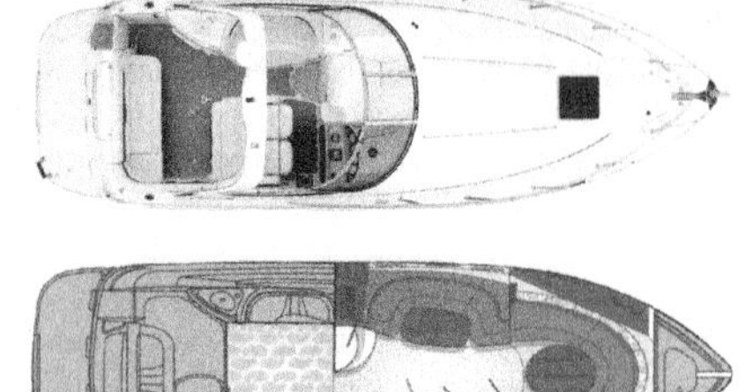

See Page 674 For Price Data

Length w/Platform	30'8"	Fuel	115 gals.
Beam	10'0"	Water	25 gals.
Draft, Up	2'1"	Waste	28 gals.
Draft, Down	2'9"	Hull Type	Modified-V
Weight	9,700#	Deadrise Aft	18°

Chaparral 300 Signature

1998–2003

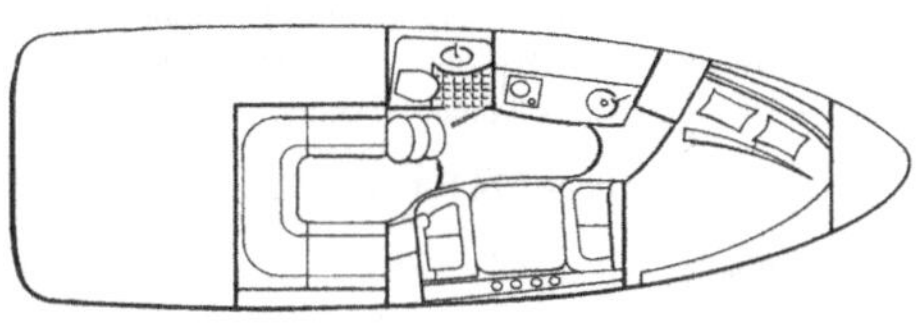

The Signature 300 is good-quality family cruiser with a well-arranged cockpit and an upscale, very comfortable interior. Like many Chaparral cruisers, she's constructed on a modified-V hull with a solid fiberglass bottom, moderate beam and an integral swim platform. While the Signature's midcabin interior is similar to many other 30-footers, the quality of the hardware, woodwork and upholstery is immediately evident. The roomy aft cabin, with its convertible settee and removable dinette table, is definitely the master stateroom in this boat with far more amenities than the forward berth. The cockpit seats six and includes a double helm seat, a U-shaped settee aft (which converts into a big sun pad), and a wet bar. The aft bench seat can be folded away to free up some cockpit space, and a gas-assist hatch provides easy access to the engine compartment. Additional features include a transom shower, walk-through windshield (there are no side decks), cockpit lighting and five opening ports. Among several engine options, twin 250hp Volvo sterndrive gas engines cruise the Signature 300 in the mid to high 20s and reach a top speed of around 40 knots.

See Page 674 For Price Data

Length w/Platform	31'3"	Clearance, Arch	11'0"
Beam	10'3"	Fuel	153 gals.
Draft, Up	2'1"	Water	30 gals.
Draft, Down	2'9"	Hull Type	Modified-V
Weight	9,800#	Deadrise Aft	20°

Chaparral 30/31 Signature

1990–97

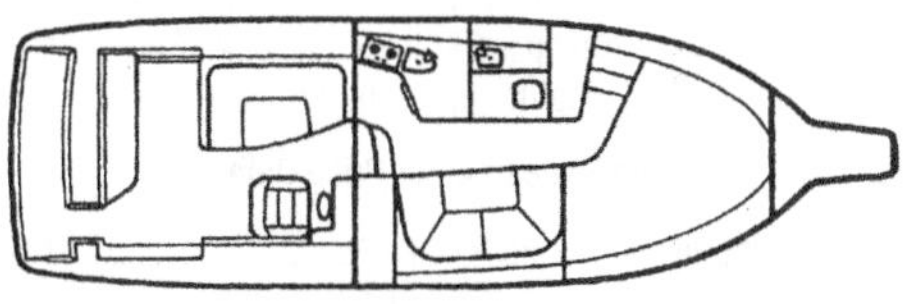

Chaparral has always enjoyed an industry reputation for quality products. No surprise, then, that the Signature 30 (called the Signature 31 from 1993–97) was considered one of the more sophisticated express boats in her class during the 1990s. Like all Chaparral models, she was built on a modified-V hull with moderate beam and a solid fiberglass bottom. Her midcabin interior is arranged in the conventional manner with double berths fore and aft and a convertible dinette in the salon. Both sleeping areas are fitted with privacy curtains, and it's worth noting that the galley can best be described as compact. On deck, the cockpit floor is flush from the transom forward—rare in a midcabin cruiser. The L-shaped lounge opposite the helm converts (with the aid of an insert) into a sun pad, and the bench seat at the transom folds away into the transom bulkhead when not in use. The helm console was updated in 1993 (among a few other upgrades). Additional features include plenty of cockpit storage, a hidden swim ladder, reasonably wide side decks, and a radar arch. A good performer, twin 230hp MerCruiser (or 250hp Volvo) sterndrives cruise the Signature 31 at 18 knots and reach 30+ knots wide open.

See Page 674 For Price Data

Length w/Pulpit	33'2"	Weight	9,750#
Hull Length	30'6"	Fuel	150 gals.
Beam	10'9"	Water	40 gals.
Draft, Up	1'11"	Hull Type	Modified-V
Draft, Down	2'9"	Deadrise Aft	17°

Chaparral 310 Signature

2004–09

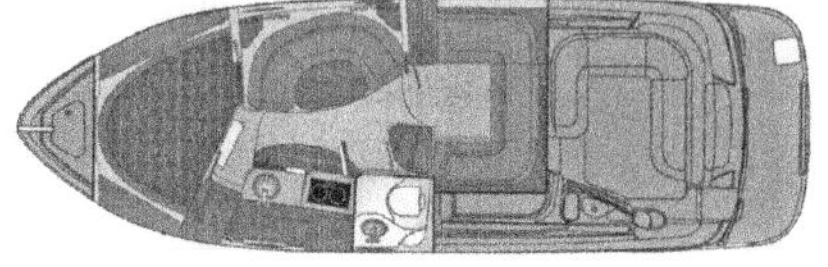

An impressive blend of modern styling and first-rate accommodations, Chaparral's Signature 310 is a well-built weekend cruiser for those willing to pay a little extra for a quality product. Chaparral builds a good boat, and the 310 stands apart from other cruisers her size for her excellent tooling and above-average finish. Built on a modified-V hull with cored hullsides and a solid fiberglass bottom, the midcabin interior sleeps six in a layout typical of most boats in this class. Cherry joinery, designer fabrics, and upscale furnishings highlight the entire cabin, and the galley is notable for its generous storage. Note also that both of the 310's hanging lockers are cedar lined—a thoughtful touch. At the helm, the tiered, non-glare dash includes space for flush-mounting a full array of electronics. As many as eight can be seated in the cockpit where a full wet bar, transom shower, and portable cooler were standard. Additional features include a transom storage locker, extended swim platform, walk-through windshield, double helm seat with bolsters, and foredeck sun pad. A good open-water performer, twin 280hp Volvo sterndrives cruise the Chaparral 310 in the mid 20s and reach a top speed of about 35 knots.

See Page 674 For Price Data

Length w/Platform	33'4"	Fuel	147 gals.
Beam	10'7"	Water	29 gals.
Draft, Up	2'1"	waste	28 gals.
Draft, Down	2'9"	Hull Type	Modified-V
Weight	11,375#	Deadrise Aft	17°

Chaparral 330 Signature

2003–09

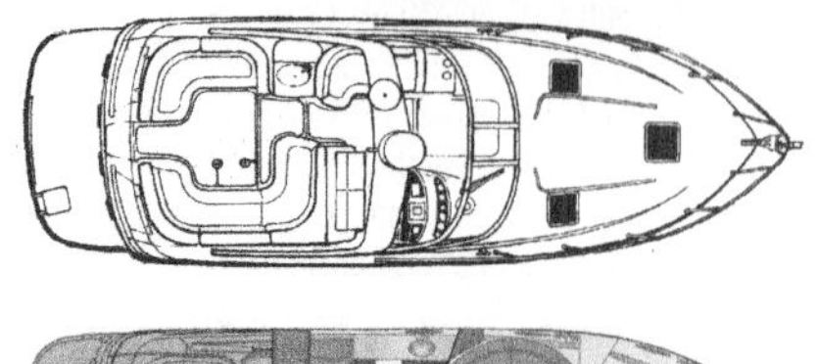

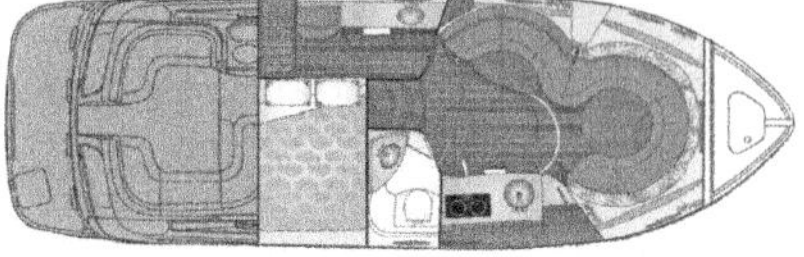

Crisp styling, tasteful cabin accommodations, and excellent performance are the hallmarks of Chaparral's Signature 330 (called the Signature 320 in 2003). This is an upscale family cruiser whose quality features and exemplary fit and finish are apparent to even inexperienced boaters. Built on a modified-V hull with cored hullsides and generous beam, the 330's main cabin is an appealing blend of cherrywood joinery, designer fabrics, and vinyl overheads. A wraparound lounge with a table forward converts to a big V-berth, and the 330's private midcabin is notable for its partial standing headroom, entryway door, and built-in vanity with sink, mirror, and upholstered seat. The galley, with its faux-granite surfaces and stainless steel sink, has enough storage for a long weekend. In the cockpit, the centerline boarding door aft allows for an unusually guest-friendly seating layout. Additional features include a cockpit wet bar, dual transom lockers, a tiered, non-glare dash, generator, and an extended swim platform. The anchor locker is on the small side and so is the fuel capacity. Twin 300hp MerCruiser sterndrives deliver a top speed in the range of 40 knots. Replaced with an all-new 330 Signature model in 2011.

See Page 674 For Price Data

Length w/Platform	35'0"	Fuel	170 gals.
Beam	11'3"	Water	45 gals.
Draft, Up	2'1"	Waste	28 gals.
Draft, Down	3'2"	Hull Type	Modified-V
Weight	13,400#	Deadrise Aft	19°

Chaparral 350 Signature

Mid-size family cruisers have always been a popular breed in the American market, and with so many to choose from it's often difficult to tell one from another. Chaparral's Signature 350 stands out, however, thanks to her above-average finish and a innovative helm layout. Chaparral has always built good boats and the 350 is certainly no exception. Constructed on a beamy modified-V hull, the cherrywood interior of this Signature is one of the most luxurious to be found in a boat her size. In a departure from the norm, a pocket door separates the forward berth from the salon—a privacy feature of genuine value to most cruisers. The galley is also well designed with plenty of counter space, and the aft cabin is very spacious with a dinette and privacy door. The 350's elevated helm platform, with its U-shaped settee and doublewide helm seat, is unique. Additional features include a walk-through windshield, a transom storage locker, excellent engine access, foredeck sun pad, and a cockpit wet bar. Among several sterndrive or inboard options, twin 315hp Volvo I/Os cruise in the low 20s (mid 30s top). Note than an updated 350 Signature model came out in 2010.

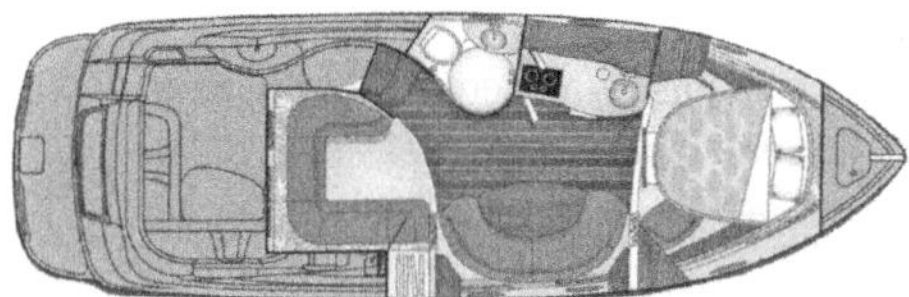

See Page 674 For Price Data

Length w/Platform	37'0"	Fuel	240 gals.
Beam	11'10"	Water	40 gals.
Draft, Up	2'1"	Waste	28 gals.
Draft, Down	2'9"	Hull Type	Modified-V
Weight	15,000#	Deadrise Aft	18°

Cheoy Lee

Quick View

- Cheoy Lee has been in the boatbuilding business for over a century although present-day operations go back to 1936 when production facilities were moved from Shanghai to Hong Kong.
- Cheoy Lee began building wooden sailing yachts in 1955, and pioneered in the production of fiberglass boats in the early 1960s.
- Family-owned for many generations, Cheoy Lee's main office is located in Hong Kong. (Their yard is on Lantau Island, a remote spot accessible only by boat.)
- Based in Fort Lauderdale, FL, Cheoy Lee Shipyards North America is a wholly owned subsidiary of the Hong Kong–based parent company.
- Always having strong ties to the United States, which has remained a major trading partner for nearly fifty years, the company has delivered nearly 5,000 vessels to date.
- Cheoy Lee maintains a service and commissioning yard on the New River in Ft. Lauderdale.

Cheoy Lee Shipyards • www.cheoyleena.com

Cheoy Lee 65 Pilothouse MY

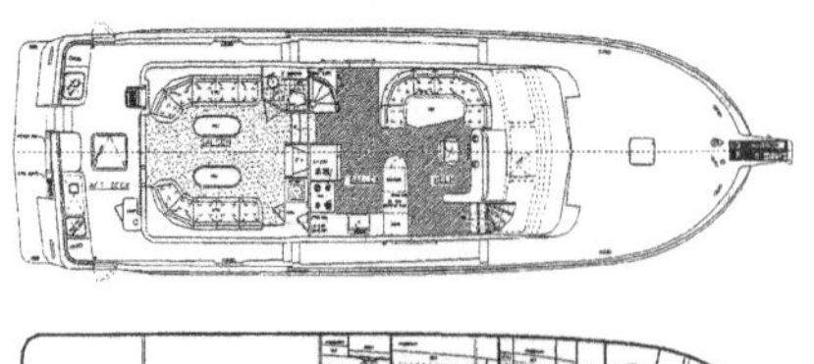

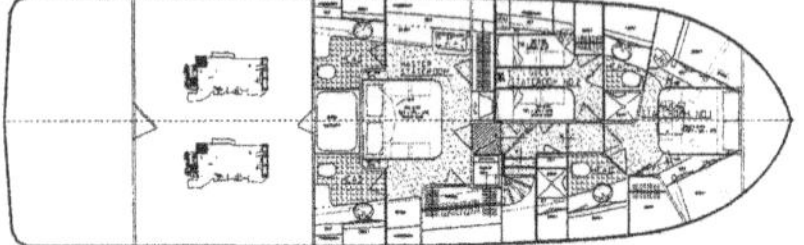

A handsome yacht with distinctive lines, the Cheoy Lee 65 Pilothouse MY is a Fexas-designed pilothouse yacht whose generous 20-foot beam affords an unusually spacious interior. Indeed, few yachts in this class can rival the Cheoy Lee 65 in terms of sheer living space. While the salon, with its day head and facing settees, is extremely spacious, the pilothouse is positively massive with a U-shaped dining settee to port and a spacious galley to starboard. (Note that the pilothouse is not open to the salon as it is in many pilothouse designs.) The full-beam master stateroom has a king-size bed as well as separate his-and-hers heads, and both guest cabins come with a private head, each with a stall shower. Topside, the flybridge is a couple of steps up from the hardtop—an unusual design that complements the 65's handsome lines. Bridge overhangs protect the small aft deck and wide side decks. Additional features include a spacious walk-in engine room, a teak aft deck sole, a flybridge wet bar, and a swim platform. A capable performer with optional 800hp Cat diesels, the Cheoy Lee 65 will cruise at 18 knots and reach a top speed of around 22 knots. Note that a cockpit version—the 72 Cockpit MY—was also available.

Not Enough Resale Data to Set Values

Length Overall	64'11"	Water	600 gals.
Beam	20'2"	Waste	150 gals.
Draft	5'0"	Headroom	6'10"
Weight	91,600#	Hull Type	Modified-V
Fuel	1,500 gals.	Deadrise Aft	NA

Cheoy Lee 66 Long Range MY

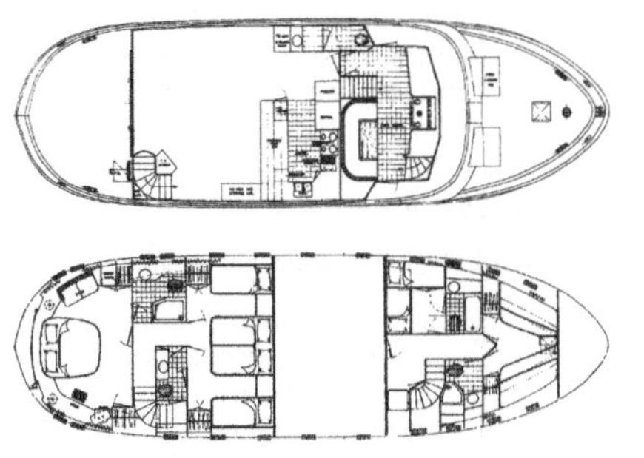

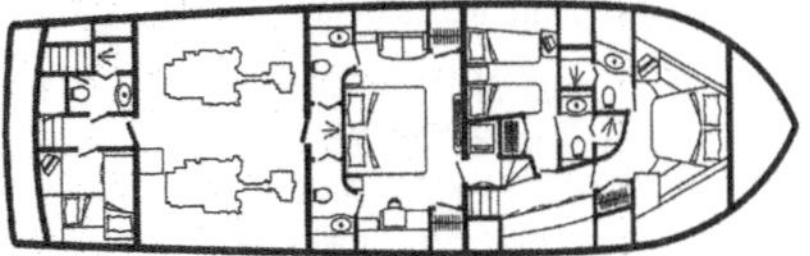

A popular yacht for many years, the first Cheoy Lee 66 Long Range MY was imported back in 1978. Twelve were sold in the U.S. through 1983, and in 1984 Cheoy Lee updated the boat's appearance with a lowered deckhouse profile and considerably less exterior teak. Hull construction is solid fiberglass, and the rounded stern of the 66 is her most distinctive design feature. The standard five-stateroom, galley-up floorplan provides overnight accommodations for up to twelve people. A four-stateroom, galley-down layout (not pictured) was also available. Like most Asian yachts, the teak interior drips with old-world elegance. Bridge overhangs protect the wide walkways of the 66, and the flybridge has seating for several guests as well as dinghy storage and a davit. Note that a WideBody model, with a full-width salon and enlarged wheelhouse, was introduced in 1985 and accounted for about half of late-model production. Twin 325hp GM (or 320hp Cat) diesels cruise at 10 knots (12–13 knots top). Cheoy Lee built this boat until 2003 on a semicustom basis. In later models, the transom incorporates a molded staircase to allow easier access to the water.

Not Enough Resale Data to Set Values

Length Overall	65'6"	Clearance	NA
Length WL	59'0"	Fuel	2,700 gals.
Beam	18'0"	Water	700 gals.
Draft	5'3"	Waste	250 gals.
Weight	87,000#	Hull Type	Displacement

Cheoy Lee 68 Sport Motor Yacht

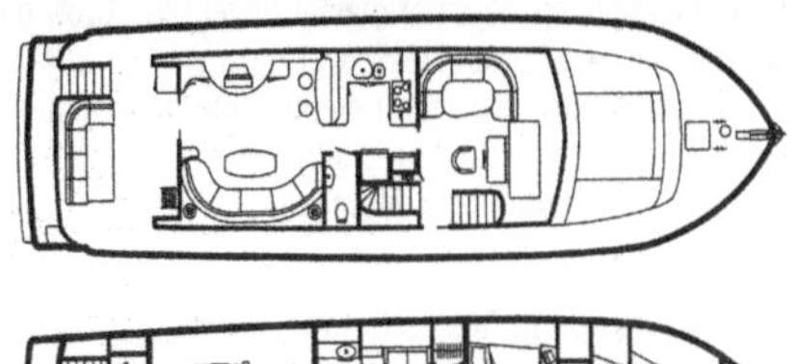

Introduced in 2004, the Cheoy Lee 68 Sport MY is a Fexas-designed luxury yacht whose impressive blend of graceful styling and excellent performance distinguished her from most of the competition. The 68 is built on a fully cored hull (except for the keel which is solid fiberglass for grounding protection) with generous beam and a shallow keel for directional stability. Her spacious three-stateroom interior is notable for its wise use of space. The dinette is in the pilothouse, where the outside view is best, and a breakfast bar separates the galley from the expansive salon. A day head is positioned forward of the salon—a great convenience that reduces traffic on the lower level. Owner and guest accommodations include an opulent full-beam master suite with his-and-hers heads, and a VIP stateroom with a queen island berth. Crew quarters are located beneath the aft deck. Topside, the flybridge can be accessed from both the cockpit and lower helm. Additional features include wide side decks, fiberglass hardtop, cherry interior woodwork, and a spacious engine room. Caterpillar 1,400 V-drive diesels cruise the Cheoy Lee 68 in the mid 20s and reach a top speed of close to 30 knots.

Not Enough Resale Data to Set Values

Length	67'11"	Fuel	1,200 gals.
Beam	18'11"	Water	430 gals.
Draft	5'5"	Waste	150 gals.
Weight	100,000#	Hull Type	Modified-V
Headroom	6'8"	Deadrise Aft	13°

Cheoy Lee 70 Sportfisherman

Sporting a high-style designer interior with a huge cockpit and a fully enclosed bridge, the sleek Cheoy Lee 70 SF remains one of the more aggressively styled big sportfishing yachts in the late-model marketplace. (Note the rakish flybridge overhang around the front windows—very distinctive indeed.) Built on a so-called "double-V" bottom (super wide chine flats extend out from a deeper V on the centerline) and fully cored from the keel up, the ride is said to be soft and dry in a variety of sea conditions. Inside, the four-stateroom layout is plush in the extreme. The raised galley forward in the salon allows room for a huge master stateroom below, and each guest stateroom has its own private head. With more than 20 feet of beam, it's hardly a surprise to note that the overall accommodations of the Cheoy Lee 70 rival those of a good-sized motor yacht. The cockpit is fitted with in-deck fish boxes, a livewell, and direct access to the engineroom. Topside, the enclosed bridge is very spacious and offers big-boat skylounge amenities including a settee and wet bar. Ahead of her time when she was introduced, a pair of 1,350hp Cat 3412 diesels will deliver a cruising speed of 22 knots and a top speed of about 26–27 knots.

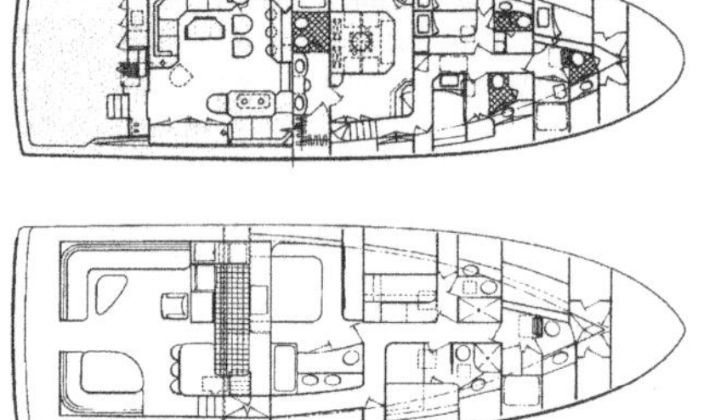

Not Enough Resale Data to Set Values

Length	70'10"	Water	400 gals.
Beam	20'9"	Clearance	18'9"
Draft	5'4"	Cockpit	NA
Weight	89,000#	Hull Type	Modified-V
Fuel	2,200 gals.	Deadrise Aft	14°

Cheoy Lee 72 Cockpit Motor Yacht

Tom Fexas created some elegant designs for Cheoy Lee before he passed away a few years back, none more striking than the 72 Cockpit Motor Yacht. This beautifully proportioned raised pilothouse yacht, with her wide 20'2" beam, took motor yacht space and luxury to the next level when she was introduced in 2003. The standard accommodations plan has three staterooms on the lower deck: a full-beam master amidships, VIP double forward, and a second guest stateroom with twin berths. Each cabin has an ensuite head, and the opulent master boasts a Jacuzzi and his-and-hers sinks as well. The 72's home-size galley—with double-door refrigerator and acres of counter space—is on the pilothouse level where a booth-style dinette is forward next to the center helm position. The salon is aft, down several steps, with facing settees, a wet bar, and day head. Note the utility space aft of master stateroom. Crew quarters aft were optional. A wide aft deck overlooks a huge cockpit with in-deck storage lockers, watertight engineroom door, and port and starboard boarding gates. Built on a fully cored hull, she'll cruise at 18 knots with Cat 1,000hp C-18 engines (low 20s top).

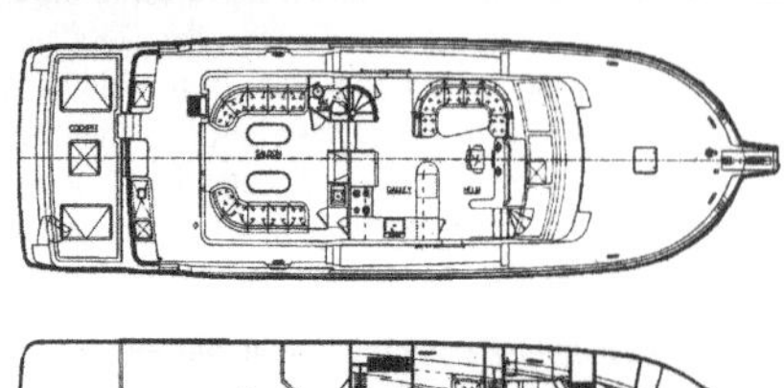

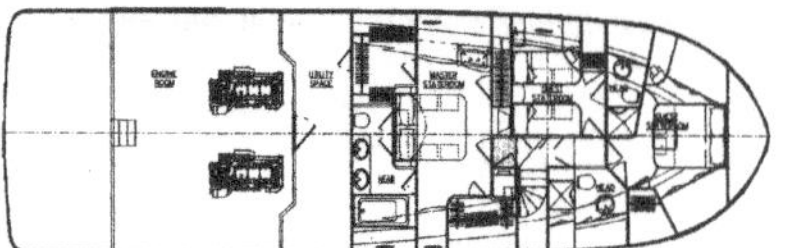

Not Enough Resale Data to Set Values

Length	71'11"	Fuel	1,850 gals.
Beam	20'2"	Water	500 gals.
Draft	5'0"	Waste	200 gals.
Weight	100,000#	Hull Type	Modified-V
Clearance	NA	Deadrise Aft	13°

Cheoy Lee 81 Sport Yacht

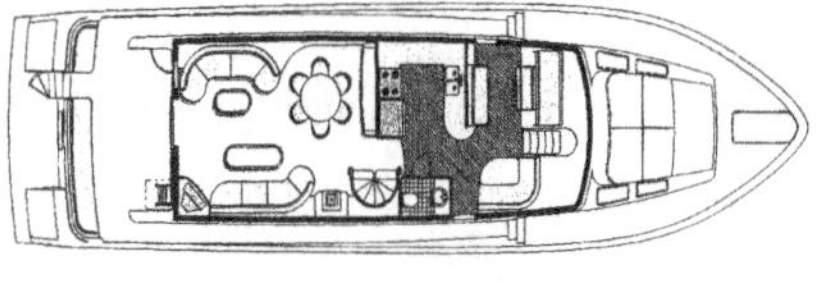

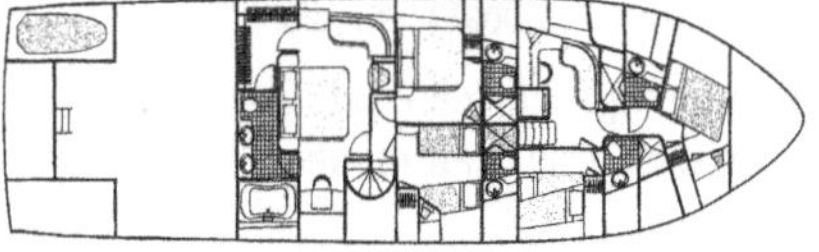

The Cheoy Lee 81 Sport Yacht is a Fexas-designed mini-mega-yacht built with all the redundant safety systems necessary to obtain the coveted ABS hull certification. Designed to be operated by a small crew, the 81 is constructed on a relatively lightweight fully cored hull with a wide 21-foot beam, rounded chines, and a shallow skeg. Because the engines are located aft, prop pockets are used to reduce the shaft angle. A semi-custom yacht, Cheoy Lee offers several floorplans including the standard five-stateroom, galley-up layout shown at right. A spiral staircase to the flybridge dominates the spacious salon, and the full-beam master stateroom includes a tub in the head and a huge walk-in wardrobe. On deck, the swim platform houses a PWC garage as well as access to the engineroom. Additional features (among many) include a flybridge hardtop, wide walkaround side decks, a large shaded aft deck, a deckhouse day head, and underwater exhausts. A beautifully styled yacht, Cat 1,400hp diesels cruise at 20 knots and reach 25–26 knots top. Note that in 2000 the addition of V-drive transmissions permitted a reduction in size of the engineroom that, in turn, resulted in an enlarged master stateroom.

Not Enough Resale Data to Set Values

Length	81'0"	Fuel	2,300–2,700 gals.
Beam	21'1"	Water	500 gals.
Draft	5'5"	Waste	250 gals.
Weight	144,000#	Hull Type	Semi-Disp.
Clearance	NA	Deadrise Aft	11°

Chris Craft

Quick View

- Founded in 1884 in Algonac, Michigan, Chris Craft was once the undisputed king of the worldwide pleasure boat industry.
- After the war Chris Craft introduced a new lineup of civilian pleasure boats in time for the massive American consumer expansion of the 1950s.
- In 1964, Chris-Craft launched the all-fiberglass Chris-Craft Commander.
- Between the 1960s and 1980s, Chris-Craft lost market share as competitors with more innovative designs and less expensive manufacturing techniques such as fiberglass hulls came on the scene.
- Chris-Craft ended production of its last mahogany-hulled boat, the Constellation, in 1971.
- Eventually the Chris Craft product line fell from public favor, and in 1989 the company assets were sold at auction to industry-giant OMC Marine.
- OMC went into bankruptcy early in 2001 production of Chris Craft boats was discontinued.
- In 2001 Chris-Craft was purchased by investment group, Stellican Ltd. Operations resumed as the new owners introduced a series of new Chris Craft models.

Chris Craft Boats • Sarasota, FL • www.chriscraft.com

Chris Craft 258/268/27 Concept

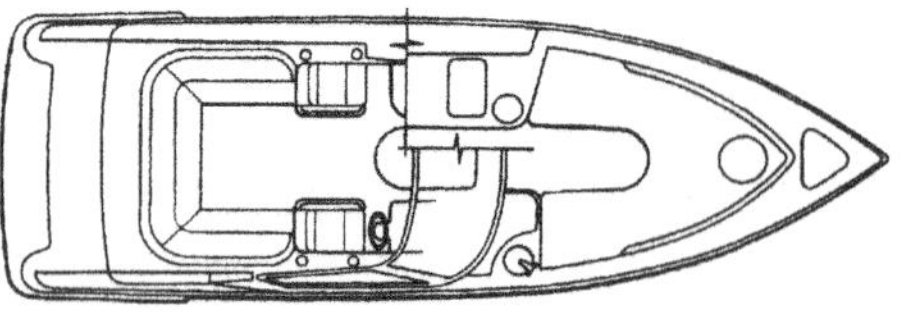

The Chris Craft 258/268/27 Concept is best described as part cruiser and part performance boat. (Note that she was called the 258 Concept in 1992, the 268 during 1993–94, and the 27 Concept in 1995–96.) A good-looking, non-trailerable cruiser with attractive sportboat lines, the Concept was built on a deep-V hull with moderate beam and a relatively steep 20 degrees of deadrise at the transom. She's a good open-water performer capable of going fast through some rough water. Since the aim of the Concept is outdoor entertainment, most of her length is devoted to an expansive cockpit layout with wraparound lounge seating for a crowd (the seat bottom pulls out to form a sun pad). A hideaway ladder folds down over the companionway door and allows access through the windshield to the foredeck—very resourceful. Below, her compact cabin features a standup head and a convertible dinette. A single 310hp sterndrive will cruise the Concept at 22 knots (36 knots top). Twin 5.0-liter sterndrives cruise at 28–29 knots (40+ knots top), and optional 5.8-liter Volvos cruise at a fast 38 knots and deliver a top speed of around 50 knots. Note that the fuel was increased to 97 gallons in 1995.

See Page 674 For Price Data

Length	27'0"	Fuel	80/97 gals.
Beam	9'0"	Water	20 gals.
Draft	3'0"	Waste	20 gals.
Weight	5,000#	Hull Type	Deep-V
Clearance	NA	Deadrise Aft	20°

Chris Craft 272/282/30 Crowne

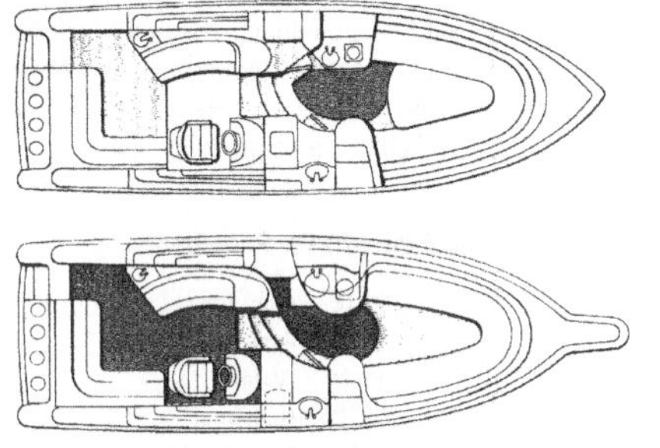

The introduction of the Crowne series in 1991 was an effort by Chris Craft to resurrect the company's declining family cruiser sales. A distinctive boat with high freeboard, the 30 Crowne (note that she was called the 272 Crowne in 1991–92, the 282 Crowne in 1993–94, and the 30 Crowne from 1995–97) owes her graceful appearance to a molded bow pulpit, a curved wraparound windshield, circular foredeck hatches, and an integrated swim platform. Belowdecks, the companionway stairs are a series of welded steps that create a more open look than the usual molded stairs. The midcabin accommodations will sleep four, and the elevated foredeck provides good headroom in the Crowne's main cabin. The U-shaped cockpit lounge can seat six, and the stylish helm console is a real eye-catcher. A wet bar was standard, and fender racks are built into the swim platform. Additional features include a foldaway helm seat, walk-through windshield, and radar arch. Twin 351-cid sterndrives cruise the 30 Crowne at 17 knots (33–34 knots top), and optional 454-cid I/Os cruise at 20 knots and top out around 40 knots. Note the rather limited fuel capacity.

See Page 674 For Price Data

Length w/Pulpit	31'6"	Weight	8,400#
Hull Length	29'5"	Fuel	100 gals.
Beam	10'0"	Water	25 gals.
Draft, Up	1'10"	Hull Type	Modified-V
Draft, Down	3'2"	Deadrise Aft	16°

Chris Craft 28 Corsair

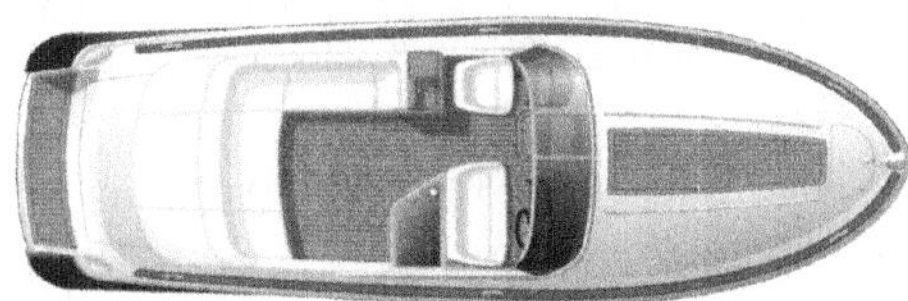

With her retro styling and curved aft tumblehome, the 28 Corsair conveys the classic Chris Craft look of yesteryear. First and foremost, the Corsair is a high-quality runabout with a level of finish seldom seen in production boats. And secondly, the Corsair's premium price gives new meaning to the term "sticker shock." Clearly, this is a boat for very affluent boaters willing to drop a bundle for a sexy, drop-dead gorgeous runabout. Built on a deep-V hull with a well-flared bow, the amenities aboard the 28 Corsair are many. The cockpit is notable, not just for its plush Ultraleather seating and custom entertainment center, but for its simplicity and comfort as well. The old-world dashboard is a nostalgic throwback to the 1950s, and an electric engine hatch provides easy access to the engine compartment. The Corsair's curved foredeck conceals a useful cuddy cabin with a V-berth and portable head. The gelcoat is flawless, and the stainless-steel windshield is a work of art. Additional features include a pressure water system, cockpit cooler storage, transom shower, and flip-up bucket seats. Twin 280hp Volvo sterndrives cruise in the mid 20s, and optional 240hp Yanmar diesels cruise at a fast 35 knots.

See Page 674 For Price Data

Length	28'0"	Clearance	5'5"
Beam	10'0"	Fuel	150 gals.
Draft, Up	1'11"	Water	35 gals.
Draft, Down	3'6"	Hull Type	Deep-V
Weight	7,500#	Deadrise Aft	20°

Chris Craft 28 Launch

Chris Craft harkened back to their mahogany roots with the introduction in 2003 of the retro-style 28 Launch, a high-quality bowrider whose meticulous detailing and classic tumblehome stern set her well apart from anything on the market. Quality like this didn't come cheap, and the premium price of the 28 Launch was enough to give pause to even the most affluent buyers. Clearly, this was a very special runabout for upscale boaters willing to drop a bundle for a sexy, drop-dead gorgeous toy. Built on a deep-V hull with a well-flared bow, the amenities aboard the 28 Launch are many. The cockpit is notable, not just for its plush Ultraleather seating and custom entertainment center, but for its simplicity and comfort as well. The old-world dashboard is a nostalgic throwback to the 1950s, and an electric engine hatch provides easy access to the engine compartment. The gelcoat is flawless, and the stainless-steel windshield is a work of art. Additional features include a pressure water system, cockpit cooler storage, transom shower, and flip-up bucket seats. A single 385hp gas MerCruiser I/O tops out at close to 40 knots; twin 300hp Mercs reach 45+ knots.

See Page 674 For Price Data

Length	28'0"	Clearance	5'5"
Beam	10'0"	Fuel	150 gals.
Draft, Up	1'11"	Water	35 gals.
Draft, Down	3'6"	Hull Type	Deep-V
Weight	7,500#	Deadrise Aft	20°

Chris Craft 300/308 Express Cruiser

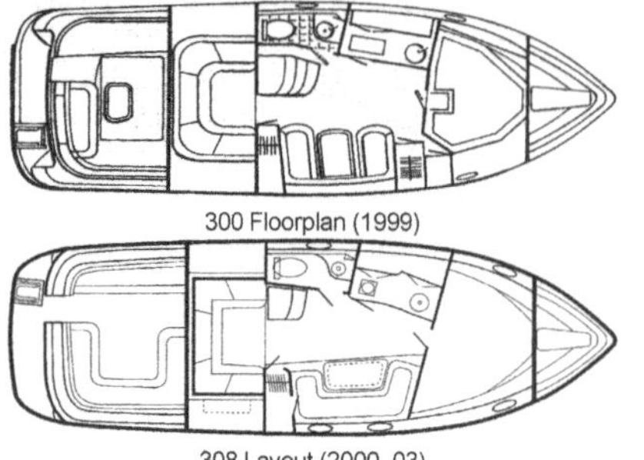
300 Floorplan (1999)

308 Layout (2000–03)

The Chris Craft 308 Express Cruiser (called the 300 Express in 1999) is a capable, entry-level family cruiser with a contemporary profile and surprisingly spacious interior accommodations. This is a boat designed to satisfy the needs of a growing family looking to move up from their too-small trailerable weekender—a full-size midcabin cruiser with good accommodations and respectable performance at an affordable price. Built on an easy-riding deep-V hull with moderate beam, a well-flared bow and reverse chines, the original midcabin interior of the 300 Express—a poorly designed layout with the refrigerator under the island berth—was completely updated for the year 2000 when she became the 308 Express. This major revision also eliminated the side decks, which permits a roomier cockpit with improved seating. Additional features of the 308 include a walk-through windshield, transom door and shower, cockpit wet bar and a well-arranged galley with adequate storage. Among several sterndrive engine options, twin 5.0-liter I/Os cruise around 20 knots (34–35 knots top), and twin 5.7-liter engines cruise at 26 knots (37–38 knots wide open).

See Page 674 For Price Data

Length	32'10"	Fuel	150 gals.
Beam	10'6"	Water	41 gals.
Draft	2'6"	Waste	35 gals.
Weight	10,000#	Hull Type	Deep-V
Clearance	7'3"	Deadrise Aft	21°

Chris Craft 320/328 Express Cruiser

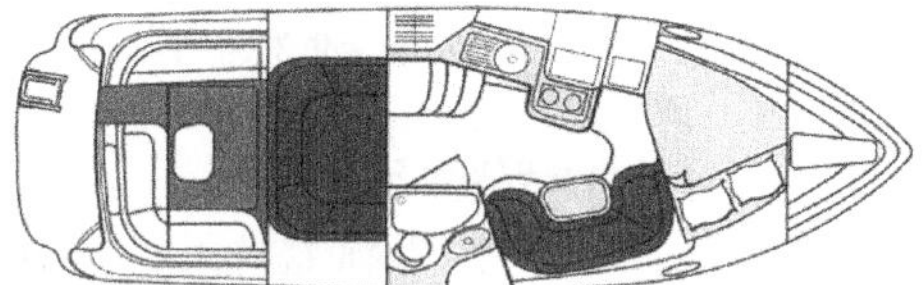

Largest boat in the Chris Craft fleet at the turn of the millennium, the 328 Express Cruiser (called the 32 Crowne in 1997 and the 320 Express in 1998–99) is a contemporary midcabin family cruiser whose moderate price will appeal to budget-minded buyers. Chris Craft enthusiasts haven't had much to cheer about in recent years when it comes to well-styled boats, but the 328 combines several nice design touches wrapped up in a conservative but still-contemporary package. She's constructed on a solid fiberglass deep-V hull with a wide beam, and her centerline helm position (as opposed to the traditional starboardside console) is somewhat unique. Belowdecks, the midcabin floorplan is quite spacious for a boat this size. The layout is fairly conventional with double berths fore and aft, a small galley and a head with shower. The Crowne's anchor arrangement is pretty slick—a concealed windlass lowers the self-stowing anchor through an opening beneath the bow. Additional features include a walk-through windshield, an electric engine compartment hatch, and transom door. Among several engine options, twin 5.7-liter Volvo I/Os cruise at 23 knots and reach a top speed of 36–37 knots.

See Page 674 For Price Data

Length	32'0"	Fuel	210 gals.
Beam	11'10"	Water	41 gals.
Draft	3'2"	Waste	35 gals.
Weight	12,000#	Hull Type	Deep-V
Clearance	9'7"	Deadrise Aft	21°

Chris Craft 33 Corsair

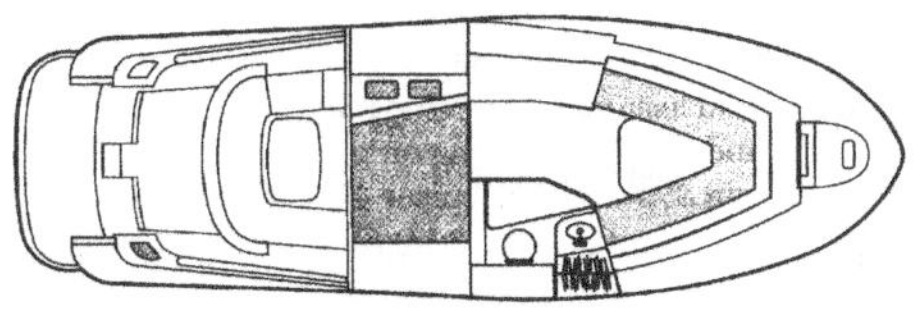

Blending classic sportboat styling with yacht-class quality, the sleek (and painfully expensive) 33 Corsair raised the bar for day-boat luxury when she was introduced in 2006. Chris Craft marketing hype described the 33 as "in a class by herself" which was true enough considering that there were few boats to compare in terms of construction quality, amenities, and price. Built on a heavyweight deep-V hull with a relatively wide 12'3" beam, this really is a beautifully styled boat with a tumblehome stern, flared topsides, and abundant teak trim. Stepping onto the wide swim platform, a teak walkthrough leads into the cockpit with its aft U-lounge (with sun pad conversion), wet bar with sink, hot-and-cold shower, and two forward (double width) helm seats. The engine compartment is accessed via a hydraulic-lift hatch lounge, but access around the motors is better suited to anorexic midgets that normal-sized men. Below decks, the Corsair's well-appointed interior—with hardwood cherry joinery and designer fixtures—features an enclosed head, a surprisingly large galley with microwave, and wraparound forward seating with a maple table that converts to a double bed. MerCruiser 375hp I/Os max out at 38–40 knots.

See Page 674 For Price Data

Length	34'11"	Fuel	207 gals.
Beam	12'3"	Water	37 gals.
Draft	3'0"	Waste	20 gals.
Weight	13,200#	Hull Type	Deep-V
Clearance	NA	Deadrise Aft	20°

Chris Craft 302/322 Crowne; 33/34 Crowne

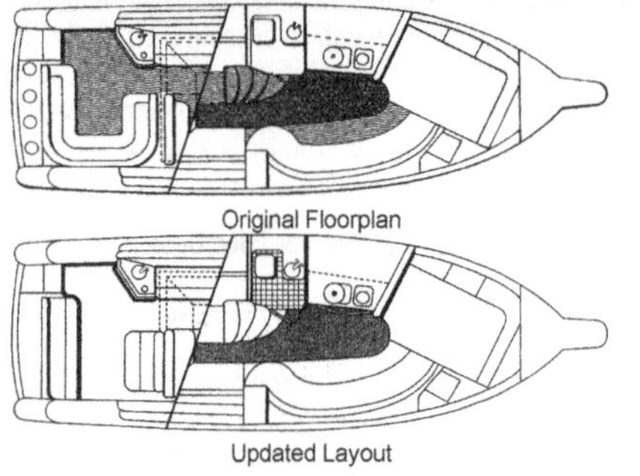
Original Floorplan

Updated Layout

Try to follow this: introduced as the sterndrive 302 Crowne (1991–92), Chris Craft offered an inboard option in 1993—the sterndrive model then became the 322 while the inboard version was called the 340. In 1995, the designations were again changed with the sterndrive becoming the 33 Crowne and the inboard model now called the 34 Crowne. All were built on solid fiberglass hulls with moderate beam and a fully integrated swim platform and bow pulpit. A centerline companionway leads down into the Crowne's spacious interior where the midcabin floorplan will sleep six adults. A curved settee—elevated from the salon sole—dominates the main cabin, and the fore and aft sleeping areas both have privacy curtains. In 1996, Chris Craft designers rearranged the cockpit, eliminating the U-shaped lounge aft of the helm in favor of a bench seat at the transom. Additional features include a cockpit wet bar, a wide swim platform with fender racks, oval ports, and (in the 340/34 model) side-dumping exhausts. The 302/322/33 Crowne, with twin 235hp OMC (or 230hp Volvos) sterndrives, will cruise in the low 20s, and the 340/34 Crowne with 300hp Volvo inboards cruise at about 25 knots.

See Page 674 For Price Data

Length w/Pulpit	34'10"	Weight	10,000#
Hull Length	32'8"	Fuel	180 gals.
Beam	11'0"	Water	35 gals.
Draft, 34	2'11"	Hull Type	Deep-V
Draft, 33	3'2"	Deadrise Aft	18°

Chris Craft 36 Corsair

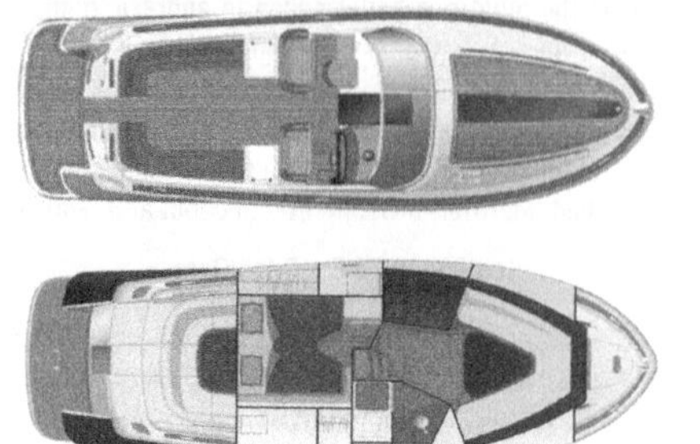

The Chris Craft 36 Corsair is a throwback to the days when mahogany Chris Craft commuter boats and runabouts characterized the boating lifestyle just after the Second World War. The demand for wooden boats may be gone—Chris Craft continued building wood boats well into the 1960s—but there are plenty of boating enthusiasts, especially those with a few years under their belts, who grow nostalgic when they see one of these new-generation Chris Craft boats with their retro styling and immaculate craftsmanship. Indeed, the 36 Corsair seems to exist just to stop traffic at the dock. With her graceful lines (note the transom tumblehome), posh cockpit seating, and teak trim there's little to compete with her when it comes to sheer eye appeal. Beneath the stunning exterior lies a luxurious twin-cabin interior that takes cruising style and elegance to the next level. Finished with solid cherry joinery, Ultraleather seating and designer galley appliances, the accommodations include a private midcabin stateroom, convertible dinette forward, full-service galley, and a large head with separate stall shower. A TV is standard in the salon. An expensive ride, Volvo 420hp gas I/Os cruise at 24–26 knots (35 knots top).

See Page 674 For Price Data

Length	38'2"	Fuel	286 gals.
Beam	12'7"	Water	50 gals.
Draft	2'10"	Waste	29 gals.
Weight	16,000#	Hull Type	Deep-V
Clearance	10'2"	Deadrise Aft	20°

Chris Craft 36 Roamer

The 36 Roamer is proof that innovative styling and quality construction are once again synonymous with the Chris Craft name. With her flawless gelcoat and graceful lines, the Roamer is an unusually distinctive boat in a world of look-alike fiberglass cruisers. She rides on a conventional modified-V hull with a well-flared bow, moderate transom deadrise, and a generous 12-foot, 6-inch beam. Belowdecks, the Roamer's elegant interior is a blend of cherrywood joinery, Ultraleather upholstery, and maple flooring. A sofa bed in the salon, an island bed in the bow, and another bed aft will sleep six, and the head includes a separate shower stall. The galley, which occupies the entire port side of the salon, is notable for its excellent storage and Corian counters. Topside, the helm is on the centerline with a double bench seat that is open to the cockpit on both sides. A sun lounge is to port, and the L-shaped cockpit seating can accommodate several guests. Engine access is excellent: the entire aft cockpit rises at the flip of a switch. A cockpit wet bar and walk-through transom were standard. Optional 370hp Yanmar diesels cruise the 36 Roamer in the mid 20s and reach close to 30 knots wide open.

Deck Plan

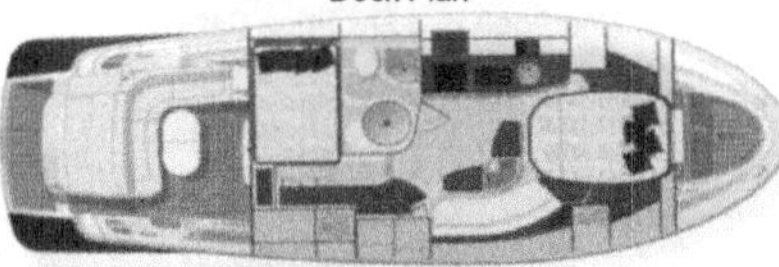
Interior Plan

See Page 674 For Price Data

Length	36'3"	Fuel	286 gals.
Beam	12'6"	Water	54 gals.
Draft	3'1"	Waste	30 gals.
Weight	17,220#	Hull Type	Modified-V
Clearance	12'10"	Deadrise Aft	17°

Chris Craft 380 Continental

Innovation is great and there's never enough of it, but innovation is not what the 380 Continental was about. This was glitz over practicality—the triumph of Chris Craft's 1990s concept of art over nautical common sense. The styling from the arch forward is contemporary enough, but the semicircular stern makes an otherwise well-proportioned boat seem a little chopped off. Not surprisingly, the circular transom also reduced the 380's usable cockpit space. Belowdecks, there are no bulkheads in the wide-open interior, so floor-to-ceiling track curtains were used to divide up the cabin into separate sleeping quarters. Note that the helm is on the centerline and the helm seat is elevated for improved visibility. A walk-through windshield provides access to the foredeck, and molded steps at the corners and a centerline transom door access the circular swim platform. Anchor handling is interesting: lacking a pulpit, the anchor is retrieved through a bow port. The Continental's extra-wide swim platform has storage lockers and a hot/cold shower. A heavy boat, standard 460-cid gas engines with V-drives cruise around 16 knots and reach 28 knots wide open.

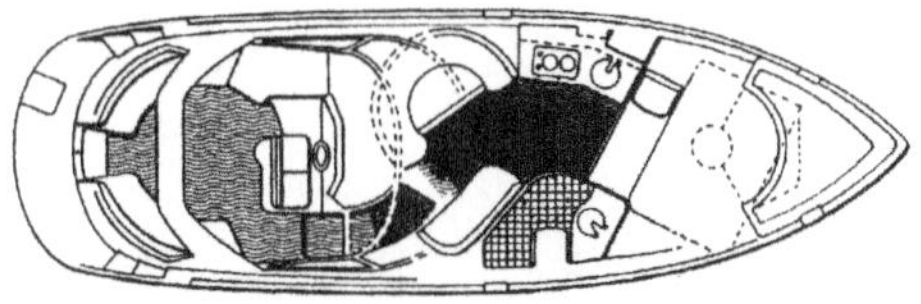

See Page 674 For Price Data

Length Overall	39'7"	Fuel	300 gals.
Hull Length	35'5"	Water	77 gals.
Beam	12'6"	Waste	20 gals.
Draft	3'1"	Hull Type	Modified-V
Weight	15,000#	Deadrise Aft	15°

Chris Craft 40/43 Roamer

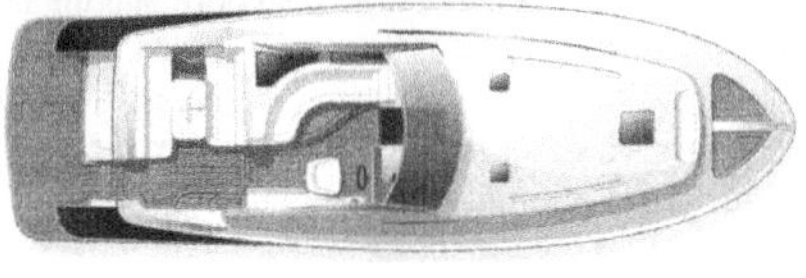

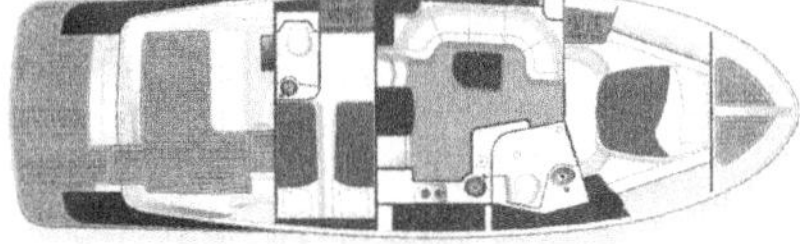

Chris Craft got it right with the 40 Roamer (called the 43 Roamer in 2003–04), a modern-day classic whose stunning lines and many custom features make her a traffic-stopper anywhere she goes. As Boating Magazine wrote at her introduction in 2003, the new Roamer 40 "harks back to those halcyon days of mahogany planking, brass fixtures, and Gray Marine engines." True enough: with her retro look—including the flared bow and foredeck rumble seat—the Roamer is nothing if not distinctive. Stepping into the oversize cockpit with its beautiful teak sole and posh lounge seating, everything about the Roamer feels elegant and romantic. The exquisite detailing of the galley, heads and staterooms complements the main cabin's efficient use of space. The salon is very roomy with cherrywood joinery and designer fixtures throughout. Stainless-steel-framed windows run the entire length of the cabin. The side decks are wide, and the hardtop was standard. On the downside, the engineroom is a very tight fit. Originally powered with 420hp inboards (about 35 knots top), Volvo IPS gas or diesel pod drives (with joystick controls) became standard in 2006. Did we say expensive?

See Page 674 For Price Data

Length	43'6"	Water	95 gals.
Beam	14'0"	Waste	35 gals.
Draft	3'2"	Headroom	6'4"
Weight	25,200#	Hull Type	Deep-V
Fuel	400 gals.	Deadrise Aft	20°

Cobalt

Quick View

- Cobalt was founded in the late 1960s by Pack St. Clair in Neodesha, Kansas.
- After a few years of mediocre sales, St. Clair had the revelation that there was a high-end niche not being filled.
- Cobalt's tri-hull models of the 1970s established the company as a quality manufacturer.
- Ensuring years saw the Cobalt brand become well known in boating circles for their series of premium open- and closed-bow runabouts.
- In 2005, Cobalt bought a factory in Vonore, TN, to produce a line of yachts in a separate company, Cobalt Yachts.
- By 2007, Cobalt sales reached its peak with about $130 in revenue. That same year, however, the company closed its Tennessee plant, laying off 110 workers.
- Cobalt has been a consistent winner in recent J.D. Power customer satisfaction rankings.

Cobalt Boats • Neodesha, Kansas • www.cobaltboats.com

Cobalt 262

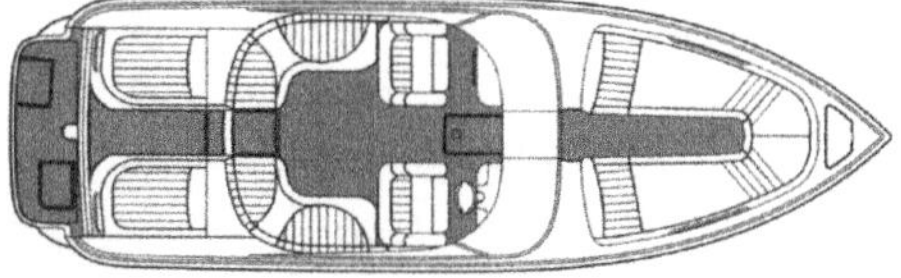

Quiet, luxurious, and meticulously finished, Cobalt runabouts have been synonymous with quality for many years. The Cobalt 262, introduced in 2000, reflects those attributes, and then some. Big trailerable bowriders are among the most popular boats on the water these days, but few surpass the 262 in comfort and eye appeal. She's built on a Kevlar-reinforced deep-V hull with an aggressive 22 degrees of transom deadrise—enough to smooth our some fairly rough water. Unlike many open-bow runabouts, the 262's cockpit incorporates a center transom walk-through, a design that provides quick and easy access to the swim platform. Filler cushions convert the aft deck into a huge sun pad, and a small head/change compartment is built into the port console. The 262 is loaded with standard features including woodgrain dash panels, a teak swim platform, bow scuff plate, flip-up bolster seats, wet locker, and a power engine hatch. A reverse sport arch was optional. A good open-water performer, a single Volvo 375hp DuoProp I/O delivers a top speed in excess of 40 knots. Note that a restyled Cobalt 262 was introduced in 2009.

See Page 674 For Price Data

Length	26'8"	Clearance	4'9"
Beam	8'6"	Fuel	70 gals.
Draft, Up	22"	Water	10 gals.
Draft, Down	39"	Hull Type	Deep-V
Weight	4,700#	Deadrise Aft	22°

Cobalt 263

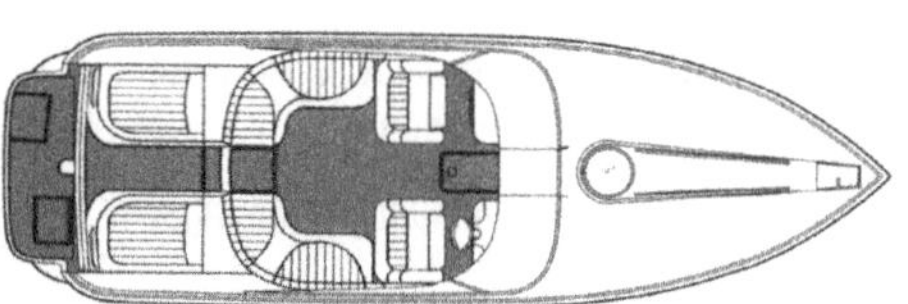

For many Cobalt enthusiasts, the 263 is the perfect day boat. Small enough to trailer, big enough for eight, and fast enough to keep the adrenaline flowing, the 263 takes open-water fun to the next level. She's built on a Kevlar-reinforced deep-V hull with an aggressive 22 degrees of transom deadrise—enough to smooth our some fairly rough water. Unlike many closed-bow runabouts, the 262's cockpit incorporates a center transom walk-through, a design that provides quick and easy access to the swim platform. Filler cushions convert the aft deck into a huge sun pad. Below, the well-appointed cabin contains a U-shaped leather settee, galley pod with sink, storage cabinets, and a portable toilet. The 263 is loaded with standard features including woodgrain dash panels, a teak swim platform, transom shower, bow scuff plate, flip-up bolster seats, and a power engine hatch. Docking lights and a reverse sport arch were optional. A good open-water performer, a single Volvo 375hp DuoProp I/O delivers a top speed in excess of 40 knots. Note that a previous Cobalt 263 was produced in 1989–1991.

See Page 675 For Price Data

Length	26'8"	Clearance	4'9"
Beam	8'6"	Fuel	70 gals.
Draft, Up	22"	Water	10 gals.
Draft, Down	39"	Hull Type	Deep-V
Weight	4,700#	Deadrise Aft	22°

Cobalt 272

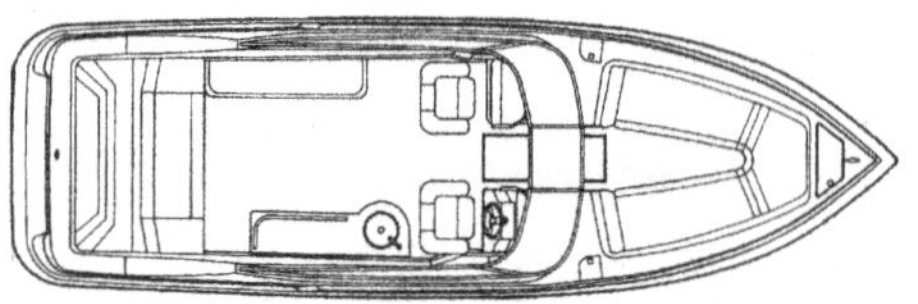

A good-looking 1990s design, the Cobalt 272 is a finely crafted bowrider whose lush amenities, deep cockpit and beautiful styling make her a standout in any marina. She's heavily built on a Kevlar-reinforced solid fiberglass deep-V hull, and an 8-foot, 6-inch beam makes her trailerable in all states and provinces. Even today, the Cobalt 272 is one of the larger bowriders around, and her upscale price placed her in the luxury-cruiser category. The helm and windshield of the 272 are well forward, resulting in a large and very comfortable cockpit. Amenities include a sun pad, a stylish wet bar with sink and cabinet, rear bench seat with storage behind, and a second bench seat that folds away into the gunwale. A large ski locker with gas-assist hatch is found in the cockpit sole, and the unique electric hideaway swim platform is a particularly innovative concept. A marine head is located inside the portside console—the door can be pulled closed for privacy and there's even a light and vents. Engine access is excellent. A variety of single sterndrive engine options were available. Among them, a 300hp Volvo delivers a top speed of close to 40 knots.

See Page675 For Price Data

Length	27'3"	Clearance	5'10"
Beam	8'6"	Fuel	97 gals.
Draft, Drive Up	1'11"	Water	10 gals.
Draft, Drive Down	3'0"	Hull Type	Deep-V
Weight	4,930#	Deadrise Aft	20°

Cobalt 282

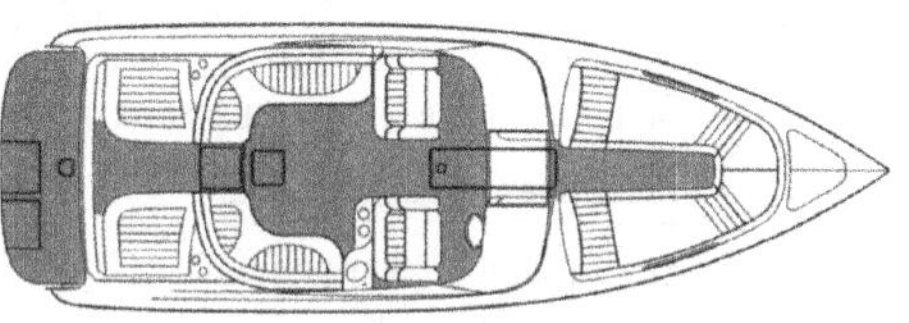

With a length of nearly 29 feet, the Cobalt 282 was near the top of the bowrider class when she was introduced in 2002. So who buys these big bowriders? People who need more space for friends and family, and people who don't want their boating activities limited to lakes and bays. Built on a deep-V hull with a 9-foot beam, the 282 can handle an offshore chop with ease while still being trailerable for those with a permit and a heavy-duty tow vehicle. (Note the unusual retro-style tail fins.) Families with young children will appreciate the 282's deep cockpit and forward seating area. Standard storage is plentiful, and bow doors reduce high-rpm wind blast. Aside from the posh cockpit seating and convenient center transom walk-through, the 282 is loaded with the kind of quality features expected in any Cobalt product. The radar arch doubles as a wakeboard tower; the flip-up helm seat makes standup driving easy; a head/storage compartment is built into the portside console. Fit and finish is nearly flawless. An air compressor (for inflatable water toys) and cockpit wet bar are standard. Expect a top speed of 40+ knots with a single 375hp MerCruiser Bravo III sterndrive.

See Page 675 For Price Data

Length	28'8"	Clearance	5'7"
Beam	9'0"	Fuel	90 gals.
Draft, Drive Up	2'0"	Water	18 gals.
Draft, Drive Down	2'9"	Hull Type	Deep-V
Weight, Single	6,750#	Deadrise Aft	22°

Cobalt 292

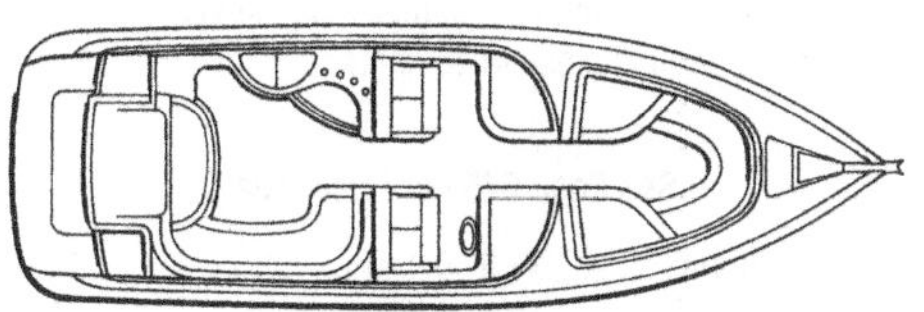

One of the larger bowriders on the market during her production years, the Cobalt 292 is among the most luxurious boats in her class with a level of finish that many other production manufacturers might well envy. She's built on the proven hull of Cobalt's popular 293 Cuddy, a deep-V affair with a relatively wide 9-foot, 6-inch beam and a fully integrated transom. Beautifully styled, the deep cockpit of the 292 is arranged with wraparound lounge seating for seven, a molded galley opposite with a sink, storage drawers and refrigerator, in-deck storage, and a walk-through transom door to the swim platform. Hidden within the portside console, the head compartment offers a toilet and over 4 feet of headroom. Like all Cobalt models, the wood dash console is a work of art. Additional features include port and starboard helm seats with flip-up bolsters, a hydraulic engine compartment hatch, leather tilt wheel, anchor locker and a cockpit ice chest. A comfortable and very quiet ride, twin 280hp Volvo sterndrives (among several engine choices) will cruise the Cobalt 292 at 27–28 knots and reach a top speed in the neighborhood of 42 knots.

See Page 675 For Price Data

Length	28'10"	Clearance	5'8"
Beam	9'6"	Fuel	130 gals.
Draft, Drives Up	2'2"	Water	31 gals.
Draft, Drives Down	3'0"	Hull Type	Deep-V
Weight, Twins	7,600#	Deadrise Aft	20°

Cobalt 293

1997–2004

Day boats in the 30-foot range had become quite popular by the late 1990s with weekend boaters more interested in an afternoon on the water than extended cruising. Among these new-breed designs, the Cobalt 293's rugged construction, graceful styling, and meticulous workmanship set her well apart from the competition. Not inexpensive, the 293 provides every comfort and convenience one could ask for in a modern day boat. The beautifully contoured cockpit comes with a wet bar with refrigeration, removable cockpit table, an extended swim platform, and a rosewood dash that—with its leather-covered steering wheel—can only be described as elegant. In a clever design, the entire transom and rear seat folds away for access to the engine compartment. There's an enclosed head in the cabin along with a V-berth/dinette and a small galley. What makes the Cobalt so special, of course, is the extraordinary fit and finish. An extremely popular model, a single 375 Volvo DuoProp I/O will reach a top speed of 35 knots. Twin 320hp Volvo DuoProps—a more popular choice—max out around 45 knots.

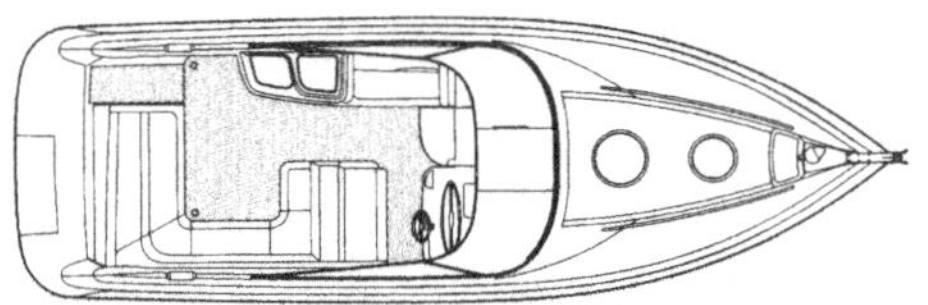

See Page 675 For Price Data

Length	28'10"	Clearance	6'2"
Beam	9'6"	Fuel	111 gals.
Draft, Drives Up	2'2"	Water	30 gals.
Draft, Drives Down	2'10"	Hull Type	Deep-V
Weight	6,950#	Deadrise Aft	20°

Cobalt 323

2006–Current

Cobalt got it right with the 323, a luxury-class cuddy cruiser with the bold styling and meticulous finish common to all Cobalt products. It's well known that Cobalts are expensive boats; this level of quality never comes cheap. Built on a Kevlar-reinforced deep-V hull, the roomy cockpit of the 323—deep enough to protect guests from high-speed wind blast—features an innovative flip-out cocktail table that stows in the port sidewall. A deluxe wet bar includes a refrigerator in addition to a stove and sink, and a large rear sun pad overlooks the 323's extended swim platform. At the entrance to the cabin, opposite the centerline door, a stainless ladder slides out for quick access to the bow. Below, the richly appointed cabin of the Cobalt 323—a match for the finest European cuddy runabouts—features a mini-galley with sink and storage, enclosed head with pull-out shower, and wraparound lounge seating forward with a removable teak table. Stainless steel is absolutely everywhere on the 323, from the windlass plate and anchor chute to the optional arch and stamped engine vents. Twin 375hp MerCruiser I/Os top at close to 45 knots.

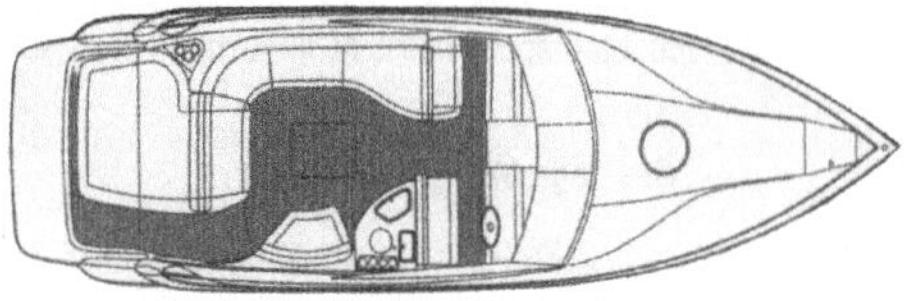

See Page 675 For Price Data

Length w/Platform	34'9"	Fuel	154 gals.
Beam	10'6"	Water	18 gals.
Draft, Up	24"	Waste	28 gals.
Draft, Down	35"	Hull Type	Deep-V
Weight	12,300#	Deadrise Aft	22°

Cobalt 343

2004–07

With her sleek profile, luxurious amenities, and high-performance stepped hull, the Cobalt 343 delivers a full blast of power and raw sex appeal. This is the kind of boat that puts the excitement back into boating—a fast, user-friendly cruiser that attracts a crowd just about everywhere she goes. Built on a slender deep-V hull with a full-length keel pad, the 343 has a cockpit capable of seating six passengers in extreme comfort. The electric centerline captain's seat, with its wraparound dash and excellent visibility, is one of the more notable features of this boat. Molded steps on either side of the cockpit provide easy access to the foredeck, and the cabin door slides on polished stainless runners. Inside, the cabin is as elegant as it is simple. An Ultraleather settee and enclosed head are standard, and while the headroom is modest, the accommodations are plush. An impressive array of standard equipment includes an air compressor, 10-disc CD changer, through-prop exhaust, power motorbox and an extended swim platform. A fast ride with twin 425hp MerCruiser engines, the Cobalt 343 will cruise in the high 30s and reach a top speed of 50+ knots.

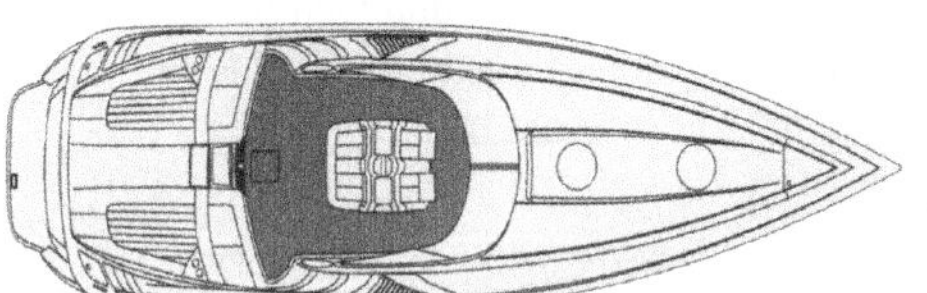

See Page 675 For Price Data

Length w/Platform	37'2"	Clearance, Top	8'2"
Hull Length	35'4"	Fuel	200 gals.
Beam	9'8"	Water	10 gals.
Draft	37"	Hull Type	Deep-V
Weight	11,750#	Deadrise Aft	24.5°

Cobalt 360

2002–05

A good-selling model for Cobalt, the 360 offers an impressive blend of sportiness, luxury, and quality. This is a very stylish sportcruiser—so stylish, in fact, that she'd be at home in just about any high-profile Mediterranean marina. Built on a Kevlar-reinforced deep-V hull, the Cobalt's expansive helm/cockpit area is as comfortable as it is innovative. Facing settees in the aft cockpit will seat five, and single sun pads (with storage under) flank the center transom walk-through. Wood and leather accents dress up the Cobalt's tiered dash where there's space to flush-mount a full array of electronic add-ons. Because of her spacious cockpit, the 360 is a day boat first and her belowdecks accommodations are modest. Headroom is limited to just 6 feet, and the small midcabin berth is probably better suited for storage than sleeping. The plush Ultraleather dinette converts to a V-berth, and while the head compartment is quite roomy the 360's compact galley is not designed for serious meal-prep activities. Cherry interior joinery and a cockpit wet bar were standard. A fast ride with 415hp MerCruiser sterndrives, the Cobalt 360 will reach a top speed of close to 50 knots.

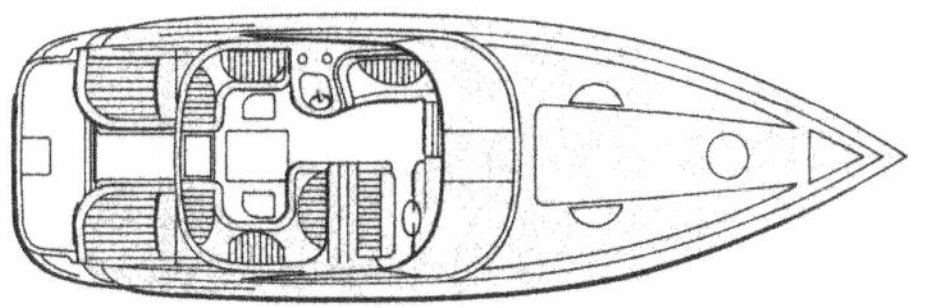

Not Enough Resale Data to Set Values

Length	36'0"	Fuel	174 gals.
Beam	10'6"	Water	35 gals.
Draft, Drives Up	2'3"	Waste	28 gals.
Draft, Drives Down	3'6"	Hull Type	Deep-V
Weight	13,710#	Deadrise Aft	22°

Cobia

Quick View

- No longer in business, Cobia had been building boats for more than 40 years before their boats were taken seriously by hard-core anglers.
- Cobias were considered "price" boats until Yamaha bought the company in 1995 and began an across-the-board improvement in quality.
- Purchased in 2005 by Maverick Boat Company, Cobia production was moved to a new facility in Marion, North Carolina.
- With the economy in recession in mid 2008, Cobia suspended operations in August of that year, laying off the Marion workforce and shifting operations to the Ft. Pierce, FL, facility where the Maverick, Hewes and Pathfinder brands are built.

Cobia Boats • Ft. Pierce, FL • www.cobiaboats.com

Cobia 250/260/270 Walkaround

1997–2007

The Cobia 270 Walkaround (called the 250 in 1997 and the 260 from 1998–2000) is an affordably priced trailerable fisherman with an efficient deck layout and a compact cabin with the basic necessities for an overnight getaway. Built on a solid fiberglass deep-V hull with an integrated bracket/dive platform, the 260 has a deep cockpit and recessed gunwales for greater stability when fighting a fish in rough seas. Wide walkways around the house make bow access easy and secure, and the Cobia's 54-square-foot cockpit affords an adequate working platform for a couple of anglers. Standard fishing amenities include built-in tackle stations, large aerated livewells, insulated fish boxes, transom door, rod holders and transom-mounted cutting boards. Cabin accommodations are fairly spartan: a V-berth forward with storage under, removable dinette table, mini-galley, two opening ports, and an enclosed head with shower. Additional features include an integral bow pulpit, a lockable electronics box at the helm, cockpit bolsters, and cockpit courtesy lights. Twin 150hp Yamaha outboards reach close to 40 knots wide open.

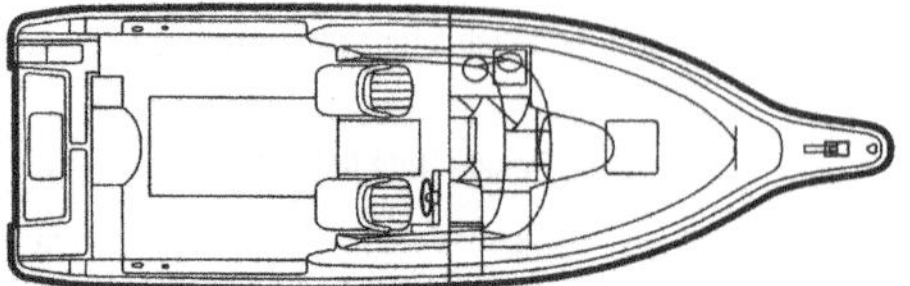

See Page 675 For Price Data

Length w/Pulpit	27'6"	Fuel	175 gals.
Beam	8'6"	Water	12 gals.
Hull Draft	1'8"	Max HP	400
Dry Weight	5,000#	Hull Type	Deep-V
Clearance	8'8"	Deadrise Aft	20°

Cobia 254/264/274 Center Console

Cobias have been known for years as inexpensive, workmanlike fishing boats for price-conscious anglers unable (or unwilling) to spend heavily for a capable, offshore boat. The Cobia 274 (called the 254 in 1997 when she was introduced and the 264 from 1998–2000) rides on the same deep-V hull used in the Cobia 270 Walkaround, a proven design with an integral transom and pulpit, reverse chines, and an outboard bracket/dive platform. She's a pretty good-looking boat overall, not flashy but handsome enough to satisfy the demands of most anglers. Fishing amenities include an oval, aerated transom livewell, four insulated fish boxes, a total of ten rod holders, and cockpit bolsters. On the downside, the transom door is on the narrow side. Like most center consoles this size, the 274 has a sub-console head compartment. Additional features include a lockable electronics box at the helm, a cooler under the bench seat forward of the console, anchor locker and high bow rails. Twin 200hp outboards cruise the Cobia 274 Center Console at 30 knots and reach a top speed of over 40 knots. Note that an all-new Cobia 274 was introduced in 2003.

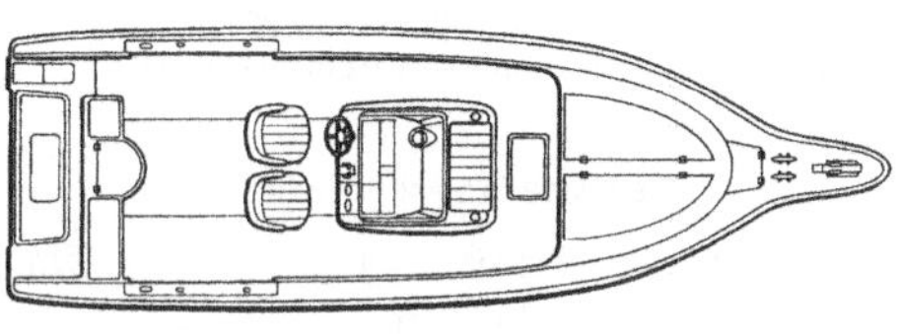

See Page 675 For Price Data

Length w/Pulpit	27'6"	Fuel	175 gals.
Beam	8'6"	Water	7 gals.
Hull Draft	1'3"	Max HP	450
Dry Weight	3,900#	Hull Type	Deep-V
Clearance, T-Top	8'10"	Deadrise Aft	20°

Cobia 274 Center Console

Introduced in 2003, the Cobia 274 Center Console (note that Cobia marketed a smaller 274 model in 2001–02) is a value-priced offshore fishboat with excellent range and good open-water performance. Hull construction is solid fiberglass, and a relatively slender 8-foot, 6-inch beam allows the 274 to be trailered without a permit. The deck layout is similar to most center consoles in her class with two insulated fish boxes aft, two more forward under the casting platform, standup livewell with high-speed pickup, and a transom door. A leaning post with 94-quart cooler is standard, and there's space at the helm for flush-mounting extra electronics. A portside door in the console reveals a sizable head compartment which is ventilated by an opening port. Additional features include removable tackle boxes in the console, low-profile bow rail, cockpit toe rails, and a safety swim ladder that can be deployed by a swimmer. Serious anglers will be impressed with the Cobia's generous 200-gallon fuel capacity—at least 20 gallons more than most other boats her size. With twin 225hp Yamaha 4-strokes, expect a top speed in the neighborhood of 45 knots.

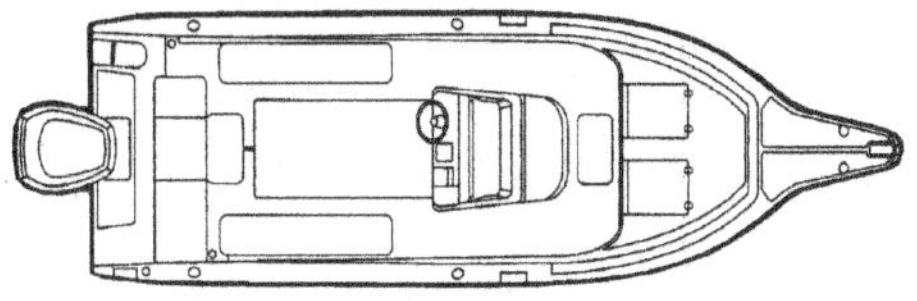

See Page 675 For Price Data

Length w/Pulpit	27'6"	Fuel	200 gals.
Beam	8'6"	Water	7 gals.
Hull Draft	1'6"	Max HP	500
Dry Weight	4,500#	Hull Type	Deep-V
Load Capacity	3,900#	Deadrise Aft	20°

Cobia 312 Sport Cabin

2003–07

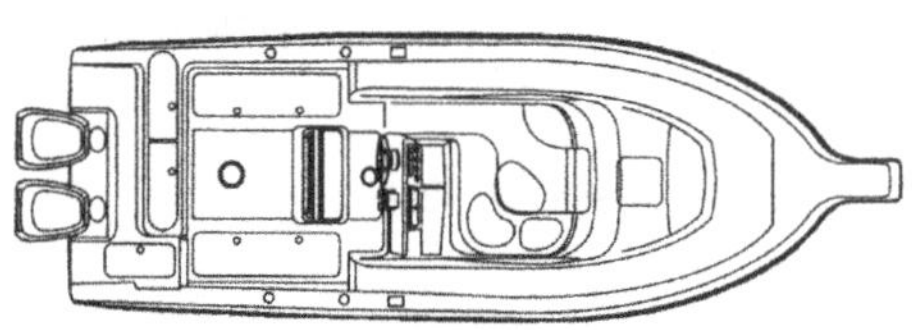

Described by Cobia as "part fishing boat and part ocean cruiser," the 312 Sport Cruiser combines the fishability of a center console with the cabin amenities of a small express. Crossover boats like this have become popular in recent years as manufacturers try to satisfy the demands of anglers who use their boats for both cruising and fishing. In the final analysis, the 312 does a good job of splitting the difference—if the cockpit is small for a 31-footer, it's still up to the needs of most serious anglers, while the modest cabin with its enclosed head and compact galley offers a level of comfort lacking in most dedicated fishing boats. Cockpit features include a 28-gallon livewell, twin in-deck 45-gallon fish/storage boxes, leaning post with 94-quart cooler, transom sink with cutting board, and raw-water washdown. Wide walkways provide excellent 360-degree fishing access, and the console comes with a tilt wheel, hydraulic steering and an angled footrest. Trim tabs, bow pulpit, a lockable electronics box, refrigerator and microwave oven are standard, and a T-top and rear cockpit seat are popular options. Twin Yamaha 225s will reach a top speed in the range of 40–45 knots.

See Page 675 For Price Data

Length w/Pulpit	30'11"	Fuel	270 gals.
Beam	9'10"	Water	20 gals.
Hull Draft	17"	Max HP	600
Dry Weight	7,300#	Hull Type	Deep-V
Clearance, Top	8'5"	Deadrise Aft	20°

Cobia 314 Center Console

2003–07

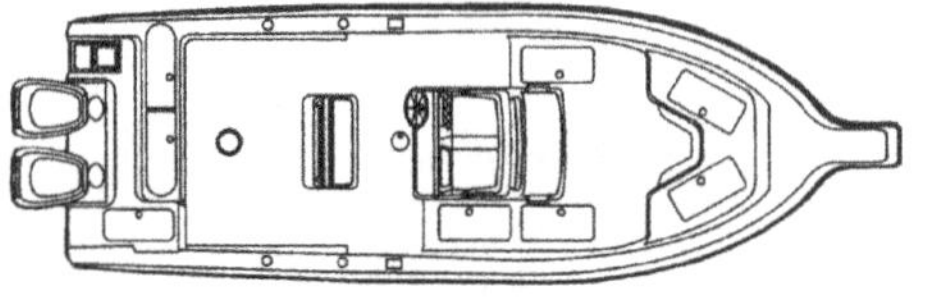

The Cobia 314 gets high marks for her roomy deck layout, solid construction, and—perhaps most important of all—an affordable price. This is Cobia's biggest boat yet, and while she competes in a market dominated by several high-end manufacturers, the 314 acquits herself well from the standpoint of features and value. Built on a solid fiberglass hull with enough freeboard to knock down spray, the 314's large 270-gallon fuel capacity and generous storage make her an excellent Bahamas cruiser. The deck layout is arranged like most big center consoles with a standard leaning post (with 94-quart cooler), transom sink and cutting boards, aerated livewell, and plenty of rod storage. Note that the entire front half of the boat has a raised deck with a step up at the console—a configuration that increases belowdecks storage, but requires some getting used to. The Cobia's large console allows for a surprisingly spacious head compartment below with a sink, shower, and even a small berth. Additional features include a transom shower, raw-water washdown, bow pulpit, and a tackle storage center. A relatively light boat for her size, twin 250hp Yamahas deliver a top speed of around 45 knots.

See Page 675 For Price Data

Length w/Pulpit	30'11"	Fuel	270 gals.
Beam	9'10"	Water	20 gals.
Draft, Engnes Up	1'5"	Max HP	600
Draft, Engines Down	2'10"	Hull Type	Deep-V
Dry Weight	7,300#	Deadrise Aft	20°

Contender

Quick View

- Contender Boats was founded in 1982 by its current owner, Joe Neber.
- Since 1984, Contender has operated continuously producing over 6000 sportfishing boats , 21' to 40' in length, in both open and cabin configurations.
- In 2008 Contender expanded its performance options by offering stepped hull options for it's four most popular larger models.
- The Contender production facility is located in Homestead Florida, where all components are manufactured in house including metal fabrication, carpentry, electrical and upholstery.
- Well built and expensive to buy, Contenders are popular boats along the East Coast where they enjoy a loyal following among veteran offshore anglers.

Contender • Homestead, FL • www.contenderoffshore.com

Contender 25 Open

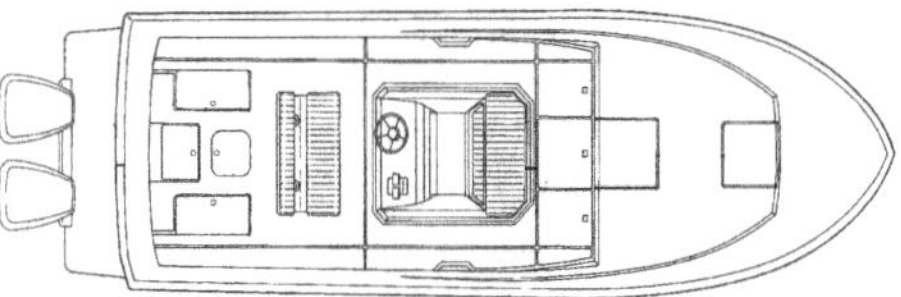

Contender's first boat, the 25 Open is a high-performance, full-transom center console fisherman whose deep-V hull, solid construction, and space-efficient deck plan made her popular with hardcore anglers. She was designed by company owner Joe Nebber with fishability her primary objective. Available with or without a cuddy cabin, the 25's cockpit layout includes two fully lined and insulated fish boxes and a circular 38-gallon livewell under the deck, aft. The Open model has an additional insulated fish box forward. An oddly-named "convertible" model has a canvas cuddy enclosure with a drop curtain and bunk cushions forward, and the cuddy has a molded fiberglass interior with V-berths and space for a portable head. Additional features include a bench seat forward of the console with storage under, lockable electronics compartment, molded inner liner, and an outboard bracket. Nearly all of these boats have been customized to some degree by their owners, and most were fitted with T-tops and rocket launchers. A rugged fishboat with proven offshore ability, twin 150hp outboards will power the Contender 25 to over 40 knots.

See Page 517 For Price Data

Length	25'3"	Fuel, Std.	150 gals.
Beam	8'3"	Water	25 gals.
Draft	1'6"	Max HP	400
Dry Weight	2,700#	Hull Type	Deep-V
Clearance	NA	Deadrise Aft	24.5°

Contender 25 Open

1998–Current

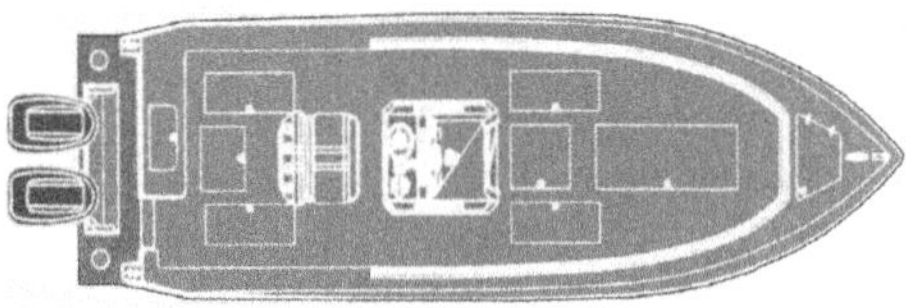

Successor to Contender's original 25 center console, the new Contender 25 offers a wider beam than her predecessor, an improved single-level deck layout, more fuel capacity, recessed trim tabs, and an integrated bracket rather than the full transom found on the original model. Built on a lightweight deep-V hull with an aggressive 24.5 degrees of transom deadrise, the Contender's hullsides are balsa-cored, and the sole and stringers are cored with Klegecell. (Note that while the 25 is easily trailered, her 8'10" beam exceeds the legal highway limit by 4 inches.) The cockpit is expertly designed with wide walkways around the console, recessed bowrails to decrease fishing line snags, and a single level cockpit to minimize trip hazards. Fishing features include two insulated in-deck 225-quart fish boxes aft, a third in-sole box forward of the console, and a 48-gallon transom livewell. An anchor locker is forward, and a choice of consoles allows for considerable owner customization. The boat can also be ordered with or without a windshield. A legendary open-water performer, twin 225hp Yamaha outboards reach a top speed of over 45 knots.

See Page 675 For Price Data

Length	27'3"	Fuel, Std.	185 gals.
Beam	8'10"	Fuel, Optional	240 gals.
Draft	1'6"	Max HP	500
Dry Weight	3,000#	Hull Type	Deep-V
Clearance	7'8"	Deadrise Aft	24.5°

Contender 27 Open

1995–2007

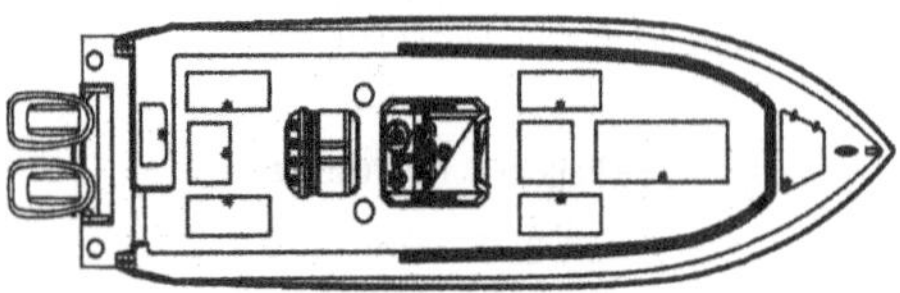

Lightweight, fast, and fun to drive, the Contender 27 is a top-quality center console with the kind of built-in fishing features that anglers love. A great-looking boat with a sleek profile, her deep-V, narrow-beam hull is an excellent open-water performer delivering a soft ride in even a rough chop. (With an 8'6" beam, the 27 is easily trailered for those with a heavy-duty tow vehicle.) High-tech foam construction is used throughout to reduce weight, and at 3,300 pounds dry, the Contender 27 is a relatively light boat for her size. The deck layout is completely uncluttered, and wide walkways around the console make it easy to maneuver a line all around the boat. Note that a recessed bow rail makes it difficult to snag a line. A storage compartment in the walk-in console can accommodate an optional marine head. Standard features include port and starboard fish boxes aft, a big 140-gallon fish box forward, a raised 48-gallon livewell at the transom, a bow anchor locker and a transom door. A popular boat sold at a premium price in her day, Yamaha 200hp outboards deliver a top speed of around 45 knots. Note that a new Contender 27 was introduced in 2008.

See Page 675 For Price Data

Length Overall	30'0"	Fuel	210 gals.
Beam	8'10"	Water	15 gals.
Hull Draft	18"	MaxHP	500
Dry Weight	4,950#	Hull Type	Deep-V
Clearance	NA	Deadrise Aft	24.5°

Contender 31 Fish Around

Contender's only walkaround model for several years, the 31 Fish Around is built on the proven hull of the Contender 31 Open—widely regarded as one of the best 31-foot offshore designs in the business. While the Fish Around lacks the expansive, uncluttered deck space of a true center console, Contender has done a good job of maximizing her fishing potential while still providing a compact cabin with overnight accommodations for two. Equally important, the Fish Around is a full 360-degree walkaround on a single level, much like a center console and better than a regular walkaround. Her deep-V hull is designed with reverse chines for a drier ride, and the hull is cored above the waterline to reduce weight. Fishing features include an abovedeck livewell, bait-prep station, two insulated in-deck fish boxes, a recessed bow rail, transom door and wide walkaround decks. An anchor locker is standard, and there's an enclosed head below along with a mini-galley and a removable dinette table. A fast and stable ride even in rough conditions, the Contender 31 Fish Around will top out at nearly 50 knots with twin 250hp outboards and cruise easily at 33 knots.

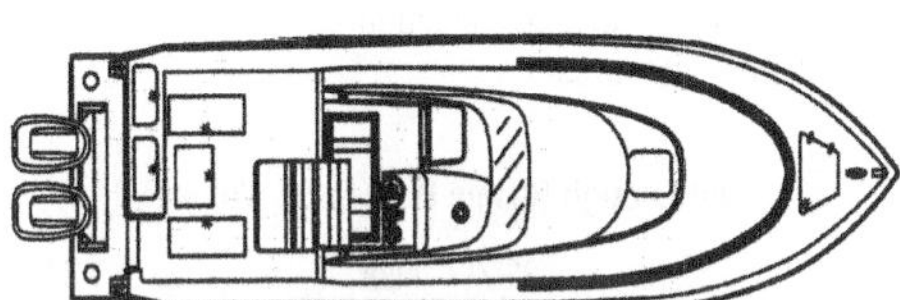

Not Enough Resale Data to Set Values

Length	32'6"	Fuel	245 gals.
Beam	9'4"	Water	40 gals.
Hull Draft	1'6"	Max HP	
Dry Weight	6,000#	Hull Type	Deep-V
Clearance	NA	Deadrise Aft	24.5°

Contender 31 Open

A proven tournament winner, the Contender 31 Open is a brawny, top-quality fisherman whose meticulous finish and high-performance capabilities placed her in the forefront of large center console fishing machines. The 31 is cored above the waterline to reduce weight, and her deep-V hull features wide reverse chines and two lifting strakes per side to provide a dry ride in a chop. A single-level cockpit makes the Contender an easier boat to move around in than most other center consoles with their raised bow-casting platforms, and a recessed bow rail reduces the chances of snagging a line. Rod holders are everywhere and the fish boxes are huge. Contender offers buyers the opportunity to customize the helm console in several ways, and the sub-console storage compartment can be fitted with a marine head and shower. Additional features include three livewells, a bait-prep center, lockable electronics storage, and an integrated dive/swim platform. A fast and stable ride in even difficult conditions, the 31 Open will top out at over 50 knots with twin 225hp Yamaha outboards and cruise at 30+ knots. Note that a cuddy version was also available.

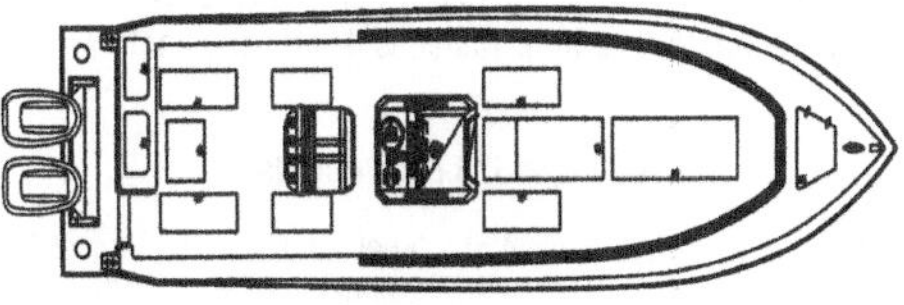

See Page 675 For Price Data

Length	31'3"	Fuel	240 gals.
Beam	9'4"	Water	NA
Hull Draft	1'6"	Max HP	500
Dry Weight	3,500#	Hull Type	Deep-V
Weight w/Engines	5,500#	Deadrise Aft	24.5°

Contender 31/32 Tournament

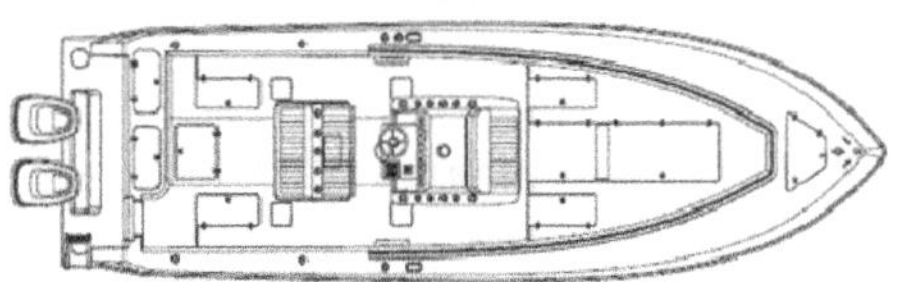

Beginning life in 2008 as the Contender 31 Tournament, the 32 Tournament rides on a single-stepped hull with an aggressive 24.5 degrees of transom deadrise. As most offshore anglers know, Contenders are semicustom boats and it's unusual to find two that are exactly alike. Suffice it to say that this Florida-built boat is designed for serious fishing. Her single-level cockpit, with recessed handrails, makes it easy to get around the entire boat without snagging a line. The helm comes with a standard bench seat/leaning post and a T-top, and the instrument panel can be customized to suit the angler's requirements. A walk-in head compartment is concealed in the beefy console. Standard features include twin 40-gallon raised livewells, pop-up cleats, walk-through transom, in-deck fish boxes fore and aft, lockabe rod storage, and K-plane trim tabs. Note the removable rear bench seat, cushioned console seat, and overbuilt T-top with electronics box. The fit and finish lavished on the Contender 31/32 is about as good as it gets in her class. A fast ride, expect a top speed in the neighborhood of 50 knots with twin Yamaha 250hp outboards.

Not Enough Resale Data to Set Values

Length	32'7"	Fuel	310 gals.
Beam	9'8"	Water	NA
Hull Draft	23"	Max HP	
Dry Weight	5,850#	Hull Type	Deep-V
Weight, Loaded	11,560#	Deadrise Aft	24.5°

Contender 33 Tournament

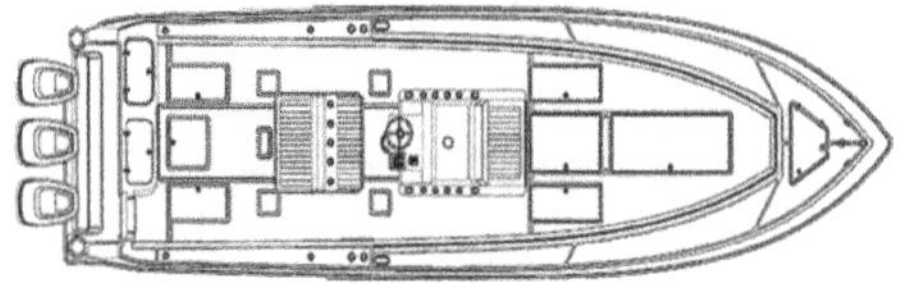

Contender's reputation for sportfishing excellence has been tested many times over by hard-core anglers up and down the east coast. For years, the company built its boats on traditional deep-V hulls, but with the 33T company founder Joe Neber chose a stepped-hull design for its increased running efficiency—no small consideration in this era of high fuel prices. The 33s uncluttered, single-level deck layout has enough working space for a half-dozen anglers and their gear. Standard features include two transom livewells (42 and 48 gallons), two insulated, in-deck fish boxes forward of the console, in-deck rod storage, and a state-of-the art console with integrated console seat and vertical rod holders along each side. Optional below-deck livewells aft of the console make it possible to house a total of four wells in this rugged fisherman. A portable head is optional in the walk-in console space. Contender offers a top-quality T-top design as well as several deluxe leaning post choices. Note that the 33 appears to have more freeboard than previous Contender models her size. Twin Yamaha 350s reach close to 45 knots top; triple 250hp Yamahas deliver 50+ knots wide open.

See Page 675 For Price Data

Length	34'5"	Fuel	400 gals.
Beam	9'8"	Water	NA
Hull Draft	24"	Max HP	1,050
Dry Weight	6,600#	Hull Type	Deep-V
Weight, Loaded	13,500#	Deadrise Aft	24.5°

Contender 35 Express

1989–2006

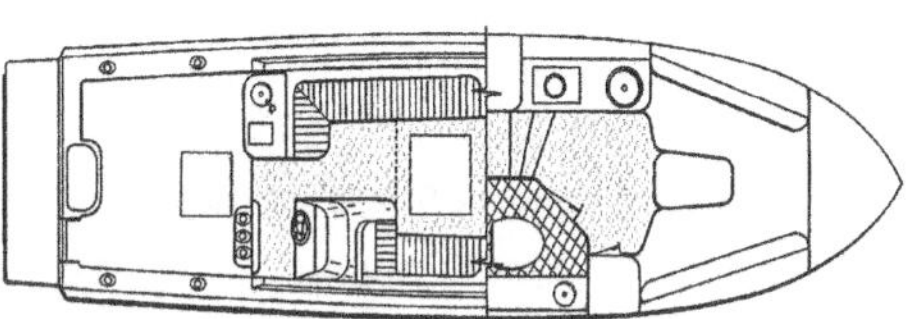

The Contender 35 is a fast, seaworthy tournament sportfisher designed to run hard in the kind of conditions that keep other boats tied up at the dock. Like all Contenders, she's built on a fully cored deep-V hull with a relatively narrow beam. At a dry weight of 5,500 pounds, the 35 is a light boat for her size, which results in a fast and fuel-efficient ride regardless of the inboard or outboard power options one might choose. Because this is a semicustom boat, several deck configurations were available from the factory including an aft side console with lounge seating forward as well as a forward helm with more cockpit space aft. The cabin sleeps four and comes with an enclosed head with shower and a small galley. Notable features include good access to the engines on inboard models (the whole center section of the deck raises hydraulically), a well-arranged helm console with tilt wheel, livewell, removable fish boxes, and rod storage below. Among several inboard and outboard engine options, twin 250hp outboards will deliver a top speed of 42+ knots, while a pair of 250hp Cummins inboard diesels cruise at a fast 30 knots (about 35 knots top).

Not Enough Resale Data to Set Values

Length	35'0'	Fuel	340 gals.
Beam	10'0"	Water	45 gals.
Hull Draft	2'0"	Max HP	
Dry Weight	5,500#	Hull Type	Deep-V
Clearance	NA	Deadrise Aft	24.5°

Contender 35 Side Console

1993–Current

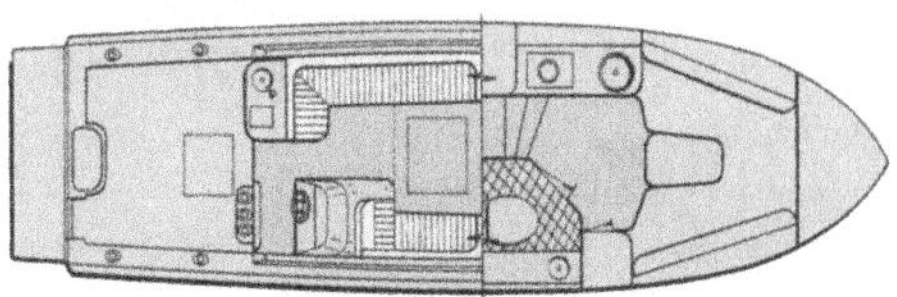

Unlike most Contenders with their design emphasis on hard-core fishing, the focus of the 35 Side Console is on versatility. Indeed, this is one Contender model built for cruising as well as fishing. Beginning with a spacious bridge deck, with its offset console and cushioned lounge seating, the 35 is perfectly suited for comfortable day cruising with family and friends. Overnight trips are no problem in this Contender; her well-appointed cabin can sleep four and includes a full-service galley with refrigerator, enclosed head with shower, and a removable dining table. In spite of her slender 10-foot beam, the cockpit has everything required for serious fishing pursuits. Standard features include a 38-gallon transom livewell, lift-out fish box, bait prep station, raw water washdown, cockpit lighting, and transom door. Note that the bridge deck lifts for access to a huge storage compartment. Bow access is a matter of climbing over the windshield—not an easy task. As is the case with all Contender models, owners are able to factory-customize their boats to the point where it's hard to find two that are alike. Twin Yamaha 250s top out around 45 knots.

Not Enough Resale Data to Set Values

Length	35'2"	Fuel	340 gals.
Beam	10'0"	Water	40 gals.
Hull Draft	24"	Max HP	
Dry Weight	7,500#	Hull Type	Deep-V
Clearance	NA	Deadrise Aft	24.5°

Contender 36 Cuddy

2003-09

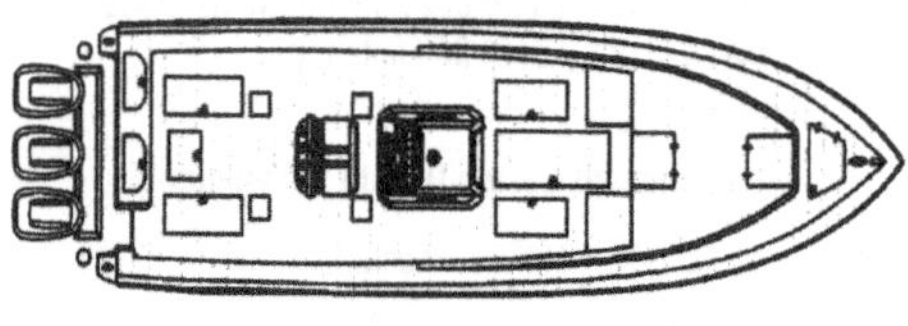

Based on the tournament-proven 36 Open Fish, the Contender 36 Cuddy is a big center console specifically designed for triple outboards. This is the kind of muscle boat capable of running far offshore in just about any kind of weather. Like all Contenders, the 36 is essentially a custom boat with practically every option chosen by the owner to fit his own particular needs. Indeed, beyond the hull and cuddy, very little is standard and no two 36 Cuddys are alike. Built with the finest materials, the lightweight deep-V hull is balsa-cored from the waterline up. Two large livewells and a padded leaning post are standard, and the console features a walk-in head compartment as well as lockable storage. An oversized V-berth and forward storage locker are found in the cabin, and aggressive nonskid in the cockpit provides secure footing for anglers. Note the molded jumpseats and in-deck storage lockers forward of the console. Additional features include Kiekhaefer trim tabs (installed on the rear of the platform rather than recessed into the hull), dual hydraulic steering, and a recessed bow rail. When fitted with three Yamaha 250 outboards, the Contender 36 delivers a top speed in the neighborhood of 50 knots.

Not Enough Resale Data to Set Values

Length Overall	36'3"	Fuel, Opt	600 gals.
Beam	10'0"	Water	45 gals.
Hull Draft	24"	Max HP	1,050
Dry Weight	7,050#	Hull Type	Deep-V
Fuel, Std	410 gals.	Deadrise Aft	24.5

Contender 36 Open

2001-07

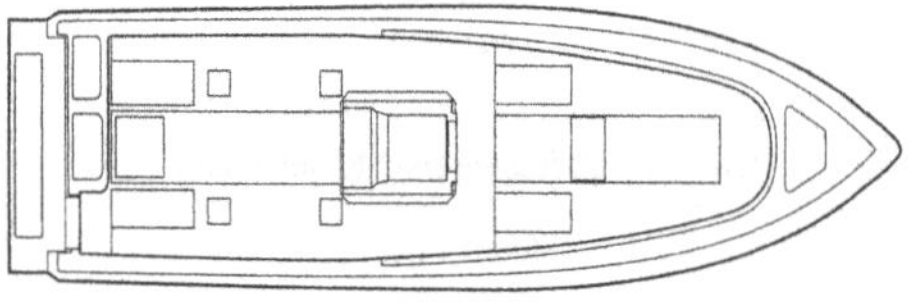

The semicustom Contender 36 is about as close as any serious angler can get to the ultimate high-performance outboard fishboat. There are no compromises here; the Contender has more beam, more livewell space, more fuel, and more fish box capacity than any boat in her class. Designed from the ground up for triple engines, the surprisingly weight-efficient deep-V hull of the 36 Open is quick to accelerate and delivers a fast and secure ride even in 4- to 5-foot seas. The cockpit, both forward and aft of the console, is huge with plenty of in-deck storage capacity. The console seems small for a boat this size but the walkways on both sides are very wide. Notable features include two oval 50-gallon transom livewells, an integrated motor bracket, transom door, a walk-in console storage/head compartment, below decks rod lockers and four insulated fish boxes. An optional coffin box forward can be raised electrically for access to a huge storage area beneath. A powerful boat with the stamina to endure serious offshore punishment, triple 250hp Yamaha outboards cruise the Contender 36 Open at an easy 35 knots (close to 50 knots max).

See Page 675 For Price Data

Length	36'2"	Fuel, Opt	600 gals.
Beam	10'0"	Water	45 gals.
Hull Draft	1'6"	Max HP	1050
Dry Weight	6,000#	Hull Type	Deep-V
Fuel, Std	420 gals.	Deadrise Aft	24.5

Cranchi Yachts

Quick View

- Cranchi was founded in 1870 by Giovanni Cranchi in his workshop on the bank of Lake Como, Italy. The company started out building boats for the local fishermen.
- In 1932 Giovanni Cranchi's grandson purchased a factory, to set up his own boatyard, and he began building his first boats.
- After the war, Cranchi wooden models became very popular. The company expanded rapidly, and by the 1990 Cranchi had become one of Italy's best-known yachtbuilders.
- Cranchis are built in state-of-the-art facilities in Piantedo and San Giorgio, Italy.
- Cranchi's were first imported into the US market in the late 1990s. As sales increased, the company established a factory office in Ft. Lauderdale (no longer in operation).

Cantiere Nautico Cranchi • San Giorgio, Italy • www.cranchi.it.

Cranchi 34 Zaffiro

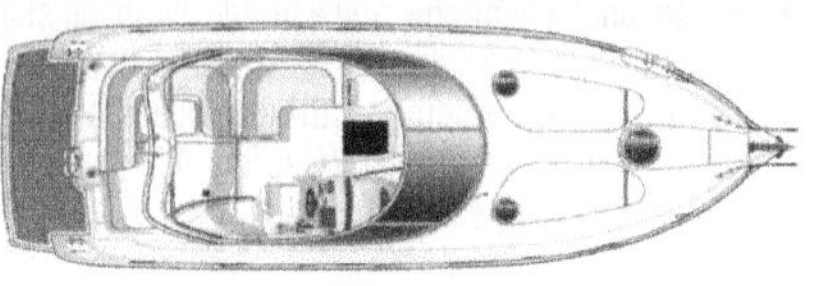

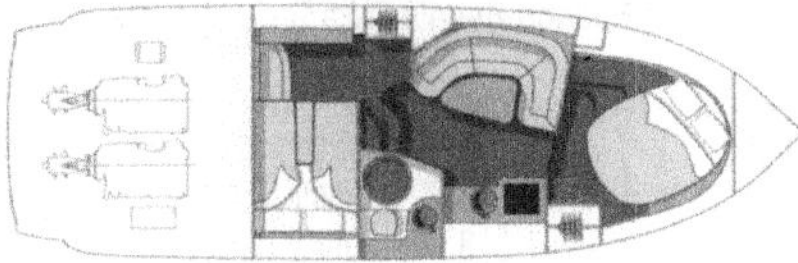

A downsized version of the Cranchi Smeraldo 36, the Zaffiro 34 is a high-quality Italian sportboat with elegant cabin accommodations, a good-running deep-V hull, and a first-class deck layout. The subdued decor of the Zaffiro's midcabin interior is a refreshing change from the high-glitz decors of so many sportboats. Unlike most of her competitors, both staterooms are fitted with privacy doors (instead of curtains), and the European appliances and rounded corners give the Zaffiro that distinctive Continental character. (On the downside, the companionway steps are way too steep.) Outside, there's plenty of guest seating with a settee opposite the helm and a big U-shaped cockpit settee with a removable cocktail table. The two-tiered helm provides space for flush-mounting the necessary electronics, and a molded wet bar is abaft the helm seat. Because the side decks are quite narrow, a walk-through windshield provides access to the bow. Additional features include a folding radar arch, adequate dry storage, and good engine access. An impressive performer with relatively small 260hp Volvo diesel sterndrives, the Zaffiro will cruise at 25 knots and reach a top speed of nearly 30 knots.

Not Enough Resale Data to Set Values

Length Overall	34'9"	Fuel	151 gals.
Hull Length	34'0"	Water	50 gals.
Beam	11'4"	Waste	40 gals.
Draft	3'0"	Hull Type	Deep-V
Weight	14,944#	Deadrise Aft	18°

Cranchi 37 Smeraldo

1998–04

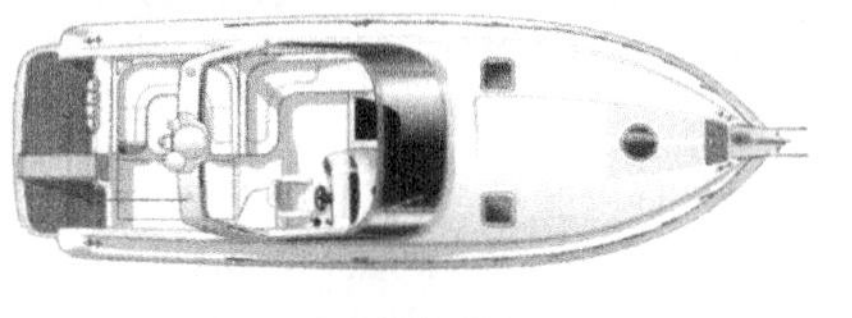

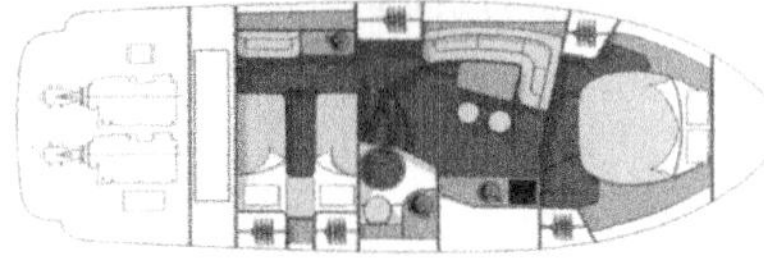

The Smeraldo 37 (called the Smeraldo 36 until 1998 when the swim platform was extended) has been a popular model in the Cranchi fleet for many years. She's built on a solid fiberglass hull with moderate beam, and with a steep 25 degrees of transom deadrise her deep-V hull makes for a particularly well-behaved ride in a chop. Her midcabin floorplan is arranged in the conventional manner with private staterooms fore and aft, a convertible portside dinette, a compact galley (a bit small by U.S. standards), and an enclosed head with shower. Aside from the meticulous finish, what sets these accommodations apart from the norm are the stylish European appliances and the rounded bulkhead doors. On deck, a comfortable L-shaped settee is opposite the helm on the bridge deck, and a U-shaped settee in the cockpit converts into a large sun pad. Hatches in the cockpit sole provide good access to the starboard engine, but getting to the portside motor means moving some furniture. Additional features include a foredeck sun pad, an elegant burlwood dashboard, and excellent storage. Among several engine options, twin 260hp Volvo diesel sterndrives cruise in the mid 20s (32–33 knots top).

Not Enough Resale Data to Set Values

Length Overall	38'6"	Clearance	9'2"
Hull Length	35'10"	Fuel	170 gals.
Beam	12'6"	Water	72 gals.
Draft	2'10"	Hull Type	Deep-V
Weight	17,218#	Deadrise Aft	19°

Cranchi 38/40 Atlantique

1995–2004

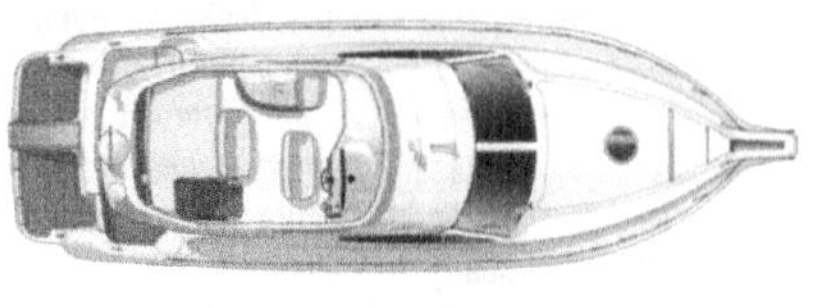

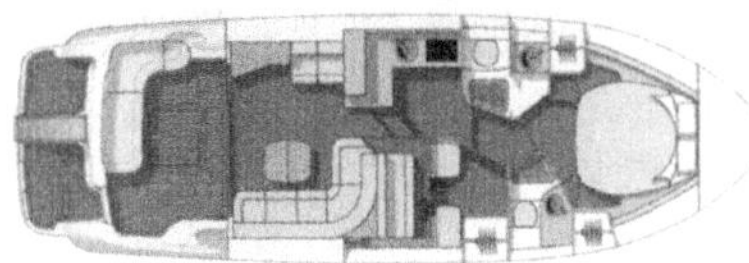

Called the Atlantique 38 until the addition of an extended swim platform in 1998 made her a 40-footer, the Atlantique 40 is a sleek European motor yacht whose luxury accommodations are very much in the Italian tradition of elegance and comfort. She's built on a soft-riding deep-V hull and, like many European yachts, she incorporates propeller tunnels to reduce shaft angles—a particularly necessary feature in the Atlantique since the engines are so aft in the hull. Her two-stateroom interior is arranged with a mid-level galley, opposite the elevated lower helm and hidden from the salon. The master stateroom is forward, and the guest cabin is fitted with twin berths that extend under the helm console. A sliding glass door opens to the Atlantique's cockpit with its built-in lounge seating, transom door and molded bridge access steps. A sun pad is aft of the helm on the flybridge, and a bridge overhang shades the cockpit. Engine access is a little awkward; the motors are located under the aft part of the salon and the gearboxes are under the cockpit. Twin 370hp Volvo diesels cruise the Atlantique 40 in the mid 20s and reach a top speed in the neighborhood of 30 knots.

Not Enough Resale Data to Set Values

Length Overall	43'2"	Fuel	278 gals.
Hull Length	38'9"	Water	93 gals.
Beam	12'7"	Waste	49 gals.
Draft	3'6"	Hull Type	Deep-V
Weight	23,128#	Deadrise Aft	19°

Cranchi 41 Endurance

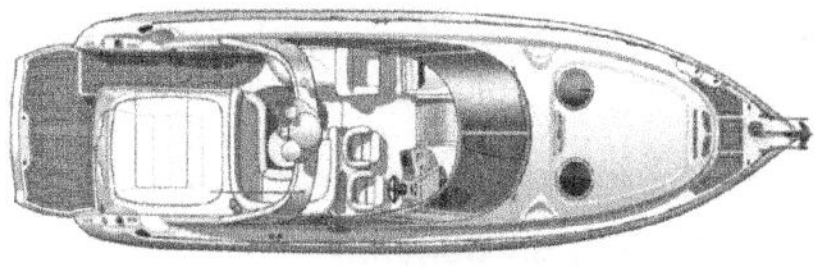

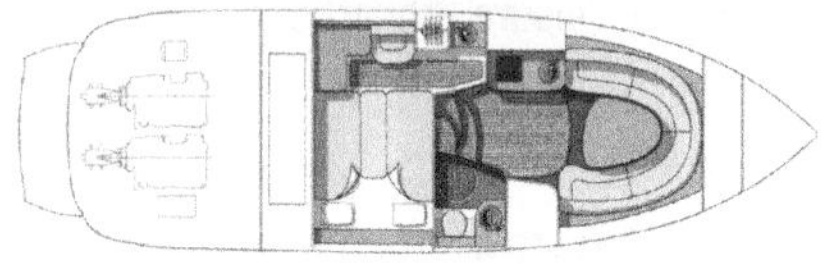

Among other attributes, the Cranchi 41 Endurance is one of the smallest sportcruisers available with a transom garage for housing a tender or PWC. She's also one of the most affordable boats in her class as well as being one of the fastest. Built on a Kevlar-reinforced stepped hull, the slender beam of the Endurance enhances performance while limiting the space available for cabin accommodations. Additionally, the transom garage pushes the cockpit forward, which further reduces interior volume. The result is a terrific day boat with a spacious cockpit and a huge aft sun pad, but whose compact interior lacks the amenities required for extended cruising. Highlighted with leather seating and teak joinery, the single-stateroom layout includes a convertible dinette forward and a small galley and head. Topside, the cockpit is arranged with U-shaped seating, wet bar, and an electric grill. Visibility from the superb helm position is excellent, but the Cranchi's side decks are narrow and the engineroom is a tight fit. A bow thruster, extended swim platform, foredeck sun pad, and teak-and-holly cabin sole were standard. A fast ride, Volvo 350hp diesel sterndrives will deliver a top speed in excess of 35 knots.

Not Enough Resale Data to Set Values

Length Overall	42'6"	Clearance	12'5"
Hull Length	39'1"	Fuel	206 gals.
Beam	11'5"	Water	40 gals.
Draft	3'1"	Hull Type	Deep-V
Weight	18,400#	Deadrise Aft	19°

Cranchi 48/50 Atlantique

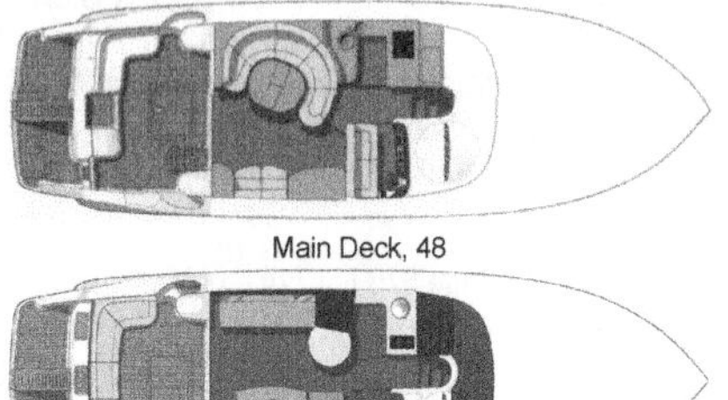

Main Deck, 48

Main Deck, 50

Cranchi's largest flybridge model, the 48 Atlantique reflects this company's reputation for quality engineering and attention to detail. Gracefully styled and projecting a classic Mediterranean profile, the Atlantique rides on a solid fiberglass deep-V hull with narrow beam and prop pockets to reduce draft. Her elegant three-stateroom floorplan is arranged with the owner's cabin at the bow and two guest staterooms aft, one with twin berths and the other with an angled double berth. On the main deck, the galley is forward in the salon, opposite the helm, which is elevated to improve visibility. A posh semicircular leather sofa dominates the salon, and the interior joinery is solid cherry, lacquered to a beautiful high-gloss finish. In the cockpit, an L-shaped settee in the corner provides comfortable seating, and a hatch in the teak sole opens to a huge lazarette large enough to be finished out as crew quarters. A bridge overhang shades most of the cockpit, and wide side decks lead to the bow and its foredeck sun pad. The engineroom, reached from either the salon or the cockpit, is unusually spacious for a European boat. Twin 480hp Volvo diesels cruise in the mid 20s; later models with 575hp Volvos are 2–3 knots faster.

Not Enough Resale Data to Set Values

Length Overall	51'7"	Fuel	402 gals.
Hull Length	49'4"	Water	148 gals.
Beam	14'2"	Waste	60 gals.
Draft	4'1"	Hull Type	Deep-V
Weight	38,582#	Deadrise Aft	18°

Crownline

Quick View

- Incorporated in 1990, Crownline began as a small family-owned builder of runabouts and cruisers based in Whittington, Illinois.
- Their first model, an 18-foot bow rider, came out early in 1991.
- By 1994 the Crownline fleet had grown to ten models, runabouts and family cruisers. By then the company had built over 10,000 boats since their 1991 start-up.
- By 1998 Crownline had grown to become the fifth largest builder of sterndrive sport boats in the world.
- In December of 2008, company management made the decision to seek strategic partners to operate Crownline and production is temporarily suspended.
- Crownline was purchased and reopened August, 2009 by Leisure Properties, LLC.

Crownline Boats • West Frankfort, IL • www.crownline.com

Crownline 262 CR

2001–04

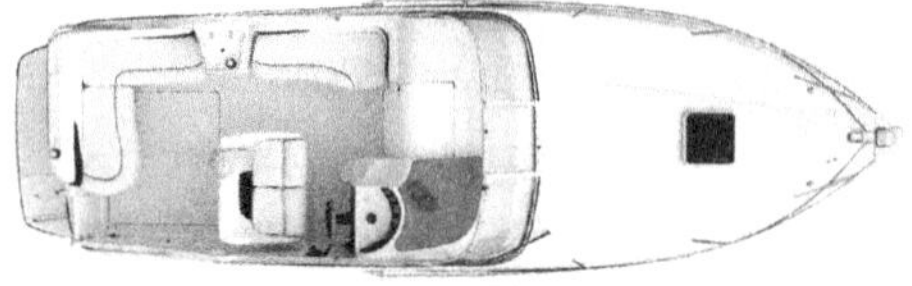

The Crownline 262 CR is a generic 26-foot family express made popular some years ago thanks to her practical layout and—perhaps more important—a very competitive price. Like most boats in her class, the 262 CR rides on a solid fiberglass modified-V hull with relatively high freeboard and a trailerable 8'6" beam. Her midcabin interior provides the amenities on expects in a big trailerable cruiser with berths for four, wraparound dinette, full-service galley with stove, microwave and refrigerator, and an enclosed head with sink. Note the Corian galley counter and pullout shower fixture in head. The 262's cockpit, with its bench seating aft, comfortable companion lounge, and double helm seat (with flip-up base) seems large for a 26-footer. Standard features include a cockpit table, woodgrain dash, cockpit shower, transom door, and wet bar with sink and storage. Engine access is excellent in those with a single engine, not so good with twin engines. On the downside, the 262's old-fashioned bolt-on swim platform detracts from her styling. Among several engine choices, a single 320hp MerCruiser Bravo III sterndrive will cruise in the low 20s (about 35 knots top).

See Page 675 For Price Data

Length	25'10"	Clearance	6'7"
Beam	8'6"	Fuel	99 gals.
Draft, Up	1'6"	Water	20 gals.
Draft, Down	2'8"	Hull Type	Modified-V
Weight	6,800#	Deadrise Aft	18°

Crownline 268 CR

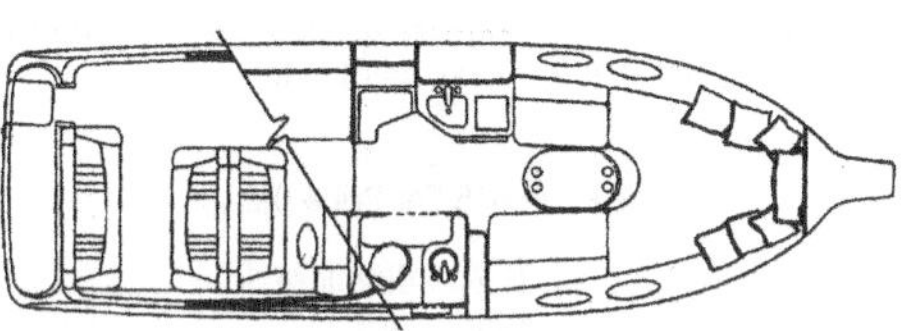

The trailerable Crownline 268 CR is basically an updated version of the earlier 250 CR (1993–96) with a new deck mold, an updated interior decor and a rearranged cockpit layout. While the 268 is a sleeker boat than her predecessor, she still suffers a little from the top-heavy appearance common to almost all small cruisers with standing cabin headroom. At 6,500 pounds, the 268 CR is no lightweight and she'll require a heavy-duty tow vehicle for over-the-road travel. Her midcabin interior includes a dinette/V-berth forward, a compact galley module, an enclosed head with shower, and four opening ports. On deck, there's seating for six in the cockpit, and a walk-through windshield with molded steps provides easy access to the bow. Note that the helm seat flips up to make a leaning post, and the aft cockpit seats can be removed to free up space. Additional features include a molded bow pulpit, recessed anchor locker, windshield vents, tilt steering, transom gate and recessed swim ladder. A single 5.7-liter MerCruiser gas engine (standard) will cruise the Crownline 268 at 20–21 knots, and an optional 7.4-liter Merc will cruise at 25 knots (35–36 knots top).

See Page 675 For Price Data

Length	26'8"	Clearance	6'11"
Beam	8'6"	Fuel	80 gals.
Draft, Up	2'0"	Water	20 gals.
Draft, Down	3'0"	Waste	17 gals.
Weight	7,100#	Hull Type	Deep-V

Crownline 270 CR

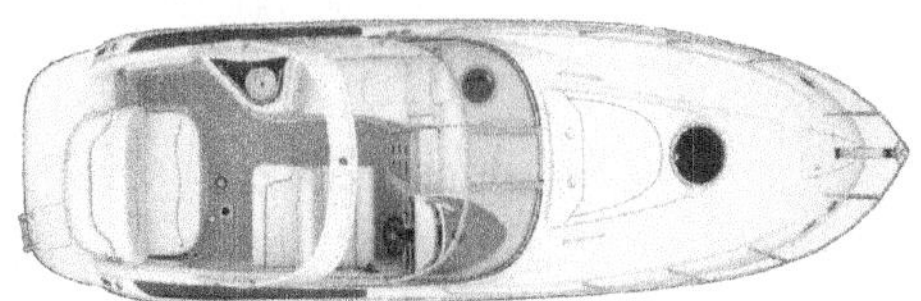

One of the largest trailerable sportcruisers available, the 270 CR offers the proven mix of performance and value typical of late-model Crownline boats. Big trailerable boats are notoriously over styled in an attempt to conceal their ungainly lines, but not so the 270 CR. Indeed, sleek styling is one of her more notable aspects (although no one is likely to confuse her for a pure-bred European sportboat). Built on a stable modified-V hull, the midcabin interior of the Crownline 270 CR includes a convertible V-berth/dinette forward, a compact galley, standup head with sink and shower, and a sizable aft cabin. Corian counters and cherry woodwork highlight the decor, and four opening ports provide adequate ventilation. In the cockpit, a wet bar is standard and the stern lounge seat—which lifts electrically for engine access—folds down to form a comfortable sun pad. Additional features include a double helm seat with flip-up bolsters, cockpit wet bar with removable cooler, snap-in cockpit carpet, and extended swim platform. A single 300hp Volvo sterndrive will cruise in the low 20s and reach a top speed of around 35 knots.

See Page675 For Price Data

Length w/Platform	28'8"	Fuel	75 gals.
Beam	8'6"	Water	25 gals.
Draft, Up	1'9"	Waste	25 gals.
Draft, Down	2'10"	Hull Type	Modified-V
Weight	7,400#	Deadrise Aft	18°

Crownline 290 CR

The affordably priced Crownline 290 CR may not win any beauty awards with her high-freeboard profile, but she has a lot to offer when it comes to cabin and cockpit accommodations. Built on a beamy modified-V hull of solid fiberglass construction, the mid-cabin floorplan of the 290 CR was originally arranged with a canted forward berth coupled with an L-shaped dinette/lounge across from the galley and a spacious head compartment. The layout was updated in 2001 with a large U-shaped dinette/double berth forward. Privacy curtains separate the sleeping areas from the main cabin, and four opening ports and three deck hatches allow for plenty of cabin ventilation. The cockpit can accommodate as many as six. The seat bottom of the doublewide helm seat flips up to create a leaning post, and a molded cockpit galley/wet bar faces the U-shaped lounge. Additional features include built-in fender storage at the transom, a walk-through windshield, removable rear bench seat, and recessed anchor storage at the bow. From a wide choice of sterndrive engine options, a pair of 250hp MerCruiser I/Os cruise the 290 CR at 22–24 knots (35+ top).

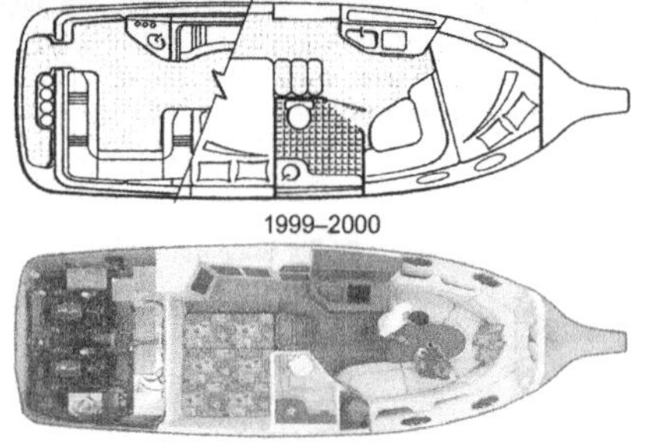
1999–2000

2001–04

See Page 675 For Price Data

Length w/Pulpit	31'2"	Clearance	8'6"
Hull Length	28'11"	Fuel	146 gals.
Beam	10'4"	Water	20 gals.
Draft, Down	2'11"	Hull Type	Modified-V
Weight	9,000#	Deadrise Aft	16°

Crownline 330 CR

The Crownline 330 CR is a modern midcabin express from a company best known for its popular series of bowriders and runabouts. Built on a conventional modified-V hull with moderate beam and transom deadrise, she was yet another entry in the highly competitive family cruiser market dominated by Bayliner, Cruisers and Sea Ray. The interior of the Crownline 330 seems surprisingly open and spacious—a visual reaction to the absence of a forward stateroom bulkhead and the cabin's extraordinary headroom. Curtains separate both sleeping areas from the salon, and the large U-shaped settee and long galley combine with some excellent fit and finish to make this a very comfortable and notably upscale interior. On deck, there's seating for seven in the cockpit along with a built-in wet bar and removable dinette. Additional features include an electrically operated engine hatch, a vented windshield with a centerline walk-through for bow access, and a separate bolt-on stern platform wide enough to handle a PWC. Standard 260hp MerCruiser sterndrives cruise at 17–18 knots and reach top speeds in excess of 30 knots. Optional 310hp Mercs cruise at 24–25 knots (about 40 knots top).

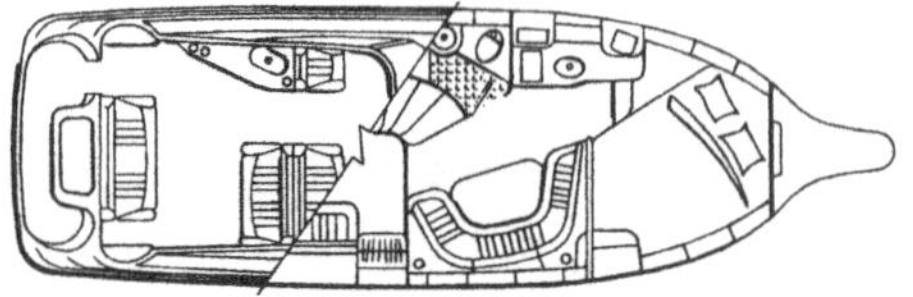

See Page 675 For Price Data

Length w/Pulpit	33'7"	Fuel	225 gals.
Beam	11'7"	Water	51 gals.
Draft, Up	1'5"	Waste	30 gals.
Draft, Down	2'11"	Hull Type	Modified-V
Weight	13,800#	Deadrise Aft	16°

Crownline 340/350 CR

Floorplan Not Available

Those who make it their business to know boats generally agree that Crownline builds a lot of boat for the money. The 340 CR (called the 350 CR beginning in 2010) meets that description well. No lightweight, she rides on a solid fiberglass modified-V hull with moderate beam and a sporty reverse transom. Unlike most boats in her class, a fiberglass hardtop is standard—an expensive extra not always available with some competitive models. Guests will enjoy the sun on the patio-sized aft cockpit or on the convertible aft bench at the transom. Below, the spacious (and well appointed) interior features a convertible settee to starboard, full-service galley with cherry cabinets to port, enclosed head with wall-mounted shower, and a centerline queen berth forward with privacy curtain. A 26" flat-screen TV is built into the aft salon bulkhead, and a large U-shaped lounge in the midcabin area converts into an adult-size double berth. Note the solid hardwood flooring throughout the cabin. Topside features include a deluxe cockpit wet bar with refrigerator, standard anchor windlass, and a transom storage locker. The teak inlaid swim platform is a nice touch. Cruise at 24–26 knots with MerCruiser 300hp Axius stern drives (optional).

See Page 675 For Price Data

Length w/Pulpit	36'0"	Fuel	193 gals.
Beam	11'10"	Water	38 gals.
Draft, Up	2'7"	Waste	30 gals.
Draft, Down	3'5"	Hull Type	Modified-V
Weight	16,300#	Deadrise Aft	18°

Cruisers

Quick View

- Cruisers, Inc. began operations in 1953 and became known around the western Great Lakes for its wood lapstrake runabouts and cruisers.
- By 1961, 300 employees worked at Cruiser's Oconto, WI, facility during peak season.
- The company began the transition to fiberglass production in 1965 and wooden boats were eliminated from the line by the end of 1966.
- In 1972 Cruisers was purchased by Mirro Marine. In 1982 Cruisers was sold to private interests, and in 1993 the company was purchased by its current owner, KCS International.
- Cruisers endured its share of financial difficulties in the early 1990s thanks to the downturn in the U.S. economy and the ill-fated 10 percent luxury tax of 1991–93.
- By the mid 1990s Cruisers returned to full production with a series of all-new family cruiser and motor yacht models as well as an expanded network of dealers.
- Cruisers Yachts has long been recognized by marine industry professionals for producing affordably priced, well-engineered motoryachts and family cruisers.

Cruisers Yachts • Oconto, WI • www.cruisersyachts.com

Cruisers 2870 Express; 280 CXi

1998–2007

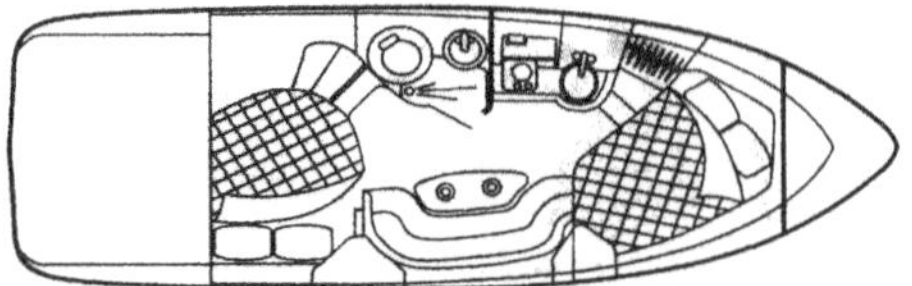

The Cruisers 280 Express (called the 2870 Express in 1998–2003) is a modern midcabin design whose appealing lines and practical layout made her a popular model for Cruisers during her production years. A fairly heavy boat at 10,000 pounds, she's built on a stable modified-V hull with a wide beam and moderate transom deadrise. Like most midcabin boats her size, the floorplan of the 280 is very open and airy with curtains (rather than bulkheads) separating the fore and aft sleeping areas from the main salon. The dinette converts into a double berth suitable for kids, and while the galley is small, it's nonetheless suitable for basic food-prep activities. The topside layout incorporates a doublewide helm seat, fore- and aft-facing cockpit settees, and a walk-through windshield with molded-in steps for easy foredeck access. Space at the helm for electronic add-ons is limited. Additional features include a removable cockpit table, sport arch, transom door and swim platform. Among several gas and diesel engine choices, a single 375hp MerCruiser will cruise the 2870 Express at 22–23 knots, and twin 225hp Volvo I/Os cruise in the mid 20s and reach a top speed of 35+ knots.

See Page 676 For Price Data

Length w/Platform	31'0"	Fuel	100 gals.
Hull Length	28'6"	Water	25 gals.
Beam	10'0"	Waste	20 gals.
Draft, Down	2'11"	Hull Type	Modified-V
Weight	10,000#	Deadrise Aft	16°

Cruisers 2870 Rogue

Introduced in 1990 as the 2870 Holiday, called the 2870 Rogue in 1991–94, and ending production in 1995 at the 2970 Rogue, this generic midcabin cruiser was a relatively popular model for Cruisers thanks to her comfortable layout and an affordable price. Like most boats of her type, the Rogue rides on a conventional modified-V hull with moderate beam and solid fiberglass construction. The floorplan is arranged with a convertible dinette/double berth forward, a configuration that leaves room for a larger galley than a boat this size might otherwise contain. Privacy curtains separate the sleeping areas from the main cabin, and sliding cabin windows and two overhead hatches provide ventilation. Topside, the cockpit can seat eight and includes a wet bar and a fold-down jump seat hidden in the back of the dual helm seat. There's a sun pad for the foredeck, but getting there is difficult since there are practically no side decks to speak of. A radar arch was a popular option, and a transom door and bow pulpit were standard. Among several engine options, twin 245hp Volvo sterndrives will provide a cruising speed of 24 knots and a top speed of 36 knots.

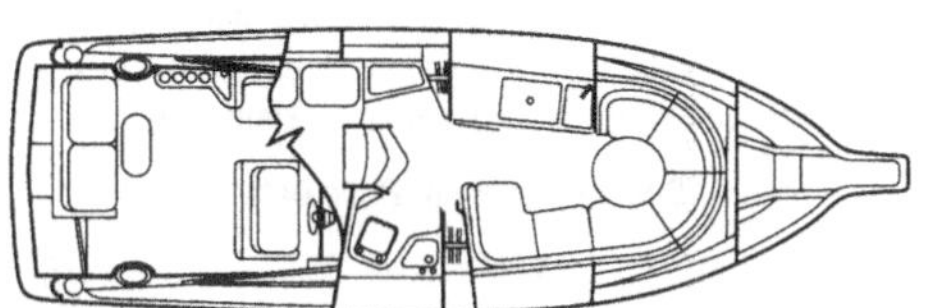

See Page 676 For Price Data

Length w/Pulpit	28'8"	Clearance	8'8"
Hull Length	26'0"	Fuel	120 gals.
Beam	9'6"	Water	30 gals.
Draft	3'2"	Hull Type	Modified-V
Weight	7,800#	Deadrise Aft	NA

Cruisers 300 CXi; 300/310 Express

The market for 30-foot express boats is extremely competitive. It's been that way for years with every major manufacturer offering his version of the perfect 30-foot family cruiser. The Cruisers 310 Express (called 300 CXi in 2007–08; 300 Express in 2009–11; 310 Express since 2012) delivers all the essentials buyers expect in a boat this size without breaking the bank. While no one would call her plain, Cruisers' no-frills approach to this boat preserves the builder's reputation for quality while still keeping the price below most competitive models. Built on a traditional modified-V hull with a 10-foot beam, her open-plan interior—with its wraparound rear seating, full-service galley, and crescent-shaped dinette—is a model of space-efficient design. The mid-settee in the salon easily converts into a double berth for guests, and there's sufficient galley storage for an extended weekend cruise. Topside, the user-friendly cockpit includes a double helm seat, companion lounge, facing rear seats, cockpit tables, removable 25-quart cooler, wet bar and sun lounge—very complete accommodations for a boat this size. Cruise efficiently at 25 knots with twin 225hp Volvo V-6 stern drives (low 30s top).

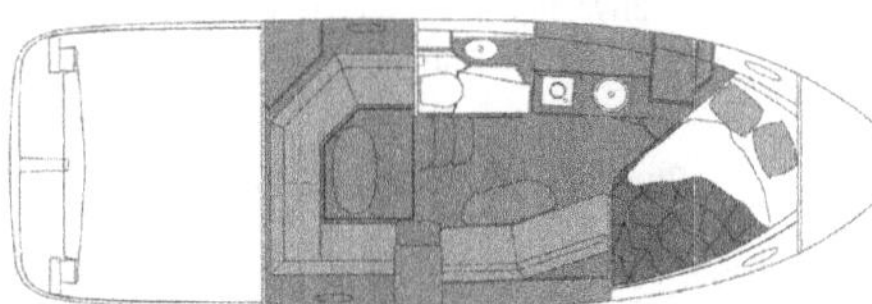

See Page 676 For Price Data

Length	31'3"	Fuel	125 gals.
Beam	10'0"	Water	30 gals.
Draft, Up	2'0"	Waste	23 gals.
Draft, Down	3'0"	Hull Type	Modified-V
Weight	10,300#	Deadrise Aft	16°

Cruisers 300 Express

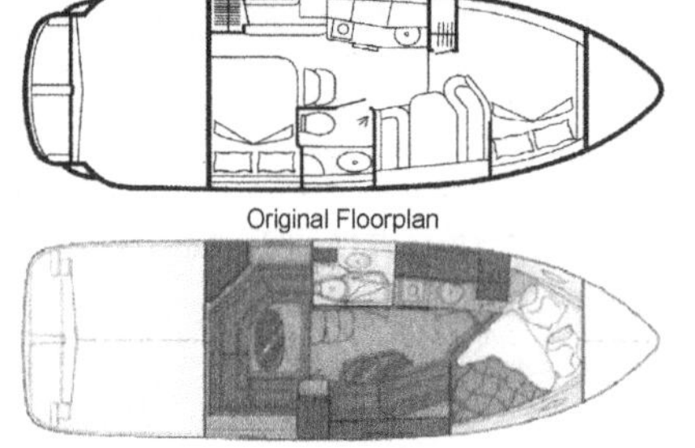
Original Floorplan

2007 Floorplan

Modern styling, roomy accommodations, and a good turn of speed combine to make the Cruisers 300 Express (called the 310 Express in 2007) competitive with the better boats in her class. A forward-facing arch is her most distinctive feature, but there's more to this boat than just a pretty face. Aside from her solid construction, the 300 Express boasts two generous sleeping areas below along with a large galley and a head/shower with full standing headroom. Privacy curtains separate the fore and aft berths from the main salon, and a blend of cherry joinery and attractive fabrics give the interior of the Cruisers 300 an upscale and very classy appearance. The cockpit is arranged with a crescent-shaped settee opposite the helm, a wet bar with removable cooler, and a comfortable transom seat. Molded steps provide easy access to the walk-through windshield, and fender storage bags snap into the concealed windlass compartment. Note that the radar arch houses cockpit lights and stereo speakers. Standard features include trim tabs, power steering, cockpit carpeting, remote-controlled spotlight, air conditioning, and a deep swim platform. Cruise at 30 knots with Volvo 320hp gas I/Os (about 40 knots top).

See Page 676 For Price Data

Length	32'3"	Fuel	150 gals.
Beam	10'6"	Water	30 gals.
Draft, Drives Up	21"	Waste	25 gals.
Draft, Drives Down	36"	Hull Type	Modified-V
Weight	11,500#	Deadrise Aft	18°

Cruisers 3075 Express

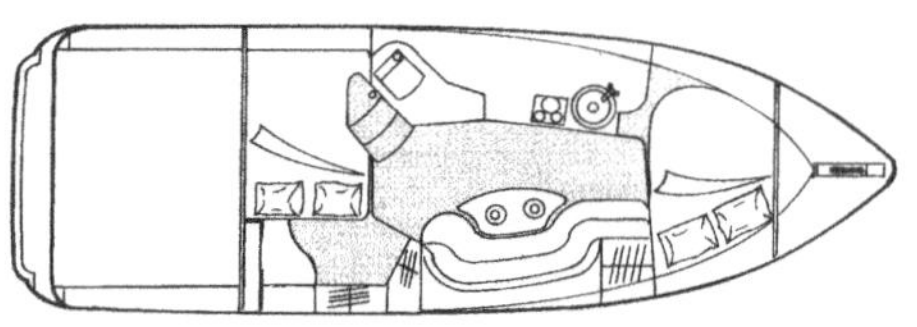

A good-looking boat with sweeping lines to mask her relatively high freeboard, the 3075 Express combines the modern styling and upscale amenities common to all late-model Cruisers yachts. Like most family cruisers, she comes with a conventional midcabin floorplan with double berths fore and aft, a small galley, and a convertible dinette. The head compartment, conveniently located to port just down from the companionway steps, is quite spacious—always a pleasant surprise in a boat this size. The primary layout for the 3075 Express features a fixed double berth aft, but owners may select an alternate layout that includes an aft settee that converts to a sleeper. Topsides, there's a doublewide seat at the helm, and molded steps next to the helm provide access via the walk-through windshield to the foredeck. A U-shaped settee at the stern converts into a big sun pad. Additional features include a cleverly designed integrated anchor platform, good engine access, and a well-arranged helm with comfortable seating. Among several sterndrive or V-drive engine options, twin 260hp MerCruisers cruise the 3075 Express at 20 knots and reach a top speed in the low-to-mid 30s.

See Page 676 For Price Data

Length w/Pulpit	33'4"	Fuel	150 gals.
Hull Length	32'1"	Water	30 gals.
Beam	10'4"	Headroom	6'3"
Draft, Down	2'9"	Hull Type	Modified-V
Weight	9,500#	Deadrise Aft	16°

Cruisers 3020/3120 Aria

1992–97

Sharing the same fully cored hull as the 3070 Rogue (1990–94), the 3120 Aria—called the 3020 Aria from 1992–94—stands out from other 30-foot express cruisers for her enormous cockpit. Indeed, about two-thirds of her overall hull length is devoted to cockpit space, resulting in a superb day boat with room for a party-size gathering. The entire stern section of the cockpit is lined with seating that folds away and disappears in the inwales. With all of the seat sections deployed, the cockpit becomes a giant sun lounge. A wet bar/galley is located in the cockpit where it's easily accessed by guests and crew. Note that a huge storage bin is located beneath the cockpit floor. Belowdecks, the Aria's compact interior features a convertible dinette/V-berth forward, storage compartments, mini-galley with sink and stove, and an enclosed head with vanity and sit-down shower. A midcabin berth was optional beneath the helm; otherwise that space is used for storage. An anchor roller, dockside water inlet, shore power and trim tabs were standard. Among several engine options, twin 260hp sterndrives cruise at 21 knots (35 top), and optional 350hp engines cruise at 25 knots (about 40 knots wide open).

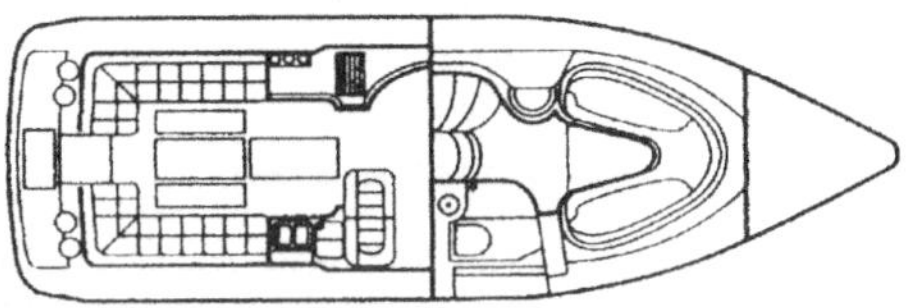

See Page 676 For Price Data

Length w/Pulpit	30'8"	Weight	8,800#
Hull Length	28'8"	Fuel	200 gals.
Beam	10'6"	Water	32 gals.
Draft, Down	3'0"	Hull Type	Deep-V
Draft, Up	2'1"	Deadrise Aft	20°

Cruisers 3175 Rogue

1995–98

Introduced in 1995, the Cruisers 3175 is a generic midcabin cruiser with twin-sterndrive power and the Euro styling features typical of many late-1990s family express boats. (Note the unique shape of the bow pulpit makes it seem like an extension of the foredeck.) Built on a deep-V hull with balsa coring in the hullsides, the interior of the 3175 is remarkably open for a 31-footer with plenty of natural lighting thanks to three overhead hatches. The floorplan is arranged with a convertible dinette/V-berth forward, a compact galley to port, a roomy head compartment with a separate stall shower, and another double berth aft. A privacy curtain separates the midcabin area from the salon, and cabin headroom is a full 6-feet, 3-inches in the galley. Topsides, visibility from the elevated helm position is excellent. Additional features include a walk-through windshield, foredeck sun pad, cockpit wet bar, dockside water inlet, trim tabs, and wraparound lounge seating in the cockpit. A radar arch was a popular option. Among several engine choices, twin 245hp/5.7-liter Volvo sterndrives cruise the Cruisers 3175 Rogue at 23 knots and reach a top speed of 38–39 knots.

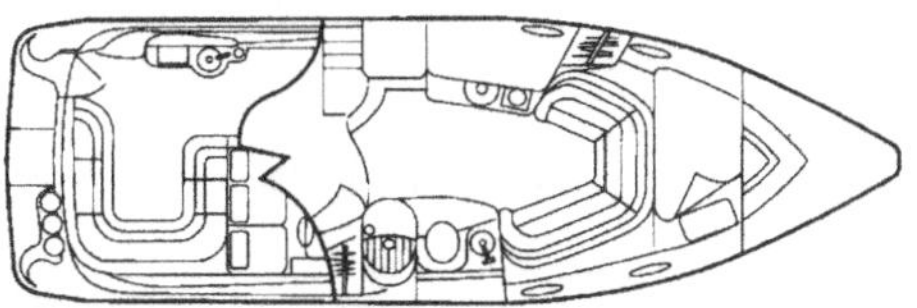

See Page 676 For Price Data

Length w/Pulpit	32'8"	Weight	9,300#
Hull Length	30'8"	Fuel	163 gals.
Beam	10'6"	Water	32 gals.
Draft, Up	2'1"	Hull Type	Deep-V
Draft, Down	3'0"	Deadrise Aft	20°

Cruisers 320 Express

Given the great number of mid-range express boats to choose from in today's market it's often difficult to distinguish one from another. So it is with the Cruisers 320 Express (called the 3275 Express in 2002–03); she doesn't set any new standards in comfort or performance and the styling is conservative at best, but there is a good deal of value here for those seeking a well-bred family boat at a reasonable price. Built on a conventional modified-V hull with an integral swim platform, the floorplan of the 320 is arranged with a convertible settee in the aft lounge area, which is very open to the salon—a notable contrast to many midcabin boats this size with cramped, cave-like aft cabins. Curtains separate the fore and aft sleeping areas from the salon, and cabin headroom—about 6 feet, 4 inches—is excellent. Topside, a windshield walk-through provides access to the bow. The anchor is deployed through a chute, and a double sun pad with a molded headrest is fitted on the foredeck. For engine access, the aft cockpit deck swings up on a pair of rams to expose the motors. Among several engine options, twin 320hp MerCruiser I/Os cruise the 320 Express at 20 knots and top out in the mid 30s.

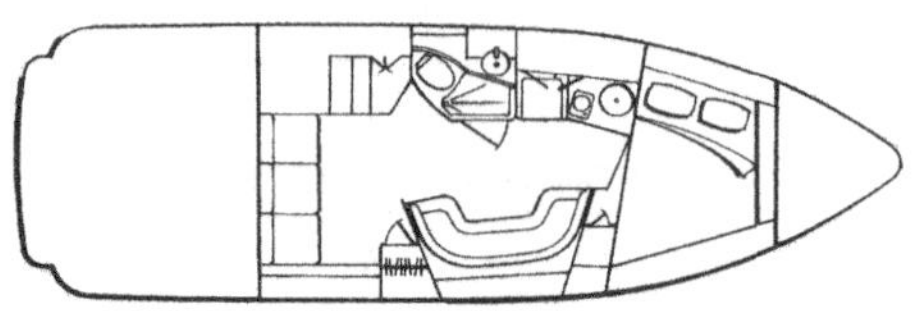

See Page 676 For Price Data

Length w/Platform	35'9"	Fuel	200 gals.
Beam	11'3"	Water	40 gals.
Draft, Up	2'0"	Waste	30 gals.
Draft, Down	2'11"	Hull Type	Modified-V
Weight	13,500#	Deadrise Aft	16°

Cruisers 3375 Esprit

Introduced in 1996, the Cruisers 3375 Esprit offered buyers a roomy 33-foot family express with a comfortable layout and a choice of sterndrive or inboard power. The Esprit is not radically different from other boats in her class—the styling is typical of a 1990s-era cruiser, and her traditional midcabin floorplan might best be described as generic. Built on a modified-V hull with balsa coring in the hullsides and bottom, a wide 11-foot, 8-inch beam allows for a spacious interior with a wide-open salon and berths for six. Privacy curtains separate the fore and aft sleeping areas from the main cabin, and while the galley is compact in size, the spacious head features a separate stall shower. Topside, the Esprit's bi-level cockpit seats six and includes a double helm seat, wet bar, and wraparound aft seating which converts into a large sun pad. Additional features include an extended swim platform, radar arch, cockpit shower, trim tabs and a transom door. Twin 260hp MerCruiser I/Os cruise the 3375 Esprit at 25 knots (about 35 knots top), while a pair of 320hp V-drive gas inboards cruise in the low 20s and reach just over 30 knots wide open.

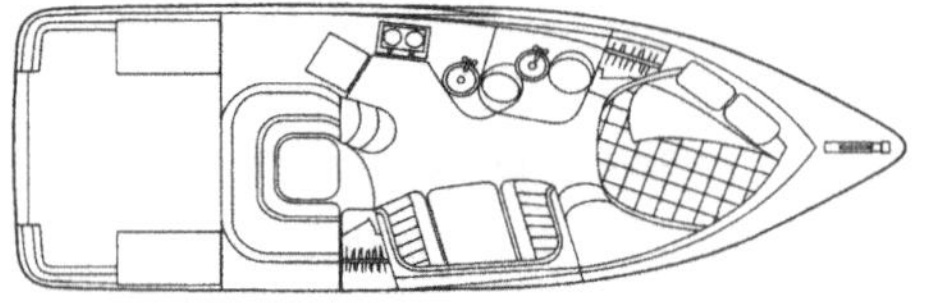

See Page 676 For Price Data

Length	35'6"	Fuel	240 gals.
Beam	11'8"	Water	50 gals.
Draft	3'0"	Waste	30 gals.
Weight	12,500#	Hull Type	Modified-V
Clearance	9'3"	Deadrise Aft	16°

Cruisers 330/350 Express

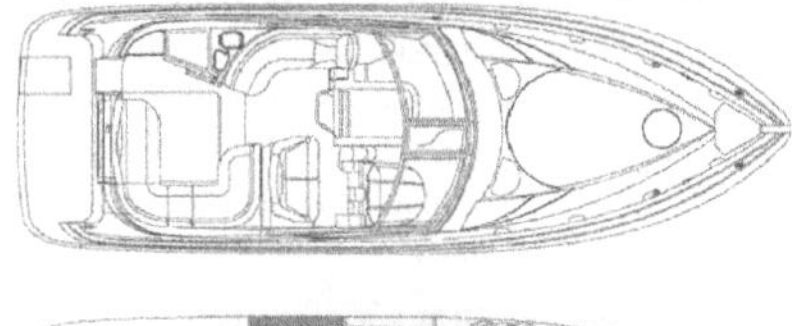

Among the better-looking boats in her class, the Cruisers 330 Express (called the 350 Express since 2011) combines modern sportboat styling with luxury-class accommodations. Indeed, this is a good example of why Cruisers Yachts continues to be a major player in the express cruiser market. The 330/350 doesn't just look good; she utilizes space as well (maybe better) than any builder in the business. Her open-plan interior is flooded with natural light, making the area feel even more spacious than it already is. With its hardwood cherry trim, faux granite counters, and six vertical portholes the accommodations are impressive for a boat this size. The U-shaped lounge aft in the salon makes a convenient place for eating or lounging and includes a spacious bookshelf and storage. Note the cushioned master berth headboard forward, and space-saving rectangular dinette. The cockpit, in addition to a deluxe wet bar and double helm seat, includes a wraparound lounge aft that converts into a big transom sun pad. Early models with Volvo 375hp V-drive gas inboards cruise at 25 knots (low 30s top). Volvo 375hp sterndrives with joystick controls became available in 2011 (30 knots cruise/40 top).

See Page 676 For Price Data

Length	35'6"	Fuel	232 gals.
Beam	11'8"	Water	40 gals.
Draft, Up	2'10"	Waste	30 gals.
Draft, Down	3'8"	Hull Type	Modified-V
Clearance	10'1"	Deadrise Aft	16°

Cruisers 3470 Express; 340 Express

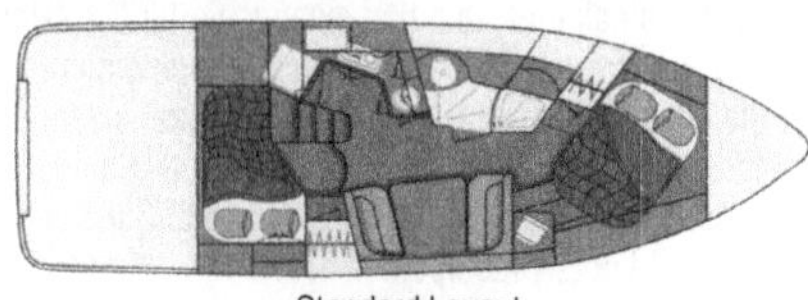
Standard Layout

Alternate Layout

Cruisers has been a strong contender in the family express market for years and the company can always be counted on to deliver a good-quality product at a competitive price. There's nothing revolutionary about the 340 Express (called the 3470 Express in 2001–03)—she's a straightforward midcabin cruiser with contemporary styling, modern construction and upscale accommodations. Indeed, the plush interior is unusually spacious for a 34-footer, and the layout is both open and inviting. Two floorplans are offered, one with a fixed berth amidships and a dinette with facing seats, and an optional arrangement with a convertible settee in the midcabin and a U-shaped dinette. Privacy curtains separate both sleeping areas from the main cabin, and the head includes a separate stall shower. Additional features include a fully cored hull, cockpit wet bar, transom door, gas-assist engine compartment hatch, foredeck sun pad and a cockpit table. Offered with inboard or sterndrive power, twin 370hp MerCruiser V-drive inboards cruise the 340 Express in the mid 20s (30+ knots top), and 375hp MerCruiser Bravo III sterndrives will top out in the high 30s.

See Page 676 For Price Data

Length	36'6"	Fuel	232 gals.
Beam	11'8"	Water	40 gals.
Draft	3'0"	Waste	30 gals.
Weight, Gas	15,500#	Hull Type	Modified-V
Weight, Diesel	16,500#	Deadrise Aft	16°

Cruisers 3570/3575 Esprit; 3572 Express

1995–2002

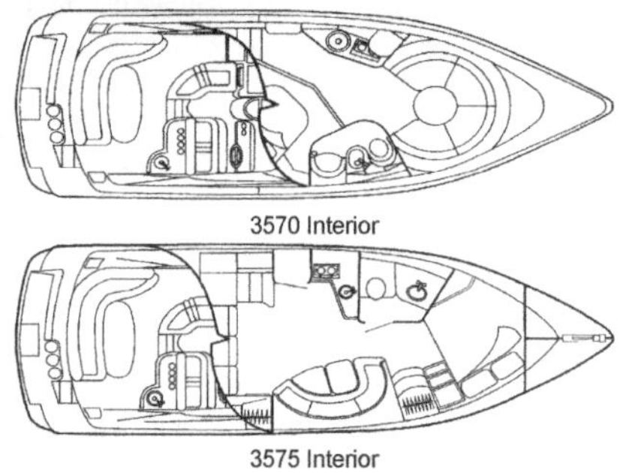
3570 Interior

3575 Interior

Innovation is an abused term in the marine industry where minor improvements are often touted as major breakthroughs. In the case of the 3570 and 3575 Esprits (same boat, different interiors), Cruisers took a design approach that gave buyers a choice of two dramatically different floorplans in the same express-boat package. The interior of the 3570 Esprit features a very unique amidships master stateroom with a queen-size berth and over 6 feet of headroom that can be closed off from the salon for privacy. A circular dinette/double berth is forward in this floorplan, and while the salon of the 3570 seems a bit compact for a 35-foot boat, the aft-stateroom configuration is innovative indeed. Interesting as this floorplan was, Cruisers introduced an alternate arrangement in 1996—the 3575 model—with a more traditional midcabin floorplan similar to most other express cruisers. Topside, the cockpit seating of the 3570/3575 is equally distinctive with elevated bridge deck seating forward and L-shaped seating at the transom. Built on a fully cored hull with prop pockets, twin V-drive 320hp MerCruisers cruise the 3570/3575 Esprit at 18 knots and reach a top speed in the neighborhood of 30 knots.

See Page 676 For Price Data

Length	39'3"	Fuel	300 gals.
Beam	13'0"	Water	70 gals.
Draft	3'5"	Waste	50 gals.
Weight	16,000#	Hull Type	Modified-V
Clearance, Arch	10'10"	Deadrise Aft	17°

Cruisers 3580/3585 Flybridge

1996–99

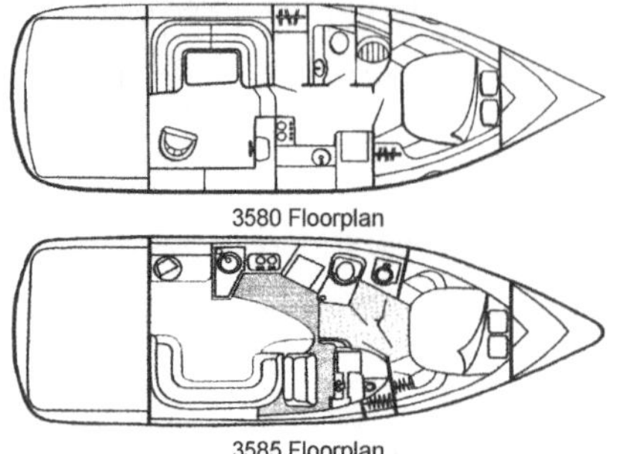
3580 Floorplan

3585 Floorplan

A stylish boat in her day with a rakish profile, the Cruisers 3580/3585 (same boat, different floorplans) was one of the first flybridge yachts to replace the traditional cockpit ladder with molded flybridge steps—a feature now common to most modern flybridge cruisers. This was, back in the mid 1990s, an innovative design in a boat of this type, and while molded steps eat up some valuable cockpit space, there's no disputing the fact that they make bridge access a whole lot more civilized. Built on a conventional modified-V hull with cored hullsides and prop pockets to reduce shaft angles, the original 3580 interior has the galley down with an optional lower helm (with poor outside visibility), while the newer 3585 floorplan introduced in 1998 has an elevated lower helm as standard with the galley forward in the salon. Both floorplans are arranged with a small midcabin that extends under the salon. Note that the side decks are quite narrow and the engine compartment, beneath the cockpit sole, is a tight fit. An optional extended swim platform is wide enough for a personal watercraft. Standard 7.4-liter V-drive gas inboards cruise the Cruisers 3580/3585 at 18 knots and reach 26–27 knots wide open.

See Page 676 For Price Data

Length Overall	39'3"	Fuel	300 gals.
Hull Length	37'4"	Water	70 gals.
Beam	13'0"	Waste	40 gals.
Draft	3'5"	Hull Type	Modified-V
Weight	18,200#	Deadrise Aft	16°

Cruisers 360/380 Express

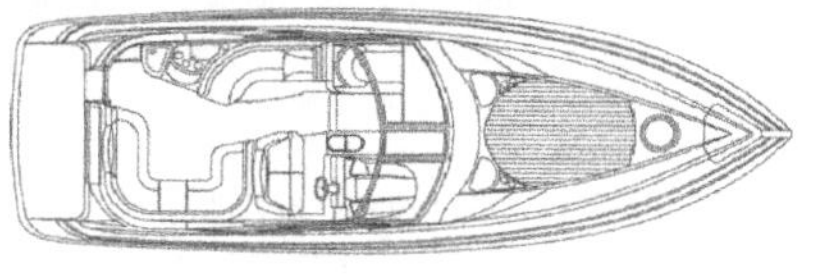

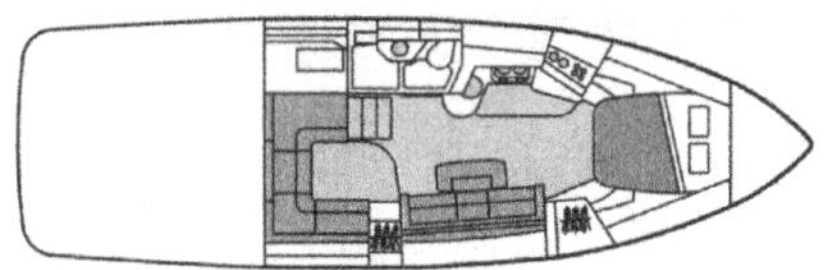

Even in a down economy when other builders are cutting back, Cruisers Yachts continues to offer innovative boats with cutting-edge styling and luxury-class features. Introduced in 2008 as the 360 Express (and called the 380 Express beginning in 2012), this richly appointed family cruiser is agile, roomy, and extremely well finished. As one expects in a boat this size, the feature list is long. Her impressively stylish, full-width salon includes a spacious galley with faux-granite countertop, forward stateroom with privacy curtain, and a U-shaped rear lounge (with table and storage) that easily converts into a double berth for guests. The head has a separate shower stall and features a countertop with Venetian-style tile backsplash. Note the cushioned master berth headboard, built-in entertainment center, and space-saving rectangular dinette. The Cruiser's roomy, guest-friendly cockpit includes a doublewide helm seat, portside chaise lounge, and circular rear settee that convert into a large sun pad. The fiberglass hardtop is standard. Early models with Volvo 375hp V-drive gas inboards cruise at 24–25 knots (30+ top). Later models with Volvo 375hp IPS pod drives run a few knots faster with better fuel efficiency.

See Page 676 For Price Data

Length	38'0"	Fuel	300 gals.
Beam	12'6"	Water	64 gals.
Draft, V-Drive	3'0"	Waste	40 gals.
Draft, I/O	3'5"	Hull Type	Modified-V
Clearance, Hardtop	11'0"	Deadrise Aft	16°

Cruisers 3670 Esprit; 3675/3775 Esprit

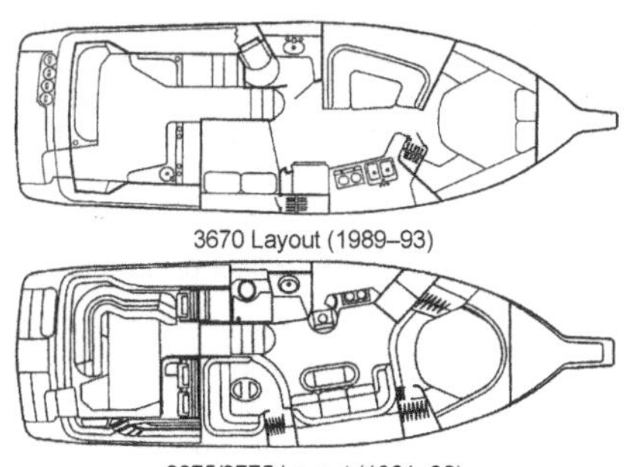
3670 Layout (1989–93)

3675/3775 Layout (1991–96)

The Cruisers 3670 and 3675 are pretty much the same boat on the outside but with different mid-cabin floorplans and cockpit arrangements. The 3670 came first in 1989 followed two years later by the 3675 (renamed the 3775 in 1995). Of the two, the 3670/3775 proved the more popular with production lasted a few years longer than the original 3670. Both were built on the same modified-V hull with prop pockets and a relatively steep 17 degrees of deadrise at the transom. Below decks, the 3670 has a U-shaped dinette to port and a walkaround double berth forward. The 3675/3775, on the other hand, had two floorplans: the first (diagram not available) was a very open arrangement with no dinette and an offset berth in the forward stateroom, while the later layout (below) brought back a small dinette as well as a centerline double berth. Where the cockpit in the 3670 has a bench seat at the transom, the 3675/3775 has wraparound lounge seating. Both came with a stainless steel arch, a cockpit wet bar, transom door, and a wide swim platform with a hidden boarding ladder and fender racks. Among several V-drive engine options, twin big-block gas engines cruise at 19 knots and reach a top speed of 29–30 knots.

See Page 676 For Price Data

Length Overall	39'5"	Weight, Diesel	17,500#
Hull Length	35'3"	Fuel	300 gals.
Beam	13'0"	Water	93 gals.
Draft	3'5"	Hull Type	Modified-V
Weight, Gas	16,400#	Deadrise Aft	17°

Cruisers 3672/3772/370 Express

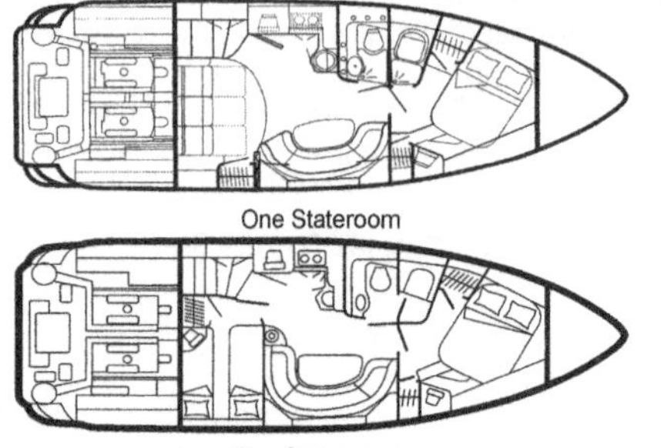

One Stateroom

Two Staterooms

With her tall freeboard and sleek appearance, the 370 Express (called the 3672 Express in 2000–02; 3772 Express in 2003) conveys the impression of being a bigger boat than her 36-foot hull length suggests. Built on a cored modified-V hull with prop pockets and an integrated swim platform, she offers a choice of cabin layouts—a rarity in production express boats these days. A very spacious single-stateroom floorplan has an aft sleeper-sofa in the salon, and an optional midcabin floorplan has a small stateroom aft with a full bulkhead and privacy door. What makes these layouts so comfortable is the single-level salon sole; in most other midcabin designs, the settee/aft berth area is a step down from the salon floor. Both interiors are tastefully finished with cherry woodwork and joinery, and both are unusually spacious thanks to the 370's wide beam. Additional features include a walk-through windshield (the side decks are very narrow), a stall shower in the head, excellent engine access, and a cockpit wet bar. Twin 370hp V-drive Crusader inboards cruise at 16 knots (around 28 knots top), and newer models with the 385hp Crusaders will run a couple of knots faster. Optional 370hp Cummins diesels cruise in the low 20s.

See Page 676 For Price Data

Length	40'2"	Fuel	300 gals.
Beam	13'0"	Water	70 gals.
Draft	3'0"	Waste	55 gals.
Weight, Gas	18,000#	Hull Type	Modified-V
Weight, Diesel	19,000#	Deadrise Aft	16°

Cruisers 3650/3750 Motor Yacht; 375 MY

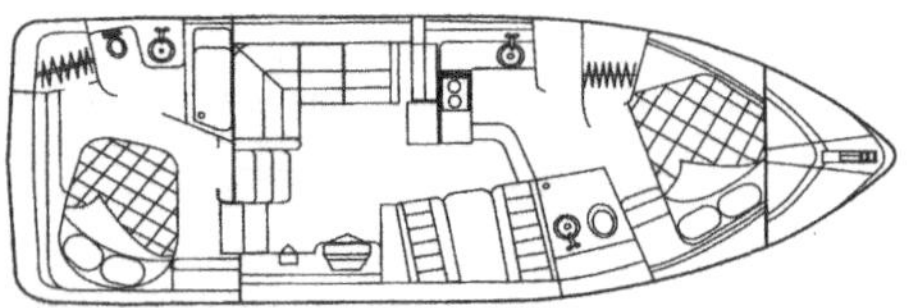

The Cruisers 3650/3750 Motor Yacht (called the 3650 MY in 1995–99; 3750 MY in 2000–03; 375 MY in 2004–05) is a contemporary aft-cabin cruiser with rakish lines and a surprisingly spacious interior. Indeed, Cruisers engineers were able to deliver the accommodations of a 40-footer in the 3650 including queen beds in both staterooms, a full dinette and galley, and a tub in the aft head compartment. This is a completely open layout with plenty of natural lighting, plenty of headroom and a very pleasant cherrywood decor. Expansive as this floorplan is, the staterooms are both on the small side and hanging locker space is limited. Topside, there's sufficient space on small aft deck for several pieces of outdoor furniture, and a big U-shaped lounge on the flybridge provides seating for five or six guests across from the helm. Despite the spacious interior, the side decks are still wide enough for secure access to the bow, and molded-in steps (instead of a ladder) make boarding from the stern platform an easy matter. In 1999 this boat was updated with improved wing doors and fiberglass weatherboards enclosing the aft deck. MerCruiser 310hp (or 370hp) gas inboards cruise at 16–18 knots (low-to-mid 20s top).

See Page 676 For Price Data

Length	40'10"	Fuel	300 gals.
Beam	13'8"	Water	68 gals.
Draft	3'2"	Waste	55 gals.
Weight, Gas	20,000#	Hull Type	Modified-V
Weight, Diesel	21,500#	Deadrise Aft	11°

Cruisers 3870 Express

The sleek lines of the Cruisers 3870 Express (called the 3870 Esprit in 1998–99) masks one of the more innovative interiors seen in a boat of this type. A scaled-down version of the company's 4270 Esprit (1998–2003), what's notable about the floorplan of the 3870 is her unique amidships stateroom with its standup dressing area, built-in TV, and a private head with shower. The wide-open salon includes a convertible sofa/dinette and a full-service galley with all the amenities. A draw curtain separates the forward island berth from the main cabin, while a bulkhead door insures privacy in the aft stateroom. Notably, the main head contains a separate stall shower. Topside accommodations include an L-shaped lounge opposite the helm, a U-shaped seating area aft, and a built-in wet bar to port. A hatch in the cockpit sole provides access to a rather compact engine compartment, and the deep swim platform is designed to support a personal watercraft. Early models with twin 310hp MerCruiser 7.4-liter gas engines (with V-drives) will cruise at 18 knots (mid-to-high 20s top), and more recent models with the 370hp MerCruiser inboards will top out at around 30 knots.

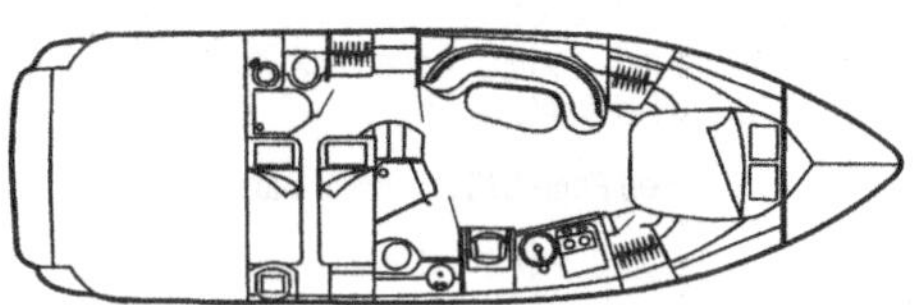

See Page 676 For Price Data

Length Overall	43'3"	Fuel	300 gals.
Hull Length	40'8"	Water	75 gals.
Beam	13'6"	Waste	50 gals.
Draft	3'0"	Hull Type	Modified-V
Weight	19,500#	Deadrise Aft	16°

Cruisers 385/395 Motor Yacht

It's a safe bet no one will ever describe the Cruisers 385 Motor Yacht (called the 395 Motor Yacht in 2007–08) as "sleek", "sexy" or "stylish". With her tall freeboard, portly profile and convoluted aft deck/transom design, the 385 is more about interior volume than pleasing lines. Like many of her contemporaries in today's motor yacht market, the side decks of the Cruisers 385 were raised to permit the inclusion of a full-beam salon. Thus, the accommodations are spacious indeed for a 38-footer. Her two-stateroom floorplan—offered with a booth-style dinette or alternate crescent-shaped dinette in the salon—is an appealing blend of high-gloss cherry joinery, Ultraleather seating, and good-quality hardware. Overlapping elliptical windows provide excellent outside visibility, and the U-shaped galley includes a double sink in addition to generous storage. Note that the forward stateroom has a single bunk as well as a double berth. Topside highlights include acrylic wing doors, U-shaped flybridge seating, an extended swim platform with boarding steps, and hardtop. The side decks are very narrow. Standard 375hp gas inboards cruise at 20 knots (high 20s top); optional Yanmar 370 diesels cruise in the mid 20s.

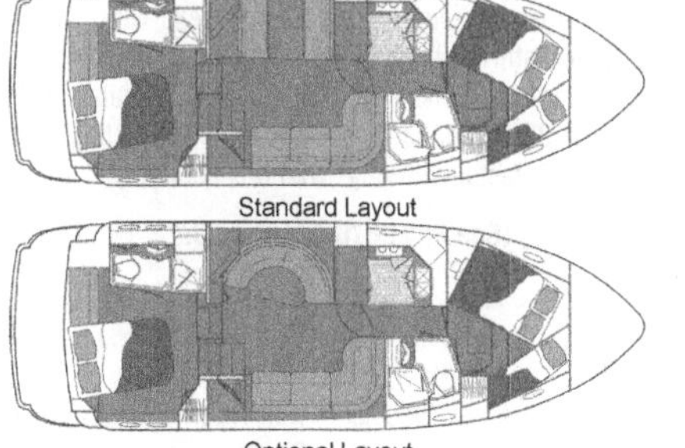
Standard Layout

Optional Layout

See Page 676 For Price Data

Length	42'2"	Fuel	300 gals.
Beam	13'8"	Water	68 gals.
Draft	3'3"	Waste	51 gals.
Weight, Gas	23,500#	Hull Type	Modified-V
Weight, Diesel	25,000#	Deadrise Aft	16°

Cruisers 3850/3950 Aft Cabin MY

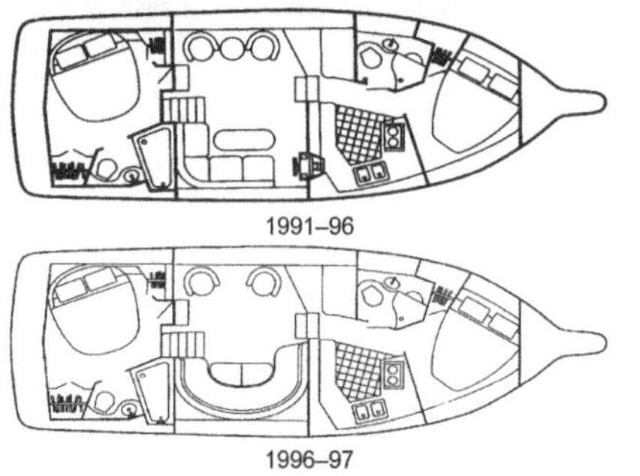
1991–96

1996–97

The Cruisers 3950 Aft Cabin (called the 3850 Aft Cabin from 1991–94) is a well-proportioned flybridge yacht whose spacious interior and rakish appearance made her a popular boat for Cruisers in the 1990s. She was built on a fully cored modified-V hull with prop pockets and a relatively wide beam. Cruiser's engineers packed some big-boat accommodations into the 3950 including two comfortable staterooms with double berths, a tub/shower in the aft head compartment, a big U-shaped galley with plenty of counter and storage space, and a built-in washer/dryer. Tastefully furnished and decorated, this is an impressive interior for a 38-foot boat. Topside, the aft deck is on the small side for a boat this size, however the innovative reverse transom with its molded boarding steps is a practical addition on a boat with this much freeboard. There's plenty of guest seating on the bridge, and a sun pad can be fitted on the foredeck. Additional features include an aft deck wet bar, wide side decks, hardtop, and good cabin storage. With big-block gas engines, the 3950 Aft Cabin will cruise at a modest 15 knots (mid 20s top). Optional 350hp Cat diesels cruise comfortably around 20 knots.

See Page 676 For Price Data

Length	41'6"	Fuel	400 gals.
Beam	14'0"	Water	100 gals.
Draft	3'4"	Waste	54 gals.
Weight, Gas	21,000#	Hull Type	Modified-V
Weight, Diesel	22,400#	Deadrise Aft	16°

Cruisers 390 Sports Coupe

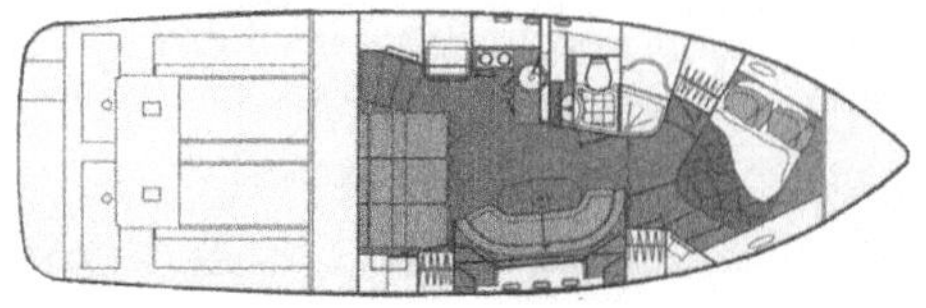

In a world of look-alike express boats, the sleek 390 Sports Coupe stands apart from the crowd. Hardtop cruisers are nothing new, of course; they've been around in one form or another for years. With the 390, however, Cruisers Yachts was able to combine modern hardtop styling with an open-plan interior more attuned to entertaining than sleeping accommodations. Add to that the versatility of a semi-enclosed helm deck—a second salon, if you will—and the result is a luxury-class day boat with world-class appeal. Offsetting the companionway to starboard on the bridge deck allows for a clever center module unit next to the helm with seating forward and a snack bar aft. A hatch in the hardtop provides ventilation on hot days, and the cockpit floor lifts electrically for engine access. Below decks, the 390's expansive salon with single stateroom forward features an aft sofa that converts to a mid-cabin berth, cherry-veneer joinery, and a large head with separate stall shower. Galley storage is modest for a boat this size. Available with V-drive inboards or Volvo's IPS Drive System. Cruise at 28 knots with Yanmar 380hp inboards (30+ top). Volvo 370hp pod drives run a few knots faster with improved fuel economy.

See Page 676 For Price Data

Length	40'2"	Fuel	300 gals.
Beam	13'0"	Water	75 gals.
Draft	3'9"	Waste	55 gals.
Weight	22,000#	Hull Type	Modified-V
Clearance	11'3"	Deadrise Aft	16°

Cruisers 3970/400/420 Express

The Cruisers 400 Express (introduced as the 3970 Express in 2003, and called the 420 Express in 2006–10) embodies the conservative styling and spacious accommodations typical of most American sportcruisers together with a choice of floorplans and a roomy cockpit with seating for a small crowd. Built on a modified-V hull with a solid fiberglass bottom, the luxury interior of the 400 Express gets high marks for headroom, storage and finish. In the area aft of the salon, Cruisers offers two different layouts. The standard plan has an aft settee open to the salon, while the optional layout encloses this area behind a bulkhead and door. High-gloss cherry woodwork and decorator furnishings highlight the interior, and both floorplans incorporate fore and aft heads with stall showers. A wet bar with refrigerator, walk-through windshield, double helm seat, and U-shaped aft lounge are standard in the bi-level cockpit. Twin 420hp V-drive gas engines cruise at 20 knots (high 20s top), and optional Yanmar 370hp diesels cruise in the low 20s. More recent models with Volvo 370hp IPS pod drives cruise economically at 25 knots.

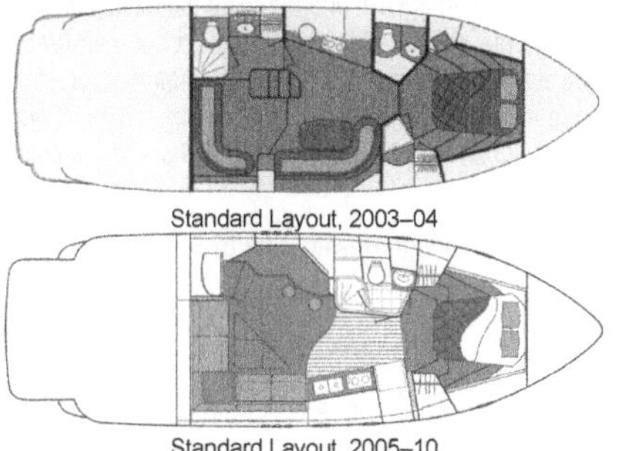
Standard Layout, 2003–04

Standard Layout, 2005–10

See Page 676 For Price Data

Length	43'0"	Fuel	300 gals.
Beam	13'6"	Water	70 gals.
Draft	3'8"	Waste	50 gals.
Weight, Gas	22,000#	Hull Type	Modified-V
Weight, Diesel	23,500#	Deadrise Aft	16°

Cruisers 405/415 Express Motor Yacht

The 405 Express Motor Yacht is what Cruiser's marketing execs called a "crossover yacht," meaning that she offers the upper-deck attributes of an express cruiser and the interior comforts of an aft-cabin motor yacht. In fact, the Cruisers 405 was an innovative yacht in 2003, and while her top-heavy profile is distracting her belowdecks accommodations are impressive indeed. Built on a fully cored hull, the 405's express-style helm and cockpit arrangement keeps the captain and passengers in the same general area. A sliding door next to the helm leads down to the salon with its faux leather upholstery, cherry woodwork, and tiered side windows. A fully equipped galley and four-person dinette are to starboard in the salon, and a hatch in the floor provides access to the engineroom. The staterooms are huge—larger than one expects in a boat this size. Both contain a queen berth and private head access, and a washer/dryer in the aft stateroom is built into the starboard corner. Note that the forward head is split with the shower and toilet in separate compartments. A good performer with optional 420hp Cat diesels, the 405 Express cruise in the low 20s and reach a top speed of 27–28 knots.

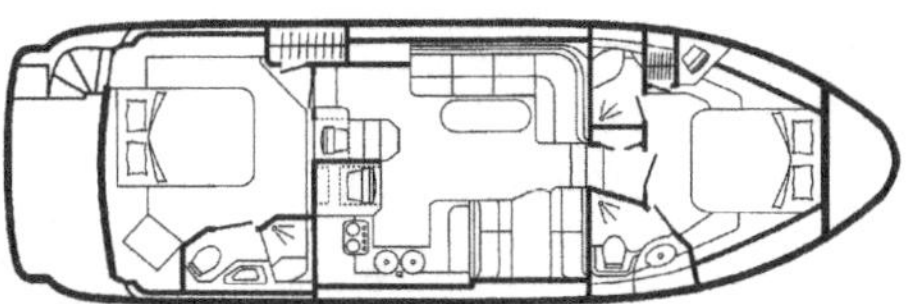

See Page 676 For Price Data

Length	42'6"	Fuel	380 gals.
Beam	13'8"	Water	100 gals.
Draft	3'6"	Waste	70 gals.
Weight	31,000#	Hull Type	Modified-V
Clearance, Arch	14'0"	Deadrise Aft	16°

Cruisers 420/430 Sports Coupe

2009–Current

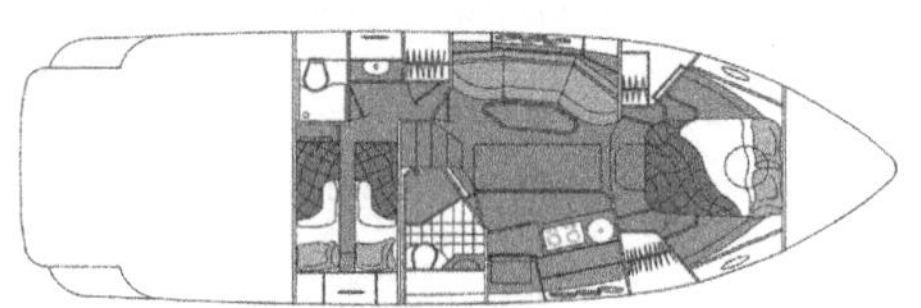

Following up on the success of the 390 Sports Coupe introduced in 2007, the Cruisers 430 Sports Coupe (called the 420 in 2009–11) takes sportyacht luxury and comfort to the next level. Like her predecessor, the 430's semi-enclosed cockpit provides a weather-protected platform for entertaining on a grand scale. Amenities include power sunroof, port-side companion seating, wet bar with sink and refrigerator, cockpit tables that convert to a sun lounge, cockpit grill, and a transom rumble seat. Access to the bow is via a side deck or split windshield. Below decks, the 420's opulent cherrywood interior—with its built-in liquor cabinet, neat 7-foot headroom, and crescent-shaped dinette—includes two large staterooms, two heads, and a home-size galley complete with wine/bottle storage and microwave/convection oven. A flat-screen TV and leather seating are standard, and the main head has a separate stall shower. Note the side-by-side chaise lounge sun pad (with adjustable backrests) on the foredeck. An electric hatch provides good access to the engines. The vertical hull ports are a nice design touch. Cruise at 24–25 knots with Volvo 370hp IPS pod drive diesels.

Not Enough Resale Data to Set Values

Length w/Platform	43'0"	Fuel	300 gals.
Beam	13'6"	Water	80 gals.
Draft	38"	Waste	50 gals.
Weight, Gas	23,000#	Hull Type	Modified-V
Weight, Diesel	23,500#	Deadrise Aft	16°

Cruisers 4270 Express

1997–2003

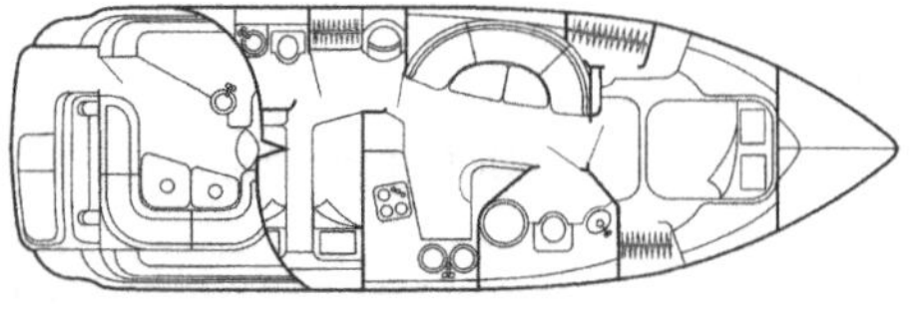

The Cruisers 4270 is a big, full-bodied express with a luxurious two-stateroom interior and cockpit seating for a small crowd. Heavily built on a fully cored hull with a wide beam and prop pockets, the sleek profile of the 4270 is accented by her long foredeck, reverse radar arch, and an extended swim platform. The expansive interior contains a unique midcabin suite with twin single berths (convertible into a queen-size bed) and a private standup head compartment—a notable departure from the cramped midcabin layouts found in most express cruisers. The U-shaped galley in this yacht is huge with wood flooring and plenty of counter and storage space. Topside, the cockpit includes removable wraparound seating, wet bar with refrigerator and icemaker, and a walk-through windshield for easy foredeck access. Additional features include a large helm console with space for flush-mounted electronics, a gas-assist engineroom hatch in the cockpit, and a concealed, remote-controlled anchor windlass. A well-finished boat, early models with optional 350hp Cat V-drive diesels cruise at 24 knots (about 28 knots top), and later models with 420hp V-drive Cats cruise at 28 knots (low 30s top).

See Page 676 For Price Data

Length	46'6"	Fuel	400 gals.
Beam	14'0"	Water	100 gals.
Draft	3'6"	Waste	50 gals.
Weight, Gas	22,000#	Hull Type	Modified-V
Weight, Diesel	23,500#	Deadrise Aft	16°

Cruisers 4285 Express Bridge

The ultimate party barge, Cruisers took waterborne entertaining to the next level in 1990 with the 4285 Express Bridge. With her spacious bridge deck, vast full-beam interior, and large cockpit with twin staircases, this is a yacht designed for socializing on a grand scale. Her fully cored hull (with prop pockets) boasts a wide 14-foot, 6-inch beam, and while the 4285 is a big 42-footer, her tall freeboard detracts from her visual appeal. Stepping below through a sliding glass cockpit door, visitors encounter an enormous interior whose single-level layout includes a U-shaped galley with serving counter and stools, wet bar with ice maker, huge double-entry head compartment, and a roomy master stateroom with island berth and walk-in closet. The command bridge, accessed via molded steps on either side of the cockpit, offers seating for 10 with wet bar, icemaker, and standard hardtop. Hatches in the cockpit sole provide access to the engines. Additional features include copious galley storage, Corian countertops, transom storage, and a cockpit shower. Cruise at 20 knots with 375hp V-drive Cats. Note that her sistership, the Cruisers 4280 Express Bridge, is same boat with two-stateroom interior.

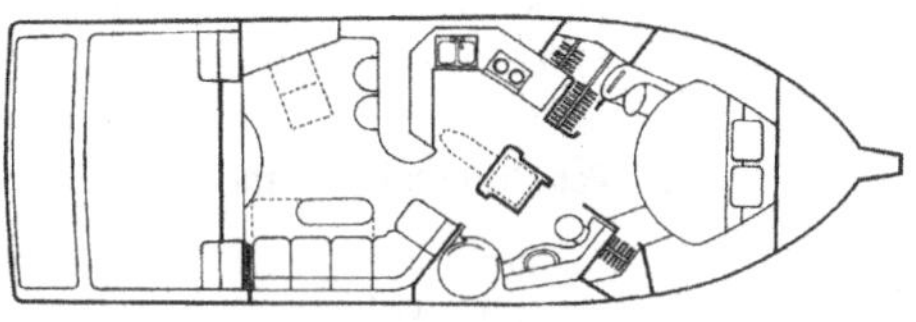

See Page 676 For Price Data

Length w/Pulpit	46'6"	Fuel	400 gals.
Beam	14'6"	Water	160 gals.
Draft	3'6"	Waste	50 gals.
Weight, Gas	23,700#	Hull Type	Modified-V
Weight, Diesel	25,200#	Deadrise Aft	16°

Cruisers 4370 Express; 440 Express

The Cruisers 440 Express (called the 4370 Express in 2003) offers upscale buyers the versatility of a big express cruiser with the interior luxury of an aft-cabin motor yacht. With her wide beam, tall freeboard and extended swim platform, the 440 is a big boat for her size. While there are several express-style yachts her size available on the market, only the 440 offers a full-size master stateroom (with private head and shower) aft of the salon. The headroom found throughout the interior is exceptional, and the decor is a lavish blend of posh upholstery, quality wall coverings, and acres of high-gloss cherry joinery. The bi-level cockpit is large enough to seat as many as eight guests in comfort. A walk-through windshield offers easy access to the foredeck, and an electric hatch in the aft cockpit sole provides entry to the engine compartment. A cockpit shower, windlass, and radar arch are standard, and a stylish fiberglass hardtop (pictured here) was optional. Among several V-drive engine options, twin Yanmar 440hp diesels cruise at 25 knots—sedate performance by European sportboat standards but suitable for the domestic market.

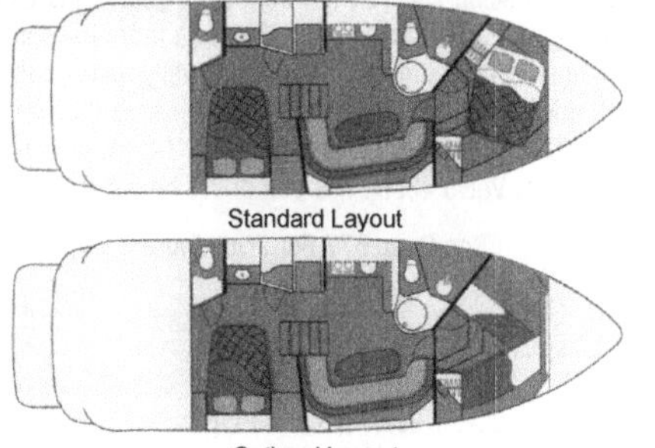

See Page 676 For Price Data

Length	46'9"	Fuel	400 gals.
Beam	14'0"	Water	95 gals.
Draft	42"	Waste	50 gals.
Weight, Gas	24,300#	Hull Type	Modified-V
Weight, Diesel	25,900#	Deadrise Aft	16°

Cruisers 4450 Express MY

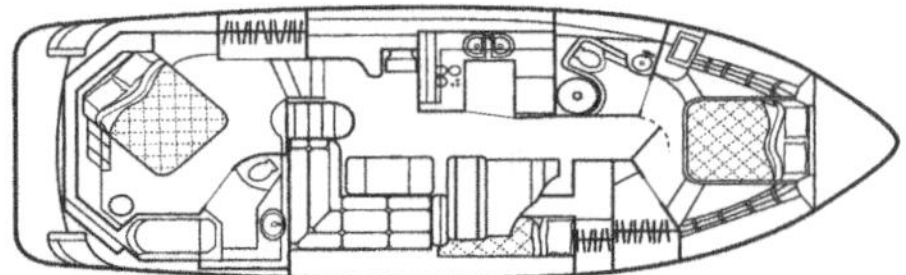

The Cruisers 4450 Express MY was an attempt to combine the interior comforts of an aft-cabin motor yacht with the open deck layout of an express cruiser—an "evolutionary step" in yachting design according to Cruisers marketing execs. Built on a beamy modified-V hull, the 4450's condo-style interior accommodations and express-like cockpit layout are likely to attract buyers looking for something a little different in their boat. Her three-stateroom interior is a departure from most aft-cabin floorplans in that the salon, galley and dinette are all on the same level (although the dinette is slightly elevated to provide headroom for the small stateroom below). The forward cabin, with a walk-in closet, is nearly as large as the owner's aft stateroom. Note that the aft head compartment includes a whirlpool tub in addition to a separate shower stall. Topside, the tiered helm and cockpit area keeps the captain and passengers in close proximity. Helm visibility is excellent, and the side decks are wide enough for secure access to the foredeck. A huge boat for her size, twin 420hp Cat diesels cruise the Cruisers 4450 at 19 knots and reach a top speed in the neighborhood of 23–24 knots.

See Page 676 For Price Data

Length	45'6"	Fuel	500 gals.
Beam	15'4"	Water	140 gals.
Draft	3'3"	Waste	100 gals.
Weight	38,000#	Hull Type	Modified-V
Clearance, Arch	14'6"	Deadrise Aft	18°

Cruisers 447 Sport Sedan

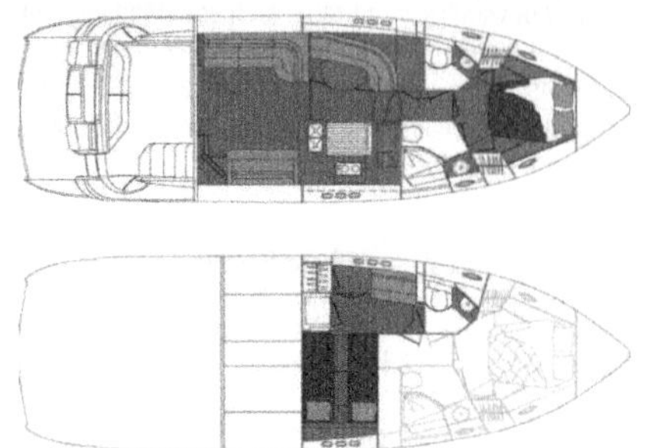

Aggressive styling defines the Cruisers 447 Sport Sedan, a luxury-class cruising yacht whose spacious, wide-open interior comes as a surprise in a boat this size. Perhaps that's because her tiered cabin windows admit so much natural lighting into the salon—indeed, the 447's cabin windows provide 360 degrees of visibility whether sitting or standing. The split-level salon is arranged with galley and dinette forward, a step above the aft salon with its facing settees and in-floor storage room. Note the sculptured salon overhead. There are two staterooms and two heads forward and below. The forward is the master and includes a queen island berth, while the full-beam guest stateroom aft has twin berths (that convert to a double), sitting area, washer/dryer space, and six opening ports. There's a staircase to the flybridge in the cockpit, and clever aft-facing seats in the transom overlook the extended swim platform. Built on a fully cored hull with more transom deadrise than most Cruisers models, the 447 actually rides on the same hull as the Rampage 45 Convertible, another boat built by parent company KCS International. Yanmar 480hp V-drive diesels cruise at 25–26 knots. Volvo 435hp IPS pod drives cruise at 30 knots.

See Page 677 For Price Data

Length	45'2"	Fuel	375 gals.
Beam	14'6"	Water	100 gals.
Draft	4'0"	Waste	48 gals.
Weight	29,500#	Hull Type	Modified-V
Clearance	16'6"	Deadrise Aft	18.5°

Cruisers 455 Express Motor Yacht

Introduced in 2004, the Cruisers 455 Express Motor Yacht is an updated version of the company's 4450 Express MY built from 1998 to 2003. Both boats share the same fully cored hull, the same tankage, and the same unusual express/motor yacht design configuration. What is different is the exterior styling; the 455's tiered cabin windows and restyled hardtop add much to her rakish personality. Belowdecks, the three-stateroom cherrywood interior is a departure from most aft-cabin floorplans in that the salon, galley and dinette are all on the same level (although the dinette is slightly elevated to provide headroom for the small stateroom below). The forward cabin, with a walk-in closet, is nearly as large as the owner's aft stateroom. Note that the aft head compartment includes a whirlpool tub in addition to a separate shower stall. Topside, the tiered helm and cockpit area keeps the captain and passengers in close proximity. Helm visibility is excellent, and the side decks are wide enough for secure access to the foredeck. A well-built yacht, twin 480hp Volvo diesels cruise the Cruisers 445 Express in the low 20s and reach a top speed just under 30 knots.

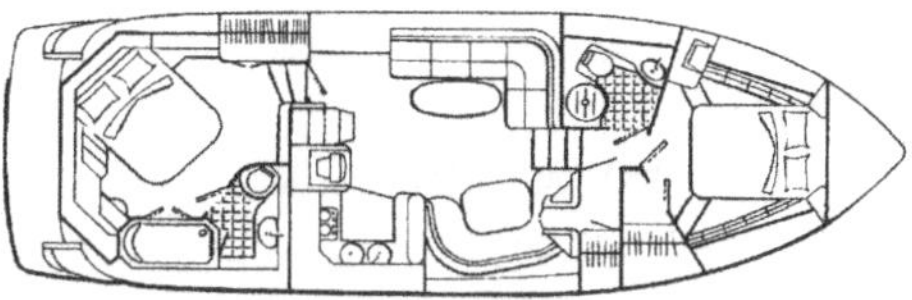

See Page 677 For Price Data

Length	45'6"	Fuel	500 gals.
Beam	15'4"	Water	140 gals.
Draft	3'3"	Waste	100 gals.
Weight	36,000#	Hull Type	Modified-V
Clearance, Hardtop	15'4"	Deadrise Aft	16°

Cruisers 477/497 Sport Sedan

Visionary thinking is "alive and well at Cruisers Yachts," proclaimed Yachting magazine in their 2006 review of the then-new 477 Sport Sedan. True enough; the 477 represented a bold departure from Cruisers' conservative Midwest styling. Called the 497 Sport Sedan in 2007, the spacious interior is highlighted by an expansive split-level salon with tiered side windows, facing leather settees with recliners, and solid cherrywood cabinets. A home-size galley with teak-and-holly flooring is forward, opposite a raised four-person dinette. A flat-screen TV built into the aft salon bulkhead can be viewed from anywhere in the room. Below decks are two large, tastefully appointed staterooms and two heads. The VIP guest cabin is unique in that it's located amidships and uses the full beam of the boat. Note the huge, step-down utility room with washer/dryer combo beneath the salon sole. The cockpit includes a cushioned transom seat (with removable table) and a wet bar with refrigerator. A staircase ascends to the climate-controlled flybridge with L-lounge seating, table, and another wet bar. The swim platform can support a PWC. Volvo 575hp V-drive diesels cruise at 24–25 knots (30+ knots wide open).

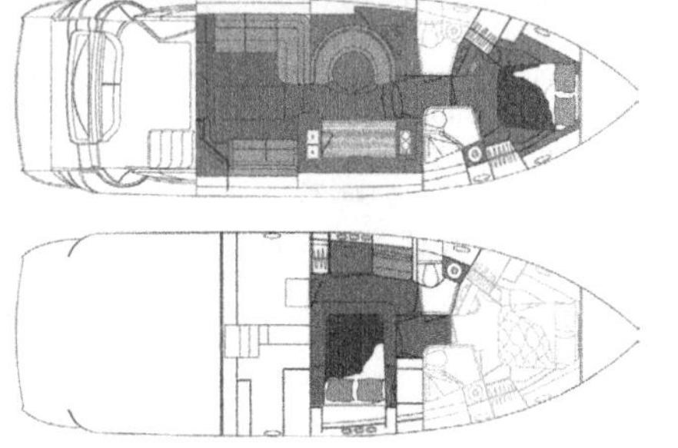

See Page 677 For Price Data

Length	50'2"	Fuel	526 gals.
Beam	15'0"	Water	150 gals.
Draft	4'1"	Waste	75 gals.
Weight	39,500#	Hull Type	Modified-V
Headroom	6'6"	Deadrise Aft	18.5°

Cruisers 5000 Sedan Sport

1998–2003

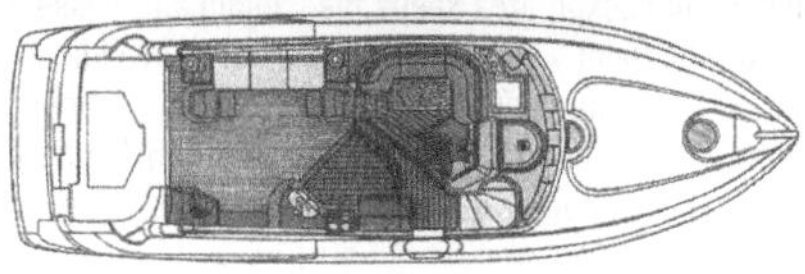

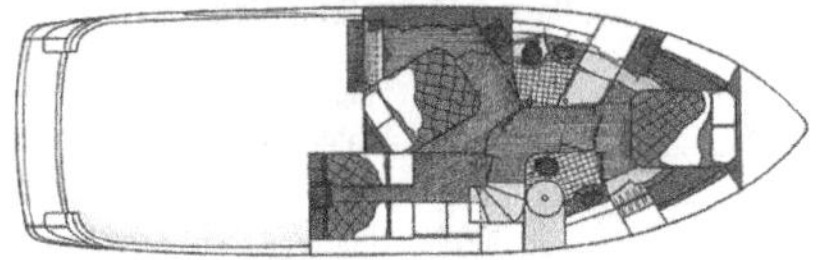

Flagship of the Cruisers fleet when she was introduced in 1998, the 5000 Sedan Sport is a stylish Euro-style motor yacht with the aggressive good looks of an Italian import. She's built on a fully cored modified-V hull with a shallow keel for improved tracking and prop pockets to reduce shaft angles. The wide-open interior of the 5000 Sedan Sport is a striking contrast to most of the imports with their sunken (hidden) galleys and tiny staterooms. Not only is the salon completely open to the galley and elevated helm/dinette, but the Sedan Sport even manages to include inside access to the flybridge—a rare convenience in a boat this size. Two of the three staterooms have double berths, and both heads have separate stall showers. On the downside, the cockpit is quite small, and the meticulous craftsmanship seen in the European imports is missing in the more affordable Sedan Sport. Additional features include rich cherrywood joinery, good engineroom access, a spacious flybridge, and a centerline lower helm. Among several V-drive engine options, twin 480hp Volvo diesels cruise the Sedan Sport at 18 knots (22–23 knots top), and 660hp Cats cruise at 25 knots (28–29 knots top).

See Page 677 For Price Data

Length	49'6"	Fuel	600 gals.
Beam	15'6"	Water	150 gals.
Draft	3'5"	Waste	100 gals.
Weight	42,000#	Hull Type	Modified-V
Clearance, Arch	16'5"	Deadrise Aft	11°

Cruisers 520 Express

2006–09

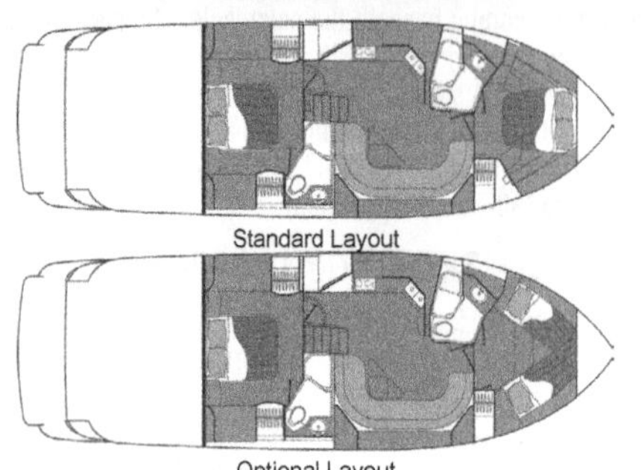
Standard Layout

Optional Layout

A spacious interior and a full array of luxury appointments characterize the Cruisers 500, a modern express yacht whose excellent performance compares well with most of her European counterparts. Built on a modified-V hull with a solid fiberglass bottom, the twin-stateroom floorplan of the 500 offers the comforts of a small motor yacht. In the salon, an opulent Ultraleather sectional with double recliners seats eight for cocktails, and the portside galley (which conceals an optional dishwasher) has a glass-encased liquor cabinet built into the end of the counter. The forward stateroom comes with either a queen- or twin-berth layout, while the full-beam master stateroom enjoys excellent natural lighting thanks to the vertical ports installed on either side of the hull. On deck, the cockpit is dominated by a huge U-shaped lounge whose rear section pulls out from the transom to form a sun pad. Visibility from the helm is excellent, and an extended swim platform can carry a small inflatable. Additional features include cherry interior joinery, walk-through windshield, fender storage, windlass, and salon entertainment center. A fiberglass hardtop was optional. Volvo 715hp V-drive diesels reach 30+ knots top.

See Page 677 For Price Data

Length	52'3"	Fuel	500 gals.
Beam	15'6"	Water	150 gals.
Draft	3'8"	Waste	75 gals.
Weight	42,000#	Hull Type	Modified-V
Headroom	6'6"	Deadrise Aft	15°

Cruisers 5370/5470 Express; 540/560 Express

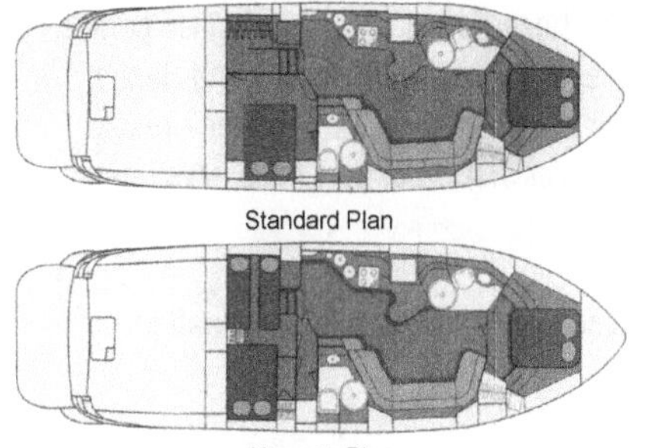

Standard Plan

Alternate Plan

Once a rarity in the world of full-production boats, 50-something express yachts were a fast-growing segment of the luxury yacht market until the Great Recession hit. This popular model (called the 5370 Express in 2002; 5470 Express in 2003; 540 Express in 2004–06; and the 560 Express in 2007–11) is the largest express-boat offering yet from Cruisers. The interior is finished entirely in cherrywood with excellent detailing, and Cruisers offers a choice of two- or three-stateroom layouts. Each stateroom has a full head with shower and a washer/dryer can be added in either configuration. (Note that the hardwood dinette table in the salon retracts electrically into the floor when not in use.) Topside, the circular lounge aft in the cockpit converts at the push of a button into a huge sun pad. Visibility from the walkaround helm is excellent and wide side decks provide secure access to the foredeck. Additional features include a fully cored hull, prop pockets, excellent access to the spacious engineroom, and an extended swim platform with a transom compartment for an optional davit. Among several engine choices, Volvo 715hphp V-drive diesels cruise at 28 knots (low to mid 30s top).

See Page 677 For Price Data

Length	58'0"	Fuel	650 gals.
Beam	16'0"	Water	150 gals.
Draft	3'10"	Waste	100 gals.
Weight	46,000#	Hull Type	Modified-V
Clearance	12'7"	Deadrise Aft	15°

DeFever

Quick View

The models described in the following pages represent a cross section of late model DeFever designs. DeFevers have been manufactured by several U.S. and Asian manufacturers over the years, some better than others. Among the better-known builders, the CTF yard in Taiwan was well known for its comprehensive series of DeFever models from 40 to 72 feet in length. DeFever designs are perhaps best characterized as sturdy long-range cruisers with a distinctive trawler (or pilothouse) profile, practical accommodations, and seakindly hulls. While the models previewed in these pages are of fiberglass construction, many older DeFevers, including the popular Alaskan series from Grand Banks, were built of wood. Clean, used DeFevers are nearly always in demand, and their resale values have held up surprisingly well over the years. Over 3,300 DeFever hulls have been built to date.

A DeFever Cruisers website (www.defevercruisers.com) contains useful information on various DeFever models.

DeFever 44 Trawler

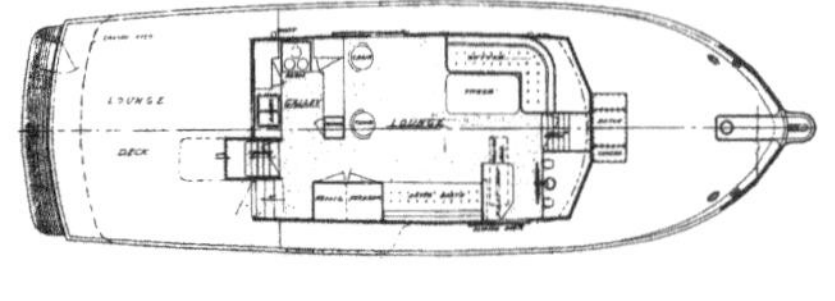

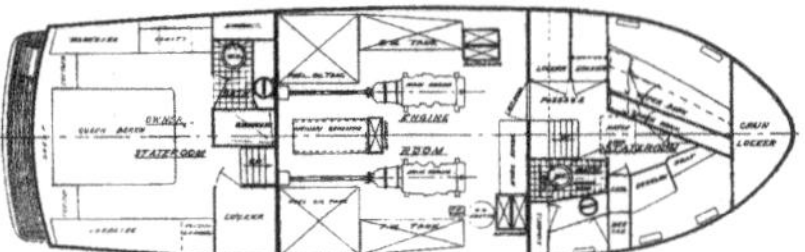

Few trawler designs have enjoyed the enduring appeal of the DeFever 44 Trawler. Nearly 100 of these sturdy yachts were built making her one of the most popular DeFever designs ever produced. The DeFever 44 is not a typical double-cabin trawler with an elevated cabintop over the aft stateroom. Rather, she's a rare flush-deck design with single-level walkaround decks—an eminently practical design that results in an attractive profile as well as generally improved accessibility. She's a heavy boat for her size, and her full-displacement hull provides a particularly comfortable ride in a chop. Belowdecks, her two-stateroom interior is arranged with the galley aft in the salon where it's easily reached from the aft deck. Visibility from the lower helm is excellent, and port and starboard doors forward in the salon provide easy access to the decks. The aft stateroom is huge with tremendous storage and cabinet space for a washer/dryer combo. A great feature of the DeFever 44 is her walk-in engineroom with workbench and near-standing headroom. Most DeFever 44s were sold with 135hp Lehman diesels that will cruise efficiently at 7–8 knots with a range of 1,500-plus miles.

See Page 677 For Price Data

Length Overall	43'9"	Clearance	NA
Length WL	38'6"	Fuel	900 gals.
Beam	14'9"	Water	350 gals.
Draft	4'7"	Waste	60 gals.
Weight	44,000#	Hull Type	Displacement

DeFever 48 Trawler

1978–92

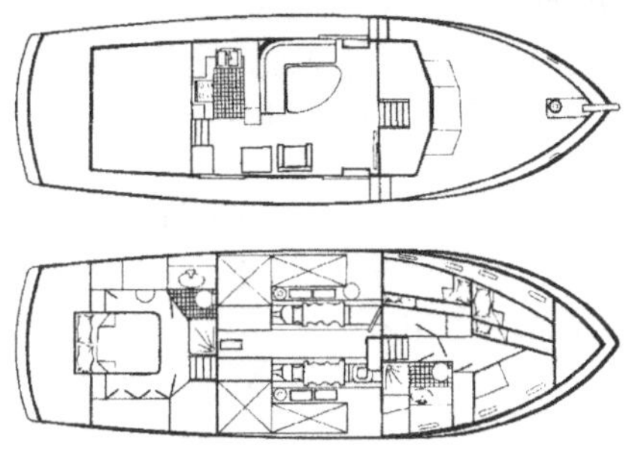

The DeFever 48 Trawler is a heavy displacement long-range cruiser built from 1978 to 1991 by the CTF yard in Taiwan. (Note that she was reintroduced in 1998 when production was moved to mainland China.) She's heavily constructed on a solid fiberglass semi-displacement hull with a long keel, a fine entry and hard aft chines. The DeFever 48 shares several design features with the smaller DeFever 44; namely, the galley arrangement (a U-shaped affair located aft in the salon) and the remarkably spacious engineroom. Inside, the DeFever is finished with teak paneling and joinery throughout—all done to high Asian standards. The floorplan includes three staterooms, two full heads, and a reasonably spacious salon with a lower helm and sliding deck doors port and starboard. Considered a trawler by most, the DeFever 48 is capable of planing speeds with engines larger than the standard twin 135hp Lehman diesels. Optional Cat 375hp diesels, found in later models, provide an almost-brisk cruising speed of 14–15 knots. With over 100 built during her initial production run, the DeFever 48 remains an extremely popular boat on the used market.

Prices Not Provided for Pre-1995 Models

Length Overall	47'3"	Headroom	6'5"
Length WL	40'10"	Fuel	950 gals.
Beam	15'4"	Water	500 gals.
Draft	4'9"	Waste	100 gals.
Weight	50,000#	Hull Type	Semi-Disp.

DeFever 49 Cockpit MY

1994–2007

The DeFever 49 Cockpit MY is basically a DeFever 44 Trawler with a 5-foot cockpit addition and extended rudders and shafts. She's not your typical sundeck trawler with an elevated cabintop over the aft stateroom. Rather, the 49 is a rare flush-deck yacht with single-level walkaround decks—an eminently practical design that results in an attractive profile as well as generally improved accessibility. The DeFever 49 is a heavy boat for her size, and her full-displacement hull delivers a notably comfortable ride in an offshore chop. Belowdecks, her two-stateroom interior is arranged with the galley aft in the salon, which makes it convenient to the aft deck. Visibility from the lower helm is excellent, and port and starboard doors forward in the salon provide easy access to the decks. The aft stateroom is huge with tremendous storage and space for a washer/dryer. A great feature of the DeFever 49 is her walk-in engineroom with its easy access and near-standing headroom. Additional features include a full teak interior, wide side decks, radar arch, hardtop, and a transom door. Among several engine options, twin 135hp Perkins diesels cruise the DeFever 49 at an economical 7–8 knots.

Main Deck Plan

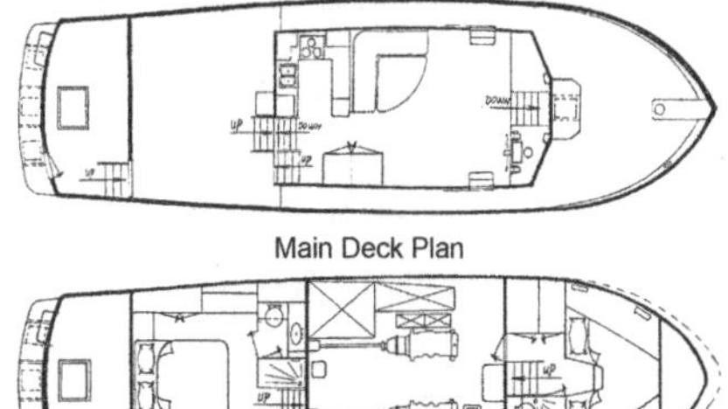

Lower Deck Plan

Not Enough Resale Data to Set Values

Length Overall	48'10"	Headroom	6'6"
Length WL	43'6"	Fuel	1,100 gals.
Beam	15'0"	Water	370 gals.
Draft	4'7"	Waste	90 gals.
Weight	53,900#	Hull Type	Displacement

Donzi

Quick View

- Donzi was founded in 1964 by boat-racing legend Don Aronow and partners Walt Walters and Jim Wynne — the inventor of the stern drive I/O power system.
- The first Donzi model was the Sweet 16, a classic high-performance design that became a best-selling classic in her own time.
- By the late 1980's Donzi expanded to include center console fishing boats, performance boats, and an entry-level series of runabouts.
- In 1989 OMC (Outboard Marine Corp.) purchased Donzi, but the marriage went south when OMC cut back on Donzi's production and changed the power from MerCruiser to Cobra.
- In 1993 Donzi was purchased by American Marine Holdings, Inc., parent company of Pro-Line Boats.
- American Marine Holdings filed for bankruptcy in January, 2012.

No longer in business.

Donzi 275 Express

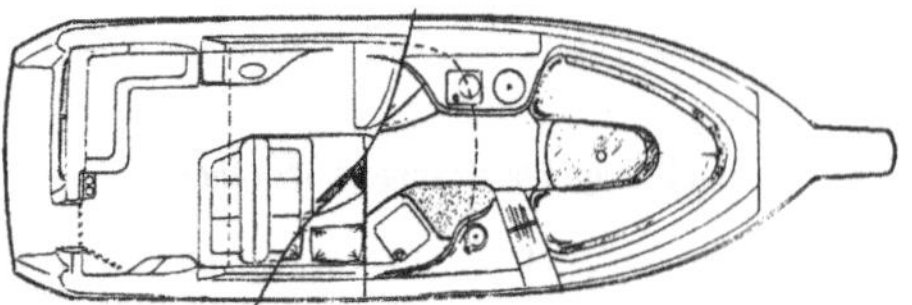

The Donzi Z27 Express (called the 275 Medallion in 1995 and the 275 LXC from 1996–98) is an entry-level family cruiser whose slender beam made her one of the larger trailerable express boats available. Affordably priced, she's built on a deep-V hull with cored hullsides, a single-piece inner liner, and a solid fiberglass bottom. Because of the limited 8-foot, 6-inch beam (required for tailoring), the interior of the Donzi Z27 is more compact than other 27-footers, most of which have wider beams. The floorplan is arranged with a convertible dinette/V-berth forward, a second double berth in the midcabin, a well-equipped galley, and a spacious standup head with hand shower. There's plenty of headroom thanks to her high freeboard and elevated foredeck. In the cockpit, a walk-through windshield with molded steps leads to the bow and an L-shaped lounge aft provides seating for five. Three hatches in the cockpit sole provide good access to the engine compartment. Additional features include windshield vents, anchor locker, and a cockpit wet bar. Among several sterndrive engine choices, a single 310hp MerCruiser I/O will cruise the Donzi Z27 at 25 knots and reach a top speed of about 32–34 knots.

See Page 677 For Price Data

Length Overall	29'3"	Clearance	7'0"
Beam	8'6"	Fuel	103 gals.
Draft, Drives Up	1'9"	Water	20 gals.
Draft, Drives Down	3'5"	Hull Type	Modified-V
Weight	6,500#	Deadrise Aft	19°

Donzi 28 ZF

1999–2001

The Donzi 28 ZF is a high-performance center console fisherman with the speed and range to travel well offshore in pursuit of remote fishing grounds. A great-looking boat, she rides on a smooth-running deep-V hull—fully cored to reduce weight—with a trailerable 8-foot, 6-inch beam. Just as several other performance-minded builders have done in recent years, Donzi fishing boats employ stepped hulls that are designed to reduce drag and improve high-end performance characteristics. No wood is used in structural components. The deck layout is arranged with insulated fish boxes that also serve as stowage compartments in the forward casting platform and a built-in 50-gallon livewell at the transom. Additional features include cockpit lighting, a sub-console head compartment with side-door entrance, transom door and shower, cockpit bolsters, a large electronics box in the console, raw-water washdowns, and a bow pulpit. A seriously fast ride, twin 225hp outboards cruise the Donzi 28 ZF at an easy 35 knots and deliver a top speed in the high 50s.

Floorplan Not Available

See Page 677 For Price Data

Length	27'8"	Fuel	180 gals.
Beam	8'6"	Water	7 gals.
Draft, Up	19"	Max HP	500
Draft, Down	30"	Hull Type	Deep-V
Dry Weight	4,500#	Deadrise Aft	22°

Donzi 29 ZF Open

2003–09

Building bigger, faster and better-performing center consoles was a a Donzi objective for many years. Introduced in 2003, the 29 ZF Open is a spacious, high-performance fishing platform with the built-in quality and features synonymous with the Donzi nameplate. (Note that the 29 ZF Cuddy is the same boat with a small V-berth cabin.) Key to the excellent performance of the 29 ZF is her twin-stepped hull—a race-proven bottom design said to deliver quick acceleration and a higher top speed. A 9-foot beam gives anglers plenty of room to work a fish, and the large console contains an enclosed head/storage compartment. The helm features a built-in electronics box, four-drawer tackle box, additional dry storage, and a Dino steering wheel. Aft, port, and starboard fish boxes drain overboard, and a big 50-gallon circular livewell is located behind the standard leaning port. There's plenty of rod storage both under and on top of the gunwales and four more in the leaning post. Additional features include cockpit bolsters, raw water washdown, recessed bow rails, anchor locker, and a transom door. A fast ride, twin 225hp Yamaha outboards will reach a top speed in excess of 45 knots.

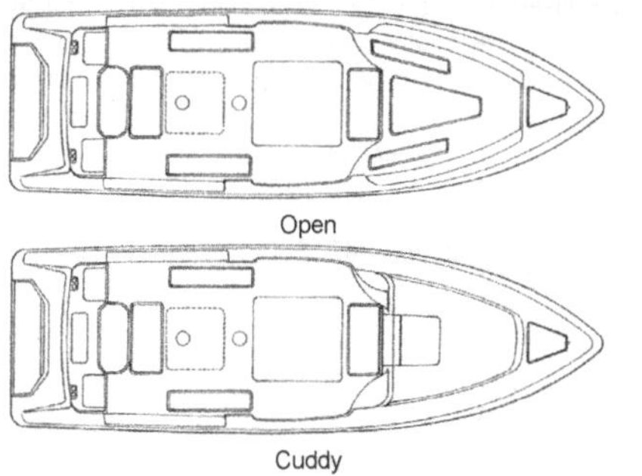
Open

Cuddy

See Page 677 For Price Data

Length Overall	28'7"	Fuel	180 gals.
Beam	9'0"	Water	7 gals.
Hull Draft	1'9"	Max HP	550
Draft, Engines Down	3'1"	Hull Type	Deep-V
Dry Weight	6,200#	Deadrise Aft	22°

Donzi 32 ZF Open

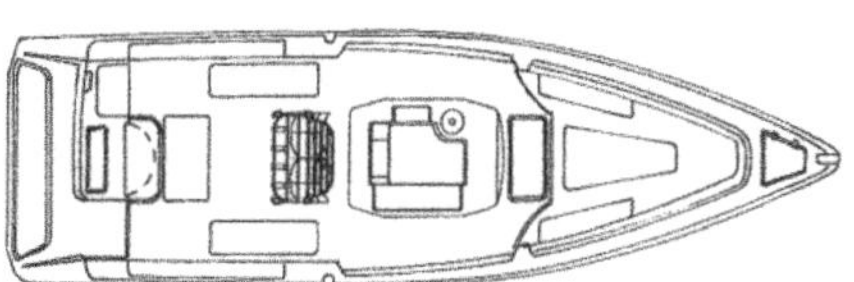

The Donzi 32 ZF is a strictly-business center console fisherman with the speed and range to travel far offshore in pursuit of those remote fishing grounds. A stylish boat with a high-performance heritage, she rides on a lightweight, deep-V hull—fully cored—with a narrow 9-foot, 2-inch beam. Just as several other performance-minded builders have done in recent years, Donzi fishing models employ stepped hulls, which are designed to reduce drag and improve handling. No wood is used in structural components. The uncluttered cockpit is arranged with three large fish boxes forward, two smaller boxes on either side of the console, and a built-in 50-gallon livewell at the transom. Note that a small head compartment with a Porta-Potti is located beneath the console. Standard features include cockpit lighting, K-Planes, rod holders, a transom door and shower, bolster cushions, a leaning post with drop-down bolsters, saltwater washdown, pop-up cleats, and a bow pulpit. A seriously fast ride, twin 250hp outboards cruise the Donzi 32 ZF at 35 knots and reach a top speed in the neighborhood of 55 knots.

See Page 677 For Price Data

Length Overall	32'1"	Fuel	290 gals.
Beam	9'2"	Water	20 gals.
Hull Draft	2'4"	Max HP	600
Dry Weight	7,600#	Hull Type	Deep-V
Clearance, T-Top	8'8"	Deadrise Aft	22°

Donzi 3250 LXC; 3250 Express

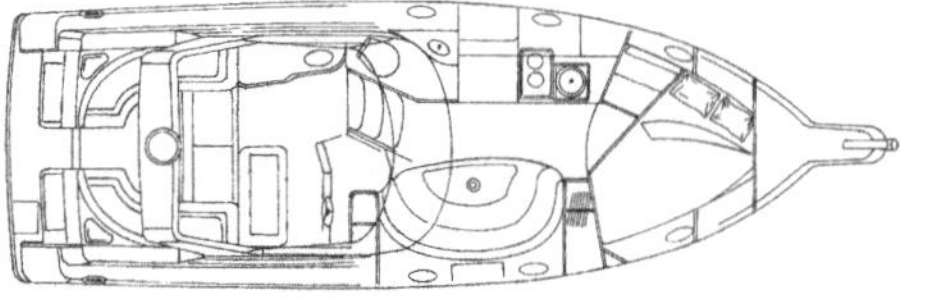

The Donzi 3250 (called the 3250 LXC in 1996–98 and the 3250 Express in 1999-2000) is an aggressively designed family cruiser whose principal appeal was an affordable price and impressive performance. (Indeed, she'll run circles around her inboard-powered counterparts although sterndrives may not appeal to everyone in a 32-footer.) Built on a deep-V hull with a wide 11-foot beam and single-piece inner liner, the interior of the Z32 sleeps four with double berths forward and a convertible semicircular dinette. The head is conveniently located just inside the companionway (where it's easily accessible from the cockpit), and a folding door provides privacy in the forward stateroom. Headroom is excellent thanks to the boat's high freeboard and raised cabintop. On deck, a cockpit wet bar is opposite the doublewide helm seat. Unlike most other family cruisers her size, the Z32 has a centerline transom door and facing settees in the cockpit (rather than an offset transom door and a big U-shaped settee). Additional features include wide side decks, an integral swim platform with transom shower, and a windlass. A good performer, twin 310hp MerCruiser I/Os cruise at 28 knots (40+ top).

See Page 677 For Price Data

Length Overall	33'8"	Clearance	NA
Beam	11'0"	Fuel	198 gals.
Draft, Drives Up	2'4"	Water	35 gals.
Draft, Drives Down	3'1"	Hull Type	Modified-V
Weight	11,500#	Deadrise Aft	19°

Donzi 35 ZF Open

1998–2011

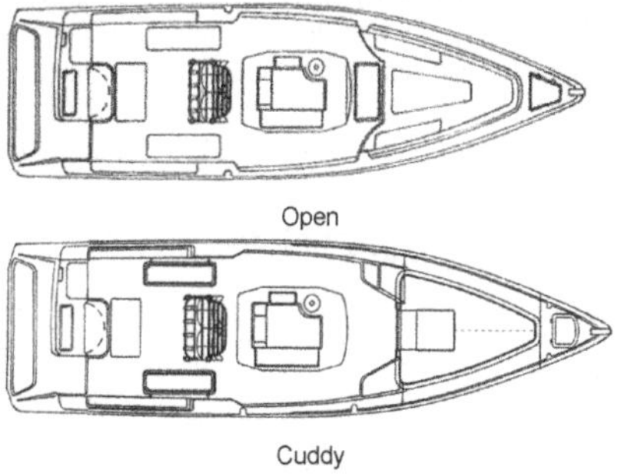

Open

Cuddy

The Donzi 35 ZF is a high-performance center console fisherman for anglers who place a premium on flat-out speed and agility. Built on a stepped-hull deep-V bottom, the 35 ZF is available in both cuddy (pictured above) and open bow versions. She's a racy boat with her droop-nose profile and colorful graphics, and her narrow 9-foot, 2-inch beam is comparable to most other high-performance fishboats found on today's market. An enclosed head with sink and shower is found in the console, and a pair of big fish boxes are built into the deck on either side of the leaning post. Forward, molded steps provide easy access to the cabintop that serves as a casting platform. Headroom is scarce in the low-profile cuddy where a V-berth, rod storage, and a convertible table are standard. Additional features include a transom livewell and sink, bolster cushions, a wide transom door, and cockpit lights. Twin 225hp outboards will deliver top speeds in the neighborhood of 43 knots (about 30 knots cruise). True performance addicts should note that the Donzi 35 ZF is capable of handling triple 225hp outboards for even higher speeds.

See Page 677 For Price Data

Length Overall	33'4"	Fuel	269 gals.
Beam	9'2"	Water	15 gals.
Hull Draft	2'6"	Max HP	750
Weight	7,950#	Hull Type	Deep-V
Clearance, T-Top	8'10"	Deadrise Aft	22°

Donzi 38 ZFX Open

2006–12

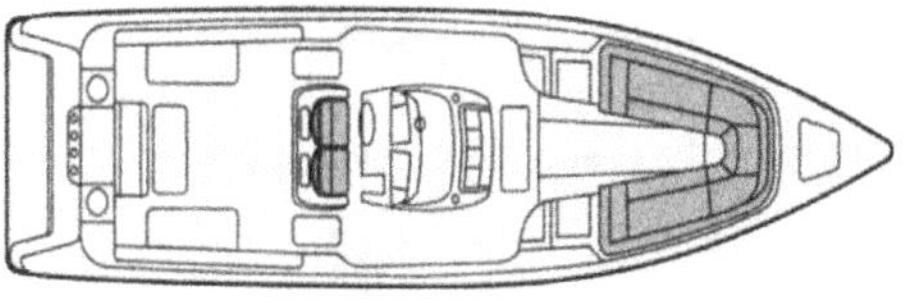

Great power comes in many flavors. In the case of the Donzi 38 ZFX Open, the form is sleek and the ride is fast. Offered in both Open and Cuddy configurations, this leading-edge sportster is built on Donzi's signature high-performance stepped hull with moderate freeboard and a slender 9'5" beam. Stepping aboard through her full transom door, the 38's hardcore fishing cockpit (with wraparound seating forward) includes a transom bait-prep center, 28-gallon livewell, raw-water washdown, two macerated fish boxes, bolster pads, transom rod holders (5), and a drop-down helm seat. Four inspection hatches provide quick access to the steering system and rigging, and the batteries, bilge pumps, and through-hulls are accessible in under-deck lockers. A hardtop with electronics locker, folding rear seat, K-planes, forward wet bar, and removable bow table were standard. With her narrow beam and relatively light weight, the 38 ZFX can be trailered behind a heavy-duty tow vehicle (with a permit, of course). Fast, versatile and innovative, triple 275hp Mercury Verado outboards deliver a top speed of well over 50 knots.

See Page 677 For Price Data

Length	38'6"	Fuel	318 gals.
Beam	9'5"	Water	28 gals.
Hull Draft	2'1"	Max HP	900
Dry Weight	10,200#	Hull Type	Deep-V
Clearance, Hardtop	5'5"	Deadrise Aft	22°

Donzi 38 ZSF

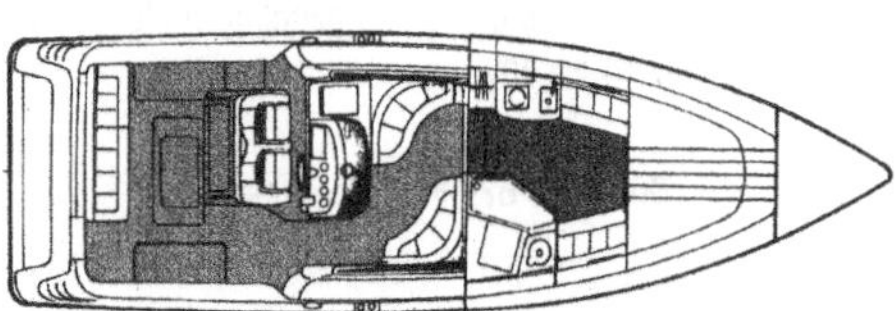

Described by Donzi as a performance center console, the 38 ZSF is an offshore fishing boat with a deck and cabin layout designed to appeal to day boaters and cruisers. Like all Donzi boats, the 38 ZSF rides on a high-performance stepped hull known for its superior rough-water handling characteristics. While she's certainly capable of serious fishing activities, the cockpit of the ZSF is a little small for a boat this size. Two in-deck fish boxes are standard, and a huge 65-gallon livewell is concealed under the aft seat. At the transom, a bait-prep station includes a cutting board and freshwater sink. Guest seating is provided by two cushioned seats forward of the helm. For overnight trips, the Donzi's compact cabin is equipped with a full galley, port and starboard seats that convert to a dinette via a slide-out table, V-berth, and a large head with sink and shower. The deep walkarounds of the 38 ZSF are wide enough for easy bow access, and visibility from the raised helm position is very good. Additional features include a foredeck sun pad, cockpit bolsters, and transom door. A fast ride with triple 250hp Mercury outboards, the 38 ZSF can hit a top speed of over 50 knots.

See Page 677 For Price Data

Length	38'6"	Fuel	420 gals.
Beam	10'6"	Water	55 gals.
Hull Draft	2'0"	Max HP	900
Dry Weight	15,000#	Hull Type	Deep-V
Clearance, Hardtop	6'6"	Deadrise Aft	22°

Donzi 39 ZSC

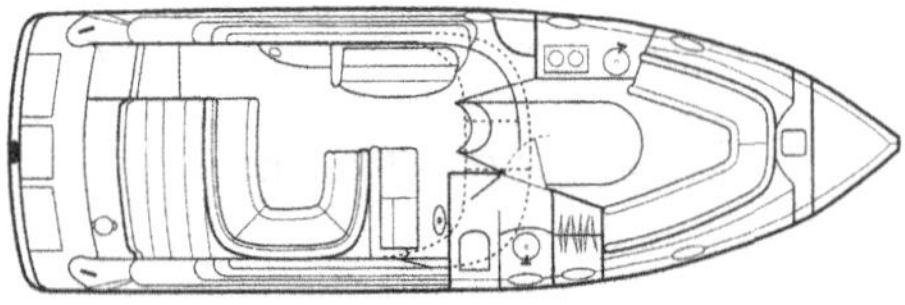

Largest boat in the Donzi fleet, the 39 ZSC is an expensive, high-powered sportcruiser with the aggressive appearance of a European import. The Donzi nameplate has long been associated with performance, and the 39 combines the company's trademark go-fast engineering with a level of creature comfort never before seen in a Donzi. Built on a stepped-hull deep-V bottom, the layout of the ZSC, with its spacious cockpit and compact interior, marks her as more day boat than family cruiser. Her lush cherrywood interior is completely open and efficiently arranged with a small sleeping berth to port (under the cockpit seat), a rather elegant galley, enclosed head and a long V-berth/dinette forward. The cockpit will seat six adults around a high-low table, and drop-down bolster seats at the helm and a portside wet bar are standard. Aft, the power-lift sun pad provides excellent access to the engine compartment. Note that the bow is reached via a walk-through in the windshield. Overall, this is an extremely well finished boat with above-average attention to detail. A fast ride with 425hp MerCruiser gas sterndrives, the Donzi 39 ZSC will reach a top speed of over 40 knots.

See Page 677 For Price Data

Length Overall	39'10"	Clearance, Arch	8'6"
Beam	12'2"	Fuel	302 gals.
Draft, Drives Up	2'3"	Water	40 gals.
Draft, Drives Down	3'3"	Hull Type	Deep-V
Weight	15,500#	Deadrise Aft	22°

Doral

Quick View

- Founded in 1972, Doral began as a builder of small runabouts in Quebec, Canada.
- By the late 1980s, the company had grown to become one of Canada's largest manufacturers of runabouts and cruisers.
- The economic recession of the early 1990s took a toll on Doral's operations and production was shut down in 1992.
- Quebec-based Cadorette Marine purchased Doral's assets and resumed production of the Doral fleet in 1993.
- Cadorette was soon purchased by French sailboat builder Jeanneau. Jeanneau went bankrupt in 1995, leaving Cadorette/Doral an orphan.
- Back in production under new ownership, Doral faltered under the weight of the Great Recession. In and out of bankrupsy for the past few years, it is believed that the last production Doral models were built in 2009.

Doral • www.doral-boat.com

Doral 270 Monticello; 270 Prestancia

Those seeking a comfortable weekend cruiser with conservative lines and better-than-average quality would do well to consider the Canadian-built Doral 270. (Note that she was called the Doral 270 Monticello in 1989–90.) Introduced in 1989, she rides built on a fully cored, modified-V hull with generous beam and a relatively modest 17 degrees of deadrise at the transom. Her midcabin interior is arranged like most boats of this size and type with double berths fore and aft, a standup head compartment, convertible dinette and a small galley with plenty of storage. While the original decor is obviously dated by today's art-deco standards, this is a very open and user-friendly layout with good headroom and storage. Topside, an L-shaped lounge across from the helm comes with a built-in wet bar, and a hidden cockpit shower is located near the transom gate. Additional features include a foredeck sun pad, molded pulpit, radar arch, and a wide swim platform. A good performer, twin 205hp V-6 MerCruiser sterndrives cruise the Doral 270 at a brisk 24 knots and reach a top speed in the neighborhood of 34 knots.

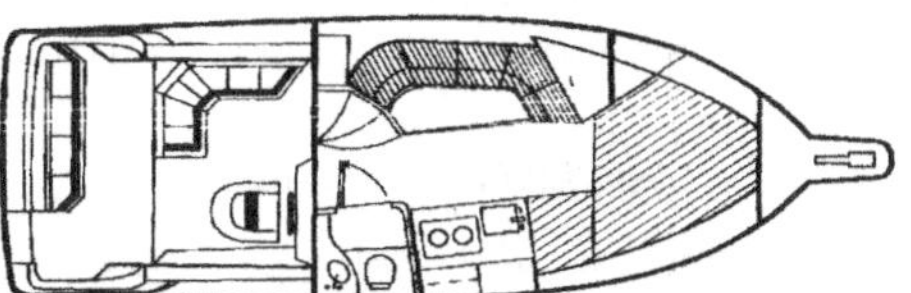

See Page 677 For Price Data

Length w/Pulpit	27'1"	Weight	7,175#
Hull Length	25'4"	Fuel	106 gals.
Beam	9'6"	Water	28 gals.
Draft, Drives Up	1'7"	Hull Type	Modified-V
Draft, Drives Down	2'9"	Deadrise Aft	17°

Doral 270 SC

1996–2002

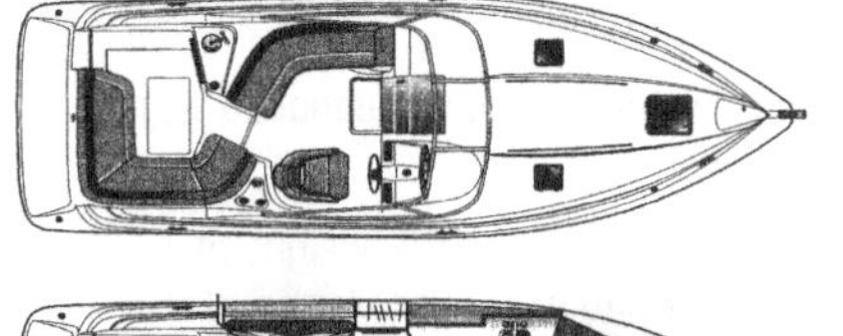

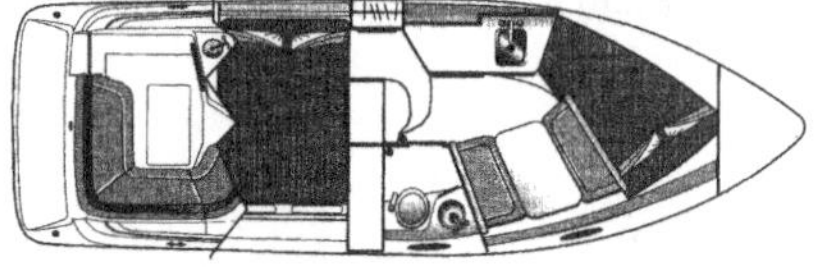

Those seeking a large trailerable family cruiser with plenty of cockpit space will find a lot to like in the Doral 270 SC. This is an excellent choice for day boaters who prefer an expansive cockpit for entertaining and sightseeing at the expense of more limited cabin accommodations. Not everyone will go for this layout of course, but it makes a lot of sense for those who seldom find themselves planning extended cruises to distant ports where the benefits of a spacious interior are most appreciated. The truth is, most folks spend the majority of their time in the cockpit, and it's here that the 270 delivers big-time with more seating and passenger amenities than one would expect in a 27-footer. A swim platform shower and built-in wet bar were standard, and the helm layout is particularly well done. If the midcabin interior is compact, there are still berths for five along with a full galley and a head with shower. On the downside, side decks are practically nonexistent. Built on a fully cored deep-V hull, a single Volvo 260hp)/) will cruise 22 knots (32–33 knots top), and a single 7.4-liter MerCruiser will cruise at 25 knots (mid 30s top).

See Page 677 For Price Data

Length	27'1"	Fuel	100 gals.
Beam	8'6"	Water	30 gals.
Draft, Drives Up	1'6"	Waste	30 gals.
Draft, Drives Down	2'6"	Hull Type	Modified-V
Weight	7,100#	Deadrise Aft	18°

Doral 28 Prestancia

2003–09

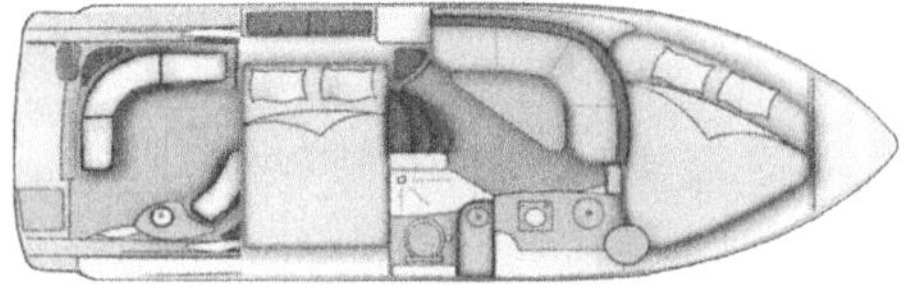

With so many midsized family cruisers to choose from these days, the Doral 28 Prestancia stands apart for her quality construction and rakish—some might say excessive—styling. Aesthetics aside, there's a lot to like about the Prestancia and it's fair to say that she's one of the biggest 28-footers around. Indeed, the cabin accommodations are surprisingly expansive for a boat this size with berths for six, a full galley, and a standup head with sink and shower. Privacy curtains separate the fore and aft sleeping areas from the main cabin, and the forward berth has an adjustable backrest for late-night readers. Note that counter space in the galley is limited, which is typical of most small cruisers. Topside, the Prestancia's cockpit is expandable; the aft lounge slides aft at the flip of a switch to increase space. On the downside, it's difficult for two people to share the double helm seat because the steering wheel is centered. A cockpit wet bar and extended swim platform were standard, and a unique mahogany lounge on the foredeck adjusts into a chair. Among several engine choices, twin 225hp MerCruiser Bravo III drives deliver a top speed of 32–33 knots.

See Page 677 For Price Data

Length w/Platform	32'2"	Fuel	110 gals.
Hull Length	27'9"	Water	30 gals.
Beam	10'1"	Waste	30 gals.
Draft, Down	3'2"	Hull Type	Modified-V
Weight	10,000#	Deadrise Aft	19°

Doral 300 Prestancia

The 300 Prestancia was a popular model in the Doral fleet during her extended 6-year production run, and used models continue to enjoy a good deal of popularity in both the Canadian and northern U.S. markets. Built in Quebec on a fully cored, deep-V hull, her 10-foot beam is quite generous considering that this is really a 28-foot boat. While she lacks the modern integrated swim platform seen in her more modern counterparts, the Prestancia's conservative lines benefit from her curved windshield, subdued hull graphics, radar arch, and fully integrated bow pulpit. With no interior bulkheads, the interior is wide open with privacy curtains for both staterooms, full galley, standup head, and a U-shaped dinette that converts into a huge 6-foot, 8-inch double berth. Seating for six is provided in the cockpit (a bench seat is hidden in the transom), and a convenient hot-and-cold shower is recessed into the transom as well. A well-finished boat inside and out, standard 4.3-liter MerCruiser I/Os cruise the 300 Prestancia at a respectable 18 knots (28 top), and optional 5.7-liter I/Os cruise at 24 knots and reach close to 40 knots wide open.

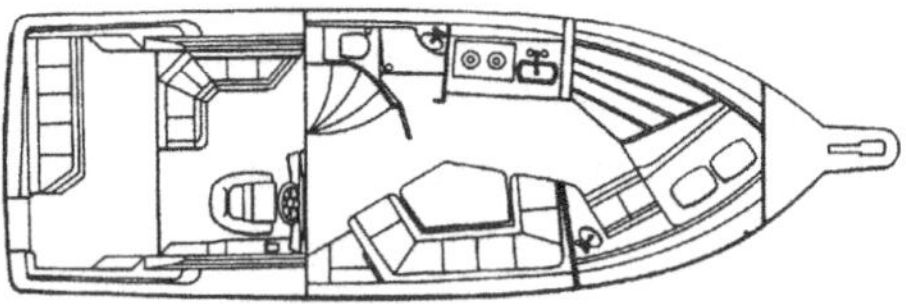

See Page 677 For Price Data

Length w/Pulpit	30'3"	Fuel	136 gals.
Hull Length	28'0"	Water	34 gals.
Beam	10'0"	Waste	26 gals.
Draft	2'11"	Hull Type	Modified-V
Weight	8,275#	Deadrise Aft	18°

Doral 300 SC

In a market crowded with 30-foot midcabin cruisers, the Doral 300 SE's oversized cockpit and distinctive styling set her apart from most competitive models her size and type. Indeed, the cockpit dimensions of the 300 SE are extravagant with lounge seating for seven or eight guests and room left over for a built-in wet bar behind the doublewide helm seat. Obviously designed with outdoor entertainment in mind, Doral engineers crafted in the 300 SE one of the most expansive cockpits to be found in a 30-foot express boat. While the belowdecks accommodations are a bit compact, her midcabin floorplan can sleep six although the forward berth is definitely a tight fit for adults. A full inner liner makes cleanup easy, and the flow-through ventilation ports in the midcabin are unique. Note that Doral also offered a sistership to the 300 SE—the 300 SC—with a larger interior and slightly reduced cockpit dimensions. Built on a fully cored hull, twin 5.7-liter MerCruisers I/Os cruise both models at 23–24 knots and reach a top speed of around 38 knots. With only 134 gallons of fuel, the cruising range is limited.

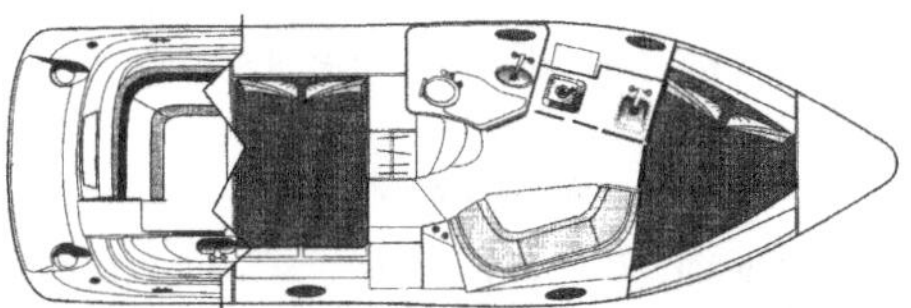

See Page 677 For Price Data

Length	30'2"	Fuel	123 gals.
Beam	10'2"	Water	30 gals.
Draft, Drives Up	1'11"	Waste	30 gals.
Draft, Drives Down	3'2"	Hull Type	Modified-V
Weight	9,642#	Deadrise Aft	18°

Doral 32 Intrigue

Dramatic styling, spacious accommodations, and a good turn of speed characterize the Doral 30 Intrigue (called the 310 SE in 2001–03), a well-built Canadian cruiser priced in the middle range of the 30-foot cruiser market. Built on a fully cored hull with a wide 11-foot, 2-inch beam, the Intrigue's interior layout—with its curved, aft-facing dinette, ample galley and stylish woodwork—offers something different from most boats in her class. The forward berth is more for kids than adults, but the aft stateroom is surprisingly large and includes a cushioned seat in the entryway. Throughout the Intrigue's interior one finds very good workmanship and many quality amenities. Topside, the cockpit can seat up to ten by extending the convertible aft bench out over the swim platform (which adds about 20 square feet to the cockpit area). There's space at the helm for flush-mounting extra electronics, and a windshield walk-through provides easy access to the foredeck. Visibility from the raised helm is excellent. A cockpit wet bar, removable table, and fender racks are standard. Among several engines offered over the years, twin 300hp MerCruisers I/Os cruise in the high 20s (38–40 knots top).

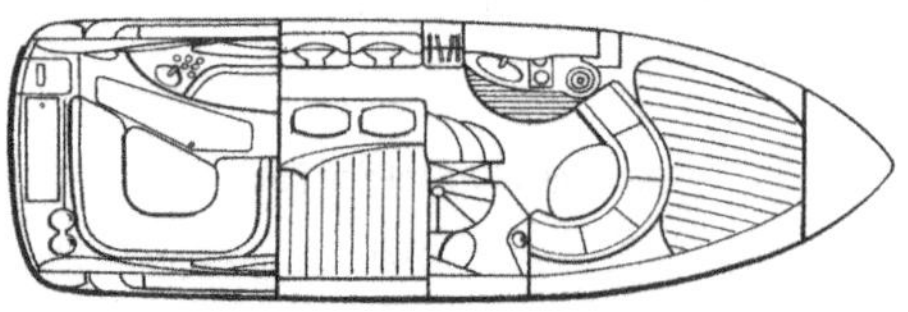

See Page 677 For Price Data

Length w/Platform	33'2"	Weight	12,500#
Hull Length	30'6"	Fuel	166 gals.
Beam	11'2"	Water	40 gals.
Draft, Down	3'7"	Hull Type	Modified-V
Draft, Up	2'5"	Deadrise Aft	19°

Doral 330 SE; 33 Elegante

The Doral Elegante (called the Doral 330 SE in 2001–03) is a heavily styled midcabin cruiser whose bold appearance and innovative interior offer something different in express-boat design. Built on a conventional modified-V hull, a forward-raked arch and fiberglass-capped windshield are her most distinctive features. Belowdecks, there are two tables in the salon; the larger one forward lowers electrically to covert the curved settee into a huge double berth. A privacy door separates the spacious midcabin—with standing headroom at the entrance—from the salon, and the galley is notable for its generous storage. Topside, the Doral's single-level cockpit is a real crowd-pleaser with wraparound seating for a small crowd. Visibility from the double helm seat is very good and a cockpit wet bar is standard. Two criticisms, however: the walk-through windshield steps next to the helm are too narrow, and the transom door is made of plastic rather than fiberglass. Additional features include excellent engine access, a foredeck sun pad, and a transom shower. Offered with several engine options, the Elegante will cruise in the low 20s with twin 320hp MerCruiser I/Os (32–33 knots top).

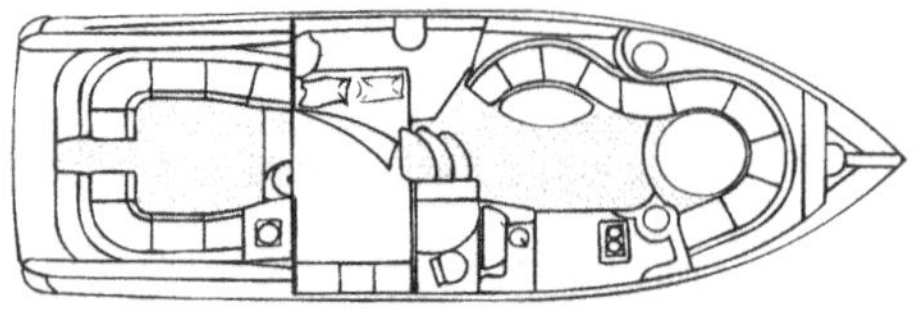

See Page 677 For Price Data

Length w/Platform	37'6"	Fuel	230 gals.
Hull Length	33'2"	Water	44 gals.
Beam	11'11"	Waste	30 gals.
Draft, Down	3'8"	Hull Type	Modified-V
Weight	15,510#	Deadrise Aft	18°

Doral 350 SC

1996–99

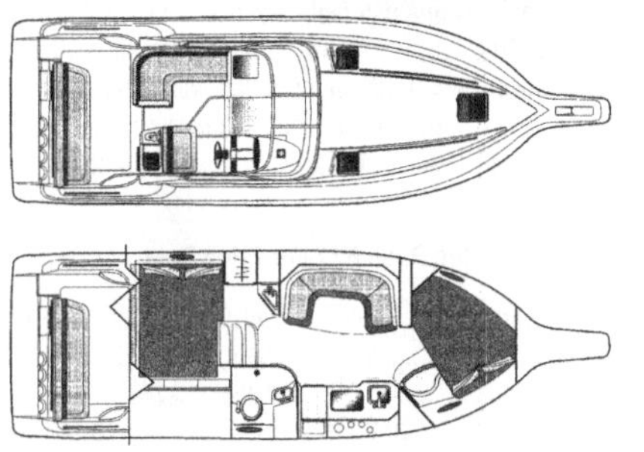

A quality-built boat with a modern express-boat profile, the Doral 350 SC combines a spacious midcabin interior with a cockpit large enough to accommodate a small group of passengers. Built on a fully cored deep-V hull, her belowdecks layout is arranged with double berths fore and aft, a large, well-equipped galley, a convertible dinette, and a standup head with shower. The 350 has more storage space than many boats her size, and three overhead deck hatches provide excellent lighting and cabin ventilation. The Doral's spacious bi-level cockpit will seat up to eight guests and comes standard with a molded wet bar and a very stylish helm with a woodgrain steering wheel and instrument panel. Fender racks were built into the transom, and wide side decks provide secure access to the bow. Note that the cockpit lounge complicates lifting the engine room hatch. Additional features include side exhausts, a large engine compartment, radar arch, and a foredeck sun pad. A good open-water performer, twin 260hp MerCruiser I/Os cruise the Doral 350 SC at 25 knots (low 30s wide top).

See Page 677 For Price Data

Length	36'10"	Fuel	210 gals.
Beam	12'0"	Water	32 gals.
Draft, Drives Up	1'8"	Waste	25 gals.
Draft, Drives Down	3'2"	Hull Type	Deep-V
Weight	12,774#	Deadrise Aft	20°

Doral 360 SE; 36 Boca Grande

1998–2009

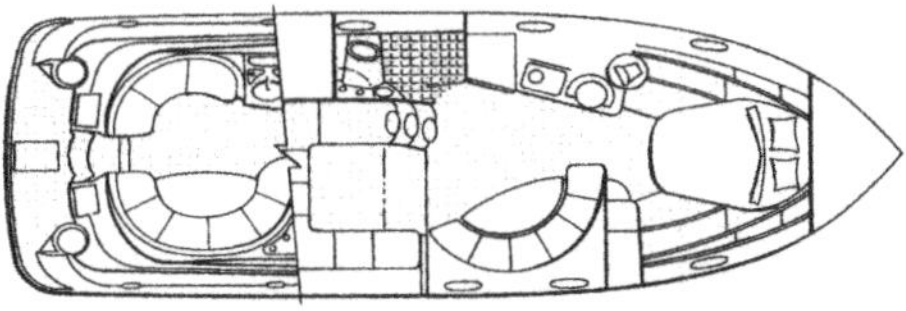

Bold styling is the hallmark of the Doral Boca Grande (called the Doral 360 SE until 2003), an eye-catching French-Canadian design whose forward-facing arch and curvaceous windshield made her a distinctive boat in a sea of look-alike family cruisers. She's constructed on a conventional modified-V hull, fully cored with a wide beam and an integral swim platform. Her midcabin interior features an accordion privacy partition for the forward stateroom (instead of a curtain), an enormous head with a Lexan shower enclosure, and excellent cabin ventilation. Note that the 360's full-size refrigerator is a rarity on a 36-footer. Topside, there's seating for up to eight in the cockpit with its doublewide helm seat, three settees and wet bar. Note that the entire aft cockpit deck rises on hydraulic rams for engine room access. Additional features include a walk-through windshield, fender storage, foredeck sun pad and cockpit wet bar. While a pair of 320hp sterndrives were standard, serious cruisers might opt for the optional 420hp 8.1-liter MerCruiser inboards with V-drives. These engines cruise the Boca Grande at 22–23 knots and reach a top speed in the low 30s.

See Page 677 For Price Data

Length w/Platform	39'3"	Fuel	258 gals.
Hull Length	36'2"	Water	50 gals.
Beam	12'6"	Waste	37 gals.
Draft	3'5"	Hull Type	Modified-V
Weight	18,800#	Deadrise Aft	18°

Doral 45 Alegria

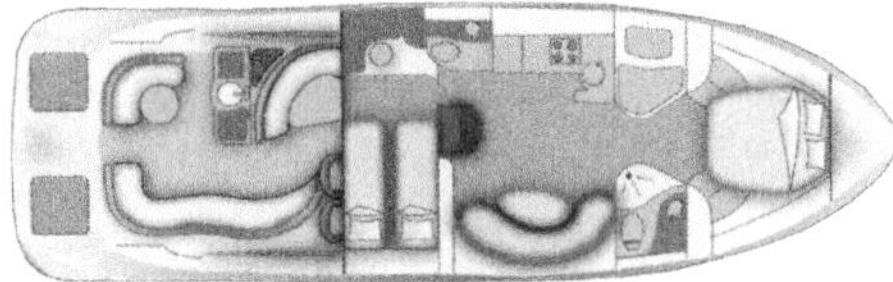

Doral's flagship model, the 45 Alegria was a state-of-the-art sport yacht when she was introduced in 2004. She was Doral's first attempt at a boat over 36 feet, a bold undertaking for a Canadian builder where the pleasure boat market is only a fraction of what it is south of the boarder. Built on a modified deep-V hull with nearly 14 feet of beam, the Alegria is a roomy boat on deck with several innovative features. The cockpit's curvy seating plan differs from most yachts in her class, and the center windshield panel retracts electrically for easy bow access. Below, the Alegria's spacious two-stateroom, two-head interior is a sophisticated blend of lacquered cherry cabinets, Ultraleather seating, and premium hardware and appliances. A fully furnished galley is to port in the salon, opposite a six-person curved leather sofa. Note the seven-foot headroom—no one will feel claustrophobic in this express. A fiberglass hardtop was standard, and a hydraulic swim platform (optional) can stow a dingy or personal watercraft. Early models with 480hp Volvo inboards top out at close to 30 knots. Newer Alegrias with 435hp Volvo IPS drives cruise at 26 knots and reach the low 30s wide open.

See Page 677 For Price Data

Length w/Platform	49'6"'	Fuel	400 gals.
Hull Length	45'3"	Water	92 gals.
Beam	13'10"	Waste	74 gals.
Weight	30,000#	Hull Type	Modified-V
Clearance	11'4"	Deadrise Aft	19°

Eagle Trawlers

Quick View

- Eagle trawlers are built by Transpacific Marine ("Transpac"), one of Taiwan's oldest boat yards with a history of producing numerous sailboat, motoryacht, and trawler designs.
- Transpac was founded in the mid 1960s when Nancy and Ennals Ives were living in Taiwan while building 38' and 40' wooden sailboats.
- In the 1990s, Transpac moved its manufacturing operation from Taiwan to Ningbo, China, where they continue production of Eagle trawlers.

Transpac Marine • Ningpo, China • www.transpacificmarine.com

Eagle 32 Pilothouse Trawler

1985–98

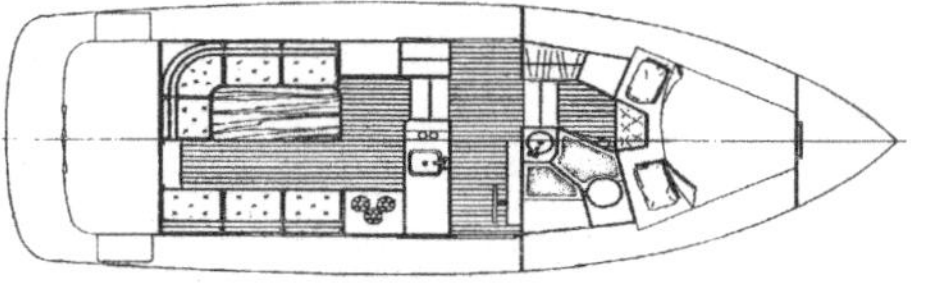

The salty lines and workboat profile of the Eagle 32 portray a sense of confidence unique to tugboat-style designs. Built in Taiwan by Transpacific Marine, her semi-displacement hull is constructed of solid glass with a full-length skeg for prop and rudder protection. Her slightly rounded transom moderates the effects of a following sea, while a hard chine and long keel provide good stability. As it is in most Asian-built boats, the interior of the Eagle is completely finished with grain-matched teak cabinetry and joinery. Visibility from the raised pilothouse is excellent, and a privacy door separates the wheelhouse from the salon for glare-free nighttime running. The stateroom is a little tight, but there's a stall shower in the head compartment and the salon dimensions are quite generous considering the wide side decks. Note that an optional upper helm station is concealed within the false smokestack. Additional features include port and starboard pilothouse deck doors and a functional mast and boom assembly. A single Lehman or Perkins 90hp diesel—or a 135hp Sabre diesel—will cruise at 7–8 knots resulting in an impressive 600-mile range with just 150 gallons of fuel.

Not Enough Resale Data to Set Values

Length Overall	32'0"	Headroom	6'4"
Length WL	28'0"	Fuel	168 gals.
Beam	11'6"	Water	125 gals.
Draft	3'4"	Waste	25 gals.
Weight	17,000#	Hull Type	Displacement

Eagle 40 Pilothouse Trawler

1994–2002

The Eagle 40 will appeal to those who are looking for something different in a double-cabin cruising trawler. Indeed, her salty lines, graceful sheer and low-profile silhouette (note the fake stack behind the pilothouse) give her the businesslike appearance of a commercial workboat. Built in Taiwan by Transpacific Marine, she rides on a solid fiberglass semi-displacement hull with a relatively wide beam, flat aftersections, and a deep prop-protecting keel. The Eagle's all-teak interior is offered with either one or two staterooms forward. The pilothouse is three steps up from the salon level and features a full-size settee with a table, port and starboard deck doors, and a hanging locker—or optional day head—to starboard. Note that a separate stall shower is found in the head in both the single- and twin-stateroom floorplans. Topside, the decks are teak and the upper helm station has a doublewide bench seat. Additional features include a functional mast and boom, a very spacious engineroom, transom door, and well-secured side decks. Among several engine options, a single 135hp Sabre diesel will cruise at 8 knots, and a 225hp Perkins diesel will deliver speeds up to 11 knots.

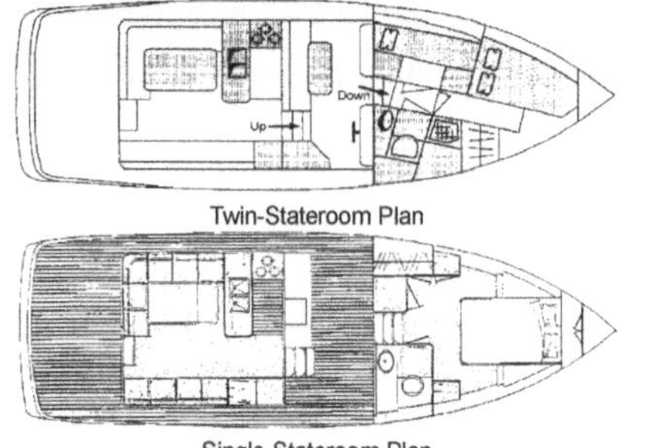

Twin-Stateroom Plan

Single-Stateroom Plan

See Page 678 For Price Data

Length Overall	40'6"	Clearance	NA
Length WL	36'10"	Fuel	400 gals.
Beam	14'6"	Water	240 gals.
Draft	4'5"	Waste	40 gals.
Weight	28,000#	Hull Type	Displacement

Eagle 53 Pilothouse Trawler

2002–Current

Introduced in 2002, the Eagle 53 Pilothouse is a blend of traditional design, spacious accommodations, and a modern semi-displacement hull capable of very efficient cruising speeds. Like all Eagles, the 53 is built in Taiwan by Transpacific Marine, a well-regarded manufacturer with many years of yachting experience. This is a classic pilothouse design with a Portuguese bridge and covered decks, and her cruise-worthy hull incorporates hard aft chines and an extended keel for increased stability. The full teak interior of the Eagle 53 is notable for its comfortable layout and generous storage. A large U-shaped galley is forward in the salon, and the pilothouse—four steps up from the salon level—includes an L-shaped settee, direct bridge access, deck doors, and a centerline helm. A choice of two or three staterooms is offered on the lower level, and an office can be added to replace the third stateroom. Additional features include wide, well-secured side decks, a spacious flybridge with seating for six, an extended swim platform, cored hullsides, and a radar arch. Among several engine options, twin 450hp Cummins diesels cruise the Eagle 53 in the neighborhood of 14–15 knots.

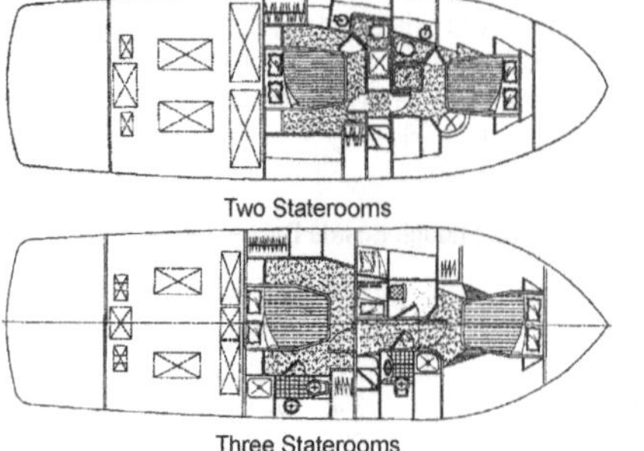
Two Staterooms

Three Staterooms

Not Enough Resale Data to Set Values

Length Overall	53'3"	Headroom	6'6"
Length WL	44'9"	Fuel	830 gals.
Beam	15'9"	Water	250 gals.
Draft	4'0"	Waste	48 gals.
Weight	43,000#	Hull Type	Semi-Disp.

Edgewater

Quick View

- Edgewater was founded in 1990 by ex-Boston Whaler executive Bob Dougherty and his son, Steven, also a lifelong boater.
- In 1995 Dougherty and his son left Edgewater, eventually starting Everglades Boats.
- Edgewater soon became a force in the small center console market as the company earned a reputation for first-class engineering and quality construction.
- In 2007, Edgewater introduced the Edgewater 265 Center Console, the company's first offshore fishing machine.
- All Edgewater boats are constructed with sufficient foam flotation to make them unsinkable.
- Edgewater today markets a full line of center console and express fishing boats, 14' to 33' in length.

EdgeWater Powerboats • Edgewater, FL • www.ewboats.com

Edgewater 260 Center Console

1996–2001

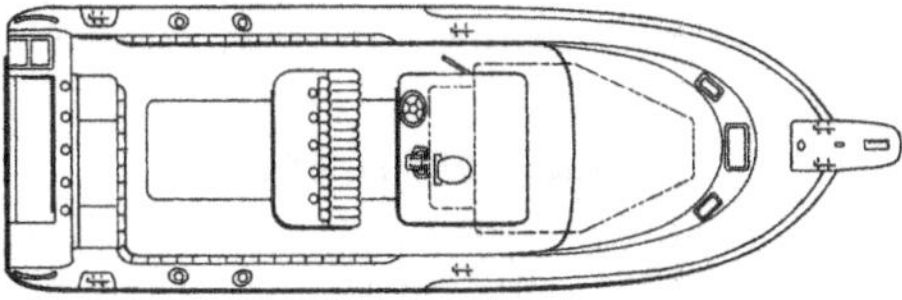

Considering her heritage, it's hardly surprising that many experienced anglers look upon the Edgewater 260 with an envious eye. The Edgewater Boat Company was founded by Bob Dougherty, chief designer for Boston Whaler for 30 years until leaving to start Edgewater (originally called Dougherty Yachts). Aside from being a solid, well-built boat, the 260 includes several innovative features of interest. Constructed on an easy-riding variable deadrise hull with low freeboard, the 260 is the only trailerable fishing boat we know of to come with a lifetime transferable hull warranty. Fishing amenities include dual bait stations (one behind the leaning post and one in the transom), an insulated fishbox, and plenty of rod holders. While many center consoles have a head inside the console, the 260 manages to include a small V-berth as well. Additional features include life jacket storage forward, saltwater washdown, a large helm console with room for flush-mounting an array of electronics, and (like Boston Whalers) positive foam flotation. Not an inexpensive boat, a pair of 150hp Yamaha outboards reach a top speed of around 40 knots.

See Page 678 For Price Data

Length w/Pulpit	28'7"	Fuel	200 gals.
Hull Length	26'7"	Water	NA
Beam	8'6"	Max HP	450
Hull Draft	1'6"	Hull Type	Deep-V
Weight	3,600#	Deadrise Aft	20°

Edgewater 265 Express

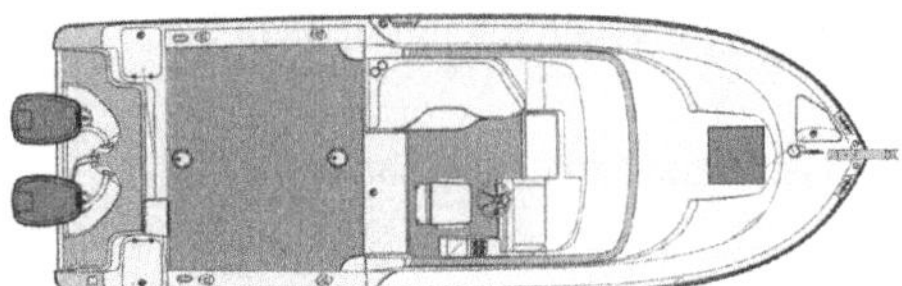

One part family cruiser and one part offshore fishing boat, a wide 9-foot, 6-inch beam makes the Edgewater 265 one of the biggest 26-foot express boats produced in recent years. (Note that most boats this size are trailerable which limits their beam to 8 feet, 6 inches.) Like all Edgewater models, the 265 rides on an unsinkable, foam-filled hull with a solid fiberglass running surface. While there's nothing unusual about her deck layout (except that it's so roomy), the midcabin berth found in the 265's cabin allows her to sleep four—a feature likely to appeal to families with kids. An enclosed head with shower, fully equipped galley with cherry cabinets, and quality hardware and fixtures combine to add a level of comfort seldom found in a small express. On deck, the spacious cockpit of the 265 Express features under-gunwale rod holders, 28-gallon lighted livewell, in-floor fish box, raw water washdown, foldaway rear seat, aft bolsters, and a transom door. The simple and well-designed helm has space for flush-mounting a pair of video displays. A factory hardtop with rocket launches is a popular option. A quick-running boat in spite of her wide beam, twin Yamaha 225s max out at close to 45 knots.

See Page 678 For Price Data

Length	26'6"	Fuel	200 gals.
Beam	9'6"	Water	30 gals.
Hull Draft	1'9"	Max HP	500
Dry Weight	5,400#	Hull Type	Deep-V
Clearance, Top	9'6"	Deadrise Aft	24°

Edgewater 265/268 Center Console

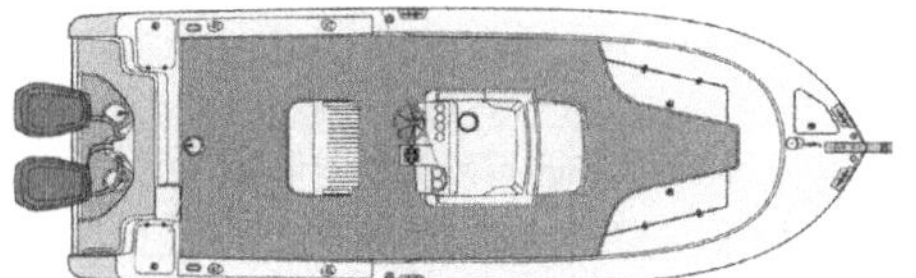

With her wide beam, deep cockpit, and unsinkable deep-V hull, the Edgewater 268 Center Console (called the 265 Center Console in 2002–06) offers anglers a pocket-size fishing rig with genuine offshore capabilities. Where the majority of boats her size are trailerable (limiting the beam to 8 feet, 6 inches), the 268's broad 9-foot, 6-inch beam ranks her at the top of her class in terms of cockpit space and storage capacity. The forward-seating layout includes a slender walk-in console with a Porta-Potti (that slides out of a storage compartment on rails), freshwater sink, and storage. Standard features include a 28-gallon livewell, aft cockpit bolsters, fresh and raw water washdowns, rod storage racks, and an acrylic transom door. There's a foldaway passenger seat along the forward edge of the transom bulkhead, and an Armstrong swim ladder on the engine platform. Note the large console storage box. Two hatches in the forward side of the bulkhead provide access to the boat's batteries located in the bilge. A leaning post and T-top with rocket launchers are popular options. A fast ride in spite of her relatively wide beam, twin Yamaha 225s deliver a top speed of about 45 knots.

See Page 678 For Price Data

Length	26'6"	Fuel	200 gals.
Beam	9'6"	Water	30 gals.
Hull Draft	1'9"	Max HP	500
Dry Weight	5,000#	Hull Type	Deep-V
Clearance, Top	6'6"	Deadrise Aft	24°

Edgewater 318 Center Console

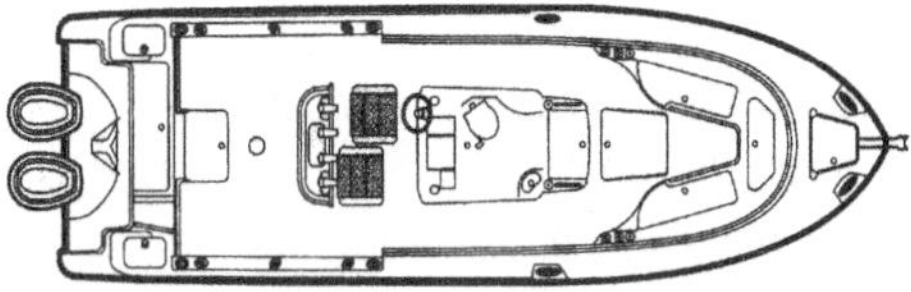

Edgewater has been a leader in high-tech construction since the mid 1990s when the company was founded. Known for their unsinkable hulls, the company's line of center console fishing boats has stood the test of time when it comes to durability and owner satisfaction. Introduced in 2006, the 318 Center Console was then the largest model in the Edgewater fleet. Her roomy cockpit with wraparound forward seating provides more than enough room for several anglers to work without bumping elbows. Two livewells are standard: a 66-gallon centerline main plus a 28-gallon lighted tank in the port corner of the transom. A deluxe leaning post with its tackle storage, foot- and backrests and 150-quart fiberglass cooler is a popular option, as is a fiberglass hardtop with rod holders and spreader lights. The 318's walk-in console includes a Porta-Potti, storage, and sink with hand-held shower. Raw and freshwater washdown systems keep the cockpit clean, and there's also a pullout transom shower and sink. The table between the bow seats goes up and down on an electric ram. Note the lockable rod storage compartments in the port and starboard bulwarks. Expect a top speed of about 45 knots with Yamaha 250s.

See Page 678 For Price Data

Length	31'10"	Fuel	300 gals.
Beam	10'2"	Water	31 gals.
Draft, Up	1'10"	Max HP	600
Draft, Down	2'10"	Hull Type	Deep-V
Hull Weight	6,500#	Deadrise Aft	24°

Egg Harbor

Quick View

- Egg Harbor was founded in 1946 by a group of experienced boat builders, Russell Post, Phil Boyd, Harold Care and C.P. Leek.
- During the 1950s, Leek purchased the remainder of the company's stock from his partners and merged Egg Harbor with his own company, Pacemaker Yachts.
- Fuqua Industries purchased Pacemaker Yachts, Inc. (including Egg Harbor) in 1965. Both companies were subsequently sold to Mission Marine & Associates in 1976.
- Egg Harbor grew throughout the 1960s and '70s, building boats from 30 to 48 feet and converting from wood construction to fiberglass during the early 1970s.
- Unable to service its debt, the company file for bankruptcy in 1990, emerging two years later when the courts approved the company's reorganization plan.
- The company acquired new ownership once again in 1996, however in October, 1997 Egg Harbor was declared insolvent and it's facilities were shut down.
- After some litigation over the rights to the Egg Harbor name, the company was purchased in 2000 by real estate developer Dr. Ira Trocki. Prduction was resumed in 2001.

Egg Harbor Yachts • Egg Harbor, NJ • www.eggharboryacht.com

Egg Harbor 35 Sport Yacht

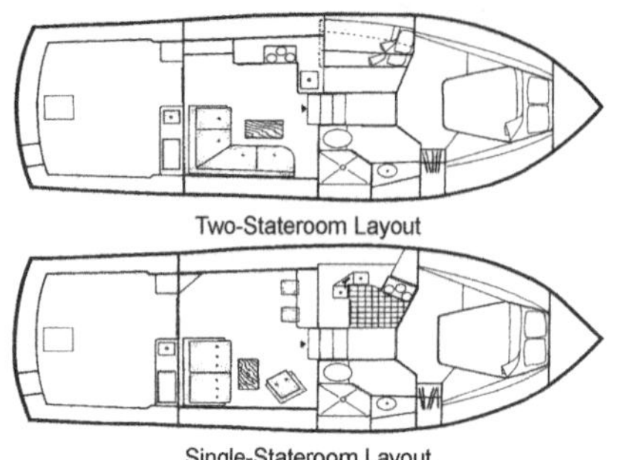

Two-Stateroom Layout

Single-Stateroom Layout

The Egg Harbor 35 Sport Yacht is one of only a few convertibles her size built in recent years. By any standard this is a handsome, beautifully designed boat, another example of why so many boating enthusiasts have held the Egg Harbor brand in such high regard over the years. Introduced in 1997, she's built on the same hull once used for the popular Egg Harbor 33 Convertible (1982–89)—a solid fiberglass modified-V design with low transom deadrise and a moderate 13-foot, 2-inch beam. Two floorplans were offered during her production years: a two-stateroom layout with the galley up, and a single-stateroom, galley-down arrangement with a serving counter overlooking the galley. A full teak interior and salon entertainment center were standard in the 35 Sport Yacht, and both floorplans feature a large forward stateroom with island berth and generous storage. Fishing features include a molded tackle center in the cockpit, transom door, and fresh and raw-water washdowns. Standard 310hp gas engines cruise the 35 Sport Yacht at 18–19 knots (about 27 knots top), and optional 350hp Cat diesels cruise at 23 knots and reach a top speed of 28–29 knots.

See Page 678 For Price Data

Length w/Pulpit	37'8"	Fuel	406 gals.
Hull Length	34'6"	Water	75 gals.
Beam	13'2"	Waste	28 gals.
Draft	3'2"	Hull Type	Modified-V
Weight	20,925#	Deadrise Aft	8°

Egg Harbor 37 Sport Yacht

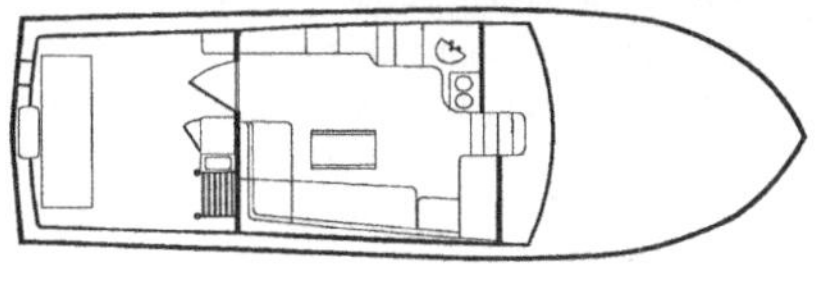

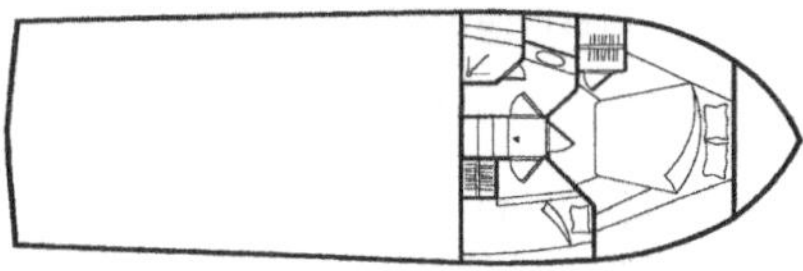

Throughout its history, Egg Harbor consistently builds good-looking boats with inviting interiors and above-average workmanship. The 37 Sport Yacht, introduced in 2001, continued that legacy into the new millennium. Built on a beamy modified-V hull with cored hullsides and a well-flared bow, she carries a little more transom deadrise than previous Egg Harbor models. The upscale interior of the Sport Yacht is an impressive display of varnished woodwork, designer fabrics, and solid brass hardware. There are two staterooms forward, and the very large head has a separate stall shower. The galley is up in this layout, to port in the salon, and a complete entertainment center (with surround sound) is built into the forward windshield area. Topside, the flybridge is large for a 37-footer with seating for five and room to walk behind both helm chairs. The big cockpit is fitted with a transom door, tackle center with sink, an in-deck fish box, direct engineroom access, and a transom livewell. Among several engine choices, twin 420hp Cat diesels cruise the Egg Harbor 37 at a very respectable 27–28 knots and reach a top speed of just over 30 knots.

See Page 678 For Price Data

Length w/Pulpit	40'8"	Fuel	400 gals.
Hull Length	37'6"	Water	80 gals.
Beam	13'6"	Waste	40 gals.
Draft	3'4"	Hull Type	Modified-V
Weight	25,800#	Deadrise Aft	12°

Egg Harbor 38 Convertible

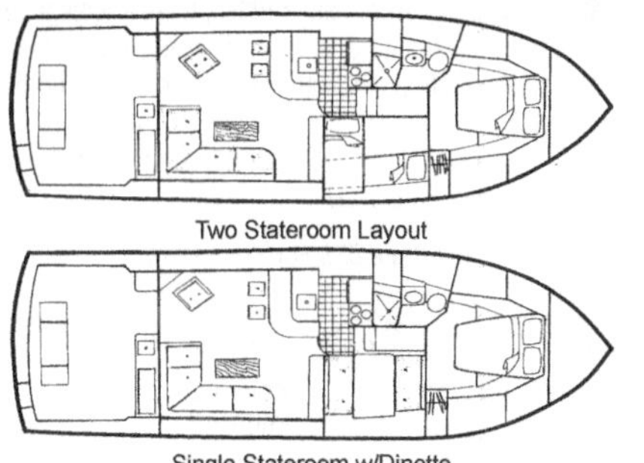
Two Stateroom Layout

Single Stateroom w/Dinette

An updated version of Egg Harbor's previous 38-foot convertible (1990–94), the new Egg 38 incorporates more contemporary styling features than her predecessor while retaining the same interior layouts and hull specifications. Built on a solid fiberglass hull with a wide 15-foot beam, this is a big 38-footer on the inside with more salon space than convertibles her size. Most were delivered with a two-stateroom interior although a single-stateroom, dinette floorplan was available. Either way, the Egg's solid mahogany (or teak) woodwork is finished to exacting standards. The serving counter (with bar stools) in both layouts is an attractive feature, as is the teak-and-holly flooring in the step-down galley. Eliminating the original 38's front windshield provides space for a salon entertainment center. The cockpit came standard with a molded tackle center, port and starboard storage cabinets, macerated fish box, fresh and raw water washdowns, and transom door. With her wide beam, engineroom access is better than most. Among several engine choices, 420hp 3126 Cats cruise at 25 knots (about 30 top). Older models with 485hp GMs will run close to the same speeds.

See Page 678 For Price Data

Length w/Pulpit	41'8"	Fuel, Diesel	506 gals.
Hull Length	38'6"	Fuel, Gas	406 gals.
Beam	15'0"	Water	115 gals.
Draft	3'10"	Hull Type	Modified-V
Weight	30,600#	Deadrise Aft	8°

Egg Harbor 42 Sport Yacht

Modern styling, luxurious accommodations, and impressive performance are the hallmarks of the Egg Harbor 42 Sport Yacht, a classic Jersey-built convertible from a company whose name has long been synonymous with quality and tradition. Built on a low-deadrise hull with a relatively wide 15-foot beam, cored hullsides, and a solid fiberglass bottom, the Sport Yacht's comfortable two-stateroom interior is arranged with an island berth in the forward stateroom and over/under bunks in the guest cabin. A breakfast bar overlooks the step-down galley, and the salon is highlighted by a sectional Ultraleather sofa and built-in entertainment center. Note the granite sole in the galley and head. As it is in all late-model Egg Harbor yachts, the varnished teak woodwork is finished to exacting standards. The 42's spacious cockpit is equipped with all the amenities expected in a yacht of this caliber, including a tackle center with sink, transom door, fish box, and direct access to the engineroom. An underwater exhaust system was standard. A stiff ride in a chop, twin 660hp Cats cruise in the high 20s and top out at over 30 knots.

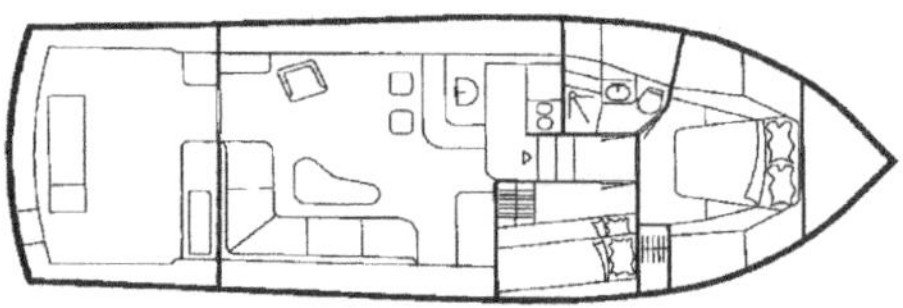

See Page 678 For Price Data

Length w/Pulpit	45'4"	Clearance	13'0"
Hull Length	42'2"	Fuel	600 gals.
Beam	15'0"	Water	115 gals.
Draft	3'10"	Waste	25 gals.
Weight	36,300#	Hull Type	Modified-V

Egg Harbor 43 Sport Yacht

Introduced in 2004, the Egg Harbor 43 Sport Yacht replaced the look-alike Egg Harbor 42 Sport Yacht produced from 2001–03. In spite of their nearly identical profiles, the 43 rides on a completely redesigned hull with considerable more transom deadrise that the 42, a little less draft, and prop pockets to reduce the shaft angles. Compared with her predecessor, the 43 is a better roughwater performer with improved headsea characteristics and a more level ride. Below, the luxurious interior of the 43 Sport Yacht is as good as it gets in a modern Egg Harbor product. The salon features a sectional sofa to starboard and a snack bar to port, and the step-down galley allows easy communication with those in the salon. There are two staterooms forward, and a dinette is optional in the salon. The high-gloss cherry woodwork is finished to a very high standard. Like all Egg Harbor convertibles, there are plenty of amenities for anglers including a transom livewell, full tackle center, and large fish box. Additional features include an engineroom sea chest, retractable flybridge electronics console, and an uncluttered engineroom. A well-finished boat, 700hp Cats cruise in the mid 20s and reach 30+ knots wide open.

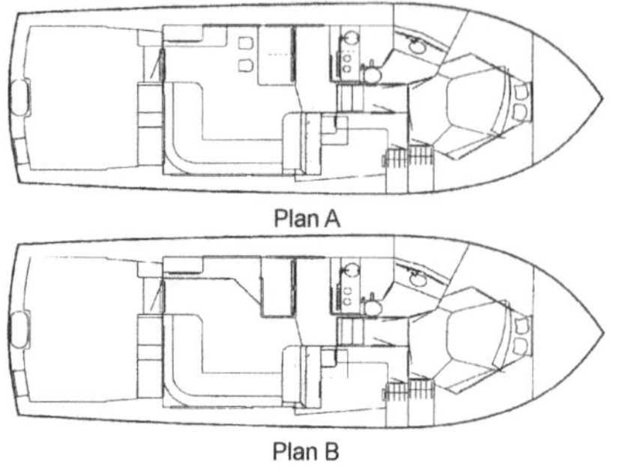

See Page 678 For Price Data

Length w/Pulpit	45'8"	Fuel	650 gals.
Hull Length	42'6"	Water	115 gals.
Beam	15'0"	Waste	40 gals.
Draft	3'6"	Hull Type	Modified-V
Weight	38,500#	Deadrise Aft	16°

Egg Harbor 52 Sport Yacht

1997–2005

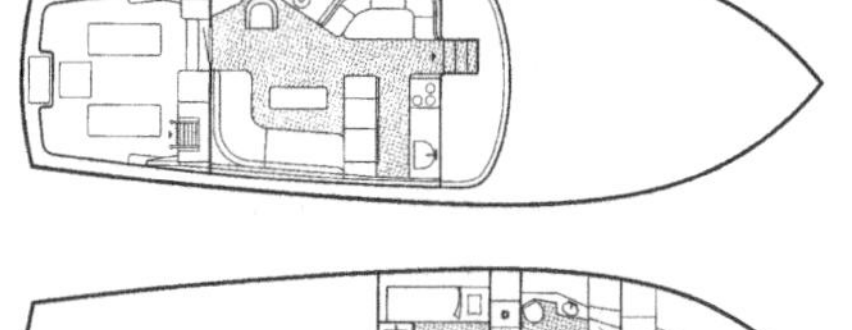

For many design enthusiasts, the Egg Harbor 52 Sport Yacht had it just about right—an impressive blend of beautiful styling, luxurious accommodations and excellent performance. Her tapered, modified-V hull has more bow flare than previous Egg Harbor models, and a sharp entry and low transom deadrise result in a dry and very maneuverable boat, quick to plane and a fast ride in open water. Her standard galley-up floorplan is arranged with the owner's stateroom amidships (note the full bath in the adjoining head) and a guest stateroom forward, both with double berths. A small third stateroom is to port, partially tucked under the dinette. The lush salon of the Egg Harbor 52, with its high-gloss teak cabinetry and designer fabrics, is quite wide which results in some fairly narrow side decks. The cockpit is one of the largest to be found in a 50-foot convertible. The same is true of the flybridge—it's massive. Additional features include two big fish boxes, a transom baitwell and transom door. Among several engine choices offered since her introduction, twin 800hp Cats cruise the Egg Harbor 52 in the mid 20s and reach 30+ knots wide open.

Not Enough Resale Data to Set Values

Length w/Pulpit	54'9"	Fuel	900 gals.
Beam	16'4"	Water	175 gals.
Draft	4'0"	Waste	60 gals.
Weight	52,000#	Hull Type	Modified-V
Clearance	13'7"	Deadrise Aft	7°

Egg Harbor 58 Convertible

1990–96

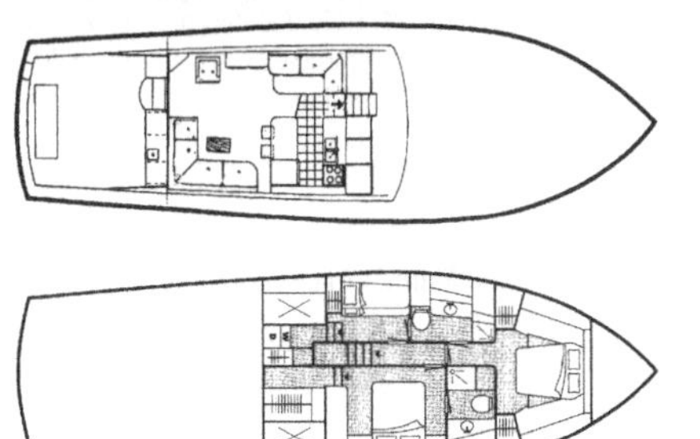

The Egg Harbor 58 is a scaled-down version of the Egg Harbor 60 Convertible introduced back in 1986. With her long foredeck, sweeping sheer, and rakish superstructure, the Egg Harbor 58 is a study in classic, Jersey-style design. She's built on a low-deadrise hull with a wide 17-foot, 6-inch beam, cored hullsides, and a solid fiberglass bottom. Below, the 58's standard interior is arranged with three staterooms on the lower level and the low-profile galley forward in the salon. The owner's suite is amidships in this layout (note that a step-down dressing room extends under the salon floor) and includes a queen bed and a tub/shower in the head. A washer/dryer is standard, situated just aft of the second guest stateroom, which can also be configured as an office. Typical of all Egg Harbor yachts, richly finished cabinets and furnishings highlight the interior. The cockpit of the Egg Harbor 58 is huge and so is the flybridge, which provides seating for a small crowd. A good open-water performer, she'll cruise in the mid-to-high 20s with 1,100hp 12V92 Detroit diesels (30+ knots top), and later models with 1,335hp MTUs cruise at a very fast 34 knots and reach a top speed of 40+ knots.

Not Enough Resale Data to Set Values

Length w/Pulpit	62'8"	Fuel	1,360 gals.
Hull Length	58'6"	Water	220 gals.
Beam	17'6"	Waste	100 gals.
Draft	5'3"	Hull Type	Modified-V
Weight	82,000#	Deadrise Aft	7°

Everglades

Quick View

- Everglades was formed in 1999 by former Boston Whaler executive (and Edgewater Boats founder) Bob Dougherty and his son, Steven.
- Everglades is best known for their patented, Rapid Molded Core Assembly Process (RAMCAP) which makes Everglades boats virtually unsinkable.
- Everglade's RAMCAP technology won the 1999 National Marine Manufacturers Association (NMMA) Innovation Award.
- In 2005, the Everglades 290 Pilot Center Console won the NMMA Innovation Award.
- Many marine industry professionals consider Everglades center consoles to be at the top of their class in terms of design innovation, construction quality, and overall fit and finish.

Everglades Boats • Edgewater, FL • www.evergladesboats.com

Everglades 260/270/275 Center Console

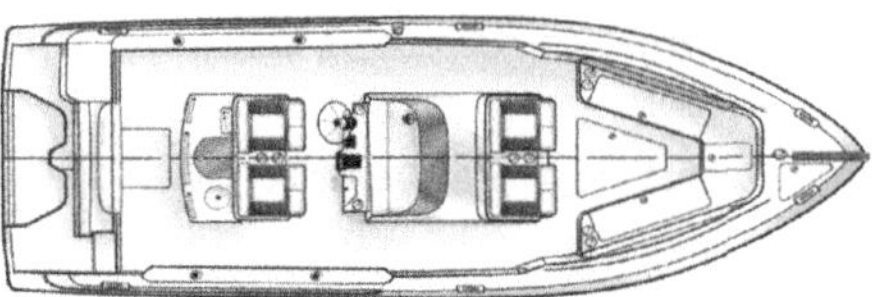

More than a few industry professionals view Everglades as the BMWs of center consoles. Hands down, these guys know how to build a top-quality product. Introduced in 2006 as the 260 Center Console (and called the 270 Center Console in 2008–10), this popular model was marketed as the 275 Center Console in 2011. Designed with plenty of space for family and friends, there are comfortable seats at the stern, helm, and forward of the console. The integrated T-top/console, with its wraparound windshield, offers outstanding helm protection in all kinds of weather. Standard features include a leaning post/bolster seat with 55-gallon livewell, bait rigging station (updated on the 275 model), lockable rod storage, a fold-down transom seat, docking lights, and powder-coated railings. The slide-out cooler is a nice touch. The transom seat lifts for access to the batteries and thru-hulls. Note that the console/hardtop design was updated in the 275 model, and the helm seats are wider. Like all Everglades boats, the foam-filled hull is unsinkable. The fit and finish of the 275 is very, very impressive. Not inexpensive, she'll attain a top speed of around 45 knots with twin Yamaha 250s.

See Page 678 For Price Data

Length	26'7"	Fuel	200 gals.
Beam	9'9"	Water	25 gals.
Draft, Up	1'8"	Max HP	600
Draft, Down	3'0"	Hull Type	Deep-V
Hull Weight	6,000#	Deadrise Aft	21°

Everglades 290/295 Center Console

2005–Current

A distinctive boat with her fully integrated hardtop/windshield, the Everglades 295 Center Console (called the 290 Center Console in 2005–10) hits all the right buttons with serious anglers. In the world of offshore fishing boats, Everglades ranks near the top when it comes to engineering and performance. The company's proprietary RAMCAP construction process insures that all Everglades boats are unsinkable. Designed with space for family and friends, there are seats at the stern, helm, and forward of the console. The combined T-top/console—with its wraparound windshield—offers outstanding helm protection in all kinds of weather. Standard features include a deluxe leaning post/helm seat with 66-gallon circulating livewell, large console compartment with marine head, sink and shower, lockable rod storage, two insulated fish boxes, slide-out cooler, tackle lockers (2), toe rails, fresh and raw water washdowns, and a foldaway transom seat. There are four rod holders in the gunwales, six in the transom, and six more across the back of the hardtop. Note the powder-coated bow rails. Exceptional fit & finish throughout. Nearly 45 knots top with twin Yamaha 250s.

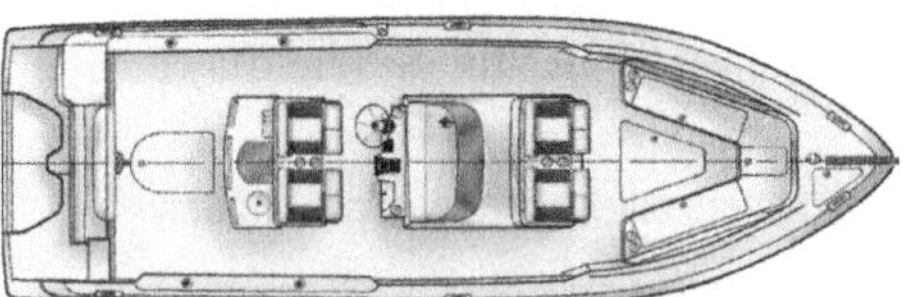

See Page 678 For Price Data

Length	28'7"	Fuel	200 gals.
Beam	9'9"	Water	25 gals.
Hull Draft	1'8"	MaxHP	700
Hull Weight	6,300#	Hull Type	Deep-V
Clearance	7'8"	Deadrise Aft	21°

Everglades 350/355 Center Console

2007–Current

A high-end fishing machine and the largest boat in today's Everglades fleet, the 355 Center Console (called the 350 Center Console in 2007–11) is stylish, fast, and loaded with amenities. Built on a deep-V hull using the company's proprietary RAMCAP construction process, the 355 is virtually unsinkable thanks to the urethane foam injected between the hull and deck. She's also innovative—the combined glass windshield/T-top has become an Everglade's trademark. Standard features include triple helm seats with flip-up bolsters, electric high-low bow table, foldaway stern seating, two livewells, forward fish box and cooler, and an aft bait freezer. A clever foldaway seat on the rear of the bait well doubles as fighting chair. The 355's large console head compartment includes a small quarter berth plus a sink, shower, and storage drawers. An anchor hatch at the bow provides access to the windlass, control switches, and a washdown hose. The powder-coated windshield frames and bow rails are a classy touch, and the hardtop has a built-in ladder for access to an optional upper helm station. This kind of quality doesn't come cheap. Triple 300hp Suzukis top out at over 40 knots.

Floorplan Not Available

See Page 678 For Price Data

Length	35'4"	Fuel	411 gals.
Beam	10'8"	Water	35 gals.
Draft, Up	2'0"	Max HP	1050
Draft, Down	3'2"	Hull Type	Deep-V
Hull Weight	9,500#	Deadrise Aft	25°

Fairline Yachts

Quick View

- Founded in 1867, Fairline began operations as a post-war builder of small powerboats for the local English market.
- The company expanded rapidly in the 1980s developing lines of high-speed cruising yachts.
- In 1988, with a worldwide economic recession on the horizon, Fairline invested hugely in a new flagship, the Squadron 62 Motor Yacht, which made its debut in 1992.
- In 2002, the 10,000th Fairline was completed, together with new production facilities at the original Oundle, England, site.
- In 2010, Fairline is put up for sale by 3i, a London-listed private equity group.
- After months of speculation regarding Fairline's future, in 2011 the company was purchased in a joint venture between an investment firm and the Royal Bank of Scotland.
- Using an extensive dealer network, Fairline has historically exported approximately 85% of its sales to Spain, Norway, France and America.

Fairline Boats • Oundle, England • www.fairline.com

Fairline 40 Targa

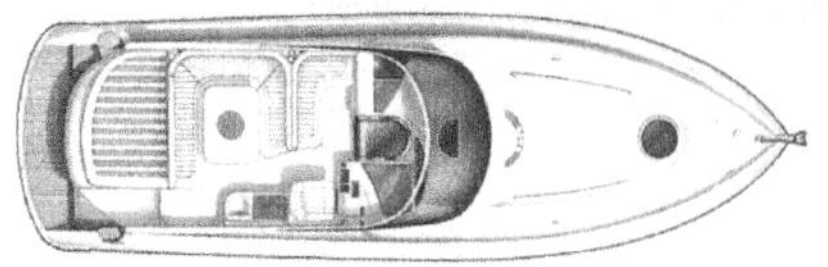

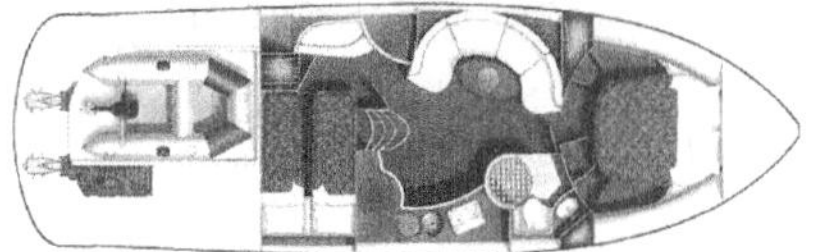

The Fairline 40 Targa is a quality European sportcruiser from a company that seldom misses the mark when it comes to building well-styled, good-running boats. Built on a deep-V hull with moderate beam, the Targa's sleek exterior conceals a dinghy garage at the stern—a useful feature seldom found in a boat this size. The cockpit, which is impeccably detailed and finished, has a convenient food-prep unit across from the U-shaped lounge with a barbecue, refrigerator and sink. Belowdecks, the midcabin interior of the 40 Targa is an impressive display of high-gloss woodwork and practical design. Headroom is excellent; there's a separate stall shower in the head, and both staterooms have doors instead of privacy curtains. The engineroom, beneath the transom garage, is roomy enough but can only be accessed if the dinghy is removed. Note that the king-size sun pad aft rises hydraulically for access to the tender storage compartment below. A bow thruster is standard—a definite plus—but the side decks are narrow and bow access is difficult. Twin 285hp Volvo diesel sterndrives cruise the 40 Targa at 27–28 knots and reach a top speed in the low 30s.

See Page 678 For Price Data

Length Overall	41'10"	Water	79 gals.
Beam	12'1"	Clearance	13'2"
Draft, Down	3'0"	Headroom	6'4"
Weight	16,000#	Hull	Deep-V
Fuel	197 gals.	Deadrise Aft	17°

Fairline 43 Phantom

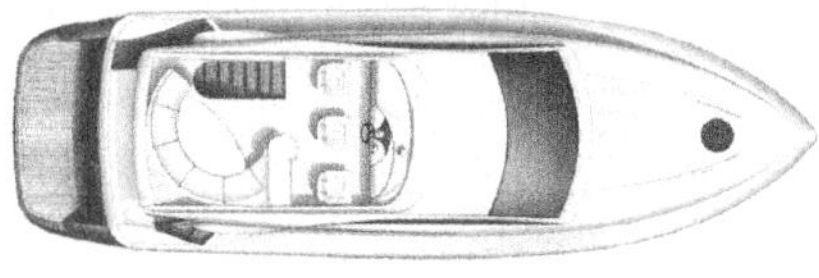

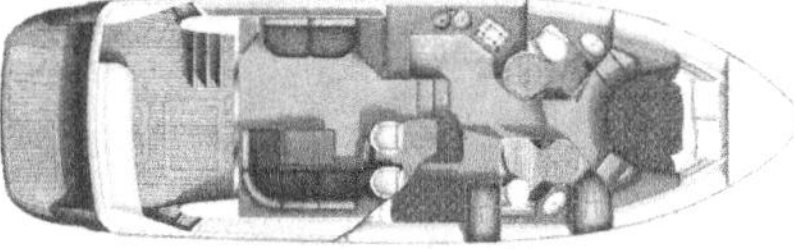

Fairline consistently builds good-looking boats with sporty lines and well-finished interiors. The 43 Phantom follows in that tradition with a sleek, eye-catching profile and a thoughtful two-stateroom floorplan that strikes a good balance between comfort and practicality. Like nearly all European flybridge yachts, the Phantom comes with an elevated lower helm—a desirable feature that in this case provides excellent visibility both fore and aft. The master stateroom is at the bow and the guest cabin is to starboard, directly below the lower helm. Both are equipped with a private head and stall shower. The galley is down, opposite the guest stateroom, where it benefits from plenty of storage. On deck, the cockpit has an integral transom seat and a huge storage lazarette under the sole, and there's an immense lounge area aft of the flybridge helm position. Additional features include cherry interior woodwork, a flybridge wet bar, port and starboard electric cabin windows, wide side decks, and a teak cockpit sole. On the downside, the engine-room is a tight fit. A good performer, 480hp Volvo diesels cruise the 43 Phantom at 27 knots and reach 31–32 knots top.

See Page 678 For Price Data

Length Overall	44'6"	Fuel	410 gals.
Hull Length	43'1"	Water	209 gals.
Beam	13'7"	Clearance	6'4"
Draft	3'6"	Hull Type	Deep-V
Weight	29,000#	Deadrise Aft	17°

Fairline 43 Squadron

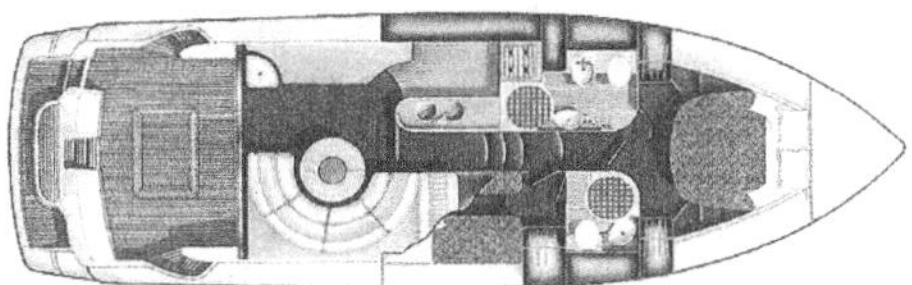

Smallest in Fairline's series of Squadron motor yachts during her mid-1990s production years, the 43 Squadron is a traditional European flybridge cruiser from one of Britian's largest powerboat manufacturers. Like most of her European competitors, she's built on a deep-V hull with moderate beam, an integrated swim platform, and propeller tunnels to reduce shaft angles and draft. While a three-stateroom layout was available, the two-stateroom floorplan (below) is generally considered more practical in a boat this size. This is a raised-pilothouse design with the helm completely open to the salon and a well-appointed sunken galley to port. The guest stateroom is tucked under the lower helm (headroom in the entry-way only), and the head adjoining the master stateroom is huge. The main area of the deckhouse is finished in light maple, and the lower-level salon windows give a good view of the outside for passengers. Both the cockpit and swim platform are teak-planked, and fender storage is built into the stylish transom. With standard 420hp Cat diesels, the 43 Squadron will cruise at 25 knots and reach 30+ knots wide open.

Not Enough Resale Data to Set Values

Length Overall	44'5"	Fuel	360 gals.
Hull Length	42'9"	Water	130 gals.
Beam	13'7"	Headroom	6'5"
Draft	3'6"	Hull	Deep-V
Weight	31,000#	Deadrise Aft	17°

Fairline 43 Targa

1998–2004

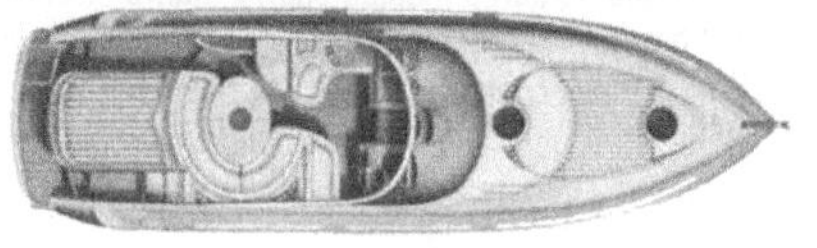

A good-selling model in the U.S., the Fairline 43 Targa's combination of sleek styling, exceptional finish, and excellent performance hits all the right buttons. There's much to admire in this boat; the styling was cutting-edge when she was introduced in 1998, and her space-efficient layout rivals many larger express boats for comfort and versatility. Built on a solid fiberglass deep-V hull with prop pockets, the slender 12'6" beam of the 47 Targa goes a long way toward explaining her exceptional open-water performance. (The wider the beam, the more power—and fuel—it takes to get up and running.) Below, the Targa's elegant two-stateroom, two-head interior is a blend of lacquered cherry cabinets, rich leather seating, and premium hardware and furnishings. The galley is timber-floored with a sweeping counter concealing a two-burner stove, oven, grill and a sink. Topside the single-level cockpit features a large dining area with wraparound seating, wet bar with sink and fridge, and an optional barbecue. Beneath the large aft sun deck lies a concealed garage for a tender. Note the teak-laid swim platform. A fast ride, twin 480hp Volvo diesels cruise at 28 knots (mid 30s top).

See Page 678 For Price Data

Length Overall	45'1"	Fuel	336 gals.
Beam	12'6"	Water	90 gals.
Draft	3'3	Waste	54 gals.
Weight	20,723#	Hull Type	Deep-V
Clearance	13'3"	Deadrise Aft	18°

Fairline 46 Phantom

1999–2005

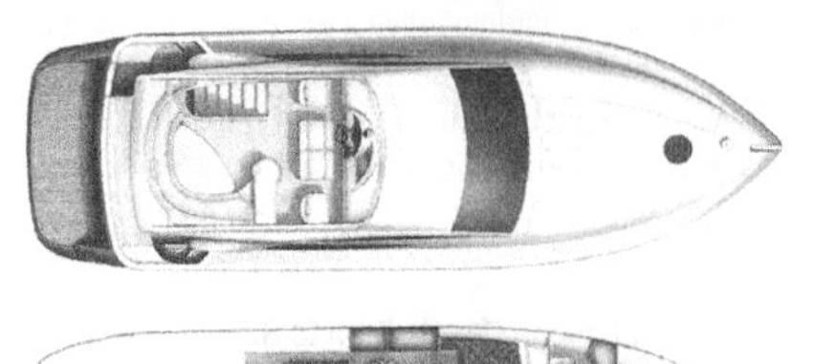

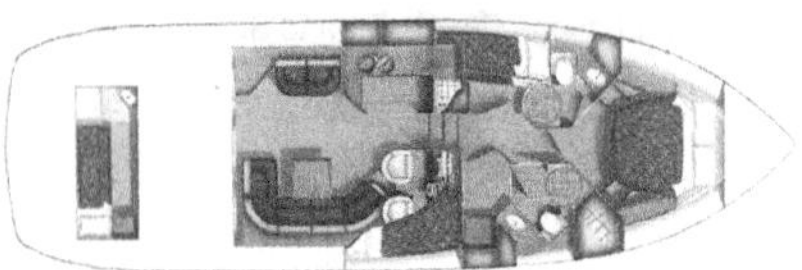

The 46 Phantom stands apart from other European flybridge yachts her size not just for her aggressive styling, but also for her spacious three-stateroom interior. It's rare to find a 46-footer with three staterooms and the Phantom can even be ordered with a fourth (crew quarters) cabin aft for a total of four staterooms and three heads. Built on an easy-riding deep-V hull with propeller pockets, the galley is up in this layout (rather than down as it is on most European flybridge boats), and there are two pedestal seats at the elevated lower helm. While the guest cabins are fairly small, the Phantom's galley—forward and to port in the salon—is large with plenty of counter space. The flybridge, which is partially shaded by a flybridge overhang, is equally spacious with four-across seating at the helm, a wet bar and a six-seat dinette aft that converts to a sun pad. Additional features include a teak cockpit sole and swim platform, molded flybridge steps, wide side decks and lacquered cherry interior joinery. A well-finished yacht with handsome lines, twin 480hp Volvo diesels cruise the Fairline 46 Phantom at 24 knots and reach a top speed of 28–29 knots.

See Page 678 For Price Data

Length Overall	47'10"	Fuel	416 gals.
Hull Length	46'0"	Water	187 gals.
Beam	14'2"	Clearance	16'6"
Draft	3'8"	Hull	Deep-V
Weight	29,000#	Deadrise Aft	19°

Fairline 47 Targa

2005–11

No ordinary express, the Fairline 47 Targa combines the spirited performance one expects in a purebred European sport cruiser with the lush amenities of a small motoryacht. Targas have long been known for their powerful lines and luxuriously equipped living areas, and the 47 Targa—introduced in 2005—took these attributes to the next level. Built on a deep-V with prop pockets and a slender 13'2" beam, the Targa's dramatic styling is coupled with a surprisingly spacious cockpit with retractable roof. In its open form, with the canvas roof retracted, there is a true sense of freedom that continues out onto the cockpit with its large sun pad. Below, the twin-cabin, twin-head interior of the 47 Targa features a comfortable main salon with a U-shaped leather settee and large galley with full-size refrigerator. The master stateroom is forward, and twin berths in aft cabin convert to double berth. Avonite counters are found in the galley and head. On the downside, cabin headroom is barely 6 feet throughout. A large stern platform has integrated garage for a tender. Good engineroom access, from the port side of the transom, is a plus. A bow thruster is standard. Cruise at 30 knots with Volvo 575hp diesels (35 knots top).

Not Enough Resale Data to Set Values

Length	47'0"	Fuel	370 gals.
Beam	13'2"	Water	80 gals.
Draft	3'6"	Waste	96 gals.
Weight	28,360#	Hull Type	Deep-V
Clearance	15'7"	Deadrise Aft	18°

Fairline 47/50 Squadron

1993–97

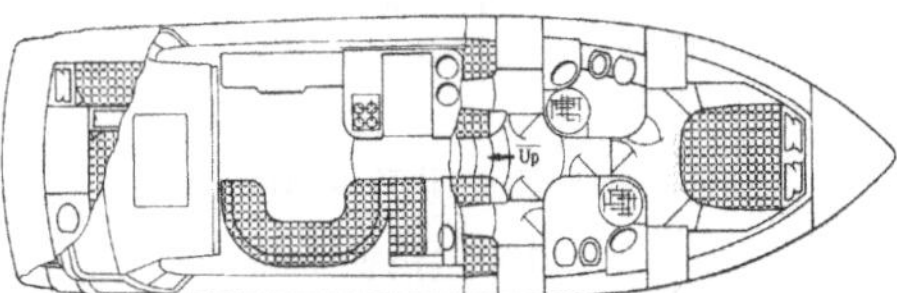

The Fairline 50 Squadron (introduced as a 47-footer, the 50 Squadron came out in 1995 with an extended swim platform) is basically a scaled-down version of the popular 56 Squadron introduced in 1993. The split-level floorplan is retained along with the same three-stateroom layout on the lower level, the principal difference being the 47/50's absence of a dinette and inside flybridge access. Like all Squadron models, hull construction is solid fiberglass, and propeller tunnels are used to keep shaft angles and draft to a minimum. Entering from the cockpit, the salon (whose dimensions are not extravagant) seems unusually wide open and comfortable, thanks in part to the fact that the galley is forward—opposite the helm—rather than farther aft in the salon. Throughout, high-gloss maple joinery and quality furnishings combine to present a very luxurious and appealing interior. Additional features include a crew cabin aft (under the cockpit sole), two large heads with circular stall showers, and a roomy flybridge with plenty of guest seating. Standard 550hp GM 6V92 diesels cruise the Fairline 47/50 Squadron in the mid 20s (about 30 knots top).

Not Enough Resale Data to Set Values

Length Overall	51'0"	Fuel	489 gals.
Hull Length	47'5"	Water	150 gals.
Beam	14'8"	Clearance	16'10"
Draft	3'8"	Hull	Deep-V
Weight	38,000#	Deadrise Aft	18°

Fairline 48 Targa

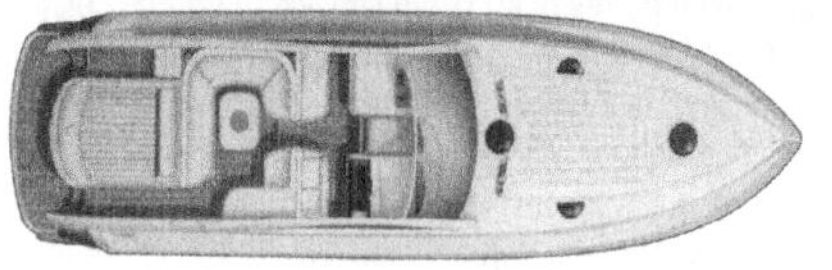

A striking yacht, the Fairline 48 Targa is a purebred Mediterranean sportcruiser whose sleek profile (dominated by a fiberglass-framed elliptical windshield) compares well with anything Sea Ray or Sunseeker has produced to date. She's built on a deep-V hull with shallow prop pockets to reduce draft, and her narrow, easily driven hull goes a long way toward explaining her good performance with relatively modest power. Fitting three staterooms in the Targa 48 was a challenge solved by placing side-by-side guest cabins below the helmdeck, each with twin single berths. While the salon is quite spacious and expertly finished, the en suite head attached to the forward stateroom is quite small and the doors to the aft cabins are narrow. On deck, the cockpit is divided into three areas: the command bridge at the front, settee and wet bar in the middle, and a centerline garage for a tender aft with a hydraulically activated door. A teak cockpit sole is standard and the side decks are wide and safe. Considered a benchmark boat in the eyes of many aficionados, twin 430hp Cats—shoehorned into a tight engineroom—will cruise the 48 Targa in the mid 20s and reach a top speed of 30+ knots.

See Page 678 For Price Data

Length	49'10"	Fuel	360 gals.
Beam	12'11"	Water	120 gals.
Draft	3'3"	Waste	40 gals.
Weight	24,600#	Hull Type	Deep-V
Clearance	NA	Deadrise Aft	19°

Fairline 50 Phantom

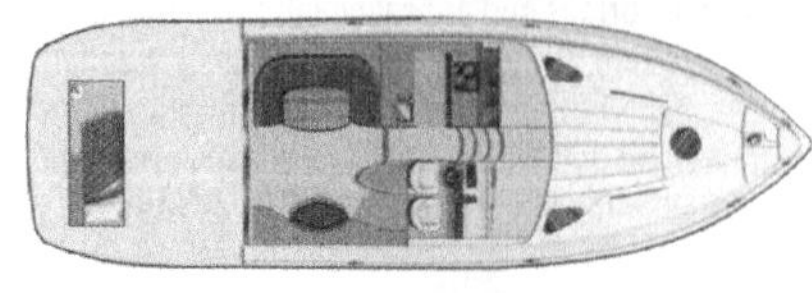

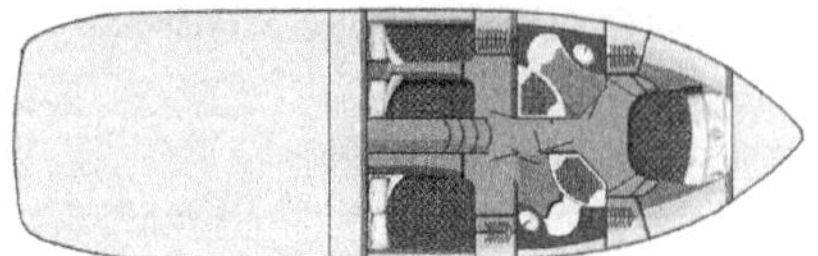

In the Phantom 50, Fairline designers kept the styling conservative while offering some innovative interior touches, a good turn of speed, and superior rough-water handling characteristics. Like all Fairline models, the Phantom is built on a solid fiberglass deep-V hull with shallow prop pockets to reduce draft. The Phantom's three-stateroom layout is arranged with the master stateroom forward and the guest staterooms aft, partially tucked under the main cabin. Both head compartments are quite large—a welcome contrast to the too-small heads found in many European yachts—and the entire floorplan seems more open than most European interiors. Topside, the Phantom's extended flybridge shades the cockpit where a hatch in the sole opens to reveal a cavernous storage area (or an optional crew cabin) below. Additional features include a washer/dryer under the companionway steps, a separate pump room for the air-conditioning units, high-gloss cherry woodwork, and a foredeck sun pad. On the downside, the engine room is a tight fit. A good performer with 675hp Volvos, the 50 Phantom will cruise in the mid 20s and reach just over 30 knots top.

Not Enough Resale Data to Set Values

Length	51'10"	Headroom	6'6"
Beam	14'9"	Fuel	523 gals.
Draft	3'11"	Water	148 gals.
Weight	34,000#	Hull Type	Deep-V
Clearance	17'0"	Deadrise Aft	18°

Fairline 52 Squadron

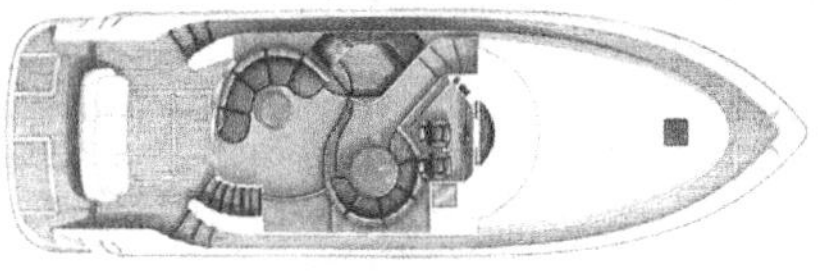

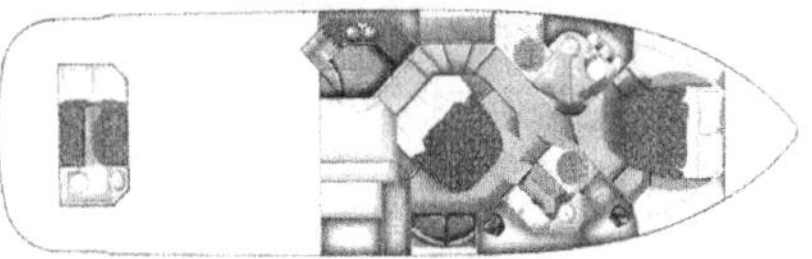

With her mini-megayacht styling, the 52 Squadron was a very innovative design and a notable departure from Fairline's previous reliance on conventional Euro-style designs. For openers, the interior layout is completely novel: the owner's cabin, with its huge berth, en suite head, and laundry room, surpasses anything seen in a sedan-style motor yacht of this type. It's notable that Fairline chose to go with a two-stateroom floorplan in the 52; most boats this size have three. The galley is down from the salon level and the dinette is up; at the highest level is a well-executed centerline helm with a wraparound dash. In the cockpit, a full-height utility locker to port houses various master switches and fuel shutoff valves (a great idea!), and the Squadron's oval flybridge design is a unique styling touch. Access to the compact engineroom—where the engines are very close together—is through a hatch in the cockpit sole. (The cockpit lazarette could be fitted out as crew quarters.) A good performer with relatively small engines, twin 600hp Cats cruise at 25 knots and deliver a top speed of about 30 knots. In the end, the Squadron's two-stateroom floorplan proved unpopular and production lasted only four years.

See Page 678 For Price Data

Length Overall	53'3"	Fuel	576 gals.
Hull Length	52'6"	Water	151 gals.
Beam	15'4"	Clearance	17'5"
Draft	3'8"	Hull	Deep-V
Weight	37,000#	Deadrise Aft	18°

Fairline 52 Targa

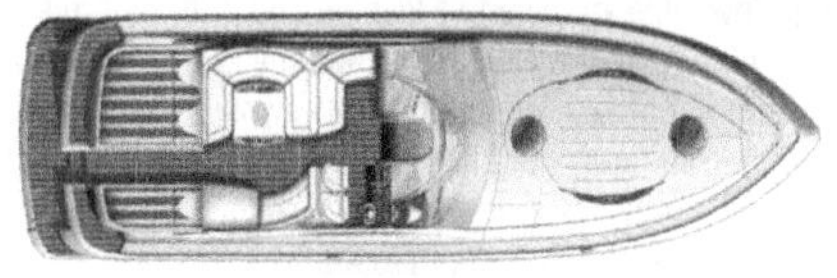

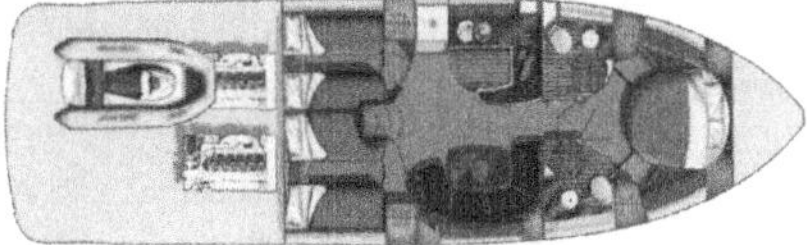

Replacing the very popular 48 Targa in 2003, the 52 Targa is further evidence (if anyone needs it) of Fairline's ability to combine comfort and performance is a modern, state-of-the-art sportcruiser. The Targa is a very impressive yacht—the finish is exemplary, and the accommodations define comfort and luxury. Her standard three-stateroom interior is arranged with the master stateroom forward and two identical guest staterooms aft. A central seating unit forms the back to the galley, and both heads are fitted with separate stall showers. Note that the galley sole is an awkward step down from the salon floor that seems unnecessary considering the Targa's tall headroom. High-gloss cherry joinery dominates the interior, and an optional den/office can replace the port guest cabin. Topside, the transom garage is big enough to handle a 12-foot tender, and access to the engineroom—under the garage—is very good. Additional features include a superb helm position, foredeck fender lockers, teak cockpit sole, and excellent cabin and cockpit storage. A good-handling yacht, the 52 Targa will cruise in the high 20s with 715hp Volvo diesels and top out at 35 knots.

See Page 678 For Price Data

Length Overall	52'5"	Headroom	6'6"
Beam	14'0"	Fuel	480 gals.
Draft	3'7"	Water	120 gals.
Weight	35,200#	Hull Type	Deep-V
Clearance	15'10"	Deadrise Aft	19°

Fairline 55 Squadron

1996–2004

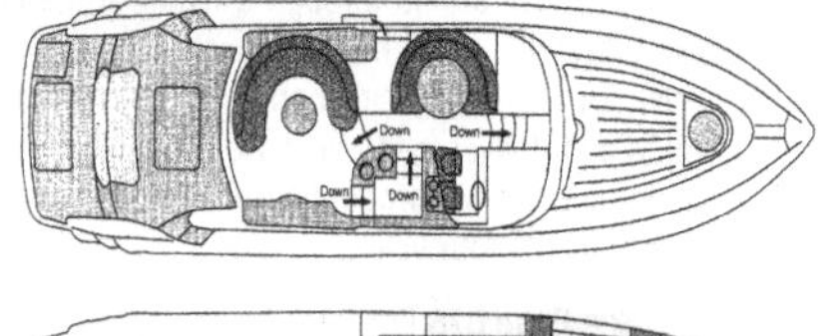

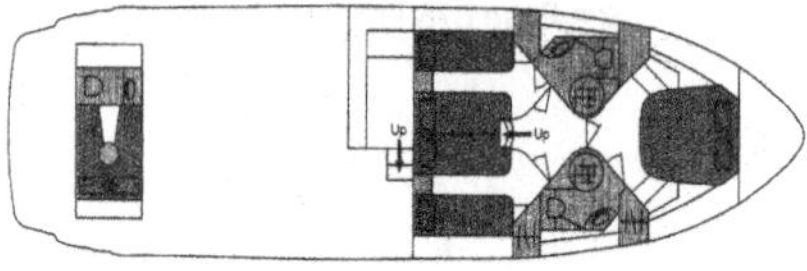

Introduced in 1996, the 55 Squadron proved to be one of Fairline's more popular motor yacht designs thanks to her sleek styling, a comfortable floorplan and excellent open-water performance. Like all of Fairline's motor yacht designs, she's built on a deep-V hull with moderate beam and propeller pockets. Her opulent three-stateroom interior is arranged with a split-level main deck layout, which features a stylish salon aft and an elevated lower helm and dinette forward. A sunken galley is to starboard, abaft the helm, and a small door off the galley opens to a spacious (and very useful) utility room. A choice of lacquered cherry or maple woodwork is available. Note that both the flybridge and engineroom can only be accessed from the salon. Additional features include an extended swim platform, a bow thruster, crew quarters (or a storage area) aft, and an unusually large flybridge. A unique set of curved aft doors open to the aft deck. On the downside, the Squadron's engineroom is a tight fit. A fast and efficient design, twin 600hp Cat (or 615hp Volvo) diesels provide a cruising speed of 24 (about 28 knots top), and a pair of 660hp Cats cruise at 26 knots and reach a top speed of 31–32 knots.

See Page 678 For Price Data

Length Overall	55'11"	Fuel	576 gals.
Hull Length	54'3"	Water	150 gals.
Beam	15'3"	Clearance	17'3"
Draft	3'8"	Hull Type	Deep-V
Weight	48,000#	Deadrise Aft	18.5°

Fairline 58 Squadron

2002–08

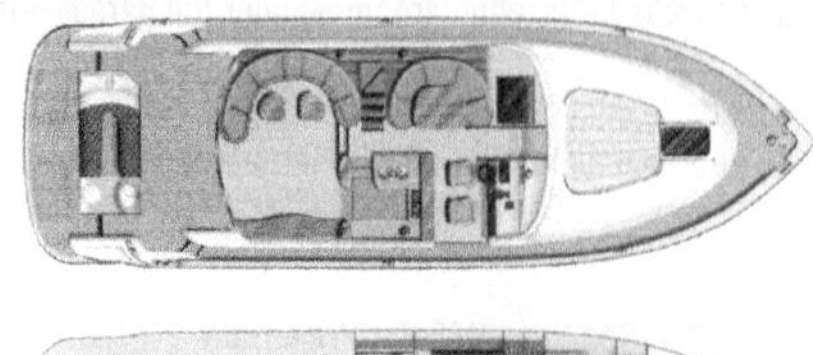

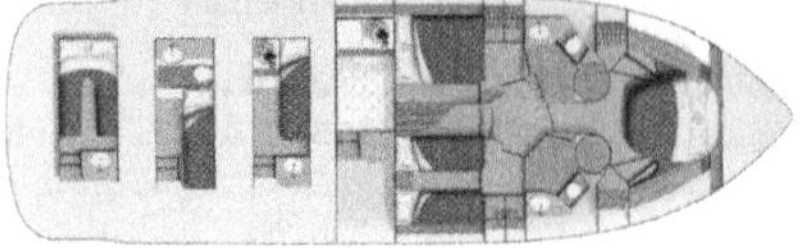

Ultra-modern in appearance (note the unique twin-pillar mast assembly) and built to very high standards, the Squadron 58 is a successful blend of contemporary European styling, sumptuous accommodations, and impressive performance. Building on the success of the popular Squadron 55, the three-stateroom floorplan of the 58 mirrors that of the 55 in nearly every respect. The dinette is on the pilothouse level, opposite the well-executed lower helm with its excellent visibility and all-weather deck door. A laundry center/utility room is accessed from the sunken galley, and the vast salon is highlighted by lacquered cherry joinery, electric windows, and stunning decor. The expansive flybridge, reached from either the salon or cockpit, has the sun pad forward of the helm—a unique location—which permits the installation of a huge settee with high-low table aft, next to a wet bar and grill. Both the cockpit and swim platform have teak decks, and the crew quarters are accessed from the cockpit settee. On the downside, the engineroom is a tight fit. Built on a solid fiberglass hull with prop pockets, the Squadron will cruise at a respectable 27 knots with 700hp Volvo diesels and reach a top speed of around 31 knots.

See Page 678 For Price Data

Length Overall	58'10"	Headroom	6'6"
Beam	16'0"	Fuel	721 gals.
Draft	4'4"	Water	247 gals.
Weight	44,000#	Hull Type	Deep-V
Clearance	19'9"	Deadrise Aft	18°

Fairline 59 Squadron

1996–99

The Fairline 59 Squadron (called the 56 Squadron until 1995 when an extended swim platform was added) is a downsized version of the successful 62/65 Squadron introduced back in 1991. A traditional European design with sleek styling and a low-profile silhouette, she rides on the same deep-V hull with propeller tunnels used in all Squadron models. The Squadron's lush three-stateroom interior is arranged with a split-level main deck area with the galley and dinette forward and the salon aft. A curved staircase behind the dinette leads up to the flybridge—a convenience not always found in a yacht this size and style—and there's also a huge storage room beneath the galley floor. Topside, the cockpit is shaded by a bridge overhang and comes with a teak sole and molded step to the side decks. (An optional crew cabin could be fitted beneath the cockpit sole.) Additional features include a foredeck sun pad, a spacious flybridge with a centerline helm, and bidets in the head compartments. Standard 600hp Cat (or Volvo) diesels cruise the 59 Squadron at 24 knots (about 27 knots top). Optional 680hp MANs cruise at 25 knots (high 20s top).

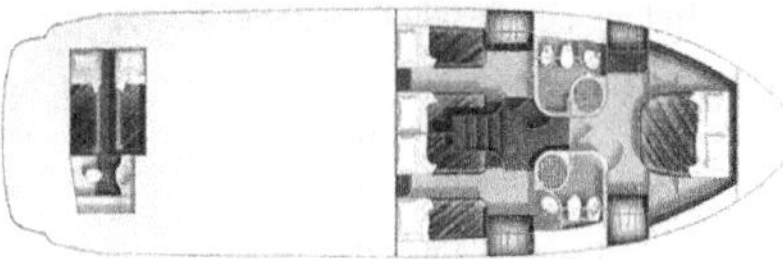

See Page 678 For Price Data

Length Overall	59'9"	Fuel	720 gals.
Hull Length	57'10"	Water	160 gals.
Beam	15'6"	Clearance	18'5"
Draft	3'10"	Hull	Deep-V
Weight	49,200#	Deadrise Aft	18.5°

Fairline 62 Squadron

1999–2002

The futuristic styling of the 62 Squadron was first seen in 1998 when Fairline introduced the smaller 52 Squadron, a cutting-edge design whose curvaceous lines won a good deal of industry attention. The 62 develops this concept even further with a creative, avant-garde interior and an equally innovative flybridge design. The luxurious floorplan, with its spacious salon and ergonomically perfect lower helm position, is arranged with a circular owner's stateroom—an unusual but quite appealing cabin configuration. The circular styling theme is most dominant in the salon with its facing curved sofas, but it's also carried up to the oval-shaped flybridge where circular guest seating is aft and a half-moon sun pad is forward of the helm console. A bridge overhang shades the cockpit, and a hatch in the built-in bench seat provides access to the crew quarters below. On the downside, both the galley and engine room are a tight fit. Built on a deep-V hull with propeller tunnels, standard 800hp Cat diesels cruise the 62 Squadron at 26 knots (28–30 knots top), and optional 1,050hp MANs cruise at a fast 28 knots (32–33 knots top).

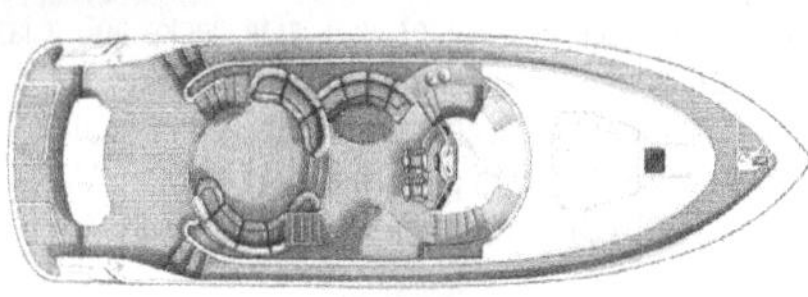

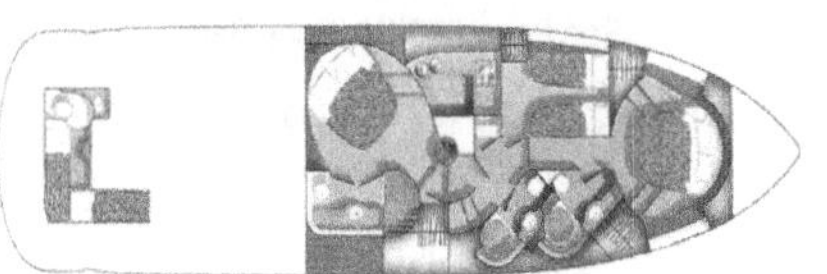

Not Enough Resale Data to Set Values

Length Overall	64'5"	Fuel	991 gals.
Hull Length	63'1"	Water	265 gals.
Beam	16'5"	Clearance	18'10"
Draft	4'6"	Hull	Deep-V
Weight	62,700#	Deadrise Aft	18°

Fairline 62 Targa

2004–07

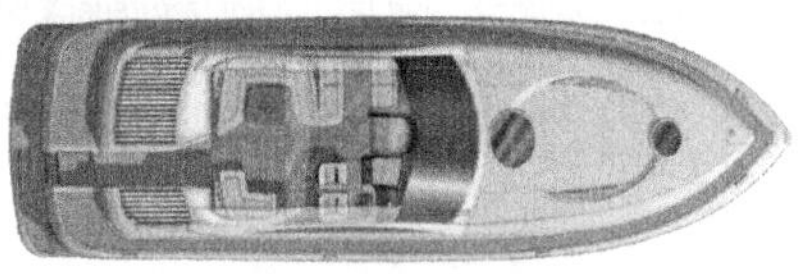

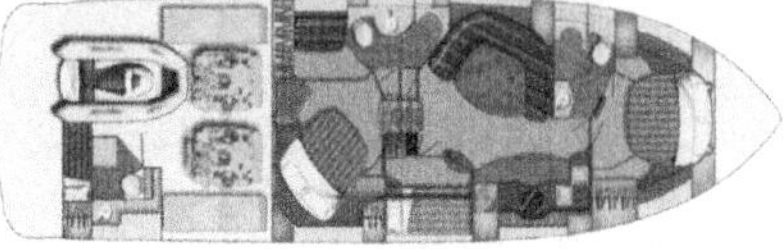

European sportcruisers are usually defined by their sleek styling, spacious cockpits, and plentiful sunbathing capabilities. Throw in a power hardtop that completely encloses the teak-soled cockpit and a lavish cherrywood interior with a full-beam master stateroom, and one might begin to accurately assess the Fairline Targa 62. A sleek profile only hints at the lavish accommodations and thoughtful amenities found aboard this muscular sportyacht. The retractable hardtop allows the bridgedeck to be transformed at the push of a button from a completely open-air deck to a fully enclosed and air-conditioned salon. Her opulent three-stateroom interior features a full-width salon with a large overhead skylight, utility room with washer and dryer, and a state-of-the-art entertainment center in the main salon. The angled berth in the master stateroom is accessible from three sides, and large windows set into the hullsides brighten the cabin considerably. Additional features include a tender garage, cockpit galley with fridge and barbecue, a huge foredeck sun pad, and teak decks. Cat 1,015hp engines cruise the Targa 62 at an honest 30 knots—impressive performance for a 60-foot boat.

Not Enough Resale Data to Set Values

Length Overall	61'11"	Fuel	780 gals.
Beam	15'7"	Water	144 gals.
Draft	4'6"	Waste	48 gals.
Weight	46,400#	Hull Type	Deep-V
Clearance	18'2"	Deadrise Aft	20°

Fairline 65 Squadron

1995–2003

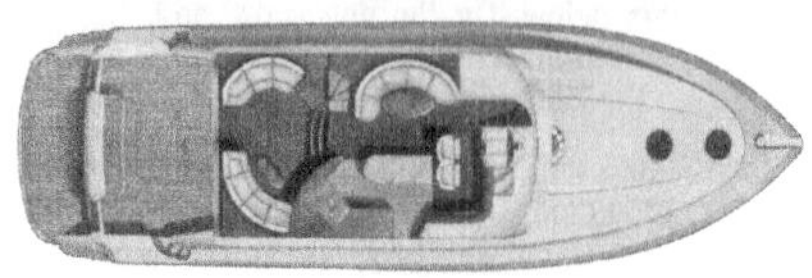

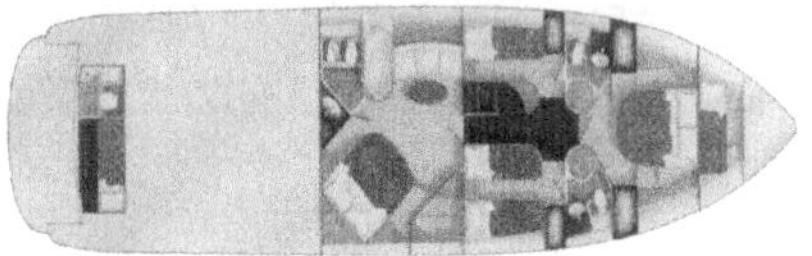

The Fairline 65 Squadron made her debut back in 1991 as a 62-footer, becoming a 65-footer in 1995 with the addition of an extended swim platform. In 1998 she was completely updated with a bold new superstructure (pictured here) and, on the inside, a slightly revised main-deck layout. A handsome yacht with a striking profile, she rides on a solid fiberglass deep-V hull with propeller tunnels and a wide beam. The lush interior of the 65 Squadron has the cooking and dining areas forward, on the pilothouse level, and the socializing area aft. (Note that the galley is enclosed and has a deck access door.) Four staterooms are on the lower level, including an opulent full-width master suite amidships, and there are also two tiny crew cabins, one at the bow and the other under the transom. Like many European motor yachts, the Squadron gives up some salon space in favor of wide side decks and a large aft deck—a good trade. The swim platform will stow an inflatable or jet ski, and the flybridge (accessed from the salon or aft deck) can seat a small crowd. A superb performer with 1,100hp MAN diesels, she'll cruise at 26 knots and reach a top speed of 31–32 knots.

See Page 679 For Price Data

Length Overall	66'10"	Clearance	NA
Hull Length	65'0"	Fuel	1,105 gals.
Beam	17'4"	Water	336 gals.
Draft	4'9"	Hull	Deep-V
Weight	71,680#	Deadrise Aft	19°

Fairline 74 Squadron

The Fairline 74 Squadron—once the largest yacht in the Fairline fleet—is an impressive blend of luxury, beauty, and performance. With her continental styling and lush interior, the Squadron can accommodate as many as ten in her standard four-stateroom, three-head layout. The formal dining area, to starboard just forward of the main salon, has seating for a dinner party of eight. The huge galley, opposite the dinette, is equipped with top-of-line appliances (including a conventional oven and grill), while the salon is arranged with a sectional sofa to port and a stunning wall-mounted bar unit to starboard. On the downside, narrow cabin windows make the interior seem a bit small for a 74-footer. A sliding steel-and-glass door opens to a spacious teak cockpit large enough to entertain a small crowd. A tender garage and small crew cabin are under the cockpit floor where a corridor leads on to the standup engineroom. Topside, the massive teak flybridge includes a grill, refrigerator and sun lounge as well as a hydraulic PWC hoist. Typical of all Fairline yachts, the joinery and detailing are exemplary. A good performer for such a big boat, MAN 1,550hp engines cruise in the high 20s (30+ knots top).

Not Enough Resale Data to Set Values

Length Overall	74'5"	Fuel	1,556 gals.
Beam	18'8"	Water	333 gals.
Draft	5'3"	Waste	100 gals.
Weight	81,200#	Hull Type	Deep-V
Clearance	24'11"	Deadrise Aft	18°

Ferretti Yachts

Quick View

- Ferretti was established in 1968 by brothers Alessandro and Norberto Ferretti.
- Initially building a line of sailboats and motor sailors, the company introduced its motor yacht series in 1980.
- The company began exporting to the U.S. in 1994, and by the late 1990s the Ferretti brand was well established in the North American market.
- In 1997, Ferretti—which had previously acquired Pershing Yachts and Riva Yachts—purchased Bertram Yachts.
- By 2004 Ferretti Yachts yearly sales had reached 160 million Euro and a 500-strong staff.
- Following a serious decline in business owing the the worldwide decession, a 2008 financial crisis left Ferretti near bankruptcy.
- Ferretti was sold in 2012 to Shandong Heavy Industry Group, the state-owned parent company of China's biggest bulldozer-maker. (WTF!)

Ferretti Yachts • Forli, Italy • www.ferretti-yachts.com

Ferretti 46/480 Motor Yacht

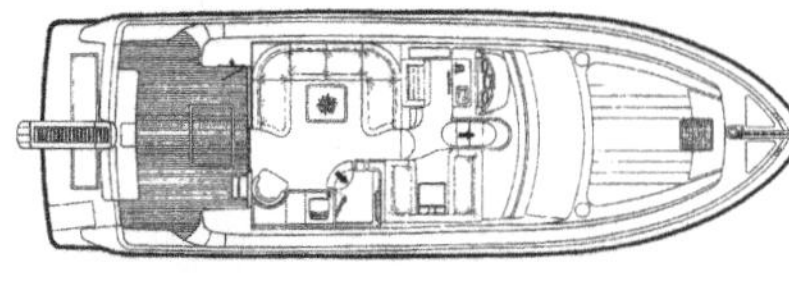

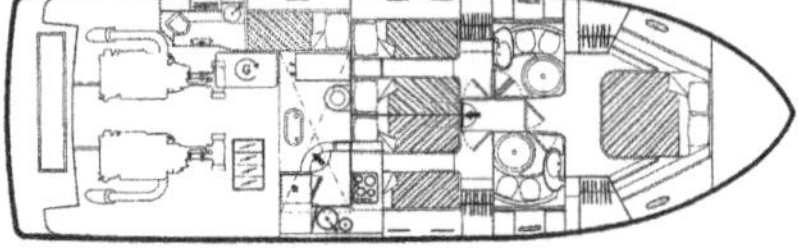

Bold styling, good performance, and luxurious accommodations are the hallmarks of the Ferretti 480 (called the Ferretti 46 until 2001 when the swim platform was extended), one of the smaller models in Ferretti's line of top-quality production yachts. Built on a modified-V hull with a wide beam, the salon layout differs from her British counterparts in that the lower helm is to port rather than starboard. The dinette is opposite the helm, and the small sunken galley in the salon is typical of European boats. As usual, the Ferretti's interior is a modern display of upscale Italian design and meticulous workmanship. Her three-stateroom floorplan is arranged with identical guest cabins, and both heads contain separate stall showers and bidets. Note that a crew cabin with head is aft and accessed from the cockpit—a big-boat luxury that makes for a smaller engine room. Additional features include a big flybridge with direct salon access (rare in a boat this size), teak cockpit sole, wide side decks and an extended swim platform. Twin 435hp V-drive Cats cruise the Ferretti 480 at 24 knots (27–28 knots top), and later models with 630hp V-drive MANs cruise in the mid 20s and top out at just over 30 knots.

Not Enough Resale Data to Set Values

Length Overall	48'7"	Clearance	10'0"
Hull Length	47'7"	Fuel	502 gals.
Beam	15'1"	Water	185 gals.
Draft	4'9"	Hull	Modified-V
Weight	44,321#	Deadrise Aft	15°

Ferretti 48 Motor Yacht

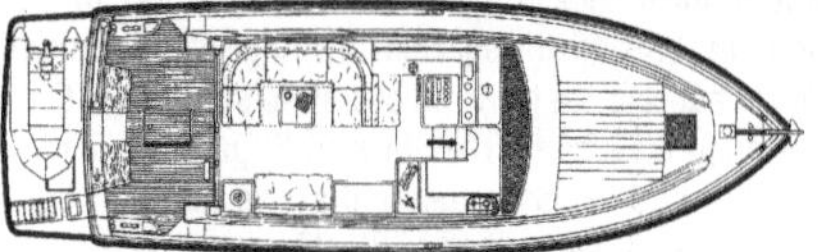
Main Deck, 2-Stateroom Layout

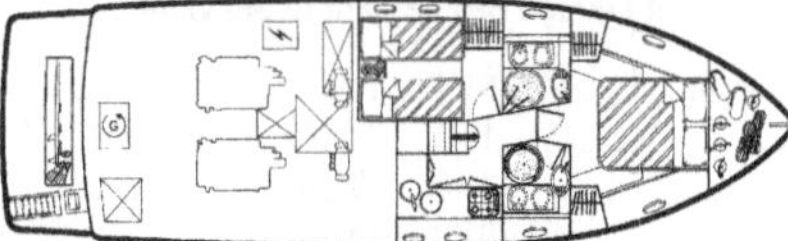
Lower Level, 2-Stateroom Layout

During her late 1990s production years, the Ferretti 48 MY (originally called the Ferretti 135) was a high-style Italian import whose sleek Mediterranean profile and high-octane performance were characteristics seldom associated with American-built motor yachts of that era. The 48's deep-V hull is cored in the hullsides and features a unique egg-crate framing system on the bottom—a high-tech method of construction then common to all Ferretti hulls. Her three-stateroom European floorplan is arranged with the dinette forward, opposite the lower helm, and a sunken galley in the salon. Both heads are fitted with circular stall showers, and a single-berth crew cabin is aft, beneath the cockpit sole. (A two-stateroom layout with the galley down was also available.) It should be noted that the level of detailing and workmanship found aboard the Ferretti 48 is extraordinary for a production yacht. Additional features include a well-appointed salon with a large U-shaped leather settee, a huge swim platform designed to stow an inflatable, and a spacious flybridge. With a pair of 435hp Cats, the Ferretti 48 will cruise at 25 knots and reach a top speed in the neighborhood of 28–29 knots.

Not Enough Resale Data to Set Values

Length Overall	48'7"	Water	172 gals.
Beam	14'0"	Clearance	14'10"
Draft	4'5"	Headroom	6'5"
Weight	40,131#	Hull Type	Deep-V
Fuel	499 gals.	Deadrise Aft	17°

Ferretti 50 Motor Yacht

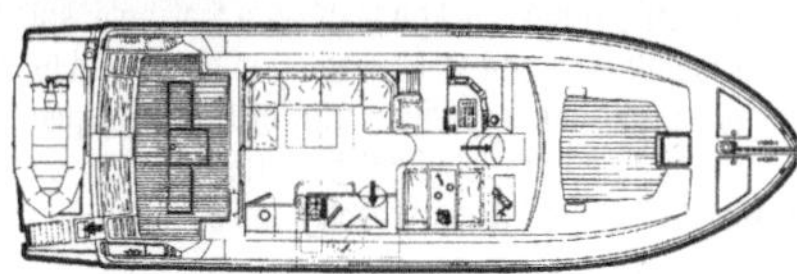

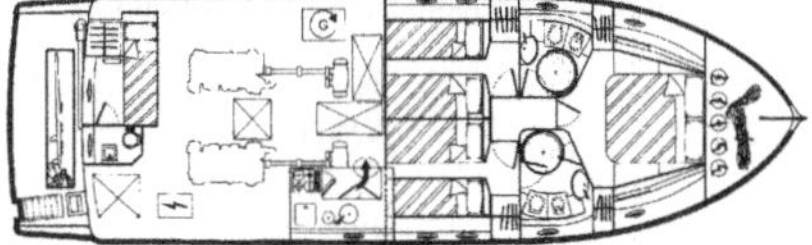

A well-finished yacht whose aggressive styling still looks good today, the Ferretti 50 (originally called the Ferretti 150) was built in Italy at a yard long recognized for its high-tech approach to boatbuilding. Constructed on an easy-riding, deep-V hull with underwater exhausts and cored hullsides, her fully integrated swim platform is designed to stow (and launch) an inflatable or jet ski. As it is with most European interiors, the three-stateroom interior of the Ferretti 50 is a departure from what American buyers are accustomed to seeing. Specifically, the galley is tucked in an alcove below the salon where it's out of the way. The result is a wide-open deckhouse with a six-person dinette opposite the lower helm serving as a second entertainment area. The interior is rich in detail and accented by stunning woodwork, creative lighting, and fine leather upholstery. Note the single-berth crew cabin with toilet aft, below the cockpit. A well-arranged flybridge, spacious staterooms and a large engine room are just a few of her more notable features. Twin 600hp V-drive Cat (or MTU) diesels cruise the Ferretti 50 Motor Yacht at 25 knots while delivering a top speed of about 29–30 knots.

Not Enough Resale Data to Set Values

Length On Deck	50'8"	Fuel	600 gals.
Hull Length	45'10"	Water	198 gals.
Beam	14'9"	Clearance	17'3"
Draft	4'3"	Hull Type	Deep-V
Weight	48,730#	Deadrise Aft	18°

Ferretti 500 Motor Yacht

2004—07

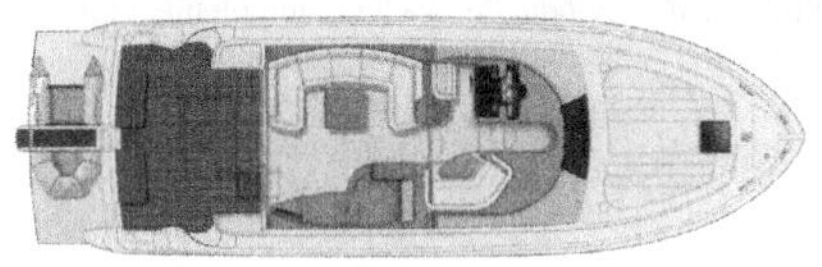

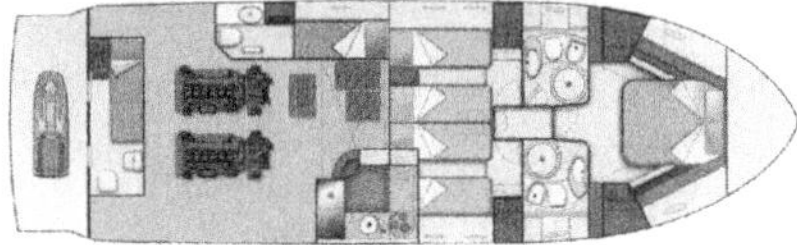

A powerful, low-profile appearance, lavish accommodations, and sophisticated engineering are the hallmarks of the Ferretti 500, an elegant 50-foot European flybridge yacht introduced in 2004 to replace the popular Ferretti 480. She rides on a modified-V hull with moderate beam, a solid fiberglass bottom, and a unique underwater exhaust system. For a boat this size a three-stateroom, two-head floorplan is the norm. The salon is opulently appointed with leather upholstery and lacquered cabinetry, and the 500's inside flybridge access is generally seen only in larger boats. If there's a downside to this posh interior, it might be found in the small, step-down galley forward in the salon. (In fairness, however, European boats do tend to have small galleys.) Note that there are two crew cabins in the Ferretti's standard layout, and a hatch in the teak-soled cockpit offers convenient access to a compact engine room. Topside, the spacious flybridge features a retractable instrument panel at the helm, an oversized sun lounge to port, and a wraparound dinette aft. The 500's PWC garage is very unusual in a boat this size. An altogether impressive yacht, 630hp MAN V-drives deliver a cruising speed of 26–27 knots.

Not Enough Resale Data to Set Values

Length Overall	51'4"	Fuel	481 gals.
Beam	15'4"	Water	180 gals.
Draft	4'10"	Waste	47 gals.
Weight	41,013#	Hull	Modified-V
Clearance	16'0"	Deadrise Aft	15°

Ferretti 530 Motor Yacht

1998–2005

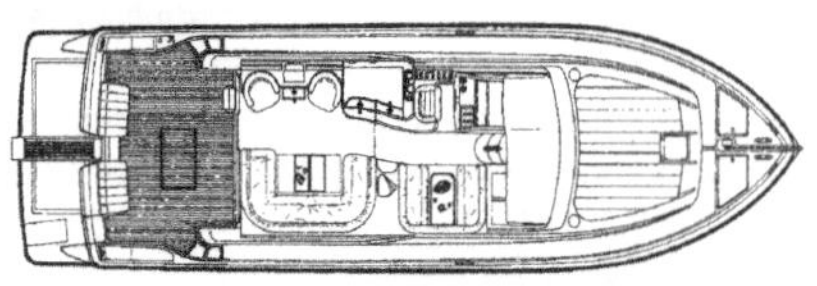

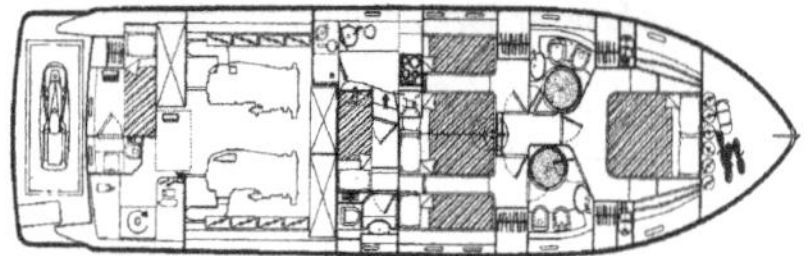

The Ferretti 530 is an example of why Ferretti stood at the pinnacle of the European motor yacht market a few years back. With her sleek Italian styling, posh amenities, and high-tech construction, the 530 made good on the Ferretti promise of luxury in the fast lane. The accommodations are a convincing display of Italian workmanship and designer furnishings. The salon is highlighted by a U-shaped leather sofa, rich cherry cabinets, and a full entertainment center. Forward of the salon, to starboard, is a raised dinette as well as a staircase to the flybridge. There are three staterooms and two heads below. The master stateroom boasts a queen island berth with mirrored headboard and flat-screen TV, while both guest cabins are fitted with twin berths and a TV. Off the sunken galley is an access door to the crew cabin, which has its own separate bathroom. The Ferretti's roomy cockpit features a teak sole, split bench seat, engineroom hatch, and stairs leading to the flybridge. A PWC can be stored inside the extended swim platform. At just 53,000 pounds, the 530 is a relatively light boat for her size. Cat 660hp diesels cruise in the mid 20s and reach a top speed of 30 knots.

Not Enough Resale Data to Set Values

Length Overall	55'1"	Fuel	670 gals.
Hull Length	53'6"	Water	211 gals.
Beam	15'4"	Waste	50 gals.
Draft	4'9"	Hull Type	Deep-V
Weight	52,920#	Deadrise Aft	19°

Ferretti 55 Motor Yacht

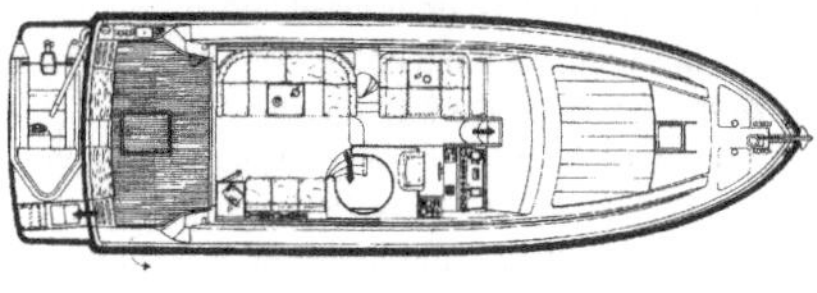

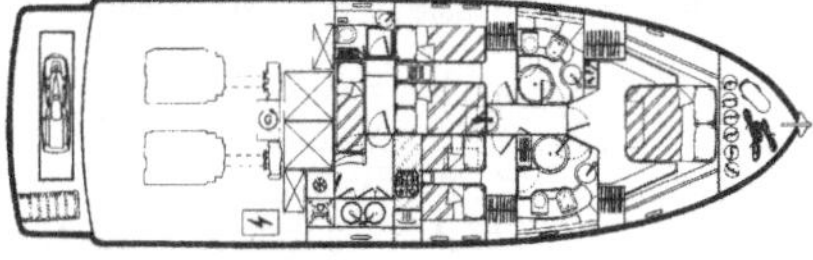

One of the early Ferretti models imported into the U.S. market during the mid 1990s, the Ferretti 55 MY (previously called the Ferretti 165) was a state-of-the-art, high-performance Italian yacht that offered American buyers something different in contemporary motor yacht design. Her hull is a medium-deadrise deep-V with moderate beam, and the huge swim platform—designed to stow a jet ski inside and a dinghy on top—is an integral part of the hull. The Ferretti's lush three-stateroom interior follows the trend seen in many European flybridge cruisers with a sunken galley between the salon aft and the elevated helm position forward. Both guest staterooms are fitted with twin berths, and the master stateroom (forward) has a walkaround queen bed. Note that a single-berth crew cabin with its own head and shower is reached from the galley. Rich mahogany woodwork, quality furnishings, and crushed leather upholstery complete the stylish interior. Additional features include a spacious flybridge with wet bar and sun lounge, laundry center, underwater exhausts, and cockpit access to the engine room. Twin 770hp V-drive MTUs cruise the Ferretti 55 at a fast 26 knots and reach a top speed of around 30 knots.

Not Enough Resale Data to Set Values

Length Overall	56'3"	Clearance	15'3"
Length WL	47'5"	Fuel	697 gals.
Beam	16'2"	Water	185 gals.
Draft	5'3"	Hull	Modified-V
Weight	61,740#	Deadrise Aft	15°

Ferretti 57 Motor Yacht

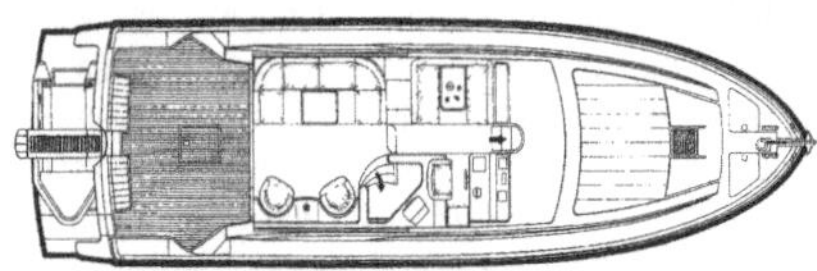

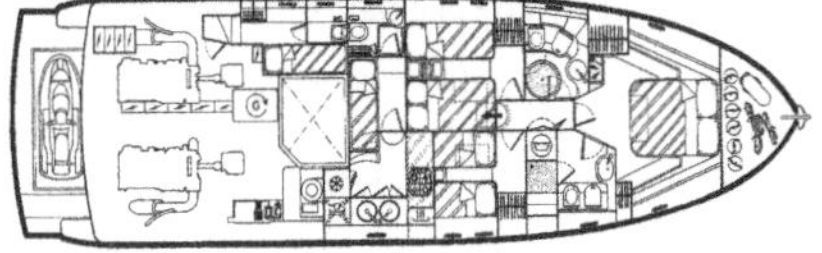

An impressive display of bold styling and state-of-the-art construction, the Ferretti 57 was a benchmark against which other European production motor yachts of her era were measured. Built on a solid fiberglass modified-V hull, the lavish interior of the Ferretti 57 is arranged with a standard lower helm with excellent visibility, a sunken galley in the salon, and four staterooms, one of which—with upper and lower berths—is accessed from the galley. (Note that a crew cabin with a single berth and head is reached from a door in the cockpit.) Unlike most European motor yachts, the Ferretti 57 has a reasonably spacious engine room (compared with other euroyachts her size) with good access to the motors. Topside, there's seating on the flybridge for a small crowd, and the bridge overhang shades the cockpit. Additional features include an underwater exhaust system, high-gloss cherry interior woodwork, a bow thruster, teak cockpit sole, and a large foredeck sun pad. A very good performer, a pair of 800hp MAN diesels cruise the Ferretti 57 at a fast 27 knots and reach a top speed in the neighborhood of 30–31 knots.

Not Enough Resale Data to Set Values

Length Overall	58'3"	Fuel	898 gals.
Hull Length	56'9"	Water	185 gals.
Beam	16'2"	Headroom	6'5"
Draft	5'3"	Hull Type	Modified-V
Weight	63,725#	Deadrise Aft	15°

Ferretti 590 Motor Yacht

2003-06

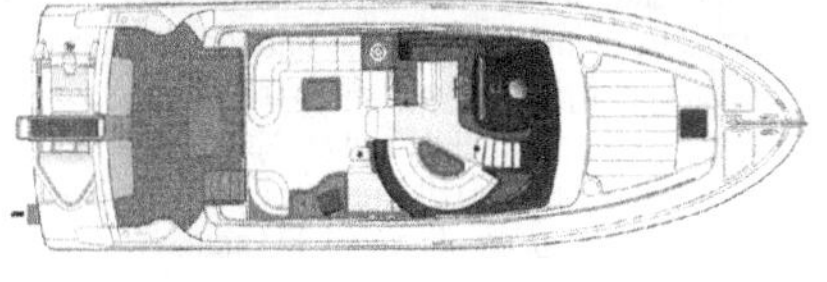

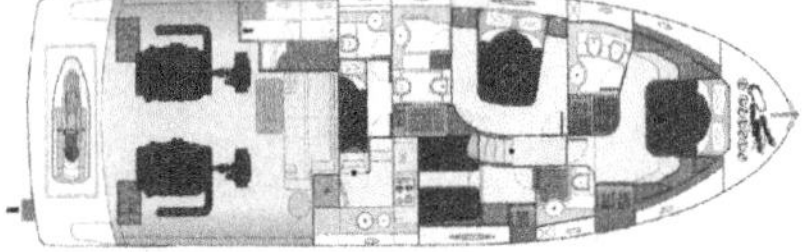

Styling and performance—signature components of every Ferretti yacht—were much in evidence in 2003 with the introduction of the Ferretti 590. The Ferretti Group was a powerful boating conglomerate in those years, and the 590 was further proof of the company's engineering and production excellence. (I hope I can finish this 2014 edition before time runs out. With Stage 4 cancer you never know—EM.) Belowdecks, the executive-class accommodations of the 590 feature a spacious main salon with L-shaped leather sofa to port and entertainment center/glass storage cabinet to starboard. The sunken galley—common in most European motoryachts of this era—is small by American standards and short on storage. There are four staterooms and heads on the lower level, including an opulent amidships master and an equally large VIP suite forward. Crew quarters are reached from a door in the galley, and there's a tiny fifth stateroom accessible from the cockpit. Note the jet bike garage within the swim platform. Additional features include a laundry center, granite galley counters, electronic engine controls, and teak decks. MAN 1,050hp engines deliver a cruising speed of 24–25 knots (about 30 knots top).

Not Enough Resale Data to Set Values

Length	60'1"	Fuel	925 gals.
Beam	17'3"	Water	180 gals.
Draft	5'2"	Waste	50 gals.
Weight	71,663#	Hull Type	Modified-V
Clearance	NA	Deadrise Aft	13°

Ferretti 60 Motor Yacht

1991-98

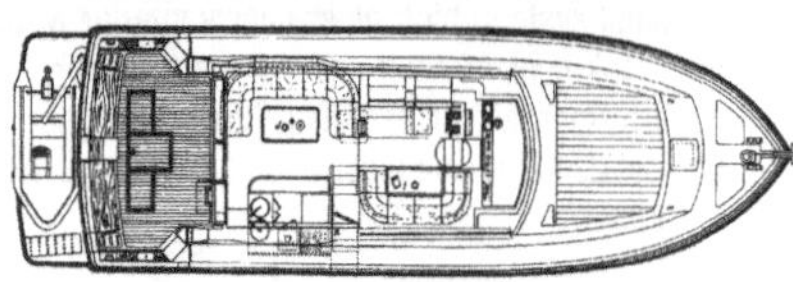

Main Deck, 4-Stateroom Layout

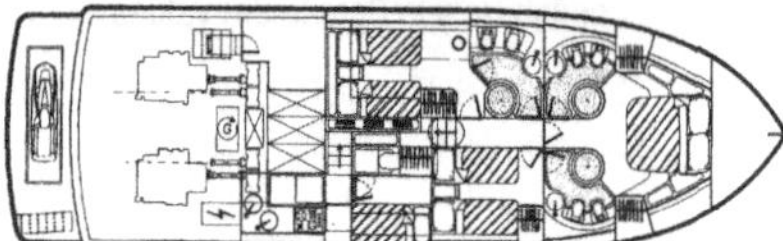

Lower Level, 4-Stateroom Layout

Introduced in 1991 and remaining in production through the 1998 model year, the Ferretti 60 (originally called the Ferretti 175) is a purebred Italian motor yacht with a distinctive Med-style appearance, luxurious accommodations and the kind of exciting performance seldom seen in an American-built motor yacht. She's built on a beamy modified-V hull, which, when combined with her low-profile superstructure, results in a yacht of exceptional stability and comfort. The Ferretti 60 can entertain owner and guests in the standard four-stateroom floorplan, each with its own head. The galley is down (accessed directly from the salon), and a full dinette is opposite the lower helm. In good weather the entire rear salon bulkhead can be opened to form a common area with the aft deck. Impeccably finished with high-gloss mahogany woodwork and top-quality furnishings, the Ferretti's interior can only be described as lavish even by today's high-glitz standards. Outside, the swim platform is designed to handle an inflatable (and a jet ski inside) and includes a hydraulic davit. Twin 1,000hp V-drive MTU diesels provide a cruising speed of 26 knots and a top speed of 31–32 knots—excellent performance indeed for a 60-foot yacht.

Not Enough Resale Data to Set Values

Length Overall	61'10"	Clearance	16'0"
Hull Length	59'6"	Fuel	898 gals.
Beam	16'9"	Water	203 gals.
Draft	5'2"	Hull	Modified-V
Weight	62,843#	Deadrise Aft	15°

Ferretti 620 Motor Yacht

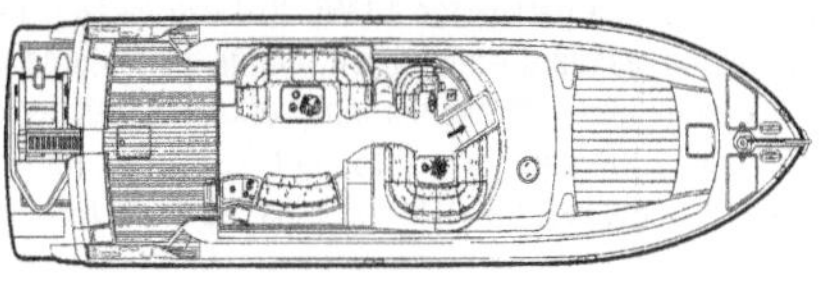

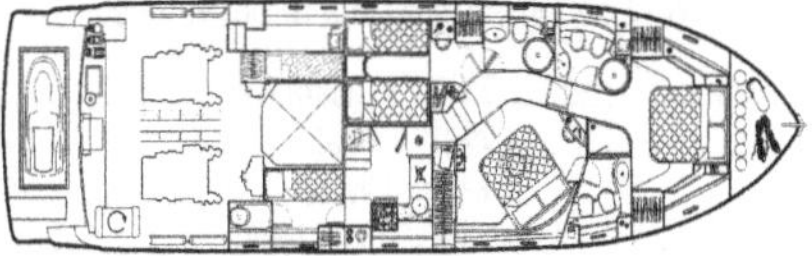

The Ferretti 620 is an updated version of the Ferretti 60 (1991–98) with updated styling and a more contemporary interior. Like all Ferrettis, the 620 is a refined, state-of-the-art yacht, and with her upscale price she was clearly aimed at the high end of the market. Built on a modified-V hull with a relatively wide beam, her lavish interior is an impressive display of Italian design elegance. The standard three-stateroom floorplan of the Ferretti 620 reflects the European bias of locating the galley down—way down—in the salon. The master suite is amidships, and each head has a separate stall shower. Note that a utility room with a washer, dryer and freezer is reached from the galley, and a separate crew cabin (with head) is accessed directly from the cockpit. The engine room, accessed from another hatch in the cockpit, is spacious and particularly well engineered. The side decks are wide, there's seating for a crowd on the roomy flybridge, and the extended swim platform can store a dinghy and PWC. A superb performer for a yacht of her size, the Ferretti 620 will cruise at a fast 29–30 knots with 1,100hp MTUs (or 1,050hp MANS) and reach a top speed of around 33 knots.

Not Enough Resale Data to Set Values

Length Overall	63'11"	Clearance	16'0"
Hull Length	61'6"	Fuel	951 gals.
Beam	16'9"	Water	211 gals.
Draft	5'2"	Hull Type	Modified-V
Weight	60,858#	Deadrise Aft	15.5°

Ferretti 680 Motor Yacht

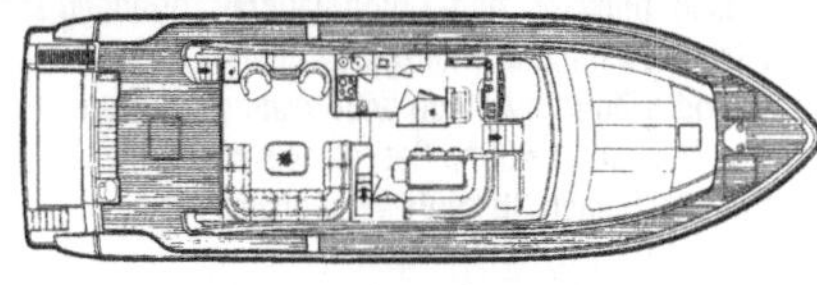

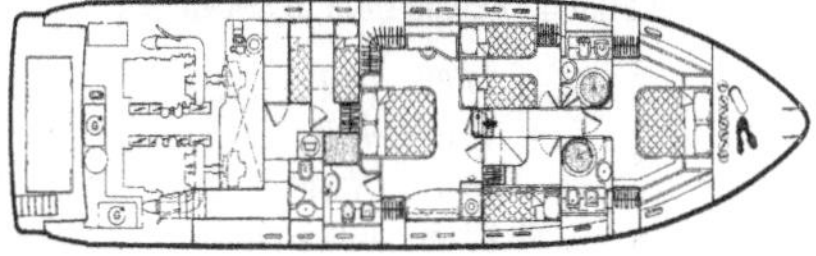

Introduced in 1999, the bold styling of the Ferretti 680 goes a long way toward dispelling the conservative image of previous Ferretti designs. A completely impressive motoryacht, the 680 was unmatched in her era for beauty and downright sex appeal. Like all Ferrettis, she rides on a beamy modified-V hull with cored hullsides and an extended swim platform. A four-stateroom floorplan is standard, although, as a semicustom yacht, Ferretti offers several alternate arrangements to meet the needs of a client. In the standard layout, a spacious full-beam owner's suite is amidships, and the galley is on the helmdeck level where it's separated from the salon. Unlike many similar yachts, the owner's stateroom in the 68 is accessed from the forward passageway rather than a private salon staircase. A beautifully finished yacht, a few of her more notable features include complete crew quarters aft, PWC storage in the swim platform, a terrific flybridge with every possible amenity, a hidden passerelle (a boarding ramp at the transom) and teak decks. An excellent performer, twin 1,360hp V-drive MANs cruise the Ferretti 680 at 27–28 knots and reach 30+ knots top.

Not Enough Resale Data to Set Values

Length Overall	69'6"	Fuel	1,102 gals.
Hull Length	67'8"	Water	277 gals.
Beam	18'6"	Clearance	18'9"
Draft	5'8"	Hull Type	Modified-V
Weight	99,225#	Deadrise Aft	12°

Ferretti 72 Motor Yacht

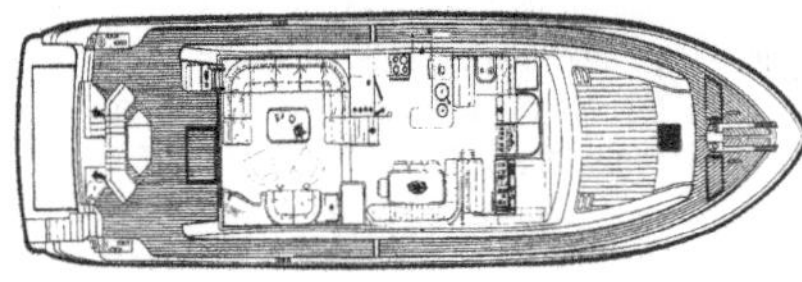

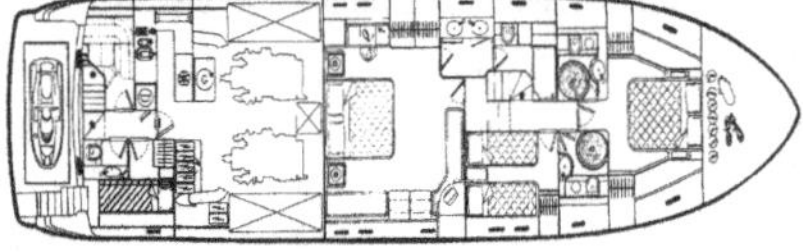

The sleek, aggressive styling of the Ferretti 72 (introduced as the Ferretti 70 in 1997) made most American motor yachts of her era look more than a little conservative. With her flowing lines, wide flybridge, and teardrop salon windows, the 72 was simply in a class by herself when it came to pure sex appeal. Built on a high-performance modified-V hull with prop pockets and a generous 18-foot beam, her lavish four-stateroom floorplan is arranged with the galley up, two steps above the salon and opposite the formal dining area. Each stateroom has its own head, and crew quarters include berths for three. Like all Ferretti yachts, the interior is a blend of fine-quality woodwork, designer furnishings, and meticulous fit and finish. The flybridge can be accessed from an aft deck staircase or through the pilothouse. Aft, the extended swim platform serves as a garage for a PWC that can be launched and retrieved by the standard bridge davit. Additional features include teak walkaround decks, an engineroom work area, teak decks, and a huge foredeck sun pad. Twin 1,150hp MTU diesels (or 1,250hp Cats) will cruise the Ferretti 72 MY at a fast 28 knots (30+ top).

Not Enough Resale Data to Set Values

Length Overall	73'3"	Clearance	20'4"
Hull Length	72'3"	Fuel	1,321 gals.
Beam	18'0"	Water	264 gals.
Draft	5'8"	Hull Type	Modified-V
Weight	97,020#	Deadrise Aft	15.5°

Ferretti 760 Motor Yacht

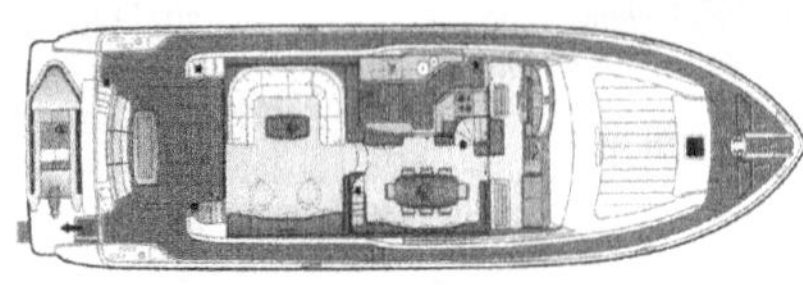

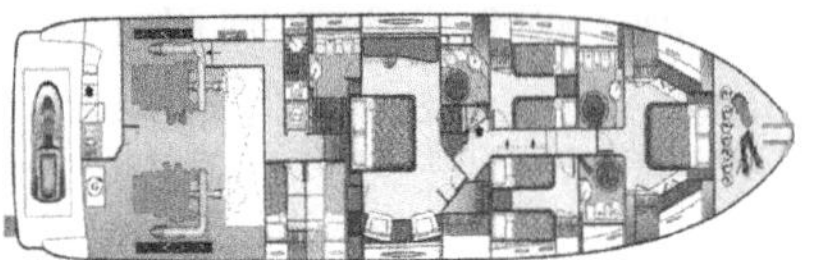

In the eyes of many industry observers, Ferretti set the standards for luxury motor yachts ever since they entered the U.S. market in the early 1990s. The Ferretti 760 delivers on that promise in a big way with an impressive blend of interior comfort, state-of-the-art construction, and outstanding performance. The accommodations include a spectacular full-beam master suite with walk-in closet, two guest cabins with twin beds and private baths, and a VIP bow stateroom with a double bed. The galley and dining area are forward of the aft salon, and a deck door in the galley makes provisioning easy and convenient. Crew quarters, accessed from the cockpit, are located forward of the spacious engine room. Topside, the 760's cockpit is large enough to include a sofa and table, and a jet-bike garage is built into the swim platform. Note that the side decks have deep bulwarks and a high handrail for added security. Additional features include high-gloss cherry interior cabinetry, teak decks, and a huge flybridge with seating for a small crowd. Twin 1,300hp MAN (or 1,400hp Cat) diesels cruise the Ferretti 760 in the mid 20s and reach 30 knots wide open.

Not Enough Resale Data to Set Values

Length	77'0"	Fuel	1,585 gals.
Beam	19'6"	Water	264 gals.
Draft	5'6"	Waste	119 gals.
Weight	98,887#	Hull Type	Modified-V
Clearance	NA	Deadrise Aft	12°

Ferretti 80/810 Motor Yacht

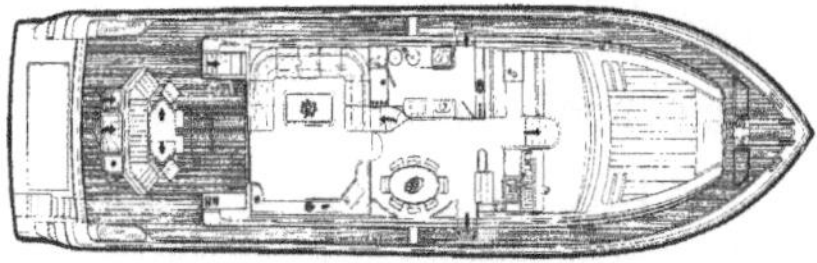
Main Deck Layout

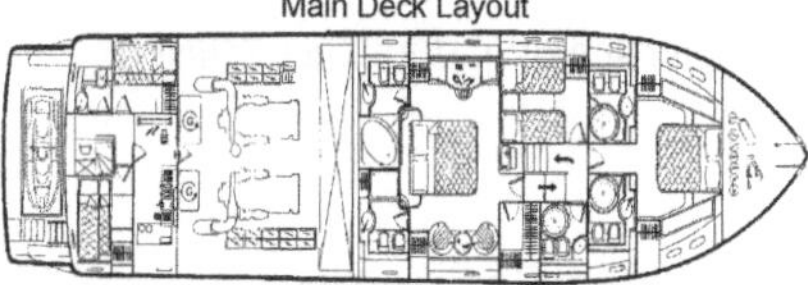
3-Stateroom Floorplan

Full-production fiberglass yachts in the 80-foot range were unheard of 30 years ago ago—the technology was there but the market was limited. With the introduction of the Ferretti 80 in 1997 (called the Ferretti 810 after 2002), Ferretti unveiled what at the time was a truly stunning example of production extravagance. Built on a high-performance hull with a wide beam, the lavish accommodations of the Ferretti 80 will appeal to upscale buyers seeking the finest in Italian styling and workmanship. Her magnificent salon, with its flawless cabinetry and huge U-shaped sofa, will accommodate as many as ten people in comfort and luxury. An enclosed galley and formal dining area are forward, a few steps up from the salon, and opposite the lower helm is a dinette with a spectacular outside view. A choice of lower-level floorplans was available (three or four staterooms), and the crew quarters can sleep four. Notable features include a massive flybridge, teak decks, a deck door at the lower helm, utility room, flybridge davit, and storage for two jet skis and an inflatable. Among several engine options offered over the years, 1,420hp MAN diesels cruise in the mid 20s (about 28 knots top).

Not Enough Resale Data to Set Values

Length Overall	81'4"	Clearance	19'7"
Hull Length	78'9"	Fuel	1,849 gals.
Beam	19'8"	Water	317 gals.
Draft	6'1"	Hull Type	Modified-V
Weight	132,300#	Deadrise Aft	15.5°

Ferretti 80/810 Raised Pilothouse

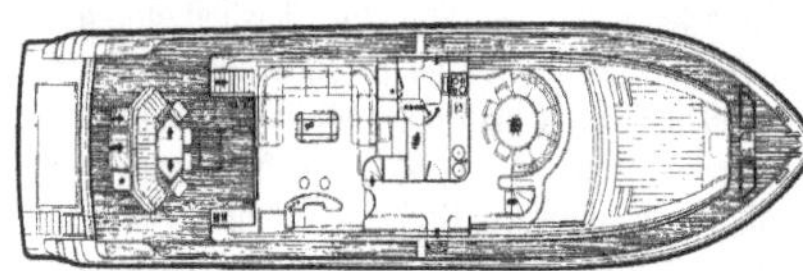
Main Deck Layout

4-Stateroom Layout

The sleek, muscular profile of the Ferretti 810 Raised Pilothouse (called the Ferretti 80 Raised PH from 1997–2002) made her one of the more distinctive motor yachts available in the late-model motor yacht market. Interestingly, the pilothouse is at the halfway point between the main deck and flybridge, a popular design feature on motor yachts from about 90 feet through 120 feet and an arrangement that permits a forward dining room with a pass-through to the galley. The huge salon will accommodate ten people and features an array of varnished cherrywood furniture and a full bar opposite the U-shaped settee. The enclosed galley is separated from the salon in this floorplan, and all four staterooms have private heads. The compact pilothouse takes nothing away from the full-width extended flybridge of the Ferretti 810 with its large U-shaped settee, wet bar, and sun lounge as well as a built-in launching crane for the dinghy. Additional features include crew quarters aft with a separate workroom, jet-bike garage, teak decks, and a huge foredeck sun pad. Twin 1,420hp MTU diesels (or 1,300hp Cats) will cruise in the mid 20s and reach a top speed of about 30 knots.

Not Enough Resale Data to Set Values

Length Overall	81'5"	Clearance	19'7"
Hull Length	78'9"	Fuel	1,849 gals.
Beam	19'8"	Water	317 gals.
Draft	6'0"	Hull Type	Modified-V
Weight	136,710#	Deadrise Aft	15.5°

Formula

Quick View

- Racing-legend Don Aronow founded Formula Boats in 1962 in Miami, Florida.
- Formula first caught public attention in 1962 with the introduction of the Formula 233, a deep-V racing boat that won notable victories on the national offshore racing circuit.
- Formula was purchased in 1964 by Alliance Machine and Foundry, owners of Thunderbird Products.
- An Atlanta-based conglomerate, Fuqua Industries, acquired Thunderbird /Formula in 1969.
- In mid 1976 Vic Porter purchased Thunderbird/ Formula from Fuqua.
- Formulas were built in California through 1981, and Florida until 1987. In 1988, Thunderbird/ Formula production was consolidated in Decatur, IN.
- Still owned by the Porter family, Formula markets a full line of performance cruisers from 26 to 40+ feet in length.

Formula Boats • Decatur, IN • www.formulaboats.com

Formula 260 Sun Sport

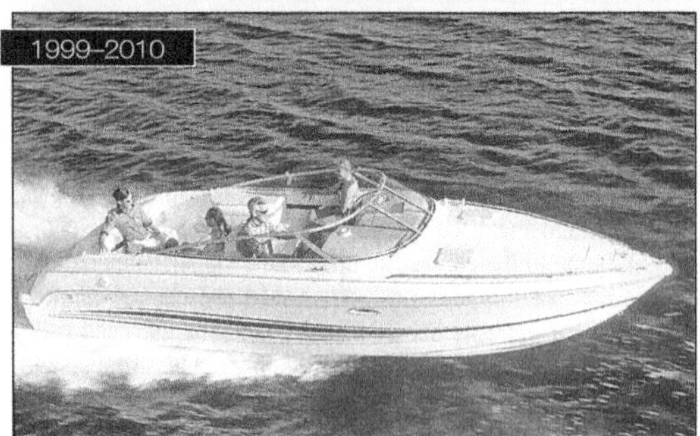

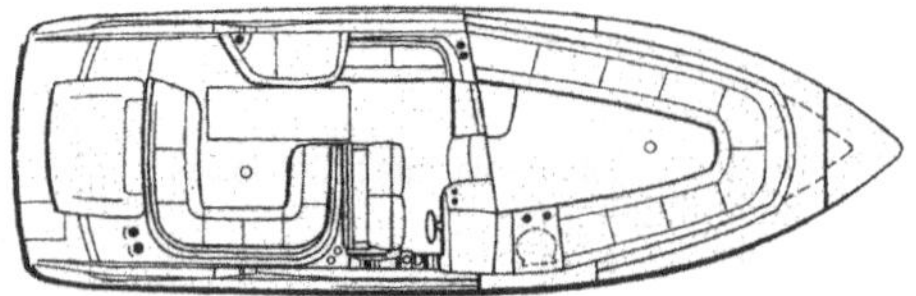

The Formula reputation for quality and performance are on vivid display in the 260 Sun Sport, a sleek closed-bow runabout with the comfort and luxury expected in a high-end day boat. Introduced in 1999, the Sun Sport comes with an array of standard features that often cost extra on other boats. She rides on a solid fiberglass deep-V hull with a trailerable 8-foot, 6-inch beam and an aggressive 22 degrees of transom deadrise. The roomy cockpit is arranged with wraparound lounge seating aft and a portside wet bar with sink, concealed trash receptacle, and Igloo cooler. Helm ergonomics—including a individually adjustable, double-wide helm seat with flip-up bolsters—are about as good as it gets in a boat this size. Molded steps lead through the windshield opening for bow access, and a removable cockpit table converts the lounge seating into a large sun pad. Smoothly finished storage units are built in for fenders, water toys and personal gear. Below, Sun Sport has a cozy cabin with a luxurious Ultraleather lounge and high-gloss, solid wood table. The big 92-gallon fuel capacity is a plus. A transom shower is standard. Cruise at 30 mph with single 310hp MerCruiser sterndrive (mid 40s top).

See Page 679 For Price Data

Length w/Platform	28'0"	Fuel	92 gals.
Hull Length	26'0"	Water	15 gals.
Beam	8'6"	Waste	2.6 gals.
Draft	2'8"	Hull Type	Deep-V
Weight	6,300#	Deadrise Aft	22°

Formula 27 PC

1994–Current

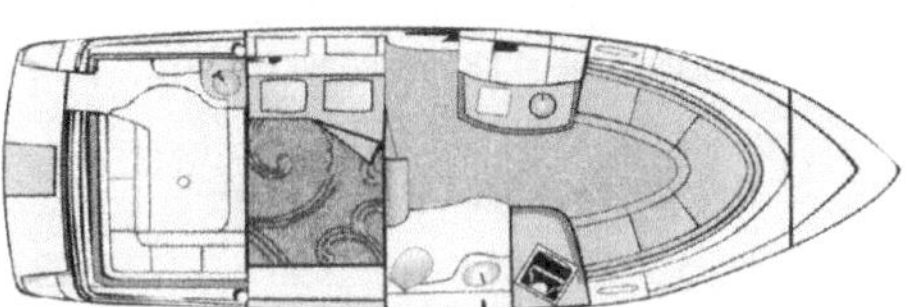

A popular boat since her introduction in 1994, the Formula 27 PC is a proven blend of quality construction, comfortable accommodations and good open-water performance. Built on a solid fiberglass deep-V hull, the 18-degree aft deadrise is a good compromise between stability and performance. Her midcabin floorplan is arranged with a built-in entertainment center facing the dinette in addition to a large head, a stylish pod-type galley, and berths for four. This is one of the more luxurious interiors to be found in a 27-footer with quality hardware and furnishings throughout. Lacking side decks (foredeck access is via a walk-through in the windshield), the full-width cockpit of the 27 PC is very spacious and comes with a doublewide helm seat, tilt wheel, wet bar, and a stowaway aft bench. Note that an electrically activated in-deck hatch provides access to the engine compartment. Additional features include a radar arch, an adjustable cocktail table for the cockpit with filler cushion, and a tilt steering wheel. A single 310hp MerCruiser (available through 1999) will cruise the Formula 27 at 22 knots (34–35 knots top), and twin 310hp MerCruisers cruise at 25 knots (about 40 knots top).

See Page 679 For Price Data

Length Overall	29'5"	Fuel	107 gals.
Hull Length	27'0"	Water	26 gals.
Beam	9'7"	Waste	30 gals.
Draft	3'1"	Hull Type	Modified-V
Weight	9,500#	Deadrise Aft	18°

Formula 280 Bowrider

1998–2008

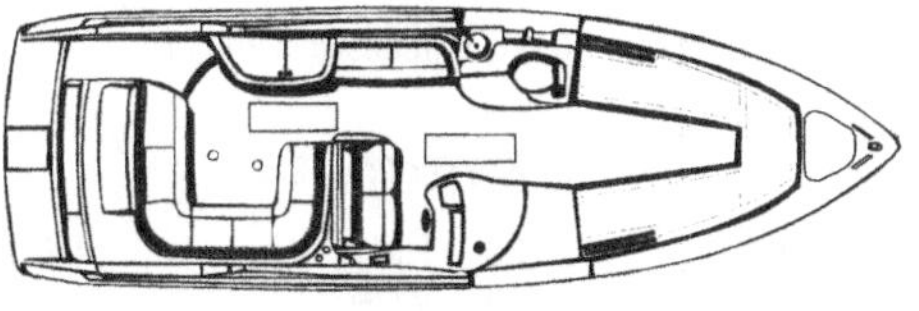

It's all about fun with the Formula 280 Bowrider, a well-built boat big enough for the ocean but small enough to trailer to local lakes and rivers. (Note, however, that because of her wide 9-foot, 2-inch beam, a permit is required for trailering.) Built on a deep-V hull, the 280 is distinguished for her attractive styling, roominess, and easy handling. She's not the least expensive big bowrider on the market, but the quality is there, and it's no secret that Formulas are built to last. Seating includes a flip-up double helm seat, double companion lounge, and a big U-shaped settee in the cockpit that converts to a sun lounge. Storage for fenders or dive tanks is located under the passenger seat, and a deluxe cockpit galley with sink and storage is standard. The 280's tiered helm position, with its Dino wheel and Kiekhaefer controls, is almost ideal, while the enclosed head includes a sink and opening port. Forward, filler cushions can turn the deep bow section into a huge sun pad. Additional features include a power engine hatch lift, stainless steel props, transom storage locker, and an extended swim platform. Offered with single or twin I/Os, twin 260hp MerCruisers deliver a top speed in the neighborhood of 45 knots.

See Page 679 For Price Data

Length Overall	29'6"	Fuel	120 gals.
Beam	9'2"	Water	120 gals.
Draft	3'0"	Waste	2.6 gals.
Weight, Single	7,300#	Hull Type	Deep-V
Weight, Twins	8,200#	Deadrise Aft	21°

Formula 280 Sun Sport

1994–2008

The Formula 280 Sun Sport is a deluxe day cruiser for those who want a boat that's long on cockpit space, handling qualities and workmanship. By any standard, the 280 is a handsome boat and her wraparound windshield and colorful hull graphics only add to her sportboat appeal. With seating for eight, the cockpit is definitely the star attraction of the Sun Sport. Aside from the big U-shaped lounge aft (which converts into a massive sun pad), there's a doublewide seat at the helm and a settee opposite. The on-deck galley makes a lot of sense on a boat like this, and there are many cockpit storage areas including fender storage under the settee. Lacking side decks, a walk-through windshield provides foredeck access, and the engine compartment (under the sun pad) is reached via a motorized hatch lift. Belowdecks, the V-shaped dinette converts into a double berth, and an enclosed head comes with a portable toilet. Among several single or twin sterndrive options, a single 310hp MerCruiser Bravo III engine will cruise the 280 Sun Sport at 21–22 knots (about 37 knots top), and twin 320hp MerCruisers cruise at 28 knots (mid 40 top)s.

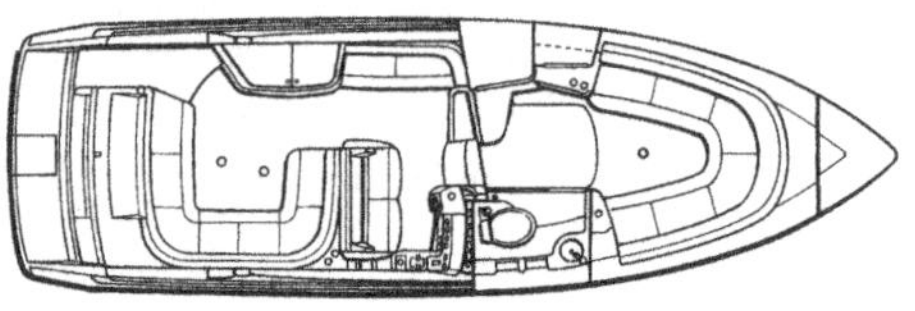

See Page 679 For Price Data

Length Overall	29'6"	Fuel	120 gals.
Beam	9'2"	Water	20 gals.
Draft	3'0"	Waste	26 gal.
Weight	8,200#	Hull Type	Deep-V
Clearance	8'6"	Deadrise Aft	21°

Formula 31 PC

1993–2004

A popular model for Formula over the years, the 31 PC enjoys top billing among late-model midcabin cruisers for her quality construction, upscale accommodations, and solid performance. Like all of Formula's PC series, the 31 is built on a modified-V hull that strikes a balance between stability and open-water performance. Belowdecks, the midcabin floorplan is organized in the conventional manner with overnight accommodations for six, a large head compartment, and privacy curtains for both staterooms. Typical of all Formula products, the hardware, fabrics, furnishings, and appliances are all first rate. The cockpit is arranged with a lounge seating opposite the double helm seat, and the U-shaped aft lounge converts into a big sun pad. Additional features include a transom shower, foredeck sun pad, cockpit wet bar, removable cocktail table, and a concealed swim ladder. A gas-assist hatch in the cockpit floor combined with a foldaway transom seat provides relatively easy access to the motors. MerCruiser 320hp engines cruise the 31 PC at 25 knots and reach a top speed in the high 30s. (Note that an updated Formula 31 PC was introduced in 2005.)

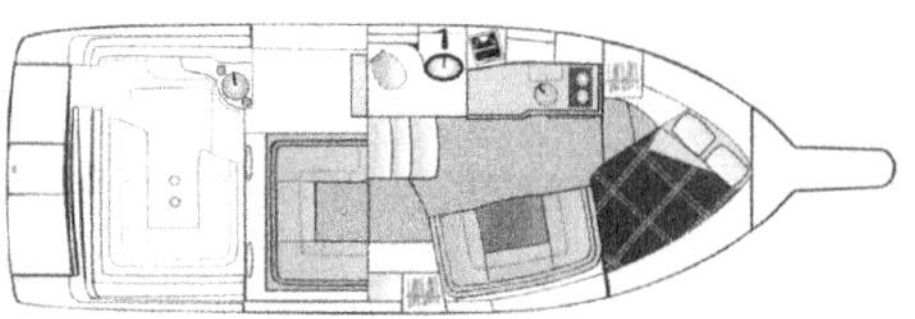

See Page 679 For Price Data

Length Overall	34'0"	Fuel	180 gals.
Hull Length	31'0"	Water	50 gals.
Beam	11'0"	Waste	40 gals.
Draft	3'2"	Hull Type	Modified-V
Weight	11,730#	Deadrise Aft	18°

Formula 31 PC

2005–Current

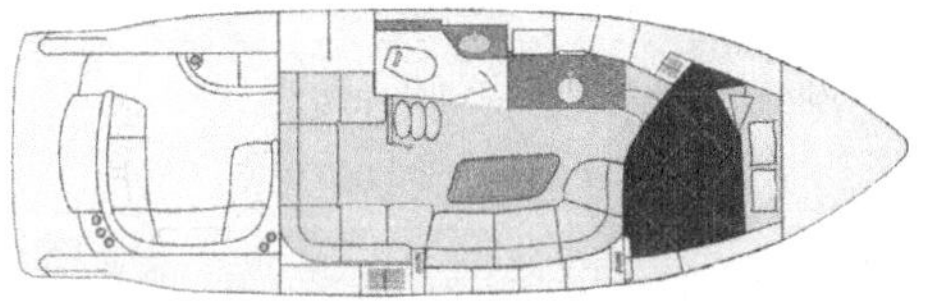

Introduced in 2005, the Formula 31 PC is an updated version of the company's original 31 PC (previous page) considered by many to be among the best express cruisers in her class. The new model retains the top-of-the-line construction features of her predecessor while adding a sporty forward-facing radar arch, an extended swim platform, and an all-new interior scheme notable for its cherry-finished cabinets and Ultraleather upholstery. The cockpit contains a comfortable U-lounge with tables that can be lowered and converted into a large sun pad. Tables and cushions can be stored along with fenders in the huge transom trunk, and twin foredeck sun pads are reached by way of an opening windshield with molded steps. Belowdecks, the 31's designer interior is as elegant as it is practical. Corian counters are found in the galley and head; a solid cherry table serves a six-person lounge; and overall fit and finish is the equal of any European sportboat. Major standard features include a windlass, trim tabs, hot and cold transom shower, 15-inch flat-screen TV/DVD, motorized engine hatch, and a premium VacuFlush toilet. Not inexpensive, twin 320hp MerCruiser sterndrives will reach a top speed of 35+ knots.

See Page 679 For Price Data

Length Overall	33'1"	Fuel	180 gals.
Beam	11'0"	Water	50 gals.
Draft, Up	2'6"	Waste	40 gals.
Draft, Down	3'4"	Hull Type	Modified-V
Weight	14,100#	Deadrise Aft	18°

Formula 310 Sun Sport

2007–Current

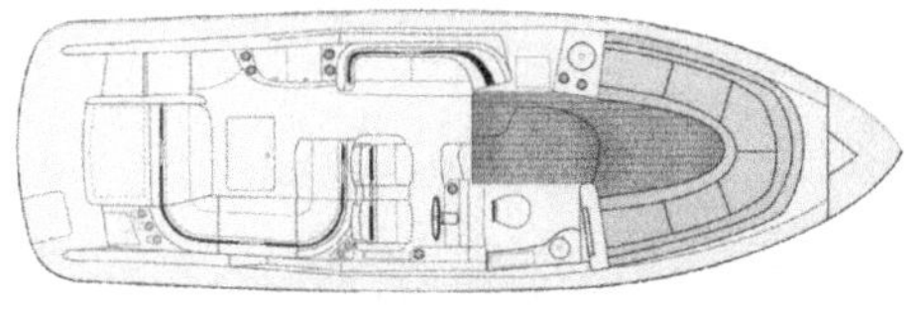

There are many who view Formula as the gold standard in the building of sport boats and runabouts. It isn't styling that sets Formulas apart, it's quality—only a few production builders can match Formula's superb finish and obsessive attention to detail. Introduced in 2007, the 310 Sun Sport offers a compelling blend of comfort and versatility. She's an excellent choice for day trips or overnighting, and her spacious cockpit has seating for ten including a clever aft-facing transom lounge that converts into sun pad. In the cabin there are deep cherry wood cabinets, solid wood tables, and a luxurious Ultraleather lounge. The enclosed head features a electric flush system with stainless steel sink and a pull-out shower. Standard features include a Corian galley counter, molded wet bar with sink, 36-quart cooler and trash receptacle, Dino tilt steering wheel, transom shower, and an extended swim platform with pull-up cleats. The transom storage trunk is a plus, and a power hatch lifts entire aft cockpit for engine access. Note the lockable under-dash storage compartment and slick LED lighting for the swim platform. Twin MerCruiser 320hp I/Os deliver 40+ knots wide open.

See Page 679 For Price Data

Length	31'0"	Fuel	130 gals.
Beam	9'6"	Water	30 gals.
Draft	3'1"	Waste	36 gals.
Weight	9,750#	Hull Type	Deep-V
Clearance	8'8"	Deadrise Aft	22°

Formula 310 Bowrider

2008–Current

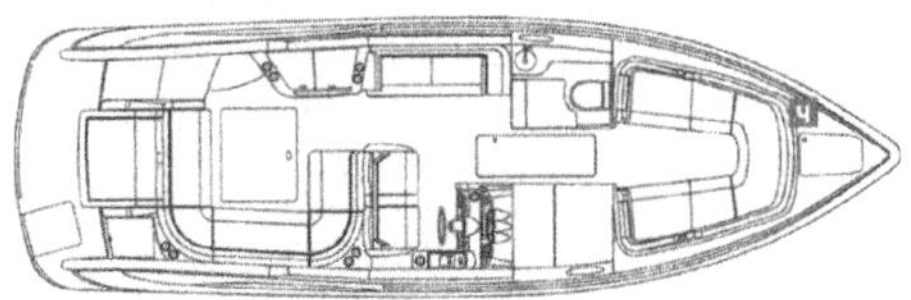

When it comes to making boats, Formula pushes all the right buttons: Its sportboats are quiet, comfortable and fuel efficient, and they're among the most reliable on the water. The 310 Bowrider delivers each of those attributes, and then some. Introduced in 2008, this big open-bow runabout combines top-notch construction with luxury-class amenities and authentic sports-car performance. She rides on a solid fiberglass deep-V hull with moderate beam and a very aggressive 22 degrees of transom deadrise. Designed to spend all day on the water, the U-shaped cockpit lounge with stowable table easily converts to a sunpad by adding the filler cushions. The forward portside lounge provides dedicated dive tank storage underneath, and the molded wet bar includes a stainless sink, Corian countertop, and a pullout refrigerator. Infloor wakeboard and ski storage is also provided. To port, the lockable head compartment features a VacuFlush toilet and a sink with Corian counter. The 310's aft-facing transom lounge also extends to a sunpad for relaxing at anchor. Note the large transom compartment for storing two fenders and assorted gear. Twin 320hp MerCruiser I/Os reach 40+ knots flat out.

See Page 679 For Price Data

Length	31'0"	Fuel	130 gals.
Beam	9'6"	Water	30 gals.
Draft, Up	1'6"	Waste	36 gals.
draft, Down	3'1"	Hull Type	Deep-V
Weight	9,875#	Deadrise Aft	22°

Formula 330 Sun Sport

1996–2006

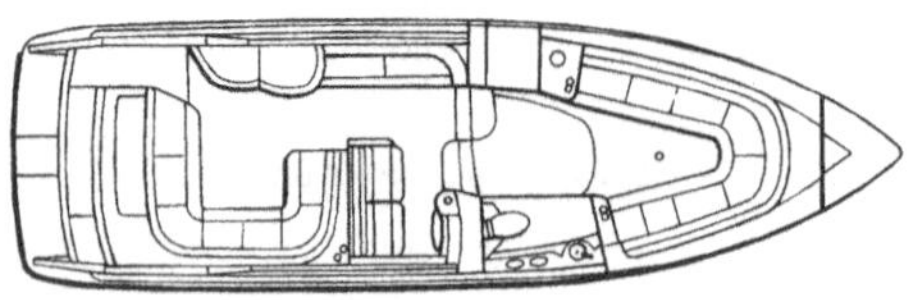

With her sleek lines and roomy cockpit, the Formula 330 Sun Sport will appeal to those seeking a high-style family sportboat with the emphasis on open-air fun. She's well constructed on a deep-V hull with generous beam (for a sportboat), and the subtle-but-colorful hull graphics do much to accent her low-slung appearance. The spacious cockpit of the Formula 330 is really what this boat is all about. Not surprisingly, it comes at the expense of a rather compact, but comfortable, interior. In spite of the limited cabin volume, the accommodations are very practical below with a U-shaped Ultraleather settee/dinette forward, an enclosed head compartment, and an entertainment center—accommodations well suited for her day boat mission. The cockpit table at the transom converts into a wide sun lounge, and a molded on-deck galley conceals a sink, a 54-quart cooler, and an optional alcohol stove. Additional features include a ski locker, dive-tank racks, a walk-through windshield and guest seating opposite the helm. A good performer with 320hp MerCruiser sterndrives, the Formula 330 Ss cruise at 28 knots and top out in the mid 40s.

See Page 679 For Price Data

Length	33'0"	Fuel	160 gals.
Beam	10'2"	Water	20 gals.
Draft	2'11"	Waste	26 gals.
Weight	9,700#	Hull Type	Deep-V
Clearance	6'0"	Deadrise Aft	20°

Formula 34 PC

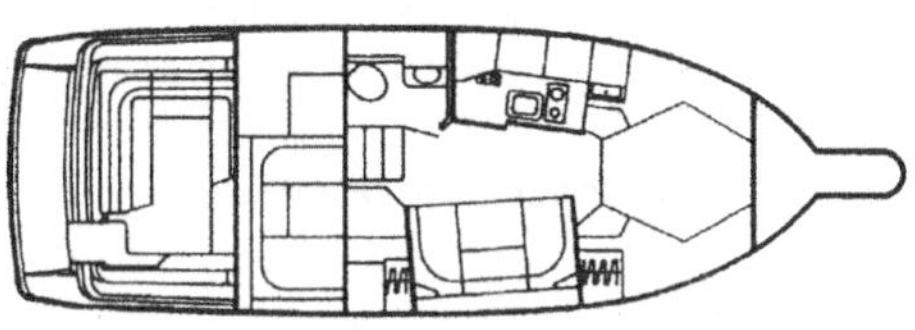

Formula got it right in 1991 with the introduction of the 34 PC, a strong-selling boat during her decade-long production run, and a boat with enduring appeal on the used market today. Like all of Formula's PC (Performance Cruiser) designs, she's built on a constant deadrise deep-V hull with moderate beam and solid fiberglass construction. The midcabin interior will sleep six and comes with an island berth in the forward stateroom and convertible facing settees in the aft cabin. Both staterooms have privacy curtains, and a bi-fold door in the head isolates the shower from the vanity. On deck, a triple-wide companion seat is opposite the helm and the entire aft section of the cockpit can be turned into a giant sunken sun pad. Additional features include well-secured side decks, a molded bow pulpit, transom shower, foredeck sun pad, and a cockpit wet bar. Generally considered a sterndrive model, V-drive inboards were optional (but never all that popular) from 1994–99. A good performer, twin 310hp Volvo or MerCruiser sterndrives cruise the 34 PC at 23–24 knots and reach a top speed in the mid 30s. Cruising speeds with twin 310hp MerCruiser inboards are a few knots slower.

See Page 679 For Price Data

Length Overall	37'0"	Clearance w/Arch	10'0"
Hull Length	34'0"	Fuel	222 gals.
Beam	12'0"	Water	60 gals.
Draft	2'6"	Hull Type	Modified-V
Weight	13,500#	Deadrise Aft	18°

Formula 34 PC

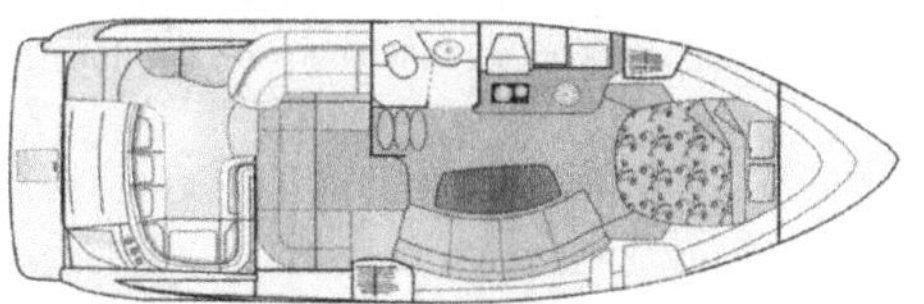

Introduced in 2004, the Formula 34 PC replaces Formula's original—and very popular—34 PC built during 1991-2002. The styling is updated and so are the cabin and cockpit accommodations, and swimmers and divers will appreciate the extended swim platform of the new 34. Built on a deep-V hull with slightly less beam than her predecessor, the Formula sleeps six in a midcabin floorplan typical of express boats this size. Privacy curtains separate both sleeping areas from the main cabin, and a luxurious Ultraleather lounge in the salon converts to a double berth for extra guests. This is a very inviting layout with lots of headroom, high-gloss cherry joinery and vinyl overheads. The galley is notable for its concealed stove, generous storage, and Corian counter. Cockpit seating includes a double helm seat, a U-shaped settee aft, and a bench seat opposite the helm. A wet bar is standard, and molded steps beside the companionway lead up to the windshield walk-through. Additional features include a reverse radar arch, power engine hatch lift, and transom storage locker. A fast ride, twin 320hp MerCruiser Bravo III sterndrives cruise the Formula 34 PC in the mid 20s and top out at over 35 knots.

See Page 679 For Price Data

Length Overall	35'7"	Fuel	206 gals.
Beam	11'6"	Water	55 gals.
Draft	3'0"	Waste	40 gals.
Weight	15,710#	Hull Type	Modified-V
Clearance	11'4"	Deadrise Aft	18°

Formula 350 Sun Sport

2008–Current

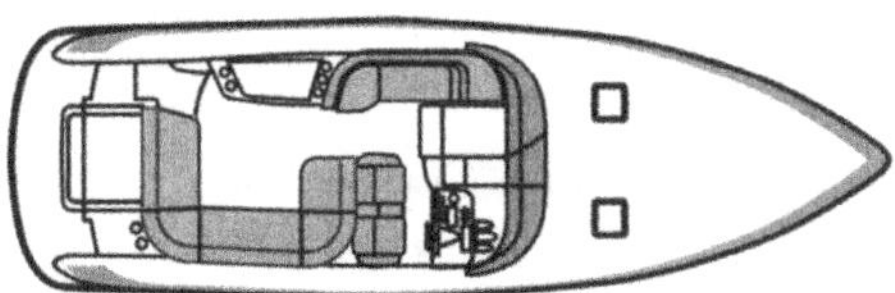

At the top in her class, the Formula 350 Sun Sport bridges the gap between a high-performance dayboat and luxury-class cruiser. This is definitely a fun-in-the-sun boat—ride and handling are superb, and the large cockpit offers every amenity required for daytime entertaining. Built on a smooth-running deep-V hull, the cockpit of the 350 Sun Sport is similar in design to most boats in her class with lounge seating aft, portside sun lounger, wet bar, and a double-wide helm seat. The difference is the quality that Formula always brings to the table: the upholstery is plush; the hardware is the best available; and the finish is mirror-smooth. The cockpit lounge seats eight, and its aft section converts to a recliner for two. A beautifully molded wet bar features a sink, Corian countertop, 36-quart cooler, and trash container. At the transom, the aft-facing lounge converts to a full-length sun pad. Forward, a windlass is tucked under a deck hatch—note the foot controls and stainless anchor chute. Helm ergonomics are exceptional. Below, the luxurious cabin of the 350 Sun Sport is as good as it gets in a boat of this type. Twin 320hp MerCruiser sterndrives reach close to 50 knots wide open. Expensive.

See Page 679 For Price Data

Length	35'0"	Fuel	172 gals.
Beam	10'9"	Water	30 gals.
Draft, Up	1'10"	Waste	37 gals.
Draft, Down	3'3"	Hull Type	Deep-V
Weight	13,470#	Deadrise Aft	21°

Formula 36 PC

1990–95

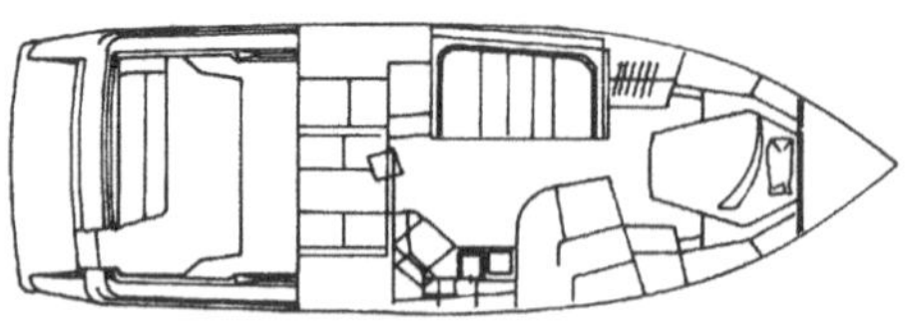

A popular model during her 6-year production run, the 36 PC is a contemporary midcabin cruiser whose attractive lines and comfortable accommodations make her a desirable boat on today's used market. She was built on a solid fiberglass deep-V hull with fairly high freeboard and prop pockets to reduce her draft requirements. Inside, the midcabin floorplan is arranged in the conventional manner, having an island bed in the forward stateroom (with a door for privacy) and facing settees in the step-down aft cabin. There's a built-in entertainment center on the aft bulkhead above the midcabin facing the salon—very innovative. In the cockpit, a big L-shaped lounge is opposite the helm, and a hydraulically operated hatch provides outstanding access to the engine compartment. Note that unlike most modern midcabin cruisers of her type and size, the Formula 36 PC has straight inboard power rather than V-drives. Standard 454-cid gas engines cruise at 17 knots and reach 26–27 knots top. Note that in 1990 (only) Formula offered an Express version of the 36 PC without the midcabin but with a huge engineroom and extra storage.

See Page 679 For Price Data

Length Overall	38'3"	Clearance	10'9"
Hull Length	36'0"	Fuel	300 gals.
Beam	13'3"	Water	60 gals.
Draft	2'8"	Hull Type	Modified-V
Weight	17,600#	Deadrise Aft	18°

Formula 37 PC

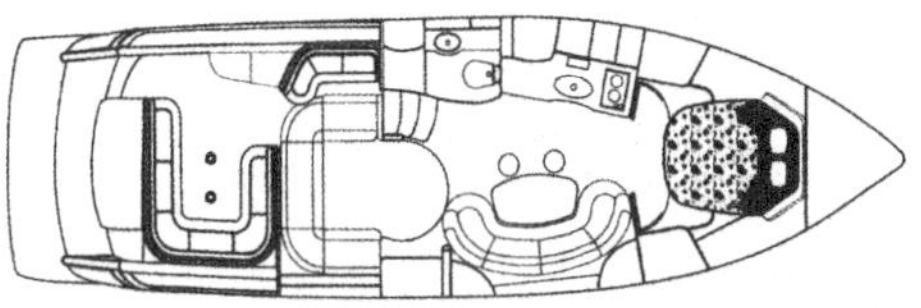

The Formula 37 PC is a top-shelf family express whose aggressive good looks (note the reverse radar arch) and sumptuous interior are designed to appeal to upmarket cruisers willing to pay a little extra for the built-in quality of a Formula product. She's built on a beamy deep-V hull with prop pockets and a relatively modest 18 degrees of deadrise at the transom. The midcabin floorplan of the 37 PC is unusually wide open and spacious thanks to the absence of any interior cabin bulkheads. Headroom is excellent, the decor is quite elegant, and the furnishings and appliances are first rate. Draw curtains rather than doors are used to separate both sleeping areas, however—a privacy issue for some. The cockpit, with its U-shaped lounge (which converts into a big sun pad), wet bar and triple-wide helm seat, can accommodate 10 passengers. Note that the entire transom and rear seat unit can be raised for excellent (and innovative) engine access. Additional features include a walk-through windshield, a huge transom locker, foredeck sun pads and an optional PWC lift. Among several sterndrive and inboard power options, twin 375hp Volvo gas engines (with V-drives) will cruise in the mid 20s and top out at just over 30 knots.

See Page 679 For Price Data

Length Overall	38'5"	Fuel	236 gals.
Beam	11'11"	Water	55 gals.
Draft	2'6"	Waste	57 gals.
Weight	16,500#	Hull Type	Modified-V
Clearance	14'4"	Deadrise Aft	18°

Formula 370 Super Sport

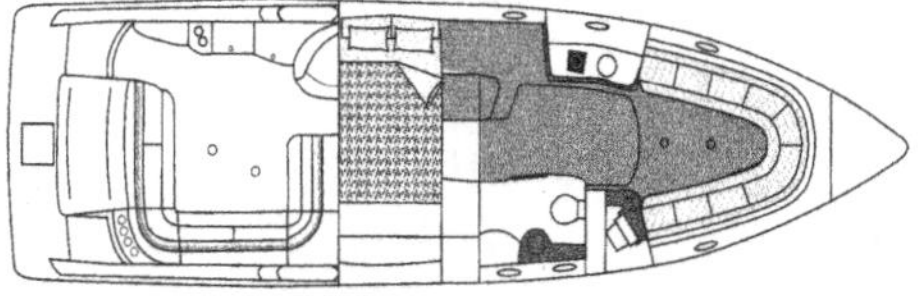

The Formula 370 Super Sport is a sleek, aggressively styled sportcruiser with an enviable combination of superior construction, first-rate accommodations and excellent open-water performance. She's basically a Euro-style sportboat with considerably more cockpit space—and less interior volume—than traditional express cruisers. Performance is important in a boat like this, and the 370's narrow beam and high-speed stepped hull deliver the fast ride and luxurious accommodations that few other sportboats can match. Her spacious and well-equipped cockpit provides seating and amenities for a small crowd. A removable cocktail table stores in a transom storage locker, and a cockpit galley comes complete with a sink, cooler and refrigerator. The cabin of the 370—among the more impressive in her class—includes a wraparound V-berth/ dinette forward, mid-berth cabin aft, and a compact galley to port with stove and refrigerator. Additional features include a walk-through windshield, transom shower, tilt steering, and a flip-up bolster seat at the helm. Like all Formula boats, the fit and finish of the 370 Super Sport is very impressive. A pair of 420hp sterndrives cruise at 30 knots (mid 40s wide open)

See Page 679 For Price Data

Length	38'6"	Fuel	238 gals.
Beam	10'6"	Water	43 gals.
Draft	3'0"	Waste	50 gals.
Weight	15,100#	Hull Type	Deep-V
Clearance	10'0"	Deadrise Aft	21°

Formula 40 PC

2002–Current

Most long-time boaters know that Formula's series of family cruisers are built to high standards, which is to say they aren't inexpensive. That's certainly true of the Formula 40 PC, a high-end express designed for those who place a priority on luxury and performance. With her sleek styling, optional hardtop, and extended swim platform, the Formula is as practical as she is handsome. It's her belowdecks accommodations, however, that set the 40 PC apart from much of the competition. Here, a tasteful blend of high-gloss cherry joinery, Ultraleather upholstery, and top-quality hardware and furnishings combine to create an impressive display of luxury and comfort. Hidden privacy doors separate the forward stateroom from the main cabin, and the Formula's tall headroom gives the impression of a much larger boat. Topside, an extended swim platform—sturdy enough to carry a jet bike—makes boarding easy. At the helm, a double flip-up seat allows the driver to drive while standing. A walk-through windshield, transom storage locker, and radar arch are standard. A good ride in a chop, twin 420hp Yanmar V-drive diesels cruise at 22–24 knots. Volvo IPS power became optional in 2009.

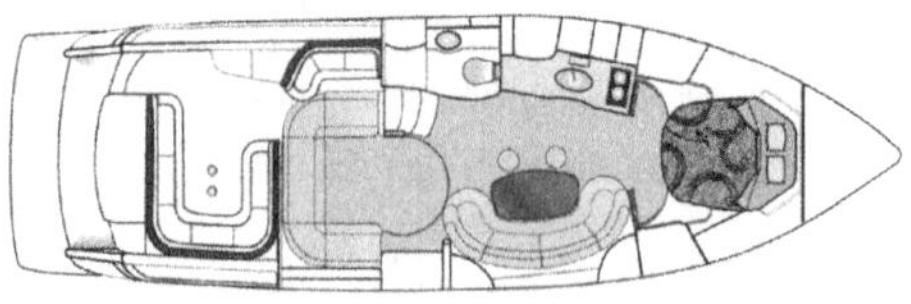

See Page 680 For Price Data

Length	42'7"	Fuel	250 gals.
Beam	12'8"	Water	55 gals.
Draft	2'11"	Waste	57 gals.
Weight	21,550#	Hull Type	Modified-V
Clearance	16'8"	Deadrise Aft	18°

Formula 400 Super Sport

1999–Current

The Formula 400 Super Sport is an American-built entry into the high-performance luxury sportboat market dominated in recent years by a handful of pricey European imports. Long and narrow, the 400 is built on Formula's "Fas3Tech" hull bottom—a double-stepped deep-V affair designed to reduce the water's grip on the hull. The result, according to company engineers, is a faster and more stable boat that runs at near-optimal running angles without the need to constantly trim the drives. Beautifully styled, the Super Sport is a superb day boat with plenty of cockpit space and a wide-open interior. With the owner's stateroom aft, a rich Ultraleather wraparound lounge forward and four overhead translucent hatches dominate the salon. On deck, the doublewide helm seat folds away for standup driving, and a walk-through windshield opens to a wide stretch of nonskid leading to the bow. Notable features include a recessed anchor storage compartment, a hinged storage locker at the transom, and good engine access. Twin 425hp gas sterndrives will achieve a top speed of close to 45 knots, while Volvo 370hp diesel I/Os top out at close to 40 knots.

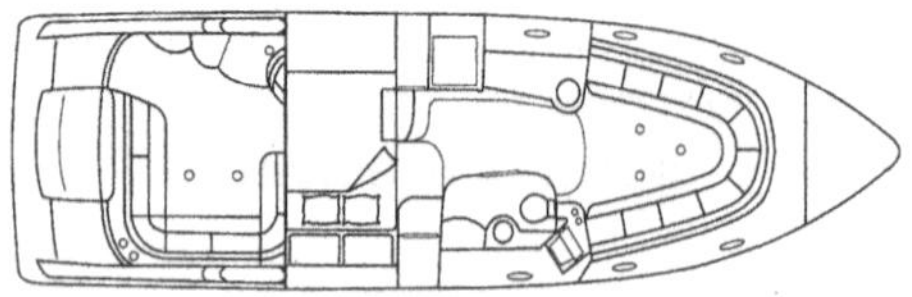

See Page 680 For Price Data

Length	41'6"	Fuel	250 gals.
Beam	11'0"	Water	50 gals.
Draft	3'0"	Waste	50 gals.
Weight, Gas	16,100#	Hull Type	Deep-V
Weight, Diesel	17,100#	Deadrise Aft	22°

Formula 41 PC

1996–2004

Flagship of the Formula fleet for several years, the 41 PC is a well-engineered express cruiser with the precise handling and quality construction typical of Formula products. This is a big boat inside and out, and a long foredeck and shapely profile make her a standout in any marina. The midcabin accommodations of the Formula 41 are impressive indeed with staterooms fore and aft and a long salon with room for a crowd. There's a separate stall shower in the double-entry head, a big galley with plenty of counter space, excellent storage, and a walkaround island berth in the forward stateroom. Outside, the cockpit is arranged with a doublewide seat at the helm and a U-shaped settee aft that converts into a huge sun pad. The lounge seat opposite the helm can be raised hydraulically to expose a big storage compartment below. A walk-through in the windshield provides access to the foredeck, and hydraulic rams lift the entire cockpit sole for engine access. Running on a deep-V hull with prop pockets, 8.2-liter gas engines cruise at 16–17 knots (around 28 knots wide open), and 450hp Cummins diesels cruise at 24–25 knots (about 30 knots top).

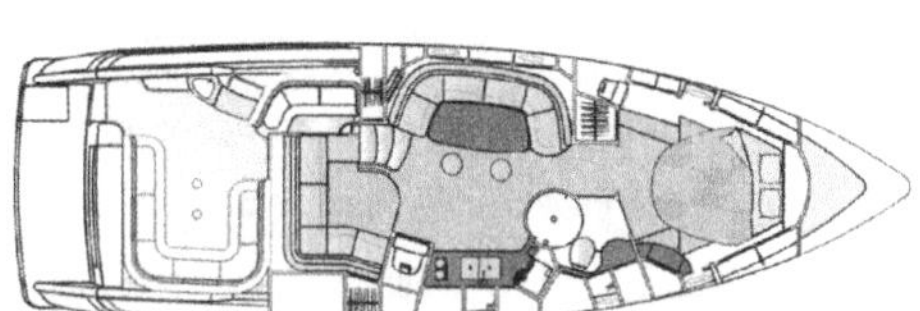

See Page 680 For Price Data

Length Overall	43'1"	Fuel, Gas	300 gals.
Hull Length	41'0"	Fuel, Diesel	350 gals.
Beam	13'6"	Water	81 gals.
Draft	2'9"	Hull Type	Modified-V
Weight	18,520#	Deadrise Aft	18°

Formula 45 Yacht

2007–Current

With her distinctive hardtop styling and versatile layout, the sleek 45 Yacht took Formula's concept of cruising luxury to the next level when she was introduced in 2007. Indeed, the 45 combines the style and sex appeal of a European sportyacht with the amenities of a small motoryacht. Boarding is easy via the extended swim platform, transom door, and twin-level cockpit. Flexiteak decking provides a nice contrast with the tan upholstery, and a walk-through windshield provides easy access to the bow. Below decks, the spacious two-stateroom interior of the 45 Yacht features a tastefully appointed salon with U-shaped leather settee, two removable dining stools, home-size galley with full-size refrigerator, and two heads. Topside highlights include bridge-deck air conditioning, outdoor galley and wet bar, and hydraulic swim platform with dinghy lift system. The entire aft cockpit section rises for access to the engines and generator. Note the power sunroof. The side decks are quite narrow. Originally offered with Volvo 575hp V-drive diesels (25–26 knots cruise), 435hp IPS pod drives soon became standard on the 45 Yacht. They'll cruise at roughly the same speed, but with better fuel efficiency.

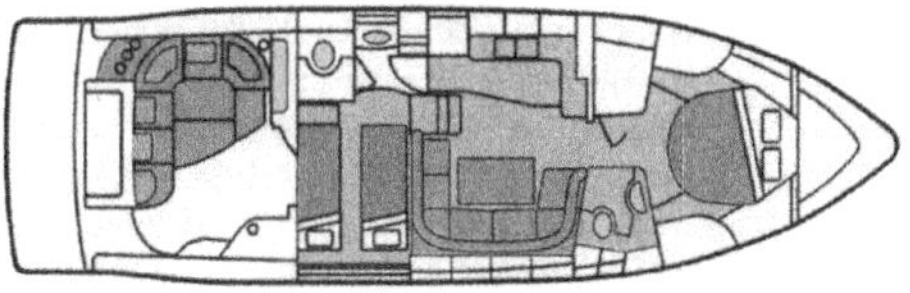

See Page 680 For Price Data

Length Overall	48'2"	Fuel	350 gals.
Beam	13'11"	Water	100 gals.
Draft	3'5"	Waste	75 gals.
Weight	32,500#	Hull Type	Modified-V
Clearance	15'5"	Deadrise Aft	18°

Formula 48 Yacht

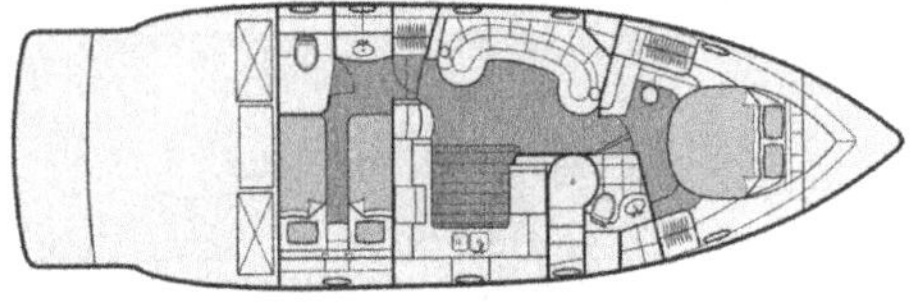

For a company whose name has long been associated with performance, the Formula 48 Yacht (called the 47 Yacht in 2003–05) is much more concerned with luxury than speed. This is Formula's largest and most expensive cruising yacht ever, and she retains the high level of quality that longtime boaters have come to expect in a Formula product. Built on a deep-V hull with prop pockets and moderate beam, the 48's lavish accommodations are both elegant and spacious. Headroom exceeds 7 feet in the salon and varnished cherrywood joinery, Ultraleather upholstery, and designer fabrics dominate the interior. The huge L-shaped galley rivals that of a small motor yacht, and the aft stateroom—which can easily double as a den—has its own private head with shower. Across from the salon, a built-in LCD television automatically tilts for the best viewing angle. The expansive cockpit of the Formula 48 provides seating for ten, and the helm layout is as good as it gets in a big express. Unlike most sterndrive-powered European sportcruisers, the Formula is an inboard design that many boaters prefer for maintenance reasons. Twin 660hp Cummins diesels cruise in the mid 20s and reach 32–33 knots wide open.

See Page 680 For Price Data

Length	51'0"	Fuel	400 gals.
Beam	14'0"	Water	100 gals.
Draft	3'8"	Waste	75 gals.
Weight	35,750#	Hull Type	Modified-V
Clearance	14'0"	Deadrise Aft	18°

Four Winns

Quick View

- Four Winns' origins date back to 1962 when the company, then called the Safe-T-Mate Boat Co., manufactured a series of small fiberglass runabouts at their facility in Cadillac, MI.
- In 1975 the Winn family (father Bill and his three sons) purchased Safe-T-Mate and began production under the Four Winns brand.
- By the mid 1980s, Four Winns had become one of the largest manufacturers of fiberglass boats in the country.
- In 1986 Four Winns was purchased by Outboard Marine Corporation (OMC).
- In 2000 OMC declared bankruptcy and operations at Four Winns were interrupted until March, 2001 when the company was purchased by Genmar Industries.
- In June, 2009, during the worst boating recession in memory, the Genmar family of boat builders (including Four Winns) declared Chapter 11 bankruptcy.
- In 2010 Platinum Equity acquires Genmar assets and resumes Four Winns production.

Four Winns Boats • Cadillac, MI • www.fourwinns.com

Four Winns 268 Vista

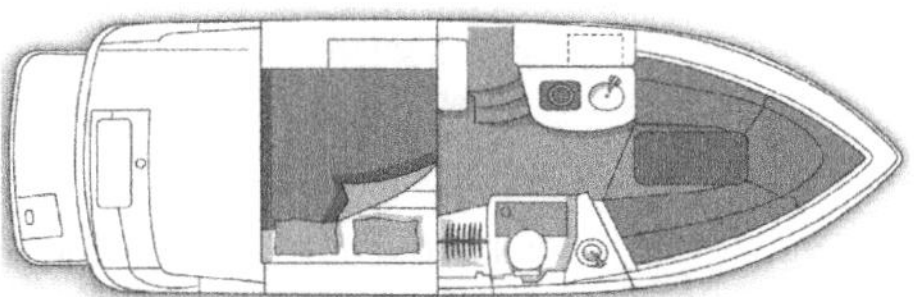

A good-looking boat, the Four Winns 268 Vista manages to retain a relatively handsome profile in spite of the high freeboard required by boats of this type for interior headroom. This is a competitively priced family cruiser with an attractive midcabin interior and a comfortable cockpit. Built on a solid fiberglass deep-V hull, the 268 is trailerable thanks to her narrow 8'6" beam, but with a combined boat and trailer weight of over 8,000 pounds, a heavy-duty tow vehicle will be required for any trailering adventures. The cockpit of the 268 has more seating than many 26-footers thanks to a huge U-shaped aft settee that converts into a big sun lounge. Visibility from the helm is very good, and a walk-through windshield with molded steps next to the helm provides easy access to the foredeck. The interior, which is quite well finished, comes with a V-berth, a full galley, dinette table and a head with shower. Additional features include an extended swim platform, transom door, foredeck sun pads and a transom storage compartment. Among several engine options, a single 280hp 5.7-liter I/O will cruise at 25 knots and reach a top speed of around 38 knots.

See Page 680 For Price Data

Length w/Platform	28'2"	Fuel	85 gals.
Hull Length	25'8"	Water	21 gals.
Beam	8'6"	Waste	21 gals.
Draft, Down	3'3"	Hull Type	Modified-V
Weight	6,470#	Deadrise Aft	17°

Four Winns 278 Vista

The Four Winns 278 Vista is a maxi-cube pocket cruiser whose stylish appearance has kept her from showing her age since she went out of production in 1998. Like many family boats her size, her modified-V hull (with a keel pad) provides a stable and comfortable ride in a variety of weather conditions. The Vista's accommodations are evenly divided between a roomy and well-arranged cockpit and the full-width cabin with its conventional midcabin floorplan. There are double berths fore and aft and both sleeping areas have a curtain for privacy. Notably, the galley has plenty of storage and counter space. There's a shower in the standup head, and the dinette table converts into a kid-sized berth. Outside, visibility from the double helm seat is excellent. Additional features include a walk-through windshield, space at the helm for flush-mounted electronics, and foldaway bench seating at the transom. Note that oval cabin ports replaced the original sliding cabin windows in 1996, and the cockpit was redesigned in 1998. A single 7.4-liter OMC sterndrive cruises at 22 knots (about 30+ knots top), and a pair of OMC 5.7-liter sterndrives cruise at 24–25 knots (35+ knots top).

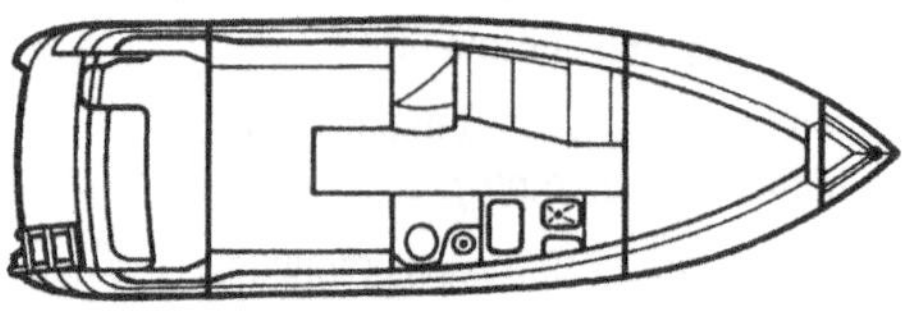

See Page 680 For Price Data

Length	27'2"	Fuel	110 gals.
Beam	9'4"	Water	38 gals.
Draft	3'3"	Waste	30 gals.
Weight	6,650#	Hull	Modified-V
Clearance	8'6"	Deadrise Aft	17°

Four Winns 278 Vista; V285

For those looking for a big trailerable cruiser—legally trailerable, that is, with no more than 8'6" of beam—the Four Winns V278 (called the V285 in 2010–12) should just about fill the bill. Trailerable express cruisers don't get any bigger than this and they probably never will. As good-looking as she is, however, the downside of the 278 Vista—or any big trailerable boat, for that matter—is her near-claustrophobic interior. That said, there's a lot to like about this boat from the standpoint of design and engineering. For the money, Four Winns builds a quality product and it shows throughout the 278. The cockpit layout makes the best use possible of the boat's slender beam with seating for four and a removable snack table that converts into a sun pad. A mini wet bar to port includes a carry-on cooler that fits under the counter. Below decks, the accommodations are tastefully appointed if not spacious. A convertible dinette in the bow sleeps two people, while a small aft cabin offers space for two more. The cherry trim is well finished, and the 278's six-foot headroom is adequate for most. Note the transom storage locker. A surprisingly good performer, a single 375hp Volvo I/O tops out at 30+ knots.

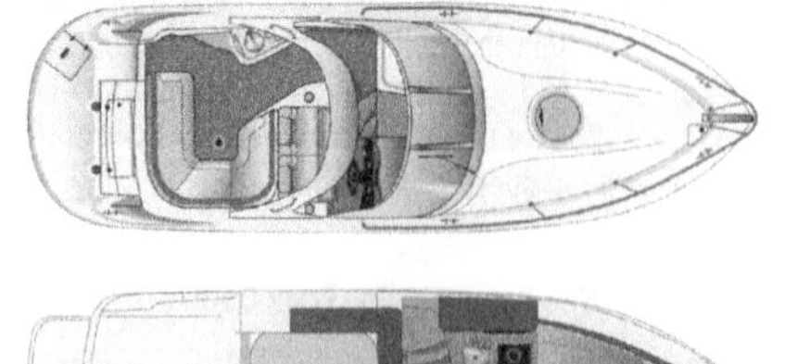

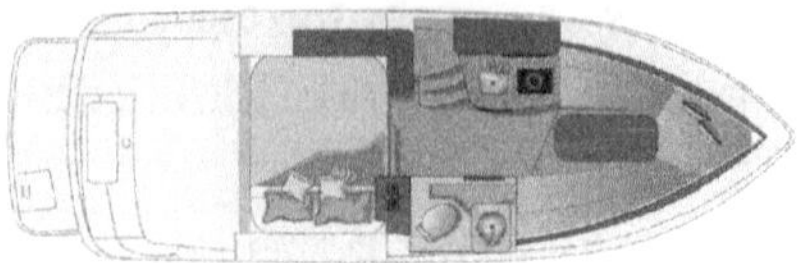

See Page 680 For Price Data

Length	28'4"	Fuel	85 gals.
Beam	8'6"	Water	21 gals.
Draft, Up	1'8"	Waste	21 gals.
Draft, Down	3'3"	Hull Type	Modified-V
Weight	7,100#	Deadrise Aft	17°

Four Winns 280 Horizon

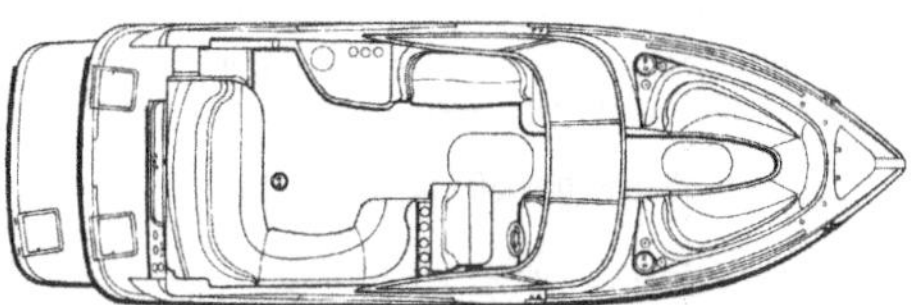

At nearly 28 feet in length, the 280 Horizon is the largest bowrider Four Winns has ever built. Big bowriders have become increasingly popular in recent years, and the Horizon, with her wide 9-foot, 4-inch beam, is bigger than most. Built on a modified-V hull, the 280 has the size and weight to handle an ocean chop while still offering the stability so important in any family runabout. Key to the popularity of this boat is her large cockpit with its wraparound seating to starboard and refreshment center (with standard refrigerator, sink, and trash bin) to port. A side settee is opposite the helm, where a flip-up double seat provides plenty of legroom for standup driving. A stylish burlwood dash displays a complete set of Faria gauges as well as a depthfinder, however there's little space for any extra electronics. An enclosed head compartment is built into the portside console, while the starboard console contains a large storage locker. Note that the 280's engine compartment is a tight fit. Additional features include a power engine hatch, transom shower, tilt steering wheel, and an extended secondary swim platform. A fast ride with twin 315hp Volvo I/Os, the Horizon will hit a top speed of around 50 knots.

See Page 680 For Price Data

Length w/Platform	27'9"	Fuel	130 gals.
Beam	9'4"	Water	12 gals.
Draft, Up	1'6"	Waste	12 gals.
Draft, Down	3'1"	Hull Type	Deep-V
Weight	7,140#	Deadrise Aft	21°

Four Winns 285 Sundowner

The Four Winns 285 Sundowner is a well-appointed day boat whose spacious cockpit can seat as many as eight in comfort. Four Winns has a reputation for building a good-quality product, and the Sundowner will easily satisfy the demands of active families more interested in practicality than glitz. Built on what Four Winns calls a "Stable-Vee" hull with a keel pad to increase speed, the Sundowner's deck plan is a model of efficiency. A wraparound lounge aft converts to a sun pad, and a portside mini-galley includes a refrigerator, sink with pressure water, and a trash bin. At the helm, a double flip-up seat provides plenty of legroom for standup driving. Note that the dash area, with its Plexiglas-covered chart flat, is tinted to reduce glare. Going below, the Sundowner's small cuddy is arranged with an enclosed head (with VacuFlush toilet) to port, a microwave cabinet opposite, and a convertible V-berth forward. On the downside, the engine compartment is a tight fit. Standard features include a power engine hatch, secondary extended swim platform, walk-through windshield, and tilt wheel. Among many engine choices, twin 270hp Volvo I/Os will deliver a top speed in excess of 50 knots.

See Page 680 For Price Data

Length w/Platform	27'9"	Headroom	5'0"
Beam	9'4"	Max Headroom	4'7"
Draft, Up	1'6"	Fuel	130 gals.
Draft, Down	3'1"	Water	12 gals.
Weight	6,380#	Hull Type	Modified-V

Four Winns 288 Vista

2004–09

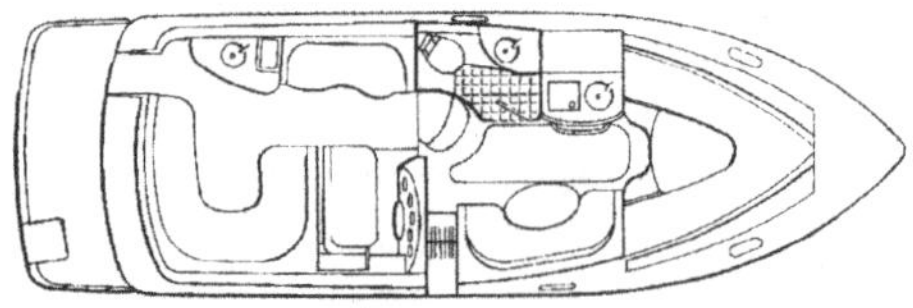

Introduced in 2004, the Four Winns 288 Vista's blend of solid construction, comfortable accommodations, and competitive price makes her a strong contender in the under-30-foot segment of today's express-boat market. Built on a modified-V hull with cored hullsides, the interior of the 288 Vista is a little larger than other boats in her class thanks to a wide 9-foot, 8-inch beam. The layout—which differs little from other midcabin cruisers—sleeps six with double berths fore and aft and a convertible Ultraleather settee in the main cabin. The midcabin area is a tight fit, but the head is large and the galley has the refrigerator located above the microwave so you don't have to bend down to reach it. For after-hours privacy, curtains separate the sleeping areas from the main cabin. Topside, the cockpit is configured with a U-shaped lounge aft, refreshment center with slide-out cooler, removable table, and an electric engine hatch. Note that the double helm seat has a flip-up bolster for the driver. An extended swim platform, aluminum radar arch, tilt steering wheel, and transom shower were standard. With twin 270hp Volvo sterndrives, the 288 Vista will cruise in the low 20s and reach 30+ knots wide open.

See Page 680 For Price Data

Length w/Platform	30'0"	Fuel	120 gals.
Beam	9'8"	Water	25 gals.
Draft, Down	3'3"	Waste	25 gals.
Weight	10,380#	Hull Type	Modified-V
Clearance, Arch	9'0"	Deadrise Aft	18°

Four Winns 298 Vista

1999–2005

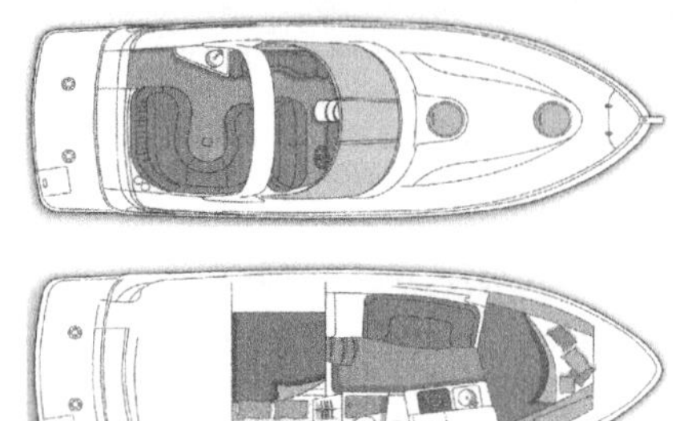

With her wide beam, generous accommodations and impressive standard equipment list, the 298 Vista became a popular model for Four Winns following her 1999 introduction. She's built on a relatively heavy modified-hull with cored hullsides, and her extended swim platform—strong enough to carry a PWC—adds much to her modern appearance. The 298's plush interior is arranged in the conventional manner with double berths fore and aft, a convertible dinette, a well-equipped galley, and a standup head compartment with a VacuFlush toilet. Note that a sliding screen door—a seldom seen accessory on any express cruiser—backs the companionway hatch. On deck, the seat cushion on the driver's side of the double helm seat flips up to create a leaning post, and molded steps in the console provide access to the foredeck via the walk-through windshield. Standard features include a removable aft seat, cockpit table, tilt wheel and full camper canvass. On the downside, the engine compartment is a tight fit, and the wide beam makes for a hard (and wet) ride in a chop. Twin 270hp Volvo 5.7-liter sterndrives cruise the 298 Vista at 25 knots and deliver a top speed of around 40 knots.

See Page 680 For Price Data

Length w/Platform	30'11"	Clearance, Arch	9'2"
Hull Length	28'0"	Fuel	140 gals.
Beam	10'6"	Water	31 gals.
Draft	3'3"	Hull Type	Modified-V
Weight	10,650#	Deadrise Aft	19°

Four Winns 318 Vista; V335

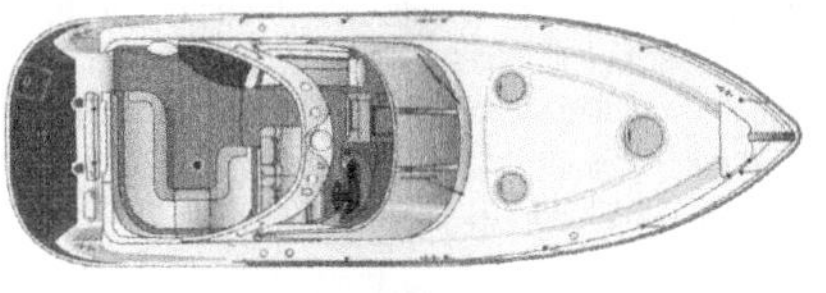

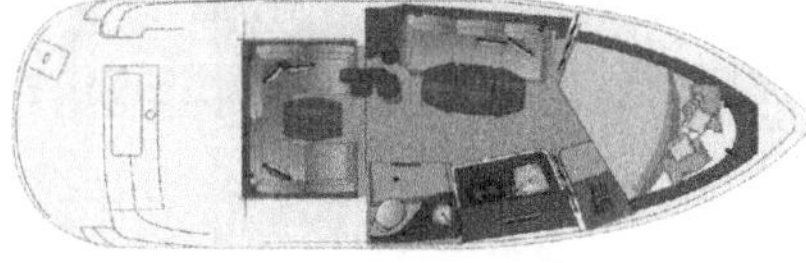

Introduced in 2006, the Four Winns 318 Vista (called the V335 in 2010–) is a spirited, high-end express whose sleek styling is a match for the best European sport cruisers. While she wasn't the largest boat in the Four Winns fleet, the 318 is certainly among the most comfortable. Built on a modified-V hull with a relatively steep 19 degrees of deadrise aft, her tastefully furnished interior—with its high-gloss cherry joinery, faux granite counter, and plush upholstery—seems large for a boat this size. The pullout galley storage is a nice touch, and the U-shaped settee in the mid-cabin features a removable table. Privacy curtains separate the fore and aft sleeping areas from the main cabin. On the downside, the companionway steps are steep and caution is required while using them underway. Topside, the user-friendly cockpit includes U-shaped rear seating (with removable dining table), portside lounger, hot-and-cold shower, and wet bar with sink and icemaker. Note the convenient transom locker for fenders, shore cord, etc. An excellent performer with Volvo 280hp gas I/Os, the 318 Vista will cruise at nearly 30 knots and deliver a top speed of 38–40 knots.

See Page 680 For Price Data

Length w/Platform	33'0"	Clearance	11'2"
Beam	10'9"	Fuel	170 gals.
Draft, Up	1'6"	Water	35 gals.
Draft, Down	3'2"	Hull Type	Modified-V
Weight	11,360#	Deadrise Aft	19°

Four Winns 328 Vista

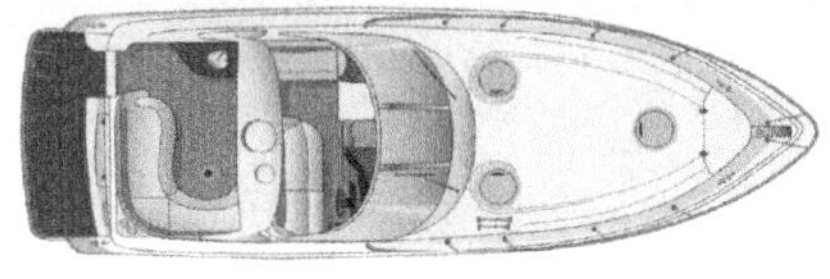

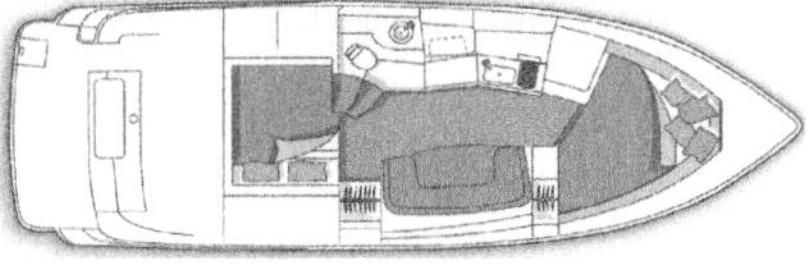

A stylish design with a graceful sheer and a tall, forward-sloped arch, the Four Winns 328 Vista is an attractively priced entry in the always-crowded midsize family cruiser market. She's built on modified-V hull with cored hullsides and a wide 11-foot, 9-inch beam. The Vista is a big boat inside and out with generous accommodations for a boat this size. Her floorplan is typical of most midcabin cruisers her size with double berths fore and aft, a large U-shaped settee, full galley (with plenty of storage drawers and cabinets), and a fair-size head with shower. Note that a sliding screen door backs the companionway hatch. In the single-level cockpit, the big U-shaped lounge aft converts into a sun pad and a molded entertainment center comes with an icemaker and sink. Molded steps in the console provide easy access to the bow via the walk-through windshield. Standard features include a large transom locker, tilt wheel, six opening ports, and an extended swim platform. Twin 280hp Volvo sterndrive engines cruise the 328 Vista at 25 knots and reach a top speed of about 35 knots. Note that the Four Winns 348 Vista is an inboard version of this boat.

See Page 680 For Price Data

Length w/Platform	35'7"	Fuel	220 gals.
Hull Length	33'5"	Water	45 gals.
Beam	11'9"	Waste	30 gals.
Draft	3'2"	Hull Type	Modified-V
Weight	12,600#	Deadrise Aft	19°

Four Winns 338/348 Vista

2000–04

The Four Winns 338 Vista (called the 348 Vista in 2002–04) is an inboard version of the Four Winns 328 Vista. Like her sistership, the 338/248 was an attractively priced entry in the very crowded midsize family cruiser market. She's built on modified-V hull with cored hullsides and a wide 11-foot, 9-inch beam. The Vista is a big boat inside and out with generous accommodations for a boat this size. Belowdecks, the floorplan is typical of most midcabin cruisers her size with double berths fore and aft, a large U-shaped settee, full galley (with plenty of storage drawers and cabinets), and a fair-size head with shower. Note that a sliding screen door backs the companionway hatch. In the single-level cockpit, the big U-shaped lounge aft converts into a sun pad and a molded entertainment center comes with an icemaker and sink. Molded steps in the console provide easy access to the walk-through windshield. Standard features include a large transom locker, tilt wheel, six opening ports and an extended swim platform. MerCruiser 320hp inboards cruise n the low 20s and reach (30+ knots top), and 320hp sterndrives cruise in the high 20s (37–38 knots wide open).

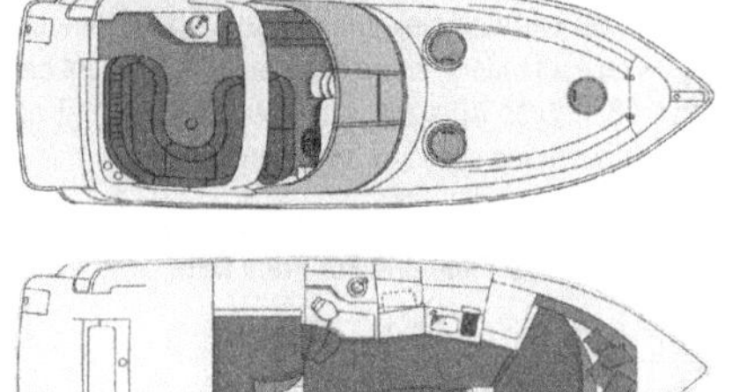

See Page 680 For Price Data

Length w/Platform	35'7"	Fuel	220 gals.
Beam	11'9"	Water	44 gals.
Draft	2'11"	Waste	30 gals.
Weight	13,100#	Hull Type	Modified-V
Clearance, Arch	9'2"	Deadrise Aft	19°

Four Winns 338 Vista; V355

2007–12

Available with sterndrive or inboard power, the Four Winns 338 Vista (called the V355 in 2010–12) combines the comforts expected in a high-end cruiser with the stable ride and upscale amenities synonymous with the Four Winns brand. There's widespread agreement within the boating industry that Four Winns delivers a lot of boat for the money. Indeed, if there were a quality gap between this Michigan-based company's products and those from Sea Ray, Formula, or Regal, it would be hard to discern in the 338 Vista. Her space-efficient cockpit, with U-shaped rear lounge, full-service wet bar, portside lounge, and doublewide helm can seat a small crowd. Below decks, the accommodations are as good as it gets in a boat this size. Interior highlights include high-gloss cherry cabinets, 20-inch flat-screen TV, teak-and-holly galley sole, faux granite counters, and leather upholstery. Bow access is via both side decks—which are very narrow—and a walk-through windshield. The fold-down, aft-facing swim platform seat in a nice touch. Engine access is a tight fit. MerCruiser 300hp gas I/Os reach nearly 40 knots top. Twin 320hp gas inboards will run a few knots slower.

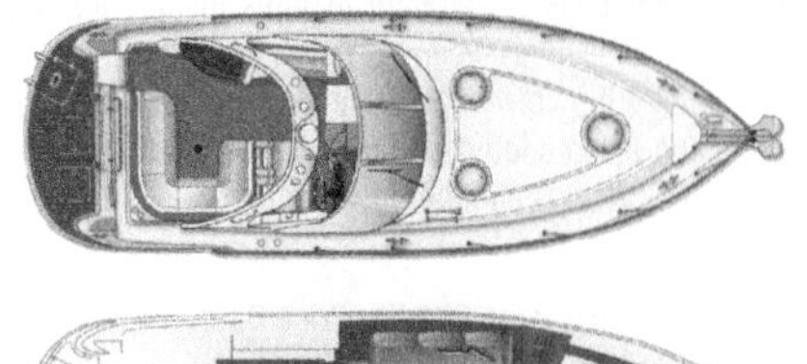

See Page 680 For Price Data

Length	35'0"	Fuel	200 gals.
Beam	11'6"	Water	45 gals.
Draft, Up	2'6"	Waste	30 gals.
Draft, Down	3'4"	Hull Type	Modified-V
Weight	12,090#	Deadrise Aft	19°

Four Winns 348 Vista; V358

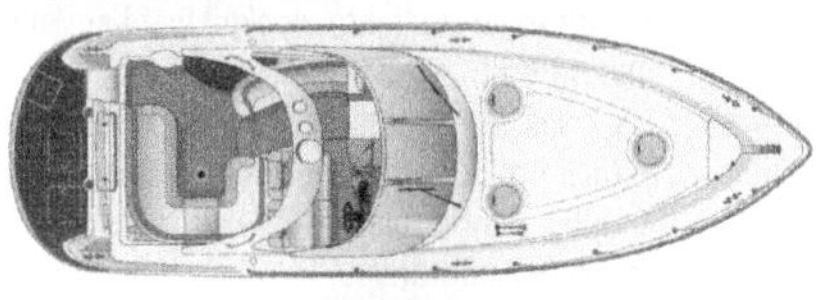

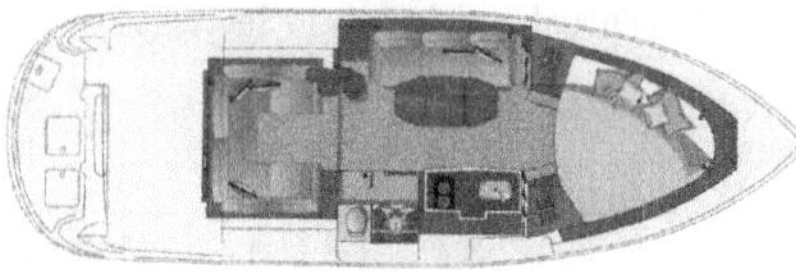

Introduced in 2005 to replace the original Four Winns 348 Vista (2001–04), this new 348 Vista (that became the V358 in 2007) is agile, solid, and easy on the eye. Four Winns' designers always manage to pack a lot of features into their express cruisers. While the cockpit and cabin accommodations of the V358 differ little from those found in most competitive models, her numerous thoughtful features make the difference. The salon table has fold-up ends making it easy to stow, and the foldout sofa converts to a double bed with no trouble at all. The sculptured cabin overhead (with indirect lighting) is a nice touch as well, something you won't see on many of her rivals. A central vacuum system was standard, and there are two hanging lockers forward rather than just one. On the downside, the companionway steps are steep, and privacy curtains are a poor second to solid stateroom doors. Topside highlights include a sporty helm layout with space for electronics, double helm seat with flip-up bolsters, extended swim platform, transom storage locker, power engine hatch, and wet bar with icemaker. Crusader 375hp inboard gas engines top out at 30–32 knots; Crusader 375hp I/Os run a few knots faster.

See Page 680 For Price Data

Length	37'0"	Fuel	230 gals.
Beam	12'0"	Water	51 gals.
Draft	3'4"	Waste	30 gals.
Weight	14,600#	Hull Type	Modified-V
Clearance	11'2"	Deadrise Aft	19°

Four Winns 378 Vista

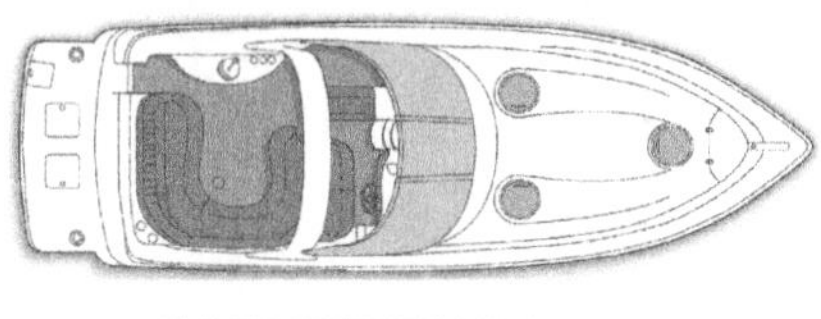

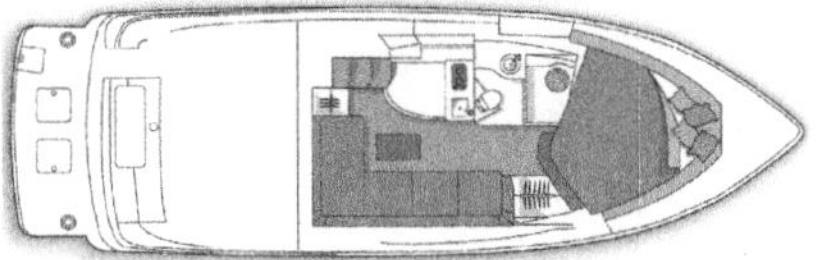

Four Winns largest boat ever, the 378 Vista joins a growing list of midsize family cruisers vying for the attention of the nation's boaters. The Vista is a well-styled boat with her flowing lines and forward-facing arch, and she has one of the larger cockpits to be found in a 37-footer. Rather than the typical midcabin interior, the 378 features an expansive salon with two convertible sofas, one along the aft bulkhead and the other along the starboard side. Privacy curtains separate the fore and aft sleeping areas from the main salon, although an aft-cabin bulkhead with door was optional. The galley offers abundant storage and counter space, enhanced by faux granite countertops and cherry cabinets. Note that air-conditioning and a central vacuum system are standard, as is the flat-screen TV installed above the galley. On deck, a walk-through windshield provides easy access to the foredeck. Cockpit seating includes a U-shaped lounge aft, double helm seat and a portside lounge, and the engine compartment is reached through a deck access panel or the standard power hatch. Twin 375hp gas inboards cruise the 378 Vista in the low 20s and top out at just over 30 knots.

See Page 680 For Price Data

Length w/Platform	41'3"	Fuel	300 gals.
Hull Length	37'9"	Water	66 gals.
Beam	12'9"	Waste	42 gals.
Draft	3'6"	Hull Type	Modified-V
Weight	21,300#	Deadrise Aft	19°

Four Winns V458; V475

2008–Current

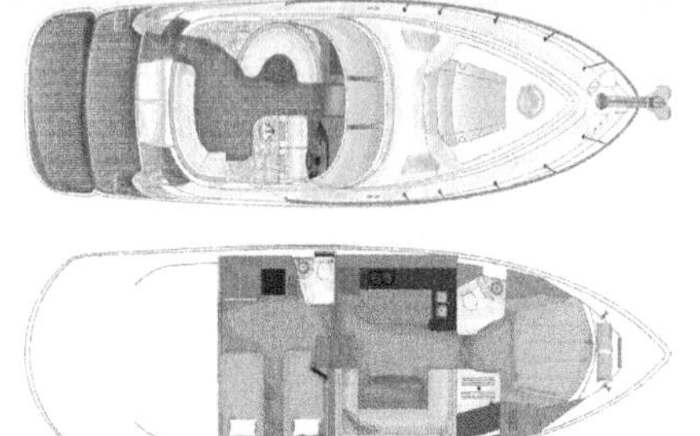

Four Winns' largest boat ever, the V475 (called the V458 in 2008–09) is an all-weather express cruiser designed from the ground up for Volvo IPS pod-drive propulsion. Pod drives were in the process of replacing traditional inboards when the V458 was introduced in 2008. Because they require less engineroom space than inboards, Four Winns designers were able to craft an unusually spacious interior in the V475 with two private staterooms, each with its own head. A home-size galley is to port in the well-appointed salon, opposite a U-shaped Ultraleather sofa/dinette. The forward master stateroom has a separate shower enclosure to starboard, and a washer/dryer cabinet is found the aft stateroom. Topside, the V475's expansive cockpit boasts standard air conditioning and seating for ten. Additional features include a fiberglass hardtop with triple skylights, cockpit wet bar with refrigerator, electric transom grill, and a huge extended swim platform. The entire aft deck rises for engine access. Lacking side decks, a windshield walk-thru provides secure foredeck access. Joystick controls make handling easy. Cruise at 25 knots (low-to-mid 30s top) with 435hp Volvo IPS pod drives.

Not Enough Resale Data to Set Values

Length w/Platform	49'4"	Fuel	380 gals.
Hull Length	44'6"	Water	101 gals.
Beam	14'0"	Waste	57 gals.
Draft	3'7"	Hull Type	Modified Deep-V
Weight	30,000#	Deadrise Aft	19°

Glacier Bay

Quick View

- 1986 - A group of entrepreneurs in Washington State, led by Glacier Bay founder Larry Graf, began engineering development of high speed, displacement catamaran hulls.
- 1987 - A full-scale 22-foot prototype catamaran is constructed alongside Graf's home in Washington during the team's after hours, weekends and holidays.
- 1990 - The first tooled production model, a Glacier Bay 248, is introduced at the Seattle International Boat Show.
- 1993 - The first commercial Glacier Bay sport fishing boats are developed for Skagway Sportfishing, an Alaska charter operation.
- 1995 - The GB 260 Canyon Runner series is introduced.
- 2007 - The NMMA and Boating Writers International (BWI) honor the 3070 Isle Runner with the 2007 Innovation Award.
- 2009 - Glacier Bay becomes an integral part of the PowerCat Group, parent company of World Cat and Carolina Cat, and production is moved to Tarboro, North Carolina.

Glacier Bay Boats • Tarboro, NC • www.glacierbaycats.com

Glacier Bay 260/2665 Canyon Runner

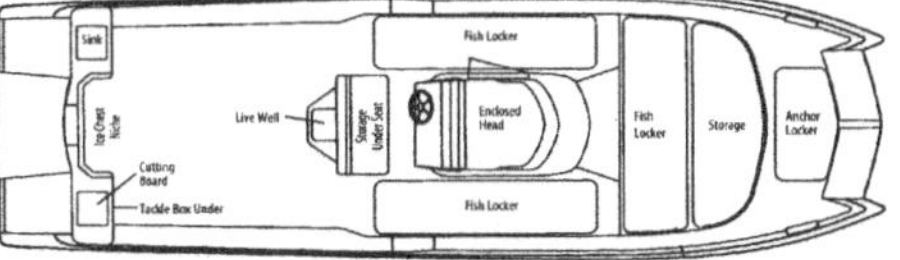

Catamarans have been gaining in popularity with anglers recently, and the Glacier Bay 260 Canyon Runner (called the 2665 in 2005–08) was one of the largest trailerable cat fishermen produced in recent years. Built in Washington, Glacier Bay was a pioneer in the catamaran market during the early 1990s. Over time, the company earned a reputation for building rugged, good-quality boats. The 260 Canyon Runner rides on a pair of sharp, thin displacement hulls that were retooled in 1999 with a finer entry and wider chines. At 4,200 pounds, she's considerably lighter than most monohull center consoles her size, and with less wetted surface to slow her down she'll attain similar speeds with far less horsepower. The great allure of catamarans for anglers, however, is their superb rough-water handling. Indeed, the Glacier Bay delivers a truly stable and comfortable ride in an offshore chop and tracking is excellent. Standard equipment included a large livewell, a sub-console head compartment, two in-deck fish boxes, a bait-prep station, and rod storage. Twin 150hp Yamaha outboards cruise at 25–26 knots at close to two miles per gallon (low 30s top).

See Page 680 For Price Data

Length	26'1"	Fuel	180 gals.
Beam	8'9"	Water	12 gals.
Hull Draft	1'8"	Max HP	300
Dry Weight	4,200#	Hull Type	Displacem
Clearance	9'6"	Deadrise Aft	NA

Glacier Bay 2670 Island Runner

1998–08

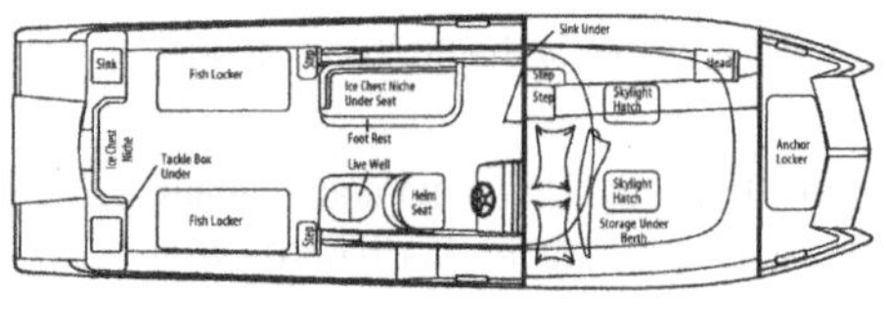

The Glacier Bay 2670 Island Runner is a good-quality walkaround catamaran with a large fishing cockpit and comfortable (for a cat) cabin accommodations. She rides on full-displacement hulls that were retooled in 1999 with a finer entry and wider chines. When it comes to fishing boats, the advantages of catamarans are well known: a better ride in poor sea conditions, reduced power requirements (due to the more efficient hulls), increased range, improved stability and more casting space at the bow. Note that the Island Runner's cabin is slightly off-center to port which puts the cabin over one of the hulls, thereby increasing the headroom below. (It also means that the starboard walkaround is wider than the portside walkaround.) Standard fishing features include an oval livewell under the helm seat, two in-deck fish boxes, coaming bolsters, tackle center and rod storage. In the cabin, a queen-size berth is over the tunnel and a spacious head compartment is located in the port hull. Among several outboard possibilities, twin Yamaha 150hp engines cruise the 260 Island Runner at 25 knots (at about two mpg) and reach a top speed of around 30 knots.

See Page 680 For Price Data

Length	26'1"	Water	22 gals.
Beam	8'9"	Waste	15 gals.
Hull Draft	1'10"	Max HP	300
Dry Weight	4,800#	Hull Type	Displacem
Fuel	180 gals.	Deadrise Aft	NA

Glacier Bay 2680 Coastal Runner

1999–2008

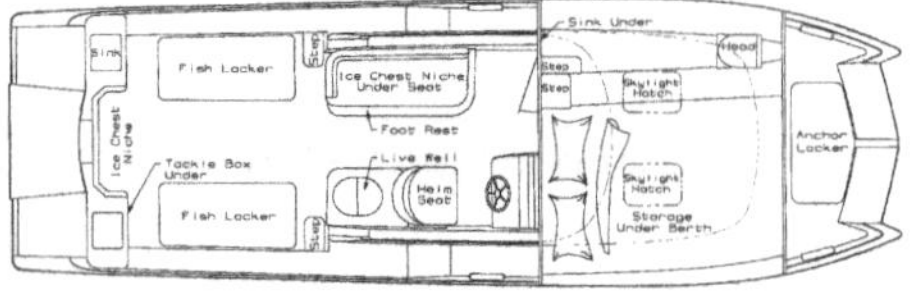

Despite their virtues, catamaran fishing boats have a boxy, awkward look about them that many anglers find hard to dismiss. The 2680 Coastal Runner is something of an exception—a good-looking cat whose graceful profile at least minimizes the reality of her rectangular catamaran shape. The Coastal Runner is the first hardtop model from Glacier Bay, and she's based on the same hull as the company's popular 26-foot center console and cuddy cabin models. Like her predecessors, she's a full-displacement catamaran (rather than a planing cat) and what she lacks in speed is made up in a softer ride and better fuel economy. What sets this boat apart from other Cats, of course, is her weatherproof pilothouse that will appeal to cold weather anglers. Note that the cuddy is slightly off-center to port which puts the cabin over one of the hulls, thereby increasing the headroom below. (It also means that the starboard walkaround is wider than the port walkway.) The cockpit is designed with built-in tackle boxes, a 32-gallon livewell, in-deck fish boxes and under-gunwale rod holders. A well-built boat, twin 150hp outboards cruise efficiently at 25 knots and reach a top speed of around 35 knots.

See Page 681 For Price Data

Length	26'1"	Water	22 gals.
Beam	8'9"	Waste	15 gals.
Hull Draft	1'9"	Max HP	300
Dry Weight	5,250#	Hull Type	Displacem
Fuel	180 gals.	Deadrise Aft	NA

Glacier Bay 2690 Coastal Runner

2000–08

With her fully enclosed pilothouse, cozy accommodations, and roomy cockpit, the Glacier Bay 2690 Coastal Runner hits all the right buttons for boaters looking for a versatile and fuel-efficient trailerable cruiser. Glacier Bay enthusiasts can argue about whether the Coastal Runner is more fishboat than family cruiser; the fact is that she's a true crossover boat with genuine appeal to both groups. Like all Glacier Bay models, the 2690 rides on a pair of foam-filled hulls whose full-displacement design insures a soft, stable ride even in challenging sea conditions. Entering the cabin via a sliding glass door, a two-person dinette —with refrigerator under the forward seat—is to port, and a small galley with sink and stove is to starboard, just behind the helm seat. Rod storage racks are overhead, and a queen berth is forward along with a 12V marine head with holding tank. Note that the cabin is slightly offset to port, which makes the starboard walkaround slightly wider than port-side walkway. Cockpit features include a 32-gallon livewell, tackle box, two in-deck fish boxes, and a transom sink and cutting board. Yamaha 150s cruise efficiently at 25 knots (about 30 knots top).

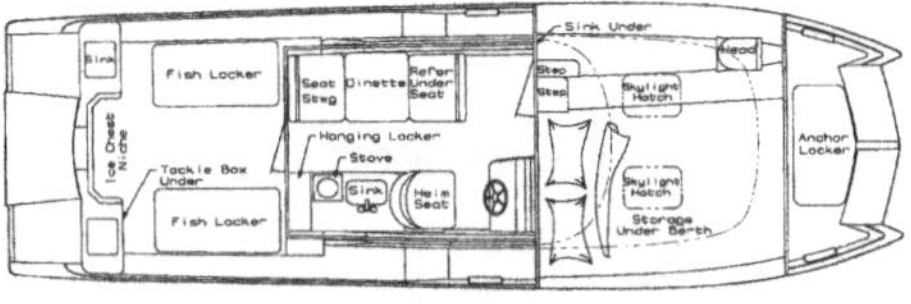

See Page 681 For Price Data

Length	26'1"	Water	22 gals.
Beam	8'9"	Waste	15 gals.
Hull Draft	1'9"	Max HP	300
Dry Weight	5,790#	Hull Type	Displacem
Fuel	180 gals.	Deadrise Aft	NA

Glacier Bay 3470 Ocean Runner

2005–08

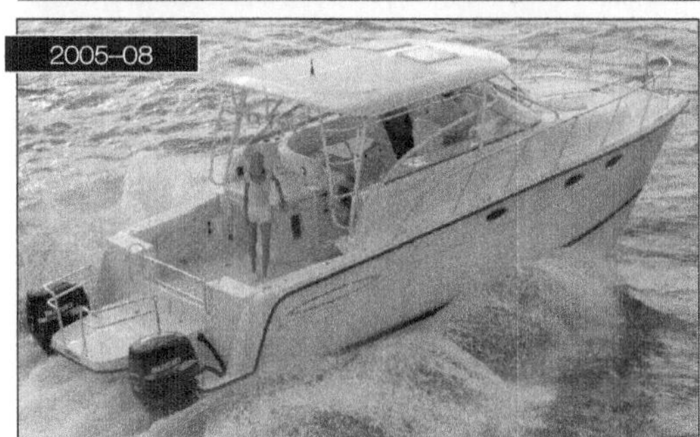

Big catamaran cruisers are a rare breed in U.S. waters—only a handfull have been built by Glacier Bay and Pro-Cat combined. The 3470 Ocean Runner (shown here with an optional hardtop) is a beefy offshore express whose chief attraction lies at the heart of any good catamaran design: a super-smooth ride and best-in-class fuel economy. Like most express boats, the Ocean Runner splits the difference between offshore fisherman and family cruiser. Her large cockpit has room enough for four anglers, and the expansive deck layout of the 3470 rivals many 40-footers in size. Fishing amenities include a 45-gallon livewell, bait prep station, tackle boxes, and under-gunwale rod storage. The bridge deck has an L-shaped settee around a dining table, across from a refreshment center with refrigerator. Note the wraparound dash at the helm. Below, the galley is in the starboard hull with a guest stateroom aft, and the master stateroom is forward in the port hull and the head—with separate stall shower—is aft. A four foot by six foot swim platform can stow an inflatable tender. No lightweight, Cummins 380hp V-drive diesels reach 28–30 knots top; twin 250hp outboards top out at close to 28 knots.

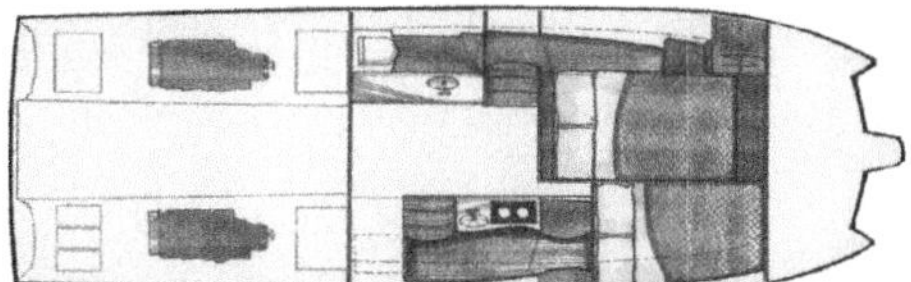

See Page 5681 For Price Data

Length	34'6""	Fuel	300 gals.
Beam	13'3"	Water	60 gals.
Hull Draft	4'0"	Waste	30 gals.
Weight	18,700#	Max HP (OB)	600
Clearance	NA	Hull Type	Displacem

Glacier Bay 3480 Ocean Runner

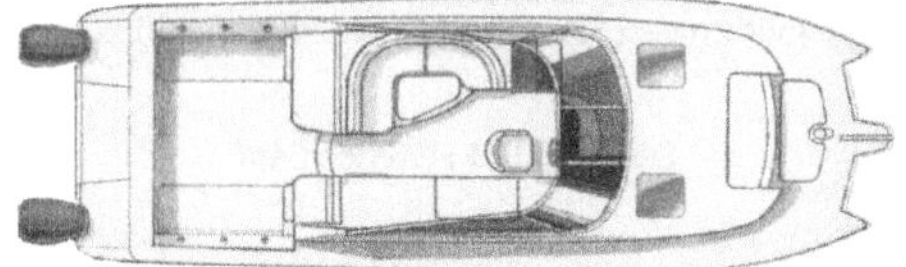

This versatile catamaran express—with her semi-enclosed pilothouse and wide 13'3" beam—is best described as part family cruiser and part fishing boat. Like most cat designs, the Ocean Runner has the deck space of a much larger boat. Indeed, her huge cockpit and spacious bridge deck dwarf those found in other express boats her size. Opening hatches in hardtop provide excellent ventilation at the helm, and the cockpit's two in-deck fish boxes and transom storage locker are cavernous. Below decks, the starboard hull contains the galley (aft) and a guest stateroom (or office) forward. The master stateroom is in the portside hull where the boat's head and shower are aft. Note the nav station in the guest stateroom. Additional features include a wide transom door, aft-facing cockpit jump seat, 45-gallon livewell, full tackle center, copious rod storage, two bow anchor lockers, and an anchor chute with roller. The displacement hulls of the 3480 Ocean Runner provide a soft, stable ride. Available with inboard or outboard power, Cummins 380hp V-drive diesels reach 28–30 knots top. Twin 250hp Yamaha outboards top out at close to 28 knots.

See Page 681 For Price Data

Length	34'6"	Fuel	300 gals.
Beam	13'3"	Water	60 gals.
Hull Draft	3'6"	Waste	30 gals.
Weight	19,400#	Max HP (OB)	600
Clearance	NA	Hull Type	Displacem

Grady-White

Quick View

- Grady-White Boats was founded in 1958 by Glen Grady and Don White.
- Eddie Smith purchased the company in 1968 and has since positioned the firm as one of the leading builders of sportfishing boats in the industry.
- The company hit it big in 1974 with the introduction of the first walkaround cabin, now a standard industry design.
- Since 1993 Grady-White boats over 20' have been built on a Hunt-designed "SeaV" hull, a variable deadrise deep-V that represents a significant improvement over earlier models.
- Best known for their series of high-quality trailerable walkarounds, 1994 saw the introduction of the company's first big center console, the 243 Chase.
- All Grady-Whites are built with positive foam flotation.
- With their enviable reputation for quality construction and strong owner satisfaction, used Grady-White models enjoy some of the best resale values in the business.

Grady-White Boats • Greenville, NC • www.gradywhite.com

Grady-White 265 Express

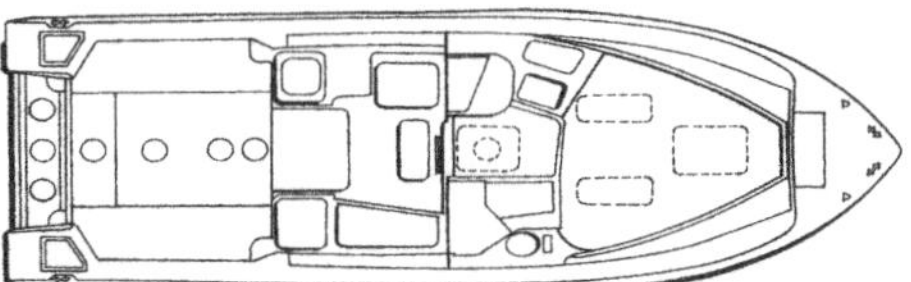

The Grady-White 265 Express, which happens to be one of the best-looking 26-footers around, is a beamy offshore fisherman with a full array of fishing features as well as a family-friendly cabin layout. Like any Grady-White, the 265 is a top-quality boat, and she was the first true express model—with narrow walkaround decks rather than deep, recessed walkways—ever built by the company. The 265 rides on a deep-V hull whose generous 9-foot, 7-inch beam is exceptional for a 26-footer. Cockpit amenities include a tackle station with sink, a 40-gallon livewell, a huge 300-quart fish box and storage bins in the corners. Note that a fold-down motorwell bulkhead is aft. On the bridge deck, bench seats flank the centerline helm, which has an overhead electronics box in the optional hardtop. The cabin of the 265 Express is surprisingly spacious and features a compact galley with refrigerator and stove, an enclosed head with shower, a wide V-berth and rod racks. A well-finished boat at a premium price, twin 250hp outboards cruise at 29 knots and deliver a top speed of around 40 knots.

See Page 681 For Price Data

Length w/Pulpit	28'6"	Fuel	250 gals.
Hull Length	25'9"	Water	20 gals.
Beam	9'7"	Max HP	500
Hull Draft	1'6"	Hull Type	Deep-V
Dry Weight	5,390#	Deadrise Aft	21°

Grady-White 268 Islander

1995–2002

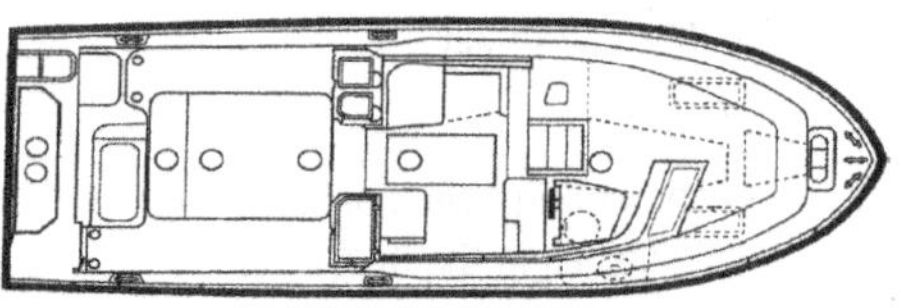

The Grady-White 268 Islander (called the 270 Islander in 2002, her last year of production) is a trailerable walkaround cuddy with the quality, comfort and performance one expects of a Grady-White product. She's constructed on a soft-riding deep-V hull with a sharp entry, cored hullsides, and an integrated drive bracket/swim platform. With nearly 60 square feet of space, the Islander's bi-level cockpit can easily satisfy the demands of two active anglers. Visibility from the elevated helm is excellent, and there's a lockable electronics box above the dash with more lockable storage under both bench and helm seats. In the cabin below are two full-sized berths, an enclosed marine head with holding tank, sink and shower, and a compact galley with sink, stove and refrigerator. While the Islander's fishboat heritage is undeniable, her deck layout provides seating for six passengers that makes her well suited for weekend outings with guests. Additional features include an aft bench seat, transom door, sliding cabin windows, and trim tabs. A popular boat, a single 250hp Yamaha will deliver a top speed of 32 knots, and twin 200hp Yamahas top out in the mid 40s.

See Page 681 For Price Data

Length w/Pulpit	26'11"	Fuel	134 gals.
Beam	8'6"	Water	32 gals.
Hull Draft	1'3"	Max HP	450
Dry Weight	4,660#	Hull Type	Modified-V
Clearance w/Hardtop	8'9"	Deadrise Aft	18°

Grady-White 263/273 Chase

1994–2011

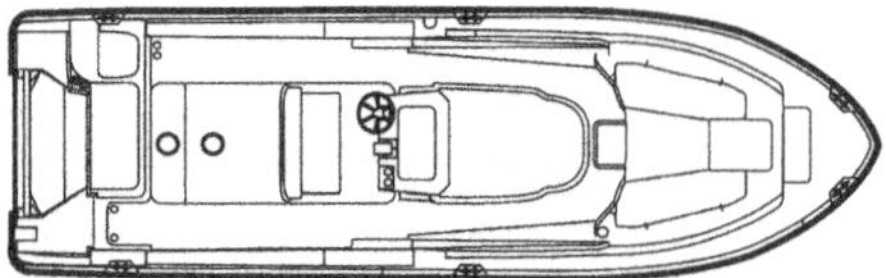

A popular boat with handsome lines and plenty of freeboard, the 273 Chase (called the 263 Chase until 2002 when the console was redesigned) is a top-of-the-line trailerable fisherman capable of serious offshore work. Gracefully styled and meticulously finished, she's built on a deep-V hull with a sharp entry, cored hullsides, positive foam flotation, and an integrated drive bracket/swim platform. With just over 50 square feet of cockpit space aft of the console, the Chase is a roomy fishing platform, and the console itself houses a standup head/storage compartment with a full 6 feet of headroom. At the helm, an electro-mechanically operated electronics enclosure raises from the top of the dash, placing the electronics at a good viewing level while protecting them from the elements when not in use. Note also that a fiberglass insert fits between the foredeck fish boxes to create a raised casting deck. Additional features include two forward fish boxes, a leaning post with seat and storage, a foldaway aft bench seat, transom door, tilt steering, lockable rod storage, and a 32-gallon aft livewell. Note the low-profile bow rail. Twin 225hp Yamaha outboards deliver a top speed of 40+ knots.

See Page 681 For Price Data

Length	26'11"	Fuel	205 gals.
Beam	8'6"	Water	10 gals.
Hull Draft	1'3"	Max HP	500
Dry Weight	4,843#	Hull Type	Modified-V
Clearance, Top	8'3"	Deadrise Aft	18.5°

Grady-White 270 Islander

2002–05

The Grady-White 270 Islander is an updated version of the company's earlier 268 Islander (1995–2002) with new cockpit and helm layouts and stylish teardrop cabin windows. The Islander is a beautifully finished trailerable fishing boat with a level of interior comfort equal to a good many family cruisers. The cockpit, with about 40 square feet of fishing space, is set up with the livewell and fish box forward, under the passenger seats—one of the few boats around with the livewell forward of the transom. The side decks are wide and deep, and a foldaway bench seat at the stern comes in handy when friends are aboard. In the cabin are two full-sized berths, an enclosed marine head with holding tank, sink and shower, and a compact galley with sink, stove and refrigerator. (The stove is notable in that it's mounted on a sliding rack—for safety, it won't slide back into the cabinet unless the burner is removed and stowed upside down.) Note the large lockable electronics box at the helm. A superb open-water performer and bone-dry in a chop, a single 250hp Yamaha will deliver a top speed of around 32 knots, and twin 200hp Yamahas will top out in the mid 40s.

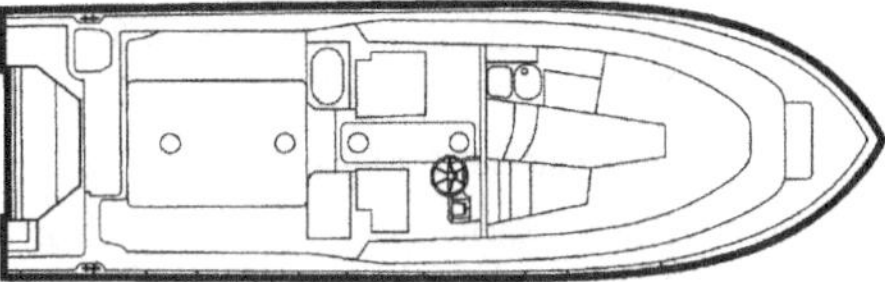

See Page 681 For Price Data

Length w/Pulpit	29'4"	Fuel	150 gals.
Hull Length	26'11"	Water	32 gals.
Beam	8'6"	Max HP	500
Hull Draft	1'5"	Hull Type	Modified-V
Dry Weight	5,594#	Deadrise Aft	18°

Grady-White 272 Sailfish

1994–2000

The 272 Sailfish (called the 252 Sailfish in 1994, her first year of production) is a redesigned version of Grady-White's popular 25 Sailfish built from 1978 through 1993. The 272 was built on an all-new hull bottom with increased transom deadrise and—because of her new integral transom bracket/swim platform—slightly longer overall length. Now a 27-footer, the Sailfish was long one of Grady-White's best selling models thanks to her quality construction, proven open-water performance and superb fishability. A wide 9-foot, 6-inch beam provides the 272 with plenty of cockpit space as well as a spacious cabin with berths for four, galley (with standard refrigerator), enclosed head, and an athwartships berth under the helmdeck. Helm visibility is excellent, and the electronics box above the instrument panel is lockable. Additional features include hydraulic trim tabs, wide, well-secured side decks, a 20-gallon transom livewell, underseat storage, transom door, cushioned fish boxes, and excellent range. A rock-solid boat engineered to the highest standards, twin 225hp Yamaha outboards top out at close to 45 knots.

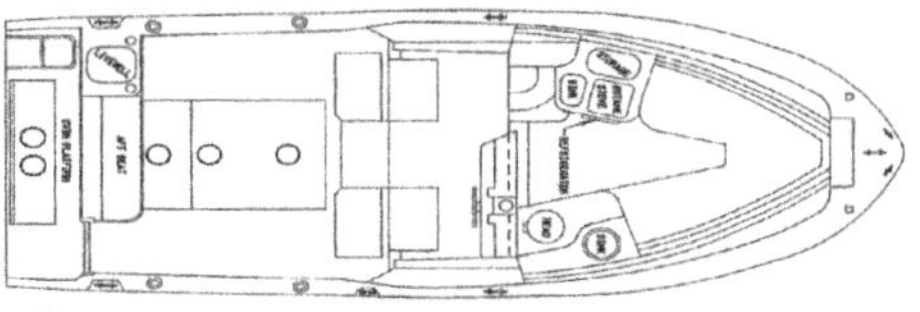

See Page 681 For Price Data

Length w/Pulpit	27'10"	Fuel	202 gals.
Beam	9'6"	Water	32 gals.
Hull Draft	1'6"	Max HP	500
Dry Weight	5,500#	Hull Type	Deep-V
Clearance, Hardtop	9'4"	Deadrise Aft	20°

Grady-White 282 Sailfish

2001–08

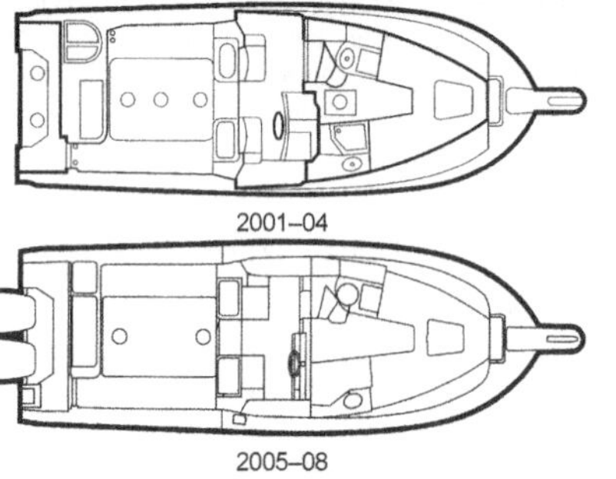
2001–04

2005–08

The Grady-White 282 Sailfish is an updated version of the company's popular 272 Sailfish, one of the best-selling offshore fishing boats ever produced. With her generous beam, rakish good looks, and impressive feature list, the 282 ranks among the best in her class for fishability and performance. Indeed, there's a lot to like about this boat if you can get past her upmarket price tag. The cockpit layout is about as good as it gets in a 28-footer, and even novice boaters will quickly appreciate the extraordinary fit and finish of the 282 Sailfish. Originally designed with an aft bench seat and transom rigging station, the cockpit was redesigned in 2005 to include an aft fish box and a space-saving foldaway rear bench seat. Below, the cabin manages to provide all the necessary amenities without being cramped. An enclosed head with sink and shower is standard, and a quarter berth extends under the helm deck at the rear of the cabin. Additional features include a bow pulpit, cockpit bolsters, heavy-duty transom door, and a superb helm layout. With over 200 gallons of fuel capacity, the 282 enjoys excellent range. Expect a top speed in the range of 35–40 knots with a pair of Yamaha 225 outboards.

See Page 681 For Price Data

Length w/Pulpit	30'2"	Fuel	207 gals.
Hull Length	28'0"	Water	32 gals.
Beam	9'6"	Max HP	600
Hull Draft	1'6"	Hull Type	Deep-V
Dry Weight	6,781#	Deadrise Aft	20°

Grady-White 283 Release; 293 Canyon

2002–Current

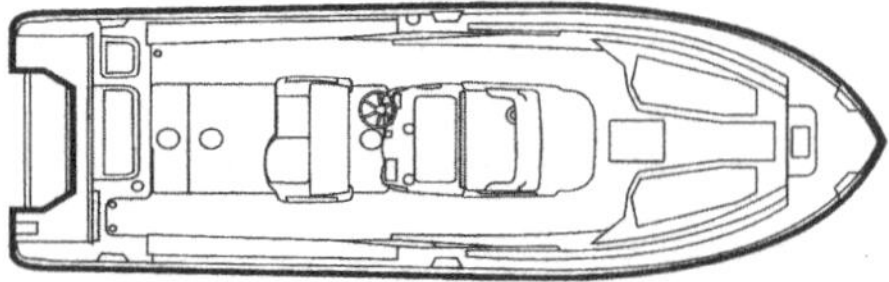

Introduced in 2002, the 283 Release (called the 283 Canyon since 2010) is a premium offshore center console with the built-in quality and handsome lines seasoned anglers have come to expect in a Grady-White product. She's built on the same deep-V hull used in the production of the 282 Sailfish, a proven bottom design with good rough-water handling qualities and a comfortable ride. With a relatively wide 9-foot, 6-inch beam, there's plenty of fishing space in the Release and her single-level deck makes for easy movement around the console. Like many center consoles her size, a lockable head compartment with sink and storage is housed in the console. Of special note is the deluxe rigging station with a sink, tackle trays, and 45-gallon livewell built into the back of the leaning post. There are two fish boxes at the bow and a third, larger one at the transom, all of which drain overboard. Additional features include a foldaway transom seat, cockpit bolsters, transom door, foam flotation, lockable rod storage under the gunwales, and a slick electrically operated pop-up electronics enclosure at the helm. Yamaha 225s deliver a top speed of close to 40 knots.

See Page 681 For Price Data

Length	28'0"	Fuel, Std.	205 gals.
Beam	9'6"	Water	20 gals.
Hull Draft	1'6"	Max HP	600
Dry Weight	5,864#	Hull Type	Deep-V
Clearance, Top	8'5"	Deadrise Aft	20°

Grady-White 300 Marlin

The Grady-White 300 Marlin began life back in 1989 as the 280 Marlin, a big, brawny walkaround fisherman with a wide beam and an integrated outboard bracket/swim platform. The new deep-V hull was introduced in 1994, and in 1995 a revised cockpit with an aft bench seat signaled the introduction of the 300 Marlin. In 2004 the transom was redesigned with a larger fish box and removable cooler box. The Marlin has always been a popular model thanks to her unmatched fishability, comfortable cabin accommodations, and top-quality engineering and construction. The cockpit is deep and uncluttered with excellent nonskid, and visibility from the raised bridge deck is excellent in all directions. There are berths for three in the upscale cabin (including a quarter berth aft) along with a standup head compartment, a full galley, and a removable dinette table. Additional features include a 30-gallon livewell, forward fish box and rigging station (300 models only), wide side decks, positive foam flotation, and a bow pulpit. A popular and venerable boat with strong resale values, twin 250 Yamaha outboards cruise the Marlin 300 at 25 knots and deliver a top speed of 35+ knots.

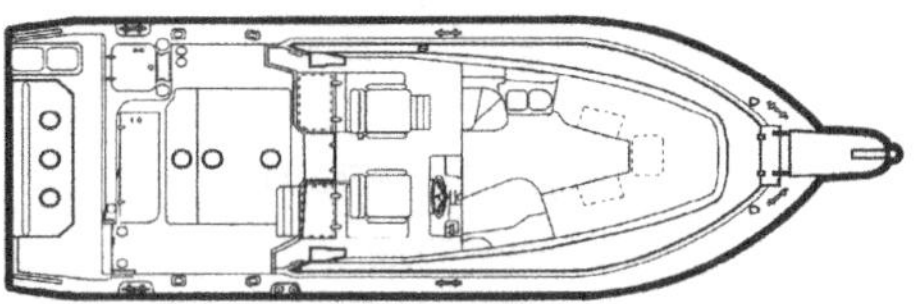

See Page 681 For Price Data

Length w/Pulpit	32'7"	Fuel	306 gals.
Hull Length	30'6"	Water	35 gals.
Beam	10'7"	Max HP	700
Hull Draft	1'7"	Hull Type	Deep-V
Dry Weight	8,221#	Deadrise Aft	19.5°

Grady-White 305 Express

Introduced in 2007, the Grady-White 305 is a premium big-water express described by one Aussie magazine as a "high-performance Range Rover on the water." Combining a spacious deck layout and unsurpassed build quality, the 305 is one hell of a boat—agile, sporty, and responsive at the helm. She can cruise with the family, of course, but the 305 Express is built for fishing. Her big, uncluttered cockpit is fitted with a 32-gallon livewell behind the helm, transom fish box, fresh/saltwater washdowns, toe rails, tackle trays, and rocket launchers on each hardtop leg. The hardtop, which is standard, comes with spreader lights and a radio box. Handrails are strategically placed throughout the boat. Note the 305's ergonomic center helm position, foldaway transom seat, pop-up electronics box, and twin cockpit showers. Below decks, her well-appointed cabin with midship berth, full-service galley, standup head and entertainment center sleeps four. The standard bow thruster is a nice touch, and a windlass is popular option. The curved windshield is a work of art. Expect a top speed in the neighborhood of 40 knots with twin Yamaha 225hp four-stroke outboards.

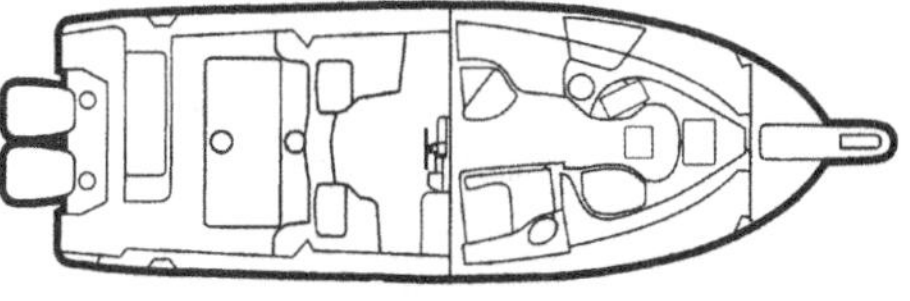

See Page 681 For Price Data

Length w/Pulpit	32'7"	Fuel	290 gals.
Hull Length	30'6"	Water	32 gals.
Beam	10'7"	Max HP	700
Hull Draft	1'7"	Hull Type	Modified-V
Dry Weight	8,850#	Deadrise Aft	17°

Grady-White 306 Bimini

1998–Current

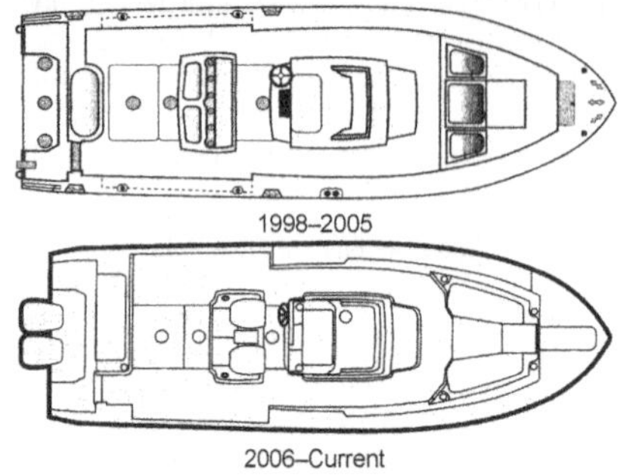
1998–2005

2006–Current

Introduced in 1998, the 306 Bimini is a top-quality offshore fisherman with a superb deck layout and a long list of built-in fishing amenities. This is a boat that will appeal to serious anglers seeking a no-compromise fishing boat, and while she's not inexpensive, she delivers big-time when it comes to performance and long-term investment value. Like all current Grady-White models, the 306 is built on a deep-V hull with a relatively wide beam, balsa-cored hull sides, and basic foam flotation. Her cockpit is huge compared with many other 30-foot center consoles, a result of moving the helm console well forward on the hull. But the most eye-catching feature of all is the innovative hydraulic ram-controlled electronics box—adjustable for viewing from various angles—that rises out of the console at the touch of a switch. Lockable rod-storage tubes are built into both gunwales, and a standup head with hand shower and storage is built into the wide console. Updates in 2006 included twin fish boxes forward (replacing the casting platform), combined helm seat/livewell, and a new transom layout with folding rear seat. About 40 knots top with twin Yamaha 250s.

See Page 681 For Price Data

Length	30'6"	Fuel	290 gals.
Beam	10'7"	Water	20 gals.
Hull Draft	21"	Max HP	700
Dry Weight	6,500#	Hull Type	Deep-V
Clearance	9'4"	Deadrise Aft	19.5°

Grady-White 330 Express

2001–Current

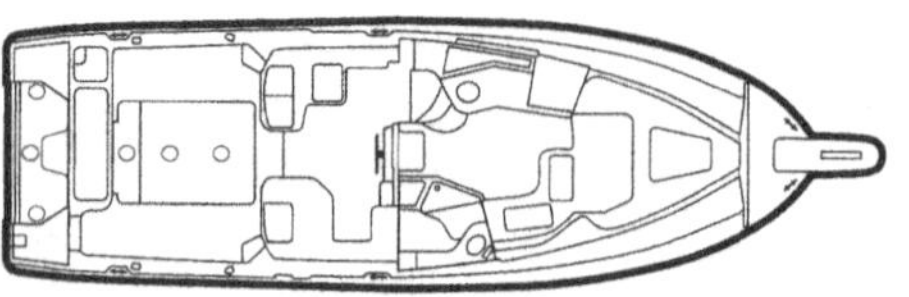

Grady-White has long specialized in building quality small- and medium-sized outboard fishing boats, but until the advent of the 330 Express in 2002 their largest offering had been a 30-footer. This new 330 Express is good news for a lot of Grady-White owners looking to move up to a larger boat, but she's not a cheap date. Fitted out with an extensive list of standard equipment—including air-conditioning, a hardtop, and a generator—the 330 is a superb, if not fast, offshore fishing machine. Her upscale midcabin interior sports such luxuries as a teak-and-holly cabin sole, a built-in entertainment center, a teak dinette table, and a full galley. With a wide 11'7" beam, there's plenty of fishing space in the cockpit, which comes with a big 270-gallon fish box at the transom, bait-rigging station, and 45-gallon livewell forward. Comfortable lounge seats surround the bridge deck helm with its very slick electrically operated pop-up electronics console. Additional features include a bow pulpit, a VacuFlush marine head, Corian counters, and two foredeck cabin hatches. Yamaha 250s reach 35+ knots top. Note that the transom was beefed up in 2009 to handle the bigger Yamaha 350s (40+ knots max).

See Page 681 For Price Data

Length w/Pulpit	35'10"	Fuel	350 gals.
Hull Length	33'6"	Water	50 gals.
Beam	11'7"	Max HP	700
Hull Draft	1'9"	Hull Type	Deep-V
Dry Weight	10,840#	Deadrise Aft	20.5°

Grady-White 336 Canyon

2008–Current

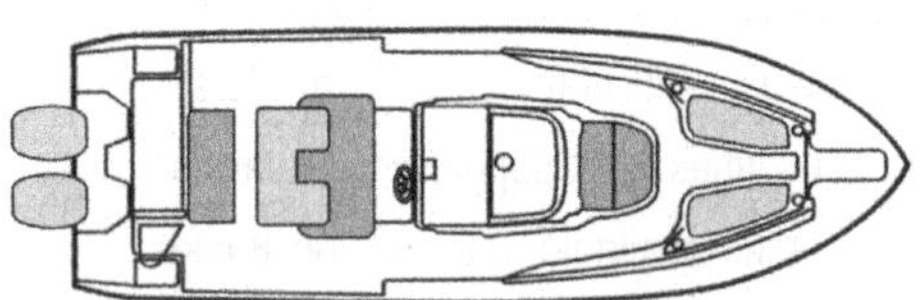

A few years ago the concept of an outboard-powered 33-footer wasn't on the table. That changed, however, with the advent of today's more powerful (and heavier) outboards from Mercury and Yamaha. Nearly overnight, the market for big outboard center consoles (and express fishermen) exploded to the point where buyers now have several models to choose from. Leading the pack is the Grady-White 336 Canyon, a muscular fishing machine whose huge 80-square-foot cockpit and leading edge features set the standards for a boat of this type. Designed to range far offshore and stay there until the day is done, key features of the Canyon Runner include a fiberglass T-top, 45-gallon livewell aft of the companion seat, bait-rigging station, foldaway rear seat, large-capacity transom fish box, and two forward fish/storage boxes. The centerline helm console (with pop-up electronics module) accommodates two big-screen video displays. Below, the roomy walk-in console compartment sports a full marine head with sink and shower, vertical rod storage, and twin berths forward. Big, powerful, and sure to impress, the 336 Canyon Runner is the real deal. About 40 knots top with twin 350s.

See Page 681 For Price Data

Length	33'6"	Fuel	350 gals.
Beam	11'7"	Water	44 gals.
Hull Draft	2'1"	Max HP	700
Dry Weight	9,200#	Hull Type	Deep-V
Clearance, Top	9'0"	Deadrise Aft	21°

Grady-White 360 Express

2005–Current

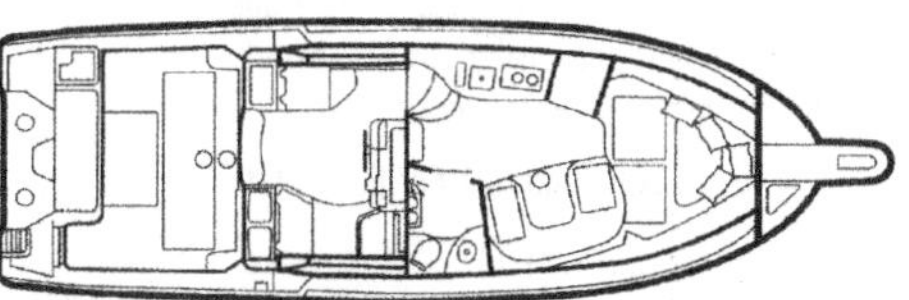

Grady-White got it right when they introduced the 360 Express in 2005. Designed for offshore anglers with very deep pockets, the 360 is a big triple-outboard fishing machine with more deck space and cabin comforts than any previous Grady-White model. Built on a Hunt-designed deep-V hull with moderate beam, the layout of the 360 is a cut above. A huge 48-gallon livewell and full rigging station—complete with freshwater sink, insulated bait box, lockable drawers and knife/plier stowage—are standard. Note that a digital thermostat controls the aft-deck refrigerator/freezer fish box. The centerline helm (with electronic controls) has a clever slide-out table/mini-dinette to starboard that, when stowed, converts into a lounge. Below decks, the 360's well-appointed cabin—with two double berths, a convertible dinette, enclosed head/shower, full-service galley, and tons of rod storage—rivals most express cruisers in space and amenities. Nearly everything is standard including a hardtop, bow thruster, air-conditioning, and generator (with separate fuel tank). The ultimate outboard express, triple Yamaha 250s will deliver a top speed of over 35 knots.

See Page 681 For Price Data

Length w/Pulpit	39'3"	Fuel	370 gals.
Hull Length	36'7"	Water	65 gals.
Beam	10'6"	Max HP	1,050
Hull Draft	2'5"	Hull Type	Deep-V
Dry Weight	14,919#	Deadrise Aft	21°

Grand Banks

Quick View

- The first wooden Grand Banks trawlers were built in 1964 at the original Grand Banks facility in Hong Kong.
- During the late 1960s and early 1970s, Grand Banks produced a series of classic DeFever-designed "Alaskan" trawlers (also wood) from 45' to 55'.
- By 1973, Grand Banks switched to fiberglass production at a new factory in Singapore.
- In 1993, Grand Banks took another traditional boat design, the lobster boat or "Downeast" cruiser, and introduced their all-new Eastbay series of luxury cruising yachts.
- In 2001, the company launched the Aleution series of raised pilothouse yachts.
- In 2005, the classic semi-displacement Grand Banks models were retired from the fleet.
- In 2007, Grand Banks introduceed the first of its Heritage series of performance trawlers.
- Grand Banks yachts are built in American Marine facilities in Singapore and Malaysia.
- Long considered among the finest production yachts available, used Grand Banks models enjoy excellent resale values.

Grand Banks Yachts • Seattle, WA • www.grandbanks.com

Grand Banks 32 Sedan

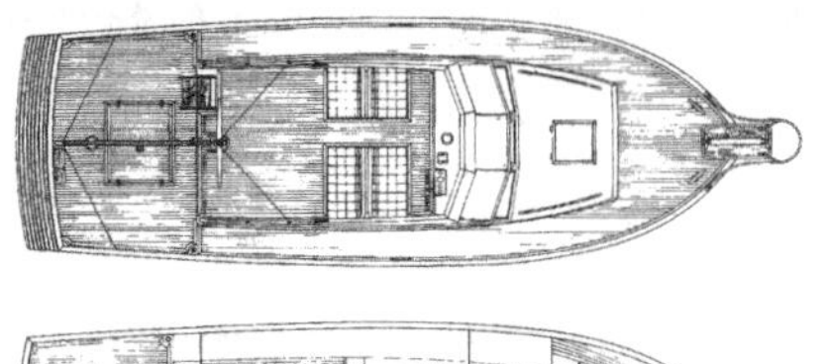

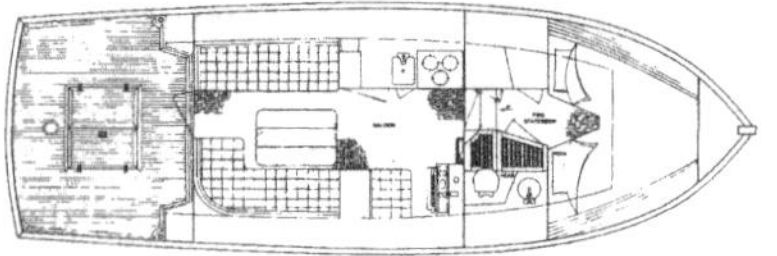

A modern classic, the Grand Banks 32 is one of the best-selling small trawler designs ever produced. A total of 861 were built during her production years and used models are always in demand. Her distinctive profile remained essentially unchanged since the original wood models were introduced back in 1965. Indeed, at a distance it's very difficult to distinguish between a pre-1973 wood Grand Banks 32 and one of the more recent fiberglass models. Powered with a single 6-cylinder Lehman diesel, owners report long hours of 7-knot cruising at 3 gallons per hour and a range of 500+ miles. A full-length skeg protects the underwater gear, and hard aft chines help to stabilize the ride. Below, the 32's straightforward and practical cabin layout—compact, yes, but very efficiently arranged—will satisfy the basic requirements of the average cruising couple. Storage is adequate, the teak woodwork is elegant, and visibility from the lower helm is very good. The aft deck is large enough for a couple of deck chairs, and wide side decks provide good foredeck access. Regardless of their age, Grand Banks 32s are dependable and seaworthy small cruisers with immense eye appeal and excellent resale values.

See Page 681 For Price Data

Length Overall	31'11"	Headroom	6'4"
Length WL	30'9"	Fuel	225/250 gals.
Beam	11'6"	Water	110 gals.
Draft	3'9"	Waste	30 gals.
Weight	17,000#	Hull Type	Semi-Disp.

Grand Banks 36 Classic

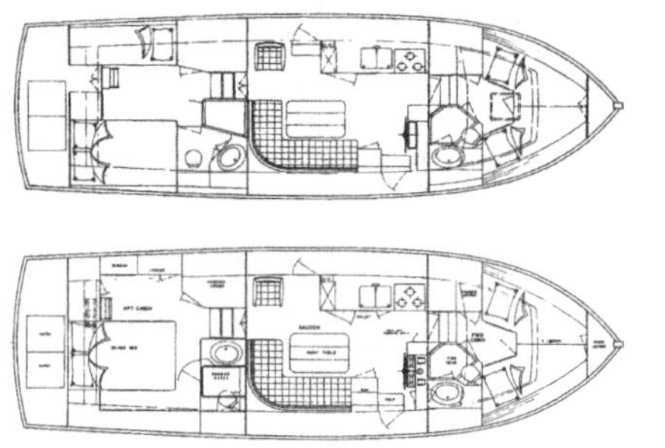

There are some boats that have been with us for so long—and are so popular—that they have attained classic status. The Grand Banks 36 is such a boat. She was the first model in the Grand Banks fleet, and over 1,200 were built during her production years. (Note that the original GB 36 was built of Philippine mahogany until mid-1973 when the transition to fiberglass was made.) A semi-displacement hull with a long keel, hard chines and a deep forefoot provide the stability that has won the 36 a reputation for seaworthiness unmatched by boats in her class. Several twin-stateroom interiors were offered over the years, all finished with handcrafted teak woodwork and all incorporating the very best in workmanship, hardware and materials. Topside, raised bulwarks provide security to the walkaround decks, and there's room for a dinghy on the aft cabintop. Notable features include teak decks, a functional mast and boom, direct cockpit access from the aft stateroom, and a spacious flybridge. Note that in 1988 the Grand Banks 36 was invisibly updated when six inches were added to the length and the beam was increased by four inches. Most GB 36s are powered by a single 120hp (or 135hp) Lehman diesel.

See Page 681 For Price Data

Length Overall	36'10"	Clearance, Mast	22'4"
Length WL	35'2"	Fuel	400 gals.
Beam	12'8"	Water	154 gals.
Draft	4'0"	Waste	40 gals.
Weight	26,000#	Hull Type	Semi-Disp.

Grand Banks 36 Europa

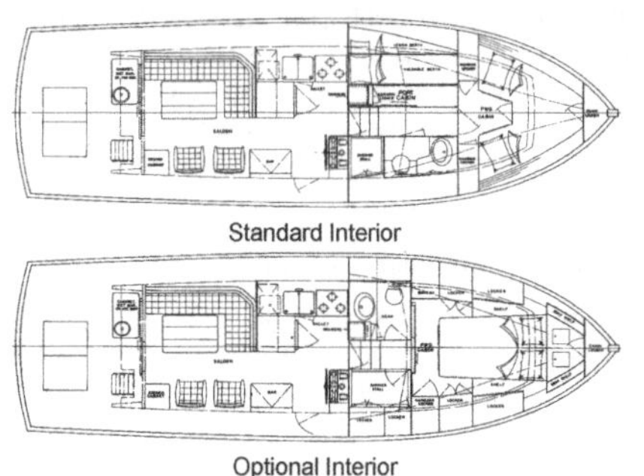
Standard Interior

Optional Interior

One of Grand Bank's most sought-after models, the 36 Europa combines graceful styling with comfortable accommodations in what is arguably one of the finest coastal cruising yachts ever produced. She's built on the same semi-displacement, hard-chined hull as the Grand Banks 36 Classic, but the Europa's flybridge extends over the aft deck and side decks resulting in a larger flybridge than most 36-footers. (Another advantage of this design is the shade afforded to the aft deck and interior at various times of the day.) Available with one or two staterooms, the Europa's full teak interior features a space-efficient salon with L-shaped dinette to port, high-low table, helm station with deck access door, and L-shaped galley with microwave, refrigerator/freezer, and overhead storage cabinets. A two-stateroom floorplan was standard (the guest cabin has a sliding pocket door for privacy), while an equally popular single-stateroom layout has a split head design with a huge walk-in shower to starboard, and an enlarged master suite with island queen berth. Note the teak decks and cabintop. A single 135hp Lehman diesel will cruise at 7–8 knots; twin 210hp Cummins diesels cruise at 10–12 knots.

See Page 681 For Price Data

Length Overall	36'10"	Headroom	6'4"
Length WL	35'2"	Fuel	400 gals.
Beam	12'8"	Water	170/205 gals.
Draft	4'0"	Waste	40 gals.
Weight	27,000#	Hull Type	Semi-Disp.

Grand Banks 38 Eastbay Express

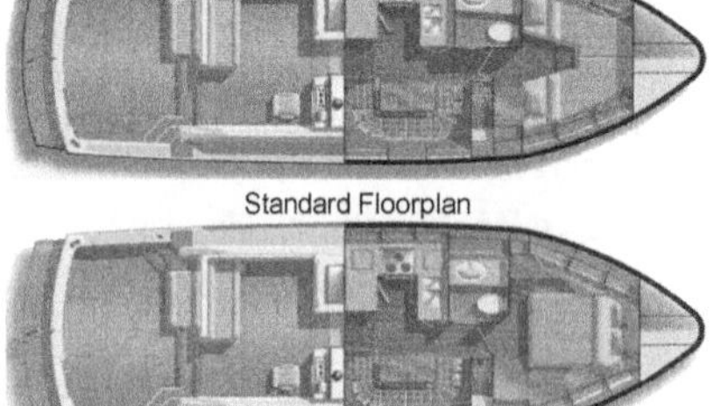
Standard Floorplan

Optional Layout

Introduced in 1994, the Eastbay 38 Express launched Grand Banks in a completely new direction. She was the first in a rapidly evolving series of Eastbay yachts whose classic Downeast lines and Hunt-designed hulls were a notable departure from Grand Bank's previous trawler heritage. Like all Eastbay models to follow, the 38 rides on a smooth-riding deep-V hull with prop pockets, a relatively wide beam, and Divinycell coring above the waterline. Her traditional teak interior was available in several single-stateroom configurations over the years, all of which reflect the upscale elegance typical of any Grand Banks product. Indeed, outstanding fit and finish and tasteful design are evident throughout the interior. Topside, helm visibility from the raised bridge deck is excellent, and there's enough space in the aft cockpit to entertain several guests. Additional features include a teak cockpit sole, good access to the motors (via a hydraulic-assist deck hatch), wide side decks, and a teak swim platform. Note that a hardtop version became available in 2002. Cat 300hp diesels cruise the Eastbay at 20 knots (mid 20s top), and 375hp Cats cruise at 23 knots (high 20s top). Over 130 were built during her production run.

See Page 682 For Price Data

Length Overall	38'0"	Fuel	344 gals.
Length WL	34'5"	Water	95 gals.
Beam	13'2"	Clearance	9'3"
Draft	3'4"	Hull Type	Deep-V
Weight	28,500#	Deadrise Aft	18°

Grand Banks 39 Eastbay SX

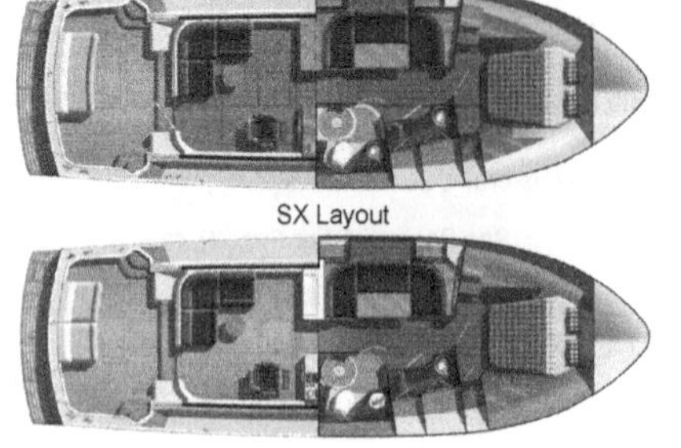
SX Layout

HX Layout

Beautifully designed yachts always speak for themselves. (Unfortunately, there aren't many of them since most builders are more obsessed with fashionable glitz than styling substance.) Introduced in 2006, the 39 Eastbay SX—the "SX" stands for Salon Express—is a graceful Downeast cruising yacht with the luxury features one expects of any Grand Banks yacht. Built on a deep-V hull with moderate beam, the standard layout for the 39SX includes a generous salon/helm deck on the main level with a Stidd helm seat and corner L-settee. Further forward is a chart table with room for a companion Stidd or convertible bench seat. Access to the engineroom is via a hatch in the cabin sole. Belowdecks, the 39SX features a U-shaped dinette, spacious galley with Corian counters, and a head with curved shower-door enclosure. Forward is a private stateroom complete with island queen berth and cedar-lined storage lockers. Note that 39 Eastbay HX model has a semi-enclosed helm deck (i.e., no salon bulkhead) with a teak sole. Yanmar 480hp diesels cruise at 24–26 knots (about 30 knots top). Note the cockpit lazarette and wide, secure side decks. Yanmar 480hp diesels cruise at 24–26 knots (about 30 knots top).

See Page 682 For Price Data

Length w/Platform	42'4"	Fuel	352 gals.
Hull Length	39'2"	Water	100 gals.
Beam	13'3"	Waste	28 gals.
Draft	3'4"	Hull Type	Deep-V
Weight	28,494#	Deadrise Aft	18°

Grand Banks 41 Heritage EU

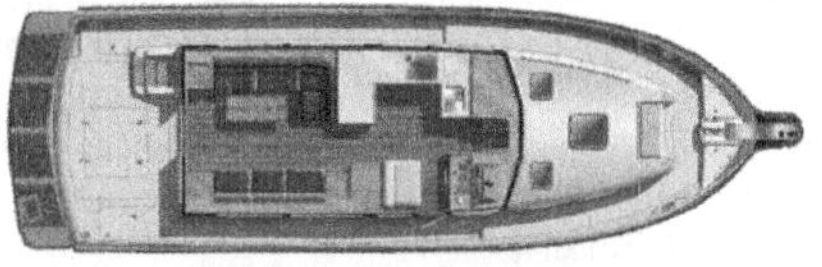

The 41 Heritage EU ("Europa") is one of the new-generation Grand Banks yachts designed to replace the classic Grand Banks 42 that was retired from production in 2005. While the styling is unmistakably Grand Banks, the Heritage is a completely different boat below the waterline where Zeus pod drives delivers the power and a new (for Grand Banks) modified-V hull provides the ride. The result is a boat the will cruise in the teens and reach a top speed of 22-24 knots. The interior of the 41 Heritage EU is similar to earlier Europa models with the extended salon housing an L-shaped dinette with settee opposite, a large U-shaped galley forward to port, and the helm to starboard. The master stateroom features a queen island berth, and twin single berths in the guest stateroom convert to a double. The teak joinery in any Grand Banks yacht is as good as it gets, period. Because pod drives require so much less engineroom space than conventional inboards, the area under the salon is used for a utility/storage room reached through a gas-assist hatch in the salon floor. Another hatch (with stairway) in the cockpit sole provides access to the Zeus drives and engines. Cruise at 15–16 knots with 425hp Cummins diesels.

See Page 682 For Price Data

Length Overall	41'4"	Fuel	500 gals.
Length WL	37'11"	Water	195 gals.
Beam	15'8"	Waste	50 gals.
Draft	3'9"	Hull Type	Modified-V
Weight	40,200#	Deadrise Aft	17.5°

Grand Banks 42 Classic

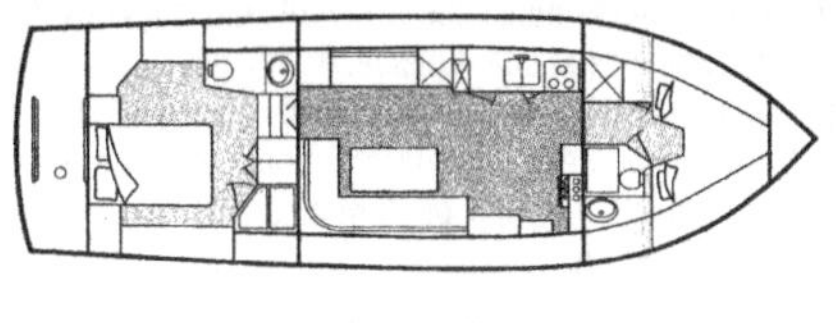

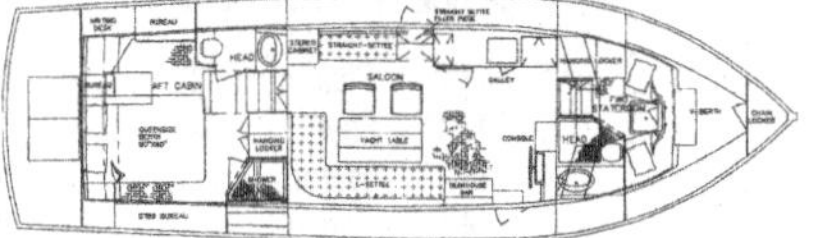

With over 1,500 delivered, the iconic Grand Banks 42 remains the most successful trawler design ever produced. Introduced in 1966, the original mahogany construction gave way to fiberglass in late 1973, and in 1991—beginning with hull #1204—the hull was lengthened and widened a few inches to add additional interior volume. The GB 42's semi-displacement hull, with its long keel, hard chines and a deep forefoot, provides a level of stability and comfort seldom matched by other boats. Several full teak interiors were offered during in the 42 Classic, all with the galley in the salon and most with port and starboard deck doors. (Note that the extra interior volume found in post-1990 models went into a larger galley and a slightly enlarged forward stateroom.) Surrounded by large cabin windows, visibility from the lower helm is excellent in all directions. A dinghy can be stored on the cabintop, and there's plenty of flybridge seating aft of the helm. Additional features include teak decks, fold-down mast and boom, and a small aft cockpit for line handling. On the downside, the engineroom is a little tight. A wide range of engine options was available over the years offering speeds up to 18 knots.

See Page 682 For Price Data

Length Overall	42'7"/43'3"	Clearance, Mast	22'6"
Length WL	41'1"	Fuel	600 gals.
Beam	13'7"/14'1"	Water	271 gals.
Draft	4'2"	Waste	50 gals.
Weight	37,400#	Hull Type	Semi-Disp.

Grand Banks 42 Europa

1979–90; 96–04

The Grand Banks 42 Europa has a history going back to 1970 when the original mahogany Europas were built for the European market. Only a few of the wood models were brought into this country, and it wasn't until 1979 the Europa was seriously marketed in the U.S. In 1991, however, the Europa was retired from the Grand Banks fleet due to lagging sales. When she was reintroduced in 1996, the Europa was built on a new, slightly larger hull allowing for an enlarged forward stateroom and stairs to replace the former flybridge ladder. As it is with all Grand Banks yachts, the Europa's interior is a blend of handcrafted teak joinery and premium hardware and fixtures. While the salon dimensions aren't extravagant for a boat this size (thanks in part to the wide side decks), large cabin windows make the interior seem open and comfortable. Built on the same semi-displacement, hard-chined hull as the Grand Banks 42 Classic, the Europa's flybridge extends over the aft deck and side decks resulting in a larger flybridge than most 36-footers. Note the teak decks and large cockpit lazarette. Among several engine choices, 210hp Cat diesels cruise at 10 knots, and twin 375hp Cats cruise at 14–15 knots.

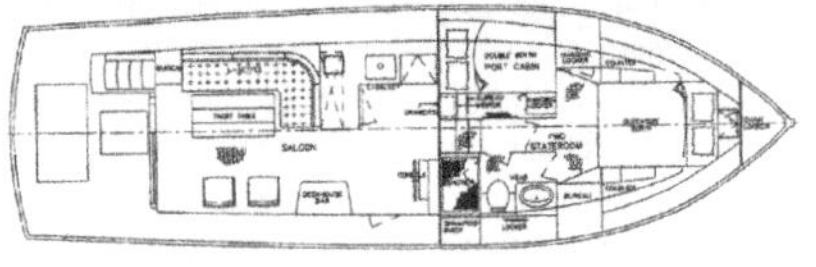
Standard Layout

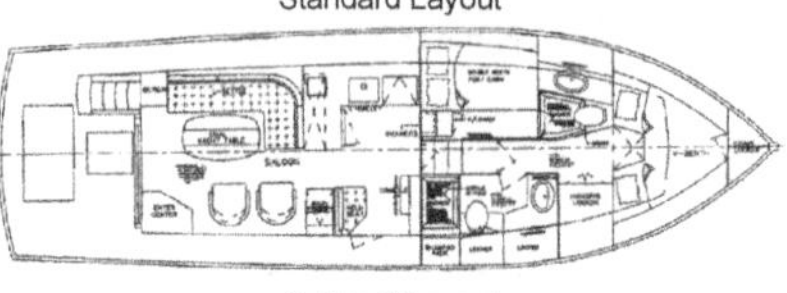
Optional Layout

See Page 682 For Price Data

Length Overall	43'3"	Clearance, Mast	22'9"
Beam (1979–90)	13'7"	Fuel	600 gals.
Beam (1996–2004)	14'1"	Water	278 gals.
Draft	4'2"	Waste	50 gals.
Weight	39,000#	Hull Type	Semi-Disp.

Grand Banks 42 Motor Yacht

1987–2004

Introduced in 1987, the Grand Banks 42 Motor Yacht is a sophisticated blend of classic styling, superb engineering, and elegant accommodations. She's built on the proven semi-displacement hull used in Grand Bank's other 42-foot trawlers with a deep forefoot, hard chines, and a long, prop-protecting keel. Two floorplans were offered in the 42 MY, a standard three-stateroom layout with the galley up, and an alternate two-stateroom arrangement with the galley down. Both came with port and starboard deck doors as well as a spacious, full-width aft cabin with a separate head and shower. With her raised afterdeck and roomy flybridge, the 42 MY offers plenty of space for on-deck entertaining. The side decks are wide and secure, and the mast and boom can be lowered for passing under low bridges. In 1991, Grand Banks redesigned the hull of all of their 42-footers, increasing the width and length by 6 inches, which added some extra space inside. Additional features include a well-finished engineroom, teak decks and cabintop, teak transom, and teak bow pulpit. Several engines options were offered over the years. Later models with Cat or Cummins diesels are capable of speeds to 18–20 knots.

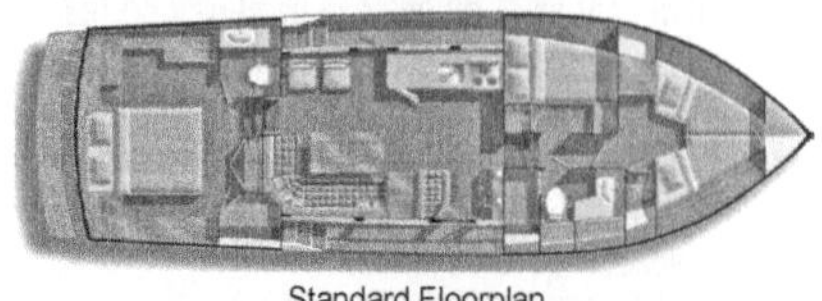
Standard Floorplan

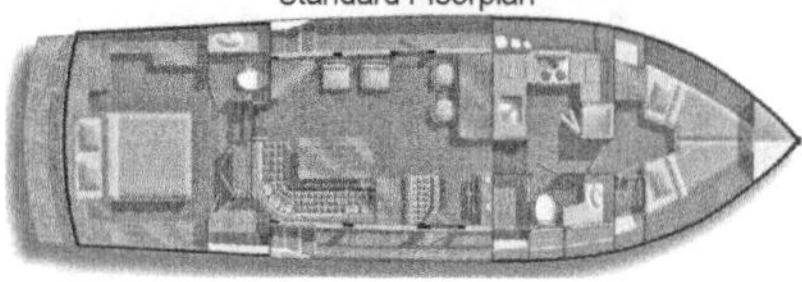
Optional Floorplan

See Page 682 For Price Data

Length Overall	42'7"/43'3"	Clearance, Mast	25'6"
Length WL	41'1"	Fuel	600 gals.
Beam	13'7"/14'1"	Water	237 gals.
Draft	4'2"	Waste	50 gals.
Weight	40,700#	Hull Type	Semi-Disp.

Grand Banks 43 Eastbay Flybridge

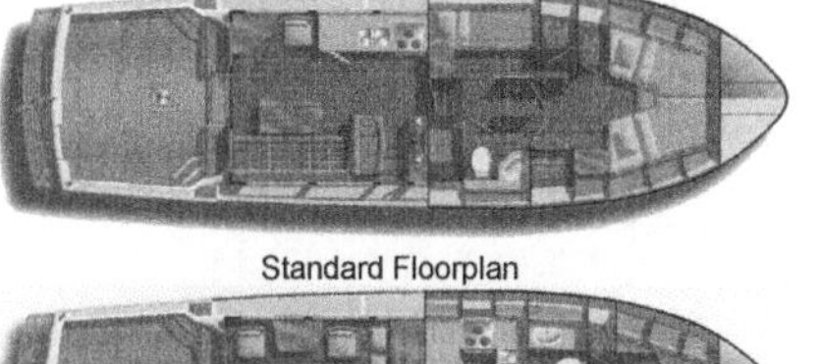

Standard Floorplan

Optional Layout

The Eastbay 43 Flybridge is an extended-cockpit version of the original Eastbay 40 Sedan of which 20 were built from 1996–97. She's a handsome Downeast-style cruiser whose upscale interior and excellent performance are a departure from the traditional go-slow Grand Banks product of old. The Eastbay's deep-V hull employs prop pockets to reduce shaft angles, a feature that also allows for relatively shallow-water running. The standard two-stateroom, galley-up floorplan has a single head with a stall shower, and an alternate two-stateroom floorplan has the galley down and two smaller heads. Typical of any Grand Banks product, the Eastbay's traditional full teak interior is meticulously crafted throughout. Note that the newer 43 with its enlarged cockpit is a better-looking and more balanced boat than the original Eastbay 40 with the added advantage of additional fuel capacity. Standard features include wide walkaround decks, a teak cockpit sole, radar mast, transom door and shower, and a well-arranged flybridge. Not inexpensive, twin 300hp Cat diesels cruise at 18–20 knots (about 22 knots top), and optional 375hp Cats cruise at 22–24 knots and deliver a top speed in the high 20s.

See Page 682 For Price Data

Length	43'0"	Fuel	450 gals.
Beam	13'4"	Water	110 gals.
Draft	3'8"	Headroom	6'6"
Weight	31,970#	Hull Type	Deep-V
Clearance	16'6"	Deadrise Aft	18°

Grand Banks 43 Eastbay Express

Standard Layout

Optional Layout

The 43 Express was yet another addition to the popular Eastbay series of classic Downeast cruisers introduced by Grand Banks back in 1994. Eastbays are premium yachts with traditional lines, meticulous finish, and impressive performance. The 43 may look traditional on the outside, but she's built on a modern Hunt-designed deep-V hull with moderate beam and prop pockets to reduce draft and shaft angles. The two-stateroom floorplan of the Eastbay 43 Express, with its hand-rubbed teak woodwork and quality furnishings, is an impressive display of nautical elegance and sophistication. There are over/under bunks in the small guest cabin, and Eastbay offered a choice of either a V-berth or a centerline double berth in the forward stateroom. The helmdeck, three steps up from the cockpit, is huge with lounge seating and a teak sole. Additional features include wide side decks, well-arranged engine room, roomy head compartment, teak swim platform, teak-and-holly cabin sole, and a total of seven opening ports for ventilation. Caterpillar 435hp diesels cruise the Eastbay 43 Express at 24 knots and deliver a top speed of 27–28 knots. Note that a hardtop model became available in 2002.

See Page 682 For Price Data

Length	43'0"	Fuel	450 gals.
Beam	13"2"	Water	110 gals.
Draft	3'8"	Waste	50 gals.
Weight	33,000#	Hull Type	Modified-V
Clearance	16'6"	Deadrise Aft	14°

Grand Banks 43 Eastbay HX

A modern display of old-world elegance, the Eastbay 43 HX combines classic Downeast styling with a modern offshore hull capable of extended offshore cruising. The Grand Banks reputation for top-shelf engineering and construction is very much on display in the 43 HX, and even novice boaters will appreciate her beautiful joinery and exemplary fit and finish. From the roomy cockpit, it's three steps up to the semi-enclosed bridge deck with its wraparound lounge seating and comfortable helm. The standard twin-stateroom interior is arranged with an L-shaped dinette and a single head compartment, while an optional layout has a large single stateroom forward, separate head and shower compartments, and a U-shaped dinette. While there are many 43-footers with more interior volume than the Eastbay, few can match her traditional elegance and none can claim her prestigious Grand Banks heritage. Additional highlights include wide side decks, teak cockpit sole, radar mast, a well-designed engineroom, and a teak swim platform. Prop pockets and employed to reduce draft and shaft angles. Twin 440hp Yanmar diesels cruise at 25 knots (28–29 knots top). Did we say expensive?

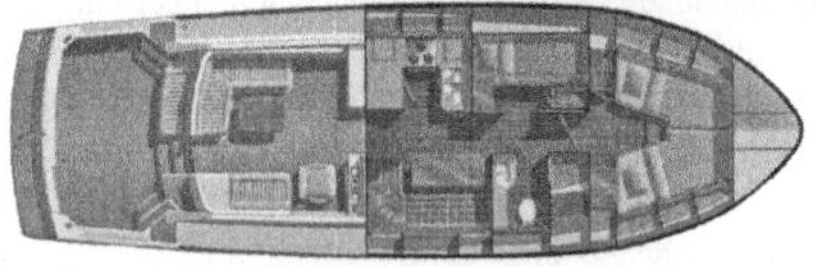
Standard HX Layout

Alternate HXLayout

See Page 682 For Price Data

Length Overall	43'0"	Clearance, Mast	14'0"
Length WL	39'5"	Fuel	450 gals.
Beam	13'2"	Water	110 gals.
Draft	3'7"	Hull Type	Modified-V
Weight	29,760#	Deadrise Aft	14°

Grand Banks 45 Eastbay SX

It says a lot about Eastbays that they continue to sell well in spite of the ongoing US recession. Like Lexus, BMW or Mercedes, quality brands never go out of style. Introduced in 2008, the 45 Eastbay SX is a timeless yacht that will likely remain in style decades into the future. Her standard two-stateroom interior features a U-settee to port surrounding a teak high-low table. Opposite sits a straight settee, just aft of the Stidd helm seat. Also in the standard arrangement, a bench seat is located opposite the helm chair, fronted by a built-in chart table. The guest stateroom has two twin berths and the master stateroom has a queen island berth and en-suite head access. An optional layout moves the galley up to the aft end of the salon with pass-through window access to the cockpit. A second head is added below as well as space for a washer/dryer. Outside huge cabin windows enhance visibility, and a power sunroof and retractable aft salon window are popular options. Note the cockpit storage lazarette, thoughtful side deck access steps, and teak swim platform. The 45 Eastbay will cruise efficiently at 25 knots with Cummins 550hp (or Caterpillar 567hp) diesels.

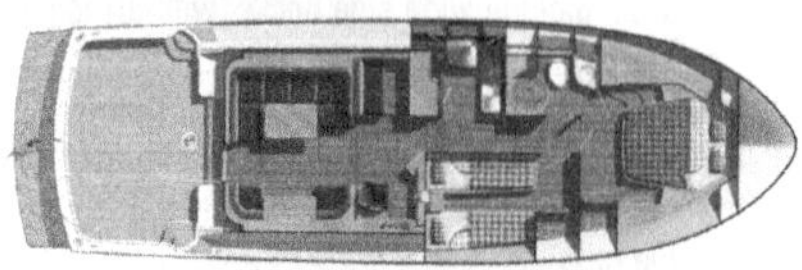
Standard Interior

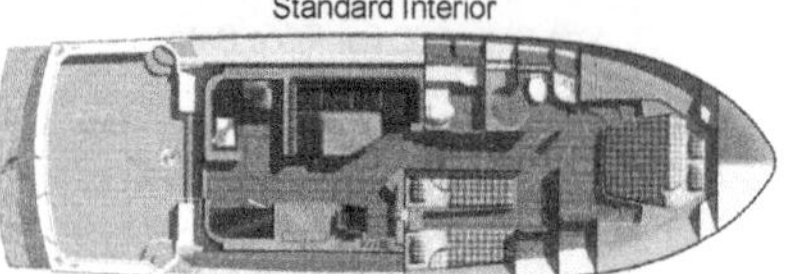
Optional Interior

Not Enough Resale Data to Set Values

Length Overall	45'9"	Fuel	512 gals.
Length WL	41'9"	Water	145 gals.
Beam	14'7"	Waste	60 gals.
Draft	3'11"	Hull Type	Modified-V
Weight	42,726#	Deadrise Aft	14°

Grand Banks 46 Classic

The Grand Banks 46 Classic ranks among the finest cruising yachts ever produced. With her timeless trawler profile, seakindly semi-displacement hull, and elegant teak interior the 46 Classic has defined cruising luxury since her introduction in 1985. Several interior layouts were offered over the years, and while a three-stateroom floorplan was standard, a galley-down, two-stateroom plan proved popular as well. The large owner's aft cabin is designed with a walkaround queen-sized bed and direct cockpit access. With her spacious salon and comfortable staterooms, the 46 offers plenty of interior space yet remains easily manageable by a crew of two. Like all Grand Banks models, the 46 Classic is an extremely well built yacht boasting a near-obsessive attention to detail. The teak joinery is flawless; the mechanical systems are first-rate, and the hull finish is mirror-smooth. (Note that the deckhouse tooling was changed at hull #43 in 1988 to provide slightly wider side decks aft.) Full walk-around decks and an aft cockpit allow the crew safe, secure movement while at sea and during docking. The large engine room has over five feet of headroom. Twin Cat or Cummins diesels deliver a top speed of 18–20 knots.

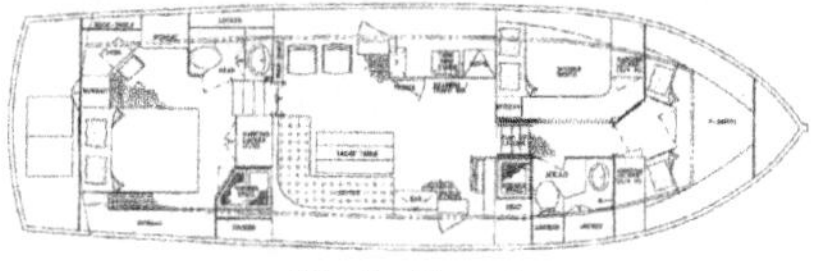
Standard Layout

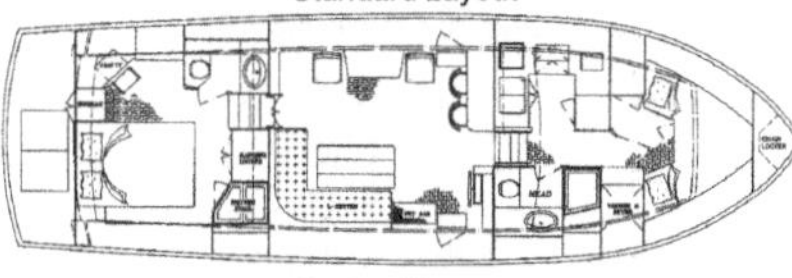
Optional Layout

See Page 682 For Price Data

Length Overall	47'1"	Clearance, Mast	23'7"
Length WL	44'10"	Fuel	630 gals.
Beam	14'9"	Water	300 gals.
Draft	4'5"	Waste	80 gals.
Weight	42,960#	Hull Type	Semi-Disp.

Grand Banks 46 Europa

An iconic yacht with many admirers, the Grand Banks 46 Europa has few peers when it comes to beauty, and fewer still in the areas of construction quality and design sophistication. She's built on the same semi-displacement, hard-chined hull as the Grand Banks 46 Classic, but the Europa's flybridge extends over the aft deck and side decks resulting in a much larger flybridge with space for a dinghy and davit. Two sliding wood-framed doors provide access to the main salon with its L-shaped settee to port, teak high-low table, helm station with deck access door, and L-shaped galley with Corian counters, holding-plate refrigeration, and overhead storage cabinets. Note the icemaker below the helm seat. Three steps down from the salon are two staterooms (including a spacious owner's suite with king-size berth) and two heads. Molded steps in the cockpit provide easy access to the flybridge with seating for eight. The engine room—accessed from the cockpit sole via a utility room plumbed for a washer/dryer—has nearly five feet of headroom. Among several engine options offered over the years, Cummins 210hp diesels cruise at 9–10 knots, and 375hp Cat diesels cruise at 13–14 knots.

Standard Galley-Up Floorplan

Optional Galley-Down Floorplan

See Page 682 For Price Data

Length Overall	47'1"	Clearance	22'0"
Length WL	44'10"	Fuel	630 gals.
Beam	14'9"	Water	300 gals.
Draft	4'5"	Waste	50 gals.
Weight	43,000#	Hull Type	Semi-Disp.

Grand Banks 47 Eastbay Flybridge

2005–Current

Anyone fortunate enough to spend time aboard an Eastbay 47 will be struck by the obvious quality of this sophisticated Downeast yacht. Like the Eastbay 58, the 47 is a flybridge-only yacht, and she takes many styling leads from her larger sibling. The beautifully crafted and spacious interior is offered with a cruise-friendly two-cabin arrangement or a single-cabin layout with a semi-open office area in place of the second stateroom. The salon is true Grand Banks elegance from the lovely teak-and-holly sole to the handmade teak cabinets and drop-down media center. A helm deck door offers quick access to the outdoors, and the L-shaped settee comes with an exquisite high-low teak table. One of the 47's most notable features is the spiral stairwell that curves its way from the cockpit up to the flybridge. Wide side decks make it easy and safe to move around, the visibility from the centerline flybridge helm position is excellent. Standard features include a premium Stidd helm chair, Corian galley counters, teak cockpit sole, and folding radar mast. Built on a deep-V hull with a solid fiberglass bottom, the Eastbay 47 will cruise at 25 knots and reach a top speed of about 30 knots with 720hp Caterpillar diesels.

Standard Floorplan

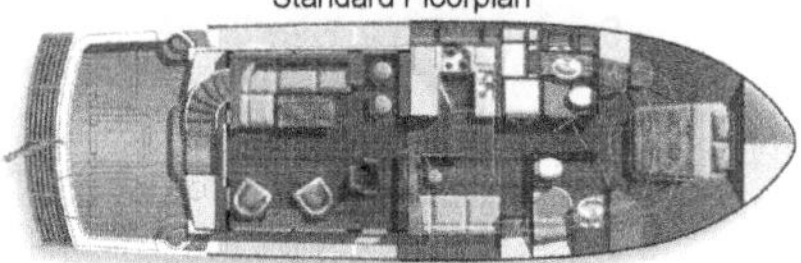
Optional Layout

See Page 682 For Price Data

Length Overall	52'4"	Fuel	700 gals.
Length WL	43'3"	Water	206 gals.
Beam	15'0"	Waste	75 gals.
Draft	3'10"	Hull Type	Deep-V
Weight	47,900#	Deadrise Aft	18°

Grand Banks 47 Heritage CL

2007–Current

Grand Banks broke with the past in 2007 with the introduction of the 47 Heritage CL ("Classic") and her sistership, the 47 Heritage EU ("Europa"). The styling is unmistakably Grand Banks, but these new models are built on modified-V hulls rather than the older semi-displacement hulls that characterized previous Grand Bank boats. Trawler enthusiasts may lament this change—semi-displacement hulls have advantages that can't easily be ignored; fuel economy, for instance—but the boating public wants performance in their trawlers these days and now they have it in the Grand Banks Heritage series. The accommodations of the 47 Heritage CL are similar to earlier Classic models with an expansive salon housing an L-shaped dinette to starboard, U-shaped galley forward to port, and lower helm seat opposite. (The step-down galley, however, differs from past Grand Banks layouts.) Both the master and guest staterooms in the standard interior are exceptionally spacious. An alternate three-stateroom interior is optional. Hatches in the aft deck access a huge storage lazarette. Note the pop-up instrument panel at the upper helm station. Cummins 500hp diesels cruise at 14–16 knots (20+ knots top).

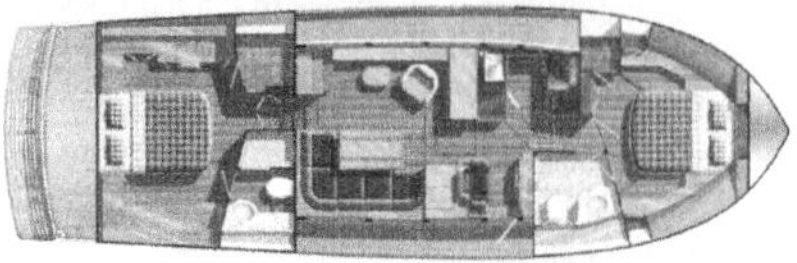
Standard Layout

Three-Stateroom Layout

See Page 682 For Price Data

Length Overall	46'10"	Fuel	600 gals.
Length WL	44'1"	Water	260 gals.
Beam	15'9"	Waste	77 gals.
Draft	3'10"	Hull Type	Modified-V
Weight	52,333#	Deadrise Aft	18°

Grand Banks 47 Heritage EU

Standard Layout

Optional Layout

Unlike the classic Grand Banks trawlers of old with their low-speed, semi-displacement hulls, the 47 Heritage EU is one of the "new-generation" Grand Banks yachts with fresh styling and more agile—and quicker—modified-V hulls. Introduced in 2007, the Heritage EU may be new under the skin but her Grand Banks pedigree is clearly evident in her signature Europa lines and meticulous, yacht-class finish. The standard salon layout for the 47EU features a U-settee to port surrounding a teak hi-low table. A settee is opposite, just aft of the Stidd helm seat. The large, open galley is arranged with an L-shaped granite countertop and microwave convection oven above the counter. Lower deck accommodations include a master stateroom forward with a queen island berth and en-suite head with shower. Farther aft is the guest cabin with twin athwartships berths. Across the companionway is a second guest head with room for a washer-dryer. Note the frameless cabin windows. The 47EU's roomy cockpit has a staircase ascending to her large flybridge with its centerline helm, wet bar, and pop-up instrument panel. Cruise efficiently at 14–16 knots with standard 500hp Cummins diesels.

See Page 682 For Price Data

Length Overall	46'10"	Fuel	600 gals.
Length WL	44'1"	Water	260 gals.
Beam	15'9"	Waste	77 gals.
Draft	3'10"	Hull Type	Modified-V
Weight	51,233#	Deadrise Aft	18°

Grand Banks 49 Classic

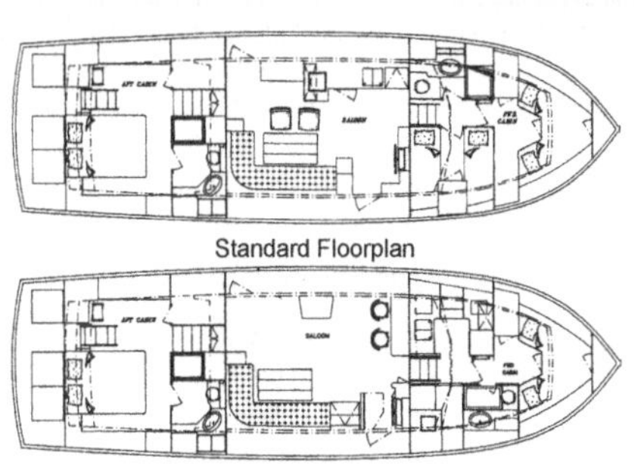

Standard Floorplan

Optional Layout

A sought-after yacht by trawler enthusiasts, the Grand Banks 49 Classic is a serious long-range cruiser with the iconic trawler profile and quality workmanship typical of all Grand Banks models. Needless to say, this is not a glitzy yacht with a Euro-style interior or fashionable "high-tech" construction. Indeed, she comes off as a little old-fashioned when compared to most other yachts, but the 49 stands apart as a proven passagemaker with a practical, time-tested interior. Highlights: the full walkaround decks are broad, secure, and easily negotiated; the standup engineroom is spacious and carefully detailed; the teak joinery is flawless inside and out; hardware, fixtures, and appliances are top quality; props and rudders are keel-protected; and her seakindly hull has a long record of handling just about every kind of weather an angry sea can dish up. Originally powered with twin 120hp Lehman diesels, more recent models came with Cat diesels from 210hp (11–12 knots top) to 435hp (17–18 knots top). A popular—and expensive—yacht in her day, about 125 Grand Banks 49 Classics were built. They continue to be highly prized on the secondary market.

See Page 682 For Price Data

Length Overall	50'6"	Clearance, Mast	26'5"
Length WL	48'9"	Fuel	1,000 gals.
Beam	15'5"	Water	500 gals.
Draft	5'1"	Waste	60 gals.
Weight	60,000#	Hull Type	Semi-Disp.

Grand Banks 49 Eastbay SX/HX

SX Layout

HX Layout

The Eastbay 49 is a top-quality hardtop express whose elegant appearance and meticulous construction represent the ultimate in classic American yachting. A handsome yacht with a long foredeck and traditional Downeast styling, she's built on a modified deep-V hull with a short keel and prop pockets for reduced draft. If the Eastbay's elegant two-stateroom interior—a blend of hand-rubbed teak joinery, a teak-and-holly cabin sole, Corian counters and custom hardware—comes up a little short in salon space, her spacious semi-enclosed helm deck (where guests will certainly prefer to congregate) provides comfortable seating for a small crowd. The beautifully finished molded hardtop is an integral part of the design, and access to the engineroom is through a hinged section of the cockpits bench seat. Additional features include wide side decks, a power-assisted center windshield panel, transom door and a teak swim platform. Note that the SX model has a fully enclosed salon while the HX version has semi-enclosed helm, i.e., no aft salon bulkhead. The large engineroom is a plus. Caterpillar 710hp Cat C-12 diesels cruise the 49 Eastbay at 25 knots (around 30 knots top).

See Page 682 For Price Data

Length Overall	54'7"	Clearance	NA
Length WL	45'8"	Fuel	775 gals.
Beam	16'0"	Water	176 gals.
Draft	4'4"	Hull Type	Deep-V
Weight	48,000#	Deadrise Aft	18°

Grand Banks 52 Europa

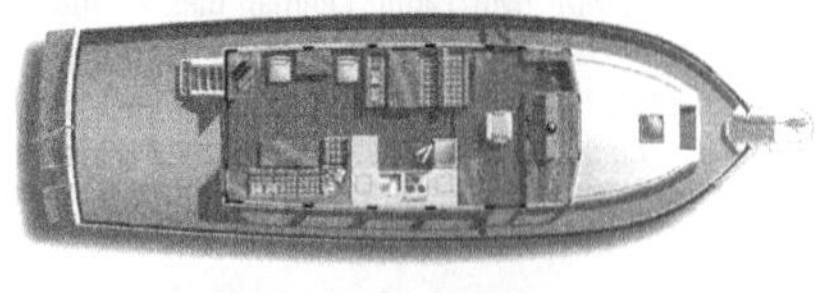

The Grand Banks 52 Europa was an evolutionary step up in size for Grand Banks when she was introduced in 1988, yet another example of the company's commitment to product development and engineering excellence. At once elegant and salty, the Europa is geared to serious long-range cruising. Built on a semi-displacement hull, buyers were able to choose the position of the engine room—it could be in front of the owner's cabin or farther aft, just forward of the crew cabin. Several floorplan configurations were available, all of which provide for three or four private staterooms. One of the most distinctive design features of the 52 Europa is the enclosed pilothouse complete with a central captain's chair and a slide-away privacy bulkhead. Like all Grand Banks yachts, the teak joinery is expertly finished, and abundant handholds are found throughout the interior. A crew cabin can be located beneath the aft deck, and molded steps provide easy access to the massive flybridge from the aft deck. Additional features include teak decks, a superb standup engine room, swim platform and wide side decks. Twin 450 Cat diesels cruise at 14–15 knots, and 660hp Cats cruise at 18 knots (20+ knots top).

See Page 682 For Price Data

Length Overall	54'1"	Clearance, Mast	29'0"
Length WL	51'9"	Fuel	1,200 gals.
Beam	15'5"	Water	500 gals.
Draft	4'10"	Waste	56 gals.
Weight	58,000#	Hull Type	Semi-Disp.

Grand Banks 54 Eastbay SX

Standard 2-Stateroom Plan

The Eastbay 54 SX incorporates the exquisite craftsmanship and classic styling for which Grand Banks has always been known. Like most quality yachts, the 54 is expensive, and she was built to standards not often found in a production yacht. She rides on a Hunt-designed deep-V hull, and at over 56,000 pounds, the Eastbay is no lightweight. Aside from her handsome lines, perhaps the most striking feature of the Eastbay 54 is her elegant raised salon with its varnished teak joinery, gleaming teak-and-holly sole, and huge wraparound windows. Visibility from the helm is excellent in all directions, and a navigation station opposite the helm is large enough for a full-size chart. The standard galley-down, two-stateroom floorplan of the 54 is notable for its spacious staterooms and huge galley. An optional three-stateroom floorplan relocates the galley in the salon. An office area with desk and washer/dryer combo is standard in either layout. On deck, the aft cockpit features built-in seating, teak decking, and lift-up engineroom access. A superb rough-water performer, 800hp Cats cruise the Eastbay 54 in the low 20s and reach nearly 30 knots wide open.

Optional 3-Stateroom Plan

See Page 682 For Price Data

Length Overall	53'9"	Clearance	16'3"
Length WL	49'6"	Fuel	935 gals.
Beam	16'0"	Water	200 gals.
Draft	4'4"	Hull Type	Deep-V
Weight	56,500#	Deadrise Aft	18°

Grand Banks 58 Classic

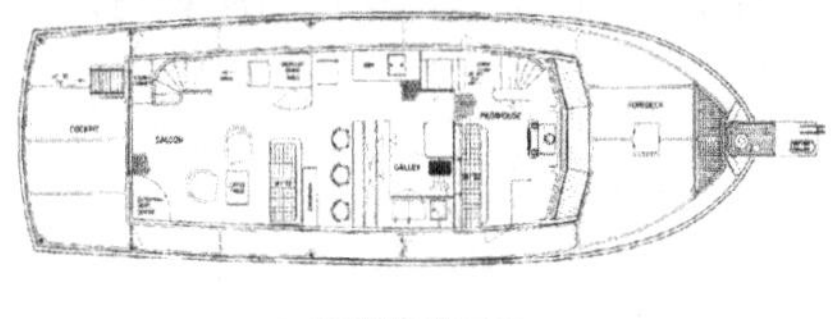

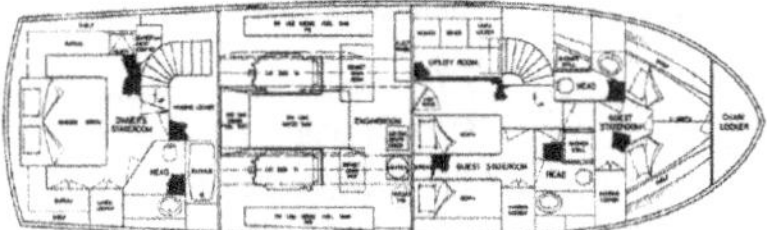

The Grand Banks 58 is a traditional flush-deck motor yacht with the distinctive styling and quality construction that Grand Banks products are known for. She's built on a solid fiberglass semi-displacement hull with a wide beam, a graceful sheer, and a deep, prop-protecting keel. This luxurious yacht was clearly designed with long-range passagemaking in mind, and her three-stateroom accommodations provide extravagant liveaboard comforts. The teak-paneled main salon/dining area is a full 210 square feet with the galley conveniently located on the main deck level. Additional features include a pilothouse chart table and settee, a huge flybridge with extended bridge overhangs, secure walkaround side decks, a spacious engine room with standing headroom, and a whirlpool in the owner's head compartment. In spite of her size, Grand Banks maintains that the 58 MY was designed to be owner-operated, and all equipment is installed for easy access. Caterpillar 375hp diesels are standard for a 9-knot cruising speed and a top speed of 11–12 knots. The cruising range at 8 knots is approximately 1,400 miles.

Not Enough Resale Data to Set Values

Length Overall	58'11"	Clearance	17'6"
Length WL	54'4"	Fuel	1,400 gals.
Beam	17'6"	Water	450 gals.
Draft	5'6"	Waste	80 gals.
Weight	100,000#	Hull Type	Semi-Disp.

Grand Banks 58 Eastbay Flybridge

2004–07

Standard Layout

Optional Layout

Luxury on a grand scale defines the Eastbay 58, a distinctive flybridge cruiser aimed at discriminating buyers with an eye for traditional styling and quality construction. This is an impressive yacht on many levels; from the spiral staircase aft to the polished anchor platform at the bow, the Eastbay gets the details right at every turn. Her three-stateroom, galley-down interior is designed for extended passages with plenty of company aboard, and an optional galley-up layout provides a fourth cabin that can easily be set up as an office. The salon is finished in warm teak joinery, and a sliding door at the helm provides easy access to the Eastbay's teak-laid decks. Access to the standup engineroom is through a large watertight door in the cockpit, and wide side decks make it easy to move around the house. Topside, the 58 boasts what is arguably the most comfortable flybridge seating available on a yacht this size. Additional features include a teak swim platform, bow thruster, premium Stidd helm seats (above and below), cockpit wet bar, and a brilliantly lit engineroom. On the downside, there's not much cockpit storage. A surprisingly good performer, 1,400hp Cat diesels will deliver a top speed of over 30 knots.

Not Enough Resale Data to Set Values

Length w/Platform	63'5"	Clearance	18'9"
Hull Length	58'8"	Fuel	1,175 gals.
Beam	17'8"	Water	280 gals.
Draft	5'4"	Hull Type	Deep-V
Weight	91,000#	Deadrise Aft	21°

Grand Banks 59 Aleutian RP

2007–Current

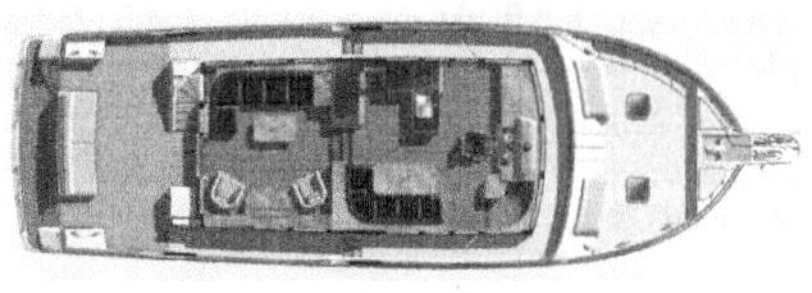

A lot of yachts boast of performance and luxury in their advertising, and for the most part those claims are justified by the facts. Few, however, can include quality in the mix, at least not the level synonymous with the Grand Banks brand. The 59 Aleutian is a case in point; a compelling raised pilothouse cruiser whose timeless styling and luxurious amenities set the standards for this class of yacht. The salon layout for the 59RP features a large U-settee to port, surrounding a teak high-low table. Two barrel chairs are opposite, and an entertainment system is contained in the forward bulkhead cabinets. In the pilothouse, the galley is to port with a U-shaped countertop and generous storage space. Opposite the galley, on a riser for greater visibility, sits an L-shaped dinette around a teak dining table with folding leaves. There are three staterooms below including an opulent full-beam master, VIP double, and a guest cabin with twin beds. The third head holds the washer/dryer. Note the pass-through between the galley and flybridge. Topside features include full teak decks, a curved cockpit stairwell, and a spacious flybridge with twin teak tables. Cat 1,000hp C18 diesels cruise at 20–22 knots (mid 20s top).

Not Enough Resale Data to Set Values

Length Overall	58'7"	Fuel	1,400 gals.
Length WL	55'4"	Water	385 gals.
Beam	18'0"	Waste	110 gals.
Draft	5'4"	Hull Type	Modified-V
Weight	90,000#	Deadrise Aft	16°

Grand Banks 64 Aleutian RP

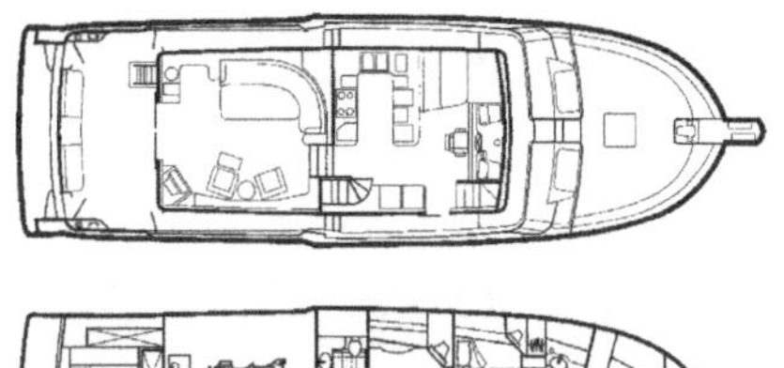

The Grand Banks 64 Aleutian is a notable departure from the time-honored series of trawlers long associated with the Grand Banks name. Aside from the fact that she's the largest Grand Banks ever, the Aleutian is faster and far more stylish than any of her predecessors. Built on an efficient semi-displacement hull with a deep keel, cored hullsides, and prop pockets, the Aleutian's handsome raised pilothouse profile is accented by a stepped sheer and a distinctive Portuguese bridge. The standard three-stateroom, three-head floorplan is designed so that the second guest cabin can be used as an office. The galley is on the pilothouse level, several steps up from the salon with its luxurious teak furnishings and Corian counters. The engine room can be accessed from either the master stateroom or the cockpit lazarette. (Note that the lazarette can house an optional crew quarters.) Additional features include a huge flybridge, wide, secure side decks, tremendous fuel capacity, and watertight engine room bulkheads and doors. Cat 1,550hp C-30 diesels cruise the 64 Aleutian at 20 knots. Note that the 70 Aleutian, introduced in 2005, is the same boat with a cockpit extension.

Not Enough Resale Data to Set Values

Length Overall	64'4"	Fuel	2,200 gals.
Length WL	59'4"	Water	440 gals.
Beam	19'10"	Waste	150 gals.
Draft	5'6"	Hull Type	Modified-V
Weight	105,000#	Deadrise Aft	14°

Hatteras

Quick View

- Hatteras began operations at High Point, NC, in 1959 with the Hargrave-designed Hatteras 41 Convertible, the first all-fiberglass sportfishing boat her size in the industry.
- In 1961 Hatteras premiered the 41 Double Cabin, the first fiberglass motor yacht.
- By the late 1960s, Hatteras was offering a full line of models including the largest production fiberglass motor yacht then available, the Hatteras 50 MY.
- The 1970s and 1980s saw Hatteras evolve into the undisputed leader of production convertibles and motor yachts in the industry.
- In 1986 Genmar purchases Hatteras from parent company AMF, Inc.
- In 1992 the Hatteras 82 Convertible became the largest production sportfisherman ever built.
- In 2001 industry-giant Brunswick purchased Hatteras Yachts from the Genmar Corporation.
- With production at a record low, parent-company Brunswick announced early in 2013 its decision to seek a buyer for Hatteras Yachts.
- A Hatteras owner's group can be found at www.hatterasowners.com.

Hatteras Yachts • New Burn, NC • www.hatterasyachts.com

Hatteras 39 Convertible

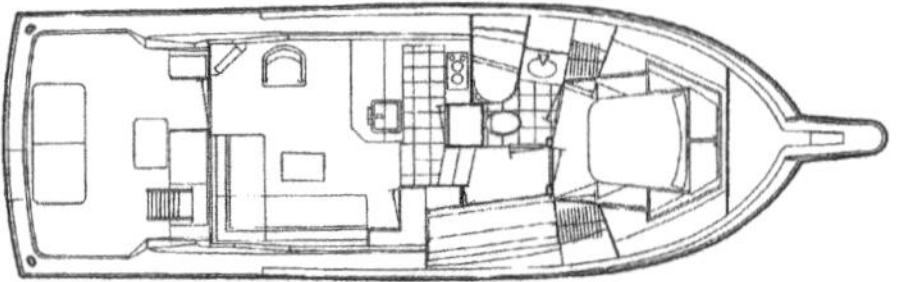

The Hatteras 39 Convertible is an updated version of the company's popular 38 Convertible (1988–93) with a restyled deckhouse and flybridge, and a slightly revised interior. She's built on a modified-V hull with cored hullsides, a solid fiberglass bottom, and a deep 4-foot, 8-inch keel. The 39's versatile interior, with its light oak joinery, is arranged with a mid-level galley—a configuration that opens up the salon considerably. The guest cabin is uniquely designed to function either as a day lounge or as a private sleeping area with a lower berth and a fold-down upper. Outside, the cockpit comes with a transom door and gate, molded tackle center, and in-deck storage box. Additional features include a well-arranged flybridge helm console, side exhausts, and five-bladed props. Note that when she was introduced in 1994, the Hatteras 39 boasted a surprisingly low price thanks to her standard 314hp Detroit 4-71 diesels—small engines indeed for a boat of this size which resulted in an unimpressive 18-knot cruising speed and just over 20 knots top. Later models with twin 465hp 6-71s cruise at a respectable 24 knots and reach a top speed of around 27 knots.

See Page 682 For Price Data

Length	39'0"	Fuel	490 gals.
Beam	13'7"	Water	120 gals.
Draft	4'8"	Waste	50 gals.
Weight	32,000#	Hull Type	Modified-V
Clearance	12'6"	Deadrise Aft	9°

Hatteras 39 Sport Express

1995–98

Tiara started the trend toward big, dual-purpose (fish or cruise) express boats with the introduction in 1991 of their 4300 Open. Viking and Bertram soon came out with 43-footers, and Hatteras followed with the 39 Sport Express in 1995. She is unquestionably a handsome boat—among the best in her class when it comes to styling. (The cruising version, with curved bridgedeck seating and a sport arch, is pictured above.) She's built on the same deep-draft hull used for the Hatteras 39 Convertible with moderate beam, a flared bow and cored hullsides. The Sport Express is a big boat on the outside with a party-size bridgedeck and a cockpit large enough to handle a full-size chair. Originally offered with curved seating opposite the helm, later models have more traditional L-shaped lounge seating. Cockpit features include an in-deck fish box, molded tackle center, transom door, and direct access to the engine room. Inside, the single-stateroom floorplan will sleep four to six and comes complete with a stall shower in the head. Twin 435hp Cats cruise at 23 knots (about 27 knots top), and 465hp Detroit 6-71s will provide a 25-knot cruising speed (28–29 knots wide open).

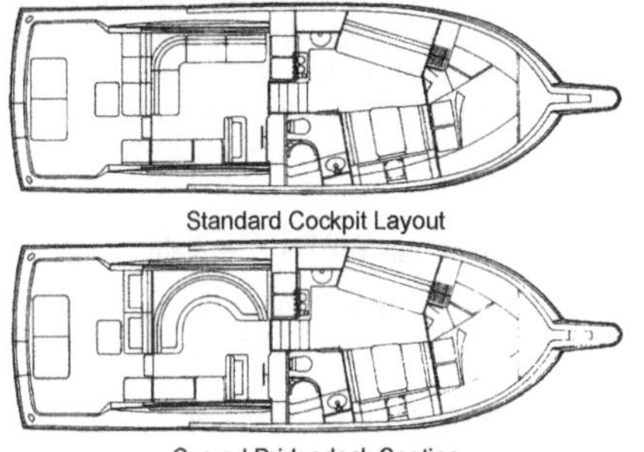
Standard Cockpit Layout

Curved Bridgedeck Seating

See Page 682 For Price Data

Length	39'0"	Fuel	458 gals.
Beam	13'7"	Water	120 gals.
Draft	4'8"	Waste	50 gals.
Weight	30,500#	Hull Type	Modified-V
Clearance	8'10"	Deadrise Aft	9°

Hatteras 40 Motor Yacht

1986–97

The last of the "small" Hatteras models, the 40 Motor Yacht (called the 40 Double Cabin until 1993) is a well-styled aft-cabin design originally conceived for export to the European market. She's built on a modified-V hull with a solid fiberglass bottom, and unlike most previous Hatteras hull designs, shallow prop pockets were used to reduce the draft and shaft angle. Several two-stateroom floorplans were offered during her production years, all arranged with the galley down and all featuring a spacious aft stateroom and a small foreword stateroom. Of the two layouts shown below, the dinette version was the most popular. Note that in late 1989, the flybridge was redesigned with a new swept-back windscreen that gave her a more streamlined appearance, but failed to offer much in the way of wind protection. (A new full-height entry door to the salon was added at the same time.) A poor performer with standard gas engines (13–14 knots cruise/20 knots top), 375hp Cat diesels eventually became standard. They'll deliver a cruising speed of 18 knots and a top speed of around 24 knots—not bad for a 38,000-pound boat. A popular model for Hatteras, 128 of these yachts were built.

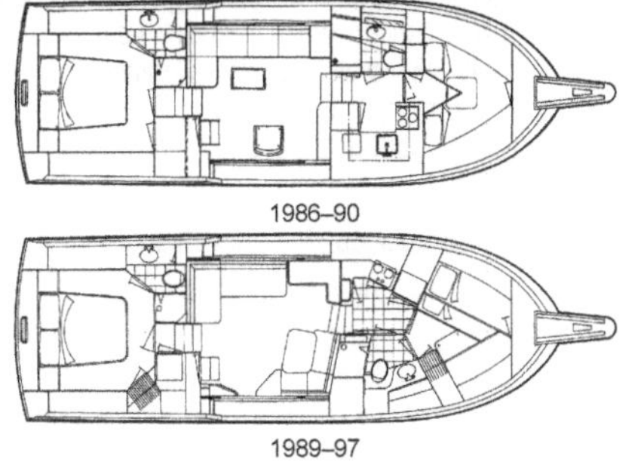
1986–90

1989–97

See Page 682 For Price Data

Length	40'10"	Fuel	359 gals.
Beam	13'7"	Water	110 gals.
Draft	4'9"	Waste	60 gals.
Weight	38,000#	Hull Type	Modified-V
Clearance	15'9"	Deadrise Aft	14°

Hatteras 42 Cockpit MY

Still a handsome yacht with a stylish reverse transom and attractive graphics, the Hatteras 42 Cockpit MY combines the convenience and versatility of a cockpit with the cruising comforts of an aft cabin design. No lightweight, she's built on a stretched version of the 40 Motor Yacht hull with modest transom deadrise, moderate beam, and an unusually deep keel section. A pair of two-stateroom, galley-down floorplans were offered during her production years, one with a built-in dinette in the salon and the other without the dinette. Both heads have separate stall showers, and the upscale decor with its light oak (or teak) woodwork and many amenities is extremely well finished. On the downside, the engine room (below the salon) is a tight fit. The side decks of the Hatteras 42 are quite wide, and the full-width aft deck is large enough for an assortment of deck furnishings. Topside, the compact flybridge is arranged with built-in seating surrounding the centerline helm position. Twin 375hp Cat diesels (or 400hp 6V53s) will cruise the Hatteras 42 Cockpit MY at 17 knots and deliver a top speed in the neighborhood of 22–23 knots.

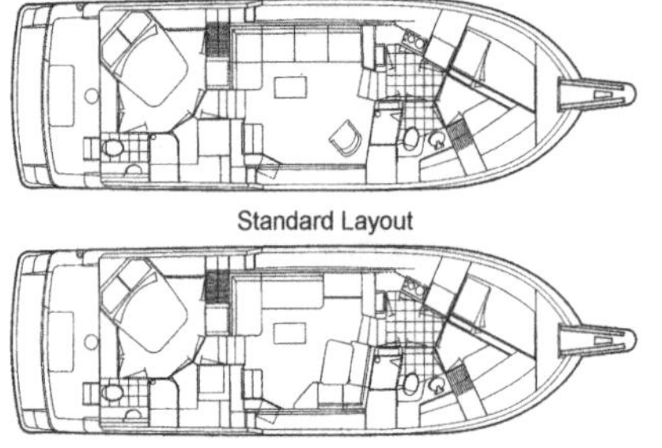

Standard Layout

Dinette Layout

See Page 682 For Price Data

Length	42'10"	Fuel	375 gals.
Beam	13'7"	Water	115 gals.
Draft	4'9"	Hull Type	Modified-V
Weight	41,000#	Headroom	6'5"
Clearance	15'9"	Deadrise Aft	NA

Hatteras 43 Convertible

Sharing the same rakish profile and step-down sheer of her larger sisterships, the Hatteras 43 Convertible is a good-looking sportfisherman with the solid construction and good open-water performance typical of most recent Hatteras designs. She's built on a conventional modified-V hull with balsa coring in the hullsides, moderate beam, and a shallow keel for directional stability. A galley-down, two-stateroom layout was standard, while an optional single-stateroom floorplan traded out the guest cabin for a large U-shaped dinette. While the salon dimensions in both layouts are somewhat compact for a 43-footer, the light ash woodwork opens up the interior significantly. A washer/dryer is located in the companionway, and there's a stylish curved shower door in the head. Outside, the 120-square-foot cockpit is tournament-grade all the way and includes direct access to the engine room—a feature seldom found in sportfisherman under 45 feet. Additional features include a large flybridge, wide side decks, transom door and a bow pulpit. A good running boat, twin 535hp 6V92 Detroit diesels cruise the Hatteras 43 Convertible at 24 knots with a top speed of about 27–28 knots.

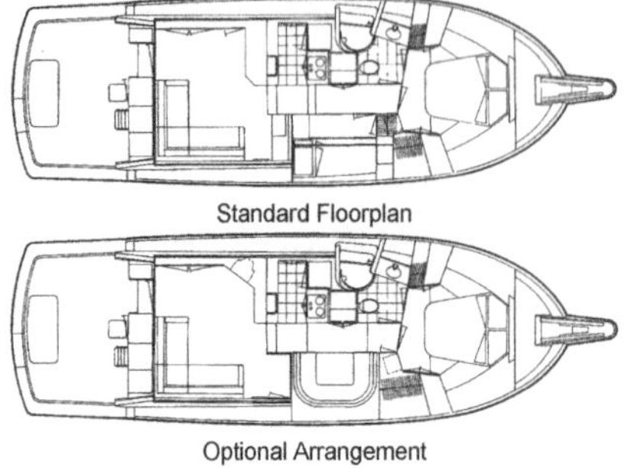

Standard Floorplan

Optional Arrangement

See Page 682 For Price Data

Length	43'2"	Fuel	500 gals.
Beam	14'3"	Water	154 gals.
Draft	4'8"	Cockpit	120 sq. ft.
Weight	40,000#	Hull Type	Modified-V
Clearance	12'4"	Deadrise Aft	10°

Hatteras 43 Sport Express

The Hatteras 43 Sport Express was designed to be an open cruiser that anglers would love. She was one of the largest open express boats in existence during the late 1990s and, because she was a Hatteras, one of the most expensive. Notably, she's built on the same hull used in the production of the popular Hatteras 43 Convertible (1991–98), a proven offshore design with moderate beam and an unusually deep keel. The huge bi-level cockpit of the 43 Sport Express came with a complete rigging station, lift-out fish boxes, livewell, transom door, and washdowns. Access to the engine room is beneath the aft-facing bench seat in the cockpit that rises for easy walk-through entry. Two interior layouts were offered with the standard plan including berths for four and a separate stall shower in the head. (An optional cabin layout with an aft head and smaller galley has a convertible settee and dinette that raised the sleeping capacity to six.) Additional features include light oak interior woodwork, a low-profile radar arch, side-dumping exhausts, and a bow pulpit. A good-running boat, twin 535hp 6-92 Detroit diesels cruise the 43 Sport Express at 26–27 knots (30+ top).

Standard Layout

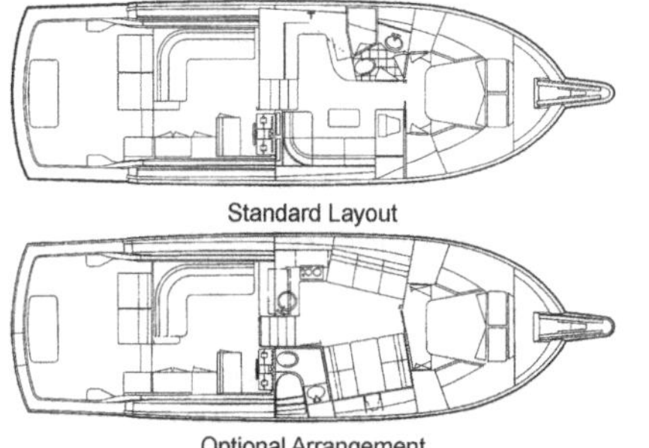

Optional Arrangement

See Page 682 For Price Data

Length	43'2"	Fuel	530 gals.
Beam	14'3"	Water	154 gals.
Draft	4'5"	Headroom	6'6"
Weight	38,000#	Hull Type	Modified-V
Clearance	9'8"	Deadrise Aft	9°

Hatteras 46 Convertible

Introduced in 1982, the Hatteras 46 Convertible (note that Hatteras built an earlier Hatteras 46-foot convertible from 1974–85) was a sophisticated blend of hard-core fishability and cruising elegance. She was heavily built on a beamy, low-deadrise hull with cored hullsides, moderate beam, and a long keel for added directional stability. Belowdecks, her two-stateroom ash interior is arranged with a mid-level dinette opposite the galley and just a single head compartment. An alternate floorplan moved the dinette up into the salon and added a second head compartment, a real necessity in a boat this size. The cockpit—among the largest of any boat this size—came with molded-in bait and tackle centers, an in-deck fish box, transom door, and direct access to a well-engineered engine room with standing headroom and excellent outboard access. Additional features include an underwater exhaust system, a standard washer/dryer, transom door and a bow pulpit. A good-running boat, a pair of 735hp 8V92s cruise the Hatteras 46 at a steady 24–25 knots and reach 28 knots wide open. Hatteras also offered 780hp MANs for the 46 Convertible that added a few more knots to the top end.

Standard Floorplan

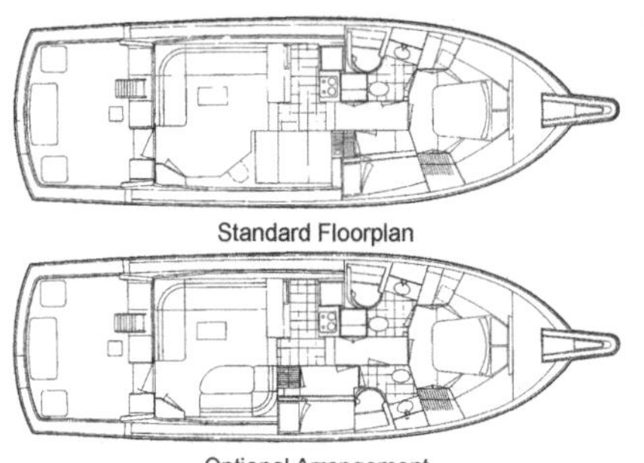

Optional Arrangement

See Page682 For Price Data

Length	46'10"	Fuel	775 gals.
Beam	15'7"	Water	188 gals.
Draft	4'6"	Cockpit	121 sq. ft.
Weight	52,000#	Hull Type	Modified-V
Clearance	13'9"	Deadrise Aft	7°

Hatteras 48 Cockpit Motor Yacht

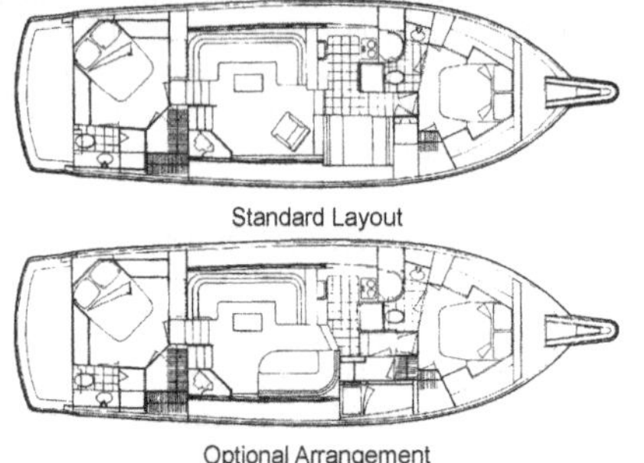

Standard Layout

Optional Arrangement

A handsome yacht with a swept-back profile and aggressive lines, the Hatteras 48 Cockpit MY is an upscale family cruiser with a wide beam and impressive accommodations. Her hull is balsa-cored from the waterline up and features a deep keel and more transom deadrise than most Hatteras designs of her era. She also has an innovative (and quiet) split exhaust system with side ports for idling and larger underwater outlets for speeds above 1,300 rpm. Below, the galley-down, two-stateroom floorplan includes walkaround berths fore and aft, a full-size convertible dinette, and stall showers in both heads. An optional three-stateroom layout moved the dinette up into the salon while adding the third cabin opposite the galley. The cockpit is far too small for any serious fishing activities, but it is suitable for line handling and getting on and off the boat. The aft deck, on the other hand, is large enough for serious entertaining. Additional features include a spacious engine room, bow pulpit, wide side decks, an aft-deck hardtop, and plenty of guest seating on the flybridge. With standard 535hp 6V-92s, the Hatteras 48 Cockpit MY will cruise at a respectable 18 knots and reach 21 knots wide open.

See Page 683 For Price Data

Length	48'11"	Fuel	667 gals.
Beam	16'0"	Water	170 gals.
Draft	5'6"	Waste	100 gals.
Weight	59,000#	Hull Type	Modified-V
Clearance	16'9"	Deadrise Aft	16°

Hatteras 48 Motor Yacht

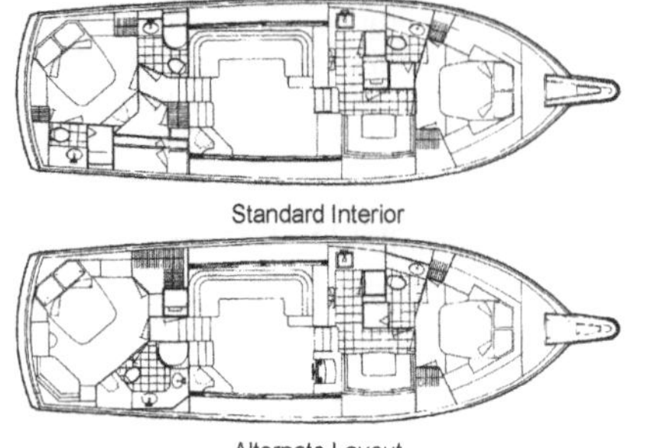

Standard Interior

Alternate Layout

A blend of conservative styling, upscale accommodations and quality construction made the 48 Motor Yacht was a popular boat for Hatteras in the early 1990s. She's built on a beamy modified-V hull with Divinycell coring in the hullsides and a notably deep keel. Offered with several floorplans over the years, most 48s were delivered with the standard three-stateroom layout with the dinette and galley down. The design of the salon and dinette area is open and airy, and the forward windshield—which functions as a skylight—creates a comfortable setting with plenty of natural lighting. One of the more prominent features of the Hatteras 48 MY is her spacious, full-width aftterdeck with its wraparound dodger, wing doors, and standard hardtop. The side decks are wide enough for easy fore and aft movement, and there's plenty of guest seating on the flybridge. No lightweight, twin 535hp 6V92 Detroit diesels were standard in early models (16 knots cruise/19 knots top). They were soon replaced with the larger 720hp 8V92s Detroits which cruise at a more acceptable 19–20 knots and reach a top speed of about 23 knots.

See Page 683 For Price Data

Length	48'9"	Fuel	764 gals.
Beam	16'0"	Water	170 gals.
Draft	5'3"	Headroom	6'6"
Weight	63,000#	Hull Type	Modified-V
Clearance	16'8"	Deadrise Aft	14°

Hatteras 50 Convertible

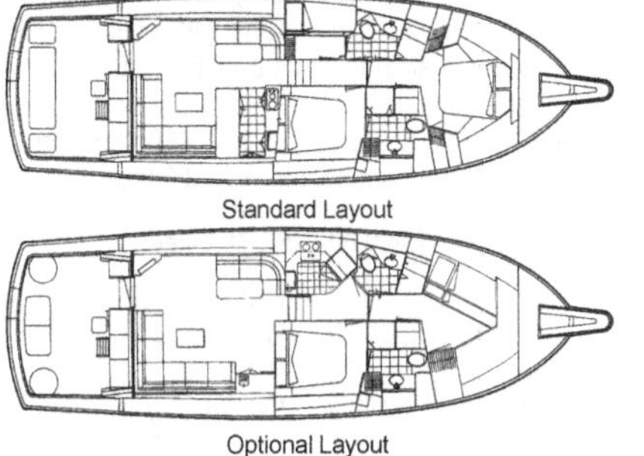
Standard Layout

Optional Layout

Hatteras nailed it in 1991 with the introduction of the 50 Convertible, the third 50-foot convertible produced by Hatteras over the years. Indeed, she turned out to be a proven tournament contender, a sportfishing icon against which other boats in her class were often judged. The Hatteras 50 was heavily built on a low-deadrise, modified-V hull with a wide beam and a fairly deep keel. Her standard three-stateroom, galley-up interior has an amidships master, two full heads, and a low-profile galley with under-counter refrigeration. For those who prefer a more expansive salon, an optional midlevel galley, available after 1997, moved the galley down. The cockpit is among the largest to be found in a 50-foot convertible. No lightweight, huge 12-cylinder diesels were required to deliver the performance expected of a modern 50-foot convertible. Early models with 1,080hp GM 12V92s cruise at 26 knots (30+ knots top). Later models with 1,400hp Cats—huge engines for a boat this size—will cruise at a fast 33 knots (high 30s top). A strong selling boat for Hatteras, in 1999 the styling was updated to keep up with the competition from Viking Yachts.

See Page 683 For Price Data

Length	50'10"	Fuel	890 gals.
Beam	16'1"	Water	184 gals.
Draft	5'4"	Waste	85 gals.
Weight	60,000#	Hull Type	Modified-V
Clearance	13'8"	Deadrise Aft	8°

Hatteras 50 Convertible

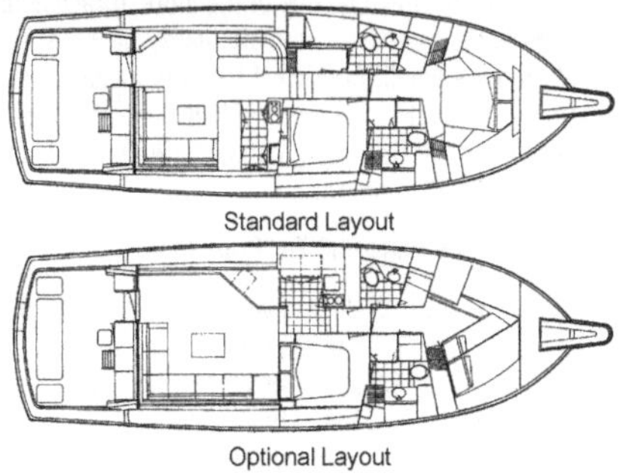
Standard Layout

Optional Layout

Aside from her sleek, new-look styling there is little to differentiate this most recent Hatteras 50 Convertible from her immediate predecessor, the hugely popular Hatteras 50 Convertible produced from 1991 to 1998. In most respects they are the same boat, but the original model was in need of a styling update in 1999 to keep up with the competition, namely, the hot-selling Viking 50 Convertible. The floorplans were retained in the updated model; a three-stateroom, two-head interior with the galley up was standard, and a two-stateroom, two-head layout with a midlevel galley and enlarged salon was optional. As before, the huge cockpit of the Hatteras 50 is among the largest to be found in a boat her size. Additional features include a state-of-the art flybridge with single-level controls, standup engineroom, wide side decks, and a full array of cockpit fishing amenities including bait freezer, fish box, oversized transom door, and fresh and raw water washdowns. Caterpillar 1,000hp C-18 diesels cruise at a fast 26–28 knots, and massive Cat 1,400hp 3412 diesels cruise at an honest 30+ knots (mid to high 30s top). Note the fuel increase in 2001.

See Page 683 For Price Data

Length	50'10"	Fuel	890/1,060 gals.
Beam	16'1"	Water	184 gals.
Draft	5'4"	Waste	85 gals.
Weight	60,000#	Hull Type	Modified-V
Clearance	13'8"	Deadrise Aft	8°

Hatteras 50 Sport Deck MY

1996–98

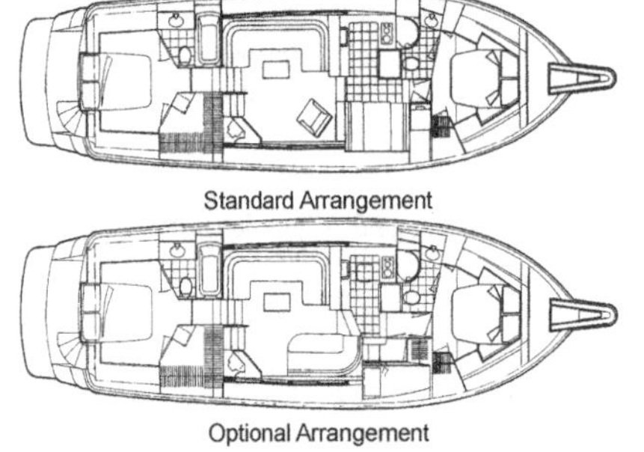

Standard Arrangement

Optional Arrangement

With her modern lines and stylish reverse transom, the Hatteras 50 Sport Deck MY is a big aft-cabin cruiser whose expensive price attracted only top-shelf buyers. She's built on a beamy modified-V hull with an unusually deep keel, cored hullsides and a solid fiberglass bottom. Two galley-down cabin plans were available: the standard two-stateroom floorplan includes a dinette opposite the galley, and an alternate layout moved the dinette into the salon to make way for a small third stateroom opposite the galley. Both floorplans include a stall shower forward and a tub/shower aft as well as a spacious and well-arranged salon. Note that the engine room has near standing headroom and excellent access to the motors. The aft deck is big for a yacht this size with room for an array of outdoor furniture. Topside, the helm is forward on the flybridge where there's lounge seating for several guests. Additional features include a broad transom with a curved staircase to the swim platform, a side-dumping exhaust system, a low-profile radar arch, walkaround double beds in the fore and aft staterooms, and excellent storage. Standard 535hp 6-92 Detroits cruise at 17 knots and reach a top speed of around 21–22 knots.

See Page 683 For Price Data

Length	50'10"	Fuel	622 gals.
Beam	16'0"	Water	170 gals.
Draft	5'6"	Headroom	6'6"
Weight	60,000#	Hull Type	Modified-V
Clearance	16'9"	Deadrise Aft	NA

Hatteras 52 Cockpit MY

1990–99

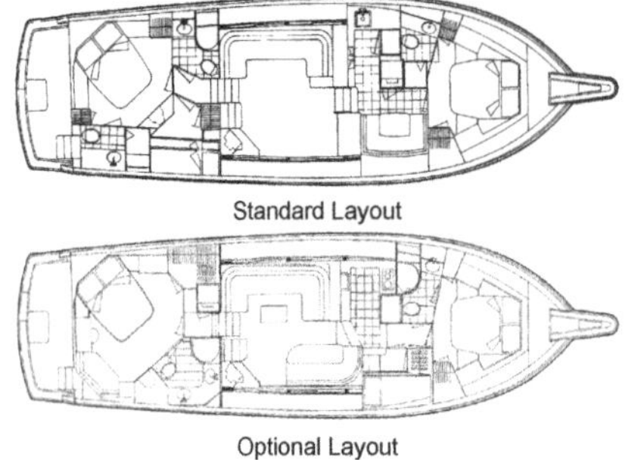

Standard Layout

Optional Layout

An impressive blend of cruising luxury and engineering excellence, the 52 Cockpit MY was one of the more successful Hatteras models produced in the recent past. The styling was considered bold in 1990, a genuine departure from the traditional Hatteras motor yacht look. Her modified-V hull carried more deadrise than previous Hatteras hulls, and a deep keel added excellent directional stability. Several floorplans were offered in the Hatteras 52 during her production years. The standard layout was a three-stateroom affair with a dinette forward and a wide-open salon—a big-boat interior made possible by locating two staterooms aft of the salon. Because this configuration made for a rather compact master stateroom, an alternate floorplan introduced in 1994 moved both guest staterooms forward of the salon while relocating the dinette into the salon. Topside, one of the more attractive features of the 52 CMY is her huge full-width afterdeck. The cockpit, on the other hand, is quite small. Additional features include a spacious engineroom, an innovative exhaust system, wide side decks, and seating for eight on the flybridge. Standard 720hp 8V92s cruise at 19–20 knots (about 23 knots top).

See Page 683 For Price Data

Length	52'11"	Fuel	994 gals.
Beam	16'0"	Water	170 gals.
Draft	5'2"	Headroom	6'6"
Weight	66,000#	Hull Type	Modified-V
Clearance	16'9"	Deadrise Aft	14°

Hatteras 52 Motor Yacht

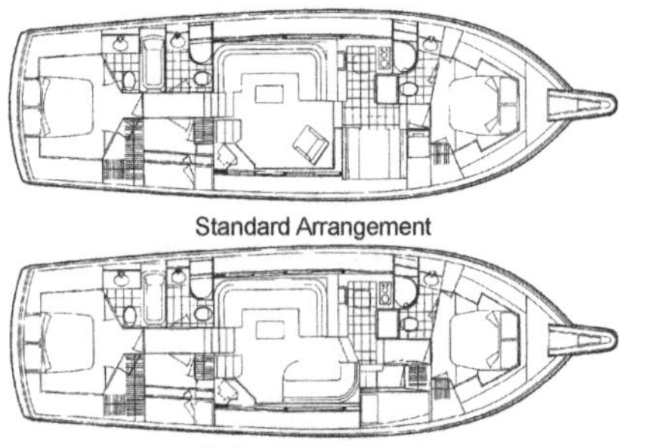
Standard Arrangement

Optional Arrangement

Aside from her handsome, slightly aggressive appearance, the most striking aspect of the Hatteras 52 Motor Yacht is her huge aft deck platform. Indeed, several 52s were built with an optional enclosure for this area creating a fully enclosed, paneled and air-conditioned living area whose dimensions actually exceed those of the main salon. At a hefty 66,000 pounds, the 52 MY is no lightweight. Add in her relatively wide beam and a low center of gravity, and the result is a particularly good riding boat with a comfortable motion. The floorplan is arranged with two of the three staterooms aft of the salon (which accounts for the huge aft deck) with a mid-level galley and dinette. Each head has a stall shower (note the tub in the owner's head compartment), and the interior woodwork is either light ash or maple throughout. Additional features include a spacious standup engine room (accessed via the galley stairs), wide side decks, an integral bow pulpit, and lounge seating for eight on the flybridge. With standard 735hp 8V92s Detroit diesels, the Hatteras 52 MY will cruise at a respectable 18–19 knots and reach a top speed in the neighborhood of 22 knots.

See Page 683 For Price Data

Length	52'9"	Fuel	994 gals.
Beam	16'0"	Water	170 gals.
Draft	5'2"	Headroom	6'6"
Weight	66,000#	Hull Type	Modified-V
Clearance	16'9"	Deadrise Aft	16°

Hatteras 54 Convertible

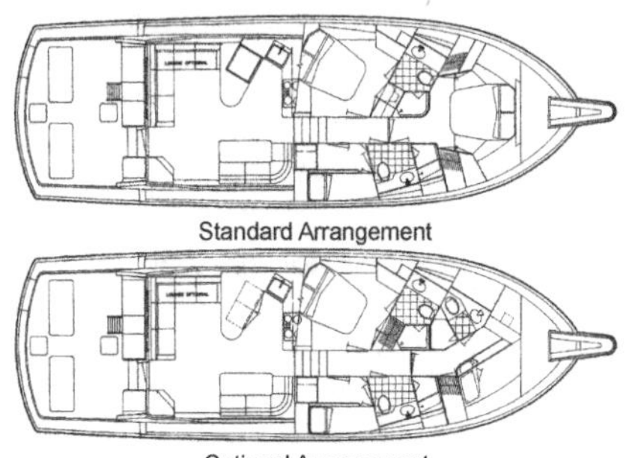
Standard Arrangement

Optional Arrangement

The Hatteras 54 Convertible replaced the popular 55 Convertible in the Hatteras fleet in 1991. A handsome boat with a bold profile, she's heavily built on a modified-V hull with a wide beam, shallow transom deadrise, and a relatively deep keel. Among her most impressive features is an innovative three-stateroom, two-head interior with its wide-open salon and spacious master and VIP staterooms. The diagonal galley configuration opens up the salon considerably, and the built-in dinette is a feature not always found in a galley-up boat this size. (Note that a three-stateroom, three-head layout was also available.) The flybridge of the Hatteras 54 is immense with a state-of-the-art helm console and plenty of guest seating. Additional features include a spacious, walk-in engineroom, a big 150-square-foot cockpit with tournament-level amenities, and a limitless selection of interior woods. Standard 870hp 12V71s cruise at just 22 knots with a top speed of 24–25 knots. Optional 1,040hp GM diesels (or 1,020hp 12-cylinder MANs) will cruise at 25 knots (28–29 knots top), and later models with 3412 Cats cruise at 28 knots (low 30s top). A new Hatteras 54 Convertible came out in 2002.

See Page 683 For Price Data

Length	54'11"	Fuel	1,320 gals.
Beam	17'4"	Water	200 gals.
Draft	5'4"	Waste	75 gals.
Weight	70,000#	Hull Type	Modified-V
Clearance	14'8"	Deadrise Aft	7°

Hatteras 54 Convertible

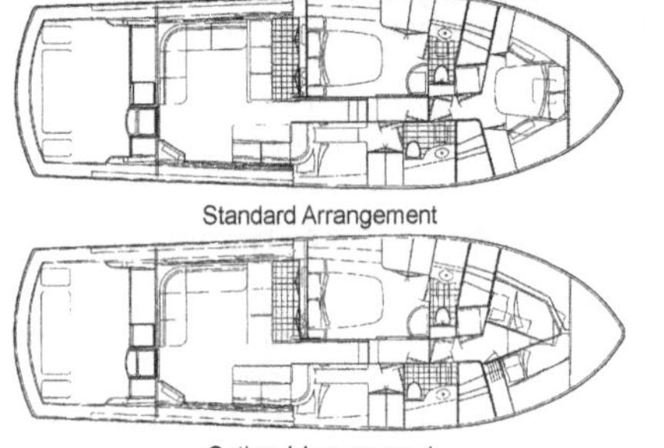

Standard Arrangement

Optional Arrangement

Introduced in 2002, the Hatteras 54 is a dramatic departure from past Hatteras convertible designs. Aside from her sleek "new-look" styling, the 54 was the first Hatteras convertible to ride on the company's then-new convex hull form with cored hullsides, shallow keel, and propeller pockets to reduce shaft angles. Belowdecks, the tasteful interior reflects the practical layout and meticulous finish common to all late-model Hatteras yachts. Three staterooms are situated on the lower level (V-berths are optional in the bow stateroom), and Hatteras made maximum use of space by extending both the master and second guest stateroom under the salon floor. Each room has its own climate control and entertainment center, and the master stateroom includes a 15-inch flat-screen TV. The galley, which is forward in the salon, comes with undercounter Sub-Zero refrigeration. With nearly 150 square feet of space, the cockpit is up to the demands of any hardcore angler. Topside, the flybridge is designed with a pair of Murray chairs and an optional electronically operated console. A fast ride, the Hatteras 54 will cruise at 30 knots with 1,400hp Cats (mid 30s top). With 1,550hp Cats she'll reach a top speed of close to 40 knots.

See Page 683 For Price Data

Length	54'0"	Fuel	1,050 gals.
Beam	17'3"	Water	200 gals.
Draft	4'2"	Waste	100 gals.
Weight	67,000#	Hull Type	Modified-V
Clearance	13'10"	Deadrise Aft	2°

Hatteras 55 Convertible

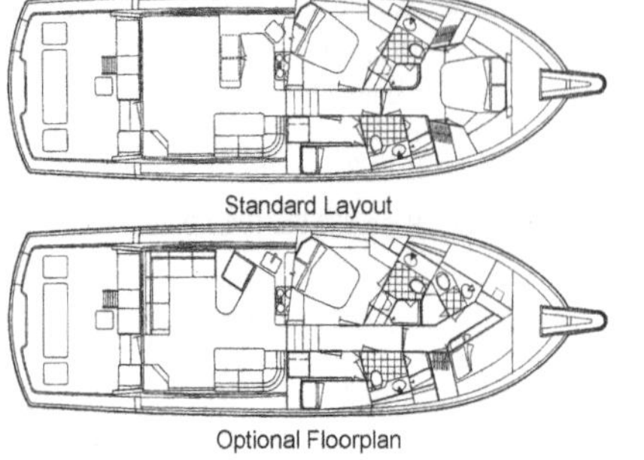

Standard Layout

Optional Floorplan

The latest Hatteras 55 Convertible (an earlier 55 Convertible from Hatteras was produced during the 1980s) is an updated version of the Hatteras 54 Convertible (1991–98) with a restyled superstructure and flybridge, a slightly modified cockpit, and shallow prop pockets. She's a rakish yacht with her low-profile appearance and huge cockpit, and she's been a popular model in the Hatteras fleet since her introduction. The standard three-stateroom floorplan (with a low-profile galley and salon dinette) is identical to the older 54, but the cockpit was redesigned with a transom fish box in place of the two in-deck units of the 54. Another upgrade is found on the massive flybridge where Hatteras engineers added a retractable electronics panel in the helm console. Note that a bridge overhang shades the forward cockpit area. A good sea boat built to the high standards normally associated with a Hatteras product, the 55 Convertible nonetheless comes up a little short in the performance department compared with her chief competitor, the Viking 55 Convertible. Standard 1,450hp 12-cylinder Cat diesels will deliver a cruising speed of 28–29 knots and a top speed of about 33 knots.

See Page 683 For Price Data

Length	55'2"	Fuel	1,320 gals.
Beam	17'4"	Water	200 gals.
Draft	5'4"	Waste	100 gals.
Weight	74,000#	Hull Type	Modified-V
Clearance	14'8"	Deadrise Aft	6°

Hatteras 60 Convertible

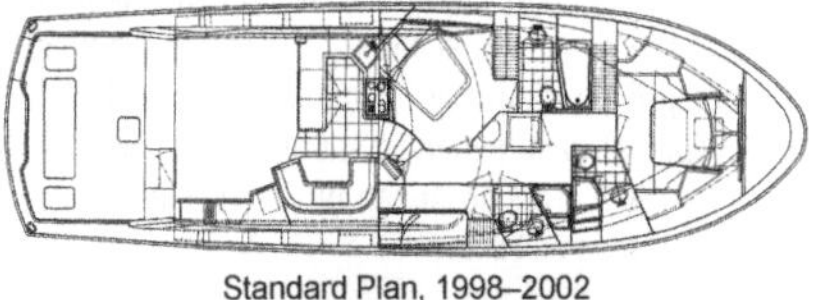
Standard Plan, 1998–2002

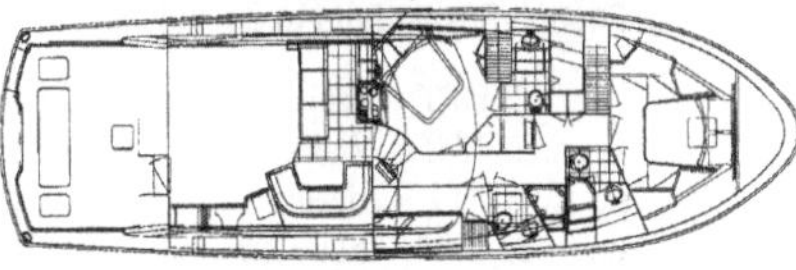
Standard Plan, 2003–06

With her long foredeck, graceful deckhouse, and massive cockpit, the Hatteras 60 Convertible (note that an earlier Hatteras 60 was built in 1977–86) is an impressive display of engineering excellence and modern convertible styling. She's built on a beefy modified-V hull with cored hullsides, propeller tunnels, and a deep keel. At least eight floorplans were offered in the Hatteras 60—far more than we have space to show. The standard layout, updated in 2003, is arranged with three staterooms with the owner's cabin amidships and a spacious VIP stateroom at the bow. Regardless of the floorplan configuration, these are lush accommodations indeed for a sportfishing boat. On deck, the huge cockpit of the Hatteras 60 is fitted with a full array of fishing amenities. The flybridge could be fully enclosed and air-conditioned for those who sought the ultimate in luxury. Additional features include frameless cabin windows, a choice of interior woodwork, and a meticulously finished engineroom. Standard 1,400hp 12-cylinder Cat diesels cruise at a fast 27–28 knots (about 33 knots top), and optional 1,480hp Cats boost the top speed to 35+ knots. Replaced in 2007 with all-new 60 Convertible.

See Page 683 For Price Data

Length	60'2"	Fuel	1,622 gals.
Beam	17'4"	Water	200 gals.
Draft	5'4"	Waste	100 gals.
Weight	74,500#	Hull Type	Modified-V
Clearance, Windshield	14'8"	Deadrise Aft	5°

Hatteras 60 Convertible

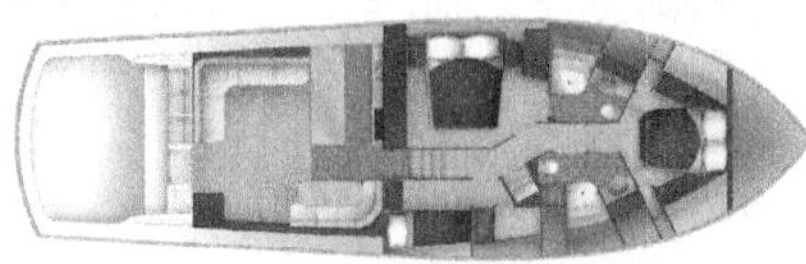
Original Floorplan

2011–Current

Claimed by Hatteras to be the first production boat to offer "a truly custom look," the distinctive styling of the 60 Convertible is a notable departure from the conservative lines of previous Hatteras models. Inside, the 60 Convertible features a luxurious salon with a comfortable L-shaped sofa with rod storage beneath, as well as an entertainment center with 42-inch plasma TV. Forward, the home-size galley features two under-counter Subzero refrigerator/freezer units. There are three staterooms and two heads below including an athwartship master with oversize queen berth. The 60's huge cockpit benefits from the boat's broad 19-foot beam. Overlooked by a mezzanine deck, access to the engineroom is on the centerline, and two large fish boxes are positioned fore and aft in the cockpit sole. Note that an updated GT60 model introduced in 2011 features a revised interior (with salon serving counter and a third head below) and a redesigned cockpit. Built on a resin-infused, modified-V hull with cored hullsides and a solid fiberglass bottom, large eight-blade propellers are tucked into deep tunnels at the stern for maximum efficiency and reduced draft. Optional Cat 1,800hp diesels cruise at a fast 33–34 knots (40 top).

Not Enough Resale Data to Set Values

Length	59'10"	Fuel	1,800 gals.
Beam	19'0"	Water	200 gals.
Draft	4'9"	Waste	100 gals.
Weight	85,000#	Hull Type	Modified-V
Clearance	13'3"	Deadrise Aft	2°

Hatteras 60 Extended Deckhouse MY

1991–97

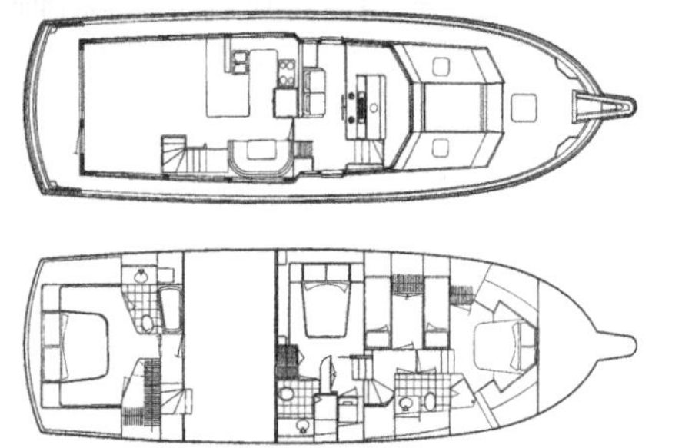

It isn't just the extended deckhouse that sets the Hatteras 60 Eetended Deckhouse MY apart from the 60 Motor Yacht. She's an entirely different yacht with a main deck galley, four staterooms, and a full-beam engine room rather than the separate walk-in rooms typical of earlier Hatteras motor yachts. Although the extended deckhouse layout widens the salon dimensions, it's notable that the 60 ED retains some modest side decks—something most extended deckhouse models lack. By eliminating the large afterdeck found in the 60 MY, the 60 ED has a more spacious deckhouse with the galley and dinette open to the salon. The wheelhouse is separated from the galley and offers direct access to the flybridge. The original four-stateroom, three-head floorplan of the 60 EDMY remained unchanged until late 1996 when Hatteras rearranged the lower-deck layout, adding a fourth head compartment and reducing the size of one of the guest cabins. Access to the master stateroom is via a private staircase in the salon, and all of the heads (in both floorplans) have separate stall showers. Standard 720hp 8V92s will deliver a cruising speed of 15–16 knots, and optional 870hp 12V71s cruise at 18 knots.

Not Enough Resale Data to Set Values

Length	60'9"	Fuel	1,033 gals.
Beam	18'2"	Water	335 gals.
Draft	5'2"	Headroom	6'5"
Weight	87,000#	Hull Type	Modified-V
Clearance	21'2"	Deadrise Aft	NA

Hatteras 6300 Raised Pilothouse

2000–03

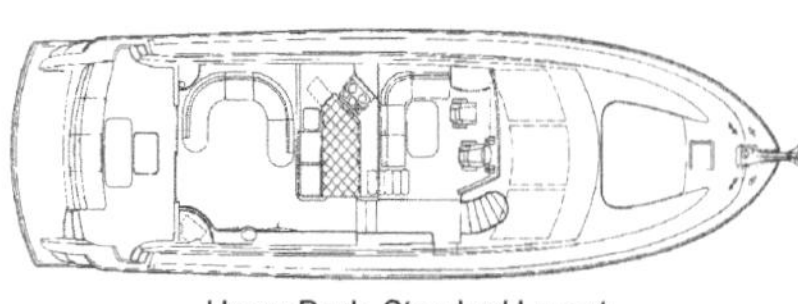

Upper Deck, Standard Layout

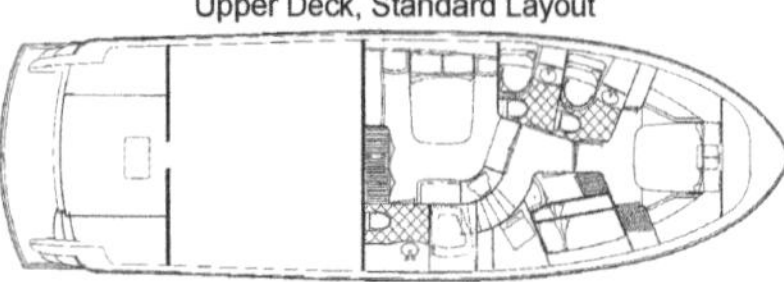

Lower Deck, Standard Layout

Introduced in 2000, the sleek styling of the Hatteras 6300 Pilothouse reflected the growing popularity of European motor yachts in the American market first seen in the mid 1990s. Heavily built on a modified-V hull with a wide beam, prop pockets and a relatively deep keel, the 6300 is no lightweight compared with other yachts her size. (Indeed, at 115,000 pounds, she's extraordinarily heavy.) While many Euro-style pilothouse yachts have both the galley and dinette on the pilothouse level, the galley in the 6300 is forward on the main deck level. With no obstructing bulkheads, visibility from the lower helm is excellent in all directions. The afterdeck is sheltered by the fully extended flybridge, and a hatch in the sole provides access to the spacious engineroom as well as the huge lazarette (or optional twin-berth crew quarters) below. Note that there is no bridge access from the afterdeck; the only entry is from the pilothouse. Also, the side decks are very narrow. The flybridge itself is best described as massive with entertaining space for a small crowd. Big 12-cylinder 1,400hp Cat 3412 diesels cruise the Hatteras 6300 at 25 knots and reach a top speed of close to 30 knots.

See Page 683 For Price Data

Length	63'0"	Fuel	1,290 gals.
Beam	18'3"	Water	280 gals.
Draft	4'11"	Waste	100 gals.
Weight	115,000#	Hull Type	Modified-V
Clearance	18'10"	Deadrise Aft	2°

Hatteras 64 Convertible

2006–Current

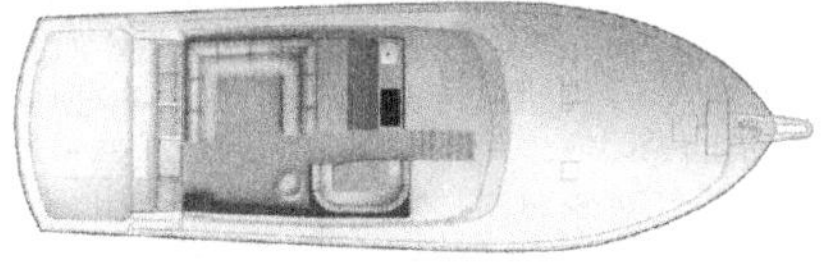

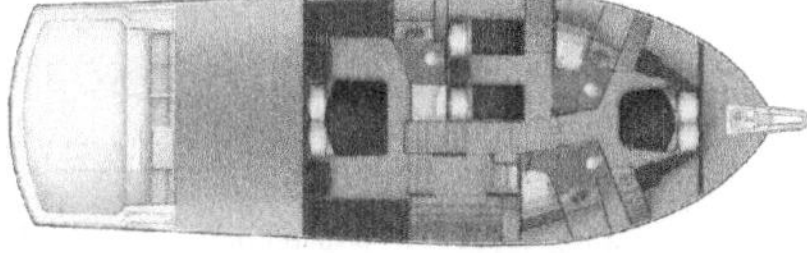

When it comes to the 64 Convertible, Hatteras pushes the right buttons: The styling is crisp, the accommodations are lush; and the finish is world-class throughout. Introduced in 2006, the 64's huge cockpit and spacious accommodations are the result of a broad 19'6" beam. She rides on a low-deadrise hull with cored hullsides and a solid fiberglass bottom. Moderate propeller tunnels are molded into the hull to reduce draft. Inside, the 64's opulent salon features a vast U-shaped sectional sofa to port, opposite a full-length cherry cabinet with built-in 42" plasma TV. The galley/dinette area is a step up from the salon and features a 4-burner ceramic cooktop, microwave/convection oven, trash compactor, disposal, and three Subzero units—two refrigerators and one freezer. There are four staterooms below including an enormous full-beam master suite with centerline king berth and en-suite head with granite counters and cherry cabinets. (Note the unique opening ports in the master stateroom.) A mezzanine deck with lounge seating overlooks the spacious cockpit. No lightweight, Cat 1,800hp C-32 engines cruise the Hatteras 64 at 28–30 knots (mid 30s top).

Not Enough Resale Data to Set Values

Length	63'10"	Fuel	1,950 gals.
Beam	19'6"	Water	343 gals.
Draft	4'10"	Waste	105 gals.
Weight	100,000#	Hull Type	Modified-V
Clearance	15'3"	Deadrise Aft	2°

Hatteras 64 Motor Yacht

2006–09

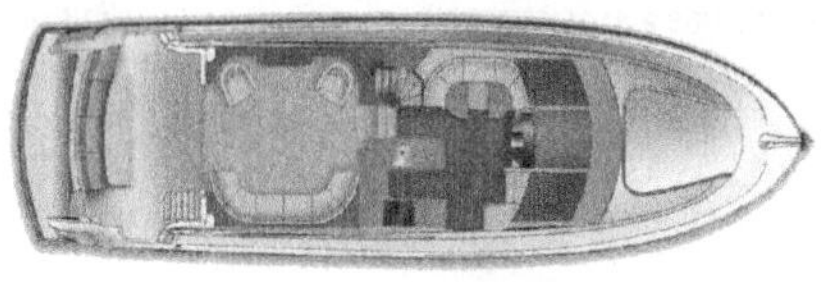

Introduced in 2006, the Hatteras 64 is a revamped version of the Hatteras 6300 Raised Pilothouse (2000–03) with an all-new interior layout. She's built on the same low-deadrise hull as her predecessor with a wide beam, a solid fiberglass bottom, and shallow propeller tunnels aft for improved efficiency and reduced draft. The standard layout consists of three staterooms and three heads with crew quarters for two. As with most modern pilothouse interiors, the galley and dinette are forward, three steps above the salon with its posh sectional lounge, twin club chairs, and cherry entertainment center. The galley features under-counter Sub-Zero refrigerator/freezer, four-burner ceramic cooktop, dishwasher, garbage disposal, and granite countertops. A lower helm is standard, and a pantograph door to starboard provides easy access to the side decks. Reached via a central stairwell in the galley, the flybridge offers lounge seating for a small crowd. Below, a full-beam master stateroom includes a king-size bed and en suite head with tub. An optional four-stateroom layout came at the expense of a smaller master. No lightweight, Cat 1,400hp engines cruise at 24–25 knots (28 knots top).

Not Enough Resale Data to Set Values

Length	64'10"	Fuel	1,515 gals.
Beam	18'3"	Water	265 gals.
Draft	4'8"	Waste	95 gals.
Weight	116,700#	Hull Type	Modified-V
Clearance, Arch	18'10"	Deadrise Aft	2°

Hatteras 65 Convertible

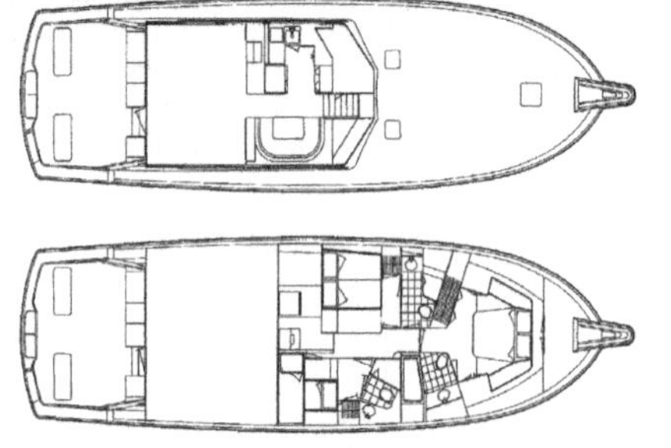

A great selling boat, the Hatteras 65 Convertible is the most popular sportfishing boat her size ever built. She's a step up from the earlier Hatteras 60 Convertible—not only are her lines more aggressive, but performance was improved as well. The hull is an extended and improved version of the 60 Convertible hull with a finer entry, balsa-cored hullsides, and prop pockets to reduce draft. Her standard three-stateroom, galley-up layout is highlighted by a spacious, beautifully appointed salon. (An alternate floorplan with an enlarged owner's stateroom and low-profile galley became available in 1996.) With 183 square feet of space, the cockpit was the largest to be found in a production boat this size. Topside, the enclosed flybridge is luxury on a grand scale. Aft controls assist with docking and backing down on a fish. Note the distinctive engineroom air intakes in the hullsides. Typical of Hatteras yachts this size, the engineroom is huge with good outboard access to the motors. Standard 1,035hp Detroit 12V92s cruise at 21 knots. Optional 1,235hp MTUs (or 1,350hp 16V92s) will cruise at 25 knots. A total of 120 of these yachts were built.

See Page 683 For Price Data

Length	65'5"	Fuel	1,674 gals.
Beam	18'0"	Water	460 gals.
Draft	5'4"	Waste	60 gals.
Weight	102,000#	Cockpit	183 sq. ft.
Clearance	21'11"	Hull Type	Modified-V

Hatteras 65 Convertible

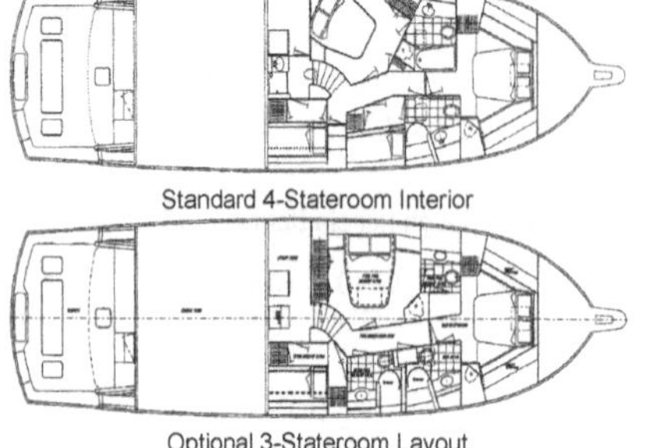

Standard 4-Stateroom Interior

Optional 3-Stateroom Layout

A restyled version of the original Hatteras 65 Convertible (1987–99), the 65 Convertible incorporates an entirely new superstructure while retaining the proven double-chine, prop-pocket hull of her best-selling predecessor. The 65's new look incorporates the rounded edges, frameless windows and a sleek raised foredeck of the sleek Hatteras 70 Convertible. An open bridge was standard, and the extended overhang shields the cockpit from sun and spray. The optional enclosed flybridge could be fitted with a spiral staircase leading to the salon. Aft controls assist with docking and backing down on a fish. Two interior arrangements were offered. The standard layout has four staterooms and three heads with a tub in the master. A three-stateroom plan also features the tub, but replaces a cabin with a larger head and greater storage. Additional features include a spacious walk-in engineroom, cockpit refrigerator/freezer, and a huge 183-square-foot cockpit with a full array of fishing amenities. A heavy boat, twin 1,400hp Cats cruise the Hatteras 65 at 22–23 knots, and optional 1,800hp V-16 Detroits cruise at 28 knots and reach a top speed of about 33 knots.

See Page 683 For Price Data

Length	65'5"	Fuel	1,800 gals.
Beam	18'0"	Water	445 gals.
Draft	6'0"	Waste	90 gals.
Weight	103,000#	Cockpit	183 sq. ft.
Clearance	18'2"	Hull Type	Modified-V

Hatteras 65 Motor Yacht

1988–96

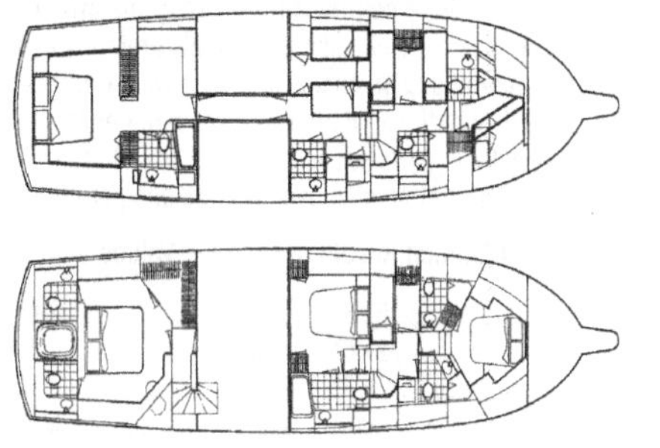

The Hatteras 65 Motor Yacht was designed as an enlarged version of the earlier Hatteras 63 MY with a fresh profile, the elimination of the sheer stripe, and a revised interior. Built on a beefy modified-V hull with a long keel, her original floorplan had four staterooms and heads with separate engine rooms. In 1989, an optional VIP layout was introduced with a more luxurious guest stateroom and a full-width engine room. In 1992, the standard floorplan was updated with queen berths in two of the three guest staterooms, a rearranged master suite with his-and-hers heads, and a single walk-in engine room. A bulkhead separates the galley and dinette from the salon, and the small aft deck is suitable for line handling. Lacking side decks, the full-width deckhouse of the 65 MY is extravagant in size and came with a choice of teak or light ash woodwork. Above, the enormous flybridge features an aft-raking windshield and U-shaped lounge seating. Twin 870hp 12V71s cruise at 17 knots (about 20 knots top), and later models with 1,075hp 12V92s cruise at 18–19 knots and reach 20+ knots top. Note that several 65 MYs have had a 9-foot cockpit addition added, turning them into the non-factory Hatteras 74 Cockpit MY.

See Page 683 For Price Data

Length	65'10"	Fuel	1,170 gals.
Beam	18'2"	Water	350 gals.
Draft	5'5"	Headroom	6'6"
Weight	99,000#	Hull Type	Modified-V
Clearance	21'5"	Deadrise Aft	NA

Hatteras 67 Extended Deckhouse Cockpit MY

1991–97

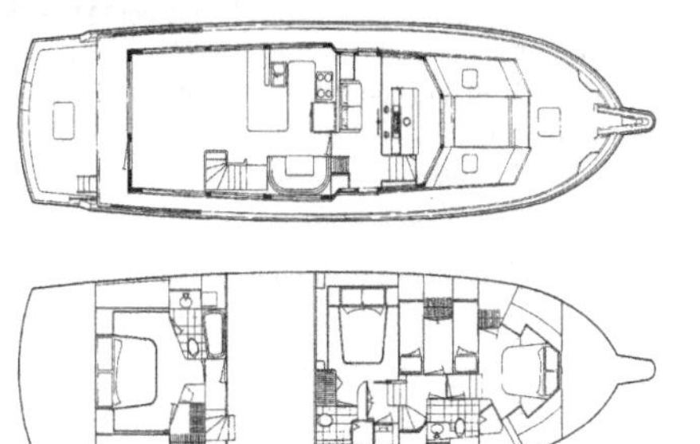

The Hatteras 67 Extended Deckhouse Cockpit MY has the distinction of being the smallest Hatteras cockpit yacht of her era with the desirable galley-up floorplan. Basically, this is simply a Hatteras 60 Extended Deckhouse MY with a cockpit addition. Heavily built with cored hullsides, a long keel, and very low deadrise aft, she retains the walkaround side decks of the 60 EDMY although they're much narrower than in previous Hatteras models. The extravagant galley-up, four-stateroom floorplan of the Hatteras 67 features light ash woodwork throughout and very generous guest accommodations. The dinette and galley are on the deckhouse level and open to the salon, while the wheelhouse—with its flybridge access—is separate. Where the original 67 had three heads, Hatteras designers added a fourth head in 1996 by reducing the size of one of the guest cabins. A small afterdeck overlooks the cockpit, and there's room on the huge flybridge for a small crowd. Additional features include a huge VIP guest stateroom, private access to the owner's aft cabin, and a transom door. Twin 870hp 12V71s cruise at 17–18 knots, and newer models with 1,040hp 12V92s cruise around 20 knots.

Not Enough Resale Data to Set Values

Length	67'2"	Fuel	1,171 gals.
Beam	18'2"	Water	372 gals.
Draft	5'3"	Headroom	6'7"
Weight	95,000#	Hull Type	Modified-V
Clearance	21'5"	Deadrise Aft	6°

Hatteras 68 Convertible

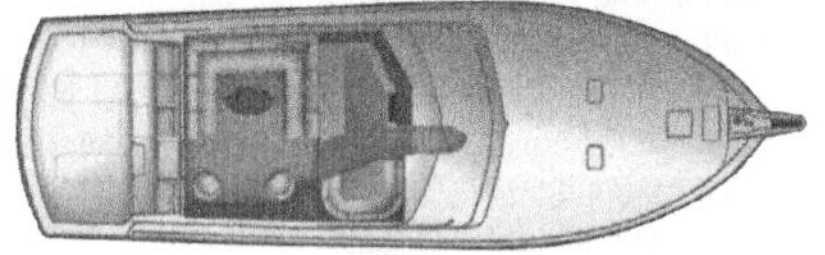

With a big mezzanine deck overlooking the cockpit and a whopping 21-foot, 6-inch beam, the Hatteras 68 Convertible is more than just a "big" 68-footer—she's gargantuan. Her broad hull form is a semi-V form with a well-flared bow and only two degrees of deadrise at the transom. Deep prop tunnels conceal an innovative trim-tab arrangement said to control running angles more efficiently than their transom-mounted counterparts. The 68 comes with a four-stateroom, four-head interior boasting a lavish full-beam master with king bed, walk-in closet, and built-in dressers. The salon, with its lacquered cherry joinery, 42-inch plasma TV, and vast U-shaped leather lounge, is actually wider than the salon of the Hatteras 80 Motor Yacht. On deck, the 68's 192-square-foot cockpit is the largest of any boat in her class, and the mezzanine deck has modular components allowing the owner to have the freezer, icebox or baitwell positioned to his preference. An open flybridge is standard, and an enclosed bridge with a rounded, one-piece windshield, is optional. A boat this size requires lots of power to deliver respectable performance. Cat 1,550hp diesels cruise at 28 knots (30+ top) burning well over 100 gallons per hour.

Not Enough Resale Data to Set Values

Length	68'6"	Fuel	2,100 gals.
Beam	21'6"	Water	400 gals.
Draft	5'3"	Waste	125 gals.
Weight	140,000#	Hull Type	Modified-V
Cockpit	192 sq. ft.	Deadrise Aft	2°

Hatteras 70 Cockpit MY

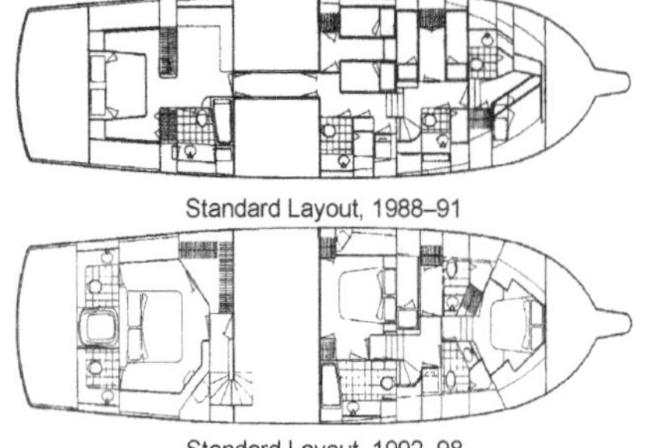
Standard Layout, 1988–91

Standard Layout, 1992–98

A very popular yacht (over 50 were built) with a handsome, euro-style profile and extravagant accommodations, the 70 Cockpit MY is among the most luxurious production yachts ever offered by Hatteras during the 1990s. She's basically a 65 Motor Yacht with a cockpit addition (the extra hull length allows for an additional 426 gallons of fuel beneath the cockpit sole). Like most modern Hatteras motor yachts, the floorplan is arranged with the galley and dinette on the deckhouse level where it's convenient to the salon. The spacious full-width salon (there are no side decks on this yacht) is extended well aft, leaving only a small afterdeck overlooking the cockpit. The wheelhouse and galley are both enclosed in this layout and separated from the salon. Originally designed with a standard four-stateroom floorplan with twin enginerooms, more recent VIP layouts have a full-width engineroom and more spacious guest accommodations. The flybridge is massive with space for a dinghy aft and enough seating for a small crowd, and the side decks are partially sheltered by overhead flybridge wings. Twin 870hp 12V71s cruise the 70 Cockpit MY at 17 knots, and later models with 1,075hp 12V92s cruise at 19 knots.

Not Enough Resale Data to Set Values

Length	70'10"	Fuel	1,596 gals.
Beam	18'2"	Water	345 gals.
Draft	5'6"	Headroom	6'7"
Weight	103,000#	Hull Type	Modified-V
Clearance	21'4"	Deadrise Aft	NA

Hatteras 70 Convertible

1998–2003

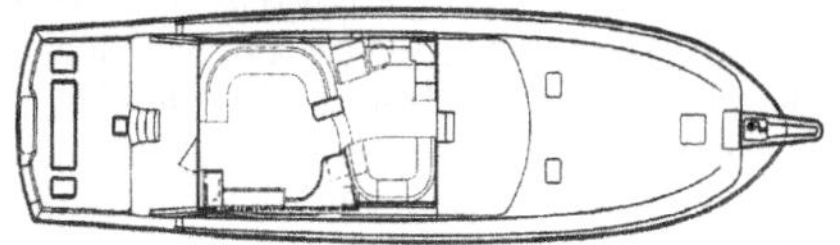

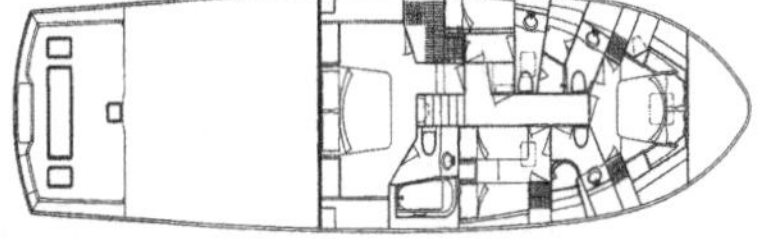

Introduced in 1998, the sleek profile and rounded enclosed flybridge of the Hatteras 70 Convertible made her one of the most elegant mega-sportfishing boats to hit the water in many years. Prop pockets are recessed into the hull to reduce draft while a long keel aids directional stability, and with a displacement of nearly 120,000 pounds, the Hatteras 70 is a heavy boat indeed. Her spacious four-stateroom interior is arranged with the galley and dinette forward, a step up from the salon. All four heads have stall showers, and the full-beam amidships owner's cabin is huge. Outside, an observation deck—sheltered by a bridge overhang—overlooks the massive 160-square-foot cockpit, and the enclosed flybridge is dominated by a state-of-the-art helm. Additional features (and the list is long) include outside controls aft on the bridge, frameless salon windows, a complete array of fishing amenities, and a spacious engine room. A bold and dramatic yacht (note the absence of any hull ports), a pair of optional 1,800hp 16-cylinder Detroit Diesels cruise the Hatteras 70 Convertible around 28 knots and reach a top speed in the neighborhood of 32–33 knots.

Not Enough Resale Data to Set Values

Length	70'3"	Fuel	2,000 gals.
Beam	18'0"	Water	365 gals.
Draft	5'4"	Waste	60 gals.
Weight	118,000#	Headroom	6'6"
Clearance	22'1"	Hull Type	Modified-V

Hatteras 70 Motor Yacht

1988–96

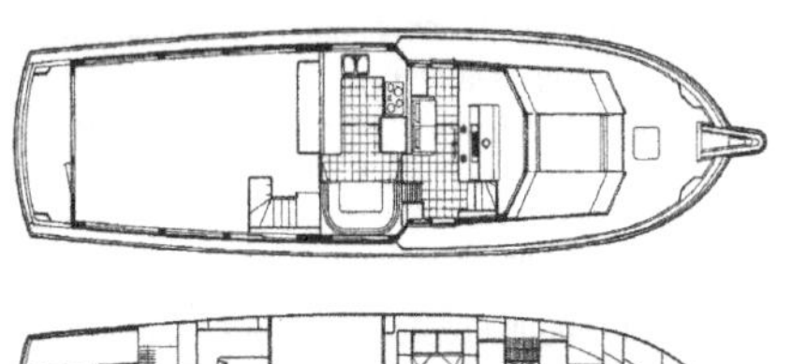

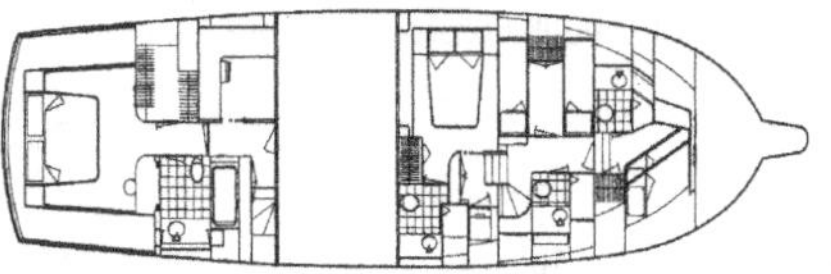

A popular yacht in the late 1980s and early '90s, the graceful profile and contemporary styling of the Hatteras 70 Motor Yacht is strikingly similar to the smaller 65 MY with the additional length used to create a more spacious salon and an enlarged master stateroom. While most Hatteras 70 Motor Yachts were delivered with semicustom interiors, a four-stateroom, three-head layout was standard with a five-stateroom arrangement offered in exchange for giving up the den/study just forward of the aft stateroom. On the upper level, the full-width salon of the Hatteras 70 is extravagant indeed and includes a formal dining area as well as a small aft deck. For privacy, both the galley and pilothouse are separate from the salon. Yielding to the demands of European buyers, a walkaround version (with a larger aft deck) became available in 1990 although few were built. Additional features include a spacious walk-in engineroom, salon access to the owner's suite, and a spacious flybridge. Twin 870hp 12V71s cruise the Hatteras 70 MY at 18 knots (21 knots top), and later models with 1075hp 12V92s cruise at 19 knots (about 22 knots wide open).

Not Enough Resale Data to Set Values

Length	70'11"	Fuel	1,596 gals.
Beam	18'2"	Water	251 gals.
Draft	5'6"	Headroom	6'4"
Weight	108,000#	Hull Type	Modified-V
Clearance	21'2"	Deadrise Aft	NA

Hatteras 70 Sport Deck MY

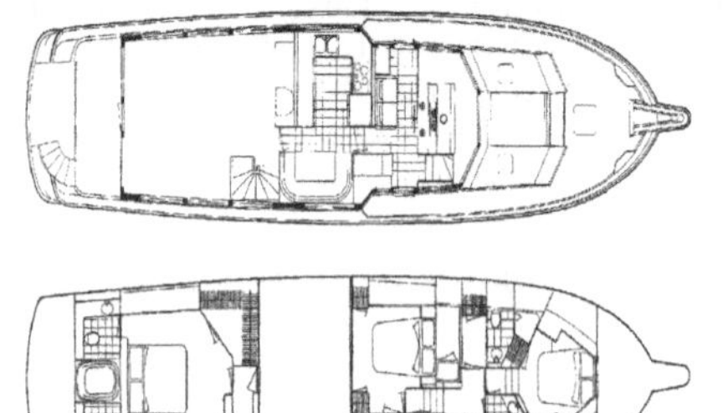

Introduced in 1995, the 70 Sport Deck combined the styling and interior accommodations of Hatteras classic yachts with a rakish, completely updated exterior appearance and an all-new reverse transom configuration. The transom design incorporates an aft platform—what Hatteras called a "sport deck"—with a curved staircase descending from the main deck. The interior is nearly identical to the late-model 65 Motor Yacht, an opulent three-stateroom affair with oak woodwork, a huge master suite, and an enclosed wheelhouse. The deckhouse galley, with its informal dinette, is aft of the wheelhouse and separated from the salon by a bulkhead to ensure privacy for owner and guests. The full-width salon of the 70 Sport Deck includes more than 240 square feet of living space—extravagant dimensions indeed for a 70-footer. Two of the three guest staterooms easily qualify as VIP suites, and the opulent master stateroom includes such luxuries as his-and-hers heads and a walk-in wardrobe. Needless to say, the list of standard equipment in this world-class yacht is impressive. No lightweight, she'll cruise at 19 knots with twin 1,100hp Detroit 12V92s with a top speed of 21–22 knots.

Not Enough Resale Data to Set Values

Length	70'10"	Water	460 gals.
Beam	18'2"	Clearance, Arch	21'4"
Draft	5'6"	Headroom	6'4"
Weight	103,000#	Hull Type	Modified-V
Fuel	1,596 gals.	Deadrise Aft	NA

Hatteras 72 Motor Yacht

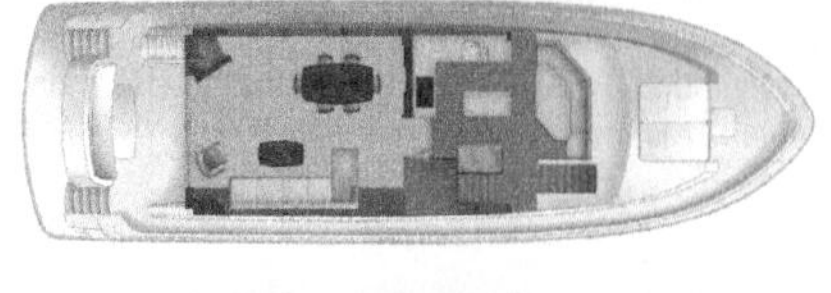

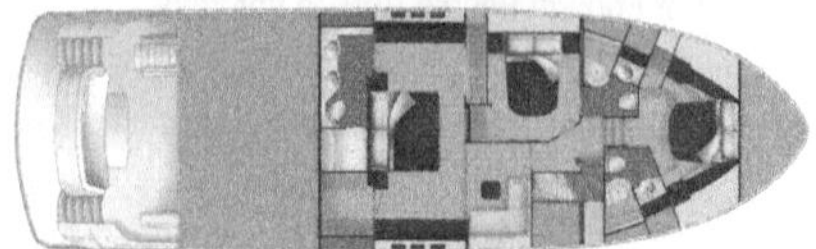

With her wide 20'2" beam, huge fuel capacity, and enormous 160,000-pound displacement, the Hatteras 72 dwarfs any European motoryacht her size in living space, cruising range, and passenger comfort. This is a big 72-footer with a truly expansive salon and a breathtaking master suite with king bed and his-and-hers heads. Forward of the salon—and on the same level—is a huge country-kitchen galley with an island and dinette. There is no lower helm in this layout although it is optional. Offered with three, four, or even five staterooms, the standard three-stateroom arrangement includes a sitting area in the full-beam master and two VIP guest cabins forward with en-suite heads. Because the Hatteras 72 was a semicustom yacht, any number of interior plans were possible. The same was true of the flybridge—it could be open or fully enclosed and air-conditioned (which most were). Note the cavernous engineroom, wide side decks, and recessed anchor windlass. It takes a lot of power to get the Hatteras 72 up and running, and even with big 1,800hp Cat C-12 engines (18–20 knots cruise) she's no performance match for her more agile—and considerably faster—European counterparts.

Not Enough Resale Data to Set Values

Length	73'4"	Fuel	2,200 gals.
Beam	20'2"	Water	300 gals.
Draft	5'4"	Waste	350 gals.
Weight	160,000#	Hull Type	Modified-V
Clearance, Arch	21'4"	Deadrise Aft	NA

Hatteras 75 Cockpit MY

2000–04

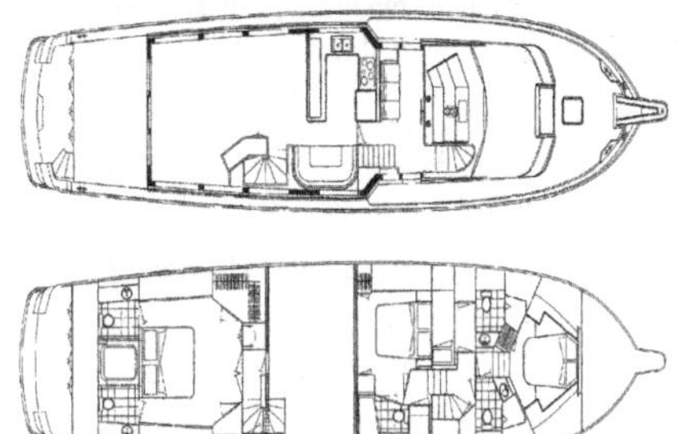

An updated version of the company's popular 74 Cockpit MY, the Hatteras 75 CMY is a widebody motor yacht whose streamlined appearance is a big step up from the conservative lines of her predecessor. For the first time on any Hatteras motor yacht, the sides of the bridge extend out to the edge of the boat making for an exceptionally large flybridge. The 75 CMY retains the spacious four-stateroom interior of the 74 CMY with an apartment-size salon, two VIP guest cabins, and an elegant owner's stateroom with private salon access and separate his-and-hers heads. The salon, with its formal dining area, is open to the galley and dinette forward. A bridge overhang shades the cockpit, and the massive flybridge of the 75 CMY features acres of lounge seating in addition to an elegant helm console. On the downside, the absence of walkaround side decks results in extra traffic passing through the salon. (Side decks were optional.) The full-beam engine room provides excellent access to the motors and ship's systems. Cat 1,400hp engines cruise at 22 knots. Note that a sistership model, the Hatteras 75 Sport Deck, eliminates the cockpit for an enlarged aft deck and master suite.

Not Enough Resale Data to Set Values

Length Overall	76'4"	Fuel	1,561 gals.
Beam	18'2"	Water	345 gals.
Draft	6'0"	Waste	215 gals.
Weight	110,000#	Hull Type	Modified-V
Clearance, Arch	21'2"	Deadrise Aft	3°

Hatteras 80 Motor Yacht

2005–12

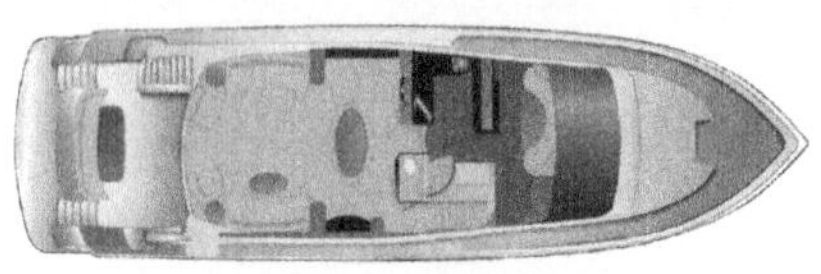

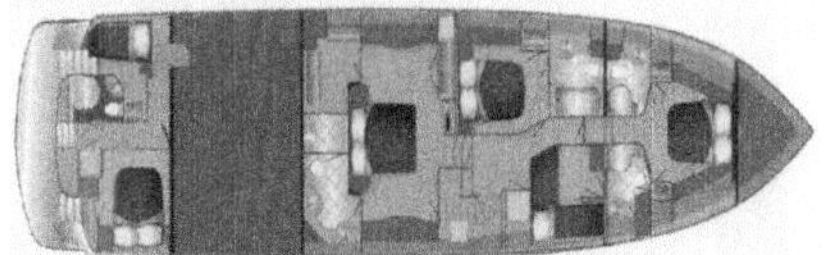

Graceful styling, lavish accommodations, and a good turn of speed characterize the Hatteras 80, one of the few U.S.-built motor yachts in this size range designed to compete with European and Asian imports. Built on a low-deadrise, modified-V hull with prop pockets and a shallow keel, the broad 21-foot, 3-inch beam of the Hatteras 80 is the equal of most 90-footers. The accommodations aboard this magnificent yacht are as extravagant as they are spacious. Dominated by a vast salon with custom furnishings and a formal dining area, the layout includes four luxurious staterooms on the lower level including an absolutely magnificent full-beam master with a king-size bed and large vertical ports in the hullsides. The VIP stateroom and guest cabins are equally luxurious, and twin crew cabins aft are accessed directly from the afterdeck. Forward of the salon, the pilothouse features comfortable lounge seating, port and starboard deck doors, and a convenient day head. Additional features include a massive, state-of-the-art engineroom, extended swim platform, 1,500-pound davit, watermaker, and Naiad stabilizers. A seriously heavy yacht, 1,550hp Cats cruise the Hatteras 80 at 22 knots (mid 20s top).

Not Enough Resale Data to Set Values

Length	79'10	Fuel	2,858 gals.
Beam	21'3"	Water	326 gals.
Draft	5'4"	Waste	388 gals.
Weight	190,000#	Hull Type	Modified-V
Clearance, Arch	21'1"	Deadrise Aft	3°

Hatteras 82 Convertible

For a brief time, the Hatteras 82 was the largest full-production convertible available in the country. Indeed, a production fiberglass yacht over eighty feet was just a dream in the early 1990s, but Hatteras identified a market for such a boat with a select group of well-heeled sport fishermen. Designed as a crewed yacht (with crew quarters beneath the afterdeck, not forward), her extravagant triple-deck profile includes a two-station enclosed skylounge bridge, four staterooms with full heads, a vast salon/deckhouse galley and entertainment area, and a huge tournament-style cockpit. Notable features of the Hatteras 82 include a circular stairwell in the salon for access to the bridge, a full-beam master suite with his-and-her heads, utility/work room, large observation (mezzanine) deck overlooking the cockpit, and an optional day head on the deckhouse level. The huge motors are almost lost in the spacious standup engineroom with its direct cockpit access. Twin 1,450hp 16V92 Detroit diesels cruise at 20 knots (about 24 knots top), and a pair of Duetz 12V-604s cruise at 24 knots and top out at around 28 knots. Note that the Hatteras 86 and 90 Convertible models are basically the same boat with larger cockpits.

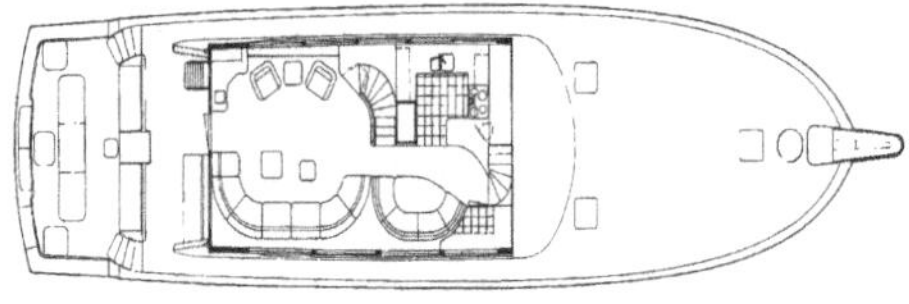

Not Enough Resale Data to Set Values

Length	82'8"	Fuel	4,210 gals.
Beam	21'5"	Water	840 gals.
Draft	6'6"	Waste	220 gals.
Weight	196,000#	Hull Type	Modified-V
Clearance	26'5"	Deadrise Aft	4°

Hinckley

Quick View

- Hinckley was founded in 1928 when Henry Hinckley began building small boats in Southwest Harbor, Maine.
- By the end of the 1950s Hinckley had become the largest producer of wooden sailing auxiliaries in the US while building a reputation for quality craftsmanship and construction.
- While Hinckley had built many powerboats over the years, the demand for sailboats was so strong that the company focused on this market exclusively until the early 1990s.
- In 1993 Hinckley broadened its product line with the introduction of the trend-setting Hinckley 36 Picnic Boat, a Downeast-style day boat with waterjet propulsion.
- An innovative company, Hinckley was experimenting in fiberglass in 1950, a decade before the rest of the industry. Hinckley introduced its own joystick control system years before the large engine manufacturers.
- Hinckley has been owned by several private equity firms in recent years. It is currently owned by Scout Partners LLC, a Rhode Island based investment company.

Hinckley Yachts • Southwest Harbor, ME • www.hinckleyyachts.com

Hinckley T29R

2003–Current

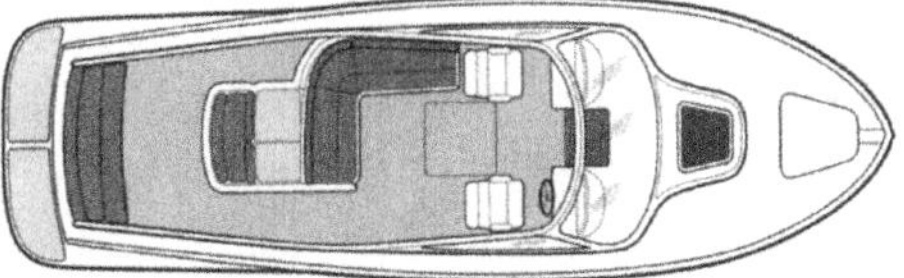

The Hinckley Talaria 29R is an expensive, jet-driven runabout whose graceful Downeast lines and meticulous finish are guaranteed to stop traffic everywhere she goes. Some have called the 29R a roadster, and it's easy to see why. The hull shape is graceful; the mahogany trim accents add the right touches of elegance; and the cockpit—with its teak helm console, Nardi steering wheel, and posh seating—is reminiscent of an old-time sports car. Built on a cored, Kevlar-reinforced hull, the cockpit of the 29R provides seating for ten with plenty of legroom and storage. The engine box, which doubles as an aft-facing passenger seat, conceals a sink with pressure water and cooler, while the high-end helm and companion chairs both have flip-up bolsters. At the stern is a full-width lounge with storage under. Forward, the cuddy is fitted with a V-berth and a VacuFlush head. Additional features include an electrically lifted engine box, joystick steering, teak swim platform, and bow thruster. Note the absence of a bow rail. A relatively light boat for her size, a single Yanmar 440hp diesel will cruise in the high 20s and top out at over 30 knots. Did we say expensive?

See Page 683 For Price Data

Length Overall	29'2"	Clearance	5'6"
Length WL	26'8"	Fuel	100 gals.
Beam	9'1"	Water	20 gals.
Draft	1'9"	Hull	Modified-V
Weight	8,200#	Deadrise Aft	19°

Hinckley 36 Picnic Boat

A breakthrough design that led to many imitators in subsequent years, the Hinckley 36 Picnic Boat is a premium, waterjet-powered runabout with the right mix of upper-class elegance, innovative design, and leading-edge performance. Her fully cored, vacuum-bagged hull weighs in at just 11,500 pounds, and with a shallow 18-inch draft the Picnic Boat can be safely operated in very shallow water. The long, open cockpit of the Picnic Boat is an excellent entertainment platform (the centerline engine box can be used as a seat or table), and the semi-enclosed helm allows her to be enjoyed even in poor weather conditions. Belowdecks, the varnished mahogany interior contains a V-berth, compact galley, and a big head compartment—upscale, if basic, accommodations for a cruising couple. On the downside, the cabin headroom is a bit less than 6 feet. Note that an optional extended pilothouse version with additional seating became available in 2001. Cruise at 20 knots with a single 350hp Yanmar diesel; 22–23 knots with a 440hp Yanmar. A seriously popular boat with strong resale values, over 400 were built before she was replaced in 2008 with a new Picnic Boat model.

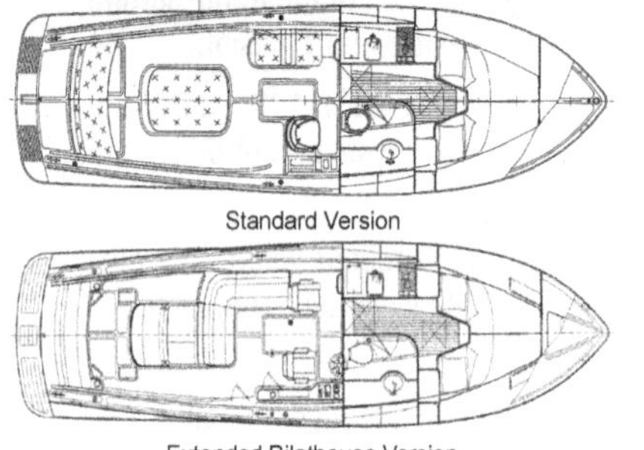

Standard Version

Extended Pilothouse Version

See Page 683 For Price Data

Length Overall	36'5"	Fuel	160 gals.
Length WL	33'7"	Water	35 gals.
Beam	10'0"	Clearance	11'4"
Draft	1'6"	Hull	Modified-V
Weight	11,850#	Deadrise Aft	15°

Hinckley Talaria 40

A beautifully styled yacht whose flawless finish is a Hinckley trademark, the Talaria 40 bears a strong resemblance to her hugely successful predecessor, the Hinckley 36 Picnic Boat. Both are essentially day boats with large cockpits and relatively small interiors, and both come with Hinckley's patented JetStick steering and control system incorporating waterjet propulsion and a bow thruster. Narrow of beam, the fully cored, shallow-draft hull of the Talaria 40 is notable for its high-tech composite construction and generous tumblehome at the transom. The pilothouse is arranged with port and starboard helm seats as well as facing L-shaped settees aft of the helm. Additional seating is found in the cockpit, beyond the shelter of the hardtop, and both the cockpit and pilothouse are on a single level. The two aft-facing cockpit settees can be raised electrically for engine access. While the Talaria's interior is small for a 40-footer, the accommodations are nonetheless elegant and certainly adequate for a weekend cruise. An exhilarating boat to drive, the price of ownership is high. Twin 440hp Yanmar diesels matched to Hamilton waterjets cruise the Talaria 40 at 28 knots and reach a top speed of 32–33 knots.

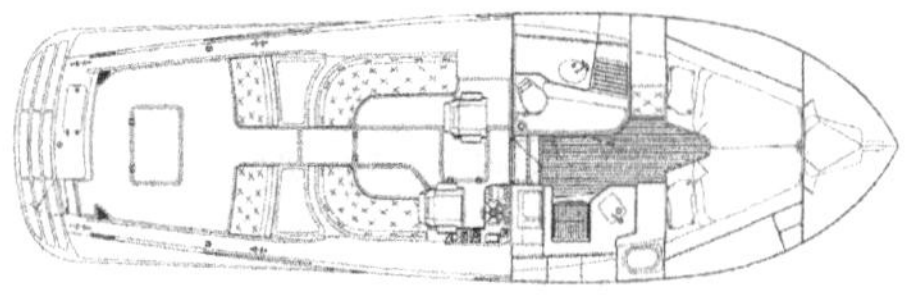

See Page 683 For Price Data

Length Overall	40'1"	Clearance	8'7"
Length WL	37'1"	Fuel	340 gals.
Beam	12'5"	Water	80 gals.
Draft	2'3"	Hull Type	Modified-V
Weight	26,000#	Deadrise Aft	16°

Hinckley Talaria 42

1990–98

The Hinckley Talaria 42 is an elegant Downeast cruiser for those able to afford the luxury of owning a finely crafted yacht from one of America's preeminent boat builders. (Note that she was introduced in 1990 as a 39-footer—two were built, basically the same as the 42 but with a smaller cockpit.) Constructed on a Kevlar-strengthened, semi-displacement hull with a long, prop-protecting keel, the superior craftsmanship of the Talaria is evident in every corner of the boat. Two floorplans were offered: a single-stateroom layout with a spacious salon and the galley down, and a two-stateroom arrangement with the galley in the salon. A lower helm is standard, and the beautiful teak interior woodwork is flawless. (Note that the cabin sole "floats" on rubber bushings to reduce vibration.) Additional features include wide side decks, an underwater exhaust system, teak cockpit sole, radar mast and a big cockpit. Among several engine options, a single 435hp Cat (or 520hp MAN) diesel will cruise at 16–17 knots and reach a top speed of around 22 knots. Of the 17 built, only one Talaria 42 was delivered with twin engines.

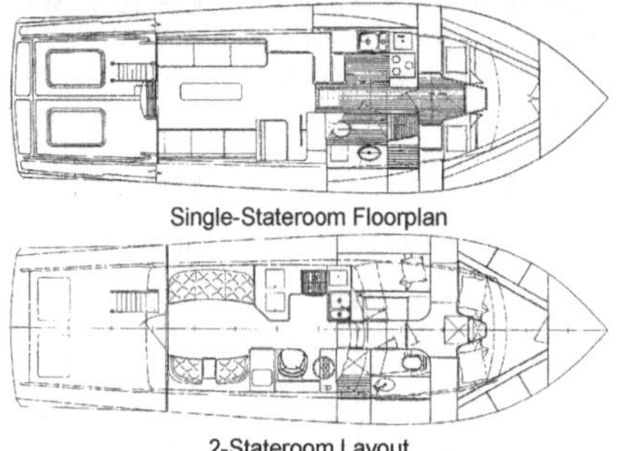
Single-Stateroom Floorplan

2-Stateroom Layout

Not Enough Resale Data to Set Values

Length Overall	41'9"	Fuel	400 gals.
Length WL	38'7"	Water	110 gals.
Beam	13'8"	Clearance	12'6"
Draft	4'4"	Hull	Semi-Disp.
Weight	22,000#	Deadrise Aft	5°

Hinckley Talaria 44 Express

1999–2008

An enlarged version of Hinckley's successful 36 Picnic Boat, the Talaria 44 is an advanced, twin-waterjet cruising yacht of the highest order. This is a beautifully crafted (and very expensive) boat, easily handled with an excellent ride and remarkable maneuverability. Built on an efficient modified-V hull with moderate beam, her high-tech construction features a Kevlar outer skin, a carbon-fiber inner skin and balsa coring in the hullsides and bottom. The heart of the Talaria is her spacious, semi-enclosed deckhouse with its plush settees, dinette table, stylish helm and visually stunning joinery. (The settees can be raised on hydraulic rams for access to the engines.) Belowdecks, the Talaria was offered with one or two staterooms. Neither floorplan can be called roomy, but the legendary Hinckley reputation for craftsmanship is on display in every corner. Notable features include a grain-matched teak interior, aft-facing cockpit seating, wide side decks (but no bow rails), shallow draft, and a JetStick control system for easy docking. Twin 440hp Yanmar diesels, matched to Hamilton waterjets, will cruise the Talaria 44 at 25 knots and reach a top speed of 30+ knots.

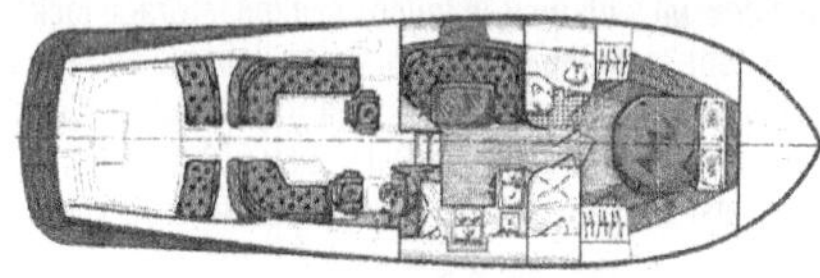
Single Stateroom

Two Staterooms

Not Enough Resale Data to Set Values

Length Overall	44'10"	Fuel	500 gals.
Length WL	41'0"	Water	100 gals.
Beam	13'6"	Waste	35 gals.
Draft	2'3"	Hull	Modified-V
Weight	29,000#	Deadrise Aft	16.5°

Hinckley Talaria 44 Flybridge

2003–Current

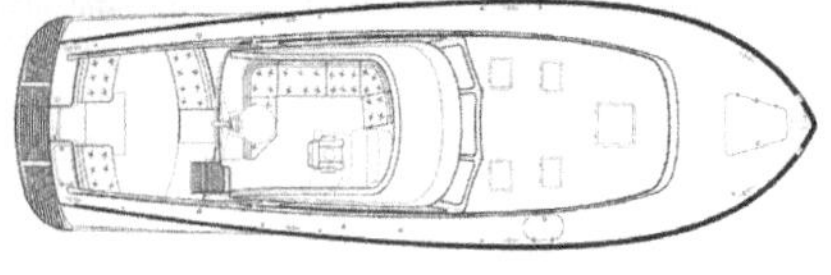

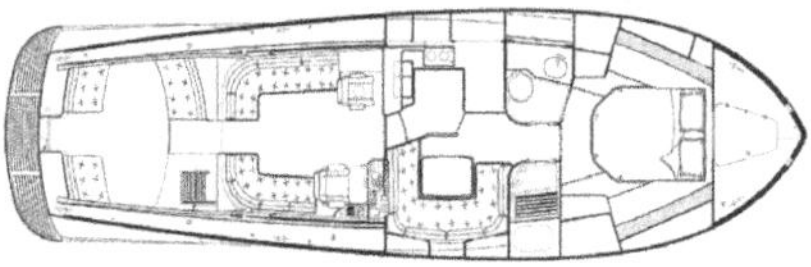

The Talaria 44 Flybridge is yet another display of Hinckley's commitment to boatbuilding excellence. This is a stunningly beautiful yacht whose blend of sensuous styling and jet-powered propulsion is as distinctive as it is unique. The heart of the 44 Flybridge is her elegant, enclosed pilothouse with its varnished cherry woodwork, teak-and-holly floor, and leather helm seat. Curved glass windows enclose the aft end of the pilothouse, and visibility from the lower helm is excellent is all directions. While Hinckley allows for several interior variations, the standard floorplan is arranged with the galley down, a split head, and two double staterooms. (Note that the shower compartment in this layout does not offer private access from the master stateroom.) The Hinckley's spacious cockpit includes built-in seating for several guests as well as a centerline transom door and six-step bridge ladder. What really sets the 44 apart, however, is her idiot-proof JetStick control system. In a word, handling is a dream—something that must be experienced to fully appreciate. Twin 440hp Yanmar diesels matched with Hamilton jet drives cruise the Talaria 44 in the mid 20s. MKII models with 550hp Cummins cruise at 28 knots.

Not Enough Resale Data to Set Values

Length Overall	44'0"	Fuel	500 gals.
Length WL	41'0"	Water	100 gals.
Beam	13'6"	Max Headroom	6'6"
Draft	2'4"	Hull	Modified-V
Weight	31,900#	Deadrise Aft	16.5°

Hinckley Talaria 55 Motor Yacht

2005–Current

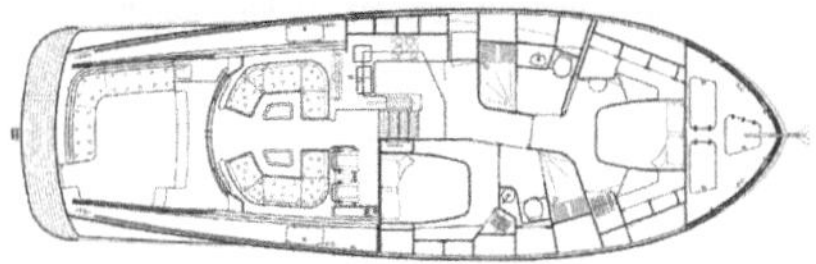

Queen of today's Hinckley fleet, the Talaria 55 Motor Yacht (note that a 55 Flybridge model is also available) takes Downeast elegance and sophistication to the next level. This is a remarkable yacht, and like all of Hinckley's Talaria models she was built with comfort as well as performance in mind. Several accommodations plans have been available since her introduction in 2005, all with two large staterooms and heads. The beautifully appointed salon of the Talaria 55 offers abundant entertainment and dining space, and electric blinds and curtains can be drawn at the touch of a button. Forward, a full-service galley features a modern drawer-style refrigerator, top-load freezer, and microwave/convection oven. Visibility from the helm is very good in spite of the long—very long—foredeck. A pair of curved sliding doors open from the salon to the 55's large cockpit with built-in lounge seating, storage lockers and a transom door. Note the extreme hull tumblehome and extra-wide side decks. An excellent performer with Hamilton waterjet propulsion and JetStick controls, twin Caterpillar 1,000hp C-18 diesels cruise the Talaria 55 at a fast 25–26 knots (30+ knots top).

Not Enough Resale Data to Set Values

Length	55'3"	Fuel	1,200 gals.
Beam	17'9"	Water	200 gals.
Draft	2'8"	Waste	100 gals.
Weight	55,000#	Hull Type	Modified-V
Clearance	NA	Deadrise Aft	16°

Horizon

Quick View

- Founded in 1987, Horizon is based in Kaohsiung, Taiwan. The company has since grown to become one of the top megayacht builders in the world.
- Horizon offers its global customers a wide range of luxury yachts from 52 to 160 feet in length.
- Over 600 Horizon yachts have been delivered.
- A world-class builder, Horizon employs hundreds of full-time craftsmen, engineers, and naval architects.

Horizon • Kaohsiung, Taiwan • www.horizonyacht.com

Horizon 70 Motor Yacht

1998–2003

A handsome yacht, an impressive blend of European styling and an affordable price—together with her excellent finish and solid construction—made the Horizon 70 Motor Yacht a viable alternative to many of the more expensive yachts in her class. She's heavily built on a conventional modified-V hull with a wide beam, cored hullsides, and a shallow keel for directional stability. Unlike most of her European counterparts with their semi-concealed galleys and cramped engine rooms, the Horizon's floorplans are arranged with the galley up, open to the salon, and her walk-in engine room is downright cavernous compared with most English and Italian designs. A semicustom yacht, several interior configurations are available from the factory. (Note that both three-stateroom floorplans shown below include crew quarters.) Notable features include high-gloss interior woodwork, a deep swim platform, radar arch, shaded aft deck, a well-arranged engine room, and a spacious flybridge with dinghy and PWC storage aft. A good performer, 1,350hp Cat diesels cruise the Horizon 70 in the low 20s (26–28 knots top).

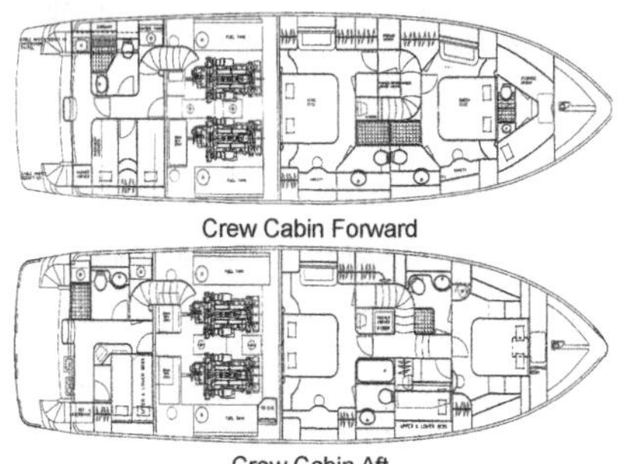

Crew Cabin Forward

Crew Cabin Aft

Not Enough Resale Data to Set Values

Length	69'4"	Fuel	1,720 gals.
Beam	18'9"	Water	400 gals.
Draft	6'0"	Waste	150 gals.
Weight	96,100#	Hull Type	Semi-Disp.
Clearance	18'6"	Deadrise Aft	12°

Horizon 70/73 Motor Yacht

An updated version of the company's original 70-foot motor yacht (previous page), the new Horizon 70 Motor Yacht features a redesigned superstructure with elliptical windows for a sleeker, more stylized look. Built on a low-deadrise hull with a wide beam, the open interior of the Horizon 70—with its mirrored salon ceiling and high-gloss cabinetry—rivals that of a much larger yacht. Horizons are semicustom boats, so each interior will differ depending on a buyer's requirements. Most 70s will incorporate a three-stateroom interior, however, with a full-beam master suite, VIP stateroom forward, and crew quarters aft. The galley and dinette are on the pilothouse level where a curved staircase provides direct flybridge access. Doors from the pilothouse provide quick access to the wide side decks, and twin staircases lead from the afterdeck down to the extended swim platform with its crew-cabin access door. A hardtop, bow and stern thrusters, and teak decks are standard, and the flybridge is large enough to stow both a dinghy and jet ski. A good performer with 1,550hp Cat diesels, the Horizon 70 will cruise in the low 20s (26–27 knots top).

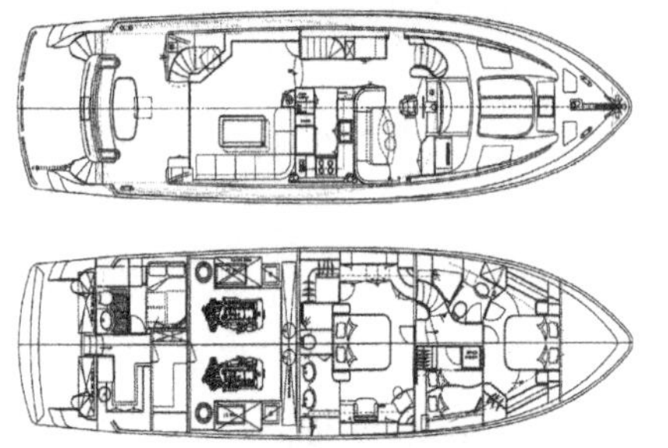

Not Enough Resale Data to Set Values

Length	73'0"	Fuel	1,750 gals.
Beam	19'0"	Water	400 gals.
Draft	6'0"	Waste	200 gals.
Weight	99,200#	Hull Type	Semi-Disp.
Clearance	20'3"	Deadrise Aft	12°

Horizon 76 Motor Yacht

Gracefully styled and competitively priced, the Horizon 76 represents a compelling blend of quality construction and luxurious accommodations. Anyone who's ever doubted the ability of Taiwan yards to deliver a quality yacht will be impressed with the level of finish found in the Horizon. Built on a beamy, vacuum-bagged hull, the lavish three-stateroom interior of the 76 is arranged with the galley and dinette on the bridgedeck level and open to the spacious salon with its rich, high-gloss woodwork. Crew quarters are aft (reached from either the swim platform or salon) and include two sleeping cabins, a full head, laundry area and access to the engine room. A flybridge overhang shades the large aft deck of the Horizon 76, and port and starboard stairways lead down to the swim platform. The flybridge is huge, and the optional Skylounge version turns this area into a small salon with an entertainment center, sofa, and dinette. Additional features include secure side decks, fore and aft boarding gates built into the bulwarks, bow thruster, and a king berth in the master stateroom. Cat 1,400hp diesels cruise at 20 knots (mid 20s top).

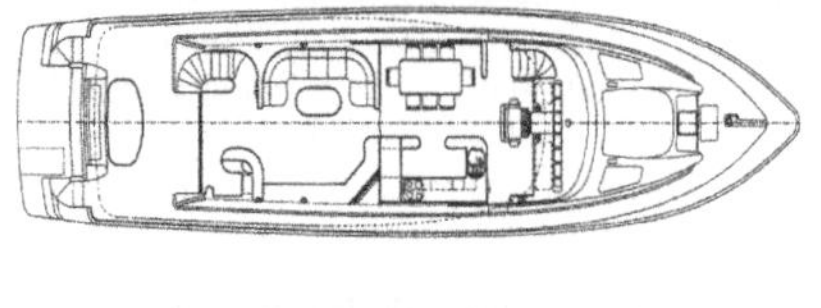

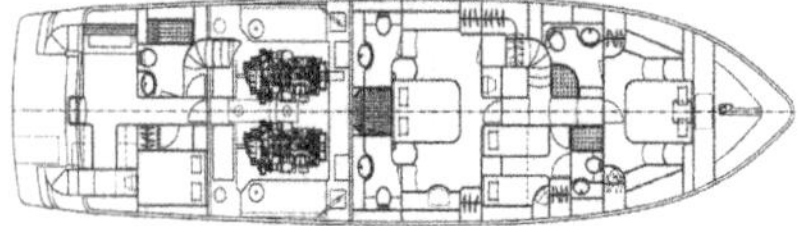

Not Enough Resale Data to Set Values

Length Overall	76'0"	Fuel	1,930 gals.
Length WL	64'2"	Water	400 gals.
Beam	18'9"	Waste	100 gals.
Draft	6'0"	Hull Type	Semi-Disp.
Weight	106,500#	Deadrise Aft	12°

Hydra-Sports

Quick View

- Hydra-Sports began building fiberglass fishing boats just outside of Nashville, TN, in 1973.
- By the mid 1980s, Hydra-Sports had become one of the best-known brands in the boating business.
- In 1998, production was moved to Columbia, SC, where Hydra-Sports focused exclusively on offshore fishing boats.
- In 2001, Hydra-Sports was acquired by Genmar. That same year operations were moved to Genmar's manufacturing facility in Sarasota, FL.
- Genmar declared bankruptcy in 2009, halting further Hydra-Sports production.
- In 2010, MasterCraft Boats purchased the Hydra-Sports and moved production to Vonore, TN.
- With sales flat and production reduced to historic lows, MasterCraft sells Hydra-Sports to a company called Hydra-Sports Custom Boats LLC.

Hydra-Sports Boats • Vonore, TN • www.hydrasports.com

Hydra-Sports Vector 2596 Center Console

2000–02

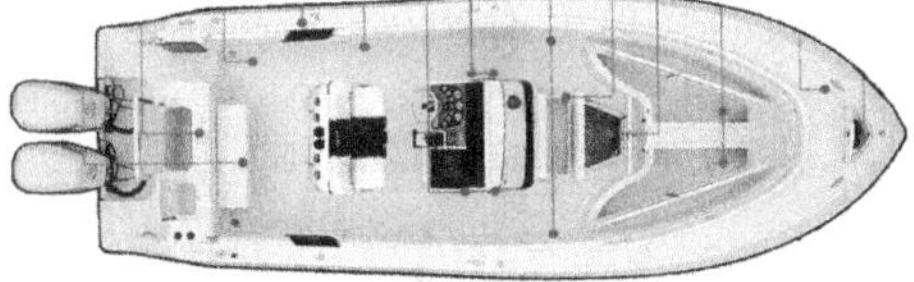

Thanks to her ultra-wide 9-foot, 7-inch beam, the Hydra-Sports 2596 is one very big center console. Indeed, most 26-foot center consoles are designed to be trailerable which mandates a beam no wider than 8-foot, 6-inches. Such a wide beam makes the 2596 an unusually spacious boat for her size and she'll prove more stable in a beam sea (albeit at the expense of head-sea performance) than most of her trailerable counterparts. Hydra-Sports has always built a quality product and the overall construction of the 2596 is to a high standard. The hull is a solid fiberglass deep-V with an integral bracket/dive platform and a Kevlar-reinforced laminate. (Note that Hydra-Sports backs their hulls with a 10-year fully transferable warranty.) A T-top and leaning post with bolster seating are standard, and a portable head is stashed in the console. Additional features include a 50-gallon livewell at the transom, lockable rod storage, a fold-away stern seat, removable cooler, and tackle storage drawers. A quality boat with a price to match, a pair of 225hp outboards cruise at 28 knots and reach 40+ knots wide open.

See Page 683 For Price Data

Length	26'2"	Fuel	236 gals.
Beam	9'7"	Water	20 gals.
Hull Draft	1'6"	Max HP	500
Weight w/225s	6,124#	Hull Type	Deep-V
Clearance, T-Top	8'6"	Deadrise Aft	23°

Hydra-Sports Vector 2796/2800

2000–05

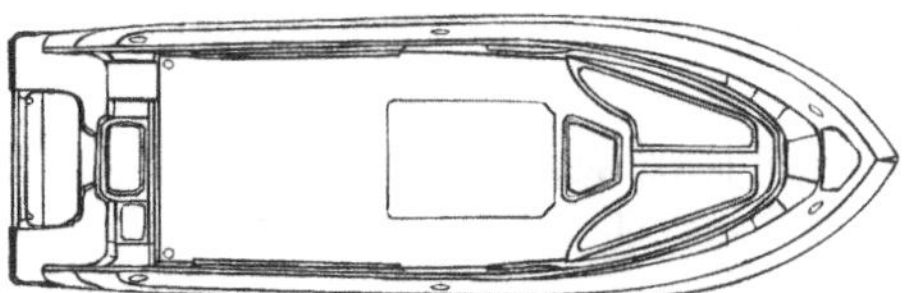

With her wide 9-foot, 8-inch beam, the Hydra-Sports 2800 Vector (called the 2796 Vector in 2000–02) is a tournament-level center console that lives up to the rigorous offshore expectations of serious anglers. This is a good-looking boat with a graceful profile accentuated by a sweeping sheer, a fully integrated bracket/swim platform, and a recessed bow rail. Like all late-model Hydra-Sports, the 2800 rides on a Kevlar-reinforced deep-V hull, and a foam-filled box stringer system makes for an unusually strong and resilient hull. Thanks to her wide beam, the cockpit is roomy enough to accommodate several anglers and their gear without being crowded. A recessed stern seat folds away when not in use, and an insulated (and lighted) baitwell is built into the transom. Additional features include a transom door, freshwater shower, a sub-console head/storage compartment, two large fish boxes forward, raw-water washdown, concealed rod storage, tackle drawers, and cockpit bolsters. A slick folding tower with an upper helm was optional. Twin Yamaha 225s reach a top speed of nearly 45 knots. With nearly 300 gallons of fuel capacity, this boat has some serious range.

See Page 683 For Price Data

Length	28'1"	Fuel	284 gals.
Beam	9'8"	Water	20 gals.
Draft, Up	1'11"	Max HP	600
Draft, Down	2'6'	Hull Type	Deep-V
Hull Weight	6,525#	Deadrise Aft	23°

Hydra-Sports Vector 2800 Walkaround

2001–05

There are less expensive choices one might make in the search a 28-foot walkaround, but for those who place a premium on construction and durability, there's a lot to like in the Hydra-Sports 2800 Walkaround. From her comfortable cabin to her deep, secure cockpit, the 2800 delivers an enviable combination of cruising and fishing features in what most would describe as a very handsome package. Built on a stout Kevlar-reinforced deep-V hull, the cockpit of the 2800 is set up with two in-deck fish boxes (macerated), a 35-gallon lighted livewell in the transom, foldaway transom seat, and a pair of aft-facing jump seats. The helm deck is a step up from the cockpit for improved visibility and extra headroom below. There are berths for three in the roomy cabin, which comes with a big double berth forward, a midships berth aft, an enclosed head with shower, and a fully equipped galley with sink, microwave, and refrigerator. Note that air conditioning and shore power are standard. Twin 225hp Yamahas cruise the Hydra-Sports 2800 Walkaround in the mid 20s and and top out around 40 knots. With nearly 300 gallons of fuel capacity, this boat has some serious range.

See Page 683 For Price Data

Length	28'2"	Fuel	284 gals.
Beam	9'8"	Water	29 gals.
Hull Draft	18"	Max HP	500
Weight w/OBs	7,225#	Hull Type	Deep-V
Clearance, Hardtop	9'0"	Deadrise Aft	23°

Hydra-Sports 2800/3100 Sportfish

A good-running boat with an integrated outboard bracket and efficient deck plan, the Hydra-Sports 3100 (note that she was called the 2800 Sport Fish from 1992–95) manages to combine all the necessary elements of a good offshore fishing boat. Hull construction is solid fiberglass, and the wide 10-foot, 7-inch beam makes for a stable fishing platform with plenty of elbow room for a couple of anglers. A bait-prep station and baitwell are built into the 3100's full-height transom, and a big lift-out fish box resides in the cockpit sole. Visibility from the raised bridgedeck is excellent, and a chart flat is built into the dash in front of the companion seat. Belowdecks is a well-arranged cabin with an enclosed head, a fully equipped galley, storage areas, and plenty of headroom. The dinette converts into a double bed, and a small aft cabin is located below the bridgedeck. Additional features include trim tabs, a large transom door, tackle drawers, molded pulpit, and cockpit washdowns. Designed to handle up to 500 horsepower, twin 225hp outboards cruise the Hydra-Sports 2800/3100 SF at 25 knots and hit 40+ knots wide open.

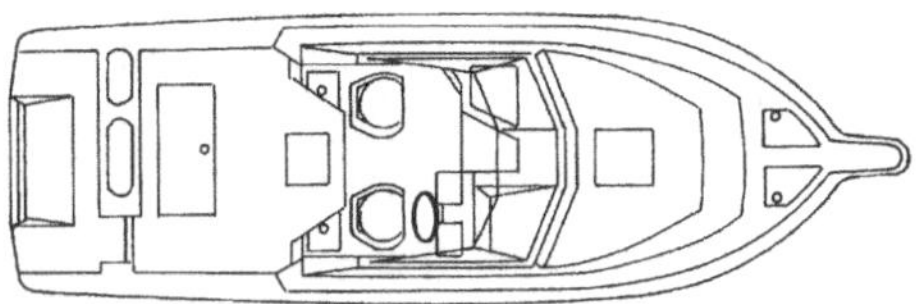

See Page 683 For Price Data

Length w/Pulpit	30'1"	Fuel	300 gals.
Beam	10'7"	Water	31 gals.
Draft	2'3"	Max HP	550
Dry Weight	7,900#	Hull Type	Deep-V
Clearance	NA	Deadrise Aft	19°

Hydra-Sports 2900 VX Express

Hydra-Sports got it right with the 2900 VX, a leading-edge express with the speed and range to reach the most distant fishing spot. Like all late model Hydra-Sports boats, the 2900 VX rides on a solid fiberglass, Kevlar-reinforced hull with moderate beam and a fully integrated transom. More fishboat than cruiser, the roomy cockpit includes a foldaway rear seat, 35-gallon livewell, insulated fish boxes, bait-prep station, and padded bolsters. The portside lounge seat on the bridge deck converts to sun pad, and there's space at the helm for flush-mounting two (small) video displays. Note the tackle box under the helm seat. Below, the well-finished interior of the 2900 VX includes a compact galley with microwave and refrigerator, enclosed head with sink and hand-held shower, and a convertible dinette forward with flip-up back rests—berths for six in a 29-foot boat! The teak-and-holly cabin sole is a nice touch, and so are the pop-up deck cleats. A walk-through windshield provides secure foredeck access. A generous 300-gallon fuel capacity delivers an impressive 400-mile cruising range. A good open-water performer, twin Yamaha 250s reach 45+ knots top.

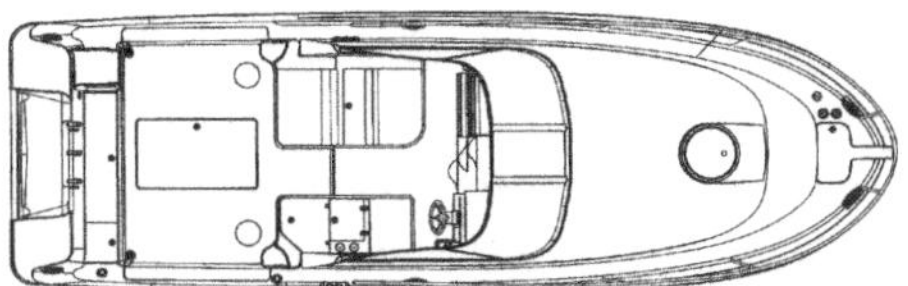

See Page 683 For Price Data

Length	29'8"	Fuel	300 gals.
Beam	9'8"	Water	27 gals.
Hull Draft	1'10"	Max HP	600
Dry Weight	8,396#	Hull Type	Deep-V
Clearance	8'9"	Deadrise Aft	23°

Hydra-Sports Vector 2900 Center Console

2006–Current

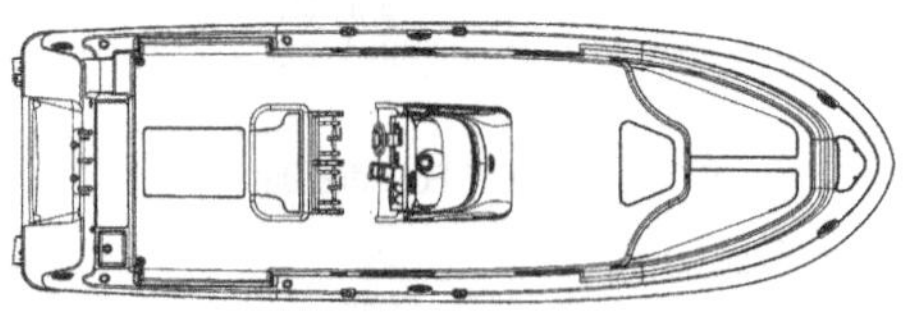

For those who value durability as much as performance, the Vector 2900 is a center console to be taken seriously. Hydra-Sports has always built a solid boat, and recent years have seen many of the company's high-quality products ascend to the upper ranks of big-water fishing rigs. Cockpit features of the 2900 include a transom rigging station with sink, foldaway rear seat, three insulated fish boxes, and lockable rod storage. A lighted, 55-gallon Kodiak livewell (with rounded corners because some bait fish can't stay alive in a rectangle) is behind the helm, and the box across the transom is designed to serve as a second livewell, fishbox, or storage box. The helm has dash space for flush-mounting two 10" video display screens. The list of standard equipment is impressive on this boat and includes a factory hardtop with electronics box, rocket launchers, and spreader lights. A roomy, walk-in console compartment contains a portable toilet, sink, and hand-held shower. Note that the windshield surrounds the entire helm—sweet. With 300 gallons of fuel capacity, the 2900 has the range to roam far offshore and stay there until the fish boxes are full. Twin Yamaha 250s top out at close to 45 knots.

See Page 683 For Price Data

Length	29'8"	Fuel	300 gals.
Beam	9'8"	Water	23 gals.
Hull Draft	1'10"	Max HP	600
Dry Weight	7,904#	Hull Type	Deep-V
Clearance	8'9"	Deadrise Aft	23°

Hydra-Sports Vector 3000 Center Console

1997–2000

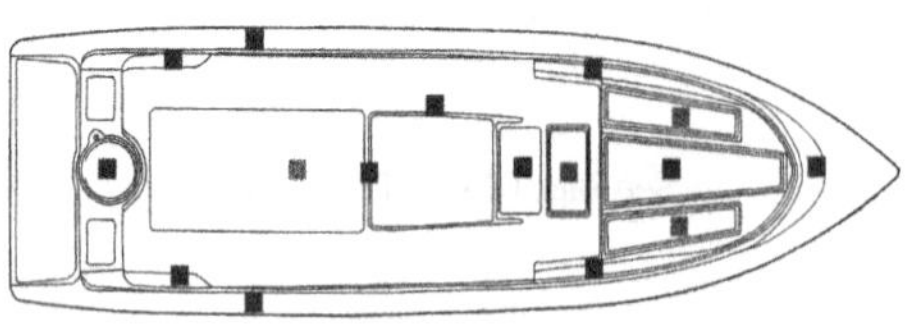

A rugged, well-engineered center console, the Hydra-Sports Vector 3000 delivers the construction and performance attributes one expects in a premium offshore fisherman. She's built on a solid fiberglass deep-V hull with a trailerable beam, a fully integrated transom platform, and Kevlar reinforcement in the keel. The deck layout of the Vector 3000 is typical of most big center consoles with the helm set far enough forward to provide plenty of fishing space aft. Like most boats of this type, the walk-in console conceals a standup head, and there's room in the dash for flush-mounting most of the necessary electronics. A large 5-foot, 6-inch fish box is located at the bow, under the casting platform, and a 50-gallon baitwell is built into the transom. A well-equipped boat in her standard configuration, additional features include an anchor locker, storage space for 20 rods around the cockpit, retractable cleats, under-gunwale tackle boxes in the aft corners, and a leaning post with drop-down bolsters. Twin 225hp outboards cruise the Hydra-Sports 3000 at 29–30 knots and deliver a top speed in the neighborhood of 45 knots.

See Page 683 For Price Data

Length	29'5"	Fuel	300 gals.
Beam	8'7"	Water	27 gals.
Draft, Engines Up	2'0"	Max HP	750
Draft, Engines Down	2'8"	Hull Type	Deep-V
Dry Weight	7,100#	Deadrise Aft	24°

Hydra-Sports Vector 3300 Center Console

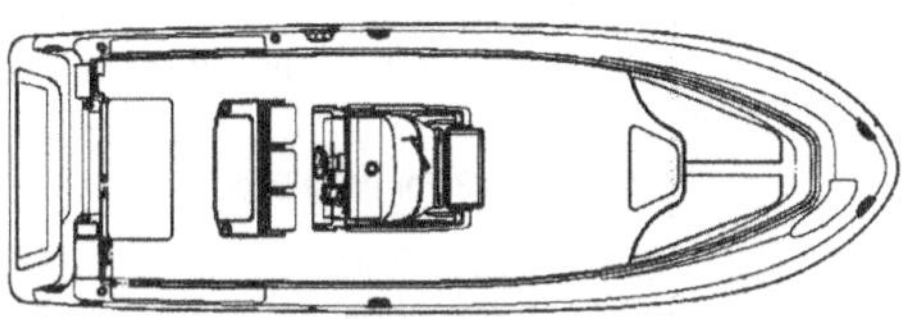

Triple outboards always look impressive, bringing forth images of high-speed performance unmatched by lesser boats. Truth is, only a few boats can actually put all that power to work with enough efficiency to justify the extra cost. The Hydra-Sports 3300 is one of those boats, a heavily built deep-V fishing machine bred for the offshore tournament wars. The 3300's generous beam creates a large, open cockpit, and her huge 55-gallon leaning-post livewell, full bait-prep station, and lockable rod storage will satisfy the demands of hardcore anglers. A pair of insulated fish boxes (with overboard drains) are forward, and a three-person, dropout bolster seat was standard. Like most modern center consoles, Hydra-Sport designers put a head inside the console, and with 6 feet, 4 inches of headroom, it's large enough to serve as a changing room. A fold-down bench seat at the transom provides additional seating. A T-top with electronics box, pop-up cleats, dual-ram steering, pullout trash receptacle, tackle storage drawers, and K-Plane trim tabs are all standard. One of the fastest boats (and smoothest-riding) on the water, triple 250hp Yamahas deliver a top speed of close to 50 knots.

See Page 683 For Price Data

Length	33'5"	Fuel	352 gals.
Beam	10'4"	Water	29 gals.
Draft, Engines Down	2'10"	Max HP	900
Hull Weight	8,620#	Hull Type	Deep-V
Clearance	7'9"	Deadrise Aft	23°

Hydra-Sports 3300 VX Express

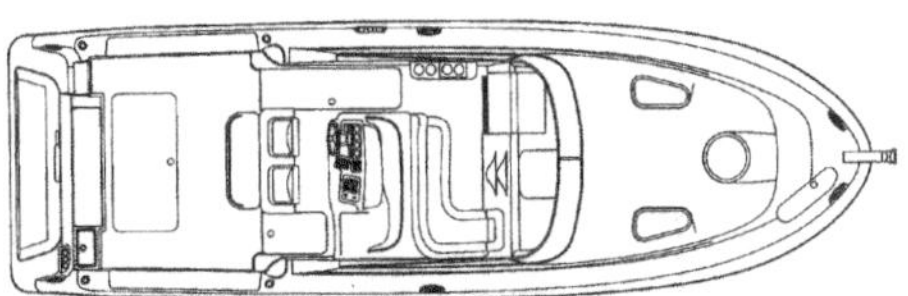

Describing the Hydra-Sports 3300 VX as an "express" is a little misleading. Yes, she has a cabin, but it's small compared to other express fishing boats her size, more suitable for an occasional overnight stay than any serious family cruising. That said, however, the 3300's mid-cabin interior is notably well finished and comes complete with a stand-up head with shower, full-service galley with microwave, a classy teak-and-holly sole, and berths for three (five if you count the flip-up pipe berths forward). If the cabin accommodations are modest in size, the deck layout is ready-made for day cruising in style and comfort. L-lounge seating is provided forward of the helm, the perfect place for guests since it's close to the driver as well being the most comfortable spot in the boat. A foldaway cockpit seat is aft, and a 55-gallon Kodiak livewell, two insulated fish boxes, cockpit shower, raw water washdown, and fiberglass hardtop with sliding overhead hatch were standard. Note that the dash flat has room for two 10" video screens. No lightweight compared with other boats in her class, the deep-V hull of the 300 VX delivers an impressive open-water ride. About 50 knots max with triple 250 Yamahas.

See Page 683 For Price Data

Length	33'5"	Fuel	352 gals.
Beam	10'4"	Water	35 gals.
Draft, Down	2'10"	Max HP	900
Hull Weight	10,500#	Hull Type	Deep-V
Clearance	9'3"	Deadrise Aft	23°

Hydra-Sports Vector 3300 Center Console

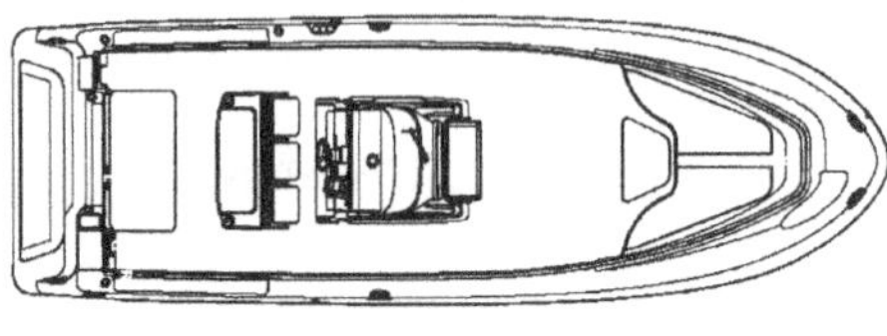

Triple outboards always look impressive, bringing forth images of high-speed performance unmatched by lesser boats. Truth is, only a few boats can actually put all that power to work with enough efficiency to justify the extra cost. The Hydra-Sports 3300 is one of those boats, a heavily built deep-V fishing machine bred for the offshore tournament wars. The 3300's generous beam creates a large, open cockpit, and her huge 55-gallon leaning-post livewell, full bait-prep station, and lockable rod storage will satisfy the demands of hardcore anglers. A pair of insulated fish boxes (with overboard drains) are forward, and a three-person, dropout bolster seat was standard. Like most modern center consoles, Hydra-Sport designers put a head inside the console, and with 6 feet, 4 inches of headroom, it's large enough to serve as a changing room. A fold-down bench seat at the transom provides additional seating. A T-top with electronics box, pop-up cleats, dual-ram steering, pullout trash receptacle, tackle storage drawers, and K-Plane trim tabs are all standard. One of the fastest boats (and smoothest-riding) on the water, triple 250hp Yamahas deliver a top speed of close to 50 knots.

See Page 683 For Price Data

Length	33'5"	Fuel	352 gals.
Beam	10'4"	Water	29 gals.
Draft, Engines Down	2'10"	Max HP	900
Hull Weight	8,620#	Hull Type	Deep-V
Clearance	7'9"	Deadrise Aft	23°

Intrepid

Quick View

- Intrepid began operations in 1983 when founder John Michel began building a 30-foot center console fishing boat from a small shop in Opalaka, FL.
- In 1990, as production of Intrepid boats grew, the company relocated manufacturing operations to the old Gulfstar facility in St Petersburg, FL.
- Intrepid's early commitment to high-tech construction earned the company an industry-wide reputation for building lightweight, high-performance hulls with superior fit and finish.
- Intrepids are semicustom boats, sold factory-direct and built to meet owner requirements.

Intrepid Powerboats • Dania, FL • www.intrepidboats.com

Intrepid 26 Center Console

The original Intrepid 26 Center Console (note that in 1997 she was replaced in the Intrepid fleet with the stepped-hull 262 Center Console) is a durable offshore fisherman whose quality construction and fast, stable ride made her a popular boat with anglers for many years. She rides on a Jim Wynne-designed deep-V hull with an integrated outboard bracket and a trailerable 8-foot, 6-inch beam. At just 2,600 lbs. (without power), the Intrepid is one of the lightest boats in her class. A good-looking boat built to high production standards, the deck layout is arranged with a 35-gallon livewell in the center of the cockpit, aft of the leaning post, with a big fish box forward and a total of six in-deck dry storage boxes. Additional storage space can be found under the console as well as beneath the padded seat forward. An anchor locker, rod holders, and under-gunwale rod racks were standard. A fast and secure ride with excellent range, twin 200hp Yamaha outboards deliver a cruising speed of 32–33 knots and a top speed of about 48 knots.

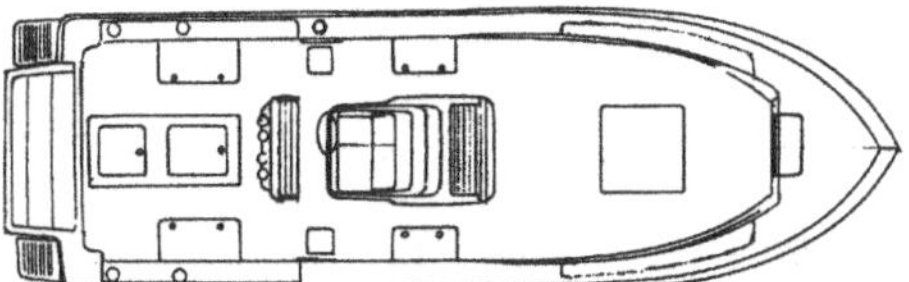

See Page 683 For Price Data

Length Overall	28'4"	Fuel, Opt.	210 gals.
Beam	8'6"	Water	25 gals.
Draft	2'0"	Max HP	450
Dry Weight	2,600#	Hull Type	Deep-V
Fuel, Std.	160 gals.	Deadrise Aft	22.5°

Intrepid 262 Center Console

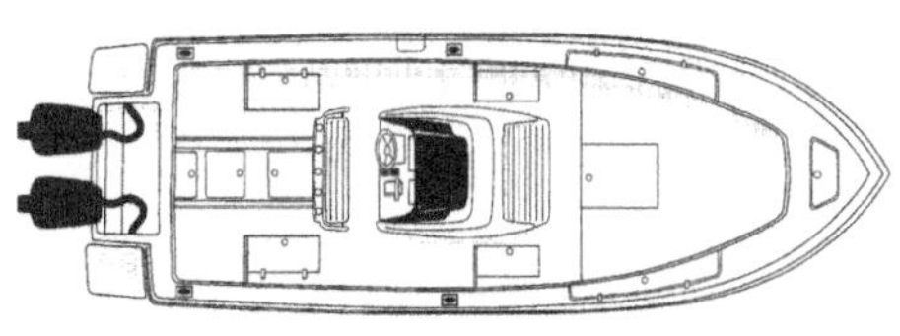

Considered by many to be among the finest 26-foot center consoles of her era, the Intrepid 262 made the cut with anglers and cruisers alike. Unlike the original Intrepid 26 Center Console (1988–96), the 262 is built on a high-performance stepped hull with a wider beam and significantly more deck space. The 262 was offered in two configurations: Plan A has a marine head forward, and Plan B replaces the head with more deck space. The deck layout is arranged with a livewell in the center of the cockpit, aft of the leaning post, a big fish box (with macerator), and four in-deck storage boxes flanking the cockpit and the center console. Additional storage compartments are located in the forward gunwales as well as beneath the cushioned seat in front of the console. An anchor locker, rod holders, trim tabs, and under-gunwale rod racks are standard. An extremely well finished boat (and priced accordingly), twin 200hp outboards cruise the Intrepid 262 Center Console at a fast 35 knots and deliver a top speed in the neighborhood of 52–54 knots. Intrepid reportedly quit building this boat only to address a backlog of orders on their larger, more profitable models.

See Page 683 For Price Data

Length	26'2"	Fuel, Std.	145 gals.
Beam	9'1"	Fuel, Opt.	190 gals.
Hull Draft	22"	Water	NA
Dry Weight	2,600#	Hull Type	Deep-V
Clearance	NA	Deadrise Aft	22.5°

Intrepid 289 Center Console

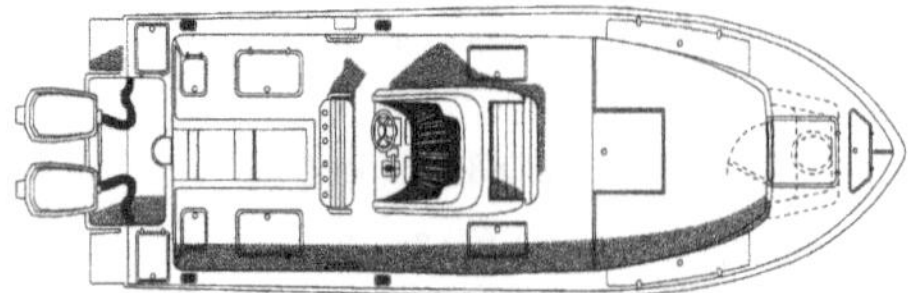

In a diverse field of offshore center consoles, the Intrepid 289 stands apart for her quality high-tech construction and high-performance stepped hull design—twin features that have placed Intrepid products at the forefront of modern fishing boat manufacturers. Vacuum bagged PVC core construction and a Kevlar-reinforced glass laminate make the 289 a strong and relatively lightweight boat for her size, and her stepped hull goes a long way toward reducing drag, particularly at higher speeds. While the deck layout is fairly straightforward—storage boxes, a large in-deck fish box, transom livewell, and a well-arranged helm—the head compartment is at the bow rather than concealed in the console as with so many other center consoles this size. Additional features include recessed oil fills, anchor locker, macerator for the fish box, trim tabs, dive platform and boarding ladder. A good-selling boat during her production years (and still much in demand on the secondary market), a pair of 200hp Mercury outboards cruise the Intrepid 289 at 30 knots and reach a top speed in the neighborhood of 45 knots.

See Page 683 For Price Data

Length w/Bracket	28'9"	Fuel	193 gals.
Beam	9'1"	Water	20 gals.
Hull Draft	2'0"	Max HP	450
Dry Weight	3,200#	Hull Type	Deep-V
Clearance	5'2"	Deadrise Aft	22.5°

Intrepid 289 Walkaround

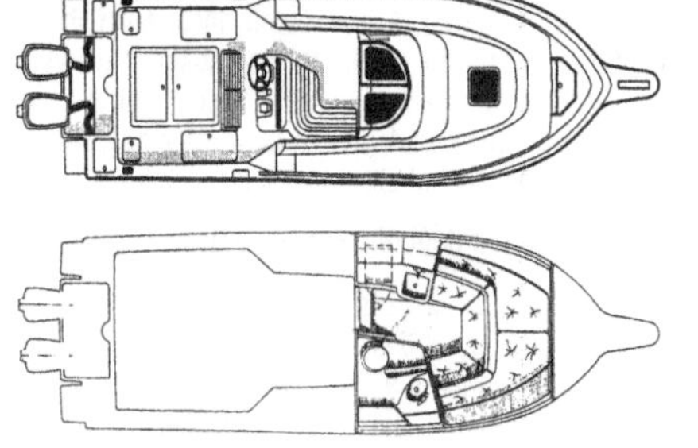

The Intrepid 289 is a lightweight walkaround fisherman whose sleek appearance, roomy interior and excellent on-deck seating will appeal to those seeking a family-style fishing boat with some weekend cruising capabilities. Like all late-model Intrepid designs, she was constructed on a high-tech lightweight hull with a stepped bottom surface for improved offshore performance. Her relatively wide beam results in some excellent accommodations below, better than one might normally expect in a walkaround this size. Aside from berths for two, the 289 boasts an enclosed head with shower, a serviceable galley with sink and cooler, and three opening cabin ports for ventilation. An L-shaped lounge seat is standard just forward of the helm console, and the cockpit is fitted with fish boxes, livewells, dry storage and a wide helm seat. Additional features include a bow pulpit and anchor locker forward, wide side decks with sturdy handrails, and a small dive platform. A very dry ride in a chop, twin 200hp Mercury outboards cruise easily at 30 knots and reach a top speed in the neighborhood of 45 knots.

See Page 684 For Price Data

Length w/Bracket	28'9"	Fuel	193 gals.
Beam	9'1"	Water	15 gals.
Hull Draft	2'0"	Max HP	450
Dry Weight	3,400#	Hull Type	Deep-V
Clearance	5'2"	Deadrise Aft	22.5°

Intrepid 300 Center Console

The Intrepid 300 is a custom-quality center console whose exhilarating 50-knot performance makes her one of the fastest boats of her type on the water. Intrepid is an industry leader when it comes to engineering and construction. All of their current models are built on stepped hulls, foam-cored to reduce weight, and finished to some of the highest standards in the business. Because Intrepids are sold factory-direct, each tends to be a semicustom boat built to meet the requirements of the buyer. As far as the 300 is concerned, she's a particularly handsome boat with a sleek profile, top-quality components, and near-flawless gelcoat. Typically, the 300's deck layout will include a two-person helm seat, custom console seat, forward seating, in-deck fish box, rod lockers, and in-deck circulating livewell. Molded steps forward provide easy access to the bow platform, and the helm console—which houses a head and sink—is designed to accommodate the latest flat-screen electronics. A removable rear bench seat and Intrepid's signature hullside dive door are popular options. Not inexpensive, twin 250hp Mercs will reach top speeds well in excess of 50 knots.

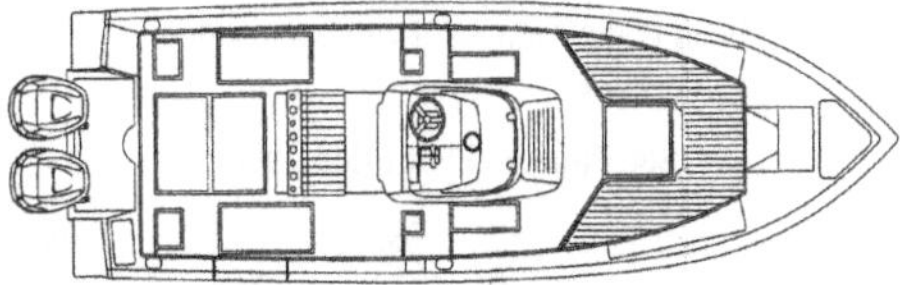

See Page 684 For Price Data

Length	30'0"	Fuel, Opt.	214 gals.
Beam	9'6"	Water	30 gals.
Draft, Up	1'10"	Max HP	500
Draft, Down	3'0"	Hull Type	Deep-V
Fuel, Std.	180 gals.	Deadrise Aft	22°

Intrepid 310 Walkaround

2004–Current

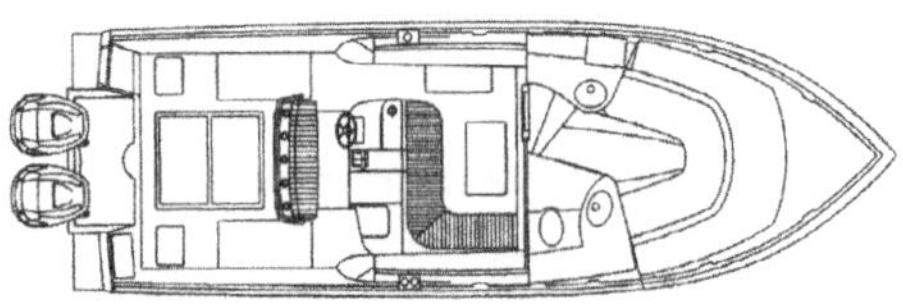

More luxury sportboat than all-out fisherman, the Intrepid 310 Walkaround offers many of the features found in larger Intrepid models in a more affordable compact package. Like her siblings, the 310 rides on a high-performance stepped hull with Divinycell coring in the topsides and a solid fiberglass bottom. While anglers will find room enough in the cockpit for fishing, the layout of the 310 is perhaps better suited for entertaining and cruising. Intrepid's signature L-shaped lounge forward of the helm offers comfortable seating for three, and few hard-core fishing boats can equal the 310's posh cabin amenities with its standard galley and enclosed stand-up head with sink, vanity, and shower. What sets this boat apart from the norm, however, is her meticulous workmanship and near-flawless finish. Because the 310 is really a semicustom boat, no two are exactly alike and each reflects the preferences of her owner. A bow pulpit, insulated fish box, trim tabs and transom door are standard, but just about everything else is optional including a removable rear bench seat and Intrepid's popular hullside dive door. A great rough-water ride, twin Yamaha 250s will hit a top speed of close to 45 knots.

See Page684 For Price Data

Length w/Pulpit	32'8"	Fuel	180 gals.
Hull Length	31'0"	Water	30 gals.
Beam	9'8"	Max HP	600
Hull Draft	2'0"	Hull Type	Deep-V
Weight	9,000#	Deadrise Aft	22.5°

Intrepid 322 Console Cuddy

1996–2003

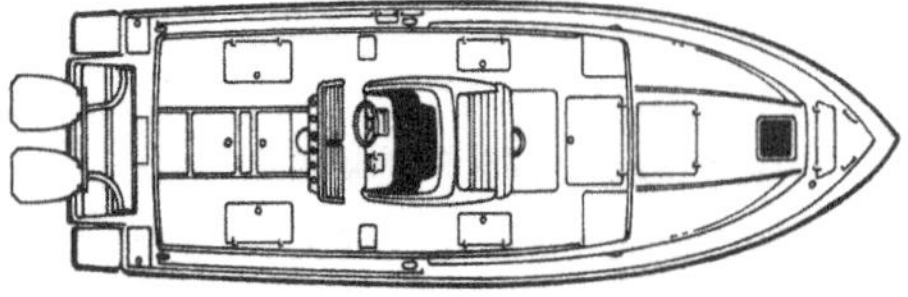

Although she bears a strong resemblance to Intrepid's earlier Intrepid 30 Cuddy, the Intrepid 322 carries a bit more beam than her predecessor, and—more importantly—she rides on Intrepid's more recent high-performance stepped-hull design. This is a well-crafted boat with lightweight foam-cored hull construction and excellent fit and finish. Her deck is flush from transom to cuddy, and fishing features include two in-deck fish boxes, transom-mounted livewells, good storage, wraparound coaming, and a well-designed console with space for flush-mounting some electronics. The generous beam of the 322 provides plenty of walkaround space between the console and gunnels, and while the cuddy is small, it does provide a couple of facing seats and sitting headroom in addition to the V-berths. (A head was optional.) An anchor locker is standard, and the gas and oil fills are hidden under clear plastic coaming hatches—a nice touch. Twin Mercury 250hp outboards cruise the Intrepid 322 at a fast (and dry) 35 knots and reach top speeds of around 50 knots. Note that the Intrepid 322 Open is the same boat without a cuddy.

See Page 684 For Price Data

Length	32'2"	Fuel, Opt	300 gals.
Beam	9'1"	Water	22 gals.
Hull Draft	2'0"	Max HP	500
Dry Weight	3,300#	Hull Type	Deep-V
Fuel, Std	240 gals.	Deadrise Aft	22.5°

Intrepid 323 Cuddy

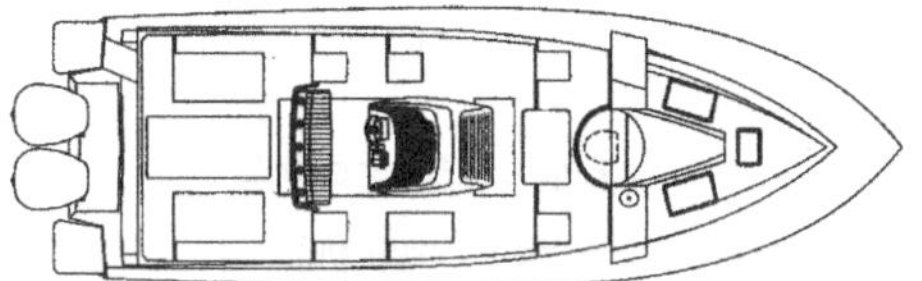

The Intrepid 323 Cuddy offers an impressive blend of quality and performance in a side-console dayboat designed mostly for cruising, but versatile enough to be set up for serious fishing. Like all late-model Intrepid products, the 323 rides on a single-step deep-V hull known for its soft ride and agile handling characteristics. There are several innovative features on this boat, beginning with a pop-up console electronics display and Intrepid's signature lounge seating forward of the console. A transom door and insulated port fish box are standard in the cockpit, and small dive platforms flank the outboard engines. Forward is a flush cuddy cabin with a V-berth, hanging locker, and a space-saving head that swivels out from under the step at the touch of a button. (A small galley pod was optional.) Standard features include cabin carpet, trim tabs, and a thru-bow anchor chute. It's important to note that Intrepids are semicustom boats, and just about everything in the way of equipment was optional. The 323's stepped hull is vacuum-bagged and fully cored. A popular model, twin 250hp Mercury outboards will deliver a top speed of about 45 knots.

See Page 684 For Price Data

Length Overall	32'2"	Clearance	NA
Beam	9'6"	Water	20 gals.
Draft	2'6"	Max HP	600
Dry Weight	9,000#	Hull Type	Deep-V
Fuel, Std.	208 gals.	Deadrise Aft	22.5°

Intrepid 33 Cuddy

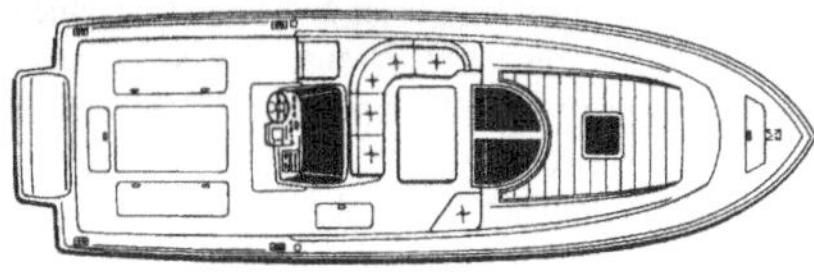

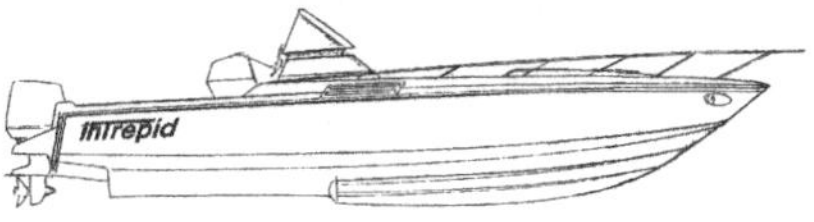

An incredibly lightweight boat for her size and one of Intrepid's most popular models during her production run, the Intrepid 33 is a high-performance day fisherman with plenty of sex appeal to go with her practical layout. Her raceboat-style stepped hull is built on a solid fiberglass bottom with Divinycell coring in the hullsides, and multidirectional pre-impregnated fabrics were used along with vacuum-bagging in the high-tech construction process. The 33's center console deck plan will appeal to those seeking plenty of guest seating in addition to good overall fishability. The layout features a semicircular settee forward of the helm and a wide-open cockpit with three in-deck storage boxes and livewell. There's room in the console for flush-mounting electronics, and swim steps are outboard of the integral engine bracket. Belowdecks, the cabin will sleep three and comes with a small galley and a private head with shower. Additional features include an anchor locker, pressure water system, raw-water washdown, and tackle station. An impressive performer, the Intrepid 32 will cruise economically at 30 knots (around 40 knots top) with twin 250hp outboards.

See Page 684 For Price Data

Length	35'6"	Fuel	250 gals.
Beam	10'6"	Water	40 gals.
Draft	2'0"	Max HP	500
Weight	5,500#	Hull Type	Deep-V
Clearance	8'0"	Deadrise Aft	22°

Intrepid 339 Center Console

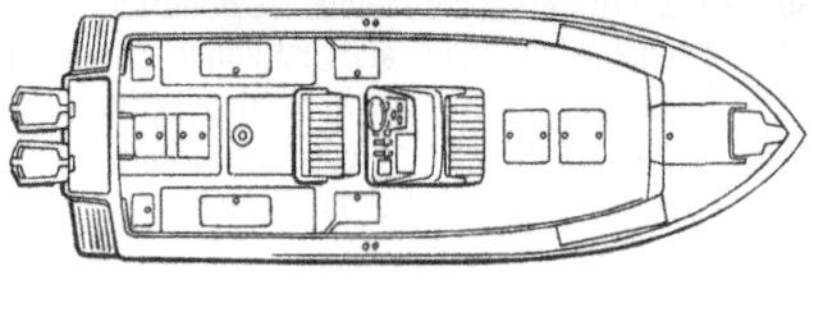

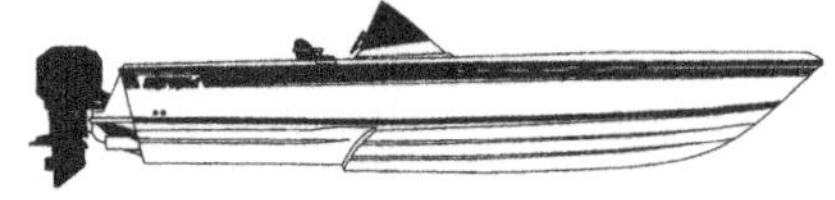

Among the larger center consoles built in recent years, the Intrepid 339 is a lightweight, high-performance fishing machine whose quality construction and balanced handling will appeal to veteran offshore anglers. Like all late-model Intrepid designs, the 339 rides on a deep-V hull with a stepped bottom—a race-proven design that reduces drag by breaking the water's grip on the hull. The hull is vacuum-bagged for strength, and foam coring is used throughout to reduce weight. The 339 isn't an overly wide boat (more beam equals less performance), but the cockpit is well arranged and the finish is as good as it gets in a production boat. The forepeak head compartment is unique (if perhaps a little curious)—enter the bow compartment, and a privacy tent deploys. Additional features of the 339 include a pair of 6-foot in-deck fish boxes, excellent storage, foldaway foredeck seating, and a superb helm console with plenty of space for flush-mounting electronics. An anchor locker, Bennett trim tabs, and twin dive platforms were standard. Note the absence of a transom door. A fast ride with twin 250hp outboards, the 339 will cruise at 32 knots and reach a top speed of 46–47 knots.

See Page 684 For Price Data

Length w/Bracket	33'9"	Fuel, Opt	295 gals.
Beam	10'0"	Water	22 gals.
Hull Draft	2'0"	Max HP	500
Dry Weight	5,000#	Hull Type	Deep-V
Fuel, Std	245 gals.	Deadrise Aft	20.5°

Intrepid 339 Walkaround

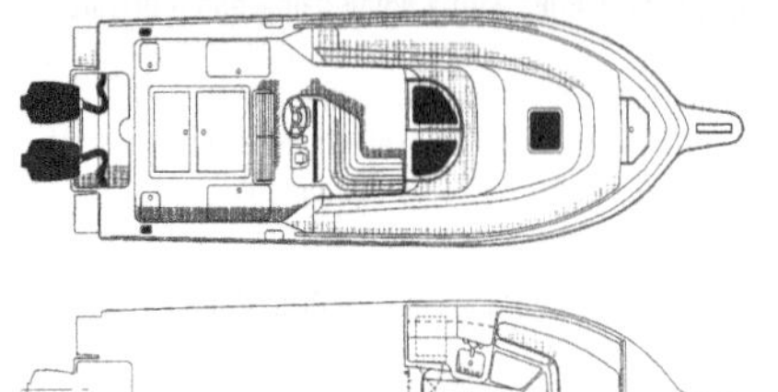

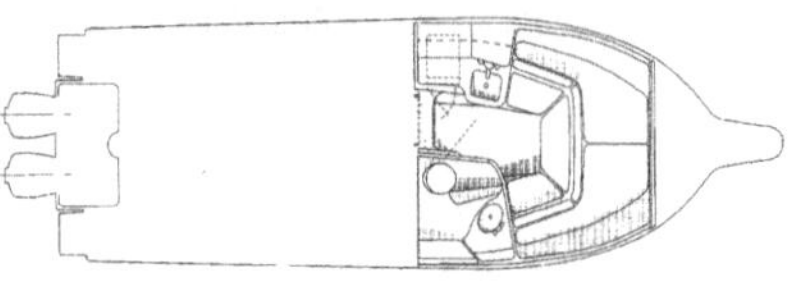

The Intrepid 339 is something different in a walkaround design. In addition to the center console and cuddy, the 339 has circular lounge seating forward of the helm—a civilized touch that family and guests will find most useful. While this pit-style entertainment area uses up some cockpit space, the extra seating turns the Intrepid into a fine family boat, which is something few walkarounds can claim. She's well built on a vacuum-bagged deep-V hull with cored hullsides and a solid fiberglass bottom. The 339 carries more beam than most high-performance fishermen, and the cockpit is roomier than you might expect in a boat of this type. Two 6-foot fish boxes and a big 35-gallon livewell are fitted beneath the sole, and a leaning post/rocket launcher, raw-water washdown, and recessed rod storage were standard. The cabin comes with V-berths, an enclosed head compartment with toilet and shower, mini-galley and overhead rod storage. The full walkaround side decks complete the utility of this versatile design. With a pair of 225hp outboards, the Intrepid 339 will cruise at 30 knots and reach 40+ knots wide open. A popular model for Intrepid, over 100 were built.

See Page 684 For Price Data

Length w/Bracket	33'9"	Fuel, Opt	295 gals.
Beam	10'0"	Water	22 gals.
Hull Draft	2'0"	Max HP	500
Dry Weight	5,500#	Hull Type	Deep-V
Fuel, Std	245 gals.	Deadrise Aft	20.5°

Intrepid 348 Walkaround

2002–04

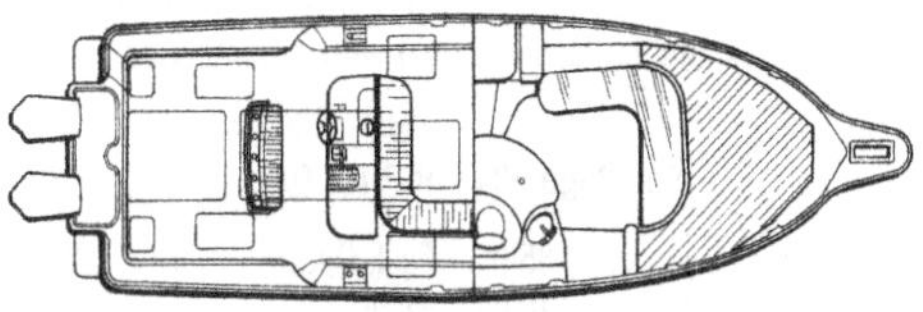

Intrepid has built a solid reputation in recent years for their series of high-performance offshore boats for buyers who place a priority on speed, handling, and unabashed sex appeal. All late-model Intrepids ride on lightweight, fully cored stepped hulls designed to reduce drag and produce exceptional speed. Like most walkarounds, the 348 is a dual-purpose boat with a fully equipped fishing cockpit and a cruise-capable interior. The centerline helm console is set well aft in the cockpit with L-shaped passenger seating forward and bench seating aft. There's plenty of space in the dash for electronics, and the helm seat retracts at the push of a button to form a leaning post. With much of the 348's length devoted to the cockpit, the interior can't be called spacious, but it is comfortable and well arranged. The V-berth rises electrically to access a storage area beneath; the head is roomy enough to take a shower; storage is adequate; and there's a microwave and sink in the galley. Additional features include wide side decks, a transom door, two large in-deck fish boxes, and a bow pulpit with anchor chute. A fast ride with 250hp outboards, the 348 will cruise in the high 20s and reach a top speed of 40+ knots.

See Page 684 For Price Data

Length	34'8"	Fuel	258 gals.
Beam	10'6"	Water	40 gals.
Hull Draft	24"	Max HP	600
Dry Weight	7,000#	Hull Type	Deep-V
Clearance w/Top	8'7"	Deadrise Aft	22.5°

Intrepid 350 Walkaround

2005–Current

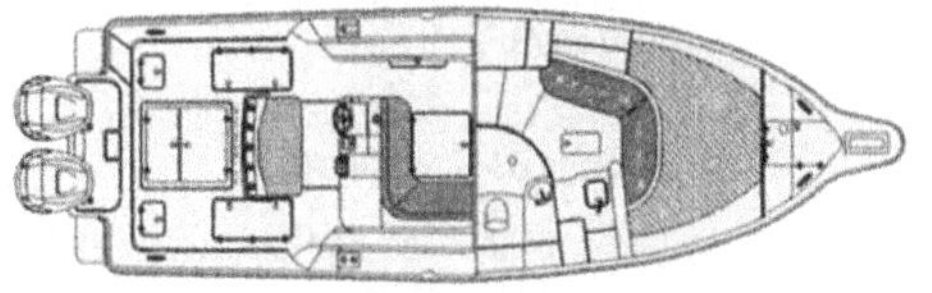

The Intrepid 350 Walkaround is a retooled version of the company's earlier 348 Walkaround (2002–04) with a slightly lengthened cockpit and new reverse transom with integral motor well and transom door. Despite her striking appearance, the 350 Walkaround is not a hard-core fishing boat. Instead, she's a high-performance cruiser with comfortable outdoor seating and efficient cabin accommodations. She's also a high-quality boat built to rigid standards. Like all modern Intrepid models, the 350 rides on a single-stepped deep-V hull with foam-cored hullsides. L-shaped lounge seating is located forward of the console, and a wraparound windshield protects the cockpit from wind and spray. An insulated fish box is aft, to port, in the cockpit along with a raw water washdown, inspection hatch, and transom door. A hullside dive door is a popular option. Below decks, the 350's cozy, well-finished cabin features convertible lounge seating, a small galley, and an enclosed head with shower. Note that Intrepids are semicustom boats; with so many factory options to choose from it's difficult to find two that are exactly alike. Twin 250hp Mercury Verado outboards deliver 40+ knots top.

See Page 684 For Price Data

Length	35'0"	Fuel, Opt.	312 gals.
Beam	10'6"	Water	40 gals.
Hull Draft	24"	Max HP	600
Dry Weight	7,500#	Hull Type	Deep-V
Fuel, Std.	258 gals.	Deadrise Aft	22.5°

Intrepid 356 Cuddy

1994–2001

One of Intrepid's most popular models during her production years, the 356 Cuddy is a versatile offshore speedster whose meticulous craftsmanship and dual-purpose layout have great appeal to family-conscious anglers. The 356 Cuddy is built on a high-performance stepped deep-V hull with moderate beam, cored hullsides, and a fully integrated outboard bracket. Like her smaller sistership, the Intrepid 339 Walkaround, the 356 Cuddy comes with lounge seating forward of the helm (but without the protective windscreen of the 339)—a comfortable entertainment area for guests. Also unlike the 339, the foredeck of the 356 is flush and without walkaround side decks. The full-size cabin comes with a compact galley, dinette/V-berths forward, and an enclosed head. (In 1998 the cabin height was slightly increased.) Additional features include an in-deck fish box, recirculating livewell, trim tabs, anchor locker, swim ladder, and a well-designed helm console with electronics storage. A good performer, twin 250hp outboards cruise the 356 at 27–28 knots and reach a top speed of 44–45 knots. Note that the Intrepid 366 is the same boat with a lengthened cockpit.

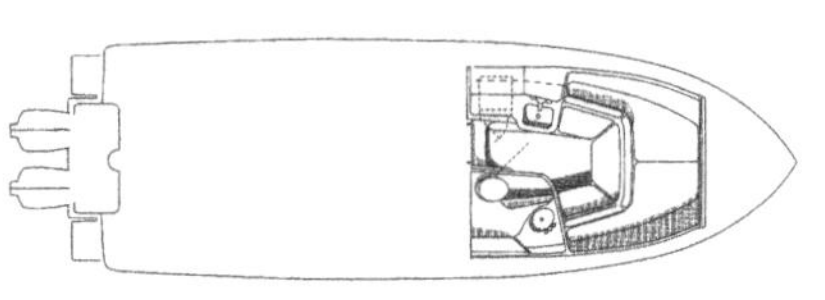

See Page 684 For Price Data

Length Overall	35'6"	Fuel, Opt.	285 gals.
Beam	10'6"	Water	50 gals.
Hull Draft	2'0"	Max HP	600
Dry Weight	6,500#	Hull Type	Deep-V
Fuel, Std.	235 gals.	Deadrise Aft	22.5°

Intrepid 366 Cuddy

1999–2003

The Intrepid 366 Cuddy is a semicustom dayboat whose exemplary finish and state-of-the-art construction made her one of Intrepid's best-selling models of recent years. The 366 is an expanded, updated version of Intrepid's popular 356 Cuddy (1994–2001) whose principal improvement is a slightly bigger cockpit. Built on a high-performance deep-V hull with moderate beam and a stepped bottom, the Cuddy retains the family-friendly deck layout of her predecessor with wraparound lounge seating forward of the helm, a large console, and a custom double helm seat with backrest. The cuddy cabin—with over 5 feet of headroom—is arranged with convertible U-shaped seating forward, a small galley with sink and ice chest, and an enclosed head with shower. Additional features include an in-deck fish box, recirculating livewell, trim tabs, anchor locker, swim ladder, and a superb helm layout with plenty of space for flush-mounting electronics. Note the twin dive platforms outboard of the engines. A fast ride even in rough-water conditions, triple 225hp outboards will deliver a top speed in the neighborhood of 50 knots.

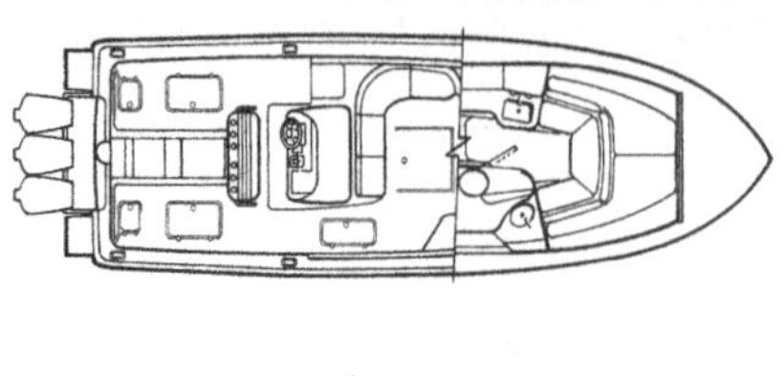

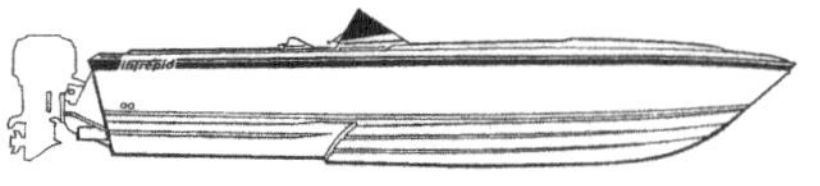

See Page 684 For Price Data

Length Overall	36'6"	Fuel, Opt.	400 gals.
Beam	10'6"	Water	30 gals.
Hull Draft	2'0"	Max HP	675
Dry Weight	6,500#	Hull Type	Deep-V
Fuel, Std.	300 gals.	Deadrise Aft	22.5°

Intrepid 370 Cuddy

2003–11

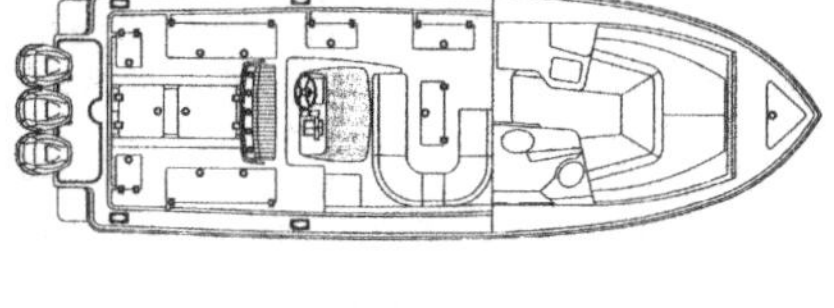

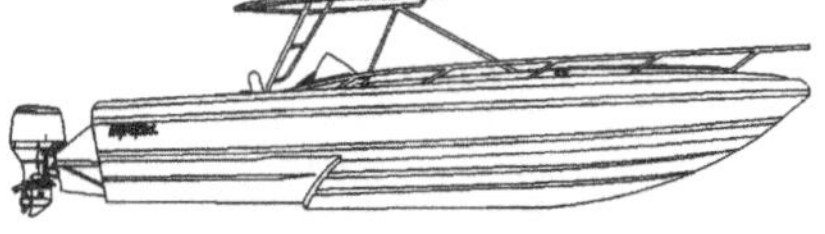

Triple outboards always look impressive, bringing forth images of high-octane performance unmatched by lesser boats. Truth is, only a few boats can really put all that power to work with enough efficiency to justify the extra cost. The Intrepid 370 Cuddy is one of those boats, a quality-built fishing/cruising machine whose smooth-riding stepped hull delivers one of the best high-speed rides in the business. Like all Intrepid models, the 370 is a semicustom boat, sold factory-direct and built to match each buyer's requirements. Aside from her muscular presence and meticulous finish, the most striking feature of the 370 is her big U-shaped seating area forward of the helm. Equally notable is her upscale cabin with its cushioned V-berth, portside galley, and roomy enclosed head with sink and shower. There's space at the helm for flush-mounting two video displays, and twin dive platforms, a recirculating livewell, and insulated fish box were standard. Intrepid's signature hullside dive door and a generator were popular options. Note that a transom door is available with twin engines only. Not inexpensive, triple 250hp Mercury outboards deliver a top speed of 50–55 knots.

See Page 684 For Price Data

Length	37'0"	Fuel	300 gals.
Beam	10'6"	Water	40 gals.
Draft, Up	2'0"	Max HP	600
Draft, Down	3'2"	Hull Type	Deep-V
Weight	11,000#	Deadrise Aft	22.5°

Intrepid 377 Walkaround

2000–08

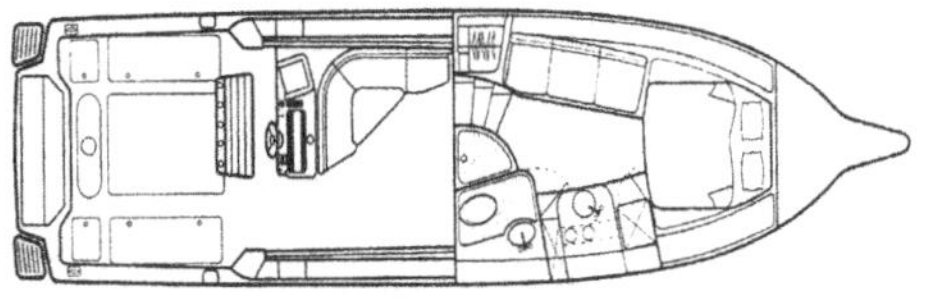

Fast and expensive, the Intrepid 377 is a semicustom rocket whose sleek profile and advanced construction set her apart from the more conventional walkaround models of lesser builders. Like all current Intrepid models, the 377 rides on a high-tech, stepped bottom hull with plenty of transom deadrise and a relatively narrow beam. The versatile deck plan of the 377 is designed to accommodate both weekend cruising and serious fishing activities. The centerline console is located well aft in the cockpit to make room for a large L-shaped settee forward, and the interior includes a compact galley, settee to port, and an enclosed head with a separate stall shower. The helm layout is superb, and an electric windlass (optional) is recessed under a hatch on the bow pulpit. Additional features include a low-profile windshield and bow rails, wide side decks, dual-cylinder hydraulic steering, good range, and a transom door. Note that a removable aft lounge seat is optional as is a dive door in the hullside to keep swimmers away from the props. A top-quality boat with near-flawless fit and finish, triple 225hp Mercury outboards will deliver a top speed of close to 50 knots.

See Page 684 For Price Data

Length w/o Pulpit	38'3"	Fuel	400 gals.
Beam	11'6"	Water	60 gals.
Hull Draft	2'4"	Max HP	900
Dry Weight	10,000#	Hull Type	Deep-V
Clearance	9'0"	Deadrise Aft	22.5°

Intrepid 390 Sport Yacht

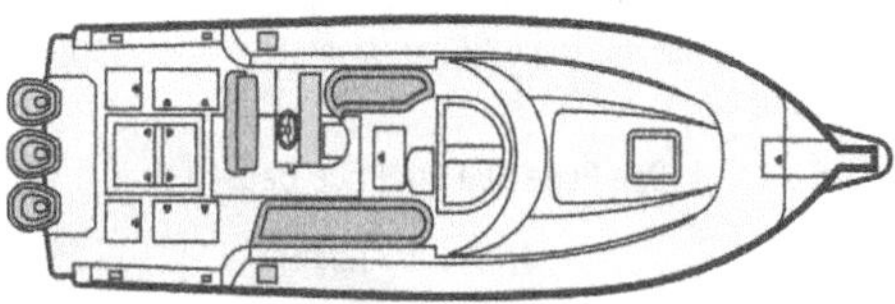

Anyone who has spent much time in the South Florida boating market is familiar with Intrepid's reputation for quality and performance. The company has been a leader in innovative design for many years, and with an extensive array of factory options it's hard to find any two Intrepids that are identical. Introduced in 2007, the 390 Sport Yacht is a bold, triple-outboard sportyacht that defines luxury in the fast lane. Built on a stepped, deep-V hull, she delivers a seriously high-octane blend of yacht-class comfort and speedboat performance. Her expansive cockpit with lounge seating forward (with electric backrests) comes standard with an insulated fish box aft, raw water washdown, livewell, and removable rear bench seat. A sleek, arch-style hardtop covers the entire forward cockpit. Below decks, the 390 Sport Yacht's posh interior with queen and convertible berths includes a roomy head with separate shower, galley with sink and microwave, and a teak-and-holly cabin sole. Note the power helm seat and distinctive shark-fin cabin windows. Intrepid's signature hullside dive door is always a popular option. Did we say fast? Expect 50-plus knots max with triple 300hp Mercury Verado outboards.

See Page 684 For Price Data

Length	41'10"	Fuel	400 gals.
Beam	12'0"	Water	60 gals.
Hull Draft	24"	Max HP	1,150
Dry Weight	15,500#	Hull Type	Deep-V
Clearance	9'0"	Deadrise Aft	20°

Intrepid 475 Sport Yacht

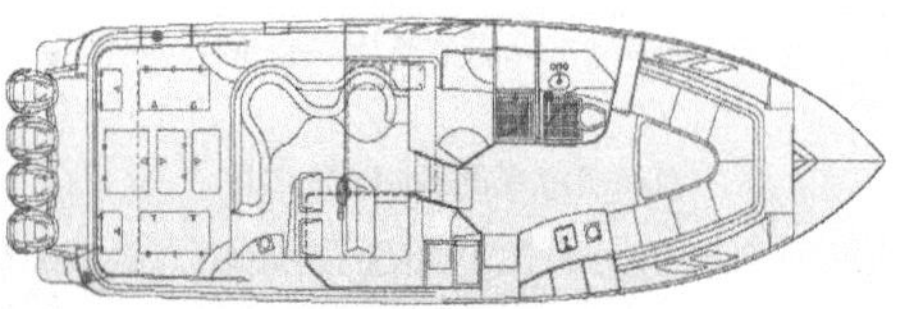

Outboard-powered boats don't get any bigger than the Intrepid 475. Flagship of today's Intrepid fleet, she occupies a narrow niche in the American performance-yacht market—the intersection of size, speed, and luxury. Indeed, with her high-tech stepped hull, exciting performance, and quad power there's nothing on the market to compete with her (so far, that is). Lounge seating for eight on the elevated bridge deck wraps around the helm with room for a full wet bar, drink cooler, and optional air-conditioning. Aft of the helm, the big 100-square-foot cockpit can be rigged for diving or fishing. The helm will accommodate two big-screen video displays in the dash, and a wraparound windshield protects against high-rpm wind and spray. Below, the 475's stylish interior consists of a dinette forward (which converts to a berth at the push of a button), two private staterooms aft, a large head with separate stall shower, and a full-service galley with side-by-side refrigerator and microwave. Headroom in the cabin is nearly seven feet. Note that the 475's outboard power results in more living and storage space than most comparably sized inboards. Four 350hp Yamaha four-strokes will top 50 knots wide open.

Not Enough Resale Data to Set Values

Length	47'6"	Fuel	480 gals.
Beam	13'8"	Water	100 gals.
Hull Draft	3'2"	Max HP	1,100
Weight	28,500#	Hull Type	Deep-V
Clearance	12'4"	Deadrise Aft	24°

Island Gypsy/Halvorsen Marine

Quick View

- Originally known as Kong & Halvorsen, Halvorsen Marine was founded in 1975 by Joseph Kong and Lars Halvorsen. Kong had been the Production Manager at Grand Banks, and Halvorsen was a well-known Australian designer of commercial and pleasure craft.
- Until 1980, most Kong & Halvorsen boats were built in Hong Kong.
- In 1990 the decision was made to shift production to new facilities in the nearby Shekou Industrial Zone (near Canton) in Mainland China.
- The Kong & Halvorsen brand was dropped in 1992 when the company name was changed to Halvorsen Marine.
- The company's series of Island Gypsy trawlers and motor cruisers are well regarded in the yachting industry thanks to their solid construction and affordable prices.
- Until recent years, Halvorsen was one of the few remaining volume importers of Asian-built trawlers into the U.S. market.

Halvorsen Marine • Australia • www.halvorsenboatsales.com.au

Island Gypsy 32 Europa

1982–2003

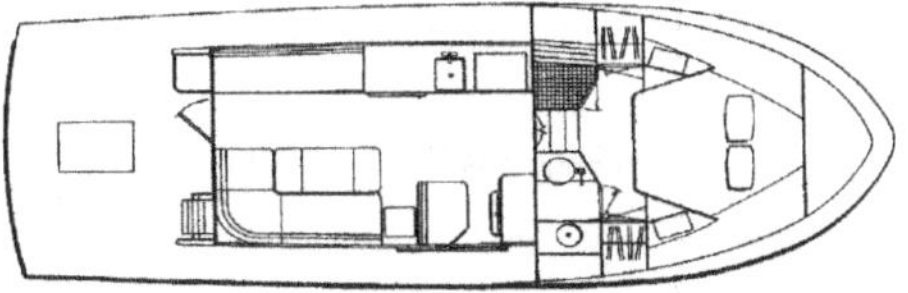

For many boating enthusiasts, the classic styling of the Island Gypsy 32 Europa is about as good as it gets in a small sedan trawler. (She is, to this writer's best information, the smallest Europa model ever produced.) Built in China in a solid fiberglass semi-displacement hull with a shallow, full-length keel, the 32 Europa's wide 12-foot beam offers considerable living space below in spite of her wide side decks. Stepping inside from the roomy cockpit, the salon/pilothouse is arranged with a convertible L-shaped dinette to starboard and a two-person settee opposite. A fully equipped galley (with oven) is forward to port, across from the lower helm. Forward is a single stateroom with a centerline island berth. A space-saving split head has a stall shower to port and the toilet/sink to starboard. As it was with all Asian-built trawlers of her era, the entire interior is finished with hand-crafted teak cabinets and trim. The aft deck and side decks of the Europa—also teak—are sheltered by bridge overhangs, and the flybridge is arranged with the helm forward and guest seating aft. A single 135hp Lehman diesel will cruise at 7 knots. Later models with a single 210hp Cummins engine will cruise at 8–9 knots.

See Page 684 For Price Data

Length Overall	32'0"	Clearance	12'4"
Length WL	29'7"	Fuel	250 gals.
Beam	12'0"	Water	120 gals.
Draft	3'8"	Waste	15 gals.
Weight	16,400#	Hull Type	Semi-Disp.

Island Gypsy 32 Sedan

1981–2001

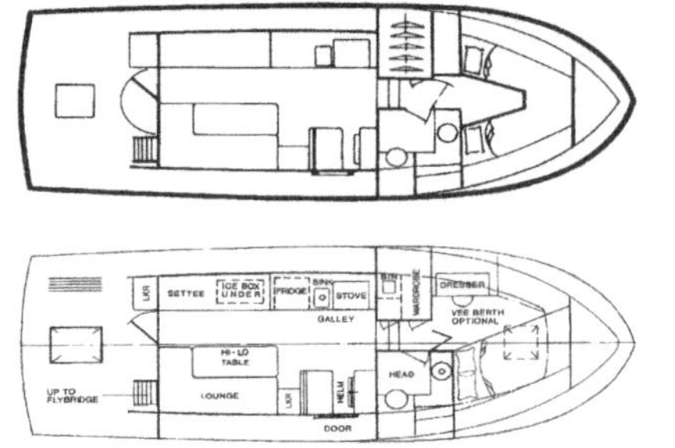

A handsome design, the Island Gypsy 32 Sedan remains among the smaller Asian-built trawlers imported into the U.S. market. She was built off and on by Halverson Marine for many years, and while the Island Gypsy 32 never enjoyed the popularity of the Grand Banks 32, she compares well with her counterpart in construction quality and finish. Built in China, the hull is solid fiberglass with hard aft chines, a full-length keel, and a skeg-mounted rudder for protection of the running gear. Stepping inside from the roomy cockpit, the salon/pilothouse area is arranged with a convertible L-shaped dinette to starboard and a two-person settee opposite. A fully equipped galley (with oven) is across from the lower helm. Forward is the stateroom—offered with V-berths or an offset double berth—as well as an adult-sized head compartment. As it was with nearly all Asian-built trawlers of her era, the interior is completely finished with hand-crafted teak cabinets and trim. Additional features include teak decks, bronze deck hardware, teak swim platform, and teak bow pulpit. A single 135hp Lehman diesel will cruise at 7 knots. Later models with a single 210hp Cummins engine will cruise at 8–9 knots.

See Page 684 For Price Data

Length Overall	32'0"	Clearance	12'4"
Length WL	29'7"	Fuel	250 gals.
Beam	12'0"	Water	120 gals.
Draft	3'8"	Waste	15 gals.
Weight	16,400#	Hull Type	Semi-Disp.

Island Gypsy 36 Classic

1979–2001

A well-built coastal cruiser with distinctive lines, the Island Gypsy 36 Classic combines timeless trawler styling with roomy accommodations and a desirable full-walkaround deck layout. She's heavily built on a solid fiberglass hull with moderate beam and a full-length, prop-protecting keel. Several two-stateroom floorplans were offered in the 36 Classic during her production years, all with the galley in the salon, either forward to port or starboard, aft of the helm seat. An L-shaped dinette in the salon converts to a double berth, and port and starboard doors provide easy deck access. A choice of V-berths or a centerline queen berth was offered in the forward guest stateroom, while twin berths or a queen berth was available in the master stateroom. Like many Asian-built trawlers, the 36 Classic came with a full teak interior as well teak decks and teak handrails. Topside, the flybridge is arranged with the helm forward and guest seating aft. Note the teak-and-holly cabin sole, folding mast and boom, bow pulpit, and teak swim platform. Many 36 Classics were delivered with a teak transom. Cruise at 7–8 knots with a single 135hp Lehman diesel. Twin diesels cruise easily at 10 knots.

Floorplan Not Available

See Page 684 For Price Data

Length Overall	36'0"	Clearance	12'6"
Length WL	32'10"	Fuel	400 gals.
Beam	13'0"	Water	200 gals.
Draft	3'6"	Waste	50 gals.
Weight	27,000#	Hull Type	Semi-Disp.

Island Gypsy 36 Europa

Few sedan trawlers of her era surpass the Island Gypsy 36 Europa for her impressive mix of versatility, range, and eye appeal—characteristics that made her one of Island Gypsy's most enduring models over the years. Distinguished by her stylish bridge overhangs and Euro-style supports, she rides on a solid fiberglass hull with moderate beam and a deep, prop-protecting keel. The Europa's two-stateroom interior (offered with V-berths or an island queen berth forward) is notable for its hand-crafted teak joinery and teak parquet flooring. Forward in the salon, the galley is to port and the lower helm is to starboard with a sliding door adjacent. Aft to starboard is an L-shaped dinette that converts to a double berth, and opposite is a settee with an insulated icebox under. Topside, the Europa's extended flybridge is among the largest in her class. A roomy cockpit is a plus, and wide side decks provide secure access to the bow. With her abundant exterior teak trim—decks, swim platform, window frames, handrails and bow pulpit—the 36 Europa will be a high-maintenance boat for those who appreciate varnished brightwork. Twin 135hp Lehman diesels cruise efficiently at 8–10 knots.

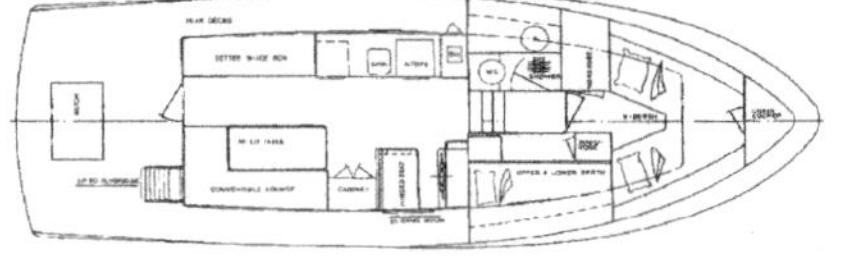
V-Berths Forward

Floorplan Not Available

Queen Berth Forward

Prices Not Provided for Pre-1995 Models

Length Overall	36'0"	Clearance	16'0"
Length WL	32'10"	Fuel	450 gals.
Beam	13'6"	Water	150 gals.
Draft	3'11"	Waste	50 gals.
Weight	25,520#	Hull Type	Semi-Disp.

Island Gypsy 36 Quad Cabin

A popular Island Gypsy model with distinctive lines (note the step-down sheer), the 36 Quad Cabin is one of several 36-foot trawler-style designs produced by the Halvorsen yard during the last several decades. She's heavily built on a solid fiberglass semi-displacement hull with moderate beam, hard chines, and a long keel that fully protects the running gear. Her unique three-stateroom interior is a rarity in a 36-foot boat. (Note that she was called the Quad Cabin because of the three-stateroom-plus-salon floorplan.) Needless to say, the two forward staterooms are on the small side, and the salon—with its combined galley, convertible dinette, and full lower helm—is rather a tight fit. Surprisingly, there's a fair amount of storage aboard, but neither head has a separate stall shower, a convenience that serious cruisers will certainly miss. Standard features include a full teak interior, twin salon deck access doors, teak decks and walkways, working mast and boom, swim platform, and a generator. Twin 120hp Lehman diesels (or 225hp Lehmans in later models) will cruise the Island Gypsy 36 Quad Cabin at 8–10 knots.

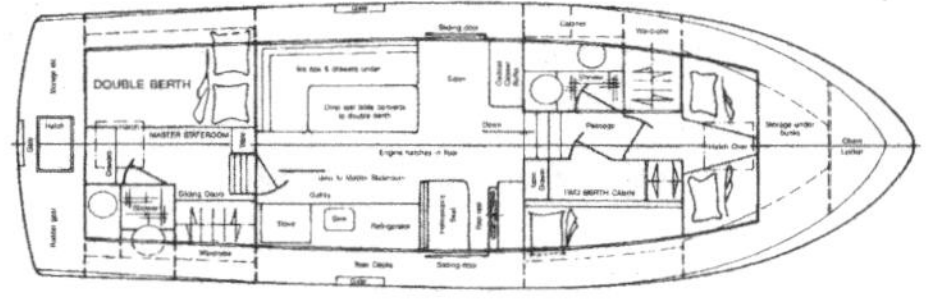

Prices Not Provided for Pre-1995 Models

Length Overall	36'0"	Clearance	16'0"
Length WL	32'10"	Fuel	450 gals.
Beam	13'6"	Water	200 gals.
Draft	3'11"	Waste	35 gals.
Weight	25,520#	Hull Type	Semi-Disp.

Island Gypsy 44 Flush Aft Deck

1979–96

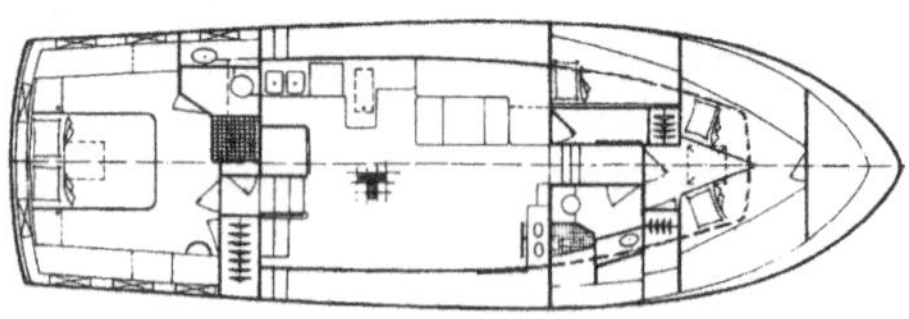

The company's most popular boat from 1978 until a factory fire destroyed the molds in 1996, the Island Gypsy 44 Flush Aft Deck is a heavily built, long-range cruiser with a traditional trawler-style profile and unusual galley-up interior. The 44 was built in China on a solid fiberglass semi-displacement hull with fairly high freeboard, hard chines, and a prop-protecting full-length keel. Inside, the three-stateroom floorplan is arranged with two small staterooms forward of the salon and a spacious master stateroom aft. The L-shaped galley is located aft in the salon, next to companionway stairs, where it's easily accessed from outside. Both heads have stall showers, and the interior is lavishly finished with Burmese teak woodwork. The decks, including the aft deck and flybridge sole are teak as are the handrails and transom. Additional features include wide side decks, folding radar mast, and a large flybridge with the helm forward. Older models with 135hp Lehman diesels cruise at 8–9 knots. Twin 210hp Cummins diesels eventually became standard (10 knots cruise/14 knots top), and 375hp Cats cruise at 16 knots. Note that production of an all-new 44 Flush Aft Deck briefly resumed in 2001.

See Page 684 For Price Data

Length Overall	44'3"	Clearance	13'7"
Length WL	38'9"	Fuel	800 gals.
Beam	15'4"	Water	400 gals.
Draft	4'3"	Waste	60 gals.
Weight	38,500#	Hull Type	Semi-Disp.

Island Gypsy 44 Motor Cruiser

1983–96

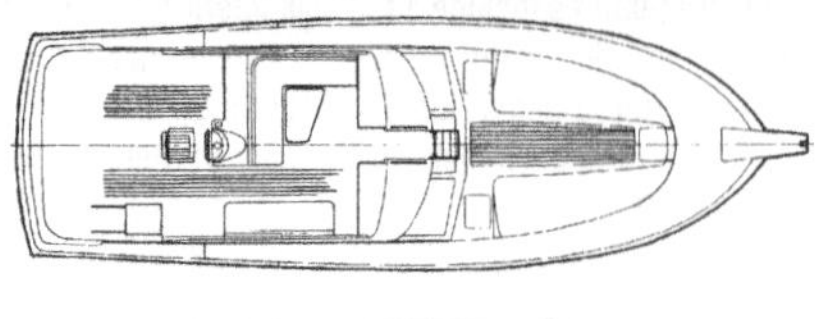

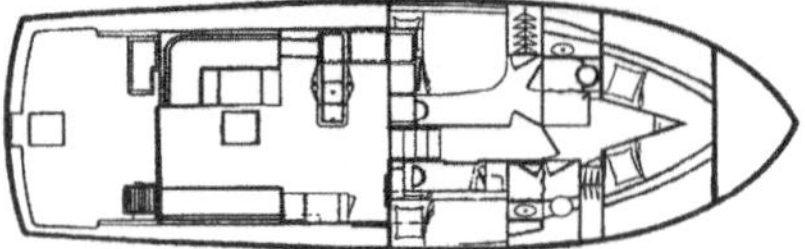

The Island Gypsy 44 Motor Cruiser is a well-regarded flybridge cruiser with just a hint of her trawler heritage. She was built in Mainland China on a solid fiberglass semi-displacement hull with hard aft chines and a full-length, prop-protecting keel. Her three-stateroom, two-head interior is rare in a boat this size—most boats under 48 feet have only two staterooms. The master stateroom with double berth and private head is amidships where the ride is most comfortable. The bow stateroom has a traditional V-berth, and single over/under berths are found in the second guest stateroom t starboard. (None of the staterooms in the Island Gypsy 44 can be described as large.) The galley is forward in the salon, opposite the lower helm. The 44's extensive interior woodwork is crafted from grain-matched Burmese teak. Topside, the helm console is aft on the bridge with guest seating forward. The extended flybridge shades the cockpit, and fold-out steps in the flybridge coaming provide convenient access to the foredeck. Teak decks and exterior trim were standard. Several engines were offered over the years. Cummins 250hp diesels cruise at 12 knots (15 knots top), and 375hp Cats cruise at 15 knots (20 knots top).

See Page 684 For Price Data

Length Overall	44'3"	Clearance	13'7"
Length WL	38'9"	Fuel	720 gals.
Beam	15'4"	Water	320 gals.
Draft	4'3"	Waste	60 gals.
Weight	38,500#	Hull Type	Semi-Disp.

Jefferson

Quick View

- Jefferson Yachts was founded in 1982 by Leon Shaw.
- Jefferson imported and marketed a series of Taiwan-built trawlers and motor yachts, all manufactured by Her Shine Marine in Kaohsiung, Taiwan.
- The first Jefferson model, the Jefferson 45 Motor Yacht, was introduced in 1982.
- The Jefferson fleet grew during the 1980s and early 1990s until their boats became some of the most popular Taiwan imports sold in the U.S.
- A downturn in the US economy—together with the 10% luxury tax of the early 1990s and increased Taiwan labor costs—resulted in a slowing market for Taiwan imports nationwide.
- Jefferson introduced its own line of U.S.-built center console fishing boats in 1994.
- With the downturn in the US economy, Jefferson declared bankruptcy in Febuary, 2012.

No longer in business.

Jefferson 35 Marlago Cuddy

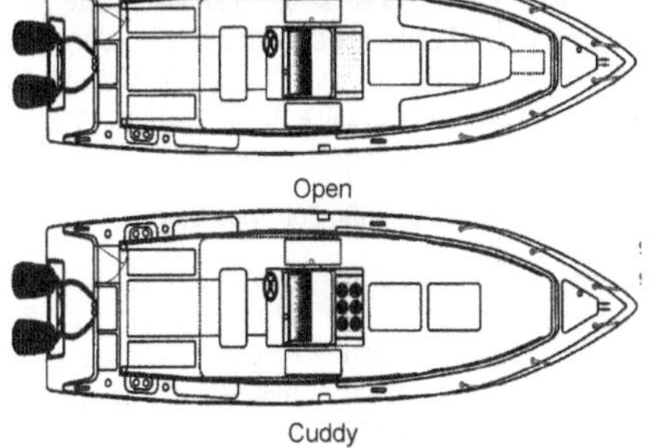

The Jefferson 35 Marlago is a high-performance center console for anglers who place a premium on speed and offshore stability. Originally built on a fully cored hull with a keel pad and a stepped transom, later models ride on a solid fiberglass bottom with the hullsides, decks, and stringers stiffened with vacuum-bagged coring. The Marlago is relatively light for a 35-footer which results in faster acceleration and higher cruising speeds with smaller engines. The cockpit features a built-in transom bait-prep center with saltwater sink, two in-deck fish boxes, transom livewell, rod lockers, and padded cockpit coaming. A rear-facing cooler seat is built into the standard leaning post, and the console houses a marine head as well as a sink and pullout shower. (Note that early models had the head between the cabin berths.) Forward, the Marlago's low-profile cuddy has a convertible dinette/V-berth and rod storage. A 50-gallon livewell that fits under the leaning post was optional. The Marlago was offered with two transom configurations: one with a transom door, bait-prep station, and livewell, or a full transom version with no transom door. An open-bow model was available beginning in 2004. Yamaha 250s deliver 45+ knots top.

See Page 684 For Price Data

Length	35'0"	Fuel, Std.	245 gals.
Beam	9'2"	Water	31 gals.
Draft, Up	1'8"	Max HP	600
Draft, Down	2'3"	Hull Type	Deep-V
Dry Weight	6,000#	Deadrise Aft	24°

Jefferson 50 Rivanna SE

2004–11

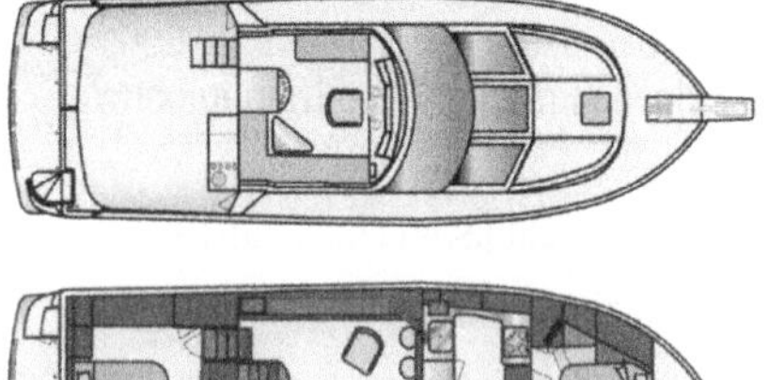

Jefferson had an enviable reputation for delivering a lot of boat for the money—something many manufacturers claim, but few actually deliver. With the 50 Rivanna, Jefferson has managed to deliver the comforts and features buyers look for in a midsize motor yacht at a surprisingly competitive price. Built on a modified-V hull with a shallow keel and solid fiberglass bottom, the standard two-stateroom, galley-down layout includes a spacious salon, a large master stateroom, and a surprisingly roomy bow stateroom with an angled double bed. The lacquered, grain-matched teak joinery found throughout the Rivanna's interior is certainly one of her more attractive features. A lower helm is optional, and the starboard sliding door in the salon provides quick deck access. A notable highlight of the 50 Rivanna is her spacious afterdeck with its standard wet bar, hardtop and wing doors. Molded steps lead down to the swim platform—a feature that makes boarding from a low dock both easy and safe—and wide side decks will be appreciated by those going forward. A modest performer with 480hp Cummins diesels, the 50 Rivanna will cruise comfortably at 18 knots (20+ knots top).

See Page 684 For Price Data

Length Overall	50'0"	Fuel	420 gals.
Beam	15'0"	Water	200 gals.
Draft	4'0"	Waste	60 gals.
Weight	37,700#	Hull Type	Modified-V
Clearance	12'10"	Deadrise Aft	12°

Jefferson 52 Marquessa

1989–2001

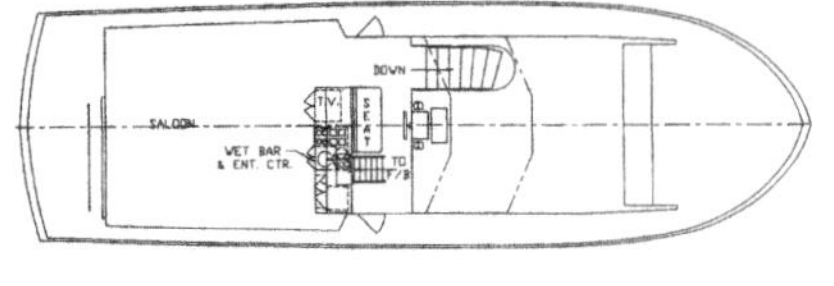

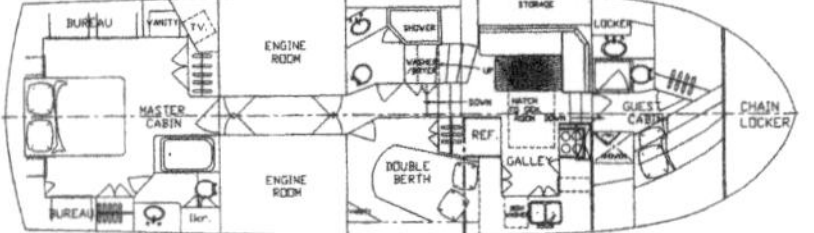

Similar in design to the old Chris Craft 501 Motor Yacht, the Jefferson 52 Marquessa is one of the smallest double-deck motor yachts ever built. Available in both an extended deckhouse version (with a full-width salon) and a standard deckhouse configuration (with an open aft deck), the Marquessa's spacious interior provides the accommodations of a much larger boat. Of the two versions, the Extended Deckhouse model was the more popular because of her greatly expanded salon. (The essential difference between this and the deckhouse version is that the side decks narrow abaft the wing doors resulting in a wider, nearly full-width salon.) With either configuration, Jefferson offered a choice of lower-level floorplans, both with three staterooms, three heads, and separate enginerooms. The wheelhouse and staterooms are trimmed in hand-rubbed teak, and a built-in entertainment center separates the lower helm from the vast salon. Additional features include port and starboard wheelhouse deck doors, a huge flybridge with seating for a small crowd, and a small tub in the aft head. Standard 550hp Detroit 6V92 diesels cruise the 52 Marquessa at 16 knots and deliver a top speed of about 20 knots.

See Page 684 For Price Data

Length Overall	52'5"	Fuel	700 gals.
Length WL	NA	Water	200 gals.
Beam	16'0"	Waste	45 gals.
Draft	4'0"	Hull Type	Modified-V
Weight	55,800#	Deadrise Aft	6°

Jefferson 52 Rivanna Cockpit MY

1994–1999

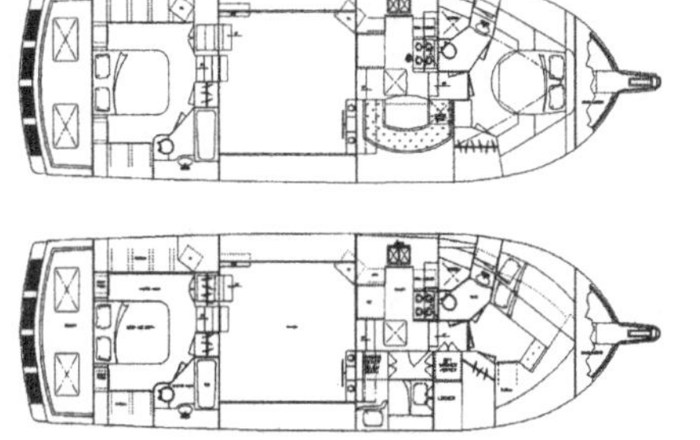

A versatile yacht with appealing lines, the very affordable price of the Jefferson 52 Rivanna Cockpit MY set her apart from most other motor yachts her size during the 1990s. Built on a conventional semi-V hull with a long keel and moderate beam, the wide-open accommodations of the Rivanna will appeal to owners who spend much of their time entertaining friends and guests. Two standard floorplans were available following her 1993 introduction, one with two staterooms and the other with three. In either plan, the fore and aft staterooms are huge with large hanging lockers and comfortable berths. A lower helm was standard, the well-crafted teak furnishings and woodwork are varnished to a high-gloss finish. Topside, the spacious aft deck comes with a wet bar and wing doors, and the flybridge is designed with the helm forward and guest seating aft. Swim, dive, or fish from small cockpit. Additional features include a hardtop, wide side decks, molded bow pulpit, and a swim platform. Among several engine options, twin 450hp Cummins diesels cruise the 52 Rivanna 52 Cockpit MY at 16 knots and reach a top speed of around 20 knots.

See Page 684 For Price Data

Length	52'4"	Headroom	6'5"
Beam	16'0"	Fuel	600 gals.
Draft	4'0"	Water	200 gals.
Weight	44,500#	Hull Type	Modified-V
Clearance, Arch	13'4"	Deadrise Aft	8°

Jefferson 56 Marquessa Cockpit MY

1991–2001

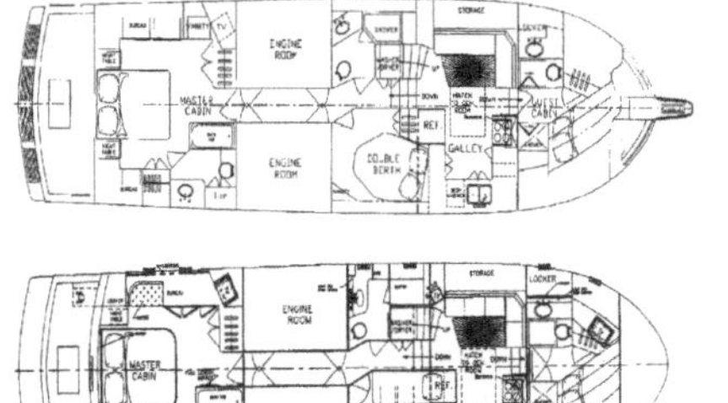

Introduced in 1991, the 56 Marquessa Cockpit MY is a spacious and altogether practical Taiwan import whose affordable price and full teak interior were among her most notable assets. Like all Jefferson yachts of her era, the Marquessa rides on a low-deadrise semi-V hull with a relatively wide beam and a long keel. Several galley-down floorplans were available which allowed owners wide latitude in customizing their boats. The lower helm is open to the salon on the deckhouse level, and there are three staterooms on the lower level. Note that the master suite—with its queen bed, double-size hanging lockers, and bathtub in the head—is reached via a corridor between separate enginerooms. The midship guest stateroom may have single berths or a double, and the bow stateroom has upper and lower berths. The Marquessa's covered aft deck is large enough for entertaining several guests, and the extended flybridge can easily accommodate a tender. Additional features include a built-in washer/dryer, a full entertainment center aft of the lower helm, and wheelhouse deck doors. Twin 550hp 6V92 Detroits cruise at 14 knots and top out around 18 knots.

See Page 684 For Price Data

Length	56'4"	Fuel	700 gals.
Beam	16'0"	Water	200 gals.
Draft	4'0"	Waste	45 gals.
Weight	57,500#	Hull Type	Modified-V
Clearance	19'6"	Deadrise Aft	6°

Jefferson 56 Rivanna Cockpit MY

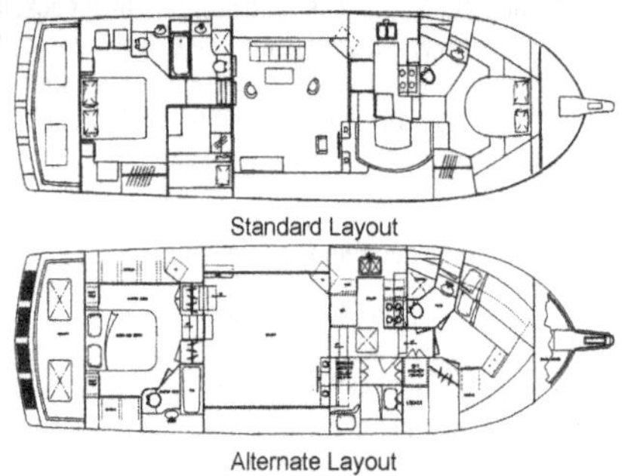

Standard Layout

Alternate Layout

The Jefferson 56 Rivanna is a traditional cockpit motor yacht whose principal characteristics are an affordable price, a huge aft deck and a wide-open interior with an abundance of handcrafted teak woodwork. Built in Taiwan on a low-deadrise, solid fiberglass hull with modest transom deadrise, the Rivanna's standard floorplan differs from most three-stateroom layouts in that the second guest cabin is aft of the salon rather than forward—a configuration that accounts for the spacious aft deck dimensions. Like many Taiwan yachts, the teak interior joinery of the Rivanna is beautifully finished throughout. A lower helm is standard, and each stateroom has a separate head compartment. (Note that several alternate floorplans have also been available.) Additional features include a spacious flybridge with seating for a small crowd, wide side decks, bow pulpit, an aft deck hardtop, radar arch and a roomy cockpit with transom door and swim platform. Among a variety of diesel engine options, twin 600hp Cats (or 635hp Cummins) will cruise the Jefferson 56 Rivanna at 18 knots and reach a top speed in the low 20s.

See Page 684 For Price Data

Length Overall	56'4"	Fuel	600 gals.
Beam	16'0"	Water	200 gals.
Draft	4'0"	Waste	45 gals.
Weight	47,000#	Hull Type	Modified-V
Clearance	16'5"	Deadrise Aft	6°

Jupiter

Quick View

- Jupiter was founded in 1989 in Jupiter, FL, and was named after that coastal community.
- The company's first boat, the Jupiter 31, went on to become one of the most popular center console boats in her class.
- The company was relocated in 1998 to the old Blackfin facility in Ft. Lauderdale
- Carl Herndon, Jupiter's president, was the founder of Blackfin Yacht Corporation and former president of Bertram Yacht.
- In 2007, Jupiter relocated to its production facility to the Florida gulf coast.
- According to the company website, each Jupiter is individually built to buyer specifications.

Jupiter Marine • Palmetto, FL • www.jupitermarine.com

Jupiter 27 Open

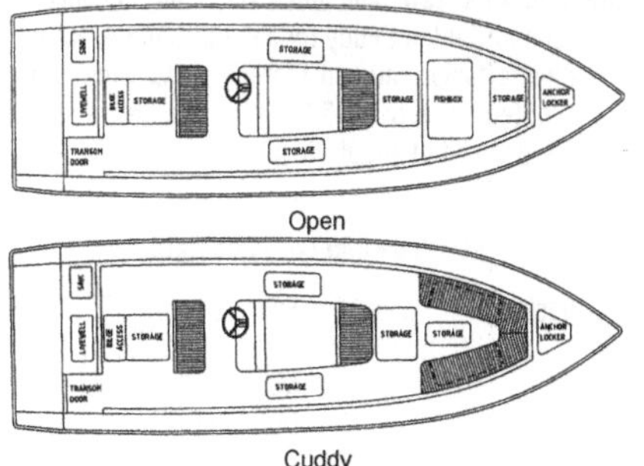

Open

Cuddy

The Jupiter 27 Open is a top-quality fishboat with a full array of premium fishing features and an extra-large console. Like her larger sibling—the very popular Jupiter 31—the 27 is built on a high-performance deep-V hull with cored hullsides and a solid fiberglass bottom. With an 8-foot, 6-inch beam, the Jupiter 27 is trailerable, a key factor in her sales success. No wood is used in the construction of the hull, and the bottom incorporates a flat lifting pad from the stern forward for high-speed efficiency. The 27 has something seldom found on a boat this size: a sub-console compartment complete with standing headroom and a V-berth that extends forward beneath the deck. There are two large electronics boxes at the helm where the wheel is mounted on the centerline. Available in Open, Forward Seating, and Cuddy configurations, standard features include a 40-gallon standing live well, 90-gallon fish box (40-gallon in the cuddy version), cockpit washdowns, pop-up cleats, bait-rigging station, and transom door. A well-finished boat, twin Yamaha 225s will top out at over 45 knots. Note that in 2002 the running surface was extended all the way aft for increased lift.

See Page 685 For Price Data

Length	27'4"	Fuel	204 gals.
Beam	8'6"	Water	37 gals.
Draft, Up	1'7"	Max HP	450
Draft, Down	2'2"	Hull Type	Deep-V
Weight w/Engines	5,820#	Deadrise Aft	24°

Jupiter 29 Forward Seating

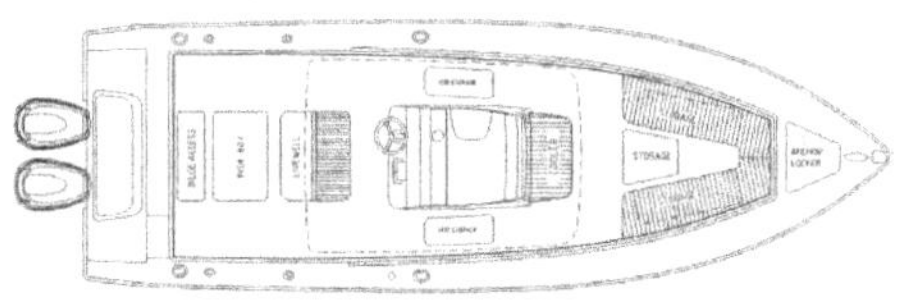

Introduced in 2006, the Jupiter 29 has the guts and brawn to go the distance in the offshore tournament wars. Jupiter has been building quality, hard-core fishing machines for years, and plenty of industry pros consider their boats among the best in the business. Built on a deep-V hull with a keel pad to boost performance and fuel efficiency, the 29's relatively high freeboard and well-flared bow insure a drier ride than many deep vees when the seas pick up. The layout features a deluxe bait-prep center with 45-gallon standup live well aft of the helm, macerated fish box, leaning post, fresh and raw water washdowns, foldaway rear seat, and lockable in-deck rod storage. There's space at the helm for twin big-screen video displays, and the console head compartment provides access to the boat's electrical panel. Cushioned bow seating (with storage under) is adequate for six adults. Note that all hatches are gasketed and dogged. With her big 285-gallon fuel capacity, the Jupiter 29 has the range to roam far offshore and stay there until the fishing is done. No lightweight at 9,430 pounds, twin Yamaha 250hp outboards reach close to 45 knots wide open.

See Page 685 For Price Data

Length	29'6"	Fuel	285 gals.
Beam	9'4"	Water	35 gals.
Hull Draft	2'9"	Max HP	600
Weight w/Engines	9,430#	Hull Type	Deep-V
Clearance	8'10"	Deadrise Aft	24°

Jupiter 31 Open

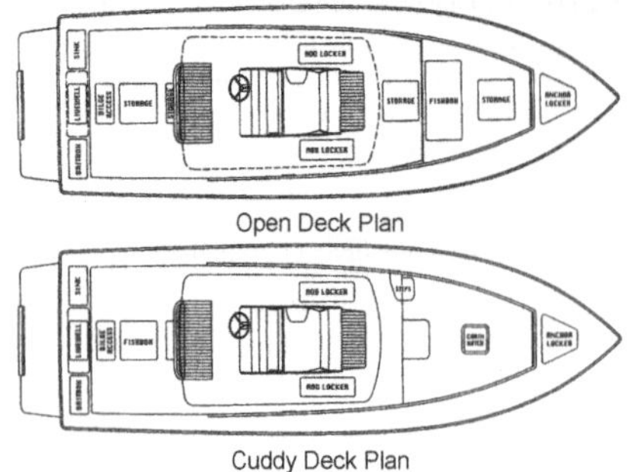
Open Deck Plan

Cuddy Deck Plan

The Jupiter 31 is a highly regarded center console fisherman with a strong following among hardcore anglers with an eye for quality. Originally a semicustom boat, she's built on a high-performance deep-V hull with a relatively wide beam, cored hullsides, and a solid fiberglass bottom. No wood is used in the construction of the hull, and the bottom incorporates a keel pad from the stern forward for high-speed efficiency. Jupiter offers the 31 in three configurations: the classic Open Fisherman, Cuddy Cabin, and the Forward Seating version introduced in 2003. Aside from her handsome lines, the most notable feature of the Jupiter 31 is her oversized console with its expansive helm and spacious sub-console head compartment. Standard fishing equipment includes a transom rigging station with sink, 30-gallon standup livewell, rod storage lockers, raw- and fresh-water washdowns, and fish boxes fore and aft. In the Cuddy model, the cabin is arranged with V-berths, dinette table, and rod storage racks. One of the most popular 31-footers ever, twin 250hp Yamahas cruise at 30+ knots and reach a top speed of about 45 knots.

See Page 685 For Price Data

Length w/Bracket	33'2"	Fuel	260 gals.
Hull Length	30'8"	Water	60 gals.
Beam	9'6"	Max HP	600
Draft, Down	2'7"	Hull Type	Deep-V
Weight	10,500#	Deadrise Aft	24°

Jupiter 34 Forward Seating

2008–Current

Jupiter has long been known in the marine industry for the high degree of quality and durability built into their boats. From the legendary Jupiter 31 to the company's largest model, the Jupiter 39, hundreds of satisfied owners can attest to Jupiter's no-compromises approach to building tough, long-lasting boats. Introduced in 2008, the Jupiter 34 was designed by the Jupiter team in conjunction with naval architects Donald Blount & Associates. Filling the gap between two popular models—the classic Jupiter 31 and the Jupiter's 39—the 34 was engineered to accommodate the new fuel-efficient Yamaha 350HP V-8 four-stroke outboards. She's available in two configurations; the standard forward seating layout or an optional Tournament model with a flush deck and oversized coffin fish box. Standard features include a deluxe leaning post/tackle center with 45-gallon livewell, fresh and raw water washdowns, foldaway transom seat, rod storage lockers, and two insulated fish boxes. Like several high-performance fishing boats, the 34 has a hull pad to boost low-speed performance. About 50 knots top with twin 350hp Yamahas; 55+ with triple 300hp Yamahas.

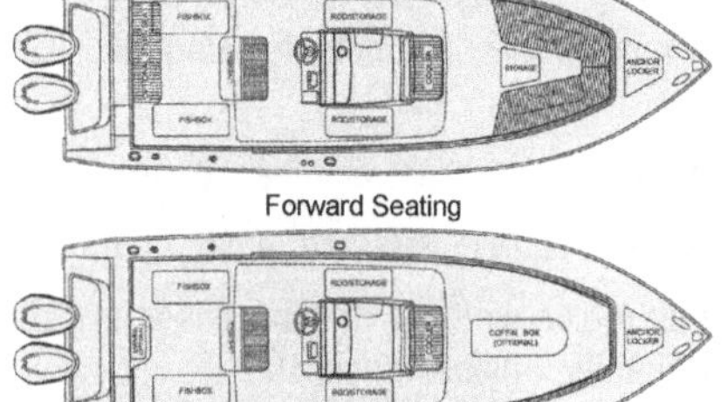

Forward Seating

Flush Floor Plan

See Page 685 For Price Data

Length	33'9"	Fuel	325 gals.
Beam	10'5"	Water	50 gals.
Draft, Up	2'0"	Max HP	700
Draft, Down	3'0"	Hull Type	Deep-V
Weight w/Engines	9,880#	Deadrise Aft	23°

Jupiter 38 Forward Seating

2005–Current

It wasn't that long ago that a "big" center console measured around 30, maybe 32 feet in length. That changed a few years back with the advent of today's big four-stroke outboards. As Randy Vance wrote at the time in Boating magazine, "Nothing has changed the boatbuilding arena like Yamaha's 350 V8 outboard." Jupiter management was quick to recognize the implications of these new engines, and in 2005 the company introduced the 38 Forward Seating. Taking big-water fishability to the next level, the 38's wide beam, centerline fuel tanks and generous freeboard make her a stable and comfortable boat. Notable features include cushioned bow seating, leaning post with 50-gallon livewell, foldout stern seat, two macerated fish boxes, two six-foot storage boxes, and two lockable rod storage boxes under the forward seating area. Side lockers offer storage for life jackets. The 38's big console head compartment includes a shower and additional rod storage. All hatches are gasketed and dogged. Twin Yamaha 250s top out in the low 40s; triple 250s hit 50+ knots, and triple 350 are good for close to 60 knots. Note that a cuddy version with V-berth, refrigerator and microwave became available in 2007.

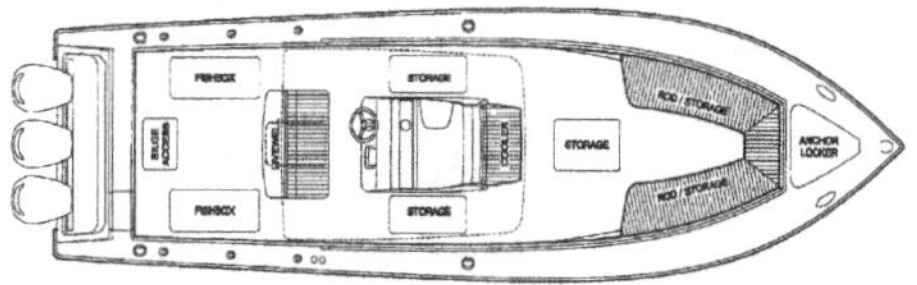

See Page 685 For Price Data

Length	38'2'	Fuel, Std/Opt	320/485 gals.
Beam	10'7"	Water	50 gals.
Draft, Up	24"	Max HP	1,050
Draft, Down	36"	Hull Type	Deep-V
Weight w/Engines	11,480#	Deadrise Aft	24°

Krogen

Quick View

- Krogen history began in 1976 when marine engineer Arthur Kadey approached naval architect James Krogen to design a 42-foot displacement trawler yacht for his personal use.
- Kadey had the boat built in Taiwan, and by 1978 the two had teamed up to form Kadey-Krogen Yachts with the idea of building and marketing the boat in the US.
- The Krogen 42 Trawler became a landmark design, remaining in production until 1998, some 203 boats later.
- The Krogen 38 Cutter—a popular sailboat design of the day— was introduced in 1980; the following year the company suffered the untimely death of co-founder Kadey.
- During the 1980s Krogen introduced several new models, the most notable being the very popular Manatee 36.
- James Krogen passed away in 1994; his son Kurt took over operations of Kadey-Krogen.
- In 2006, company ownership was acquired by John Gear, Larry Polster, and Tom Button.
- Kadey-Krogen is headquartered in Stuart, FL,, with regional offices in Annapolis and Seattle. The company markets its boats only through its regional offices.

Kady-Krogen Yachts • Stuart, FL • www.kadeykrogen.com

Krogen 39 Trawler

1998–Current

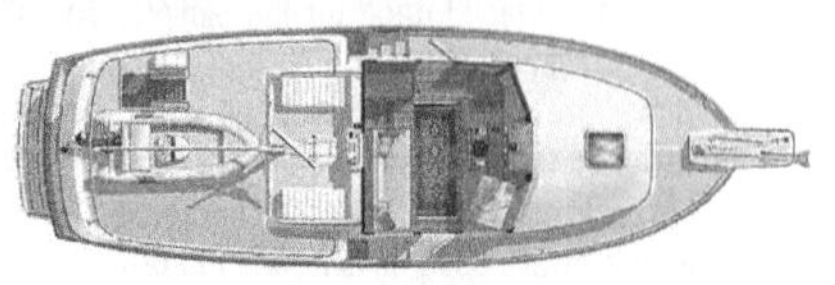

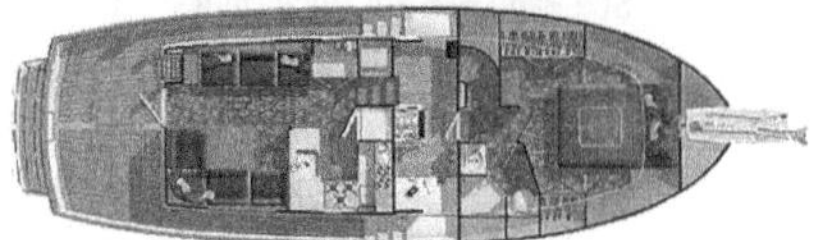

Based on the popular Krogen 42 and designed for the cruising couple, the Krogen 39 is a single-stateroom trawler whose salty profile and seakindly hull design will appeal to traditionalists seeking a real trawler rather than a semi-displacement imitation. Built in Taiwan on a ballasted, full-displacement hull, the Krogen 39's teak interior is arranged like most pilothouse trawlers with the galley in the salon. Instead of a second stateroom below the pilothouse, however, the Krogen has a walk-in engineroom with a workbench and excellent engine access. Both the stateroom and head compartment are very roomy, and port and starboard deck doors in the wheelhouse provide easy deck access. Topside, there's space on the extended hardtop for a 10-foot dinghy, and bridge overhangs provide weather protection to the side decks as well as the aft deck. Additional features include a transom door and swim platform, a flybridge with a centerline helm, and a fold-down mast and boom assembly for launching a small dinghy. A single 121hp John Deere diesel will cruise the Krogen 39 at 7–8 knots with a cruising range of over 2,000 nautical miles.

See Page 685 For Price Data

Length Overall	43'8"	Ballast	2,000#
Length WL	36'8"	Fuel	700 gals.
Beam	14'3"	Water	300 gals.
Draft	4'3"	Waste	35 gals.
Weight	33,470#	Hull Type	Displacement

Krogen 42 Trawler

1977–97

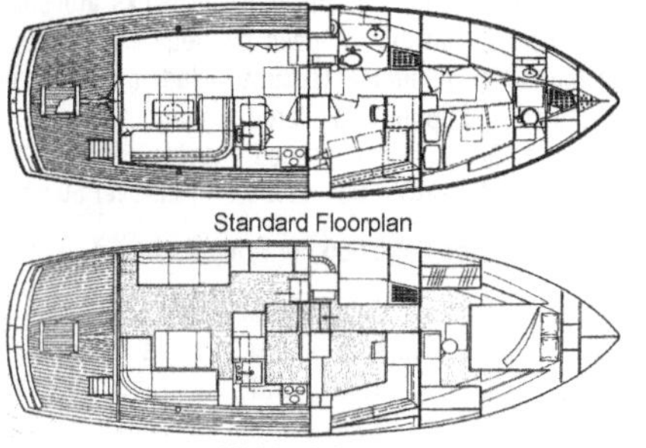
Standard Floorplan

Widebody Layout

The Krogen 42 is one of the few production trawler-style cruising yachts built on a full displacement hull. (Note that the hull was fully cored until 1995; hull construction then became solid fiberglass.) As such, she displays all of the characteristics normally associated with such long-range designs including a comfortable ride, excellent seaworthiness, and the easy rolling motion typical of any soft-chine boat. The Krogen is a particularly salty-looking vessel with a distinctive profile and an upright bow. Inside, the focal point of the boat is the functional pilothouse with watch berth located a few steps up from the salon level. Until hull #65 (1985), the Krogen 42s were built with glass-over-plywood decks; thereafter the 42s were built with cored decks and superstructures. An extremely popular boat with experienced cruisers, she's been the subject of constant refinements over the years and remains one of the most sought-after models on the used boat market. A single Lehman diesel was standard, and at her 8-knot hull speed the Krogen 42 has a range of 2,000+ miles. A popular boat with a loyal following, 206 were built including five with twin engines. Note that a Widebody model with a full-width salon was introduced in 1989.

See Page 685 For Price Data

Length Overall	42'4"	Ballast	2,500#
Length WL	39'2"	Fuel	700 gals.
Beam	15'0"	Water	360 gals.
Draft	4'7"	Waste	40 gals.
Weight	39,500#	Hull Type	Displacement

Krogen 44 Trawler

2004–Current

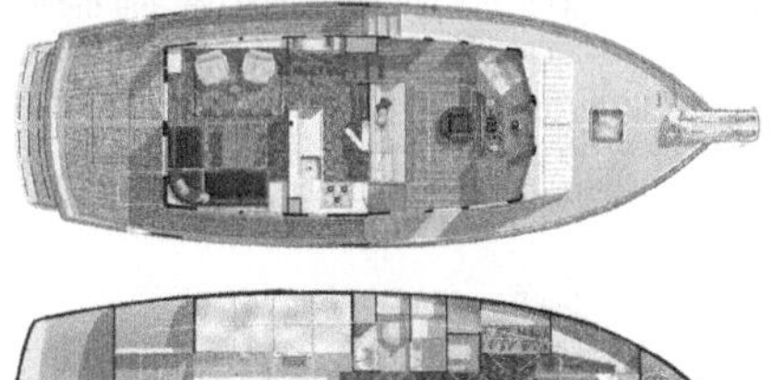

Based on the classic Krogen 42 Trawler, the Krogen 44 offers more space than her predecessor (thanks to a slightly wider beam) while incorporating several significant design and engineering refinements. Unlike many so-called "trawlers" with their hard-chine, semi-displacement hulls, the 44 is a true displacement vessel, a ballasted, soft-chine passagemaker built of premium materials by a company known for its quality control. One of the more notable upgrades buyers will notice in the Krogen 44 is the use of weathertight aluminum doors and sliding aluminum windows instead of teak doors and teak window frames. A more subtle and not-so-obvious upgrade is that the pilothouse, flybridge and boat deck are a single mold instead of fastened together, providing a much stronger structure. While the interior layout of the 44 is similar to the old 42, the pilothouse is significantly larger with room for a fixed helm chair. The aft deck is larger as well with room for a table and several chairs. With her salty lines, seakindly hull and comfortable interior, the 44 will have broad appeal for the serious, long-range cruising crowd. She'll cruise efficiently at 7–8 knots with a single 156hp John Deere diesel engine.

See Page 685 For Price Data

Length Overall	49'0"	Ballast	2,500#
Length WL	40'11"	Fuel	850 gals.
Beam	15'6"	Water	350 gals.
Draft	4'6"	Waste	52 gals.
Weight	43,140#	Hull Type	Displacement

Krogen 48 North Sea

1996–2008

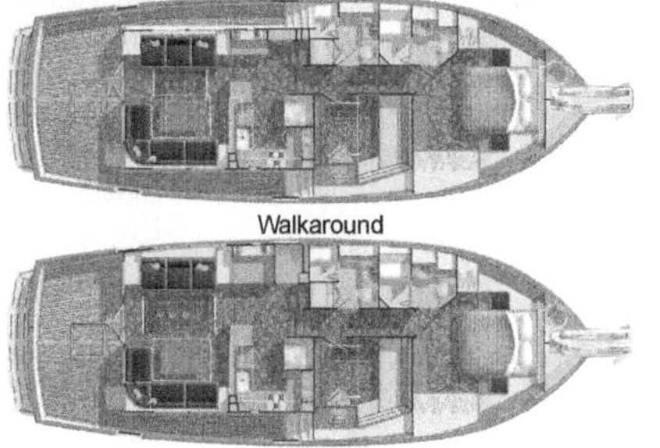
Walkaround

Widebody

Trawler purists will find much to like in the Krogen 48 North Sea, a sturdy raised pilothouse trawler with a ballasted, full-displacement hull and the long-range capability required of a true oceangoing vessel. Built in Taiwan, the 48 is a semicustom yacht in that she's offered with a choice of several two- and three-stateroom interiors. The standard model comes with full walkaround side decks, while the Widebody version eliminates the port sidedeck. In either version, the galley is forward in the salon, and the teak-trimmed pilothouse is arranged with a centerline helm, dual deck doors, and an L-shaped settee that converts to a berth. (Note that the walkaround layout does not allow room for stairs from the pilothouse to the bridge.) An elegant parquet sole graces the salon where facing settees provide comfortable seating for several guests. Topside, the cockpit and side decks are shaded by bridge overhangs, and the extended flybridge will accommodate an inflatable tender. Additional features include a full teak interior, fold-down mast and boom, and a large engineroom accessed from the galley. At an 8-knot cruising speed, the single 210hp Cat diesel provides a range of nearly 2,000 nautical miles. Over 50 were built.

See Page 685 For Price Data

Length Overall	53'0"	Ballast	4,500
Length WL	45'5"	Fuel	1,000 gals.
Beam	16'8"	Water	400 gals.
Draft	5'0"	Waste	125 gals.
Weight	56,450#	Hull Type	Displacement

Krogen 48 Whaleback

1993–2003

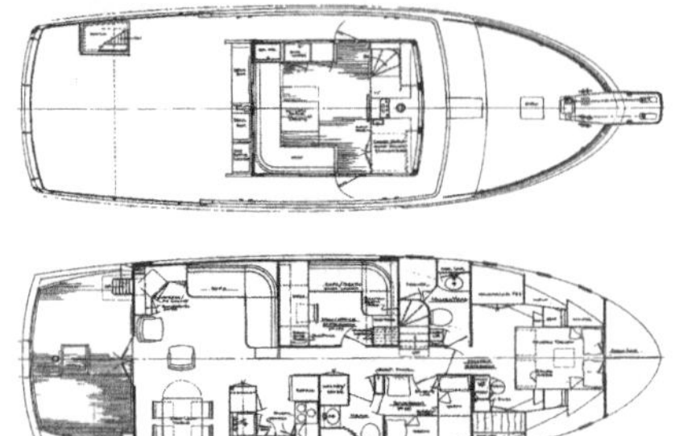

A distinctive design with a flush foredeck and Portuguese bridge, the 48 Whaleback is a full-displacement cruising trawler with a deep entry, rounded bilges, and a ballasted, prop-protecting keel. With well over 16 feet of beam and no side decks, the interior dimensions of the Whaleback are downright extravagant for a boat this size. The floorplan—arranged on a single level from the cockpit to the forward stateroom—includes three staterooms (one of which doubles as a den) and two full heads in addition to an expansive salon and generous galley. All of the cabinets, trim, and paneling are fashioned of grain-matched teak. The pilothouse, with its distinctive reverse-raked windshield, features full 360 degrees of visibility in addition to a spacious chart table, an L-shaped settee, port and starboard deck access doors, and a wet bar. There's room on the extended upper deck for dinghy storage, and the mast and boom are fully functional. Note the protected walkway surrounding the pilothouse. At an economical 8-knot cruising speed, a single 210hp Cat diesel delivers a cruising range of approximately 2,000 miles. About 30 were built until production ended in 2003.

See Page 685 For Price Data

Length Overall	48'5"	Ballast	4,500#
Length WL	45'5"	Fuel	1,020 gals.
Beam	16'8"	Water	540 gals.
Draft	5'0"	Waste	100 gals.
Weight	56,200#	Hull Type	Displacement

Krogen 58 Trawler

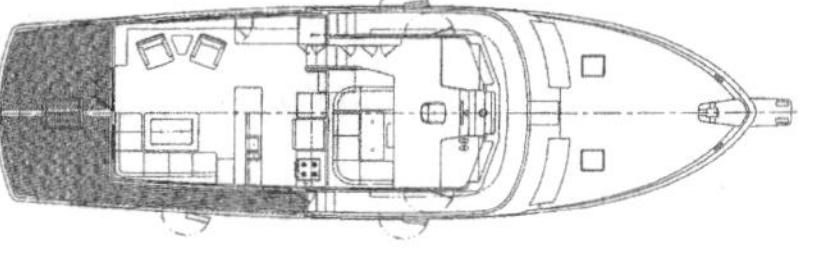

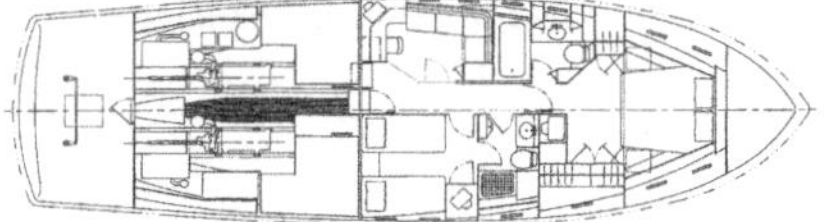

The Krogen 58 is a full-displacement, twin-engine trawler with an Alaskan-style profile and genuine long-range capability. Built in Taiwan to Krogen's high production standards, the 58 rides on a ballasted, full-displacement hull with cored sides and a long keel flanked by twin skegs that protect the running gear. With her raised pilothouse profile and sturdy Portuguese bridge, the no-nonsense appearance of the Krogen 58 is very appealing. Note that the deckhouse is asymmetrical: the salon extends to the port gunwale, which creates more interior space while leaving room for a secure sidedeck to starboard. A galley access door is a nice convenience, and the reverse pilothouse windshield reduces glare. Unlike most pilothouse designs, the master stateroom in the 58 is forward while the two guest staterooms are aft with the portside cabin doubling as an office. The engineroom, accessed by doors in the lazarette or forward on the lower level, is remarkably spacious with excellent headroom and a workbench. Cherry interior woodwork, weathertight doors, a folding mast, and a bow thruster are standard. At an efficient 8-knot cruising speed, the twin 154hp Deere diesels will provide a cruising range of 2,000 miles.

See Page 685 For Price Data

Length Overall	63'3"	Ballast	7,000#
Length WL	52'3"	Fuel	1,760 gals.
Beam	18'1"	Water	400 gals.
Draft	5'3"	Waste	100 gals.
Weight	96,830#	Hull Type	Displacement

Larson

Quick View

- Larson has a history going back to 1913 when Paul Larson built several wooden boats in a small warehouse in Little Falls, MN.
- As Larson grew to become a leader in the wooden runabout field, the Larson brand soon became well known throughout the western Great Lakes market.
- In 1954, Larson switched from wood to fiberglass production.
- During the 1960s and 1970s, Larson became one of the largest manufacturers of small boats in the industry.
- In 1978, Larson was acquired by Minstar, later to become Genmar Industries.
- In June of 2009, Genmar—corporate owner of Larson Boats—declared bankruptcy.
- Larson was sold at auction to corporate turn-around firm Platinum Equity in January, 2010. Platinum then sold Larson to a partnership headed by ex-Genmar owner Irwin Jacobs.

Larson Boats • Little Falls, MN • www.larsonboats.com

Larson 274 Cabrio

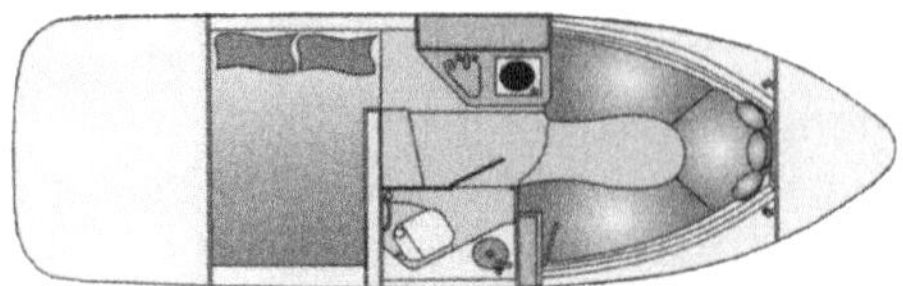

At 27 feet in length, the Larson 274 Cabrio is one of the larger trailerable midcabin cruisers available on the used-boat market. She differs from other boats of her type in that she rides on a notched hull that is said to improve both efficiency and performance. The Cabrio's compact interior offers 6 feet, 2 inches of headroom along with berths for four, full galley, and a head with shower. The galley is highlighted with a faux granite counter, a single-burner electric stove, and under-counter refrigerator. The cabinets are trimmed in bright maple, and the galley sole is covered with an easy-to-clean wood grain composite. There's a big double in the midcabin where a curtain provides privacy from the main cabin. Topside, the cockpit is arranged with a double helm seat forward, a wet bar, and facing seats aft. Note that the Cabrio's 2-foot swim platform offers plenty of room for carrying an inflatable tender. Additional features include a tilt wheel, radar arch, transom door, CD player, and walk-through windshield. A good performer with a single 250hp Volvo Duoprop sterndrive engine, the 274 Cabrio will cruise in the mid 20s and top out at over 30 knots.

See Page 685 For Price Data

Length Overall	28'0"	Fuel	85 gals.
Beam	8'6"	Water	12.5 gals.
Draft, Drive Up	2'0"	Waste	4 gals.
Draft, Drive Down	2'10"	Hull Type	Modified-V
Weight	6,000#	Deadrise Aft	14°

Larson 280/290 Cabrio

A popular model for Larson, the 280 Cabrio (called the 290 Cabrio in 1997–2001) is well-appointed express whose roomy accommodations and affordable price struck a good balance between comfort and value. She was built on what Larson calls a Duo DeltaConic hull, which incorporates a notched bottom design said to improve both lift and top-end performance. Below, the Cabrio sleeps six in three double berths. The list of standard equipment included an electric refrigerator, alcohol/electric stove, and an enclosed head with vanity and shower. With a wide 10-foot beam, there's a surprising amount of room below and Formica cabinets and oak trim present an upscale impression. Above deck, the cockpit is arranged with a removable L-shaped lounge and a doublewide, back-to-back seat at the helm. Additional features include a tilt wheel, reasonably wide side decks, a power-assist engine hatch, and a walk-through transom. Several sterndrive power options were available. Among them, a single 310hp MerCruiser will reach a top speed in excess of 35 knots, and twin 250hp Mercs will top out at 40+ knots.

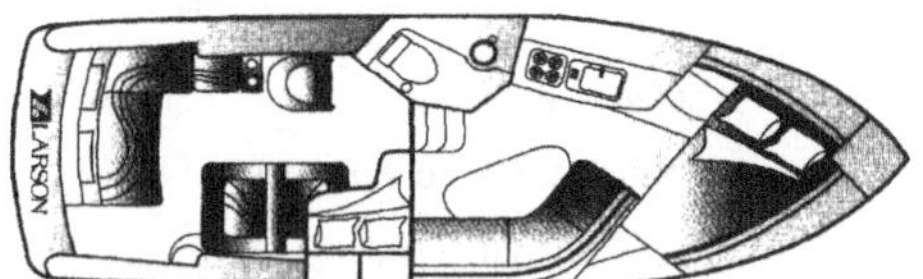

See Page 685 For Price Data

Length w/Pulpit	28'11"	Fuel	125 gals.
Beam	10'0"	Water	33 gals.
Draft	2'10"	Waste	33 gals.
Weight	7,500#	Hull Type	Modified-V
Clearance, Arch	9'4"	Deadrise Aft	18°

Larson 300/310 Cabrio

The affordably priced Larson 300 Cabrio (called the 310 Cabrio in 1995–98) was the largest model in the Larson fleet for much of the 1990s. Basically, the Cabrio is a redesign of an earlier Larson model—the Contempra DC-300 (1988–90)—with a streamlined profile and an upgraded cabin layout. Built on a stable DeltaConic hull with a relatively wide beam, the original midcabin interior of the Cabrio has a large island berth area in the bow, two hanging lockers, a double berth aft, and a convertible dinette that might sleep a single (small) adult. In 1994, an all-new floorplan with an angled berth forward opened up the salon considerably, allowing space for a full-size dinette and a slightly enlarged galley. On deck, the Cabrio's cockpit is arranged with a doublewide (reversible) helm seat, a covered wet bar (very slick), and a gas-assist engine access hatch in the sole. A bow pulpit, windshield vents, and a cockpit shower were standard. Among several engine options, twin 205hp 5.0-liter MerCruiser sterndrives cruise the Larson 300/310 Cabrio at about 20 knots (about 30+ knots top), and a pair of 235hp MerCruisers will deliver a top speed in the high 30s.

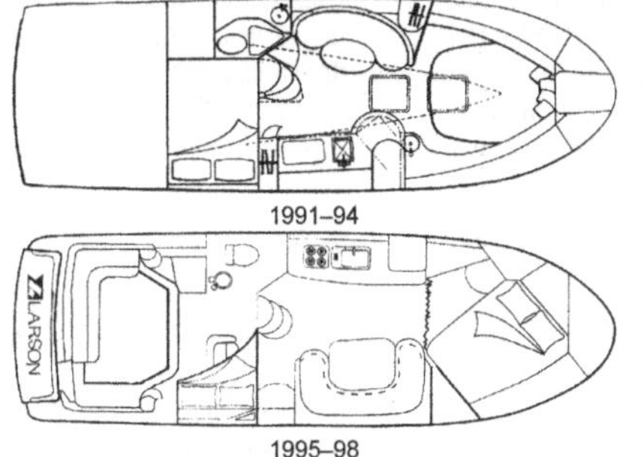

See Page 685 For Price Data

Length w/Pulpit	32'6"	Clearance	7'4"
Hull Length	29'11"	Fuel	170 gals.
Beam	10'6"	Water	30 gals.
Draft	2'10"	Hull Type	Modified-V
Weight	9,500#	Deadrise Aft	14°

Larson 310 Cabrio

Larson's reputation for delivering a lot of boat for the money was on full display with the introduction in 2003 of the 310 Cabrio, a roomy midcabin cruiser whose moderate price included an impressive inventory of standard equipment. Built on a solid fiberglass hull with a notched bottom, the Cabrio's wide-open interior is dominated by a curved lounge that extends from the head compartment all the way around to the galley. A dinette table is to port, and the midcabin is tucked behind the companionway steps, which leaves it open to the salon. Privacy curtains separate the sleeping areas from the main cabin, and the head contains a separate stall shower—a luxury on any 30-foot boat. On deck, the cockpit has a U-shaped settee aft as well as a wet bar, and the driver's side of the double helm seat has a drop-down bolster for standup driving. A large transom locker stores fenders and dock lines, etc. There are no side decks on the Cabrio, so a walk-through windshield—with no handrail—provides access to the foredeck. A tilt wheel, radar arch, and transom shower were standard. Among several sterndrive options, twin 280hp Volvo gas engines cruise in the low 30s and reach a top speed of 40+ knots.

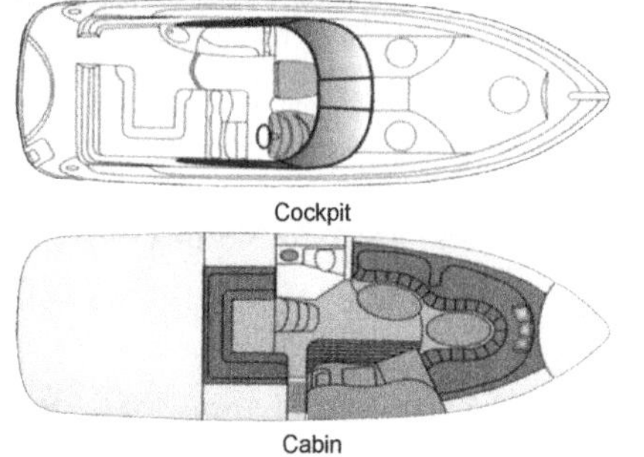
Cockpit

Cabin

See Page 685 For Price Data

Length	31'0"	Fuel	160 gals.
Beam	10'6"	Water	46 gals.
Draft, Up	1'8"	Waste	37 gals.
Draft, Down	2'10"	Hull Type	Modified-V
Weight	10,400#	Deadrise Aft	14°

Larson 330 Cabrio

Neither high-tech nor expensive, the Larson 330 Cabrio is an economy-class cruiser with generous cabin accommodations, plenty of storage, and a well-arranged cockpit. Like all recent Cabrio models, the 330 rides on a stepped hull, a bottom design said to reduce drag and improve performance by breaking the water's grip on the hull. The interior of the 330 will sleep six with an angled double berth forward, a large midcabin berth, and a convertible dinette. The galley contains plenty of storage cabinets and counter space, and a roomy head compartment has overhead storage and a large vanity, but no shower stall. Topside, a double helm seat, wet bar, and U-shaped settee are standard in the cockpit. Lacking side decks, a windshield walk-through provides access to the bow. A radar arch and transom door are also standard, and a filler turns the cockpit into a large sun pad. Note that an extended swim platform has been a popular option. On the downside, the engine compartment is a tight fit. A fast ride with twin 300hp MerCruiser sterndrives, the 330 Cabrio will cruise in the mid 20s and reach a top speed of around 40 knots.

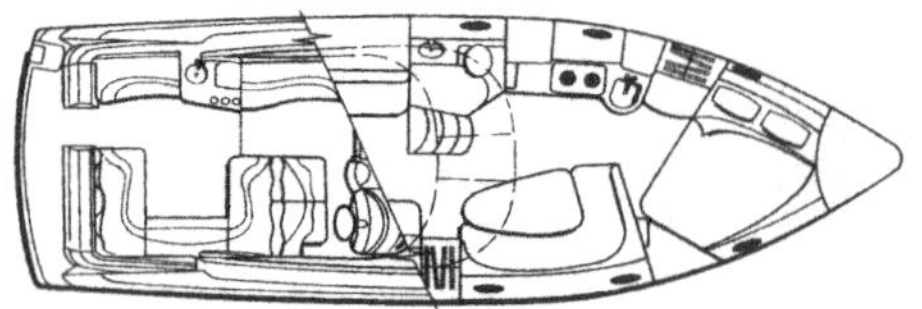

See Page 685 For Price Data

Length	32'0"	Fuel	240 gals.
Beam	11'6"	Water	46 gals.
Draft, Up	2'0"	Waste	37 gals.
Draft, Down	2'10"	Hull Type	Modified-V
Weight	12,500#	Deadrise Aft	14°

Larson 350 Cabrio

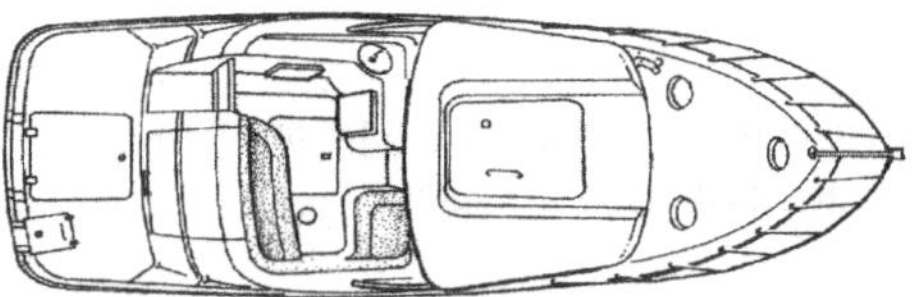

Larson is one of those builders with a history of providing a lot of boat for the money. They occupy one of those sweets spots in the American boating market, the intersection of price and value that manufacturers seldom achieve. Introduced in 2006, the 350 Cabrio is a roomy wide-body express with the features and amenities of a more expensive boat. She rides on Larson's signature "Duo Delta Conic" hull, a stepped-bottom design that delivers brisk performance as well as good fuel economy. Below decks, the 350's mid-cabin interior is nicely appointed with high-gloss cherry cabinets, faux granite counters, and soft-vinyl wall coverings. The curved galley provides more working space than most cruisers her size, and a circular glass enclosure converts part of the head compartment into a shower stall. Larson broke new ground with the 350 Cabrio by offering the hard top as a standard feature. Her user-friendly cockpit includes a curved chaise lounge to port and convertible seating aft. Note the walk-through windshield—there are no side decks on the 350 Cabrio. The transom storage locker is a nice touch. Cruise at 25–26 knots with 320hp MerCruiser I/Os (about 40 knots wide open).

See Page 685 For Price Data

Length	36'4"	Fuel	230 gals.
Beam	12'0"	Water	46 gals.
Draft, Down	3'1"	Waste	37 gals.
Weight	14,000#	Hull Type	Modified-V
Headroom	6'6"	Deadrise Aft	18°

Larson 370 Cabrio

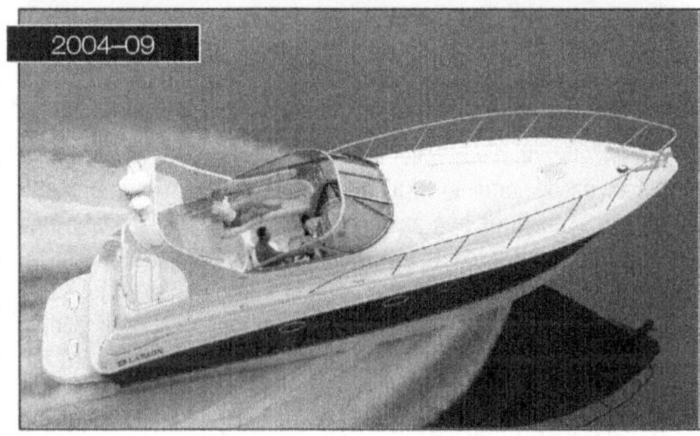

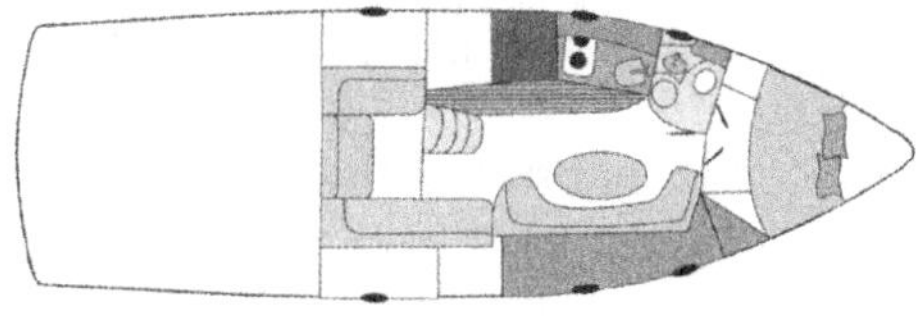

Larson's biggest boat ever, the 370 Cabrio builds on the company's long history of providing a lot of boat for the money. There's nothing high-tech or cutting-edge about the 370—hull construction is solid fiberglass; fit and finish is adequate considering the price; and the styling is on a par with most the competition. The Cabrio's base price, however, is refreshingly attractive and she comes with enough standard equipment to make her a true turnkey boat. Starting with a well-designed cockpit and including a spacious interior, the Cabrio offers most of the amenities of her higher-priced counterparts with little sacrifice in quality. Her midcabin floorplan is typical of boats her size with berths for six, a spacious galley, and a double-entry head compartment. A solid door separates the master stateroom from the salon, and attractive cherrywood laminates are applied liberally throughout the interior. A wet bar is standard in the cockpit along with wraparound aft seating, carry-on cooler, and a removable cocktail table. Also standard are a genset, radar arch, microwave, VacuFlush toilet, windlass, and air conditioning. Twin 375hp Volvo I/Os cruise at 25 knots (about 30 knots wide open).

See Page 685 For Price Data

Length	36'11"	Fuel	266 gals.
Beam	13'0"	Water	35 gals.
Draft, Up	2'6"	Waste	35 gals.
Draft, Down	3'4"	Hull Type	Modified-V
Weight	16,800#	Deadrise Aft	22°

Lazzara

Quick View

- Brothers Dick and Brad Lazzara formed the Lazzara Yacht in 1991, but the company's roots go back to the 1960s when father Vince Lazzara established sailboat-builder Columbia Yachts.
- Following the sale of Columbia in 1967, Lazzara and sons established Gulfstar Yachts which went on to market a series of successful fiberglass motoryachts and motor-sailers.
- In 1987 Gulfstar merged with Viking Yachts to form the Viking-Gulfstar line of motoryachts, but the luxury tax of 1990 caused the venture to fail.
- The brothers sold their interest in Gulfstar to Viking and, in 1990, founded Lazzara Yachts.
- By 1992 the company's first yacht, the Lazzara 76, was launched.
- Lazzara continued to build highly personalized yachts through it's 106, 110, and 116 product lines. No two 100 footers built by Lazzara have been the same.

Lazzara Yachts • Tampa, FL • www.lazzarayachts.com

Lazzara 68 Motor Yacht

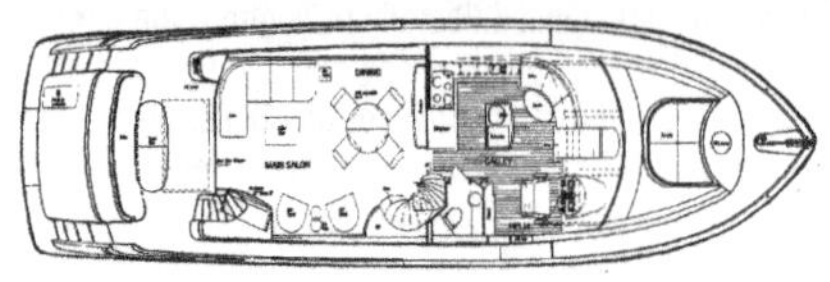

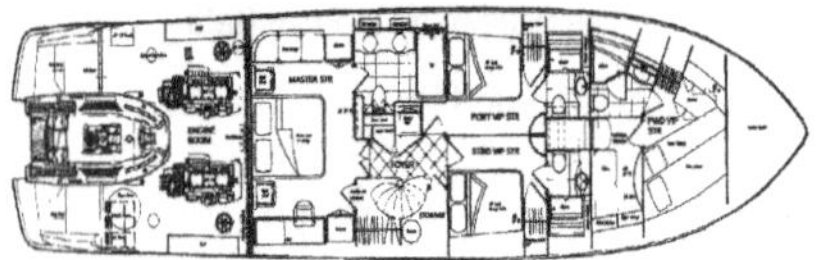

The Lazzara 68 combines the aggressive styling and exciting performance of a European motor yacht in a domestic, all-American package. Since launching their first yacht in 1993, Lazzara has become well known in the industry for their quality engineering and lavish accommodations. The 68 is the smallest Lazzara ever built, but she'll easily compete with larger boats thanks to an impressive inventory of features and amenities. Her standard four-stateroom interior includes a large, full-beam master suite and three comfortable VIP staterooms, each with its own head. The beautiful salon contains a formal dining area as well as a spiral staircase leading up to the bridge, and an open galley and lounge are forward adjacent to the lower helm station. Topside, the spacious flybridge provides seating for ten, a full wet bar, and a 70-square-foot aft sun pad. In a further display of her megayacht-like features, a garage for a tender or PWC is hidden behind the hydraulically actuated transom door. Additional features include high-gloss cherrywood joinery, engineroom workbench and toolbox, bow and stern thrusters, and teak decks. Caterpillar 1,000hp diesels cruise the Lazzara 68 in the mid 20s (27–28 knots top).

Not Enough Resale Data to Set Values

Length	68'6"	Fuel	1,300 gals.
Beam	18'2"	Water	300 gals.
Draft	4'2"	Waste	100 gals.
Weight	104,000#	Hull Type	Modified-V
Clearance	22'8"	Deadrise Aft	12.5°

Lazzara 76 Motor Yacht

1993–2003

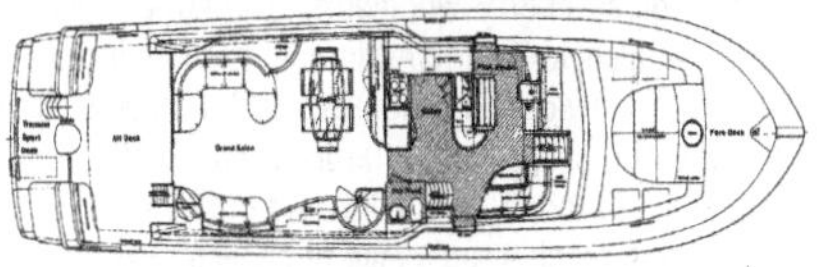

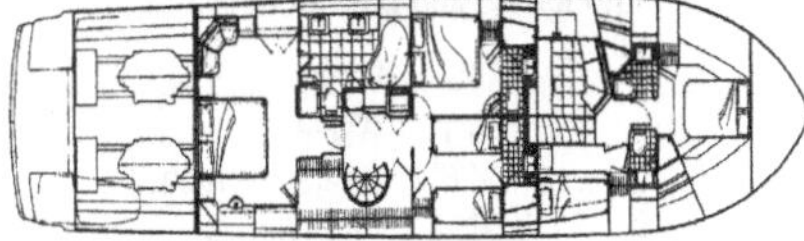

A state-of-the-art design when she was introduced in 1993, the Lazzara 76 Motor Yacht is a sleek Euro-style luxury yacht that incorporates a host of innovative features. Built on a low-deadrise hull with a wide beam and propeller pockets, the hull, deck, superstructure—even the interior floors—are fully cored to reduce weight. The floorplan is arranged with five staterooms on the lower level including a huge owner's suite and two spacious guest staterooms. There are two main deck configurations: the Standard layout has walkaround side decks while the Grand Salon features a full-width salon and no side decks. Either way, the galley can be isolated from the salon by closing off the breakfast bar, and both layouts include a formal dining area and day head. A circular staircase in the salon leads up to the bridge with its stylish hardtop. Additional features include a den/office forward, a transom garage, foredeck sun lounge, and an aft engineroom housing a pair of 1,150hp MTUs. (Note that 1,000hp MTUs were used on the first five hulls.) A good performer, she'll cruise in the low 20s (mid 20s top) with her V-drive diesels. Note that the Lazzara 80 Cockpit MY, introduced in 1996, is the same boat with a cockpit extension.

Not Enough Resale Data to Set Values

Length	76'11"	Water	350 gals.
Beam	19'1"	Waste	100 gals.
Draft	4'6"	Clearance, Arch	23'6"
Weight	94,000#	Hull Type	Modified-V
Fuel	1,750 gals.	Deadrise Aft	14°

Lazzara 80 Open Bridge

2003–06

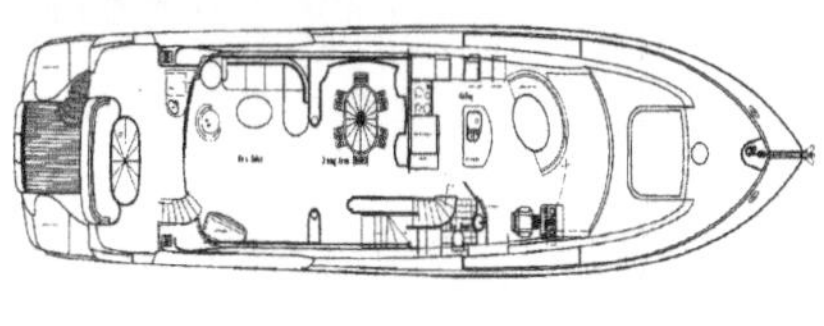

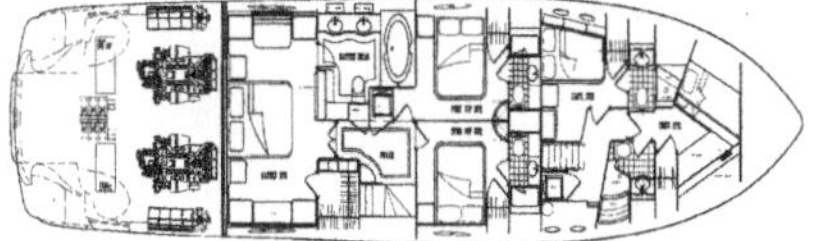

Introduced in 2004, the Lazzara 80 E is a redesigned version of the company's existing 80 SC Skylounge model with an all-new flybridge, deck, and interior. Her open flybridge, with its swept-back radar arch, lowers the profile of the 80 E nearly 4 feet compared with her sistership, giving her a sleeker, more balanced appearance. This is a leading-edge yacht in every respect, a display of aggressive styling and high-tech construction usually associated with only the finest European yachts. With her wide 20-foot beam, the 80 E is roomier than anything in her class. The spacious salon and dining area have all the amenities expected in a modern 80-footer including a pop-up plasma TV, etched-glass cabinets, and stunning curved glass doors that open electrically to the teak afterdeck. Guest and owner staterooms are reached via a salon staircase, and the master suite contains a bar, full entertainment center, and a huge his-and-hers marble bathroom with a hot tub. Additional highlights include bow and stern thrusters, tender garage with automatic launching system, upper and lower helms, and modern navigational systems. A superb performer with 1,550hp Cat engines, she'll cruise at 25–26 knots (30+ top).

Not Enough Resale Data to Set Values

Length	80'7"	Water	400 gals.
Beam	20'1"	Waste	200 gals.
Draft	4'6"	Clearance, Arch	24'7"
Weight	115,000#	Hull Type	Modified-V
Fuel	2,000 gals.	Deadrise Aft	11°

Lazzara 80 SC

2001–07

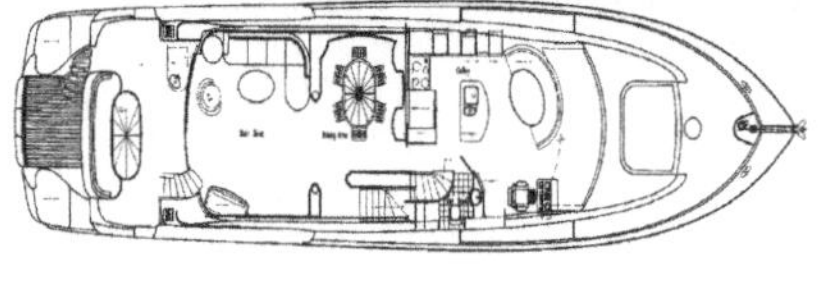

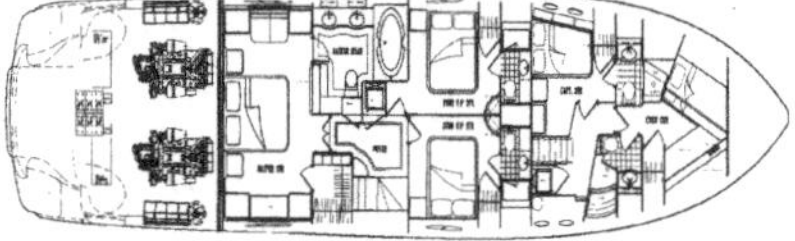

An impressive blend of sophisticated engineering, quality construction, and lush accommodations, the Lazzara 80 SC is a mini-megayacht whose distinctive tri-deck styling gives her the appearance of a considerably larger yacht. The interior can only be described as opulent, and the enclosed skylounge is a special place indeed. With no lower helm, the main deck level of the Lazzara 80 is devoted to a cavernous salon (with a formal dining section) and an equally spacious galley/dinette area forward. There are three large staterooms below—a full-beam master and two identical VIP cabins—and a washer/dryer in the foyer is for the use of guests. With the engineroom well aft in the hull, the two-stateroom crew quarters are forward and accessed directly from the galley. Both the salon and skylounge have expansive windows, plasma TVs, and high-gloss cherry woodwork. The large engineroom is reached through a cockpit door. Additional features include a cockpit livewell, power skylounge windows, master suite Jacuzzi, main deck day head, and a spacious afterdeck. An excellent performer with standard 1,300hp MTUs, the Lazzara 80 SC will cruise in the mid 20s knots and reach a top speed of close to 30 knots.

Not Enough Resale Data to Set Values

Length	80'7"	Water	400 gals.
Beam	20'1"	Waste	200 gals.
Draft	4'6"	Clearance, Arch	24'7"
Weight	117,000#	Hull Type	Modified-V
Fuel	2,000 gals.	Deadrise Aft	11°

Legacy Yachts

Quick View

- The first Legacy model—the Legacy 40 Sedan—was introduced in 1995 when sailboat-builder Freedom Yachts of Middletown, RI, conceived the Legacy series to tempt sailors considering a switch to power.
- Following the successful introduction of the Legacy 40, the company unveiled the 34 Sedan and 34 Express models in 1996, the Legacy 28 Express in 1999, and the Legacy 32 and 42 Express models in 2005–06.
- Highly regarded for their quality construction, Legacy quickly established itself as one of the country's leading builders of production Downeast-style cruising yachts.
- Legacy ended production and closed its Middletown, RI, factory in September, 2008.
- Legacy assetts were acquired by Ohio-based Tartan/C&C Yachts in early 2010.

No longer in production.

Legacy 28 Express

1999–2006

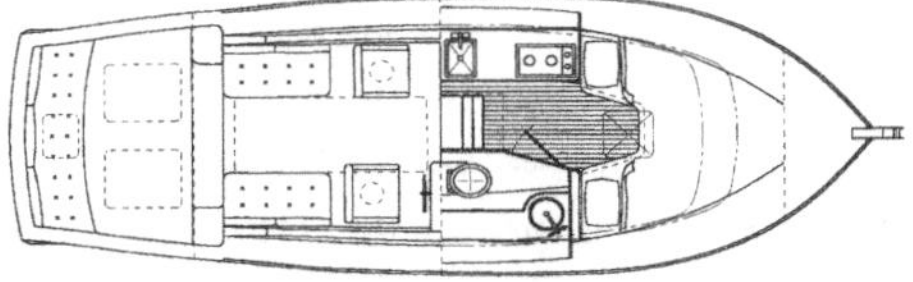

The Legacy 28 Express joins the ranks of a handful of premium small cruisers whose traditional styling and top-quality construction set them well apart from the norm. Built on a conventional hard-chine hull with moderate beam, a short keel and a fairly flat stern, the Legacy provides a remarkably smooth ride in a variety of sea conditions. Her upscale interior features with a V-berth forward, a small-but-efficient galley, four large opening ports, enclosed head with shower, and an abundance of grain-matched cherry woodwork. Visibility from the helm is excellent, and wide side decks make it easy to reach the bow. The inboard-facing bench seats (as opposed to L-shaped seating) on the bridgedeck are a compromise. Additional features include a full-width transom seat, a quiet underwater exhaust system, and a notably ergonomic helm position. On the downside, the Legacy's low-deadrise bottom isn't too fond of a chop. An expensive boat in her day, a single 250hp Yanmar diesel will cruise the Legacy 28 Express in the low 20s (about 25 knots top), while a 300hp Yanmar will cruise at 25 knots and top out at close to 30 knots.

See Page 685 For Price Data

Length	28'0"	Water	30 gals.
Beam	9'6"	Waste	25 gals.
Draft	2'2"	Headroom	6'0"
Weight	6,500#	Hull Type	Modified-V
Fuel	120 gals.	Deadrise Aft	5°

Legacy 34 Express

1996–2006

A scaled-down version of the Legacy 40, the Legacy 34 is a Downeast-style cruiser from Freedom Yachts, builder of Freedom sailboats. The 34 is a handsome small yacht which is no big surprise considering that her designer, Mark Ellis, has drawn many popular Downeast yachts over the years. The Legacy is built on a fully cored hull with moderate beam, a sharp entry, and—in the single-screw version—a keel of sufficient depth to offer prop and rudder protection. The interior of the Legacy 34 will easily suit the needs of the cruising couple, and the above average fit and finish is an indication of how well this boat is put together. Extra-large cabin windows provide all-around visibility, and the varnished mahogany woodwork and teak-and-holly sole add much to the traditional feel of the boat. Notable features include a deck door at the helm, wide side decks, a separate stall shower in the head, and a gas-assist engineroom hatch. With a single 440hp Cummins diesel the Legacy will cruise at a comfortable 16–18 knots (20-plus knots top) with a fuel burn of better than 1 nautical mile per gallon. Twin-diesel options ranging from 315 to 440hp will cruise in the mid to high 20s.

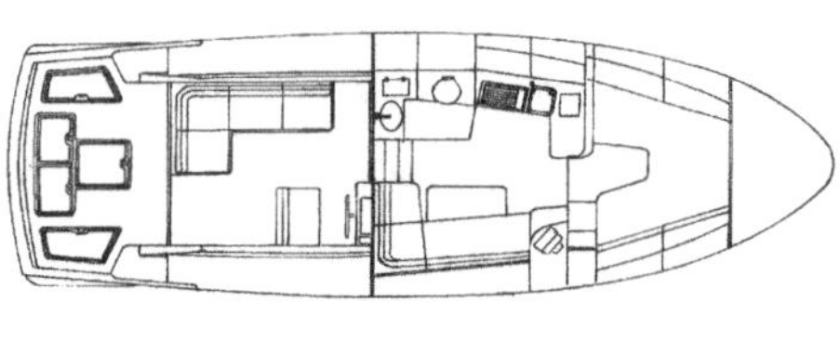

See Page 685 For Price Data

Length	34'0"	Water	94 gals.
Beam	12'5"	Waste	35 gals.
Draft	3'6"	Headroom	6'5"
Weight	15,800#	Hull Type	Modified-V
Fuel	251 gals.	Deadrise Aft	17°

Legacy 40 Express

1995–2006

A handsome Downeast-style cruiser, the 40 Sedan introduced in 1995 was Legacy's first entry into the powerboat market. She's built on an easily driven, fully cored hull with a sharp entry, moderate transom deadrise, and a deep skeg that protects the prop and rudder in the single-screw version. Not inexpensive, the finely crafted interior of the Legacy 40 is a blend of mahogany woodwork and trim with top-quality fixtures. Her standard galley-down floorplan (which can be altered to fit the requirements of buyers) includes two comfortable staterooms, each with a double berth. While the salon dimensions are modest compared with some 40-foot sedans, the large windows and lovely teak-and-holly cabin sole create a very comfortable and traditional environment indeed. Additional features include a roomy cockpit, wide side decks, and folding radar mast. Among several engine options available over the years, a single 420hp Cat diesel will cruise an early-model Legacy 40 at 17–18 knots, and later models with twin 370hp Cummins cruise at 22–23 knots. Note that a single-stateroom Express model is also available.

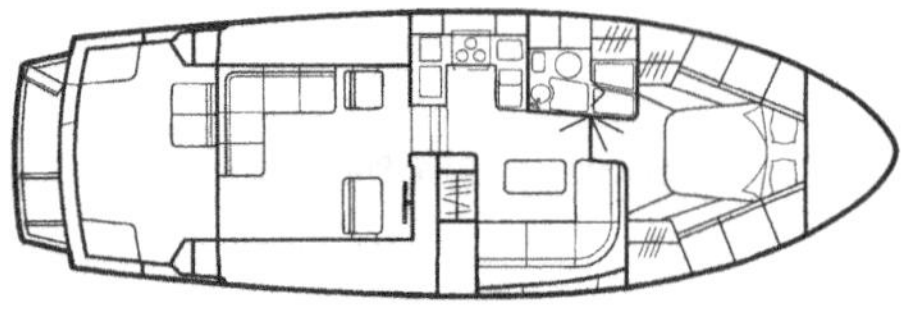

Not Enough Resale Data to Set Values

Length Overall	39'4"	Fuel	410 gals.
Length WL	36'0"	Water	120 gals.
Beam	13'7"	Waste	40 gals.
Draft	3'8"	Hull Type	Modified-V
Weight	22,000#	Deadrise Aft	17°

Luhrs

Quick View

- The Luhrs story began in the 1930s at the height of the depression when Henry Luhrs, Sr. opened a small boat-building company in New Jersey.
- Luhr's production-line manufacturing methods helped propel the companys growth, and by 1960 Luhrs and his sons, John and Warren, were producing more than 1,000 boats a year.
- In 1965, the company—then one of the largest in the industry—was sold to Bangor Punta, a railroad and lumber conglomerate.
- In 1969 Luhr's sons purchased a small New Jersey builder called Silverton Sea Skiffs.
- In 1980 the Luhrs brothers started two new companies, Mainship Yachts and Hunter Marine.
- John and Warren purchased the Luhrs name from Bangor Punta in 1981 and began production of an new series of sportfishing boats in St. Augustine, FL.
- Luhrs grew rapidly during the 1980s and 1990s, becoming one of the best known US manufacturers of offshore sportfishing boats.
- Morgan Industries, parent company of Luhrs Marine Group, filed for bankruptcy in 2012.

No longer in business.

Luhrs 250 Open

1993–1996

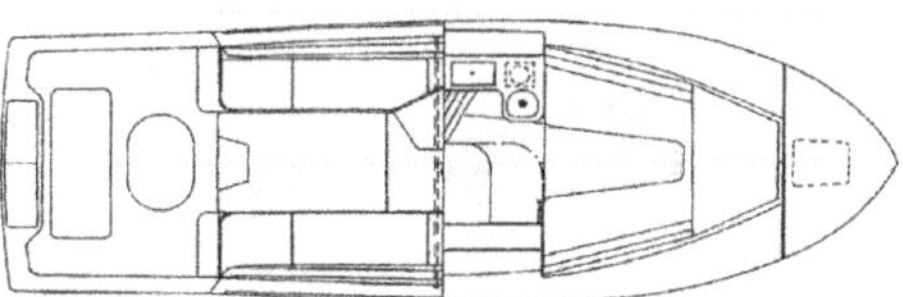

The Luhrs 250 Open is an inboard-powered fisherman with a spacious cockpit and overnight accommodations for four. She's built on a solid fiberglass modified-V hull with a wide beam and a well-flared, Carolina-style bow. Inboard power is rare in a boat this size, but the 250 will appeal to anglers seeking the reliability (and economy) of inboard engines as well as the open-cockpit, full-transom design that inboards allow. Her practical deck layout is arranged with the port and starboard lounge seating—enough for six adults—on an elevated bridgedeck, a couple of steps up from the cockpit level. An oval livewell is built into the transom, and a lazarette beneath the cockpit sole provides extra storage space. Four rod holders come with the (standard) soft-top half tower. Belowdecks, the dinette seats flip up to provide two upper berths, and a curtain encloses the head area for privacy. (Note that this is not an enclosed head compartment.) Additional features include a small galley area with space for a cooler, a swing-away helm seat, and tackle drawers. A single 320hp gas inboard will cruise at 18 knots (high 20s top), and twin 280hp gas inboards cruise at 26 knots (low 30s top).

See Page 686 For Price Data

Length	25'1"	Fuel	193 gals.
Beam	9'3"	Water	20 gals.
Draft	2'3"	Waste	20 gals.
Weight	7,800#	Hull Type	Modified-V
Clearance	8'6"	Deadrise Aft	15°

Luhrs 28 Open

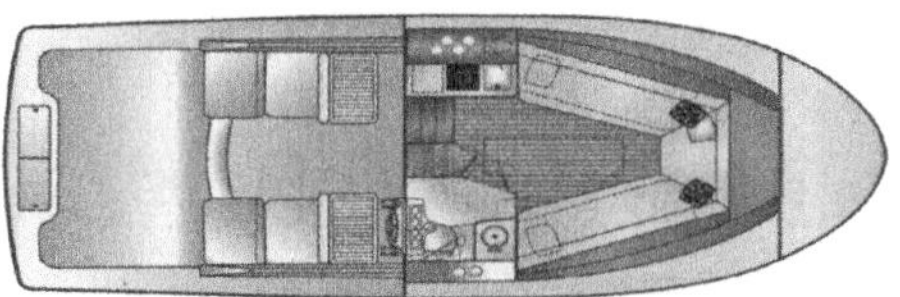

There are very few small inboard fishing boats being built these days, so the introduction of the Luhrs 28 Open in 2005 came as good news for offshore anglers who prefer the reliability of inboard power. With her handsome lines and expansive cockpit, the 28 offers an impressive mix of fishing and family-friendly features. For openers, a broad 11-foot, 6-inch beam makes this a big 28-footer allowing the well-appointed interior to provide the comfort and versatility of a somewhat larger boat. Seat backrests convert to pipe berths to accommodate a crew of four, and overhead racks can store up to eight rods. The full-feature cockpit of the 28 Open comes equipped with a transom fish box, insulated livewell to port, and bait-prep center with cutting board and tackle drawers. The bridge deck lifts for access to electrical panel, fuel tanks, and the engines. Additional features include fresh and saltwater washdowns, cockpit lazarette with rudder and pump access, and space at the helm for electronics. Built on a modified deep-V hull with a solid fiberglass bottom, twin 330hp gas engines cruise at 20 knots, and Yanmar 260hp diesels cruise at 24 knots. With 300 gallons of fuel, this boat has outstanding range.

See Page 686 For Price Data

Length w/Pulpit	31'10"	Fuel	300 gals.
Hull Length	29'10"	Water	55 gals.
Beam	11'6"	Waste	15 gals.
Draft	2'8"	Hull Type	Modified-V
Weight	10,000#	Deadrise Aft	19°

Luhrs 290 Open

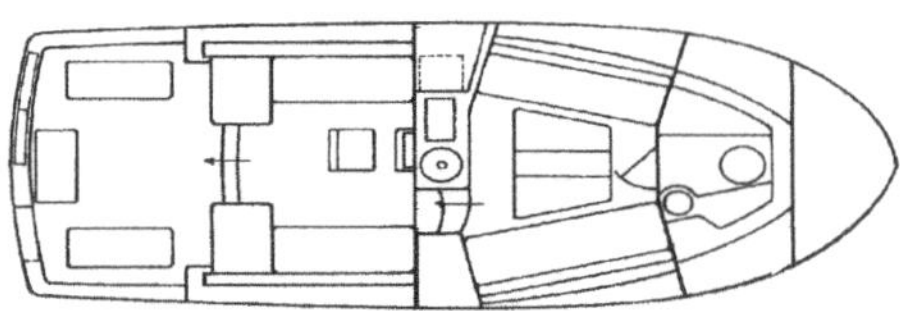

A good-selling model with classic South Florida styling, the Luhrs 290 Open will appeal to offshore anglers seeking a pocket fishing platform at an affordable price. She's built on a relatively lightweight modified-V hull with cored hullsides, a well-flared bow, and a wide 11-foot, 6-inch beam. Her cockpit is large enough for a full-size chair and includes two in-deck fish boxes, a transom door, and a smaller fish box built into the transom. The helm is located on the centerline (where visibility is excellent), and the entire bridge deck lifts up for easy access to the step-down engine compartment. The cabin of the 290 is somewhat unique: the head is forward and there are swing-up pilot berths over the port and starboard settees. A small galley is aft and the interior is nicely trimmed with teak. Notable features include a standard tower with buggy top and controls, electronics box, transom door, bait-prep station, bow pulpit, and side-dumping exhausts. Among several engine options offered over the years, twin 270hp inboard gas engines cruise the 290 Open at 16–17 knots (25+ knots top), and optional 230hp Yanmar or Volvo diesels cruise at an efficient 20–21 knots. (Note that she was called the 29 Open in 2001–2002.)

See Page 686 For Price Data

Length w/Pulpit	31'10"	Fuel	302 gals.
Hull Length	29'10"	Water	55 gals.
Beam	11'6"	Waste	20 gals.
Draft	2'0"	Hull Type	Modified-V
Weight	10,000#	Deadrise Aft	16°

Luhrs 300 Tournament

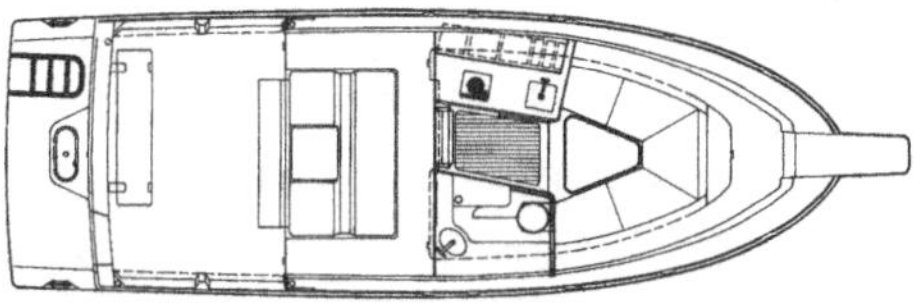

The Luhrs 300 Tournament is an updated version of the earlier Luhrs 290 Tournament (1989–90) with several notable improvements, including a windshield (which the 290 somehow lacked), and a fully integrated swim platform. A good-looking boat, she's built on a deep-V hull with average beam, a well-flared bow, and cored hullsides. The cockpit is large enough to handle a fighting chair and comes standard with an in-deck fish box, tackle drawers, bait-prep center, and two built-in seats with rod gimbals. The helm is set behind a center-vent windshield, and there's space in the console for flush-mounting electronics. A baitwell is located on the transom platform, and the full-length helm seat features a hydraulic lift mechanism for easy access to the (tight) engine compartment. Cabin accommodations include a dinette that converts to a double berth, a small galley, and a standup head with shower—a generous layout for a walkaround boat. Additional features include a bow pulpit, transom door, fish/dive platform, and wide walkarounds. Twin 270hp gas engines were standard (18–19 knots cruise/25+ top), and a pair of 170hp Yanmar diesels (18 knots cruise/20+ top) were a popular option.

See Page 686 For Price Data

Length w/Pulpit	34'6"	Fuel	250 gals.
Hull Length	31'6"	Water	40 gals.
Beam	10'9"	Waste	20 gals.
Draft	2'6"	Hull Type	Modified-V
Weight	12,000#	Deadrise Aft	18°

Luhrs 30/31 Open

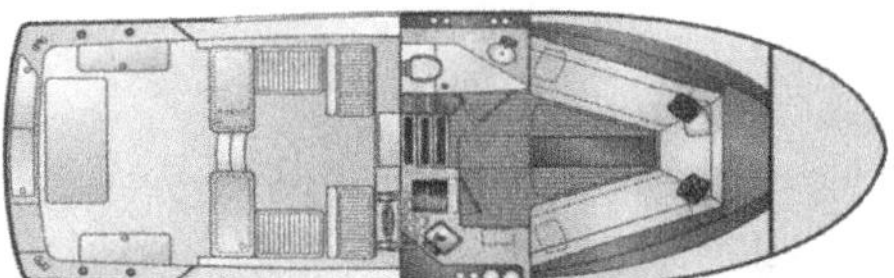

The Luhrs 30 Open (called the Luhrs 31 Open in 2006–09) is one of a handful of inboard express fishing boats her size built in recent hears. (Most fishboats in this size range are outboard-powered for reasons having to do with their higher speeds.) The 30/31 Open rides on a solid fiberglass deep-V hull whose prop pockets reduce both shaft angles and draft. The raised bridge deck offers excellent seating and helm visibility, and the cockpit is large enough to accommodate four anglers without bumping elbows. There are two insulated fish boxes in the cockpit, one in the sole and the other in the transom. A complete bait-prep center is forward, a cooler is to port, and a 45-gallon livewell is starboard. Below, the compact cabin is highlighted with a cherry-and-ash sole, quality hardware, and Corian counters. The forward settees convert to four single berths, and the head is quite large although it lacks an opening port. A hardtop, windlass, cockpit washdowns, and electronics box were standard. Standard gas inboards cruise at 25 knots (low 30s top), and optional 315hp Yanmar diesels cruise in the mid 20s (about 30 top). Newer models with Volvo 260hp IPS drives cruise at 22 knots.

See Page 686 For Price Data

Length Overall	34'4"	Fuel	300 gals.
Hull Length	31'5"	Water	50 gals.
Beam	11'10"	Waste	25 gals.
Draft	2'6"	Hull Type	Deep-V
Weight	13,500#	Deadrise Aft	20°

Luhrs 320 Convertible

1988–99

A popular model, the 320 Convertible was the first of Luhr's hugely successful Tournament series of moderately priced and highly styled fishing boats. (Note that the 320 was built on a fully cored hull until 1991 when Luhrs went to a solid fiberglass bottom and cored hullsides.) Good looks and a low price are a potent combination in the boating industry, and when an attractive light oak interior was added to the mix, the sales success of the 320 Convertible was assured. Belowdecks, an island berth is fitted in the single stateroom, and the salon is open to the mid-level galley. (Note that the original dinette layout was replaced in 1992 with facing settees.) The uncluttered cockpit of the 320 Convertible comes with molded tackle centers, a transom door, and washdowns. In a smart marketing decision, Luhrs made the half tower standard. While the flybridge on any 32-foot boat will be small, the bridge layout on the 320 managed up to five in reasonable comfort. Additional features include an in-deck fish box, a fighting chair plate in the cockpit sole, bow pulpit, and a fairly roomy engine compartment. Standard 320hp gas inboards cruise right around 20 knots and reach a top speed of 29–30 knots.

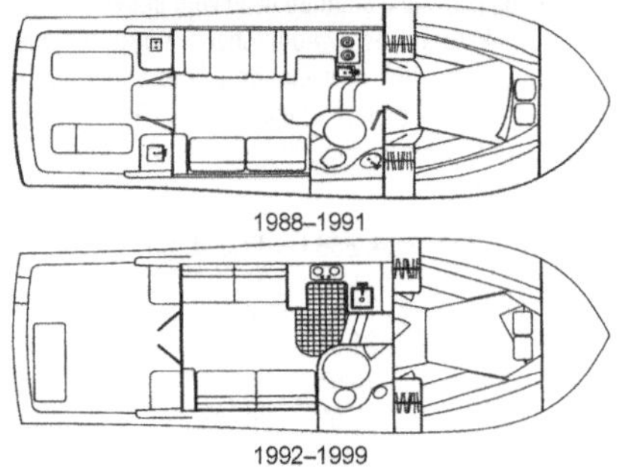
1988–1991

1992–1999

See Page 686 For Price Data

Length w/Pulpit	34'8"	Fuel	272 gals.
Hull Length	31'6"	Water	60 gals.
Beam	13'0"	Waste	30 gals.
Draft	3'1"	Hull Type	Modified-V
Weight	15,000#	Deadrise Aft	18°

Luhrs 320 Open

1994–2008

The Luhrs 32 Open (called the 32 Open from 2000–08) is a very handsome open express with a good deal of value built into her affordable base price. Designed as a smaller alternative to the 38 Open, the 32 is built on a deep-V hull with cored hullsides, a wide beam, and a considerable amount of flare at the bow. The deck plan is arranged with a walkaround center console and flanking bench seats on the bridge deck level, and a big fishing cockpit aft with a transom door, molded tackle center, and standup livewell. Inside, the 32 Open has berths for five with a V-berth/dinette forward and a convertible settee whose hinged backrest becomes a pilot berth at night. The teak woodwork, Corian countertops, and upscale fabrics make this an attractive and easily cleaned interior. The list of standard equipment is impressive: full tower with controls, hardtop with electronics box, enclosure panels, and cockpit washdowns. Among several engine choices, standard 5.7L gas engines cruise the Luhrs 320 Open around 20 knots and reach a top speed of 28–30 knots. Optional 315hp Yanmar diesels cruise at a fast 28 knots (mid 30s top).

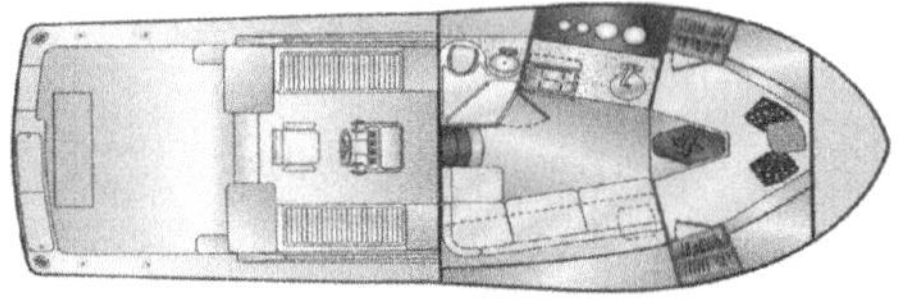

See Page 686 For Price Data

Length w/Pulpit	34'8"	Fuel	340 gals.
Hull Length	31'6"	Water	60 gals.
Beam	13'0"	Waste	30 gals.
Draft	3'1"	Hull Type	Modified-V
Weight	15,000#	Deadrise Aft	18°

Luhrs 34 Convertible

The smallest flybridge model in the Luhrs fleet when she was introduced in the fall of 1999, the 34 Convertible is an affordably priced flybridge sedan with a comfortable interior and a roomy cockpit with plenty of built-in fishing amenities. There aren't many production 34-foot convertibles being built these days so the 34 fills a much-neglected niche in the market. Constructed on a beamy modified-V hull with cored hullsides, the single-stateroom interior of the Luhrs 34 is arranged with the galley aft in the salon and a split head—the toilet and stall shower compartments are separate—which eases congestion in the morning. The starboard salon settee slides out to create a double berth and the backrest can be flipped up for another berth. The flybridge will seat four, and molded steps lead up to the bridge rather than a ladder. Additional features include cockpit engineroom access, transom door, tackle center, transom fish box, and a molded hardtop. Note that the engineroom is a tight fit. Standard 320hp gas engines cruise the Luhrs 34 Convertible at 18 knots, and optional 350hp Yanmar diesels cruise around 22 knots and reach a top speed close to 30 knots.

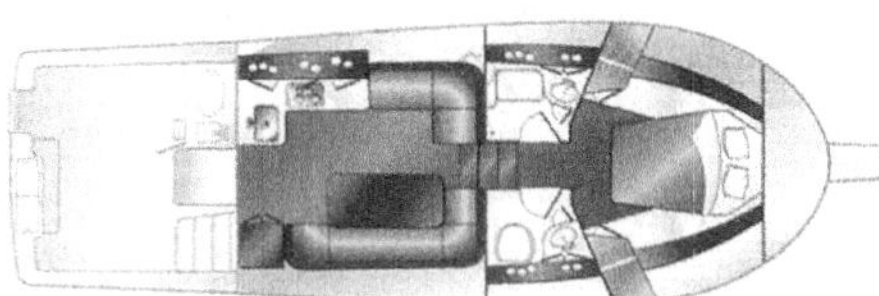

See Page 686 For Price Data

Length w/Pulpit	36'10"	Fuel	300 gals.
Beam	13'1"	Water	90 gals.
Draft	3'4"	Waste	40 gals.
Weight	18,000#	Hull Type	Modified-V
Clearance	16'5"	Deadrise Aft	18°

Luhrs 350 Convertible

Considered a particularly handsome boat when she was introduced in 1990, the Luhrs 350 Convertible is a solid, midsized fishing boat equally suitable for hardcore fishing or family cruising. Aside from her aggressive profile and custom-style appearance, the 350 was affordably priced as well—no small factor in the eyes of any boating enthusiast. Her original single-stateroom floorplan is arranged with the mid-level galley open to the salon and an island berth in the bow stateroom. An updated two-stateroom floorplan introduced in 1995 has the galley in the salon and a smaller forward stateroom. Either way, the interior of the 350 is large for a 35-footer and it's quite surprising to find a cockpit big enough for a fighting chair and a full tackle center. Note that a half tower and transom door were standard, and the flybridge was redesigned in 1995. Twin 310hp gas engines cruise the Luhrs 350 Convertible at 17 knots with a top speed of around 25–26 knots. Optional Cat 350hp (or Volvo 370hp) diesels cruise around 24 knots and reach 28 knots top. Note that the 350 Convertible is not one of Luhr's better riding boats in a chop.

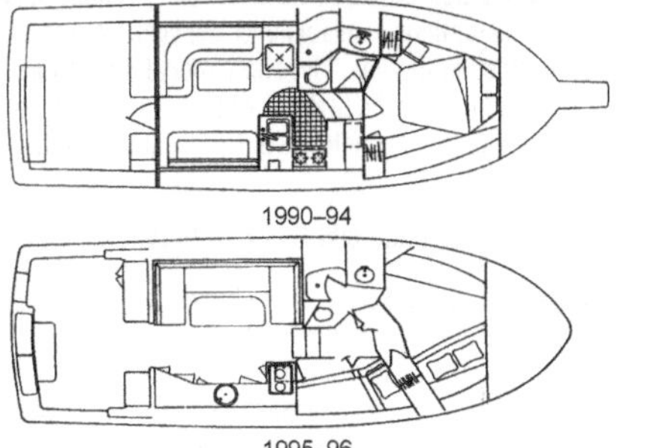

See Page 686 For Price Data

Length w/Pulpit	38'6"	Fuel	390 gals.
Hull Length	35'0"	Water	93 gals.
Beam	12'10"	Waste	40 gals.
Draft	3'4"	Hull Type	Modified-V
Weight	20,000#	Deadrise Aft	18°

Luhrs 36 Convertible

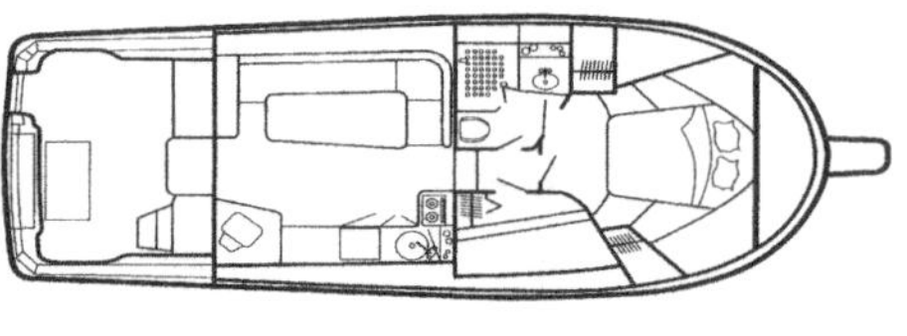

The Luhrs 36 Convertible's most notable feature when she came out in 1998 is the molded staircase leading from the cockpit up to the flybridge. Rather than negotiating a near-vertical ladder, these steps make bridge access easy and a good deal safer for everyone. Built on a beamy deep-V hull with a well-flared bow, the 36 boasts a very spacious interior although it comes at the expense of a rather small cockpit (at least compared with other sportfishing boats her size). The two-stateroom, galley-up floorplan is arranged with a queen berth forward and a settee in the guest cabin that converts into over/under single berths. A separate shower stall is found in the head, and an L-shaped settee/dinette is to port in the spacious salon. The engineroom is accessed through a hatch in the salon sole. Topside, the 36 does give up some flybridge space to accommodate the stairway, but not much. Fishing features include a transom door, a transom fish box, and a molded bait-prep center to port. Note that the side decks are narrow. A factory half tower was standard. Among several engine choices, optional 440hp Yanmar diesels cruise at 22 knots and deliver a top speed in the mid-to-high 20s.

See Page 686 For Price Data

Length w/Pulpit	38'11"	Fuel	400 gals.
Hull Length	36'2"	Water	94 gals.
Beam	13'10"	Waste	30 gals.
Draft	3'3"	Hull Type	Modified-V
Weight	22,000#	Deadrise Aft	18°

Luhrs 36 SX; 36 Open

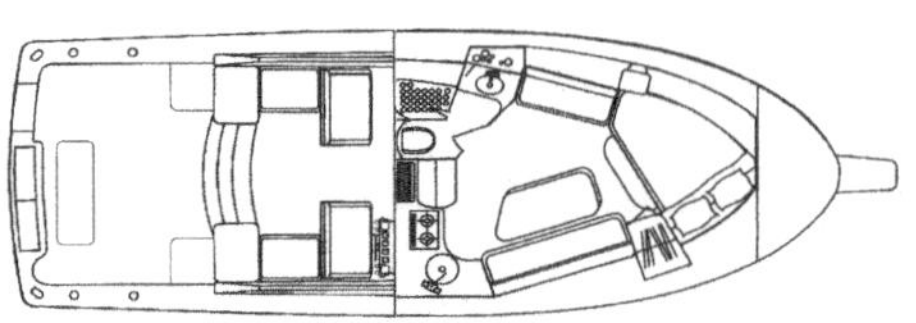

Serious anglers looking for a well styled, moderately priced express fisherman with good open-water performance will find a lot to like in the Luhrs 36 Open. (Note that she was called the 36 SX from 1997–2001.) Constructed on a beamy deep-V hull with cored hullsides and a well flared bow, the deep cockpit of the Luhrs 36 is large enough for a full-size fighting chair and comes with transom fish box, a portside transom door, rod holders and a split tackle center/sink forward. The bridge deck, a few steps up from the cockpit sole, can be raised hydraulically for excellent access to the engines. The spacious interior—with its teak woodwork, separate stall shower, full galley, and berths for four—is attractively finished and easily suited for family cruising. Additional features include a bow pulpit, doublewide helm and companion seats, reasonably wide side decks and a well-arranged helm console. Among many gas and diesel engine options available over the years, a pair of 420hp gas engines cruise in the low 20s, and optional 420hp Cats cruise at 26–27 knots. Note that the first few of these boats (built in 1997) came with a center-console helm layout and a standard radar arch.

See Page 686 For Price Data

Length w/Pulpit	38'11"	Headroom	6'4"
Hull Length	36'2"	Fuel	400 gals.
Beam	13'10"	Water	94 gals.
Draft	3'5"	Hull Type	Modified-V
Weight	22,000#	Deadrise Aft	18°

Luhrs 380/40/38 Convertible

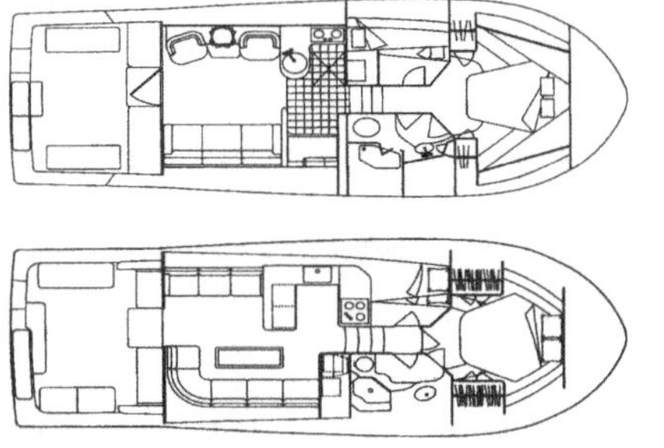

Like all of Luhr's recent products, the 380 Convertible (called the 40 Convertible in 1999–2003; 38 Convertible in 2004–08) delivered an impressive blend of solid construction, roomy accommodations, and a very competitive price. She's built on a beamy deep-V hull designed with generous flare at the bow and balsa coring in the hullsides. The half-tower was standard, and her tournament-style flybridge and the large cockpit with molded tackle centers will satisfy the demands of most serious anglers. Several two-stateroom floorplans were offered during her production years, all with a spacious salon, a roomy master stateroom, and a well-appointed decor. Storage is excellent, and the head compartment comes with a separate stall shower. The 380 came with a good deal of standard equipment including air conditioning, generator, rocket launchers, bait well, and in-deck fish boxes. A popular model, 370hp gas engines were standard until 1991, but the vast majority of these boats were sold with diesel power. Among several choices, a pair of 485hp Detroit diesels cruise at 23 knots (27–28 knots top), and 420hp Cat (or 440hp Yanmar) diesels cruise at 19–20 knots (mid 20s top).

See Page 686 For Price Data

Length w/Pulpit .... 40'10"
Hull Length .... 37'9"
Beam .... 14'11"
Draft .... 3'7"
Weight .... 30,000#

Fuel .... 423 gals.
Water .... 94 gals.
Waste .... 36 gals.
Hull Type .... Modified-V
Deadrise Aft .... 18°

Luhrs 380/40/38 Open

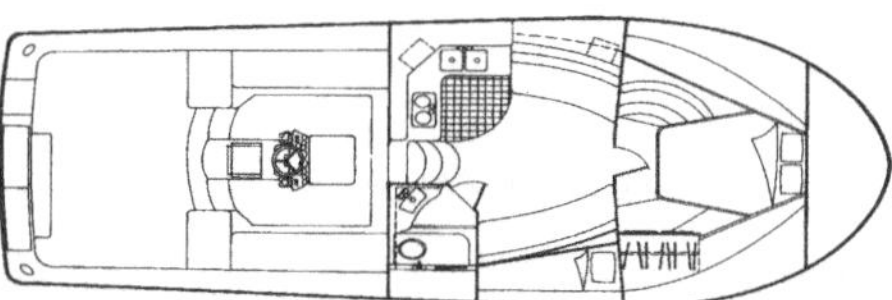

Luhrs came up with a real beauty in the 380 Open (called the 40 Open in 1999–2004; 38 Open in 2004–07), a big, feature-packed fishing machine with a very inviting price tag. Open sportfishing boats have been growing in length and popularity in recent years, and the competition between manufacturers in this marketing segment is very competitive. Built on a wide, low-profile hull with cored hullsides, the 380 Open is a roomy boat with plenty of space for guests and crew. Her large bi-level cockpit layout includes a unique centerline helm console flanking full-length lounge seats with rod storage under, a molded transom fish box, and port and starboard tackle centers, which double as bait-watching seats. Below, the interior is notable for its spacious layout and stylish decor—impressive accommodations indeed for a serious fishboat. Additional features include a standard tuna tower, hydraulic bridge deck lift mechanism for superb engineroom access, pop-up electronics display at the helm and side exhausts. A good-running boat with excellent range, optional 420hp Cat (or 420hp Yanmar) diesels cruise around 26 knots and deliver a top speed in the neighborhood of 30 knots.

See Page 686 For Price Data

Length w/Pulpit .... 40'10"
Hull Length .... 37'9"
Beam .... 14'11"
Draft .... 3'7"
Weight .... 30,000#

Fuel .... 563 gals.
Water .... 80 gals.
Waste .... 36 gals.
Hull Type .... Modified-V
Transom Deadrise .... 18°

Luhrs 41 Convertible

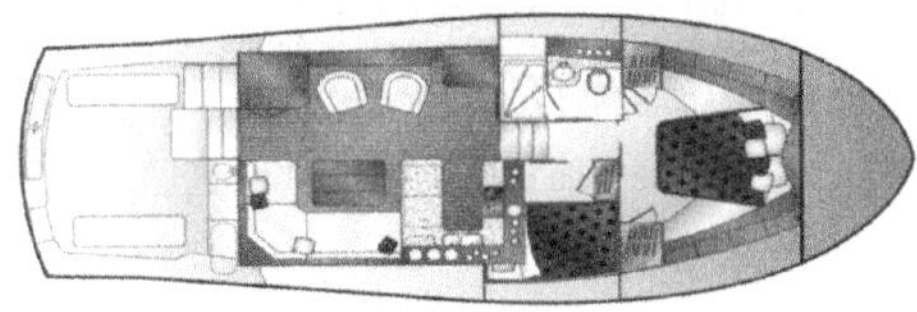

Offshore anglers will find a lot to like in the Luhrs 41 Convertible, beginning with her rakish good looks and including a spacious interior and good open-water performance. Heavily built on a modified-V hull with prop pockets and a wide 15-foot, 9-inch beam, the two-stateroom interior of the Luhrs 41 includes a large master stateroom forward with an island berth and two big hanging lockers. The U-shaped galley is forward in the salon, which has an electrically operated Ultraleather sofa, twin barrel chairs, and a full entertainment center with a flat-screen TV. A handsome teak-and-holly cabin sole replaces the carpet found in many older Luhrs models. (An optional washer/dryer unit can be installed in a salon cabinet.) Topside, the 85-square-foot cockpit has two large fish boxes in the sole and two smaller boxes in the transom. A tackle center is forward with livewell and sink, and a portside stairway leads up to the bridge with an L-shaped bench seat forward of the helm console. A factory hardtop was standard. Note that the engineroom of the Luhrs 41 is particularly well arranged. Cummins 580hp diesels cruise in the high 20s and reach around 30 knots wide open.

See Page 686 For Price Data

Length w/Pulpit	44'6"	Fuel	600 gals.
Hull Length	42'3"	Water	130 gals.
Beam	15'9"	Waste	40 gals.
Draft	3'6"	Hull Type	Modified-V
Weight	33,000#	Deadrise Aft	18°

Luhrs 41 Open

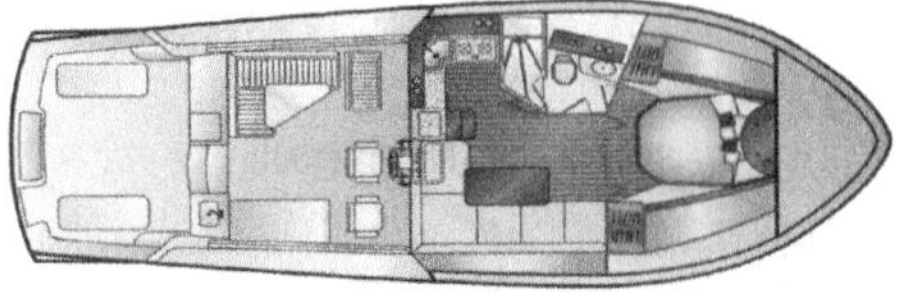

Introduced in 2006, the Luhrs 41 Open is among the larger express sportfishing boats built in recent years. Based on the hull of the 41 Convertible, the 41 Open has the same Carolina-style flared bow and distinctive hull tumblehome at the transom. With a broad 15'9" beam, the 41 Open is a big boat for her size. Her 100-square-foot fishing cockpit came standard with a 50-gallon livewell in the transom, molded bait-prep station with tackle drawers, sink and water faucet, two 45-gallon in-deck fish boxes with macerators, and four gunwale-mount rod holders. Note the separate pump room aft of engineroom. Belowdecks, the 41 Open's well-appointed interior uses the galley counter as the first step into the cabin—maybe not such a good idea. An L-shaped dinette, which electrically slides out to form a double berth, seats six and features storage for seven rods behind the seat back. The forward stateroom has a queen-sized island berth with storage under and two hanging lockers. An open-air galley was available for the bridge deck, and the standup engineroom is unusual in a boat this size. Prop pockets reduce draft and shaft angles. Cruise at 26–27 knots with Cummins 580hp diesels (about 30 knots top).

See Page 686 For Price Data

Length w/Pulpit	44'6"	Clearance	22'0"
Hull Length	42'3"	Fuel	600 gals.
Beam	15'9"	Water	130 gals.
Draft	3'6"	Hull Type	Modified-V
Weight	33,000#	Deadrise Aft	18°

Luhrs 44 Convertible

The Luhrs 44 Convertible is an impressive blend of style, performance, and value. She is, in fact, significantly less expensive than most of her competitors, especially considering her extensive list of standard equipment. Built on a low-deadrise, modified-V hull with a deep keel and plenty of beam, the layout of the Luhrs 44 is a bit unusual in that the galley and entertainment center are aft in the salon and the seating areas are forward. With her long foredeck, the house is shorter in length than most other convertibles her size, resulting in somewhat modest salon dimensions. The staterooms, however, are quite spacious, and there's space in the companionway for an optional washer/dryer. Note that the head is split with the toilet separated from the shower by a solid sliding door. In the cockpit, Luhr's signature BridgeWalk stairway makes bridge access easy, but at the expense of some valuable cockpit space. Standard features include a hardtop with spreader lights, 13.5 kw genset, Mathers electronic controls, bait freezer, engine crash pumps, and a huge 60-gallon livewell. Expect a cruising speed in the low-to-mid 20s with optional 635hp Cummins diesels (about 30 knots top).

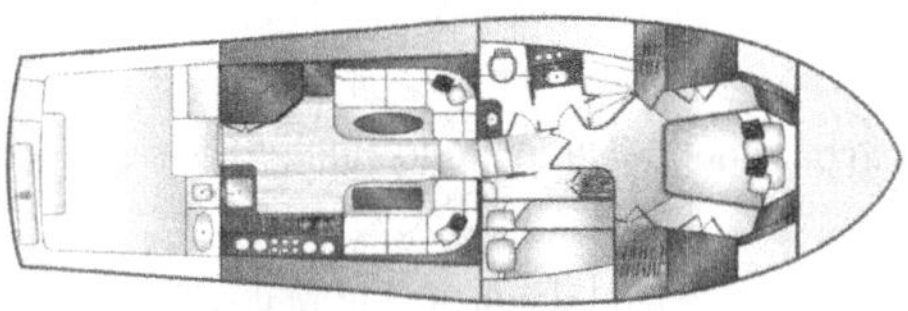

See Page 686 For Price Data

Length w/Pulpit	46'4"	Clearance	18'4"
Hull Length	43'2"	Fuel	700 gals.
Beam	16'0"	Water	125 gals.
Draft	4'6"	Hull Type	Modified-V
Weight	33,500#	Deadrise Aft	12°

Luhrs 50 Convertible

A well-styled boat with the sleek profile typical of most late-model Luhrs designs, the Luhrs 50 Convertible is a competitively priced tournament fisherman with a super-wide 18-foot beam and a molded stairway ascending to the flybridge from the cockpit. She's constructed on a modified-V hull with a flared bow and shallow keel, and her graceful sheer, sleek windows and extended bridge overhang have become hallmarks of modern Luhr's styling. The spacious three-stateroom interior of the Luhrs 50 is arranged with the owner's cabin forward, and a unique feature of the deckhouse galley is an island work area flanked by an L-shaped counter. The huge 155-square-foot cockpit comes complete with fish boxes, a livewell, freezer, washdowns and tackle center—all standard. The molded flybridge steps will be a convenience to some, but they enter the bridge forward of the helm resulting in a slightly awkward flybridge layout. Additional features include a hardtop with enclosure, cockpit access to the engine room, and maple or cherry interior trim. Twin 800hp Cat diesels cruise at 26–27 knots (30+ knots top), and optional 1,350hp 12-cylinder Cats cruise at 31–32 knots (about 35 knots wide open).

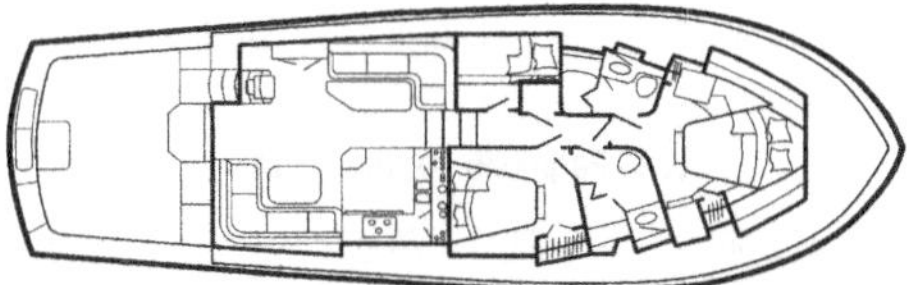

See Page 686 For Price Data

Length	50'10"	Fuel	1,000 gals.
Beam	18'0"	Water	200 gals.
Draft	5'0"	Headroom	6'5"
Weight	48,000#	Hull Type	Modified-V
Clearance	18'0"	Deadrise Aft	12°

Mainship

Quick View

- Mainship, a subsidiary of the Luhrs Maine Group which also owned Silverton, was a spin-off of the popular Mainship 34 Trawler introduced by Silverton in 1978.
- In response to the fuel crisis of the 1970s and '80s, Mainship built more than 1,200 trawlers from 30 to 40 feet in length.
- The line was expanded to include several sedan cruiser and double-cabin models, and by the early 1990s Mainship was offering a full line of express cruisers and motor yachts.
- Mainship built a reputation over the years for delivering good value thanks to efficient production methods and their policy of including an extensive list of standard equipment with each boat.
- In the 1990s, Mainship reintroduced its trawler line with two new models: a 35- and 39-footer, delivering more than 300 boats in five years.
- Morgan Industries, parent company of Mainship, Luhrs, Silverton, and Hunter Sailboats filed for bankruptcy in May, 2012.
- David Marlow, president/owner of Marlow Yachts, purchased the assets of Mainship late in 2012. The new company's first model was introduced in February, 2013.

Marlow/Mainship • www.mainship.com

Mainship 30 Pilot

1998–2007

Mainship got it right with the 30 Pilot, a Downeast-style cruiser whose practical layout and affordable price catapulted her into the ranks of classic small-boat designs. Built on a solid fiberglass, semi-displacement hull with a prop-protecting skeg, the Pilot is suited to a variety of uses. A large cockpit makes her a competent fish or dive platform, and her economical operation and comfortable accommodations appeal to weekend cruisers. Don't look for a lot of glitz in the Pilot—this is a basic boat with modest amenities and average workmanship. The cabin was originally arranged with a V-berth/dinette forward, a good-sized head, and a teak-and-holly cabin sole. In 2003, the updated Series II Pilot featured a cherry interior and a revised cabin layout with a V-berth that folds in half when not in use. (Note that the Series II also incorporates a shortened keel, propeller tunnel, and a five-blade prop.) Early models with a single 170hp Yanmar diesel will cruise at 14 knots (16–17 knots top), and those with a 230hp Yanmar will cruise at 16 knots (19–20 knots top). Series II models with a 315hp Yanmar will cruise at a steady 18 knots and reach a top speed in the low 20s.

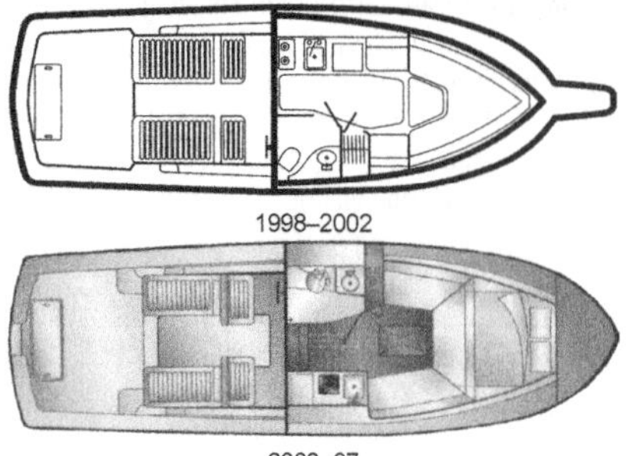
1998–2002

2003–07

See Page 686 For Price Data

Length w/Pulpit	33'1"	Weight	10,000#
Hull Length	30'0"	Fuel	175 gals.
Beam	10'3"	Water	40 gals.
Draft, Original Hull	2'11"	Waste	13 gals.
Draft, Series II	2'3"	Hull Type	Semi-Disp.

Mainship 30 Pilot Sedan

The Mainship 30 Pilot Sedan is a hardtop version of popular Mainship 30 Pilot. The big difference, of course, is the Sedan's semi-enclosed helm and bridge deck. Built on a solid fiberglass, semi-displacement hull with a prop-protecting skeg, the Pilot is suited to a variety of uses. A large cockpit makes her a competent fish or dive platform, and her economical operation and comfortable accommodations appeal to weekend cruisers. Don't look for a lot of glitz in the Pilot—this is a basic boat with modest amenities and average workmanship. The cabin was originally arranged with a V-berth/dinette forward, a good-sized head, and a teak-and-holly cabin sole. In 2003, the updated Series II Pilot featured a new cherry interior and a revised cabin layout with a V-berth that folds in half when not in use. (Note that the Series II also incorporates a shortened keel, propeller tunnel, and a five-blade prop.) Early models with a single 170hp Yanmar diesel will cruise at 14 knots (16–17 knots top), and those with a 230hp Yanmar cruise at 16 knots (19–20 knots top). Series II models with a 315hp Yanmar cruise at a steady 18 knots and reach a top speed in the low 20s.

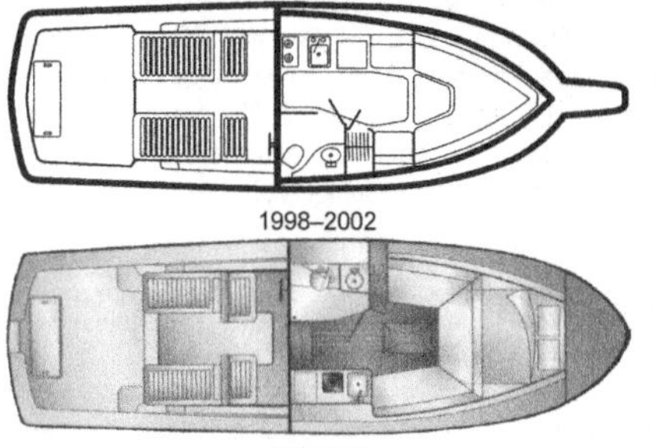
1998–2002

2003–07

See Page 687 For Price Data

Length w/Pulpit	33'1"	Weight	11,000#
Hull Length	30'0"	Fuel	175 gals.
Beam	10'3"	Water	40 gals.
Draft, Original Hull	2'11"	Waste	13 gals.
Draft, Series II	2'3"	Hull Type	Semi-Disp.

Mainship 31 Sedan Bridge

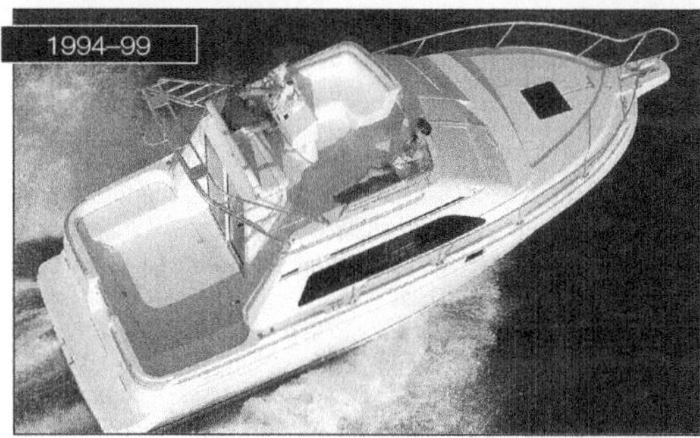

While the chief attraction of the 31 Sedan Bridge may have been her attractive styling and affordable price, those who step below will be immediately impressed with the spacious interior packed into this small cruiser. Like all sedan-bridge designs, the sunken floorplan is made possible by locating the engines aft, under the cockpit, rather than placing them beneath the salon sole. The result is a wide-open interior arranged more or less on a single level from the salon forward. There are two staterooms in this layout—no small achievement in a 31-foot boat. The galley is opposite the dinette in the main salon, and a double-entry head offers private access to the forward stateroom. Outside, molded steps lead up to the flybridge with its wraparound guest seating and portside helm position. With very narrow side decks, a walk-through in the bridge coaming provides direct access to the foredeck. The cockpit comes with a transom door, and the entire cockpit sole lifts up to get at the engines. Additional features include a swim platform, molded cockpit seating, hidden swim ladder, and a bow pulpit. Twin 340hp V-drive gas engines cruise at 19–20 knots (about 30 knots top).

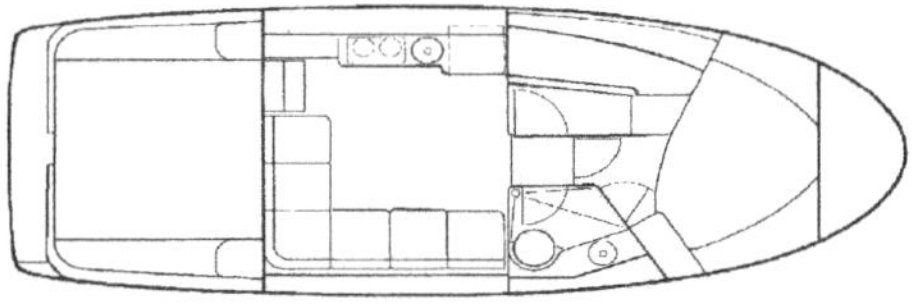

See Page 687 For Price Data

Length Overall	33'3"	Clearance	14'4"
Hull Length	31'3"	Fuel	200 gals.
Beam	11'10"	Water	50 gals.
Draft	2'10"	Hull Type	Modified-V
Weight	16,000#	Deadrise Aft	13°

Mainship 34 Motor Yacht

Mainship engineers went all-out with the 34 Motor Yacht in an effort to create the interior volume of a 40-footer in a 34-foot boat. Built on a solid fiberglass hull with a wide beam, this moderately priced family cruiser is aimed at those who want the absolute maximum living space possible in a small motor yacht. Not only are double berths found in both staterooms, but both heads have separate stall showers—no small feat in a boat this size. Not surprisingly, the salon dimensions are quite modest, although the wide beam and the absence of wide side decks provides a good deal of width. Note that the engineroom, accessed via hatches in the salon sole, is a tight fit. Topside, lounge seating surrounds the center-console helm, and a walk-through in the forward bridge coaming provides easy access to the foredeck. Additional features include an aft deck wet bar, hardtop, molded steps to the bridge and swim platform, molded-in side boarding steps, and a radar arch. No award-winner when it comes to sex appeal (or performance, for that matter), standard 320hp gas inboards cruise the Mainship 34 MY at 15 knots and reach a top speed of 26–27 knots. This was a very popular model for Mainship.

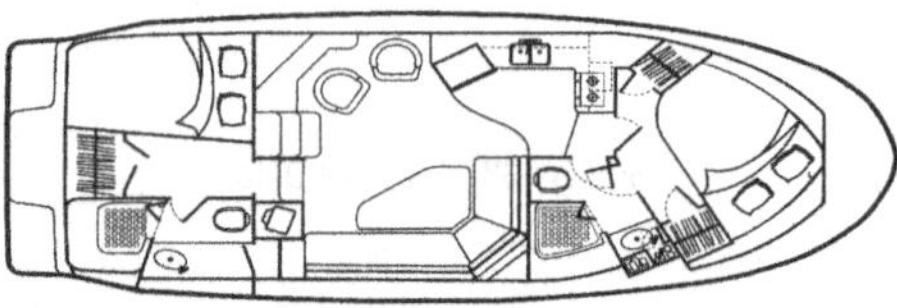

See Page 687 For Price Data

Length w/Pulpit	36'5"	Fuel	300 gals.
Hull Length	34'6"	Water	70 gals.
Beam	13'8"	Waste	30 gals.
Draft	3'2"	Hull Type	Modified-V
Weight	18,500#	Deadrise Aft	16°

Mainship 34 Pilot Sedan

The Mainship 34 Pilot is an enlarged version of the hugely popular Mainship 30 Pilot, a stylish Downeast cruiser introduced by Mainship in 1998. Where the 30 is essentially a dayboat, the larger interior of the 34 provides the volume required for extended cruising. The first 34 Pilots were express models; in 2001 the Sedan version—with an extended hardtop—came out, offering owners the added security of a semi-enclosed pilothouse. Well-appointed accommodations consist a roomy main salon with galley and convertible dinette, enclosed head with shower, and a single stateroom forward with bi-fold privacy door. A TV on a swivel platform is mounted forward in the cabin. In the cockpit, facing bench seats behind the helm and companion seats can double as extra berths. A centerline hatch in the cockpit provides access to the engine. Additional features include a standard bow thruster, tilt-away helm, transom door, and wide side decks. The 34 rides on a semi-displacement hull with moderate beam and a long, prop-protecting keel. A single 350hp Yanmar diesel will cruise the 34 Pilot at 14 knots (burning just 8–10 gallons per hour) and reach a top speed of 16–17 knots. Twin 240hp Yanmar diesels cruise at 18 knots.

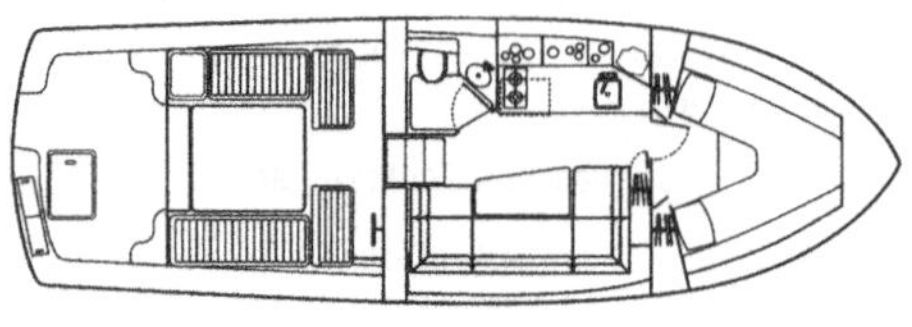

See Page 687 For Price Data

Length w/Pulpit	36'1"	Clearance	9'0"
Hull Length	34'0"	Fuel	250 gals.
Beam	12'3"	Water	70 gals.
Draft	3'3"	Waste	20 gals.
Weight	16,000#	Hull Type	Semi-Disp.

Mainship 34 Trawler

Designed for comfortable coastal cruising, the Mainship 34 Trawler combines a salty profile with sturdy construction and a practical single-stateroom interior. Many will see the 34 as the ideal boat for the cruising couple—easily handled in tight quarters, easy to maintain, and reasonably easy on the wallet. Built on a semi-displacement hull with a full keel, the galley-down layout of the Mainship 34 results in a notably spacious salon. A serving counter (with two stools) overlooks the galley, and a convertible sleeper-sofa is available to accommodate overnight guests. The U-shaped galley has all the amenities required for preparing meals including generous storage and Corian counters. Forward, the stateroom has a centerline double berth and space for an optional TV, and the double-entry head compartment includes a separate stall shower. Note that a lower helm was optional. On deck, a flybridge overhang shelters the Mainship's wide walkways. Note that the engineroom access hatch beneath the flybridge stairway is a tight fit. A single 240hp Yanmar diesel will cruise efficiently at 8 knots (12–13 knots top). Twin 315hp Yanmars reach 16–18 knots top. (The modest fuel capacity limits range with twin engines.)

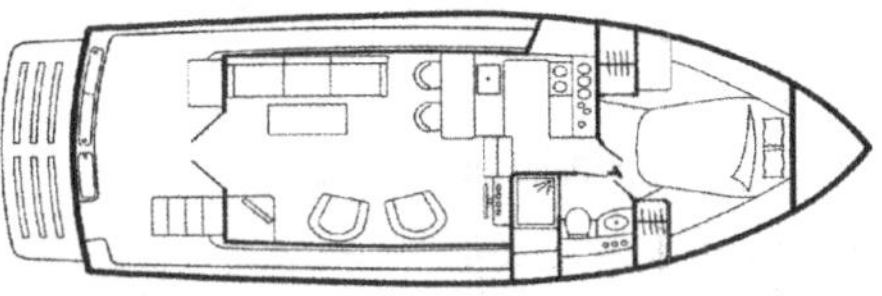

See Page 687 For Price Data

Length w/Pulpit	38'10"	Headroom	6'4"
Beam	14'3"	Fuel	250 gals.
Draft	3'4"	Water	70 gals.
Weight	20,000#	Waste	34 gals.
Clearance	15'0"	Hull Type	Semi-Disp.

Mainship 350/390 Trawler

The Mainship 350 Trawler (called the Mainship 390 in 1999–2005) is a stylish, moderately priced coastal cruiser with classic trawler lines and a good turn of speed. Unlike a true trawler with a full-displacement hull, the 350/390 is built on a faster modified-V hull with flat aftersections and a shallow, full-length keel. She's a very roomy boat inside thanks to her wide 14-foot, 2-inch beam, and the floorplan manages to include double berths in both staterooms as well as a separate stall shower in the head. (Note that the guest stateroom is partially tucked beneath the galley.) Visibility from the lower helm is excellent, and a deck door provides easy access to the foredeck. Aft, a sliding glass door opens to the covered cockpit where a series of molded steps (instead of a ladder) ascends to the extended flybridge. Additional features include deep, well-protected side decks, an integral swim platform, transom door, a full teak interior, and radar mast. Among several engine choices, a single 300hp Cat diesel will cruise the Mainship 350/390 at 10–12 knots (about 14 knots top), and twin 230hp Yanmars cruise at 14 knots (18–19 top).

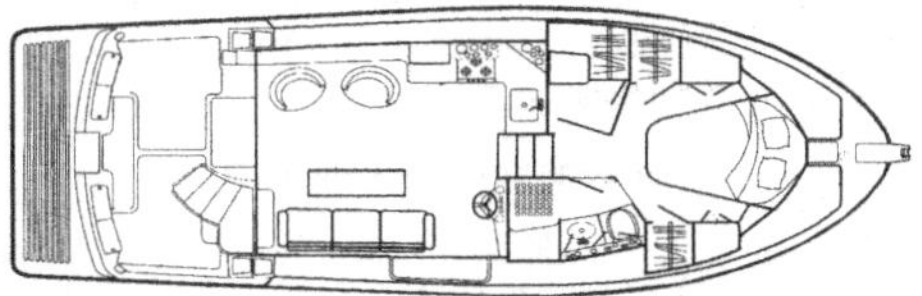

See Page 687 For Price Data

Length Overall	39'9"	Clearance	18'8"
Hull Length	34'9"	Fuel	300 gals.
Beam	14'2"	Water	130 gals.
Draft	3'8"	Waste	30 gals.
Weight	22,000#	Hull Type	Modified-V

Mainship 37 Motor Yacht

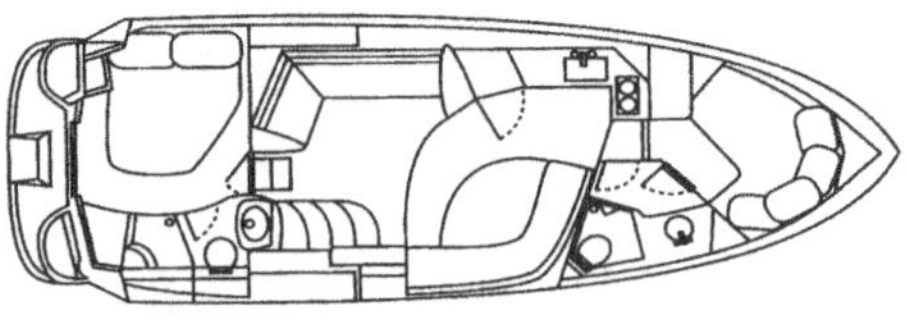

The Mainship 37 Motor Yacht was quite an innovative design when she came out in 1995 with several unique features. Most small motor yachts this size have an open front windshield, but not the Mainship. This allows for a very unusual interior configuration with the step-down galley and dinette completely merged into the salon. The result is a truly cavernous main cabin area with a sculptured overhead and extraordinary headroom throughout. While the salon windows are located at head-level, there's an unusual starboardside window at the dinette level opposite the galley. Given the extravagant salon dimensions, it's hardly a surprise that the staterooms are small. The aft deck is also small, but the flybridge is huge with a centerline helm console and wraparound seating for eight. Because of her narrow side decks, a walk-through in the forward flybridge coaming provides direct access to the foredeck. A hardtop was a popular option, and the molded boarding steps on either side of the aft deck are quite unique. A heavy boat with lots of freeboard, twin 370hp gas inboards cruise the 37 Motor Yacht at 14–15 knots with a top speed in the low 20s.

See Page 687 For Price Data

Length w/Pulpit	39'6"	Fuel	300 gals.
Hull Length	37'9"	Water	100 gals.
Beam	13'5"	Clearance	13'6"
Draft	3'7"	Hull Type	Modified-V
Weight	21,000#	Deadrise Aft	17°

Mainship 395 Trawler

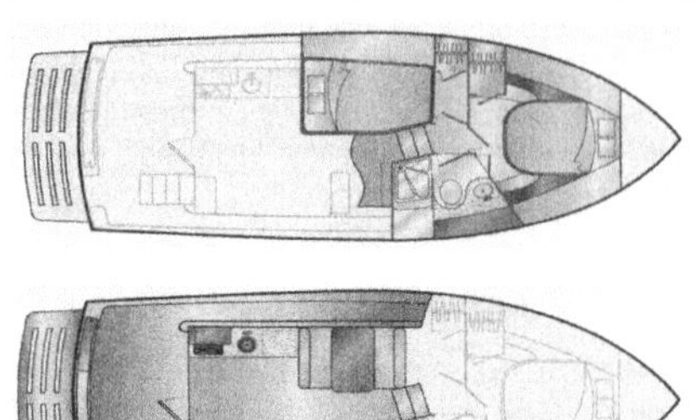

The Mainship 395 Trawler is a fuel-efficient, moderately priced performance trawler with classic lines, space-efficient accommodations, and a good turn of speed. Unlike a true displacement trawler, the 395 is built on a faster semi-displacement hull with flat aftersections and a shallow, full-length keel—a hull design that provides high efficiency at slower speeds, yet can be run at planing speeds as well. She's a surprisingly big boat inside thanks to a broad 14'3" beam, and the floorplan manages to include double berths in both staterooms as well as a separate stall shower in the head. (Note that the guest stateroom is partially tucked beneath the raised dinette in the salon.) The galley is aft in the salon where it can be easily accessed from the cockpit. Visibility from the lower helm is excellent, and the center windshield panel swings open for ventilation. Aft, a sliding glass door opens to the covered cockpit where a series of molded steps ascend to the flybridge. Additional features include bow and stern thrusters, transom door, and flybridge seating for six. Power options included a V-drive single Yanmar 380hp diesel (8–10 knots cruise) or twin Yanmar 220hp diesels (about 15 knots at cruise).

See Page 6879 For Price Data

Length Overall	39'5"	Fuel	250 gals.
Hull Length	37'5"	Water	70 gals.
Beam	14'3"	Waste	35 gals.
Draft	3'3"	Hull Type	Semi-Disp.
Weight	20,000#	Deadrise Aft	8°

Mainship 40 Sedan Bridge

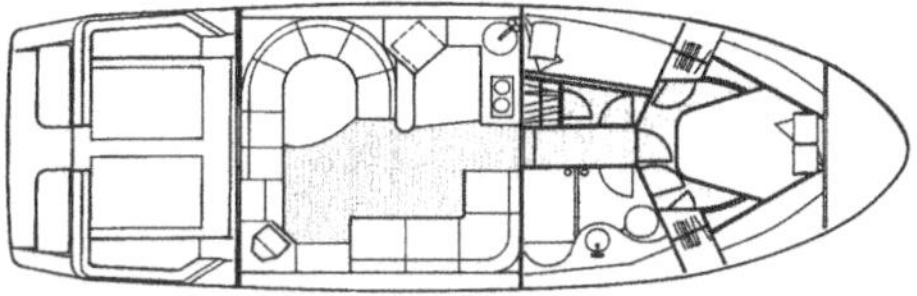

Introduced in 1993, the Mainship 40 Sedan Bridge is an inexpensive family boat whose spacious interior and large flybridge make her an excellent choice for day cruising and entertaining. She was built on a solid fiberglass, modified-V hull with moderate beam, and her low-profile appearance is the result of locating the engines under the cockpit sole. The single-level interior of the 40 Sedan Bridge—a step down from the cockpit level—is arranged with two staterooms forward and a spacious, full-beam salon with lounge seating for eight. A big U-shaped galley is forward in the salon, and a walkaround double berth is found in the master stateroom. This is an expansive floorplan for a 40-footer, however the furnishings are mostly inexpensive and the finish is less than impressive. The cockpit has built-in bench seating, a transom door, and twin hatches in the sole for engine access. Topside, the flybridge has an island helm console with wraparound lounge seating. Lacking side decks, the foredeck is reached via a door in the forward flybridge coaming. Standard 320hp V-drive gas engines cruise the Mainship 40 at a sedate 16 knots and deliver a top speed in the mid 20s.

See Page 687 For Price Data

Length	40'7"	Fuel	310 gals.
Beam	13'6"	Water	93 gals.
Draft	3'5"	Headroom	6'4"
Weight	20,000#	Hull Type	Modified-V
Clearance	17'0"	Deadrise Aft	18°

Mainship 400 Trawler; 41 Expedition; 414 Trawler

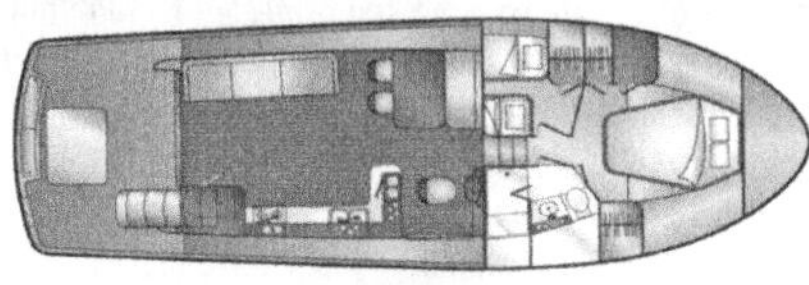
2003–09 Interior

Revised Interior

The Mainship 400 Trawler (called the 41 Expedition in 2009; 414 Trawler in 2010–12) is an updated version of the company's popular 350/390 Trawler, with the extra length used to enlarge the main deck salon. She rides on the same semi-displacement hull as her predecessor, with flat aftersections and a shallow, full-length keel. The expansive two-stateroom interior of the Mainship 400 is arranged with an island berth in the master stateroom and single berths in the mid-stateroom, which is partially tucked under the salon sole. A dinette—something the 390 sorely lacked—seats four, and the large galley is equipped with a built-in microwave, flat-screen TV, and Corian counters. In the cockpit, the straight, molded stair steps to the bridge are an improvement over the 390's curved staircase. For many, the spacious flybridge of the Mainship 400—with its grill, dinette table, and wet bar—is among the highlights of the boat. Additional features include a washer/dryer, a convenient deck access door at the lower helm, covered cockpit, wide side decks, and high-gloss cherrywood interior joinery. A single 385hp Cat (or 370hp Cummins) diesel will cruise efficiently at 12 knots and reach a top speed of 15–16 knots.

See Page 687 For Price Data

Length w/Pulpit	41'4"	Clearance	19'2"
Hull Length	38'4"	Fuel	300 gals.
Beam	14'2"	Water	130 gals.
Draft	3'8"	Waste	47 gals.
Weight	24,000#	Hull Type	Semi-Disp.

Mainship 430 Aft Cabin Trawler

1999–2006

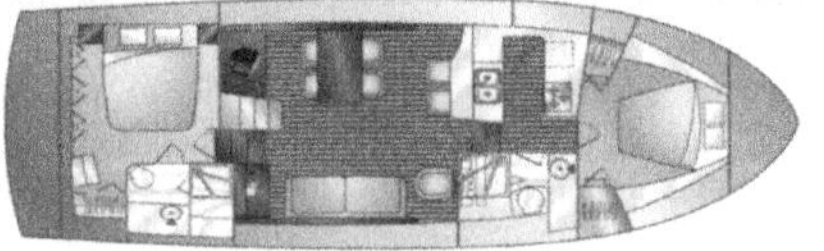

Two Staterooms

Three Staterooms

The Mainship 430 Trawler is a handsome, affordably priced aft cabin cruiser with very spacious accommodations and a good turn of speed. Indeed, the 430 is one of a growing number of "fast trawlers" introduced in recent years whose modified-V hulls are capable of planing-speed performance. With her wide 15-foot, 6-inch beam, the 430 is a big boat inside. Several two- and three-stateroom floorplans were offered during her production years, all with two heads and all with an athwartships double berth in the small aft cabin. Port and starboard doors in the salon open to deep, walkaround side decks, and a door in the owner's cabin provides direct access to the cockpit—a big convenience. A lower helm is standard in the salon but visibility from this position isn't great. Topside, lounge seating aft of the helm will seat six. The small cockpit makes line handling easy. Additional features include a traditional teak interior, stall showers in both heads, washer/dryer space under the forward salon steps, folding radar mast, transom door and a bow pulpit. Standard 300hp Cat 3126 diesels cruise the Mainship 430 Trawler at 13 knots and reach a top speed of 16–17 knots.

See Page 687 For Price Data

Length w/Pulpit	47'9"	Clearance	18'8"
Hull Length	43'0"	Fuel	500 gals.
Beam	15'6"	Water	250 gals.
Draft	3'8"	Waste	50 gals.
Weight	36,000#	Hull Type	Semi-Disp.

Mainship 43/45/479 Trawler

2006–12

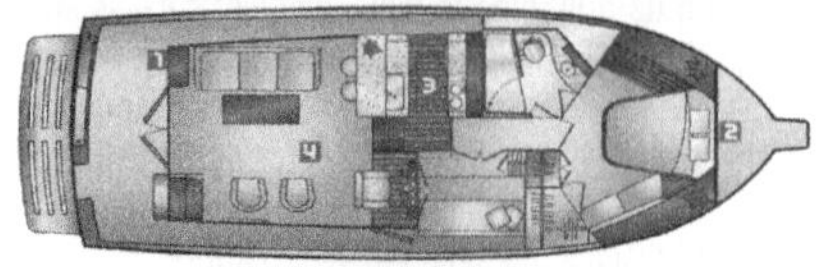

43/45 Interior

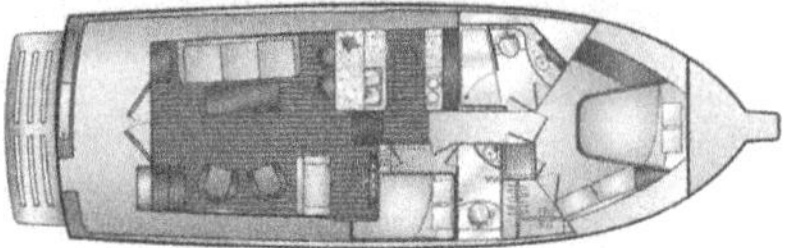

479 Interior

Introduced in 2006, the Mainship 43 Trawler (called the 45 Trawler in 2008–09; 479 Trawler in 2010–12) remained the flagship of Mainship's fleet until the company closed down in early 2012. As explained on the Mainship web site, her semi-displacement hull permits owners to "cruise with the efficiency of a traditional trawler or sprint to your destination like a modern express." That describes most of today's performance trawlers—boaters love the classic trawler "look," they just don't like the slow hull speed of a real displacement trawler. The two-stateroom interior of the Mainship 43/45, updated in the 479 model to include a double bed in the guest cabin as well as a second head, is arranged with a step-down galley forward of the salon and a queen island bed in the master stateroom. A broad 15'6" beam allows for an expansive salon, and wide side decks are covered and protected by high bulwarks. Note the sliding deck access door at the lower helm—a must when short-handed. On the downside, the cockpit is small and some have complained of a high running angle. With her 777-gallon fuel capacity, the 43/45/479 Trawler has excellent range. Cruise at 18 knots (low 20s top) with Yanmar 440hp V-drive diesels.

See Page 687 For Price Data

Length Overall	47'9"	Clearance	18'8"
Hull Length	43'0"	Fuel	777 gals.
Beam	15'6"	Water	200 gals.
Draft	3'8"	Waste	56 gals.
Weight	40,000#	Hull Type	Semi-Disp.

Mainship 45 Pilot

One of the last models introduced by Mainship before they went out of business in 2012, the 45 Pilot is a sturdy coastal cruiser whose wide 15'6" beam gives her the cabin accommodations of a larger boat. Seductive Downeast styling is one of the 45 Pilot's most appealing features—she's arguably one of the more distinctive boats her size on the water. Built on a semi-displacement hull with a solid fiberglass bottom, the Pilot's spacious two-stateroom interior is dominated by a well-appointed pilothouse/salon with cherry woodwork and a teak-and-holly sole. A serving counter with two bar stools overlooks the step-down galley, and visibility from the helm is extraordinary thanks to the large cabin windows. The pilothouse deck door is a plus, and two electrically operated skylights—plus an opening center windshield—provide plenty of cabin ventilation. Below, the master stateroom is huge and includes a sofa and walk-in closet. The private guest stateroom is to starboard with a full bed and private head. A hardtop overhang partially shades the windshield and cockpit, and a bow locker stows the windlass, anchor and chain. Yanmar 440hp diesels cruise at 16–17 knots. Excellent range—close to 1,000 miles at 8 knots.

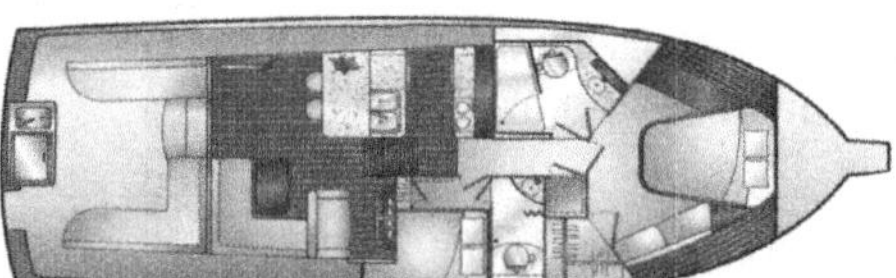

Not Enough Resale Data to Set Values

Length w/Pulpit	47'9"	Clearance	10'7"
Hull Length	43'0"	Fuel	777 gals.
Beam	15'6"	Water	200 gals.
Draft	3'8"	Waste	56 gals.
Weight	38,000#	Hull Type	Semi-Disp.

Mainship 47 Motor Yacht

Introduced in 1990 and updated in 1993 with a new interior, the Mainship 47 was of the least expensive motor yachts in her class during her production years. With her distinctive appearance (note the unusual window treatment and aggressive bridge overhang), the Mainship 47 is a contemporary motoryacht design that came with a good deal of standard equipment. She rides on a beamy, modified-V hull with cored hullsides and a moderate 15 degrees of transom deadrise. Originally offered with three staterooms, an alternate floorplan introduced in 1993 has two staterooms with the galley and dining area aft in the salon and a small office/communications center forward. The salon is very spacious and so is the forward stateroom, but the aft cabin (and the aft deck above) is small for a boat this size. A utility room housing the washer/dryer and workbench is forward of the engineroom. Additional features include an underwater exhaust system, foredeck sun pad and light oak interior woodwork. Twin 485hp 6-71s cruise the Mainship 47 MY in the low 20s and reach a top speed of about 25 knots.

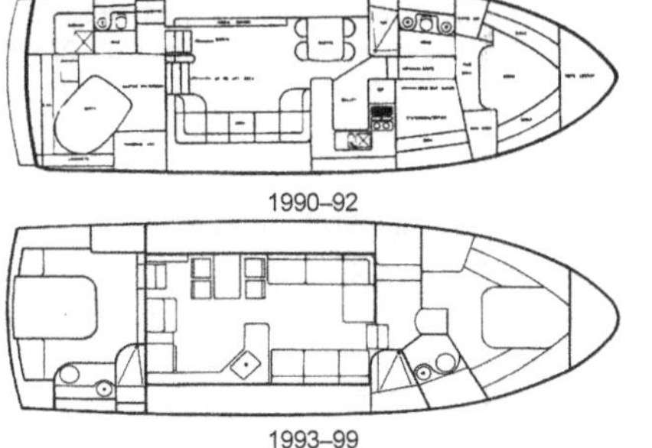

See Page 687 For Price Data

Length	46'10"	Fuel	600 gals.
Beam	15'5"	Water	200 gals.
Draft	3'10"	Waste	50 gals.
Weight	44,000#	Hull Type	Modified-V
Clearance	19'6"	Deadrise Aft	12°

Mako

Quick View

- Mako Marine was founded in 1967 by Robert Schwebke in the Miami superb of Hialeah.
- Schwebke sold the company in 1970 and bought it back again in 1976.
- Mako was one of the pioneers of the center console boat, promoting them nationally and converting great numbers of anglers to the utility of the design.
- Mako started the concept of the factory-sponsored fishing tournament, now an accepted marketing event in the calendars of several major boating manufacturers.
- Mako experienced a sales decline during the early 1990s, a recessionary period that had a severe impact on the boating industry, and the company temporarily shut down in 1994.
- In 1994 a New York investment company acquired Mako's debt and took control of the company. Mako went public in 1995, and a year later a majority interest was acquired by Tracker Marine.
- Tracker moved Mako production from Miami to North Carolina in late 2004.

Mako Boats • www.mako-boats.com

Mako 261 Center Console

1987–95

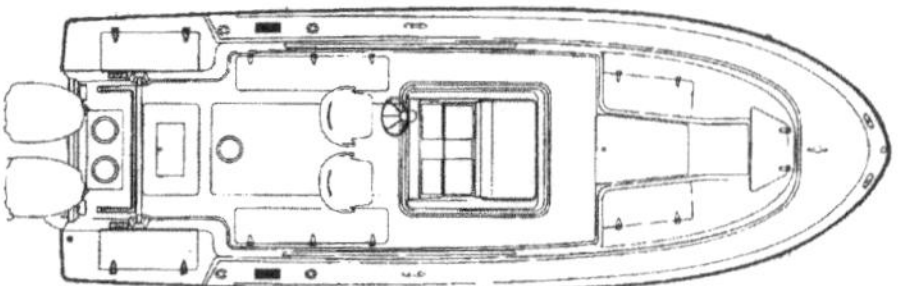

One of Mako's more popular models for many years, the 261 Center Console is a trailerable offshore fisherman with a no-nonsense layout and superb open-water handling characteristics. Heavily built on a solid fiberglass deep-V hull, the 261 delivers one of the more comfortable rides available in a boat this size. The cockpit can handle a mounted chair, and there's a large enclosure in the console for electronics. Storage is excellent with three big fish boxes forward and two in-deck compartments flanking the console. Additional features include recessed trim tabs, lift-out fish boxes at the transom corners, plenty of rod storage, and wide, flat gunwales all around. A factory T-top was a popular option, and most were equipped with a leaning post with rocket launchers. On the downside, there's no room in the small console for a portable head. Twin 200hp Yamahas will deliver top speeds in the neighborhood of 42–44 knots and an efficient cruising speed of 28 knots. Range is excellent, around 250–275 miles. A sistership model, the Mako 261B, is basically the same boat with a full transom and bracket-mounted outboards.

See Page 687 For Price Data

Length	26'0"	Fuel	200 gals.
Beam	8'6"	Water	25 gals.
Hull Draft	16"	Max HP	400
Dry Weight	3,900#	Hull Type	Deep-V
Clearance	NA	Deadrise Aft	23°

Mako 282 Center Console

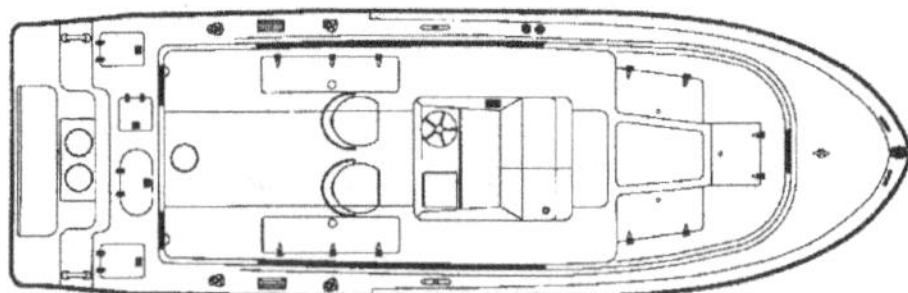

Mako got it right in 1998 with the introduction of the Mako 282 Center Console, a good-looking fisherman with an impressive blend of range, speed, and fishability. Loaded with a full array of standard fishing features, her uncluttered cockpit has enough working space for as many as six anglers to work without feeling confined. The wide helm console of the 282 has room for most necessary electronic add-ons, and unlike most other center consoles you access the interior (with its marine head, batteries, and storage bins) from the front rather than the side. Note that in 1998 the transom tooling was updated to provide a walk-through door and a foldaway transom seat. Standard fishing features include a standup 46-gallon livewell and sink in the transom, two in-deck fish boxes, and center casting platform storage box, flush-mounted rod holders, and two recessed rod lockers. There's also lockable storage at the bow—a useful feature for valuable gear. A heavily built boat able to take a pounding when the seas pick up, twin 225hp Yamaha outboards cruise the Mako 282 Center Console in the high 20s and reach a top speed of close to 45 knots.

See Page 687 For Price Data

Length w/Pulpit	31'1"	Fuel	235 gals.
Hull Length	28'1"	Water	10 gals.
Beam	8'6"	Max HP	450
Hull Draft	16"	Hull Type	Deep-V
Dry Weight	4,500#	Deadrise Aft	23°

Mako 284 Center Console

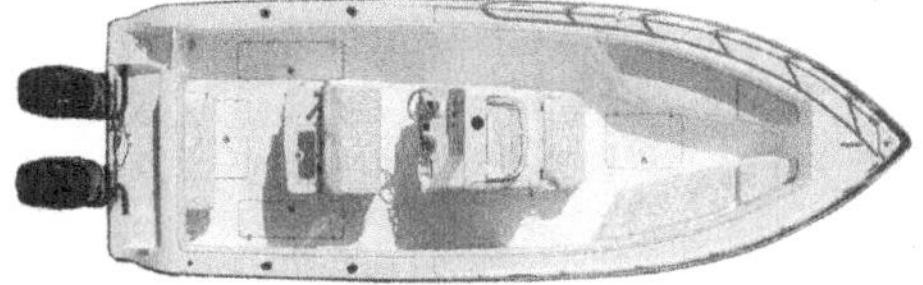

The market for 28-foot center consoles is among the most competitive in the business. This is the sweet spot for many offshore angers, the intersection of price and performance where builders fight hard for attention. The Mako 284 was introduced into this crowded market in 2005, two years before the economy tanked and the boat business went south. Built on a solid fiberglass deep-V hull, her wide 9'10" beam provides cockpit space for several anglers and their gear. Behind the helm is a large bait prep station with a 50-gallon livewell, removable cutting board, tackle storage, and freshwater sink. The leaning post has lockable storage and a backrest, and there's space at the helm for flush-mounting a pair of 10" video displays. The 284's console head compartment houses a sink and access to the boat's battery switch and wiring panel. Cushioned bow seating will accommodate four adults. Most everything about the 284 is solid and business-like, and it's easy to see why she became a popular model for Mako. Her deep-V hull handles a chop without pounding, and a sharp entry and well-flared bow contributes to a dry ride. Twin 250hp Mercury outboards deliver a top speed of about 45 knots.

See Page 687 For Price Data

Length	28'4"	Fuel	235 gals.
Beam	9'10"	Water	14 gals.
Draft, Up	1'9"	Max HP	600
Draft, Down	3'2"	Hull Type	Deep-V
Dry Weight	6,000#	Deadrise Aft	21°

Mako 293 Walkaround

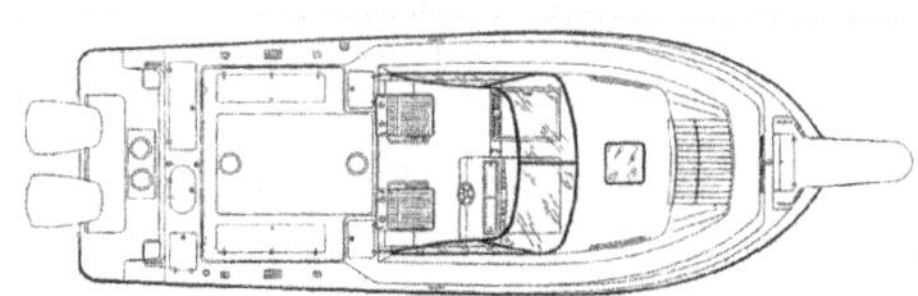

The Mako 293 Walkaround (called the 263 Walkaround in 1993–94) is a big walkaround cuddy with just about every feature an angler could ask for on a boat this size. She's built on a deep-V hull with a solid fiberglass bottom and cored hullsides, and there's enough foam packed into the hull to provide positive flotation. The deck layout boasts a full-height transom with a built-in livewell, shower, transom door, and two storage bins. There are two big fish boxes in the cockpit sole and tackle drawers are located behind the helm and companion seats. Rod storage is under the gunwales. The side decks are wide, deep, and well secured, and bench seating is built into the forward cabin trunk. Below, the Mako's roomy midcabin floorplan sleeps four and includes a full galley, high-low dinette table, and an enclosed head with shower. Additional features include an elevated helm station, dive platform, recessed trim tabs, teak cabin sole, molded bow pulpit, and anchor locker. A good performer, the Mako 293 Walkaround will cruise efficiently in the high 20s with a pair of 250hp Mercury outboards and reach a top speed in the neighborhood of 40 knots.

See Page 687 For Price Data

Length w/Pulpit	30'10"	Fuel	240 gals.
Hull Length	28'7"	Water	40 gals.
Beam	9'6"	Max HP	500
Hull Draft	1'7"	Hull Type	Deep-V
Weight	6,100#	Deadrise Aft	23°

Mako 314 Cuddy

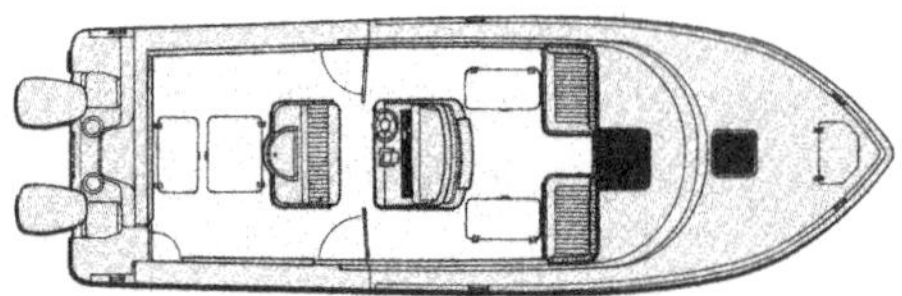

The Mako 314 Cuddy is a big, beamy, outboard-powered center console from a company with a long history of building rugged and dependable sportfishing boats. There's nothing high-tech about the 314; she's heavily built on a solid fiberglass hull, and her 10-foot, 6-inch beam is wider than many other center consoles her size. With her high bow rail and flat cabintop, the entire forward section of the 314 is one big casting platform. There's a large storage area in the console for life jackets and fenders, etc., and the cuddy cabin is quite spacious with a dinette/V-berth forward, an enclosed head compartment with shower, and a compact galley with sink, stove, and refrigerator. Port and starboard jump seats are forward of the helm, which also features a fold-down front console seat. Standard fishing amenities include three in-deck fish boxes, a 35-gallon transom livewell, a leaning post with tackle center, and lockable rod storage. The Mako 314 Cuddy will cruise at 25 knots with a pair of 225hp outboards and reach a top speed of 33–34 knots. Note that the engines are not as close together as most center consoles this size, which results in improved close-quarter handling characteristics.

See Page 687 For Price Data

Length	31'3"	Fuel	300 gals.
Beam	10'6"	Water	39 gals.
Draft, Up	1'7"	Max HP	500
Draft, Down	3'2"	Hull Type	Deep-V
Dry Weight	7,500#	Deadrise Aft	21°

Mako 333 Attack

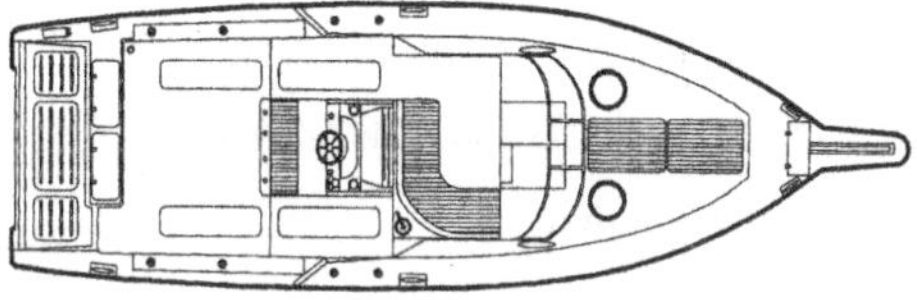

The largest model Mako has built to date, the 333 is a departure from the company's previous models in that she possesses some comfortable cruising accommodations—something previous Makos have never provided. She's heavily built on a deep-V hull with moderate beam and a steep 24.5 degrees of deadrise at the transom. The deck layout is arranged with a curved L-shaped lounge on the bridge deck, forward of the command console. The cockpit is quite large (in spite of the deck space dedicated to non-fishing pursuits) and includes two in-deck fish boxes, a huge 60-gallon transom livewell, coaming bolsters, rod storage, and a sturdy transom door. The entire helm deck rises on electric rams to provide access to a huge storage area for additional rod storage, a generator, dive tanks, etc. Below, the 333's tastefully appointed cabin comes with a V-berth forward, a double berth aft (under the bridge deck), a small galley with microwave and refrigerator, and an enclosed head compartment with an electric head and shower. When fitted with twin 250hp outboards, she'll cruise in the low 20s and reach a top speed 35+ knots.

See Page 687 For Price Data

Length w/Pulpit	36'0"	Fuel	350 gals.
Hull Length	33'9"	Water	35 gals.
Beam	10'6"	Max HP	750
Hull Draft	1'9"	Hull Type	Deep-V
Weight	11,500#	Deadrise Aft	24.5°

Marine Trader

Quick View

- Founded by Don Miller in 1968, during the 1970s and 1980s Marine Trader imported a growing range of Taiwan-built sailboats, trawlers and motoryachts.
- The company concluded sailboat production in 1995, focusing on motoryachts.
- From the 1970s up to the mid 1980s, Marine Trader made a significant impact on the U.S. trawler market, selling hundreds of boats in every major boating region in the country.
- By the year 2000, Marine Trader had imported over 3,000 boats into the U.S. market, more than any other importer in the country.
- Marine Trader models were built by several Taiwan manufacturers over the years.
- Based in Toms River, NJ, Marine Trader ended production some years ago (date unknown).
- A Marine Trader owner's group can be found at http://mtoa.net.

No longer in business.

Marine Trader 34 Double Cabin

1972–2001

An industry classic, the Marine Trader 34 Double Cabin is the best-selling small trawler ever imported and sold in the U.S. Built by CHB in Taiwan, there were other distributors besides Marine Trader and she may be recognized on the West Coast as the La Paz, Eagle, or CHB 34 DC. She enjoyed her best years during the 1970s when powerboats, with their big fuel-guzzling engines, were out of favor. There were several updates to the 34 over the years. Prior to 1975 she was built with a plywood house and a fiberglass cloth overlay. Until 1985 the decks were teak-planked and fastened through fiberglass to a balsa sub-deck—a constant source of deck leaks—and after 1985 the 34 was constructed of solid fiberglass. The flybridge was revised in 1991, and the teak window frames were eliminated in 1992. Below decks, the all-teak interior is arranged with small staterooms fore and aft, two heads and a very practical passageway from the aft stateroom to the cockpit. A lower helm is standard, and a sliding salon door provides easy access to the deck. No one will ever confuse the Marine Trader 34 with a Grand Banks when it comes to quality. A single 135hp Lehman diesel will cruise at 7 knots burning just 2–3 gallons per hour.

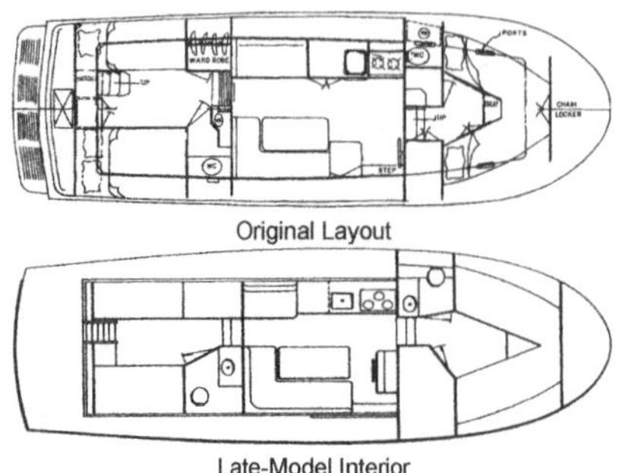

Original Layout

Late-Model Interior

See Page 687 For Price Data

Length Overall	33'6"	Headroom	6'4"
Length WL	30'3"	Fuel	300 gals.
Beam	11'9"	Water	150 gals.
Draft	3'6"	Waste	40 gals.
Weight	17,000#	Hull Type	Semi-Disp.

Marine Trader 34 Sedan

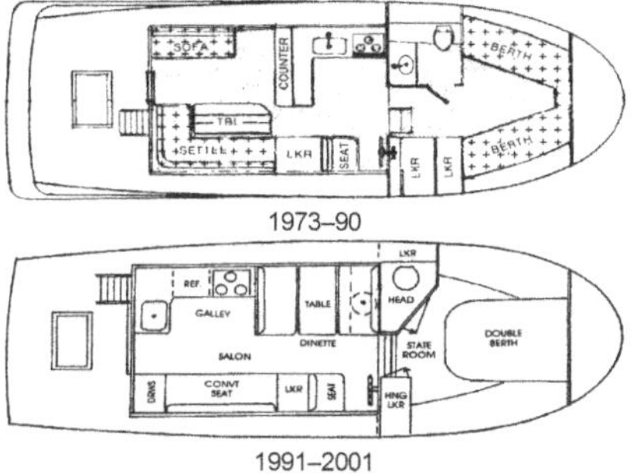

1973–90

1991–2001

In one form or another, the Marine Trader 34 Sedan has been a fixture in the marine marketplace since 1973. Inexpensive to buy and economical to operate, the 34 is the quintessential cheap Taiwan trawler. Built on a beamy hull of solid fiberglass construction, the superstructure is fiberglass as well, although for the first few years it was glass-over-plywood construction, which caused a lot of dry rot problems. The 34 Sedan has been updated several times over the years, most notably in 1991 when the flybridge was restyled and the interior revised, and in 1995 when the teak decks and window frames were eliminated. Despite the modifications, she still retains the classic trawler design elements including full walkaround decks, a salty profile, a full teak interior, and an extended flybridge whose supporting stanchions give the boat a true motoryacht appearance. A teak bow pulpit, swim platform, and a mast and boom assembly are standard. Most 34 Sedans have been powered with a single 135hp Lehman diesel (120hp in older models) which cruise efficiently at 7 knots burning 2–3 gph. An optional 210hp Cummins can deliver up to 12 knots top. The cruising range of this boat can exceed 750 miles.

See Page 687 For Price Data

Length Overall	33'6"	Clearance	12'0"
Length WL	30'3"	Fuel	300 gals.
Beam	11'9"	Water	150 gals.
Draft	3'6"	Waste	40 gals.
Weight	19,600#	Hull Type	Semi-Disp.

Marine Trader 38 Double Cabin

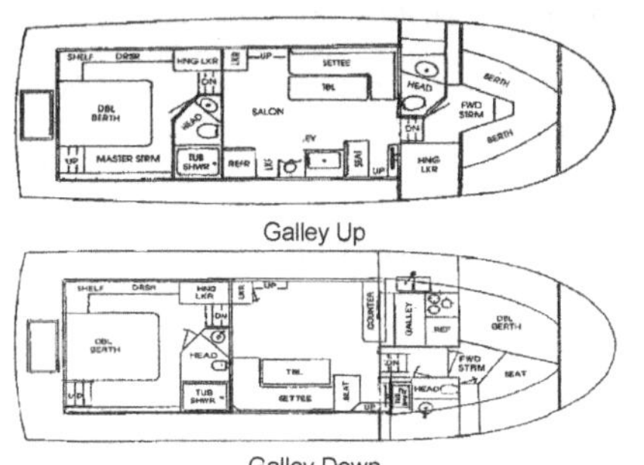

Galley Up

Galley Down

The Marine Trader 38 Double Cabin, introduced back in 1980, proved to be a popular boat with budget-minded buyers drawn to her classic trawler profile, economical operation, and lavish teak interior. Like most Asian trawlers of her era, she rides on a solid fiberglass hull with hard aft chines, a well-flared bow, and a long, prop-protecting keel. Today's 38 looks much like the original prototype despite the many modifications and updates made over the years. While a galley-up layout was first offered, the later galley-down floorplan proved more popular because of its more open salon. Either way, the cockpit can be accessed directly from the aft stateroom (a very useful feature indeed), and port and starboard deck doors in the salon provide quick access to the decks. Topside, the flybridge is arranged with the helm forward and two back-to-back guest seats. On the downside, no one will ever confuse the Marine Trader 38 with a Grand Banks when it comes to quality. Nearly all of these boats were powered with a single 120/135hp Lehman diesel, and fuel consumption at 7–8 knots is only 3 gallons per hour. Later models with twin 210hp Cummins diesels (optional) will cruise at 12 knots.

See Page 687 For Price Data

Length Overall	38'0"	Clearance	NA
Length WL	34'8"	Fuel	300 gals.
Beam	12'10"	Water	250 gals.
Draft	4'0"	Waste	50 gals.
Weight	22,000#	Hull Type	Semi-Disp.

Marine Trader 40 Sundeck

1983–2000

Introduced in 1983, the Marine Trader 40 Sundeck is a roomy aft-cabin cruising yacht notable for her affordable price and economical operation. Like most Marine Trader models, the 40 rides on a solid fiberglass hull with hard aft chines, a well-flared bow, and a long, prop-protecting keel. Her standard two-stateroom interior—completely finished with well-crafted teak joinery—is arranged with the galley down, which allows for a wide-open salon. If the bow stateroom is a little small, the owner's aft stateroom is huge with plenty of built-in storage drawers, a big hanging locker, and a large head with a built-in tub. A serving bar opposite the lower helm overlooks the galley, and port and starboard deck doors in the salon provide easy access to the decks. Topside, the full-width sundeck is among the largest to be found on a boat this size. Additional features include an aft-deck hardtop, teak handrails, bow pulpit, and a teak swim platform. Twin 135hp Lehman diesels (a single Lehman is standard) will cruise the Marine Trader 40 at an economical 7–8 knots with a top speed of about 10 knots. Note that the Marine Trader 44 Yachtfish (1986–Current) is the same boat with a cockpit addition.

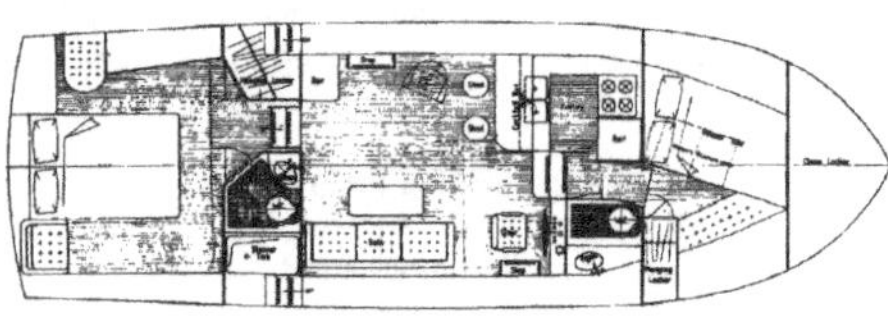

See Page 687 For Price Data

Length Overall	39'4"	Clearance	NA
Length WL	36'5"	Fuel	350 gals.
Beam	12'11"	Water	250 gals.
Draft	4'0"	Waste	50 gals.
Weight	25,000#	Hull Type	Semi-Disp.

Marine Trader 46 Double Cabin

1990–99

Among the least expensive boats of her type on the market, the Marine Trader 46 Double Cabin is a traditional Taiwan-built trawler whose spacious interior and comfortable ride have great appeal to entry-level buyers on a budget. Like all Marine Trader models, the 46 was built on a solid fiberglass, semi-displacement hull with hard aft chines and a deep, prop-protecting keel. Belowdecks, the galley-down floorplan of the 46 is arranged with centerline double berths in both staterooms and a full dinette opposite the galley. A lower helm was standard, and port and starboard deck doors in the salon provide easy access to the decks. In the aft cabin, a companionway door opens directly into the cockpit—a very convenient feature indeed. While the exterior decks and handrails are teak, the window frames are aluminum to reduce leaks. Additional features include a mast and boom assembly, excellent storage, bow pulpit, and swim platform. On the downside, the so-so finish reflects her low price. Twin Lehman 135hp diesels cruise the Marine Trader 46 at 7–8 knots, and optional 210hp Cummins diesels cruise at 11–12 knots and reach a top speed in the neighborhood 15 knots.

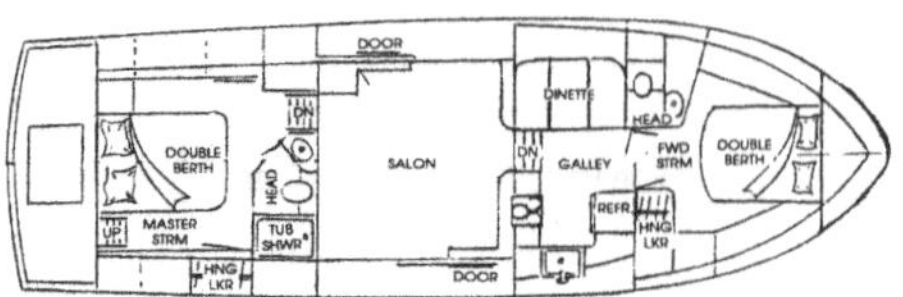

Not Enough Resale Data to Set Values

Length	46'2"	Fuel	600 gals.
Beam	14'7"	Water	220 gals.
Draft	3'8"	Headroom	6'3"
Weight	35,000#	Hull Type	Semi-Disp.
Clearance	14'2"	Deadrise Aft	NA

Marlow Yachts

Quick View

- Marlow Yachts began operations in 2001 with the introduction of the Marlow 65 Explorer.
- Originally built in Tainan, Taiwan, Marlow yachts are currently produced at a new, state-of-the-art factory in Xiamen, China.
- All Marlow motoryachts feature the company's signature "Strut Keel" technology, a design that employs twin keels at the stern in addition to a shallow, single-centered keel.
- With over 60 semicustom pilothouse yachts delivered to date, Marlow Yachts has developed an enviable reputation within the industry for sophisticated construction, meticulous finish and impressive customer satisfaction.

Marlow Yachts • Palmetto, FL • www.marlowyachts.com

Marlow 57 Explorer

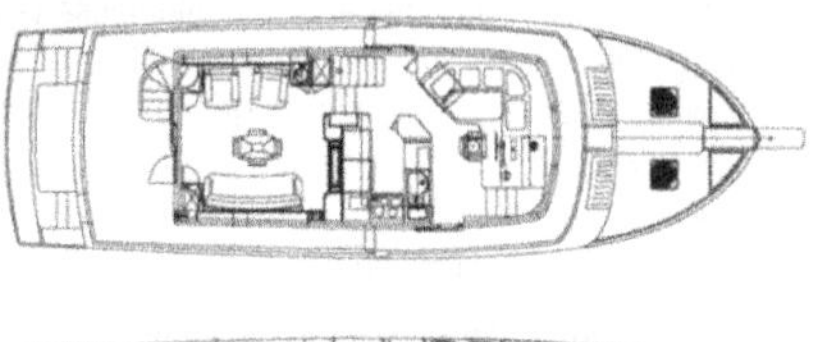

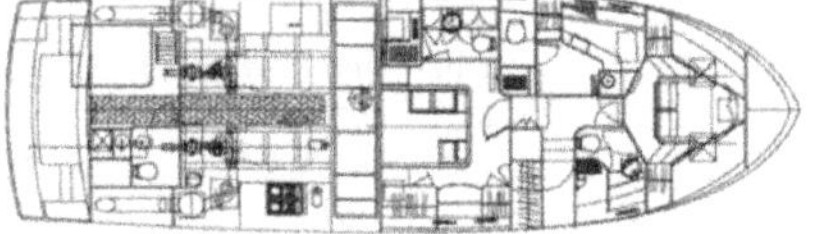

The Marlow 57 Explorer is a spacious and elegant pilothouse yacht designed for long range cruising in comfort, luxury, and security. That description can be applied to many high-end motoryachts, it's true; what sets the Marlow apart, however, is her exceptional finish and unique twin strut keels. Built on a Kevlar-reinforced fully cored hull, the three-stateroom interior of the Marlow 57 features an opulent full-beam master suite, VIP cabin forward, and a portside guest stateroom that can be configured as an office. The aft crew quarters are very large for a yacht this size. Forward of the salon, the U-shaped galley—with granite counters, Sub-Zero refrigeration, etc.—and curved dinette are on the pilothouse level. The overhead grabrails in salon are a nice touch. The engine room, with over six feet of headroom, is accessed from the aft deck. A Portuguese bridge wraps around the wheelhouse for added security. Note the reverse stern with protected swim platform. Additional features include teak decks (including the flybridge), teak and holly flooring throughout, washer/dryer, and prop pockets. Cruise at 18 knots with 575hp Cat diesels. A Command Bridge model (i.e., enclosed flybridge) is also available.

Not Enough Resale Data to Set Values

Length Overall	62'2"	Fuel	1,500 gals.
Beam	18'2"	Water	310 gals.
Draft	4'11"	Waste	120 gals.
Weight	69,000#	Hull Type	Semi-Disp.
Clearance	17'8"	Deadrise Aft	14°

Marlow 61 Explorer

2004–Current

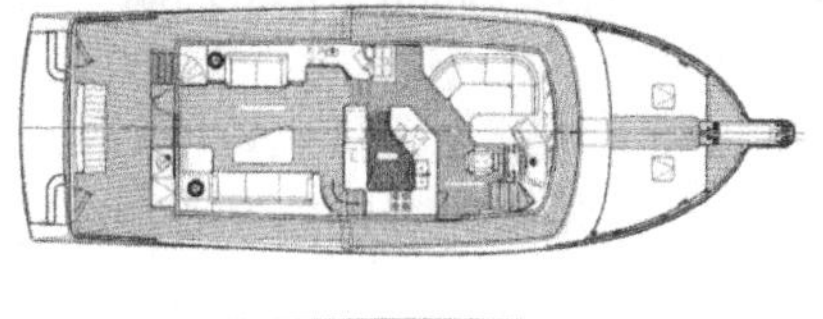

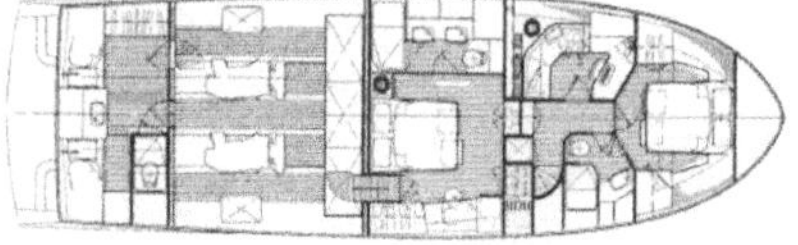

Brokers who specialize in semicustom motor yachts are nearly unanimous in their praise of Marlow boats. Introduced at the 2004 Miami Boat Show, the 61 Explorer combines rugged pilothouse styling with a unique twin-keel bottom designed for prop protection and downsea directional stability. Built on a Kevlar-reinforced fully cored hull, the elegant main salon of the Marlow 61 has Ultraleather seating along both sides with a wet bar and wine cooler forward, to port, and an entertainment center forward. The pilothouse, three steps above the salon, features a gourmet galley, dining area for six, and a large helm area. Note the natural marbles and granites used in the galley. Below, there are three staterooms and three full heads on the lower level including a spacious full-beam master with king-size bed, VIP stateroom with king bed, and upper/lower berths in the second guest stateroom. The flybridge and boat deck are accessed via a floating staircase from the port side of the pilothouse and a staircase from the cockpit. The engine room is reached from the aft crew cabin. A Portuguese bridge protects the pilothouse. Cruise at 12–14 knots (about 20 knots top) with 700hp Cat engines.

Not Enough Resale Data to Set Values

Length	61'5"	Fuel	1,400 gals.
Beam	18'2"	Water	300 gals.
Draft	4'2"	Waste	150 gals.
Weight	77,000#	Hull Type	Semi-Disp.
Clearance	NA	Deadrise Aft	14°

Marlow 65 Explorer

2001–Current

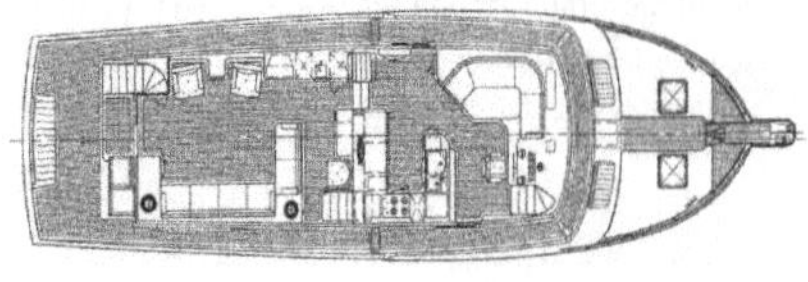

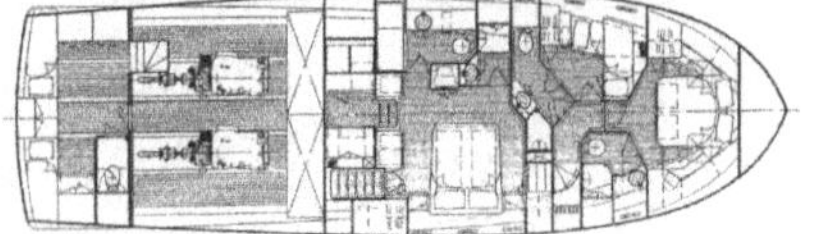

A handsome yacht with a go-anywhere appearance, the Marlow 65 Explorer is a limited-production pilothouse yacht with a couple of interesting features worthy of note. Foremost among these is her bottom design, which utilizes a shallow center keel as well as foil-shaped struts running along each prop shaft—a "twin keel" configuration said to improve tracking while permitting the boat to run aground without damage to the running gear. The three-stateroom interior of the Marlow 65 differs from many pilothouse yachts her size in that the master stateroom has its own private entryway from the salon rather than shared access from the pilothouse. A step-down utility area aft of the master suite can serve as a laundry (or storage) center, and a spacious twin-berth crew cabin, with direct access to the engine room, is reached from the aft deck. With the galley and dinette on the pilothouse level, the Explorer's long salon seems spacious indeed. Additional features include a separate pump room, sea chests (to reduce through-hull fittings), wide side decks, a Portuguese bridge, and a spacious flybridge with plenty of guest seating. Twin 800hp Cat diesels cruise at 20 knots and reach a top speed of 24–25 knots.

Not Enough Resale Data to Set Values

Length	65'10"	Fuel	1,400/1,800 gals.
Beam	18'4"	Water	400 gals.
Draft	4'5"	Waste	150 gals.
Weight	83,000#	Hull Type	Semi-Disp.
Clearance	18'0"	Deadrise Aft	14°

Marlow 70 Explorer

2003–Current

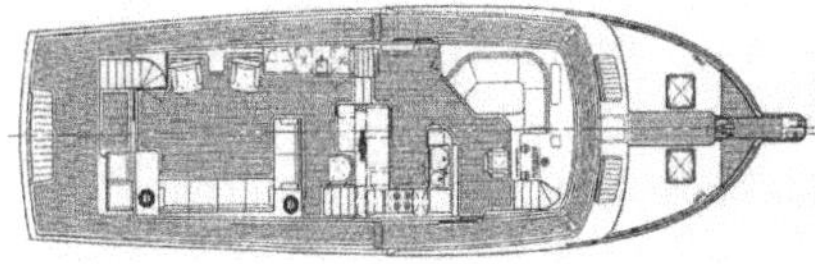

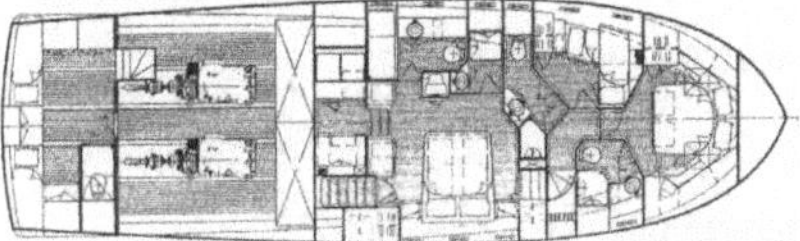

A popular yacht, the 70 Explorer combines the handsome pilothouse lines of all Marlow yachts with state-of-the-art construction and an opulent three-stateroom interior. She's built on a modern Kevlar-reinforced, fully cored hull using Marlow's "Strut Keel" technology, a design which employs twin keels at the stern in addition to a shallow, single-centered keel. The standard (but highly customizable) three-stateroom interior of the Marlow 70 features a private entryway to the master stateroom from the salon rather than shared access from the pilothouse. A step-down utility area aft of the master suite can serve as a laundry (or storage) center, and a spacious twin-berth crew cabin—with direct access to the engine room—is reached from the aft deck. With the galley and dinette on the raised pilothouse level, the Explorer's long salon seems spacious indeed. Lavish finishes include hand-crafted teak joinery, teak-and-holly sole, granite countertops and more. Additional features include a separate pump room, sea chests (to reduce through-hull fittings), teak decks, a Portuguese bridge, and a spacious flybridge with every conceivable amenity. Twin 800hp Cat diesels cruise at 20 knots and reach a top speed of 24–25 knots.

Not Enough Resale Data to Set Values

Length	71'3"	Fuel	1,900 gals.
Beam	18'4"	Water	400 gals.
Draft	4'5"	Waste	150 gals.
Weight	85,000#	Hull Type	Semi-Disp.
Clearance	18'2"	Deadrise Aft	NA

Marlow 78 Explorer

2004–Current

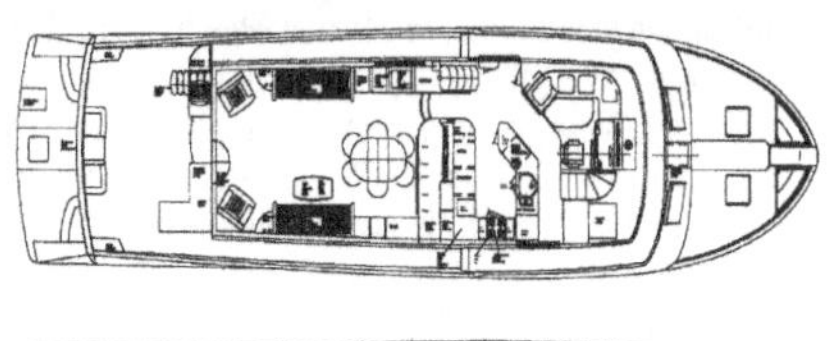

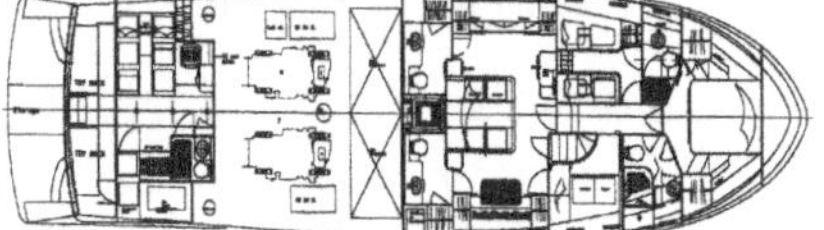

The Marlow 78 Explorer is a heavily built pilothouse yacht whose thoughtful design, meticulous finish and modern construction result in an exceptionally luxurious and seaworthy yacht. Marlows have an unusual bottom design with both prop shafts enclosed in twin keel struts, giving more protection to the props. The 78's raised pilothouse layout features an elegant salon/dining area, country-kitchen galley forward, and four staterooms below including an enormous, full-beam master suite. A large crew cabin is aft, and the entire interior is trimmed in top-quality Burmese teak joinery and teak-and-holly flooring. A few of her more notable highlights include an ocean-crossing, 3,000-gallon fuel capacity, wave-breaking Portuguese bridge with storage lockers, protected side decks, spacious cockpit with molded transom seats, and an extended swim platform. An interior stairwell leads to the crew quarters and standup engineroom. The 78's massive flybridge can entertain a small crowd. Note that 78E (shown above) has an integrated swim platform while the 78C has a conventional transom. Her composite, Kevlar-reinforced hull is cored throughout. Cat 1,500hp diesels cruise at 18–20 knots (low 20s top).

Not Enough Resale Data to Set Values

Length	78'2"	Fuel	3,000 gals.
Beam	20'4"	Water	550 gals.
Draft	4'10"	Waste	200 gals.
Weight	100,000#	Hull Type	Semi-Disp.
Clearance	18'2"	Deadrise Aft	NA

Marquis Yachts

Quick View

- Marquis Yachts was formed in 2002 as a division of Wisconsin-based Carver Yachts. Their first model, the Marquis 59 Pilothouse, was launched in 2003.
- The Italian design team of Nuvolari-Leonard has been responsible for the styling and interior layout of all Marquis yachts.
- Over the years the Marquis product line has grown to include ten different models ranging in size from 42 feet to 72 feet in length.
- There are currently more than 500 Marquis yachts cruising the world's lakes, oceans, rivers and seas.

Marquis Yachts • Pulaski, WI • www.marquisyachts.com

Marquis 40 Sport Coupe; 420 SC

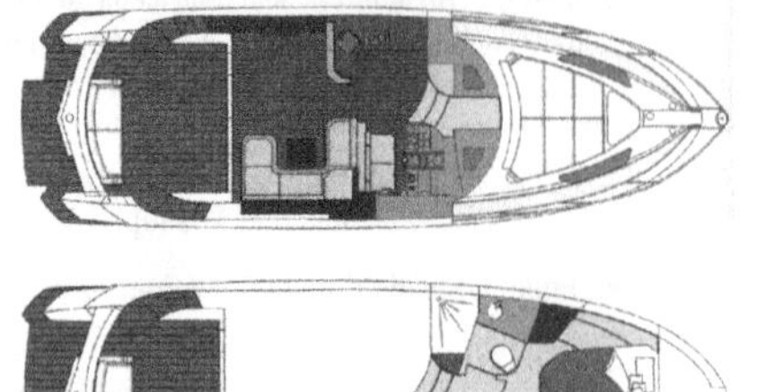

Introduced in 2008, the Marquis 40 Sport Coupe (called the 420 SC in 2009–12) is one of the first boats designed to take advantage of the space-saving features of Volvo IPS pod drives. The bold and dramatic styling of the 40 SC is the result of Marquis' partnership with the Italian Naval Architectural firm of Nuvolari-Lenard. Perhaps the most innovative feature of the boat is what Marquis calls a "sliding transom" that glides aft with a push of a button to create more than 60 square feet of cockpit space. Below, the two-stateroom, single-head interior of the Marquis 40 features a queen berth in the forward master stateroom and single berths in the starboard-side guest cabin. The salon, with its sweeping windows, U-shaped sofa and disappearing 26" TV, is a modern blend of hardwood cabinets, lacquered trim, and designer fabrics. (An electric table in the salon drops to cocktail level or raises to dinette height.) The euro-stlye galley is up and to port, opposite the two-seat helm station. Note the huge power retractable sunroof with integrated shade. Helm visibility could be better. Volvo 435hp IPS pod drives with joystick controls cruise the Marquis 40 SC at 28 knots (mid 30s top).

See Page 688 For Price Data

Length	43'7"	Fuel	300 gals.
Beam	13'11"	Water	140 gals.
Draft	3'7"	Waste	45 gals.
Weight	31,000#	Hull Type	Modified-V
Clearance	13'9"	Deadrise Aft	16°

Marquis 50 Sport Bridge

2009–Current

Keeping with Marquis tradition, the 50 Sport Bridge (called the 500 Sport Bridge since 2011) is the creation of yacht-design studio Nuvolari-Lenard of Venice, Italy. Her bold lines, megayacht-style interior, and impressive triple-IPS power offer something truly different from most domestic motoryachts her size. Built on a semi-V hull with a solid fiberglass bottom and moderate beam, perhaps the most innovative feature of the 50 SB is what Marquis calls a "sliding transom" that glides aft with a push of a button to create additional cockpit space. The well-appointed interior features dark Zebrano wood, black granite counters, and cherry flooring throughout. Below, the three-stateroom, two head layout includes a forward master suite with en suite head, VIP queen to port, and twin single berths in the second guest cabin. Note that the galley, salon, cockpit, and swim platform are all on the sale level, a feature quickly appreciated when the aft salon doors are opened to unite the areas. An optional hydraulic swim platform makes lowering the tender in and out of the water an easy task. Triple Volvo 435hp IPS pod drives (with joystick controls) cruise the Marquis 50 SB at over 30 knots (high 30s top).

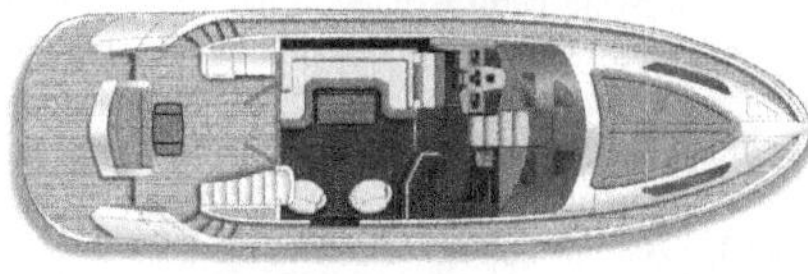

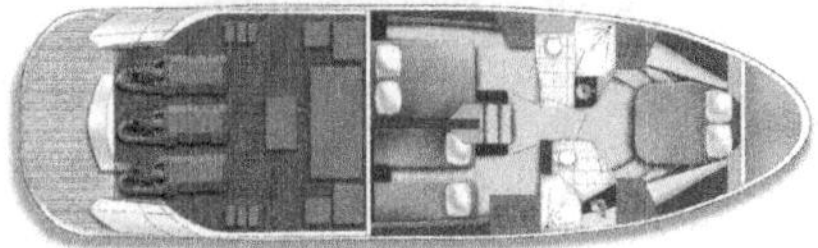

Not Enough Resale Data to Set Values

Length	50'7"	Fuel	506 gals.
Beam	15'7"	Water	160 gals.
Draft	3'9"	Waste	90 gals.
Weight	46,300#	Hull Type	Modified-V
Clearance	16'8"	Deadrise Aft	16.5

Marquis 55 LS; 560

2007–Current

The Marquis 55 LS (called the 560 since 2009) is marketed as a blend of Italian styling and American craftsmanship. True enough: the design work was done in Venice, Italy, by Novolari-Lenard, and all Marquis yachts—a division of Carver Yachts—are built in Pulaski, Wisconsin. Introduced in 2007, the 55 LS is an appealing and well-constructed motoryacht whose graceful lines stand in dramatic contrast to Carver's usual slab-sided designs. Her spacious and richly appointed interior is similar in layout to many other motoryachts her size, with a full-beam salon, home-size galley and dedicated dinette forward, and three staterooms and two heads on the lower level. Note that the guest head is split with the shower to port and toilet to starboard. A lower helm is standard—to port, which is somewhat uncommon. The flybridge can be reached from interior steps or a staircase in the cockpit, and a watertight door in transom opens to a spacious lazarette and engineroom. Additional features include bow and stern thrusters, a large flybridge with pop-up helm display, and distinctive hullside windows. The side decks are narrow. Volvo 715hp diesels cruise the Marquis in the low 20s (27–28 knots top).

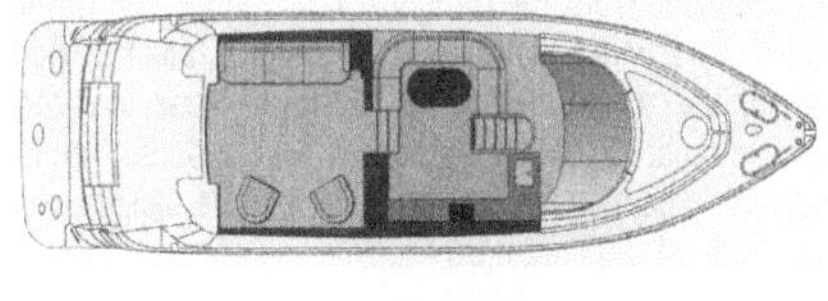

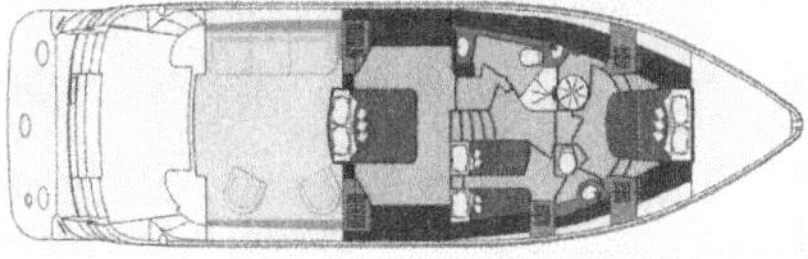

Not Enough Resale Data to Set Values

Length	57'4"	Fuel	836 gals.
Beam	16'0"	Water	200 gals.
Draft	4'11"	Waste	100 gals.
Weight	62,000#	Hull Type	Modified-V
Clearance	18'5"	Deadrise Aft	14°

Marquis 59 Pilothouse

2003–08

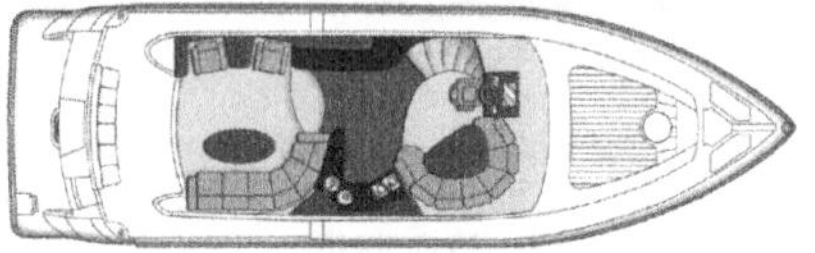
Main Deck Plan

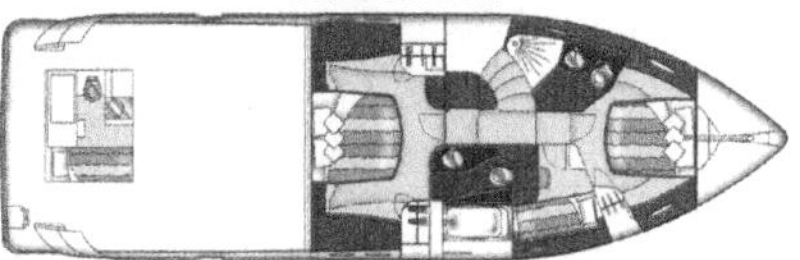
Lower Level Plan

Flagship of the Carver fleet in 2003 (before Marquis became a separate brand, that is), the Italian styling of the Marquis 59 was a sharp contrast from Carver's past emphasis on conservative, American-bred styling. Riding on a moderate-deadrise hull with cored hullsides and a solid fiberglass bottom, the Marquis' lavish accommodations rival her European counterparts in both luxury and design. The split-level salon stretches unbroken from the sliding entryway doors to the pilothouse windshield. Ultraleather settees and cherry cabinets highlight the aft salon while the galley and dinette are forward, on the pilothouse level. A lower helm is optional, and the full-service galley's boasts solid granite counters and Sub-Zero refrigeration. On the lower level, the master stateroom is aft and includes a king bed as well as two big hanging lockers. An island berth is fitted in the VIP bow stateroom, and over/under bunks are in the tiny port guest cabin. On deck, a curved staircase in the cockpit leads to the huge flybridge with lounge seating, wet bar, and davit. Note the standup engineroom and hydraulic swim platform. Twin 825hp MANs cruise in the low 20s. Called the Marquis 600 after 2009.

See Page 688 For Price Data

w/Platform	59'6"	Fuel	800 gals.
Beam	16'6"	Water	200 gals.
Draft	5'5"	Waste	80 gals.
Weight	58,500#	Hull Type	Modified-V
Clearance, Arch	16'3"	Deadrise Aft	14°

Marquis 65 Pilothouse

2005–10

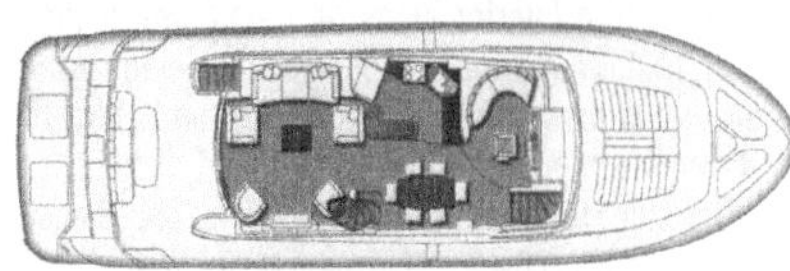

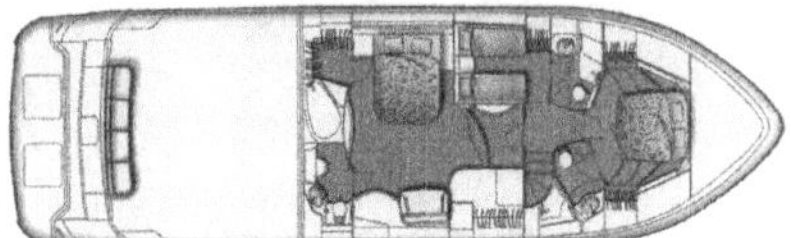

A stunning sales success with over 80 built, the Marquis 65 took motoryacht design and luxury to the next level when she was introduced in 2005. There were many Italian-styled yachts available at the time, but none matched the beauty and sex appeal of the Marquis 65. Looking from the stern, the main deck's visual scope reaches all the way forward, through the salon, dining room, galley, and pilothouse to the seascape ahead. With large windows along each side, the effect is airy and expansive. A formal dining area forward of the salon holds an oval table for six, while the home-size galley to port features such luxuries as granite counters and floors. A lower helm was optional. There are three staterooms and heads below, including an opulent amidships master with king-size berth, walk-in closet, and his-and-hers heads. Aft, two-person crew quarters are accessed from the transom. Throughout, the furnishings, decor and workmanship are to a very high standard. Additional features include a hydraulic swim platform, bow/stern thrusters, and—unlike most European motoryachts—a spacious engineroom with standing headroom. MTU 1,500hp V-drive diesels cruise the Marquis 65 at 24–26 knots (30+ top).

See Page 688 For Price Data

Length	69'11"	Fuel, Std/Opt	1,200 gals.
Beam	17'11"	Water	200 gals.
Draft	6'0"	Waste	150 gals.
Weight	94,000#	Hull Type	Modified-V
Clearance	24'5"	Deadrise Aft	13°

Maxum

Quick View

- Maxum, a division of Brunswick Corp., was created in 1988 as a low-cost compliment to Brunswick's fast-growing Bayliner brand.
- Most Maxum hulls were the same as those of Bayliner, with different decks and interiors to differentiate the brand.
- Maxums were marketed as an upscale version of Bayliners—more expensive than Bayliners, but not as costly as Brunswick's premium Sea Ray models.
- Headquartered in Arlington, WA, by 2005 Maxum had grown to become the 12th largest manufacturer of sportboats and express cruisers in the country.
- Maxum became well known in the early 2000s when the company introduced a boat at the Miami Boat Show with a bow thruster and twin stern thrusters—a breakthrough docking system that made it easy for beginners to dock a single-engine sterndrive boat.
- With the economic downturn, Bruiswick discontinued the Maxum brand in late 2009.

No longer in business.

Maxum 2600/2700 SE

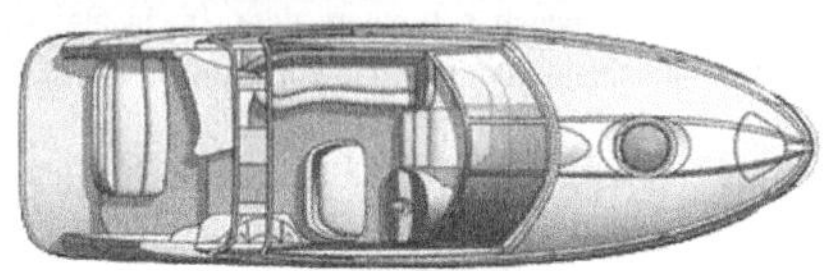

The market for big trailerable cruisers is as competitive as any in the marine industry. This is the sweet spot for many buyers, the intersection of size, comfort, and price where over 20 manufacturers slugged it out for market share a few years back when the marine industry was healthy. Introduced in 2006, the Maxum 2600 SE (called the 2700 SE in 2008–09) is a single-engine family express with stylish lines, agile handling qualities, and a generic mid-cabin interior. No, she doesn't have the "space of a 30-footer" as Maxum's marketing hype claimed, but she does have an unusually large cockpit for a boat this size. Belowdecks, the inviting cabin—with cherry wood trim, enclosed head with shower, and a U-shaped lounge forward—will sleep four adults in reasonable comfort. The Corian galley counter and built-in microwave are nice, but galley storage is minimal. The Maxum's open transom design and extended swim platform make boarding easy, and the optional sport arch folds down for trailering. Note the swivel double helm seat with flip-up bolster. The tiered, easy-to-read dash gauges are also a plus. Cruise in the mid 20s (35 knots top) with a single 320hp MerCruiser I/O.

See Page 688 For Price Data

Length	27'0"	Fuel	85 gals.
Beam	8'6"	Water	20 gals.
Draft, Up	1'11"	Waste	20 gals.
Draft, Down	3'4"	Hull Type	Modified-V
Weight	6,784#	Deadrise Aft	17°

Maxum 2700 SCR

The majority of 27-foot express cruisers built for the American market during the past three decades have been trailerable models. In practically every state in the country, that means the beam cannot exceed 8'6" in width. The Maxum 2700 SCR, however, is not trailerable and that makes her different from most boats her size. Indeed, with her wide 9'8" beam the accommodations aboard the 2700 SCR dwarf those of most other 27-footers. Introduced in 1993, this wide-body cruiser became a popular model for Maxum during her four-year production life. Beginning with a roomy, user-friendly cockpit with facing rear seats and a triple helm seat, and extending into the spacious interior with convertible dinette and berths for six, the 2700 SCR is a comfortable and well-equipped boat. The booth-style dinette isn't crowded; the head isn't too small (as it is in many small cruisers), and galley storage exceeds anything in her class. On the downside, Maxums of this vintage were inexpensive boats so don't expect much in the way of leading-edge finish. Note that while her wide beam compromises performance, it also improves stability. Twin 280hp MerCruisers I/Os max out at close to 35 knots.

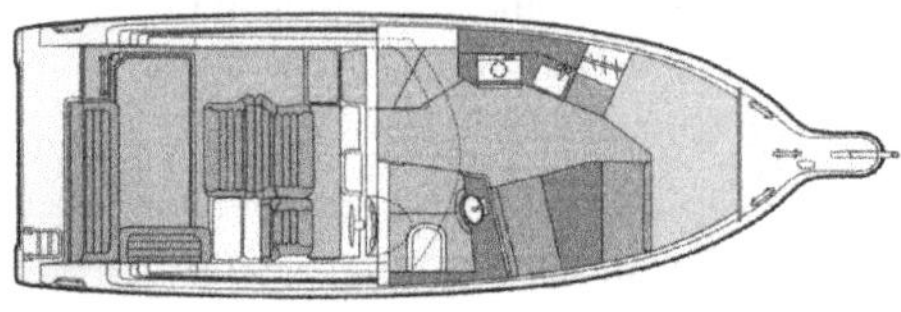

See Page 688 For Price Data

Length	28'9"	Fuel	102 gals.
Beam	9'8"	Water	30 gals.
Draft, Up	1'10"	Waste	16 gals.
Draft, Down	3'3"	Hull Type	Modified-V
Weight	6,450#	Deadrise Aft	18°

Maxum 2700 SE

Spacious accommodations are a strong point of the Maxum 2700 SE (called the 2700 SCR in 2001–02), a beamy, maxi-volume express cruiser with contemporary styling and a lengthy list of standard features. Built on a solid fiberglass modified-V hull, the high freeboard of the 2700 permits a very expansive interior with an impressive 6 feet, 4 inches of headroom in the salon. The midcabin floorplan is arranged in a conventional manner with a convertible V-berth/dinette forward, an efficient galley to port with built-in microwave, an enclosed head with electric toilet and shower, and an athwartships double berth aft with privacy curtain. On deck, a sun lounge is opposite the doublewide helm seat and there's enough cockpit seating for eight adults. A gas-assist hatch in the cockpit sole provides easy access to the engine. Additional features include a wet bar, transom door, freshwater shower, walk-through windshield, four opening ports and stereo/CD player. Among several engine options, a single 320hp MerCruiser sterndrive will cruise the Maxum 2700 SE at 20 knots and reach 30+ knots top. Note the limited 84-gallon fuel capacity.

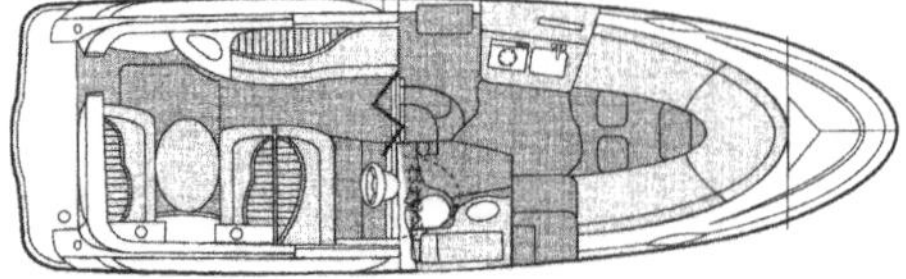

See Page 688 For Price Data

Length	28'1"	Fuel	84 gals.
Beam	9'5"	Water	30 gals.
Draft, Up	1'10"	Waste	20 gals.
Draft, Down	3'3"	Hull Type	Modified-V
Weight	7,400#	Deadrise Aft	16°

Maxum 2800/2900 SCR; 2900 SE

A good-selling model, this widebody cruiser (called the 2800 SCR in 1997–2000; 2900 SCR in 2001–02; 2900 SE in 2003–06) was among the more the more affordable midsize cruisers available during her production years. Hull construction is solid fiberglass, and her deep-V hull delivers a stable and comfortable ride in spite of her high freeboard. The 2800/2900 is a surprisingly big boat on the inside because her full-width cabin eliminates the side decks in order to take maximum advantage of the beam. The floorplan is arranged in the usual way with double berths fore and aft, a convertible dinette, compact galley, and an enclosed head with standing headroom. Privacy curtains separate the sleeping areas from the main cabin. There's seating for six in the cockpit with facing settees aft and a doublewide seat at the helm. Note that her modest 102-gallon fuel capacity limits the cruising range. Twin hatches in the cockpit sole provide good access to the engine(s). A single 260hp MerCruiser sterndrive will top out in the mid-to-high 20s. Later models with a 320hp MerCruiser I/O will hit a top speed of 30+ knots, and twin 220hp MerCruisers cruise at 22 knots (mid 30s top).

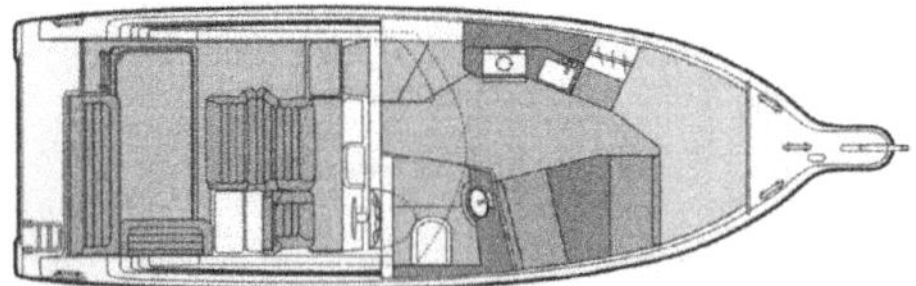

See Page 688 For Price Data

Length	29'10"	Fuel	102 gals.
Beam	9'9"	Water	30 gals.
Draft, Up	1'10"	Waste	16 gals.
Draft, Down	3'3"	Hull Type	Modified-V
Weight	9,100#	Deadrise Aft	18°

Maxum 2900 SE

Introduced at the onset of the Great Recession, the Maxum 2900 SE joined over a dozen other express cruisers her size fighting for recognition in a very competitive—and fast declining—market. (Indeed, two years later Maxum was out of business.) Aiming for the right balance of style and versatility at the lower end of the price scale, the 2900 SE boasts a roomy cockpit with twin rotating forward seats and a three-position rear seat that converts to a sun pad. A transom door, removable table, and shower were standard, and a cockpit grill was a popular option. Below, the decidedly Spartan interior includes an offset double berth forward with privacy curtain, convertible dinette to starboard, standup head with shower, and fully equipped galley with microwave, stove and refrigerator. On the downside, the decor is plain and there's precious little galley storage. The teak-and-holly cabin sole is a nice touch. A tight entry makes the midcabin berth difficult to access. In 2009, the 2900 SE became the first Maxum model to have Mercury's new Axius sterndrive system with joystick controls. Twin 300hp MerCruiser I/Os cruise at 25 knots (low 30s top). Later models with the 260hp MerCruiser/Axius package reach up to 35 knots.

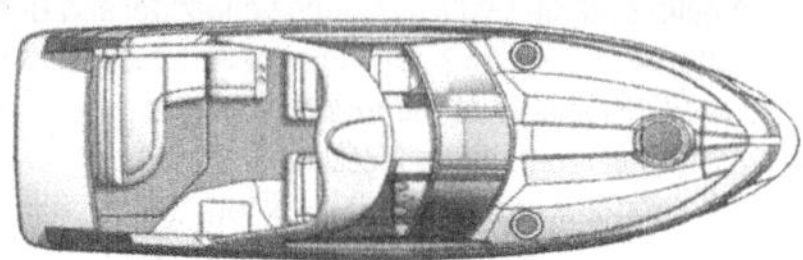

See Page 688 For Price Data

Length	30'0"	Fuel	125 gals.
Beam	9'11"	Water	30 gals.
Draft, Up	2'3"	Waste	30 gals.
Draft, Down	3'3"	Hull Type	Modified-V
Weight	10,187#	Deadrise Aft	18°

Maxum 3000 SCR

1997–2001

The Maxum 3000 SCR is a budget-priced family express whose contemporary styling and comfortable interior make her a lot of boat for the money. Like her sisterships in the Maxum fleet, she's built on a solid fiberglass deep-V hull with a molded pulpit and integrated transom. Her midcabin floorplan is arranged in the conventional manner with a convertible U-shaped lounge aft and a double berth in the forward stateroom. Both cabins have foldaway accordion privacy doors—a definite improvement over the privacy curtains so often found in other midcabin designs. By offsetting the forward berth, Maxum designers created a very open interior in the SCR, larger in fact than the actual dimensions might suggest. Storage is plentiful, and three overhead hatches and six opening ports provide excellent lighting and ventilation. A gas-assist hatch in the cockpit sole provides good access to the engine compartment. Additional features include a walk-through windshield, wet bar, and a foredeck sun pad. A little light on fuel for a boat this size, twin 220hp MerCruiser sterndrives cruise the 3000 SCR in the mid 20s (about 35 knots top), and a single 310hp MerCruiser will cruise in the low 20s (about 30 knots wide open).

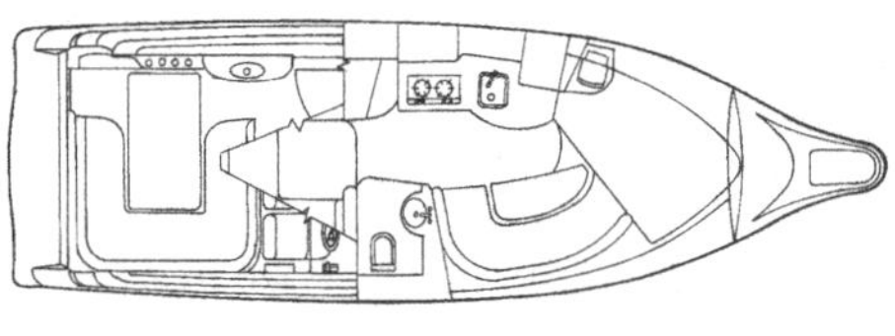

See Page 688 For Price Data

Length	32'9"	Fuel	150 gals.
Beam	9'11"	Water	40 gals.
Draft, Up	1'10"	Waste	30 gals.
Draft, Down	3'7"	Hull Type	Modified-V
Weight	11,500#	Deadrise Aft	18°

Maxum 3100 SE

2002–08

During a decade-long production history Maxum built its reputation by delivering affordable, well-styled boats to an entry-level, budget-minded public. The Maxum 3100 SE (called the 3100 SCR in 2002) fit into this mold nicely—a modern sterndrive cruiser with a midcabin interior and a very competitive price. She's built on a solid fiberglass, modified-V hull with moderate beam and reverse chines to dampen spray. Belowdecks, privacy curtains separate the fore and aft sleeping areas from the main cabin. Between them is an expansive salon with a semicircular lounge/dinette (which converts to a double berth) to starboard, an enclosed head with sink and shower, and a full galley to port with abundant storage. There are six opening ports for ventilation, and the absence of any interior bulkheads makes for a very open floorplan. The cockpit has a doublewide helm seat, an L-shaped lounge opposite, and U-shaped seating aft complemented by a sink and cooler space. An opening windshield provides access to the foredeck with its twin sun pads. A capable performer, twin 260hp MerCruiser sterndrives cruise the 3100 SE in the mid 20s and reach 33–34 knots top.

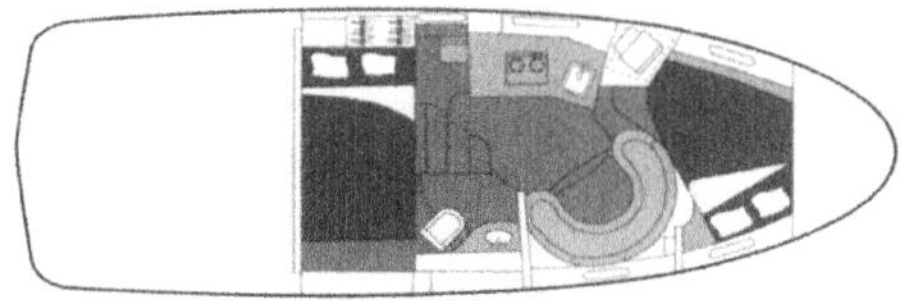

See Page 688 For Price Data

Length	30'9"	Fuel	150 gals.
Beam	10'6"	Water	35 gals.
Draft, Up	2'1"	Waste	30 gals.
Draft, Down	3'5"	Hull Type	Modified-V
Weight	11,000#	Deadrise Aft	18°

Maxum 3200 SCR

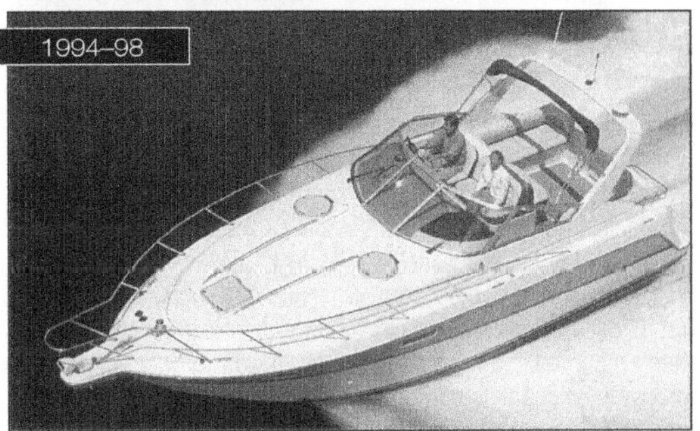

Largest boat in the Maxum fleet when she was introduced in 1994, the 3200 SCR is a low-cost sterndrive cruiser with functional deck and cabin layouts and an impressive list of standard features. During her production years, she was among the least expensive boats of her type on the market. Hull construction is solid fiberglass, and the Maxum's 11-foot beam—together with the lack of any side decks—results in an unusually spacious interior for a 32-footer. The midcabin layout is arranged in the usual manner with double berths fore and aft, a convertible dinette, complete galley, and a standup head with sink and shower. A curtain forward and a folding door aft separate the sleeping areas from the salon, and headroom is excellent, even in the small aft cabin. On deck, the cockpit is arranged with facing settees aft and a doublewide seat at the helm (which folds out into a lounge). A windshield walk-through provides access to the foredeck sun pad and bow platform. Note that there's little space around the console for extra electronics. Among several sterndrive engine options, twin 250hp MerCruisers cruise the Maxum 3200 SCR at 20 knots and reach a top speed of 30+ knots.

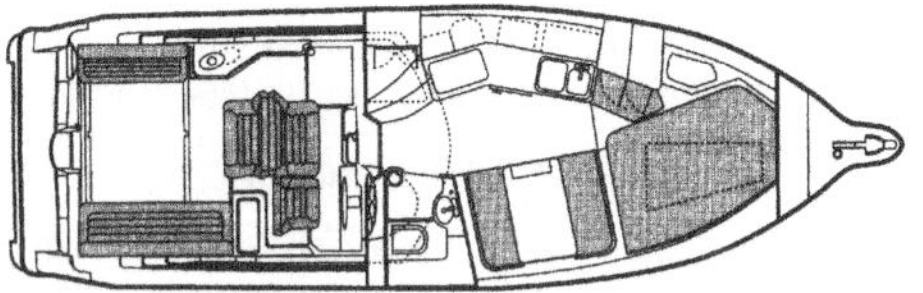

See Page 688 For Price Data

Length	34'9"	Fuel	186 gals.
Beam	11'0"	Water	36 gals.
Draft, Up	2'3"	Waste	30 gals.
Draft, Down	3'8"	Hull Type	Modified-V
Weight	10,800#	Deadrise Aft	17°

Maxum 3300 SCR; 3300 SE

A stylish boat with a reverse arch and long, sexy foredeck, the Maxum 3300 SCR (called the 3300 SE in 2003–07) was one of the more affordable family cruisers her size during the early 2000s. Like her sisterships in the Maxum fleet, she's built on a straightforward modified-V hull with an integral swim platform and bow pulpit. The midcabin interior is arranged with an offset double berth forward, a convertible dinette to starboard and a full galley (with Corian countertops and a hardwood floor) opposite. The head is aft, across from the entryway where it's easily accessed from the cockpit. There are plenty of storage bins and lockers below, and three overhead hatches and three opening ports provide good cabin ventilation. The cockpit of the 3300 is set up a little different than most with facing settees aft, a centerline transom door, and an aft-facing lounge behind the (triple-wide) helm seat. A cockpit entertainment bar was standard, and a walk-through windshield provides access to the foredeck sun pad. Among several sterndrive engine options, twin 320hp MerCruisers cruise the 3300 SCR in the low-to-mid 20s and reach a top speed of 35+ knots.

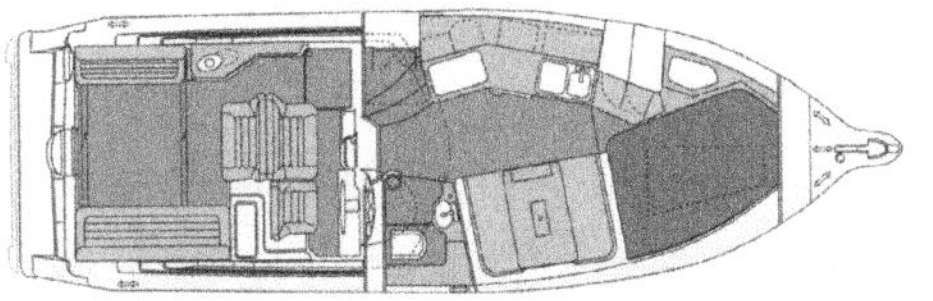

See Page 688 For Price Data

Length	35'7"	Fuel	179 gals.
Beam	11'5"	Water	36 gals.
Draft	3'6"	Waste	30 gals.
Weight	11,300#	Hull Type	Modified-V
Clearance	10'6"	Deadrise Aft	17°

Maxum 3500 SCR; 3500 SY

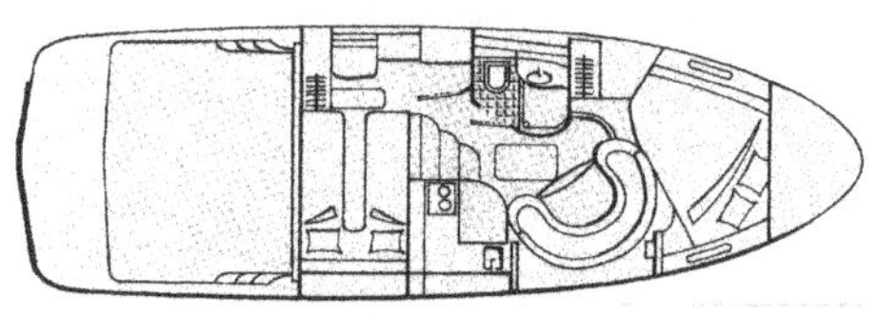

Affordable pricing was the hallmark of Maxum boats from the day the company introduced its first model in the late 1980s. In a highly competitive market, the 3500 SCR (called the 3500 Sport Yacht in 2003–08) stood out for her blend of contemporary styling, roomy accommodations, and rugged construction—a durable boat offered at a moderate price compared with more the upscale products from Sea Ray, Formula, and Cruisers. Built on a beamy modified-V hull, the absence of side decks allows for a particularly expansive interior. The floorplan features an offset double berth forward (with privacy curtain) followed by a semicircular lounge to starboard, and a full-service galley aft with refrigerator and microwave. Twin single berths in the private midcabin can easily be converted to a double berth. In the cockpit, a U-shaped seating area converts into a sun pad, and visibility from the elevated helm is excellent. A hatch in the bridge deck sole provides good access to the engine space. A transom shower, walk-through windshield, and wet bar were standard. Early models with 310hp MerCruiser V-drive inboards cruise in the low 20s (30 knots top). Later models with 370hp MerCruisers cruise in the mid 20s (35+ knots top).

See Page 688 For Price Data

Length	34'11"	Fuel	240 gals.
Beam	12'2"	Water	40 gals.
Draft, Up	2'2"	Waste	40 gals.
Draft, Down	3'1"	Hull Type	Modified-V
Weight	15,510#	Deadrise Aft	15°

Maxum 3700 SCR

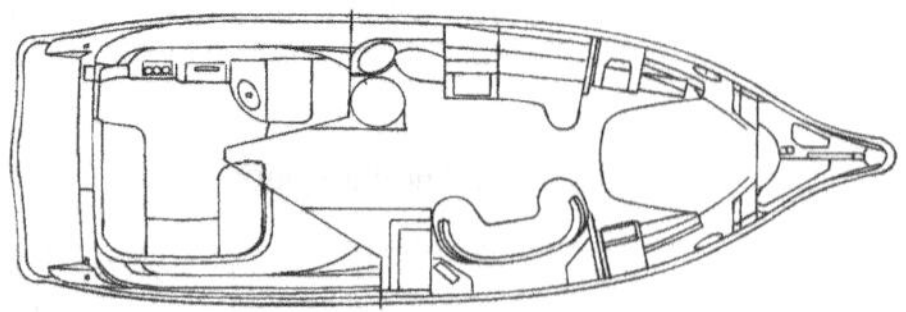

Patterned after the popular 4100 SCR, the Maxum 3700 SCR is an affordably priced express cruiser whose wide-open interior and sporty appearance will appeal to a cross section of budget-minded family cruisers. She's built on a solid fiberglass modified-V hull with an integrated swim platform and moderate beam, and at just over 20,000 pounds, she's a relatively light boat for her size. The midcabin interior of the 3700 SCR—essentially a scaled-down version of the larger 4100 SCR—is extremely open thanks to the absence of a fixed bulkhead separating the stateroom from the salon. A large and well-equipped galley is to port, and the twin berths in the aft cabin easily convert into a queen bed. Headroom is about 6 feet, 4 inches in the main cabin, and a circular stall shower is located in the head. On deck, the bi-level cockpit of the 3700 SCR comes with a doublewide helm seat, wet bar, transom door, and an aft lounge that converts into a sun pad. Twin 380hphp V-drive MerCruiser inboards cruise the Maxum 3700 SCR at 18 knots (26–27 knots top), and optional 370hp Cummins diesels cruise in the mid 20s and top out at close to 30 knots.

See Page 688 For Price Data

Length	39'3"	Fuel	244 gals.
Beam	13'0"	Water	65 gals.
Draft	3'7"	Waste	50 gals.
Weight	20,700#	Hull Type	Modified-V
Clearance	12'11"	Deadrise Aft	15°

Maxum 3700 SY

In a market crowded with midsize express boats, the Maxum 3700 SY (stands for "Sport Yacht") stood out for her sleek styling, beefy construction, and notably competitive price. Maxum excelled at delivering a lot of boat for the money during the company's decade-long history, and the 3700 Sport Yacht offered a good mix of comfort and performance at a price below most of the competition. Hull construction is solid fiberglass, and a wide 13-foot beam allows for an expansive interior as well as a large cockpit area. The belowdecks layout is similar to many midcabin boats this size with berths for six, a large head with separate shower, and a full galley with Corian counters and plenty of storage. A faux teak-and-holly sole is installed in the galley area, and cherry woodwork is liberally applied throughout the cabin. For privacy, the forward stateroom has a privacy door while the aft stateroom uses a curtain. The cockpit, with its U-shaped lounge aft and double helm seat, will seat as many as eight in comfort. Standard 320hp MerCruiser inboards cruise the 3700 Sport Yacht at 18 knots and reach a top speed in the mid 20s. Optional 370hp MerCruisers will reach a top speed of around 30 knots.

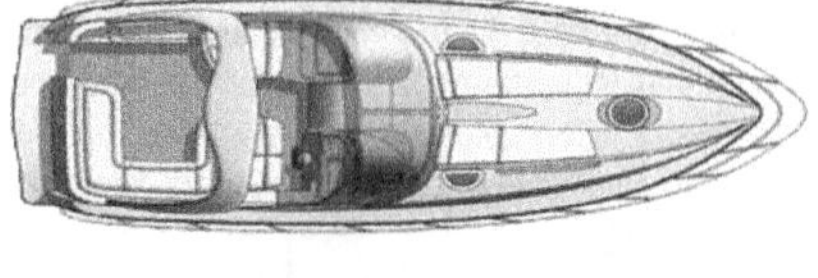

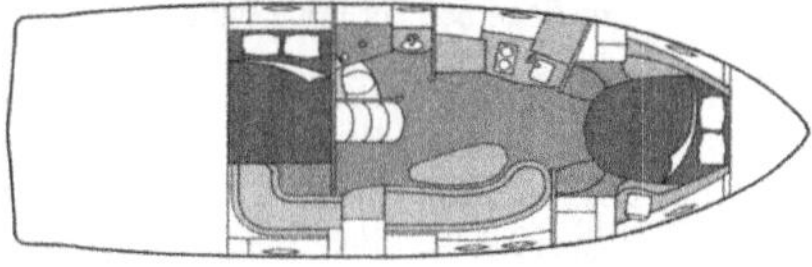

See Page 688 For Price Data

Length	37'2"	Fuel	300 gals.
Beam	13'0"	Water	80 gals.
Draft, Up	2'4"	Waste	45 gals.
Draft, Down	3'6"	Hull Type	Modified-V
Weight	17,800#	Deadrise Aft	15°

Maxum 3900/4100 SCR

The Maxum 4100 SCR (called the 3900 SCR in 1996) is a well-styled cruiser whose roomy interior and low price appealed to budget-minded buyers. Like all Maxum models, she's constructed on a solid fiberglass hull, and a reverse arch and huge swim platform add considerably to her pleasing profile. The 4100 SCR was one of the larger express boats available in the late 1990s, and it's no surprise that her cockpit accommodations are generous indeed. There's seating for eight with double bench seats forward and facing settees aft, each with a removable table. A wet bar was standard, and a pair of gas-assist hatches in the cockpit sole provide access to the engine compartment. At each corner of the transom are molded steps leading to the side decks—a useful feature. Belowdecks, the midcabin interior of the 4100 SCR is arranged with a convertible U-shaped lounge in the midcabin and an island berth forward. The salon sofa also converts, and folding doors provide privacy for the fore and aft sleeping areas. Note that fit and finish is rather poor. Twin 400hp V-drive gas inboards cruise at 22 knots (26–27 knots top), and optional 370hp Cummins diesels cruise at 20 knots (about 23 knots top).

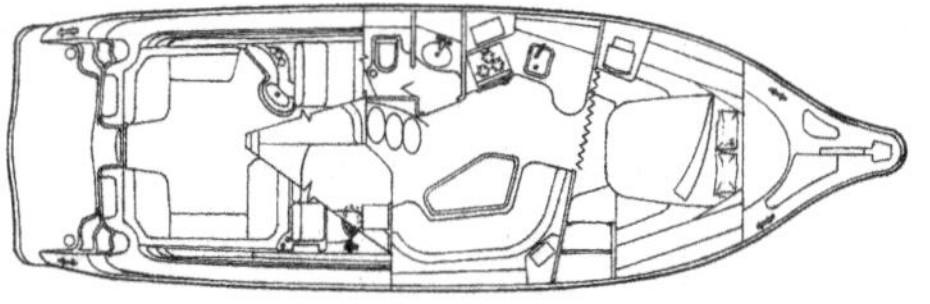

See Page 688 For Price Data

Length	43'7"	Fuel	330 gals.
Beam	13'6"	Water	77 gals.
Draft	3'2"	Waste	45 gals.
Weight	18,800#	Hull Type	Modified-V
Clearance	13'4"	Deadrise Aft	16°

Maxum 4100 SCA

1997–2001

A low-cost yacht whose curvaceous styling and spacious interior offers great appeal for entry-level buyers, the Maxum 4100 SCA is what many marine industry observers call a lot of boat for the money. She rides on a relatively lightweight modified-V hull with a wide beam and a shallow keel for directional stability. The two-stateroom interior of the Maxum 4100 is arranged with the galley down and a mid-level dinette forward of the salon. Walkaround queen berths are found in the both staterooms, and the forward head has a circular shower stall while the head and shower units in the aft stateroom are separate. On deck, molded steps lead from the aft deck down to the swim platform, and the flybridge has guest seating forward of the helm along with a wet bar and a triple helm seat. Additional features include cherry interior trim, wide side decks, and an aft-deck hardtop with wing doors. On the downside, the engineroom is a tight fit, and the level of fit and finish is unimpressive. A modest performer with standard 400hp gas engines (15–16 knots at cruise), optional 370hp Cummins diesels cruise at 20 knots and reach a top speed of around 22 knots. Note the modest fuel capacity.

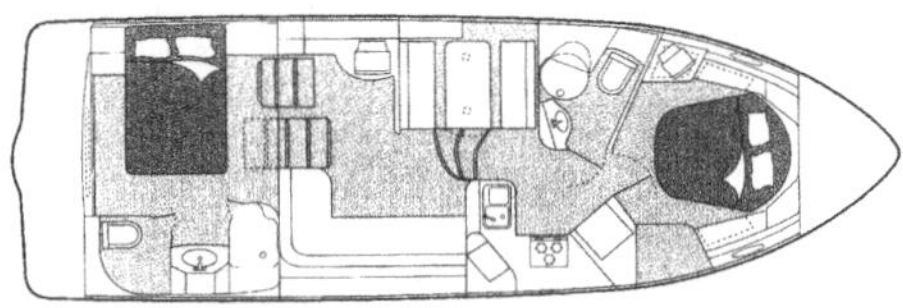

See Page 688 For Price Data

Length	41'8"	Fuel	300 gals.
Beam	13'10"	Water	90 gals.
Draft	3'9"	Waste	76 gals.
Weight	30,000#	Hull Type	Modified-V
Clearance	18'2"	Deadrise Aft	10°

Maxum 4100 SCB

1997–2001

A scaled-down version of the larger Maxum 4600 SCB, a low price and a sleek pilothouse profile made the Maxum 4100 SCB a good-selling boat during her production years. Sedan-style designs like the 4100 SCB have become increasingly popular with buyers in recent years thanks to their sporty appearance, open floorplans, and large cockpits. The two-stateroom layout of the SCB has the salon and galley on a single level with an elevated dinette (or optional lower helm) opposite the galley. Both staterooms share a single double-entry head with a separate stall shower, and the salon includes a built-in entertainment center and a large U-shaped sofa. In the cockpit, which is shaded by the extended flybridge, molded steps lead up to the bridge deck and a transom door and shower were standard. Additional features include a cockpit wet locker, a deep swim platform, and a roomy bridge with a wet bar and sun pad. Note that the engineroom is tight, and overall fit and finish is inconsistent. A modest performer with 400hp gas engines (15–16 knots cruise), optional 370hp Cummins diesels cruise the 4100 SCB at 18 knots and reach a top speed of around 22 knots.

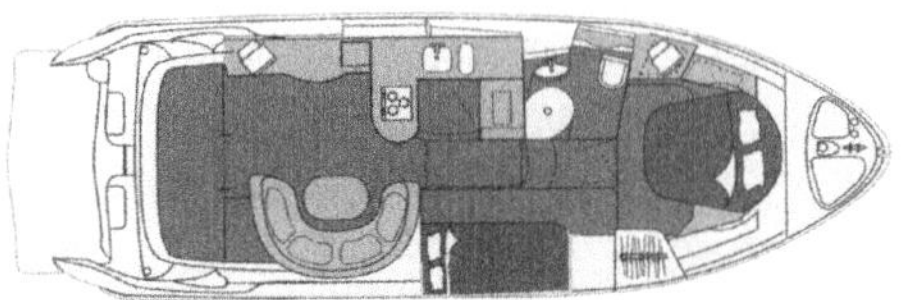

See Page 688 For Price Data

Length	42'2"	Fuel	380 gals.
Beam	13'11"	Water	100 gals.
Draft	3'9"	Waste	75 gals.
Weight	28,770#	Hull Type	Modified-V
Clearance	18'0"	Deadrise Aft	13°

Maxum 4200 SY

2002–08

With her "floating" fiberglass hardtop, the Maxum 4200 Sport Yacht (called the Maxum 4200 SCR in 2002) is a very distinctive yacht indeed. Without the hardtop, the 4200 might easily be confused with a European sportboat; with it, however, the visual impact is striking. Built on a beamy modified-V hull with an integrated swim platform, the two-stateroom, two-head interior of the 4200 is much more spacious than most of her European counterparts. High-gloss cherry joinery, teak-and-holly flooring, and Ultraleather upholstery combine to give the salon a rich and fairly elegant ambiance (although the fit and finish is something less than impressive). Privacy doors separate both staterooms from the salon, and the forward head is fitted with a separate stall shower. In the cockpit, the arching side windows and elevated hardtop provide plenty of protection from sun and wind. Molded steps in the transom corners lead up to the side decks, and the aft seating section rises hydraulically for engine access. An affordably priced boat with many standard features, twin 450hp Cummins V-drive diesels cruise the Maxum 4200 in the low-to-mid 20s and reach 27–28 knots top.

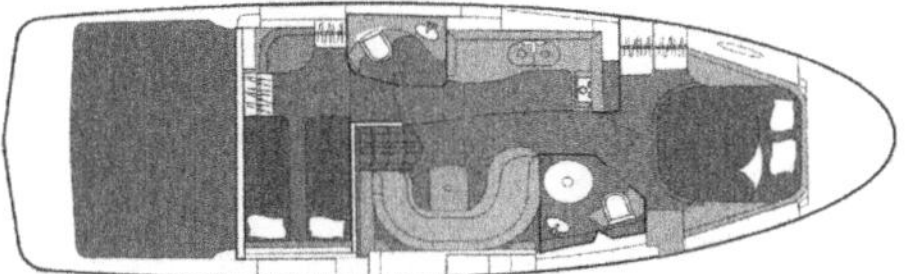

See Page 688 For Price Data

Length	42'9"	Fuel	480 gals.
Beam	13'10"	Water	130 gals.
Draft	3'8"	Waste	70 gals.
Weight	35,700#	Hull Type	Modified-V
Clearance, Hardtop	12'0"	Deadrise Aft	18°

Maxum 4600 SCB

1997–2001

A heavy dose of European styling and a super-attractive price combined to make the 4600 SCB an early marketing success for Maxum. Indeed, her appeal to budget-minded buyers is undeniable in spite of a generally marginal level of fit and finish. At just over 30,000 pounds, the 4600 is a relatively lightweight boat for her size. She rides on a solid fiberglass hull with moderate beam and a shallow keel for directional stability. The Maxum's two-stateroom floorplan is arranged with the galley up, a step down from the salon level, with a choice of either an elevated dinette or a lower helm to starboard. Both head compartments are fitted with separate stall showers, and a good deal of cherry paneling and trim are applied throughout the stylish interior. On deck, the compact cockpit is shaded by a flybridge overhang. A ladder leads up to the flybridge with ample guest seating and wet bar aft of the helm, and the wide swim platform can store a PWC. Early models with 400hp gas inboards cruise at 16–17 knots cruise (24 knots top). Optional 370hp Cummins cruise at 18 knots (about 22 knots top), and a pair of 450hp Cummins cruise at 20 knots and reach a top speed of 23–24 knots.

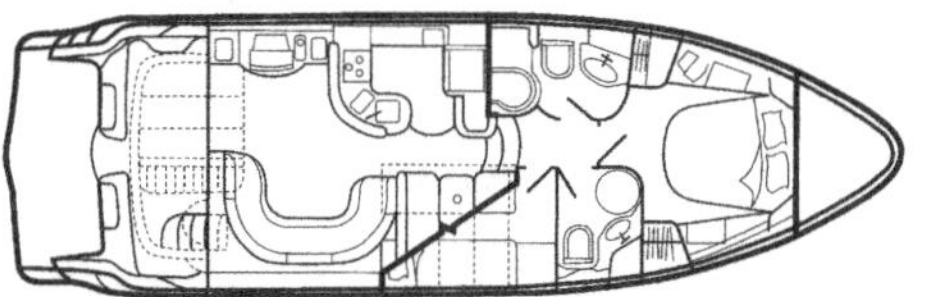

See Page 688 For Price Data

Length	45'11"	Fuel	418 gals.
Beam	14'4"	Water	100 gals.
Draft	4'0"	Waste	75 gals.
Weight	30,400#	Hull Type	Modified-V
Clearance, Arch	14'2"	Deadrise Aft	9°

McKinna

Quick View

- McKinna delivered their first boat, a 48-foot pilothouse design, in 1995.
- Eighteen months later the McKinna 57 Pilothouse was introduced.
- By the end of 1999, McKinna's production had increased to 30 boats per year ranging in size from 47 to 60 feet.
- McKinna models have been built in Taiwan for years by Lien Hwa Boats, of the largest and most experienced Asian yards. More recent McKinna models have been produced in different yards.

McKinna Yachts • www.mckinnayachts.com

McKinna 47 Sedan; 481 Sedan

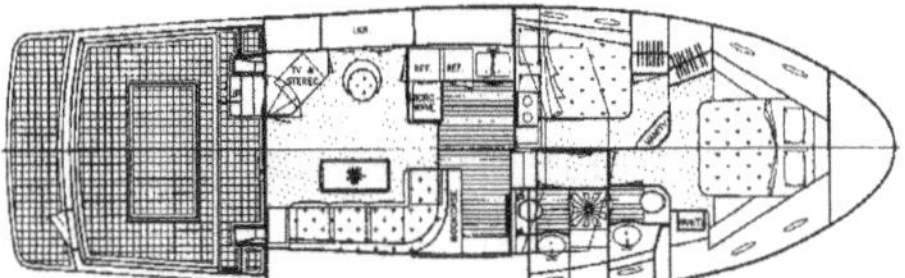

The McKinna 47 is a Taiwan-built sedan that's conservative profile masks a surprisingly space-efficient interior. She rides on a conventional modified-V hull with a well-flared bow, a shallow keel for stability, and a relatively wide 15-foot beam. Her spacious galley-up floorplan is arranged with two staterooms, both with queen-size berths and built-in vanities, and two heads that share a common shower stall. An L-shaped sofa dominates the salon where the large, wraparound cabin windows provide excellent natural lighting and outside visibility. A lower helm is optional and the interior is finished out in handcrafted maple woodwork. While the McKinna is clearly designed with cruising in mind, her large cockpit—partially shaded by the bridge overhang—is suitable for a couple of light-tackle anglers. Topside, the flybridge is huge with the helm forward and seating for eight. Additional features include wide side decks, a transom door, a teak cockpit sole and freshwater washdowns fore and aft. Standard 330hp Cummins diesels cruise at 18 knots (about 22 knots top), and optional 370hp Cummins cruise at 21 knots (24–25 knots wide open).

See Page 688 For Price Data

Length Overall	50'0"	Fuel	700 gals.
Beam	15'0"	Water	200 gals.
Draft	3'10"	Waste	40 gals.
Weight	29,700#	Hull Type	Modified-V
Clearance	19'6"	Deadrise Aft	18°

McKinna 57 Pilothouse

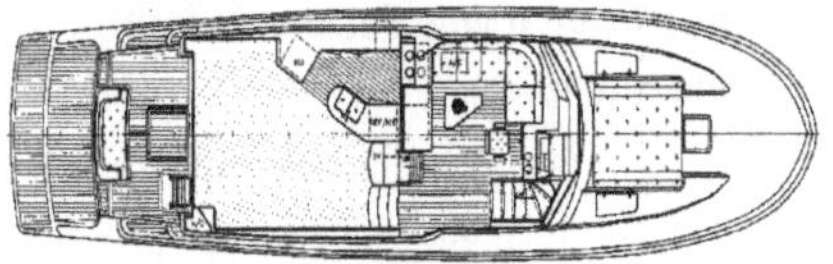

Salon Galley Layout

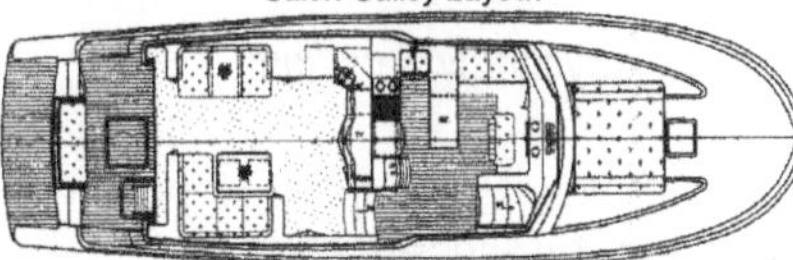

Three Staterooms

The McKinna 57 is a raised pilothouse cruising yacht whose combination of distinctive styling, roomy accommodations, and affordable price set her apart from many competitive motoryachts of her era. Built in Taiwan by Lien Hwa Shipyards, the McKinna 57 rides on a semi-displacement hull with a moderate 15-foot, 5-inch beam, shallow keel, and a solid fiberglass bottom. Several two- and three-stateroom floorplans were available in the 57 with a choice of maple, teak, or light oak interior joinery. Most were delivered with the galley forward in the spacious, full-beam salon. The raised pilothouse boasts an L-shaped dinette, watertight deck door, and direct flybridge access. Cockpit features include a teak sole, combined grill and wet bar, dual transom doors, and an access hatch to the engineroom. Note that to preserve space, the cockpit does not have a flybridge ladder or steps. Topside, the flybridge has a large settee, wet bar, and sun pads. Additional features include Corian galley counters, companionway washer/dryer cabinet, bow thruster, and an extended teak swim platform. A heavily built yacht, optional MAN 600hp (or Cummins 640hp) diesels cruise the McKinna 57 at 20 knots (low 20s top).

See Page 688 For Price Data

Length Overall	62'0"	Fuel	850 gals.
Beam	15'5"	Water	270 gals.
Draft	4'2"	Waste	100 gals.
Weight	52,500#	Hull Type	Semi-Disp.
Clearance	NA	Deadrise Aft	18°

McKinna 65 Pilothouse

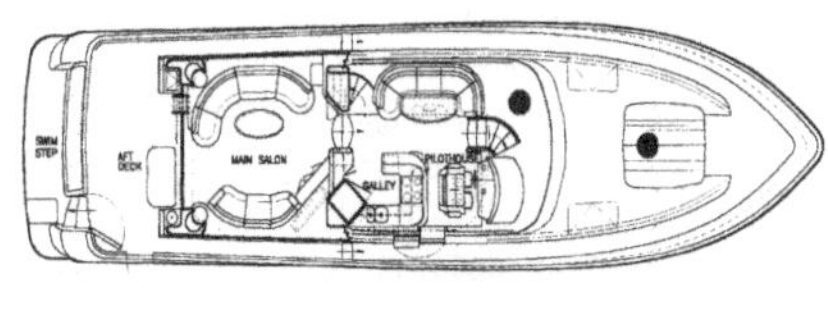

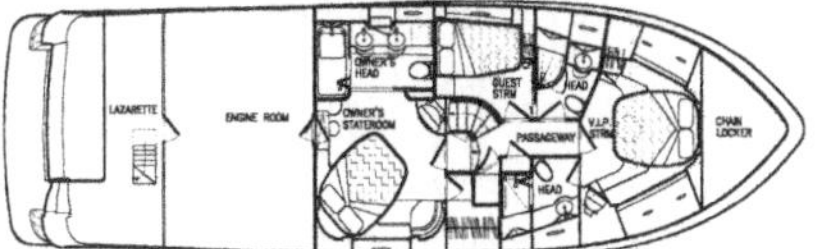

The McKinna 65 is an elegantly designed pilothouse yacht whose graceful profile stands in contrast to the exaggerated styling of her Euro-style counterparts. Heavily built on a modified-V hull with prop pockets and a relatively wide beam, the high-gloss interior of the McKinna 65 is an impressive display of grain-matched woodwork and luxurious furnishings. Included in the three-stateroom layout is a amidship master suite with a diagonally positioned berth. The galley and dinette are on the pilothouse level, a few steps up from the spacious salon with its facing settees and built-in 42-inch plasma TV. The flybridge, which can be reached only from a pilothouse staircase, seats eight and extends well aft with space for a tender. Adding to the sense of luxury are the teak decks and flybridge sole. Note the engine room, accessed from the aft deck, is a little tight. Additional features include wide side decks, bow thruster, foredeck sun lounge, extended swim platform, laundry center, underwater exhaust system, and a sliding deck door at the lower helm. Optional 800hp Caterpillar diesels cruise the McKinna 65 at 20 knots (24–25 top).

Not Enough Resale Data to Set Values

Length Overall	67'6"	Fuel	1,100 gals.
Beam	17'3"	Water	280 gals.
Draft	3'7"	Headroom	6'8"
Weight	70,000#	Hull Type	Modified-V
Clearance	NA	Deadrise Aft	NA

Meridian Yachts

Quick View

- Meridian Yachts is a component of the Sea Ray Group, an operating unit within the Brunswick Boat Group.
- Meridian was formed in 2003 when Brunswick management decided to give Bayliner's bigger yachts a new name.
- Side Note: Bayliners had long suffered from the reputation of being "price" boats, and as Bayliner models grew to include yachts as large as 57 feet it was decided to form Meridian to market these products without the Bayliner name.
- In late 2008—a time of plant closings throughout the marine industry—Brunswick closed Meridian's Arlington, WA, manufacturing facility and relocated production to Palm Coast, FL.
- A Meridian owner's group can be found at www.meridianyachtowners.com.

Monterey Boats • Williston, FL • www.montereyboats.com

Meridian 341 Sedan

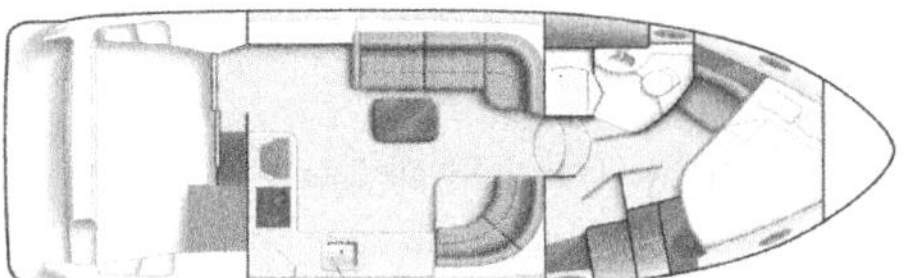

When she joined the Meridian fleet in 2003 the 341 Sedan was among the most affordable boats of her type on the market. This was Meridian's entry-level offering, and there was a lot to like about her from the standpoint of features and value. In fact, the 341 wasn't really a "new" model; she was originally marketed as the Bayliner 3488 Command Bridge. She became the Meridian 341 in 2003 when Bayliner went out of the big-boat business and Meridian Yachts was formed. Sharing the same hull, cabin accommodations, and flybridge layout as her predecessor, the 341 is a simple and very practical boat. Her two-stateroom interior is highlighted with cherry woodwork, cedar-lined hanging lockers, and leather upholstery. The head is fitted with a separate stall shower, and wraparound cabin windows provide plenty of natural lighting. In the cockpit, molded steps make bridge access very easy. Additional features include a transom door, radar arch, excellent cabin headroom, and an extended flybridge. Note the narrow side decks. Twin 320hp MerCruiser inboards cruise the Meridian 341 at 20 knots and reach a top speed of 28–29 knots. Note that an all-new 341 Sedan model was introduced in 2005.

See Page 689 For Price Data

Length	35'3"	Fuel	224 gals.
Beam	11'8"	Water	92 gals.
Draft	3'2"	Waste	30 gals.
Weight	17,000#	Hull Type	Modified-V
Clearance	13'6"	Deadrise Aft	7.5°

Meridian 341 Sedan

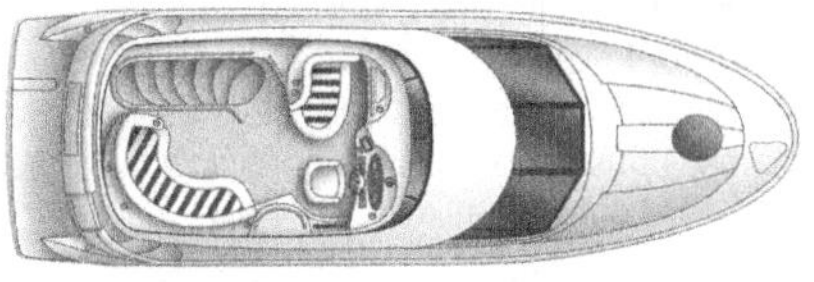

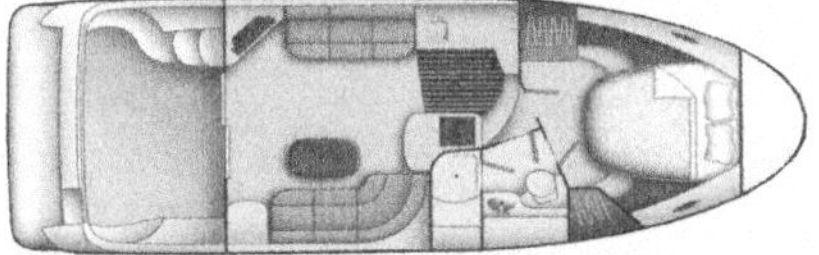

Introduced in 2005, the Meridian 341 Sedan is not an updated version of the company's original 341 Sedan built in 2003–04. This is a completely different boat with greater beam than her predecessor, more dramatic styling, and a revised two-stateroom interior. Built on a low-deadrise hull with a solid fiberglass bottom, the 341's tiered cabin windows create the impression of great space in the salon. The galley is forward, on the same level as the salon, and the well-appointed decor is an attractive blend of leather seating, vinyl wall coverings, and cherry joinery. A head with a stall shower is to starboard, accessed from either the master stateroom or the passageway. If the interior of the 341 Sedan seems unusually spacious for a 34-footer, the cockpit is tiny and the side decks are practically nonexistent. A molded staircase leads up to the extended flybridge with its wet bar and guest seating. Additional features include a transom door, radar arch, fore and aft freshwater washdowns, VacuFlush toilet, and stern and bow thrusters. A lower helm was optional. A modest performer with 320hp gas inboards, she'll cruise at 18 knots and reach 26–27 knots wide open.

See Page 689 For Price Data

Length	35'10"	Fuel	250 gals.
Beam	12'6"	Water	90 gals.
Draft	4'0"	Waste	35 gals.
Weight	18,254#	Hull Type	Modified-V
Clearance	14'1"	Deadrise Aft	11°

Meridian 368 Motor Yacht

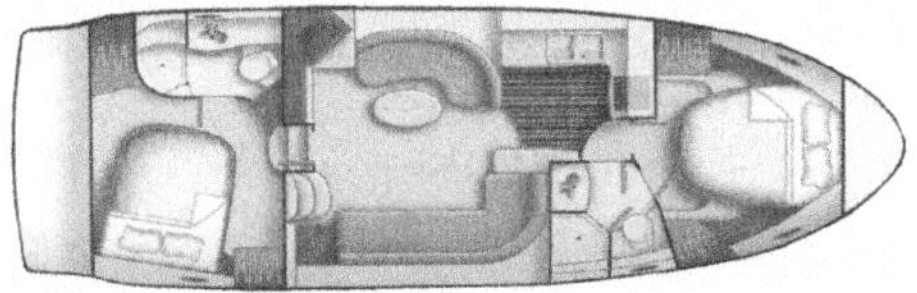

The Meridian 368 does an admirable job of delivering many of the features found in a full-size motor yacht in a compact 36-foot hull. Equally important, she did it at a price point designed to appeal to entry-level buyers. For openers, this is a coastal cruiser and not an offshore passagemaker. Range is limited thanks to the 368's modest fuel tankage, and her low-deadrise hull is no picnic in an offshore chop. When it comes to amenities, however, the Meridian is in her element. Beginning with a spacious salon and including two comfortable staterooms, a well-appointed galley with cherry joinery, and two full heads, the accommodations of the 368 rival those of a much larger boat. The salon's tiered windows admit plenty of natural lighting while providing a panoramic view of the outdoors, and a large picture window in the master stateroom overlooks the extended swim platform. On the bridge, the helm is forward and a wet bar and lounge seating were standard. Additional features include bow and stern thrusters, teak-and-holly galley floor, opening salon windows, and salon entertainment center. Standard 370hp gas engines cruise at 18–19 knots, and optional 330hp Cummins diesels cruise in the mid 20s.

See Page 689 For Price Data

Length	37'8"	Fuel	250 gals.
Beam	13'7"	Water	90 gals.
Draft	3'6"	Waste	50 gals.
Weight	24,250#	Hull Type	Modified-V
Clearance	13'6"	Deadrise Aft	13°

Meridian 381 Sedan

The Meridian 381 Sedan is a slightly revised version of the Bayliner 3788 Motor Yacht that was first introduced in 2001. (She became the Meridian 381 in 2003 when Bayliner went out of the big-boat business and Meridian Yachts was formed.) With her modern styling and expansive interior, the affordable price of the 381 makes her an appealing yacht for entry-level buyers on a budget. Built on a low-deadrise hull with a wide beam and shallow keel, the two-stateroom, galley-up interior of the 381 is highlighted with solid-cherry woodwork, faux leather upholstery, and earth-tone fabrics. For a 38-footer, the salon seems exceptionally open and inviting with facing settees aft and a full-size dinette forward. Below, an island berth is located in the master stateroom, while the guest stateroom is partially tucked under the salon floor. In the cockpit, molded steps provide easy access to the flybridge. (Note that the extended flybridge shades most of the cockpit.) A radar arch, transom door, and teak-and-holly galley floor were standard. Twin 320hp MerCruiser gas inboards cruise the 381 Sedan at 15–16 knots and top out in the mid 20s.

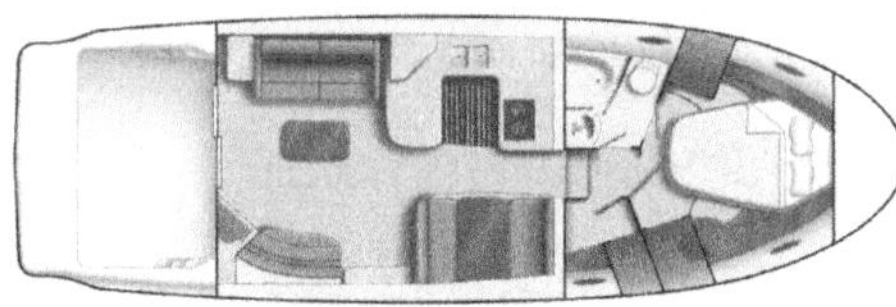

See Page 689 For Price Data

Length	38'6"	Fuel	300 gals.
Beam	13'7"	Water	125 gals.
Draft	3'4"	Waste	37 gals.
Weight	22,275#	Hull Type	Modified-V
Clearance	14'1"	Deadrise Aft	10°

Meridian 391 Sedan

Since the company's founding in 2003, Meridians have been known for their edgy styling. Boat styling is a moving target, however, and what's sexy today may appear dated in a few short years. Introduced in 2006, the sweeping lines of the Meridian 391 distinguish her from other boats in her class. With her short foredeck and long superstructure, the below decks accommodations are spacious indeed. Adding to that impression are the tiered side windows and large front windshield—the outside views are panoramic, but it's a little like being in a giant fishbowl. The two-stateroom floorplan of the 391 Sedan consists of a step-down galley forward of the salon, opposite an elevated dinette. The guest stateroom—which has a queen bed—extends beneath the dinette so headroom here is minimal. Note that the head is split in this layout with the shower stall on one side and the sink/toilet on the other. A lower helm is optional in place of the dinette. In the cockpit, the flybridge staircase lifts for access to the engineroom. Lounge seating on the huge bridge can accommodate a small crowd. Standard 370hp gas engines cruise at 18 knots; optional 380hp Cummins diesels cruise at 20+ knots.

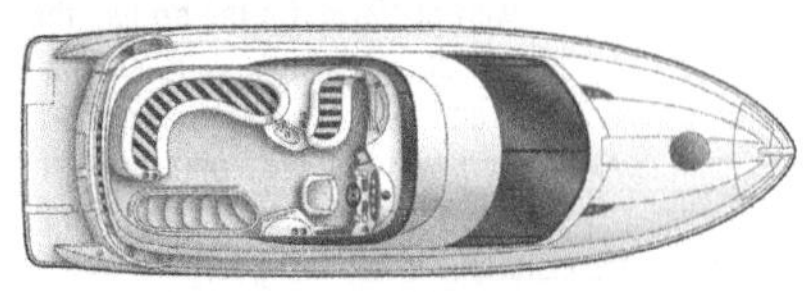

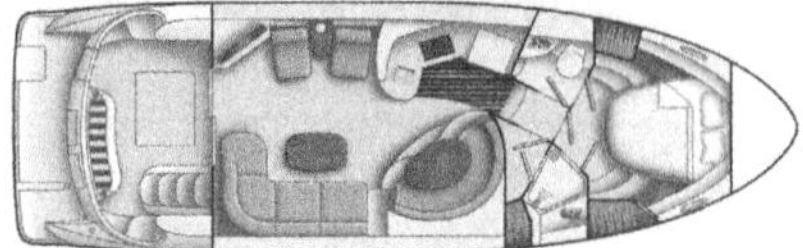

See Page 689 For Price Data

Length	40'11	Fuel	350 gals.
Beam	13'11"	Water	125 gals.
Draft	3'3"	Waste	40 gals.
Weight	25,000#	Hull Type	Modified-V
Clearance	14'0"	Deadrise Aft	10°

Meridian 408 Motor Yacht

2003–08

With her tall freeboard and full-bodied profile, the Meridian 408 may not be the prettiest motor yacht on the block but she definitely delivers the goods when it comes to accommodations and comfort. The 408 was one of the first really new Meridian designs—most early Meridian models were ex-Bayliners—and her condo-style interior rivals that of a small apartment. Built on a low-deadrise hull with a wide beam, the Meridian's expansive full-width salon is easily her most notable feature. Tiered windows provide near 360-degree visibility, and the built-in entertainment center aft includes a flat-screen TV. The galley is down a couple of steps from the salon, and high-gloss cherry woodwork is applied throughout. With her huge salon and spacious bow stateroom, it's hardly a surprise to find that the master stateroom is a bit small for a 40-footer. Here, the head and shower compartments are separated—and the bed is athwartships—to save space. Topside, a wet bar is standard on the small aft deck, and the bridge is arranged with guest seating aft of the centerline helm. Optional 370hp Cummins diesels cruise the Meridian 408 at 18–20 knots and top out in the mid 20s. Note the modest fuel capacity.

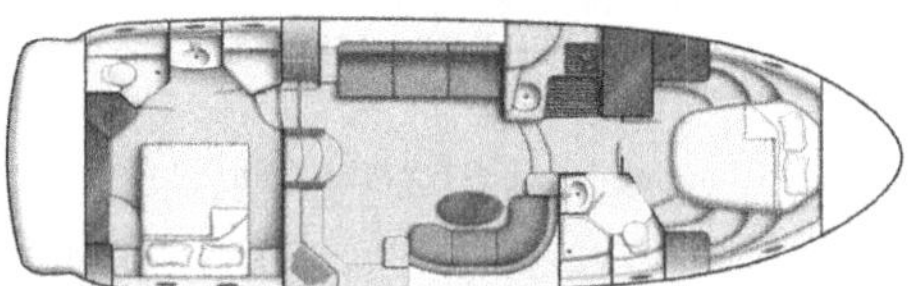

See Page 689 For Price Data

Length	42'2"	Fuel	330 gals.
Beam	14'4"	Water	90 gals.
Draft	3'10"	Waste	55 gals.
Weight	29,000#	Hull Type	Modified-V
Clearance	14'4"	Deadrise Aft	10°

Meridian 411 Sedan

2003–07

Introduced in 2003, the Meridian 411 is a competitively priced sedan cruiser whose crisp styling and comfortable accommodations remain her most impressive features. Like other Meridian models, the 411 rides on a solid fiberglass hull with generous beam and a relatively flat bottom. Her two-stateroom interior compares favorably with other boats of her type and size, and while the overall finish may lack the polish of a more expensive yacht, the layout is practical and well organized. The expansive salon is arranged with the galley and dinette forward, a step up from the aft salon with its facing settees and entertainment center. The dinette converts to a double berth in the usual fashion, and a hatch in the salon floor provides access to a very well arranged engineroom. Topside, there's seating for eight and a built-in wet bar on the large flybridge. Additional features include an extended swim platform, cherry interior joinery, radar arch, and reasonably wide side decks. Note that a lower helm station was optional. Twin 370hp Cummins diesels cruise the Meridian 411 Sedan in the low 20s and reach a top speed of 26–28 knots. A popular model, over 300 were sold.

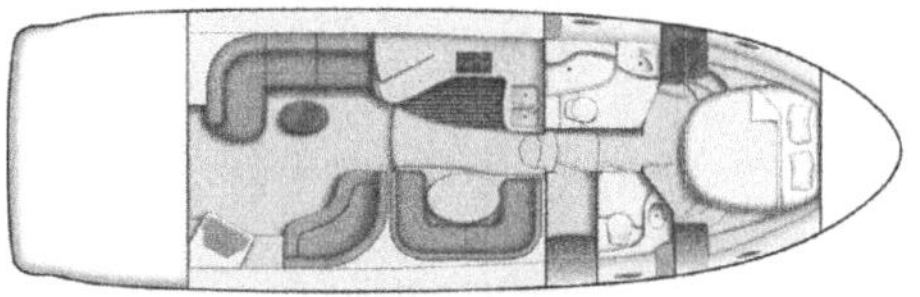

See Page 689 For Price Data

Length	46'0"	Fuel	400 gals.
Beam	14'2"	Water	150 gals.
Draft	3'9"	Waste	55 gals.
Weight	25,000#	Hull Type	Modified-V
Clearance	15'0"	Deadrise Aft	7°

Meridian 441 Sedan

2008–Current

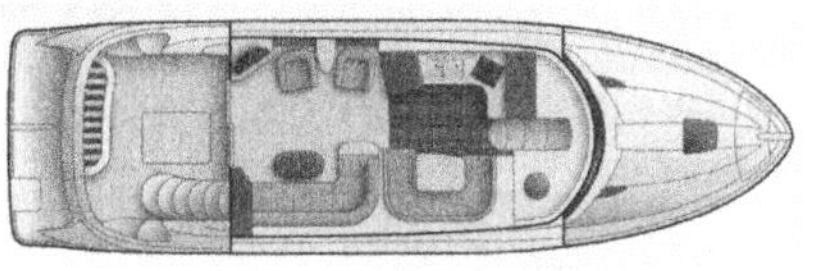

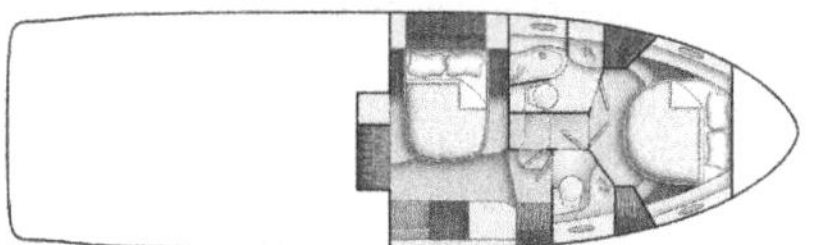

With her sleek styling and upscale accommodations, the Meridian 441 Sedan is a modern, luxury-class motoryacht whose appeal will extend from liveaboards to coastal cruisers. Built on a modified-V with shallow deadrise aft, the 441's rakish profile is accented by tiered cabin windows and an aggressive hardtop design. Below decks, her two-stateroom, two-head layout provides a large master suite forward with a queen-size island berth. The spacious amidships guest stateroom, which spans the yacht's beam, features a double berth, vanity and settee. The split-level salon of the 441 Sedan is arranged with the galley and dinette forward, a step above the aft salon. Wraparound windows provide copious natural lighting; the outside views are panoramic indeed. Note the sculptured salon overhead. An optional lower helm is available in place of the dinette, and a washer/dryer is located in the guest stateroom. Access to the 441's extended flybridge, with wraparound lounge seating, is via a stairway from the cockpit. (The standup engineroom is reached from the cockpit as well.) No racehorse with 425hp Cummins inboard diesels, the 441 will cruise at a leisurely 20 knots (low 20s top).

See Page 689 For Price Data

Length	47'2"	Fuel	432 gals.
Beam	14'3"	Water	150 gals.
Draft	3'1"	Waste	55 gals.
Weight	31,233#	Hull Type	Modified-V
Clearance	NA	Deadrise Aft	7°

Meridian 459 Cockpit MY

2004–08

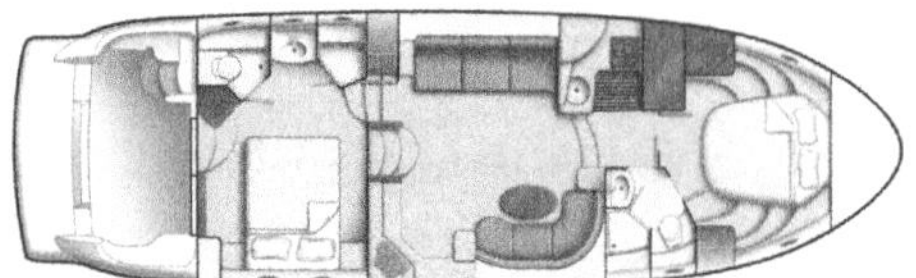

The Meridian 459 is a cockpit version of the Meridian 408 Motor Yacht introduced in 2003. Built on a low-deadrise hull with a wide beam, the Meridian's expansive two-stateroom interior is her most notable feature. Tiered windows provide near 360-degree visibility in the salon, and the built-in entertainment center aft includes a flat-screen TV. The galley is down a couple of steps from the salon, and high-gloss cherry woodwork is applied throughout. With her big salon and spacious bow stateroom, it's hardly a surprise to find that the master stateroom is on the small side for a yacht this size. Here, the head and shower compartments are separated—and the bed is positioned athwartships—to save space, and a sliding glass door provides direct access to the large cockpit. Topside, a wet bar and bench seating are standard on the small aft deck, and the bridge is arranged with guest seating aft of the centerline helm. Additional features include an extended swim platform, hardtop, and cockpit storage lockers. Fuel capacity is modest for a boat this size. Cummins 425hp diesels cruise at 20 knots and reach a top speed of 23–24 knots.

See Page 689 For Price Data

Length	47'8"	Fuel	330 gals.
Beam	14'4"	Water	90 gals.
Draft	3'10"	Waste	55 gals.
Weight	30,700#	Hull Type	Modified-V
Clearance	14'4"	Deadrise Aft	10°

Meridian 490 Pilothouse

2003–08

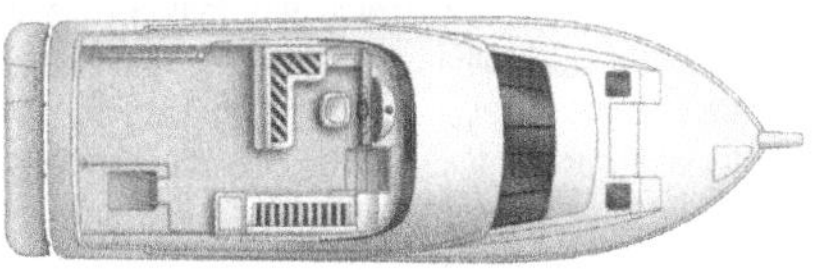

One of the first Meridian yachts to be introduced, the 490 Pilothouse wasn't really a "new" model; she was originally marketed as the Bayliner 4788 Pilothouse. She became the Meridian 490 in 2003 when Bayliner went out of the big-boat business and Meridian Yachts was formed. The 490 was already a huge sales success before Meridian took over having found the sweet spot in the market where price and value intersect. She continued her popularity as the 490 Pilothouse, remaining in production with Meridian for another six years before being retired from the fleet. Whether sold as a Bayliner or Meridian, the price of this yacht was always affordable compared with competitive models. Her three-stateroom cherrywood interior features a spacious full-beam salon, big U-shaped galley, two full heads, and a raised pilothouse with flybridge access. The third stateroom, accessed from master stateroom, has a settee with hinged upper/lower berths allowing it to double as a dressing room. Note the companionway washer/dryer location. The extended flybridge easily stows a dinghy. On the downside, the cockpit is small and the engineroom is a little tight. Cruise efficiently at 20 knots with Cummins 330hp diesels.

See Page 689 For Price Data

Length w/Pulpit	54'0"	Fuel	444 gals.
Beam	15'1"	Water	200 gals.
Draft	3'4"	Waste	48 gals.
Weight	29,990#	Hull Type	Modified-V
Clearance	18'2"	Deadrise Aft	NA

Meridian 540 Pilothouse

2003–06

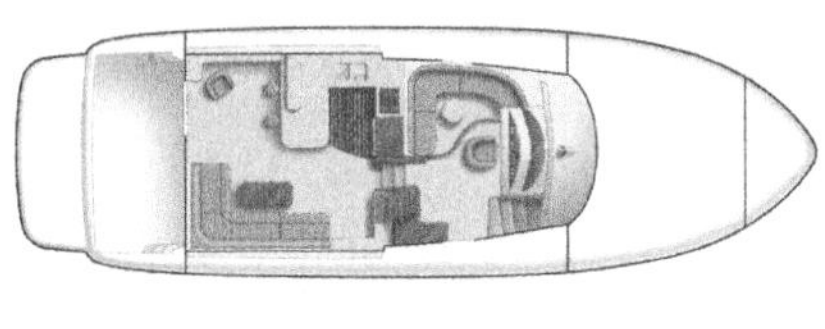

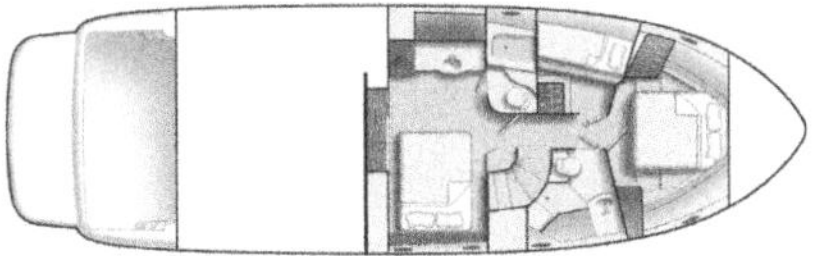

The Meridian 540 Pilothouse offers buyers a level of comfort and luxury usually associated with more expensive yachts. Pilothouse boats have become increasingly popular in recent years due to their handsome lines and all-weather cruising capabilities. In the case of the 540, Meridian designers delivered a notably handsome yacht whose graceful lines incorporate the best in modern pilothouse styling. Built on a modified-V hull with a wide 16-foot, 3-inch beam, the three-stateroom interior is as spacious as it gets in a yacht this size. The focal point of the 540 is her large pilothouse with its wraparound dinette, flybridge stairway, and centerline helm position. Large windows offer a panoramic view from the salon, and both the master and forward staterooms are fitted with queen berths. Clever storage solutions, a full complement of home-style appliances, and a well-appointed decor make the Meridian's interior as practical as it is inviting. Additional features include a flybridge davit, extended swim platform, bow and stern thrusters, and flybridge wet bar. Note that the engineroom is accessed directly from the cockpit. A modest performer with Cummins 635hp diesels, the Meridian 540 will cruise at 20+ knots.

See Page 689 For Price Data

Length	56'9"	Fuel	700 gals.
Beam	16'3"	Water	200 gals.
Draft	4'10"	Waste	76 gals.
Weight	50,554#	Hull Type	Modified-V
Clearance	19'3"	Deadrise Aft	12°

Meridian 580 Pilothouse

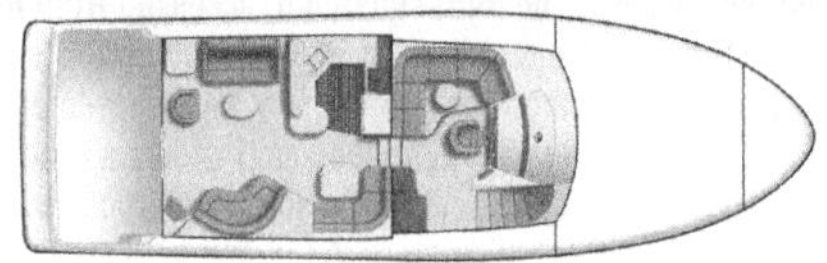

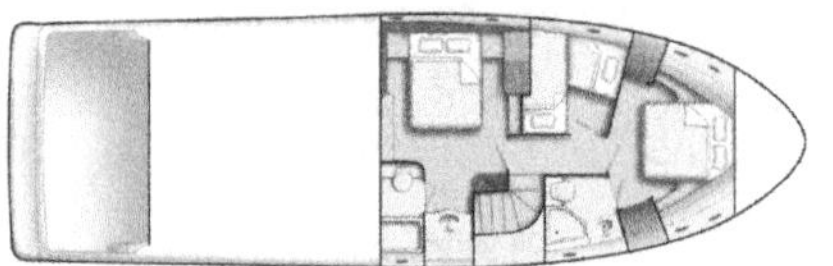

Flagship of the Meridian fleet, the 580 Pilothouse is one of the most affordable yachts her size on the market. Actually, the 580 wasn't really a new model for Meridian; she was called the Bayliner 5788 Command Bridge during the late 1990s, becoming the Meridian 580 in 2003 when Bayliner went out of the big-boat business and Meridian Yachts was formed. The 580's styling is more graceful than the older Bayliner 5788 (note the nonfunctional air intakes above the salon windows), and her three-stateroom interior has been updated in both decor and salon configuration. Like most pilothouse yachts, the galley and dinette are positioned forward in the salon. Visibility from the raised pilothouse is excellent, and there are two full heads on the lower level along with a full-beam master stateroom and VIP double. The interior of the 580 is finished with varnished teak or cherry joinery, faux-granite counters, and earth-tone fabrics. Additional features include flybridge dinghy storage, foredeck sun pad, cockpit engineroom access, and an extended swim platform. Cummins 635hp diesels cruise the Meridian 580 at a modest 18 knots and top out in the low 20s.

See Page 689 For Price Data

Length	59'5"	Fuel	800 gals.
Beam	17'4"	Water	218 gals.
Draft	4'11"	Waste	74 gals.
Weight	59,920#	Hull Type	Modified-V
Clearance	19'7"	Deadrise Aft	10°

Mikelson Yachts

Quick View

- Based in San Diego, CA, Mikelson was founded in 1984 by partners Dick Peterson and Pat Sullivan.
- The company made its name in the indistry with a series of well regarded Fexas-designed convertibles and yachtfishermen.
- Until recent years, all Mikelson models were imported from Taiwan where the boats were manufactured by Bluewater Marine under the company's close control.
- Sold primarily into the West Coast market, Mikelson yachts have a well-deserved reputation for their excellent performance and stylish appearance—design characteristics often associated with Tom Fexas designs.
- Mikelson currently offers a 6-boat series of quality long-range sportfishing boats from 43 to 75 feet in length.

Mikelson Yachts • San Diego, CA • www.mikelsonyachts.com

Mikelson 43 Sportfisher

1997–Current

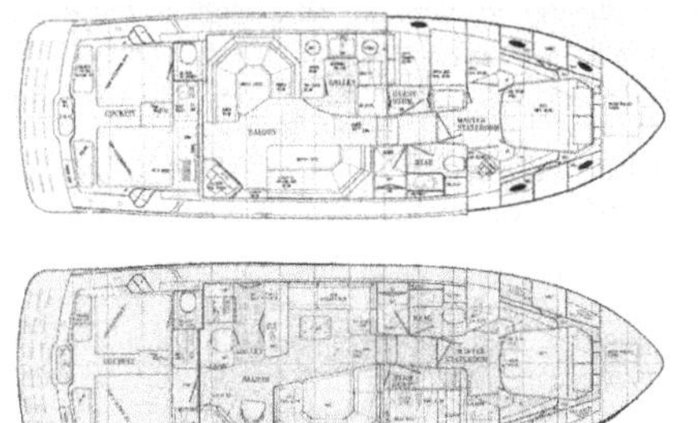

Mikelson's entry-level fishing boat, the 43 Sportfisher's excellent performance, solid construction, and versatile layout have made her a sales success since she was introduced in 1998. Mikelson has built an impressive reputation in recent years with their expanding line of durable West Coast convertibles, and the 43 Sportfisher retains the same rakish styling and practical design features seen in the company's larger boats. Built in Taiwan on a modified-V hull with a wide beam and prop pockets to reduce shaft angles, the 43's standard two-stateroom interior is arranged with an island berth in the master stateroom and over/under single bunks in the guest cabin. The salon dinette is a nice touch (only a few boats this size have one), and the interior is fully finished with rich cherry woodwork. Aside from the well-equipped cockpit (transom bait tank, bait-prep center, etc.), the flybridge is a real attention-getter with its circular settee and wraparound helm console. Note the wide side decks and sturdy railings. Engine access, via hatches in the cockpit sole, is excellent. Twin 450hp Cummins diesels cruise at 24 knots (29–30 knots top). Newer models are offered with 480hp Zeus pod drives. Over 60 have been sold.

See Page 689 For Price Data

Length w/Pulpit	48'8"	Fuel	600 gals.
Hull Length	43'10"	Water	200 gals.
Beam	15'10"	Waste	60 gals.
Draft	3'10"	Hull Type	Modified-V
Weight	35,000#	Deadrise Aft	14.5°

Mikelson 50 Sportfisher

1992–2009

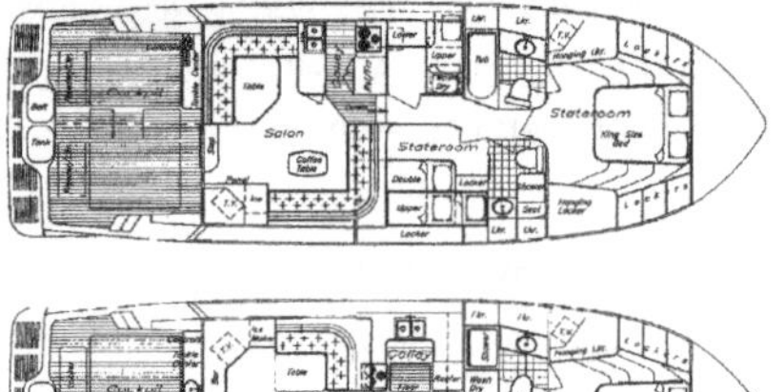

The Mikelson 50 Sportfisher evolved from the Mikelson 48 Sedan, an innovative West Coast cruiser whose sleek, low-profile appearance, highly efficient hull, and unique under-cockpit engine location set her apart from just about every other boat her size on the market. Following up on the sales success of the 48 Sedan, the 50 Sportfish model came out in 1992 with an enlarged cockpit and a conventional transom rather than the reverse transom of the original 48. Built on a fully cored hull with rounded bilges and a wide beam, the 50 is a light boat for her size—a feature that results in some surprising performance figures with relatively small engines. Offered with two or three staterooms, the spacious interior dimensions rival those of a larger boat. One of the more interesting features of the Mikelson 50 is her huge flybridge with its circular dinette and fore and aft helm consoles. Additional features include wide side decks, teak or cherry interior, excellent engine access, and a double bait tank built into the transom. A good-selling model (over 80 Mikelson 50s were sold), twin 540hp Cummins V-drive diesels cruise at 22 knots and reach 24–25 knots top. With 1,000 gallons of fuel this is a seriously long-range boat.

See Page 689 For Price Data

Length	50'5"	Fuel	1,000 gals.
Beam	16'8"	Water	250 gals.
Draft	3'10"	Waste	80 gals.
Weight	45,000#	Hull Type	Modified-V
Clearance	NA	Deadrise Aft	12°

Mikelson 59 Nomad

2004–Current

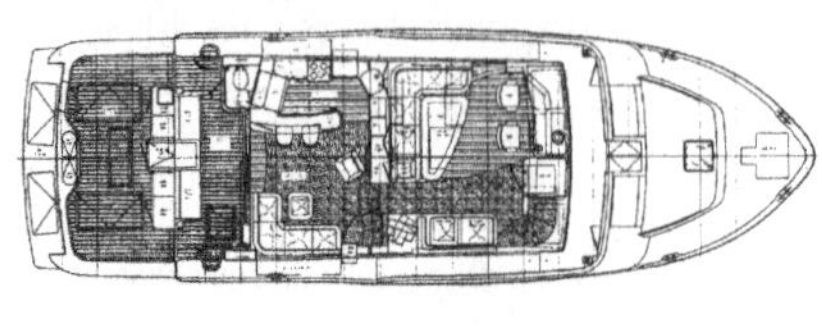

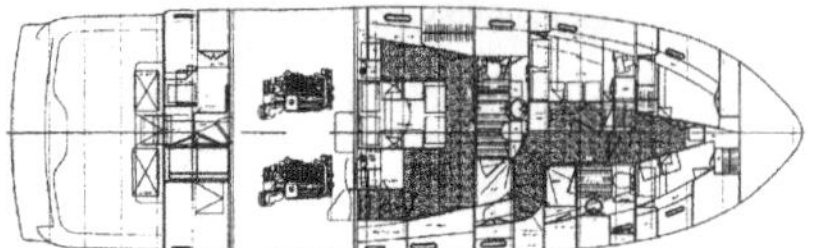

The Mikelson 50 Nomad is a long-range fishing boat whose distinctive pilothouse design is unlike any other production sportfishing boat currently on the market. This is a yacht engineered for extended cruising, an objective she achieves through a unique hull design capable of impressive fuel efficiency at relatively high speeds. Built on a modified-V hull with a deep keel, propeller pockets and a broad beam, each Nomad interior can be custom designed for the owner, and several floorplan options are available. In the standard three-stateroom configuration, the cavernous full-beam amidships master stateroom—with its private salon access—rivals the owner's suite of an 80-footer. The pilothouse is also huge, and a portside door leads to a wraparound Portuguese bridge. Aft sliding salon doors open to the Nomad's large afterdeck that, in turn, overlooks the teak-planked cockpit with its two huge livewells and large-capacity fish boxes. Note the absence of a traditional flybridge. Additional features include a very spacious engine room, aft crew quarters with washer/dryer, and an extended hardtop with dinghy storage. Cruise at 12–15 knots with Cummins 635hp diesels.

Not Enough Resale Data to Set Values

Length Overall	61'4"	Fuel	2,000 gals.
Beam	18'6"	Water	350 gals.
Draft	5'6"	Waste	150 gals.
Weight	80,000#	Hull Type	Modified-V
Clearance	NA	Deadrise Aft	11°

Mikelson 60 Sportfisher

1992–99

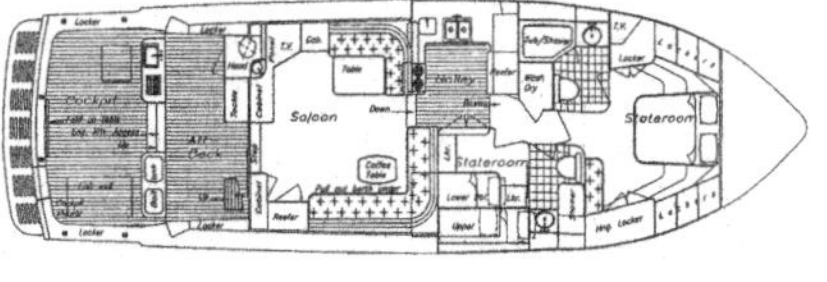

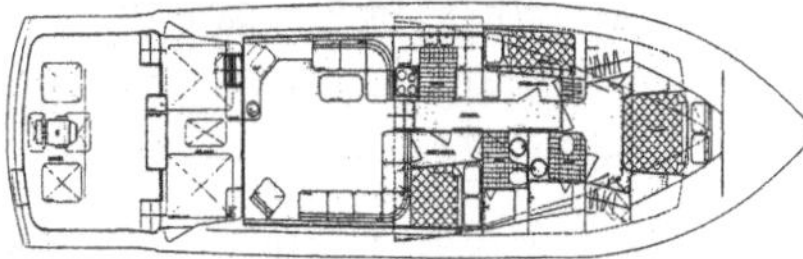

Designed by Tom Fexas and built in Taiwan, the Mikelson 60 is an innovative West Coast fisherman with a rakish profile and plenty of built-in sex appeal. She was built on a lightweight, fully cored hull with a wide 17-foot, 2-inch beam, prop pockets, and moderate transom deadrise—a notably efficient hull requiring relatively small engines for her size. Several floorplans were available: the standard galley-down layout has three staterooms, and alternate arrangements had two staterooms with an enlarged galley. Either way, the wide-open salon comes with built-in settees and plenty of teak cabinetry and woodwork. Stepping outside, an unusual aft deck platform overlooks the giant-size cockpit. The flybridge is also huge with a wraparound helm console forward and lounge seating for a small crowd aft. The engines are located under the aft deck where they're accessed via hydraulically operated hatches in the sole. The Mikelson 60 also has a rather unique underwater exhaust system with a transom bypass for quiet operation. A good performer with 735hp 8V92s, she'll cruise in the low 20s and reach 26–27 knots wide open. Note that the Mikelson 56 Sportfish (1990–97) is essentially the same boat with a smaller cockpit.

See Page 689 For Price Data

Length	59'1"	Fuel	1,000 gals.
Beam	17'2"	Water	300 gals.
Draft	4'4"	Headroom	6'5"
Weight	55,000#	Hull Type	Modified-V
Clearance	NA	Deadrise Aft	14.5°

Mikelson 61 Pilothouse Sportfisher

2000–08

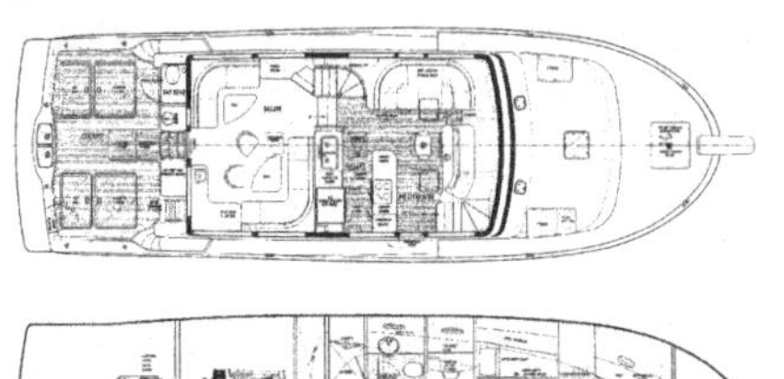

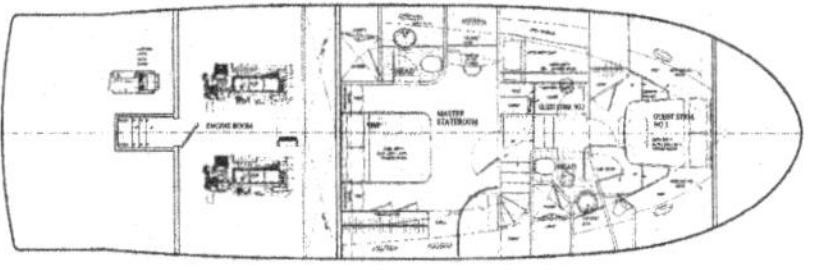

Even with the growing popularity of pilothouse motor yachts in recent years, Mikelson's decision to introduce a pilothouse sportfisherman was an innovative concept. This is a good-looking yacht—a completely different style from standard convertible designs—with the luxury interior accommodations of a pilothouse motor yacht and the king-size cockpit dimensions of a good fishing boat. With nearly 19 feet of beam, the Mikelson 61 is an unusually spacious boat and her three-stateroom interior includes a huge, full-width master stateroom beneath the pilothouse. Both the galley and dinette are on the pilothouse level, and the expansive salon will entertain a small crowd. The cockpit, a few steps down from the salon level, is equally large and includes a handy day head as well as direct engine room access. Topside, the extended flybridge (accessible from either the cockpit or the pilothouse) can accommodate a dinghy. Additional features include a sliding deck door at the lower helm, very wide side decks, cherry interior cabinetry, a huge engine room, and a fiberglass hardtop. Twin 800hp Cat diesels cruise at 20 knots (mid 20s top). Larger 1,400hp Cats are good for speeds up to 30 knots.

Not Enough Resale Data to Set Values

Length	61'0"	Fuel	1,600 gals.
Beam	18'11"	Water	250 gals.
Draft	4'9"	Cockpit	165 sq. ft.
Weight	66,650#	Hull Type	Modified-V
Clearance	NA	Deadrise Aft	NA

Mikelson 64 Sportfisher

1997–2001

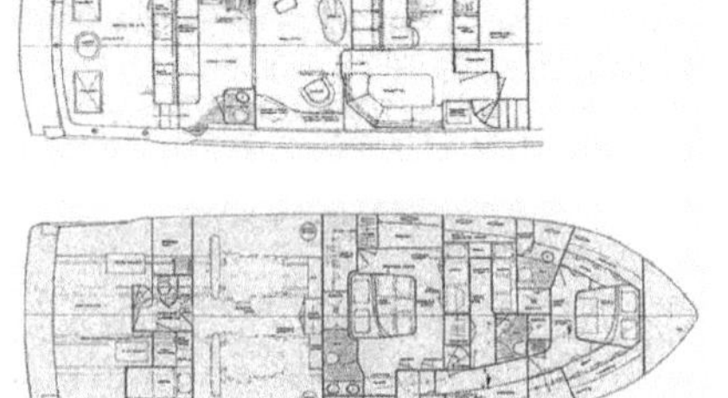

The Mikelson 64 is a long-range West Coast fisherman with unusually spacious accommodations and an aggressive, low-profile appearance. This is a big yacht—indeed, her 19-foot-plus beam is by far the widest of any boat this size. Based on the company's successful 72- and 78-foot yachts (and built in Taiwan), the 64 compromises little in the way of comfort and luxury. Her standard three-stateroom, three-head interior includes a full-beam master amidships with a centerline king bed, and the wide beam of the 64 translates into a huge salon with an aft-facing settee on the lower level and the galley and dinette forward on the upper level. Like her larger sistership, an observation deck (with a day head) overlooks the 210-square-foot cockpit which is fully rigged with baitwells, two fish boxes, tackle center and a control station. Beneath the observation deck is a crew cabin with head and an access door to the engine room. Topside, the flybridge features a wraparound helm, a circular settee, refrigerator and aft controls. Built on an efficient, fully cored modified-V hull, twin 1,300hp Caterpillar 3412 diesels cruise the Mikelson 64 at 25 knots and reach a top speed of just over 30 knots.

See Page 689 For Price Data

Length	64'9"	Fuel	1,500 gals.
Beam	19'5"	Water	350 gals.
Draft	5'0"	Headroom	6'5"
Weight	87,000#	Hull Type	Modified-V
Clearance	NA	Deadrise Aft	6°

Mikelson 70 Sportfisher

2001–Current

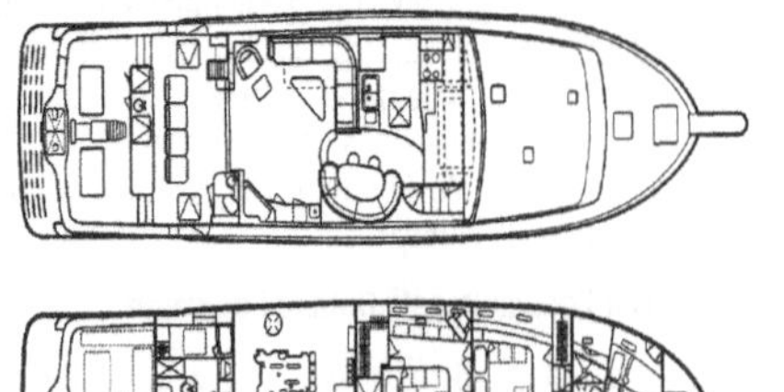

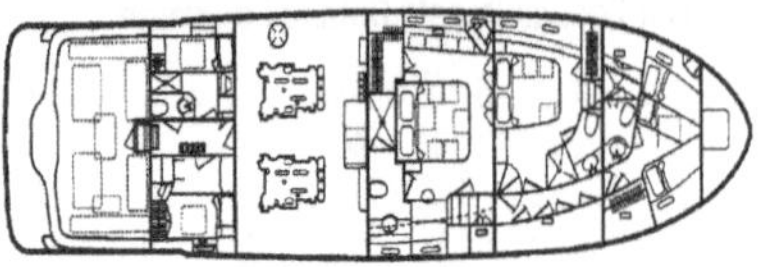

Built in Taiwan and marketed to West Coast anglers, the Mikelson 70 is a luxury sportfishing yacht whose distinctive appearance sets her well apart from conventional East Coast convertibles. Aside from her rakish profile, the most distinctive feature of the Mikelson 70 is her unique afterdeck—what Mikelson calls the "Lanai Deck"—a 90-square-foot platform overlooking the cockpit with lounge seating and a day head. Below, the Mikelson's interior is arranged with five staterooms, three forward of the engine room and twin crew cabins aft (accessed from the cockpit). With the galley and dinette forward on the pilothouse level, the main salon of the Mikelson 70 is huge. The midships guest stateroom is nearly as large as the master stateroom, and each stateroom contains an ensuite head. Topside, the Mikelson's large flybridge has fore and aft steering stations as well as lounge seating for six. Additional features include a spacious engine room, cherry interior woodwork, swim platform, transom bait tanks, and wide side decks. Built on a fully cored hull with prop pockets, the Mikelson 70 will cruise in the mid 20s and top out at close to 30 knots with 1,400hp Caterpillar diesels.

Not Enough Resale Data to Set Values

Length	69'10"	Fuel	2,200#
Beam	19'10"	Water	350 gals.
Draft	5'0"	Headroom	6'6"
Weight	95,000#	Hull Type	Modified-V
Clearance	NA	Deadrise Aft	NA

Mikelson 72/78 Sportfisher

1994–2001

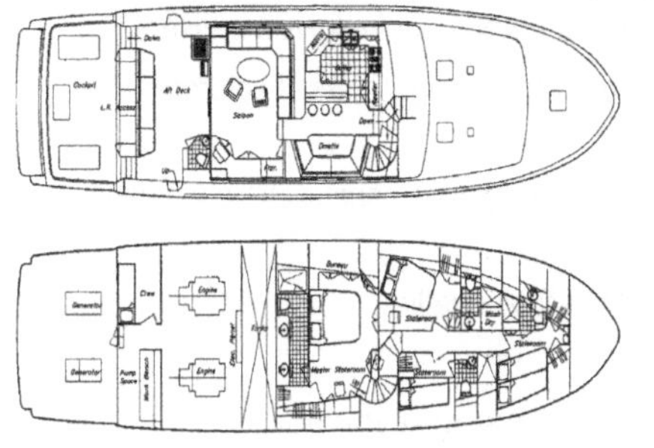

Built by Knight & Carver in San Diego, the Mikelson 78 (originally produced in 1994–95 as a 72-footer; the 78 has a longer cockpit) is a long-range sportfisher with a rakish profile and motor yacht-style accommodations. She's built on a fully cored hull with a very wide beam, and her sleek appearance makes her a clear standout among today's crop of mostly conservative production 65-foot-plus sportfishermen. While Mikelson promotes its ability to custom-design each 78 to an owner's requirements, the standard floorplan has the galley forward and elevated from the salon. This allows for the placement of an absolutely huge full beam master stateroom beneath the galley floor. Each of the other three staterooms has a double bed and all four heads have stall showers. An observation deck (with the standup engine room below) overlooks the spacious cockpit, and the flybridge—which may be enclosed—is the largest of any boat in her class and can even be ordered with a day head. Twin 1,100hp 12-cylinder MTUs cruise at 20 knots and deliver a top speed of 24–25 knots. With nearly 4,000 gallons of fuel and an easily driven hull, the 78 Sportfish has a range of some 1,400 miles.

Not Enough Resale Data to Set Values

Length, 72	72'6"	Weight, 78	105,000#
Length, 78	77'6"	Fuel, 72	3,000 gals.
Beam	20'6"	Fuel, 78	3,700 gals.
Draft	5'6"	Water	420 gals.
Weight, 72	95,000#	Hull Type	Modified-V

Monterey

Quick View

- Monterey began operations in 1985 when brothers Charles and Jeff Marshall (both ex-employees of Chaparral Boats) formed a new company to produce a series of ski boats.
- Relocating to Archer, Florida, the Monterey line grew steadily during the late 1980s as production expanded and their boats reached an ever-wider national audience.
- In 1989 the company introduced their first family cruiser; by the mid 1990s Monterey was offering a complete line of ski boats, runabouts, and express cruisers.
- In 1994, Monterey expanded its model selection introducing its first Explorer deck boat.
- In 2000, the company relocated to Williston, FL and completed construction of a new, state-of-the-art facility and world headquarters.
- By 2005, Monterey was producing some 2,000 boats annually.

Monterey Boats • Williston, FL • www.montereyboats.com

Monterey 262 Cruiser

1997–2002

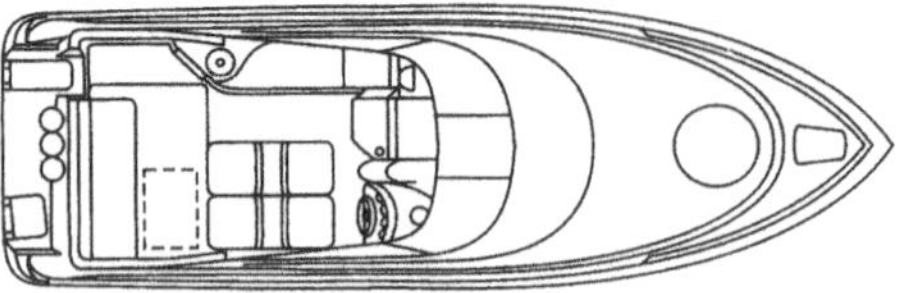

The Monterey 262 is a well-designed and heavily built trailerable cruiser with a number of attractive features that set her apart from some of her better-known counterparts. Few 26-footers with standing cabin headroom can be described as sleek—their elevated foredeck usually give them a decidedly bulky appearance; however, the 262's wraparound (walk-through) windshield, oval ports, and integral bow pulpit add a good deal of sex appeal to her profile. While the cockpit is about average in size, the built-in reclining lounge opposite the helm is a nice touch, and the helm seat can be flipped up and turned into a leaning post for standup driving. (It can also be folded down with its aft-facing jump seats to form a sun lounge.) A wet bar was standard, and the transom seat folds away into the transom when more cockpit space is required. Belowdecks, the mid-cabin floorplan of the Monterey 262 is arranged in the conventional manner with a dinette/V-berth forward, a small galley, standup head compartment, and a double berth aft beneath the raised bridge deck. A single 300hp Volvo 7.4-liter I/O will cruise the 262 Cruiser at 20 knots and reach a top speed of around 35–36 knots.

See Page 689 For Price Data

Length	26'5"	Fuel	70 gals.
Beam	8'6"	Water	21 gals.
Draft, Up	1'6"	Waste	21 gals.
Draft, Down	2'10"	Hull Type	Deep-V
Weight	5,500#	Deadrise Aft	20°

Monterey 265/276 Cruiser

1993–99

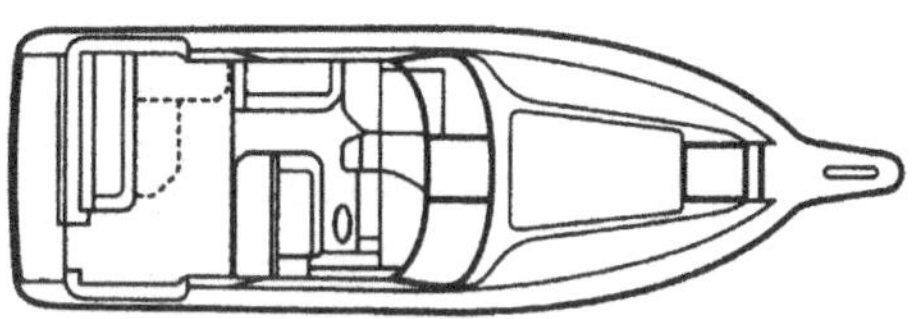

The Monterey 276 Cruiser (called the 265 Cruiser in 1993–94) is a value-priced weekend cruiser with roomy accommodations, a practical deck plan, and good open-water performance. She's constructed on a solid fiberglass, deep-V hull with an integral swim platform and a relatively wide 9-foot, 6-inch beam. Her midcabin interior is arranged in the usual way with a convertible dinette/U-shaped settee, a compact galley with sink, refrigerator, and stove, an enclosed head with shower, and twin settees in the midcabin that convert into a big double berth. There's near-standing headroom in the main cabin, and a large hanging locker provides plenty of storage. Topside, the Monterey's roomy bi-level cockpit has a double helm seat forward and bench seating at the transom. Additional features include a walk-through windshield (the side decks are quite narrow), foredeck sun pad, cockpit wet bar and sport arch. A single 310hp MerCruiser sterndrive will cruise the Monterey in the mid 20s and reach a top speed of just under 40 knots. Twin 190hp Mercs (or Volvos) will cruise in the high 20s and top out at 40+ knots.

See Page 689 For Price Data

Length w/Pulpit	29'0"	Fuel	100 gals.
Hull Length	26'10"	Water	32 gals.
Beam	9'6"	Waste	21 gals.
Draft, Down	3'0"	Hull Type	Deep-V
Weight	6,500#	Deadrise Aft	20°

Monterey 270 Cruiser

2006–08

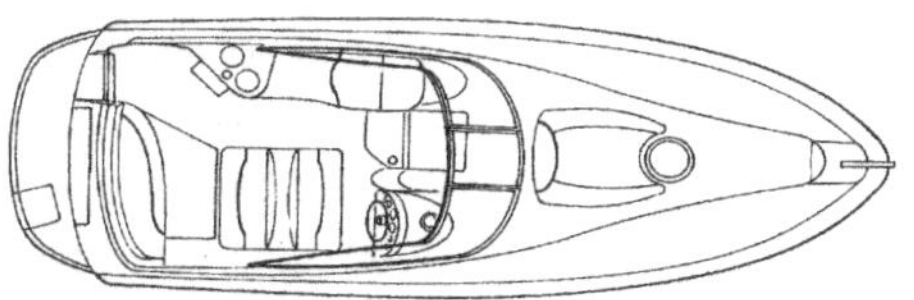

Year after year, the market for big, trailerable express cruisers remains among the most competitive in the business. With the 2006 introduction of the 270 Cruiser, Monterey offered an attractive, somewhat less expensive alternative to similar 27-footers from Sea Ray, Regal and Four Winns. In nearly every respect—styling, features, construction, etc.—the 270 compares well with her more costly counterparts. Built on a modified-V hull with 18 degrees of transom deadrise, the layout makes good use of the limited space available on a small cruiser such as this. The cockpit offers a fair amount of elbow space (considering her modest 8'6" beam) with seating for six and a wet bar with sink and removable cooler. The double helm seat converts to a lounge for sunning. The cabin is another example of good space management with a U-shaped dinette large enough for five adults at mealtime, or two adults when the area is converted to a berth. Two more people can sleep in the 270's aft cabin—a squeeze for adults, but the kids will enjoy this sanctuary. Note the transom storage locker and foredeck sun pad. A walk-through windshield provides bow access. A single Volvo 320hp gas I/O will cruise at 20+ knots (low 30s top).

See Page 689 For Price Data

Length	29'0"	Fuel	89 gals.
Beam	8'6"	Water	21 gals.
Draft, Up	1'10"	Waste	21 gals.
Draft, Down	3'4"	Hull Type	Modified-V
Weight	7,400#	Deadrise Aft	18°

Monterey 282 Cruiser

2001–06

Monterey always packs a lot of features into their sportcruisers, and the Monterey 282 has everything a family needs to enjoy a long weekend afloat. Built on a deep-V hull with a wide 10-foot beam, the 282 is a comfortable boat below and her floorplan—with its booth-style dinette—is quite different from most midsize cruisers. Although the galley is on the small side with little counter space, the big dinette is both functional and very innovative in design. The head is also quite large and comes with a hinged seat over the toilet, which makes changing clothes (or taking a shower) very comfortable. An athwartships double berth is forward, and twin settees in the midcabin convert into a large double berth. (Note that the dinette can also be converted into a berth for a couple of kids.) Topside, the cockpit is arranged with an aft-facing seat behind the double helm, wet bar with storage to port, and a removable rear seat. A transom door opens to a big swim platform where dock lines and fenders can be stored in a transom box. A fast ride with optional 260hp MerCruiser sterndrives, the Monterey 282 will cruise at close to 30 knots and reach a top speed of 40+ knots.

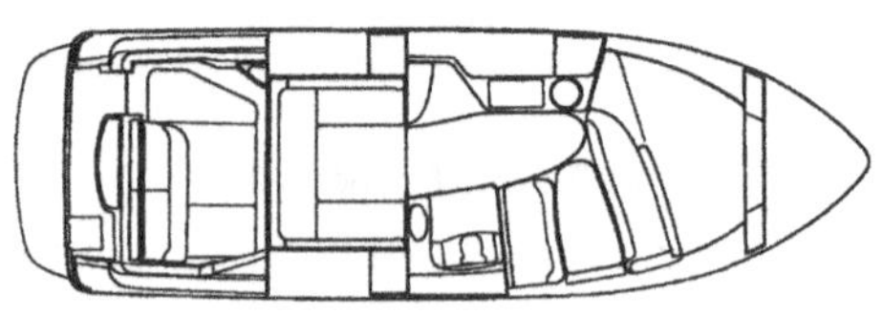

See Page 689 For Price Data

Length w/Platform	30'10"	Fuel	142 gals.
Hull Length	28'9"	Water	38 gals.
Beam	10'0"	Waste	18 gals.
Draft, Down	3'1"	Hull Type	Modified-V
Weight	10,000#	Deadrise Aft	19°

Monterey 286/296 Cruiser

1993–2000

A well-styled cruiser by the standards of her day, the 296 Cruiser was Monterey's first entry into the highly competitive market for 30-foot sterndrive family weekenders. (Called the 286 Cruiser in 1993–94, the cockpit was revised in 1995 when she became the 296 Cruiser.) Hull construction is solid fiberglass, and her deep-V bottom provides a stable, comfortable ride in most weather conditions. The interior of the 296 is arranged in the usual fashion with double berths fore and aft, a convertible dinette, enclosed head and shower, and generous storage. Two bench seats in the midcabin provide seating, and between them is a fold-down table that converts the seats into the roomiest berth in the boat. Originally designed with a single helm chair, a double helm seat (with an aft-facing bench seat) became standard in 1995. Additional features include a walk-through windshield, a wide swim platform with fender racks, good main cabin headroom, a sport arch, and a molded bow platform. Among several sterndrive engine options, twin 250hp Volvos cruise in the high 20s and reach a top speed in excess of 40 knots. Note that the 140-gallon fuel capacity is pretty slim for a 29-foot boat.

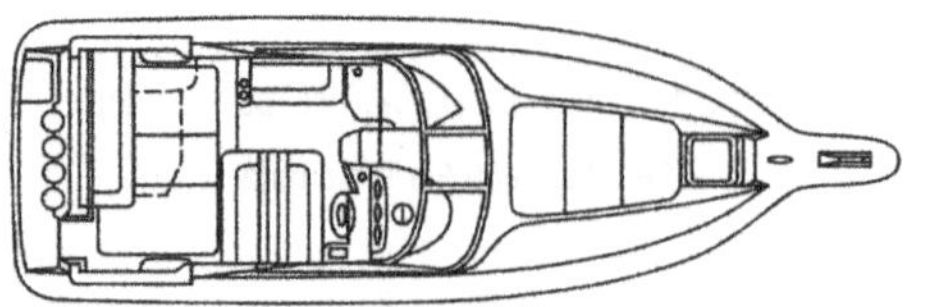

See Page 689 For Price Data

Length w/Pulpit	31'6"	Fuel	140 gals.
Hull Length	28'10"	Water	44 gals.
Beam	10'0"	Waste	21 gals.
Draft, Down	3'1"	Hull Type	Modified-V
Weight	8,000#	Deadrise Aft	19°

Monterey 290 Cruiser; 300 SCR

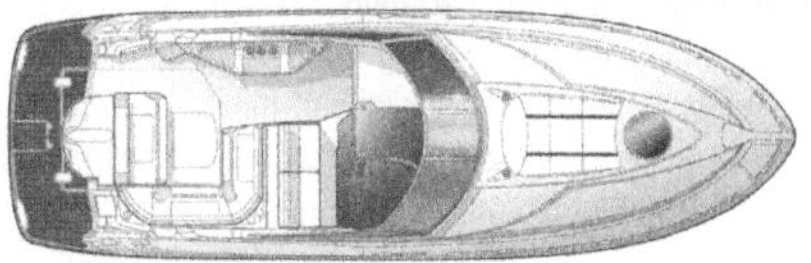

Monterey has a history of building solid, long-lasting cruisers that most brokers view as a lot of boat for the money. That certainly seems true of the 290 Cruiser (called the 300 SCR since 2009), a well built family express with the sleek styling and spirited performance that have made Monterey boats so popular over the years. Like most express boats her size, the 290 rides on a modified-V hull with a solid fiberglass bottom and a conservative 10-foot, 3-inch beam. (That moderate beam is a plus when it comes to performance; when the beam-to-length ratio exceeds 3:1, it takes more power to drive a hull through the water, and agility starts to decline.) The user-friendly cockpit of the 290 Cruiser features a cockpit table and wet bar with sink in addition to a double helm seat and lounge seating aft. The extended swim platform makes boarding easy, and a walk-through windshield provides access to the bow. Below, the cherry-trimmed interior includes a circular dinette forward (that converts to a double berth), midcabin settee/berth aft, standup head with shower, and a compact galley. Note the bow sun pad and standard transom shower. A good performer, Volvo 270hp I/Os reach close to 40 knots wide open.

See Page 689 For Price Data

Length	31'4"	Fuel	142 gals.
Beam	10'3"	Water	38 gals.
Draft, Up	1'9"	Waste	18 gals.
Draft, Down	3'1"	Hull Type	Modified-V
Weight	10,000#	Deadrise Aft	19°

Monterey 298 Sport Cruiser

To many, the Monterey 298 Sport Cruiser is one of the best-looking sportboats on the market. She's a closed-bow version of the company's popular 298 SS bowrider with surprisingly complete cabin accommodations to go with her exhilarating performance. Built on a deep-V hull, the focal point of the 298 is her large cockpit with its aft bench seat that folds down to increase the size of the existing sun pad. A contoured lounge is opposite the helm, and a forward-raked radar arch and flashy hull colors add to her sex appeal. Below, the 298 offers 5 feet, 5 inches of headroom in the main cabin, and incorporates a compact midcabin aft that stretches beneath the cockpit floor. Amenities include a full galley with cherrywood cabinets, a convertible dinette forward, and a fully enclosed head with shower. The extended swim platform comes with a recessed boarding ladder, and a flip-up seat at the helm permits standup driving. Additional features include a walk-through windshield, transom shower, cockpit wet bar, and good engine access. Twin 280hp Volvo gas sterndrives cruise in the low 30s and reach a top speed of 45 knots.

Floorplan Not Available

See Page 689 For Price Data

Length w/Platform	31'10"	Fuel	142 gals.
Hull Length	29'7"	Water	15 gals.
Beam	9'6"	Waste	18 gals.
Draft, Down	3'1"	Hull Type	Deep-V
Weight	8,500#	Deadrise Aft	22°

Monterey 298 Super Sport

From the comfortable bow seating to her well-planned cockpit, the Monterey 298 SS is one very spacious boat. In fact, she's one of the largest bowriders ever produced by a major U.S. manufacturer. Built on a deep-V hull with a wide 9-foot, 6-inch beam, the focal point of the 298 is her large cockpit with its aft bench seat that folds down to increase the size of the existing sun pad. A contoured lounge is opposite the helm, abutting a small console with wet bar and sink, and the doublewide helm seat has a flip-up bolster for standup driving. An unusual feature of the 298 SS is the double berth concealed within the portside console. An enclosed head is in the opposite console, and both of these compartments are fitted with an opening port for ventilation. There's plenty of storage under the back-to-back helm seats, and the sun pad lifts up to reveal the engine compartment. Standard features include an extended swim platform, docking lights, pull-up cleats, transom shower, fender storage, and VacuFlush toilet. An excellent open-water performer, twin 280hp Volvo gas sterndrives cruise in the low 30s and reach a top speed of 45 knots.

Floorplan Not Available

See Page 690 For Price Data

Length w/Platform	31'10"	Fuel	142 gals.
Hull Length	29'7"	Water	15 gals.
Beam	9'6"	Waste	18 gals.
Draft, Down	3'1"	Hull Type	Deep-V
Weight	8,000#	Deadrise Aft	22°

Monterey 302 Cruiser

The Monterey 302 is a stylish, affordably priced family cruiser with the features and amenities one expects in a modern express boat. Like all Monterey sportboats, she rides on a solid fiberglass deep-V hull with moderate beam and reverse chines to reduce spray. The 302's midcabin interior differs from most others in her class in one important respect: instead of being open to the salon with just a curtain for privacy, the 302's aft stateroom is fully enclosed with a solid bulkhead and cabin door. The salon may seem a little less open, but many will agree that the true privacy this layout affords is worth it. Topside, there's a doublewide companion seat (with a reversible backrest) at the helm, a wet bar, a removable transom bench seat and an extended swim platform (optional). The side decks are narrow so the foredeck is best is accessed from the walk-through windshield. Additional features include a reverse arch, transom storage locker, tilt steering, foredeck sun pad and a removable cockpit table. A good performer, twin 280hp MerCruiser sterndrives will deliver a cruising speed of 25 knots and a top speed of just under 40 knots.

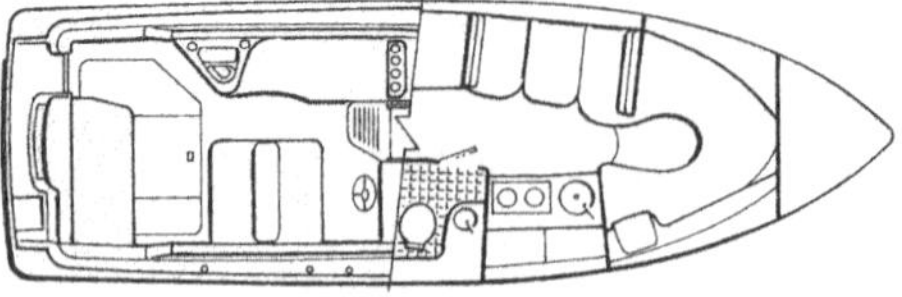

See Page 690 For Price Data

Length w/Platform	32'1"	Fuel	160 gals.
Hull Length	30'5"	Water	45 gals.
Beam	10'6"	Waste	28 gals.
Draft, Down	3'1"	Hull Type	Modified-V
Weight	10,700#	Deadrise Aft	19°

Monterey 322 Cruiser

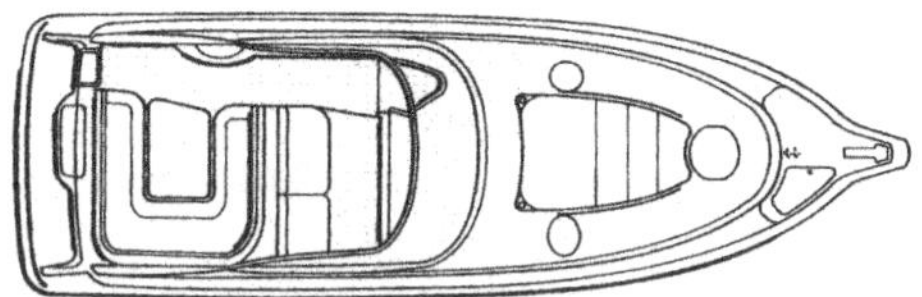

Like her smaller sisterships in the Monterey fleet, the 322 Cruiser is a well-executed blend of crisp styling, solid construction, and comfortable cabin accommodations. She's a good-looking boat with her reverse arch and wraparound windshield, and she lacks the bloated, tall-freeboard appearance seen in many other express cruisers her size. Built on a deep-V hull with moderate beam, the midcabin floorplan of the Monterey is an attractive mix of Corian counters, a curved earth-tone sofa, and premium fixtures. The midcabin is particularly spacious, and privacy curtains separate both sleeping areas from the salon. Three overhead hatches and five opening ports provide adequate cabin ventilation. In the cockpit, visibility from the elevated helm is excellent. There's seating for six at the U-shaped lounge behind the helm, and a wet bar was standard. Note that a walk-through windshield provides access to the bow. Additional features include a foredeck sun pad, a molded pulpit, anchor locker, fender racks at the transom, and a foldaway transom seat. MerCruiser 320hp gas sterndrives cruise the Monterey 322 in the mid 20s and reach a top speed of about 40 knots.

See Page 690 For Price Data

Length w/Platform	36'3"	Fuel	210 gals.
Hull Length	32'8"	Water	44 gals.
Beam	10'10"	Waste	30 gals.
Draft, Down	3'4"	Hull Type	Modified-V
Weight	12,000#	Deadrise Aft	18°

Monterey 330/340 Sport Yacht

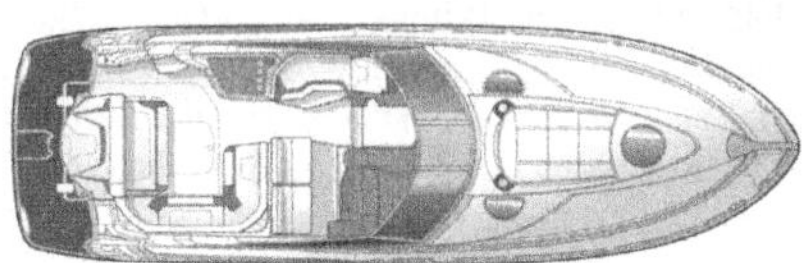

With her stylish lines and user-friendly layout, the Monterey 330 Sport Yacht (called the 340 Sport Yacht since 2010) is a top-shelf family cruiser with the right mix of comfort and performance. Thirty-something express boats have grown in popularity in recent years, and the 330 Sport Yacht was the largest boat in the Monterey fleet when she was introduced in 2007. Her open cockpit design comprises an aft lounge for three that has three different positions: a forward-facing seat, an aft-facing seat, and a two-person sun pad. A portside lounger is opposite the helm, and the deluxe wet bar includes a sink and refrigerator. While there are molded steps leading up the side decks, the best access to the foredeck is through the opening windshield. The sporty dash layout is a real attention-getter. Below decks, the 330's spacious interior is tastefully appointed with cherry mica joinery, premium galley appliances, Ultraleather seating, and a long-lasting synthetic wood floor. A flat-screen TV is standard, and fit and finish throughout the cabin is excellent. A hatch in the cockpit floor lifts on hydraulic rams for access to the motors. Cruise at 25 knots with twin 320hp Volvo sterndrive engines (high 30s top).

See Page 690 For Price Data

Length	35'3"	Fuel	210 gals.
Beam	11'3"	Water	42 gals.
Draft, Up	2'1"	Waste	28 gals.
Draft, Down	3'4"	Hull Type	Modified-V
Weight	14,200#	Deadrise Aft	17°

Monterey 350/360 Sport Yacht

2005–Current

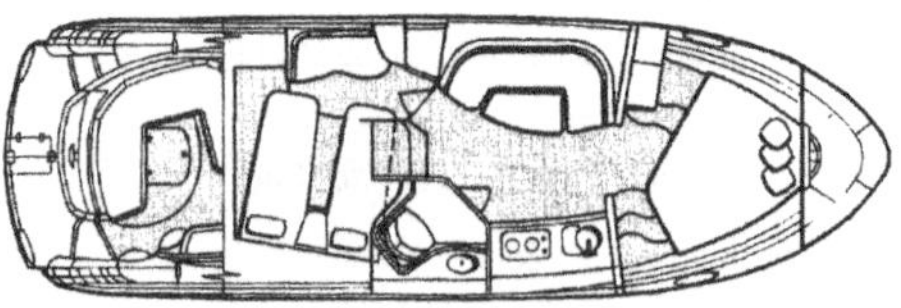

Introduced in 2005, the 350 Sport Yacht (called the 360 SY after 2009) combines bold styling and very aggressive performance in a luxurious, reasonably priced package. Many express cruisers in this size range are designed with inboard power, but for flat-out speed it's difficult to match the performance of the Monterey's sterndrive power. Stepping aboard, one of the most striking features of the 350 SY is the massive eurostyle helm with its matte gray finish and Faria gauges. A U-shaped lounge in the aft cockpit offers seating for six and converts to a sun pad with the insertion of a filler, and the standard wet bar comes with a sink and 48-quart cooler. Belowdecks, the layout differs from many other cruisers in her class in that the midcabin is a true stateroom with standing headroom and a solid cherrywood door rather than just a privacy curtain. The salon is carpeted except for the area in front of the galley, which is finished with cherry-and-holly flooring. Engine access is through an electric hatch in the cockpit sole. On the downside, the single helm seat precludes the mate from joining the skipper. A fast ride with optional 420hp Volvo sterndrives, the 350 SY will reach a top speed in excess of 40 knots.

See Page 690 For Price Data

Length Overall	37'0"	Fuel	230 gals.
Beam	11'6"	Water	48 gals.
Draft, Up	2'4"	Waste	38 gals.
Draft, Down	3'6"	Hull Type	Modified-V
Weight	16,500#	Deadrise Aft	17°

Monterey 400 Sport Yacht

2008–Current

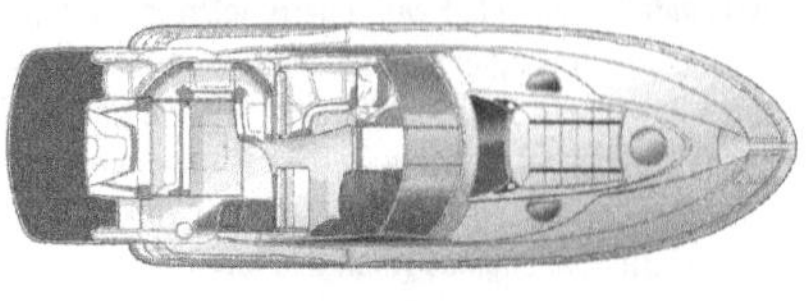

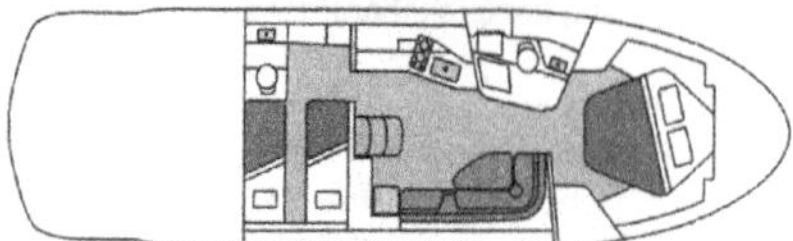

Flagship of the Monterey fleet, the 400 Sport Yacht was designed from the ground up for Volvo's IPS pod-drive propulsion system. Pod drives were the future when the 400 Sport Yacht was being developed; their performance and handling advantages over conventional inboard power have been game-changers for the industry. The Monterey's two-stateroom, two-head interior is notable—many express boats this size have a single head. With her luxurious cherry wood trim, synthetic wood flooring, posh Ultraleather seating, and designer furnishings, the accommodations aboard the 400 Sport Yacht are the equal of the best European imports. The single berths in the aft midcabin easily convert to a double with a filler, and a home theater system with flat-screen TV is standard in the salon. In the cockpit, a unique foldout table deploys from the aft portside lounge providing an alternative to the belowdecks dinette on warm summer evenings. A hardtop, cockpit wet bar, and windlass are standard,. Engine access is as good as it gets in a boat of this type. Joystick controls permits precise low-speed control. Cruise efficiently at 26–28 knots (35 top) with 370hp Volvo IPS diesels.

Not Enough Resale Data to Set Values

Length w/Platform	41'0"	Fuel	330 gals.
Beam	12'6"	Water	75 gals.
Draft	3'9"	Waste	40 gals.
Weight	22,000#	Hull Type	Modified-V
Clearance	10'7"	Deadrise Aft	17°

Navigator

Quick View

- Jule Marshall, who founded Navigator Yachts in 1988, was well known during the 1970s and 1980s as the owner (and founder) of Californian Yachts.
- Marshall sold Californian in the mid-1980s, and by 1988 he was back in the yacht-building business with Navigator Yachts.
- Starting with a single 33-foot model, Navigator grew rapidly in the following years to become one of the largest builders of production pilothouse motor yachts in the U.S.
- According to the company website, Navigator has produced over 1,000 pilothouse yachts since 1988.
- Navigator was sold at the end of 2012 to a private equity group.
- A Navigator owner's group can be found at www.navyachtowners.net.

Navigator Yachts • Perris, CA • www.navigatorachts.com

Navigator 44 Classic

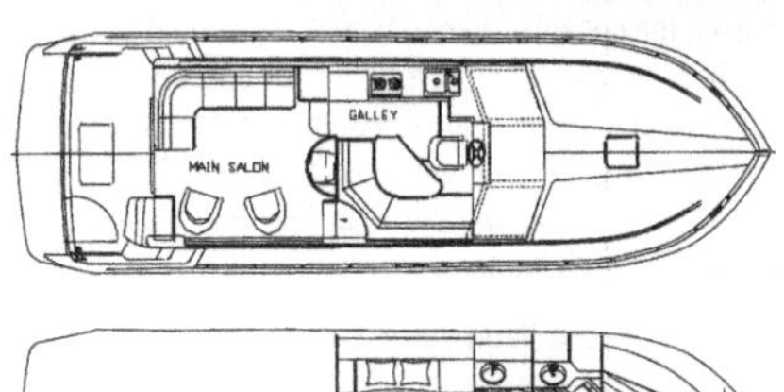

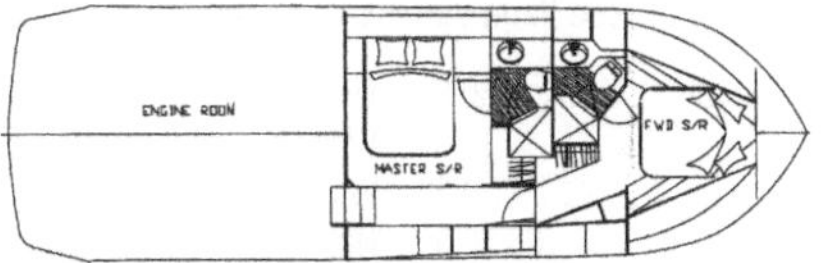

Introduced in 2002, the Navigator 44 Classic is a blend of traditional pilothouse design, rugged construction, and practical cabin accommodations. Navigator developed a reputation since its founding in the late 1980s for delivering a lot of boat for the money, and the 44 Classic is easily one of the more affordable boats of her type available in today's used market. Built on a solid fiberglass hull, her two-stateroom interior is arranged with the galley and dinette on the pilothouse level, two steps up from the salon. A lower helm is standard, a huge L-shaped sofa and centerline entertainment center dominate the salon. A corridor to starboard in the salon leads to the staterooms, both of which have double berths and private en suite heads. The interior is fully carpeted and highlighted with lacquered cherry joinery, vinyl overheads, and Corian counters. The side decks on the 44 Classic are nearly a foot wide so movement around the boat is easy and safe. Unlike most pilothouse designs, however, there is no deck access door at the lower helm. A modest performer with Volvo 318hp diesels, she'll cruise at 18 knots and reach a top speed in the low 20s.

See Page 690 For Price Data

Length	44'0"	Headroom	6'5"
Beam	15'0"	Fuel	500 gals.
Draft	4'5"	Water	130 gals.
Weight	34,500#	Waste	70 gals.
Clearance	19'3"	Hull Type	Modified-V

Navigator 48 Classic

1997–2007

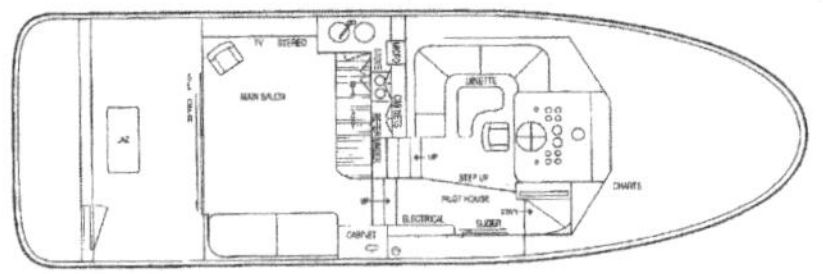

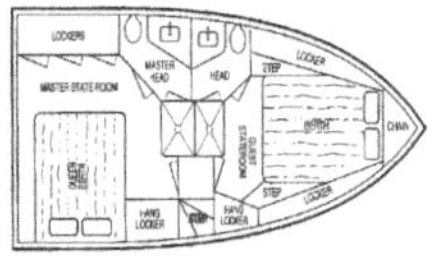

The Navigator 48 Classic is a stretched version of the original Navigator 46 Classic (1995–97) with the extra length used to create a larger cockpit. A very competitively yacht, the 48 was a good-selling yacht following her introduction in 1997 thanks to her comfortable interior and an efficient, smooth-riding hull. The great appeal of a pilothouse yacht, of course, is the ability to operate in poor weather from the confines of a well-positioned lower helm. In that regard, visibility from the Classic's raised pilothouse—with its wraparound dinette, centerline helm, direct flybridge access, and starboard deck door—is excellent in all directions. Buyers can choose from the standard two-stateroom or alternate three-stateroom layout, and the entire interior of the 48 Classic is finished with attractive cherry woodwork. In the cockpit, a hatch provides direct access to the large engineroom, and the flybridge is designed to accommodate a dinghy and davit. Wide side decks make it easy to get around on deck, and a radar arch and transom door were standard. Among several diesel engine options, standard 318hp Volvos cruise the 48 Classic at 17–18 knots and reach a top speed of around 22 knots.

See Page 690 For Price Data

Length Overall	52'8"	Fuel	500 gals.
Beam	15'0"	Water	130 gals.
Draft	4'5"	Waste	70 gals.
Weight	37,000#	Hull Type	Modified-V
Clearance	NA	Deadrise Aft	15°

Navigator 50 Classic

1993–2000

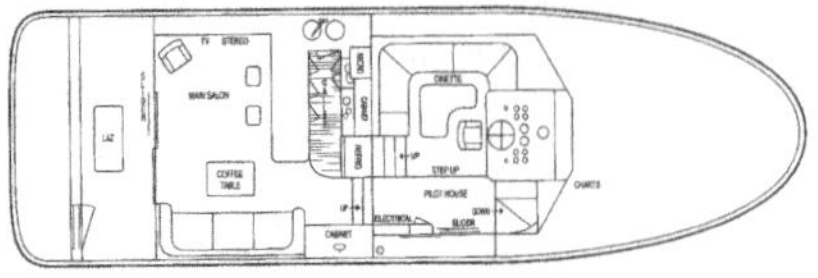

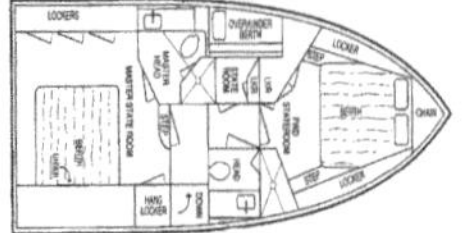

One of Navigator's more popular models, the 50 Classic is basically an enlarged version of the Navigator 46 Classic with more spacious master stateroom and salon dimensions, but with the same-size cockpit. She's built on a solid fiberglass modified-V hull with moderate beam, a well-flared bow and an integral swim platform. Her two-stateroom floorplan is arranged with a full-beam master stateroom aft and a roomy guest cabin forward. Both staterooms have double berths and both heads are fitted with separate stall showers. As it is with most traditional raised pilothouse designs, the galley is located forward in the salon. Visibility from the pilothouse, with its full dinette, centerline helm, flybridge stairs and sliding deck door, is excellent. The engineroom is reached via a hatch (and ladder) in the cockpit sole. Note that there's no flybridge access from the cockpit—very unusual. Additional features include reasonably wide side decks, a roomy flybridge with a cockpit overhang for storing a tender, transom door, radar arch, and a bow pulpit. A good performer with relatively modest 340hp Volvo diesels, the Navigator 50 Classic will cruise at 18–19 knots and reach a top speed of just over 20 knots.

See Page 690 For Price Data

Length Overall	50'0"	Fuel	600 gals.
Beam	15'0"	Water	170 gals.
Draft	4'3"	Waste	70 gals.
Weight	38,000#	Hull Type	Modified-V
Headroom	6'6"	Deadrise Aft	15°

Navigator 53 Classic

1995–2006

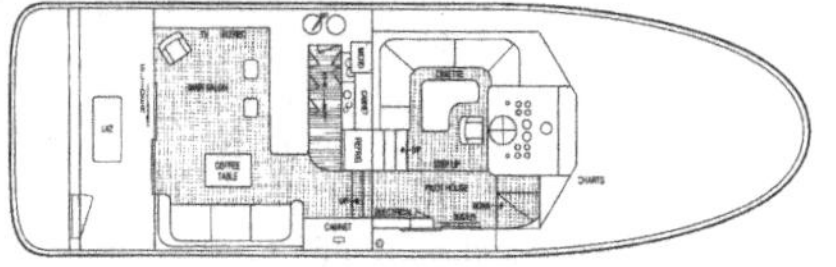

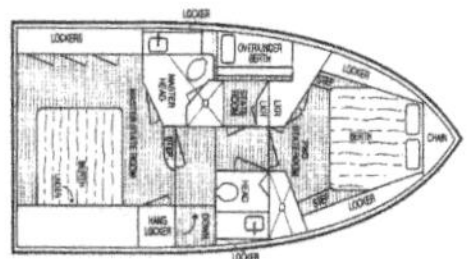

Navigator had a winning design with the 53 Classic, a handsome pilothouse cruising yacht introduced in 1995 with the right mix of features and price. Indeed, the 53 remains a good value today compared with other yachts her size and while the fit, finish and overall quality aren't in the Hatteras or Viking league, the Navigator nonetheless delivers a lot of boat for the money. Built on an easy-riding modified-V hull with a slender 15-foot beam, the three-stateroom interior of the 53 Classic is arranged with the galley forward in the salon and a U-shaped dinette in the pilothouse. The full-beam salon is spacious and very comfortable, and both heads contain separate stall showers. The cockpit is huge with just over 100 square feet of usable space, but the fact that you can't access the flybridge from the cockpit is notable. Topside, wraparound lounge seating aft of the helm will seat a small crowd. Additional features include an integral swim platform, pilothouse deck access door, a spacious engineroom and excellent helm visibility. Twin 370hp Volvo diesels cruise the Navigator 53 Classic at 15–16 knots and deliver a top speed of around 20 knots.

See Page 690 For Price Data

Length Overall	53'0"	Fuel	600 gals.
Beam	15'0"	Water	170 gals.
Draft	4'6"	Waste	70 gals.
Weight	42,500#	Hull Type	Modified-V
Headroom	6'6"	Deadrise Aft	15°

Navigator 56 Classic

2000–05

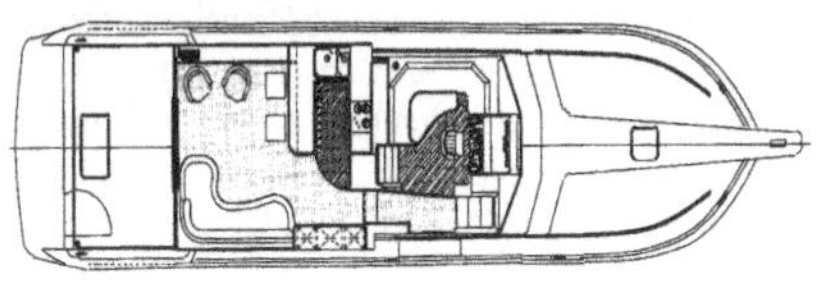

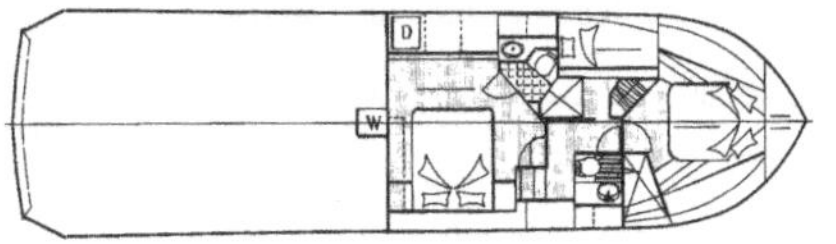

Navigator prospered in recent years by delivering capable—if basic—yachts at prices well below many competitive yachts. The 56 Classic follows in that tradition, a conservative pilothouse design with graceful lines and a practical three-stateroom layout. A slightly stretched version of the 53 Classic, she's built on a modified-V hull with a solid fiberglass bottom and an integrated swim platform. Her 15-foot beam is narrow compared with other boats her size, but it's an easily driven hull capable of good economy at normal cruising speeds. The Navigator's three-stateroom floorplan is arranged with the galley forward in the salon and the dinette on the pilothouse level. Both heads have a separate stall shower, and Corian counters are standard in the galley and heads. Maple and cherry woodwork are used throughout the interior—not the best joinery, but certainly adequate. The engineroom, reached via a hatch in the galley sole, provides easy access to the motors. Note that because of the full-width salon, there are no side decks. A pilothouse deck door, bow pulpit, transom door, and radar arch were standard. Volvo 430hp diesels cruise at 17 knots (20–21 top).

See Page 690 For Price Data

Length Overall	56'0"	Fuel	600 gals.
Beam	15'0"	Water	170 gals.
Draft	4'6"	Waste	40 gals.
Weight	45,500	Hull Type	Modified-V
Clearance	NA	Deadrise Aft	15°

Navigator 5600 Pilothouse

1994–99

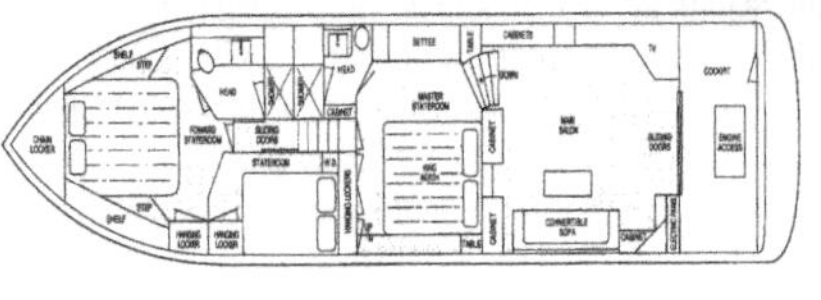

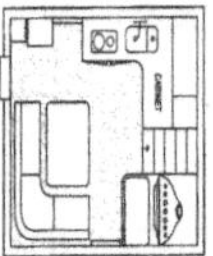

An enlarged version of the popular Navigator 5300 Pilothouse, the additional length of the 5600 Pilothouse is most visible in a larger salon and an improved exterior profile. Her roomy three-stateroom interior will appeal to many couples that plan to operate the boat by themselves. The floorplan differs from most other raised pilothouse designs in that the galley is located in the pilothouse instead of the salon. This, together with the fact that there are no side decks, results in a surprisingly spacious salon in spite of her relatively narrow beam. For privacy, the master stateroom is accessed directly from the salon (rather than from the forward companionway), and because there is no pilothouse bulkhead the helmsman has a good view aft. A dinette is opposite the galley in the wheelhouse, and a nearby ladder leads up to the bi-level flybridge with its wraparound guest seating and dinghy storage. Additional features include two pilothouse deck doors, a well-arranged engineroom (accessed from a cockpit hatch), transom door, a shaded cockpit and large cabin windows. No flybridge access from the cockpit. Volvo 380hp diesels cruise at 17–18 knots (about 20 top). Replaced in 2000 with new Navigator 56-foot model.

See Page 690 For Price Data

Length Overall	56'0"	Fuel	600 gals.
Beam	15'0"	Water	200 gals.
Draft	5'6"	Waste	70 gals.
Weight	50,000#	Hull Type	Modified-V
Clearance	NA	Deadrise Aft	15°

Navigator 5800 Pilothouse

1999–2001

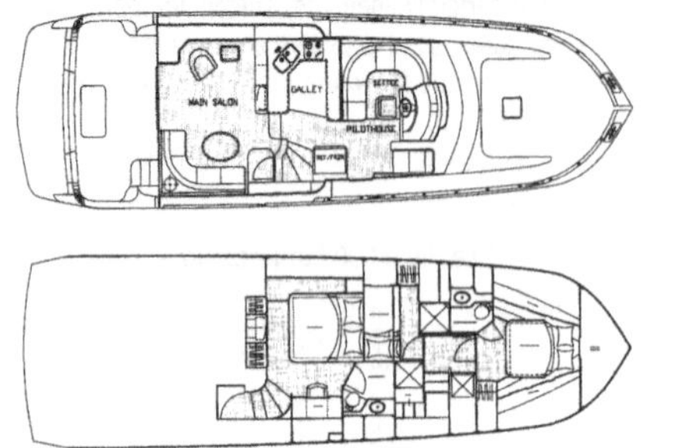

The Navigator 58 is a spacious, moderately priced pilothouse cruiser with softer lines than earlier Navigator designs and an innovative three-stateroom layout. Like all Navigator yachts, the 58 rides on a solid fiberglass modified-V hull, and her wide 17-foot, 4-inch beam creates a very expansive and open interior. The Navigator's floorplan is arranged with the galley on the pilothouse level rather than in the salon as it is in many pilothouse layouts. This gives the impression of a small salon compared with other yachts her size, but many will favor this arrangement since it effectively separates the galley from the primary entertainment/lounge area. Note that the master stateroom is separate from the guest cabins and has a private access stairway from the salon. Visibility from the pilothouse, with its wraparound dinette and single deck access door, is good in nearly all directions. Additional features include inside and outside flybridge access, a spacious engineroom, washer/dryer, a large swim platform, foredeck seating and maple interior woodwork. A pair of 485hp GM 6-71 diesels cruise the Navigator 58 MY at a respectable 18 knots and reach a top speed of 20+ knots.

See Page 690 For Price Data

Length Overall	58'0"	Fuel	800 gals.
Beam	17'4"	Water	200 gals.
Draft	4'9"	Waste	70 gals.
Weight	64,000#	Hull Type	Modified-V
Headroom	6'6"	Deadrise Aft	NA

Navigator 6100 Pilothouse

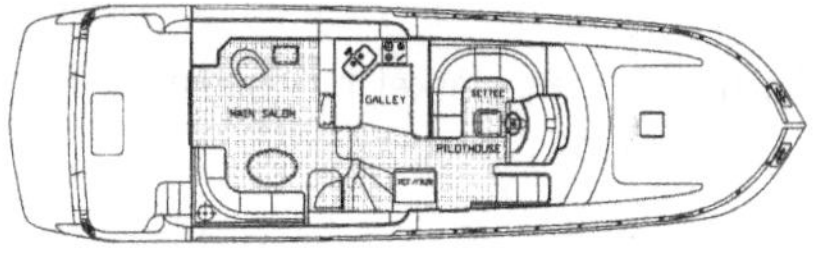

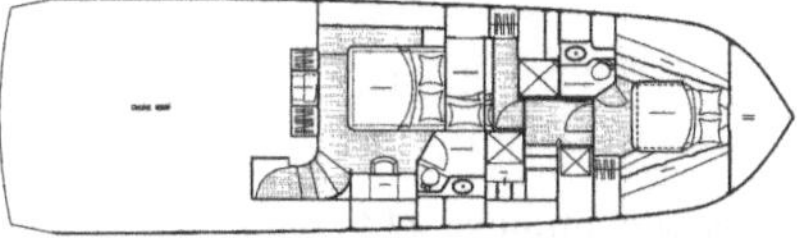

Largest yacht in the Navigator fleet, the 6100 Pilothouse offers a compelling blend of traditional pilothouse styling and a versatile layout. This is not a flashy, high-performance yacht with a pretentious personality. Instead, the Navigator 6100 is a traditional pilothouse cruising yacht whose competitive price reflects the manufacturer's conservative approach to boatbuilding. Constructed on a solid fiberglass modified-V hull with an integrated swim platform, the Navigator's spacious three-stateroom layout is arranged with the galley and dinette on the pilothouse level, two steps up from the full-beam salon. The owner's stateroom is private in the 6100, reached via a salon stairwell and fitted with a king-size bed and vanity. As it is with most pilothouse designs, visibility from the lower helm is very good. On deck, a hatch in the cockpit sole provides access to the standup engineroom, and the flybridge can be reached from both the cockpit and pilothouse. Additional features include high-gloss cherry interior joinery, port and starboard transom doors, and Corian counters in the galley and heads. The Navigator 6100 will cruise at 18 knots with 675hp Volvo diesels and reach a top speed in the low 20s.

See Page 690 For Price Data

Length Overall	61'6"	Fuel	800 gals.
Beam	17'4"	Water	200 gals.
Draft	4'9"	Waste	70 gals.
Weight	66,000#	Hull Type	Modified-V
Headroom	6'5"	Deadrise Aft	15°

Neptunus

Quick View

- Neptunus was founded in 1970 by a Dutch yachting enthusiast who, unable to find the type of boat he wanted, decided to build his own boat—a 37-foot twin-keel cruiser called the Neptunus 107.
- The success of the Neptunus 107 (over 300 were sold) led to the development of larger boats, and by the early 1980s Neptunus had expanded into the greater European market.
- In 1989, Neptunus make the move into the North American market by building a production facility in Ontario, Canada. (Note that all Neptunus models sold in th U.S. are built at the Canadian yard.)

Neptunus Yachts • Ontario, Canada • www.neptunusyachts.com

Neptunus 51/55 Sedan

1993–98

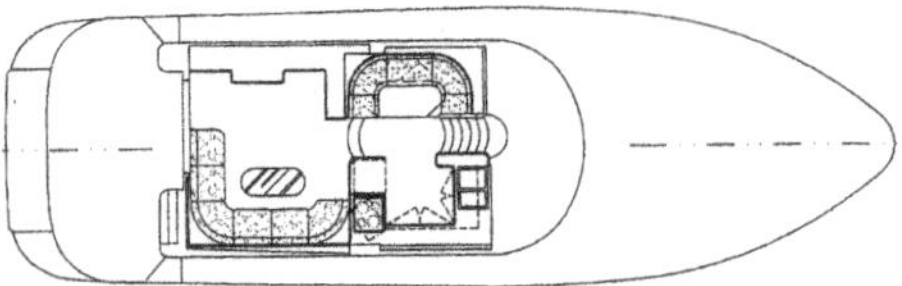

Since 1989, Neptunus—a Holland-based manufacturer—has been building yachts for the North American market at a facility in Ontario, Canada. Among several models, the Neptunus 55 Sedan (called the Neptunus 51 from 1993–96) proved quite popular with North American buyers during the late 1990s. Her angular lines are typical of many European motor yachts of her era; a rakish design with a sweptback profile, an extended flybridge, and a split-level salon with the galley and dinette forward. Essentially a semi-custom yacht, several interior arrangements were offered in the 51/55 although a three-stateroom, two-head layout is typical. A lower helm was optional, and the interior is finished in attractive light ash woodwork. The cockpit is completely shaded by the extended flybridge, and wide walkways make it easy to get around the deck. Topside, the flybridge is arranged with the centerline helm forward with a wet bar and lounge seating aft. The transom platform can accommodate an 11-foot tender. Twin 550-hp 6V92 Detroits cruise the Neptunus 51/55 in the low 20s (about 25 top), and 735-hp 8V92s cruise in the mid 20s and top out at close to 30 knots.

Not Enough Resale Data to Set Values

Length Overall	55'0"	Fuel	750 gals.
Hull Length	52'0"	Water	160 gals.
Beam	15'7"	Waste	70 gals.
Draft	4'8"	Hull Type	Modified-V
Weight	50,600#	Deadrise Aft	13°

Neptunus 56 Flybridge

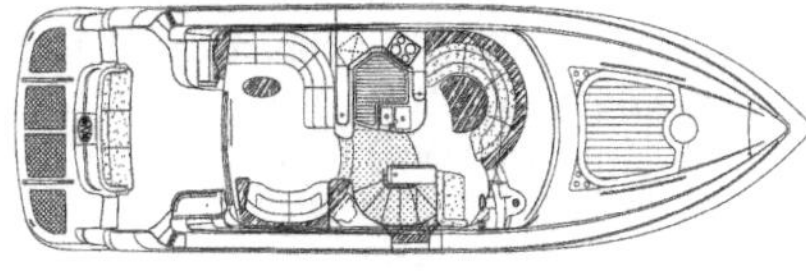

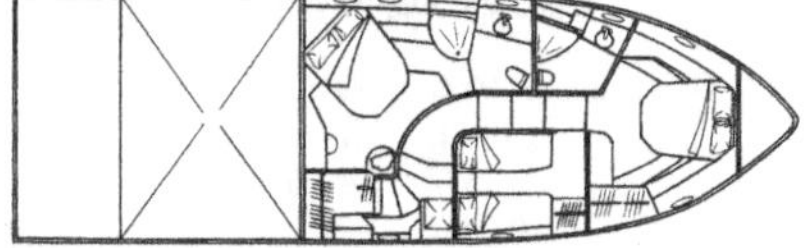

The first thing one notices about the Canadian-built Neptunus 56 is the unusual styling; this is definitely not your typical motor yacht design. Pictured here with the optional hardtop, it's difficult to escape the opinion that the 56 is a bit overstyled. She's built on a deep-V hull with moderate beam, prop pockets, and a solid fiberglass bottom. The floorplan differs from most European designs in that the staterooms on the lower level are accessed from a staircase across from the galley rather than a passageway further forward, adjacent to the lower helm. This allows for a huge dinette opposite the helm, much larger than the dinettes found in other pilothouse motor yachts this size that are often quite small. With the U-shaped galley open to the salon and dinette, the Neptunus has a very social main deck layout, richly accented with high-gloss cherry joinery and furnished with many luxury amenities. The cockpit—mostly shaded by a bridge overhang—is very spacious with a transom lounge and engineroom access hatch. The side decks, however, are narrow. A bow thruster and washer/dryer were standard. A good performer, 800hp Cats cruise the Neptunus in the mid 20s and reach a top speed of 27–28 knots.

Not Enough Resale Data to Set Values

Length	57'0"	Fuel	820 gals.
Beam	16'2"	Water	180 gals.
Draft	4'4"	Waste	110 gals.
Weight	52,000#	Hull Type	Deep-V
Clearance	16'7"	Deadrise Aft	19°

Neptunus 58/60 Sedan

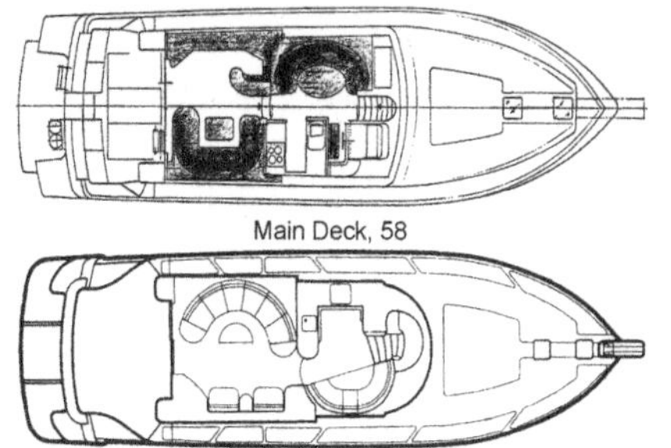
Main Deck, 58

Main Deck, 60

The Neptunus 60 Sedan (called the 58 Sedan from 1992–96) is a Canadian-built Euro cruiser whose attractive styling and upscale accommodations made her a popular model for Neptunus during her production years. Built primarily for the U.S. market on a semi-custom basis, the 60 Sedan rides on a solid fiberglass modified-V hull with an integral swim platform and relatively high freeboard. Neptunus completely redesigned the interior of this yacht in 1997 by eliminating the lower helm and enlarging both the salon and galley. The revised floorplan has three staterooms with the master suite forward, two full heads, and a spacious VIP cabin with a double berth. A large semicircular sofa dominates the salon, and the cockpit—shaded by a bridge overhang—has built-in bench seating and direct access to the well-arranged engine room. Additional features include an extended swim platform, a spacious flybridge with a centerline helm and lounge seating aft, wide side decks, and (beginning in 1997) cherry interior woodwork. A strong performer, 735-hp Detroit diesels cruise the Neptunus 60 Sedan in the low 20s and reach a top speed of 26–27 knots.

Not Enough Resale Data to Set Values

Length	60'0"	Water	200 gals.
Beam	16'8"	Waste	110 gals.
Draft	4'5"	Headroom	6'5"
Weight	57,200#	Hull Type	Modified-V
Fuel	950 gals.	Deadrise Aft	14°

Neptunus 65 Motor Yacht

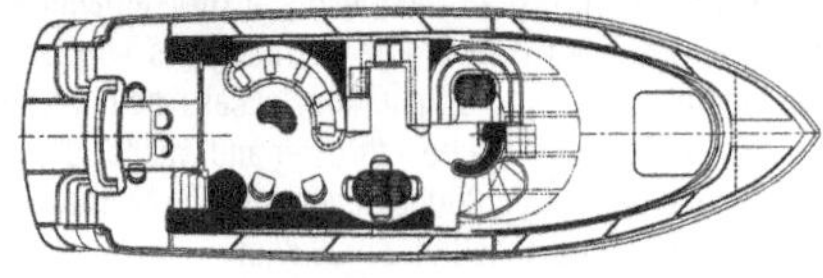

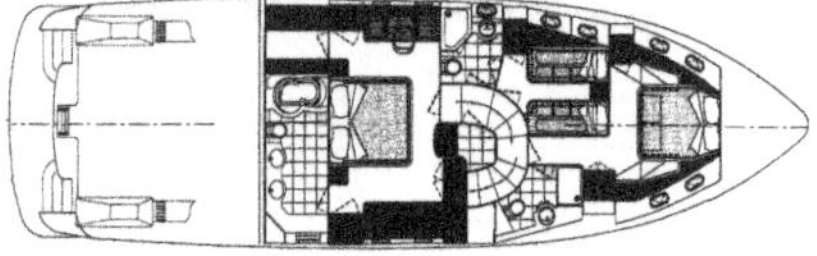

The Neptunus 65 is a semicustom mini-megayacht with the imposing profile of a larger, tri-deck motor yacht. (Note that the superstructure was completely revised during the 2000 model year.) She's heavily built on a solid fiberglass hull with prop pockets to reduce draft, and a near 19-foot beam provides the Neptunus 65 with one of the roomiest interiors in her class. Her three stateroom floorplan is arranged with the galley forward in the salon. A lower helm is optional; in its place, a U-shaped dining settee with panoramic views is forward of the galley. On the lower level, the amidships master stateroom is huge (note that the ensuite head compartment is aft of the stateroom bulkhead). The extended flybridge of the Neptunus 65 provides space for tender storage and an open-air settee abaft the pilothouse. Additional features include engine room access from the swim platform, jet-ski storage (under the starboard transom stairs), a huge lazarette, and wide walkaround side decks. Standard 1,100-hp 12V92 Detroit diesels cruise the Neptunus 65 MY at 20 knots (low 20s top).

Not Enough Resale Data to Set Values

Length Overall	65'4"	Water	300 gals.
Beam	18'11"	Waste	200 gals.
Draft	5'0"	Headroom	6'5"
Weight	88,000#	Hull Type	Modified-V
Fuel	1,400 gals.	Deadrise Aft	NA

Nordhavn

Quick View

- Nordhavn is owned by Pacific Asian Enterprises (PAE), a company formed in 1976 to import and market the Transpac 49, CT yachts, and Mason sailing yachts from Taiwan.
- In 1989 the company introduced their first trawler design, the Nordhavn 46.
- Just as a backlog of orders was beginning to develop, in 1991 the industry was hit with the 10% luxury tax. PAE did not sell a single new boat to an American during this period.
- Building on their reputation for quality construction, the company introduced the Nordhavn 62 in 1995, and in 1997 the Nordhavn 50 was was unveiled—both to excellent reviews.
- Recent years have seen the Nordhavn brand evolve as one of the premier producers of quality diplacement trawlers, many with ocean-crossing capability.
- Resale values on used Nordhavn models have been consistently strong in all boating markets.
- A Nordhavn owner's group can be found at http://groups.yahoo.com/group/NordhavnOwners.

Nordhavn • Dana Point, CA • www.nordhavn.com

Nordhavn 35 Coastal Pilot

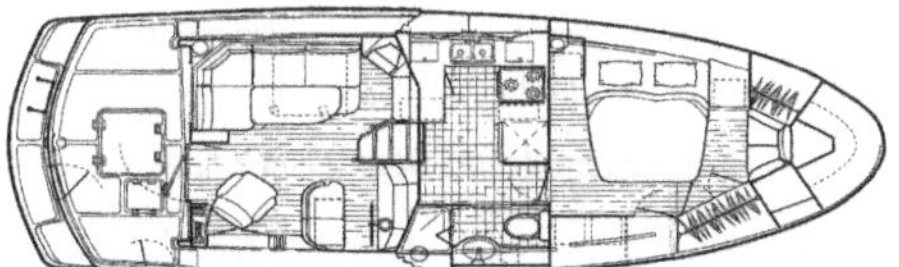

With her sturdy, ship-like appearance, the Nordhavn 35 will appeal to experienced cruisers who appreciate the virtues of functional design and uncompromising construction. She's built on a semi-displacement hull with rounded bilges, a deep forefoot, and a full-length keel with an attached rudder. The accommodations of the 35 are designed for the cruising couple. The single stateroom is very spacious, and the galley-down configuration allows for an open and comfortable salon. Everything about this boat seems overbuilt, and the engineroom—reached from a door in the galley—is designed for easy access to all important service points. The Nordhavn 35 also excels in storage space throughout the interior and outside in the huge cockpit lazarette. Helm visibility from the elevated wheelhouse is excellent. Additional features include a mast and boom assembly, a bow thruster, wide side decks, and commercial-grade doors and windows. Early models with a single 350hp Yanmar diesel will cruise at 7–8 knots. Note that beginning with hull #9, hull and drive train modifications boosted the cruising speed to 11–12 knots when powered by a single 370hp Yanmar.

See Page 690 For Price Data

Length Overall	35'4"	Clearance	NA
Length WL	33'4"	Fuel	590 gals.
Beam	13'2"	Water	165 gals.
Draft	3'6"	Waste	40 gals.
Weight	25,000#	Hull Type	Semi-Disp.

Nordhavn 40

1999–Current

The Nordhavn 40 is a ballasted, full-displacement cruiser, heavily built and capable of extended bluewater passages. This is a yacht for the serious cruising enthusiast, a beamy, rugged-looking vessel with high freeboard and a well-conceived layout. Unlike other models in the Nordhavn fleet, the 40 is built in California (by Pacific Seacraft) rather than in Taiwan. Her spacious two-stateroom interior has the galley forward in the roomy full-beam salon, and the amidships raised pilothouse is fitted with a fold-down helm seat, watch berth and port and starboard deck doors. The engineroom, which is located beneath the salon sole, is easily accessed from a door in the guest cabin. Notable features of the Nordhavn 40 include a beautiful teak interior, commercial-quality hardware and systems, a Portuguese bridge with a walk-through to the foredeck, and a functional mast and boom. On the downside, the cockpit is small and the narrow side decks around the salon are for cleaning duties only. Note that a dry stack exhaust and keel cooling system are standard. A single 140hp Lugger diesel provides a cruising speed of 7 knots with a cruising range of around 2,500 miles.

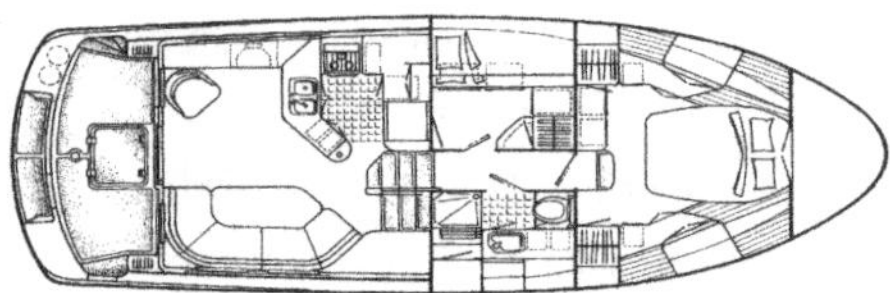

See Page 690 For Price Data

Length Overall	39'9"	Ballast	2,500#
Length WL	35'5"	Fuel	920 gals.
Beam	14'6"	Water	250 gals.
Draft	4'9"	Waste	70 gals.
Weight	50,000#	Hull Type	Displacement

Nordhavn 43

2004–Current

The Nordhavn 43 is a beefy, go-anywhere trawler whose robust construction and practical layout will appeal to serious ocean-going cruisers. The 43 incorporates the same modified full-displacement hull of her siblings in the Nordhavn fleet, a design that delivers excellent seakeeping qualities and features full stern sections and a deep keel. Belowdecks, the two-stateroom interior has several clever design touches that add to the boat's comfort at sea. Note that the salon is slightly offset to port, so the only walkway from the cockpit forward is on the starboard side of the house. Two large settees are found in the salon, and a single private berth is aft in the raised pilothouse where port and starboard watertight Dutch doors provide access to the Portuguese bridge. On the lower level, the full-beam master stateroom is located amidships, and the guest stateroom is located as far aft as possible for maximum comfort while underway. The Nordhavn's meticulous engineroom provides excellent service access to the engine and pumps. Note the drystack exhaust system and optional 27hp "get-home" diesel with folding prop. A single 165hp Lugger diesel offers a cruising range of 2,500–3,000 miles at 7 knots.

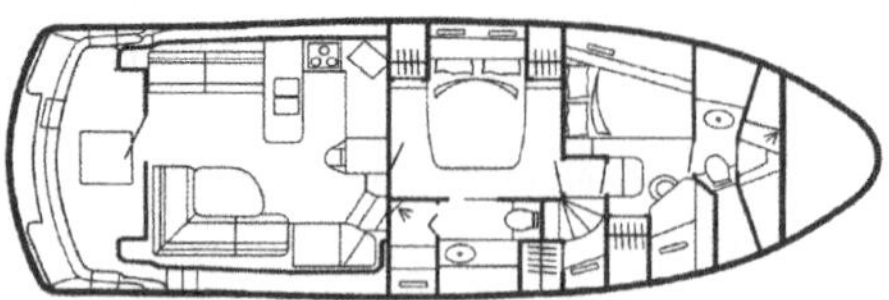

Not Enough Resale Data to Set Values

Length Overall	43'0"	Clearance, Mast	30'4"
Length WL	38'4"	Fuel	1,200 gals.
Beam	14'10"	Water	300 gals.
Draft	4'11"	Waste	50 gals.
Weight	54,540#	Hull Type	Displacement

Nordhavn 46

1989–2005

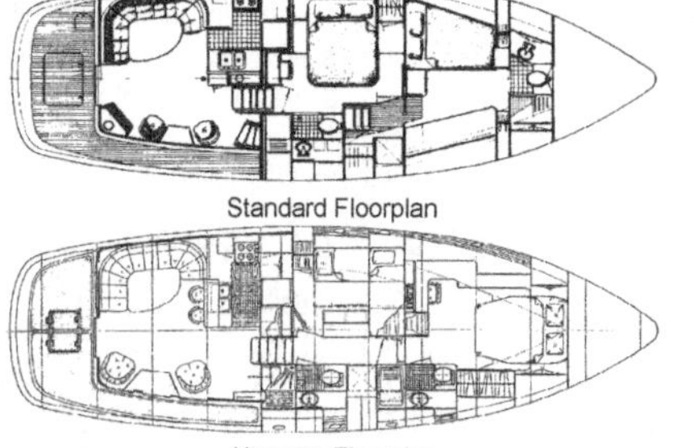

Standard Floorplan

Alternate Floorplan

An extremely popular yacht, the Nordhavn 46 is a classic pilothouse trawler with a ballasted, full-displacement hull and the sturdy profile of a North Sea workboat. Indeed, she's a distinctive boat with a Portuguese bridge (or breakwater) in front of the wheelhouse and forward-sloping windows in the wheelhouse itself. While the Nordhavn's two-stateroom interior may be somewhat confining compared with traditional 46-foot trawlers, it conforms well to the requirements of serious cruising in a displacement-type hull. Most of the accommodations are near the center of the boat where the motion is most comfortable. The owner's stateroom is below the pilothouse—way down, it seems. In the standard layout, the forward stateroom is reached separately from the pilothouse; however, an alternate floorplan has both staterooms accessed from the salon. Additional features include a dry exhaust system, substantial bulwarks all around, a single sidedeck (the salon extends to the portside rail), and large well-secured windows in the salon. Powered with a single 140hp Lugger diesel, the Nordhavn 46 will cruise at 8 knots at 3 gallons per hour for a range of 1,800–2,000 miles. Over 80 were built.

See Page 690 For Price Data

Length Overall	45'9"	Ballast	4,800#
Length WL	38'4"	Fuel	1,000 gals.
Beam	15'5"	Waree	280 gals.
Draft	5'0"	Waste	50 gals.
Weight	60,000#	Hull Type	Displacement

Nordhavn 47

2003–Current

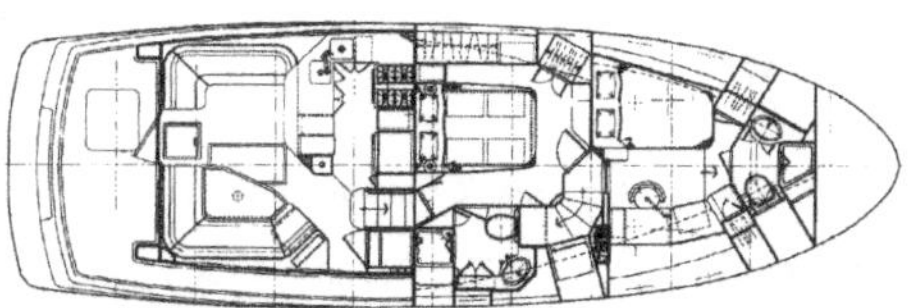

The Nordhavn 47 is a ballasted, full-displacement trawler designed to carry its owners in safety and comfort just about anywhere in the world. Like all Nordhavn yachts, the 47 is built to unusually high standards with commercial-grade doors and windows, a redundant electrical system, and solid fiberglass hull construction. The heart of the Nordhavn 47 is her ship-like pilothouse, five steps up from the salon, with its unsurpassed visibility, L-shaped dinette, watch berth, and handsome wraparound helm. The galley is forward in the well-appointed salon, and both staterooms have private en suite heads. The 47's standup engineroom, reached from the master stateroom, is about as good as it gets in a production yacht. A 40hp Yanmar auxiliary diesel is abaft of the main engine, and heat from the engine is released through a keel cooler. Topside, a dry stack expels exhaust 20 feet above the deck, and high bulwarks provide plenty of security on the side and aft deck. A beautifully crafted yacht in every respect, a single 173hp Lugger diesel will cruise the Nordhavn 47 at 8 knots. With nearly 1,500 gallons of fuel, the cruising range is said to approach 3,000 nautical miles.

See Page 690 For Price Data

Length Overall	51'0"	Ballast	6,000#
Length WL	43'4"	Fuel	1,450 gals.
Beam	16'1"	Water	400 gals.
Draft	5'6"	Waste	120 gals.
Weight	85,000#	Hull Type	Displacement

Nordhavn 50

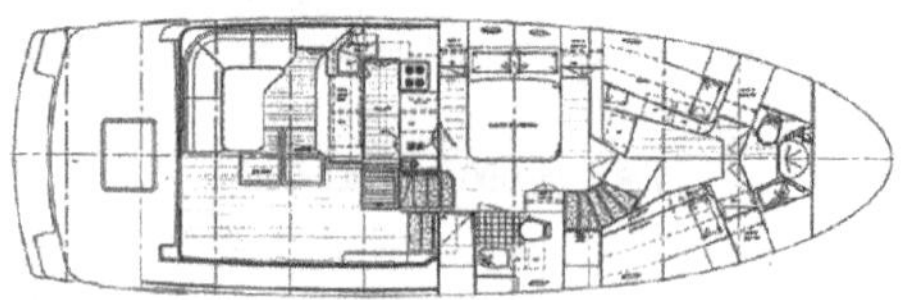

Built in Taiwan to high production standards, the Nordhavn 50 is a rugged bluewater passagemaker with genuine ocean-crossing capabilities. She's constructed on a full-displacement hull with a deep keel, a high-freeboard bow, and an innovative bulbous bow extension (beneath the waterline) that increases both fuel efficiency and hull speed. The house is set well forward to increase interior volume. The standard two-stateroom floorplan of the Nordhavn 50 is similar to many pilothouse boats with the master stateroom amidships (with direct engineroom access) and the galley forward in the salon. (Note that a three-stateroom floorplan is available.) A full-width nav station is in the pilothouse along with a dinette and deck access doors. Additional features include a small cockpit with transom door and a huge lazarette, a wraparound Portuguese bridge in front of the pilothouse, wide and well-secured side decks, standing headroom in the engineroom, and an integral swim platform. A quality boat in every respect (and priced accordingly), a single 300hp Lugger diesel will deliver an efficient cruising speed of 7–8 knots and a top speed of about 10 knots. Range at lower speeds is in the neighborhood of 3,000 miles.

See Page 690 For Price Data

Length Overall	51'2"	Ballast	6,600#
Length WL	44'2"	Fuel	1,320 gals.
Beam	16'0"	Water	260 gals.
Draft	5'2"	Waste	50 gals.
Weight	80,000#	Hull Type	Displacement

Nordhavn 55

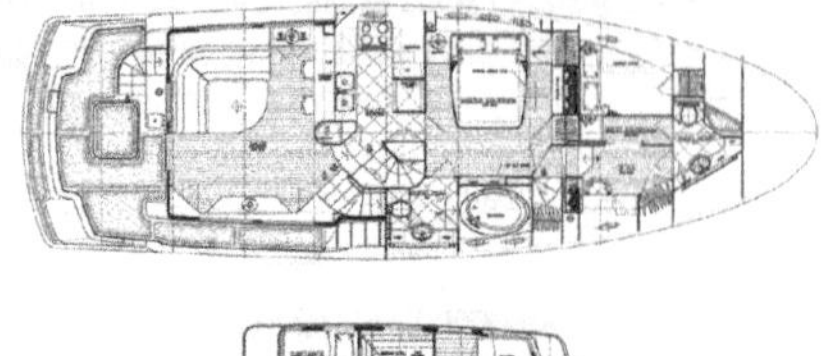

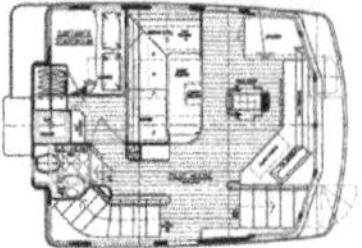

The stately Nordhavn 55, with her with towering profile and rugged construction, targets ocean cruisers obsessed with quality and security. Nordhavns are as good as it gets when it comes to full-displacement production trawlers, and the 55 sets the standard for design and engineering excellence. Her asymmetrical cabin allows for a wider main salon and galley, leaving the only side deck on the starboard side. With home-style appliances, abundant storage cabinets, and plenty of counter space, the galley will please the most demanding chef. The owner's stateroom is on the same level as the galley, located amidships, where the boat's motion is least objectionable during passages or while at anchor. Forward is a spacious guest cabin with a double berth, office area, and private head with stall shower. The 55's commercial-like pilothouse, with private stateroom and head, provides full 360-degree visibility. A flybridge is standard, providing the perfect place to operate the boat in good weather. With her high bow and generous freeboard, the Nordhavn punches through heavy seas with ease. Range is about 3,000 miles at 8 knots with a single 330hp John Deere diesel.

Not Enough Resale Data to Set Values

Length Overall	56'1"	Clearance, Mast	27'8"
Length WL	50'1"	Fuel	2,250 gals.
Beam	18'0"	Water	600 gals.
Draft	6'6"	Waste	120 gals.
Weight	115,000#	Hull Type	Displacement

Nordhavn 57

1999–2007

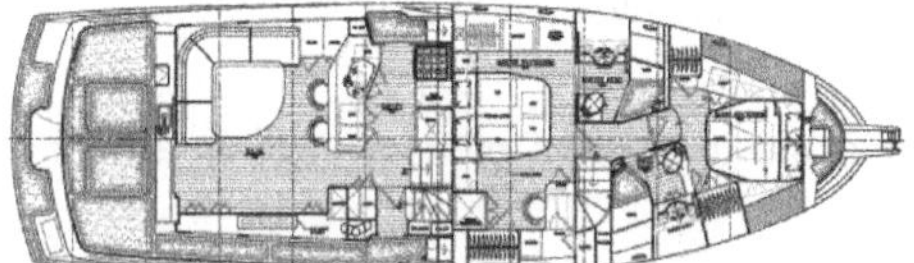

Conservatively styled, heavily built, and engineered for redundancy and confidence at sea, the Nordhavn 57 is unlike any other long-range yacht her size on the market. This is a serious passagemaker with a bulbous bow beneath the waterline (to increase hull speed), a full-displacement hull, and an unusually wide full-length keel that allows for a standing engineroom beneath the salon. Her three-stateroom, two-head layout is arranged with the galley in the salon and a full-beam master stateroom amidships, under the pilothouse. Note the superstructure is designed with a wide sidedeck to starboard and a narrower walkway to port. There's a deck access door in the galley and two additional deck doors in the pilothouse, five steps up from the salon. On deck, high protective bulwarks and a Portuguese bridge around the wheelhouse provide plenty of deck security. The ship-like engineroom is accessible from the cockpit lazarette, an exterior door on the starboard walkway or the salon. Note the 70hp auxiliary get-home diesel in case of an emergency. A seaworthy yacht of uncompromising quality, the Nordhavn's single 340hp Lugger diesel delivers almost 3,500 miles of range at 8 knots.

Not Enough Resale Data to Set Values

Length Overall	57'6"	Clearance	21'0"
Length WL	52'8"	Fuel	2,000 gals.
Beam	17'7"	Water	300 gals.
Draft	6'8"	Waste	60 gals.
Weight	120,000#	Hull Type	Displacement

Nordhavn 62

1995–Current

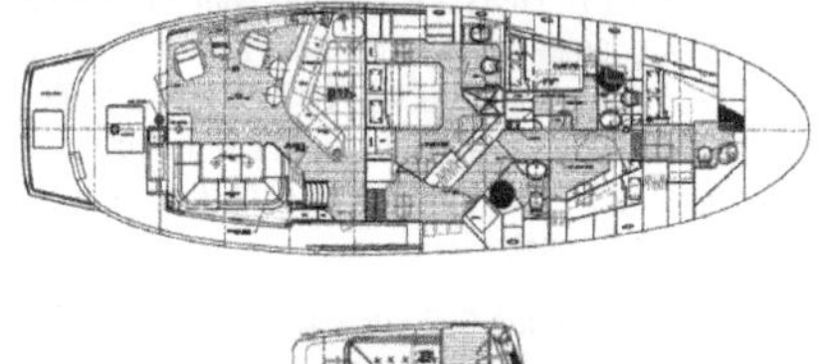

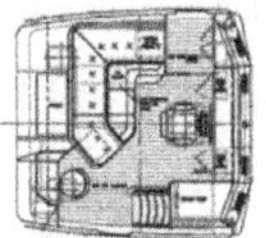

The Nordhavn 62 is a sophisticated and heavily built long-range cruising yacht capable of transoceanic voyages in safety and comfort. Looking for all the world like a small freighter, the Nordhavn (built in Taiwan by the well-regarded Ta Shing yard) is constructed on a ballasted full-displacement hull with watertight bulkheads, a long, deep keel, and an efficient bulbous bow. The entire superstructure of the Nordhavn is aft; her long foredeck is nearly flush, and the high bow—with its reserve buoyancy—will be difficult to bury in a head sea. The belowdecks accommodations are practical and luxurious. Three staterooms are included in the standard layout, and the separate crew quarters are reached via a hatch in the foredeck. The enclosed pilothouse, accessed from the salon, includes a head and bunk beds. Notable features include high bulwarks surrounding the decks, a spacious engineroom, keel cooler, dry stack exhaust, a Portuguese bridge coaming around the pilothouse, and a fully equipped workshop. A single 340hp Luger diesel will cruise the Nordhavn 62 efficiently at 9 knots while burning just 6.5 gallons per hour. Range at this speed is around 3,000 miles. At lower speeds the range may exceed 4,500 miles.

Not Enough Resale Data to Set Values

Length Overall	62'8"	Ballast	10,000#
Length WL	55'6"	Fuel	2,652 gals.
Beam	19'4"	Water	525 gals.
Draft	6'10"	Waste	100 gals.
Weight	150,000#	Hull Type	Displacement

Nordic Tugs

Quick View

- Nordic Tugs was formed in 1979 when naval architect Lynn Senour designed the company's first product, the Nordic Tug 26.
- Introduced at the 1980 Seattle Boat Show, the Nordic Tug 26 (priced at just $30,000!) proved an immediate success with 37 reported sold at the show, and 54 sold by the end of the month.
- In 1982, the Northwest Marine Trade Association (NMTA) dubbed Nordic Tugs "one of the biggest success stories of a largely depressed pleasure boat construction scene."
- Nordic Tugs expanded its product line to include a 32-foot model (1985), 37' and 42' models (mid-to-late '90s), and a 52-footer (2003).
- In August, 2010, Nordic Tugs closed its Burlington, WA manufacturing plant due to the ongoing effects of the U.S. recession.
- In October, 2010, the company announced plans to resume production after a 3-month pause.
- A list of Nordic Tug owner's groups can be found at the Nordic Tugs web site.

Nordic Tugs • Burlington, WA • www.nordictug.com

Nordic 26 Tug

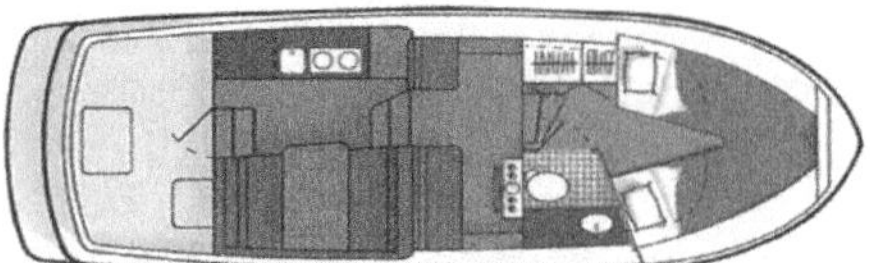

The Nordic 26 is a salty and very distinctive character boat with an upright profile (note the plumb bow and fake stack) and a well-arranged interior suitable for the cruising couple. More than just an eye-catching design, however, she's well constructed and quite able to head offshore for extended coastal cruising. Construction is solid fiberglass, and her full-keel, semi-displacement hull features a rounded transom and a wide 9'6" beam. Two floorplans were available—one with V-berths and the other with an offset double berth—and the original L-shaped lounge in the salon was replaced in 1995 with a dinette. The pilothouse is raised two steps from the salon (engine access is below), and the shaded aft deck is large enough for a couple of deck chairs. With a 50hp diesel, the Nordic 26 Tug will cruise at 7 knots burning about a gallon per hour. Speeds to 14 knots are available with an optional 100hp diesel engine. A popular boat, a total of 172 were built. Note that the Nordic 2-26 model, introduced in 1995, has a slightly raked stack and wider catwalks in addition to the booth-style dinette. Out of production in 1997, reintroduced in 2009. Cruise at 6–7 knots with 100hp Yanmar diesel.

See Page 690 For Price Data

Length Overall	26'4"	Clearance	9'8"
Length WL	25'2"	Fuel	100 gals.
Beam	9'6"	Water	40 gals.
Draft	3'3"	Waste	20 gals.
Weight	7,500#	Hull Type	Semi-Disp.

Nordic 32 Tug

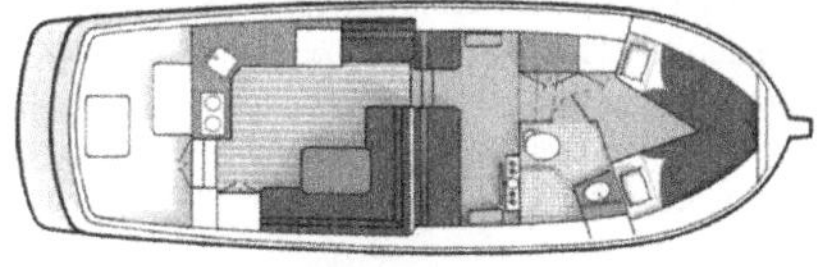

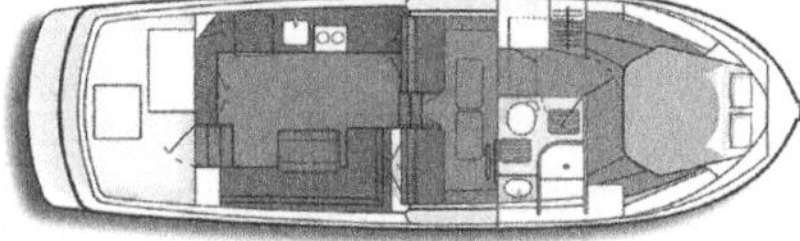

The most popular boat of her type ever built, the Nordic 32 is a full-keeled, semi-displacement cruiser whose classic tugboat profile and quality construction have endeared her to yachting enthusiasts for many years. Indeed, with her plumb bow, rounded stern, and false smokestack, the 32 is an unquestionably eye-catching design. Until recently, two interior configurations were available: one with an angled double berth in the stateroom and the galley forward in the salon, and the other with V-berths forward and an L-shaped galley aft in the salon. In both arrangements, teak paneling and a teak-and-holly cabin sole highlight the interior, and the salon settee converts in a double berth for overnight guests. The Nordic received an extensive makeover in 2002. The result of the reengineering was the 32+ with an island berth in the forward stateroom, a new galley layout with under-counter refrigeration, and a swim platform that extends the hull and waterline length. In 2008 the hull was revised to include a prop pocket. Several diesel engines have been available over the years. Cruise at 12 knots with single 220hp Cummins diesel; 14 knots with 270hp Cummins.

See Page 690 For Price Data

Length Overall	34'2"	Headroom	6'4"
Beam	11'0"	Fuel	200 gals.
Draft	3'6"	Water	100 gals.
Weight	16,000#	Waste	30 gals.
Clearance	10'4"	Hull Type	Semi-Disp.

Nordic 37 Tug

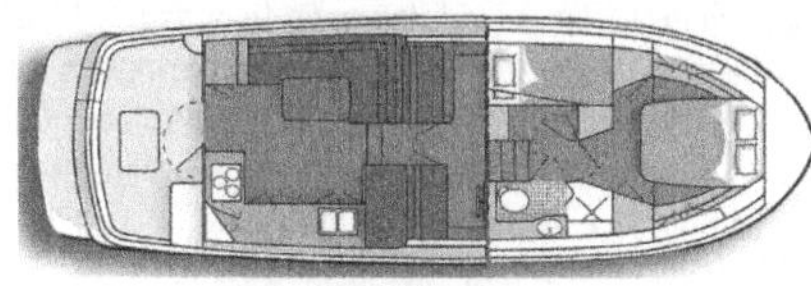

Two Staterooms

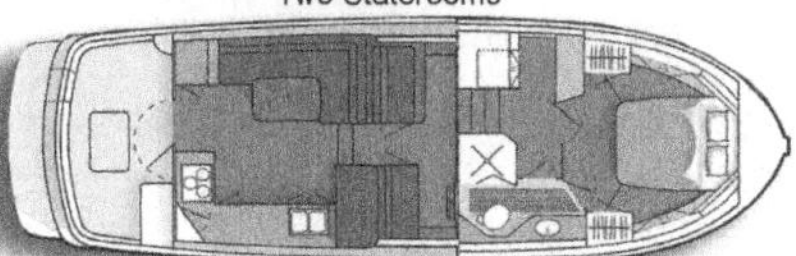

Single Stateroom

Bridging the gap between the company's 32-foot and 42-foot models, the Nordic 37 shares the same salty tugboat profile as her sisterships in the Nordic fleet with a plumb bow, false smokestack, and a stylish reverse transom. She rides on a solid fiberglass, semi-displacement hull with a slender beam and a full, prop-protecting keel. The raised pilothouse floorplan of the 37 Tug was originally arranged with two staterooms forward including an island berth in the master stateroom and over/under berths in the guest cabin. In 2003, an alternate single-stateroom layout greatly enlarged the master stateroom while also adding more floor space in the shower. In both configurations, the Nordic's full-beam salon is open to the wheelhouse and aft deck, and solid teak joinery and quality fabrics highlight the interior. Additional features include a large engineroom, convertible salon dinette, storage lazarette, transom door, and bow thruster. A single 330hp Cummins diesel will cruise the Nordic 37 at 12–14 knots and reach a top speed of around 18 knots. At her 8-knot hull speed she'll cruise for over 1,000 miles burning only 3 gallons per hour. Note that a flybridge option became available in 2004.

See Page 690 For Price Data

Length Overall	39'2"	Clearance	12'4"
Length WL	37'4"	Fuel	320 gals.
Beam	12'11"	Water	144 gals.
Draft	4'4"	Waste	32 gals.
Weight	22,600#	Hull Type	Semi-Disp.

Nordic 42 Tug

1996–Current

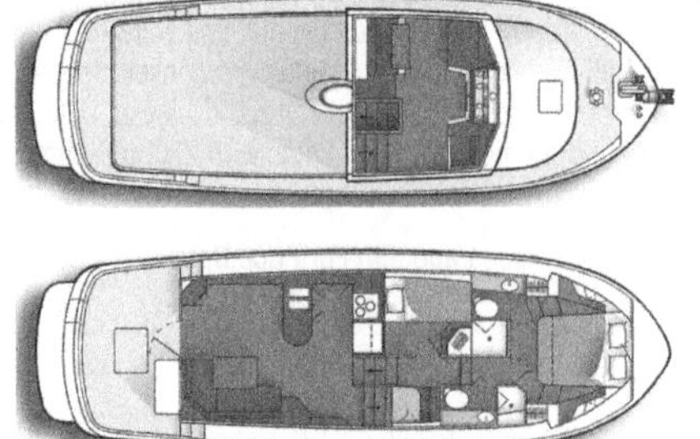

Serious cruisers will find a lot to like in the Nordic 42, a well-built passagemaker whose tugboat profile is a real attention-getter in a world of cookie-cutter production boats. She's heavily built on a solid fiberglass, semi-displacement hull with a wide 14-foot beam and a deep, prop-protecting keel. Her floorplan is quite innovative in that the guest stateroom and guest head are reached directly from the salon, while the forward stateroom and head are reached from the wheelhouse—a layout that affords excellent cabin separation and privacy. (The staterooms in most pilothouse designs are accessed only from the wheelhouse.) The Nordic's all-teak interior is very handsome indeed, and a laundry center is tucked beneath the stairs leading up to the pilothouse. The cockpit, partially shaded by a flybridge overhang, includes a molded seat/storage locker, while the fake stack on the cabintop houses a radar reflector. Additional features include twin pilothouse deck doors, walkable side decks, bow thruster, and a spacious engineroom. A single 540hp Cummins diesel will cruise at 10 knots and deliver a top speed of 15–16 knots. Note that a flybridge became optional in 2006.

See Page 690 For Price Data

Length Overall	46'3"	Headroom	6'6"
Length WL	40'2"	Fuel	600 gals.
Beam	13'10"	Water	200 gals.
Draft	4'7"	Waste	50 gals.
Weight	31,400#	Hull Type	Semi-Disp.

Nordic 52/54 Tug

2004–Current

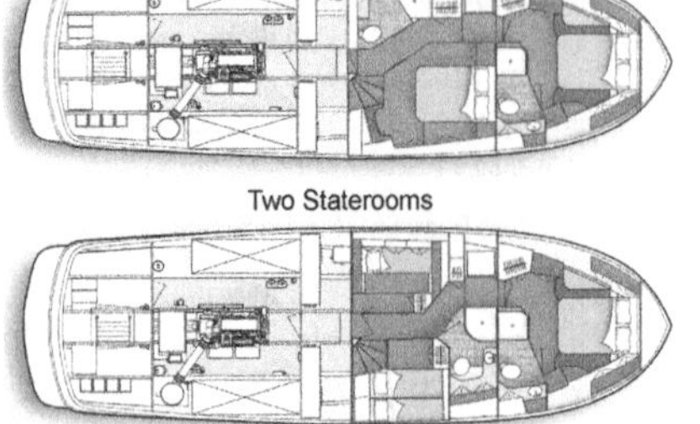

Two Staterooms

Three Staterooms

With her sturdy profile and prominent bow—the bow pulpit rides nearly 9 feet above the waterline—the Nordic 54 Tug is an imposing yacht up close. Introduced in 2004 (and called the Nordic 52 until 2009) this is Nordic's largest yacht to date. Built on a semi-displacement hull with a deep, prop-protecting keel, she was originally designed for twin engines; three were built before Nordic engineers redesigned the hull for single-screw power which then became standard. A spacious, teak-trimmed salon with leather settee, removable dinette table and flat-screen TV highlights the interior of the 54 Tug. A large galley with dishwasher and under-counter refrigeration is forward of the salon. The 54's raised pilothouse resembles that of a small ship with a state-of-the-art helm, U-shaped dinette, and watertight deck doors. On the lower level buyers can choose from a two-stateroom floorplan with an amidships master, or a three-stateroom layout with the master suite forward. Additional features include a washer/dryer, cockpit storage lazarette, an enormous engineroom, and wide, well-secured side decks. A flybridge is a popular option. Cruise at 9–10 knots with a single 610hp Cummins engine (about 15 knots top).

Not Enough Resale Data to Set Values

Length Overall	56'10"	Clearance, Mast	21'9"
Length WL	52'6"	Fuel	1,300 gals.
Beam	16'10"	Water	300 gals.
Draft	5'3"	Waste	130 gals.
Weight	68,000#	Hull Type	Semi-Disp.

Ocean Yachts

Quick View

- Ocean Yachts was founded in 1977 by a group of ex-Pacemaker employees headed by Jack Leek. Their first boat was the Ocean 40 Super Sport.
- The 1980s saw Ocean Yachts establish itself in the marketplace for their Super Sport series of David Martin-designed offshore convertibles.
- By the latter part of the decade Ocean had expanded to include Sunliner motor yachts to compliment their sportfishing boats.
- The Ocean 53 SS was one of the first convertibles to break the 40-knot barrier in 1994.
- Ocean Yachts positioned themselves as a more affordable alternative to products from Viking, Hatteras and Bertram.
- During the 1990s and continuing into recent years, Ocean was one of the largest manufacturers of sportfishing yachts, 37' to 73', in the industry.

Ocean Yachts • Egg Harbor, NJ • www.oceanyachtsinc.com

Ocean 37 Billfish

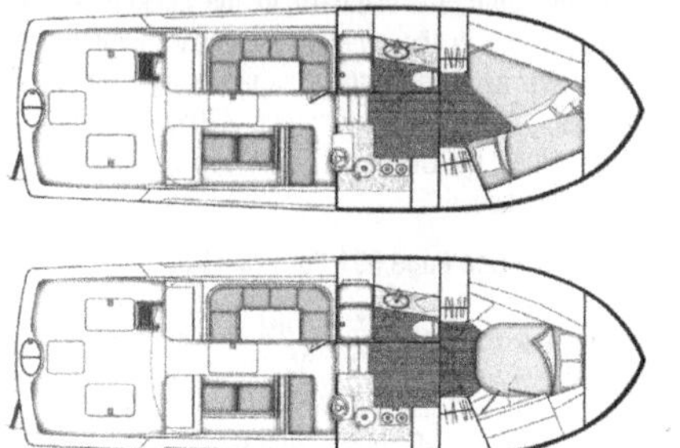

Introduced in 2009, the Ocean 37 Billfish is a throwback to the classic, custom-built fishing boats of the 1960s. Her vintage Palm Beach styling belies her modern engineering and construction, however, and the 37 Billfish incorporates the same modern amenities found in every Ocean Yacht. Unlike flybridge convertibles with their enclosed (and luxurious) salons, Ocean designers eliminated the aft cabin bulkhead in the 37 Billfish that allows the skipper to join in the fishing action. This open main deck design makes the Billfish unique in today's market—she's currently the only dual-helm flybridge boat produced without a fixed salon bulkhead. In keeping with her sportfishing heritage, the main-deck layout of the Billfish is functional, efficient, and easy to clean. Insulated fish boxes and a bait prep center are standard in the cockpit, and the U-shaped dinette converts when necessary to a double bed. Forward and below, the well-appointed interior is finished with high-gloss cherry joinery, wood-planked flooring, and premium appliances. The engineroom is surprisingly large, and prop pockets in the hull reduce draft. Yanmar 480hp diesels cruise at 24–26 knots; Volvo 435hp IPS drives cruise at 28–30 knots.

See Page 691 For Price Data

Length	37'8"	Fuel	400 gals.
Beam	13'10"	Water	75 gals.
Draft	2'6"	Waste	35 gals.
Weight	23,500#	Hull Type	Modified-V
Clearance	15'5"	Deadrise Aft	13°

Ocean 38 Super Sport

1992–95

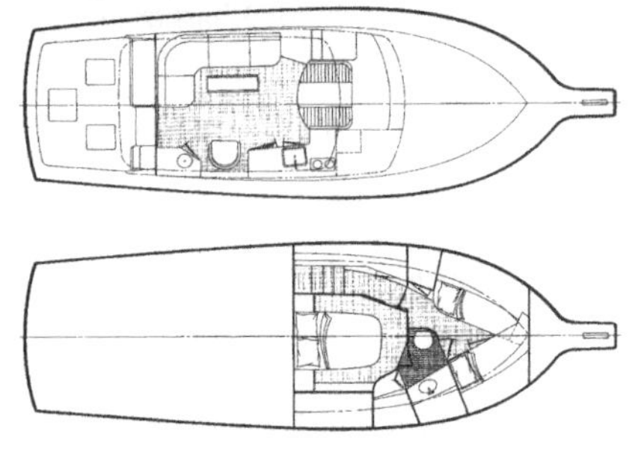

The newer Ocean 38 SS looks a lot like the original 38 SS (1984–91) on the outside but she's an entirely different boat below. Built on a slightly wider (and heavier) hull with a sharper entry and cored hullsides, the newer 38 has a smaller cockpit than her predecessor but a much larger interior. Indeed, the two-stateroom floorplan is innovative and completely unique for a boat of this size. Stepping into the salon, one is confronted with a surprisingly spacious and efficient layout with the dinette positioned forward (beneath the windshield panels) and an open galley to starboard. The companionway is all the way to port (there's a 7-foot rod locker in the outside wall) and leads down to a midships master stateroom of truly remarkable proportions. Compared to other fishing boats her size, the cockpit of the Ocean 38 is a little small. A fiberglass console contains a tackle locker, freezer and sink, while an in-deck fish box, transom door and teak covering boards were standard. (Note that a hardtop was also standard.) The engine room, however, is a tight fit. The Ocean 38 SS came standard with a choice of 425hp Cats (22–23 knots cruise/28 knots top) or 430hp Volvo diesels (26 knots cruise/30 knots top).

See Page 691 For Price Data

Length	38'9"	Fuel	400 gals.
Beam	14'2"	Water	80 gals.
Draft	3'8"	Waste	35 gals.
Weight	27,000#	Hull Type	Modified-V
Clearance	15'4"	Deadrise Aft	12°

Ocean 40 Sport Fish

1999–2005

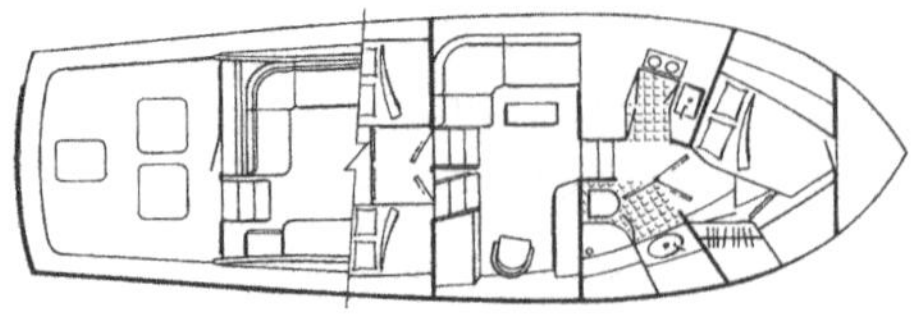

An innovative cabin layout and a notably affordable price are among the attributes of the Ocean 40 Sport Fish, a good-looking open sportfisherman whose highly elevated bridgedeck and spacious midcabin interior set her apart from most other express fishing boats of her type. She's built on the same proven modified-V hull used in the production of her sistership, the Ocean 40 SS, with a sharp entry, a shallow keel and a relatively wide 14-foot, 2-inch beam. Rather than being a dedicated fishing boat, the 40 Sport Fish is better described as a capable fisherman with a comfortable cruising interior. Raising the helm several extra feet from the cockpit provides the headroom for the private midcabin, but veteran anglers will note that communication between the helm and cockpit is compromised. A transom baitwell, tackle lockers and a transom door are standard in the cockpit; there's near-standing headroom in the otherwise compact engine room, and the bridgedeck is arranged with L-shaped lounge seating aft of the centerline helm. A good performer, twin 420hp Cat (or 440hp Yanmar) diesels cruise the Ocean 40 Sport Fish at 22 knots and reach 30+ knots wide open.

See Page 691 For Price Data

Length	40'4"	Fuel	390 gals.
Beam	14'2"	Water	90 gals.
Draft	3'8"	Waste	40 gals.
Weight	26,500#	Hull Type	Modified-V
Clearance	12'6"	Deadrise Aft	14°

Ocean 40 Super Sport

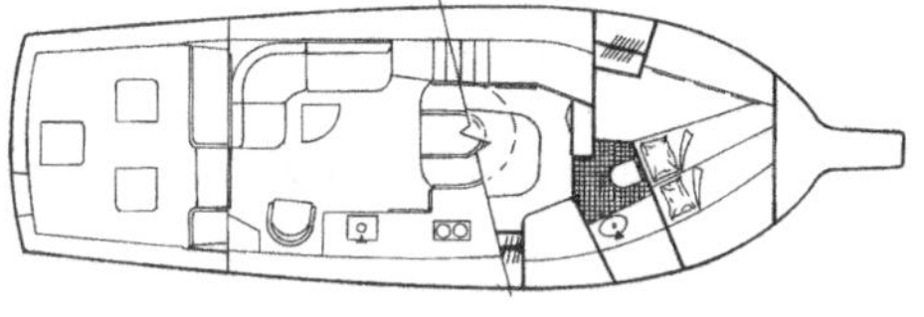

Ocean Yachts has never been shy over the years when it comes to introducing innovative design concepts in their Super Sport convertibles. In the 40 SS introduced in 1997, designer David Martin created yet another high-performance sportfisherman with a unique two-stateroom, galley-up interior that will almost certainly catch most observers by surprise. Located forward in the salon, a step up from the floor is a four-person dinette—an unusual feature in a 40-foot convertible. While this layout is unusual to be sure and may not appeal to everyone (since it moves the companionway well off to port), the upside is the huge amidships stateroom beneath this dinette with its surprising 7-foot headroom. Like all Ocean Yachts, the teak interior is tastefully decorated and well finished throughout. On deck, the cockpit comes standard with a molded tackle center, saltwater washdown, and transom door. (Note the athwartships flybridge ladder.) Additional features include cockpit engineroom access, an integral bow pulpit, and a well-arranged helm console. Built on a low-deadrise hull with moderate beam, twin 420hp Cat (or 440hp Yanmar) diesels cruise at 24 knots and reach a top speed of 30+ knots.

See Page 691 For Price Data

Length	40'4"	Fuel	408 gals.
Beam	14'2"	Water	90 gals.
Draft	3'8"	Cockpit	80 sq. ft.
Weight	27,500#	Hull Type	Modified-V
Clearance	15'5"	Deadrise Aft	14°

Ocean 42 Super Sport

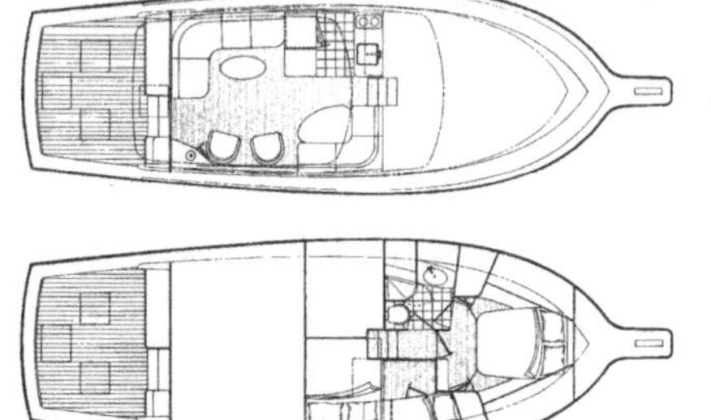

The Ocean 42 was one of so-called "new generation" of Super Sport models when she was introduced in the early 1990s. (Note that an earlier Ocean 42 SS model ran from 1980–83.) She has a more streamlined appearance than previous Ocean convertibles, as well as less exterior teak trim and a revised hull with additional transom deadrise (for a better rough-water ride) and a shallower, slightly longer keel. The varnished teak interior of the Ocean 42 is arranged with a walkaround double berth in the bow (master) stateroom, and a double (and slide-out single) berth in the guest stateroom. The galley is forward in the salon, opposite the L-shaped dinette, and a full wet bar is aft, adjacent to the sliding salon door. Note that a hatch in the galley sole leads to a machinery and storage area. Not surprisingly, the cockpit came with a full array of fishing amenities including a bait freezer, transom door, tackle locker and a large in-floor fish box. Additional features include a stylish hardtop, bow pulpit, teak covering boards, and a well-arranged engineroom. Twin Caterpillar 425hp diesels were standard in the 42 SS (24 knots cruise/27 knots top), and 485hp Detroit 6-71s (26 knots cruise/30 knots top) were optional.

See Page 691 For Price Data

Length	42'0"	Fuel	466 gals.
Beam	15'0"	Water	100 gals.
Draft	3'7"	Cockpit	100 sq. ft.
Weight	35,466#	Hull Type	Modified-V
Clearance	15'4"	Deadrise Aft	5°

Ocean 42 Super Sport

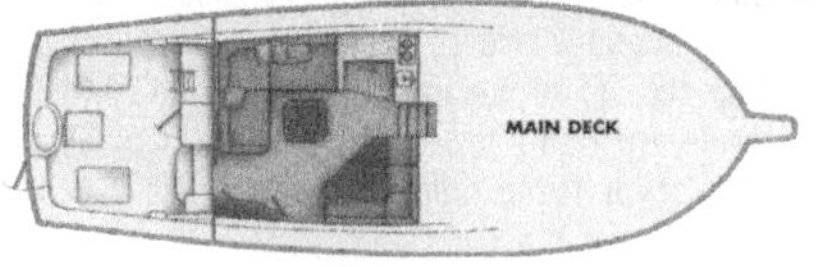

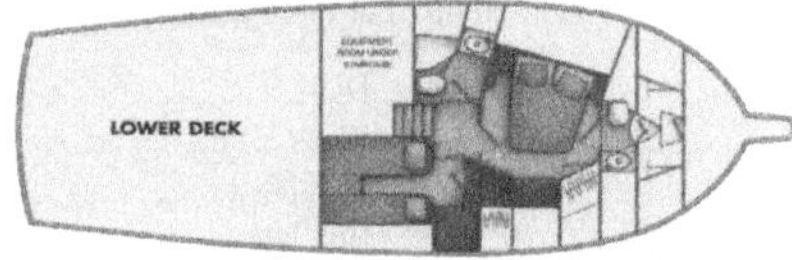

For over 30 years, Ocean Yachts has produced a series of stylish and affordable Super Sport models for generations of offshore boating enthusiasts. Known for their luxurious interiors and spirited performance, Super Sports have thrived over the years in one of the most demanding—and competitive—segments of the boating market. Introduced in 2006, the 42 Super Sport (note that a previous 42 SS model was built in 1991–95) is a versatile, luxury-class convertible equally suited for tournament-level fishing or extended family cruising. Her clever two-stateroom interior features a well-appointed salon/dinette/galley area on the deckhouse level and two full heads below (most 42-footers have only one). The galley is on the small side for a boat this size, but the master stateroom layout, with an athwartships queen and forward head compartment, is as comfortable as it is innovative. Note the big storage room under the galley, and washer/dryer combo in the guest stateroom. Cockpit amenities include a transom livewell, in-deck fish boxes, and direct engineroom access. An underwater exhaust system reduces noise and cockpit fumes. Cat 510hp diesels cruise at 25–26 knots (30 knots top).

See Page 691 For Price Data

Length	42'1"	Fuel	430 gals.
Beam	15'4"	Water	100 gals.
Draft	3'11"	Headroom	6'6"
Weight	34,151#	Hull Type	Modified-V
Clearance	15'5"	Deadrise Aft	NA

Ocean 43 Super Sport

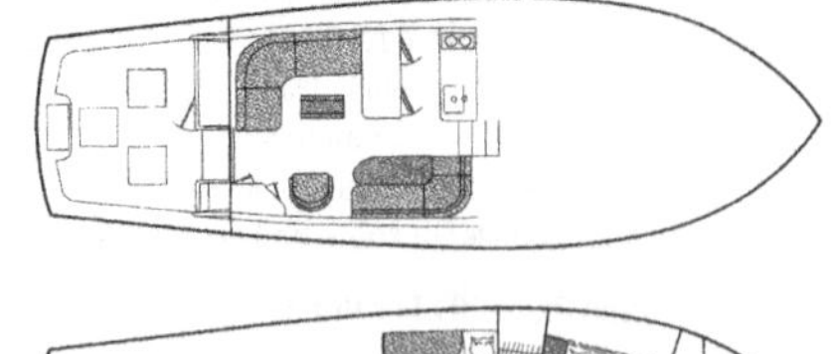

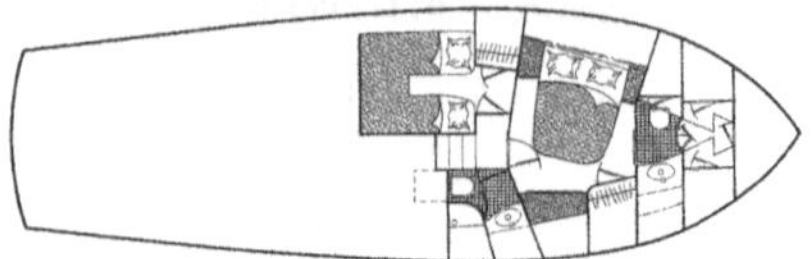

Like most Ocean models, the 43 Super Sport is a lot of boat for the money. Aggressively priced, the 43 delivered more than just a rakish profile and better-than-average performance; she also boasts a well-finished interior with a spacious salon and an innovative master stateroom layout. Built on a tapered, modified-V hull with a shallow keel and a well-flared bow, the 43 SS came with a long list of standard equipment and relatively few options. Her spacious two-stateroom floorplan is arranged with a private head in the master stateroom (located in the bow of the boat) and twin single berths in the guest cabin. The wide-open salon is created by extending the house well forward on the foredeck and tucking the guest stateroom under the galley. The cockpit has a freezer, a huge fish box, transom livewell, washdowns, tackle storage lockers, and a transom door. Additional features include a central vacuum system, wide side decks, engineroom washdown, and a bow pulpit. Note that the engineroom is a tight fit. Among several engine options, twin 480hp Volvo (or 500hp Yanmar) diesels cruise the 43 Super Sport at 25 knots and reach a top speed in excess of 30 knots.

See Page 691 For Price Data

Length	43'10"	Fuel	438 gals.
Beam	15'2"	Water	94 gals.
Draft	3'7"	Headroom	6'6"
Weight	37,000#	Hull Type	Modified-V
Clearance, Hardtop	15'5"	Deadrise Aft	7°

Ocean 44 Motor Yacht

1992–99

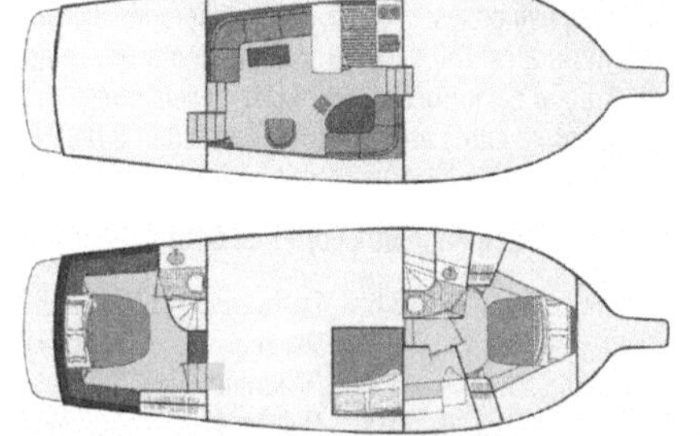

A competitively priced yacht with a rakish profile and impressive performance, the Ocean 44 MY is notable for her innovative three-stateroom interior. Most motor yachts in this size range have two-stateroom floorplans with the galley down. The Ocean 44, however, boasts three staterooms—each with a double berth—in a very unusual configuration. While the fore and aft staterooms are fairly generic, the starboard guest stateroom is quite unique in that it extends beneath the main salon dinette. Indeed, this second guest cabin is considerably larger than it appears at first glance, although it does consume some valuable engine room space. The galley is on the deckhouse level in this layout, and both heads are fitted with stall showers. Topside, the full-width aft deck comes with a wet bar and wing doors, and the flybridge is arranged with the helm forward and lounge seating for six. Additional standard features included a radar arch, built-in washer/dryer, bow pulpit and swim platform. Built on a low-deadrise, modified-V hull, optional 485hp 6-71 diesels cruise the Ocean the 44 MY at 24 knots (27–28 knots top). Note that the Ocean 48 Cockpit MY (1993–99) is the same boat with a cockpit extension.

See Page 691 For Price Data

Length	44'0"	Max Headroom	6'6"
Beam	15'0"	Fuel	466 gals.
Draft	3'7"	Water	100 gals.
Weight	40,000#	Hull Type	Modified-V
Clearance	12'0"	Deadrise Aft	5°

Ocean 45 Super Sport

1996–99

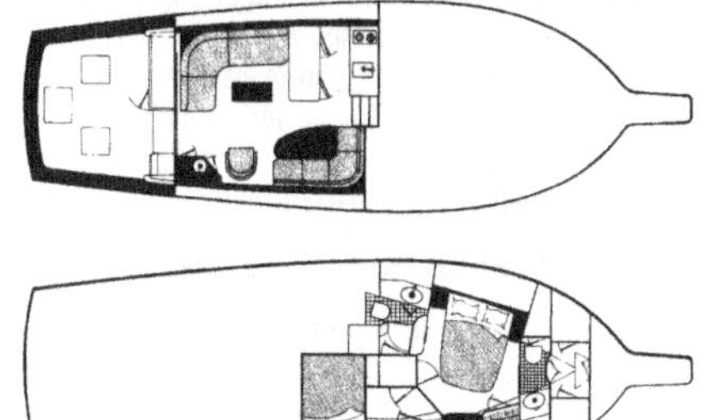

One of the more affordable boats her size during the late 1990s, the Ocean 45 Super Sport is a high-style convertible whose beautifully finished interior and excellent performance made her popular with hardcore anglers as well as family cruisers. Like all Ocean models, she's built on a low-deadrise, modified-V hull whose tapered design narrows considerably at the transom. The result is a fast and efficient hull form, although the cockpit dimensions are smaller than one might expect in a 45-footer. Belowdecks, the two-stateroom floorplan of the 45 Super Sport is unique. The spacious master stateroom, with its angled double bed, is forward, and the en suite head compartment is in the bow—very unusual indeed. Also unusual is the guest stateroom with its slide-out single bunk and a double bed that extends beneath the salon dinette. On the deckhouse level, the salon, galley and dinette all combine to form a large and comfortable living area. Additional features include cockpit tackle centers, an offset bridge ladder, teak covering boards, transom door, and a spacious flybridge. A good-running boat with 485hp Detroit 6-71s, the 45 Super Sport will cruise around 26 knots and reach a top speed of 31–32 knots.

See Page 691 For Price Data

Length	44'8"	Fuel	466 gals.
Beam	15'2"	Water	100 gals.
Draft	3'7"	Headroom	6'6"
Weight	37,000#	Hull Type	Modified-V
Clearance	15'4"	Deadrise Aft	1.5°

Ocean 46 Super Sport

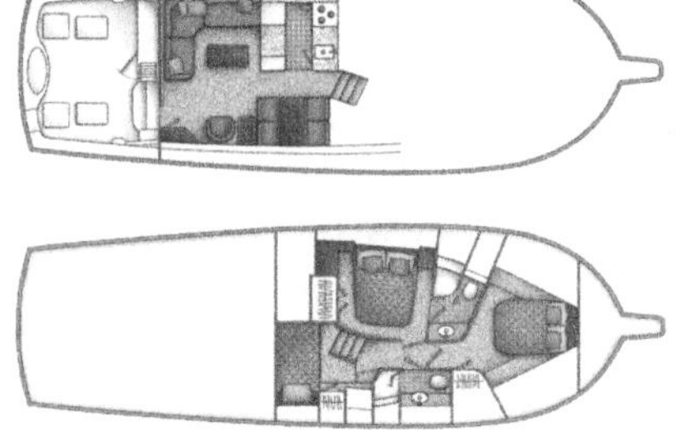

In the early 1980s Ocean Yachts produced the original 46 Super Sport which went on to become the company's most popular mid-sized model ever. The new 46 resembles her predecessor in speed and performance, but with increased beam and additional transom deadrise, she's a more comfortable and better-riding boat. While creative space management has been an Ocean trademark for several years, it still comes as a surprise to find a three-stateroom layout in a 46-foot boat—most convertibles this size have two-stateroom floorplans. Focal point of this innovative interior is the well-appointed salon with its teak joinery, leather sofa, and vinyl wall coverings. Both heads are fitted with stall showers, and buyers can choose either a full-size double berth or crossover berths in the forward stateroom. (Note that the small aft stateroom contains only a single berth.) The cockpit comes with all the necessary features including fish boxes, livewell, and engineroom access. Corian galley counters, a central vacuum system, and a bow pulpit were standard. A good performer, 825hp MTU diesels cruise the Ocean 46 at an honest 30 knots and reach a top speed of 34–35 knots.

See Page 691 For Price Data

Length	46'6"	Fuel	620 gals.
Beam	15'10"	Water	125 gals.
Draft	4'2"	Headroom	6'5"
Weight	42,561#	Hull Type	Modified-V
Clearance	16'4"	Deadrise Aft	14°

Ocean 48 Cockpit Motor Yacht

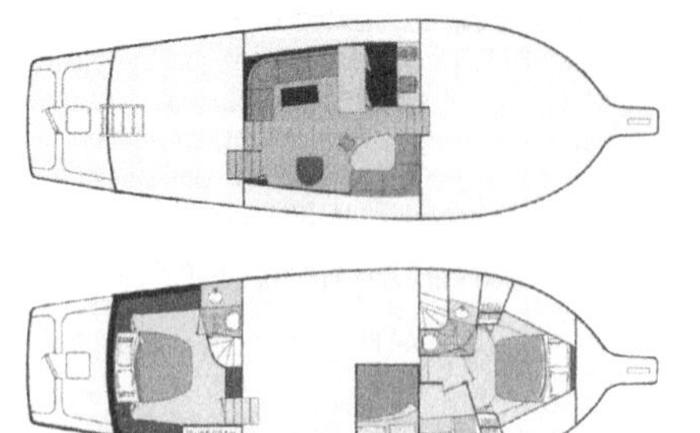

A good-selling boat, the Ocean 48 Cockpit Motor Yacht is a cockpit version of the company's 44 Motor Yacht (1992–99). She rides on the same low-deadrise hull as her sistership, and shares an identical three-stateroom interior made notable for its spacious salon. Most motor yachts in this size range have only two staterooms. The 48, however, has three—each with a double berth—in a very unusual configuration. While the fore and aft staterooms are fairly generic, the starboard guest stateroom is unique in that it extends beneath the main salon dinette. Indeed, this second guest cabin is considerably larger than it appears at first glance, although it does consume some valuable engineroom space. The galley is on the deckhouse level in this layout, and both heads are fitted with stall showers. Topside, the full-width aft deck comes with a wet bar and wing doors, and the flybridge is arranged with the helm forward and lounge seating for six. Additional standard features included a cockpit transom door, built-in washer/dryer, bow pulpit, and swim platform. Built on a low-deadrise, modified-V hull, optional 485hp 6-71 diesels cruise the 48 Cockpit MY in the mid 20s and reach a top speed of just under 30 knots.

See Page 691 For Price Data

Length	48'0"	Max Headroom	6'6"
Beam	15'0"	Fuel	466 gals.
Draft	3'7"	Water	100 gals.
Weight	42,500#	Hull Type	Modified-V
Clearance	12'0"	Deadrise Aft	5°

Ocean 48 Sport Fish

1997–2001

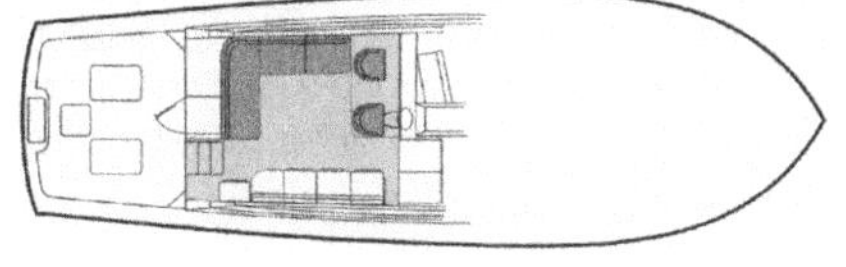

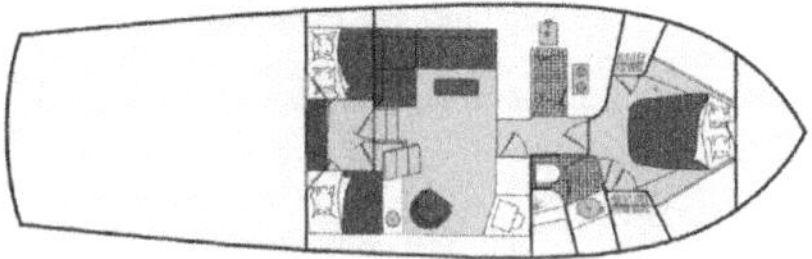

A handsome yacht with aggressive lines and a sleek profile, the Ocean 48 Sport Fish brought something new to the late 1990s market for big express-type sportfishing boats with her innovative two-stateroom interior. Most boats of this type are bare-knuckle fishing machines whose single-stateroom interiors are designed to accommodate the needs of dayboaters. Thus, the genuine cruising capabilities of the 48 Open are unique for a serious express fisherman. Built on the same modified-V hull used for the Ocean 48 Convertible, designer David Martin created the space for the midcabin stateroom of the 48 Sport Fish by substantially elevating the bridgedeck. (Note that there is a single berth as well as a double berth in the aft stateroom.) For fishing, the cockpit is equipped with a transom door, two huge in-deck fish boxes, a rod storage cabinet, tackle center, and a transom baitwell. Additional features include a standup engine room, a centerline helm with elevated seats (for excellent visibility), a full teak interior, and a separate stall shower in the head. Twin 625hp 6V-92 diesels cruise the 48 Sport Fish at 28 knots (30+ knots top), and later models with 660hp Cats cruise at 30 knots (34–35 knots top).

Not Enough Resale Data to Set Values

Length	48'8"	Fuel	685 gals.
Beam	16'0"	Water	150 gals.
Draft	4'0"	Headroom	6'6"
Weight	42,500#	Hull Type	Modified-V
Clearance, Hardtop	15'6"	Deadrise Aft	NA

Ocean 48 Super Sport

1995–2003

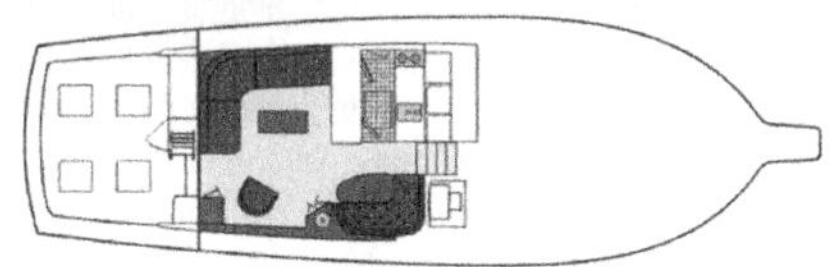

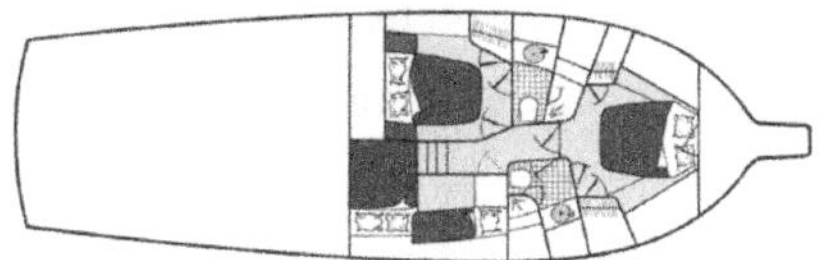

Latest in a series of 48-foot convertibles from Ocean Yachts, the most recent 48 Super Sport has a wider beam than her predecessors with a more rakish profile (the house is carried farther forward on the deck), greater bow flare, and a deeper forefoot for an improved headsea ride. Like all Ocean designs, her low-deadrise, tapered hull is quick to accelerate and fast across the water—performance characteristics common to most Jersey-style fishing boats over the years. A pair of galley-up floorplans are offered in the Ocean 48, one with three staterooms and the other with two. Both layouts have walkaround queen berths in the master stateroom, and both have two heads with separate stall showers. The cockpit comes fully equipped with a bait-prep station, freezer, engine controls, transom door, teak covering boards, and an in-deck fish box. Additional features include cockpit engineroom access, wide side decks, and a spacious, well-arranged flybridge. Among several engine choices, early models with 535hp 6V-92s cruise at 24 knots (about 28 knots top), and later models with 660hp Cats (or 680hp MANs) cruise at 28 knots (30+ knots top).

See Page 691 For Price Data

Length	48'8"	Fuel	685 gals.
Beam	16'0"	Water	150 gals.
Draft	4'2"	Waste	60 gals.
Weight	45,000#	Hull Type	Modified-V
Clearance	15'6"	Deadrise Aft	2°

Ocean 50 Super Sport

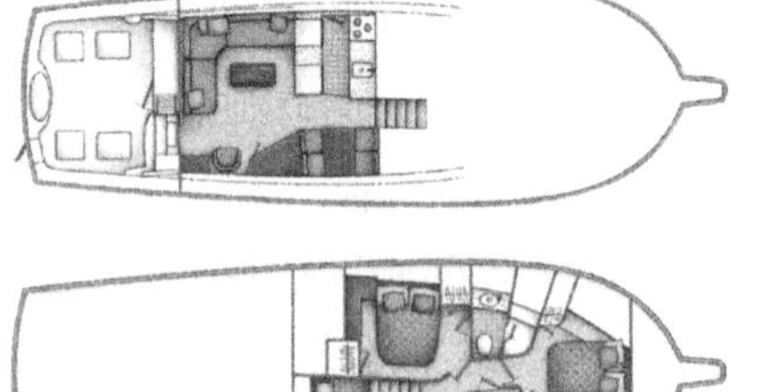

Introduced in 2004, the Ocean 50 Super Sport replaced the popular 48 Super Sport (1995–2003), one of the builder's best-selling models of recent years. The 50 is slightly wider than her predecessor, and she has more transom deadrise for improved rough-water performance without sacrificing speed. Ocean has always had a reputation for excellent space utilization, and the three-stateroom, two-head interior of the 50 Super Sport delivers a balanced blend of comfort and luxury. An L-shaped sofa and built-in entertainment center dominate the salon that is highlighted by grain-matched teak (or maple) woodwork, vinyl overheads, and deep pile carpeting. A flat-panel TV/DVD is found in the master stateroom, a washer/dryer unit is located in the companionway, and the forward guest stateroom is available with a large island berth or an upper-and-lower berth arrangement. For the angler, the Ocean 50 comes standard with a standup livewell, bait-prep center, in-deck fish box, and transom door. The engineroom offers good outboard access to the motors. A fast ride, MTU 825hp diesels cruise the Ocean 50 SS at 28–30 knots (about 33 knots top).

See Page 691 For Price Data

Length	50'6"	Cockpit	123 sq. ft.
Beam	16'9"	Fuel	780 gals.
Draft	4'5"	Water	150 gals.
Weight	54,038#	Hull Type	Modified-V
Clearance	18'0"	Deadrise Aft	14°

Ocean 52 Super Sport

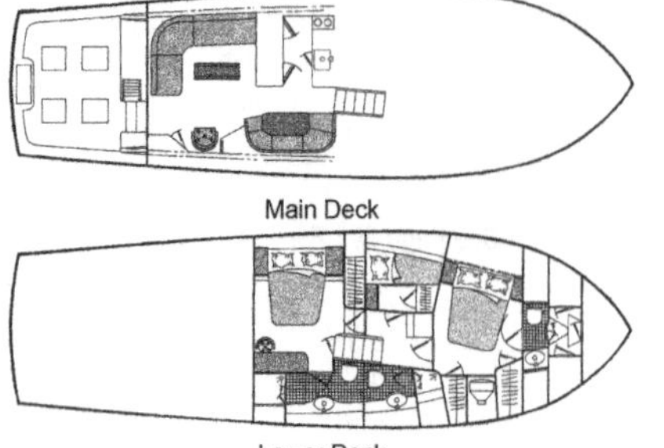
Main Deck

Lower Deck

Built on the same hull as the proven 53 Super Sport, the Ocean 52 Super Sport is a well-designed tournament fishing yacht with an affordable blend of performance, fishability and cruising elegance. David Martin, who designed most all of Ocean's hulls over the years, is well known for creating exceptionally roomy and innovative interiors. In the case of the 52 SS, the lush accommodations include three staterooms and three full heads—a big floorplan indeed for a 52-footer. The forward cabin has a walkaround double berth and a private head in the forepeak, while the full-width master stateroom is aft, down a few steps from the hallway, where it's located beneath the elevated galley and dinette. Ocean offers a choice of teak or maple interior joinery, and the decor is a sophisticated mix of designer fabrics and plush carpeting. On deck, the cockpit comes with all of the fishing amenities expected in a serious tournament machine. Additional features include a well-designed helm console, a built-in washer/dryer, and a fiberglass hardtop. On the downside, the engineroom is a tight fit. Twin 800hp Cats, 825hp MANs, or 825hp MTUs will all cruise the Ocean 52 in the high 20s with a top speed of around 33 knots.

See Page 691 For Price Data

Length	52'7"	Fuel	860 gals.
Beam	16'4"	Water	150 gals.
Draft	4'4"	Headroom	6'5"
Weight	56,000#	Hull Type	Modified-V
Clearance, Hardtop	17'4"	Deadrise Aft	8°

Ocean 53 Super Sport

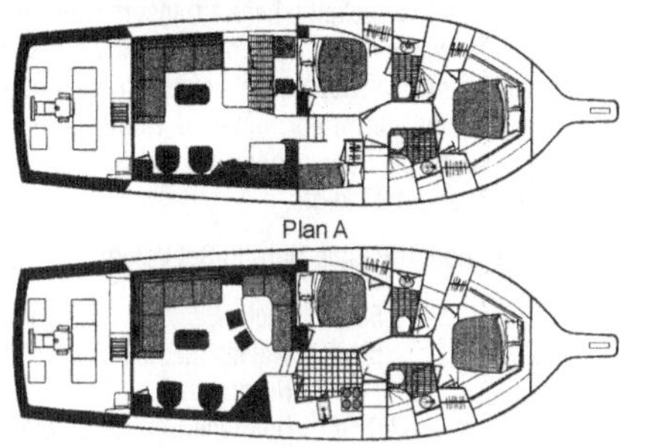
Plan A

Plan B

Replacing the very popular 55 Super Sport in 1991, the 53 Super Sport was built on an all-new Ocean hull design with a sharper entry and slightly increased transom deadrise. The hull changes make the Ocean 53 a generally better headsea boat than her predecessor with a notably drier ride. Several floorplans were offered over the years, and while three-stateroom layouts have been the most popular, a two-stateroom, galley-down version with a dinette delivers an extremely spacious salon. Although the deckhouse dimensions are slightly smaller than the 55 Super Sport model she replaced, there's plenty of room for entertaining, and the luxurious furnishings and teak woodwork create a very inviting atmosphere. A transom door was standard in the cockpit, and the fish box was repositioned behind the chair for improved access to the rudder posts. Competitively priced, additional features include a factory hardtop, a well-arranged (but not overly spacious) engineroom, and cockpit controls. Note the absence of the exterior teak trim seen in most previous Ocean models. Twin 760hp 8V92 Detroits cruise at 26 knots (29–30 top), and optional 820hp MANs (very popular) cruise at a fast 30 knots (33–34 knots top).

See Page 691 For Price Data

Length	53'0"	Fuel	860 gals.
Beam	16'4"	Water	200 gals.
Draft	4'4"	Cockpit	118 sq. ft.
Weight	52,000#	Hull Type	Modified-V
Clearance	16'3"	Deadrise Aft	8°

Ocean 54 Super Sport

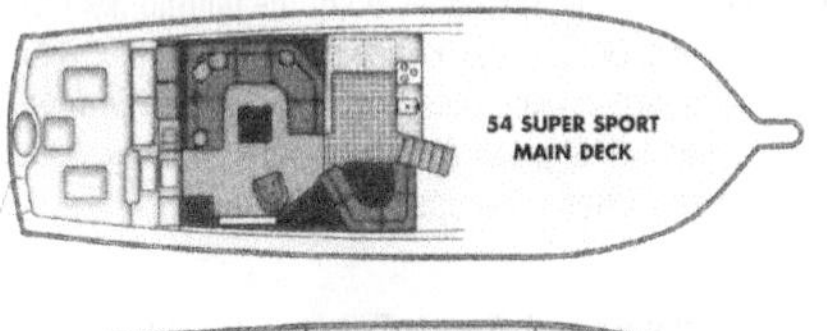

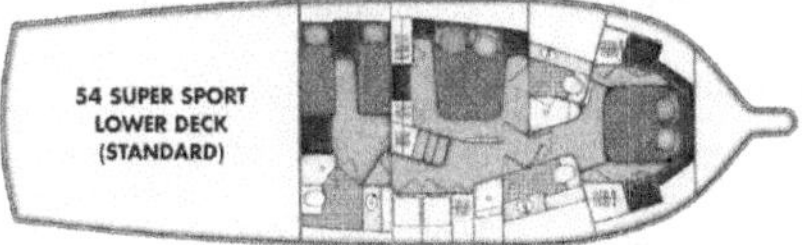

For years, Ocean Yachts has occupied the sweet spot in the super-competitive convertible market—the intersection of muscular styling, lush accommodations, and leading-edge performance. With the 2007 introduction of the 54 Super Sport, Ocean raised the bar for boats in her class by delivering a high-quality yacht with the features and value of larger Ocean models. Below decks, her innovative interior with lacquered cherry joinery features a truly elegant split-level salon dominated by a big U-shaped leather settee to port and a built-in entertainment center opposite. A full-service galley and wraparound dinette are forward, a step above the aft salon. There are three staterooms and three full heads on the lower level including a midship master suite and VIP double forward. Aft and athwart, the crew or second guest stateroom has side-by-side twin berths. A mezzanine deck, with under-sole freezer and engineroom access, overlooks the 54's large cockpit with its standard transom livewell, fresh and raw water washdowns, and insulated fish boxes. Prop pockets in the hull reduce draft and improve running efficiency. MAN 1,0500hp engines cruise at 25 knots (about 30 knots top).

See Page 4691 For Price Data

Length	54'6"	Fuel	1,000 gals.
Beam	16'10"	Water	200 gals.
Draft	4'0"	Waste	50 gals.
Weight	61,000#	Hull Type	Modified-V
Clearance	17'5"	Deadrise Aft	13.5°

Ocean 56 Super Sport

Simply put, the Ocean 56 Super Sport is a downsized version of the popular Ocean 60 Super Sport with slightly reduced cockpit dimensions. The hull is the same (only shortened), the flybridge is identical, and the spacious three-stateroom interior of the 56 Super Sport is a virtual clone of the 60's Plan A. A beautifully styled yacht, the 56 was offered at a surprisingly affordable price compared with others in her class. Belowdecks, the lush interior is a blend of deep-pile carpeting, varnished teak joinery, and designer fabrics. The three-stateroom, three-head floorplan, with its full-beam master stateroom beneath the elevated galley, is as practical as it is innovative. The galley and dinette are a step up from the salon on the deckhouse level, and headroom is a full 6 feet, 5 inches throughout the interior. Even with its reduced size, there's still plenty of fish-fighting space in the cockpit where a transom livewell, tackle center with freezer, washdowns, and rod storage were standard. Topside, the flybridge has a wraparound helm with rod storage and seating for six. A good performer, optional 1,050hp 10-cylinder MAN diesels cruise the 56 Super Sport at a fast 32 knots and deliver a top speed of about 35 knots.

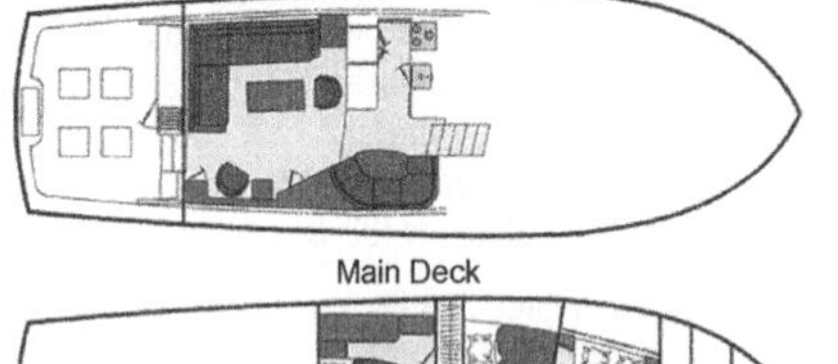

Not Enough Resale Data to Set Values

Length	56'0"	Fuel	900 gals.
Beam	16'10"	Water	220 gals.
Draft	4'5"	Headroom	6'5"
Weight	63,000#	Hull Type	Modified-V
Clearance, Hardtop	16'8"	Deadrise Aft	10°

Ocean 57 Odyssey

Introduced in 2004, the Ocean 57 Odyssey is a reworked version of the Ocean 57 Super Sport with an enclosed bridge, a cruise-friendly cockpit, and a transom storage garage large enough for a 10-foot RIB. Ocean is marketing the Odyssey as a motoryacht, and while her three-stateroom interior is identical to the 57 Super Sport, few would disagree that her accommodations are as luxurious as they are practical. Each stateroom has its own head, and the galley and dinette are forward on the deckhouse level, partially separated from the salon by a cherry-paneled bulkhead. A washer/dryer is standard under the companionway steps forward of the galley. A circular staircase in the salon—and a ladder in the cockpit—provides access to the enclosed flybridge with its L-shaped settee and tinted, wraparound windows. (Note that a second steering station is positioned abaft the pilothouse.) One of the highlights of the 57 Odyssey is her spacious engineroom with its excellent outboard service access and cockpit entry door. A good performer with 1,015hp Cat diesels, the 57 Odyssey will cruise in the mid 20s and reach a top speed of 30+ knots.

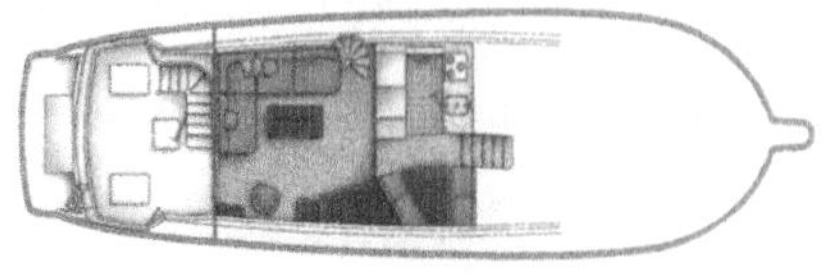

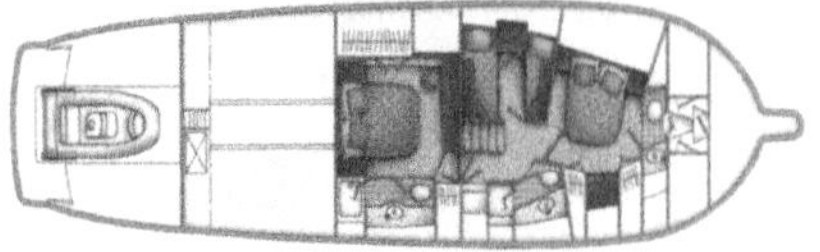

Not Enough Resale Data to Set Values

Length Overall	63'8"	Headroom	6'5"
Beam	16'10"	Fuel	893 gals.
Draft	4'10"	Water	200 gals.
Weight	71,000#	Hull Type	Modified-V
Clearance	17'7"	Deadrise Aft	NA

Ocean 57 Super Sport

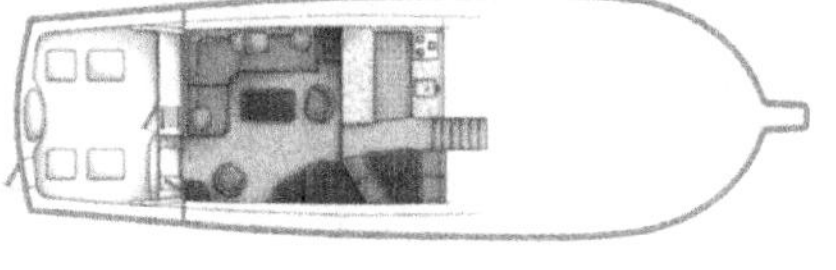

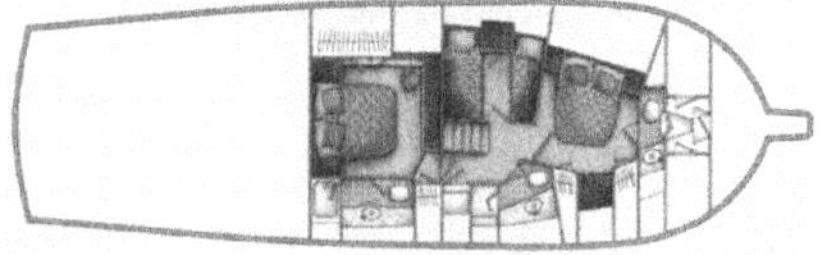

The Ocean 57 Super Sport is an updated version of the Ocean 56 Super Sport (1999–2002) with a reworked running surface, additional transom deadrise, a redesigned helm console, and improved engineroom access. Ocean has built a reputation over the years for delivering a lot of boat for the money, and the 57 offers a compelling blend of luxury and performance in addition to value. Her lush three-stateroom interior—unchanged from the 56 Super Sport—compares well with her more expensive competitors in both design and layout. Like many convertibles her size, the salon is set on two levels with the galley and dinette forward. Both the master and forward guest staterooms have en suite heads, and a washer/dryer is positioned just aft of the day head. The high-gloss cherry woodwork found throughout the 57's interior is remarkably well finished. The cockpit includes all the expected fishing amenities, and there's seating for a small crowd on the huge flybridge. (Note that an enclosed bridge was optional.) Standard 1,015hp Cats cruise at 28–30 knots, and optional 1,300hp Cats cruise in the low 30s and reach 35+ knots top.

Not Enough Resale Data to Set Values

Length	57'0"	Headroom	6'8"
Beam	16'10"	Fuel	1,047 gals.
Draft	4'10"	Water	200 gals.
Weight	66,269#	Hull Type	Modified-V
Clearance	17'5"	Deadrise Aft	14°

Ocean 60 Super Sport

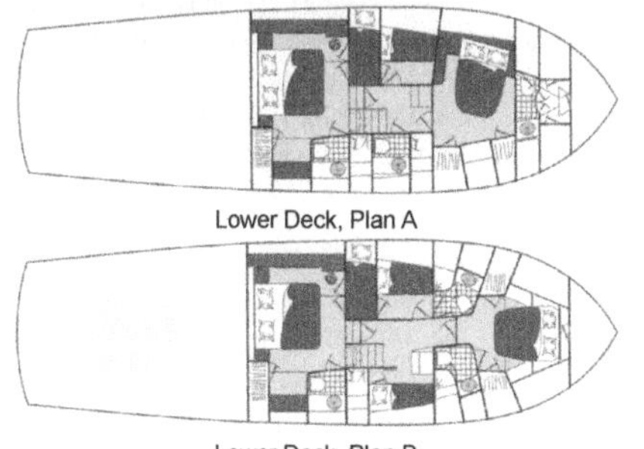

Lower Deck, Plan A

Lower Deck, Plan B

A fast ride, the Ocean 60 Super Sport is an angular, Jersey-style convertible whose rakish styling and lavish accommodations will appeal to upmarket anglers who place a premium on luxury and performance. Like all Ocean designs, the 60 Super Sport rides on an efficient modified-V hull, tapered at the stern with a deep forefoot and plenty of flare at the bow. A pair of floorplans, one with three staterooms and the other with four, were offered in the 60 SS—both sharing the same main deck layout with the dinette and galley a step up from the salon. The lower-level layouts are notable in that both locate the full-width master stateroom aft, beneath the forward part of the salon. A laundry center was standard, and the VIP guest suite in the three-stateroom floorplan is huge. The spacious cockpit of the Ocean 60 came with all of the amenities one expects in a yacht of this type (including direct access to the engineroom), and the large flybridge is designed with wraparound lounge seating, refrigerator, and hardtop. Standard 1,350hp MANs cruise the Ocean 60 Super Sport at an impressive 32 knots and reach a top speed of 35+ knots.

See Page 691 For Price Data

Length	60'0"	Fuel	1,140 gals.
Beam	17'0"	Water	240 gals.
Draft	4'8"	Headroom	6'6"
Weight	72,000#	Hull Type	Modified-V
Clearance	17'0"	Deadrise Aft	10°

Ocean 62 Super Sport

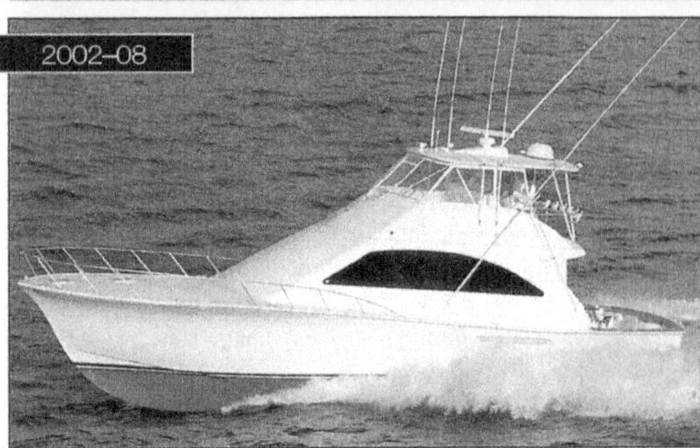

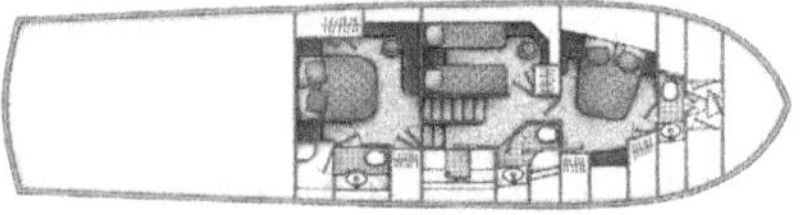

Three Staterooms

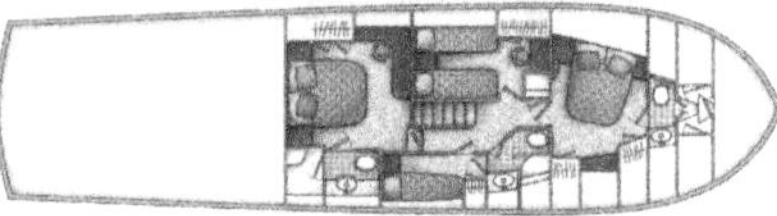

Four Staterooms

Ocean's 62 Super Sport is yet another in the company's series of competitively priced, high-performance sportfishing yachts. Offered with either a closed or open flybridge, she rides on an updated modified-V hull design with more deadrise than previous Ocean models. The 62 Super Sport looks a lot like the Ocean 60 Super Sport (1996–2001), the boat she replaced in the 2002 Ocean lineup, with the same graceful lines and tapered hull shape. The main deck layout is arranged with the galley and dinette forward, a step up from the salon. (Note that in the Enclosed Bridge version, a spiral staircase just aft of the galley leads up to the bridge.) Buyers can choose from three or four staterooms on the lower level. In the three-stateroom version, a laundry room replaces the starboard guest cabin. The cockpit is equipped with port and starboard rod lockers, a transom livewell, in-deck fish boxes, and a bait center with freezer and sink. The standup engineroom, reached from the cockpit, provides good service access to the motors. Twin 1,400hp Cat diesels cruise the 62 Super Sport at a fast 32 knots (about 35 knots top). Optional 1,500hp MTUs will hit 38 knots wide open.

Not Enough Resale Data to Set Values

Length	62'0"	Fuel	1,450 gals.
Beam	17'5"	Water	255 gals.
Draft	5'0"	Waste	100 gals.
Weight	82,000#	Hull Type	Modified-V
Clearance	17'11"	Deadrise Aft	14°

Ocean 65 Odyssey

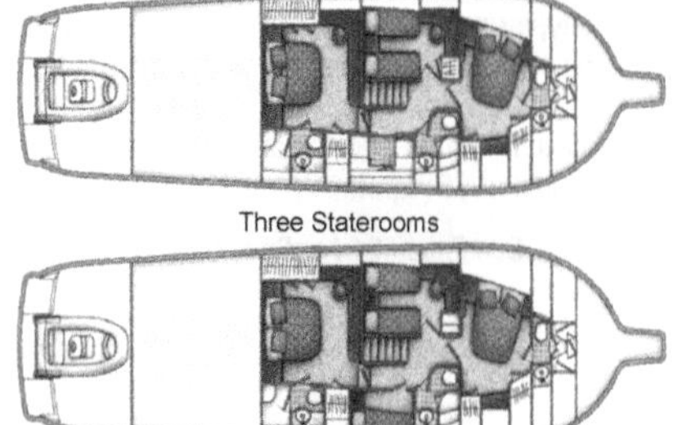

Three Staterooms

Four Staterooms

The Ocean 65 Odyssey is a reworked version of the company's 62-foot Super Sport convertible with an enclosed flybridge, a cruise-friendly cockpit, and a transom storage garage large enough for a 10-foot RIB. Ocean is marketing the Odyssey as a motor yacht, and while her interior is nearly identical to the 62 Super Sport, few would disagree that her accommodations are as luxurious as they are practical. There are four staterooms in the standard layout (including a starboard crew cabin), and both the master and forward VIP staterooms are served with en suite heads. The galley and dinette are forward on the main deck level, separated from the salon by a teak-paneled bulkhead. A circular staircase in the salon—and a ladder in the cockpit—provides access to the enclosed bridge with its dinette, entertainment center, and wraparound windows. (Note that a second steering station is positioned abaft the pilothouse.) Additional features include an extended flybridge platform, spacious engineroom, and molded cockpit seating. A good performer with 1,015hp Cats, the 65 Odyssey will cruise in the mid 20s and reach a top speed of over 30 knots.

Not Enough Resale Data to Set Values

Length Overall	67'6"	Headroom	6'5"
Beam	17'5"	Fuel	1,100 gals.
Draft	5'0"	Water	350 gals.
Weight	87,000#	Hull Type	Modified-V
Clearance, Hardtop	18'1"	Deadrise Aft	12°

Ocean 66 Super Sport

1993–99

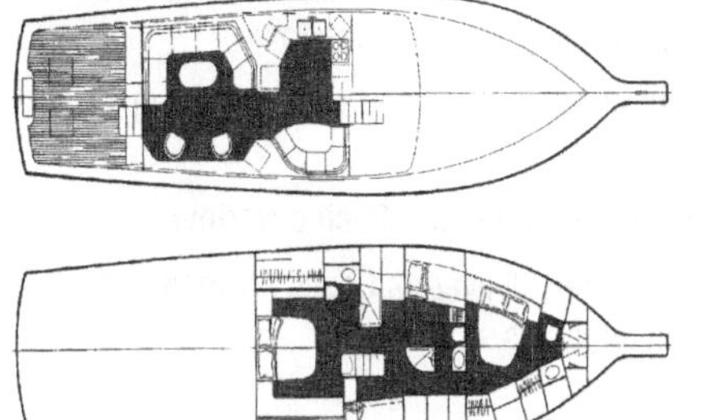

Sportfishing luxury on a grand scale describes the 66 Super Sport, the largest boat in the Ocean fleet during the 1990s and still a handsome yacht today in spite of her age. She's basically an improved (and easier riding) version of the earlier 63 Super Sport with a deeper forefoot, a reshaped transom, additional fuel, and a newly configured flybridge. The 66 is built on a tapered modified-V hull with cored hullsides and a nearly flat 3 degrees of transom deadrise. Belowdecks, her lavish (and innovative) floorplan is arranged with the galley and dinette forward and a step up from the huge salon. There are four staterooms on the lower level with the full-beam master suite located beneath the galley. The cockpit comes with molded tackle centers, cockpit controls, in-deck fish box, and direct engineroom access. Topside, the factory hardtop and built-in radar arch were standard, and the massive flybridge includes three pedestal seats, a wet bar, and lounge seating for a crowd. Additional features include teak covering boards, laundry center with washer/dryer, central vacuum system, and a bow pulpit. Standard 1,040hp 12V-92s cruise the Ocean 66 at 25 knots and deliver a top speed in the high 20s.

See Page 691 For Price Data

Length	66'0"	Fuel	1,400 gals.
Beam	17'8"	Water	300 gals.
Draft	5'0"	Cockpit	135 sq. ft.
Weight	80,000#	Hull Type	Modified-V
Clearance	17'10"	Deadrise Aft	3°

Ocean 70 Super Sport

2000–04

Main Deck (Closed Bridge)

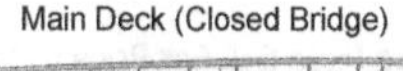

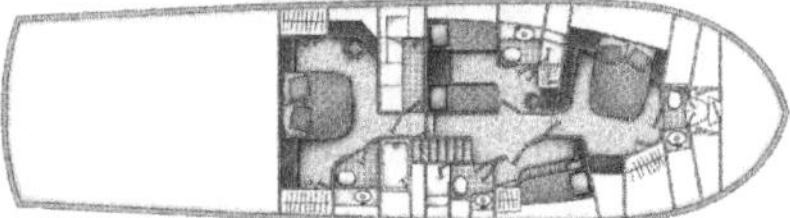

Lower Deck

The Ocean 70 Super Sport was the largest and most luxurious model in the company's history when she was introduced in 2000. She's built on a very beamy modified-V hull with prop pockets (to reduce draft) and more transom deadrise (for a softer ride) than previous Ocean designs. The lavish four-stateroom floorplan of the 70 SS is arranged with the full-beam master stateroom aft, under the galley and dinette area, which is similar to the layouts found in most all of Ocean's latest models. A VIP stateroom is in the forepeak, and a utility room with a washer/dryer and freezer is located between the master stateroom and the second guest cabin. In a practical design touch, the flybridge is reached from either the cockpit or the salon. The cockpit, with over 150 square feet of space, comes with a full complement of fishing amenities. Additional features includes an enclosed flybridge (an open bridge is optional), a bathtub in the master stateroom head, and three guest heads, each with a separate stall shower. An excellent performer, 1,400hp Cats cruise at 28 knots (32–33 knots top), and optional 1,800hp Detroits cruise the 70 SS at a fast 30+ knots.

Not Enough Resale Data to Set Values

Length	70'0"	Fuel	1,865 gals.
Beam	19'8"	Water	370 gals.
Draft	5'0"	Headroom	6'6"
Weight	112,000#	Hull Type	Modified-V
Clearance, Hardtop	18'4"	Deadrise Aft	14°

Ocean Alexander

Quick View

- Ocean Alexander was founded in 1978 by Taiwan businessman Alexander Chueh.
- The company's first boat, a 50-foot pilothouse yacht designed by naval architect Ed Monk, Jr, established the Alexander brand in the U.S. market.
- In the mid 1980s Ocean Alexander launched a series of contemporary motor yachts to meet the growing popularity of pilothouse boats.
- Ocean Alexander is notable in that the company marketed their boats under the company brand. (Note that many Taiwan builders in the 1980s and 1990s sold their boats to various importers who, in turn, marketed them under various names.)
- During the 1980s and 1990s Ocean Alexander directed its efforts to becoming a leader in the pilothouse motoryacht category.
- Ocean Alexander has long enjoyed an enthusiastic market in the Pacific Northwest.
- With over 30 years of experience and 1,500-plus vessels delivered, Ocean Alexander is one of the world's major builders of production motoryachts.

Ocean Alexander Yachts • www.oceanalexander.com

Ocean Alexander 390 Sundeck

1985–99

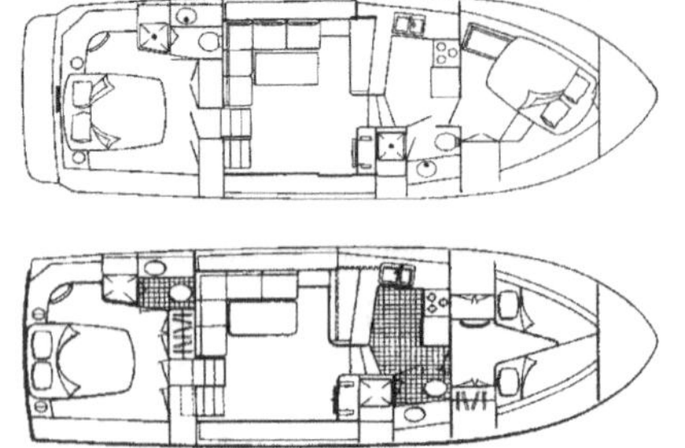

The introduction of the 390 Sundeck in 1986 marked the beginning of what became a successful series of midsize Alexander sundeck models. She was built on a modified-V hull with cored hullsides and a relatively wide beam, and it's worth noting that the 390—like all Alexander yachts of her era—was not an inexpensive boat compared with other Taiwan imports. Belowdecks, her galley-down floorplan is arranged with double berths in both staterooms (V-berths were optional in the bow stateroom), and there are separate stall showers in both head compartments. The salon dimensions are more than adequate for a boat of this size, and the interior was completely finished with handcrafted teak or light oak woodwork. Topside, the helm console is located well forward on the flybridge, and the full-width aft deck is large enough for entertaining a small group of friends. Most 390s were sold with a radar arch and hardtop. Several engine options were offered over the years including 275hp Lehmans, 250hp GMs, 306hp Volvos, and 300hp Cummins. Depending upon the engines, cruising speeds range from 15–17 knots, and top speeds are around 19–21 knots.

See Page 515 For Price Data

Length	39'3"	Fuel	300 gals.
Beam	13'11"	Water	150 gals.
Draft	3'2"	Waste	18 gals.
Weight	24,800#	Hull Type	Modified-V
Clearance	14'0"	Deadrise Aft	12°

Ocean Alexander 420/422 Sport Sedan

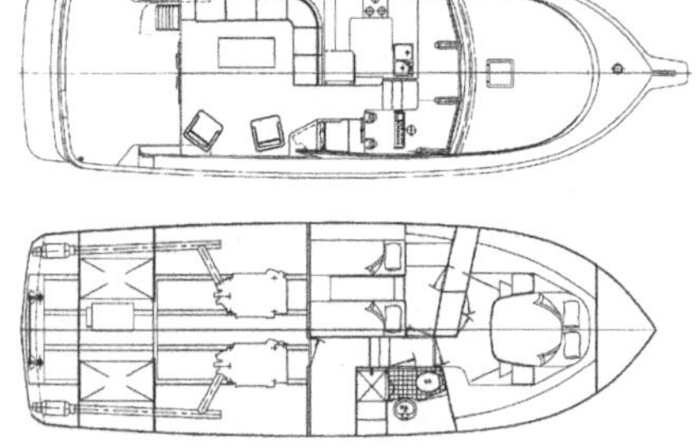

Introduced in 1994 as a replacement for the company's earlier 42 Sedan, the 420 Sport Sedan (called the 422 Sport Sedan in 1996–2001) has a more rakish profile than her predecessor together with a reworked hull bottom with propeller tunnels to reduce draft and shaft angles. From the large cockpit, a pair of sliding glass doors open to the single-level salon where an L-shaped settee is to port and a raised galley forward, opposite the lower helm. Two staterooms and a single head are forward, but in the standard floorplan there is no direct entry to the head from the owner's stateroom—an unusual arrangement in a boat this size. Note the step-down storage room (with an engineroom access door) behind the head compartment. One of the more attractive features of the 420/422 Sport Sedan—or any Ocean Alexander yacht for that matter—is the handcrafted interior teak joinery. From the cockpit, molded steps at the corners lead to the wide side decks and a transom door opens to the swim platform. Among several engine options, twin 375 Cat diesels deliver a cruising speed of 22 knots and a top speed of about 26 knots. More recent models with twin 420hp Cats deliver about the same speeds.

See Page 691 For Price Data

Length	42'0"	Fuel	500 gals.
Beam	14'4"	Water	150 gals.
Draft	3'3"	Headroom	6'4"
Weight	33,100#	Hull Type	Modified-V
Clearance	NA	Deadrise Aft	NA

Ocean Alexander 420/440 Sundeck

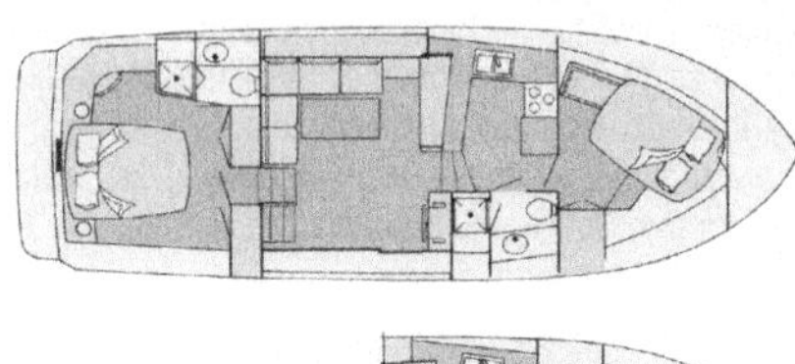

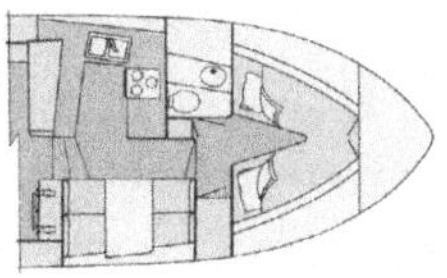

Good-selling models for Ocean Alexander during their production years, the 420 and 440 Sundeck yachts differ only in the larger cockpit dimensions of the 440 model. Both share the same modified-V hull with cored hullsides, a shallow keel and moderate transom deadrise, and both incorporate the sleek European styling characteristics that made Alexander boats so popular during the 1990s. Inside, the two-stateroom, galley-down layout is offered with either an offset double berth or V-berths in the forward stateroom. Both heads are fitted with stall showers, and a lower helm was standard in the salon. The interior woodwork—mostly teak although light oak was occasionally used—is extremely well crafted as it is in all Alexander yachts. The full-width afterdeck can accommodate several deck chairs, and the flybridge is arranged with seating for six. Additional features include a well-organized engine room, hardtop and radar arch, wide side decks, and generous storage. Twin 250hp GM and Cummins engines cruise the 420 or 440 at 15 knots (about 18 knots top), and 350hp or 375hp Cats cruise at 20 knots and reach a top speed of 23–24 knots.

See Page 690 For Price Data

Length, 420	42'3"	Fuel	300 gals.
Length, 440	43'9"	Water	150 gals.
Beam	13'11"	Waste	68 gals.
Draft	3'2"	Hull Type	Modified-V
Weight	27,000#	Deadrise Aft	NA

Ocean Alexander 423 Classico

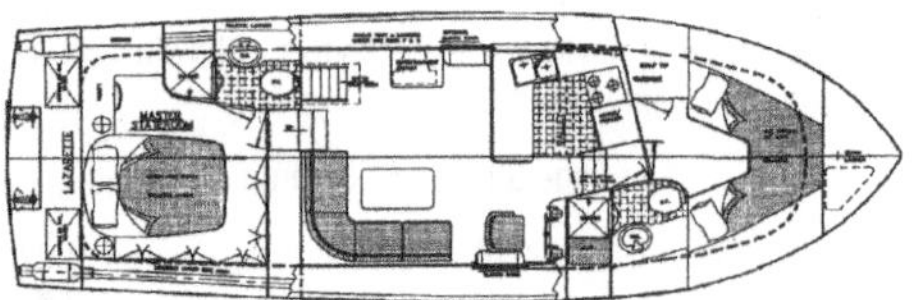

The 423 Classico is a well-crafted cruising yacht with a trunk cabin profile, full walkaround decks, and a straightforward two-stateroom interior layout. For most of the 1990s, Alexander's Classico series of trawler-style yachts appealed to owners who enjoyed the look and feel of a traditional trawler but wanted something better than typical low-speed trawler performance. With her wide beam, the Classico is a roomy boat for her length, and her cutaway keel and prop pockets provide protection for the running gear in the event of grounding. Her stylish profile is accented with a rakish bridge overhang, and the Classico's house is set well forward on the foredeck in order to expand the salon and galley dimensions. The staterooms in the standard floorplan are arranged with V-berths forward and a walkaround queen bed aft. The galley is forward in the salon, and a lower helm and deck access door were standard. Among several engine options, twin 220hp Cummins diesels cruise at an efficient 11 knots (15–16 knots top), and 420hp Cat diesels cruise at 18 knots and reach a top speed of 22–23 knots.

See Page 6916 For Price Data

Length	42'3"	Fuel	550 gals.
Beam	14'8"	Water	160 gals.
Draft	3'10"	Waste	60 gals.
Weight	34,200#	Hull Type	Modified-V
Clearance	NA	Deadrise Aft	10°

Ocean Alexander 426 Classico

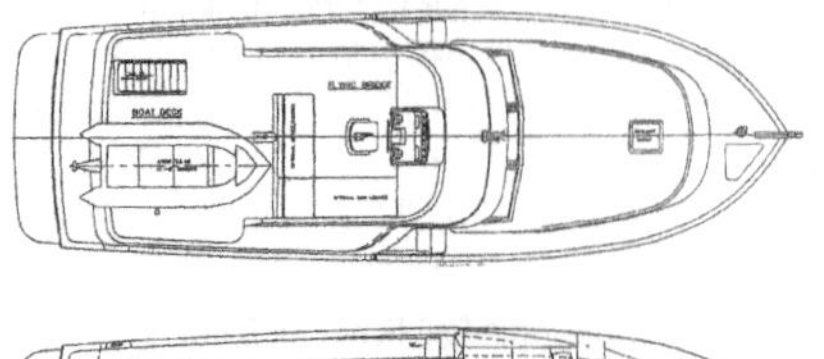

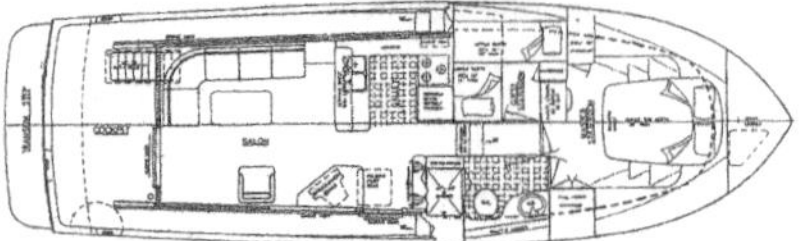

The renewed popularity of trawler-style yachts during the 1990s continued with the introduction of the Alexander's 426 Classico, a stylish sedan cruiser from the design board of the highly regarded Ed Monk, Jr. (Note that she was called the 423 Classico in her first year of production.) She's built on a modified-V hull with a shallow, prop-protecting keel, prop pockets, and a wide beam. Her standard galley-up floorplan includes two staterooms with a centerline queen berth in the owner's cabin and single berths in the guest stateroom. The head comes with a separate stall shower, and a sliding deck door at the lower helm provides convenient access to the foredeck. The salon dimensions of the 426 Classico are quite generous in spite of the wide side decks. In a departure from most sedan layouts, there's a second portside deck door abaft the galley in the salon—a nice touch. Topside, the extended flybridge can accommodate an 11-foot inflatable. Additional features include a full teak interior, radar arch, and a transom door. Twin 220hp Cummins diesels cruise the 426 Classico at an efficient 11 knots and reach 15–16 knots top. Optional 350hp Cats diesels cruise at 17 knots (about 20 knots top).

See Page 691 For Price Data

Length	42'3"	Fuel	600 gals.
Beam	14'8"	Water	200 gals.
Draft	4'0"	Waste	60 gals.
Weight	35,000#	Hull Type	Modified-V
Clearance	12'8"	Deadrise Aft	10°

Ocean Alexander 430/460 Classico MKI

With her stout, ship-like appearance, the Ocean Alexander 430 and 460 Classicos (the 460 has a larger cockpit) project the image of serious bluewater cruisers. Indeed, the 430/460 seem massive compared with other boats their size—an impression heightened by a Portuguese bridge, generous freeboard, and unusually tall bulwarks on either side of the pilothouse. They're built on the same proven hull used in the production of Alexander's 423 and 426 Classico models with soft chines, cored hullsides, and prop pockets. The floorplan is similar to that of many pilothouse designs with the galley in the salon and a midships master stateroom. The spacious full-width salon on the 463/460 is beautifully finished with handcrafted teak joinery, and visibility from the enclosed pilothouse is excellent. On deck, a centerline gate in the Portuguese bridge provides access to the bow, and molded steps on the port side of the pilothouse lead up to the cabintop where a dinghy can be stored. A cockpit storage lazarette, transom door, and a hinged mast with radar platform were standard. Note that a flybridge was optional. Standard 220hp Cummins diesels will provide a cruising speed of 10 knots and a top speed of 13–14 knots.

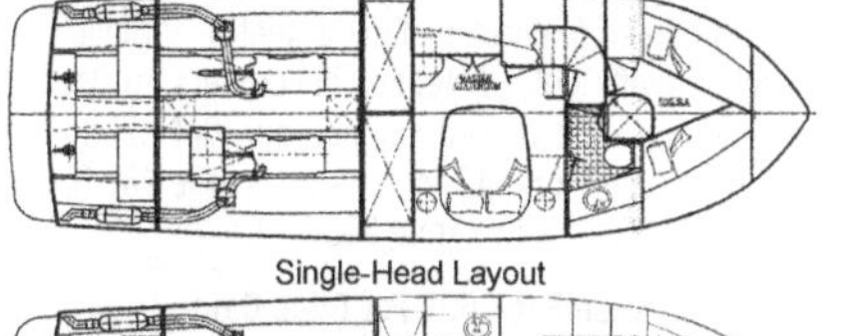

Single-Head Layout

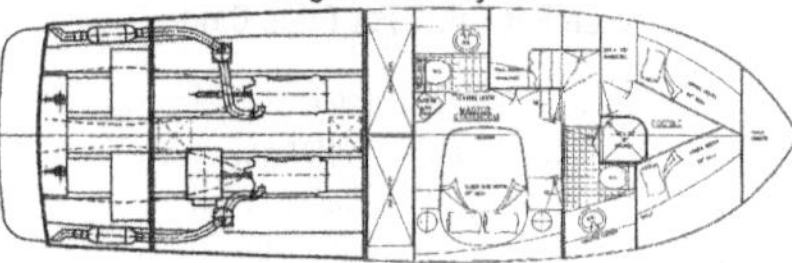

Two-Head Layout

See Page 691 For Price Data

Length, 460	45'8"	Weight, 460	42,500#
Length, 430	43'6"	Fuel	600 gals.
Beam	14'8"	Water	200 gals.
Draft	4'2"	Waste	60 gals.
Weight, 430	38,900#	Hull Type	Semi-Disp.

Ocean Alexander 456 Classico

The Ocean Alexander 456 Classico is a solid, heavily built cruiser whose handsome lines and quality construction made her a popular boat throughout the 1990s. She's built on a beamy semi-displacement hull with cored hullsides and a cutaway keel that protects the running gear. With the house set well forward on the hull, the Classico is a very roomy boat inside. Her two-stateroom interior is arranged in the conventional manner with a centerline queen berth aft, a mid-level galley, and V-berths forward. Both heads have stall showers, and the teak joinery applied throughout the interior is finished to a very high standard. Note the port and starboard deck doors in the salon. Topside, the flybridge comes with L-shaped lounge seating aft of the helm, and there's space for a dinghy on the aft cabintop. The deep, step-down cockpit of the 456 has a transom door—a thoughtful touch. Additional features include a radar arch, full walkaround decks, bow pulpit and swim platform. No lightweight, standard 220 Cummins (or 210hp Cat) diesels cruise the 456 Classico at 10–11 knots and reach a top speed of about 15 knots.

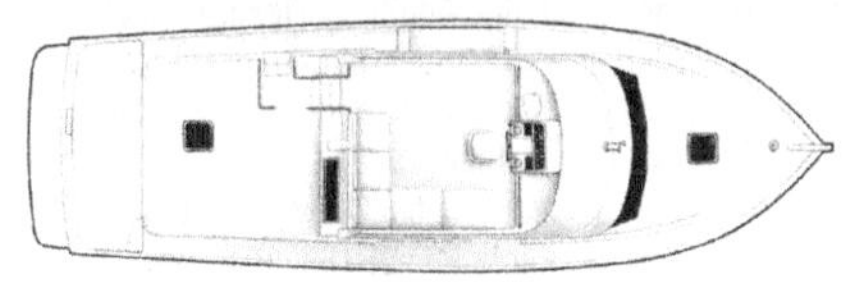

See Page 691 For Price Data

Length	45'6"	Fuel	550 gals.
Beam	15'8"	Water	250 gals.
Draft	4'0"	Waste	40 gals.
Weight	40,000#	Headroom	6'3"
Clearance	12'9"	Hull Type	Semi-Disp.

Ocean Alexander 480 Sport Sedan

1994–2003

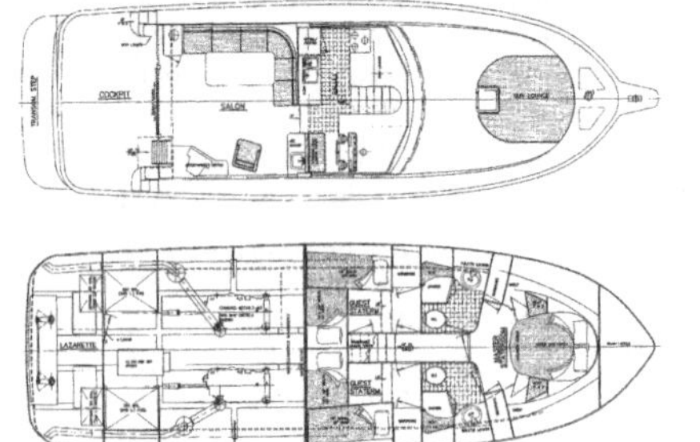

A successful blend of sporty Mediterranean styling and versatile pilothouse accommodations, the 480 Sport Sedan made the cut with yachting enthusiasts drawn to Ocean Alexander's long-standing reputation for quality. She's built on a lightweight semi-V hull with a relatively wide 15'6" beam, balsa-cored hullsides, and propeller pockets—the first (but not the last) Alexander model to incorporate pockets to reduce shaft angles and draft. The split-level salon/pilothouse floorplan of the 480 is arranged with the galley forward, opposite the lower helm position. An L-shaped sectional sofa to port dominates the salon with it's wet bar, entertainment center, and large cabin windows. Note the handsome Burmese teak woodwork. There are three staterooms below including a large master suite forward with island berth, and matching guest staterooms with single berths. Both heads are fitted with separate stall showers. Additional features include a sunken foredeck sun pad, roomy cockpit (with molded steps at the corners for deck access), and a spacious, well-arranged engineroom. Cat 420hp diesels—small engines indeed for a 48-footer—cruise the 480 Sport Sedan at a respectable 20–22 knots (mid 20s top).

See Page 691 For Price Data

Length	48'6"	Fuel	500 gals.
Beam	15'6"	Water	180 gals.
Draft	2'9"	Waste	40 gals.
Weight	36,000#	Hull Type	Modified-V
Clearance	NA	Deadrise Aft	NA

Ocean Alexander 486/510 Classico

1993–2003

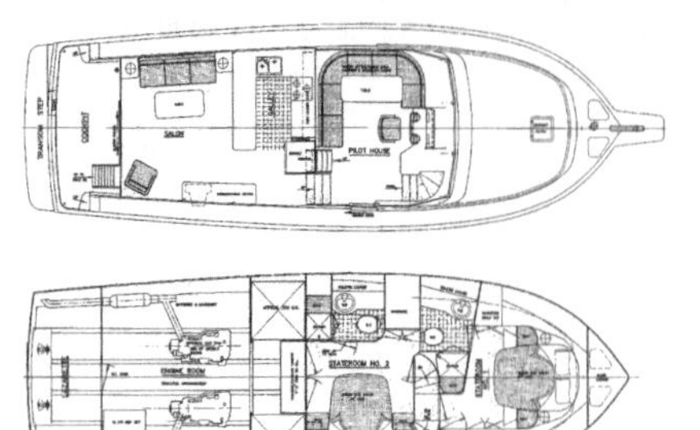

The Ocean Alexander 486 and 510 Classicos (the 510 has a larger cockpit) are a pair of sturdy raised-pilothouse designs with the businesslike appearance of serious Northwest passagemakers. They're heavily built on a modern semi-displacement hull with cored hullsides and a keel deep enough to protect the props—basically a stretched version of the smaller 456 Classico hull. Many pilothouse boats this size have three-stateroom layouts, but the 486/510 has only two, both of which are very spacious (and about equal in size) with walkaround double berths, excellent storage, and roomy heads with separate stall showers. Aft of the pilothouse are the galley and salon with large cabin windows, teak parquet flooring, and sliding glass doors opening to the cockpit. The side decks are wide and well protected, and there's space on the extended flybridge for a dinghy. Additional features include a laundry center in the forward stateroom, pilothouse deck access door, molded flybridge steps, and transom door. Note the handsome teak interior woodwork. A handsome yacht, 420hp (or 450hp) Cat diesels—small engines indeed for a boat this size—cruise either boat at an economical 14–15 knots (about 18 knots top).

Not Enough Resale Data to Set Values

Length, 486	48'0"	Clearance	NA
Length, 510	50'6"	Fuel	700 gals.
Beam	15'8"	Water	260 gals.
Draft	4'0"	Hull Type	Semi-Disp.
Weight	48,000#	Deadrise Aft	NA

Ocean Alexander 51/53 Sedan

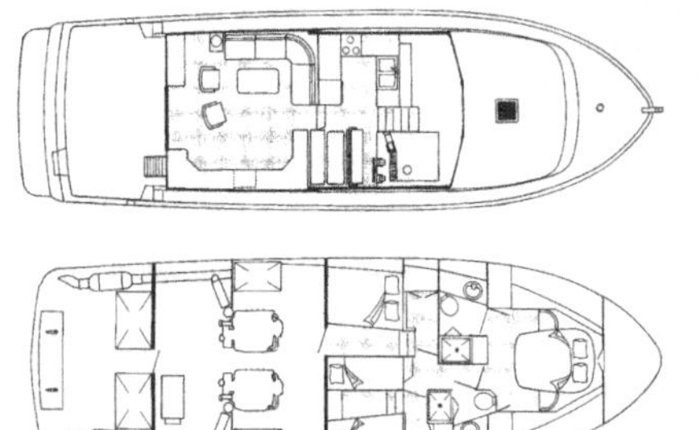

The Ocean Alexander 51/53 is a traditional raised pilothouse motor yacht whose attractive lines and comfortable interior made her a relatively popular model during her production years. Offered in two versions, the 51 Sedan (pictured above) has a conventional squared-off transom, while the 53 model introduced in 1991 has a Euro-style reverse transom that ads an extra two feet to her overall length. Instead of locating the galley on the salon level—the traditional layout in pilothouse floorplans—the 51/53 has the galley to port on the pilothouse level in the European fashion. The result is a huge salon with extravagant entertaining capabilities. The master stateroom is forward in this layout, and both guest cabins are located beneath the pilothouse sole. Additional features include a large cockpit with a transom door, wide side decks, a foredeck sun pad, radar arch, and a spacious flybridge with plenty of guest seating. Early models with 400hp 6V53s cruise the Alexander 51 Sedan at 16 knots (just under 20 knots top). Later models with 550hp 6V92s cruise at about 20 knots, and optional 735hp 8V92s cruise in the mid 20s and reach a top speed in the neighborhood of 28 knots.

Not Enough Resale Data to Set Values

Length, 51	51'1"	Clearance	12'6"
Length, 53	53'0"	Fuel	500 gals.
Beam	16'4"	Water	250 gals.
Draft	3'2"	Waste	60 gals.
Weight	45,500#	Hull Type	Modified-V

Ocean Alexander 52 Sedan

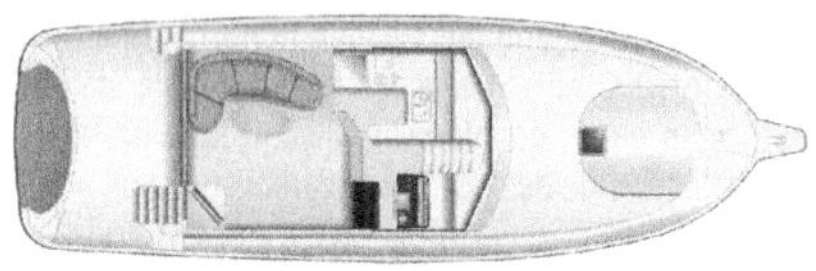

Opt. Lower Helm

Lower Level

Graceful styling and a versatile layout—note the eurostyle reverse transom and extra-large cockpit—characterize the Alexander 52 Sedan, an modern pilothouse yacht from a company known for its world-class products. Like many recent Ocean Alexander designs, the 52 Sedan rides on an efficient low-deadrise hull with generous beam and propeller pockets. The split-level salon/pilothouse floorplan of the 52 is arranged with the galley forward, opposite the U-shaped dinette (or optional lower helm). An L-shaped sectional sofa to port dominates the salon with it's high-gloss woodwork, entertainment center, and large cabin windows. Note the sunburst ceiling panel in the salon overhead. There are three staterooms below including a large master suite forward with island berth, a VIP stateroom to port, and second guest cabin opposite with over/under single berths. Both heads have separate stall showers. The spacious cockpit of the 520—with its teak sole, full wet bar, and molded cockpit steps—is far more spacious that any similar yacht. Wide side decks are a plus, and the swim platform has port and starboard entry gates. Yanmar 480hp diesels cruise at 20 knots (low 20s top).

Not Enough Resale Data to Set Values

Length	52'0"	Fuel	600 gals.
Beam	15'6"	Water	180 gals.
Draft	4'0"	Waste	40 gals.
Weight	36,000#	Hull Type	Modified-V
Clearance	NA	Deadrise Aft	10°

Ocean Alexander 520/540 Pilothouse

The Alexander 520 and 540 Pilothouse are basically the same boat—the 520 has a conventional transom and the 540 has a Euro-style reverse transom which adds some pizzazz to her appearance. They're built on a modified-V hull with cored hullsides, moderate beam, and a shallow keel for directional stability. Several floorplans were available in the 520/540 over the years. The original three-stateroom interior has the master suite forward, and an alternate two-stateroom layout (available in more recent models) has the master stateroom amidships. Either way, the galley is forward in the salon, and the raised pilothouse is arranged with a centerline helm, direct flybridge access, and port and starboard deck doors. The cockpit of the 520/540—partially shaded by a bridge overhang—is large enough for casual entertaining and comes with a transom door for easy water access. Additional features include a huge flybridge with dinghy storage, wide side decks, well-crafted teak interior woodwork, and excellent storage. Among several engine options, twin 425hp Cats (or 440hp Yanmar) diesels cruise at 15–16 knots and reach a top speed of just under 20 knots.

Three Staterooms

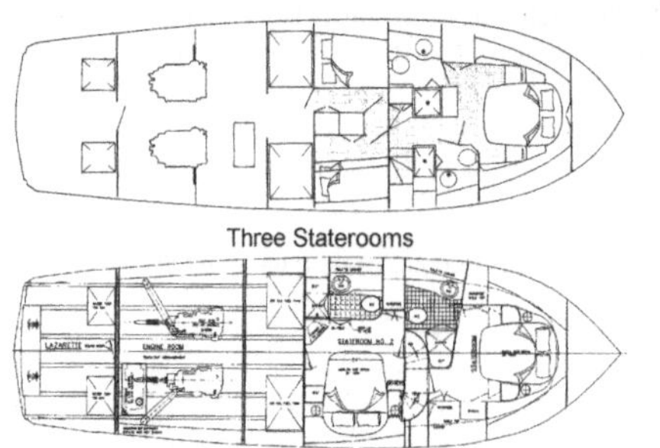

Two Staterooms

Not Enough Resale Data to Set Values

Length	52'5"	Fuel	600 gals.
Beam	15'6"	Water	300 gals.
Draft	4'7"	Waste	40 gals.
Weight	41,500#	Headroom	6'4"
Clearance	14'0"	Hull Type	Modified-V

Ocean Alexander 546 Yachtfisher

The Alexander 546 Yachtfisher is a modern tri-level cockpit yacht who's versatile layout and spacious accommodations are well suited for cruising and entertaining. There's much to like about the 546: The styling is crisp; workmanship is world-class; and her Monk-designed hull is a model of weight-efficient construction. Introduced on a limited-production basis in 1995, the Yachtfisher's luxurious three-stateroom interior boasts a full-beam main salon with deluxe wet bar, entertainment center, and flybridge access stairs. Forward, three steps down from the salon, is a home-size galley (with tremendous storage), L-shaped dinette, and lower helm. The huge master stateroom is entered from the aft end of the galley and features a king-size berth, vanity with swivel chair, and generous storage. The forward VIP stateroom is also very spacious, while the second guest cabin to port is fitted with over/under single berths. All three heads have separate stall showers. Note the Corian galley counters, hardwood flooring, and walk-in engineroom. Wide side decks and a cavernous cockpit lazarette are a plus. Detroit 6V-92 625hp (or Cat 660hp) diesels cruise at 14–15 knots (around 18 knots top).

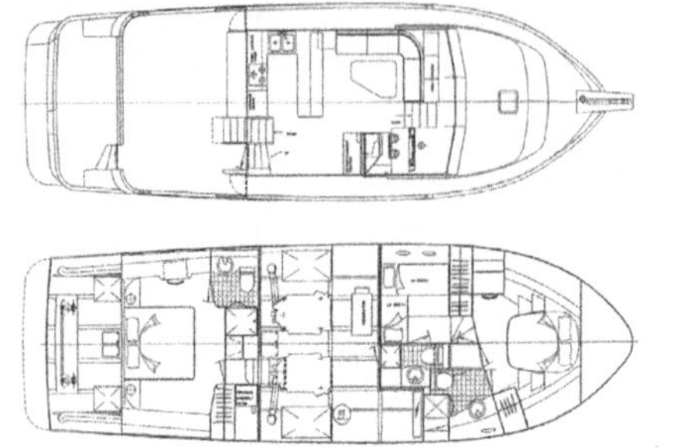

Not Enough Resale Data to Set Values

Length w/Pulpit	55'10"	Fuel	700 gals.
Beam	16'4"	Water	240 gals.
Draft	4'1"	Waste	75 gals.
Weight	49,000#	Hull Type	Modified-V
Clearance, Arch	25'0"	Deadrise Aft	NA

Ocean Alexander 548 Pilothouse

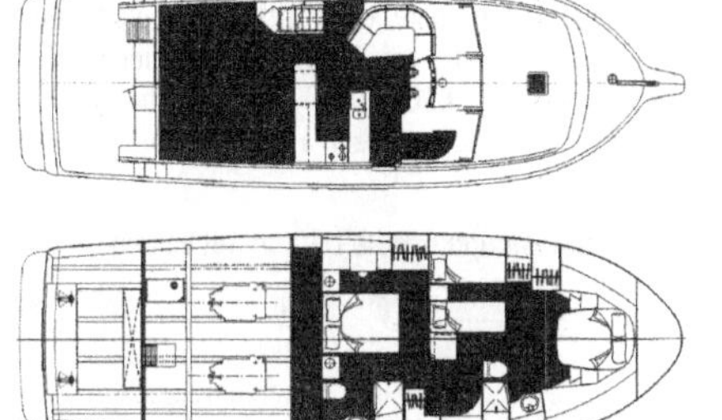

An imposing yacht with world-class amenities, the Alexander 548 will appeal to upscale buyers looking for a heavily built long-range cruiser from a top-tier builder. A broad 17'6" beam provides this yacht with a tremendous amount of living space. Her split-level interior begins with a spacious salon with sectional sofa, wet bar, entertainment center, and high-gloss teak paneling and cabinets. The pilothouse, three steps up from the salon, boasts a large U-shaped galley with granite counters, side-by-side refrigerator and garbage disposal, circular dinette forward, and a centerline helm position with excellent outside visibility. Note the inside flybridge steps aft of the dining area—a feature not always found in a boat this size. There are three staterooms and two full heads below including an opulent master with king-size berth, and an equally impressive VIP stateroom forward with queen berth. Note the spacious walk-in engineroom with standing headroom. Wide side decks and a large cockpit with transom door and lazarette storage under are a plus. Detroit 485hp Detroit 6-71 diesels deliver a cruising speed of 18 knots (22–23 knots top). Later versions with twin 660hp Cats cruise at 20 knots.

Not Enough Resale Data to Set Values

Length	55'7"	Fuel	1,000 gals.
Beam	17'6"	Water	260 gals.
Draft	4'0"	Waste	80 gals.
Weight	52,000#	Headroom	6'5"
Clearance	NA	Hull Type	Modified-V

Ocean Alexander 58/64 Pilothouse

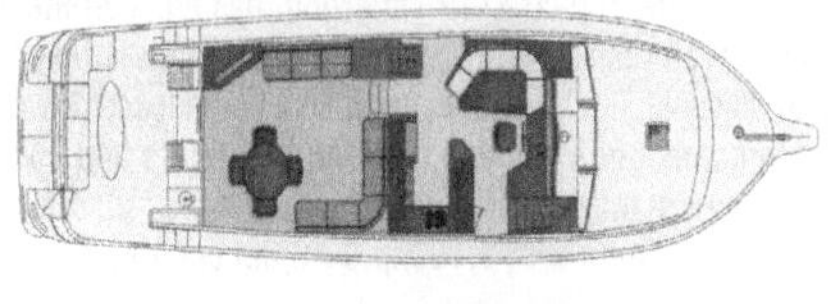

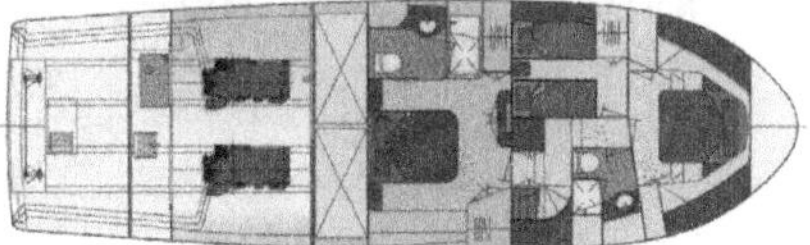

A successful model for Ocean Alexander, the 58/64 Pilothouse combines the sleek styling and executive-class accommodations one expects in a modern, high-end luxury yacht. She's called the 58/64 Pilothouse because two transom configurations were offered: one with an integral swim platform, and the other with a Eurostyle transom with port and starboard curved stairways to the platform, a larger cockpit, and a longer bridge overhang. Built on a semi-V hull with a nearly full-length keel and propeller pockets, the 58/64's lavish three-stateroom interior is an impressive blend of high-gloss woodwork, designer fabrics, and premium furnishings. The galley and dinette are on the pilothouse level, forward of the spacious salon with its Ultraleather seating, built-in entertainment center, and formal dining area. A utility room with washer/dryer is positioned between the master stateroom and standup engineroom. On deck, the spacious cockpit of the Alexander 64 is shaded by a bridge overhang. Full walkaround side decks with high bulwarks make getting around easy. Note the large cockpit lazarette. Caterpillar 800hp (or MTU 825hp) diesels cruise the 58/64 Pilothouse at 20 knots (low 20s top).

Not Enough Resale Data to Set Values

Length w/Pulpit	64'3"/69'8"	Fuel	1,000/1,500 gals.
Beam	17'6"	Water	260/300 gals.
Draft	4'0"	Waste	100 gals.
Weight	69,500/73,500#	Hull Type	Semi-Disp.
Clearance	NA	Deadrise Aft	NA

Ocean Alexander 610 Pilothouse

1997–2002

A stretched version of the Ocean Alexander 548, the Ocean Alexander 610 is a contemporary pilothouse design whose handsome lines and quality workmanship are an easy match for most of her high-style European counterparts. Built on a modified-V hull with a shallow keel and prop pockets, the three-stateroom floorplan of the Ocean Alexander 610 will appeal to those who dislike the sunken galleys, small heads, and cramped enginerooms of most European designs. Because the galley and dinette are forward on the deckhouse level, the salon of the 610 is very expansive indeed. The pilothouse is three steps up from the salon and comes with a centerline helm, direct bridge access, and port and starboard deck doors. Typical of all Ocean Alexander products, the interior teak joinery is finished to high standards. Additional features include a spacious engineroom with near standing headroom, underwater exhausts, a teak cockpit sole, radar arch, bow pulpit, and a large flybridge with seating for a small crowd. No racehorse, twin 735hp 8V-92 Detroit diesels (or 660hp Cats) will cruise the 610 Pilothouse at a respectable 20 knots and reach a top speed of 22–23 knots.

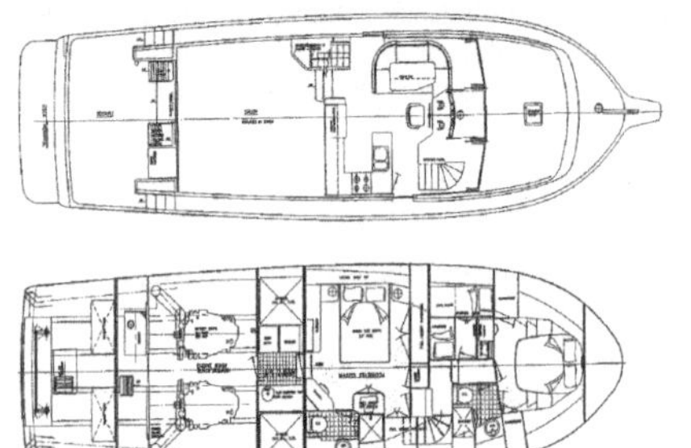

Not Enough Resale Data to Set Values

Length	61'0"	Fuel	1,000 gals.
Beam	17'6"	Water	300 gals.
Draft	4'0"	Headroom	6'9"
Weight	69,300#	Hull Type	Modified-V
Clearance	NA	Deadrise Aft	NA

Ocean Alexander 74 Motor Yacht

2007–11

The seductive Alexander 74 is a premium blend of tasteful styling, spacious accommodations, and state-of-the-art construction. Ocean Alexander has pretty much set the standard in recent years for motoryachts in this size range. In the case of the 74, her lavish three-stateroom (plus crew quarters) layout takes pilothouse luxury to the next level. The interior is finished in high-gloss varnished wood with leather-upholstered seating. The salon is large and roomy with satin-finished cherry cabinets, a large settee area, and custom entertainment center. A "powder room" head is to port going forward to the pilothouse. The galley is larger—and probably better equipped—than those of most homes. Below, the full-beam master suite has an island king bed, vanity, and his-and-hers heads with a common stall shower. The guest stateroom has twin beds, and the forward VIP stateroom has a centerline queen. The cockpit features two small settees to port and starboard, each with a small cocktail table. Between them a hatch leads down to the crew accommodations and engineroom. Stabilizers and bow/stern thrusters were standard. A Skylounge model was also available. Cruise at 16–18 knots with 1,100hp C-18 Cat engines.

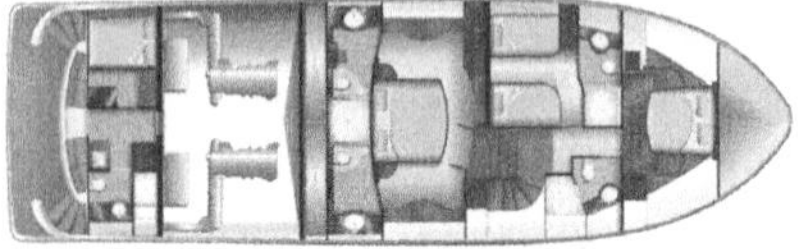

Not Enough Resale Data to Set Values

Length	77'6"	Fuel	2,000 gals.
Beam	20'0"	Water	350 gals.
Draft	5'11"	Waste	200 gals.
Weight	144,000#	Hull Type	Semi-Disp.
Clearance	NA	Deadrise Aft	NA

Offshore Yachts

Quick View

- The Offshore Yachts story dates back to 1948 when company founder Richard Hunt built his first laminated fiberglass pleasure boat.
- In the 1950s, Hunt pioneered in fiberglass boat manufacturing in the U.S. Navy before developing his own line of fiberglass cruisers.
- In 1984, naval architect William Crealock produced hull designs for a new generation of Offshore cruising yachts.
- Offshore Yachts became well known during the 1980s for its popular 48 Yachtfisher, a Crealock-designed cruiser built in Taiwan.
- Distributed in the U.S. by Offshore West in California, Offshore Yachts offers a full line of well-regarded cruising yachts, 52' to 90' in length.

Offshore Yachts • www.offshorewest.com

Offshore 48 Pilothouse

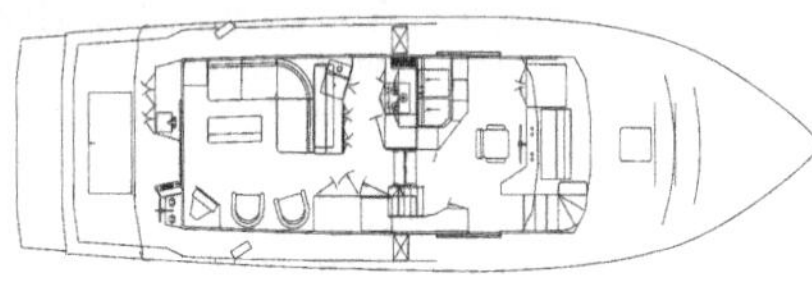

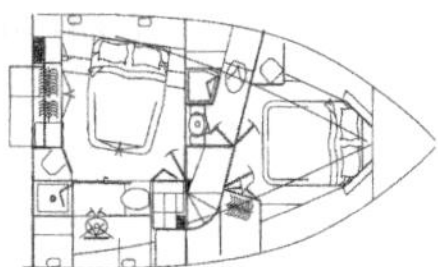

Designed by well-known naval architect William Crealock, the Offshore 48 Pilothouse is an outstanding blend of traditional lines, comfortable accommodations, and efficient open-water performance. Offshore's trademark full walkaround decks are evident in the 48, as are the large, low windows for good sit-down visibility from the pilothouse. Built on a smooth-riding semi-V hull with a shallow keel, the two-stateroom interior of the Offshore 48 provides comfort and privacy for both owners and guests. The galley is located on the salon level, and the pilothouse is arranged with a centerline helm, sliding deck doors, and a stairway to the flybridge. Hatches in the both the galley and cockpit floors provide access to the engineroom. The handcrafted teak joinery, quality hardware, and durable fabrics used throughout the interior reflect the high level of workmanship seen in all Offshore models. Topside, the flybridge is designed with the helm forward and lounge seating aft. A radar arch, bow pulpit, and swim platform were standard. Standard 420hp Cat diesels cruise the Offshore 48 Pilothouse at a sedate 16 knots and reach a top speed of 19–20 knots.

See Page 691 For Price Data

Length	48'6"	Fuel	600 gals.
Beam	15'6"	Water	300 gals.
Draft	4'4"	Waste	50 gals.
Weight	47,000#	Hull Type	Modified-V
Clearance	NA	Deadrise Aft	11°

Offshore 48 Sedan

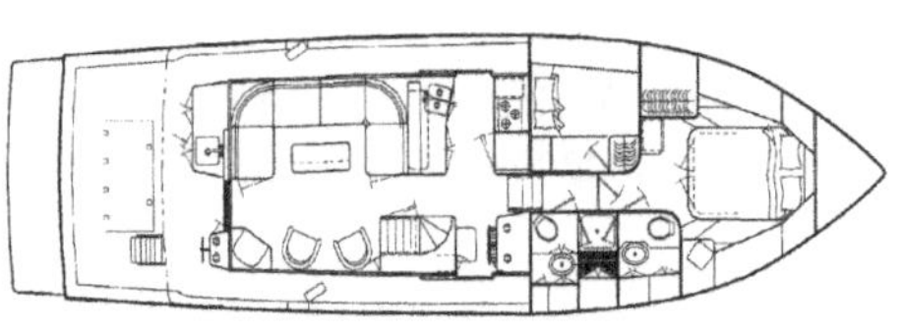

The Offshore 48 Sedan is a distinctive and well-conceived sedan with several features of interest to experienced cruisers. While she's not designed with the mega-volume interior found in some other yachts her size, the Offshore does place a priority on outdoor recreation as her generous deck areas suggest. Not only are the walkarounds wide and the cockpit spacious, but the flybridge dimensions are extremely generous for a 48-footer. Constructed on a modified-V hull with balsa coring from the waterline up, the interior is arranged with the salon and galley on the same level. A stairway abaft the lower helm leads up to the bridge, and two staterooms and two heads are forward. Varnished teak woodwork and trim are used throughout, and the wrap-around cabin windows make the salon seem more expansive than it really is. Flybridge overhangs provide weather protection for the cockpit and side-deck walkways. Among several diesel options, 375hp Cats cruise the Offshore 48 at 16 knots (about 20 knots top), and later models with the 420hp Cats will run a knot or so faster.

See Page 691 For Price Data

Length	48'6"	Fuel	600 gals.
Beam	15'6"	Water	300 gals.
Draft	3'6"	Waste	50 gals.
Weight	41,500#	Hull Type	Modified-V
Clearance	15'2"	Deadrise Aft	11°

Offshore 48 Yachtfish

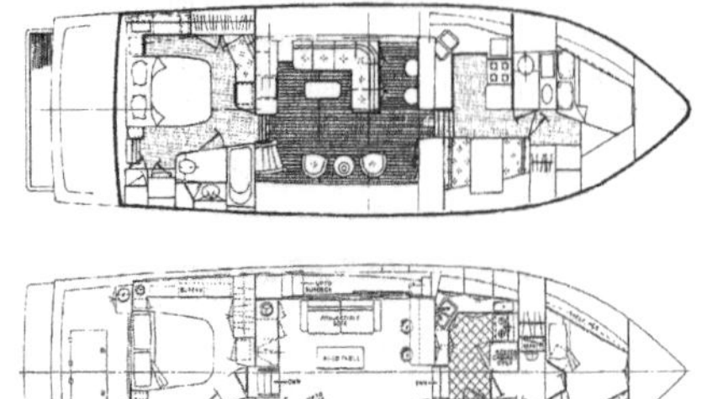

The Offshore 48 Yachtfisher (built by Tung Hwa in Taiwan) is a traditional double-cabin design with a trawler-style appearance and a practical cruising layout. Her low-freeboard modified-V hull is cored from the chine up, and her 15-foot, 6-inch beam is about average for a boat this size. Inside, the 48's two-stateroom, galley-down floorplan was available with or without a salon dinette. A serving counter overlooks the galley, and the wide-open salon seems big for a boat this size. Additional features include a full teak interior, deck doors port and starboard in the salon, and an entryway door from the cockpit to the aft cabin—a convenient feature. The walkaround side decks are quite wide and protected with raised bulwarks. Although she's called a Yachtfisher, the cockpit is too small for any serious fishing and is better suited for boarding and swimming. The full-width aft deck overlooks the cockpit, and the flybridge is arranged with the helm forward and lounge seating aft. Among several diesel options, 375hp Cats cruise the Offshore 48 at 16 knots (about 20 knots top), and later models with 435hp Cats cruise at around 18 knots. A popular boat, over 140 are said to have been built.

See Page 691 For Price Data

Length	48'3"	Fuel	600 gals.
Beam	15'6"	Water	300 gals.
Draft	3'6"	Headroom	6'4"
Weight	41,000#	Hull Type	Modified-V
Clearance	15'2"	Deadrise Aft	11°

Offshore 52 Sedan

An ideal cruising yacht for those who appreciate the versatility of a sedan layout, the Offshore 52 Sedan combines a spacious interior and an efficient, seakindly hull in what most observers will agree is a handsome, well-finished yacht. Built in Taiwan, her modified-V hull incorporates a very wide 16-foot, 10-inch beam with a cutaway keel and generous flare at the bow. Below, her three-stateroom floorplan is arranged with the galley forward in the salon, opposite the lower helm. (Note the sliding deck door in the galley—very convenient for bringing provisions aboard.) A salon stairway abaft the lower helm provides access to the flybridge, and solid teak cabinets, a teak-and-holly cabin sole, and vinyl overheads highlight the interior. Two of the three staterooms are fitted with double berths, and both heads have separate stall showers. Additional features include a good-size cockpit with transom door and storage bins, wide side decks, a large engine room, and a spacious flybridge with room for a dinghy. A modest performer, twin 485hp 6-71 Detroits cruise the 52 Sedan at 14–15 knots and reach about 18 knots top. Later models with 450hp Cummins—or 435hp Cats—will cruise at similar speeds.

Standard 3-Stateroom Layout

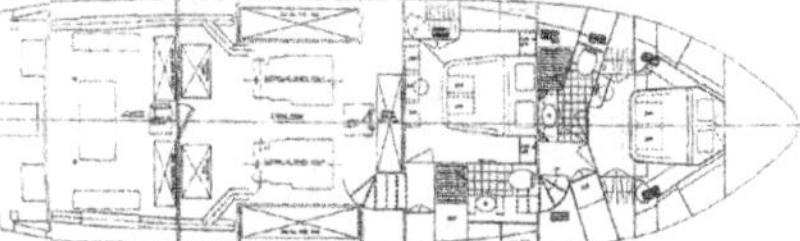
Optional 2-Stateroom Layout

Not Enough Resale Data to Set Values

Length	52'0"	Fuel	700 gals.
Beam	16'10"	Water	400 gals.
Draft	3'10"	Waste	50 gals.
Weight	52,000#	Hull Type	Modified-V
Clearance	NA	Deadrise Aft	12°

Offshore 52/54 Pilothouse

A handsome profile and a superb cruising layout characterize the Offshore 54 Pilothouse, a well-built Taiwan import designed by highly regarded naval architect William Crealock. She's built on a low-deadrise semi-V hull with cored hullsides, generous beam, and a long, prop-protecting keel. While a two-stateroom floorplan is available, the three-stateroom arrangement has proven the more popular. In this layout, each cabin is completely private; the owner's stateroom is accessed from the salon, and the guest stateroom is reached from the pilothouse. The dinette is on the pilothouse level where port and starboard sliding doors provide easy deck access and a ladder leads up to the flybridge. The grain-matched teak interior of the Offshore 54 is exceptional. Note that bridge overhangs shelter the cockpit as well as the wide side decks. Additional features include cockpit access to the engineroom, a large flybridge with dinghy storage, a cockpit transom door, and a radar arch. Twin 450hp Cummins diesels cruise the 54 Pilothouse at 14 knots (18 knots top), and later models with 660hp Cats cruise at 18 knots. The Offshore 52 Pilothouse is the same boat with a traditional transom.

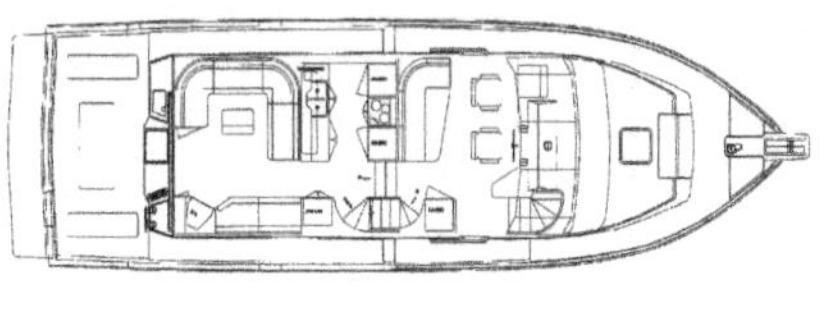

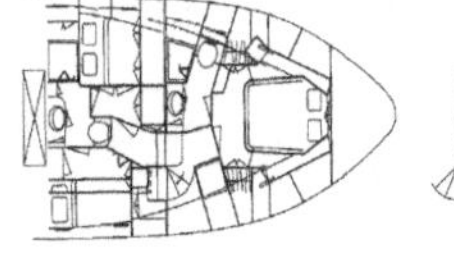

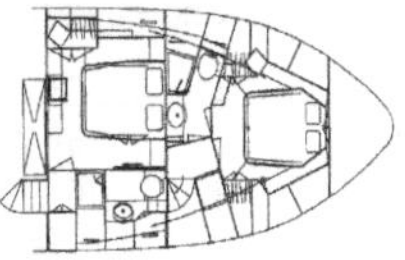

Not Enough Resale Data to Set Values

Length, 52	56'3"	Fuel	1,000 gals.
Length, 54	57'3"	Water	300 gals.
Beam	15'10"	Waste	70 gals.
Draft	4'1"	Hull Type	Modified-V
Weight	57,000#	Deadrise Aft	12°

Offshore 55/60 Pilothouse

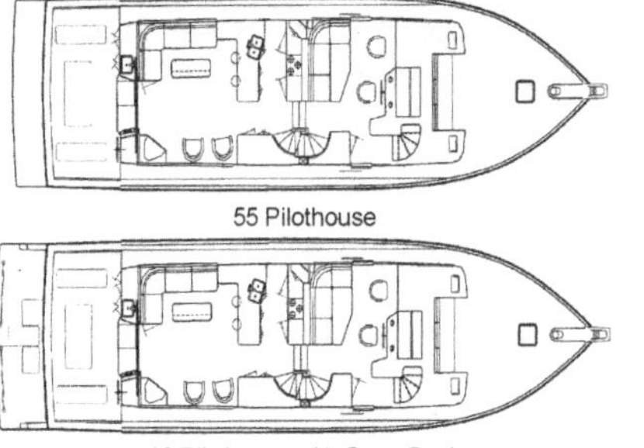

55 Pilothouse

60 Pilothouse with Sport Deck

Pilothouse yachts have a strong following in the Pacific Northwest where the advantages of an inside helm can be appreciated year-round. The Offshore 55 Pilothouse and her more recent sistership, the Offshore 60 Pilothouse (introduced in 1998), differ only in the 60's extended transom platform and increased fuel capacity. These are highly finished yachts, built in Taiwan and designed for yachtsmen who value substance over glitz. The three-stateroom interior of the 55/60 is arranged with the pilothouse three steps up from the salon. The master suite is reached from a private salon staircase, while another staircase from the pilothouse leads to a foyer with a concealed washer/dryer. The galley is forward of the salon, and solid teak cabinetry, quality furnishings, and vinyl overheads highlight the interior. Flybridge overhangs shade the wide side decks and much of the cockpit, and the extended swim platform of the 60 is ideal for water activities. Early models with 485hp Detroit 6-71s cruise the Offshore at 16–17 knots (about 19 knots top), and later models with 660hp Cats cruise at a leisurely 20 knots and reach a top speed in the low 20s.

Not Enough Resale Data to Set Values

Length, 55	55'0'	Weight, 60	63,000#
Length, 60	59'6"	Fuel, 55	700 gals.
Beam	16'10"	Fuel, 60	1,000 gals.
Draft	5'0"	Water	400 gals.
Weight, 55	61,500#	Hull Type	Modified-V

Offshore 58/62 Pilothouse

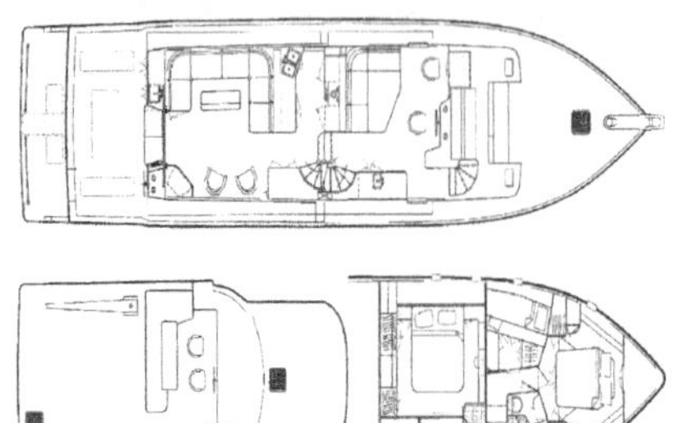

The Offshore 58 Pilothouse and her sistership, the 62 Pilothouse, are a pair of luxurious cruising yachts whose only difference is the extended swim platform of the 62. With a seakindly hull and a comfortable three-stateroom interior, the 58/62 offers all of the features one associates with traditional cruising elegance. A low silhouette, a wide beam and a low center of gravity give the Offshore a notably stable ride, while the hull's deep forefoot reduces pounding in a headsea. Below, the roomy pilothouse is open to the main salon, and the lack of bulkheads between these areas—together with the large windows—make for an expansive interior. The full-beam master stateroom, accessed by an amidships stairwell, features a king-size bed and an entertainment center. The engineroom is reached from a hatch in the cockpit, and flybridge overhangs protect the wide side decks. Additional features include teak interior joinery, twin pilothouse deck doors, and flybridge dinghy storage. Early models with 550hp 6V92s cruise at a modest 15 knots (17–18 knots top), and later models with 800hp Cats cruise at 18 knots (20–21 knots top).

Not Enough Resale Data to Set Values

Length, 58	58'0"	Fuel	1,000 gals.
Length, 62	62'6"	Water	400 gals.
Beam	16'10"	Waste	85 gals.
Draft	4'8"	Hull Type	Modified-V
Weight	65,000#	Deadrise Aft	12°

Phoenix

Quick View

- Phoenix Marine began production in 1977 with the introduction of the Phoenix 29 Convertible.
- The line quickly expanded over the years, and by the late 1980s Phoenix manufactured a series of Jim Wynne-designed models from 27 to 38 feet in length.
- The economic recession of the early 1990s—together with the ill-fated 10 percent luxury tax imposed on boats costing over $100,000—took its toll on Phoenix Marine, and the company went into bankruptcy in 1994.
- Following a brief period of ownership by American Marine Holdings (which owned Pro-Line and Donzi Marine), Phoenix was purchased in 2000 by Ft. Lauderdale-based Jupiter Marine.
- The Phoenix brand was retired by Jupiter in 2001.

No longer in business.

Phoenix 27 Tournament

Built on the same hull as the Phoenix 27 Weekender (1979–94), the 27 Tournament is a traditional raised-deck express with a clean and uncluttered fishing layout. She's built on a beamy deep-V hull with prop pockets and a steep 21 degree of transom deadrise. Her bi-level cockpit eliminates the engine boxes found in the Weekender while providing much-improved helm visibility. Belowdecks, the cabin accommodations are centered around a convertible dinette forward and a small galley to port. There's standing headroom in the head, and the interior is tastefully finished with teak trim and off-white mica laminates. Additional features include a molded bow pulpit, transom door and gate, an in-deck fish box, raw water washdown, lockable rod storage under the cockpit coaming, and good access to the engines. Among several gas and diesel engine options offered over the years, a pair of 260hp gas engines cruise at 23 knots cruise (29–30 knots top), and Volvo 200hp diesels cruise at 25 knots and top out at just under 30 knots. Twin 250hp outboards cruise at 25 knots and reach a top speed of around 40 knots.

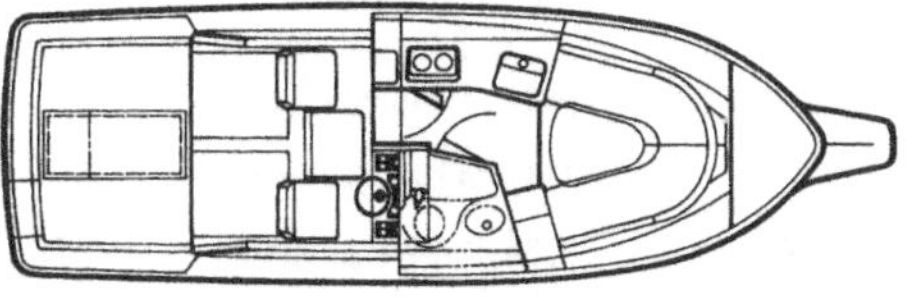

See Page 692 For Price Data

Length w/Pulpit	30'3"	Clearance	7'6"
Hull Length	27'3"	Fuel	220 gals.
Beam	9'10"	Water	24 gals.
Draft	2'0"	Hull Type	Deep-V
Weight	8,200#	Deadrise Aft	20°

Phoenix 29 SFX Convertible

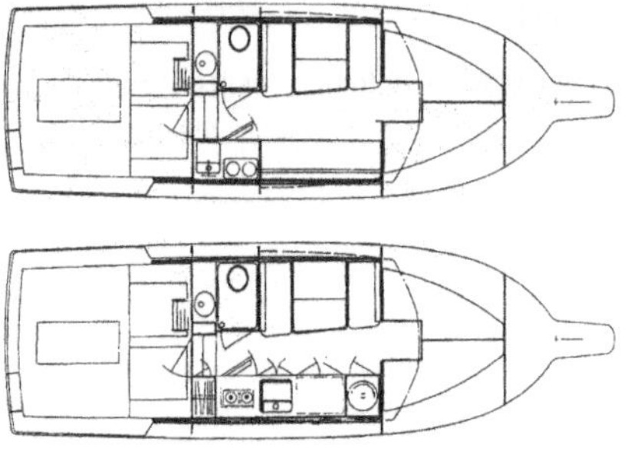

The Phoenix 29 SFX is an updated and restyled version of the earlier Phoenix 29 Convertible (1977–87). She replaced the conservative profile of her predecessor with the more aggressive lines of the larger Phoenix 33 Convertible. Indeed, the oversized flybridge of the SFX seems almost too large for a 29-footer. Phoenix introduced a number of desirable features in this model including a transom door, molded pulpit, aluminum rails, and a revamped and updated interior layout with berths for six. Stoutly built, an all-new hull featured a slightly wider beam at the waterline, a redesigned entry, and extra strakes for improved lift and stability. Notably, the absence of a forward stateroom bulkhead results in a more open and spacious interior. Borrowing again from the 33 Convertible, a unique air duct system is used to rid the cockpit of exhaust fumes while underway. Among several engine options offered during her production years, twin 270hp gas engines cruise the 29 SFX at 22 knots (29–30 knots top). Optional 200hp Volvo diesels cruise at 25 knots (around 30 knots top), and Volvo 225hp diesels cruise at 27 knots and top out at just over 30 knots.

See Page 692 For Price Data

Length w/Pulpit	31'11"	Clearance	9'6"
Hull Length	29'0"	Fuel	180 gals.
Beam	10'0"	Water	50 gals.
Draft	2'4"	Hull Type	Deep-V
Weight	9,450#	Deadrise Aft	22°

Phoenix 32 Tournament

With her graceful profile, excellent deck layout, and solid construction, the 32 Tournament was one of the more appealing designs produced by Phoenix in the late 1990s. She's built on a beamy modified-V hull with a solid fiberglass bottom and prop pockets to reduce the shaft angles. Like all Phoenix models, a one-piece inner liner was chemically bonded to the hull. There are sleeping accommodations for four adults below, and the head is fitted with a separate stall shower—a convenience usually absent in hardcore express boats this size. The backlighted rod locker next to the companionway is impressive, but the cabin headroom is quite low. On deck, visibility from the centerline helm is excellent, and three hatches in the bridge deck provide access to the somewhat crowded engine compartment. (Note that the center hatch, along with the helm seat, lifts hydraulically from the front.) Cockpit fishing amenities include a molded bait-prep station and tackle center, freezer, fish box, and transom door. Among several engine choices offered over the years, twin 350hp Cat (or 370hp Volvo) diesels cruise at 26 knots and reach a top speed of around 30 knots.

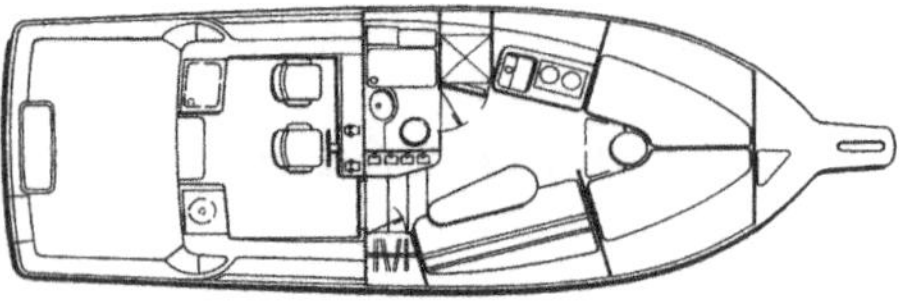

See Page 692 For Price Data

Length w/Pulpit	34'8"	Weight, Diesel	19,320#
Hull Length	32'1"	Fuel	320 gals.
Beam	12'0"	Water	76 gals.
Draft	2'9"	Hull Type	Modified-V
Weight, Gas	16,360#	Deadrise Aft	17°

Phoenix 33 Convertible; 33/34 SFX

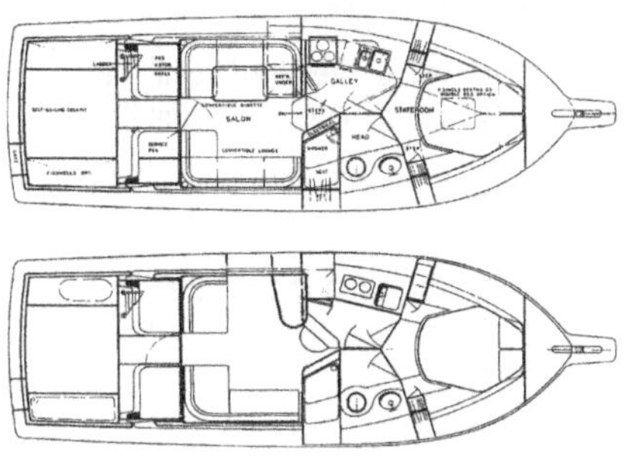

The Phoenix 34 SFX Convertible (called the Phoenix 33 Convertible in 1987–94) was a popular model for Phoenix during the 1990s thanks to her sturdy construction, a big fishing cockpit, and a very space-efficient interior layout. The hull—strengthened with a full-length inner liner—is essentially a deep-V with propeller pockets to allow the engines to be moved aft without increasing the shaft angle. Several floorplans were offered during her production years, all with the galley down from the salon and all with a stall shower in the head. These are particularly well-finished interiors with quality fabrics and furnishings throughout. On deck, cockpit freeboard is fairly low, and nearly all of the 144-square-foot area is usable fishing space. Engine boxes make access to the motors easy, and a transom door, in-deck storage, and washdowns were standard. The flybridge is big for a 34-footer with seating for five and lockable rod storage. Among several gas and diesel engine options, a pair of 320hp gas engines cruise the Phoenix 34 SFX at 19 knots and top out in the high 20s. Later models with 350hp Cat 3116 diesels cruise at 22 knots and reach 30+ knots top.

See Page 692 For Price Data

Length w/Pulpit	36'9"	Weight, Diesel	23,600#
Hull Length	33'9"	Fuel	300 gals.
Beam	13'0"	Water	70 gals.
Draft	2'9"	Hull Type	Modified-V
Weight, Gas	20,810#	Deadrise Aft	17°

Phoenix 37 Convertible; 38 SFX

Bold styling and rugged construction characterize the 38 SFX Convertible, the largest boat in the late-model Phoenix fleet. (Note that she was called the Phoenix 37 Convertible until 1995.) She's built on the same hull as the company's earlier 38 Convertible (1982–88) with full-length inner liner, prop pockets to reduce shaft angles, and a shallow keel for directional stability. Her two-stateroom, galley-up interior is arranged with an island berth forward and stacked single berths in the guest stateroom. Teak or white ash interior woodwork were offered, and a glassed-over deckhouse windshield was optional. With her large and uncluttered cockpit, the 38 SFX is designed to meet the needs of serious fishermen. A transom door was standard along with cockpit bolsters, a molded tackle center, livewell, rod storage, and two in-deck fish boxes. Air intake vents forward of the bridge channel air into the cockpit to reduce diesel fumes—a clever idea. Twin 375hp Cat diesels cruise at 22–23 knots, and 485hp 6-71s cruise at 26–27 knots. Newer models with a pair of 435hp Cats cruise at a 25 knots and top out in the high 20s.

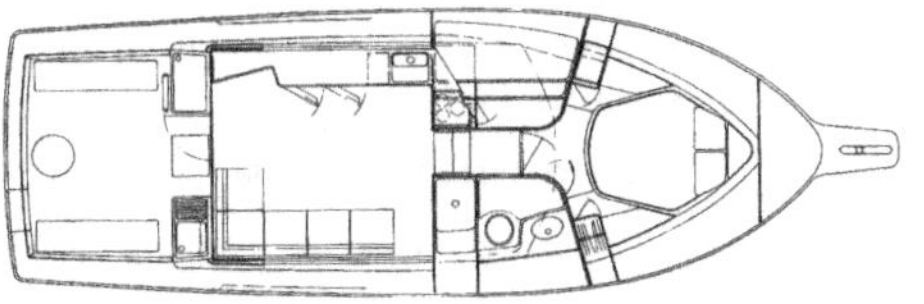

See Page 692 For Price Data

Length w/Pulpit	41'11"	Clearance	12'7"
Hull Length	37'10"	Fuel	440 gals.
Beam	14'0"	Water	100 gals.
Draft	3'7"	Hull Type	Deep-V
Weight	30,800#	Deadrise Aft	18°

Post

Quick View

- Founded in 1957 by Russell Post, Post Marine was a limited-production builder of traditional Jersey-style sportfishing boats.
- Early Post models were built of wood, but the boat that established the company's name was the Post 42 Sportfisherman introduced in 1974.
- A handsome design built on a solid fiberglass hull, the Post 42 became one of the most admired mid-range sportfishing boats on the market.
- In over four decades of production, Post yachts were recognized for their traditional mahogany-and-teak interiors, high production standards, and tournament-level fishability.
- Privately owned and marketed through a limited number of dealers, Post built only a small number of boats annually..
- A victim of the Great Recession, Post Yachts declared bankruptcy in March, 2011.

No longer in business.

Post 42 Sport Fisherman

1997–2009

The Post 42 was designed as an affordable alternative to the more expensive Post 43. Powered with less costly engines, she's built on a low-deadrise semi-V hull with a shallow keel and a wide 15-foot, 9-inch beam. Like many convertibles her size, the 42 comes with a conventional two-stateroom interior, however the rich appointments, excellent joinery, and quality furnishings set her apart from much of the competition. The salon features a built-in entertainment center and facing settees, and Post engineers even managed to squeeze a laundry center into the companionway. Topside, the Post's extended flybridge is bigger than it looks with seating for eight, rod storage, and a well-arranged helm console. Because the bridge ladder is recessed into the bait-prep console, the cockpit—partially shaded by the bridge overhang—is less cluttered than most other convertibles. Notable features include teak interior joinery, a top-notch engineroom (accessed from under the deckhouse step), two in-deck fish boxes, transom door, and bow pulpit. Twin 430hp Volvo (or 435hp Cat) diesels cruise the Post 42 in the mid 20s (28–29 knots top), and Volvo 480hp diesels cruise in the high 20s and top out at over 30 knots.

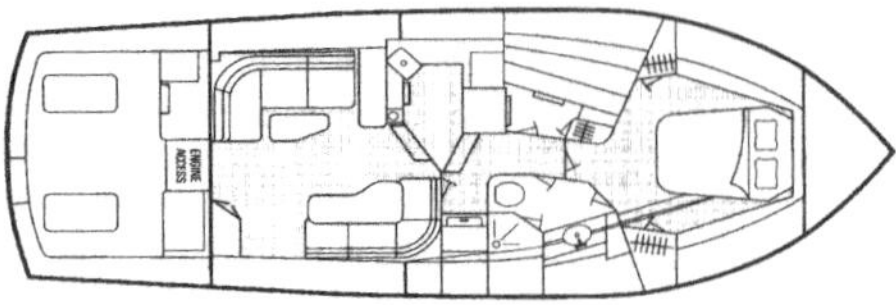

See Page 692 For Price Data

Length	42'10"	Fuel	529 gals.
Beam	15'9"	Water	114 gals.
Draft	4'0"	Waste	31 gals.
Weight	42,996#	Hull Type	Modified-V
Clearance, Hardtop	16'11"	Deadrise Aft	7°

Post 43 Sport Fisherman

The Post 43 is an updated version of the classic Post 42 Sport Fisherman (1975–83) with a revised interior and a slightly larger cockpit. Introduced in 1984, she rides on a low-deadrise, semi-V hull with a deeper forefoot than the 42 as well as a second spray rail and increased transom deadrise—changes that contribute to improved headsea performance and a measurably improved ride. Below, her two-stateroom layout is a blend of traditional teak woodwork, quality furnishings, and designer fabrics. A centerline pedestal berth dominates the forward stateroom, while the guest stateroom is arranged with stacked single berths. The galley is down, across from the guest cabin, and the salon includes an L-shaped convertible settee and a full teak entertainment center forward. Topside, a molded tackle center (which serves as a base for the bridge ladder), in-deck fish boxes, and transom door were standard in the cockpit. Note that the Post 43 III—introduced in 1989—included several standard equipment updates. Twin 485hp 6-71s cruise the Post 43 in the mid 20s with a top speed of 27–28 knots. Optional 550hp 6V92s cruise in the high 20s and reach a top speed around 30 knots.

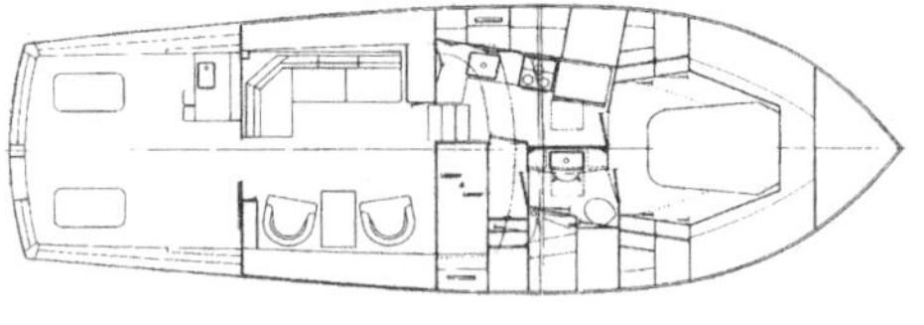

Prices Not Provided for Pre-1995 Models

Length	43'8"	Fuel	500/550 gals.
Beam	15'9"	Water	120 gals.
Draft	3'6"	Cockpit	125 sq. ft.
Weight	33,000#	Hull Type	Modified-V
Clearance	13'7"	Deadrise Aft	8°

Post 43 Sport Fisherman

The second Post 43 model (the original Post 43 ran from 1984 to 1989) is essentially the same boat as the Post 44, the boat she replaced in 1995, but with an updated, much-improved interior. Like all Posts, the 43 rides on a low-deadrise hull with moderate beam and a shallow keel for directional stability. With her sharp entry and flat aftersections, the 43 is quick to accelerate and a fast boat across the water. Below, the expansive salon of the Post 43 is much larger than the earlier 44, the result of space saved by eliminating one of the heads. A full dinette is forward in the salon, and a serving counter overlooks the mid-level galley. An island berth dominates the large master stateroom, and solid teak cabinets, plush furnishings, and vinyl overheads highlight the interior. Traditionally, Post models have had compact enginerooms, but by locating the fuel tanks aft in the 43—rather than between the engines—headroom is increased and serviceability enhanced. Additional features include a superb helm console, excellent storage, cockpit engineroom access, and a transom door. A fast ride with optional 535hp 6V-92s, she'll cruise in the high 20s and reach a top speed of about 30 knots.

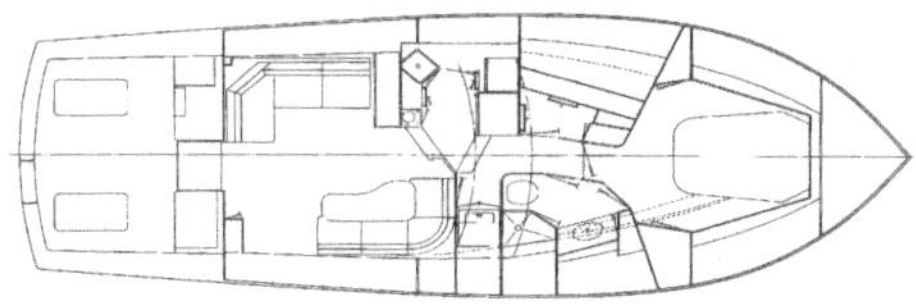

See Page 692 For Price Data

Length	43'9"	Water	120 gals.
Beam	15'9"	Clearance	13'7"
Draft	3'6"	Cockpit	125 sq. ft.
Weight	40,000#	Hull Type	Modified-V
Fuel	543 gals.	Deadrise Aft	7°

Post 46 Sport Fisherman

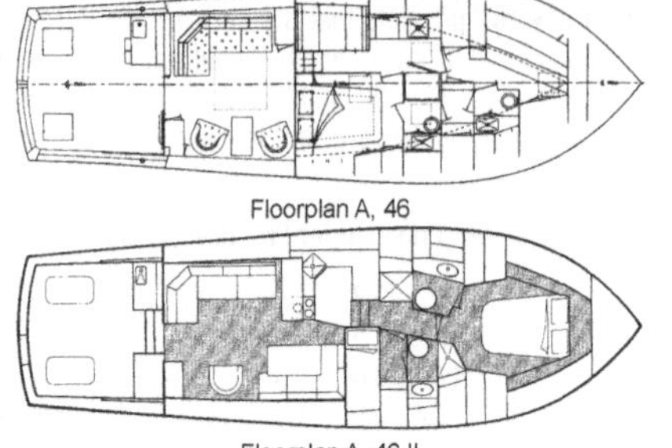
Floorplan A, 46

Floorplan A, 46 II

The original Post 46 was introduced back in 1978 as a stretched version of the popular Post 42. Hull construction is solid fiberglass and her tapered form and low transom deadrise resulted in a boat quick to accelerate and fast over the water. In 1988, Post introduced the 46 II model with a little more transom deadrise and a deeper forefoot for improved headsea performance. Several two-stateroom floorplans were offered in the Post 46/46 II during her production years, and all are notable for their quality joinery and furnishings. What really distinguishes the 46 from the offerings of other builders is, of course, her sensuous and graceful styling, long a Post trademark. Cockpit access to the engineroom of the 46 II became standard in 1992, and in 1995 a much-improved standup engineroom resulted from moving the fuel tanks aft. Among several engine options, early models with 410hp 6-71 Detroit diesels cruise at 21 knots. Later models with 485hp 6-71s cruise at 23–24 knots, and 625hp 6V92 diesels cruise at around 25 knots. A well-regarded boat, used Post 46 models are nearly always in demand. Note that the Post 47 is an updated 46 II with a wider flybridge and revised interior choices.

See Page 692 For Price Data

Length	46'9"	Fuel	620 gals.
Beam	15'9"	Water	120 gals.
Draft	3'10"	Waste	31 gals.
Weight	44,000#	Hull Type	Modified-V
Clearance, Windshield	13'7"	Deadrise Aft	3°/7°

Post 47 Sport Fisherman

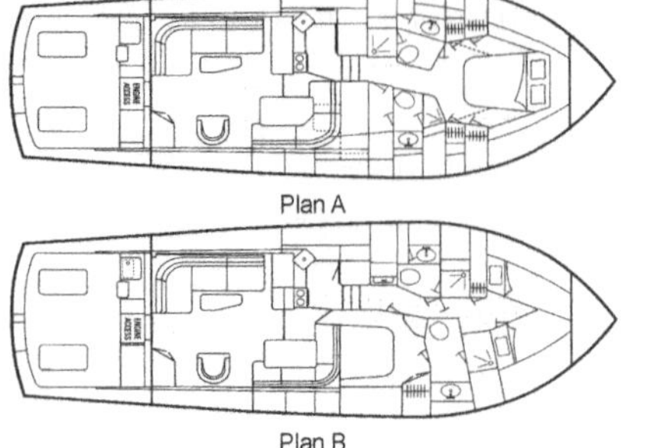
Plan A

Plan B

The Post 47 is a further refinement of the popular Post 46, one of the most highly regarded sportfishing boats produced in recent years. Although her hull and running surface are identical to her predecessor, the flybridge of the 47 is wider and longer than the old 46, which allows for an expanded console and additional guest seating. Aside from a graceful and alluring profile, the luxurious two-stateroom, mid-galley floorplans offered in the 47 both come with separate stall showers in each head and space near the companionway for a washer/dryer installation. While the interior teak joinery is very good, the exterior is teak-free (unlike earlier Posts). The cockpit is huge, one of the largest in her class. The flybridge ladder is recessed between the cockpit tackle lockers to preserve space, and the engine room is reached from under the deckhouse step. Topside, the centerline helm provides console space full a full array of installed electronics. Built on a low-deadrise hull with a shallow keel. twin 625hp Detroit 6V92s cruise the Post 47 at 25 knots (29–30 knots top), and optional 680hp MANs cruise at 28 knots and reach a top speed in the neighborhood of 32 knots.

See Page 692 For Price Data

Length	46'9"	Fuel	635 gals.
Beam	15'9"	Water	120 gals.
Draft	4'2"	Waste	31 gals.
Weight	49,668#	Hull Type	Modified-V
Clearance, Hardtop	16'11"	Deadrise Aft	7°

Post 50 Convertible

A great-looking boat with a long foredeck and muscular profile, the Post 50 combines the elegance of a yacht-style interior with the brute force of a well-bred offshore fishing machine. She's built on a low-deadrise modified-V hull with cored hullsides, a wide beam, and a solid glass bottom. Unlike other Post designs, the 50's hull is not tapered at the transom that helps account for her very large cockpit. Several three-stateroom, two-head floorplans were offered over the years. Like all Post models, the interior woodwork and detailing are finished to high standards, and the lush decor is very impressive. The cockpit—nearly 150 square feet—comes with a full array of fishing gear including a molded tackle center, cockpit controls, transom door, and direct access to the engineroom (where headroom was dramatically improved in 1995 when the fuel tanks were moved aft). Note that in 1997 the flybridge was widened to the full width of the deckhouse. Among several engine options offered over the years, 735hp 8V92s cruise in the high 20s (30+ knots wide open), and later models with 860hp MANs boost the cruising speed to a fast 30 knots and reach a top speed in the mid 30s.

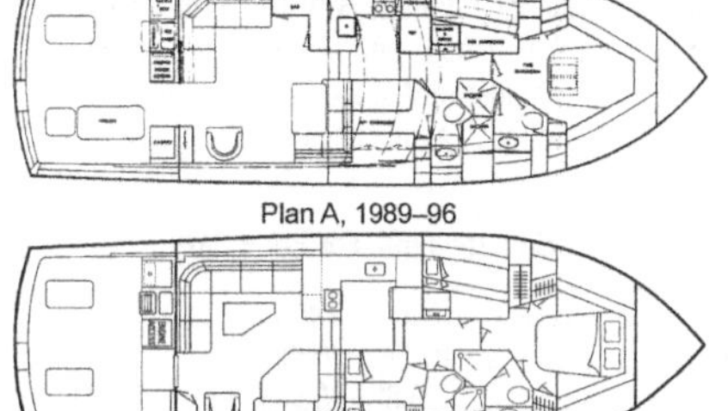

Plan A, 1989–96

Plan A, 1997–09

See Page 692 For Price Data

Length	50'7"	Fuel	870 gals.
Beam	16'11"	Water	240 gals.
Draft	4'6"	Waste	42 gals.
Weight	57,122#	Hull Type	Modified-V
Clearance, Hardtop	17'2"	Deadrise Aft	7°

Post 53 Convertible

The Post 53 Convertible was the Jersey-based company's final model introduction prior to going out of business in 2009—the last in a series of semicustom sportfishing boats stretching back to the late 1950s. Sharing the classic styling and excellent quality of her predecessors, the 53 rides on a low-deadrise modified-V hull with a solid fiberglass bottom and a wide 16'11" beam. Her tournament-ready cockpit boasts standard features such as a top-loading freezer, lift-out in-deck fish boxes, transom livewell, tackle storage and a bait-prep center. Below, the 53's three-stateroom layout and spacious salon and galley are equipped with tons of storage, making her ideal for family cruising. The master stateroom is to port with a walkaround queen bed and private head with separate stall shower. The guest stateroom is forward, also with an island queen, while a smaller stateroom with over/under bunks is to starboard. Note high-gloss teak cabinetry, frameless windows, Corian galley counters, and companionway washer/dryer. Topside, the front of the helm console opens to reveal a large rod storage locker. The engineroom is as good as it gets in a convertible this size. MTU 1,200hp engines cruise at 30 knots (about 35 knots top).

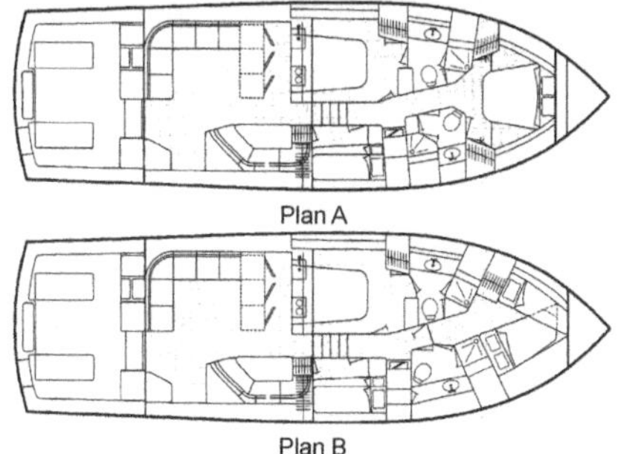

Plan A

Plan B

Not Enough Resale Data to Set Values

Length	52'10"	Fuel	926 gals.
Beam	16'11"	Water	240 gals.
Draft	5'0"	Waste	80 gals.
Weight	59,000#	Hull Type	Modified-V
Clearance	NA	Deadrise Aft	7°

Post 56 Convertible

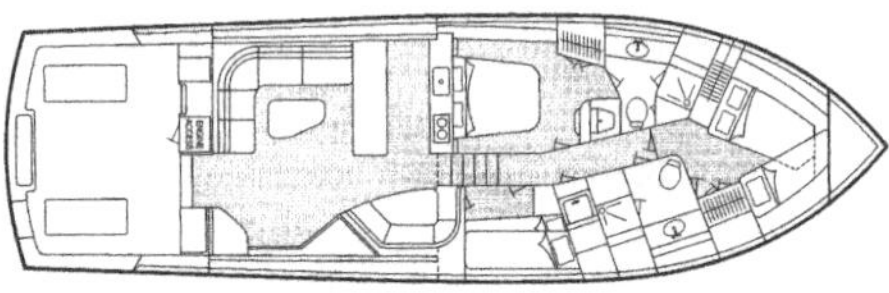

Derived from the Post 50 Convertible, the 56 Convertible is the largest boat Post ever built during their many years in business. Like her sisterships in the Post fleet, she's built on a good-running modified-V hull with very modest transom deadrise, cored hull-sides, and a solid fiberglass bottom. The three-stateroom, two-head layout of the Post 56 is fairly standard for a convertible this size with a midships owner's cabin and the galley forward in the salon, opposite the dinette. Under-counter refrigeration maximizes counter space in the galley, and a washer/dryer unit is accessed from the hallway. Lacquered teak joinery—grain-matched and hand-fitted—is used throughout the interior, a Post trademark for many years. The cockpit, which measures more than 12 feet in length, is fitted with tackle storage, bait freezer, two fish boxes, transom livewell, and direct access to the spacious and well-engineered engineroom. The flybridge is huge with plenty of guest seating, rod storage beneath the console, and single-lever controls. A fast ride with 1,300hp 12-cylinder MANs, the Post 56 Convertible will cruise at 31–32 knots and reach a top speed of 35+ knots.

See Page 692 For Price Data

Length	55'11"	Fuel	1,200 gals.
Beam	16'11"	Water	250 gals.
Draft	5'6"	Waste	80 gals.
Weight	66,830#	Hull Type	Deep-V
Clearance, Hardtop	17'6"	Deadrise Aft	7°

Pro-Line

Quick View

- Ray Atwood and his son Dan started Pro-Line Boats in 1968 as a small regional builder of dedicated fishing boats.
- The company experienced a period of steady growth through the 1970s and 1980s, and in 1989 Pro-Line was purchased by a private investor group headed by Ken Hall.
- In subsequent years, Pro-Line became well known in the industry as a volume, low-cost builder of popular center console and walkaround fishing boats.
- When Pro-Line purchased Donzi Marine in 1993, Hall created a holding company (American Marine Holdings) which went on to purchase Phoenix Marine in 1995.
- During the 1990s, Pro-Line had grown to become one of the largest builders of trailerable and offshore fishing boats ranging in size from 17 feet to 34 feet in length.
- American Marine Holdings, owner of Baja Boats, Donzi Marine, Fountain Powerboats, and Pro-Line Boats filed for bankruptcy in January, 2012.
- Following a 12-month shutdown, Pro-Line returned to production in 2013 from facilities in Washington, NC.

Pro-Line Boats • Washington, NC • www.prolineboats.com

Pro-Line 26 Sport

The Pro-Line 26 Sport is a full-featured trailerable center console who's sensible deck plan and clean lines will appeal to anglers looking for a capable offshore fishing boat at a moderate price. No longer in business, Pro-Line prospered in later years by giving customers dependable and well-finished boats that compared well with more expensive offerings from their upmarket competitors. Built on a deep-V hull with cored hullsides and a solid fiberglass bottom, the cockpit of the 26 Sport is arranged with a pair of in-deck 45-gallon fish boxes, a leaning post with a built-in baitwell, an aft bench seat, freshwater sink, tackle storage and a transom door. There's plenty of storage forward, under the casting deck, and a head/storage compartment is enclosed within the large console. Additional features include a bow pulpit, anchor locker, trim tabs, under-gunwale rod racks, console seat, coaming bolsters and rod holders. Considered a lot of boat for the money, a single 225hp Mercury outboard delivers a top speed of just over 30 knots, and twin 150s max out at over 40 knots.

Floorplan Not Available

See Page 692 For Price Data

Length	27'0"	Fuel	170 gals.
Beam	8'6"	Water	15 gals.
Hull Draft	1'4"	Max HP	400
Dry Weight	4,500#	Hull Type	Deep-V
Clearance	NA	Deadrise Aft	19°

Pro-Line 26 Super Sport

The market for trailerable center consoles in the 26–27-foot range is among the most competitive in the industry. With entries from over a dozen major builders—and even more from smaller semicustom manufactures—the 26 Super Sport stands out for her stylish lines and space-efficient deck layout. Her uncluttered cockpit has fishing space fore and aft and features a casting deck/bow seating forward, wide walkways, in-deck fish boxes, raw water washdown, rod storage racks, freshwater shower, foldaway transom seat, and a lighted livewell built into the transom. The factory T-top includes an electronics box, rocket launchers, overhead storage, and spreader lights. The console has a walk-in enclosed head below, and a molded bench seat forward with cushioned backrest. Note the large dash flat at the helm for a big-screen video display. Excellent storage for a 26-footer, a resource always in short supply. Built on a solid fiberglass deep-hull with a slender 8'6" beam, the 26 Super Sport is quick to accelerate and a smooth ride across the water. Twin 150hp Honda outboards deliver a top speed of about 40 knots.

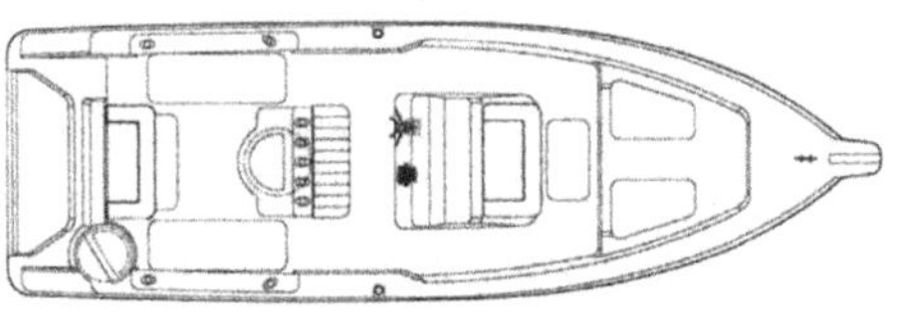

See Page 692 For Price Data

Length	26'4"	Fuel	156 gals.
Beam	8'6"	Water	15 gals.
Hull Draft	1'6"	Max HP	450
Hull Weight	4,400#	Hull Type	Deep-V
Cockpit	92 sq. ft.	Deadrise Aft	22°

Pro-Line 2610 Walkaround; 27 Walk

The Pro-Line 2610 (called the 27 Walk beginning in 2000 when an integrated transom became standard) is a popular wide-beam walkaround with a large fishing cockpit and a cabin big enough for comfortable cruising. The 2610 stands out because of her broad 9'6" beam—most 26-footers are designed to be legally trailerable which limits beam no more than 8'6" in width. Available with sterndrive or outboard power, the 65-square-foot cockpit of the Pro-Line 2610 carries a full load of fishing features including two in-deck fish boxes, removable, transom bait station with 35-gallon livewell, built-in tackle drawers, and a walk-thru transom door. Below, the cabin accommodations include a fully equipped galley with stove and refrigerator, dinette that converts to a comfortable double berth, and an enclosed head compartment with a standup shower. A tall windshield provides good wind and spray protection at the helm, and wide side decks make getting around easy and safe. A factory hardtop was a popular option. Twin 225 Yamaha outboards deliver a top speed of about 40 knot, and a single 310hp Volvo I/O will top out in the mid 30s.

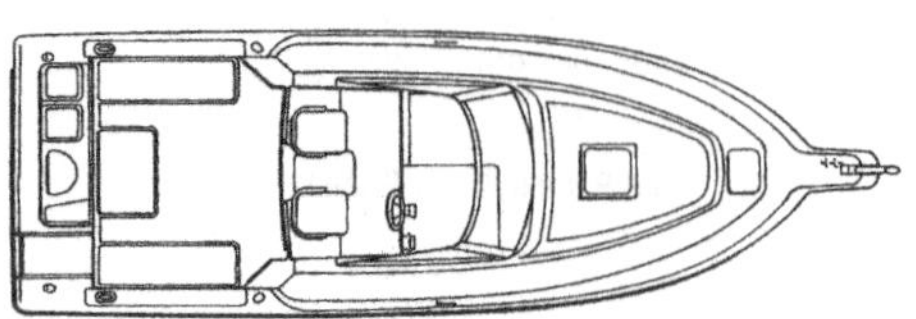

See Page 468 For Price Data

Length	29'1"	Fuel	200 gals.
Beam	9'10"	Water	30 gals.
Hull Draft	1'9"	Max HP	500
Hull Weight	5,900#	Hull Type	Deep-V
Clearance	7'9"	Deadrise Aft	19°

Pro-Line 27/29 Express

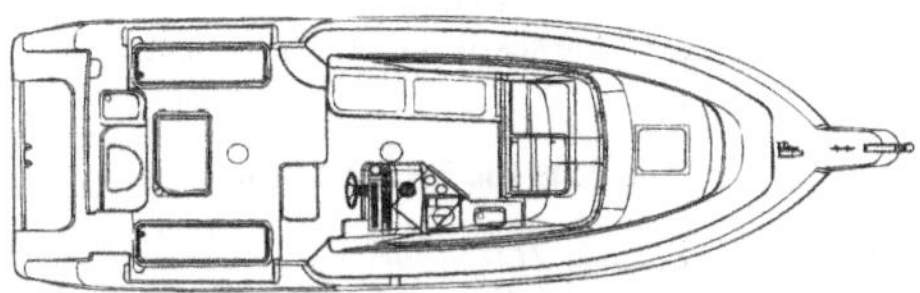

Innovation may be an overused term in the marine industry, but few would deny that the term can properly be applied in describing the Pro-Line 27 Express. (Note that she was called the 29 Express from 2005.) This is a what many in the business call a "crossover" boat, a combination fishboat/day cruiser that meets the needs of serious anglers who want a boat they can also use for occasional family cruising. Note that while Pro-Line calls this boat an express, her deep, recessed walkways are those of a traditional walkaround design. What sets the 27 Express apart from similar boats in her class is the location of the galley. Rather than putting it down in the cabin where space is limited, it's outdoors on the extended bridgedeck, just forward of the helm, where it's convenient to everyone. A bench seat opposite the helm and a transom seat in the cockpit provide plenty of guest seating, and a V-berth and portable head are found in the compact cabin. Fishing features include a 35-gallon transom livewell, tackle drawers, two in-deck fish boxes and a transom door. Twin 200hp Mercury outboards reach a top speed of close to 40 knots.

See Page 692 For Price Data

Length w/Pulpit	29'1"	Water	30 gals.
Beam	9'10"	Cockpit	80 sq. ft.
Hull Draft	1'9"	Max HP	500
Dry Weight	5,900#	Hull Type	Deep-V
Fuel	200 gals.	Deadrise Aft	19°

Pro-Line 27/29 Sport

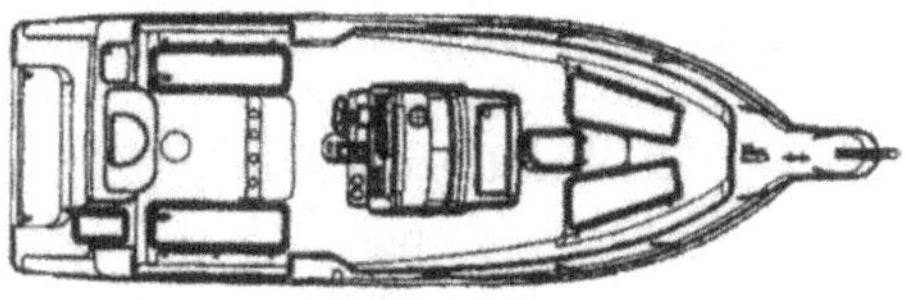

The Pro-Line 27 Sport began life back in 1993 when she was introduced as the Pro-Line 2700 Sportsman, a full-transom center console with bracket-mounted outboards. So popular was this boat that when Pro-Line decided to replace her in 2000, they completely updated the old Sportsman, adding a new integrated transom and redesigning the helm console. With nearly 10 feet of beam, the 27 Sport is more than a foot wider than most other center consoles in this class. All-fiberglass construction makes her an easy boat to clean and maintain, and the center console contains a head compartment with near-standing headroom. The Sportsman's 115-square-foot cockpit provides plenty of room to fish, and the raised casting deck at the bow allows anglers to easily fight fish around the pulpit. Standard fishing features include a transom bait station with livewell and sink, in-deck fish boxes, transom door, and tackle drawers. Dry storage is plentiful with three large storage bins under the raised casting deck. Note that a bow pulpit and leaning post were standard. A stable boat thanks to her wide beam, twin 225hp Mercury outboards will reach a top speed in excess of 45 knots.

See Page 692 For Price Data

Length w/Pulpit	29'1"	Fuel	200 gals.
Beam	9'10"	Water	15 gals.
Hull Draft	1'8"	Max HP	500
Dry Weight	5,200#	Hull Type	Deep-V
Clearance	NA	Deadrise Aft	19°

Pro-Line 2700 Sportsman

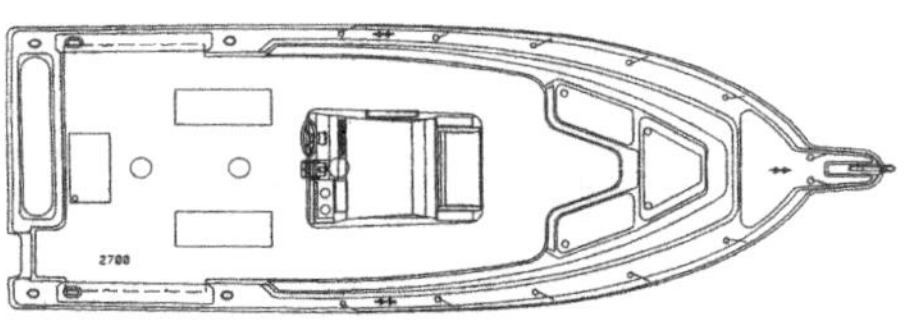

A sturdy, uncomplicated boat, the Pro-Line 2700 Sportsman achieved a good deal of buyer satisfaction in the 1990s with her affordable price and roomy, well-arranged cockpit. With nearly 10 feet of beam, the Sportsman is more than a foot wider than most other center consoles in this class. All-fiberglass construction makes her an easy boat to clean and maintain, and the center console contains a head compartment with near-standing headroom. The Sportsman's 115-square-foot cockpit provides plenty of room to fish, and the raised casting deck at the bow allows anglers to easily fight fish around the pulpit. While the high gunwales add a measure of cockpit security, it's a long reach down to the water. Standard fishing features include a transom bait station with livewell and sink, three in-deck fish boxes (two aft and one forward of the console), transom door, and tackle drawers. Dry storage is plentiful with three large storage bins under the raised casting deck. Note that a bow pulpit and leaning post were standard. A stable boat thanks to her relatively wide beam, twin 225hp Mercury outboards will reach a top speed in excess of 45 knots.

See Page 468 For Price Data

Length	27'6"	Fuel	200 gals.
Beam	9'10"	Water	15 gals.
Hull Draft	1'8"	Max HP	500
Dry Weight	4,750#	Hull Type	Deep-V
Clearance	8'4"	Deadrise Aft	19°

Pro-Line 2810 Walkaround

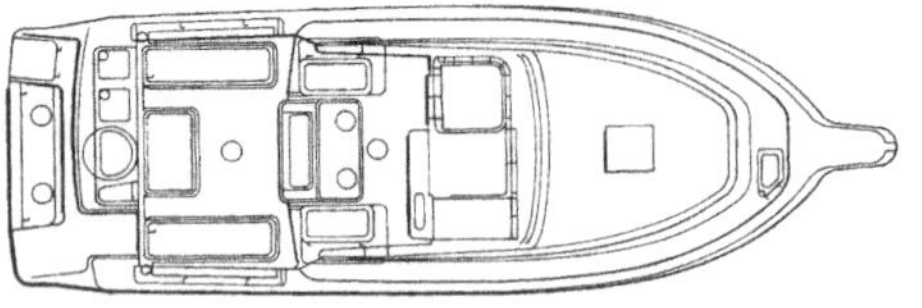

The Pro-Line 2810 Walkaround (called the 28 Walk in 2000) was aimed at serious anglers who wanted a roomy fishing boat with a comfortable, family-friendly interior. Built on a solid fiberglass hull with a relatively wide beam, the full bow section and relatively high forward freeboard of the 2810 account for much of her interior volume. She's a fishing boat first, however, and the cockpit—with about 70 square feet of space—offers a pair of fish boxes in the sole and plenty of storage for rods under the gunwales. A walk-through transom features a standup livewell, a bait-prep center and a shower. At the helm, the molded electronics box above the dash is huge, and the entire console tilts back for access to the wiring. While the side decks of the 2810 aren't as deep as those found in many walkarounds, they are wide and foredeck access is safe and secure. Below, the cabin is arranged with a convertible V-shaped dinette/double-berth forward, a one-piece molded galley, a rod storage locker (nice touch), and an enclosed standup head with shower. Powered with a pair of 225hp Mercury outboards, the Pro-Line 2810 will reach a top speed in the neighborhood of 40 knots.

See Page 468 For Price Data

Length w/Pulpit	29'6"	Fuel	200 gals.
Beam	10'2"	Water	21 gals.
Hull Draft	2'1"	Max HP	500
Hull Weight	6,500#	Hull Type	Deep-V
Cockpit	72 sq. ft.	Deadrise Aft	21°

Pro-Line 29 Grand Sport

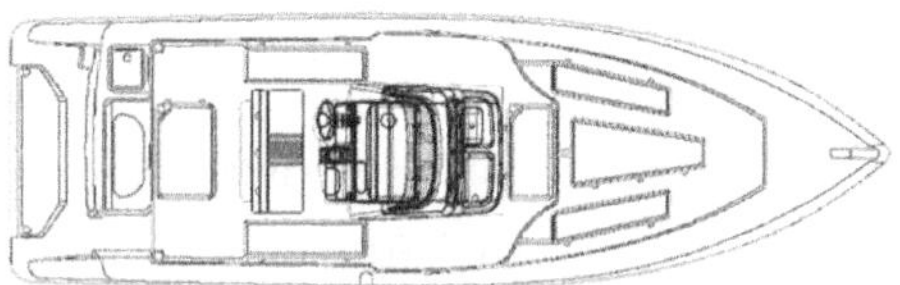

With her high freeboard and prominent bow, the Pro-Line 29 Grand Sport offers something different in a mid-size center console boat. She is, as Pro-Line enthusiasts often claim, a big 29-footer, and her deep cockpit spells extra security for all concerned. Others argue that the Grand Sport's extremely tall gunwales have no real purpose, serving only to block the view from the helm. (Indeed, Pro-Line designers had to put a 4-inch pedestal at the helm just to see over the bow.) Regardless of one's take on these matters, the Grand Sport is a very roomy boat with plenty of fishing space in both the cockpit and bow area. The dash features a huge electronics flat and can support several large-screen units, while the walk-in head compartment is among the largest in her class. Standard features include a leaning post with backrest and 50-gallon livewell, two large in-deck fish boxes, foldaway transom seat, fresh and saltwater washdowns, fold-away rear seat, and transom door. Low-profile bow rails and pop-up cleats prevent line snags. Note that the entire console hinges forward for wiring access. Twin 250hp Merc outboards deliver a top speed in the neighborhood of 45 knots.

See Page 692 For Price Data

Length	29'4"	Fuel	240 gals.
Beam	9'8"	Water	15 gals.
Hull Draft	1'10"	Max HP	500
Hull Weight	6,310#	Hull Type	Deep-V
Clearance	7'11"	Deadrise Aft	22°

Pro-Line 29 Super Sport

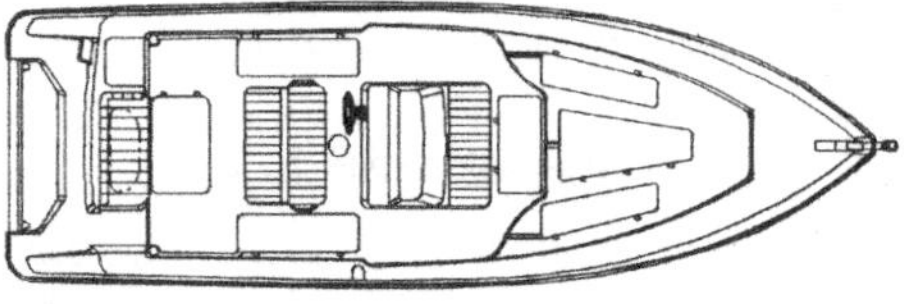

Savvy boaters and marine industry professionals alike tend to view Pro-Lines as a lot of boat for the money. For years, Pro-Line—which went out of business early in 2012—delivered affordably priced fishing boats that were well built, well equipped, and easy on the eye. Introduced in 2005, the 29 Super Sport is a high-performance fishing rig for big-water anglers focused on speed and agility. She rides on a solid fiberglass deep-V hull with generous freeboard and a slender 9-foot beam. Notable features include a raised bow casting platform, large-capacity fish box, leaning post with tackle station, lockable rod storage, enclosed head compartment, console cooler, fresh and raw water washdowns, and bow storage lockers. A big 45-gallon livewell is located beneath the transom seat. The 2900's tall windshield offers good high-speed wind and spray protection. Not only can her deep-V hull take a pounding, but the narrow beam makes her more fuel-efficient than her wide-beam counterparts. With a trailer weight of just over 7,000 pounds, she can be towed behind most any full-size SUV or pickup. Expect a top speed in the neighborhood of 45 knots with twin Mercury 250 outboards.

See Page 692 For Price Data

Length	28'7"	Fuel	192 gals.
Beam	9'0"	Water	15 gals.
Hull Draft	1'7"	Max HP	500
Hull Weight	5,300#	Hull Type	Deep-V
Cockpit	101 sq. ft.	Deadrise Aft	22°

Pro-Line 2950 Mid Cabin

Boaters who enjoy cruising as well as fishing will find numerous features for both activities aboard the Pro-Line 2950 Mid-Cabin. Introduced in 1992, the 2950 remained in production until 1999 when Pro-Line replaced her with the 30 Walk—basically the same boat with an integrated bracket/dive platform. Like all Pro-Lines of recent years, the 2950 is a blend of affordability, comfort, and performance. With nearly 11 feet of beam, she's wider than most other boats in her class, and her big 80-square-foot cockpit is backed up by a transom bait station with livewell, built-in tackle box, freshwater sink, and a transom door. The high freeboard of the 2950 provides great cockpit security, but it's a long reach over the gunwale down to the water. Below, there are berths for three in the cabin: the V-berth sleeps two adults, and the midships berth will sleep two kids or a single adult. Additional features include a triple-wide helm seat, four opening ports, a molded bow pulpit, and very deep walkarounds. Offered with inboard, sterndrive, or outboard power, a pair of 250hp Yamaha outboards cruise the 2950 Mid-Cabin in the high 20s and reach a top speed of over 40 knots.

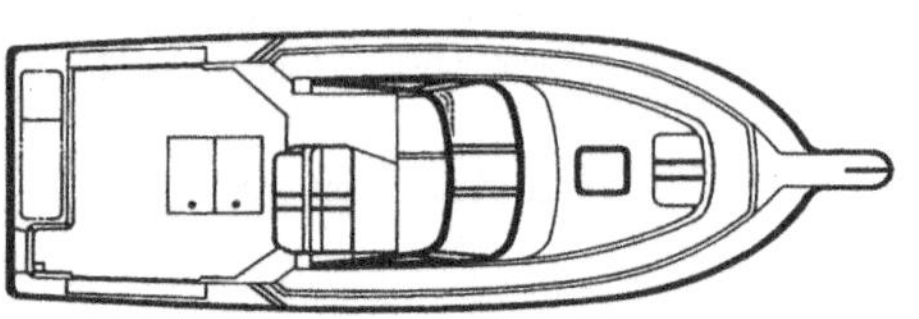

See Page 693 For Price Data

Length	30'0"	Fuel	220 gals.
Beam	10'9"	Water	42 gals.
Hull Draft	1'10"	Max HP	500
Hull Weight	7,500#	Hull Type	Deep-V
Cockpit	80 sq. ft.	Deadrise Aft	19°

Pro-Line 30 Walkaround

The Pro-Line 31 Walk began life back in 1992 when she was introduced as the 2950 Mid-Cabin, a value-priced fishboat with a wide beam and bracket-mounted outboards. A popular model for many years, she was completely updated in 2000—including a new integrated bracket/dive platform—when Pro-Line reintroduced her as the 30 Walk. Called the 31 Walk since 2005, the most distinguishing features of this boat are her deep walkarounds, a spacious cockpit, and an excellent open-water ride. Visibility from the raised bridge deck is excellent, and the well-equipped cockpit is fitted with a jump seat, in-deck fish box, rod storage, tackle drawers, and transom door. A bait-prep station is built into the transom complete with a 45-gallon livewell and sink. Belowdecks, the cabin sleeps three with V-berths forward, a compact galley, enclosed head, and a mid-berth aft. Additional features include a molded bow pulpit, generous storage, four opening cabin ports, and foredeck seating. A rugged boat with low maintenance requirements, a pair of 250hp Yamaha outboards cruise the Pro-Line 31 Walk in the high 20s and reach a top speed of over 40 knots.

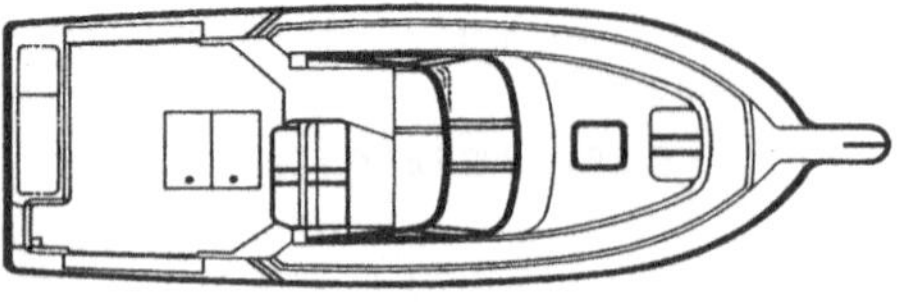

See Page 693 For Price Data

Length	32'6"	Fuel	300 gals.
Beam	10'10"	Water	39 gals.
Hull Draft	1'10"	Max HP	600
Hull Weight	7,600#	Hull Type	Deep-V
Cockpit	84 sq. ft.	Deadrise Aft	19°

Pro-Line 30 Express

Considering the number of anglers who use their boats for family activities as well as serious fishing pursuits, it's hardly news that manufacturers have been offering some interesting crossover designs in recent years. The Pro-Line 30 Express (called the 31 Express in 2005) is such a boat—a capable offshore fishing platform that doubles as a weekend cruiser with extra cockpit seating for guests and a unique topside galley. While she looks at first like a traditional walkaround design, the helm console has been moved aft on the lengthened bridge deck to make room for an open-air galley to starboard, directly across from an extended L-shaped lounge. This innovative deck layout turns the 30 into an excellent boat for entertaining friends, although it was necessary to sacrifice some cockpit space to make it all work. Below, the compact cabin is arranged with a full double berth forward, a standup head with shower to port, and a storage bin aft with a wine rack. Additional features include a big 45-gallon livewell, two in-deck fish boxes, cockpit shower, bow pulpit, and a transom door. Twin Yamaha 225hp four-stroke outboards cruise the 30 Express in the high 20s and reach a top speed of just over 40 knots.

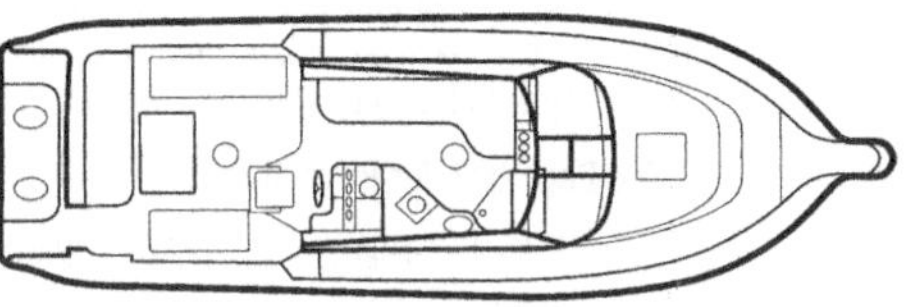

See Page 693 For Price Data

Length	32'6"	Fuel	312 gals.
Beam	10'10"	Water	30 gals.
Hull Draft	1'10"	Max HP	500
Hull Weight	7,700#	Hull Type	Deep-V
Cockpit	102 sq. ft.	Deadrise Aft	19°

Pro-Line 30/31 Sport

With nearly 11 feet of beam, the Pro-Line 31 Sport (called the 30 Sport until 2005) is one of the bigger 30-foot center consoles on the market. Indeed, lots of open deck space and spacious interior allows anglers and divers the freedom to bring along a large party of friends and gear without feeling cramped. Built on a solid fiberglass, deep-V hull with an integrated dive platform and bow pulpit, the wide beam of the 31 Sport makes her an exceptionally stable fishing platform when trolling or drift fishing. Perhaps her most notable feature, however, is the enormous console which houses a spacious, standup head compartment with a sink and sleeping berth—a compact mini-cabin with adequate overnight accommodations for a single angler. There's plenty of rod storage with four in-gunwale holders and under-gunwale racks. Additional features include pop-up cleats, cockpit lighting, transom door, lockable electronics storage, recessed trim tabs, insulated fish boxes, and a big 45-gallon transom livewell. A good performer with twin 250hp Mercury outboards, the Pro-Line 31 Sport will cruise easily in the high 20s knots and reach a top speed of just over 40 knots.

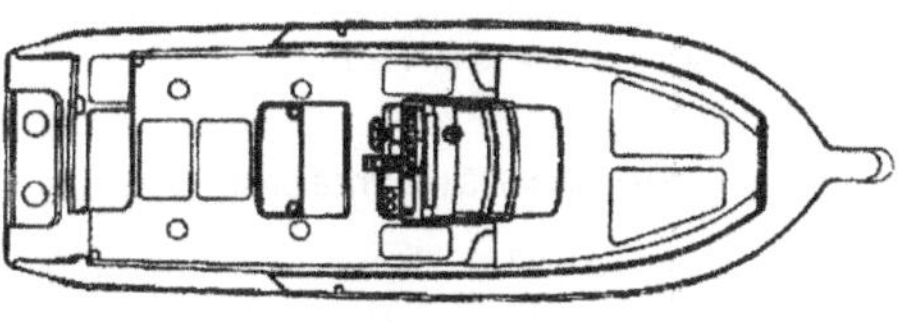

See Page 693 For Price Data

Length	32'6"	Fuel	300 gals.
Beam	10'10"	Water	39 gals.
Hull Draft	1'10"	Max HP	600
Dry Weight	7,000#	Hull Type	Deep-V
Cockpit	145 sq. ft.	Deadrise Aft	19°

Pro-Line 32 Express

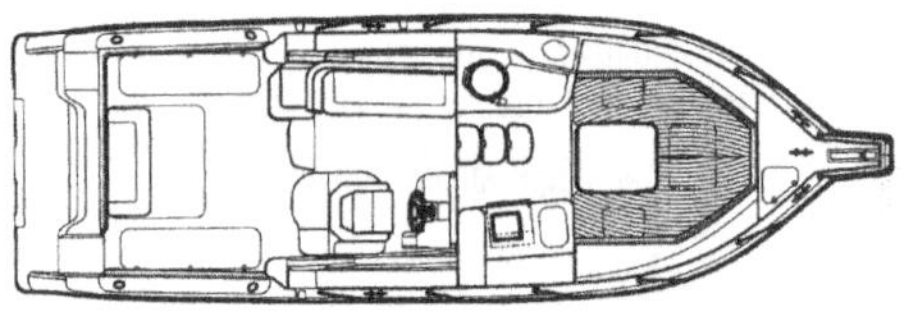

Among the more popular boats in her class, the versatile Pro-Line 32 Express strikes the right balance between full-on fishing boat and comfortable family cruiser. The market for mid-size express boats is very competitive, and several big-name boat manufacturers battle it out for supremacy in this segment every year. What set the 32 Express apart, however—note that she went out of production in 2012 when Pro-Line went out of business—was her affordable price and spacious layout, the result of her wide 10'10" beam. Indeed, when matched hull-to-hull against other express boats her size, the 32's favorable price point and roomy accommodations were hard to ignore. Standard fishing features include two in-deck fish boxes, 35-gallon livewell, tackle drawers, and fresh and raw water washdowns. A rear bench seat folds into the transom when not in use to free up valuable cockpit space. Below decks, a roomy mid-cabin interior with full-service galley, enclosed head with shower, and convertible dinette sleeps four. A large lazarette in the cockpit sole can accommodate an optional generator. With her big 300-gallon fuel capacity, the 32 Express has excellent range. About 40 knots top with Mercury 250hp outboards.

See Page 693 For Price Data

Length	32'4"	Fuel	300 gals.
Beam	10'10"	Water	39 gals.
Hull Draft	1'11"	Max HP	600
Hull Weight	9,500#	Hull Type	Deep-V
Clearance, Top	10'2"	Deadrise Aft	22°

Pro-Line 3250 Express; 32 Express

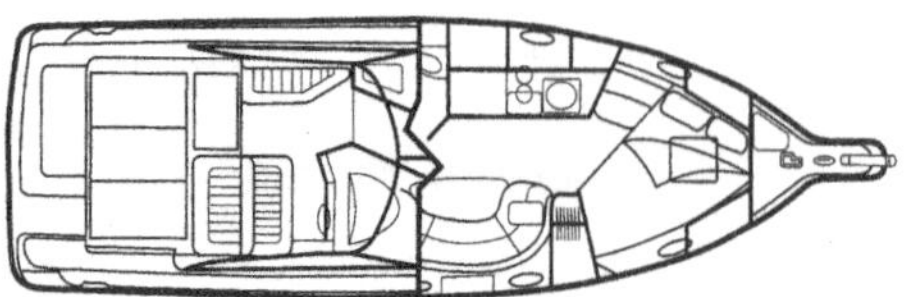

The Pro-Line 32 Express (called the 3250 Express in 1997–99) combines the features of a good fishing boat with a spacious cabin that offers real comfort and elegance below. Express boats like the 32 are popular with anglers who want family-friendly cruising accommodations, and while the 32 does indeed have a comfortable interior, her moderate 11-foot beam offers less in the way of cabin volume than many of her wider-beam counterparts. The midcabin floorplan is arranged with double berths fore and aft, a convertible U-shaped dinette, and a small head compartment with shower. Two opening ports and a pair of deck hatches provide ventilation, and the aft stateroom can be closed off with an accordion door. On deck, there's space in the dash for an array of electronics, and fish boxes are located beneath the bridge deck settee and the aft-facing cockpit seat. Fishing features include a transom bait station with livewell and sink, bolster padding, tackle drawers, lockable rod storage, and transom door. A good performer, twin 310hp MerCruiser (or Volvo) sterndrives cruise at the Pro-Line 32 in the high 20s and reach a top speed of 40+ knots.

See Page 693 For Price Data

Length	33'8"	Fuel	250 gals.
Beam	11'0"	Water	35 gals.
Hull Draft	2'1"	Waste	15 gals.
Weight	12,000#	Hull Type	Deep-V
Clearance	7'4"	Deadrise Aft	19°

Pro-Line 33 Express

The 33 Express (called the 3310 Sportfish in 1999) is a rugged inboard-powered canyon runner—the very first inboard design from Pro-Line—whose upmarket price tag comes as a surprise considering the company's reputation for producing affordable, budget-friendly boats. Heavily built on a deep-V hull with cored hullsides and a molded inner liner, the 33 is obviously meant for fishing although her passenger-friendly bridge deck and comfortable interior work well for occasional family cruising. An impressive list of standard fishing amenities includes both transom and in-deck fish boxes, a 35-gallon livewell, bait-prep center, fresh- and saltwater washdowns, bolster cushions, and a transom door. Belowdecks, the interior of the 33 Express is arranged with a convertible dinette/V-berth forward, a full galley and enclosed head to port, and a cleverly shaped pedestal dining table lowers to create a huge berth. Like several other high-end express fishermen, the entire bridge deck rises hydraulically for access to the engines. Twin 350hp Cat (or Yanmar) diesels cruise the Pro-Line 33 Express in the high 20s and reach a top speed in the mid 30s.

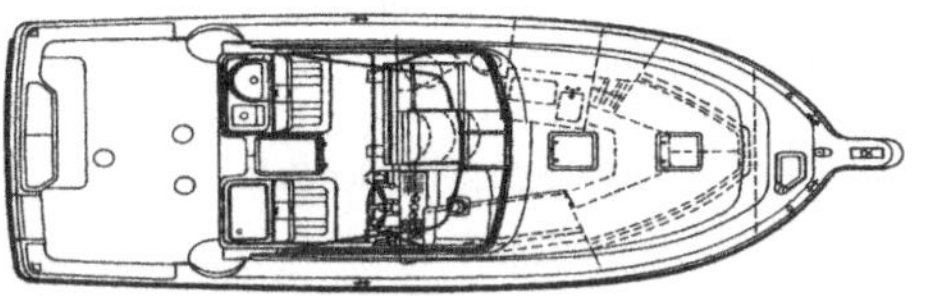

See Page 693 For Price Data

Length	33'0"	Fuel	300 gals.
Beam	12'6"	Water	40 gals.
Draft	3'5"	Waste	20 gals.
Weight	11,200#	Hull Type	Deep-V
Clearance	7'8"	Deadrise Aft	19°

Pro-Line 33 Walkaround

The Pro-Line 34 Walk (called the 33 Walk in 2003–04) is a full-featured walkaround fishing boat whose comfortable cabin allows her to double as an occasional family cruiser. This is Pro-Line's largest walkaround model, and aside from her handsome lines and roomy deck plan, the 34's competitive price makes her one of the better values around for a boat of this type. Built on a solid fiberglass hull, the 75-square-foot cockpit of the 34 Walk comes standard with two in-deck macerated fish boxes, coaming bolsters, lockable rod storage, and a tackle station with sink. Live-bait anglers will appreciate the Pro-Lines's big 40-gallon oval livewell located under the lift-up transom seat. Below, the compact cabin includes a full galley, standup head and shower, and a mid-berth under the helm. A convertible dinette is forward, and three overhead deck hatches admit plenty of outside lighting. Additional features include a well-designed helm with space for extra electronics, deep walkways, a molded bow pulpit, windlass, and a transom door. A good performer, she'll reach a top speed of close to 40 knots with a pair of 225hp Mercury outboards.

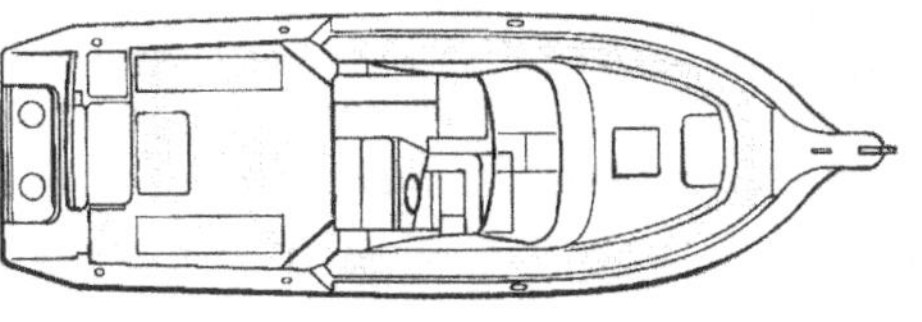

See Page 693 For Price Data

Length	33'8"	Fuel	285 gals.
Beam	11'0"	Water	39 gals.
Hull Draft	2'1"	Max HP	600
Dry Weight	12,000#	Hull Type	Deep-V
Clearance	6'10"	Deadrise Aft	19°

Pro-Line 3400 Super Sport Cuddy

1998–2001

Built using the original Donzi 33 hull, the Pro-Line 3400 Super Sport is a high-performance offshore center console for serious anglers with a lust for speed. Indeed, the 3400's ability to handle up to 675 horsepower allows her to be rigged with triple 225hp outboard motors. Her proven deep-V hull carries a relatively narrow 9-foot, 2-inch beam, and the entire boat is Divinycell cored to keep the weight down. Like any good center console design, the 3400 was built with an impressive array of fishing amenities including a recirculating livewell, two in-deck fish boxes, leaning post with rod holders, a lockable electronics box, coaming bolsters, under-gunwale rod storage, and a tackle station. Beneath the center console is a standup head compartment with freshwater sink and a shower. Additional features include a molded bow pulpit, a bench seat forward of the console, cockpit lighting, and a transom door. Note that her sistership, the 3400 Super Sport Cuddy, is the same boat with a V-berth for overnighting. A fast and stable ride with twin 250hp outboards, the Pro-Line 3400 Super Sport will cruise at 30 knots and reach over 45 knots wide open.

Floorplan Not Available

See Page 693 For Price Data

Length	34'10"	Fuel	300 gals.
Beam	9'2"	Water	30 gals.
Hull Draft	2'1"	Max HP	675
Dry Weight	7,500#	Hull Type	Deep-V
Cockpit	112 sq. ft	Deadrise Aft	22.5°

Pro-Line 35 Express

2006–11

Big outboard-powered express boats have become very popular in recent years thanks to the new generation of high-horsepower, 4-stroke outboards. Built for the sportfishing enthusiast who also wants a boat capable of a comfortable weekend cruise, the Pro-Line 35 Express combines hard-core fishing features with a spacious, well-appointed cabin. She rides on a modified deep-V hull with cored hullsides and decks and a solid fiberglass bottom. Topside, the boat has high stainless rails and a bow pulpit with anchor roller, standard windlass, and line locker to starboard. Cockpit features include two insulated, in-deck fish boxes, tackle storage center, dual washdowns, and foldaway stern seat. An L-shaped bench on the bridge deck provides plenty of room to stretch out and relax while trolling, and a lighted 45-gallon livewell is built into the back side of the helm station. Pop-up cleats are a plus, but side decks are on the narrow side. Below, the midcabin interior of the 35 Express includes a flat-screen TV, standup head with pull-out shower, galley with microwave and fridge, and a small dinette opposite the galley. Mercury Twin 250hp outboards top out at 40 knots; triple 225s reach close to 50 knots top.

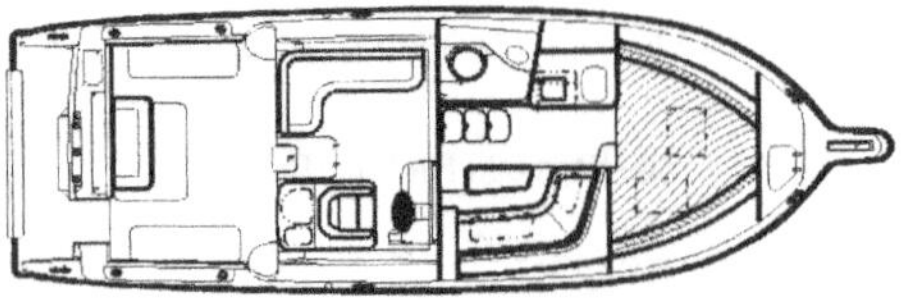

See Page 693 For Price Data

Length	35'6"	Water	60 gals.
Beam	12'6"	Waste	21 gals.
Hull Draft	2'1"	Max HP	900
Hull Weight	11,200#	Hull Type	Deep-V
Fuel	320 gals.	Deadrise Aft	19°

Pursuit

Quick View

- Pursuit traces its roots back to 1955 when Leon Slikkers left his job at the Chris Craft plant in Holland, MI, and began the Slickcraft Boat Company.
- The company was sold to the AMF Corp. in 1969, and Slikkers stayed on as president until 1973 when he resigned.
- In 1974 Slikkers founded S2 Yachts and began building cruising and racing sailboats. The Pursuit series of fishing boats followed in 1977, and in 1979 the Tiara series was introduced.
- The 1980s and 1990s were an era of steady growth for Pursuit as the company gradually grew its line of high-quality center console and express fishing boats.
- Built in Ft. Pierce, Florida, Pursuit is an industry leader in innovative fishing boat design and manufacturing excellence.
- Pursuit boats are generally viewed as among the best fishing boats in the industry.

Pursuit Boats • Ft. Pierce, FL • www.pursuitboats.com

Pursuit 2600 Center Console Inboard

1994–97

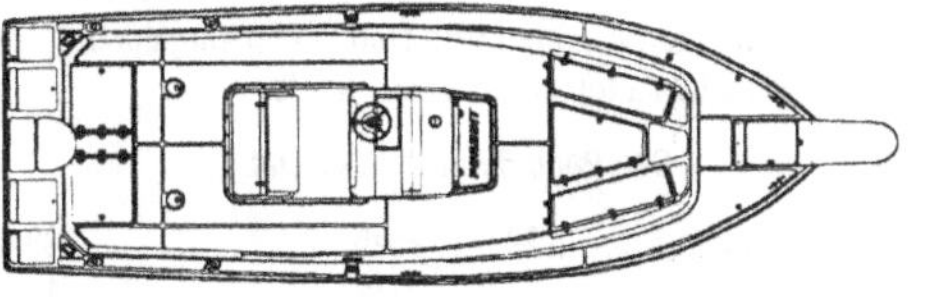

The reliability, ease of maintenance, and economy of an inboard engine still outweighs any similar benefits that outboard motors can offer. Of course you can't go as fast with a single inboard as you can with a pair of outboards, but with the engine amidships and deep in the hull, the added stability and improved balance and handling of an inboard design is quite remarkable. That said, the 2600 Center Console combines the best features of a small inboard fisherman with Pursuit's high production standards in a first-rate offshore fishing package. With a wide 9-foot, 7-inch beam, the 2600 is a big boat for her size with more cockpit space than one normally expects in a 26-footer. The list of standard features is impressive: transom livewell and bait rigging station, a big fish box, tackle storage, a tilt-away console with an enclosed head and sink under, and in-deck dry storage and rod locker forward. (Note that the hull is designed with a prop pocket.) The standard 320hp gas inboard cruises at 25 knots and delivers about 32 knots wide open. Several inboard diesel options were also available.

Not Enough Resale Data to Set Values

Length w/Pulpit	28'7"	Fuel	160 gals.
Hull Length	26'5"	Water	20 gals.
Beam	9'7"	Waste	20 gals.
Hull Draft	2'4"	Hull Type	Deep-V
Hull Weight	6,000#	Deadrise Aft	20°

Pursuit 2670 Center Console; C 260

2005–07

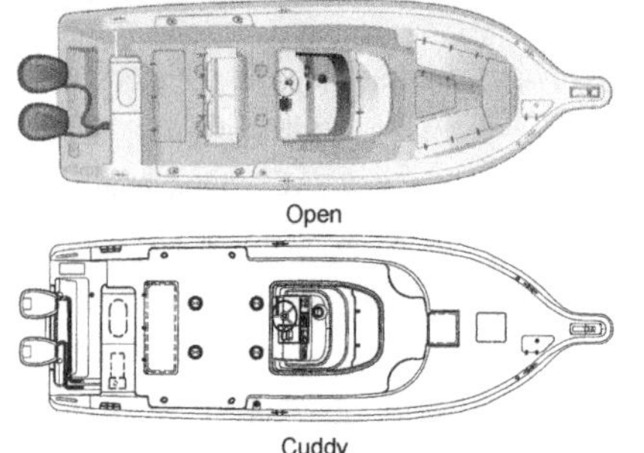
Open

Cuddy

Pursuit got it right with the 2670 Center Console (called the C 260 in 2007), a rock-solid fishing machine from one of the country's top builders of offshore center consoles. Offered in open-bow or cuddy configurations, the 2670 is a good-looking fishboat with a large cockpit and an impressive array of high-end features. Her well-designed helm offers a wealth of digital information arranged for maximum visibility, and the standard leaning post includes a four-rod rocket launcher, tackle trays, and stowage. The 2670's factory T-top comes with a lifejacket storage area sewn into the underside, and a wraparound acrylic windshield protects the helm. Note that the sub-console compartment does not contain a head. In cuddy models, the cabin contains a double berth, marine head, storage, and rod racks. Aft, the transom has a deep 49-gallon livewell and bait prep station in addition to bilge access. There's a large fishbox in the floor, and rod storage under each of the padded gunnels. Built on a traditional deep-V hull with a wide 9-foot, 3-inch beam, the 2670 tracks well and handles rough water with confidence. Expect a top speed of close to 40+ knots with twin 200hp Yamaha outboards.

See Page 693 For Price Data

Length w/Pulpit	28'5"	Fuel	188 gals.
Hull Length	26'5"	Water	18 gals.
Beam	9'3"	Max HP	450
Hull Draft	1'8"	Hull Type	Deep-V
Dry Weight	5,800#	Deadrise Aft	21°

Pursuit 2670 Cuddy Console

2002–05

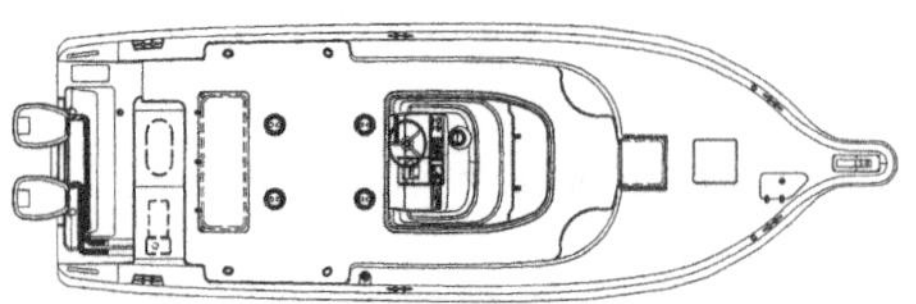

Pursuit's 2670 Cuddy Console provides the 360-degree fishability of a traditional center console with the added benefit of a small cuddy cabin to escape the elements and/or provide secure storage for tackle and other marine gear. Traditionally styled and built to Pursuit's high production standards, the 2670 runs on deep-V hull with balsa coring in the hullsides and a solid fiberglass bottom. An integral bow pulpit is standard, and the tilt-away helm console—with its cast aluminum wheel—contains space below for dry storage or several scuba tanks. The cockpit is fitted with a macerated in-deck fish box, and a 49-gallon lighted livewell, cutting board, tackle drawers and a rigging station with sink are all built into the transom. Just aft of the cabin are a pair of molded steps for access to the bow and casting platform, which is protected by a low-profile bow rail. Although the cabin is small, it comes with a large V-berth, an electric head, and storage racks for 16 rods. Additional standard features include a leaning post with rocket launcher, cockpit bolsters and lighting, recessed trim tabs, and a transom door. Powered with twin 200hp Yamaha outboards, the 2670 will attain a top speed of 40+ knots.

See Page 693 For Price Data

Length w/Pulpit	28'5"	Fuel	188 gals.
Hull Length	26'5"	Water	18 gals.
Beam	9'3"	Max HP	400
Hull Draft	1'8"	Hull Type	Deep-V
Dry Weight	5,400#	Deadrise Aft	21°

Pursuit 2670 Denali; LS 265

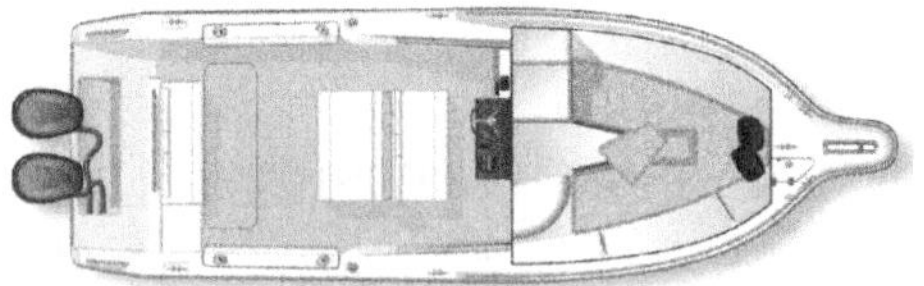

More pleasure boat than hardcore fisherman, the Pursuit 2670 (called the LS 265 Denali in 2007) will appeal to experienced boaters who have an eye for quality and long-term value. Unlike conventional express cruisers with their glitzy styling, cluttered cockpits, and overstuffed interiors, the Denali offers beautiful styling, a spacious, wide-open cockpit, and a simple interior with V-berths and a concealed head. This is an ideal boat for day boaters who enjoy fishing, swimming, and cruising with friends and family. Her deep-V hull can run any inlet with confidence, and the Denali's meticulous finish is as good as it gets in a small production boat. The centerpiece of the 2670 is the aft-facing bench seat in the center of the cockpit, which pulls out and converts into a full-length sun pad. The centerline helm position—unusual in any boat—is notable for its exceptional visibility and intelligent dash layout. For anglers, a 12-gallon livewell, in-sole fish box with pumpout, tackle lockers, cockpit sink, and cabin rod storage are all standard. The 2670 Denali will reach a top speed of 45 knots with a pair of Yamaha 225 outboards. (Note that the 2665 Denali is the same boat with sterndrive power.)

See Page 693 For Price Data

Length w/Pulpit	28'0"	Fuel	188 gals.
Hull Length	26'5"	Water	18 gals.
Beam	9'3"	Max HP	450
Draft	3'0"	Hull Type	Deep-V
Weight	7,355#	Deadrise Aft	21°

Pursuit 2855 Express Fisherman

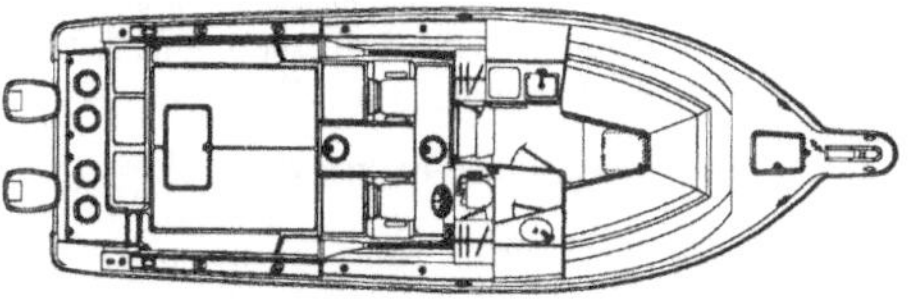

Introduced in 1993, the Pursuit 2855 Express Fisherman is a rugged offshore fisherman whose solid construction and comfortable ride make her a pleasure to fish in fair weather or foul. She was a good-looking boat in her day with crisp styling and integrated bracket/dive platform, and like all Pursuits the workmanship and finish are well above average. The cockpit of the 2855 is completely unobstructed and includes a transom door as well as a bait and tackle-rigging station in the transom bulkhead. A pair of molded fish boxes are located behind the companion seats, and the helm console is wide enough for flush mounting most necessary electronics. The only significant feature missing from the cockpit is horizontal rod storage under the gunwales. Belowdecks, the 2855 will sleep four (the dinette converts to a double berth and the seat backs swing up to form pilot berths) and includes a compact galley area and a standup head with shower. Additional features include fairly wide side decks, a molded bow pulpit, balsa coring in the hullsides, and a windshield center vent. Twin 250hp outboards reach a top speed of close to 40 knots.

See Page 693 For Price Data

Length w/Pulpit	33'3"	Fuel	300 gals.
Hull Length	31'0"	Water	30 gals.
Beam	10'3"	Max HP	500
Hull Draft	1'9"	Hull Type	Deep-V
Weight	6,500#	Deadrise Aft	20°

Pursuit 2860/2865 Denali

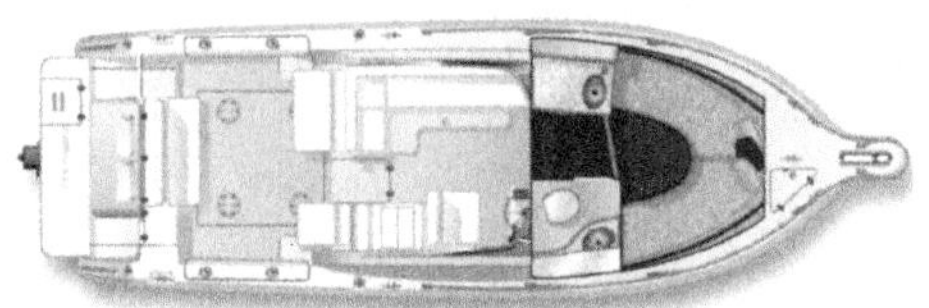

The Pursuit 2860 is an upmarket sterndrive pleasure boat whose practical layout will appeal to anglers and day cruisers alike. Only a few 28-footers can claim the built-in versatility of the Denali—this is a boat equally well adapted to fishing, swimming, or leisurely weekend cruising. Built on a seaworthy deep-V hull with moderate beam and an integrated swim platform, the focal point of the Denali is her spacious bridge deck with its posh L-shaped lounge seating, wet bar, and well-designed helm. The aft cockpit is large enough for several anglers and their gear, and the transom contains a freshwater sink, insulated fish box/cooler, and raw-water washdown. Belowdecks, the Denali's well-appointed cuddy cabin contains berths for two with a teak-and-holly sole, removable table, galley with sink, refrigerator and stove, and an enclosed head with shower. Updated in 2002, the revised 2865 Denali featured a pair of aft-facing seats in the cockpit, a restyled transom, and a new curved windshield. Built-in tackle drawers, a bow pulpit, dash glove box, and an electric helm seat were all standard. Among several single engine options, a Volvo 375hp gas I/O will reach a top speed of 35+ knots.

See Page 693 For Price Data

Length w/Pulpit	32'10"	Fuel	148 gals.
Hull Length	28'0"	Water	30 gals.
Beam	9'6"	Waste	20 gals.
Draft, Drives Down	3'0"	Hull Type	Deep-V
Weight	7,600#	Deadrise Aft	21°

Pursuit 2870 Center Console; C 280

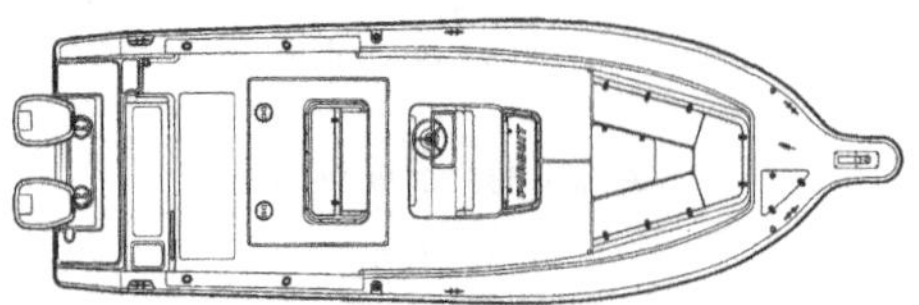

The 2870 Center Console (called the 2870 CC in 1997–2006; C 280 in 2007–08) is a rugged offshore fisherman with the built-in quality one expects in a Pursuit product. With a wide 9'6" beam, she delivers one of the larger fishing platforms in her class, and a generous fuel capacity gives her the long-range capability that big-water fishermen demand. Built on a deep-V hull with cored hullsides, the 2870's layout affords anglers the ability to fight fish from virtually anywhere on the boat. The tilt-away console is large enough to accommodate a good array of flush-mounted electronics and, like most center consoles in today's market, a fully enclosed head compartment with toilet, sink, and a pressurized water system is concealed within the console. The leaning post has a freshwater sink and tackle-storage space as well as a 35-gallon livewell, and the transom rigging station contains a large fish box, sink and raw water washdown. Additional features include a transom door, bow pulpit with anchor roller, an insulated in-deck fish box, a lockable electronics cover, and lockable bow storage. Twin 225hp Yamahas reach a top speed of 40+ knots. Note that all-new Pursuit C 280 model was introduced in 2009.

See Page 693 For Price Data

Length w/Pulpit	30'0"	Fuel	234 gals.
Hull Length	28'0"	Water	20 gals.
Beam	9'6"	Max HP	450
Hull Draft	1'9"	Hull Type	Deep-V
Weight w/T250s	7,150#	Deadrise Aft	22°

Pursuit 2870 Offshore Center Console

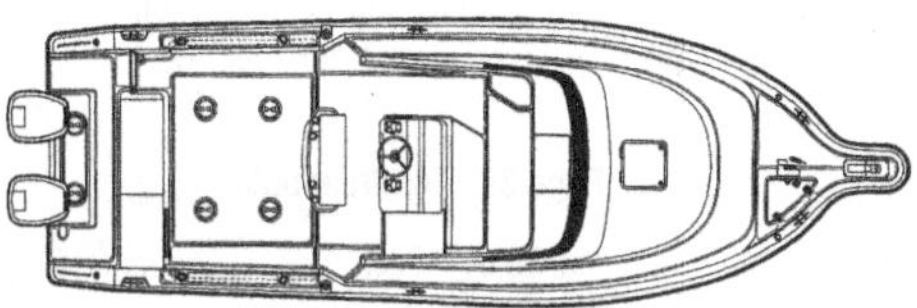

The Pursuit 2870 Offshore Center Console is a true crossover boat in that she combines the recessed walkways and efficient cabin layout of a walkaround design with the centerline helm position of a traditional center-console fisherman. The result is a very innovative boat able to satisfy the demands of anglers and cruisers alike. Built on a proven deep-V hull, there is much to like about the layout of the 2870 Offshore. The cockpit is intelligently arranged with a large in-floor fish box, rod holders, and a transom bait and rigging station with cutting board and sink. The leaning post incorporates a 26-gallon livewell, and the aft-facing jump seat next to the helm sits atop a five-drawer tackle center. Note the huge sub-deck storage compartment just aft of the console for batteries, water tanks, and oil reservoirs. A tilt-away helm provides easy access to wiring and gauges. Belowdecks, the compact cuddy cabin contains all the basics including a removable table, mini-galley with sink and stove, and marine head. A good performer, twin 225hp Yamahas reach a top speed of 40+ knots. Note that the Pursuit 2800 Offshore Center Console (1996–98) is the same boat with sterndrive power.

See Page 693 For Price Data

Length w/Pulpit	30'0"	Fuel	234 gals.
Hull Length	28'0"	Water	20 gals.
Beam	9'6"	Max HP	450
Hull Draft	1'8"	Hull Type	Deep-V
Hull Weight	5,950#	Deadrise Aft	22°

Pursuit 2870 Walkaround

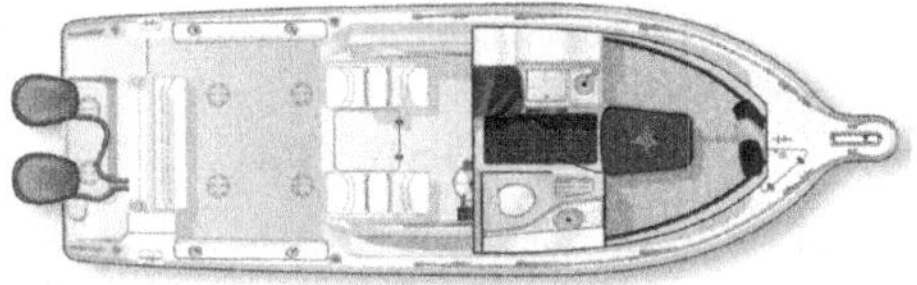

Considered by many to be among the best in her class, the Pursuit 2870 Walkaround is a top-quality offshore fisherman for anglers with an keen eye for engineering and workmanship. Easy on the eye (but a little tough on the wallet), the 2870 rides on a proven deep-V hull with moderate beam and a fully integrated transom. Her deep cockpit is rigged for serious fishing with a large insulated fish box, circulating livewell, and a transom bait-prep center with cutting board and sink. Excellent nonskid provides anglers with a steady grip when the seas pick up, and deeply recessed walkways make it easy to get around the cabin. Twin aft-facing cockpit seats and a rear bench seat offer plenty of guest seating. The well-appointed cabin—which is quite spacious for a 28-footer—includes a convertible dinette, teak-and-holly sole, galley with sink and stove, and enclosed head compartment. An athwartships single berth under the helmdeck doubles as a convenient storage area. A good rough-water performer, twin 225hp Yamahas reach a top speed of 40+ knots. Note that the Pursuit 2800 Walkaround (1996–98) is the same boat with sterndrive power.

See Page 693 For Price Data

Length w/Pulpit	30'0"	Fuel	234 gals.
Hull Length	28'0"	Water	20 gals.
Beam	9'6"	Max HP	500
Hull Draft	1'8"	Hull Type	Deep-V
Dry Weight	7,570#	Deadrise Aft	22°

Pursuit C 280

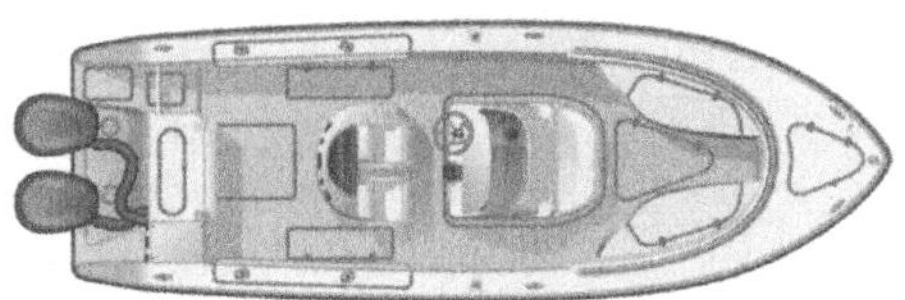

For demanding offshore fishermen with an eye for quality, owning a Pursuit says a lot about how they view their boating priorities. It's not just about styling (although the C 280 easily ranks among the best-looking 28-foot center consoles on the water); for most, it's about the satisfaction of owning a top-quality boat backed by a company that's been doing things right for over three decades. The C 280's appeal is immediately apparent in her graceful sheer, flawless gel coat, and extraordinary fit and finish. Aft of the helm in the seat base is a 52-gallon lighted livewell just opposite of the transom rigging station with removable tackle drawers, cutting surface and molded tool holders. A foldaway stern seat and two 29-gallon in-deck, insulated fish boxes with macerators were standard. There's also an additional 45-gallon insulated fish box in the transom. The head compartment within the console contains a manual head with holding tank, pumpout and macerator. There's space at the helm for two big-screen video displays. The bow anchor chute is a nice touch. Yamaha 250s max out around 45 knots. Note that a previous C 280 model ran from 2007–08.

See Page 693 For Price Data

Length	28'0"	Fuel	220 gals.
Beam	9'6"	Water	20 gals.
Draft, Up	1'7"	Max HP	500
Draft, Down	2'10"	Hull Type	Deep-V
Weight w/250s	7,300#	Deadrise Aft	24°

Pursuit OS 285

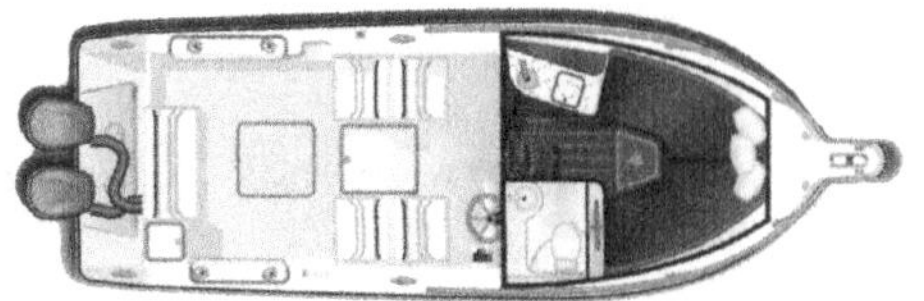

For over 30 years, Pursuit has been one of the leading builders of high-end sportfishing boats. Pursuits consistently rank with the best names in the business for quality and durability, so it was no surprise that when the OS 285 was introduced in 2008 she received an enthusiastic reception from industry pros up and down the East Coast. Built on a deep-V hull with moderate beam and a sharp entry, the large cockpit of the OS 285 features a molded-in stern seat with an insulated storage compartment in the seat base. Across from the stern bench are port and starboard aft-facing seats whose bases conceal a cooler and 32-gallon livewell. A bait rigging station and sink are to starboard, opposite the transom door. Below decks, the 285's cozy, well-appointed cabin includes a convertible dinette forward, athwartships mid-berth aft, galley with microwave, coffee maker and refrigerator, and an enclosed head with hand-held shower. A tall windshield (with side vents) protects the helm from high-rpm windblast. Standard features include a fiberglass hardtop (with PFD storage), teak cabin flooring, cockpit bolsters, and deluxe helm/companion seats with armrests. Twin Yamaha 250s top out at 40+ knots.

See Page 693 For Price Data

Length w/Pulpit	30'8"	Fuel	232 gals.
Beam	9'6"	Water	30 gals.
Hull Draft	1'9"	Max HP	600
Weight w/T250s	7,570#	Hull Type	Deep-V
Clearance, Top	8'4"	Deadrise Aft	22°

Pursuit 3000 Express

1998–2003

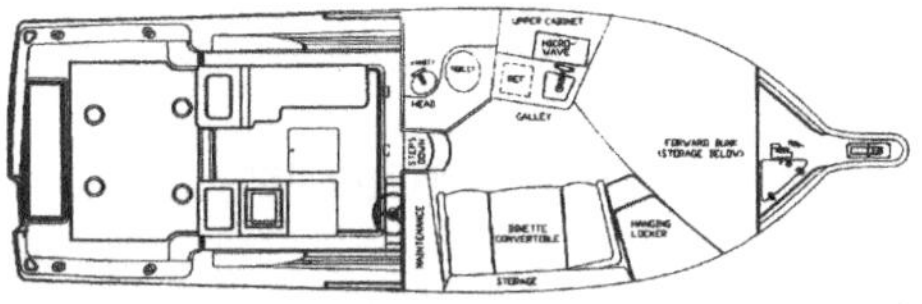

A popular model from a company that seldom misses the mark when it comes to design and engineering, the Pursuit 3000 Express is an upmarket midsize fisherman with a comfortable interior and a well-arranged deck layout. This was the replacement boat for Pursuit's long-running 3100 Express Fisherman; the 3000's narrower beam, sharper entry, and additional transom deadrise make her a better rough-water performer than her predecessor. While the cockpit can't be described as massive, anglers will appreciate the excellent nonskid (a Pursuit trademark) and the fine detailing. A transom door, in-deck fish box, bait-prep center and coaming bolsters are standard, and a drop-down seat at the transom provides extra seating. The cabin—a handsome display of luxury fabrics and teak trim—sleeps four adults. Additional features include a classy helm with space for extra electronics, a full-height windshield (excellent visibility), side exhausts, and wide side decks. An electric lift system raises the entire bridge deck for engine access. Twin 320hp Crusader gas inboards cruise the 3000 Express at 25 knots (about 35 knots top), and optional 250hp Cummins diesels cruise at 25 knots and reach a top speed of 30 knots.

See Page 693 For Price Data

Length w/Pulpit	32'8"	Fuel	210 gals.
Hull Length	30'10"	Water	30 gals.
Beam	10'6"	Waste	18 gals.
Draft	2'10"	Hull Type	Deep-V
Weight	10,600#	Deadrise Aft	21°

Pursuit 3000 Offshore

1995–2004

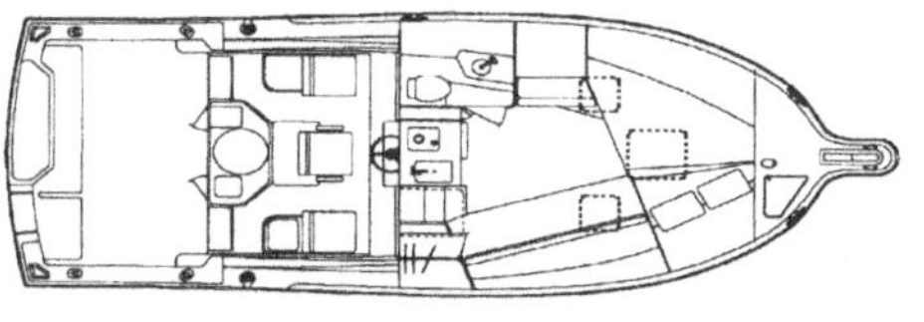

A popular model with a custom "Palm Beach" profile that many anglers love, the Pursuit 3000 Offshore was one of the preeminent offshore fishing boats in her class following her introduction in 1995. She's built on a smooth-running modified-V hull with a relatively wide beam, a substantial 19 degrees of transom deadrise, and a well-flared bow. The cockpit—about 60 square feet in size—came with a full array of top-notch fishing amenities including a transom door, a centerline bait station (with an abovedeck livewell), two cushioned storage boxes, and a big transom fish box. Note that the helm is located on the centerline, a design that opens up the interior by moving the companionway to starboard. The entire bridge deck can be hydraulically raised for engine access. There are berths for four below in the spacious cabin—two pilot berths to starboard and a double berth forward—as well as a roomy head, a backlit rod storage showcase, and a complete galley. An impressive, well-engineered boat with a price to match, twin 375hp Crusader gas inboards cruise in the high 20s (about 35 knots top), and optional 230hp Volvo diesels cruise in the mid 20s and top out at about 30 knots.

See Page 693 For Price Data

Length w/Pulpit	31'2"	Fuel	250 gals.
Hull Length	29'1"	Water	40 gals.
Beam	12'0"	Waste	20 gals.
Draft	2'9"	Hull Type	Modified-V
Weight	11,500#	Deadrise Aft	19°

Pursuit 3070 Center Console

2001–07

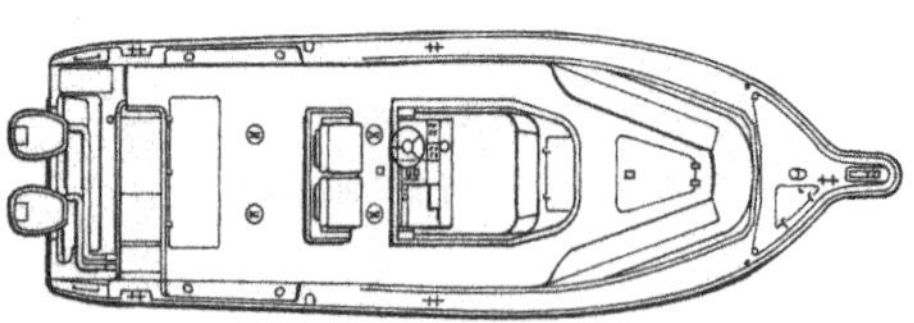

The Pursuit 3070 Center Console (called the C 300 in 2007) is a beamy deep-V fisherman with all of the built-in quality and precision engineering Pursuit owners have come to expect over the years. This is a handsome boat with a graceful sheer as well as a strictly-business personality. Built on the same hull as the popular 3000 Express (as well as the 3070 Offshore Center Console), the large cockpit of the 3070 is the result of her wide 10-foot, 6-inch beam. The big console, with space at the helm for flush-mounting electronics, houses an enclosed head compartment (with an electric head) with a classy teak-and-holly sole and an opening port. Fish boxes are located under the forward seats and aft, where a 5-foot insulated in-deck box will hold a full day's catch. Principal features include refrigerated bait drawers in the transom, an adjustable leaning post, circulating baitwell, stern seat, and a transom rigging station. While the 3070 Center Console carries more beam than many other 30-foot center consoles, it comes at the cost of compromised headsea performance. Twin 250hp Yamahas cruise an honest 30 knots and reach a top speed of around 40 knots.

See Page 693 For Price Data

Length w/Pulpit	32'8"	Fuel	310 gals.
Hull Length	30'10"	Water	30 gals.
Beam	10'6"	Max HP	500
Draft, Down	3'3"	Hull Type	Deep-V
Dry Weight	8,945#	Deadrise Aft	21°

Pursuit 3070 Offshore Center Console

1999–2006

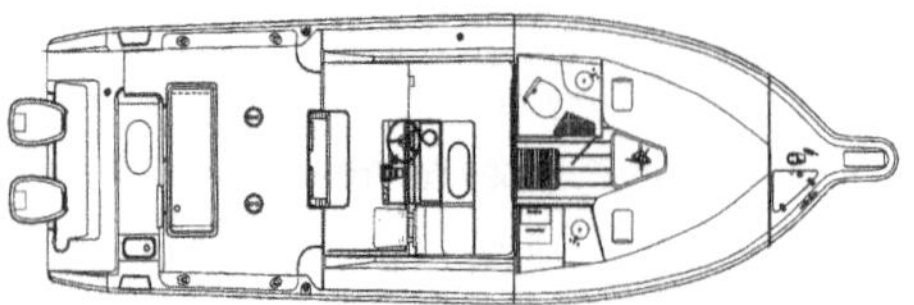

The Pursuit 3070 Offshore Center Console is a true crossover boat combining the recessed walkways and efficient cabin of a walkaround design with the centerline helm position of a traditional center-console fisherman. The result is a very innovative boat able to satisfy the demands of anglers and cruisers alike. There is much to like about the layout of the 3070 Offshore beginning with her comfortable bridge deck seating and including a roomy cockpit with 44-gallon livewell, bait-prep center with freshwater sink and cutting board, tackle storage, and large 5-foot in-floor fish box. Looking for under-gunwale rod storage? Forget it—the leaning post tilts forward at the push of a button to expose lighted racks under the bridge deck for up to 12 rods. Below decks, the 3070's compact cabin includes a V-berth and mid-cabin berth, enclosed head with shower, teak-and-holly sole, and small galley with sink, stove and refrigerator. Beginning in 2003, a full wraparound windshield replaced the cut-down windscreen of previous years. Not an inexpensive boat, twin 250hp Yamaha outboards top out at just over 40 knots.

See Page 693 For Price Data

Length w/Pulpit	32'8"	Fuel	310 gals.
Hull Length	30'10"	Water	30 gals.
Beam	10'6"	Max HP	500
Draft, Down	3'3"	Hull Type	Deep-V
Dry Weight	8,100#	Deadrise Aft	21°

Pursuit 3070 Offshore Express

2002–07

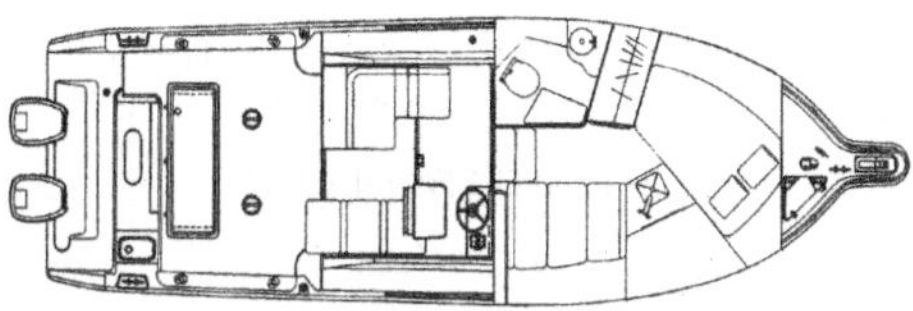

Introduced in 2002 and lasting just two years in production, the Pursuit 3070 Express was one of an increasing number of big express boats offered with standard outboard power. Most express fishing boats over 30 feet are inboard-powered, and while inboards offer better low-speed maneuverability (as well as an uncluttered transom), outboards are faster and they can be trimmed up to run in shallow water. Built on a deep-V hull, the 3070 Express is a handsome boat with an efficient deck layout and a full array of fishing amenities. The cockpit features a transom livewell, foldaway transom seat, cutting board, and sink. An aft-facing jump seat is built into the back of the helm for watching baits. On the raised bridgedeck, a portside L-lounge seats three, and the entire aft section of the bridgedeck raises on mechanical rams to reveal a cavernous storage compartment. Belowdecks, the compact cabin is arranged with a V-berth forward and a small mid-berth aft, a complete galley, teak-and-holly cabin sole, and a standup head with shower. Twin 250hp Yamaha outboards deliver a top speed of about 40 knots.

See Page 694 For Price Data

Length w/Pulpit	32'8"	Fuel	310 gals.
Hull Length	30'10"	Water	30 gals.
Beam	10'6"	Max HP	500
Hull Draft	1'6"	Hull Type	Deep-V
Dry Weight	9,640#	Deadrise Aft	21°

Pursuit 3100 Express

1993–97

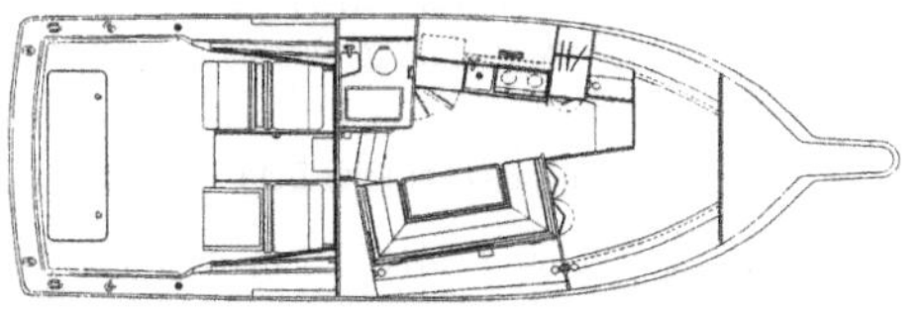

The Pursuit 3100 Express is pretty much the same boat as the original Tiara 3100 Open (1979–91), a conservative and well-built boat with an upscale interior and relatively roomy cockpit. Built on a solid fiberglass modified-V hull with a wide beam and side-dumping exhausts, the 3100 Express is one of those boats that can easily double as a comfortable family cruiser since her interior accommodations are more upscale than one usually expects in a true fishing boat. While there's no midcabin, there are berths for four (with the dinette converted) along with a full-sized galley, adequate storage, a roomy head compartment, and a beautiful teak-and-holly cabin sole. The 3100's spacious single-level cockpit provides an excellent fishing platform with plenty of room for a mounted chair. A bait and tackle center fits behind the helm seat, and a circulating livewell (optional) can be fitted in the cockpit sole. Additional features include cockpit bolsters, wide side decks, bow pulpit, and swim platform. More family cruiser than fishing boat, the 3100 has a reputation for being a stiff ride in a chop. Standard 300hp gas inboards cruise at 20–21 knots (around 30 knots top).

See Page 694 For Price Data

Length w/Pulpit	33'9"	Fuel, Std	206 gals.
Hull Length	31'1"	Fuel, Opt	276 gals.
Beam	12'0"	Water	36 gals.
Draft	2'9"	Hull Type	Modified-V
Weight	11,000#	Deadrise Aft	16°

Pursuit C 310

2007–Current

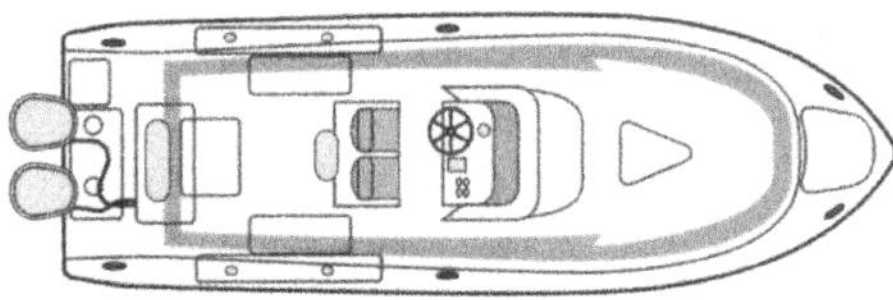

For offshore anglers shopping for a quality center console in the 30-foot range, the Pursuit C 310 will probably be on the short list of likely candidates. For some, this may be their last boat, and they want it to last. Pursuit has been building high-end center consoles for many years, and the company has of record of producing leading-edge products with proven layouts and solid customer support. Introduced in 2007, the C 310 is a tournament-level fishing machine with the premium amenities anglers expect in a Pursuit product. The helm and companion seats feature flip-up bolster-style bases for driving while seated or standing. Built into the aft section of the helm seat base is a 52-gallon lighted, recirculating livewell for easy access from the transom-mounted rigging station complete with tool holder, cutting surface, and tackle drawers. There are two insulated, in-deck fish boxes, and a third fish box is built into the transom. Rod holders are everywhere. Note that a lockable rod rack under the forward seat swings out for use. Other comforts include an anchor windlass with remote, folding transom seat, pop-up cleats, marine head with holding tank and macerator, and courtesy lights. Yamaha 250s top out at 45 knots.

See Page 694 For Price Data

Length	31'2"	Fuel	260 gals.
Beam	9'6"	Water	20 gals.
Draft, Up	1'10"	Max HP	500
Draft, Down	2'8"	Hull Type	Deep-V
Weight w/T250s	8,500#	Deadrise Aft	24°

Pursuit OS 315 Offshore

2008–Current

American boaters have a love affair with big, outboard-powered express boats like the Pursuit OS 315. Designed to split the difference between hardcore fishing and comfortable family cruising, several builders compete in this popular market sector with models ranging from the affordable to seriously expensive. Introduced in 2008, the Pursuit OS 315 ranks near the top of her class not just for cost, but quality as well. Like all Pursuit models, she rides on a deep-V hull with moderate beam and a relatively sharp entry. Her enclosed helm, integral hardtop, and vented windshield afford unobstructed visibility and excellent weather protection while on the water. For fishing, the 315's cockpit is fitted with a 32-gallon recirculating livewell, tackle drawers, and a large insulated cooler in the stern seat base. An L-shaped lounge on the bridge deck provides comfortable seating for four. The 315's upscale cabin features a single adult berth amidships, full-service galley to port, and an enclosed stand-up head opposite. The forward dinette converts to a double bed in the usual fashion. With her 284-gallon fuel capacity, the OS 315 has very good range. Yamaha 250hp outboards max out at 36–38 knots.

See Page 694 For Price Data

Length w/Pulpit	32'8"	Fuel	284 gals.
Beam	10'8"	Water	30 gals.
Hull Draft	1'6"	Max HP	600
Weight w/T250s	11,000#	Hull Type	Deep-V
Clearance, Top	9'3"	Deadrise Aft	20°

Pursuit 3100 Offshore

2004–05

Introduced in 2004, the Pursuit 3100 Offshore is a redesign of the company's popular 3000 Express, a strong-running fishing boat that's also a capable cruiser. The resemblance between the two boats is unmistakable, but it's the Offshore's stylish single-piece windshield and modern vacuum-bagged construction that sets her apart from her predecessor. Built on a deep-V hull with prop pockets, the 3100's uncluttered cockpit is arranged with a fold-down rear seat, and large in-deck fish box forward of the transom. A livewell is located just aft of the portside lounge seat, while a sink and icemaker is positioned abaft the helm seat. For engine access, the entire aft section of the bridge deck raises on electronic rams. Below, the 3100 sleeps four with an angled double berth forward and a starboard dinette that converts into a second berth. A teak-and-holly sole adds a stylish tone to the cabin, and the compact galley comes with a microwave and refrigerator. Like all Pursuit products, the finish of the 3100 Offshore can only be described as exemplary. Standard 320hp gas inboards cruise in the mid 20s, and optional 315hp Yanmar diesels cruise at just over 30 knots.

See Page 694 For Price Data

Length w/Pulpit	34'6"	Fuel	192 gals.
Hull Length	32'4"	Water	30 gals.
Beam	10'6"	Waste	18 gals.
Draft	3'3"	Hull Type	Deep-V
Weight	10,322#	Deadrise Aft	21°

Pursuit 3370 Offshore; OS 335

2004–08

When she was introduced in 2004, the 3370 Offshore (called the OS 335 in 2007–08) was the largest outboard-powered express Pursuit had yet built. It wasn't so long ago that most express boats this size were inboards. The advent of Yamaha's monster 350hp four-stroke outboard changed everything, however, allowing manufactures to build much bigger boats with outboard power. The 3370 is basically an outboard version of the company's 3100 Offshore with the additional two feet used to hang the outboards. Built on a deep-V hull, the Offshore's stylish one-piece windshield and sophisticated vacuum-bagged construction are just two of the features that set her apart from the competition. The cockpit has three foldaway seats, two facing aft and a larger one in the transom for cruising. Tackle drawers and a removable fish box were standard, and the transom features a cutting board and 45-gallon livewell. The well-appointed cabin—with diagonal berth forward, convertible dinette to starboard, portside galley, and mid-berth aft—sleeps four adults and two children. An agile and spirited performer, twin 300hp Mercs deliver just over 40 knots top.

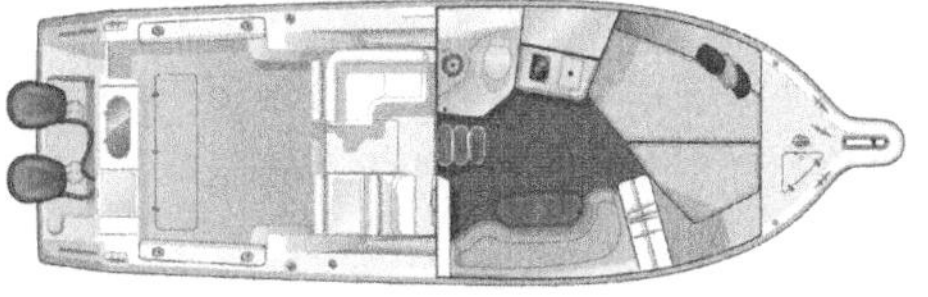

See Page 694 For Price Data

Length w/Pulpit	35'1"	Fuel	310 gals.
Beam	10'6"	Water	30 gals.
Draft	2'4"	Max HP	600
Weight w/T250s	10,670#	Hull Type	Deep-V
Clearance	9'7"	Deadrise Aft	21°

Pursuit 3400 Express

The 3400 Express is a serious offshore fishing machine with all the built-in amenities hardcore anglers have come to expect in a Pursuit product. She's built on a beamy modified-V hull with a solid fiberglass bottom, cored hullsides and prop pockets to reduce the shaft angle. Originally, the deck plan incorporated a centerline helm flanked by L-shaped lounges. The companionway was to starboard, and the interior had the galley aft. In 1999 the deck tooling was completely changed with a new starboard-side helm position with an L-shaped lounge to port. With the companionway now on the centerline, an all-new interior floorplan was devised with a full dinette, although the stall shower of the original layout was lost. As before, the entire bridge deck raises up for access to the motors. The cockpit comes with a molded bait station and tackle center, transom-mounted fish box, and a transom door with gate. Additional features include wide side decks, a molded bow pulpit, and side-dumping exhausts. A good-running boat, twin 370hp Cummins diesels cruise the 3400 Express in the mid 20s (30+ knots wide open).

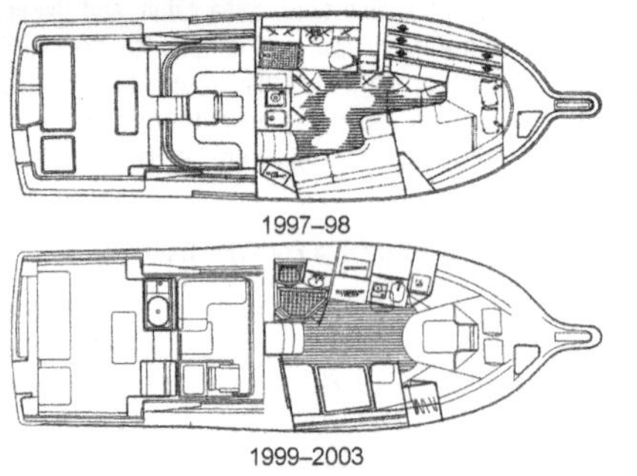
1997–98

1999–2003

See Page 694 For Price Data

Length w/Pulpit	36'4"	Fuel	350 gals.
Hull Length	33'9"	Water	60 gals.
Beam	12'9"	Waste	30 gals.
Draft	2'2"	Hull Type	Modified-V
Weight	14,000#	Deadrise Aft	18°

Pursuit 345 Drummond Runner

A unique boat from a company known for its marketing savvy, the Pursuit 345 Drummond Runner is a multipurpose express whose innovative center-island galley raised the bar for dayboat comfort and versatility. Locating the galley in the cockpit isn't a new idea, but Pursuit designers took the concept to the next level by incorporating into the island a sink, side-loading refrigerator, microwave, single-burner stove, and storage drawers, and then adding a folding sun lounge aft for two passengers. Not surprisingly, moving the galley into the cockpit frees up space in the cabin. Boasting a full-size V-berth, folding settee, and a very large head compartment, there's more elbow space in the 345's cabin than one expects in a boat this size. In addition to the cruising layout described above, the Drummond Runner was also available in a sportfish configuration with bait prep center, live well, tackle storage, and in-deck fish boxes. Additional features include an electric helm seat, Corian galley counter, built-in transom seat, windlass, and a fiberglass hardtop with canvas enclosure. Built on an aggressive deep-V hull with a notched bottom and integral transom, twin 250hp Yamaha outboards reach close to 40 knots wide open.

Standard Plan

Sportfish Plan

See Page 694 For Price Data

Length	34'5"	Fuel	300 gals.
Beam	9'6"	Water	30 gals.
Hull Draft	1'10"	Max HP	600
Weight w/T250s	10,395#	Hull Type	Deep-V
Clearance, Top	8'0"	Deadrise Aft	24.5°

Pursuit 3480 Center Console; C 340

Over the past decade, the market for large center consoles has grown faster than any other segment of the boating industry. With the introduction in 2005 of the 3480 Center Console (called the C 340 in 2007–10), Pursuit joined the likes of Contender, Boston Whaler, Grady-White and Regulator in offering an expensive, high-quality fishing machine designed for serious offshore work. Built on a slender deep-V hull with a notched transom, the most notable fishing feature of the 3480 is her single-level deck—with nothing to trip over, anglers can move more quickly around the boat while fighting a fish. A recessed bow rail makes it easy to cast a net, and the door to the head inside the console is in front, not the side, providing very easy access. Note that there are two forward and two aft fish boxes beneath the sole. Interestingly, the interiors of both livewells are painted blue, which is said to keep bait alive longer. Consistent with all Pursuit boats, the diamond non-skid is excellent and the helm layout is large enough for plenty of electronics. Additional fishing features include 360-degree cockpit bolsters, toe kicks around both livewells, bait-prep station, and rod holders everywhere. Yamaha 250s will deliver over 40 knots top.

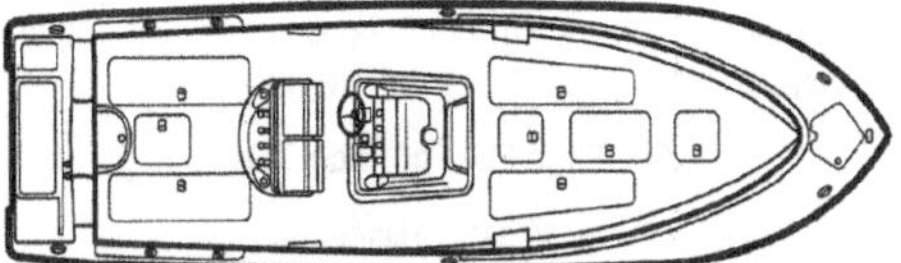

See Page 694 For Price Data

Length	34'5"	Fuel	375 gals.
Beam	9'6"	Water	30 gals.
Hull Draft	1'10"	Max HP	600
Weight w/T250s	9,300#	Hull Type	Deep-V
Clearance, Top	9'4"	Deadrise Aft	24.5°

Pursuit OS 375; 385 Offshore

Flagship of today's Pursuit fleet, the OS 385 Offshore (called the OS 375 Offshore until 2012) hits the right buttons with deep-pocket boaters obsessed with quality. With her triple-outboard power, versatile deck layout, and luxury-class accommodations, the OS 385 is as good as it gets in an express boat this size. There is much to admire in this handsome express, beginning with her stylish, fully integrated hardtop and windshield (engineered to support an optional factory tower) and including her spacious fishing cockpit and extensive equipment list. The plush interior is a mixture of light-colored joinery, designer fabrics, and premium galley appliances. The V-berth shape is a little different, but the mid-berth is comfortable for two adults and there's plenty of storage throughout. The galley is huge, and the head includes a separate stall shower. Fishing amenities include a lighted 50-gallon recirculating livewell, two in-deck fish boxes, tackle storage, and a 300-quart refrigerated fish box in the transom. Note the fold-down transom seats. Bridge air-conditioning, an 8kW generator, and a bow thruster are standard. Fit and finish is remarkable. A fast ride, triple Yamaha 350s deliver 45+ knots wide open.

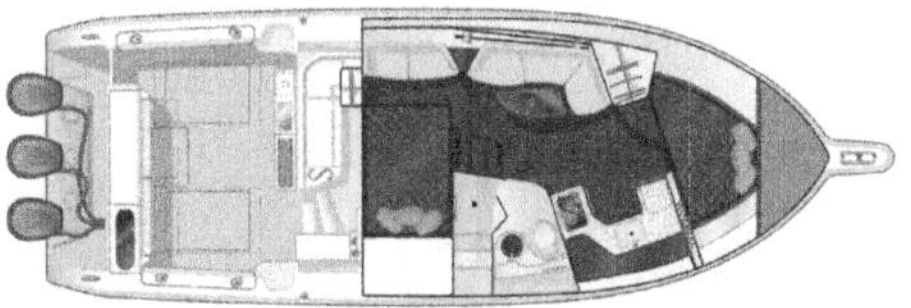

See Page 694 For Price Data

Length w/Pulpit	39'2"	Fuel	370 gals.
Hull Length	36'11"	Water	65 gals.
Beam	13'0"	Max HP	1,050
Hull Draft	3'6"	Hull Type	Modified-V
Weight, 3/350	18,450#	Deadrise Aft	18°

Pursuit 3800 Express

Queen of the Pursuit fleet during her production years, the 3800 Express is a premium (as in expensive) midsized fisherman from a company whose reputation for quality is seldom questioned. She is, by any standard, a particularly handsome boat with a semicustom profile seen in subsequent Pursuit models. She rides a beamy modified-V hull with considerable bow flare and cored hullsides. With the bridge deck of the 3800 raised a couple of steps from the cockpit level, visibility from the helm—with its tall windshield—is exceptional. A comfortable L-shaped settee is to port, opposite the double helm seat, and the entire helm deck can be raised at the push of a button for complete access to the engines. The cockpit is fitted with a full array of fishing amenities including a bait-prep center, a 50-gallon livewell, in-deck storage, and a foldaway transom seat. For a fishing boat, the rich interior of the 3800 Express is downright lush with a beautiful inlaid dinette table, a teak-and-holly cabin sole, and an upright rod display locker just inside the companionway. Among several engine options, a pair of 450hp Cummins (or 480hp Volvo) diesels cruise in the mid 20s (30+ top).

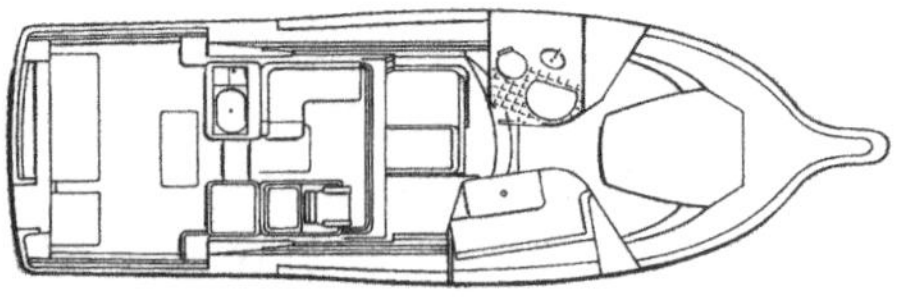

See Page 694 For Price Data

Length w/Pulpit	40'11"	Headroom	6'2"
Hull Length	38'6"	Fuel	438 gals.
Beam	14'2"	Water	110 gals.
Draft	3'11"	Waste	40 gals.
Weight	21,800#	Hull Type	Modified-V

Rampage

Quick View

- Rampage boats were originally built by Tillotson-Pearson, the Rhode Island-based manufacturer of Freedom, Alden, and J-Boat sailboats.
- The Rampage 31, a good-running express fisherman introduced in 1985, established the Rampage name with East Coast anglers.
- Additional designs were brought out in subsequent years, and by 1990 Rampage offered a full line of models from 24 to 40 feet.
- Rampage was purchased by Cruisers, Inc., in 1990, and production was moved to Oconto, WI.
- Owing to Cruisers' own financial problems of the early 1990s, the Rampage line virtually ceased to exist during much of the 1990s.
- In 1993 both Cruisers and Rampage were purchased by current owner KCS Industries.
- Production resumed in 1999 with the introduction of the Rampage 30 and 38 Express. The current Rampage fleet runs from 30' to 45'.

Rampage Yachts • Oconto, WI • www.rampageyachts.com

Rampage 30 Express

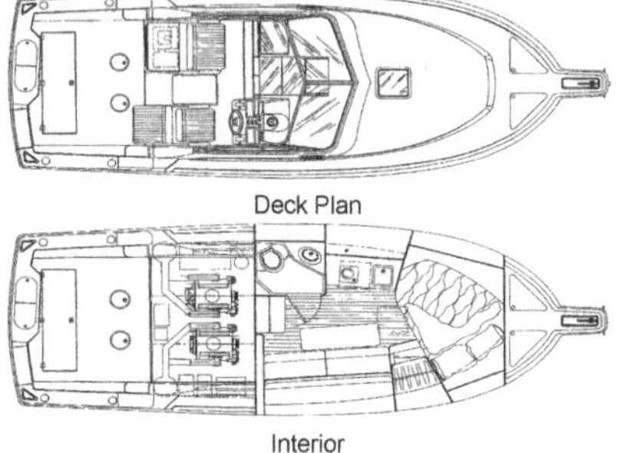
Deck Plan

Interior

The Rampage 30 is one of the new-generation Rampage designs introduced in 1999 by the company's new owner, KCS Inc. (which also owns Wisconsin-based Cruisers Yachts). Built on a fully cored hull with a relatively wide beam, the Rampage 30 is a rugged and well-finished boat that compares well with other high-end express fishermen her size. The cockpit comes with a 38-gallon transom livewell, a big in-deck fish box, transom door and gate, and a lockable tackle center. For engine access, the entire bridge deck can be raised on a hydraulic lift. Belowdecks, the cherrywood interior of the Rampage 30 is surprisingly plush for a fishing boat with berths for four and premium furnishings and hardware. Carpeting is standard, but an optional teak-and-holly sole adds even more class to this upscale interior. Additional features include a tilt-away helm, bow pulpit, lighted engine compartment, underwater exhausts, and plenty of rod storage. While not inexpensive, the Rampage 30 compares well with other premium express fishermen in her class. Twin 315hp Yanmar diesels cruise in the mid 20s (30+ knots top).

See Page 694 For Price Data

Length w/Pulpit	31'0"	Fuel	250 gals.
Beam	11'3"	Water	31 gals.
Draft	2'10"	Waste	20 gals.
Weight	12,000#	Hull Type	Modified-V
Clearance	7'0"	Deadrise Aft	19°

Rampage 30 Open/Offshore

Rampage got it right with the 30 Offshore (called the 30 Open when she was introduced in 2002), a high-end diesel express with the DNA of a pocket battlewagon. Notable for her classic "Palm Beach" styling and excellent finish, the Offshore features a large cockpit area with a transom door (with top lid), full coaming bolsters, 38-gallon lighted baitwell, insulated fish box that is both removable and macerated, and fresh and raw water washdowns. The lockable tackle center has a gasketed top, large slide-out storage drawers with dividers, and a molded fiberglass sink with spray nozzle and removable cutting board. An electrically actuated engine hatch makes engine inspections easy. Note the Offshore's center helm position. Below, the settee lounge converts to upper and lower sleeping bunks with rod storage beneath. The offset double berth forward has a queen-sized mattress with storage under, and the galley comes complete with refrigerator, electric stove, microwave, storage drawers and cabinets. Built on a fully cored hull with moderate beam, 315hp Yanmar diesels cruise in the mid 20s (30+ top).

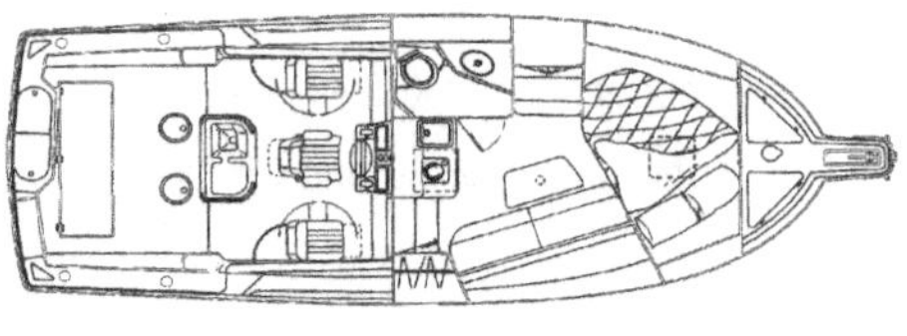

See Page 694 For Price Data

Length w/Pulpit	31'0"	Fuel	250 gals.
Hull Length	28'9"	Water	31 gals.
Beam	11'3"	Waste	20 gals.
Draft	2'10"	Hull Type	Modified-V
Weight	12,000#	Deadrise Aft	19°

Rampage 33 Express

The Rampage 33 is a premium express fishing boat whose spacious layout offers as much or more in the way of comfort than any boat in her class. Built on a modified-V hull with prop pockets and a full 13-foot beam, the Rampage draws a mere 29 inches of draft. Her center-helm design features a tilt-out pod that affords excellent visibility and access. Aft of the helmdeck, the 70-square-foot cockpit can be configured with a 45-gallon livewell and bait-prep center for fishing, or wet bar and foldaway bench seating for cruising. Belowdecks, the well-appointed interior of the Rampage 33 can sleep six; the forward V-berth/dinette area converts to four single bunks, and the starboard sofa folds out to form a queen berth. High-gloss cherry joinery and Corian galley counters highlight the decor, and an optional entertainment center contains a DVD and 15-inch flat-screen TV. Note that the 33's engine compartment is huge with excellent service access all around the engines. Additional features include cabin rod storage, large in-deck fish box, bow pulpit, wide 8-inch side decks, and L-shaped lounge seating next to the helm. Not inexpensive, 460hp Cat diesels cruise in the high 20s (32–33 knots top).

See Page 694 For Price Data

Length w/Pulpit	35'6"	Fuel	367 gals.
Hull Length	33'0"	Water	60 gals.
Beam	13'0"	Waste	45 gals.
Draft	2'5"	Hull Type	Modified-V
Weight	17,200#	Deadrise Aft	18°

Rampage 38 Express

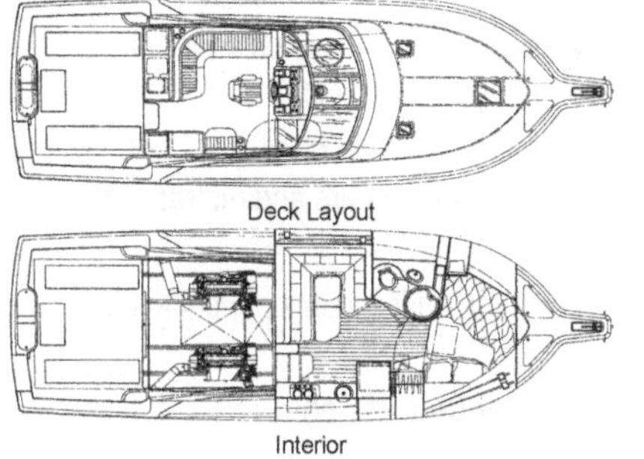
Deck Layout

Interior

The introduction of the Rampage 38 (and her smaller sistership, the Rampage 30) in 1999 marked the reappearance of the Rampage nameplate after an absence of nearly 10 years. A handsome boat, she's built on a fully cored hull with a relatively wide beam and an efficient 19 degrees of transom deadrise. The deck layout of the Rampage 38 has a center helm pod forward with an L-shaped lounge to port and wet bar opposite. Aft, the cockpit is equipped with two removable in-deck fish boxes, a custom 55-gallon livewell (with a window), a molded tackle center with sink and cooler, and a transom door and gate. The entire bridge deck lifts on a pair of hydraulic rams to reveal a spacious and well-designed engine compartment. Below, the cabin of the 38 will accommodate four with a double berth forward and a convertible U-shaped dinette to port. Additional features include excellent cabin headroom, a separate stall shower in the head, power windshield center vent, hinged helm (for access to the wiring), tilt steering, and cherry-wood interior trim. Cummins 450hp engines cruise the Rampage 38 Express in the mid 20s; 575hp Cat engines cruise at 30+ knots.

See Page 694 For Price Data

Length w/Pulpit	39'6"	Fuel	400/512 gals.
Hull Length	36'11"	Water	60 gals.
Beam	13'9"	Waste	39 gals.
Draft	3'6"	Hull Type	Modified-V
Weight	24,000#	Deadrise Aft	19°

Rampage 45 Convertible

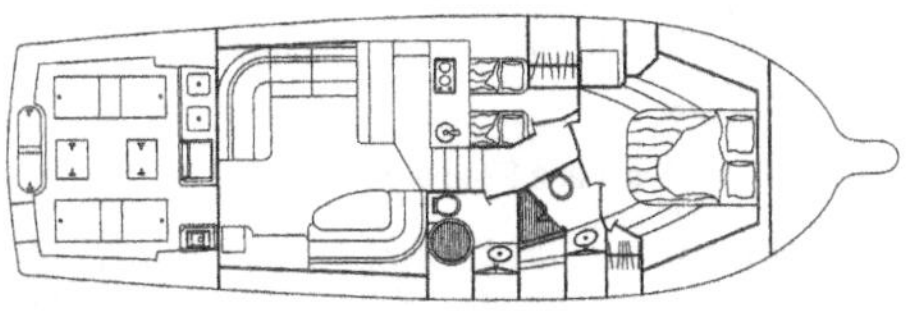

A good-looking boat, the Rampage 45 bears a strong resemblance to several late-model Hatteras designs—no small compliment in today's crowded, cookie-cutter convertible marketplace. She rides on a beamy modified-V hull with a well-flared bow, cored hullsides, and propeller pockets to reduce draft and shaft angles. Inside, the cherry-trimmed interior of the Rampage 45 boasts a spacious main salon with L-shaped lounge seating to port (with rod storage under), U-shaped galley with Corian counters and under-counter refrigeration, and three-person dinette to starboard. Forward, the master stateroom is fitted with an island berth, and the portside guest cabin has single berths that convert to a queen. While both heads are fitted with separate stall showers, the circular shower door in the day head is a bit difficult to use. The huge, tournament-class fishing cockpit of the Rampage 45 came standard with a 36-gallon livewell, complete tackle center, engineroom access door, and two in-deck fish boxes. Topside, the flybridge has with single-lever helm controls and bench seating forward of the console. Cat 800hp diesels cruise the Rampage 45 at 26–28 knots (low 30s top).

See Page 694 For Price Data

Length w/Pulpit	48'8"	Fuel	700 gals.
Hull Length	45'10"	Water	100 gals.
Beam	16'0"	Waste	60 gals.
Draft	4'0"	Hull Type	Modified-V
Weight	36,000#	Deadrise Aft	10°

Regal

Quick View

- Founded in 1969 by Paul Kuck, Regal grew to become one of the largest privately held boat manufacturers in the country.
- The first Regal boat was a 21-foot cuddy, followed by a 16-foot tri-hull and 14-foot runabout, all produced out of a small, leased production facility in Orlando in 1969.
- For the next 15 years Regal enjoyed a period of rapid growth. By the early 1990s the fleet had expanded to include a full range of runabouts, sportboats and express cruisers, 17' to 38'.
- The Regal World Headquarters in Orlando, FL, contains nearly half a million square feet including a state-of-the-art Yacht Center and a 7-acre, 20-foot deep test basin. The Valdosta, GA, facility encompasses an additional 150,000 square feet of production space.
- By 2004, Regal boats were distributed by over 180 of the top dealers and distributors in the business with locations in more than 45 countries.
- Regal remains a family-owned business, now operated by the decendents of Paul Kuck.

Regal Boats • Orlando, FL • www.regalboats.com

Regal 2665 Commodore

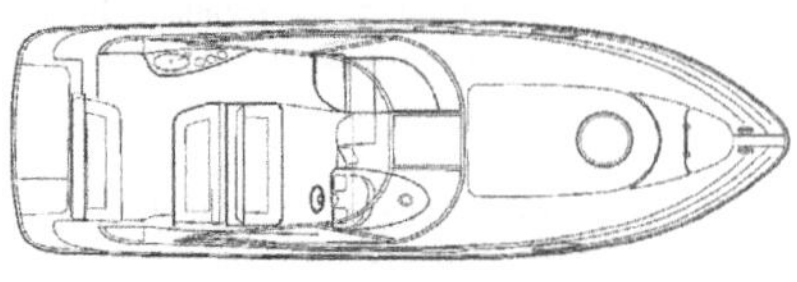

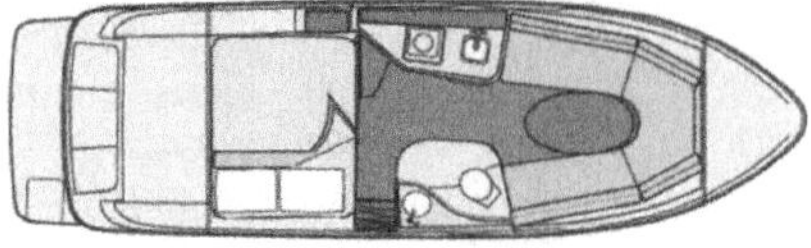

A popular model during her production years, the Regal 2665 Commodore is a well built 26-footer that combines a roomy, user-friendly cockpit with comfortable cabin accommodations. The market for trailerable family cruisers this size is extremely competitive—close to two dozen manufacturers fight it out each year for a share of this lucrative market. Aside from her well-balanced layout, the Commodore's upscale amenities and above-average finish set her a notch or two above much of the competition. The cockpit is arranged with facing bench seats aft of the helm, and the flip-up rear seat converts to a sun pad. A small refreshment center to port has a sink and space below for a carry-on ice chest. The helm features a well-arranged dash and sports a deluxe Dino tilt wheel. Below decks, the Commodore's cozy midcabin interior has all of the essentials required for a weekend getaway including a standup head, convertible dinette, fair-sized hanging locker, and a very complete galley. Note that the original stepped hull of the 2665 Commodore was replaced in 2004 with a new deep-V hull. Cruise at 25 mph (40+ mph top) with a single 320hp Volvo sterndrive.

See Page 694 For Price Data

Length w/Platform	29'2"	Fuel	74 gals.
Beam	8'6	Water	18 gals.
Hull Draft	1'7"	Waste	18 gals.
Weight	6,850#	Hull Type	Deep-V
Clearance	9'2"	Deadrise Aft	20°

Regal 260 Valenti; 272 Commodore

1991–96

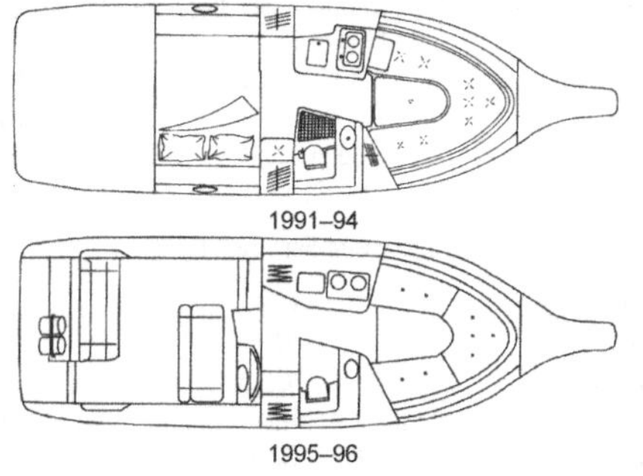

1991–94

1995–96

The 272 Commodore (called the 260 Valenti in 1991–92) was a popular family cruiser in the 1990s with traditional lines and a surprisingly spacious interior. Like most boats of her type and length, the 272 has a lot of unattractive freeboard—a necessity for standing cabin headroom. Featuring a molded bow pulpit and an integrated swim platform in addition to a curved windshield, the 272 was constructed on a fully cored, deep-V hull with a wide 9-foot, 2-inch beam. Her midcabin interior—slightly revised and updated in 1995—is arranged with a semicircular dinette/double berth forward, a standup head with vanity, and a spacious queen-size berth aft. Privacy curtains separate both sleeping areas from the main cabin, and the decor is a blend of quality furnishings and off-white joinery. On deck, the cockpit is arranged with a triple-wide helm seat forward and bench seating aft. A large, electrically operated hatch in the cockpit sole provides good access to the engine compartment. Among several sterndrive engine options, twin 180hp Volvos cruise the 272 Commodore at 22 knots (high 30s top), while a single 300hp MerCruiser will cruise at 20 knots and top out around 35 knots.

See Page 694 For Price Data

Length w/Pulpit	28'6"	Fuel	105 gals.
Beam	9'2"	Water	27 gals.
Draft, Up	1'6"	Waste	17 gals.
Draft, Down	3'6"	Hull Type	Deep-V
Weight	6,800#	Deadrise Aft	21°

Regal 2660/2765 Commodore

1999–2005

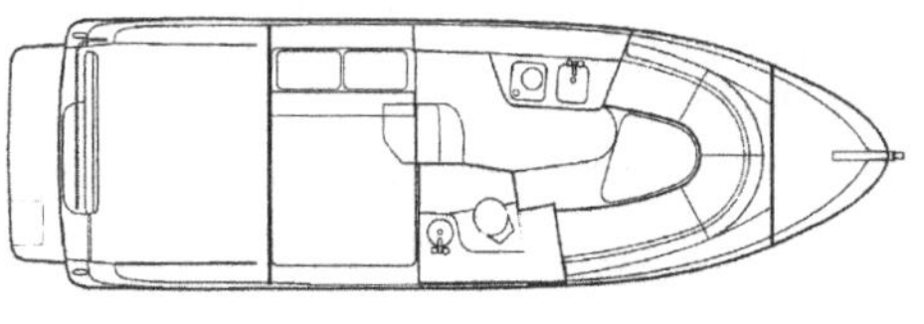

Regal's largest trailerable cruiser, the 2765 Commodore (called the 2660 Commodore from 1999–2001) has all the amenities a cruising family will need for comfortable overnight outings. Several manufacturers produce similar models, but the 2765's notched hull sets her apart from the others. (Notched hulls—originally designed for high-performance racing boats—are said to be more efficient than conventional V bottoms and able to attain higher top speeds.) The midcabin floorplan will comfortably sleep four adults, and while it can't be described as spacious, the cabin includes a compact head compartment, good ventilation, and a complete galley. On deck, the cockpit is arranged with a removable rear bench seat, a sun lounge opposite the helm (with a reversible backrest), swivel helm seat and a refreshment center with a removable cooler. Lacking side decks, molded steps next to the helm lead to an opening windshield. Note the large bolt-on swim platform. A single 310hp MerCruiser sterndrive will cruise the Regal 2765 at 20 knots (35–36 knots top). Twin 220hp MerCruiser I/Os cruise in the low-to-mid 20s (40+ top).

See Page 694 For Price Data

Length	29'10"	Fuel	76 gals.
Beam	8'6"	Water	28 gals.
Draft, Down	2'9"	Waste	28 gals.
Weight	6,950#	Hull Type	Deep-V
Clearance	7'2"	Deadrise Aft	21°

Regal 2760/2860 Commodore

1998–2005

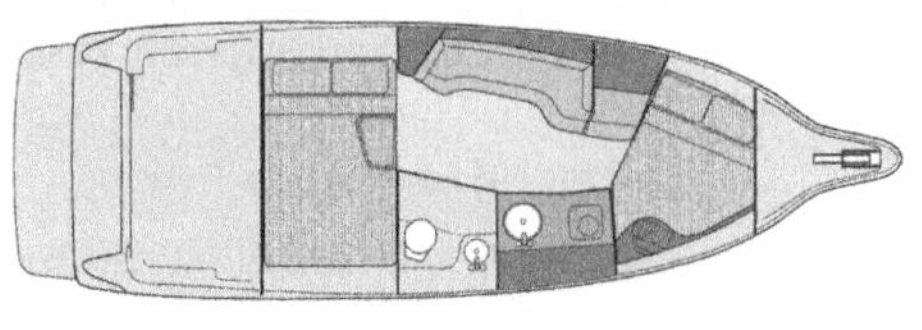

The Regal 2760 Commodore (called the 2860 Commodore in 2002–05) is a well-built express with innovative cockpit seating and a space-efficient interior. She's unlike other boats of her type and size in that she rides on a stepped hull, a race-bred design said to improve performance by ventilating the bottom. Like most modern express cruisers, the Commodore incorporates a midcabin floorplan with berths for six. The fore and aft sleeping areas, each with a double berth, are separated from the main cabin by a privacy curtains. (Note that the elbowroom in the aft cabin is at a premium.) In a departure from the norm, the refrigerator is under the forward berth, which frees up some storage space beneath the galley counter. Topside, the cockpit is arranged with a doublewide seat at the helm, an L-shaped settee opposite, and a bench seat at the transom. A walk-through windshield provides access to the big foredeck sun pad. Additional features include a molded bow pulpit, radar arch, cockpit wet bar, tilt wheel, and a transom door. Among several engine options, twin 220hp MerCruisers I/Os cruise at 22–23 knots and reach a top speed in the mid-to-high 30s.

See Page 694 For Price Data

Length w/Pulpit	31'0"	Fuel	103 gals.
Beam	9'11"	Water	27 gals.
Draft, Down	3'3"	Waste	17 gals.
Weight	8,350#	Hull Type	Deep-V
Clearance	8'10"	Deadrise Aft	21°

Regal 2860 Window Express

2006–11

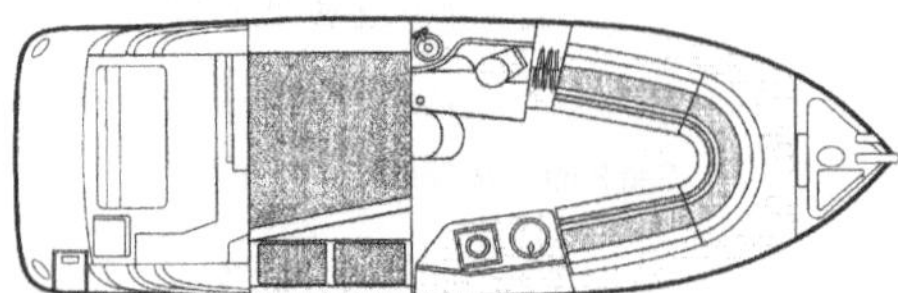

Every once in a while something new in the way of boat design comes along that catches the public imagination. Such was the case in 2006 when Regal introduced their new 2860 Window Express. As the name implied, a "window" was integrated into the cabin overhead, a feature that didn't exist in other boats. The effect of this increased natural lighting in the cabin was well described when Boating Magazine's Peter McDonald wrote in a review of the 2860, "I've never set foot in a midsize cruiser that felt so welcoming belowdecks." Built on a modified-V with moderate beam and a keel pad, the cockpit of the Window Express is arranged in the normal fashion with an L-lounge to port, transom bench seat, and a refreshment center with cooler, sink and storage behind the helm. A large storage locker built into the transom has space for fenders, toys, and docking lines. Note the pull-up cleats on the swim platform. Below, the midcabin interior of the Regal 2860—an appealing blend of cherry cabinets, Corian galley counter, and designer fabrics—is a match for the best boats in her class, especially with the increased natural lighting. Twin 220hp MerCruiser I/Os cruise at 25 knots (38–40 knots top).

See Page 694 For Price Data

Length	29'5"	Headroom	6'3"
Beam	9'6"	Fuel	100 gals.
Draft, Down	3'3"	Water	35 gals.
Weight	9,000#	Hull Type	Modified-V
Clearance	10'2"	Deadrise Aft	18°

Regal 290/300 Commodore

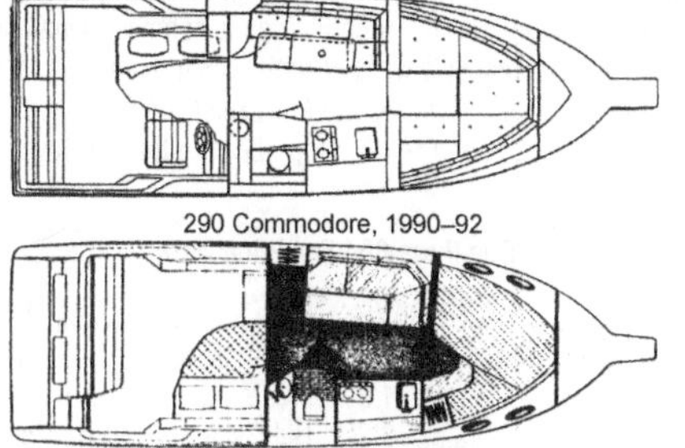

290 Commodore, 1990–92

300 Commodore, 1993–94

Regal nearly always gets it right with their express cruisers. They're not the least expensive boats on the market, but quality never comes cheap and Regal doesn't cut a lot of corners. The Regal 290 Commodore (called the 300 Commodore in 1993–94) is a case in point; an updated version of Regal's very popular 277/280 Commodore built from 1982 to 1989, the 290/300 is virtually the same boat as her predecessor but with a new integral swim platform replacing the bolt-on platform of the 277/280 models. The result is a more stylish boat with leaner lines and considerably enhanced eye appeal. Below decks, her well-appointed interior is similar to most express cruisers her size with double berths fore and aft, convertible dinette, full-service galley with microwave, and an enclosed head with shower. Note that in 1993, when she became the 300 Commodore, an offset double berth in the forward stateroom replaced the V-berth found in the 290 Commodore. Built on a solid fiberglass hull with moderate beam, several single and twin sterndrive power options were offered over the years. Among them, a pair of 300hp MerCruisers cruise at 25 knots (high 30s/low 40s top).

Prices Not Provided for Pre-1995 Models

Length w/Pulpit	32'5"	Fuel	140 gals.
Hull length	30'0"	Water	35 gals.
Beam	10'0"	Waste	21 gals.
Draft, Down	3'2"	Hull Type	Modified-V
Weight	9,200#	Deadrise Aft	16°

Regal 292/2960/3060 Commodore

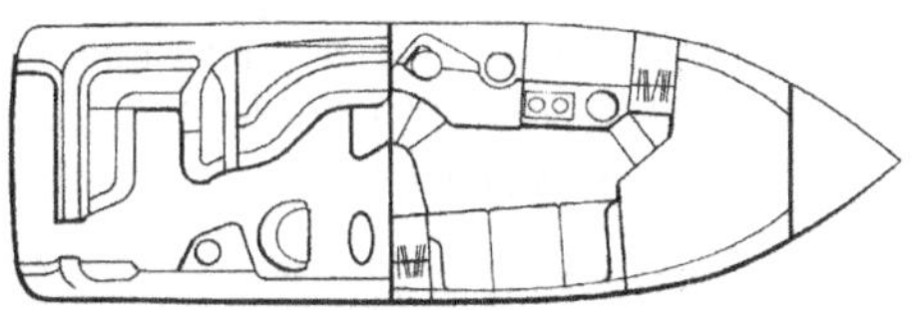

The Regal 292 Commodore (called the 2960 Commodore in 2000–2001; 3060 Commodore in 2002–03) is an upmarket sterndrive cruiser with an attractive blend of crisp styling and comfortable accommodations. She was built on a solid fiberglass hull with a relatively wide beam, a sharp entry, and innovative trim tab pods beneath the swim platform. In the European fashion, she was one of a growing number of 1990s sportboat designs with no bow pulpit. Her plush, full-beam interior (there are no side decks) includes double berths fore and aft and a convertible dinette in the salon—berths for four adults and two kids. There are privacy curtains for both staterooms, and the rich furnishings and Corian countertops lend a touch of luxury seen only in better-quality boats. The cockpit has a U-shaped lounge aft that converts into a sun pad, a transom door, and a wet bar. Additional features include a walk-through windshield, radar arch, and—after 2002—an optional extended swim platform. Among several engine choices, twin 260hp MerCruiser I/Os cruise at 22 knots (high 30s top), and twin 280hp Volvo gas engines cruise at 24 knots (about 40 knots top). Note that a new 3060 Commodore was introduced in 2004.

See Page 694 For Price Data

Length Overall	31'10"	Fuel	150 gals.
Beam	10'4"	Water	35 gals.
Draft, Up	1'8"	Waste	30 gals.
Draft, Down	3'2"	Hull Type	Deep-V
Weight	9,500#	Deadrise Aft	18°

Regal 3060 Window Express

Aggressive styling is the hallmark of the Regal 3060 Window Express, a sporty midcabin express introduced in 2004. Built on a modified-V hull with an extended swim platform, the sleek profile of the 3060 is accented by her rakish cat-eye cabin windows and sharply angled arch. The helm area keeps things sociable by positioning a circular lounge adjacent to the driver's seat. A fold-away bench seat in the cockpit provides additional seating, and there's a light switch inside the transom door for boarding at night. Belowdecks, the Regal 3060 has the distinction of being the only express cruiser in her class with a big overhead cabin window, a design innovation that bathes the forward part of the cabin in an avalanche of natural lighting. The well-appointed interior compares well with other midcabin boats her size with berths for four, removable dinette table, full galley, and a good-sized head with sink and shower. Additional features include a companionway screen, swivel helm seat, cockpit wet bar with cooler, trim tabs, and hot/cold transom shower. Twin 270hp MerCruisers I/Os cruise the Regal 3060 at 25 knots and reach a top speed in the low-to-mid 40s.

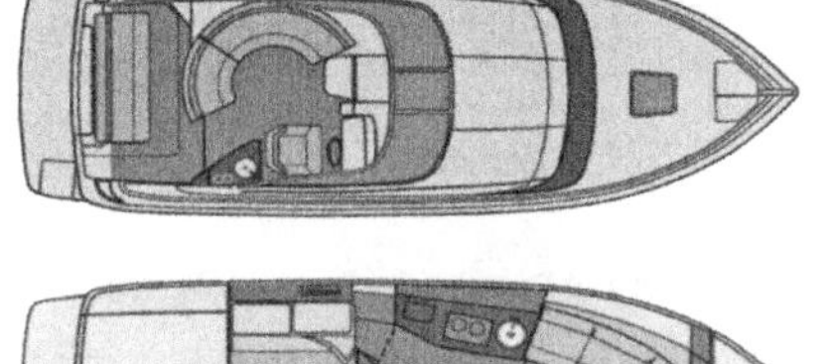

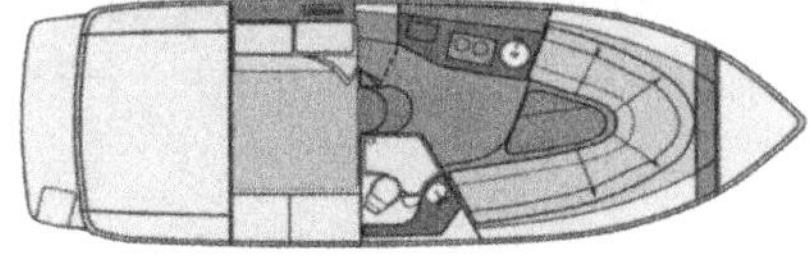

See Page 694 For Price Data

Length	30'10"	Fuel	151 gals.
Beam	10'6"	Water	30 gals.
Draft, Up	1'8"	Waste	28 gals.
Draft, Down	3'2"	Hull Type	Modified-V
Weight	11,000#	Deadrise Aft	18°

Regal Ventura 9.8; 322/3260 Commodore

The Regal 3260 Commodore (called the Ventura 9.8 in 1993–94 and the 322 Commodore from 1995–99) was a notably popular model for Regal. (Indeed, it's a rare event when a major manufacturer keeps a boat in production for a full decade.) Built on a deep-V hull with cored hullsides, the deluxe interior of the 322/3260 Commodore is a blend of high-end furnishings and quality components. The floorplan is arranged with an angled double berth forward, a posh Ultraleather sofa/dinette in the salon, and handsome U-shaped aft cabin seating that converts into a queen-size bed. (Note that in the inboard version a queen bed is permanent.) On deck, the cockpit is set up with a doublewide helm seat forward, wraparound guest seating aft, a built-in wet bar, and a transom door. An electric engine hatch provides access to the motors. Additional features include a radar arch, walk-through windshield, foredeck sun pad, and large transom lockers. A fast boat with 300hp MerCruiser sterndrives, the Regal 322/3260 will cruise at 25 knots and top out in the low 40s. With 300hp V-drive inboards, the cruising speed is around 22 knots with a top speed in the mid 30s. Note that engine access for inboard models is a tight fit.

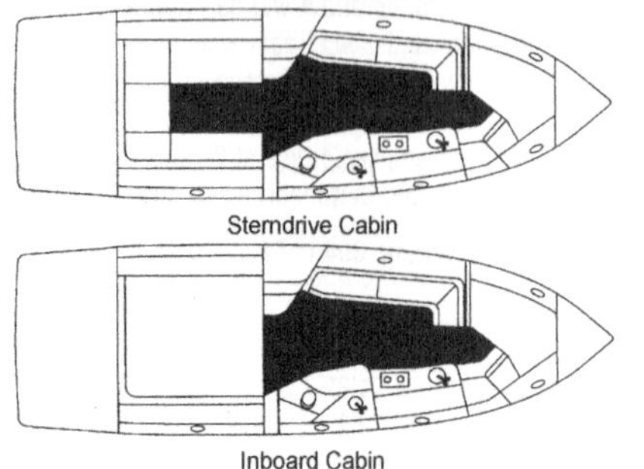

Sterndrive Cabin

Inboard Cabin

See Page 695 For Price Data

Hull Length	32'0"	Fuel	172 gals.
Beam	11'2"	Water	50 gals.
Draft	3'2"	Waste	30 gals.
Weight	11,800#	Hull Type	Modified-V
Clearance, Arch	10'1"	Deadrise Aft	19°

Regal 3350 Sport Cruiser

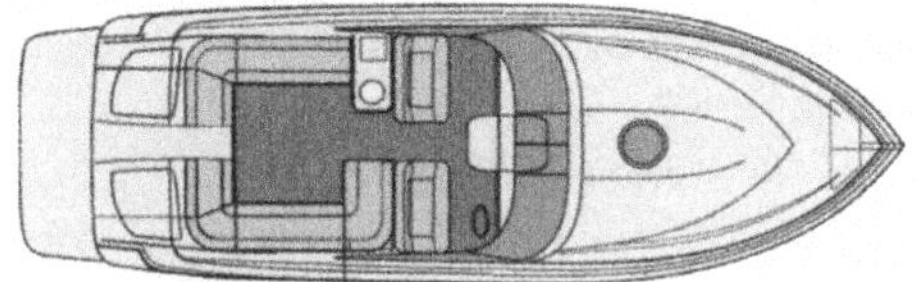

Sportboats are all about performance and fun, but many fall short of expectations. Packaged in a bubble of high-octane marketing hype, some so-called sportboats are really nothing more than warmed-over runabouts. Not so with the Regal 3350: this is a well-conceived performance cruiser designed from the bottom up for spirited boating. Built on a deep-V hull with a board beam, the vast cockpit of the 3350 offers more seating than just about any boat in her class. Both the helm and companion seats are doublewide with flip-up bolsters, and the huge U-shaped aft lounge—which converts into a giant sun pad—is bisected by a centerline transom door. (A pair of cockpit tables can be stored in a designated compartment.) While the cockpit is obviously the social center of the 3350, the interior is still large enough to offer a luxurious retreat for after-hours relaxing. Lounge seating wraps around the cabin with the bow section serving as a dinette or roomy double berth. Leather upholstery and a cherry-and-holly sole are standard, however the head is small and headroom is modest. A fast ride with 320hp Volvo sterndrives, expect a top speed in excess of 40 knots. Note the modest 186-gallon fuel capacity.

See Page 695 For Price Data

Length	34'8"	Headroom	5'2"
Beam	11'4"	Fuel	186 gals.
Draft, Up	1'8"	Water	30 gals.
Draft, Down	2'11"	Hull Type	Deep-V
Weight	11,400#	Deadrise Aft	19°

Regal 3360 Window Express

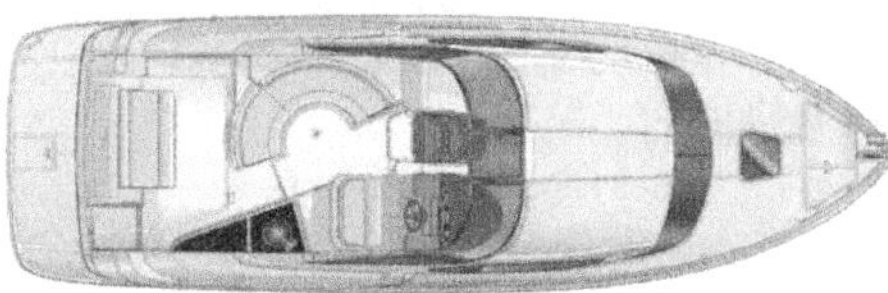

Innovation is an overused term in the boating industry, but Regal was breaking some new ground in 2006 when they introduced the 3360 Window Express. As the name implied, a "window" was integrated into the cabin overhead, a feature that didn't exist in other express boats her size. Experienced from below, the result was (and is) a dramatic improvement in natural lighting throughout the cabin. Built on a modified-V hull, the deck layout of the 3360 is available with a standard C-shaped forward lounge or optional L-lounge with convertible backrest. A wet bar with sink, refrigerator and storage is to starboard in the cockpit, and the real seat folds into the transom when not in use. The sporty helm, with its tiered instruments and burlwood trim, has space for flush-mounting a small video display. Below, the midcabin interior of the Regal 3360 is an appealing blend of leather seating, cherry joinery, hardwood flooring, and designer fabrics. Note the handy floor locker in the galley area. Additional features include a walk-through windshield, power engine compartment hatch, flip-up helm seat, extended swim platform, and a transom storage locker. Volvo 320hp I/Os cruise at 25 knots and reach 36–38 knots top.

See Page 695 For Price Data

Length	34'8"	Fuel	180 gals.
Beam	11'4"	Water	50 gals.
Draft, Down	2'11"	Waste	28 gals.
Weight	13,500#	Hull Type	Modified-V
Headroom	6'4"	Deadrise Aft	19°

Regal 3560/3760 Commodore

2003–10

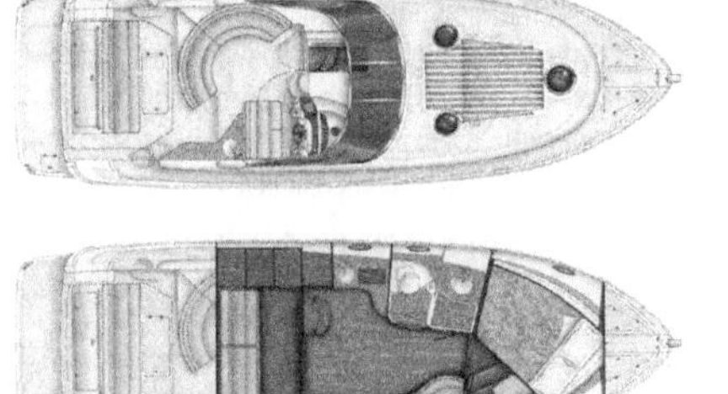

In a market crowded with midsize family cruisers, the Regal 3560 Commodore (called the 3760 Commodore in 2007–10) ranked near the top of her class in luxury, performance, and cost. Built on a conventional modified-V hull, the strong point of this yacht is her spacious interior with its high-gloss cherry joinery, Corian counters, and leather upholstery. A solid wood pocket door insures privacy in the forward stateroom, and the salon flows seamlessly into the midcabin, creating a large area for entertaining. The starboard settee folds out to become a double berth, and the refrigerator is positioned above the galley counter so you don't have to bend down every time you want a cold one. An elegant cherry-and-holly floor is standard, as is a flat-screen 15-inch TV/DVD in the main cabin. Abovedeck, the cockpit is arranged with a horseshoe lounge opposite the helm and a foldaway seat aft. Note that the single helm seat precludes the mate from joining the skipper. Offered with inboard or sterndrive power, Volvo 420hp Duoprop sterndrives cruise at a fast 28–30 knots (40+ knots top), and 420hp MerCruiser inboards cruise in the mid 20s and reach a top speed of close to 35 knots.

See Page 695 For Price Data

Length Overall	38'0"	Fuel	276 gals.
Hull Length	34'8"	Water	67 gals.
Beam	12'2"	Waste	30 gals.
Draft	3'0"	Hull Type	Deep-V
Weight	15,200#	Deadrise Aft	19°

Regal 3780/3880/4080 Commodore

2001–11

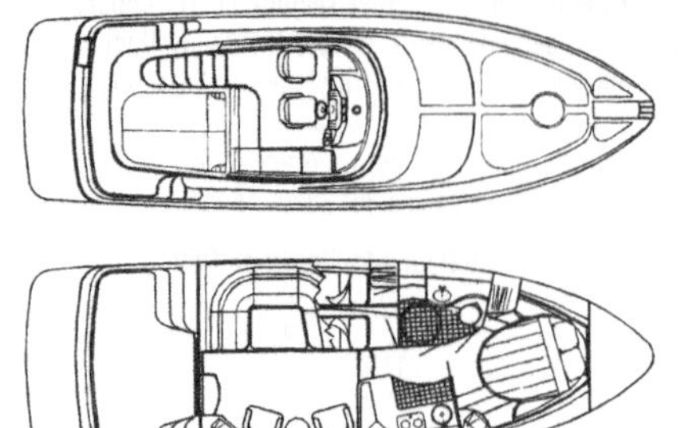

Regal's first-ever flybridge yacht, the 3780 Commodore (called the 3880 Commodore in 2001–06; 4080 Commodore in 2007–11) was a notable departure from the company's 30-year history of producing family runabouts and express cruisers. In the mid 1990s, the rakish styling of the Commodore would have been striking; today it's pretty much the norm for mid-range flybridge sedans. The high side decks of the 3880 may not add much to her appearance but they allow for a full-beam salon with the kind of living space seen only in a larger boat. The galley is down, opposite a small guest stateroom that extends under the salon. Hatches in the salon sole lift to reveal deep storage bins, and a bar counter divides the salon from the galley. Topside, the Commodore's flybridge is big for a boat this size with seating for six and a double sun pad aft. Additional features include cockpit engineroom access, foredeck sun pads, molded flybridge steps, and a foldout cockpit seat. Note the overhead cockpit storage in the flybridge overhang. Twin 420hp V-drive gas engines cruise at 20 knots (about 28 knots top), and optional 370hp Cummins diesels also cruise at 22–23 knots (about 30 top).

See Page 695 For Price Data

Length Overall	40'1"	Fuel	252 gals.
Beam	13'0"	Water	80 gals.
Draft	3'3"	Waste	40 gals.
Weight	19,300#	Hull Type	Modified-V
Clearance, Arch	16'9"	Deadrise Aft	18°

Regal 380/400/402 Commodore

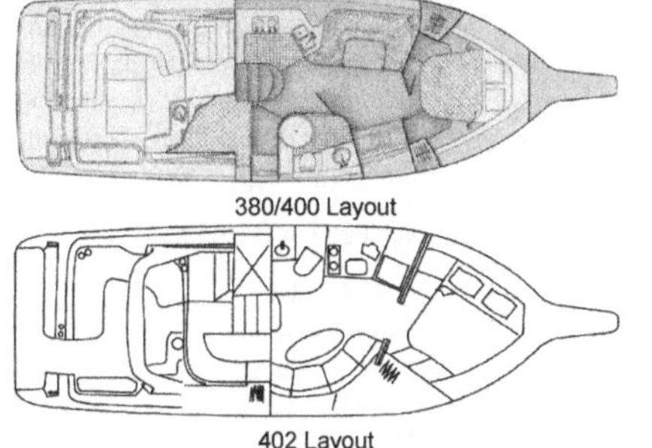

380/400 Layout

402 Layout

Regal is one of those manufacturers prone to renaming the same boat every so often just to keep it fresh in the minds of dealers and customers. Such is the case with this popular family cruiser: Called the 380 Commodore in 1991–92, she was re-branded as the 400 Commodore in 1993–94, and in 1995—with a new interior and redesigned cockpit—she became the 402 Commodore. Always a popular model, she rides on a modified-V hull with a solid fiberglass bottom and prop pockets to reduce draft. Belowdecks, the floorplans of all three models feature privacy doors for both staterooms, a full galley, and a separate stall shower in the head. The 402 Commodore has an offset double berth in the forward stateroom as well as a leather salon sofa, while the aft galley location in the 380 and 400 models makes it easily accessed from the cockpit. Note the standing headroom in the aft cabin—a rare luxury in a boat this size. Additional features include an electric engine compartment hatch, side exhausts, and a roomy cockpit with seating for eight. Standard 310hp MerCruiser gas engines cruise at 18–19 knots (27–28 knots top), and optional Cummins 330hp diesels cruise at 26 knots (about 30 knots top).

See Page 695 For Price Data

Length w/Pulpit	42'0"	Fuel	265 gals.
Hull Length	39'5"	Water	125 gals.
Beam	13'1"	Waste	65 gals.
Draft	3'0"	Hull Type	Modified-V
Weight	16,000#	Deadrise Aft	17°

Regal 3860/4060 Commodore

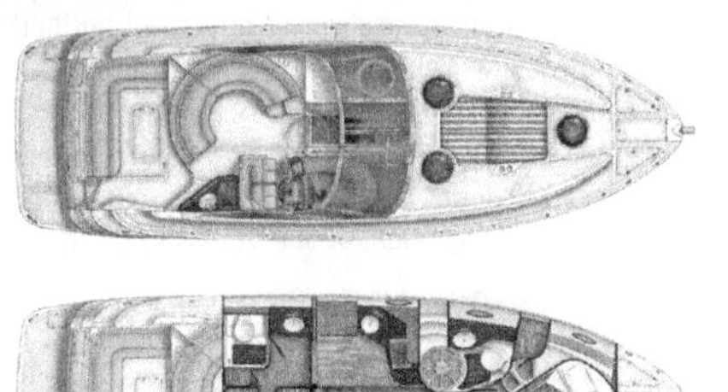

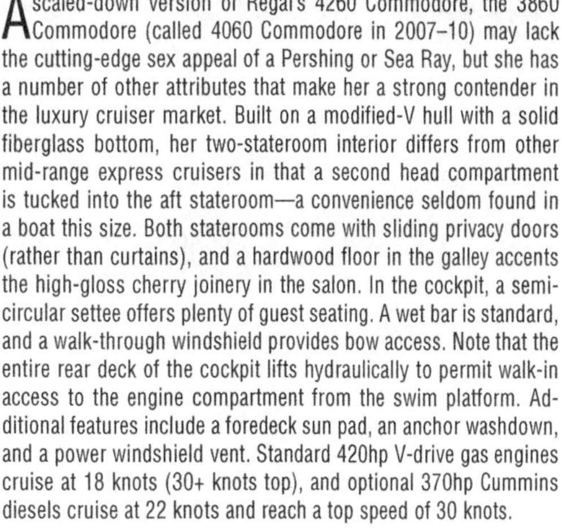

A scaled-down version of Regal's 4260 Commodore, the 3860 Commodore (called 4060 Commodore in 2007–10) may lack the cutting-edge sex appeal of a Pershing or Sea Ray, but she has a number of other attributes that make her a strong contender in the luxury cruiser market. Built on a modified-V hull with a solid fiberglass bottom, her two-stateroom interior differs from other mid-range express cruisers in that a second head compartment is tucked into the aft stateroom—a convenience seldom found in a boat this size. Both staterooms come with sliding privacy doors (rather than curtains), and a hardwood floor in the galley accents the high-gloss cherry joinery in the salon. In the cockpit, a semi-circular settee offers plenty of guest seating. A wet bar is standard, and a walk-through windshield provides bow access. Note that the entire rear deck of the cockpit lifts hydraulically to permit walk-in access to the engine compartment from the swim platform. Additional features include a foredeck sun pad, an anchor washdown, and a power windshield vent. Standard 420hp V-drive gas engines cruise at 18 knots (30+ knots top), and optional 370hp Cummins diesels cruise at 22 knots and reach a top speed of 30 knots.

See Page 695 For Price Data

Length w/Platform	40'1"	Fuel	277 gals.
Beam	13'0"	Water	75 gals.
Draft	3'3"	Waste	40 gals.
Weight	19,000#	Hull Type	Modified-V
Clearance, Arch	11'9"	Deadrise Aft	18°

Regal 4160/4260/4460 Commodore

Flagship of the Regal fleet for several years, the 4160 Commodore (called 4260 Commodore in 2002–05; 4460 Commodore in 2006–09) is a high-style luxury sport yacht with a spacious, well-arranged interior and a particularly innovative cockpit layout. She rides on a beamy deep-V hull with propeller pockets, and her aggressive profile owes much to a gracefully integrated bow pulpit and a unique fore-and-aft arch design. Boarding from one of two transom gates, one is struck by the cockpit configuration—the aft section is small, but the elevated bridge deck is huge with a large U-shaped settee and table opposite the helm. This is a very social layout since most of the guest seating is centered near the double-wide helm rather than aft as it is on most express cruisers. The Regal's plush two-stateroom interior is notable in that both cabins have pocket doors for privacy (rather than curtains) and each has its own head. Additional features include a walk-through windshield, cockpit wet bar, a power-assist windshield vent, foredeck sun pad, and a large transom storage locker. A good performer with optional 450hp Cummins (or 480hp Volvo) diesels, the Commodore will cruise at 28 knots (30+ top).

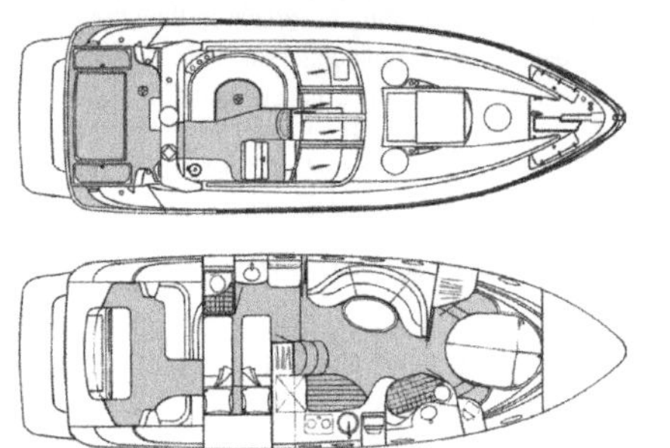

See Page 695 For Price Data

Length w/Platform	44'4"	Fuel	328 gals.
Hull Length	40'10"	Water	101 gals.
Beam	14'0"	Waste	48 gals.
Draft	2'11"	Hull Type	Deep-V
Weight	20,375#	Deadrise Aft	20°

Regal 52 Sport Coupe

Regal entered the 50-foot-plus sportyacht market in a big way in 2008 with the introduction of the 52 Sport Coupe, a bold, Italian-style express with the right mix of luxury, comfort and performance. Designed specifically for Volvo IPS pod drives, Regal (along with Tiara) was a leader in embracing this new power system in a boat this size. She rides on a modified-V hull with cored hullsides, tall freeboard, and a wide 15'4" beam. The Sport Coupe's expansive main deck is loaded with amenities including an integral hardtop with electric sunroof, tiered side windows, wraparound cockpit seating, and a tender garage. Below decks, the luxurious two-stateroom interior features a huge salon finished with high-gloss cherry joinery, deluxe leather seating, and acres of teak-planked flooring. The VIP stateroom is forward, and the galley/dinette area is located between the vertical portholes providing plenty of natural lighting. An enormous full-beam master stateroom dwarfs anything in her class. A washer/dryer combo is located in the galley. Note that the 52's versatile design offers a choice of several interior layouts to choose from. Cruise at 25 knots (30 top) with fuel-efficient 435hp Volvo IPS diesels.

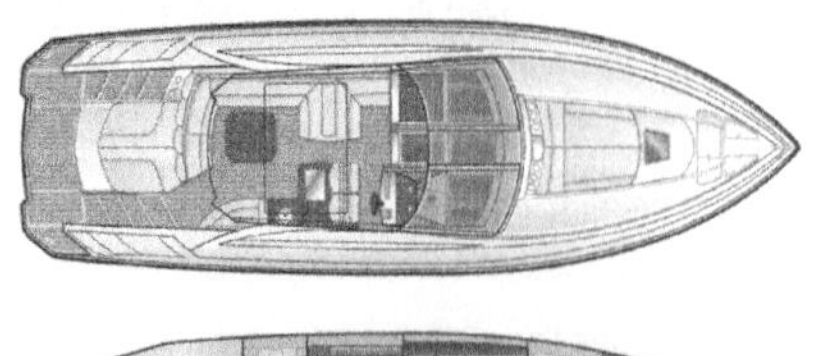

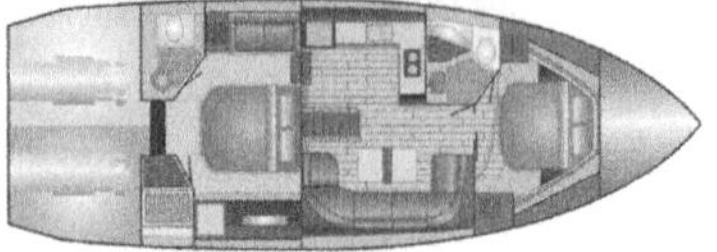

See Page 695 For Price Data

Length	53'0"	Fuel	450 gals.
Beam	15'4"	Water	125 gals.
Draft	3'10"	Waste	65 gals.
Weight	34,400#	Hull Type	Modified-V
Clearance	12'0"	Deadrise Aft	15°

Regulator

Quick View

- Founded in September, 1988 by avid fisherman and marine-industry veteran Owen Maxwell, Regulator launched its first model, the Regulator 26 Center Console, in 1990.
- During the 1990s—a period of steady growth for Regulator—the company developed an enviable reputation for building high-quality offshore fishing boats at a premium price.
- By 2002, Regulator had nearly 100 employees and produced about 200 boats per year from its recently-expanded headquarters in Edenton, NC.
- As it has with most of the marine industry, the recession took a toll on Regulator, and in 2008 the company slashed its workforce and scaled back operations at its Edenton plant.
- Since 2009 Regulator's sales have been slowly recovering, and in 2012 the company introduced the Regulator 34 Center Console, the largest model in Regulator's fleet.

Regulator Boats • Edenton, NC • www.regulatormarine.com

Regulator 26 Center Console

1991–Current

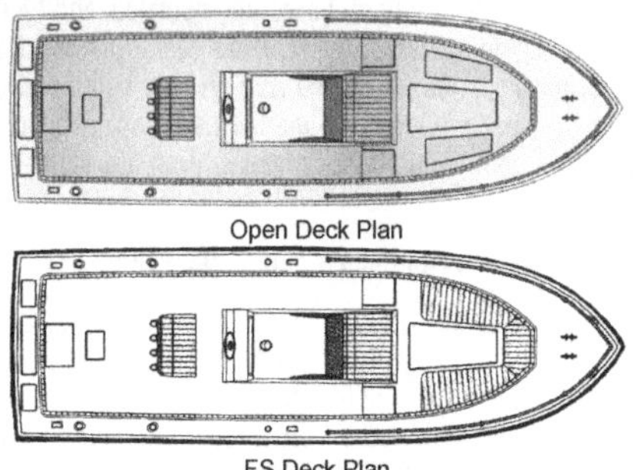

Open Deck Plan

FS Deck Plan

The Regulator 26 Center Console is a trailerable, high-performance fisherman whose quality construction, great ride and classic good looks set the stage for future models in the Regulator fleet. Not inexpensive, she's constructed on a solid fiberglass deep-V hull with a sharp entry, wide reverse chines, and a single-piece grid-type stringer system for superior structural support. The Regulator's standard deck plan is arranged in the traditional manner with the large center console housing a standup head compartment below. Lockable storage protects the electronics, and the leaning post comes with rod holders and built-in tackle storage. Forward, a pair of in-deck fish boxes flank a huge center compartment that can be fitted with rod racks or left empty for storage. Additional features include an in-deck live well, seawater washdown, transom fish boxes, a cooler under the console seat, and a large insulated fish box under the raised bow deck. Note that the Regulator 26 FS model has cushioned seating with storage under forward of the console. A classic sportfishing design (over 1,500 have been sold), twin Yamaha 200s cruise at 30 knots (40+ top).

See Page 695 For Price Data

Length	25'10"	Fuel, Std./Opt.	176/200 gals.
Beam	8'6"	Water	19 gals.
Draft, Up	2'0"	Max HP	500
Draft, Down	2'7"	Hull Type	Deep-V
Dry Weight	5,000#	Deadrise Aft	24°

Regulator 26 Express

1993–98

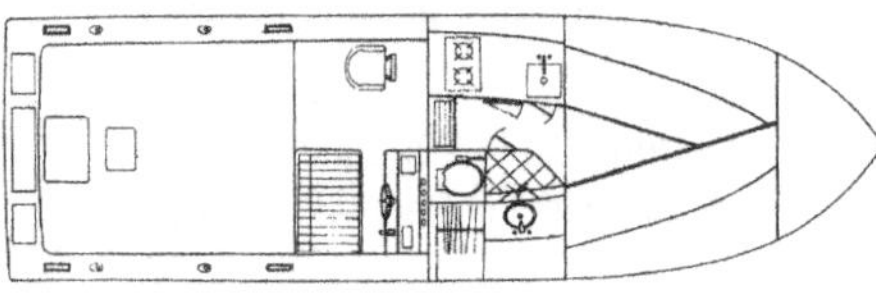

The rugged good looks of the Regulator 26 are a good deal more than just skin deep; superb craftsmanship, a great open-water ride and long list of standard equipment make her one of the premium trailerable fishermen her size on today's market. Heavily built on a solid fiberglass deep-V hull with a sharp entry, reverse chines and a single-piece grid-type stringer system for structural support, the overall fit-and-finish of the 26 are to standards well above average in a small production boat. The single-level cockpit is designed for serious fishing and comes with an in-deck 50-gallon baitwell, two transom bait boxes, underseat coolers, and in-deck lockable rod storage for up to six full-size rods. Molded steps lead up to the wide side decks, and a high bow rail makes the foredeck (which is completely covered with nonskid) a safe platform to work. With only a pair of pedestal chairs forward, the cockpit will easily accommodate four anglers. The interior is basic with berths for two, a stand-up head and a small galley. Offered with outboard or single sterndrive power, a pair of 200hp Yamahas cruise at 28 knots (around 40 knots top), and a 216hp Volvo diesel I/O will cruise at 25 knots (about 30 knots top).

See Page 695 For Price Data

Length	25'10"	Headroom	6'0"
Beam	8'6"	Fuel	218 gals.
Draft, Up	24"	Water	19 gals.
Draft, Down	31"	Hull Type	Deep-V
Dry Weight	5,400#	Deadrise Aft	24°

Regulator 28 FS

2011–Current

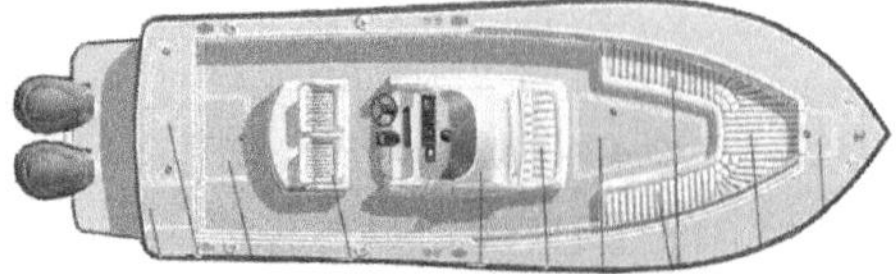

Introduced in 2010, Regulator describes the 28 FS (FS stands for "forward seating") as a descendant of the Regulator 26, the company's most popular model and one of the best small fishing boats ever produced. Like the 26, the 28 FS has an outboard bracket that, according to designer Lou Codega, "takes full advantage of the sharp bow entry and deep-V design." With her generous 9'5" beam, the Regulator 28 is a roomy boat with space for several anglers and their gear. Her single-level deck means no cockpit obstructions when fighting a fish. Regulator offers this boat with several leaning post/livewell options, all of which contain a built-in tackle center. Standard features include a full-width 272-quart transom fishbox, large-capacity 456-quart in-deck fishbox forward, saltwater washdown, lockable (lighted) rod storage, cockpit bolsters, and a 33-gallon freshwater system. All fish boxes are insulated, and there's an insulated cooler under the forward console seat. Note the 28's wide gunwales, foldaway rear seat, and pull-up bow lights and cleats. The walk-in console contains a marine head, opening port, and standing headroom. Twin 300hp Yamahas reach 50+ knots.

Not Enough Resale Data to Set Values

Length	27'7"	Fuel	235 gals.
Beam	9'5"	Water	33 gals.
Draft, Up	2'0"	Max HP	
Draft, Down	2'8"	Hull Type	Deep-V
Dry Weight	8,260#	Deadrise Aft	24°

Regulator 29 FS

2006–Current

Regulator builds a tough boat, a reputation that stems from the original Regulator 26—one of the most popular fishing boats her size ever produced—and continues today with the company's entire line of deep-V center consoles. Regulator describes the 29 FS (forward seating) as a "bluewater fishing machine that meets the demands of sportsmen who desire superior performance and reliability in a rugged, well built center console boat." Few industry pros would argue with that characterization. Built on a solid fiberglass deep-V hull with moderate beam, the 29 FS carries her outboards on the transom rather than on a bracket as the 26 does. Storage space is plentiful aboard the 29 FS with a 520-quart, insulated fishbox forward in the cockpit that doubles as a rod locker. The 200-quart insulated lockers that flank either side can be used for fish boxes or dry storage. Standard features include a combined leaning post/tackle center, 30-gallon in-deck livewell, pop-up cleats, fresh and raw water washdowns, cushioned bow seating, and a console head compartment with marine toilet. With her 285-gallon fuel capacity, the 29 FS has excellent range. Yamaha 250s reach 45 knots.

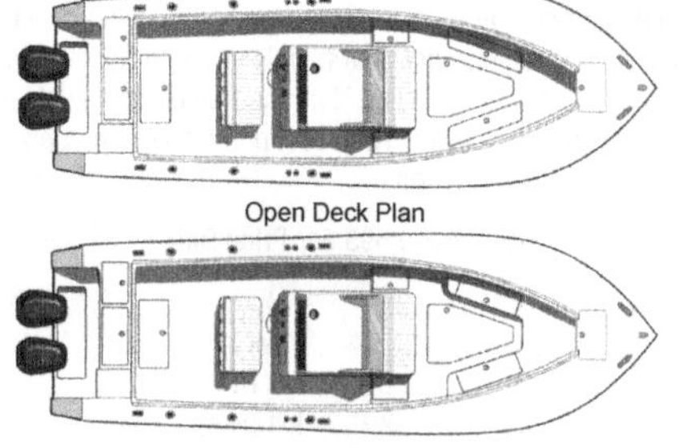
Open Deck Plan

Forward Seating

See Page 695 For Price Data

Length	29'0"	Fuel	285 gals.
Beam	9'6"	Water	20 gals.
Draft, Up	2'0"	Max HP	500
Draft, Down	2'7"	Hull Type	Deep-V
Hull Weight	6,900#	Deadrise Aft	24°

Regulator 32 FS

1999–Current

The Regulator 32 FS (for "Forward Seating") is a heavily built offshore fisherman whose quality construction, soft ride, and aggressive good looks will find an appreciative audience among hardcore anglers. Unlike many high-performance center consoles her size, the Regulator's wide beam results in a more stable fishing platform than her narrow-beam counterparts with considerably more cockpit space. Storage capacity—which is copious for a boat this size—includes a 645-quart forward in-deck fishbox (which doubles as locking storage for eight rods), a 50-gallon transom livewell, and a 130-quart fishbox also in the transom. The standard helm seat with flip-up bolsters contains a livewell and bait rigging station. Offered with our without bow seating over the years, the forward seating layout is now standard. The console contains a standup head compartment with sink, shower, and opening port. With her generous 310-gallon fuel capacity, the 32 has the ability to range well offshore and stay there until the fishing is done. Built on a deep-V hull with a well-flared bow and reverse chines, twin 250hp Yamaha outboards will take the Regulator 32 to a top speed in excess of 40 knots.

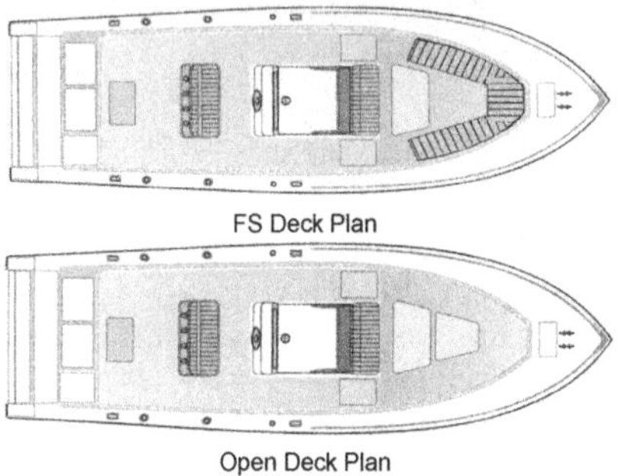
FS Deck Plan

Open Deck Plan

See Page 695 For Price Data

Length	32'0"	Fuel	310 gals.
Beam	10'5"	Water	38 gals.
Draft, Up	2'0"	Max HP	700
Draft, Down	2'8"	Hull Type	Deep-V
Dry Weight	7,400#	Deadrise Aft	24°

Regulator 34 SS

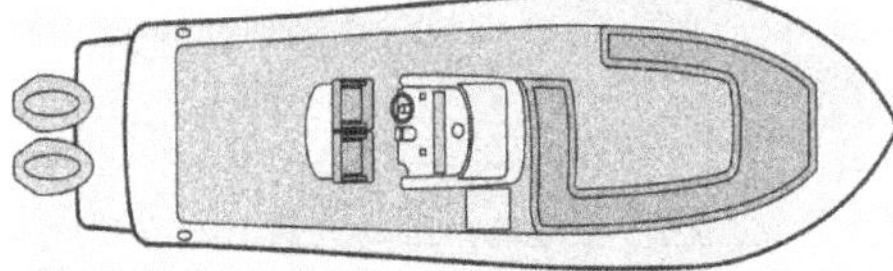

The Regulator 34 SS (for "Starboard Seating") differs from most big center consoles in that the lounge seating forward of the console wraps around the starboard side of the bow. While that eliminates the walkaround capability common to most center console boats, it opens the door to the other unique feature of the 34 SS: an enlarged console cuddy complete with standing headroom, compact galley, sink with pullout shower, electric head (with 13-gallon holding tank), and a sleeping berth for two tucked under the forward deck. These are luxurious amenities for a fishing boat—the forward seating can accommodate up to 12 guests!—but most anglers would agree that it's rare to use the entire length of the boat to fight a fish. The 34's large cockpit boasts an 85-gallon transom fish box, foldaway rear seat, saltwater wash down, transom door, and 360-degree coaming pads. The livewell, bait sink, and cutting board are built into the tackle station at the aft side of the leaning post, and there's space to flush-mount two 12" video displays in the dash. Note the frameless windshield and Armstrong engine bracket. Twin 350hp Yamahas (the only power option) reach 45+ knots top.

See Page 695 For Price Data

Length w/Bracket	38'6"	Fuel	380 gals.
Beam	10'11"	Water	35 gals.
Draft, Up	2'3"	Max HP	700
Draft, Down	2'7"	Hull Type	Deep-V
Weight w/Engines	11,115#	Deadrise Aft	24°

Rinker

Quick View

- In the 1930s, dairy farmer Lossie Rinker starts building fishing, and later racing boats, out of his workshop on the White River in Indiana. (The company was then called Rinkerbuilt.)
- In 1958, Rinkerbuilt introduces fiberglass in the manufacturing process, long before most competitors, along with innovations such as multiple gelcoat colors and back-to-back seating.
- In the 1970s the company expanded with a popular line of small tri-hulls.
- The 1980s bring a new name ("built" is dropped as the suffix) and new designs as the now 40-year old company continues to grow.
- In 1985 Rinker introduced its first express cruiser, a 25-footer that laid the groundwork for the company's current Fiesta Vee series.
- Still family owned and operated after three generations in business, Rinkers are distributed nationwide as well as in several foreign countries.
- Rinker has the distinction of being the oldest American boat brand in continuous production.

Rinker Boats • Elkhart, IN • www.rinkerboats.com

Rinker 260/265 Fiesta Vee

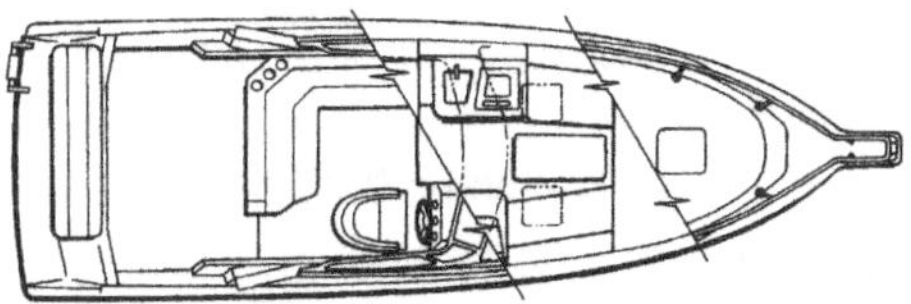

The Rinker 260/265 Fiesta Vee is an economy-priced midcabin family cruiser with an attractive profile to go with her trailerable 8-foot, 6-inch beam. Indeed, she's one of the larger trailerable boats available although you'll need a heavy-duty tow vehicle to take advantage of her mobility. Introduced as the 260 Fiesta Vee in 1991, Rinker engineers updated the styling, enlarged the galley, and raised the deck four inches in 1994 when the model name was changed to the 265 Fiesta Vee. Hull construction is solid fiberglass, and her deep-V bottom provides a stable and comfortable ride in a chop. The compact accommodations are efficiently arranged with a dinette/V-berth forward and a standup head compartment amidships. The midcabin offers good headroom at the entrance, an athwartships double berth, and a small port for ventilation. Outside, a sizeable L-shaped settee is opposite the helm and a molded-in bench seat is set against the transom. A good-selling boat during her production years, a single 5.7-liter I/O will cruise the 265 at 21 knots (about 33 knots top), and an optional 7.4-liter MerCruiser cruises at 32 knots with a top speed of 42–43 knots.

See Page 695 For Price Data

Length w/Pulpit	28'11"	Fuel	75 gals.
Beam	8'6"	Water	33 gals.
Draft, Drive Up	1'9"	Waste	27 gals.
Draft, Drive Down	2'11"	Hull Type	Deep-V
Weight	5,725#	Deadrise Aft	20°

Rinker 266 Fiesta Vee

1996–99

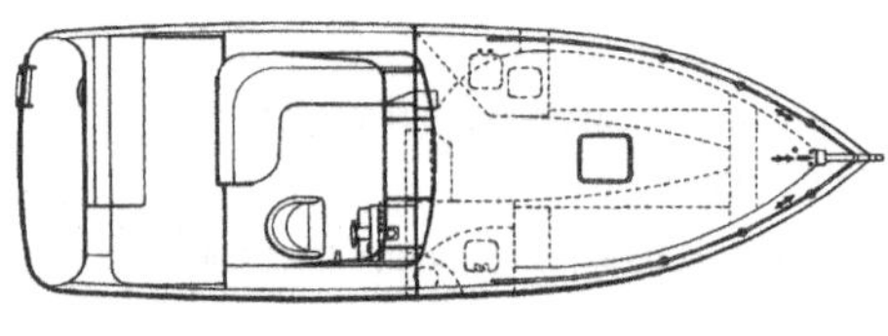

Trailerable family cruisers with standing cabin headroom generally have a fat, overstuffed appearance due to their elevated foredecks and helms. The Rinker 266 Fiesta Vee comes off looking a little better than most, however, thanks to her streamlined deck profile and some clever cabin graphics. Like all Rinker models, the 266 is a fairly straightforward boat, affordably priced and conservatively built on a solid fiberglass deep-V hull. At over 6,000 lbs., she's no lightweight and she'll require a heavy-duty tow vehicle for any serious traveling. Belowdecks, the Fiesta Vee's cabin is surprisingly spacious thanks to the absence of walkaround decks. The midcabin floorplan is quite typical with a convertible dinette/V-berth forward, a small mid-berth aft, an enclosed head with shower, and a compact galley. Notably, there's a full interior liner that makes cleanup quick and easy. The bi-level cockpit has a large L-shaped lounge opposite the helm, a walk-thru windshield, and a transom seat with storage under. On the downside, the engine hatch is difficult to lift and a gas-assist strut would have been a useful touch. A single 250hp MerCruiser I/O will cruise the 266 at 18 knots and reach a top speed of 31–32 knots.

See Page 695 For Price Data

Length	27'5"	Fuel	75 gals.
Beam	8'6"	Water	33 gals.
Draft, Drive Down	3'0"	Waste	27 gals.
Weight	6,150#	Hull Type	Deep-V
Clearance	6'8"	Deadrise Aft	20°

Rinker 270 Fiesta Vee

1999–2006

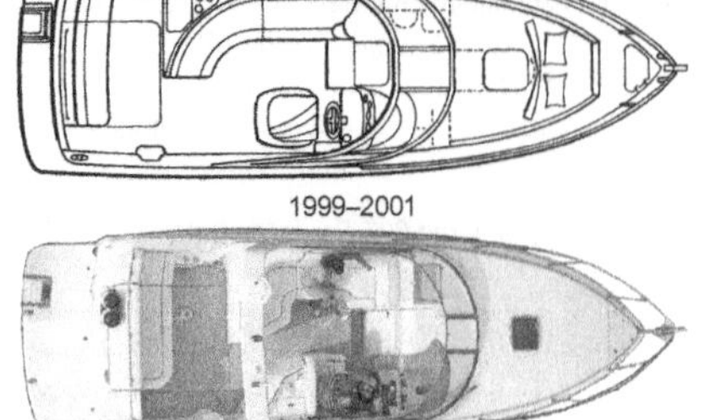

1999–2001

2002–06

Bargain hunters looking for a big 27-foot family cruiser with a midcabin layout and a low price will want to check out Rinker's 270 Fiesta Vee. Indeed, this is a boat that offers a lot of bang for the buck, and as long as one isn't too obsessed with fine detailing the Fiesta Vee should satisfy the demands of most entry-level buyers. Built on a solid fiberglass modified-V hull, the 270 is not trailerable like many 27-footers thanks to her generous 9-foot, 1-inch beam. The interior is arranged like most midcabin cruisers her size with a convertible dinette/V-berth forward, complete galley, enclosed head with shower, and a double berth aft with a curtain for privacy. The single-level cockpit—updated in 2002 with a wet bar and double helm seat—has lounge seating aft and a transom door. Standard features include a walk-through windshield, electric engine hatch (which is actually part of the rear seat) windshield wiper, and transom shower. Among many sterndrive engine choices, a single 320hp MerCruiser 6.2L will cruise the 270 Fiesta Vee in the low 20s and top out at 35+ knots. With just 100 gallons of fuel capacity, don't plan any long trips.

See Page 695 For Price Data

Length w/Platform	30'4"	Fuel	100 gals.
Hull Length	27'10"	Water	33 gals.
Beam	9'1"	Waste	27 gals.
Draft, Drives Down	3'0"	Hull Type	Modified-V
Weight	7,350#	Deadrise Aft	18°

Rinker 280 Fiesta Vee

1993–99

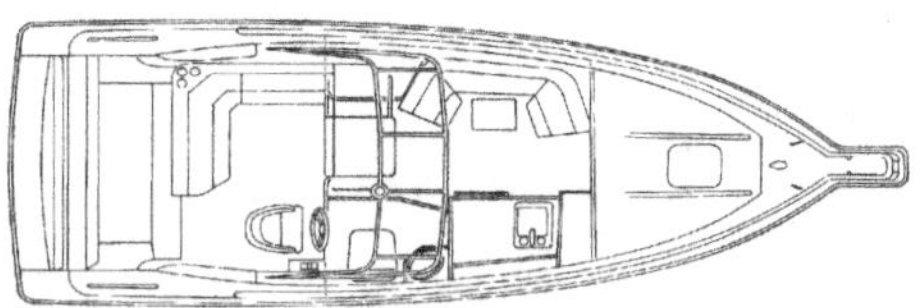

Like all Rinker models, the 280 Fiesta Vee is a budget-priced, no-glitz package with a lot of standard features that other manufacturers consider as extra-cost options. Hull construction is solid fiberglass, and her 10-foot beam is about average for an express cruiser her size. She's a good-looking boat with her integral swim platform and curved windshield, and despite the low price, the overall fit and finish is surprisingly good. The 280's midcabin floorplan is typical of family cruisers her size with double berths fore and aft, convertible dinette, and a compact galley. Privacy curtains separate the sleeping areas from the salon. Headroom is excellent throughout, and there are plenty of storage bins and lockers. On deck, the cockpit is arranged with a big L-shaped settee opposite the helm and bench seating at the transom. Note that the side decks are narrow and foredeck access is no easy matter, especially underway. The fuel capacity is pretty light as well. Twin 180hp 4.3-liter sterndrives cruise the Rinker 280 around 20 knots (about 30 knots top), and optional 235hp 5.7-liter Mercs cruise in the mid 20s and reach 35+ knots wide open. Note the modest fuel capacity.

See Page 695 For Price Data

Length w/Pulpit	30'2"	Fuel	120 gals.
Beam	10'0"	Water	33 gals.
Draft, Drives Up	1'10"	Waste	27 gals.
Draft, Drives Down	3'0"	Hull Type	Deep-V
Weight	8,680#	Deadrise Aft	20°

Rinker 280/290 Express Cruiser

2007–Current

Introduced in 2007, the Rinker 280 Express Cruiser (called the 290 Express Cruiser since 2012) combines a low, entry-level price with the fuel-efficiency that comes with single-engine power. For decades, Rinker has built their name on delivering affordable, well-equipped boats. Indeed, they have long occupied that sweet spot in the American boating market, the intersection between price and value. Built on a solid fiberglass modified-V hull with tall freeboard and a slender 9'1" beam, the user-friendly cockpit of the 280 Express consists of wraparound rear seating, a refreshment center with sink and storage, portside lounger, and a double helm seat with flip-up bolster. Note the aft facing "rumble seat" built into the transom—nice touch. Lacking side decks, a walk-through windshield provides access to the bow. Below decks, the cozy mid-cabin interior of the Rinker 280 might best be described as no frills and basic. Where some 28-footers with greater beam might sleep six, the 280 sleeps four. There's more galley storage than some boats her size, however, and mid cabin double berth has its own flat screen TV/DVD. A single 375hp MerCruiser I/O will cruise at 24–25 knots (mid 30s top).

See Page 695 For Price Data

Length	31'8"	Fuel	100 gals.
Beam	9'1"	Water	33 gals.
Draft, Up	2'0"	Waste	27 gals.
Draft, Down	3'0"	Hull Type	Modified-V
Weight	7,640#	Deadrise Aft	18°

Rinker 290 Fiesta Vee; 300 Express Cruiser

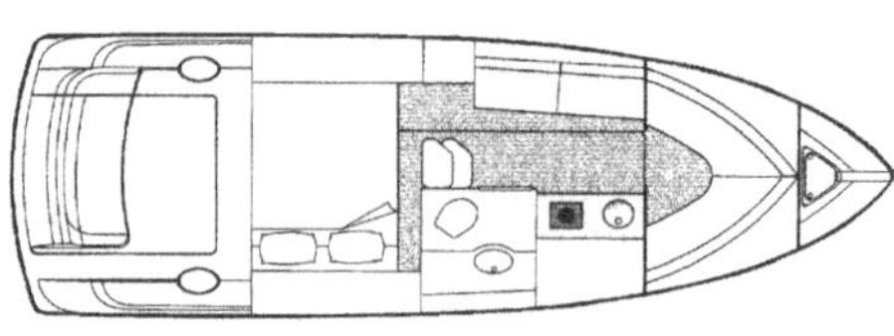

The Rinker 290 Fiesta Vee (called the 300 Express Cruiser in 2005–09) is an entry-level family cruiser whose low price and impressive inventory of standard equipment made her one of the better boating values of her era. For a so-called "price boat," the 290/300 delivers most of the features found in more expensive boats. While the materials and finish may not compare with a Sea Ray or Regal, the Rinker is a capable entertainment platform with a comfortable cabin layout and plenty of cockpit seating. Built on a solid fiberglass hull, the interior is arranged in the typical fashion with a forward V-berth (which is a little narrow), a double midcabin berth, and a convertible settee. The TV/VCR is positioned for easy viewing, and cherry laminate cabinets and faux granite counters accent the full-service galley. Topside, an L-lounge opposite the helm and a bench seat at the transom will seat several passengers in comfort. An electric hatch provides good access to the engine compartment. A radar arch, extended swim platform, windlass and tilt steering wheel were all standard. Twin 260hp MerCruiser I/Os cruise the Rinker 290/300 in the mid 20s and reach a top speed of over 35 knots.

See Page 696 For Price Data

Length	33'2"	Fuel	150 gals.
Beam	10'6"	Water	33 gals.
Draft, Up	1'10"	Waste	47 gals.
Draft, Down	3'0"	Hull Type	Modified-V
Weight	11,100#	Deadrise Aft	18°

Rinker 300 Fiesta Vee

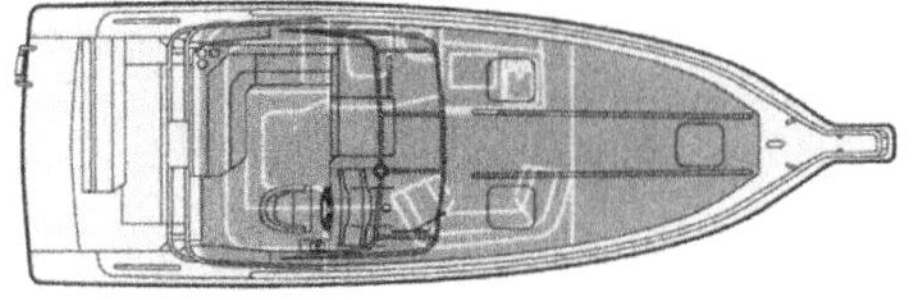

A good-selling model for Rinker during the 1990s, the 300 Fiesta Vee owed her popularity to a very affordable price, a comfortable interior, and surprisingly good performance. Hull construction is solid fiberglass, and the Fiesta Vee's generous 10-foot, 6-inch beam results in spacious cabin accommodations well suited to the needs of a small family. Her midcabin floorplan is arranged in the normal manner with double berths fore and aft, a convertible dinette in the salon, fully equipped galley, and a very spacious head compartment. Storage—including the aircraft-style overhead lockers—is excellent. Note that the midcabin, with its removable table, is a separate seating area during the day, while a privacy curtain separates it from the main salon at night. With its integrated swim platform and bow pulpit, the 300 Fiesta Vee looks like a larger boat. Lounge seating in the cockpit can easily accommodate six adults, however narrow side decks makes a trip to the foredeck a bit of a challenge. Note, too, that the fit and finish is unimpressive. Among several engine choices, twin 260hp 5.7-liter MerCruiser sterndrives cruise the Rinker 300 in the low 20s while delivering a top speed in excess of 35 knots.

See Page 696 For Price Data

Length w/Pulpit	33'11"	Fuel	140 gals.
Beam	10'6"	Water	34 gals.
Draft, Drives Up	1'8"	Waste	25 gals.
Draft, Drives Down	2'10"	Hull Type	Modified-V
Weight	10,000#	Deadrise Aft	18°

Rinker 310/312 Fiesta Vee; 320 Express

2000–09

One of the most affordable boats in her class during her production years, the Rinker 310 Fiesta Vee (called the 312 Fiesta Vee in 2003–04; 320 Express in 2005–09) is a stylish family cruiser that might best be described as a lot of boat for the money. Rinker has a reputation for building solid, well-equipped boats at prices much lower than the competition, and the 320 will appealed to entry-level buyers suffering sticker-shock from their last visit to a Sea Ray dealer. Built on a beamy modified-V hull with relatively high freeboard, the Fiesta Vee is a notably spacious boat inside with excellent headroom and plenty of storage. The midcabin floorplan will sleep six, and while the decor is a little plain compared with some of her more upscale counterparts, the accommodations are arranged in a practical and very utilitarian manner. In the cockpit, a comfortable U-shaped settee is opposite the helm with a mini-galley and transom seating is aft. Additional features include a radar arch, transom door, swim platform, fender storage, and an electric engine access hatch. A good performer, twin 260hp 5.0-liter sterndrive engines cruise the Fiesta Vee at 20 knots and reach a top speed of 35+ knots.

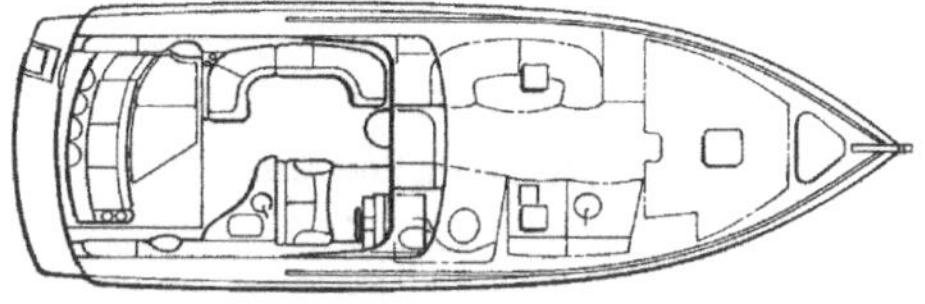

See Page 696 For Price Data

Length	34'8"	Fuel	165 gals.
Beam	11'4"	Water	39 gals.
Draft, Up	1'10"	Waste	45 gals.
Draft, Down	3'0"	Hull Type	Modified-V
Weight	12,360#	Deadrise Aft	18°

Rinker 330/340 Express Cruiser

2008–Current

In keeping with the company's reputation for delivering a lot of boat for the money, Rinker's 330 Express Cruiser (called the Rinker 340 Express Cruiser since 2010) strikes the right balance between affordability and value. She has most of the features found in the more expensive boats in her class (Sea Ray, Regal, Four Winns, etc.), but the high-end amenities are fewer and the finish less refined. Like all Rinker express models, the 330 rides on a solid fiberglass hull with moderate beam and relatively high freeboard. The styling is contemporary—slightly on the conservative side—and the accommodations are similar to most express cruisers her size. The cockpit consists of wraparound rear seating, a refreshment center with sink and storage, a portside lounger, and a double helm seat with flip-up bolster. Note the aft facing "rumble seat" built into the transom—nice touch. Lacking side decks, a walk-through windshield provides access to the bow. Belowdecks, the 330's well-appointed interior includes a double bed forward, convertible midcabin lounge, full-service galley, and a convertible dinette—comfortable accommodations for six. Cruise at 24–25 knots (about 35 top) with twin 280hp Volvo I/Os.

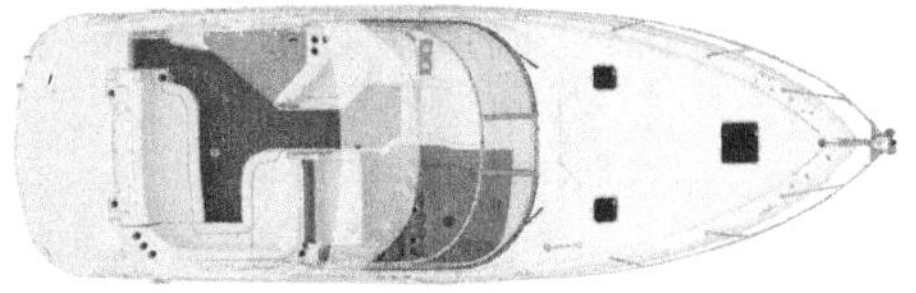

See Page 696 For Price Data

Length	35'8"	Fuel	168 gals.
Beam	11'4"	Water	40 gals.
Draft, Up	1'10"	Waste	47 gals.
Draft, Down	3'0"	Hull Type	Modified-V
Weight	14,100#	Deadrise Aft	18°

Rinker 330/340/342 Fiesta Vee

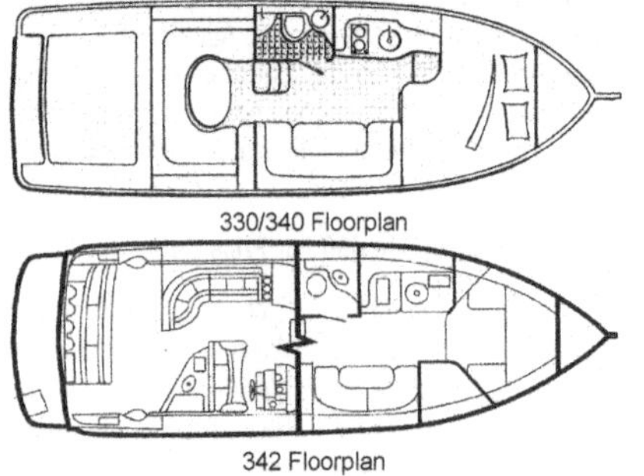
330/340 Floorplan

342 Floorplan

The Rinker 330 Fiesta Vee (called the 340 Fiesta Vee in 2000–01; 342 Fiesta Vee in 2002–06) is a midsize family cruiser whose crisp styling, roomy interior and attractive price make her a popular choice for budget-minded boaters. Built on a beamy semi-V hull, the Fiesta Vee's original midcabin floorplan was arranged a little different from the norm in that the galley refrigerator is forward, under the double berth. On the downside, sitting headroom in both the fore and aft berths was very low in early models. Significantly, Rinker updated the boat for 2000 (when she became the 340 Fiesta Vee) with a lowered floor in the salon and new, taller, foredeck tooling that increased cabin headroom and overall living space. An all-new floorplan was introduced in 2002—along with an extended swim platform and additional fuel—when she became the 342 Fiesta Vee. The cockpit, with seating for six to eight, includes a full wet bar with sink and refrigerator. Additional features include a walk-through windshield, electric engine hatch, extended swim platform, and transom shower. Among several sterndrive options, twin 280hp Volvo gas sterndrives cruise the Fiesta Vee in the low-to-mid 20s and reach a top speed of around 35 knots.

See Page 696 For Price Data

Length w/Platform	37'0"	Fuel	200/235 gals.
Beam	12'0"	Water	51 gals.
Draft, Drives Down	2'11"	Waste	45 gals.
Weight	14,280#	Hull Type	Modified-V
Clearance	9'8"	Deadrise Aft	18°

Rinker 350/360 Express Cruiser

The Rinker 360 Express Cruiser (called the Rinker 350 Express Cruiser in 2008) strikes the right balance between size, affordability and value. She has most of the features found in the more expensive boats in her class (Sea Ray, Regal, Four Winns, etc.), but the high-end amenities are fewer and the finish less refined. Like all Rinker express models, the 360 rides on a solid fiberglass hull with moderate beam and relatively high freeboard. The styling is contemporary—slightly on the conservative side—and the accommodations are similar to those found in competitive express cruisers her size. The cockpit consists of wraparound rear seating, a refreshment center with sink and storage, a portside lounger, and a double helm seat with flip-up bolster. Note the aft facing "rumble seat" built into the transom—a great place to take a break from swimming or diving. Lacking side decks, a walk-through windshield provides access to the bow. Belowdecks, the 360's well-appointed interior includes a double bed forward, convertible midcabin lounge, full-service galley, and convertible dinette—comfortable accommodations for six adults. MerCruiser 300hp engines cruise at 22–23 knots (mid 30s top).

See Page 696 For Price Data

Length	37'11"	Fuel	235 gals.
Beam	12'0"	Water	51 gals.
Draft, Up	1'10"	Waste	45 gals.
Draft, Down	3'0"	Hull Type	Modified-V
Weight	15,550#	Deadrise Aft	18°

Rinker 360/370/380 Express Cruiser

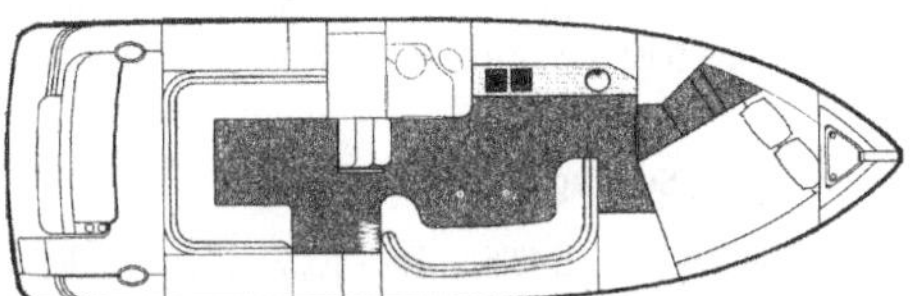

The Rinker 360 Fiesta Vee (called the 370 Express in 2007–08; 380 Express in 2009) make good on the Rinker promise of a lot of boat for the money. Indeed, with her crisp styling, brisk performance and comfortable accommodations, the 360 Express easily holds her own against many of the more expensive boats in her class. Built on a solid fiberglass hull with relatively modest beam, the interior of the Rinker 360 differs from the typical midcabin boat in that the forward stateroom is separated from the salon by a solid wood bulkhead door rather than just a curtain. The salon galley is large enough for serious meal-preparation activities, and the midcabin—partially obstructed by the companionway steps—is unusually spacious. The head compartment is also quite large and includes a separate shower enclosure. On deck, the cockpit has a full wet bar with sink, icemaker, refrigerator, and built-in blender. A flip-up helm seat allows for standup driving, and molded steps access the walk-through windshield. The entire aft deck can be raised on hydraulic rams to reach the engines. A good performer, twin 375hp MerCruiser sterndrives deliver a top speed of just over 40 knots.

See Page 696 For Price Data

Length	39'4"	Fuel	235 gals.
Beam	12'3"	Water	51 gals.
Draft, Up	2'0"	Waste	45 gals.
Draft, Down	3'0"	Hull Type	Modified-V
Weight	18,400#	Deadrise Aft	18°

Rinker 390/400 Express Cruiser

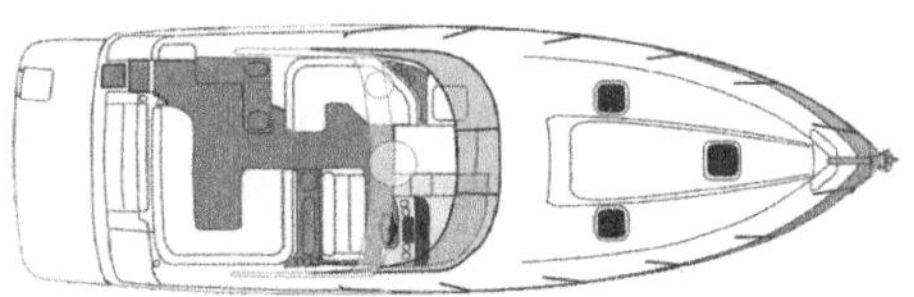

Rinker got it right with the 400 Express Cruiser (called the 390 Express Cruiser when she was introduced in 2006), a value-priced sterndrive cruiser with all the features one expects in a modern family express this size. She's built on a solid fiberglass hull with moderate beam and a relatively steep 18 degrees of transom deadrise. The 400's tall freeboard results in an exceptionally spacious interior with nearly seven feet of cabin headroom. The master stateroom is forward in this layout and includes a queen island berth and flat-screen TV. But it's the huge aft stateroom that comes as a surprise, a feat made possible by Rinker's decision to use space-saving sterndrive power in this boat rather than more conventional inboard (V-drive) power. Both staterooms come with privacy doors rather than curtains—a real plus. Satin-finished cherry joinery is applied throughout the interior that also features a Corian galley counter and teak flooring. The split-level cockpit, with seating for a small crowd, includes a full-service wet bar with icemaker, double helm seat with flip-up bolster, walk-through windshield, and transom shower. MerCruiser 375hp I/Os cruise at 25 knots (35+ top). Axius Drives became optional in 2008.

See Page 696 For Price Data

Length Overall	41'6"	Fuel	300 gals.
Beam	13'0"	Water	69 gals.
Draft, Drives Up	1'10"	Waste	45 gals.
Draft, Drives Down	3'2"	Hull Type	Modified-V
Weight	19,680#	Deadrise Aft	18°

Rinker 390/410/420 Express Cruiser

Rinker's largest boat ever, the 410 Express (called the 390 Fiesta Vee in 2004; 410 Express in 2005–06; 420 Express in 2007) is a roomy midcabin cruiser whose affordable price included an impressive array of standard features. Built on a modified-V hull with a solid fiberglass bottom, the highlight of this big express is her spacious interior with its 7-foot headroom, full-size sofa, and copious storage. Privacy doors separate the fore and aft staterooms from the main salon, and both staterooms come with built-in TVs. (Note that the aft stateroom has a separate berth for one child.) In the alcove just off the head is a full-size washer/dryer combination, while the galley features not just the expected microwave, but a real oven. Topside, the cockpit comes with a double helm seat, wet bar with refrigerator, icemaker and blender, and a U-shaped aft lounge that converts into a big sun pad. Additional features include cherry interior joinery, transom storage locker, and a gas grill that slides into a base of the extended swim platform. Twin V-drive 425hp gas engines cruise at 22–23 knots (about 30 knots top), and 380hp Cummins diesels cruise at 25–26 knots (also 30 knots top).

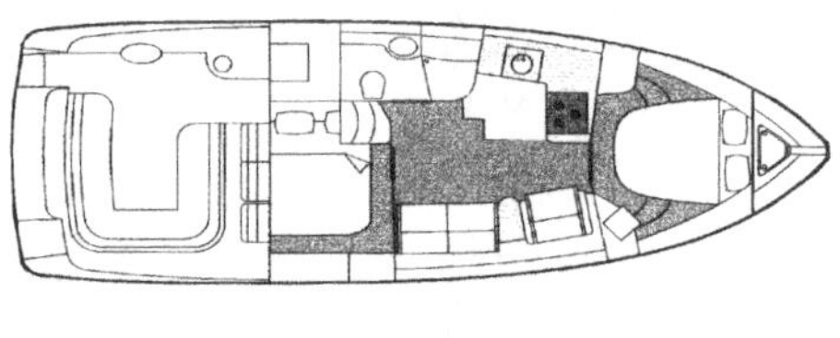

See Page 696 For Price Data

Length w/Platform	43'6"	Fuel	300 gals.
Beam	13'10"	Water	100 gals.
Draft	3'2"	Waste	88 gals.
Weight	24,500#	Hull Type	Modified-V
Clearance	12'10"	Deadrise Aft	18°

Riviera

Quick View

- Riviera was founded in 1981 by Bill Barry-Cotter, a name well-known in Australian offshore racing boat circles.
- By 1985 Riviera had grown to become the largest builder of production boats in Australia.
- Riviera began exporting to the U.S. in the late 1980s. Despite high shipping costs, a favorable exchange rate allows Rivieras to be competitive with domestic sportfishing boats.
- By 2000 Riviera was selling over 300 boats annually, half of which was exported to a dealer network spanning 30 countries.
- Riviera purchased Stuart Yacht in 2006 which then became Riviera's U.S. sales headquarters.
- With sales falling due to the worldwide recession, Riviera filed for bankruptcy in late 2009.
- Riviera resumes production in 2010.
- In 2012, Riviera was purchased by Longhurst Holding, an Australian investment company.

Riviera Yachts • Queensland, Australia • www.riviera.com.au

Riviera 33 Convertible

1992-97

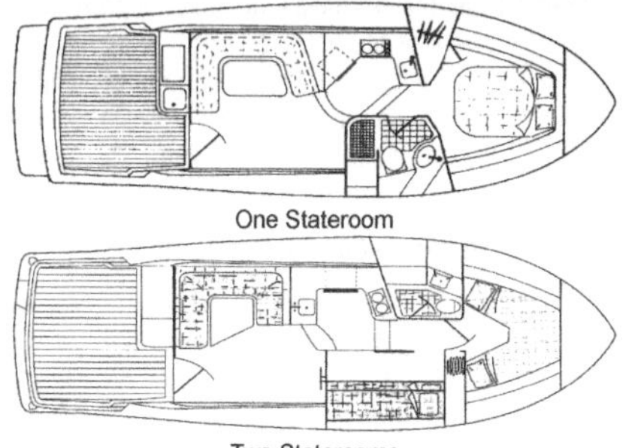

One Stateroom

Two Staterooms

Only a handful of small convertibles have been built in recent years and the Riviera 33—a Bertram look-alike from Australia—certainly ranks among the most handsome of the lot. Introduced into the American market in 1992, her appeal had much to do with a very affordable price, the result of the dollar's favorable exchange rate during most of the 1990s. Hull construction is solid fiberglass, and like all Riviera models, she has a collision bulkhead forward and two watertight bulkheads aft. Lower helms disappeared from sportfishermen years ago, but not from Rivieras. In both the single- and twin-stateroom interiors, the salon steering station is a welcome alternative (although it was often deleted by U.S. buyers). Engine access on the Riviera is unique for a boat this size: the cockpit sink swings out revealing a set of steps leading below. Topside, the flybridge is huge for a 33-footer with bench seating forward of the helm. Additional features include overhead grab rails in the salon, a transom door, and teak interior woodwork. Among several engine options, twin 315hp Cummins diesels cruise in the low 20s (26–28 knots top).

See Page 696 For Price Data

Length	33'0"	Fuel	296 gals.
Beam	12'6"	Water	84 gals.
Draft	2'7"	Waste	25 gals.
Weight	20,500#	Hull Type	Modified-V
Cockpit	NA	Deadrise Aft	16°

Riviera 33 Convertible

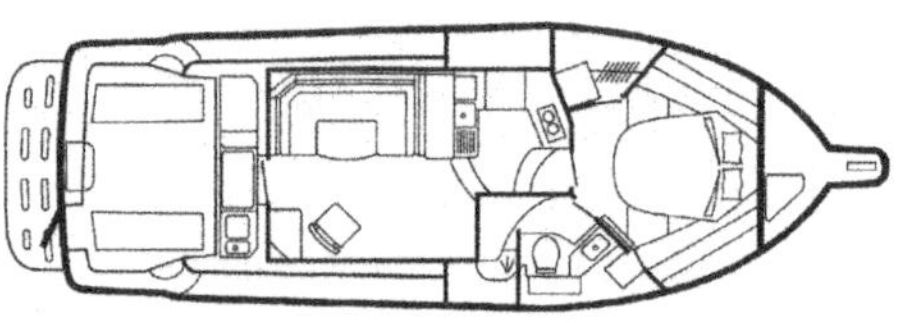

Small flybridge convertibles are rare in today's fishing-boat market—most domestic manufacturers find it far more profitable to concentrate their efforts on larger, more expensive models. With the Aussie-built Riviera 33, however, buyers had the opportunity to purchase a quality, smartly styled small convertible at a surprisingly affordable price. Built on a solid fiberglass hull with prop pockets and underwater exhausts, the Riviera's forward collision bulkhead offers a level of security seldom found in a boat of this type. Her single-stateroom interior is available with or without a lower helm. While the salon dimensions are modest, a U-shaped settee doubles as a comfortable dinette and wraparound windows admit plenty of natural lighting. A hatch in the salon's teak and holly sole offers inside engineroom access; the main entry is found in the cockpit. On the flybridge, twin helm chairs and a forward bench seat can accommodate several guests. The 33's lighted cockpit has a tackle station with freshwater sink to starboard, top-loading refrigerator cabinet to port, in-deck fish box, and a transom bait-prep center. Note the raw water washdown in the anchor locker. Twin 310hp Volvo diesels cruise at 22 knots (high 20s top).

See Page 696 For Price Data

Length w/Pulpit	37'3"	Fuel	264 gals.
Beam	12'7"	Water	103 gals.
Draft	3'3"	Waste	18 gals.
Weight	19,800#	Hull Type	Modified-V
Clearance	14'5"	Deadrise Aft	15°

Riviera 34 Convertible

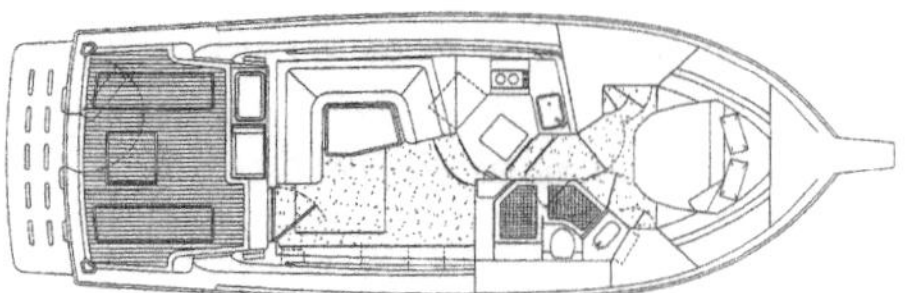

A handsome Bertram-like profile, solid construction, and good open-water performance distinguish the Riviera 34, an Australian-built sportfisherman whose low price attracted a lot of attention in the late 1990s. She rides on a solid fiberglass hull with a generous 13-foot, 4-inch beam, and at nearly 20,000 pounds the 34 is no lightweight. The single-stateroom interior of the Riviera is arranged with the galley down, separated from the salon by a serving counter. A lower helm was a popular option, and wraparound cabin windows admit plenty of outside natural lighting. This is a spacious interior with a wide, open salon, a large stateroom with a full-size island berth, and a separate stall shower in the head. Topside, the cockpit came with a molded bait-prep console with freezer and sink, transom door, and direct access to the engineroom. Additional features include a tournament-style flybridge with bench seating forward of the helm, a large storage compartment under the galley sole, wide side decks, and a bow pulpit. A well-conceived boat, twin 330hp Cummins diesels cruise the Riviera 34 in the mid 20s and reach close to 30 knots top.

See Page 696 For Price Data

Length	34'0"	Water	84 gals.
Beam	13'4"	Clearance	NA
Draft	2'7"	Headroom	6'4"
Weight	19,400#	Hull Type	Modified-V
Fuel	296 gals.	Deadrise Aft	17°

Riviera 36 Convertible

With her rakish flybridge and long foredeck, it's hard to believe that the Riviera 36 isn't a purebred American sportfisherman. This Australian import is definitely a looker—certainly one of the better-looking 36-footers around—and a favorable exchange rate made her something of a bargain as well. Hull construction is solid fiberglass, and she was designed with a collision bulkhead forward as an extra margin of safety. A lot of anglers like the 35–36-foot size range since you can get a good-size cockpit as well as a two-stateroom interior without breaking the bank. (Note that a single-stateroom floorplan with an enlarged cockpit became available in 1999.) In either layout, a lower helm is optional. A transom door and an engine room access hatch are standard in the cockpit, and the big tournament-style flybridge has bench seating forward of the rather plain-Jane helm console. The Riviera 36 has a cruising speed of 24 knots with a pair of 315hp Cummins diesels and a top speed of around 27–28 knots. Optional 350hp Cummins (or Cat) diesels cruise at 26 knots (about 30 knots top).

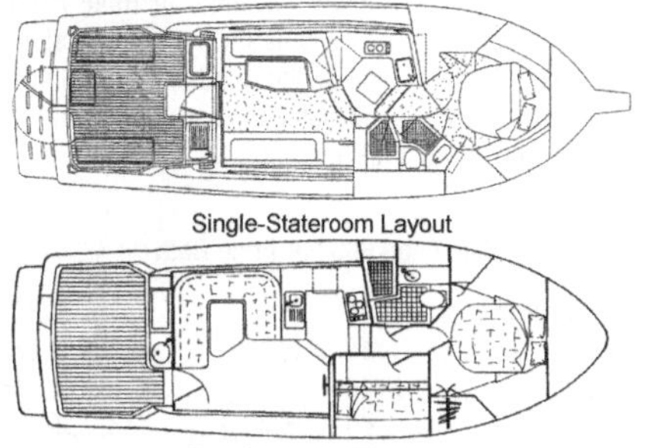
Single-Stateroom Layout

Two-Stateroom Floorplan

See Page 696 For Price Data

Length	36'0"	Water	119 gals.
Beam	13'5"	Clearance	NA
Draft	3'5"	Headroom	6'4"
Weight	22,800#	Hull Type	Modified-V
Fuel	324 gals.	Deadrise Aft	16°

Riviera 3600 Sport Yacht

Introduced in 2007, the conservative lines of the Riviera 3600 Sport Yacht set her apart from the more aggressively styled European sportboats her size. Boating tastes vary, of course; Sunseekers and Sea Rays tend satisfy those who want to stand out in the crowd, while sport cruisers from Tiara and Riviera appeal to the more sedate among us. Built on a modified-V hull with prop pockets to reduce draft, the Riviera 3600's two-stateroom interior features a fully enclosed salon/pilothouse rather than the open maindeck layout seen in many hardtop yachts. Large side windows provide good helm visibility, and the salon furnishings include a convertible leather settee in addition to a full-service galley, pop-up TV (under the windshield) and teak-and-holly flooring. There are two private staterooms below—the master is forward with a centerline queen bed while the guest stateroom, aft and to port, has over/under twin berths. In the cockpit, the settee built into the transom converts into a sun pad. The engineroom, reached via a cockpit hatch, is tight. Note the underwater exhaust system. Cruise in the mid 20s with 370hp Volvo diesels (about 30 knots top). The MK II version, introduced in 2009, features Volvo IPS pod drives.

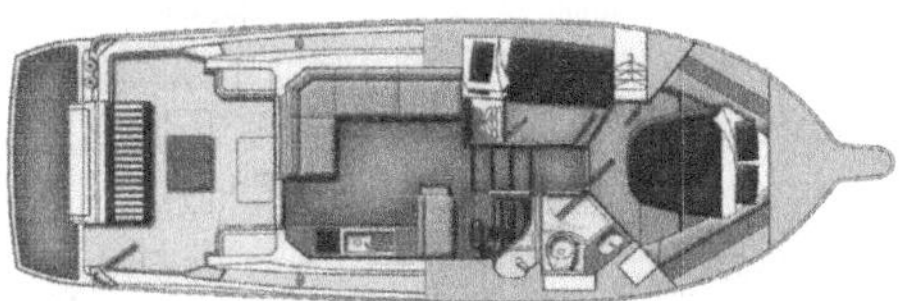

See Page 696 For Price Data

Length w/Pulpit	38'6"	Fuel	212 gals.
Beam	12'7"	Water	103 gals.
Draft	3'3"	Waste	18 gals.
Weight	20,300#	Hull Type	Modified-V
Clearance	NA	Deadrise Aft	15°

Riviera 37 Convertible

2001–08

Smart styling, solid construction, and comfortable accommodations are the hallmarks of the Riviera 37, an Australian-built convertible designed for serious fishing or extended family cruising. Like all Riviera models, the 37 rides on a stable modified-V hull whose solid fiberglass construction includes a watertight collision bulkhead forward and separate compartments throughout the hull. Below, the standard two-stateroom interior of the Riviera 37 is arranged with the galley down and a single head with separate stall shower. A lower helm is available (which accounts for the open front windshield), and varnished teak woodwork, a large salon dinette, and a teak-and-holly galley sole highlight the interior. Access to the spacious engineroom is gained from the big cockpit where a transom door, insulated fish box, and molded tackle center were standard. On the flybridge, there's seating for three passengers forward of the helm console. A bow pulpit, swim platform, and generator were standard. Twin 370hp Cummins diesels cruise the Riviera 37 in the mid 20s and reach a top speed of about 30 knots. Note the relatively modest fuel capacity.

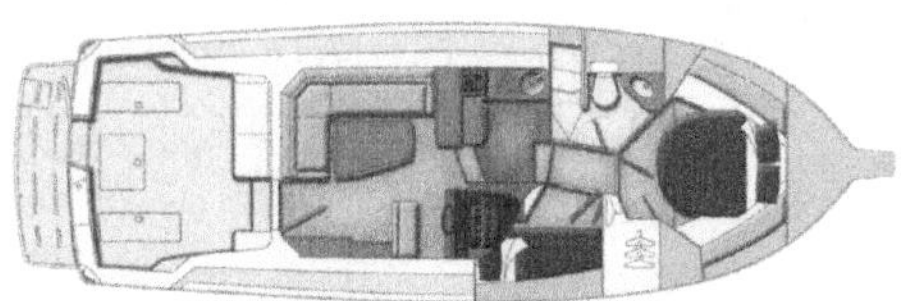

See Page 696 For Price Data

Length w/Pulpit	42'11"	Fuel	370 gals.
Hull Length	37'11"	Water	122 gals.
Beam	13'10"	Waste	18 gals.
Draft	3'5"	Hull Type	Modified-V
Weight	24,000#	Deadrise Aft	18°

Riviera 40 Convertible

2001–06

Considering the conservative styling of previous Riviera models, the sweeping—almost sculptured—lines of the Riviera 40 Convertible marked the beginning of Riviera's "new-look" convertible styling on display in new Riviera model introductions in recent years. Like her sisterships, the 40 is built on a beamy solid fiberglass hull with a well-flared bow and a short, shallow keel. Her two-stateroom interior is spacious for a 40-footer, and the varnished joiner work and quality fabrics add a touch of luxury to an otherwise unpretentious decor. A lower helm is optional, and there are three single berths in the guest stateroom. The door in the cockpit provides access to the engineroom, and a pair of in-deck fish boxes, a transom door, livewell (with a window) and molded tackle centers were standard. On the flybridge, an L-shaped settee forward of the helm will seat six adults. Additional features include a bow pulpit, wide side decks, and front cabin windows. Twin 450hp Cummins or Cat (or 430hp Volvo) diesels cruise in the mid 20s and reach a top speed of close to 30 knots, and 535hp Cummins diesels cruise in the high 20s and reach 30+ knots wide open.

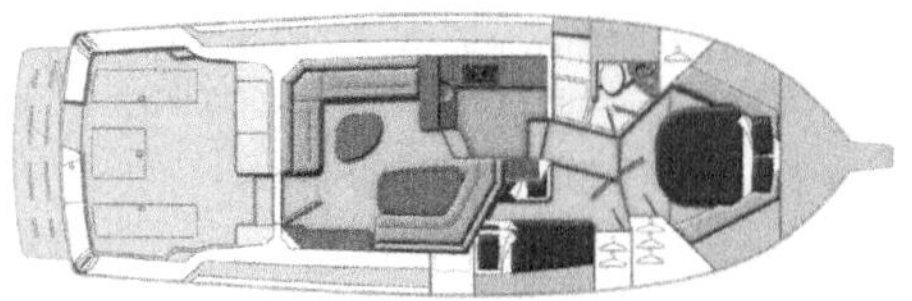

See Page 696 For Price Data

Length w/Pulpit	46'4"	Fuel	473 gals.
Hull Length	42'11"	Water	122 gals.
Beam	14'11"	Waste	18 gals.
Draft	4'1"	Hull Type	Modified-V
Weight	29,800#	Deadrise Aft	15°

Riviera 4000 Offshore

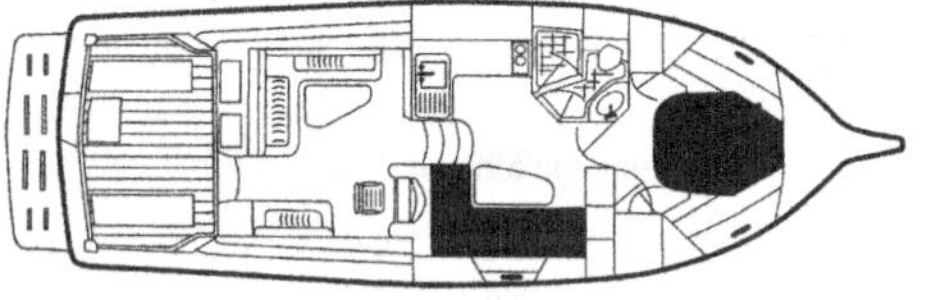

Riviera's first-ever express when she was introduced in 1998, the 4000 Offshore is a well built family cruiser with conservative lines (note the absence of an integrated swim platform) and a surprisingly spacious interior. She's constructed on a solid fiberglass modified-V hull with a wide 14-foot, 4-inch beam and a shallow keel for directional stability. Below decks, the oak-finished interior provides a sleeping capacity for four people, including a large forward cabin with an island berth. The salon dinette converts to double berth, and the Riviera's large head compartment includes a separate shower stall. A mirror-backed cocktail cabinet separates the dining area from the forward stateroom. On deck, the cockpit has a double helm seat, a second dinette with a molded-in freezer and sink, and a hydraulic midship hatch for engineroom access. (Note that the Riviera has a spacious engineroom—something that wouldn't be possible with a conventional midcabin interior.) Additional features include a cockpit transom door, radar arch, swim platform, and a bow pulpit. Among several engine options, a pair of 450hp Cummins (or 435hp Cat) diesels cruise the 4000 Offshore in the mid 20s (close to 30 knots top).

See Page 696 For Price Data

Length w/Pulpit	44'7"	Fuel	394 gals.
Hull Length	41'0"	Water	119 gals.
Beam	14'4"	Headroom	6'4"
Draft	3'11"	Hull Type	Modified-V
Weight	25,353#	Deadrise Aft	15°

Riviera 42 Convertible

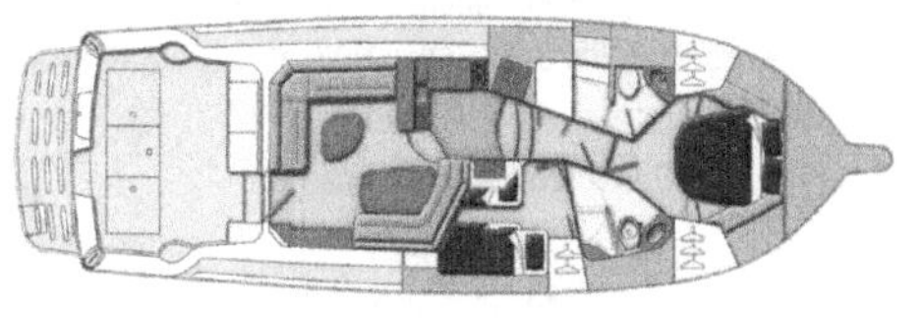

The Riviera 42 is an Austrialian-built flybridge convertible whose solid construction and sleek styling have great appeal for American buyers. Riviera is the only foreign fishboat builder to have succeeded in winning the hearts of American anglers thanks in large measure to the company's reputation for reliability and strong resale values. Built on a solid fiberglass hull with a wide beam and forward collision bulkhead, the two-stateroom, two-head interior of the Riviera 42 is available with or without a lower helm. A unique triple-bunk guest cabin to starboard has side-by-side bunks as well as an upper berth, and the master stateroom comes with an island berth and private ensuite head. High-gloss cabinetry, a salon dinette, and a well-equipped galley combine to make this interior as comfortable as it is practical. Above, the Riviera's flybridge is somewhat unique in that the helm is to starboard with the companion seat on the centerline—a design that means the driver doesn't have to get up to let someone pass behind him. A sun shade shelters the cockpit where a bait-prep center, in-sole fish box, cooler/freezer, and trash receptacle are standard. Cruise in the low 20s with 480hp Cummins diesels (26–28 knots top).

See Page 696 For Price Data

Length w/Pulpit	50'10"	Fuel	476 gals.
Hull Length	42'11"	Water	122 gals.
Beam	14'11"	Waste	40 gals.
Draft	4'2"	Hull Type	Modified-V
Weight	30,900#	Deadrise Aft	15°

Riviera 43 Convertible

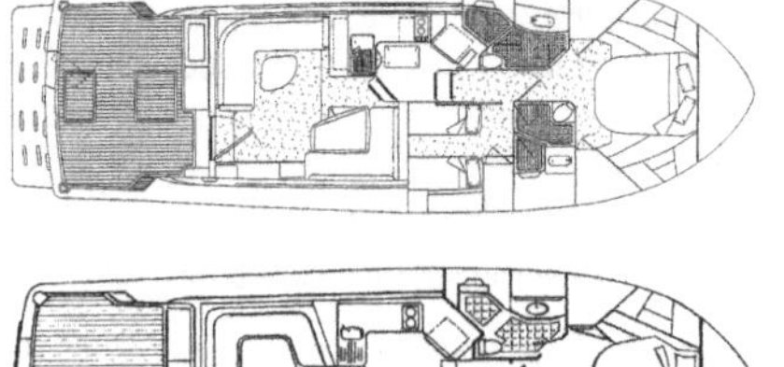

Introduced to the American market in 1996, the 43 Convertible quickly become one of Riviera's most popular models thanks to her handsome, Bertram-like styling, solid construction, and a low price made possible by the favorable exchange rates of the 1990s. Built on a beamy, solid fiberglass hull with a forward collision bulkhead and a shallow keel for directional stability, the Riviera 43's standard two-stateroom interior layout features two full heads (with stall showers) and twin beds in the guest stateroom. A huge storage bin is under the island berth in the master stateroom, and an L-shaped dinette is forward in the salon. An entertainment center is above the dinette, and solid teak cabinets and vinyl overheads highlight the interior. The Riviera's roomy cockpit came with a freezer, storage cabinets, and sink as well as direct access to a spacious, well-arranged engineroom. Topside, the flybridge is large for a 43-footer with an L-shaped lounge forward and a removable table. Among several diesel engine options, 420hp Cats (or 430hp Cummins) will cruise in the low 20s (26–28 knots top), and 610hp Volvos cruise in the mid 20s and reach a top speed of around 30 knots.

See Page 696 For Price Data

Length w/Pulpit	48'6"	Water	164 gals.
Beam	15'8"	Clearance	16'8"
Draft	4'2"	Headroom	6'6"
Weight	35,300#	Hull Type	Modified-V
Fuel	580/832 gals.	Deadrise Aft	16°

Riviera 47 Convertible

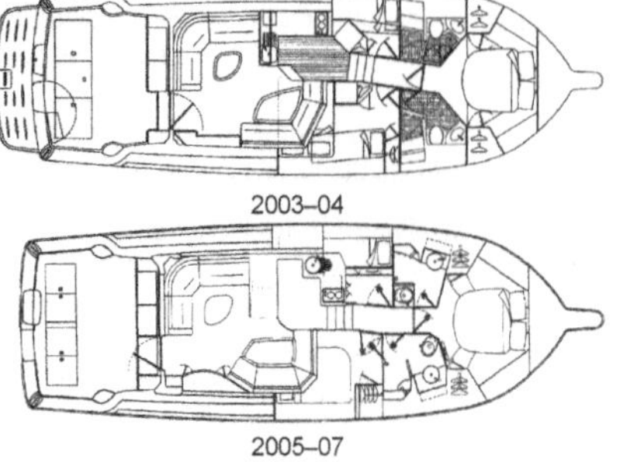
2003–04

2005–07

Riviera has earned an enviable reputation in recent years for delivering stylish, well-built yachts at very competitive prices. Introduced in 2003, the Riviera 47 split the difference between fishing boat and family cruiser by combining a cockpit big enough for serious fishing and interior accommodations for up to three couples. Like all Riviera models, the 47 rides on a stable modified-V hull whose solid fiberglass construction includes a watertight collision bulkhead forward and separate compartments throughout the hull. Notably, the 47 is one of just a few convertibles under 50 feet to feature three private staterooms. The galley-up floorplan includes a dinette to starboard as well as leather salon seating, quality galley appliances, and built-in entertainment center. A transom livewell, tackle center, and fish box are standard in the cockpit, and wide side decks provide secure access to the foredeck. Topside, an L-shaped lounge and table are forward of the helm console. Additional features include overhead rod storage in the salon and a well-arranged (but compact) engineroom. Cummins 660hp diesel inboards cruise the Riviera 47 Convertible in the mid-to-high 20s (30+ knots top).

See Page 696 For Price Data

Length w/Pulpit	53'1"	Fuel	977 gals.
Hull Length	49'10"	Water	164 gals.
Beam	16'1"	Waste	40 gals.
Draft	4'5"	Hull Type	Modified-V
Weight	43,200#	Deadrise Aft	16°

Riviera 51 Convertible

2004–12

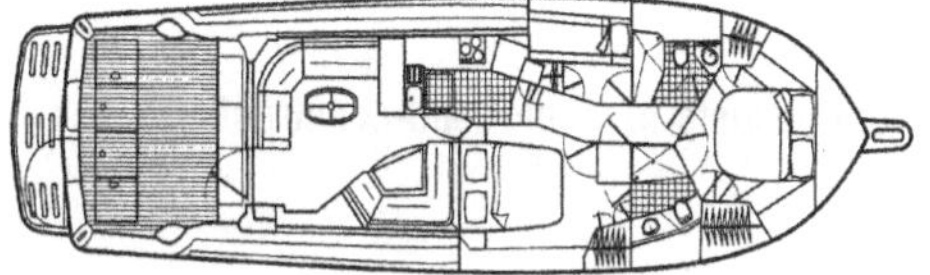

Rivieras are held in high regard among offshore anglers for their tremendous eye appeal, common-sense layouts, and near-bulletproof construction. The 51 Convertible reinforces that reputation for quality and toughness while setting a new standard for luxury not previously associated with boats from this Australian manufacturer. Built on a semi-V hull with moderate beam and a solid fiberglass bottom, the Riviera's elegant cherrywood interior is roomy, comfortable, and impressively appointed. The salon and dinette blend easily into a single open space, and the forward VIP stateroom is nearly as spacious as the master. For kids or crew, a second guest cabin has upper and lower berths. One of the highlights of the Riviera 51 is her spacious flybridge with its starboard helm position, wet bar, and L-shaped lounge seating. The teak-soled cockpit offers a full array of fishing amenities, and the engine room—while snug—offers good access to all maintenance points. Additional features include an overhead rod-storage compartment in the salon, washer/dryer, hardtop, forward collision bulkhead, and bow thruster. A modest performer with MTU 825hp diesels, she'll cruise at 26–28 knots (30+ top).

Not Enough Resale Data to Set Values

Length w/Pulpit	58'2"	Fuel	977 gals.
Hull Length	54'8"	Water	227 gals.
Beam	16'2"	Waste	40 gals.
Draft	4'6"	Hull Type	Modified-V
Weight	48,060#	Deadrise Aft	14°

Riviera 58 Enclosed Bridge

2003–06

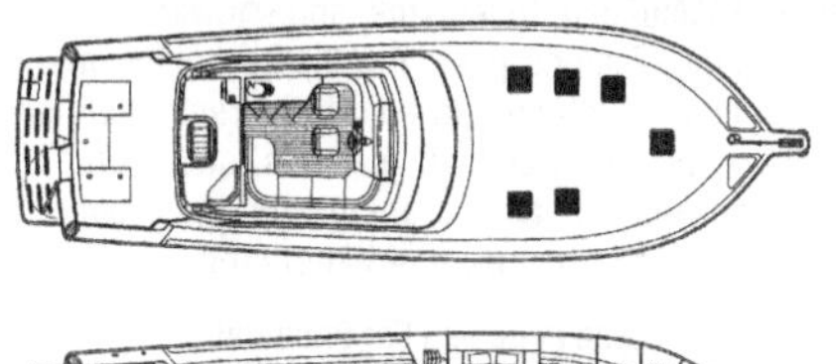

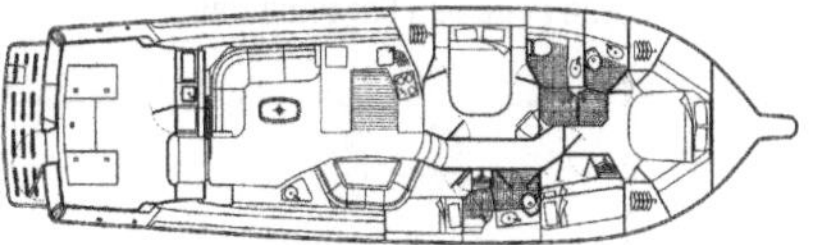

The Riviera 58 Convertible isn't just the largest model in the Riviera fleet, she's also the largest production boat of her kind ever made in Australia. Designed for long-range cruising or fishing, she's constructed to the same tough standards as all Rivieras including a forward collision bulkhead and separate watertight compartments throughout the hull. Building an enclosed bridge on a 58-foot hull might easily result in a top-heavy profile, but the Riviera's lines are balanced and very pleasing. Belowdecks, her luxurious four-stateroom interior is a conservative blend of earth-tone fabrics, vinyl overheads, and high-gloss cherry cabinetry. The galley is forward in the spacious salon, and the fourth stateroom—amidship on the starboard side—can easily be configured as an office. Although geared toward family cruising, the cockpit is fitted with a small transom livewell, in-deck fish boxes, and tackle storage. One of the highlights of the 58 is, of course, her enclosed, air-conditioned flybridge with its many amenities and outstanding visibility. A relatively light boat for her size, 1,500hp Cats cruise the Riviera 58 at just over 30 knots making her one of the quickest boats in her class.

Not Enough Resale Data to Set Values

Length w/Platform	64'5"	Headroom	6'6"
Hull Length	61'0"	Fuel	1,110 gals.
Beam	17'9"	Water	215 gals.
Weight	67,200#	Hull Type	Modified-V
Draft	5'2"	Deadrise Aft	10°

Robalo

Quick View

- One of the oldest builders of fishing boats in the country, Robalo (which in Spanish means "snook") was founded in Everett, Washington, in 1968.
- Robalo was one of the early manufacturers of center console fishing boats in the 1960s.
- The company was acquired by industry-giant AMF (which then owned Hatteras, among other brands) in the early 1970s.
- Robalo languished under AMF's ownership during the 1970s. In 1991, Brunswick's US Marine division purchased Robalo and began expanding the line.
- In 2001, US Marine sold Robalo to Marine Products Corp., parent company of Chaparral Boats.
- Robalo's are widely admired by sportfishing enthusiasts for their solid construction and above-average finish.

Robalo Boats • Nashville, GA • www.robalo.com

Robalo 260 Center Console

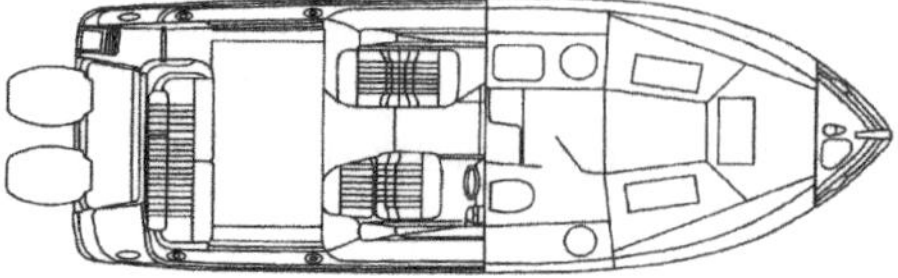

Robalo builds a serious fishboat and they're not inexpensive. That's especially true of the 260 Center Console, a tournament-grade fishing machine loaded with high-end features. Built on a Kevlar-reinforced hull with aggressive transom deadrise and a wide 9-foot beam, the 260 is bigger than most other 26-footers. Robalo really gets it when it comes to cockpit layouts. The foredeck features a cushioned seating area with a table; remove the cushions and add the filler to make a large casting deck just below the recessed bow rail. The bow also includes three insulated, locking fish boxes on hydraulic lifts, one in-deck and two integrated into the casting platform. A foldaway rear seat frees up cockpit space when fishing, and the console head compartment contains a VacuFlush toilet, sink, and shower. Standard features include a leaning post with flip-up bolster and cooler, bait prep center with cutting board and removable bait box, full cockpit bolsters, cockpit toe rails, and storage for 20 rods (6 lockable). A terrific open-water ride, twin Yamaha 225 outboards reach close to 45 knots top.

See Page 696 For Price Data

Length	26'5"	Fuel	205 gals.
Beam	9'0"	Water	26 gals.
Draft, Up	1'8"	Max HP	500
Draft, Down	2'10"	Hull Type	Deep-V
Weight w/OB	6,075#	Deadrise Aft	23°

Robalo 2620 Center Console

A good-looking center console with an integrated bracket/dive platform and a molded pulpit, the Robalo 2620 is an affordable offshore fisherman with an impressive list of standard equipment. Robalo always had a reputation for building solid, durable boats—their 10-year limited hull warranty spoke for itself—and the cored stringer system and fiberglass cockpit liner of the 2620 only adds to her strength. (Note that her 8-foot, 11-inch beam is wider by 5 inches than the legal limit for trailering.) Like most modern center-console designs her size, a marine head is concealed within the console. A leaning post is standard; the passenger seat at the transom is removable, and the cockpit is surrounded with knee-level coaming bolsters. Additional features include an aerated live well, two fish boxes (under the elevated forward deck), fresh and raw water washdowns, under-gunwale rod storage, anchor locker, and a portable cooler stored under the seat in front of the console. Twin 200hp outboards reach a top speed of 40 knots. Note that she was updated in 2000 with improved below-deck storage access and redesigned tackle storage.

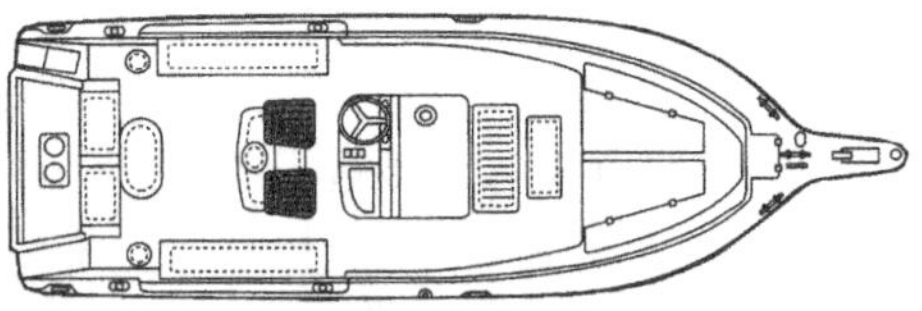

See Page 4696 For Price Data

Length	27'5"	Fuel	200 gals.
Beam	8'11"	Water	25 gals.
Draft, Up	1'4"	Max HP	500
Draft, Down	2'6"	Hull Type	Deep-V
Dry Weight	5,350#	Deadrise Aft	20°

Robalo 2640 Walkaround

A well-built walkaround for anglers or families who don't fit the open-fishboat profile any more, the Robalo 2640 combines the advantages of a roomy, uncluttered cockpit with the overnight comforts of an efficient cuddy cabin. Robalo builds a solid boat—their 10-year limited hull warranty speaks for itself—and the cored stringer system and full inner liner of the 2640 only adds to her strength. (Note that her 8-foot, 11-inch beam is wider by 5 inches than the legal limit for trailering.) The Robalo's uncluttered cockpit is fitted with two in-deck fish boxes, aft-facing jump seats, transom shower, a circular livewell and a removable bench seat at the transom. Additional fishing features include cockpit bolsters, under-gunwale rod storage, tackle storage, and fresh and raw water washdowns. Note the stylish wraparound windshield. Below, the cabin will sleep two with a dinette/V-berth forward, mini-galley, and an enclosed head with shower. Twin 200hp outboards cruise the Robalo 2640 Walkaround at 27 knots and reach a top speed of 42–43 knots.

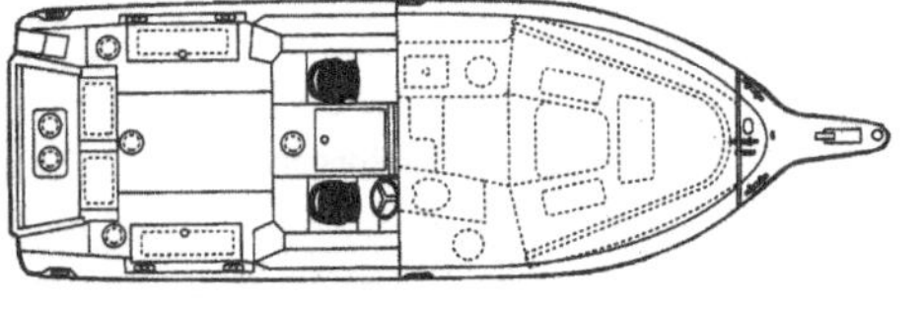

See Page 696 For Price Data

Length w/Pulpit	27'5"	Fuel	162 gals.
Beam	8'11"	Water	25 gals.
Hull Draft	1'6"	Max HP	450
Weight	6,200#	Hull Type	Deep-V
Clearance w/Hardtop	8'11"	Deadrise Aft	20°

Robalo 265 Walkaround

2003–Current

The appeal of a good express boat like the Robalo 265 can be summed up in a single word: versatility. Half fishing boat and half weekend cruiser, express boats are a great choice for anglers with active families. Belying her small size, the 265 Walkaround is built to handle big water with confidence. Like all late model Robalo boats, the 265 rides on a Kevlar-reinforced hull, a costly manufacturing process that makes for a near-bulletproof hull. Fishing features include a 33-gallon transom livewell, 40-gallon fish box aft of the helm chair, large cockpit fish box, and bait prep center. Below, the 265's well-appointed cabin boasts a small galley with refrigerator and microwave, an enclosed head with shower, convertible V-berth/dinette, and rod holders. The glossy maple woodwork and teak-and-holly cabin sole are nice features. On deck, a full-width transom seat flips out of the way for access to the livewell. A raw-water washdown is standard. There's space at the helm for electronic add-ons. Note the premium cockpit upholstery and near-flawless gelcoat. The hull is foam-filled and unsinkable. Yamaha 250s top out around 50 mph.

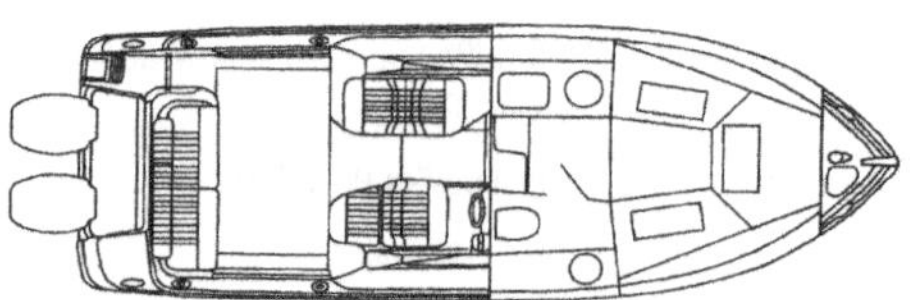

See Page 696 For Price Data

Length	26'1"	Fuel	180 gals.
Beam	9'0"	Water	23 gals.
Draft, Up	1'8"	Max HP	500
Draft, Down	2'10"	Hull Type	Deep-V
Weight w/OB	6,675#	Deadrise Aft	23°

Robalo 2660 Cuddy Cabin

1983–95

One of the larger offshore trailerable fishing boats, Robalo's 2660 Cuddy had one of the longest production runs of any boat in her class. She was the top-of-the-line model in the Robalo fleet for many years and, like any successful walkaround design, the 2660 presents a balance of good fishing capabilities and efficient cabin accommodations. Built on a foam-filled deep-V hull with a fiberglass inner liner, the traditional outboard well and squared-off windshield of the 2660 give her a dated appearance compared with modern walkaround designs. The cockpit—large enough to comfortably accommodate a couple of anglers—comes with a pair of removable in-deck fish boxes, an aerated livewell, raw water washdown, tackle storage, recessed rod holders and a fresh-water shower. Below, the cabin sports a convertible dinette, small galley pod and an enclosed head. New deck tooling in 1994 repositioned the cabin further forward, increasing cockpit space as well as cabin headroom, and fishboxes were added beneath the pedestal seats. A good performer thanks to her narrow beam, twin 200hp outboards reach a top speed of around 40 knots.

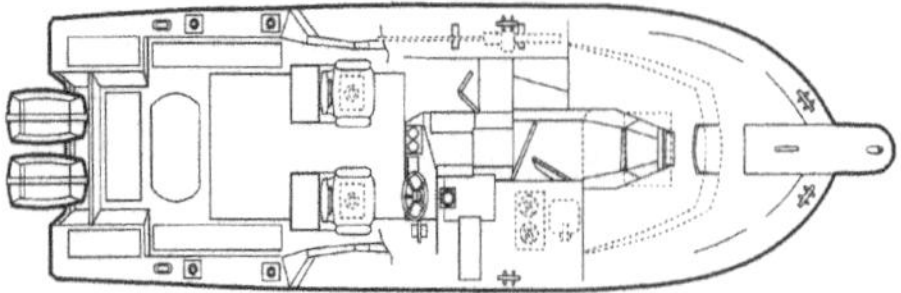

See Page 696 For Price Data

Length w/Pulpit	27'8"	Fuel	200 gals.
Beam	8'6"	Water	20 gals.
Draft, Up	1'8"	Max HP	400
Draft, Down	2'10"	Hull Type	Deep-V
Dry Weight	5,370#	Deadrise Aft	25°

Robalo 300 Center Console

Flagship of the current (2013) Robalo fleet, the 300 Center Console is a hardcore fishing boat for anglers able to afford the top-notch quality Robalo brings to the table. Like all late-model Robalo boats, the 300 is built on a Kevlar-reinforced deep-V hull, and her broad 10'6" beam allows plenty of fishing space for two anglers. Notably, the 300's uncluttered, single-level cockpit and wide walkways make getting around easy. Wraparound bow seating—which converts to a large casting platform—is enhanced with a standard dinette table and filler cushion. At the helm, bolster bucket seats with flip-up front cushions have arm rests for long-distance runs. A deluxe leaning post includes a 94-quart removable ice chest behind the bolster. Aft, a full-width transom seat folds into the transom for added fishing space. A vertical rod storage rack is found in walk-in head, and a transom service hatch provides easy access to the batteries. Two livewells, one 25-gallon and one 50-gallon—both with blue LED lighting—are standard. Good range with 300-gallon fuel capacity. Yamaha 250hp outboards top out at 40+ knots.

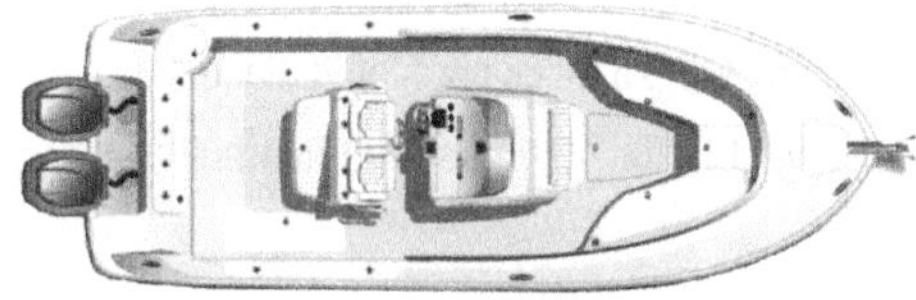

See Page 696 For Price Data

Length	29'2"	Fuel	300 gals.
Beam	10'6"	Water	30 gals.
Draft, Up	1'8"	Max HP	600
Draft, Down	2'10"	Hull Type	Deep-V
Dry Weight	7,500#	Deadrise Aft	21°

Robalo 305 Walkaround

More than a few boating enthusiasts—and plenty of brokers, as well—have a good opinion of Robalo boats. Overpriced? Maybe, but quality is never cheap, and Robalo styling, features and finish are probably a match for any of the high-end brands. The Robalo 305 is a case in point: Introduced in 2007, the 305 sports a wide 10-foot, 6-inch beam, premium fishing amenities, and cabin accommodations for six. The standard hard top sports six rod holders, an electronics box, and integrated lifejacket storage. The 305's large cockpit includes two insulated livewells (55 gallons combined), both with red LED lighting. A folding aft bench seat, and a jump seat behind the captain's chair are standard, and two insulated fish boxes provide nearly 200 gallons of storage. Note that the L-shaped lounge opposite helm has a clever 3-position backrest. Wide walkways and sturdy handholds offer excellent foredeck access. The Robalo's well-appointed cabin includes a full-service galley with maple cabinets and a teak-and holly sole. Both V-berth backrests tilt up and lock, converting to bunk beds. On the downside, the mid-berth is better suited to kids than two adults. Yamaha 250hp outboards top out at close to 40 knots.

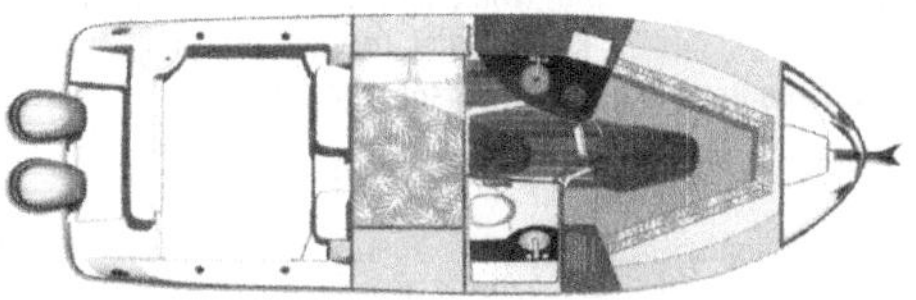

See Page 696 For Price Data

Length	29'2"	Fuel	300 gals.
Beam	10'6"	Water	40 gals.
Draft, Up	1'8"	Max HP	700
Draft, Down	2'10"	Hull Type	Deep-V
Dry Weight	9,600#	Deadrise Aft	21°

Sabre

Quick View

- The Sabre story began in 1970 when the company's founder, Roger Hewson, set out to build a 28-foot sailing yacht in the small town of South Casco, ME.
- Introduced in 1971 at the Newport Boat Show, the Sabre 28 was a resounding success; during the next fifteen years 588 Sabre 28's were built.
- With the decline of the sailing industry in the late 1980s, in 1989 Sabre sought to broaden its market and created the first Sabre 36 "Fast Trawler".
- The success of their first model led to the introduction of the Sabreline 34 in 1990.
- Today more than half of Sabre's production is dedicated to power boats ranging in size from 38' to 52' in length.
- Sabre's manufacturing facilities are located in Raymond, ME, 25 miles north of Portland.
- Sabre Yachts has been producing sail and motor yachts for 40 years, and has built over 4,000 hulls to date.

Sabre Yachts • South Casco, ME • www.sabreyachts.com

Sabreline 34 Sedan

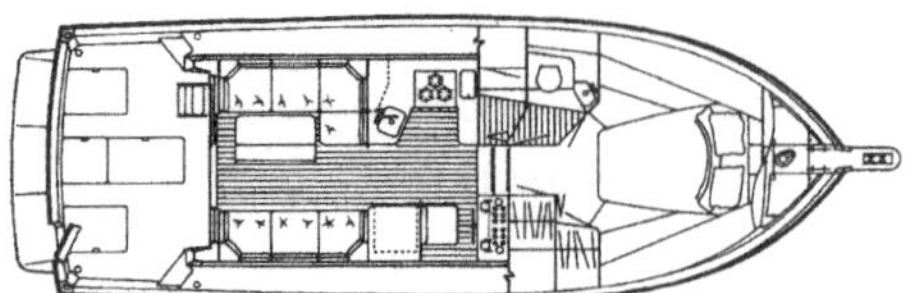

A timeless Downeast profile, quality construction, and a beautiful teak interior characterize the Sabreline 34, a modern trawler-style sedan from Sabre Yachts. She's built on the same modified-V hull used in the production of the original Sabreline 36 with moderate beam and a shallow keel for directional stability. Like all Sabre boats (sail or power), there's no shortage of craftsmanship or attention to detail in the way she's put together. Her traditional teak (later changed to cherry) interior is arranged with the galley forward in the salon opposite the lower helm and a walkaround island berth in the stateroom. Everything is carefully arranged with an eye toward practicality and comfort. The large salon windows all open (so does the center windshield forward), and ventilation in this boat is exceptional. The 34 isn't a beamy boat so the interior dimensions are somewhat compact. Notable features include excellent engine access and a stall shower in the head, which also has a wet locker (nice touch). A popular model, the Sabreline 34 will cruise at 18 knots with twin 220hp Cummins diesels and reach a top speed of 20–21 knots. Later models with 300hp Yanmars cruise in the low 20s (around 25 knots top).

See Page 696 For Price Data

Length w/Pulpit	37'6"	Fuel	250 gals.
Hull Length	34'0"	Water	160 gals.
Beam	12'6"	Waste	25 gals.
Draft	3'3"	Hull Type	Modified-V
Weight	17,800#	Deadrise Aft	14°

Sabre 34 Hardtop Express

Once the province of custom New England builders, the market for Downeast cruising yachts has grown rapidly in recent years—proof, if any were needed, that classic styling never grows old. Sabre Yachts has long been a leader in this market, producing a series of Downeast-style yachts distinguished by their handsome lines and yacht-class accommodations. Introduced in 2006, the Sabre 34 Hardtop Express combines the versatility of an open-deck express with the luxury of a premium cruising yacht. She's built on an Airex-cored modified-V hull with shallow prop pockets and a generous 13'3" beam. Her elevated helm deck offers clear sight lines from the Stidd helm chair, and the convertible backrest at the forward end of the L-shaped settee creates a companion seat. A full-service galley is located to starboard, aft of the helm seat. Forward and below, the 34's posh cabin with convertible settee, queen bed forward, and large head with separate stall shower is perfect for the cruising couple. Note the sliding cabin windows, wide side decks, and excellent helm visibility. The engine compartment is a little tight. Cruise at 25 knots (30+ top) with twin 370hp Volvo inboard diesels.

See Page 696 For Price Data

Length	34'6"	Fuel	275 gals.
Beam	13'3"	Water	80 gals.
Draft	3'0"	Waste	30 gals.
Weight	20,000#	Hull Type	Modified-V
Clearance, Mast	12'8"	Deadrise Aft	16°

Sabreline 36 Aft Cabin

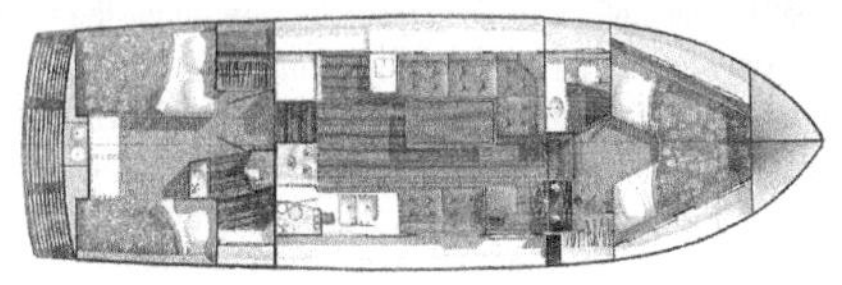

Marketed as a "fast trawler," the Sabreline 36 is a well-crafted family cruiser with comfortable accommodations, a traditional profile, and a good turn of speed. While she may look like a trawler on the outside, the Sabreline rides on a high-performance, modified-V hull rather than a displacement or semi-displacement hull used in conventional trawlers. The result is a boat that gives a smooth transition from displacement planing speeds. The Sabreline's interior is fairly conventional, using the typical salon/pilothouse design with staterooms fore and aft. A double berth was optional in the master stateroom, and the L-shaped dinette converts into a double berth for extra overnight guests. Topside, wide walkaround decks make getting around easy, and the flybridge is arranged with the helm forward and guest seating aft. Additional features include twin salon deck doors, large cabin windows, a roomy engineroom, underwater exhausts, and a fold-down radar mast. Twin 250hp GM diesels cruise the Sabreline 36 at 16 knots (about 20 knots top), and later models with a pair of 315hp Cats cruise at 18 knots and reach 23–24 knots top.

See Page 697 For Price Data

Length w/Pulpit	40'1"	Fuel	300 gals.
Hull Length	36'0"	Water	225 gals.
Beam	12'6"	Waste	40 gals.
Draft	4'3"	Hull Type	Modified-V
Weight	20,000#	Deadrise Aft	14°

Sabreline 36 Express

Traditional styling, comfortable accommodations, and quality construction are the hallmarks of the Sabreline 36 Express, a Downeast classic whose timeless lines will turn heads in any marina. Built on a fully cored hull with moderate beam, the bottom was redesigned in 2000 (the MKII version) by increasing the transom deadrise from 14 to 18 degrees and eliminating the skeg of the earlier model. While the Sabreline's bi-level cockpit is roomy enough for some light-tackle fishing—and the bridge deck has adequate seating for family and friends—it's the elegant interior that captures the hearts of purists. Here, a blend of varnished hardwood joinery, solid panel doors, and a teak-and-holly sole create a warm and completely inviting living area. Notable features of the Sabreline 36 include wide side decks, a transom door, side exhausts, radar mast, and a well-arranged engineroom. On the downside, there's no shower stall in the head. Early hull models with 300hp Cat diesels cruise at 20 knots (around 24 knots top), and later MKII versions with 315hp Yanmars cruise in the mid 20s (around 28 knots top), and optional 370hp Yanmars cruise in the mid 20s and top out at 30+ knots.

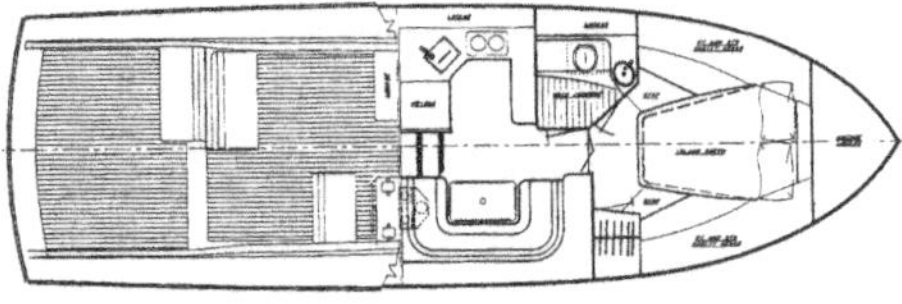

See Page 697 For Price Data

Length w/Pulpit	40'1"	Clearance, Mast	12'0"
Hull Length	36'0"	Fuel	300 gals.
Beam	12'6"	Water	100 gals.
Draft	3'4"	Hull Type	Modified-V
Weight	18,500#	Deadrise Aft	14°/18°

Sabreline 36 Sedan

Traditional design and boatbuilding excellence are joined in the Sabreline 36 Sedan, a Maine-built cruising yacht whose classic styling will endure for decades to come. She's built on the same fully cored, vacuum-bagged hull used for Sabreline's popular 36 Express with prop pockets and a substantial 18 degrees of transom deadrise. The cherrywood interior of the Sabreline 36 might best be described as understated elegance—a practical galley-down, single-stateroom layout, finely finished and tastefully appointed. Wraparound windows surround the salon where a fully equipped lower helm (with a deck access door) is standard and a convertible L-shaped settee is to port. Forward, the spacious stateroom has a centerline queen berth and direct access to the double-entry head with its circular shower enclosure. The cockpit has a transom door and a wet bar as well as three storage lockers under the sole, and the flybridge is well arranged with the helm forward and guest seating aft. Note that the Sabreline's large engineroom provides good service access to the motors. Expect a cruising speed of 25–26 knots with optional 370hp Yanmar diesels (close to 30 knots top).

See Page 697 For Price Data

Length	36'0"	Fuel	300 gals.
Beam	12'6"	Water	100 gals.
Draft	3'4"	Waste	30 gals.
Weight	19,500#	Hull Type	Modified-V
Clearance, Mast	19'0"	Deadrise Aft	18°

Sabre 38 Express

2005–10

The Sabre 38 Express (originally called the Saberline 38 Express) combines classic Downeast styling and lively performance in a hardtop cruising yacht of exceptional beauty. Built on vacuum-bagged hull with a wide 13-foot, 8-inch beam and prop pockets, the focal point of the 38 Express is her semi-enclosed pilothouse with its swivel helm and companion seats, folding teak table, and full wet bar with refrigerator and ice maker. Stepping below, the handcrafted cherry interior of the 38 Express offers all the conveniences and amenities sophisticated cruisers demand, from a recessed entertainment center with flat-screen TV and DVD player to a beautiful inlaid dinette table crafted in cherry and bird's-eye maple. A sliding door separates the master stateroom from the salon, and the compact but functional galley is positioned close to the companionway steps where it's convenient to the helm deck. The hardtop has a pair of screened hatches for ventilation and the side windows slide open. The wide side decks of the Sabreline are notable in that they permit excellent access to the foredeck area—a safety feature often overlooked in modern yachts. Yanmar 440hp diesels cruise at 25–26 knots (30+ top).

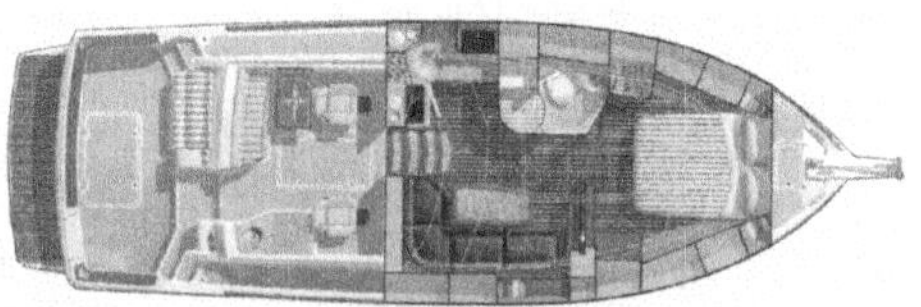

See Page 697 For Price Data

Length	36'8"	Fuel	350 gals.
Beam	13'8"	Water	100 gals.
Draft	3'4"	Waste	30 gals.
Weight	21,500#	Hull Type	Modified-V
Clearance, Mast	13'5"	Deadrise Aft	18°

Sabre 42 Hardtop Express

2004–Current

Introduced in 2004, the Sabre 42 Express (called the Sabreline 42 until 2007) embodies the graceful styling, luxurious accommodations, and high-quality construction common to all Sabre yachts. The 42 is a particularly handsome yacht, and her low-profile cabintop conceals a considerable amount of living space below. Built on a modified-V hull with a wide beam and prop pockets, the focal point of the 42 Express is her semi-enclosed pilothouse with its swivel helm and companion seats, folding teak table, and full wet bar. Below decks, the traditional two-stateroom interior is highlighted with varnished cherrywood cabinetry, leather upholstery, and a beautiful teak-and-holly sole. The master stateroom can be fitted with a pedestal berth or V-berths. The guest stateroom contains a double berth, and both cabins share a large head with a circular shower stall. On the downside, the galley is small for a 42-foot yacht. A transom door, radar mast, and bow pulpit are standard. Note that the hull of the Sabre 42 is built with vacuum-bagged PVC foam core making it light and extremely strong. Yanmar 440hp inboard diesels cruise at 22–23 knots. Newer models with 850hp Zeus pod drives cruise efficiently at 28 knots.

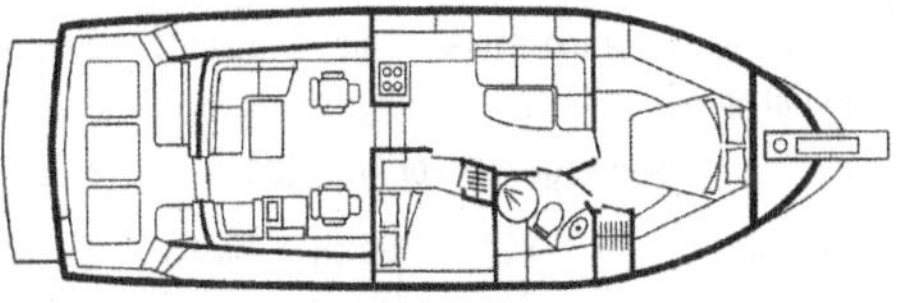

See Page 697 For Price Data

Length	42'3"	Fuel	450 gals.
Beam	14'4"	Water	160 gals.
Draft	3'9"	Waste	60 gals.
Weight	29,000#	Hull Type	Modified-V
Clearance, Mast	13'3"	Deadrise Aft	16°

Sabreline 42 Sedan

The Sabreline 42 is an impressive blend of traditional Downeast styling, quality construction, and modern performance—attributes that established Sabrelines as among the best production yachts in the industry. With her upright profile, extended hardtop and big cabin windows, the Sabreline 42 looks like a trawler but her modified-V hull (with prop pockets) allows her to perform more like a sport fisherman. The richly appointed interior, with its varnished cherry paneling and teak-and-holly sole, is arranged with the galley down from the salon and includes a single head and good storage. Visibility from the lower helm is excellent, and the master stateroom can be ordered with a centerline double berth or V-berths. Note that the guest cabin, opposite the galley, is fitted with double French doors. On deck, a staircase—rather than a vertical ladder—leads from the large cockpit to the flybridge. Additional features include a deck access door at the lower helm, wide side decks, and a spacious engineroom. Twin 420hp Yanmar diesels cruise the Sabreline 42 in the low 20s (26–27 knots top), and 465hp Yanmars cruise in the mid 20s and reach a top speed of around 30 knots.

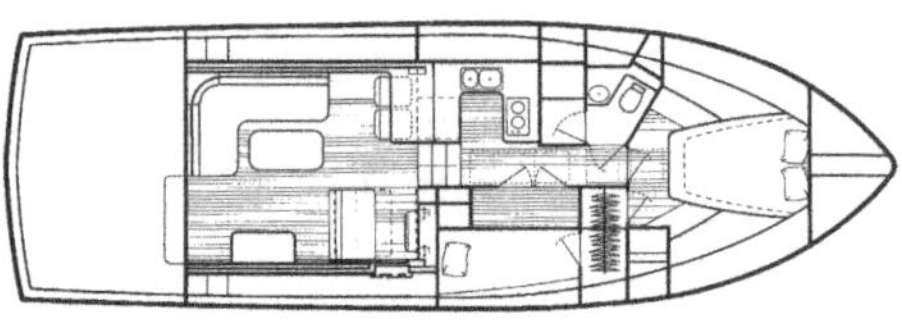

See Page 697 For Price Data

Length	42'3"	Fuel	450 gals.
Beam	14'4"	Water	160 gals.
Draft	3'9"	Waste	60 gals.
Weight	30,000#	Hull Type	Modified-V
Headroom	6'6"	Deadrise Aft	16°

Sabreline 43 Aft Cabin

Most production trawlers of the past few decades have been built on low-speed, semi-displacement hulls that generally require large engines to exceed 14–15 knots. The Sabreline 43 differs from that norm in that she's constructed on a modified-V hull that allows her to run efficiently at much higher speeds than one usually expects of a trawler-style design. Performance aside, the Sabreline 43 is a quality-built double-cabin cruiser with full walkaround decks and extremely comfortable accommodations. The standard galley-down floorplan is available with V-berths or a double berth in the forward stateroom, a lower helm is standard, and both heads are fitted with separate stall showers. Deck access is excellent: there are port and starboard access doors in the salon, a companionway door aft, and a cockpit door in the master stateroom. Solid teak cabinets and a teak-and-holly cabin sole highlight the interior, and prop pockets combine with a shallow keel to protect the running gear. Topside, the spacious flybridge is arranged with an L-shaped dinette abaft the helm. Twin 370hp Yanmar diesels cruise the Sabreline 43 at 16 knots and deliver a 20-knot top speed.

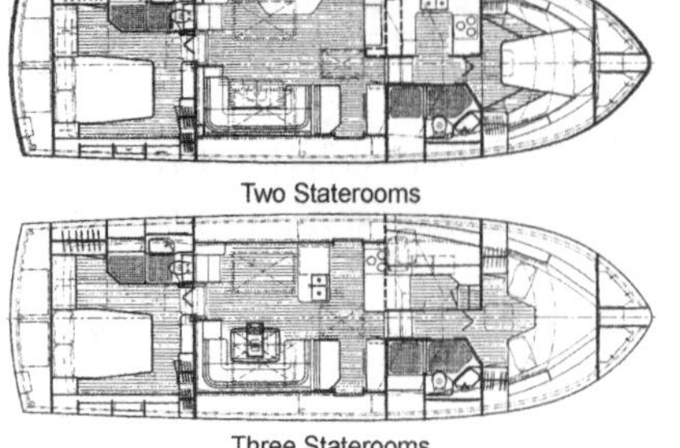
Two Staterooms

Three Staterooms

See Page 697 For Price Data

Length w/Pulpit	48'1"	Clearance, Mast	17'9"
Hull Length	43'6"	Fuel	520 gals.
Beam	15'0"	Water	250 gals.
Draft	4'0"	Hull Type	Modified-V
Weight	38,500#	Deadrise Aft	14°

Sabreline 47 Aft Cabin

1997–2007

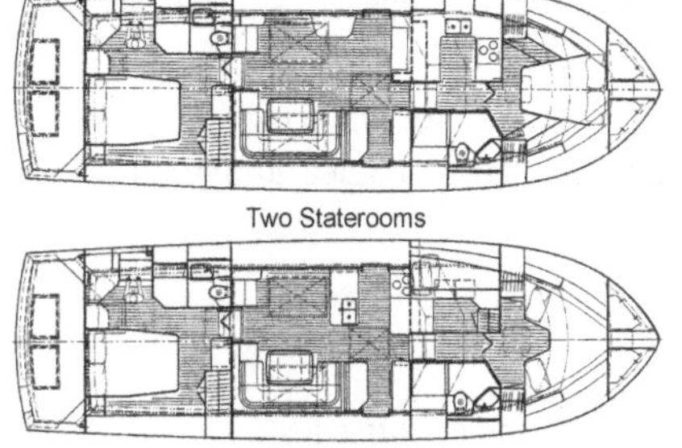

Two Staterooms

Three Staterooms

A handsome yacht with a modern trawler profile, the Sabreline 47 Aft Cabin is a lengthened version of the Sabreline 43 Aft Cabin with the extra hull length used to enlarge the 47's aft stateroom and cockpit dimensions. Like all Sabreline models, she rides on a fully cored semi-V hull (rather than a semi-displacement hull normally found on most trawler-style designs) with moderate beam, a well-flared bow, and a shallow keel. While she isn't a notably spacious boat below (thanks in part to her wide side decks), the 47's two-stateroom, galley-down interior is a classic blend of solid teak (or mahogany) cabinets, quality hardware, and attractive vinyl overheads. There are two sliding deck doors in the salon, and the aft cabin—with a total of nine opening ports—provides direct access to the large cockpit. Additional features include side-dumping exhausts, a spacious flybridge with the helm forward (to starboard), folding radar mast, full lower helm, a particularly well-arranged engineroom, and separate stall showers in both heads. A comfortable ride, twin 350hp Cat diesels cruise at 15–16 knots. Later models with 420hp Cats cruise at 17–18 knots, and twin 500hp Yanmars cruise at 20 knots.

See Page 697 For Price Data

Length w/Pulpit	52'1"	Clearance, Mast	23'4"
Hull Length	47'6"	Fuel	605 gals.
Beam	15'0"	Water	300 gals.
Draft	4'5"	Hull Type	Modified-V
Weight	43,000#	Deadrise Aft	14°

Sabre 52 Salon Express

2007–Current

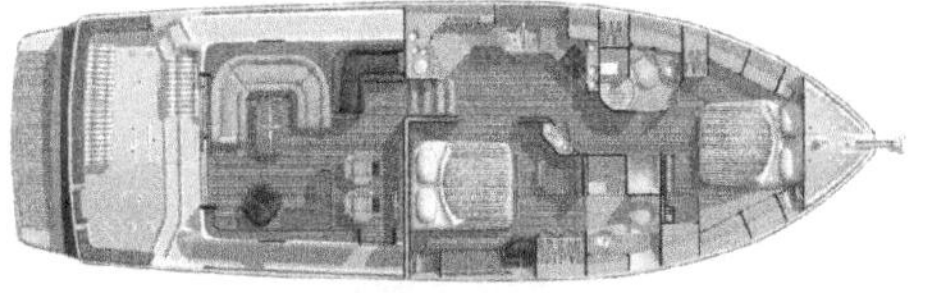

The Sabre 52 Salon is an executive-class cruising yacht who's timeless styling and sophisticated engineering place her in the forefront of yachting excellence. Sabre's reputation for craftsmanship is well known—the company has been building quality Downeast yachts since the late 1980s. Built on a modified-V hull with prop pockets and Divinycell-cored hullsides, the 52's two-stateroom interior is highlighted by an expansive pilothouse/salon area with satin-finished cherry woodwork, U-shaped leather sofa, and big 360-degree cabin windows. Note the Stidd helm seats, sliding deck door, and beautifully finished entertainment cabinet. A power sunroof is standard, and a teak and holly sole runs the full length of the boat. The galley is down and to port, opposite the master stateroom with its queen island berth, en-suite head, and unique Shoji-style pocket doors. The guest stateroom is forward and also includes a queen berth and private head. The cockpit, partially shaded by the extended hardtop, features a transom seat, aft-facing bench seat, and an access hatch to the engineroom. Wide side decks are a plus. Cruise at 26–28 knots with 865hp Cat diesels. Offered with 700hp Volvo IPS drives since 2010.

Not Enough Resale Data to Set Values

Length	53'2"	Fuel	800 gals.
Beam	16'0"	Water	200 gals.
Draft	4'3"	Waste	80 gals.
Weight	46,000#	Hull Type	Modified-V
Clearance	11'5"	Deadrise Aft	15°

Scout

Quick View

- Founded in 1989 by Steve Potts, Scout Boats began building 14- and 15-foot fishing boats from a small facility in Summerville, South Carolina.
- From the beginning Scout boats have thrived on a reputation for quality engineering and construction—factors responsible for the company's sustained growth in recent years.
- Scout pioneered the first reverse-shoebox hull/deck design, and their wood-free manufacturing process is a Scout trademark, as it produces rot-free composite stringers and transoms.
- Producing some 1,500 boats a year by the mid 2000s, Scout Boats has (according to its website) weathered the Great Recession and continues to introduce new models going forward.

Scout Boats • Summerville, SC • www.scoutboats.com

Scout 260/262 Sportfish

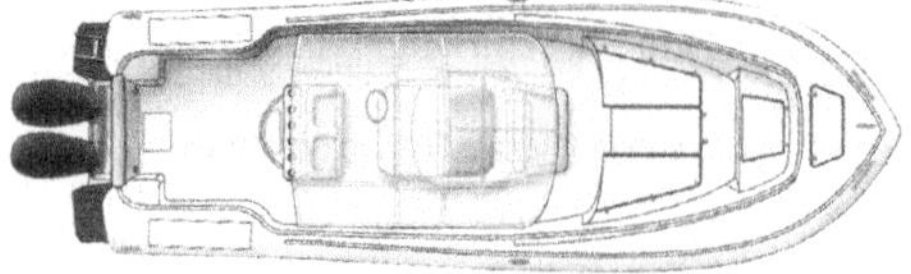

With her roomy cockpit and cool retro-style appearance, the Scout 262 Sportfish (called the 260 Sportfish in 2006) ranks among the better 26-foot center consoles on the water. Scout is known for introducing models with market-first innovations, and the 262 Sportfish was no exception. One of her more interesting features is a wave gate/fold-down stern seat that provides easy access to the transom, swim platforms, and engines. The wide 8'10" beam of the 262 Sportfish is rare in a 26-footer (most boats this size opt for a trailerable 8'6" beam), and her innovative gunwale fish boxes are unique to Scout boats. Standard features include a factory T-top (very classy), aft rigging station with sink and 27-gallon corner livewell, removable stern seat, and console head compartment with opening port. An electronically actuated sliding window at the helm protects the boat's electronics package, and an optional leaning post came with a huge 55-gallon livewell. A "Guy Harvey Package" included a special hull color and graphics, and the 262 SFX model features cushioned bow seating. Twin Yamaha 150s max out at over 40 knots.

See Page 697 For Price Data

Length	26'2"	Fuel	145 gals.
Beam	8'10"	Water	10 gals.
Draft, Up	1'4"	Max HP	350
Draft, Down	2'5"	Hull Type	Deep-V
Hull Weight	3,900#	Deadrise Aft	21°

Scout 280 Abaco

Scout has been building small fishing boats since 1990 and the Abaco, at the time of her introduction, was the company's first try at a model larger than 20 feet. (Note that she was called the 260 Cabrio in 2000, and the 260 Abaco in 2001.) Built on a beamy deep-V hull, the graceful styling of the Abaco gives her the appearance of a semicustom boat. There's bench seating for four and two captain's chairs (which convert to leaning posts) on the raised helmdeck, and cockpit amenities include a 35-gallon lighted livewell, two large in-deck fish boxes, bait prep center, and under-gunwale rod storage. While the cabin is adequate for an overnight stay, the absence of windows makes for a somewhat dark interior. Too, the V-berths are a tight fit although the athwartships single berth under the helm is long enough to stretch out on. Additional features include cockpit coaming bolsters, fresh and raw water washdowns, aft-facing jump seats, and a standard hardtop. It's notable that the fiberglass hull stringers run straight through the reverse transom and into the engine mount, transmitting the stress generated by the engines throughout the entire hull. Twin 200hp Yamaha outboards deliver a top speed of 40+ knots.

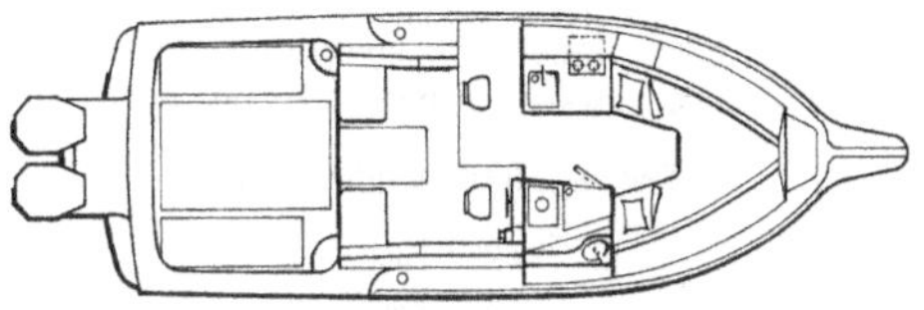

See Page 697 For Price Data

Length w/Pulpit	28'6"	Fuel	210 gals.
Beam	9'5"	Water	25 gals.
Hull Draft	20"	Max HP	600
Weight	5,100#	Hull Type	Deep-V
Clearance	10'0"	Deadrise Aft	21°

Scout 280 Sportfish

The Scout 280 Sportfish is a beamy center console fisherman whose quality construction and excellent fit and finish will appeal to experienced anglers. She rides on a solid fiberglass deep-V hull, and it's notable that the fiberglass stringers run straight through the reverse transom and into the engine mount, transmitting the load generated by the engines throughout the hull. No wood is used in the construction, and the Scout's reverse chines make for dry ride in a chop. Like most modern center consoles in this size range, the console houses an enclosed head compartment with standing headroom and an opening port. Standard features of the Scout 280 include a T-top with electronics box, spreader lights, a 30-gallon transom livewell, leaning post with full tackle center, cockpit bolsters, and an electric motor-actuated dash panel that protects the electronics. On the downside, the lack of a transom door is notable. At just 4,100 pounds (less engines), the Scout 280 is quite light for her size, which helps account for her good performance with twin 200hp Yamaha outboards—a cruising speed of around 28 knots and a top speed in excess of 40 knots.

See Page 697 For Price Data

Length w/Pulpit	28'6"	Fuel	210 gals.
Beam	9'5"	Water	20 gals.
Hull Draft	20"	Max HP	600
Dry Weight	4,300#	Hull Type	Deep-V
Clearance, T-Top	8'0"	Deadrise Aft	21°

Scout 282 Sportfish XSF

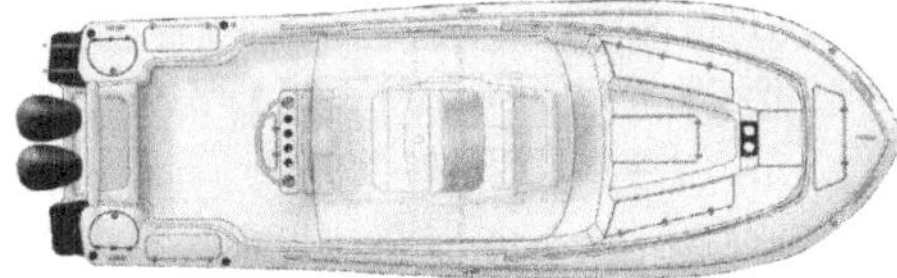

What's not to like about a Scout? Their boats are nearly always the best styled in their class; the finish is top-notch; and strong resale values help justify their premium cost. All of these characteristics—and more—apply to the 282 Sportfish, a classy 28-footer whose Carolina-style bow flare, broker sheer, and rounded aft hull tumblehome are unique in a production center console boat. Standard features include cushioned forward seating, forward 416-quart insulated fish box and 165-quart stern fish box, port and starboard 35-gallon livewells, bait prep station with sink and tackle storage, and a console head compartment with sink and opening port. Rod storage on the boat includes four flush-mount rod holders aft, two more in the bow, horizontal rod storage, and rocket launchers mounted on the factory T-top. Additional standard features include dual swim platforms, cockpit courtesy lights, and a locking electronic storage compartment in the dash. Note the 282's recessed bow rails, pop-up cleats, and unusual gunwale fish boxes. Excellent range for a boat this size. Yamaha 250s deliver close to 50 knots wide open.

See Page 697 For Price Data

Length	28'2"	Fuel	205 gals.
Beam	9'6"	Water	20 gals.
Draft, Up	1'6"	Max HP	600
Draft, Down	3'0"	Hull Type	Deep-V
Dry Weight	5,100#	Deadrise Aft	22°

Sea Ray

Quick View

- Sea Ray was founded in 1959 by C.N. "Connie" Ray when he bought a small fiberglass shop in Detroit that made (among other products) a 16-foot family runabout.
- Sensing that the future in boating was in fiberglass, by the early 1960s Ray had concentrated on boatbuilding exclusively and was soon offering a line of small cruisers and sportboats.
- The 1970s saw Sea Ray emerge as a powerhouse in the boating industry, and by the early 1980s Sea Ray had become the second-largest production builder (behind Bayliner) in the industry.
- When Ray sold the company to the Brunswick Corp. in 1986 (for a cool $350 million), Sea Ray was selling around 14,000 boats a year ranging in size from an 18-foot runabout to an industry-leading 39-foot express cruiser.
- The acquisition of Sea Ray made Brunswick the world's largest producer of pleasure boats, twice the size of the nearest competitor.
- Based in Knoxville, TN, today's Sea Ray has grown to embrace nine national and international manufacturing facilities; it is by far the leading brand of boats in the U.S.

Sea Ray Boats • Knoxville, TN • www.searay.com

Sea Ray 260 Bowrider

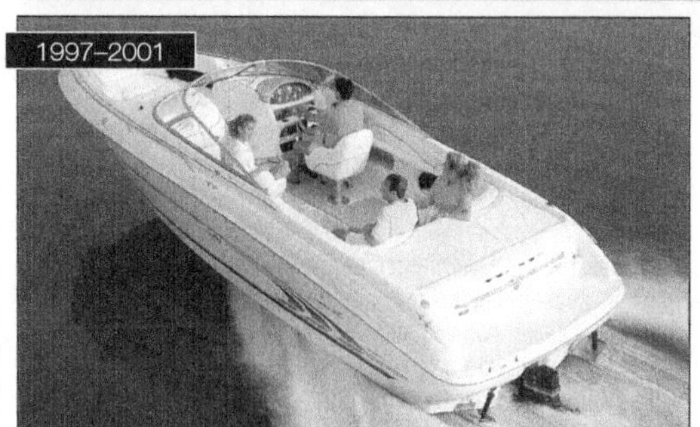

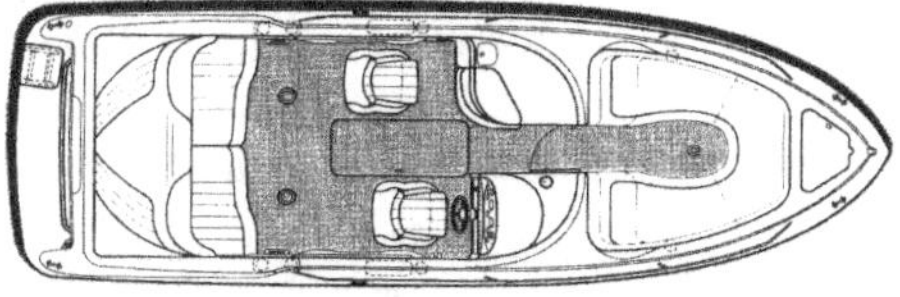

Big open-bow runabouts have long been a staple of the marine industry as boaters continue to embrace their passenger-friendly layouts, sporty styling and spirited performance. Bowriders once had a reputation for being utilitarian boats with lots of passenger seating but few creature comforts. With the 260, however, Sea Ray took passenger comfort to the next level by including a lockable head compartment in the portside helm console—unusual in a boat of this size in the late 1990s. Built on a solid fiberglass deep-V hull, the 260 Bowrider's trailerable 8-foot, 6-inch beam provides a roomy cockpit with swivel bucket seats forward and an aft bench seat with storage under. Just behind the rear seat is a sun pad that lifts on gas-assist struts for access to the engine compartment. Forward, inserts convert the bow seats into a second sunpad. The burled helm of the Sea Ray 260 is a sporty touch, and the integrated swim platform conceals a stainless steel boarding ladder. Additional features include a built-in ice chest, trash receptacle, ski locker, and tilt steering. A single 310hp MerCruiser sterndrive delivers a top speed of 35+ knots.

See Page 697 For Price Data

Length	25'6"	Clearance	5'7"
Beam	8'6"	Fuel	75 gals.
Draft, Up	1'11"	Water (Opt.)	10 gals.
Draft, Down	3'5"	Hull Type	Deep-V
Weight	4,450#	Deadrise Aft	19.5°

Sea Ray 260 Bowrider Select

1998–2001

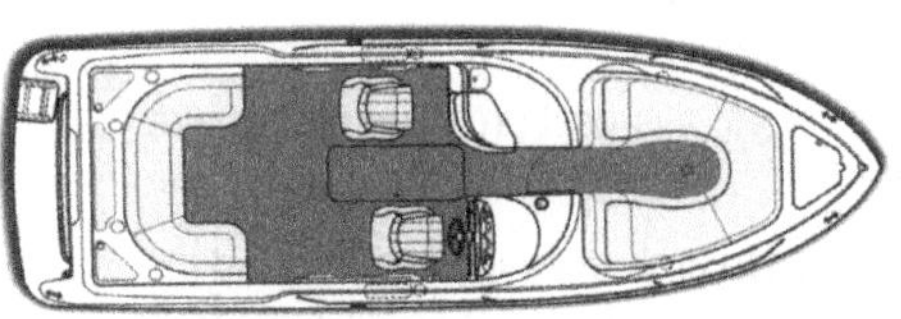

Bowriders have a reputation for being utilitarian boats with lots of passenger seating but few creature comforts. By design, of course, that's what a bowrider really is—a sportboat with open bow seating in place of a cuddy cabin. With the Sea Ray 260, however, there's more: a surprisingly roomy enclosed head compartment opposite the helm that transforms this dayboat into a much more practical and comfortable day cruiser. Built on a solid fiberglass deep-V hull, the 260 Bowrider's trailerable 8-foot, 6-inch beam provides a roomy cockpit with swivel bucket seats forward and an aft bench seat with storage under. Just behind the seat is a sun pad which can be raised with gas-assist struts for access to the engine compartment. (Note that a "Signature Select" model has a curved U-shaped lounge seat in the stern and no sun pad.) Up front is the wraparound bow seating with a filler that converts this area into a large sunning platform. The simulated burlwood helm of the 260 is very attractive, and a walk-thru windshield provides easy access to the bow seats. A single 310hp MerCruiser sterndrive delivers a 25-knot cruising speed (about 40 knots top).

See Page 697 For Price Data

Length Overall	25'6"	Clearance	5'7"
Beam	8'6"	Fuel	75 gals.
Draft, Up	1'11"	Water	10 gals.
Draft, Down	3'2"	Hull Type	Deep-V
Weight	5,200#	Deadrise Aft	19.5°

Sea Ray 260 Overnighter

1998–2001

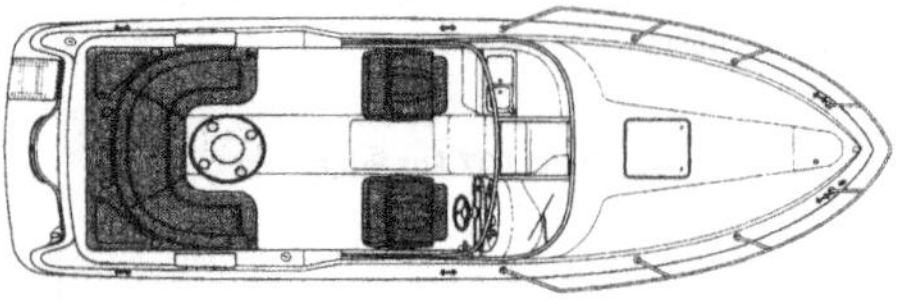

Sea Ray's 260 Overnighter is a fun-in-the-sun family runabout whose sexy profile and above-average finish will appeal to buyers with an eye for quality. Like other day cruisers of her type, the 260 is mostly cockpit and she's designed for those who do most of their boating on day trips with only an occasional need for overnighting. Depending on the seating arrangements—there are four additional cockpit plans besides the standard layout pictured below—the Overnighter accommodates three couples in a spacious cockpit that includes a refreshment center, swim platform and a concealed swim ladder. The stylish helm has a burlwood instrument panel with a tilt wheel, and the wraparound windshield (with a centerline walk-through) adds much to the boat's sleek appearance. The entire aft deck and seat lifts on a hydraulic ram for engine (and storage) access. Below, the small cabin consists of a V-berth, head compartment, four opening ports and removable table. Note that an 8-foot, 6-inch beam makes her trailerable without a permit. A single 310hp MerCruiser I/O will cruise the Sea Ray 260 Overnighter at 24 knots and reach a top speed of 37–38 knots.

See Page 697 For Price Data

Length	25'6"	Clearance	5'5"
Beam	8'6"	Fuel	75 gals.
Draft, Up	1'11"	Water	10 gals.
Draft, Down	3'2"	Hull Type	Deep-V
Weight	5,000#	Deadrise Aft	19.6°

Sea Ray 260 Sundeck

2007–Current

For many boating enthusiasts, Sea Ray is the gold standard for deck boats and bowriders. It's not always easy to tell the two types apart—they look quite alike at first glance, and it's not until a closer look reveals the deckboats's fuller bow section and front boarding gate the the differences become apparent. Built on a solid fiberglass hull with a trailerable 8'6" beam, Sea Ray designers gave the 260 Sundeck slightly more freeboard than standard deckboats so she'll be dryer in big-water conditions. The versatile cockpit—completely revised in 2010—provides comfortable seating for several guests. There are port and starboard lounge seats at the bow with molded armrests, grab bars, drink holders and storage beneath. The portside console houses a small head compartment, and ski/wakeboard storage is found in the cockpit floor. There's plenty of storage in the 260, more than might be expected in a boat this size. A hinged aft seat provides good engine access. Additional features include a cockpit table, tilt steering wheel, two built-in coolers (one a carry-on), freshwater shower, transom door, and an extended swim platform. A single 300hp MerCruiser I/O delivers 35+ knots top.

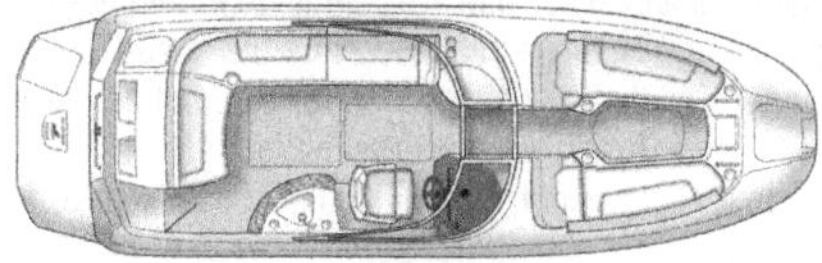
2007–09

2010–Current

See Page 697 For Price Data

Length	26'4"	Fuel	65 gals.
Beam	8'6"	Water	18 gals.
Draft, Up	25"	Waste	10 gals.
Draft, Down	40"	Hull Type	Deep-V
Dry Weight	5,168#	Deadrise Aft	21°

Sea Ray 260 Sundancer

1999–2004

An extremely well styled boat, the Sea Ray 260 Sundancer set the class standards in her day for feature-rich accommodations and leading-edge design. Sea Ray builds a good boat—the level of quality ranks among the best of any production builder of midcabin designs—and the gelcoat, hardware and finish of the Sundancer are impressive. (Note that while her 8-foot, 6-inch beam makes her legally trailerable, it'll take at least a 3/4-ton truck to get the job done as the boat and trailer package will weigh in at close to 9,000 pounds.) Below decks, the sliding cabin door has steps to the foredeck molded in, an innovative idea that saves space at the helm. Headroom below is adequate for most adults, and a full galley was standard along with a good-size head compartment and a reasonably spacious mid-stateroom. In the cockpit, the rear seat folds out of the way when not in use. Additional features include a gas-assist engine hatch, wet bar, a flip-up bolster seat at the helm, and transom storage. A single 310hp MerCruiser sterndrive (optional) will cruise the 260 Sundancer at 22 knots and reach a top speed of 34–35 knots. A huge sales success, used models remain very popular.

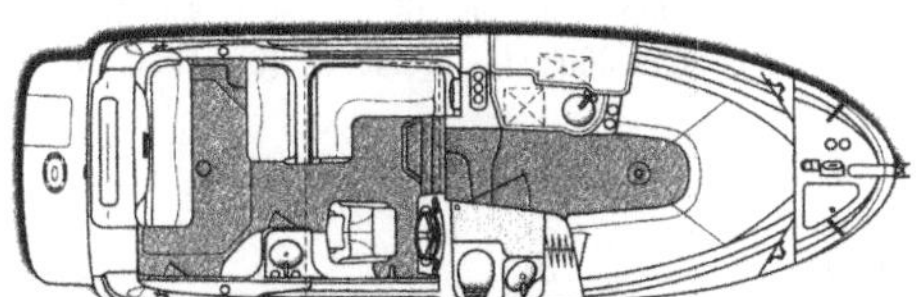

See Page 697 For Price Data

Length	28'0"	Fuel	85 gals.
Beam	8'6"	Water	28 gals.
Draft, Up	1'10"	Waste (Opt.)	28 gals.
Draft, Down	2'11"	Hull Type	Deep-V
Weight	6,200#	Deadrise Aft	19°

Sea Ray 260 Sundancer

2005–08

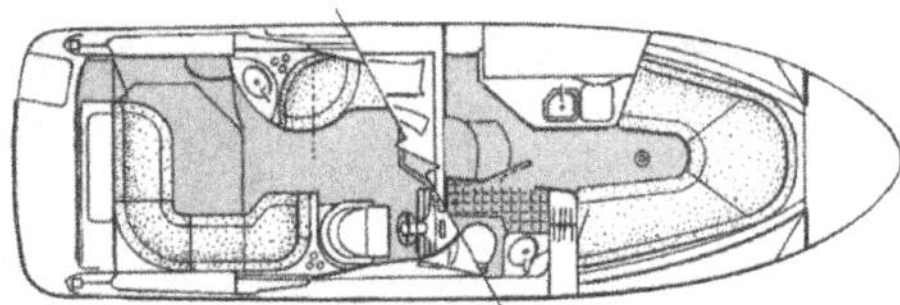

An updated version of the original 260 Sundancer introduced in 1999, this second-generation 260 benefits from freshened styling, a revised cockpit layout, and minor cosmetic and hardware upgrades in the cabin. The effect was to make an already popular boat just a little more appealing to the masses of Sea Ray enthusiasts. As 26-foot cruisers go, the 260 was at (or near) the top of the chart during her production years when it came to price. Quality never comes cheap, however, and there's much to admire about the 260 in her sturdy construction and best-in-class finish. In the cockpit, wraparound rear seating leaves room for passengers to easily move about, and the wet bar features a sink, storage, and removable cooler. An electric engine compartment hatch provides good engine access. Below decks, the 260 Sundancer boasts big-boat amenities and style, with a parchment-colored headliner and high-gloss wood laminate cabinets. Note the Vacu-Flush toilet in the head. The midberth is big enough for two, but access is tight. The deep transom storage compartment with gas-assisted lid is a nice touch. No lightweight, a single 300hp MerCruiser I/O tops out at 30+ knots.

See Page 697 For Price Data

Length	28'8"	Fuel	84 gals.
Beam	8'6"	Water	28 gals.
Draft, Up	1'10"	Waste	28 gals.
Draft, Down	3'4"	Hull Type	Deep-V
Weight	7,900#	Deadrise Aft	21°

Sea Ray 250/260 Sundancer

2009–Current

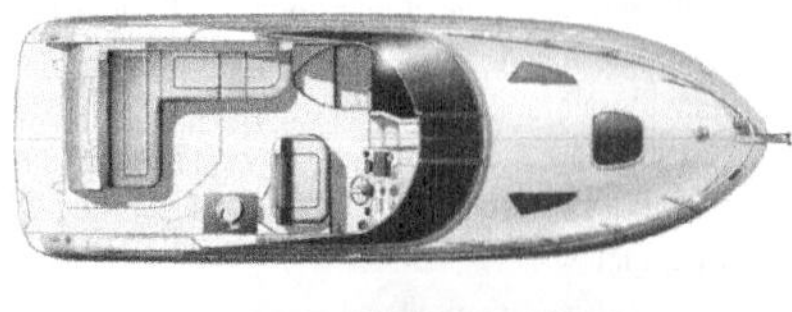

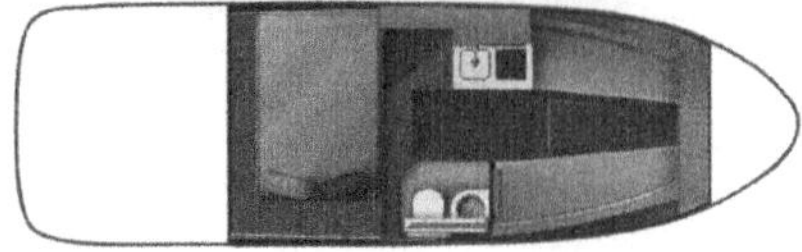

In a market crowded with full-size trailerable cruisers, Sea Ray's long-running series of 260 Sundancers continue to set the standards for owner popularity and best-in-class resale values. Like her predecessors, this latest 260 Sundancer (called the 250 Sundancer when she was introduced in 2009) is well styled, versatile, and built to last. Mid-cabin interiors are the rule in boats this size, but the Sundancer stands out for her high-gloss cherry cabinets, premium amenities, and top-notch fit and finish. Featuring a convertible V-berth/dinette forward, galley with dual-voltage refrigerator, sink, and microwave, and an enclosed head with shower, the cabin of the 260 Sundancer provides basic accommodations for two adults and two children. Topside, a doublewide helm seat rotates to face aft when the boat is at rest, and the standard wet bar has space for a carry-on cooler below. Note that Sea Ray's signature "SmartCraft" instrument package (with built-in engine diagnostics) is standard. On the downside, fuel capacity—just 75 gallons—is modest for a boat this size. No lightweight, the 260 Sundancer will cruise at 25 knots with an optional 300hp MerCruiser I/O (35+ knots top).

See Page 697 For Price Data

Length w/Pulpit	26'7"	Fuel	75 gals.
Beam	8'6"	Water	20 gals.
Draft, Up	1'11"	Waste (Opt.)	18 gals.
Draft, Down	3'5"	Hull Type	Deep-V
Weight	6,950#	Deadrise Aft	19°

Sea Ray 270 Amberjack

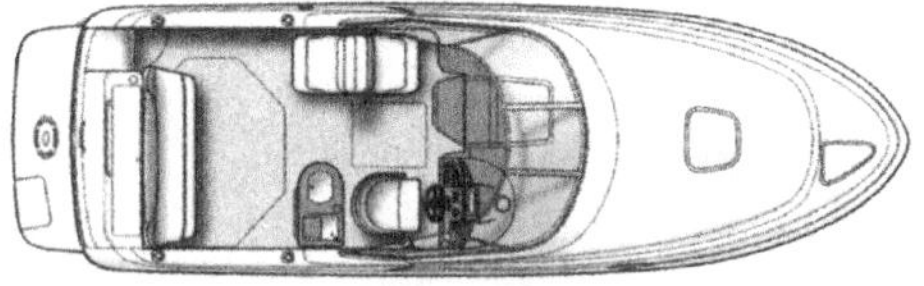

Sea Ray has been marketing their series of Amberjack fishing boats for years. These are not hardcore fishing boats; for the most part, Amberjacks are repurposed Sea Ray cruisers, with fishing amenities replacing the cockpit wet bars and lounge seating found in the company's Sundancer and Weekender models. Introduced in 2005, the 270 Amberjack (note that an earlier 270 Amberjack was produced in 1986–90) rides on a solid fiberglass deep-V hull with a trailerable 8'6" beam. Her single-level cockpit came standard with a fold-down rear seat, transom fish/storage box, port and starboard rod storage, and four rod holders. An optional fishing package included a bait-prep station with sink, 25-gallon livewell, and raw water washdown. Below decks, the Amberjack's compact interior with high-gloss cherry cabinets, full-service galley, and standup head with shower sleeps two. A walk-through windshield provides access to the bow. An aluminum arch with rocket launchers was a popular option. The easy-lift cockpit hatch provides good engine access. With just 100 gallons of fuel capacity, range is limited. A single 320hp MerCruiser I/O delivers a top speed in excess of 30 knots.

See Page 697 For Price Data

Length	30'0"	Fuel	100 gals.
Beam	8'6"	Water	28 gals.
Draft, Up	15"	Waste	28 gals.
Draft, Down	3'8"	Hull Type	Deep-V
Weight	7,325#	Deadrise Aft	21°

Sea Ray 270 Select EX

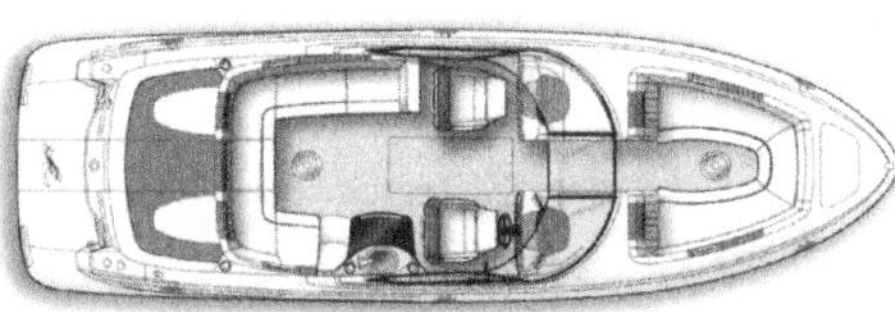

Taking bowrider luxury and styling to the next level, the Sea Ray 270 Select EX (or 270 SEX) proved a major sales success for Sea Ray following her introduction in 2005. With her roomy cockpit, gull-wing sun pads, deluxe wet bar, and enclosed head the 270 Select has the size and comfort families demand in a modern, multipurpose dayboat. Unlike many of her competitors, the Select rides on a modified deep-V hull with a wave-calming 21 degrees of transom deadrise. In other words, this is a boat capable of handling deep water—something many popular bowriders are best advised to avoid. With a modest 9-foot beam, the 270 Select isn't the roomiest boat her size on the market although no one would call her layout anything less than comfortable. The head compartment under the portside helm console is lockable, and storage compartments are found beneath the bow and cockpit lounges. Note the backrests in the forward cockpit seating, and the large ski/wakeboard locker in the cockpit sole. A transom shower and power engine hatch are standard. Cruise in the high 20s with a single 320hp MerCruiser sterndrive (36–38 knots top).

See Page 697 For Price Data

Length	28'6"	Fuel	94 gals.
Beam	9'0"	Water	21 gals.
Draft, Up	1'9"	Waste	10 gals.
Draft, Down	3'1"	Hull Type	Modified-V
Weight	5,555#	Deadrise Aft	21°

Sea Ray 270 Sundancer

1994-97; 1999

A good-selling boat, the 270 Sundancer (note that there were two earlier versions of the 270 Sundancer) is built on the same solid fiberglass hull used for her immediate predecessor, but with a revised deck profile and an updated cockpit layout. With a relatively narrow (for a 27-footer) 8-foot, 6-inch beam, this is a trailerable boat, but only with a 3/4-ton truck. The companionway is on the centerline in this model, and the old bi-fold companionway door of the previous model was replaced with a sliding acrylic door that's easier to operate. Below, the Sundancer's midcabin floorplan features a convertible dinette/V-berth forward, a complete galley with generous counter space, and a standup head with sink and shower. The mid-stateroom includes a double bunk, sliding windows, and a privacy curtain. On deck, a double helm seat with an aft-facing seat, refreshment center, and foldaway rear seat were standard. A single 330hp 7.4-liter MerCruiser sterndrive will cruise the Sundancer in the low 20s and reach a top speed of about 35 knots. Out of production in 1998, she was briefly reintroduced into the Sea Ray fleet for 1999 as the 270 Sundancer "Special Edition."

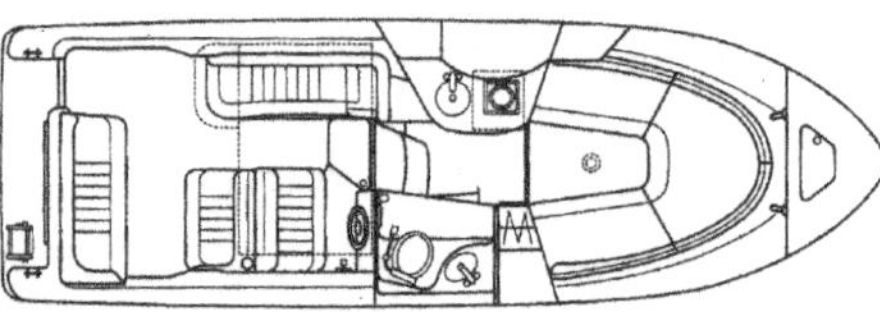

See Page 697 For Price Data

Length w/Pulpit	29'11"	Fuel	100 gals.
Beam	8'6"	Water	24 gals.
Draft, Up	1'11"	Waste	20 gals.
Draft, Down	3'0"	Hull Type	Deep-V
Weight	6,400#	Deadrise Aft	20°

Sea Ray 270 Sundancer

1998–2001

There have been several 270 Sundancer models in Sea Ray fleet going back to the early 1980s. Unlike her two predecessors, however, this most recent version of the 270 Sundancer is not trailerable—a notable difference that results in a roomier (and heavier) boat. Built on a deep-V hull with a wide 9-foot, 2-inch beam, the 270 Sundancer is a well-styled cruiser with clean lines and simple hull graphics. With her wider beam, the interior is spacious for a 27-footer with comfortable accommodations for as many as six. There's a V-berth forward, a double berth in the mid-stateroom, a full galley (but not much counter space), and a standup head with sink and shower. In the cockpit, a portside settee is opposite the helm and a cooler is located under the aft-facing jump seat. Note that the foredeck steps are molded into the cabin door—a useful feature that opens up space at the helm. Additional features include a transom storage bin, cockpit shower, an extended swim platform, and a gas-assist engine hatch. A single 310hp MerCruiser sterndrive will cruise the 270 Sundancer at 20 knots (about 32–33 knots top), and twin 190hp Mercs will top out in the mid-to-high 30s.

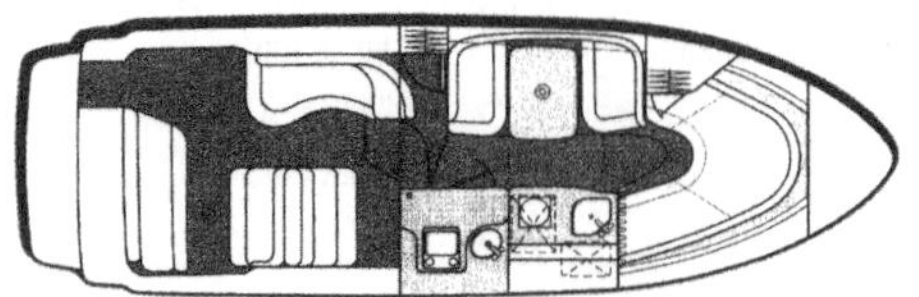

See Page 697 For Price Data

Length w/Platform	29'10"	Fuel	100 gals.
Beam	9'2"	Water	28 gals.
Draft, Up	1'11"	Waste	28 gals.
Draft, Down	3'5"	Hull Type	Deep-V
Weight	7,500#	Deadrise Aft	21°

Sea Ray 270 Sundeck

2002–07

One of the bigger deckboats on the market when she was introduced in 2002, the Sea Ray 270 Sundeck might easily be confused with a full-blown sportboat were it not for her broad bow area with its lounge seating and walk-through boarding gate. The 270 differs from other deckboats in that she includes a berth under the starboard helm console. (It's open to question whether sleeping quarters make much sense in a dayboat of this type, but the area is always useful for stowage.) The passenger-side console houses a lockable head with sink and opening port, and a well-positioned cockpit galley includes a second sink as well as an insulated cooler and faucet with pullout sprayer. An L-shaped settee spans the transom and port side of the cockpit, and the rear section rises to reveal the engine compartment. An extended swim platform is standard. Technically, a permit is required to tow the Sea Ray 270 since her 8-foot, 10-inch beam exceeds the legal 8-foot, 6-inch width restriction; realistically, however, the chances of getting stopped are pretty slim. Among several sterndrive engine options, a single 375hp MerCruiser Bravo III will hit a top speed of over 40 knots.

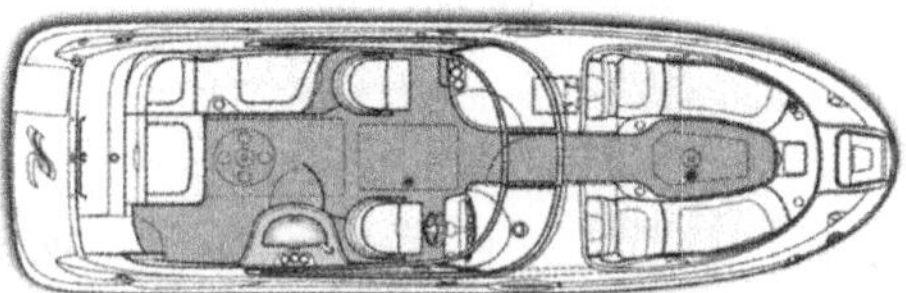

See Page 697 For Price Data

Length	26'6"	Clearance	6'4"
Beam	8'10"	Fuel	85 gals.
Draft, Up	1'8"	Water	24 gals.
Draft, Down	3'0"	Hull Type	Modified-V
Weight	5,800#	Deadrise Aft	21°

Sea Ray 280 Bowrider

1996–2001

One of Sea Ray's most popular runabouts, the 280 Bowrider was the largest bowrider available from any manufacturer when she was introduced in 1996. Built on a smooth-running deep-V hull and weighing in at a hefty 6,400 pounds, the 280 has the size and bulk to handle offshore waters in relative comfort. The interior is arranged in the conventional manner with U-shaped lounge/sun pad forward and wraparound lounge seating aft in the cockpit. A wet bar with cooler, glass rack, and trash receptacle is positioned behind the helm, and a lockable head compartment with sink and shower is below the portside helm console. A tilt wheel and flip-up bolster seat are standard at the helm. An electrically operated engine hatch under the U-shaped aft seat lifts to reveal a well-finished engine compartment. Additional features include a fresh water washdown system, large in-floor ski stowage locker, dockside power, and a transom shower. An extended, add-on swim platform was optional. Among several sterndrive power choices offered with the 280 Bowrider, twin 260hp (or 270hp) MerCruisers deliver a top speed of 45–50 knots, while a single 310 MerCruiser I/O will reach the mid 30s top.

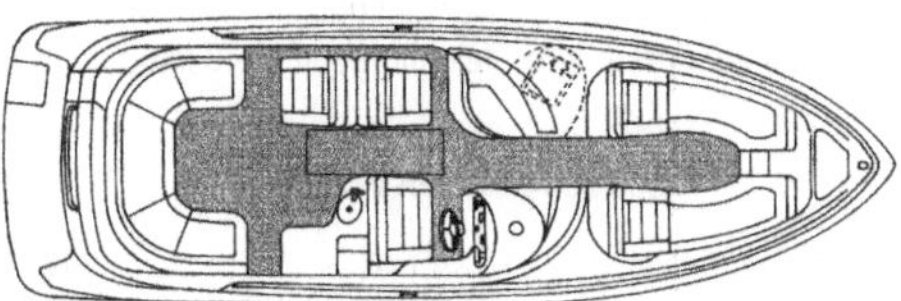

See Page 697 For Price Data

Length	27'6"	Clearance	NA
Beam	9'6"	Fuel	127 gals.
Draft, Up	2'2"	Water	24 gals.
Draft, Down	3'5"	Hull Type	Deep-V
Weight	6,400#	Deadrise Aft	21°

Sea Ray 280 Sun Sport

1996–2001

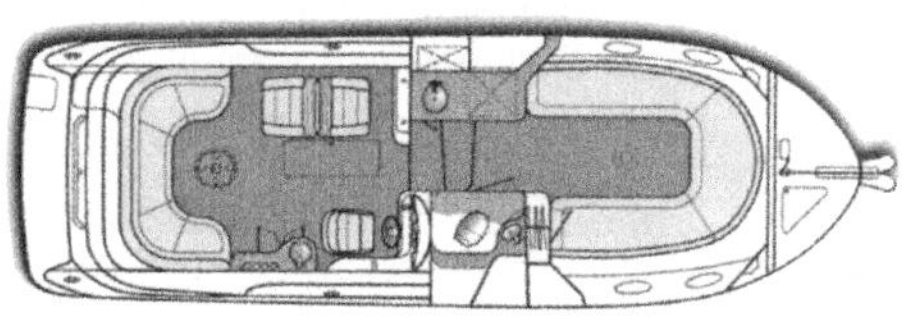

The Sea Ray 280 Sun Sport offers the versatility and performance one expects in a modern sport cruiser together with a healthy dose of old-fashioned sex appeal. The popularity of the Sun Sport derives from her ability to do several things well. A functional cabin makes the 280 a good overnighter, and her generous 9-foot, 6-inch beam provides the cockpit space required to accommodate several guests in comfort. The 280's big cockpit still leaves enough space below for an expansive U-shaped dinette (with a removable table) as well as an enclosed head with VacuFlush toilet and pullout shower. A wet bar with cooler, glass rack, and trash receptacle is just behind the helm seat, and an electrically operated engine hatch under the U-shaped aft seat lifts to reveal a well-finished engine compartment. The sporty helm console is a plus, and the flip-up bolster seat is essential in any high-speed sportboat. An extended swim platform and transom shower were standard, and a radar arch was a popular option. Among several sterndrive power choices offered with the 280 Bowrider, twin 260hp (or 270hp) MerCruisers deliver a top speed of 45–50 knots, while a single 310 MerCruiser I/O will reach the mid 30s top.

See Page 697 For Price Data

Length	27'6"	Fuel	127 gals.
Beam	9'6"	Water	24 gals.
Draft, Up	2'2"	Waste	20 gals.
Draft, Down	3'5"	Hull Type	Deep-V
Weight	8,200#	Deadrise Aft	21°

Sea Ray 280 Sundancer

2001–09

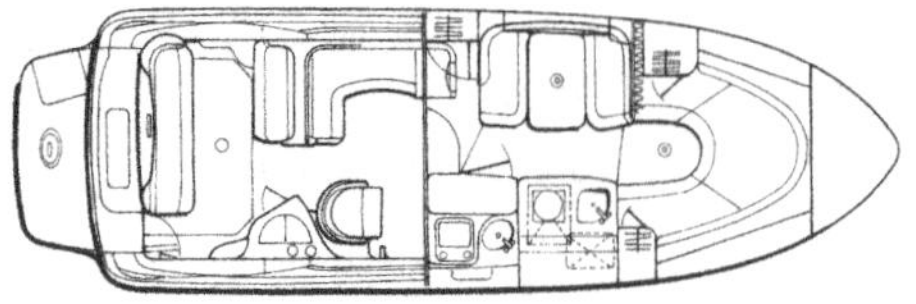

Those looking for a small midcabin family cruiser will find a lot to like in the Sea Ray 280 Sundancer. The styling is crisp—a Sea Ray trademark these days—and the interior makes the most out of available space with berths for four adults (and two kids), decent headroom, a full galley, and a V-berth that converts into a second dinette. Built on a deep-V hull with a moderate beam and an integrated swim platform, the Sundancer's curved radar arch is an appealing design touch that's showing up on a good many express boats these days. The single-level cockpit is arranged with a sun pad opposite the helm, an aft-facing bench seat, wet bar, and a retractable rear bench seat that folds up into the transom when it's necessary to get into the engine compartment. A large storage locker is built into the transom, and molded steps at the helm provide easy access to the walk-through windshield. On the downside, the midcabin and head dimensions are fairly small, and the engine compartment hatch is heavy. Powered with twin 260hp MerCruiser sterndrives, the 280 Sundancer will cruise in the mid-to-high 20s and reach a top speed in the neighborhood of 40 knots.

See Page 697 For Price Data

Length w/Platform	31'1"	Fuel	100 gals.
Beam	9'5"	Water	28 gals.
Draft, Up	1'10"	Waste	28 gals.
Draft, Down	3'3"	Hull Type	Deep-V
Weight	8,630#	Deadrise Aft	21°

Sea Ray 280 Sundancer

2010–Current

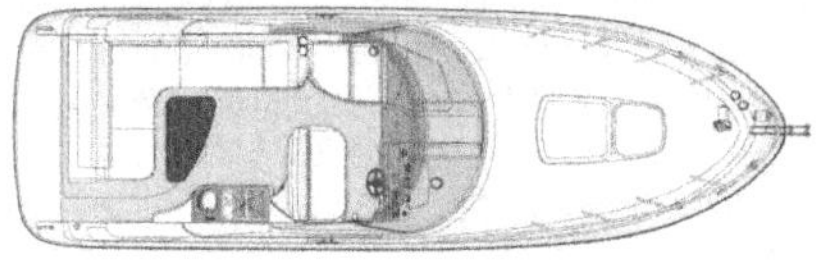

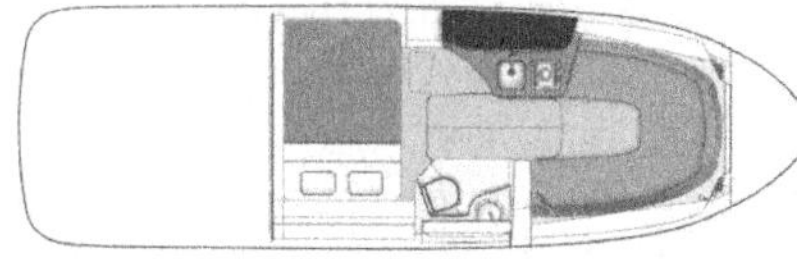

Third in a series of 280 Sundancer models, Sea Ray designers took midsize express-boat luxury to the next level with the 2010 introduction of this stylish family cruiser. With her sleek lines, upscale amenities, and single-engine economy, the 280 is yet another example of why Sea Ray so dominates the market for quality express cruisers. Built on a deep-V hull with moderate beam and relatively tall freeboard, the 280 Sundancer's user-friendly cockpit features a curved portside L-shaped lounger with storage below, removable carry-on cooler, electrically actuated engine hatch, and a wet bar with sink, ice maker and Corian countertop. As with most boats this size, a walk-through windshield provides easy bow access. Note the dash flat for flush-mounting a video display. Below decks, the Sundancer's well-appointed interior includes a convertible dinette, midcabin berth, standup head, and full galley with sink, stove and refrigerator. Most have been sold with the optional sport arch. The 280 Sundancer can be easily towed with a full-size pickup or SUV (overwide permit required). She'll cruise at 25 knots (35 top) with a single 320hp MerCruiser I/O.

See Page 698 For Price Data

Length w/Platform	28'8"	Fuel	84 gals.
Beam	8'10"	Water	28 gals.
Draft, Up	2'0"	Waste	28 gals.
Draft, Down	3'5"	Hull Type	Deep-V
Weight	8,211#	Deadrise Aft	19°

Sea Ray 280/300 Weekender

1991–95

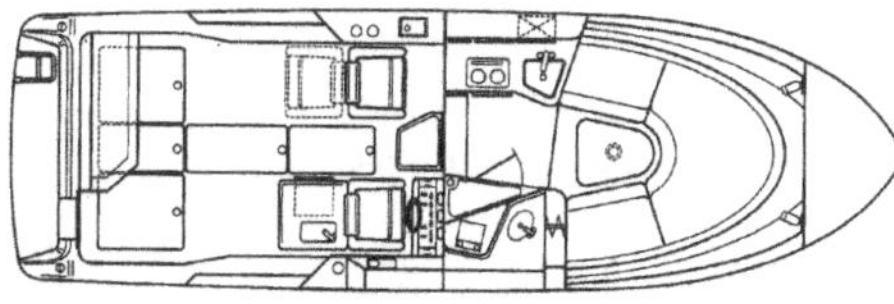

Attractive sportboat styling, a big, single-level cockpit, and cabin accommodations for two characterize the Sea Ray 300 Weekender (called the 280 Weekender in 1991), a popular day cruiser from the early 1990s. Aside from her solid construction, the Weekender's main draw is her large cockpit with its side-panel storage, a portside cooler, drink holders, and transom door. A removable bench seat at the stern was a popular option, and twin hatches in the aft cockpit floor provides good access to the engines. Below, the Weekender's interior is arranged with a convertible dinette/V-berth forward, a small galley, and a standup head with sink and shower—comfortable accommodations for two adults. Built on a deep-V hull with a generous 10-foot, 6-inch beam and an integrated swim platform, the 300 Weekender came with a choice of inboard or sterndrive power. Among several engine options, twin 250hp MerCruiser inboards (with V-drives) will cruise in the mid 20s (30+ knots top), and the 250hp MerCruiser sterndrives will top out at close to 40 knots. Note that inboard models have prop pockets and side exhausts.

See Page 698 For Price Data

Length w/Pulpit	31'11"	Fuel	200 gals.
Hull Length	29'9"	Water	28 gals.
Beam	10'6"	Waste	28 gals.
Draft	2'8"	Hull Type	Deep-V
Weight	7,800#	Deadrise Aft	21°

Sea Ray 290 Amberjack

2000–09

Sea Ray, with their on-again, off-again series of Amberjacks, has made halting efforts over the years to market fishing boats to veteran anglers. The 290 Amberjack isn't a serious fishing machine by any means; she is, however, a capable family cruiser/fisherman with the emphasis on comfortable accommodations. Built on a deep-V hull with a relatively wide beam, the Amberjack's fishing amenities are comprised of molded bait-prep station (with livewell) behind the helm, cockpit rod storage, and an optional aluminum arch with rocket launchers. The 290's interior is plush for a fishing boat with a convertible dinette, head with shower, and a well-equipped galley with a built-in microwave. Note that the mid-berth is very shallow and suitable for only a single adult. Additional features include a removable aft bench seat, power vent windshield, transom door and swim platform, and freshwater washdown. Among many engine choices, twin 260hp MerCruiser sterndrives cruise the Amberjack in the low 20s (about 35 knots top), and 300hp sterndrives cruise in the mid 20s (40+ knots wide open). With 300hp V-drive inboards, she'll cruise in the low 20s and top out around 30 knots.

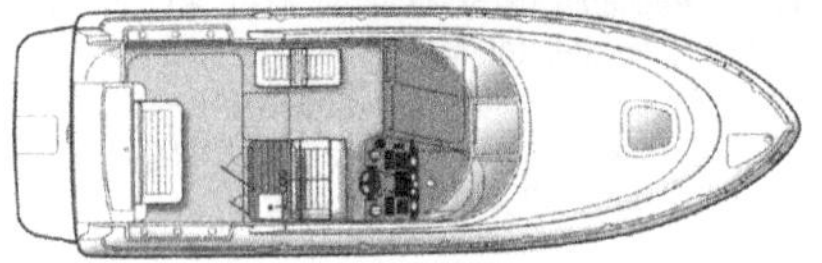

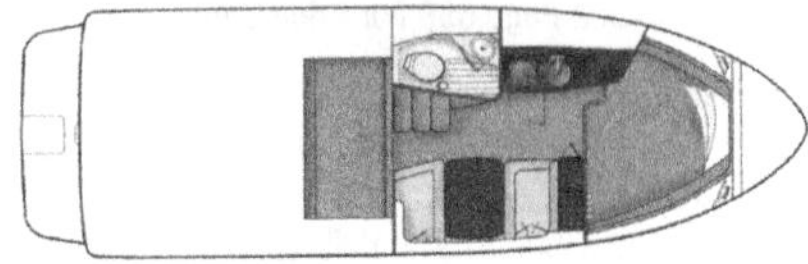

See Page 698 For Price Data

Length w/Platform	31'4"	Fuel	250 gals.
Beam	10'6"	Water	30 gals.
Draft, Up	2'5"	Waste	28 gals.
Draft, Down	2'10"	Hull Type	Deep-V
Weight	12,215#	Deadrise Aft	21°

Sea Ray 290 Bowrider

2001–04

The market for super-size runabouts was undergoing explosive growth in the early 2000s when Sea Ray introduced the 290 Bowrider. She was the company's largest open-bow model ever, and her wide 9'8" beam offered interior space for a small crowd. Built on a modified deep-V hull, the 290 has the size and bulk to handle offshore waters with ease. Two cockpit seating plans were available: the standard layout has U-shaped seating aft, a back-to-back companion seat, and a centerline transom walk-through, while an alternate plan features a large sun pad aft, a starboard walk-through, and bucket seats forward. A cockpit wet bar is standard in either arrangement as are an electric engine compartment hatch and an in-floor ski storage locker. In the bow, a table and filler cushions turn the forward seating area into a huge sun pad. A lockable head in the portside helm console comes with a VacuFlush head, sink, and pullout shower. Additional features include a flip-up bolster seat, transom shower, and an extended swim platform. A good-looking runabout with plenty of sex appeal, twin 260hp MerCruiser sterndrives deliver a top speed of around 45 knots.

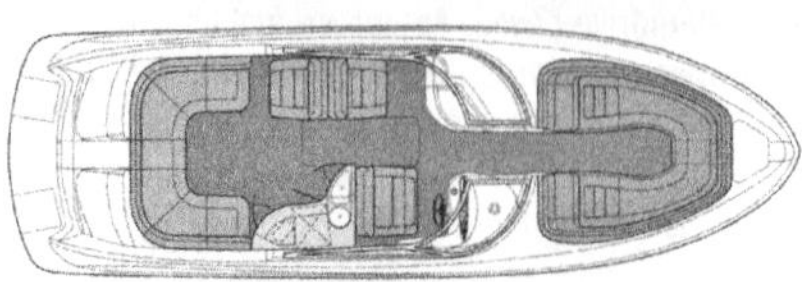

Standard Seating

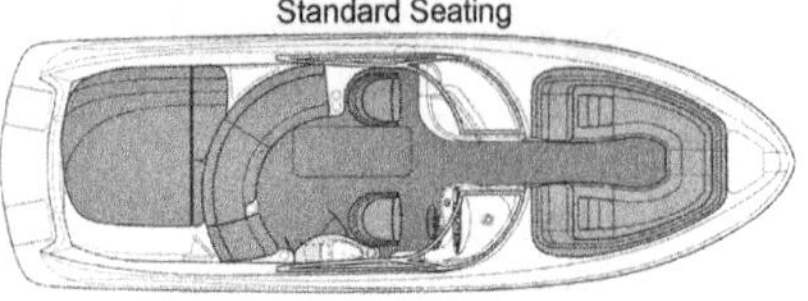

Optional Seating

See Page 698 For Price Data

Length	29'6"	Fuel	130 gals.
Beam	9'8"	Water	24 gals.
Draft, Up	2'0"	Waste	20 gals.
Draft, Down	3'1"	Hull Type	Deep-V
Weight	7,700#	Deadrise Aft	21°

Sea Ray 290 Select EX

An upmarket version of original Sea Ray 290 Bowrider (2001–04), the 290 Select EX combines a sophisticated blend of sports-car performance, luxury-class comfort, and head-turning sex appeal. The 290 was Sea Ray's largest bowrider ever, and her wide 9'8" beam offers an enormous amount of seating space. Built on a modified deep-V hull with a wave-calming 21 degrees of transom deadrise, the 290 has the size and bulk to handle offshore waters with ease. Like her predecessor, there are two cockpit tables for entertaining that can be easily stowed when underway. A deluxe refreshment center includes a wet bar with bottle rack, trash bin, and optional refrigerator. The stylish, high-gloss burl dash is a plus, and a lockable head in the portside helm console comes with a VacuFlush head, sink, and pullout shower. As with most bowriders, removable cushions convert the entire forward seating area into a vast sun pad. A power engine compartment hatch is standard. Note the swim platform storage lockers. An extended swim platform was a popular option. A single 375hp MerCruiser I/O tops out at 40 knots; twin 260hp Mercs reach 45+ wide open.

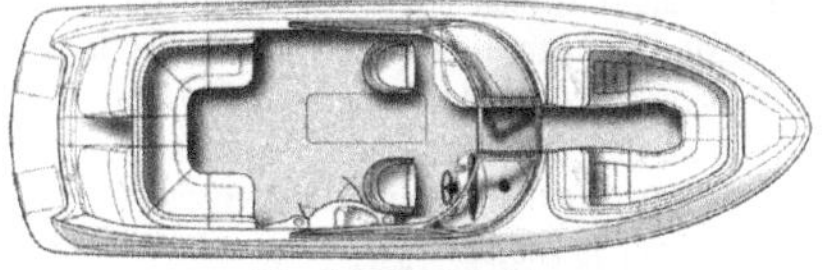
Standard Seating Plan

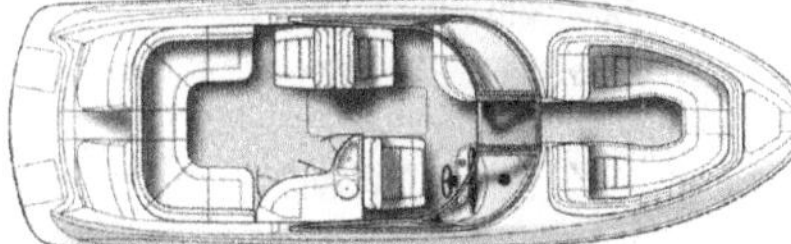
Optional Seating Plan

See Page 698 For Price Data

Length	29'6"	Fuel	130 gals.
Beam	9'8"	Water	24 gals.
Draft, Up	2'0"	Waste	20 gals.
Draft, Down	3'6"	Hull Type	Deep-V
Weight	7,700#	Deadrise Aft	21°

Sea Ray 290 Sun Sport

Classic good looks, roomy accommodations, and brisk performance characterize the Sea Ray 290 Sun Sport, a well-finished sportboat from a company with a long history in developing high-end runabouts. Built on a deep-V hull with a wide beam, the Sun Sport's rakish persona is accented by colorful graphics and a forward-sloping radar arch. Two cockpit seating plans were available: the standard seating includes a large sun pad aft, a starboard transom walk-through, and bucket seats forward, while the optional arrangement provides U-shaped seating aft, a back-to-back companion seat, and a centerline transom walk-through. A cockpit wet bar is standard, and a large lighted ski storage area is located in the cockpit sole. A lockable sliding cabin door with integral steps provides easy access to the foredeck. Below, the 290's well-finished cabin includes a convertible dinette/V-berth forward, compact galley with sink and refrigerator, and an enclosed head with pullout shower and premium VacuFlush head. The 290 Sun Sport will top out at 40+ knots with a pair of 260hp MerCruiser I/Os, and twin 320hp Merc I/Os will hit a top speed of just over 45 knots.

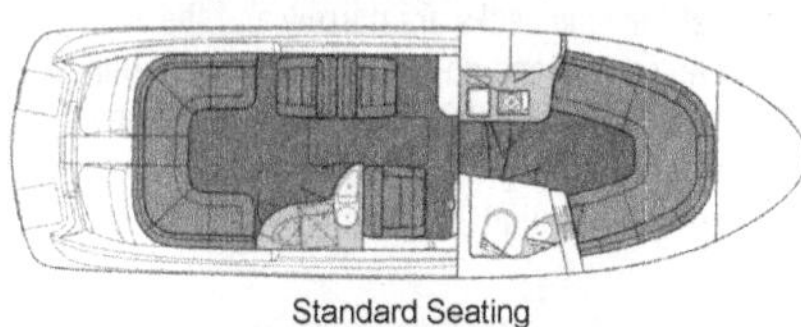
Standard Seating

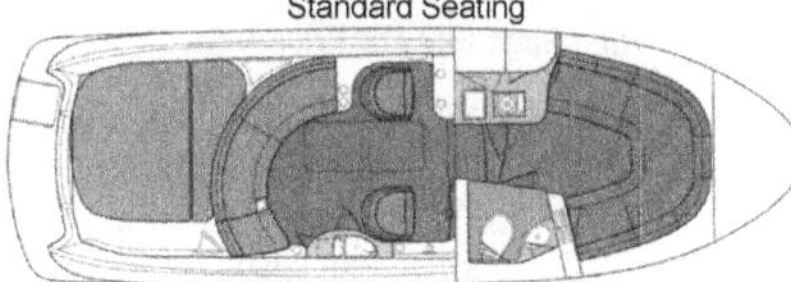
Optional Seating

See Page 698 For Price Data

Length	29'6"	Fuel	130 gals.
Beam	9'8"	Water	24 gals.
Draft, Up	2'2"	Waste	20 gals.
Draft, Down	3'1"	Hull Type	Deep-V
Weight	8,300#	Deadrise Aft	21°

Sea Ray 290 Sundancer

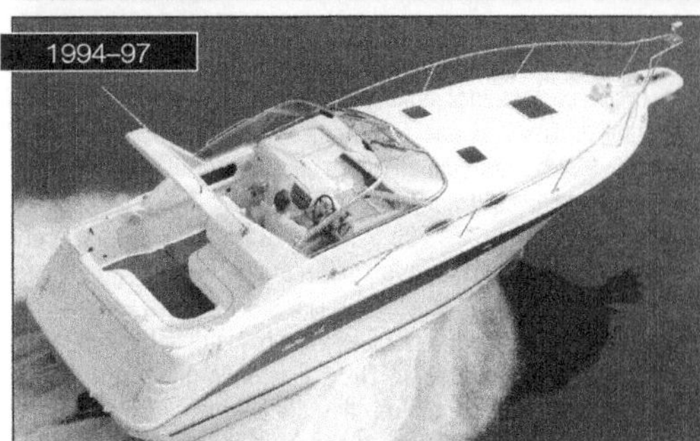

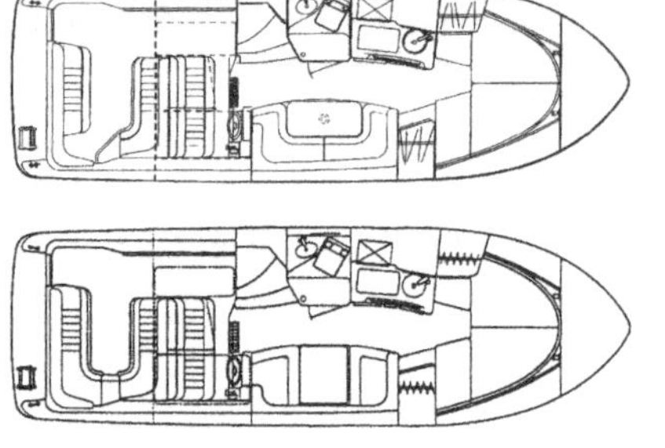

Sea Ray nearly always gets it right when it comes to their series of family cruisers, and the introduction of the 290 Sundancer in 1994 is a good illustration of why this company has long dominated the market for upmarket express boats. Loaded with amenities, this versatile weekender is a 1990s blend of crisp styling, comfortable accommodations and good performance. She rides on a solid fiberglass hull with a sharp entry and a moderate 9-foot, 8-inch beam. Two floorplans were offered in the 290, one with a U-shaped dinette and the other with a conventional dinette with facing seats. Both staterooms are fitted with double beds and privacy curtains, and storage space—with two large hanging lockers—is notable. On deck, the 290's cockpit is arranged with an elevated triple-wide helm seat, and a U-shaped lounge aft converts into a sun pad. There's a protected chart flat at the helm (very nice), and the faux-burlwood instrument panel is well laid out. On the downside, the engine compartment is a tight fit. A single 300hp MerCruiser sterndrive will cruise the 290 Sundancer at 20 knots (30+ knots top), and a pair of 190hp sterndrives cruise in the mid 20s and reach a top speed of about 35 knots.

See Page 698 For Price Data

Length w/Pulpit	32'1"	Fuel	130 gals.
Beam	9'8"	Water	24 gals.
Draft, Up	2'0"	Waste	24 gals.
Draft, Down	3'9"	Hull Type	Deep-V
Weight	8,500#	Deadrise Aft	21°

Sea Ray 290 Sundancer

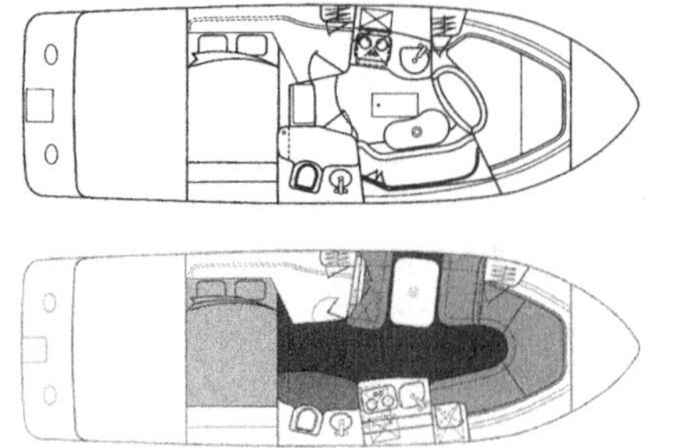

A handsome boat with sculptured lines and first-rate accommodations, the Sea Ray 290 Sundancer (note that an earlier 290 Sundancer was built in 1994–97) offers just about everything one could desire in a quality midsize family cruiser. Sea Ray always builds a solid boat, and at over 10,000 pounds, the Sundancer is no lightweight. The interior was originally offered in two configurations: Plan A has a convertible dinette forward, and Plan B has a double berth forward with the dinette table in front of the starboard-side settee. In 1999 a new cabin layout replaced the original floorplans. Topside, the cockpit includes a portside sun lounge and a removable aft bench seat in addition to a very stylish helm console. Standard features include a cockpit shower and wet bar, excellent storage, a drop-down helm seat, and a transom door. Note that the side decks are narrow and the engineroom is a tight fit. Among several engine options, a single 310hp MerCruiser sterndrive will cruise the 290 Sundancer at 18–19 knots (about 25 knots top), and twin 260hp MerCruisers cruise in the low 20s and reach a top speed of around 35 knots.

See Page 698 For Price Data

Length	31'8"	Fuel	130 gals.
Beam	10'2"	Water	28 gals.
Draft, Up	2'3"	Waste	28 gals.
Draft, Down	3'1"	Hull Type	Deep-V
Weight	10,500#	Deadrise Aft	21°

Sea Ray 290 Sundancer

2006–08

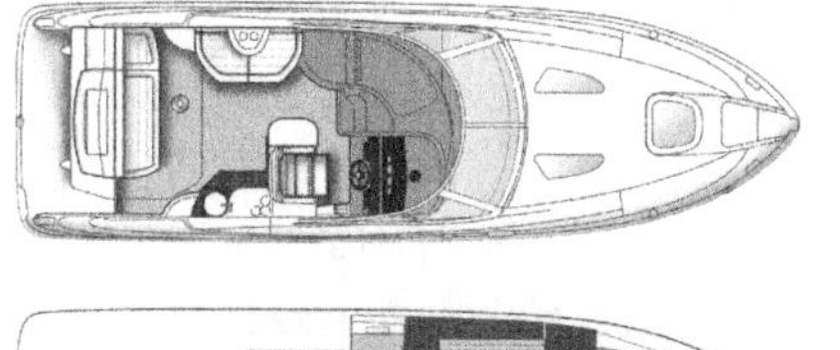

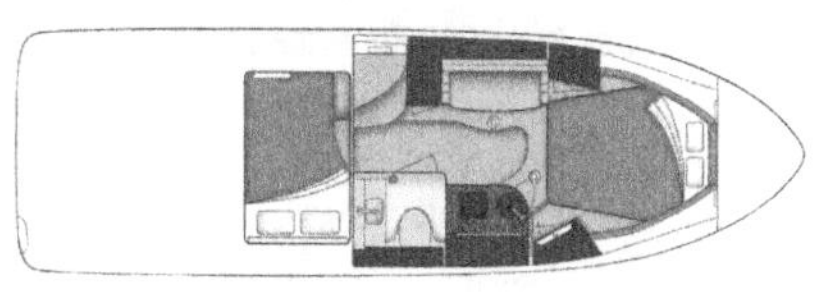

The distinctive, cutting-edge styling of the Sea Ray 290 Sundancer still resonates with boaters today, years after her 2006 introduction. Sea Ray designers created a uniquely American blend of sweeping lines and graceful accents in the 290 Sundancer, and the chances are good that this boat will retain her rakish good looks well into the future. Built on a deep-V hull with moderate beam and tall freeboard forward, the Sundancer's accommodations are at once practical and luxurious. Her expansive cockpit—less crowded than most, but with less seating as well—includes a wet bar with Corian counter, a stainless steel sink, drink holders and a designated space for the carry-on cooler. A transom shower and transom storage locker were standard, and the 290's sculptured, forward-reaching radar arch was a popular option. Below decks, the Sundancer's midcabin interior, with solid cherry cabinets and big U-shaped dinette, features an innovative double berth forward that easily converts into an aft-facing settee. A very popular model, she'll cruise at 20 knots with a single 375 MerCruiser sterndrive. Twin 260hp I/Os cruise in the mid 20s (about 40 knots top).

See Page 698 For Price Data

Length Overall	31'1"	Fuel	125 gals.
Beam	9'6"	Water	28 gals.
Draft, Drives Up	2'4"	Waste	28 gals.
Draft, Drives Down	3'3"	Hull Type	Deep-V
Weight	9,250#	Deadrise Aft	21°

Sea Ray 300 Sundancer

1994–97

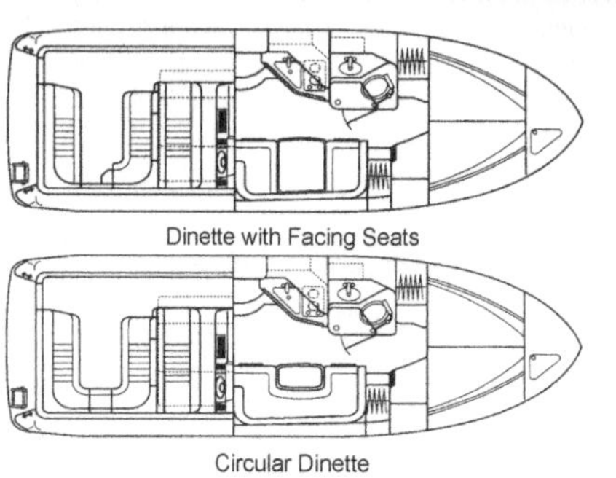

Dinette with Facing Seats

Circular Dinette

With her oval port lights, low-profile arch, and sculptured lines, this third version of Sea Ray's 300 Sundancer series was one of the best-looking sportboats in the market during the late 1990s. She's built on the same easy-riding deep-V hull used in the production of the previous 300 Sundancer model (1992–93), but with a restyled profile, an updated interior, additional (and badly needed) fuel capacity, and a revised cockpit layout. Accommodations for six are provided below in two different floorplan configurations, both with a standup head with shower, full galley, two hanging lockers, and a convertible dinette. On deck, visibility from the triple helm seat is very good, and a protected chart flat is built into the dash. A filler converts the U-shaped cockpit seating aft of the helm into a large sun pad. Additional features include a walk-through transom, molded bow pulpit, radar arch, and good engine access. The 300 Sundancer was available with a choice of inboard or sterndrive power. A very popular model for Sea Ray, twin 250hp MerCruiser V-drive inboards cruise at 19–20 knots (about 30 knots top), and the less-popular sterndrive versions of the same engines cruise in the low 20s and top out at close to 35 knots.

See Page 698 For Price Data

Length w/Pulpit	33'1"	Fuel	200 gals.
Hull Length	30'6"	Water	35 gals.
Beam	10'6"	Waste	28 gals.
Draft	2'11"	Hull Type	Deep-V
Weight	10,200#	Deadrise Aft	21°

Sea Ray 300 Sundancer

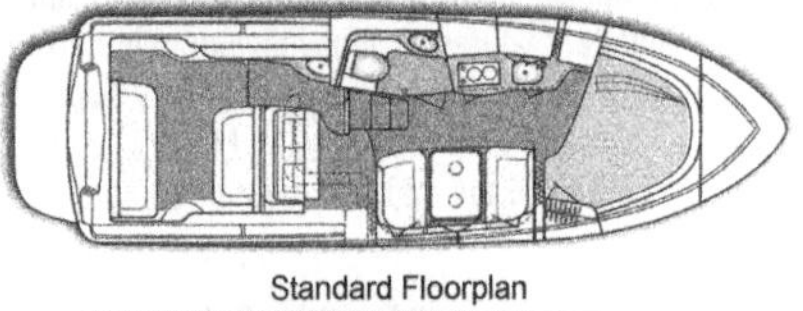

Standard Floorplan

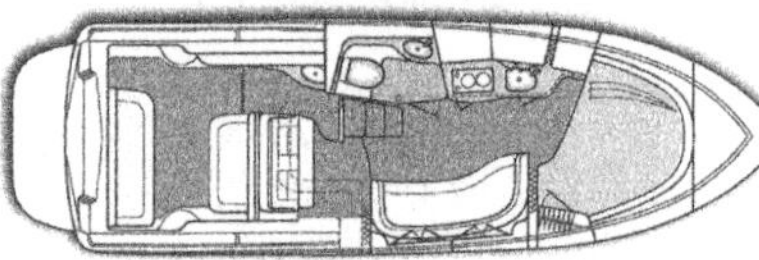

Optional Floorplan

Lots of manufacturers build 30-foot midcabin express cruisers, but few have been at it as long as Sea Ray and probably no company does it better. This is the forth in a series of 300 Sundancer models Sea Ray has produced since 1985, and an extended 30-inch swim platform made her the most stylish of the pack. Like her predecessors, the newest Sundancer rides on a deep-V hull with moderate beam and a solid fiberglass bottom. Buyers can pick from two interior floorplans. The standard layout has a dinette that converts into a berth, while the optional configuration features a curved sofa bed with a matching table. Both plans include an enclosed head and shower, a double berth forward, and of course a midberth aft. Privacy curtains separate the sleeping areas from the main cabin, which is highlighted by three overhead hatches and attractive burlwood cabinets. The cockpit comes with a wet bar and a removable table in addition to a fore-and-aft facing bench seats, and the entire cockpit sole rises on hydraulic rams to reveal the engine compartment. The sporty tiered helm is particularly well arranged. No lightweight, twin 260hp MerCruiser sterndrives cruise the 300 Sundancer at 20 knots (mid 30s top).

See Page 698 For Price Data

Length w/Platform	33'4"	Fuel	170 gals.
Beam	10'5"	Water	35 gals.
Draft, Up	2'0"	Waste	28 gals.
Draft, Down	3'4"	Hull Type	Deep-V
Weight	12,000#	Deadrise Aft	21°

Sea Ray 310 Sun Sport

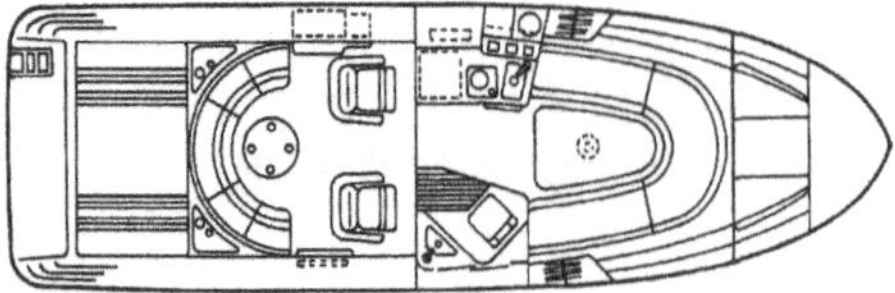

Considered a very stylish boat by the standards of her era, the Sea Ray 310 Sun Sport had the look and feel of a true Mediterranean-bred sportboat. She's still a distinctive boat with her reverse arch and colorful hull graphics, and the Sun Sport's sleek, low-profile appearance delivered a healthy dose of 1990's sex appeal. She's built on a lightweight, relatively narrow deep-V hull, and her low foredeck results in very modest cabin headroom. Because she's a dayboat and not a cruiser the accommodations below are fairly basic. A U-shaped dinette forward—which can seat up to six—converts into a double bed, and there's a small mini-berth/storage shelf in the forepeak. The Sun Sport's small cockpit is arranged with horseshoe-shaped seating aft of the helm and twin bucket seats forward. A full-width sun pad is located over the engine compartment, and drink holders are everywhere. Note that the Sun Sport's original tubular radar arch was replaced with a more stylish fiberglass arch in 1993. Performance is excellent: she'll cruise at 30 knots with twin 350hp MerCruiser sterndrives and reach a top speed in the neighborhood of 45 knots.

See Page 698 For Price Data

Length	31'2"	Fuel	160 gals.
Beam	9'6"	Water	20 gals.
Draft, Up	2'2"	Waste	11 gals.
Draft, Down	3'1"	Hull Type	Deep-V
Weight	8,100#	Deadrise Aft	21°

Sea Ray 310 Sundancer

With her striking profile and comfortable interior, the Sea Ray 310 Sundancer was designed for upscale boaters willing to pay top dollar for a quality midsize express. This is a well-crafted boat, better finished than previous Sea Ray models and incorporating high-grade hardware, appliances, and furnishings. When the 310 was introduced in 1998, she came with an unusual floorplan that required those using the forward kidney-shaped berth to climb over the circular dinette seat. Sea Ray dumped that plan in 1999, replacing it with a more conventional layout with an angled double berth forward and a conventional dinette with facing seats. In both configurations, a roomy midcabin offers true seclusion thanks to a real door instead of a curtain. The Sundancer's large cockpit has everything for relaxing and entertaining including a triple helm seat (with a flip-up seat for the driver), U-shaped aft seating, and wet bar with removable cooler. For engine access, the entire bridge deck rises electrically at the push of a button. Among several engine choices, twin 260hp MerCruiser V-drive inboards cruise the 310 Sundancer at 18 knots (26–27 knots top), and 260hp MerCruiser sterndrives will top out in the mid 30s.

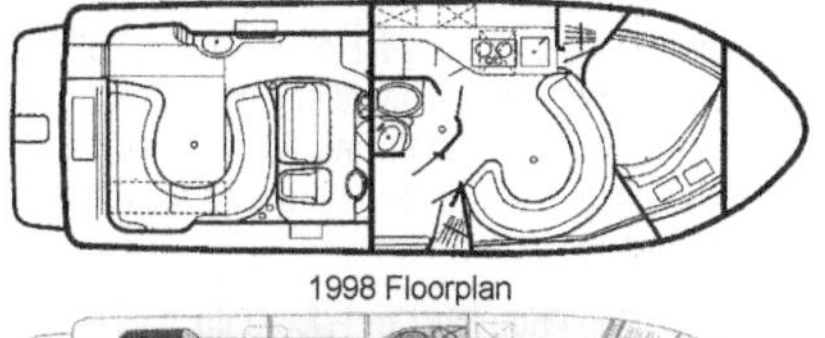
1998 Floorplan

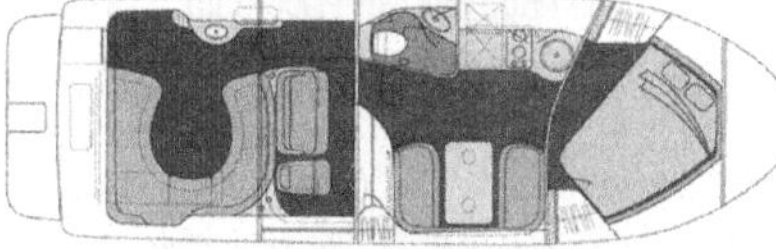
1999–2002

See Page 698 For Price Data

Length w/Platform	33'10"	Weight	12,000#
Hull Length	31'6"	Fuel	200 gals.
Beam	11'2"	Water	35 gals.
Draft, Drives Up	1'11"	Hull Type	Deep-V
Draft, Drives Down	3'7"	Deadrise Aft	23°

Sea Ray 310 Sundancer

Few segments of the American boating industry are as competitive as the market for midsize, 30-something express cruisers. This is the sweet spot for many boaters, the intersection of size and value where several manufacturers slug it out for valuable market share. The Sea Ray 310 Sundancer—latest in a series of 310 Sundancer models reaching back to 1990—combines leading-edge styling with the luxury one expects in a modern Sea Ray yacht. Like most of her Sundancer siblings, the 310 rides on a deep-V hull with moderate beam, cored hullsides, and a solid fiberglass bottom. Below decks, the midcabin accommodations are a rich blend of satin-finished cherry cabinets, hardwood flooring, leather upholstery, and designer galley appliances. Privacy curtains separate the sleeping areas from the main salon, and a 19" flat-screen TV can be viewed from anywhere in the cabin. Note that the 310 Sundancer's modest 10-foot beam—slender compared with many express cruisers her size—dramatically improves handling, performance, and fuel-efficiency. Cruise at 25 knots (high 30s top) with twin 260hp Mercury Bravo III drives. Axius drives with joystick controls are optional.

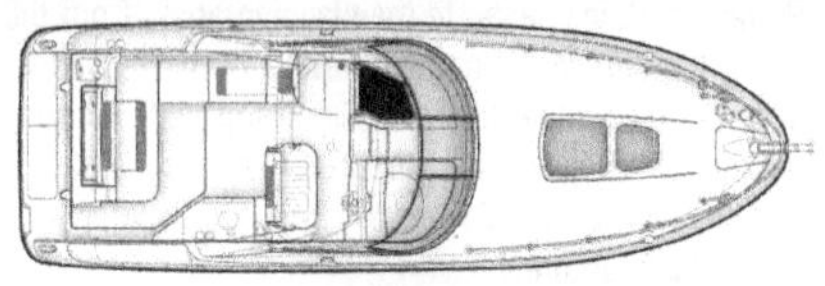

See Page 4698 For Price Data

Length	31'0"	Fuel	125 gals.
Beam	10'0"	Water	28 gals.
Draft, Up	2'6"	Waste	28 gals.
Draft, Down	3'5"	Hull Type	Deep-V
Weight	11,630#	Deadrise Aft	21°

Sea Ray 310/330 Express Cruiser

1990–95

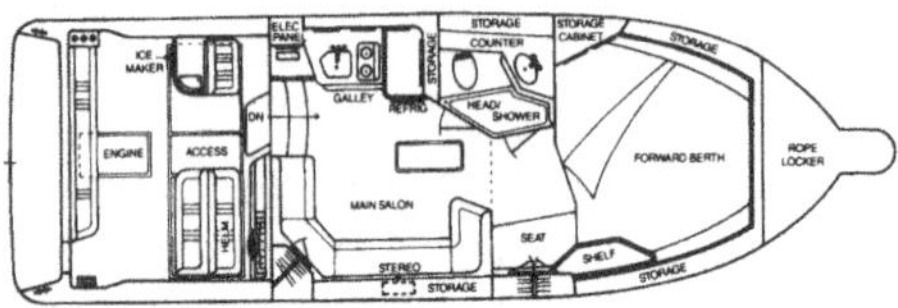

Introduced as the 310 Express Cruiser in 1990–91, the Sea Ray 330 Express was a good-selling boat in the early 1990s thanks to her crisp styling and a very roomy interior. Like most Sea Rays of her era, she was built on a solid fiberglass hull with an integrated swim platform and a generous 11-foot, 5-inch beam. (Note that inboard models incorporated prop pockets and side-dumping exhausts.) While she eschews the midcabin floorplan popular in most express boats, the wide-open salon of the 310/330 EC is unusually spacious for a boat this size. The salon is dominated by a huge wraparound sofa (which converts into a sleeper by night), and a privacy curtain separates the stateroom from the main cabin. Because the interior is so large, the cockpit of the 310/330 is on the small side. The companion and double helm seats hold three adults, while an aft-facing bench seat has room for two more. A foldaway transom seat and radar arch were popular options. Among several sterndrive and inboard engine choices, twin 300hp MerCruiser sterndrives cruise in the mid 20s and reach a top speed of over 30 knots. Note that oval ports replaced the original sliding cabin windows in 1994.

See Page 698 For Price Data

Length w/Pulpit	35'4"	Weight	10,000#
Hull Length	32'10"	Fuel	200 gals.
Beam	11'5"	Water	40 gals.
Draft, Inboard	2'3"	Hull Type	Deep-V
Draft, I/Os	3'0"	Deadrise Aft	21°

Sea Ray 310/330 Sundancer

2007–Current

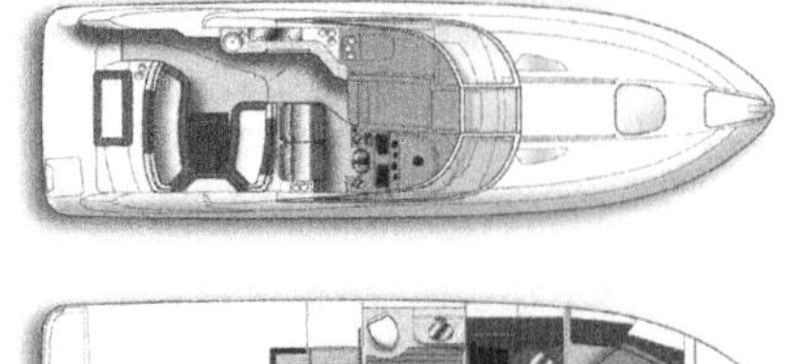

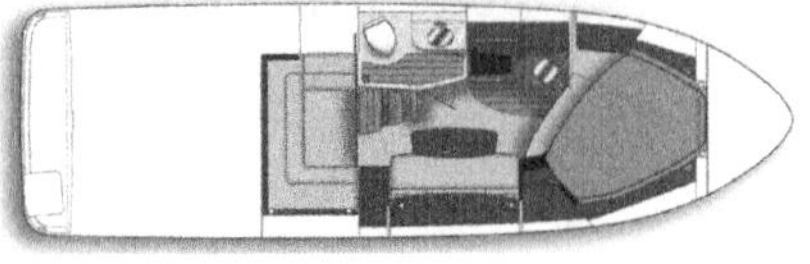

Among the many reasons why Sea Ray practically owns the market for high-end express cruisers, innovative styling probably ranks at the top of the list. Indeed, the compelling lines of the 330 Sundancer (called the 310 Sundancer in 2007–09) are as good as it gets in a modern express yacht. Like most Sundancer models, the 330 rides on a deep-V hull with moderate beam, cored hullsides, and a solid fiberglass bottom. Her spacious cockpit features wraparound lounge seating aft, an extra-large wet bar with optional grill and refrigerator, and a slick foldaway transom seat that creates aft-facing seating on the swim platform. A power engine hatch provides easy access to the engineroom. Below decks, her midcabin accommodations are a compelling blend of cherrywood cabinets, maple flooring, Ultraleather seating, and designer galley appliances. Privacy curtains separate the sleeping areas from the main salon, and a flat-screen TV can be viewed from anywhere in the cabin. Note the innovative fiberglass arch top with aft sunshade. Twin MerCruiser 300hp V-drive inboards (gas) cruise at 25 knots; 320hp Merc I/Os cruise at 28+ knots. The Axius Drive System with joystick controls is optional.

See Page 698 For Price Data

Length	33'4"	Fuel	200 gals.
Beam	10'5"	Water	35 gals.
Draft, Up	2'5"	Waste	28 gals.
Draft, Down	3'3"	Hull Type	Deep-V
Weight	14,000#	Deadrise Aft	21°

Sea Ray 320 Sundancer

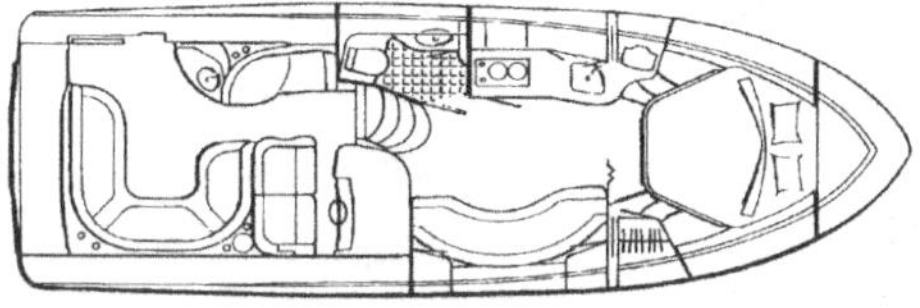

Sea Ray has been setting the standards for express cruisers for some 30 years, so it was hardly a surprise that the 320 Sundancer introduced in 2003 delivered just the right blend of style, comfort, and performance. Sea Ray's dedication to quality is clearly evident in this boat, from the sporty burlwood dash to her near-flawless gelcoat and premium hardware. Below decks, the 320's interior is brightly lit and completely open. High-gloss cherry panelling and mirrored accents highlight a decor rich in luxury and sophistication. The salon settee converts to a double berth; an island berth is forward, and the midcabin area aft of the companionway steps serves as a secondary conversation area. Curtains separate both sleeping areas from the main salon, and faux granite counters and Formica cabinets are found in the galley. The Sundancer's cockpit layout is arranged with U-shaped seating aft for four, a stylish dual helm seat with flip-up bolster, and a full wet bar. On the downside, the side decks are quite narrow, and engine access is a little difficult. Available with inboard or sterndrive power, the 320 Sundancer will cruise in the mid to high 20s with either 300hp Mercury V-drive inboards or 260hp MerCruiser I/Os.

See Page 698 For Price Data

Length w/Platform	35'6"	Fuel	200 gals.
Beam	11'5"	Water	40 gals.
Draft	2'9"	Waste	28 gals.
Weight	13,200#	Hull Type	Deep-V
Clearance	10'2"	Deadrise Aft	21°

Sea Ray 330 Express Cruiser

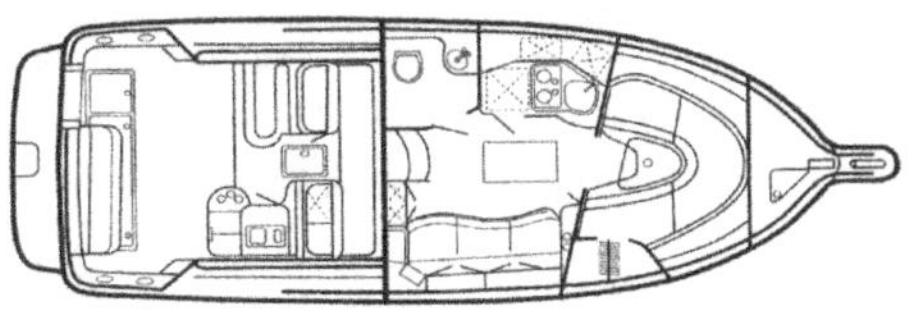

A good-looking express whose bold 1990's styling has stood the test of time, the Sea Ray 330 Express Cruiser splits the difference between part-time fishing boat and weekend family cruiser. With her super-wide 13-foot, 5-inch beam, the 330 is a big 33-footer with a large cockpit and very spacious interior. Built on a fully cored deep-V hull with prop pockets to reduce shaft angles, the vast cockpit of the 330 is well-suited for everything from entertaining to fishing with lots of storage, a deluxe bait-prep/entertainment center with wet bar, and an insulated in-floor fish box. Below decks, her well-appointed interior features a salon sofa that electrically converts into a bed, full-service galley with microwave, and a forward stateroom (with privacy door) that converts into a dinette with dedicated table storage. A power adjustable double helm seat was standard, and the entire bridge deck can be raised electrically for engine access. Additional features include a centerline windshield vent, reverse radar arch, wide side decks, and cockpit side storage. Twin 370hp MerCruiser inboards cruise the 330 Express at 20 knots and top out at close to 30 knots.

See Page 698 For Price Data

Length w/Platform	38'0"	Fuel	275 gals.
Hull Length	33'6"	Water	50 gals.
Beam	13'5"	Waste	28 gals.
Draft	3'0"	Hull Type	Deep-V
Weight	16,500#	Deadrise Aft	19.5°

Sea Ray 330 Sundancer

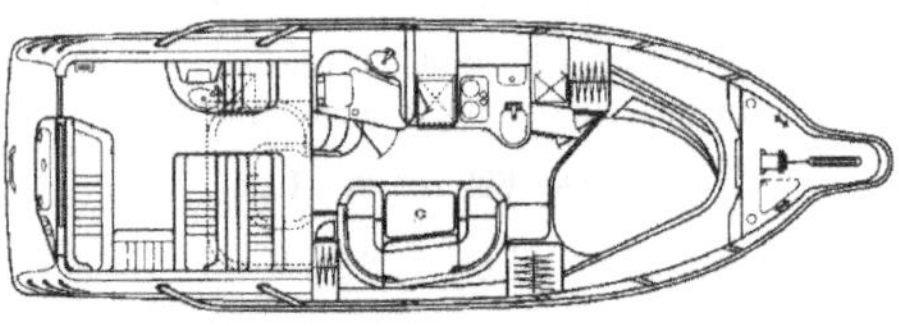

An updated version of Sea Ray's earlier 310/330 Sundancer (1990–94), the Sea Ray 330 is a more stylish boat than her predecessor with a softer profile, increased fuel capacity, and a redesigned hull bottom. The styling is low and lean—a company trademark in recent years—and it's notable that the hull of the 330 incorporates less transom deadrise than most other Sea Ray hulls. Belowdecks, the interior follows the standard Sundancer formula with a midcabin berth aft, full galley, convertible dinette, standup head with shower, and a double berth forward. Privacy curtains separate the sleeping areas from the main cabin, and three hanging lockers provide plenty of storage. In the cockpit, a four-person bench seat across the transom faces a smaller, aft-facing one behind the helmsman, and the gap can be filled to produce a large sun pad. Additional features include a transom door, cockpit wet bar, good engine access, transom storage locker, and wide side decks. Available with sterndrive or inboard power, twin 330hp MerCruiser sterndrives cruise the 330 Sundancer in the high 20s and reach a top speed of 35+ knots, and twin 310hp V-drive inboards cruise in the mid 20s and top out in the low 30s.

See Page 698 For Price Data

Length w/Pulpit	35'10"	Weight	11,200#
Hull Length	33'6"	Fuel	225 gals.
Beam	11'5"	Water	40 gals.
Draft, Inboards	2'1"	Hull Type	Modified-V
Draft, I/Os	3'0"	Deadrise Aft	17°

Sea Ray 330/350 Sundancer

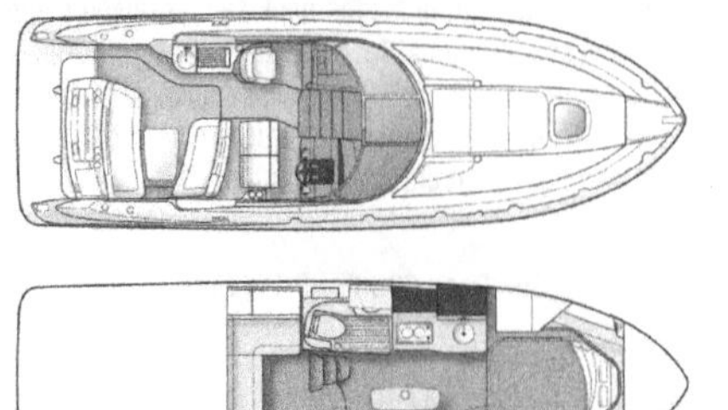

In a down economy quality products nearly always endure better than those whose principal appeal is price alone. Sea Ray ranks among the best names in the business for quality and they, along with other high-end brands like Tiara, Viking, Boston Whaler and Grady-White will survive a tough economy with innovative, cutting-edge products designed to stand the test of time. That description surely fits the Sea Ray 350 Sundancer—called the 330 Sundancer in 2008–09, and successor to the original 350 Sundancer model built in 2008–09. (Get that? Sea Ray doesn't make this stuff easy.) With her graceful styling and yacht-class amenities, this blue-chip yacht set the class standards when she came out in 2008 for express-boat luxury and sex appeal. Below decks, her midcabin accommodations are a compelling blend of cherrywood cabinets, maple flooring, Ultraleather seating, and designer galley appliances. Privacy curtains separate the sleeping areas from the main salon, and a flat-screen TV can be viewed from anywhere in the cabin. Note the innovative fiberglass arch top with aft sunshade. Offered with sterndrive or V-drive inboard power. Twin 370hp MerCruiser gas inboards cruise at 25 knots (mid 30s top).

See Page 698 For Price Data

Length	35'6"	Fuel	225 gals.
Beam	11'6"	Water	40 gals.
Draft, Up	2'9"	Waste	28 gals.
Draft, Down	3'6"	Hull Type	Deep-V
Weight	15,400#	Deadrise Aft	21°

Sea Ray 340 Amberjack

2001–03

A versatile boat capable of serious fishing activities as well as comfortable family cruising, the Sea Ray 340 Amberjack (called the 330 Express Cruiser in 1997–2001) is one of the roomiest boats in her class thanks to a super-wide 13-foot, 5-inch beam. Indeed, this is a big 33-footer with a wide-open cockpit and a very spacious interior. Built on a fully cored deep-V hull with prop pockets, the original Express Cruiser floorplan was arranged with a V-berth in the forward stateroom and a sofa in the salon. In 2001—when she became the 340 Amberjack—the interior was redesigned to include an angled double berth forward and a full-size dinette in the salon. In both layouts the stateroom is separated from the salon by two sliding doors. Cockpit amenities include an in-deck livewell and fish box, a foldaway bench seat at the transom, and a clever dual-purpose bait-prep station/wet bar behind the helm seat. The entire bridge deck can be raised electrically for engine access. Additional features include a centerline windshield vent, radar arch, wide side decks, and rod storage in the cabin sole. Twin 370hp MerCruiser inboards cruise at 20 knots and top out at close to 30 knots.

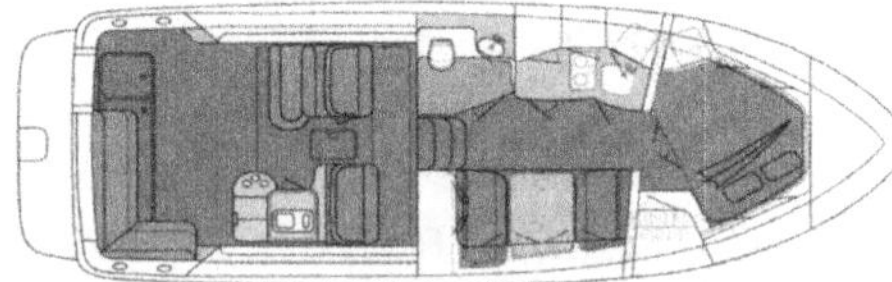

See Page 698 For Price Data

Length w/Platform	38'0"	Fuel	275 gals.
Hull Length	33'6"	Water	50 gals.
Beam	13'5"	Waste	28 gals.
Draft	3'0"	Hull Type	Deep-V
Weight	16,500#	Deadrise Aft	19.5°

Sea Ray 340 Sundancer

1999–2002

A popular boat for Sea Ray, the 340 Sundancer (note that an earlier 340 Sundancer was produced from 1984–89) is a good example of why Sea Ray continues to lead the market for midcabin express boats. Attractively styled and built to high standards, the 340 is a superb entertainment platform with a wide-open interior and a cockpit large enough to accommodate a small crowd. Two floorplans were available, both with the forward stateroom open to the main cabin and a mid-stateroom disguised as a sunken conversation area by day. Privacy curtains separate the sleeping areas from the salon, and a hidden TV/VCR pulls out and swivels so it can be viewed from anywhere in the boat. Rich cherry woodwork and posh furnishings highlight the Sundancer's interior, but storage is hard to come by. Topside, an adjustable helm seat overlooks a tiered dash configuration, and facing bench seats, a cockpit table, and wet bar make the cockpit a comfortable place for guests. On the downside, the engine compartment is a tight fit and the side decks are narrow. Twin 320hp MerCruiser V-drive inboards cruise the 340 Sundancer at 20 knots and reach a top speed of around 30 knots.

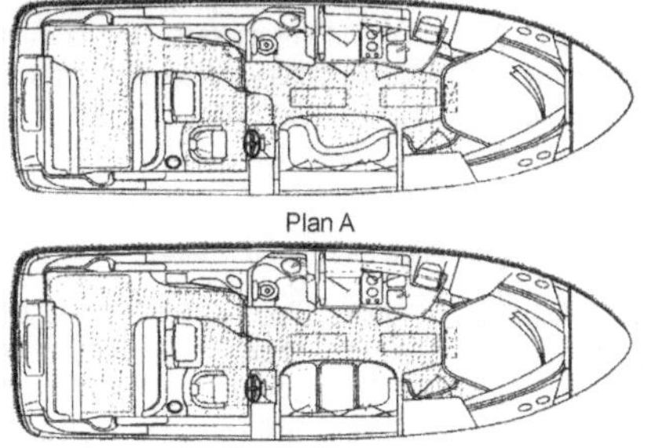
Plan A

Plan B

See Page 698 For Price Data

Length w/Platform	33'6"	Fuel	225 gals.
Beam	11'5"	Water	40 gals.
Draft	2'5"	Waste	28 gals.
Weight	13,000#	Hull Type	Modified-V
Clearance	NA	Deadrise Aft	17°

Sea Ray 340 Sundancer

Introduced in 2003, the Sea Ray 340 Sundancer replaced the previous 340 Sundancer (1999–2002)—a popular model in the Sea Ray fleet for several years. Wider in the beam than her predecessor, with a newly designed cockpit and a deep-V hull, the sleek styling of the 340 Sundancer conceals an interior that seems remarkably spacious for a 34-foot boat. The cabin is well lit with seven ports and overhead hatches, and the upscale decor is accented with rich cherry cabinets and earth tone fabrics and upholstery. The layout is typical of most Sundancer interiors with a pedestal berth forward and convertible settees in the salon and midcabin area. Corian counters and quality hardware are found in the galley, and privacy curtains separate the sleeping areas from the main cabin. Semicircular lounge seating is aft in the cockpit, and an electric hatch lifts to reveal a rather compact engine compartment. The helm is notable for its excellent design and good visibility. A premium express finished to very high standards, MerCruiser 370hp V-drive inboards cruise the Sea Ray 340 Sundancer at 24–25 knots and reach a top speed in the low 30s.

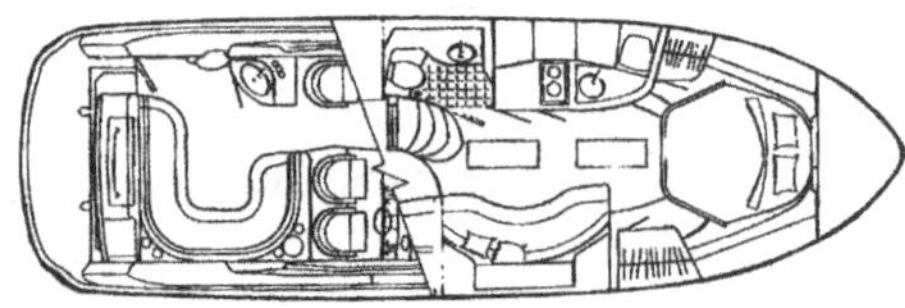

See Page 698 For Price Data

Length	37'6"	Fuel	225 gals.
Beam	12'0"	Water	45 gals.
Draft, Up	2'3"	Waste	28 gals.
Draft, Down	3'1"	Hull Type	Deep-V
Weight	15,500#	Deadrise Aft	21°

Sea Ray 350/370 Express Cruiser

Like most Sea Ray models, the 350 Express Cruiser (called the 370 Express Cruiser in 1993–95) has aged well over the years. Styling trends are a moving target, of course, but looking at a boat as old as the 350/370 Express is to appreciate the skills of past-generation Sea Ray designers. Built on a deep-V hull with prop pockets and a wide 12-foot, 4-inch beam, the interior of the Express Cruiser differs from Sea Ray's Sundancer models in that there is no mid-stateroom below the helm. A huge semicircular sofa that converts to a sleeper for two dominates the wide-open salon. Forward, through a privacy curtain, the stateroom has an angled double bed as well as a mirrored vanity. The head contains a separate stall shower, and an optional TV/VCR swivels out for easy viewing from anywhere in the cabin. Topside, the spacious single-level cockpit has a double helm seat forward, an aft-facing double cockpit seat, wet bar, and a bench seat at the transom. Note that in 1994 the original sliding cabin windows were replaced with oval ports. Standard 310hp MerCruiser inboards cruise at 20 knots and reach a top speed of 28–29 knots.

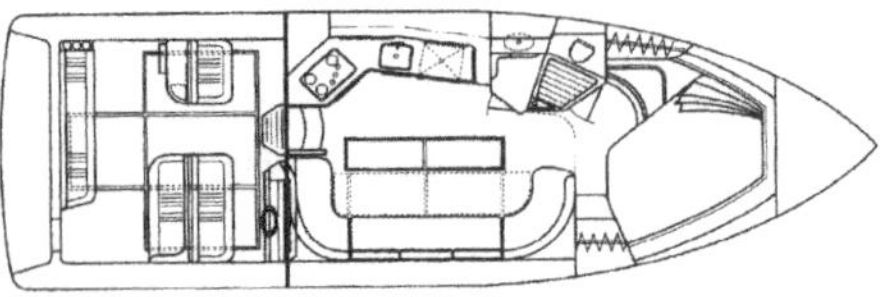

See Page 698 For Price Data

Length w/Pulpit	39'5"	Fuel	250 gals.
Hull Length	36'10"	Water	70 gals.
Beam	12'4"	Waste	20 gals.
Draft	2'5"	Hull Type	Deep-V
Weight	13,100#	Deadrise Aft	21°

Sea Ray 350/370 Sundancer

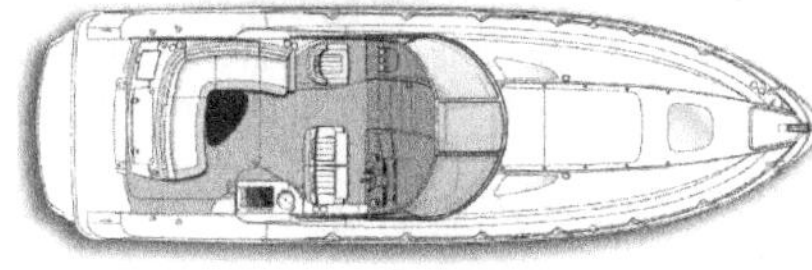

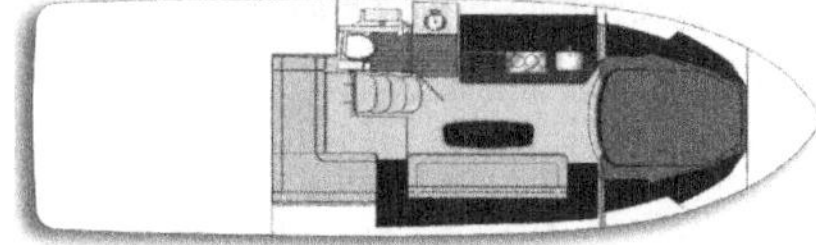

With her seamless hardtop, large hull windows, and sweeping sheerline the Sea Ray 370 Sundancer (called the 350 Sundancer in 2008–09) strikes the right balance of innovative design and next-generation styling. Introduced in 2008, the 370 became yet another Sundancer sales success in spite of a severely depressed boating economy. Nearly all late-model Sundancers are built on deep-V hulls with cored hullsides and a solid fiberglass bottom. While Sundancers are generally known for their cutting-edge styling, the 370's especially lush cabin accommodations are a match for the most expensive European sportyachts. With 6'7" of cabin headroom and a huge mid-stateroom, the interior is that of a considerably larger boat. The 370's comfortable cockpit can seat a small crowd and includes a deluxe wet bar with refrigerator, teak cockpit table, power engine-room hatch, and a clever aft-facing transom seat that folds out of the lazarette and overlooks the swim platform. The swivel helm and companion seats are a nice touch. Cruise at 24–26 knots with 375hp gas I/Os, and about 20 knots with V-drive inboards. Axius power with joystick control is also available.

See Page 698 For Price Data

Length	37'6"	Fuel	225 gals.
Beam	12'0"	Water	50 gals.
Draft, Up	2'3"	Waste	28 gals.
Draft, Down	3'3"	Hull Type	Deep-V
Weight	18,064#	Deadrise Aft	21°

Sea Ray 36 Sedan Bridge

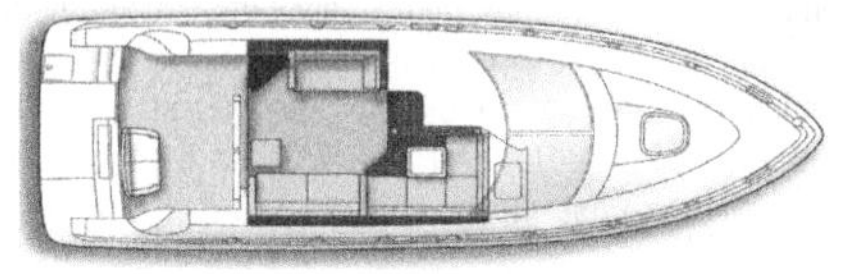

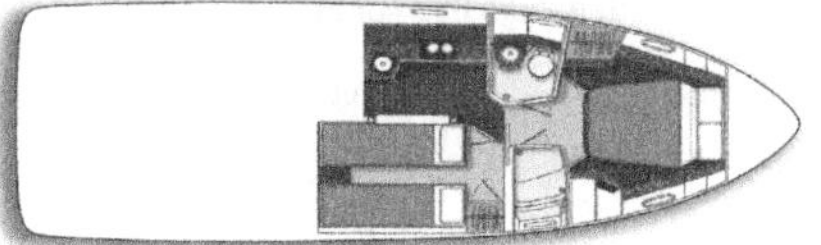

With her seamless hardtop, sleek profile and spacious interior, the 36 Sedan Bridge made good on the Sea Ray promise of cutting-edge styling and luxury-class accommodations. At 36 feet, she falls into one of those elusive sweet sports in the boating market—not too big for gas engines (which kept the price down), and not too small to have the two-stateroom floorplan most families require for a weekend on the water. Built on a modified-V hull with a generous 13-foot beam, the galley-down interior of the 36 Sedan Bridge is an appealing blend of cherrywood cabinets, Ultraleather seating, Corian counters, and designer galley appliances. An elevated dinette is forward in the salon, and wraparound cabin windows provide panoramic views of the water. A queen island bed is in the master stateroom, and twin single beds are in the guest cabin. Note the space-saving split head configuration—sink and toilet to port, shower stall to starboard. An in-floor galley compartment offers much-needed storage space. Topside, the helm console has space for flush-mounting electronics. The engineroom is a seriously tight fit. Gas 370hp inboards cruise at 20 knots; optional 380hp Cummins diesels cruise at 22+knots.

See Page 698 For Price Data

Length	38'4"	Fuel	300 gals.
Beam	13'0"	Water	75 gals.
Draft	3'4"	Waste	35 gals.
Weight	22,000#	Hull Type	Modified-V
Clearance	18'0"	Deadrise Aft	17°

Sea Ray 360 Sundancer

2002–06

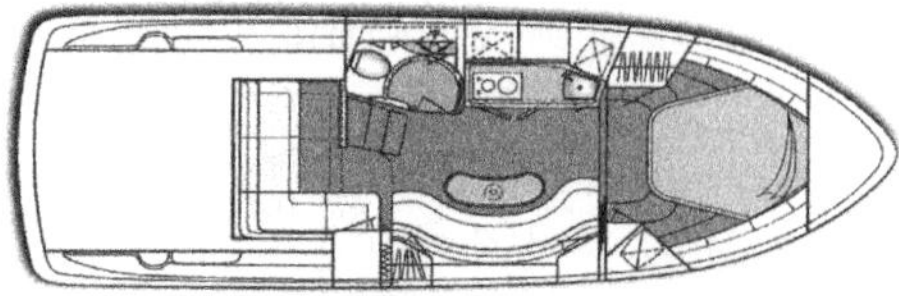

Knowledgeable cruisers will be hard-pressed to find a more capable midsized express than the Sea Ray 360 Sundancer. Gracefully styled and impressively finished, the 360 delivers a careful balance of performance and comfort, albeit at a rather upscale price. Built on a deep-V hull with moderate beam, the Sundancer's midcabin interior gets high marks for its quality furnishings and fixtures. This is a comfortable layout with plenty of storage, a built-in entertainment center, a plush Ultraleather lounge, and excellent headroom. A two-part pocket door provides privacy for the forward stateroom, and both the salon sofa and midcabin lounge convert easily into double berths. At the helm, a bucket seat with a flip-up bolster allows for standup driving and there's space in the tiered, burled dash for electronics. Engine access is excellent; the entire cockpit floor rises on hydraulic rams to completely expose the motors and V-drives. Additional features include an extended swim platform, an underwater exhaust system, transom storage locker, and cockpit wet bar. MerCruiser 8.1-liter 370hp V-drive gas engines cruise the 360 Sundancer at 18 knots and reach a top speed of 30+ knots.

See Page 698 For Price Data

Length w/Platform	39'0"	Fuel	250 gals.
Beam	12'6"	Water	55 gals.
Draft	3'1"	Waste	35 gals.
Weight	18,500#	Hull Type	Deep-V
Clearance	11'4"	Deadrise Aft	21°

Sea Ray 370 Express Cruiser

1997–2000

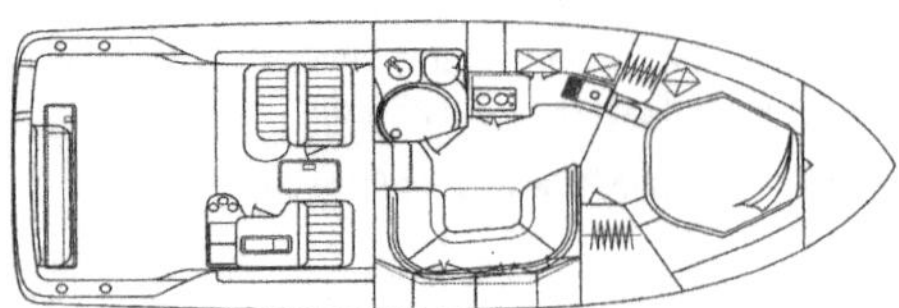

The 370 Express Cruiser was an effort by Sea Ray to develop a serious, tournament-level fishing boat. In that regard, she followed the approach Tiara so successfully pioneered with their 3600 and 3700 Open models—a top-quality express with a big, well-designed cockpit and a lavish, family-friendly interior. Not inexpensive, the Sea Ray 370 is a big boat thanks to her wide 14-foot, 2-inch beam. The cockpit offers lots of space for fishing, and there's plenty of room for a fighting chair or for storing loose gear such as coolers. A bait-prep center with sink is positioned for easy access, and a pair of lift-out fish boxes were standard. The 370's machinery space is reached via a centerline hatch, and for complete access the bridge sole can be raised at the push of a button. Below, the plush interior will sleep four with a double berth in the private bow stateroom, and a lounge to starboard that pulls out into a double berth. Additional features include rod storage beneath the cabin sole, a fold-up transom seat, prop pockets, and a fully cored hull. Optional 340hp Caterpillar diesels cruise the 370 Express Cruiser in the mid 20s and deliver a top speed of around 30 knots.

See Page 698 For Price Data

Length w/Platform	41'4"	Fuel	350 gals.
Hull Length	37'0"	Water	70 gals.
Beam	14'2"	Waste	28 gals.
Draft	3'3"	Hull Type	Deep-V
Weight	18,000#	Deadrise Aft	19.5°

Sea Ray 370 Sedan Bridge

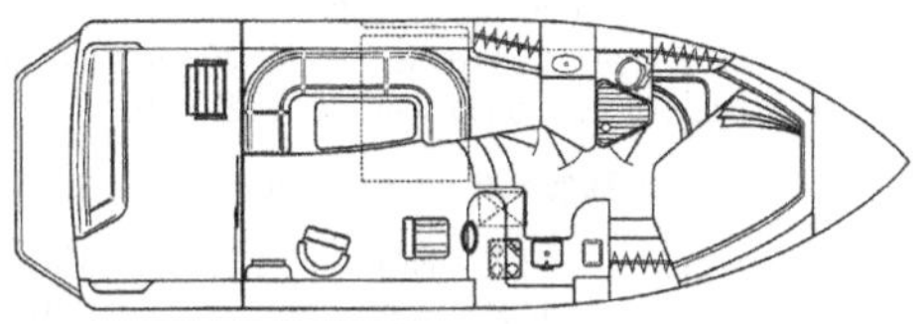

With her long foredeck and relatively small cockpit, the 370 Sedan Bridge is a maxi-volume family cruiser with conservative lines and a very spacious interior. She's built on solid fiberglass deep-V with prop pockets, moderate beam, and side-dumping exhausts. Below, the two-stateroom floorplan of the 370 features an expansive salon with a full-length settee, removable dinette table, breakfast bar, and large wraparound cabin windows. An angled double berth resides in the bow stateroom, and the portside guest cabin has another double berth extending below the salon sole. Oak trim and earth-tone wall coverings highlight the interior, and the double-entry head has a separate stall shower. Topside, the cockpit includes a transom door and optional bench seating, while the flybridge is arranged with L-shaped lounge seating aft of the helm. On the downside, the side decks are rather narrow. Additional features include a radar arch, swim platform, tilt steering wheel, and a bow pulpit. A lower helm station was optional. Standard 310hp MerCruiser gas inboards cruise the 370 Sedan Bridge at 18 knots and deliver a top speed in the mid to high 20s.

See Page 698 For Price Data

Length w/Platform	40'10"	Fuel	250 gals.
Hull Length	36'10"	Water	70 gals.
Beam	12'4"	Waste	20 gals.
Draft	2'7"	Hull Type	Deep-V
Weight	14,600#	Deadrise Aft	21°

Sea Ray 370 Sundancer

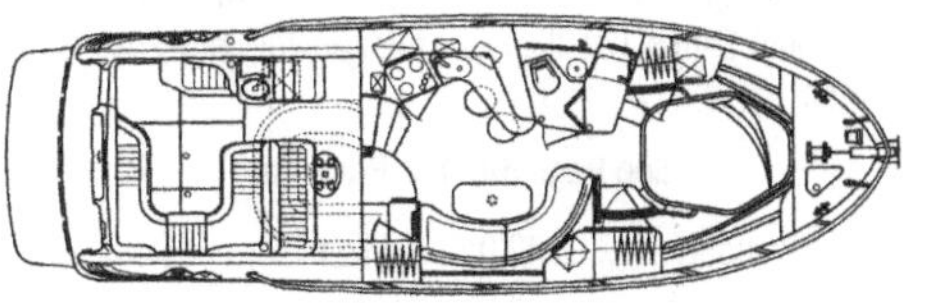

For years, Sea Ray has dominated the market for midcabin cruisers with their state-of-the-art styling and innovative features. The introduction in 1995 of the 370 Sundancer was yet another in the company's evolving series of Sundancer models, each a little nicer than the last, and each a little more expensive. Built on a fully cored hull, the Sundancer's interior seems unusually spacious, perhaps because the aft stateroom—with its U-shaped settee and removable table—is wide open to the main cabin. A sliding privacy door closes off the forward stateroom by night, and the salon sofa converts to a double bed for extra guests. This is, in fact, a very well executed layout, and the built-in breakfast bar, faux granite countertop, and sculptured overhead panels are worthy of note. Topside, the 370's cockpit can easily handle a crowd, and a wet bar with sink, cooler, trash bin, and cutting board were standard. Additional features include an underwater exhaust system, a distinctive two-tier swim platform, good engine access, and very secure side decks. Twin V-drive 310hp gas inboards cruise the 370 Sundancer at 18 knots (about 30 knots top), and 300hp Cummins diesels cruise in the low 20s.

See Page 699 For Price Data

Length w/Pulpit	40'1"	Fuel	275 gals.
Hull Length	37'6"	Water	70 gals.
Beam	12'7"	Waste	28 gals.
Draft	2'8"	Hull Type	Deep-V
Weight	17,000#	Deadrise Aft	20°

Sea Ray 370/380 Aft Cabin

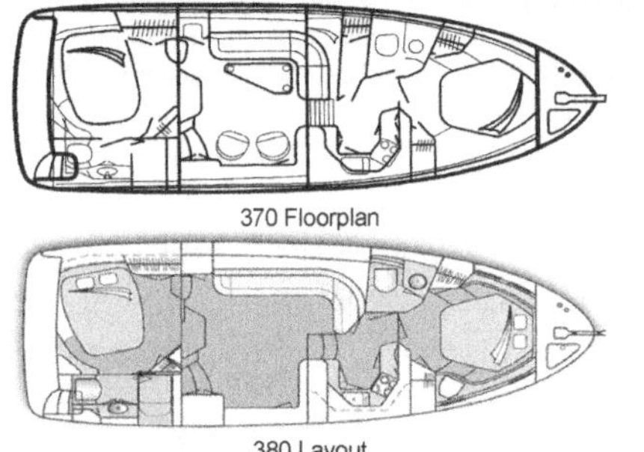
370 Floorplan

380 Layout

One of Sea Ray's infrequent aft-cabin models, the 370 Aft Cabin (called the 380 Aft Cabin in 2000–01) combined a rakish profile with comfortable accommodations and good offshore performance. She rides on a fully cored hull with shallow prop pockets, underwater exhausts, and a wide 14-foot, 3-inch beam. Aft-cabin boats under 40 feet usually have rather ungainly lines in order to incorporate a big master stateroom, and the 370/380 does in fact have a slightly "full-bodied" look about her. Her appeal lies below, however, where Sea Ray designers were able to incorporate a spacious and very inviting interior. Both staterooms include double berths, and a third mini-stateroom opposite the galley can be configured as a utility room. (Note that in 2000 this third cabin was eliminated in favor of an enlarged salon.) Topside, the aft deck has a built-in wet bar as well as wing doors, while the flybridge is arranged with the helm forward and lounge seating for four. On the downside, the engineroom—accessed via a gas-assist hatch in the salon sole—is a tight fit, and the side decks are narrow. Twin 380hp gas engines cruise at 20 knots (close to 30 knots top), and 340hp Cat diesels will reach a top speed of 22–23 knots.

See Page 699 For Price Data

Length	38'2"	Fuel	300 gals.
Beam	14'3"	Water	100 gals.
Draft	3'1"	Waste	55 gals.
Weight	23,800#	Hull Type	Modified-V
Clearance, Arch	16'4"	Deadrise Aft	19.5°

Sea Ray 380 Sundancer

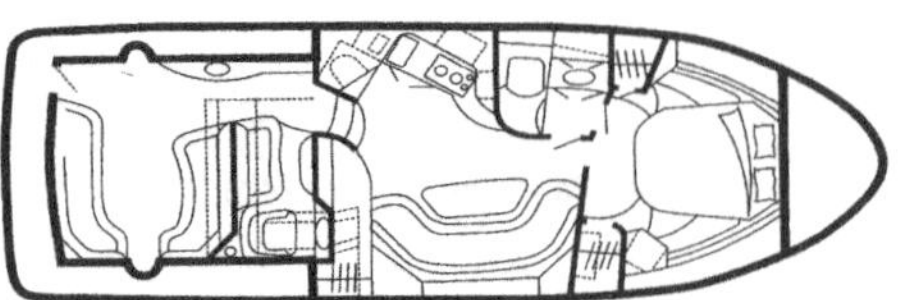

Great styling has long been a Sea Ray trademark, and while few American sportboats are as glamorous as their European counterparts the quality found in late-model Sundancers is second to none. Built on a fully cored deep-V hull with a wide beam, few imports can match the spacious interior of the 380 Sundancer with her superb galley (including a full-size refrigerator), excellent storage, and wide-open floorplan. The layout is typical of most Sundancers with double berths fore and aft and a sofa in the salon that converts to a double berth for extra guests. The midcabin stateroom serves as a conversation area during the day, and then electrically converts into a bed at night. A door separates the forward stateroom from the main cabin, while a curtain provides privacy for the midcabin. On deck, the spacious cockpit provides wraparound seating for six to seven and comes with a wet bar, fender storage, and a removable table that converts into a sun pad. An electric hatch provides access to a rather compact engine compartment. Standard 370hp V-drive inboards cruise at 18 knots (mid 20s top), and optional 340hp Cat diesels cruise in the mid 20s (about 30 knots top).

See Page 699 For Price Data

Length w/Platform	42'0"	Fuel	275 gals.
Hull Length	38'0"	Water	70 gals.
Beam	13'0"	Waste	42 gals.
Draft	3'4"	Hull Type	Deep-V
Weight	18,300##	Deadrise Aft	19.5°

Sea Ray 38/390 Sundancer

Sea Ray didn't get to where they are today by cutting corners. Well, they used to go short on fit and finish but that was years ago; these days the Sea Ray brand is golden with most boaters. The 38 Sundancer (called the 390 Sundancer in 2010–11) is a case in point. Introduced in 2006, she rides on a deep-V hull with cored hullsides, prop pockets, and a solid fiberglass bottom. While Sundancers are generally known for their cutting-edge styling—note the vertical hull ports and seamless hardtop with aft sunshade—the lush accommodations of the 38 Sundancer are a match for the best European sportyachts her size. With 6'7" of cabin headroom, a huge mid-stateroom, and a private bow stateroom with flat-screen TV, the interior has the look and feel of a small motoryacht. The Sundancer's wide-open cockpit with centerline walk-through provides facing lounge seating for a small crowd. The swivel helm seat with flip-up bolster is a nice touch. A transom storage locker, power engineroom hatch, foredeck sun pads, underwater exhausts, and anchor washdown system were standard. MerCruiser 420hp gas inboards cruise at 20 knots; optional 380hp Cummins diesels cruise at 25–26 knots.

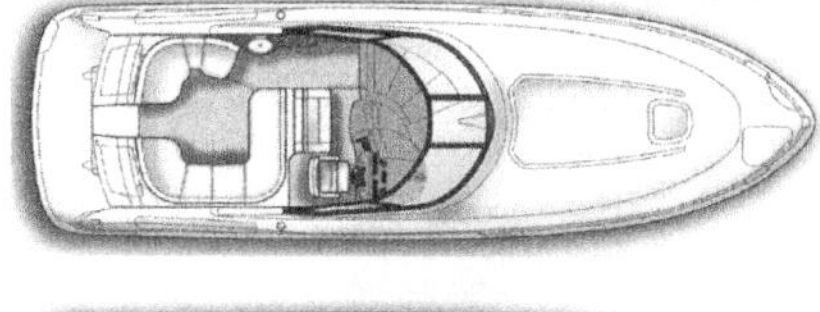

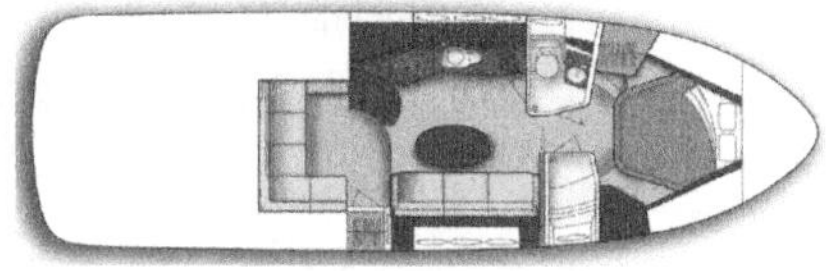

See Page 699 For Price Data

Length Overall	39'0"	Fuel	250 gals.
Beam	12'6"	Water	55 gals.
Draft	3'1"	Waste	35 gals.
Weight	19,400#	Hull Type	Deep-V
Clearance	12'1"	Deadrise Aft	21°

Sea Ray 390 Motoryacht; 40 MY

Building on their reputation for design innovation, Sea Ray's 390 Motor Yacht differs from traditional motor yachts in that the helm and aft deck of the 390 are on the same level. The advantage of this layout is that it keeps the captain in the social center of the boat rather than isolated on a flybridge; the disadvantage is seen in the 390's ungainly, full-bodied profile. From the standpoint of comfort, however, the 390 receives high marks for her spacious interior and luxurious accommodations. The light-filled salon is accented with high-gloss cherry cabinets and leather upholstery, and a high/low table with stools and a breakfast bar provide dining space. The galley, which is down from the salon level, benefits from the natural light that flows from an overhead skylight. An optional washer/dryer is found under the steps that lead from the galley to the salon. Topside, an extended hardtop shelters the small aft deck with its wet bar, acrylic wing doors, and bench seating. A stairway—with a safety railing—leads down to the swim platform. Standard 370hp gas inboards cruise at 18 knots (25–26 knots top), and optional 446hp Cummins diesels cruise in the low 20s (about 25 knots top).

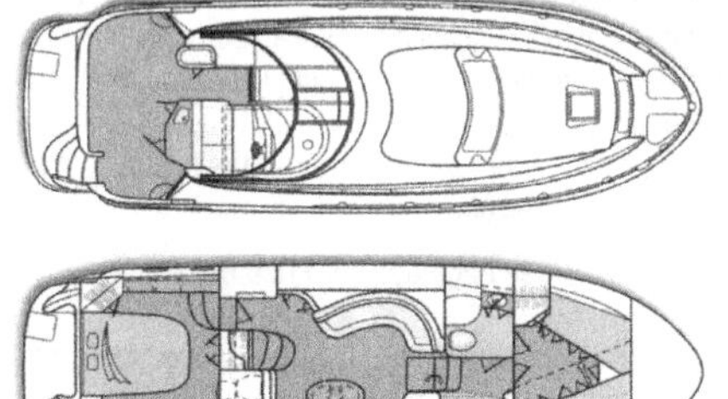

See Page 699 For Price Data

Length w/Platform	41'9"	Fuel	300 gals.
Beam	14'3"	Water	100 gals.
Draft	3'0"	Waste	54 gals.
Weight	26,500#	Hull Type	Modified-V
Clearance	13'8"	Deadrise Aft	15°

Sea Ray 390/40 Sundancer

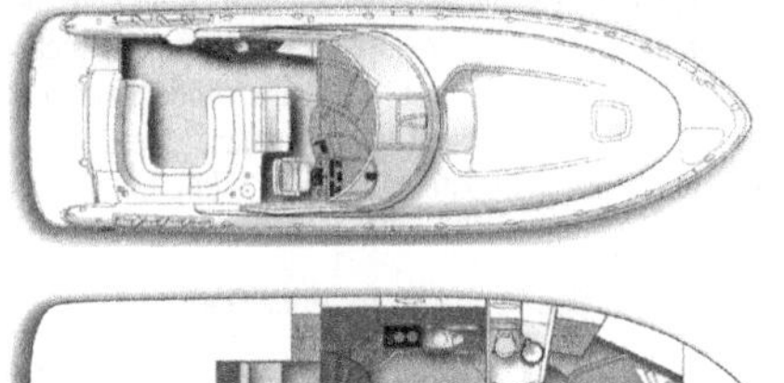

Among several big express cruisers available in today's market, the Sea Ray 390 Sundancer (called the 40 Sundancer in 2006–09) is notable for her sleek styling and distinctive fiberglass hardtop. Sea Ray has been building good-quality family cruisers since the 1980s but it's only been in the last few years that the company has become a recognized leader in sportboat styling and design. Built on a deep-V hull with prop pockets and a solid fiberglass bottom, the lavish interior of the 390 Sundancer is a blend of high-gloss cherrywood cabinets, Ultraleather upholstery, and vinyl wall coverings. A flat-screen TV is built in above the galley countertop, and by splitting the head into two compartments—toilet to port and shower to starboard—the salon dimensions are those of a slightly larger boat. For privacy, a sliding door separates the master stateroom from the salon. The 390/40's cockpit is similar to other Sundancer layouts with a U-shaped seating area aft, flip-up helm seat, and Corian-topped wet bar with sink and faucet. The entire cockpit sole can be raised on hydraulic rams for access to the engines. With standard 370hp V-drive gas engines she'll cruise in the low 20s (about 30 knots top).

See Page 699 For Price Data

Length w/Platform	41'0"	Fuel	275 gals.
Beam	13'2"	Water	70 gals.
Draft	3'4"	Waste	42 gals.
Weight	19,300#	Hull Type	Deep-V
Clearance	13'3"	Deadrise Aft	19°

Sea Ray 400 Express Cruiser

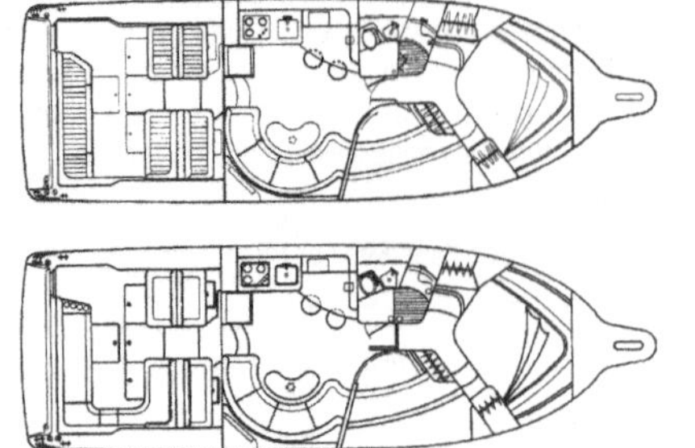

With her bold styling, huge cockpit, and luxurious interior the Sea Ray 400 Express Cruiser was considered a state-of-the-art boat when she was introduced back in 1992. This was the long-awaited replacement model for the 390 Express Cruiser (1984–91), and while she has less beam than her predecessor, she was a big step up in luxury and appearance. Built on a deep-V hull with a solid fiberglass bottom, the two-stateroom interior of the 400 Express offers comfortable accommodations for six. The master stateroom includes a pedestal island berth as well as a TV/VCR and a privacy door, and a circular pocket door closes off the starboard sitting room, converting it into a private stateroom with a full-size bed and convertible upper bunk. A separate shower stall is found in the head, and the large galley includes a breakfast bar and generous storage. On deck, double helm and companion seats are forward in the cockpit, while U-shaped seating aft converts into a sun pad. An extended swim platform was a popular option in later models. Twin 340hp Mercury inboards cruise at 18 knots (mid 20s top), and optional Cat 340hp diesels cruise in the mid 20s and reach a top speed of 28–29 knots.

See Page 699 For Price Data

Length w/Pulpit	45'7"	Fuel	300 gals.
Hull Length	40'4"	Water	100 gals.
Beam	13'0"	Waste	30 gals.
Draft	3'3"	Hull Type	Deep-V
Weight	18,000#	Deadrise Aft	19°

Sea Ray 400 Sedan Bridge

1996–2003

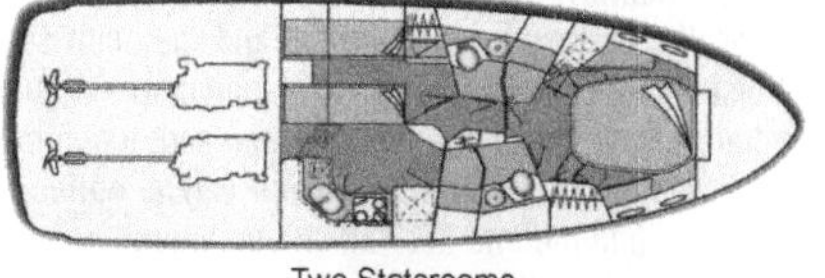
Two Staterooms

Three Staterooms

Sea Ray got it right with the 400 Sedan Bridge, a super-popular cruising yacht with a near perfect mix of European styling, upscale accommodations, and luxury-class amenities. Introduced in 1996, Sea Ray went on to sell hundreds of these yachts before production ended in 2003. Below decks, the interior of the 400 Sedan Bridge is an appealing display of high-gloss cherry joinery, Ultraleather salon seating, and quality hardware and appliances. Most were delivered with a two-stateroom, galley-down floorplan with dinette and two full heads. (An alternate three-stateroom, galley-up interior was optional.) In both layouts the master stateroom is forward with a pedestal queen berth, cedar-lined hanging lockers, TV/VCR, and en-suite head. (Note that the salon sofa converts to a bed at the touch of a button.) Cockpit amenities include aft bench seating, icemaker, molded flybridge steps, and transom door with gate. On the downside, the engineroom is a tight fit. Built on a fully cored hull with moderate beam, prop pockets, and underwater exhausts, 370hp MerCruiser inboards cruise the Sea Ray 400 Sedan Bridge at 20 knots (high 20s top), and optional 340hp Cat diesels cruise at 22 knots (about 25+ knots top).

See Page 699 For Price Data

Length w/Platform	44'0"	Fuel	350 gals.
Hull Length	41'6"	Water	120 gals.
Beam	14'3"	Waste	28 gals.
Draft	3'4"	Hull Type	Modified-V
Weight	22,000#	Deadrise Aft	18.5°

Sea Ray 400 Sundancer

1997–99

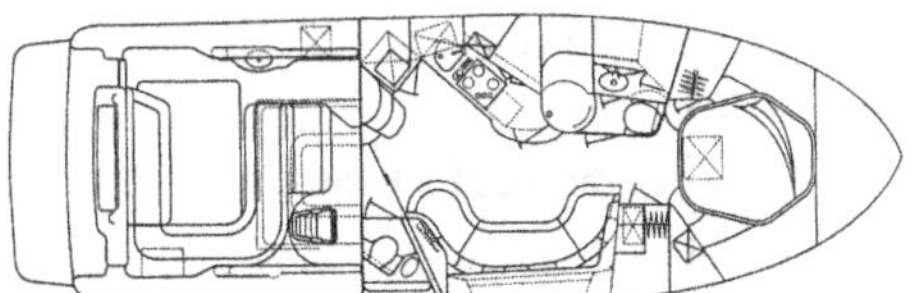

Long on styling and loaded with cruising amenities, the Sea Ray 400 Sundancer set the class standards in her day for sportcruiser luxury and elegance. She's built on a deep-V hull with a solid fiberglass bottom, moderate beam, and prop pockets to reduce the shaft angles of her V-drive engines. The midcabin floorplan of the 400 Sundancer is arranged in the conventional manner with the owner's stateroom forward, an open galley in the main cabin, and a midcabin stateroom/lounge with a privacy door. Note that there's a second head adjoining the midcabin—a very desirable feature indeed. The forward head has a stall shower, and the level of fit and finish throughout is second to none. Topside, the huge U-shaped cockpit lounge will seat a small crowd, and the entire aft section of the cockpit sole rises electrically without moving the aft seat for engine access. Foldaway boarding steps, a radar arch, and a transom storage locker were standard. An extended swim platform was a popular option in later models. Twin 340hp V-drive inboards cruise at 18 knots (mid 20s top), and optional Cat 340hp diesels cruise in the mid 20s (close to 30 knots top).

See Page 699 For Price Data

Length w/Platform	44'4"	Fuel	330 gals.
Hull Length	41'6"	Water	100 gals.
Beam	13'8"	Waste	28 gals.
Draft	3'4"	Hull Type	Deep-V
Weight	22,500#	Deadrise Aft	19°

Sea Ray 410 Express Cruiser

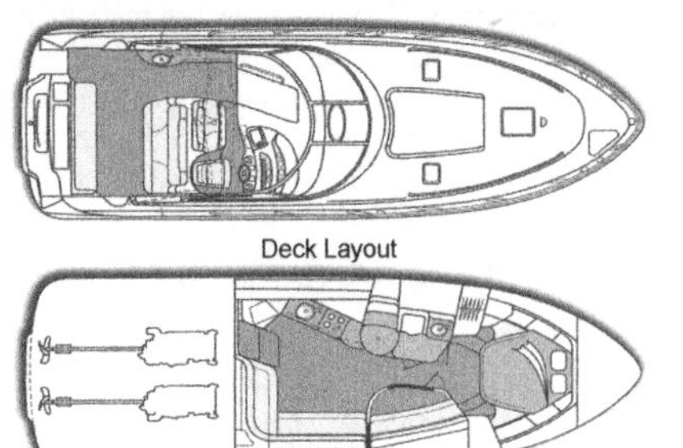
Deck Layout

Interior Floorplan

The signature attribute of Sea Ray cruisers over the past 20 years has been bold, cutting-edge styling. That was certainly on display in 2000 when Sea Ray introduced its new 410 Express Cruiser, an executive-class sportyacht with as much sex appeal as any of the European imports. Built on a fully cored hull with a wide beam, the 410's two-stateroom floorplan provides luxurious accommodations for six. The forward stateroom has a full-size pedestal bed as well as private head access, and a circular pocket door closes off the starboard sitting room, converting it into a private stateroom with twin bunks. The galley is huge with generous counter space and plenty of storage. High-gloss cherry woodwork, faux granite countertops, and decorator fabrics highlight the interior. Topside, the 410 Express Cruiser provides a large cockpit area as well as wide walkways to the foredeck. The forward cockpit sole lifts electrically for easy engine access, and the helm seat has a flip-up bolster so the captain can drive standing up. Additional features include a cockpit wet bar, foredeck sun pad, transom storage locker, and side exhausts. Among several engine options, 420hp Cat diesels cruise in the mid 20s (28–30 knots top).

See Page 699 For Price Data

Length w/Platform	45'6"	Fuel	335 gals.
Hull Length	41'6"	Water	100 gals.
Beam	13'10"	Waste	42 gals.
Draft	3'4"	Hull Type	Deep-V
Weight	21,000#	Deadrise Aft	19°

Sea Ray 410 Sundancer

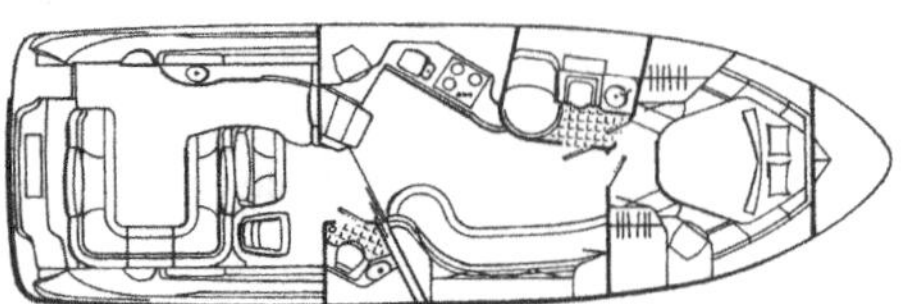

Sea Ray introduced the 410 Sundancer in 2000 as the replacement boat for the company's popular 400 Sundancer built in 1997–99. Great styling has long been a Sea Ray trademark, and while few American sportboats are as glamorous as their European counterparts the graceful lines of the 410 Sundancer will surely stand the test of time for many years to come. Built on a fully cored hull with a wide beam, the interior features a large bow stateroom with a full-size pedestal bed, TV/VCR, and private access to the forward head. The mid-stateroom, which is open to the salon, has an electrically convertible sleeper/sofa, and the well-organized galley includes plenty of storage and counter space. Both staterooms have doors rather than privacy curtains, and there are two heads in this layout, one for each stateroom. Topside, the cockpit has U-shaped seating with a sun pad, table, and a full wet bar. For engine access, the entire aft section of the cockpit sole can be raised at the flip of a switch. A modest performer with standard 370hp V-drive MerCruisers (16 knots cruise/mid 20s top), optional Cat 340hp V-drive diesels cruise the 410 Sundancer in the mid 20s and reach a top speed of 28–29 knots.

See Page 699 For Price Data

Length w/Platform	45'6"	Fuel	335 gals.
Hull Length	41'6"	Water	100 gals.
Beam	13'10"	Waste	42 gals.
Draft	3'2"	Hull Type	Deep-V
Weight	21,000#	Deadrise Aft	19°

Sea Ray 420 Aft Cabin

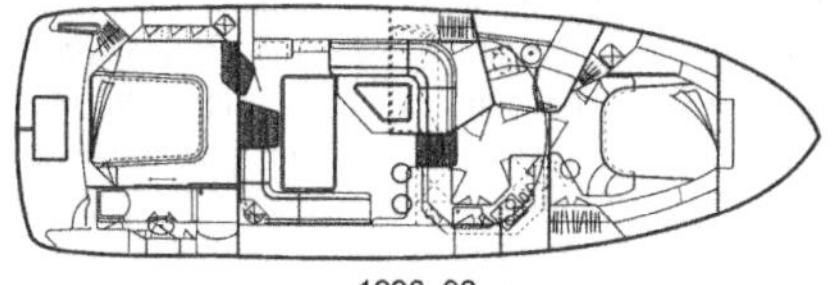
1996–98

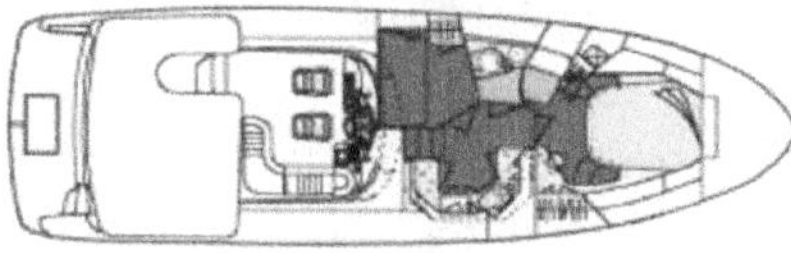
1999–2002

Creative styling, a spacious interior, and quality construction made the 420 Aft Cabin a popular yacht in the Sea Ray fleet during her production years. Aft-cabin yachts often look more like condos than boats, but the sleek profile of the 420 speaks volumes about Sea Ray's ability to incorporate European styling influences in an American-built yacht. Built on a fully cored hull with prop pockets and underwater exhausts, the 420 has more interior space than seems possible in a yacht her size. The three-stateroom floorplan is arranged with double beds in the fore and aft staterooms, while the second guest stateroom—which can also be configured as a laundry room—extends under the salon sole. The galley is down, which allows space in the salon for an L-shaped dinette. Topside, a fiberglass panel surrounds the aft deck, and molded steps descend to the wide swim platform. Additional features include a spacious flybridge, wide side decks, radar arch, transom storage compartment, and an aft deck wet bar. On the downside, the engineroom is a tight fit. Among several engine choices, twin 420hp Cat (or 430hp Cummins) diesels cruise in the mid 20s and reach 27–28 knots top.

See Page 699 For Price Data

Length	45'5"	Fuel	350 gals.
Beam	14'3"	Water	120 gals.
Draft	3'1"	Waste	55 gals.
Weight	27,000#	Hull Type	Modified-V
Clearance	15'6"	Deadrise Aft	18.5°

Sea Ray 420/44 Sedan Bridge

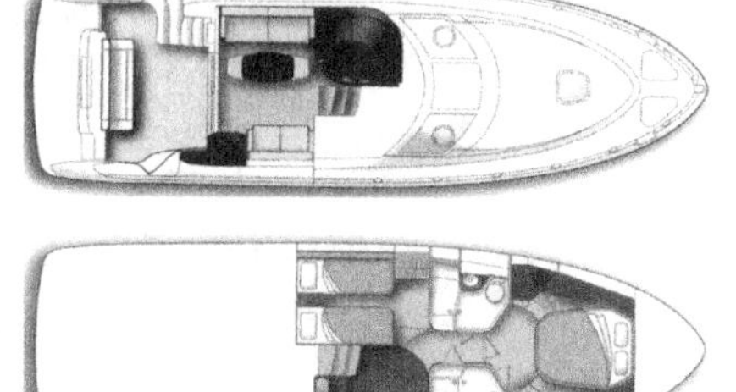

The Sea Ray 420 Sedan Bridge (called 44 Sedan Bridge in 2006–09) combines the bold, cutting-edge styling and lush accommodations boating enthusiasts have come to expect in late-model Sea Ray yachts. By any standard, the 420 is a strikingly handsome design both inside and out. Wood floors, oversized windows, and plush Ultraleather sofas are just a few of the luxuries found in the spacious cabin. A raised dining area provides a panoramic view of the outdoors, and deep-pile carpeting and high-gloss cherry cabinets highlight the decor. Below, a small guest cabin to port has twin single beds, while the forward master stateroom features a queen-size island berth and a 13-inch TV/DVD player. A lower helm was optional as was a washer/dryer, which is hidden under the galley stairs. Both head compartments are fitted with shower stalls. A sliding glass door opens to the cockpit with its walk-through transom, transom bench seat, and molded flybridge stairs. Offering good visibility fore and aft, the extended flybridge includes a large U-shaped aft seat with removable table. Cummins 480hp diesels cruise the 420 Sedan Bridge in the mid 20s and reach about 30 knots top.

See Page 699 For Price Data

Length Overall	45'5"	Fuel	350 gals.
Beam	14'3"	Water	120 gals.
Draft	3'6"	Waste	42 gals.
Weight	28,500#	Hull Type	Modified-V
Clearance	NA	Deadrise Aft	18°

Sea Ray 420/440 Sundancer

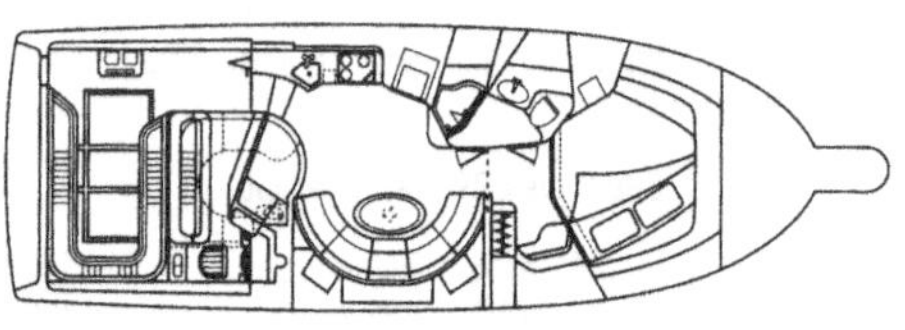

One of the largest American-built express yachts of her era, the 420 Sundancer (called the 440 Sundancer in 1992–95) took Sea Ray styling and luxury to the next level when she was introduced in 1990. With her powerful lines, spacious cockpit, and expansive two-stateroom interior the 420/440 Sundancer was further evidence of Sea Ray's dominance in the express cruiser market. She's built on a deep-V hull with a solid fiberglass bottom and a wide 13-foot, 11-inch beam. (Note that the 440's hull has prop pockets while the original 420 hull did not.) Below decks, the Sundancer's wide-open interior is a blend of curved bulkheads, white Formica cabinets, and light oak woodwork. Pocket doors provide privacy for both staterooms, and the step-down mid cabin features a vanity and concealed portable head. Topside, the cockpit is arranged with a triple companion seat at the helm, wet bar, and U-shaped lounge seating aft. In 1994 the original sliding cabin windows were replaced with oval ports. Twin 330hp MerCruiser V-drive gas inboards cruise at 17–18 knots (low-to-mid 20s top), and 300hp Cat (or Cummins) diesels cruise at 20 knots. Optional 425hp Cats top out in the high 20s.

See Page 699 For Price Data

Length w/Pulpit	47'1"	Fuel	400 gals.
Hull Length	44'0"	Water	100 gals.
Beam	13'11"	Waste	28 gals.
Draft	3'3"	Hull Type	Deep-V
Weight	20,000#	Deadrise Aft	19°

Sea Ray 420/44 Sundancer

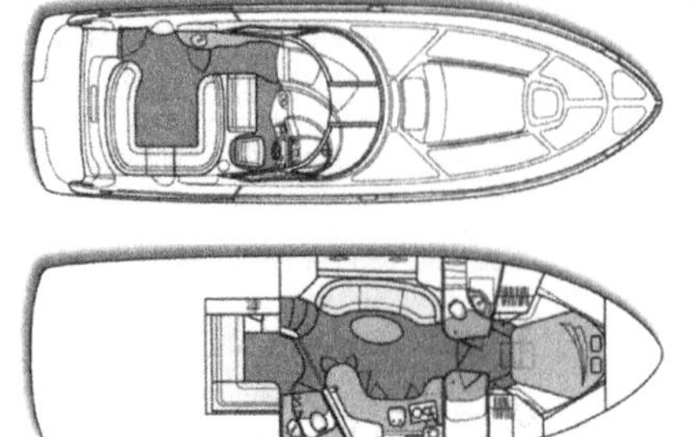

Yet another Sea Ray sales success story, the 420 Sundancer (called the 44 Sundancer in 2006–08) set the gold standard for express yacht styling and luxury during her production years. Indeed, her muscular lines compared well with the best Mediterranean sportcruisers of her era, and a large cockpit and spacious interior made many of her European counterparts seem small in comparison. Built on a deep-V hull with prop pockets and a relatively wide 14-foot beam, the luxurious two-stateroom, two-head floorplan of the 420 Sundancer is an impressive blend of high-gloss cherry joinery, Ultraleather seating, and designer fabrics. Privacy doors (not curtains) separate both staterooms from the salon, and the Sundancer's full-service galley includes an under-counter refrigerator/freezer in addition to Corian counters and hardwood flooring. Topside, a flip-up bolster seat is standard at the helm, and the entire cockpit sole can be raised at the push of a button for engine access. Note the extended swim platform, split forward head, and underwater exhaust system. A good performer with Cummins 450hp V-drive diesels, the 420 Sundancer will cruise in the mid 20s and top out around 30 knots.

See Page 699 For Price Data

Length Overall	45'0"	Fuel	335 gals.
Beam	14'0"	Water	100 gals.
Draft	3'6"	Waste	42 gals.
Weight	22,500#	Hull Type	Deep-V
Clearance	11'3"	Deadrise Aft	19°

Sea Ray 43/470 Sundancer

2009–Current

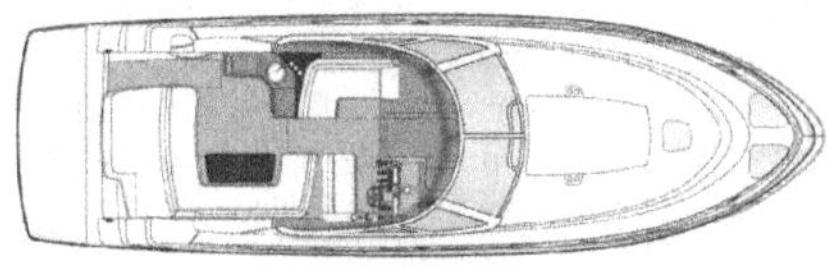

Designed specifically for Zeus pod drives, the Sea Ray 470 Sundancer (called the 43 Sundancer in 2009) combines the powerful styling and lush accommodations common to all recent Sundancer models with the efficiency and performance gains provided by Zeus pod-drive propulsion. Built on a deep-V hull with cored hullsides and a wide 14-foot beam, the spacious two-stateroom, two-head interior of the 470 Sundancer is an appealing blend of high-gloss cherry cabinets, Ultraleather seating, hardwood flooring, and premium galley appliances. Both staterooms are private, and the forward head is split with the toilet and sink to port and the shower to starboard. A 26" drop-down TV/DVD is standard in the salon. The 470's sleek fiberglass hardtop—which shades a good part of the cockpit—includes dual power sunroofs as well as power side windows. Note the built-in chart table under helm seat. Additional features include a power engine compartment hatch, Euro-style aft sun pad, deluxe cockpit wet bar with refrigerator, underwater exhaust system, and a large extended swim platform. Joystick control makes docking easy. Cruise at 25 knots (low 30s top) with optional 480hp Cummins diesels.

See Page 699 For Price Data

Length Overall	47'3"	Fuel	350 gals.
Beam	14'0"	Water	100 gals.
Draft (Zeus)	4'0"	Waste	42 gals.
Weight	28,500#	Hull Type	Deep-V
Clearance	14'2"	Deadrise Aft	19°

Sea Ray 440 Express Bridge

1993–98

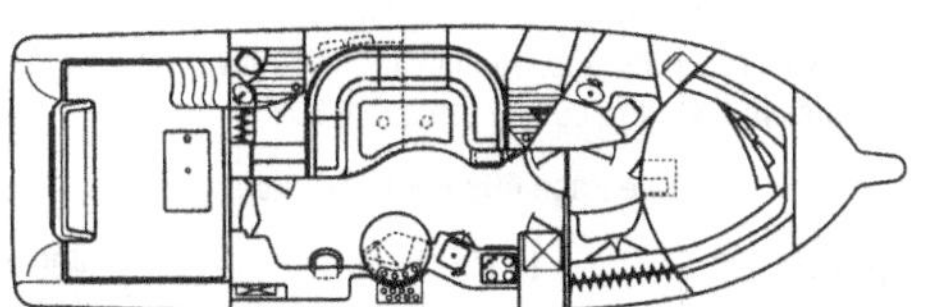

Distinctive styling and an enormous full-beam interior are just two of the many features that made the 440 Express Bridge a popular model for Sea Ray in the mid 1990s. Like most "express bridge" designs with their space-saving V-drive power and low deckhouse profiles, the 440's sunken salon utilizes the entire width of the hull to create a huge, wide-open floorplan laid out on a single level. With the engines under the cockpit there's even room for an innovative midcabin stateroom—complete with a second head—beneath the molded cockpit bridge steps, something not seen in any previous express bridge models. Built on a fully cored hull with moderate beam and prop pockets to reduce the shaft angles, the 440's huge, party-time flybridge is arranged with the wraparound helm console/settee on the centerline and additional bench seating forward. A walk-through gate in the flybridge coaming provides access to the foredeck with its built-in bench seating. The cockpit features a full bench seat at the transom as well as dual transom doors and a gas-assist hatch for engine access. Optional 340hp Cat diesels cruise the 440 Express Bridge at 20 knots and deliver a top speed of 23–24 knots.

See Page 699 For Price Data

Length w/Pulpit	47'1"	Fuel	400 gals.
Hull Length	44'0"	Water	100 gals.
Beam	13'11"	Waste	60 gals.
Draft	3'3"	Hull Type	Deep-V
Weight	28,000#	Deadrise Aft	19°

Sea Ray 450 Express Bridge

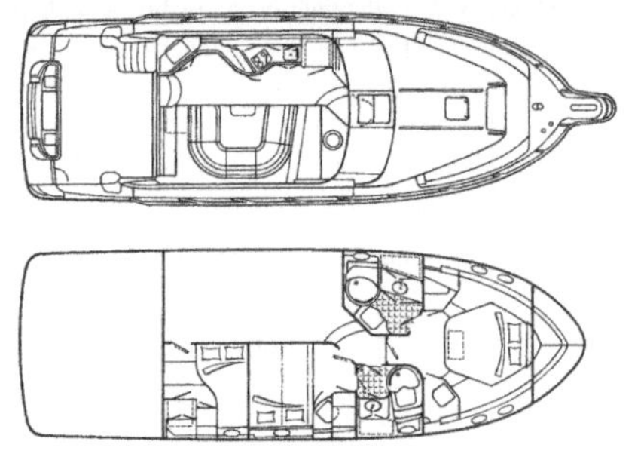

Sea Ray moved the innovation bar up a notch when they introduced the 450 Sedan Bridge in 1998. It wasn't just her sleek styling that drew attention; the real innovation is below where Sea Ray designers were able to incorporate a unique floorplan whose raised salon dinette conceals two staterooms below. The aft stateroom, which is accessed via a private entryway next to the salon door, includes a full-length bed with a hanging locker and built-in washer/dryer. Guests in the amidships stateroom have direct access to one of two heads, and the forward stateroom is fitted with a pedestal bed as well as a full entertainment center. High-gloss cherry cabinets, faux granite countertops, and vinyl overheads highlight this upscale interior. Topside, the party-time flybridge has an L-shaped centerline helm with a wet bar and seating for a small crowd. A door in the forward bridge coaming provides quick access to the foredeck. Underwater exhausts, a radar arch, and a foldaway cockpit seat were standard, and an extended swim platform is a popular option. Twin 420hp V-drive Cats (or 430hp Cummins) diesels cruise the Express Bridge at 20 knots and top out in the mid 20s.

See Page 699 For Price Data

Length Overall	51'4"	Fuel	400 gals.
Hull Length	45'6"	Water	100 gals.
Beam	14'8"	Waste	60 gals.
Draft	3'5"	Hull Type	Modified-V
Weight	29,500#	Deadrise Aft	15°

Sea Ray 450 Sundancer

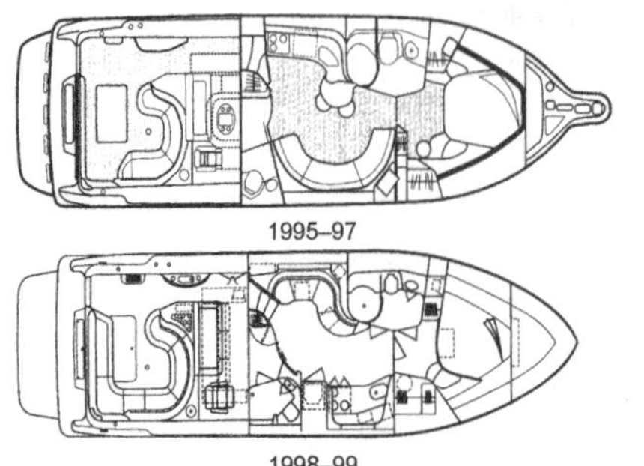

1995–97

1998–99

The Sea Ray 450 Sundancer was one of the largest sportcruisers available when she was introduced in 1995. Her bold styling has held up well over the years, and with a wide 14-foot beam the interior of the Sundancer provides comfortable accommodations in very elegant surroundings. Like most late-model Sea Ray yachts, the 450 rides on a fully cored hull with prop pockets and a steep 20 degrees of transom deadrise. Sea Ray offered two floorplans for the 450 during her 5-year production run, both with private staterooms fore and aft, two full heads, and a convertible salon sofa. Faux granite countertops highlight the galley, and high-gloss oak cabinets are found throughout the interior. In the cockpit, a circular aft-facing seat, U-shaped seating and cocktail tables convert into a huge sun pad. A wet bar and transom door were standard, and a gas-assist hatch in the cockpit sole provides good access to the engine compartment. Additional features include a reverse sport arch, transom storage locker, underwater exhaust system, and an extended swim platform. A good-running boat, twin 340hp V-drive Cat diesels cruise the 450 Sundancer in the low 20s, and 420hp Cats cruise in the mid 20s and top out at 30+ knots.

See Page 699 For Price Data

Length w/Pulpit	48'1"	Fuel	400 gals.
Hull Length	45'6"	Water	100 gals.
Beam	13'11"	Waste	60 gals.
Draft	3'7"	Hull Type	Deep-V
Weight	23,500#	Deadrise Aft	20°

Sea Ray 450 Sundancer

2010–Current

Beginning in 2006, pod drive propulsion systems have evolved from a novel engineering concept to a marine industry game changer. Led by Tiara Yachts, builders have begun to introduce new models specifically designed for pod drive power. The 450 Sundancer is one of these new-breed designs, a high-impact sportyacht whose innovative interior offers something different from previous Sundancer models—a media room, complete with 37" TV, leather settee and cocktail tables. Because the Zeus pod drives used in the 450 require less engineroom space than traditional V-drive inboards, Sea Ray engineers were able to create a much larger amidships area aft of the salon—space dedicated a second stateroom in previous Sundancer models but now used for the 450's media room. In other respects, the 450 Sundancer follows the pattern of previous Sundancer model introductions: cutting-edge styling, sumptuous accommodations, and yacht-class construction. Features include a hardtop with retractable sunroof, huge cockpit with full-service wet bar, and joystick controls. The entire aft cockpit floor lifts for engine access. Cruise at 25 knots (30+ top) with 364hp Cummins diesels with Zeus drives.

Not Enough Resale Data to Set Values

Length w/Platform	45'5"	Fuel	292 gals.
Beam	13'2"	Water	70 gals.
Draft, Axius Drives	3'2"	Waste	42 gals.
Draft, Zeus Drives	3'10"	Hull Type	Deep-V
Weight, Zeus	27,205#	Deadrise Aft	19°

Sea Ray 460 Sundancer

1999–2005

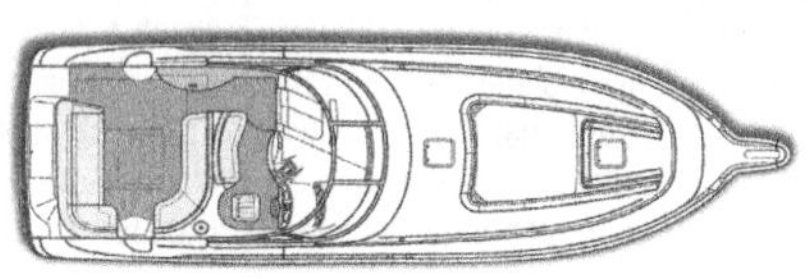

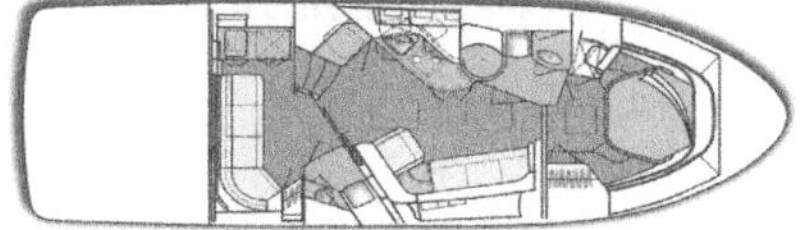

One of the largest domestic express yachts available when she was introduced in 1999, the Sea Ray 460 Sundancer is an impressive blend of American sportboat styling, luxury-class accommodations, and state-of-the-art construction. While the styling was perhaps more conservative than most European express yachts of her era, a wide beam and an expansive two-stateroom, two-head floorplan provide the 460 with cabin dimensions that European imports—with their relatively narrow beams—could only envy. Sea Ray interiors have always been among the best in the business, and the accommodations of the 460 are impressive in every respect. The mid-stateroom, complete with an enclosed head and standard washer/dryer, offers complete privacy behind sliding pocket doors. (Note that the settees in both the salon and mid-stateroom convert to double berth at the touch of a button.) In the cockpit, the facing aft settees convert electrically into a huge sun pad. A gas-assist hatch provides easy access to the engineroom. An extended swim platform was standard. Twin 430hp V-drive Volvo (or Cummins) diesels cruise the 460 Sundancer in the low 20s (27–28 top).

See Page 699 For Price Data

Length Overall	51'4"	Fuel	400 gals.
Hull Length	45'6"	Water	100 gals.
Beam	14'8"	Waste	60 gals.
Draft	3'7"	Hull Type	Modified-V
Weight	28,000#	Deadrise Aft	15°

Sea Ray 47 Sedan Bridge

Sea Ray's series of Sedan Bridge models have been popular since the original 340 Sedan Bridge came out back in 1983. Characterized by their low-profile appearance and inboard V-drive power, modern Sedan Bridge models combine the versatility of a flybridge yacht with the accommodations of a high-end luxury cruiser. Built on a modified-V hull with cored hullsides and prop pockets to reduce shaft angles, the two-stateroom interior of the Sea Ray 47 differs from most sedan floorplans in that the galley is positioned aft in the salon rather than forward, a design that reduces a lot of foot traffic through the salon. The dinette is forward, two steps up from the salon level, where guests can enjoy a panoramic view of the water. Below decks, an opulent, full-beam master stateroom is amidships while the VIP guest stateroom is forward. Both are fitted with queen island beds and flat-screen TVs. The party-time flybridge of the 47 Sedan Bridge—accessed via wide bridge steps—is arranged with the helm aft and lounge seating forward. A fiberglass hardtop and extended swim platform were standard. Cummins 600hp V-drive diesels cruise at 25 knots (about 28–30 top).

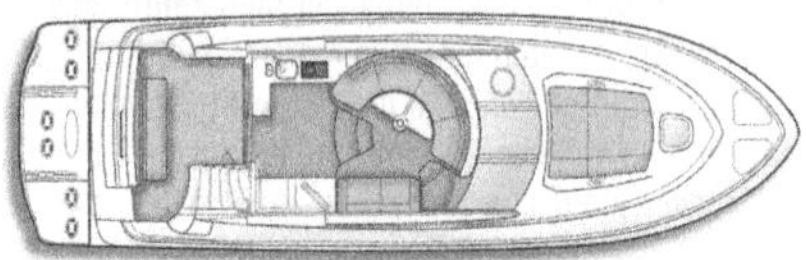

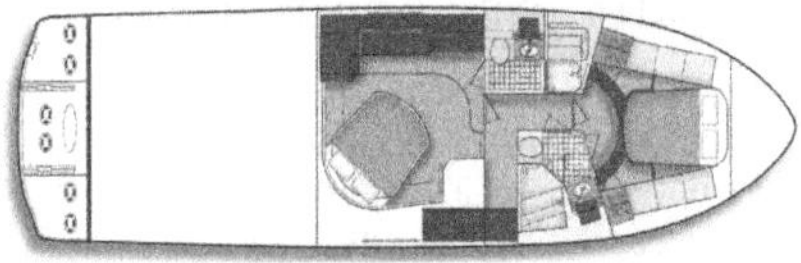

See Page 699 For Price Data

Length	50'8"	Fuel	530 gals.
Beam	14'8"	Water	117 gals.
Draft	4'2"	Waste	60 gals.
Weight	37,500#	Hull Type	Modified-V
Clearance	NA	Deadrise Aft	19°

Sea Ray 48 Sundancer

Bold and innovative styling has been a Sundancer trademark for many years, an assertion that few marine industry pros would likely dispute. That was certainly in evidence in 2005 with the introduction of the 48 Sundancer, a remarkably handsome hardtop cruiser whose sweeping lines and distinctive hullside ports reset the styling standard for boats in her class. Built on a beamy deep-V hull with a solid fiberglass bottom and prop pockets to reduce shaft angles, the opulent two-stateroom interior of the 48 Sundancer is a sophisticated blend of high-gloss cherry cabinets, Ultraleather seating, hardwood floors and designer galley appliances. Both staterooms are private, and the forward head is split with the toilet and sink to port and the shower to starboard. A 26" flatscreen TV/DVD is standard in the salon, and the aft head has a separate stall shower. The 48's sleek fiberglass hardtop—which shades a good part of the cockpit—includes dual power sunroofs as well as power side windows. An optional hydraulic swim platform can support a dinghy. Cruise in the low 20s with 540hp Cummins V-drive diesels (28–29 knots top). Zeus pod drives became available in 2008.

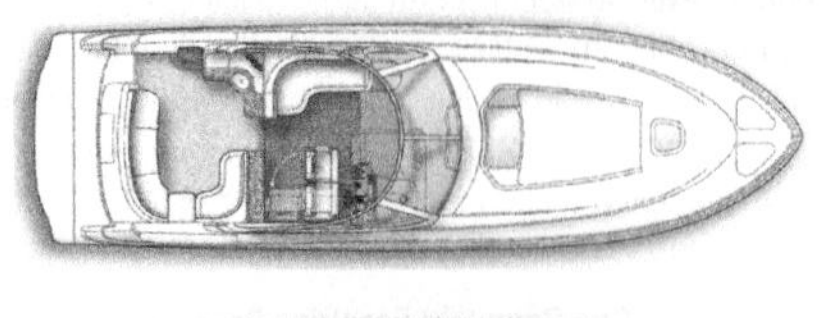

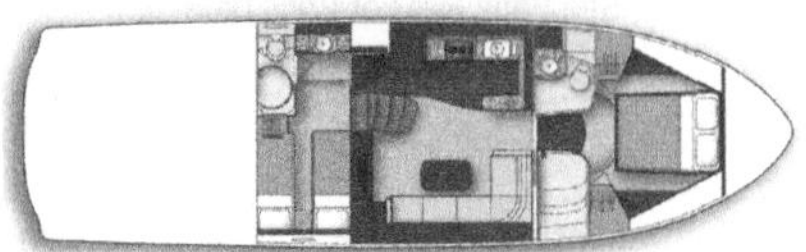

See Page 699 For Price Data

Length w/Platform	50'8"	Fuel	400 gals.
Beam	14'8"	Water	110 gals.
Draft	4'0"	Waste	60 gals.
Weight	33,600#	Hull Type	Deep-V
Clearance	NA	Deadrise Aft	19°

Sea Ray 480 Motor Yacht

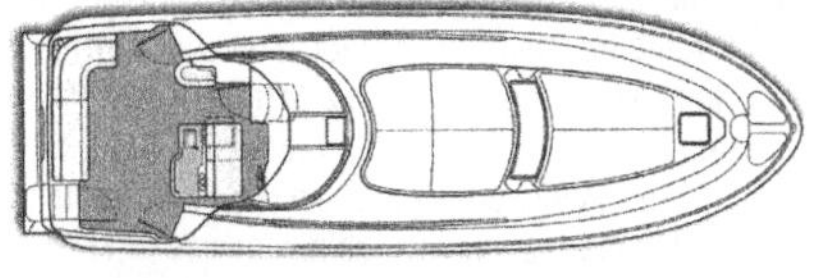

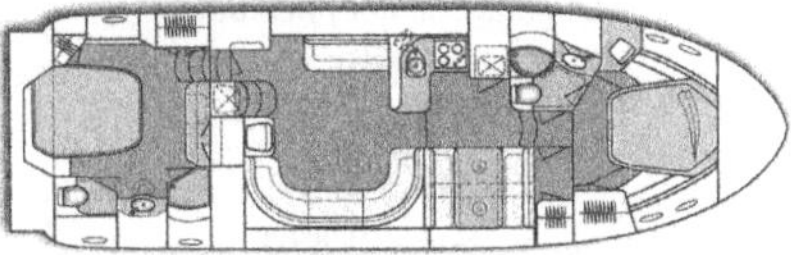

The Sea Ray 480 is a throwback to the era of the classic flush-deck motor yachts that dominated the market during the 1970s and early 1980s. (Flush-deck yachts are distinguished by having the primary helm and aft deck on the same level.) Practical in design and more sociable than flybridge yachts, the 480 allows owner and guests to enjoy the ride together in the comfort and security of the protected aft deck. Belowdecks, the comfortable interior of the Sea Ray 480 is roomy and luxurious. A long, U-shaped Ultraleather lounge dominates the salon with its recessed lighting, elliptical windows, and built-in entertainment center. Both the galley and dinette are open to the salon, and there are two staterooms forward, one with a double berth and the other, stretching beneath the salon sole, with twins. Note that a washer/dryer combo is fitted in a utility space under the galley stairs. Wing doors, a stylish and functional hardtop, and an aft deck wet bar were standard. On the downside, the engineroom, accessed via a hatch in the salon sole, is a tight fit. Twin 535hp Cummins diesels cruise the Sea Ray 480 in the low 20s (27–28 knots top), and 640hp Cats cruise in the mid 20s (about 30 knots top).

See Page 700 For Price Data

Length w/Platform	50'5"	Fuel	500 gals.
Beam	15'3"	Water	120 gals.
Draft	3'11"	Waste	60 gals.
Weight	38,500#	Hull Type	Modified-V
Clearance	15'0"	Deadrise Aft	15°

Sea Ray 480 Sedan Bridge

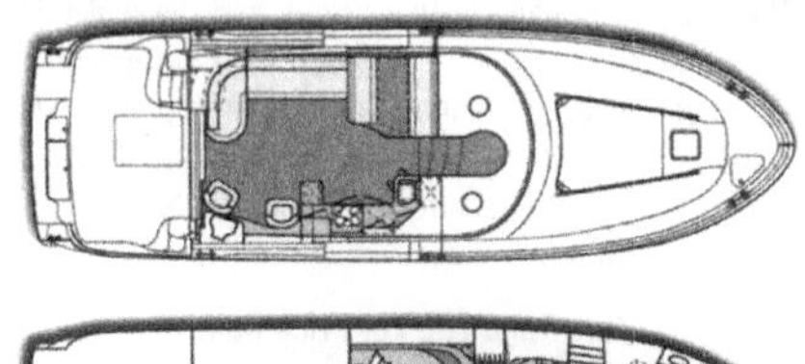

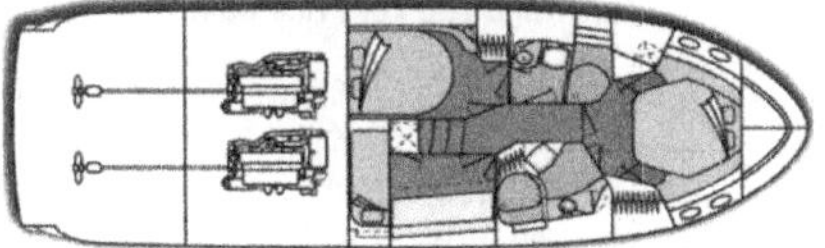

Sea Ray got it right with the 480 Sedan Bridge, one of the best-looking sedan cruisers of her era. Built on a fully cored hull with prop pockets to reduce the shaft angles, the 480 boasts a surprisingly large interior for a boat this size. Step through the sliding glass doors to a spacious salon with its electrically convertible sofa, dinette, and built-in entertainment center. Opposite, the large galley is designed with an island-style breakfast bar and under-counter refrigeration. There are three staterooms on the lower level including a full-size berth in the portside stateroom, twin bunks (and a washer/dryer combo) in the starboard stateroom, and a spacious master stateroom forward with an entertainment center. On deck, molded cockpit steps lead up to the bridge where wraparound lounge seating is located forward of an extremely well designed helm console. Additional features include high-gloss interior joinery, an extended swim platform, transom storage, wide side decks, and a fiberglass hardtop. Standard 535hp 6V-92 diesels cruise the 480 Sedan Bridge in the low 20s (27–28 knots top), and optional 660hp Cats cruise in the high 20s and top out at over 30 knots.

See Page 700 For Price Data

Length w/Platform	51'2"	Fuel	500 gals.
Beam	15'3"	Water	140 gals.
Draft	3'9"	Waste	68 gals.
Weight	40,400#	Hull Type	Modified-V
Clearance	NA	Deadrise Aft	15°

Sea Ray 480/500 Sundancer

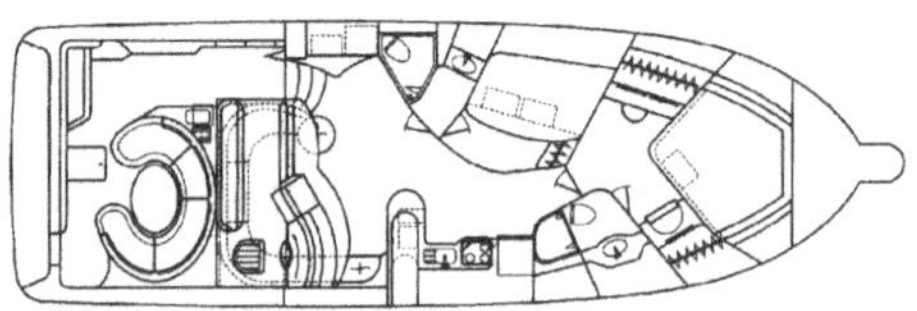

Sea Ray's largest Sundancer model ever when she was introduced, the 480 Sundancer (called the 500 Sundancer in 1992–99) was one of the most impressive express yachts on the market during the 1990s. With her long foredeck and sleek profile, the 480/500 combined luxury and extravagance in what was once a state-of-the-art package. Her sheer size is impressive enough, but it's the expansive, high-style interior that caused first-time viewers to catch their breath. Here, laid out on a single level and presenting a panorama of curved bulkheads and designer furnishings, the Sundancer's accommodations rival those of a small motor yacht. There are two private staterooms, two heads (each with a stall shower), a plush U-shaped sofa aft, and a wide-open salon with excellent headroom throughout. The cockpit—with its triple companion seat, full wet bar, and circular lounge seating—can seat a small crowd. Additional features include a reverse sport arch, wide side decks, and a huge engineroom. Early models with 485hp 6-71 V-drive diesels cruise in the low 20s (about 25 knots top). Later models with 735hp 8V92s cruise at nearly 30 knots. Note that oval ports replaced the original sliding cabin windows in 1994.

See Page 700 For Price Data

Length w/Platform	55'8"	Fuel	500 gals.
Hull Length	50'1"	Water	150 gals.
Beam	15'0"	Waste	68 gals.
Draft	4'0"	Hull Type	Modified-V
Weight	34,500#	Deadrise Aft	17°

Sea Ray 500/52 Sundancer

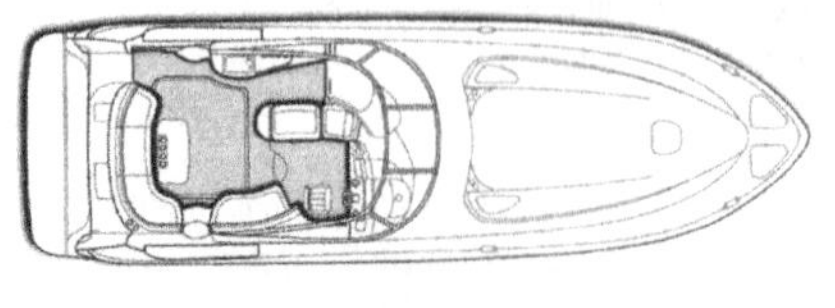

While the Sea Ray 500 Sundancer may lack the jaw-dropping sex appeal of the best European yachts, it's safe to say that she takes a back seat to few other yachts of her type when it comes to executive-class luxury and leading-edge design. Built on a deep-V hull with prop pockets to reduce the shaft angle, the Sundancer's innovative cockpit layout is notable. Arranged with a unique rotating lounge, the cockpit forms a single entertaining area rather than the divided space found in other express yachts. Another major change is found below; instead of the ubiquitous midcabin floorplan, both of the Sundancer's staterooms are forward. While there's a foldout bed option aft, this area is now part of the main salon making it even grander than before with posh Ultraleather sofas, 6-foot, 8-inch headroom, and built-in 22-inch flatscreen TV/DVD. There are two heads in this layout, and the galley includes plenty of storage as well as a hardwood floor. An extended swim platform, cherry interior cabinets, and a hardtop were standard. An extremely well finished yacht, 640hp Cummins V-drive diesels cruise the Sea Ray 500 Sundancer at 26–28 knots and reach a top speed of over 30 knots.

See Page 700 For Price Data

Length	53'4"	Fuel	560 gals.
Beam	15'3"	water	150 gals.
Draft	4'2"	Waste	68 gals.
Weight	40,015#	Hull Type	Deep-V
Clearance	14'0"	Deadrise Aft	19°

Sea Ray 500/52/520 Sedan Bridge

2005–Current

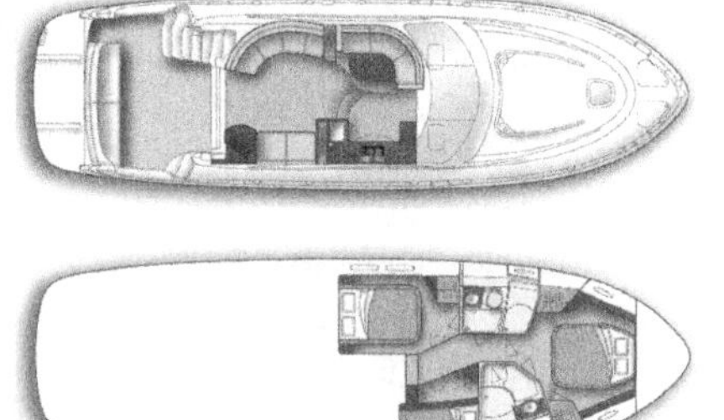

The modern styling and spirited performance of the Sea Ray 500 Sedan (called 500 Sedan Bridge in 2005; 52 SB in 2006–09; 520 SB starting in 2010) compare well with her European counterparts from Azimut, Fairline, and Sealine. There are differences, of course; the Sea Ray lacks the standard lower helm found in most European yachts, and her flybridge—with its fiberglass hardtop and secure seating—is superior in just about every respect to any of the imports. Below decks, the three-stateroom interior of the 500 Sedan Bridge is arranged with an elevated dinette forward of the salon, a spacious galley area, and a large master stateroom at the bow. Both heads are fitted with separate stall showers, and a "utility room" under the galley sole houses an optional washer/dryer combination. The main salon, with its Ultraleather upholstery, entertainment center, and high-gloss cherry cabinets can seat a small crowd in luxury and comfort. A hatch in the cockpit sole leads to the engineroom, and the swim platform is large enough to stow a tender. Additional standard features include a flybridge wet bar, salon entertainment center, and anchor washdown. Cummins 640hp diesels cruise in the mid 20s (30+ top).

See Page 700 For Price Data

Length w/Platform	52'3"	Fuel	500 gals.
Beam	15'3"	Water	140 gals.
Draft	4'3"	Waste	68 gals.
Weight	42,000#	Hull Type	Modified-V
Clearance	15'8"	Deadrise Aft	15°

Sea Ray 510 Sundancer

2000–03

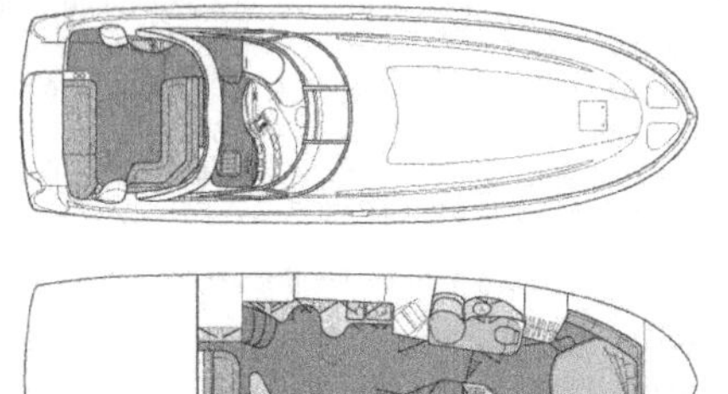

An impressive display of Sea Ray's world-class design and engineering skills, the 510 Sundancer is a purebred American sportyacht with muscular lines and lavish, world-class accommodations. Unlike her narrow-beam European counterparts (Sunseeker, Cranchi, Pershing, etc.) with their slender interiors, the Sundancer's wide-beam hull results in a surprisingly spacious interior positively loaded with luxury features. The two-stateroom layout is dominated by a vast main salon with high-gloss cherry joinery, deep pile carpeting, and a posh Ultraleather sofa with electrically operated slide-out bed. To port is a home-size galley with Corian counters, hideaway mini-bar and copious storage. Forward, the large master stateroom features an island double berth, vanity with sink, and private en-suite head. (Both heads have separate stall showers.) The cockpit, with its wraparound helm console, retractable sun pad and stylish hardtop, offers seating for a small crowd. Additional features include a washer/dryer combo, central vacuum system, underwater exhausts, and anchor washdown. Twin 660hp V-drive Cats cruise at 25 knots (about 30 top), and 770hp Cats cruise in the high 20s (low 30s top).

See Page 700 For Price Data

Length w/Platform	53'6"	Fuel	600 gals.
Hull Length	50'6"	Water	150 gals.
Beam	15'8"	Waste	68 gals.
Draft	4'3"	Hull Type	Deep-V
Weight	38,500#	Deadrise Aft	18°

Sea Ray 540 Cockpit MY

2001–02

The Sea Ray 540 Cockpit MY is a well-styled pilothouse cruiser with a compelling blend of luxury-class accommodations, versatile layout, and quality construction. Built on a modified-V hull with moderate beam and prop pockets, the 540's three-stateroom interior is arranged with the master stateroom aft, under the pilothouse, and a large guest stateroom at the bow. Notably, the 540 was one of the few U.S. boats in her size range to offer an optional lower helm station—a common feature in European flybridge yachts. Note the absence of a fixed dinette; instead, a movable high/low table can be used in the salon. A washer/dryer is fitted in the master stateroom, and the engineroom—accessed from the cockpit—is spacious and well arranged. Besides the cockpit steps, the bridge can be reached from an interior staircase—a luxury seldom found in a 54-footer. The flybridge came with a full hardtop, and the dinette aft of the helm electrically converts into a double sun pad. An extended swim platform and flybridge air conditioning were popular options. Standard 640hp Cat diesels cruise at 20 knots and reach a top speed of around 25 knots. Optional 800hp Cats will run a couple of knots faster.

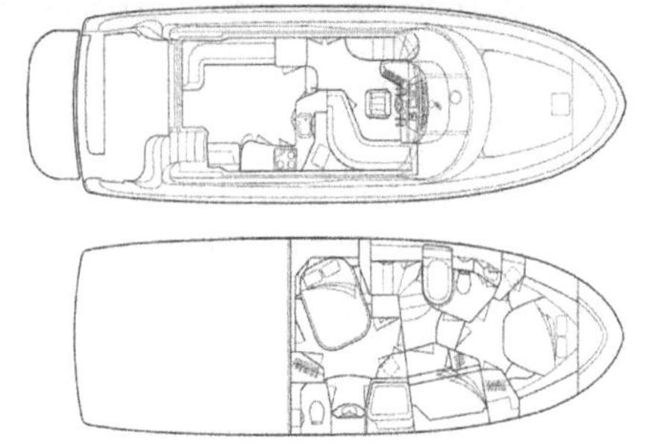

Not Enough Resale Data to Set Values

Length w/Platform	54'0"	Fuel	800 gals.
Hull Length	50'6"	Water	200 gals.
Beam	15'6"	Waste	68 gals.
Draft	4'9"	Hull Type	Modified-V
Weight	49,000#	Deadrise Aft	18°

Sea Ray 540 Sundancer

1998–2001

Introduced in 1998, the Sea Ray 540 Sundancer is a mega-volume sportcruiser whose muscular good looks and luxurious accommodations can still turn heads. This boat offers a seemingly endless list of high-tech features, and her extravagant interior is a study in comfort, beginning with the huge Ultraleather sofa that converts electrically into a slide-out bed. The Sundancer carries most of her beam forward, which creates plenty of living space below. The master stateroom is amidships and has a queen bed as well as a private head compartment. Forward, the guest stateroom has a full-size berth and space for a washer/dryer combo. The galley is open in the salon, and storage cabinets are abundant throughout the boat, all finished in high-gloss cherry woodwork. In the cockpit, two immense L-shaped settees, which can accommodate a small crowd, convert at the push of a button into a massive sun pad. Additional features include a foredeck sun pad, a superb helm console, and a hydraulic high-low swim platform to facilitate the launch of a tender. Twin 640hp Cat diesels cruise in the mid 20s (30+ knots top), and 745hp 8V-92s cruise in the high 20s and reach a top speed of 32–33 knots.

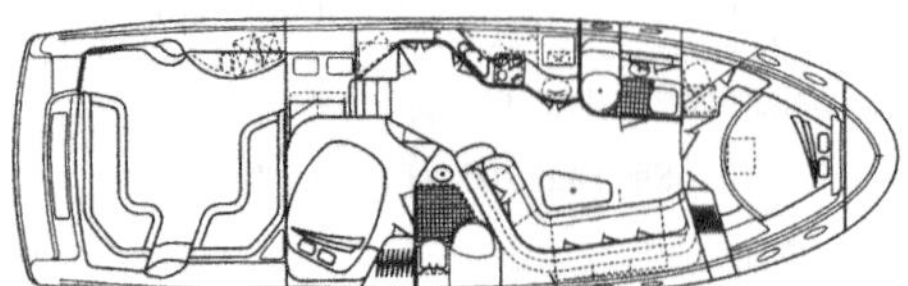

See Page 700 For Price Data

Length w/Platform	57'8"	Fuel	600 gals.
Hull Length	54'11"	Water	150 gals.
Beam	15'11"	Waste	68 gals.
Draft	3'11"	Hull Type	Modified-V
Weight	39,000#	Deadrise Aft	17°

Sea Ray 540 Sundancer

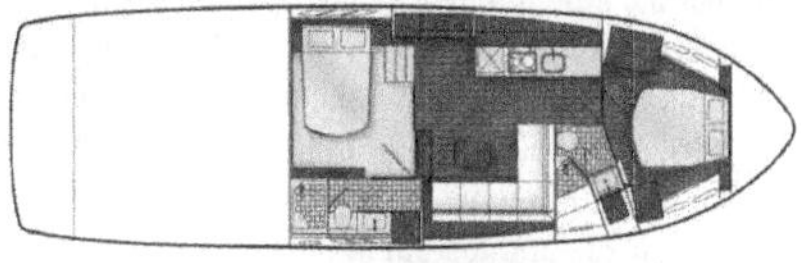

Two Staterooms

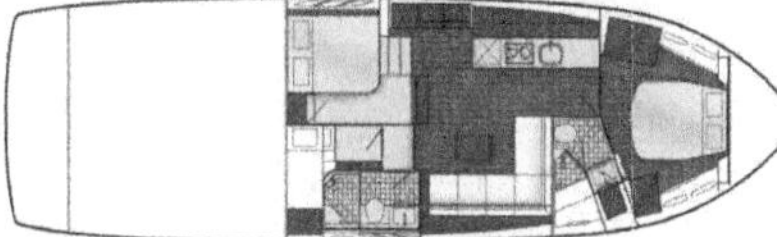

Three Staterooms

You're getting into some rarified air with the 540 Sundancer, an executive-class luxury yacht that took Sea Ray styling and performance benchmarks to the next level when she was introduced in 2010. Sea Ray is the only American builder with any real experience building big express cruisers like this. They led the way back in 1991 with the introduction of the 63 Super Sun Sport, and recent years have seen several 50-foot-plus Sundancer models added to the Sea Ray fleet. The 540 Sundancer, introduced in 2010, is among the new-generation Sundancers to employ Zeus pod-drive propulsion—an engineering game-changer whose impact in the boating industry cannot be overestimated. Highlights include a palatial cherrywood interior with a choice of two- or three-stateroom layouts, a sleek fiberglass hardtop with retractable sunroof, giant cockpit with circular lounge seating, full wet bar with refrigerator, and eurostyle sun pad aft. Note the 540's hardwood cabin flooring, generous salon headroom, Ultraleather seating, and designer galley hardware. Hullside windows provide significant natural lighting below. Joystick control makes docking easy. Cruise at 25 knots (30+) with 715hp Cummins diesels.

Not Enough Resale Data to Set Values

Length w/Platform	54'9"	Fuel	600 gals.
Beam	15'3"	Water	150 gals.
Draft	4'2"	Waste	68 gals.
Weight	50,000#	Hull Type	Deep-V
Clearance	16'4"	Deadrise Aft	21°

Sea Ray 55/580 Sundancer

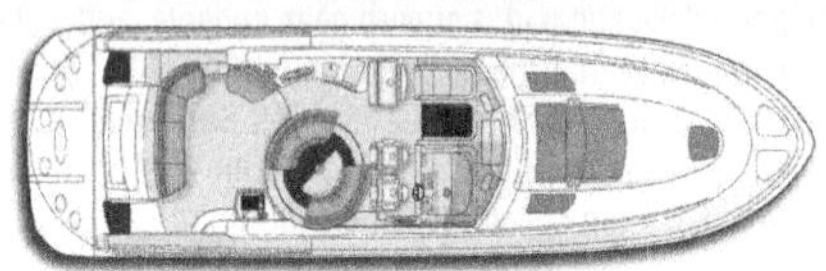

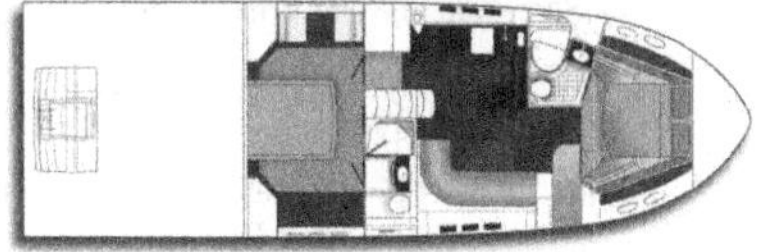

The 580 Sundancer (called the 55 Sundancer in 2008–09) took the Sea Ray concept of yachting elegance and sophistication to the next level when she was introduced in 2008. The market for a supersize sportcruiser like the 580 is always limited; few boaters can afford a yacht like this to begin with, especially during the past few years since the advent of the Great Recession. For those lucky one percent with the resources, however, the 580 Sundancer represents something close to the ultimate when it comes to making a statement. Her lavish two-stateroom interior—an eye-popping blend of dark cherrywood cabinets, Ultraleather seating, Corian counters, and hardwood floors—includes a home-size galley with serving counter, opulent full-beam owner's suite (with a queen bed that tilts and massages), and two full heads. A twin-section cockpit lounge slides around a table on circular tracks—very innovative. Note the massive standup engineroom, cockpit galley with wet bar & grill, and twin retractable sunroofs in the hardtop. Hullside windows provide significant natural lighting in the master stateroom. A hydraulic swim platform is a popular option. Man 900hp V-drive diesels cruise at 25–26 knots (about 30 knots top).

See Page 700 For Price Data

Length Overall	60'0"	Fuel	825 gals.
Beam	15'11"	Water	200 gals.
Draft	4'6"	Waste	70 gals.
Weight	53,500#	Hull Type	Modified-V
Clearance	17'9"	Deadrise Aft	17°

Sea Ray 550 Sedan Bridge

The Sea Ray 550 Sedan Bridge is a stretched version of the company's earlier 500 Sedan Bridge model. The 550 differs from her predecessor in that she has a larger cockpit, an improvement that allowed Sea Ray to market her as both a cruising yacht and fishing boat. She's built on a fully cored modified-V hull, and her 15-foot beam is moderate compared with many of today's mega-beam yachts. Most boats this size come with just two staterooms, but Sea Ray engineers were able to create a three-stateroom interior in the 550 without compromising the size of the salon. Indeed, the salon, galley, and dining area are completely open, and the galley counter serves as a convenient breakfast bar. Both heads have separate stall showers, and space for a washer/dryer combo is provided beneath the salon floor. Topside, the flybridge of the 550 is another big attraction—it's huge with entertaining space for a small crowd. Unlike the 500 Sedan Bridge, the cockpit of the 550 is large enough for some serious fishing activities. Among several engine options, twin 650hp 8V-92 Detroits cruise the 550 Sedan Bridge in the mid 20s (about 30 knots top), and 735hp Detroits cruise in the high 20s and top out in the low 30s.

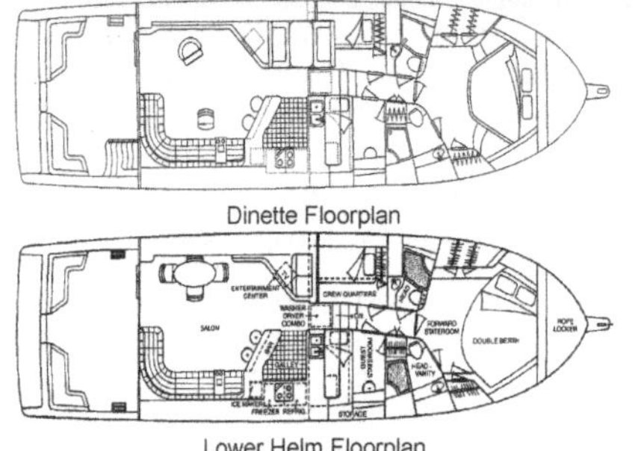
Dinette Floorplan

Lower Helm Floorplan

See Page 700 For Price Data

Length Overall	57'10"	Fuel	700 gals.
Hull Length	54'10"	Water	200 gals.
Beam	15'0"	Waste	40 gals.
Draft	4'2"	Hull Type	Modified-V
Weight	45,000#	Deadrise Aft	17°

Sea Ray 550 Sundancer

The Sea Ray 550 Sundancer is basically an updated version of the company's earlier 540 Sundancer (1998–2001) with a revised interior, a restyled hardtop, and an overhead skylight to add some natural lighting to the salon. Built on a modified-V hull with a solid fiberglass bottom, the 550's luxurious two-stateroom layout is highlighted by its beautiful high-gloss cherry woodwork, a long, curved Ultraleather sofa to port (which converts electrically into a slide-out bed), and a curved galley to starboard with a built-in 42-inch plasma TV and a Lexan wine rack. Both staterooms include double berths, and the small refrigerator at the base of the companionway steps can be replaced by a washer/dryer combo. In the spacious cockpit, the two L-shaped settees convert at the push of a button into a massive sun pad. Additional features (among many) include a foredeck sun pad, a superb helm console, and a standard bow thruster. Note that the engineroom is a tight fit. Twin 640hp Cat inboard diesels cruise the Sea Ray 550 Sundancer in the mid 20s (about 30 knots top), and a pair of 765hp MANs cruise at 28 knots and reach a top speed in the neighborhood of 32–33 knots.

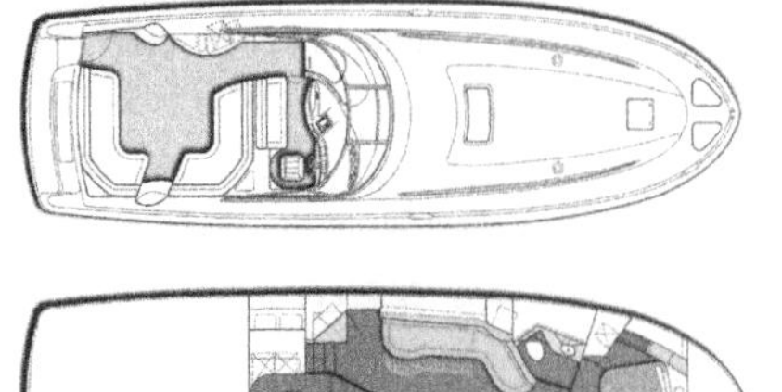

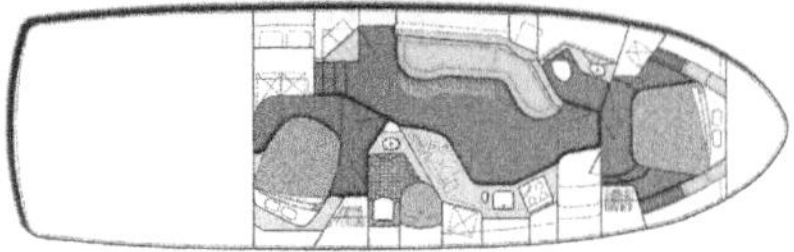

See Page 700 For Price Data

Length	57'8"	Fuel	600 gals.
Beam	15'11"	Water	150 gals.
Draft	4'0"	Waste	68 gals.
Weight	39,000#	Hull Type	Modified-V
Clearance	13'4"	Deadrise Aft	17°

Sea Ray 560 Sedan Bridge

1998–2004

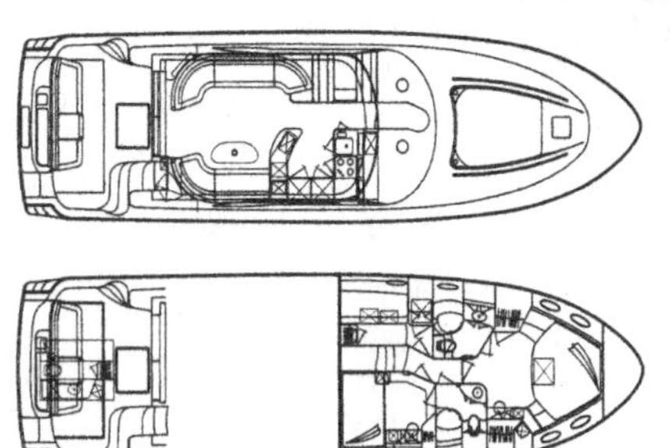

A popular model, the Sea Ray 560 Sedan Bridge was the equal of many European flybridge yachts of her era when it came to quality, performance, and styling. The Sedan Bridge is no European impersonator, however; she rides on a modified-V hull (rather than a deep-V), and while a lower helm was available it wasn't the standard feature as it is on most imports. The plush three-stateroom interior of the 560 is arranged with the master suite forward and a VIP stateroom to port. A full dinette is opposite the helm (elevated to provide better headroom in the third stateroom), and facing sofas provide plenty of salon seating. In the cockpit, a molded staircase leads to the flybridge with its wraparound helm and standard hardtop. A large hatch in the cockpit sole provides access to the engines, and a bench seat at the transom folds away to free up cockpit space. Additional features include a fully cored hull, prop pockets, livewell, fish box, a transom storage locker, and a hydraulic high-low swim platform (to facilitate the launch of a tender). Twin 640hp Cat diesels cruise the Sea Ray 560 in the low 20s (about 28 knots top), and optional 1,050hp MANs cruise in the high 20s and top out at 33–34 knots.

See Page 700 For Price Data

Length	58'6"	Fuel	800 gals.
Beam	16'0"	Water	200 gals.
Draft	4'6"	Waste	68 gals.
Weight	50,000#	Hull Type	Modified-V
Clearance	NA	Deadrise Aft	15°

Sea Ray 58/580 Sedan Bridge

2006–Current

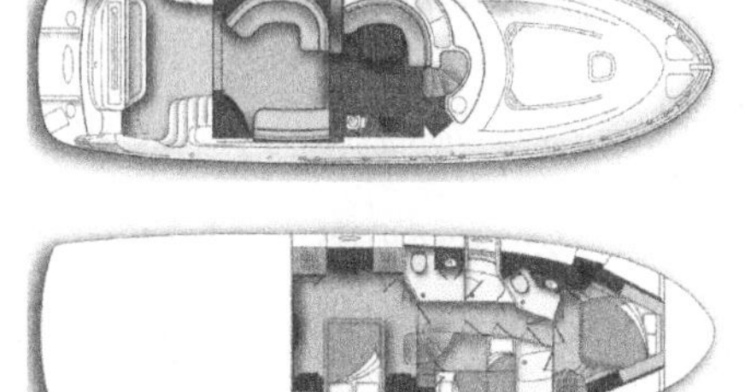

The streamlined styling of the Sea Ray 550 Sedan Bridge is further evidence—if any were needed—of the "Europeanization" of American motor yacht design. Fortunately, her beauty is more than skin deep, and the 550 compares well in both comfort and build quality with her high-end competitors. There are differences, of course; the Sea Ray lacks the standard lower helm found in most European yachts, but her flybridge, with its standard fiberglass hardtop, secure seating, and well-arranged helm, is superior in just about every respect to any of the imports. Belowdecks, the opulent three-stateroom interior of the 550 Sedan Bridge is arranged with curved salon seating aft, galley and dinette forward, and a spacious full-beam master stateroom amidships. Separate head and shower compartments serve the two guest cabins, and high-gloss cherrywood woodwork is found throughout the interior. The swim platform, which is large enough to handle a small tender, can be fitted with an optional launching davit that stores out of sight in the transom. A good performer for a boat this size, she'll cruise at 24–26 knots with 900hp MAN diesels and reach a top speed of just over 30 knots.

See Page 700 For Price Data

Length w/Platform	58'7"	Fuel	700 gals.
Beam	16'0"	Water	150 gals.
Draft	4'3"	Waste	68 gals.
Weight	51,500#	Hull Type	Modified-V
Clearance	18'8"	Deadrise Aft	17°

Sea Ray 580 Super Sun Sport

A cutting-edge yacht when she came out in 1997, the Sea Ray 580 Super Sun Sport has the high-impact sex appeal of a purebred European sportcruiser. Indeed, with her muscular profile, integrated hardtop, and stylish reverse transom—with its PWC garage and flanking walkways—the Super Sun Sport remains a handsome express yacht even by today's styling standards. She's built on a fully cored hull with prop pockets and a relatively wide 15-foot, 9-inch beam. Below decks, the opulent salon is dominated by a full-length Ultraleather sofa that converts into a double bed at the touch of a button. The master stateroom, with its private head and queen-size bed, is aft while the guest stateroom is forward. Both heads have separate stall showers, and the home-style galley features acres of counter space and copious storage. Cockpit highlights include a big U-shaped lounge aft of the helm, full wet bar, hidden foldout boarding steps, and sun lounge atop the PWC compartment. Note that there are two entrances to the engine compartment, one via a cockpit deck hatch and the other by lifting the floor of the garage. Among several diesel engine options, twin 776hp Cats (or 735hp Detroits) will cruise in the high 20s (low 30s top).

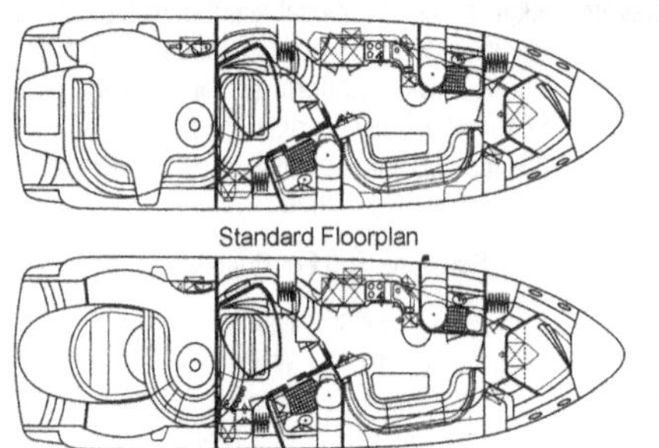

Standard Floorplan

Alternate Floorplan

See Page 700 For Price Data

Length w/Platform	60'10"	Fuel	700 gals.
Hull Length	58'11"	Water	200 gals.
Beam	15'9"	Waste	68 gals.
Draft	4'1"	Hull Type	Modified-V
Weight	48,000#	Deadrise Aft	17°

Sea Ray 60/610 Sundancer

Sea Ray's flagship yacht, the 610 Sundancer (called the 60 Sundancer in 2006–09) combines motoryacht comfort and luxury with sportyacht performance. This isn't the biggest express yacht Sea Ray has ever built, but it's certainly the most sophisticated and visually impressive. As might be expected, her feature list is practically endless. Prominent among them, however, is a fully enclosed pilothouse/salon—what Sea Ray calls a "cockpit sunroom"—with twin overhead sun roofs, facing leather settees, entertainment center and state-of-the-art helm. Forward and below, the 610's spacious three-stateroom cherry interior (with 7-foot-plus headroom) includes a full-beam master suite aft with hullside windows, full-service galley with serving counter, two full heads, and hardwood flooring throughout. A small crew cabin with transom entry is optional. The cockpit, with port and starboard transom doors, includes a wet bar with refrigerator, grill and aft bench seating. The engineroom is huge. A hydraulic lift swim platform, transom storage locker, bow and stern thrusters, and foredeck sun pad are standard. MAN 1,100hp V-drive diesels cruise at a fast 28 knots (33–34 knots top).

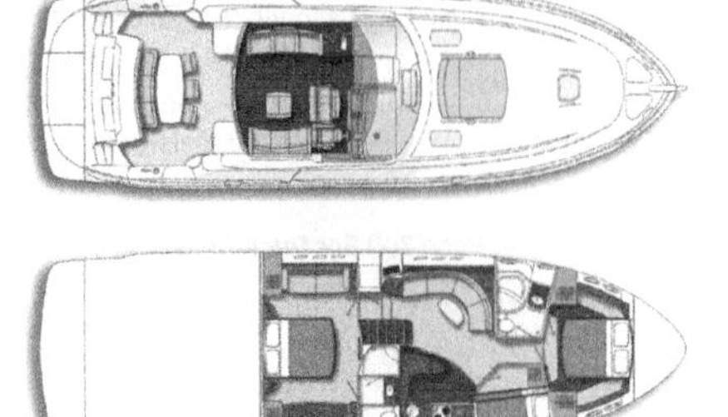

See Page 700 For Price Data

Length	61'6"	Fuel	900 gals.
Beam	16'9"	Water	200 gals.
Draft	4'2"	Waste	70 gals.
Weight	55,700#	Hull Type	Modified-V
Clearance	NA	Deadrise Aft	17°

Sea Ray 630 Sundancer

1996–2000

Introduced in 1996, the 630 Sundancer took Sea Ray's concept of luxury in the fast lane to an unprecedented level. She wasn't just the largest Sea Ray yacht produced to date, she was the only one to employ surface drives to reduce drag and boost top speed. Built on a fully cored hull with moderate beam and an integrated transom, the 630 Sundancer remains a visually impressive yacht even by today's standards. Below, a luxurious leather sofa containing an electrically operated slide-out bed is the focal point of the roomy salon. The master stateroom is forward with a centerline queen, and both VIP staterooms have private heads and separate showers. Note the salon day head and home-size galley with hardwood flooring, serving bar and stools. A giant 27-foot cockpit sets the stage for every conceivable amenity from the circular, raised sun pad aft to the deluxe entertainment center with wet bar, refrigerator, icemaker and CD changer. Additional features include Corian counters and sinks, central vacuum system, foredeck sun pad, bow thruster, and twin transom doors. Expect a top speed of close to 45 knots with 3412 Caterpillar diesels matched to Arneson surface drives.

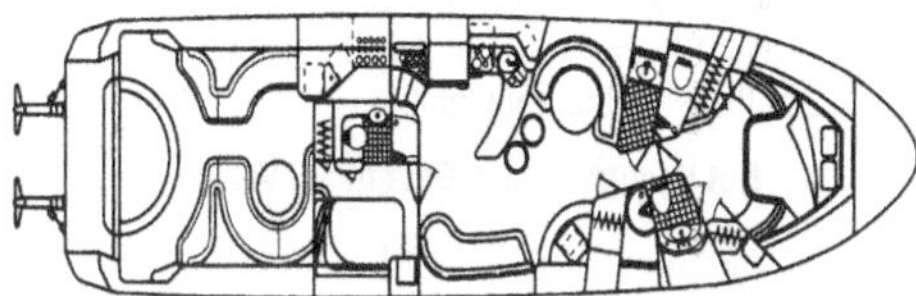

See Page 700 For Price Data

Length w/Platform	68'8"	Fuel	1,061 gals.
Hull Length	62'6"	Water	200 gals.
Beam	15'9"	Waste	65 gals.
Draft, Inboards	3'11"	Hull Type	Deep-V
Weight	64,000#	Deadrise Aft	19°

Sea Ray 630 Super Sun Sport

1991–2000

The 630 Super Sun Sport and her sistership, the 630 Sundancer set American sportyacht standards in their day for size and luxury. While they look alike on the outside, the Sundancer uses Arneson surface drives to reduce draft and drag—an installation that results in a much higher top speed. Both are built on fully cored, deep-V hulls with moderate beam (the Sun Sport has prop pockets) and an integrated transom. Sharing similar floorplans, the massive salon is dominated by sculptured overhead panels and a long contoured leather sofa. The master stateroom is all the way forward, and a day head is in the salon. Note the crew quarters in the Sun Sport hidden beneath the transom and accessed via the cockpit sun pad. Additional features include a reverse arch, two transom doors, circular lounge seating in the cockpit, and a well-arranged engineroom with push-button access. An excellent performer with 1,075hp 12V92 diesels, the Sun Sport will cruise at 30 knots (32–33 knots top). The Sundancer model, available during 1995–99, can reach a top speed of nearly 45 knots with 1,300hp surface-drive Cats—super-impressive performance for a 63-foot yacht.

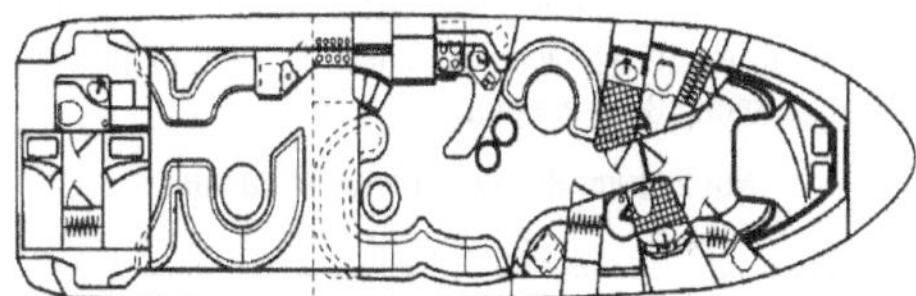

See Page 700 For Price Data

Length w/Platform	64'6"	Fuel	800 gals.
Hull Length	62'6"	Water	200 gals.
Beam	15'9"	Waste	70 gals.
Draft	5'0"	Hull Type	Deep-V
Weight	54,500#	Deadrise Aft	19°

Sea Ray 650 Cockpit Motor Yacht

Until the introduction of the limited-production 680 Sun Sport in 2001, the 650 Cockpit Motor Yacht was the largest boat Sea Ray had ever produced. Built on a fully cored hull with a wide 18-foot beam, she was an impressive yacht in her day with a rakish profile and an innovative floorplan. What makes the layout unusual is the aft engineroom, a configuration that allows the master suite to be located amidships—rather than aft, as in most motor yachts—where the beam is the greatest. There are three guest staterooms forward along with two full heads and a walk-in utility room. The full-width salon of the 650 is arranged with the galley and breakfast bar forward and a formal dining area to port. A passageway leads to the enclosed pilothouse with its centerline helm and watch berth. Outside, the cockpit has room for a few deck chairs and provides easy access to the engineroom below. While the flybridge can handle a small crowd, it doesn't compare with the party-size platforms found on most other 65-footers. A good-running boat, 870hp (or 900hp) 12V71s cruise at 20 knots (24 knots wide open), and 12-cylinder 1,000hp MTUs cruise at 23 knots (27–28 top). A total of 12 of these yachts were built.

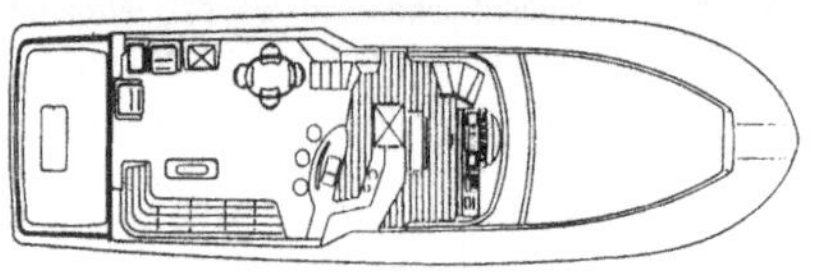
Deckhouse Layout

Lower Level Floorplan

Not Enough Resale Data to Set Values

Length	64'6"	Fuel	1,000 gals.
Beam	18'1"	Water	275 gals.
Draft	4'10"	Waste	264 gals.
Weight	76,000#	Hull Type	Modified-V
Clearance	25'3"	Deadrise Aft	18°

Sea Ray 680 Sun Sport

The biggest Sea Ray ever, the 680 Sun Sport showcased the company's world-class engineering and production skills during the early 2000s. Built on a balsa-cored hull with a wide 18'6" beam, the 680's fully enclosed pilothouse and spacious three-stateroom accommodation plan deliver a one-of-a-kind blend of sportyacht comfort and luxury. The upper salon, with its curved Ultraleather sofa, wet bar, entertainment center, and retractable side windows is clearly the focal point of the boat. Below, a more intimate salon is furnished with a leather sofa and matching loveseat. The portside galley includes SubZero refrigeration and copious storage, while the amidships master stateroom features a walkaround queen-size bed and private head with circular shower. Crew quarters (with transom access) are aft. Note that the Sun Sport lacks the transom garage of the Viking Sport Cruisers V-65 or Sunseeker's Predator 68—yachting contemporaries of her era. (An optional hydraulic swim platform provides PWC storage instead.) Additional features include a retractable sunroof, teak cockpit flooring, leather helm seats, and an electrically actuated sun pad. Cat 1,400hp engines cruise at 25 knots (30+ knots top).

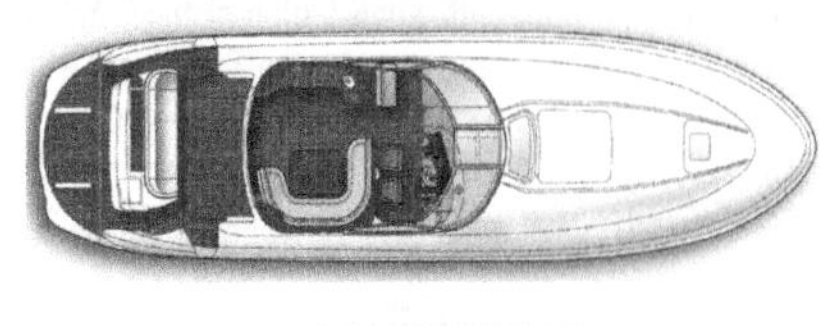

Not Enough Resale Data to Set Values

Length	70'5"	Fuel	1,000 gals.
Beam	18'6"	Water	200 gals.
Draft	4'9"	Waste	100 gals.
Weight	75,000#	Hull Type	Deep-V
Clearance	13'8"	Deadrise Aft	19°

Sealine

Quick View

- Sealine was founded in 1972 by aircraft engineer Tom Murrant. The first Sealine boats were displayed to the public in 1978 at the Southampton Boat Show.
- Sealine boats stood out from the crowd almost from the start by offering colored gelcoats where most other boatbuilders were churning out white or brown hulls.
- By the 1990s, Sealine had grown to become one of England's big-four builders along with Princess Yachts, Fairline Yachts, and Sunseeker Yachts.
- By 2002, with an international sales and dealer network, Sealine was producing 300 luxury yachts a year, mostly for export.
- Sealine withdrew from the US market in 2001 when the company was bought by giant US firm Brunswick to avoid competition with the new owner's U.S. brands
- A division of Brunswick for more than 10 years, Sealine was sold to the UK-based Oxford Investment Group in August, 2011.
- Sealine re-entered the U.S. market in 2012 with a sales office in Ft. Lauderdale.

Sealine Yachts America • Dania, FL • www.sealine.com

Sealine F37 Flybridge

The Sealine F37 is an affordably priced sportcruiser with a distinctive (some might say excessive) styling, a well-arranged interior, and excellent performance. Like all Sealine models, the F37 is constructed on a solid fiberglass hull with moderate beam, and at just 21,000 pounds, she's a very weight-efficient yacht. The Sealine's two-stateroom, galley-down floorplan is fairly standard in this size range, although it is notable that there are two heads in this layout rather than just one—a definite plus when cruising with others, although it makes for a small guest stateroom. Visibility from the lower helm is excellent, but headroom both here and in the salon is less than might be desired. The cockpit, with its teak staircase, overhead table/canopy storage, and unique foldout bench seat, is well shaded by a bridge overhang. The side decks are quite wide, and the spacious flybridge is arranged with a centerline helm, a starboard side sun lounger, and a vast sun pad aft. Unfortunately, like all Sealines (and most European boats in general) the engine room is very small. A good performer with 260hp Volvo diesels, the Sealine F37 cruises in the low-to-mid 20s (nearly 30 knots top).

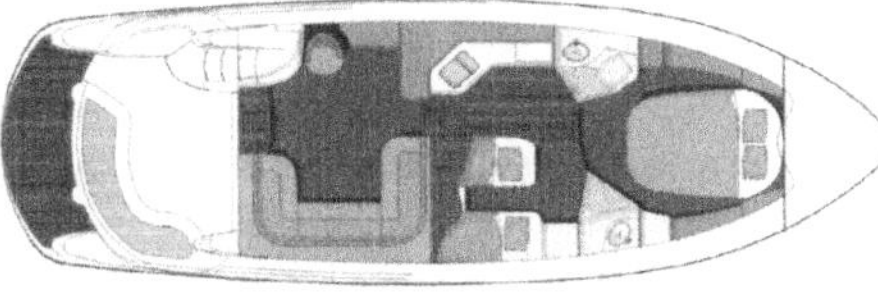

Not Enough Resale Data to Set Values

Length	38'6"	Fuel	264 gals.
Beam	12'5"	Water	103 gals.
Draft	3'5"	Headroom	6'4"
Weight	21,000#	Hull Type	Modified-V
Clearance	14'0"	Deadrise Aft	18°

Sealine S37 Sports Cruiser

1996–2003

The Sealine S37 Sports Cruiser is a full-bodied family express with conservative lines and generous interior accommodations. Built the old-fashioned way on a solid fiberglass hull, the Sports Cruiser's deep-V hull insures a smooth and comfortable ride in a chop. Clearly, she lacks the sleek, sweptback profile of a Sea Ray or Sunseeker, but the seven-berth layout of the Sealine S37 and her separate head and shower compartments make a lot of sense in a family cruiser. In this boat, it's possible to take a shower without tying up the head at the same time. Further, both compartments can be accessed from the salon as well as the forward stateroom—very unusual. There's a standup dressing area in the midcabin, and four angled aluminum-framed doors close off the salon from the staterooms and head areas. On deck, the bi-level cockpit has a big semicircular settee/sun lounge aft of the helm, a wet bar to port, and a transom door that opens to a small swim platform with a teak sole. Note that the side decks are quite narrow and engines access, via a gas-assist hatch in the cockpit floor, is tight. Optional Volvo 250hp diesels cruise the Sealine S37 in the mid 20s and reach a top speed of over 30 knots.

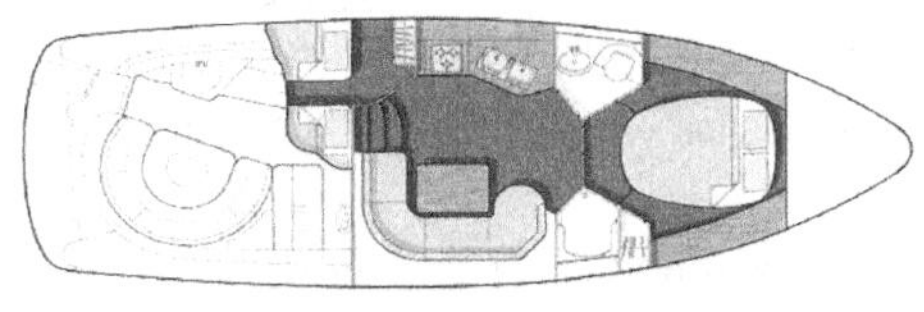

Not Enough Resale Data to Set Values

Length	37'1"	Clearance	12'6"
Beam	12'2"	Fuel	237 gals.
Draft, Drives Up	2'5"	Water	29 gals.
Draft, Drives Down	3'1"	Hull Type	Modified-V
Weight	15,000#	Deadrise Aft	18°

Sealine C39 Coupe

2003–05

Sealine launched the C39 Coupe in 2003 with three different drive systems: sterndrives, Arneson surface-drive diesels, and a closed-tunnel drive system called Trimax that, like the Arneson, uses surface drive propellers. Beyond the propulsion choices, the C39 is a very distinctive boat in her own right. Unlike the usual open-backed hardtop sportcruisers from Sunseeker and Sea Ray, etc., the fully enclosed C39 provides complete protection from the elements. The tall, rounded house is unique; it creates a spacious salon area with excellent headroom and superb visibility from the raised two-seat helm position. A compact-but-complete galley is located opposite the convertible dinette, and power side windows and a big overhead sunroof provide plenty of ventilation. Below, the living quarters consist of two staterooms and two heads, both with a stylish washbasin, but neither of which has a separate shower stall. The cockpit, which can be extended 25 inches at the push of a button, includes a separate life raft compartment. Arneson or Trimax surface drives will both reach a top speed of close to 35 knots with a pair of 310hp Volvo diesels.

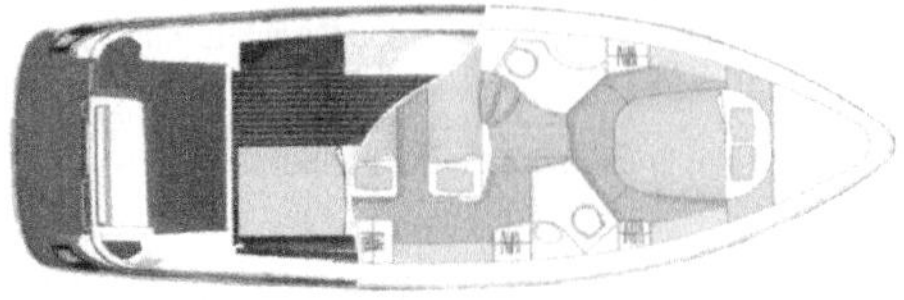

Not Enough Resale Data to Set Values

Length	39'3"	Clearance, Arch	13'10"
Beam	12'3"	Fuel	276 gals.
Draft, Up	2'1"	Water	96 gals.
Draft, Down	3'4"	Hull Type	Modified-V
Weight	18,700#	Deadrise Aft	18°

Sealine S41 Sports Yacht

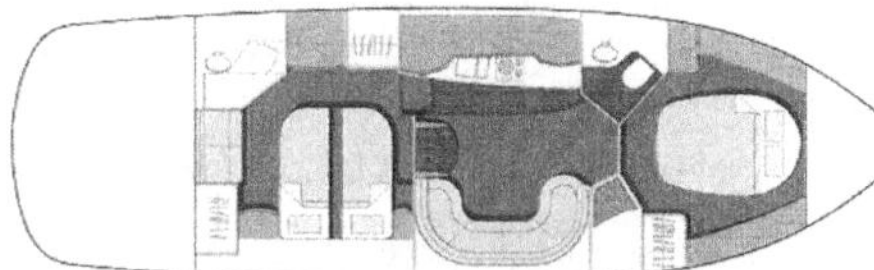

In many ways, the Sealine S41 is quite unlike any other European sportboat on the market. It's not just the partial hardtop with its sliding roof panel that sets her apart—what Sealine calls a Solar Protection System; the real surprise is found below where the S41's two-stateroom floorplan delivers a motor yachtsize aft cabin with full standing headroom, a walkaround queen berth and a private head. By any standard, this is an impressive layout for an express cruiser, one made possible by locating the engines aft and using sterndrive power rather than inboards. On deck, the bi-level cockpit is very spacious with plenty of seating, a dedicated life raft locker, wet bar and sun pad. An overhead storage bin in the hardtop stores the cockpit table and the two-part enclosure. Note that there have been some reports that the hardtop, which has no forward supports, may flex at higher speeds. Additional features include a teak cockpit sole, an electric sunroof, twin bolster seats at the helm and a surprisingly large galley. The engine room is a tight fit. Twin 300hp Volvo diesel I/Os cruise the Sealine S41 in the mid 20s (about 30 knots top). Note that the Sealine S43 Sports Yacht is the same boat with inboard power.

Not Enough Resale Data to Set Values

Length	42'3"	Fuel	306 gals.
Beam	13'4"	Water	84 gals.
Draft	3'7"	Waste	34 gals.
Weight	21,500#	Hull Type	Modified-V
Clearance, Mast	14'2"	Deadrise Aft	18°

Sealine F42/5 Flybridge

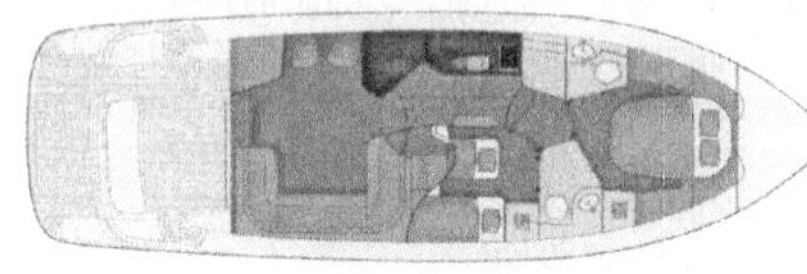
Two Staterooms

Three Staterooms

The Sealine F42/5 (so named because of her innovative extendable cockpit) is one of the few flybridge sedans her size available with a three-stateroom interior. That said, the standard two-stateroom layout will probably prove more popular because of the more spacious salon. Regardless of which interior is selected, the 42/5 gets high marks with experienced owners for her quality engineering and construction. Of the many notable features of the Sealine 42/5, perhaps the most practical is the ability to extend the cockpit by nearly 3 feet at the touch of a button. There's an enormous storage lazarette below the cockpit, and molded steps lead up to the extended flybridge with seating for eight and swivel helm seat. Although the engine room, accessed via hatches in the salon sole, seems small, most of the secondary pumps, etc., are located in the lazarette which adds a measure of serviceability. Visibility from the lower helm is excellent, but the side decks are narrow and care is necessary in going forward, especially while underway. Twin 480hp Volvo diesels cruise the Sealine 42/5 Flybridge in the mid-to-high 20s and reach a top speed of just over 30 knots.

Not Enough Resale Data to Set Values

Length	42'4"	Fuel	372 gals.
Beam	13'10"	Water	165 gals.
Draft	3'4"	Waste	60 gals.
Weight	27,600#	Hull Type	Modified-V
Clearance, Mast	14'3"	Deadrise Aft	16°

Sealine 43 Flybridge

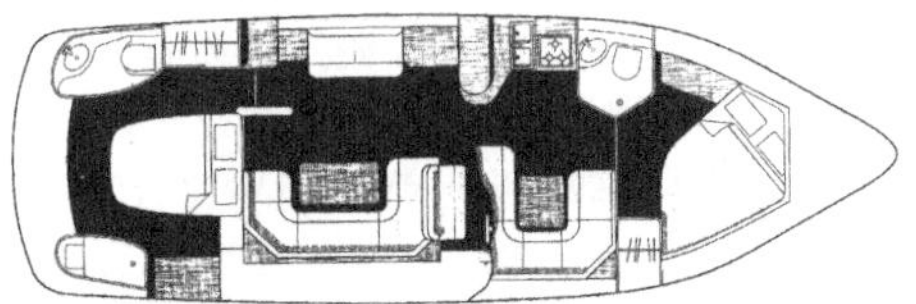

Introduced in the UK in 1991 as the Sealine 390 and first seen in the U.S. in 1996, the Sealine F43 Flybridge (called the 410 Statesman in 1993–98 and the 43 Flybridge since 1999 when the swim platform was extended) has remained a popular boat over the years thanks to a comparatively moderate price and a very innovative aft-cabin floorplan. The F43 is constructed on a solid fiberglass modified-V hull with moderate beam and an integrated swim platform. Her galley-down, aft-cabin floorplan has the master stateroom aft, under the cockpit. To make this configuration work the molded seating around the cockpit perimeter is cleverly designed to provide full standing headroom around the centerline bed in the cabin below. A lower helm is standard in the salon, and there are separate toilet and shower compartments in the master stateroom. Outside, the cockpit is partially sheltered by a bridge overhang, and an overhead compartment in the overhang stores the removable cockpit table. Note that the side decks on the F43 are quite narrow and the engine room is a tight fit. Twin 370hp Volvo (or Cummins) diesels cruise in the low-to-mid 20s and and top out at close to 30 knots. Over 400 were built.

Not Enough Resale Data to Set Values

Length	43'5"	Fuel	350 gals.
Beam	13'8"	Water	120 gals.
Draft	3'8"	Headroom	6'2"
Weight	26,000#	Hull Type	Modified-V
Clearance	13'11"	Deadrise Aft	17°

Sealine F44 Flybridge

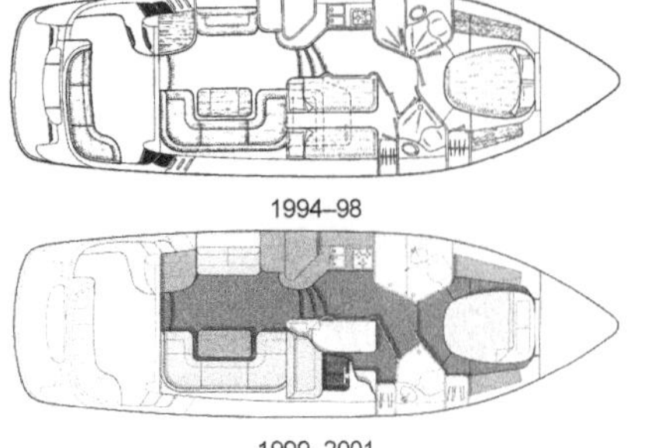

1994–98

1999–2001

Sealines have often been noted for their excessive styling, and the 44 Flybridge (called the 420 Statesman until 1998 when the swim platform was extended) is by any standard a very distinctively styled yacht. Built in England, she rides on a solid glass modified-V hull with moderate beam, a fully integrated swim platform, and prop pockets to reduce shaft angles. The Sealine's two-stateroom, galley-down floorplan was slightly upgraded in 1999 when the berths in the guest cabin were rearranged. The cockpit comes with a built-in lounge seat, transom door, and molded steps to the side decks. A useful feature of the 44 Flybridge (as well as many other Sealine models) is an overhead compartment above the cockpit that houses a canvas cockpit enclosure. To port, a curved stairway leads to the flybridge where a large sun pad it located aft of the helm. Additional features include foredeck fender storage, a huge storage bin beneath the cockpit and side exhausts. On the downside, the engineroom is a tight fit. Twin 370hp Volvo (or Cummins) diesels cruise in the low 20s (25+ knots top), and a pair of 450hp Cummins cruise in the mid to high 20s and reach a top speed in excess of 30 knots.

Not Enough Resale Data to Set Values

Length	44'0"	Fuel	350 gals.
Beam	13'8"	Water	120 gals.
Draft	3'6"	Waste	40 gals.
Weight	26,500#	Hull Type	Modified-V
Clearance	15'6"	Deadrise Aft	16°

Sealine T46 Motor Yacht

1999–2003

With her spacious aft cabin floorplan (a rarity in European motor yachts), the Sealine T46 Motor Yacht incorporates the sleek, low-profile styling typical of many European flybridge designs with the greater volume and privacy of an American-style interior layout. Indeed, there is much to like about this floorplan with its elevated lower helm, large staterooms and—rare for any European yacht—a reasonably spacious galley. (Note that an optional three-stateroom layout eliminates the dinette.) Visibility from the lower helm is excellent, however the Sealine's engine room—accessed by removing panels in the salon sole—is an extremely tight fit. On deck, molded seating surrounds the cockpit, and the flybridge overhang conceals a drop-down canopy for aft deck weather protection. Additional features include a giant foredeck locker, teak decks, a roomy flybridge with wraparound guest seating and sun pad, a large circular escape hatch/window in the owner's stateroom (where the bed faces aft), and a deep swim platform. A good performer with 430hp Volvo (or 450hp Cummins) diesels, the T46 Motor Yacht will cruise in the low-to-mid 20s and reach a top speed of about 30 knots.

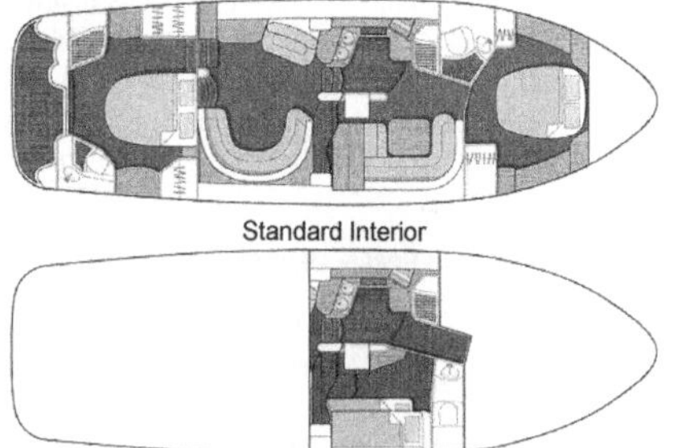

Standard Interior

Optional Three-Stateroom Layout

Not Enough Resale Data to Set Values

Length	45'6"	Fuel	424 gals.
Beam	14'2"	Water	120 gals.
Draft	4'1"	Headroom	6'3"
Weight	31,700#	Hull Type	Deep-V
Clearance	16'2"	Deadrise Aft	20°

Sealine T47 Motor Yacht

2000–05

Aggressive styling, good performance, and a raft of innovative features combine to make the Sealine T47 one of the better yachting values available in the U.S. market. The accommodations are excellent; instead of three staterooms, the T47 has two, and both are large and comfortable. The galley is on the lower level to increase salon space, and an extra double berth folds out from the salon settee. The high-gloss cherry woodwork throughout the T47's interior is particularly impressive—better than in any previous Sealine model. Sightlines from the lower helm are excellent, and there's an ingenious storage compartment with sliding trays in the galley sole. The crew cabin, under the teak-laid cockpit and accessed from the settee, is larger than expected and contains a washer/dryer in addition to a toilet and single berth. A cockpit entertainment center features a barbecue and refrigerator, and an overhead compartment stores the cockpit enclosure. Topside, the flybridge seats six comfortably and includes a sun pad. On the downside, working space between the motors is tight. Built on a deep-V hull with prop pockets, twin 480hp Volvo diesels cruise the T47 at 25 knots and reach a top speed of around 30 knots.

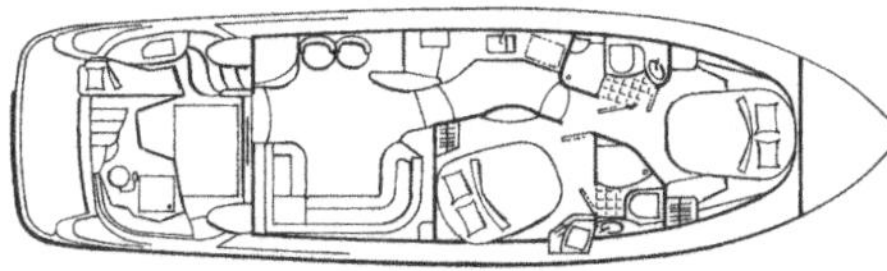

Not Enough Resale Data to Set Values

Length Overall	46'9"	Fuel	514 gals.
Beam	14'2"	Water	160 gals.
Draft	3'10"	Headroom	6'6"
Weight	28,650#	Hull Type	Deep-V
Clearance	15'6"	Deadrise Aft	18.5°

Sealine T51 Motor Yacht

1998–2004

Flagship of the Sealine fleet for several years, the T51 Motor Yacht is a UK-built flybridge cruising yacht whose graceful lines are particularly evident in the long sweep of her extended flybridge. She's built on a deep-V hull with a sharp entry, a relatively narrow beam, and an integral swim platform. Unlike many European motor yachts, the Sealine T51 does not employ prop pockets to reduce the shaft angles. With her main-deck superstructure set well forward, the Sealine is a spacious yacht both inside and out. Her three-stateroom, two-head floorplan is arranged with both guest cabins located beneath the elevated helm deck. While the roomy salon can seat a small crowd, the galley is on the small side with limited storage space. Outside, hatches in the teak cockpit sole access a huge lazarette as well as a companionway to the compact engineroom. Additional features include a spacious flybridge with sun pad and U-shaped settee, electric deckhouse windows, bow thruster, and overhead storage lockers in the cockpit. A very good performer, twin 600hp Cat (or 635hp Cummins) diesels cruise the Sealine T51 Motor Yacht at 25 knots and reach a top speed in the neighborhood of 30 knots.

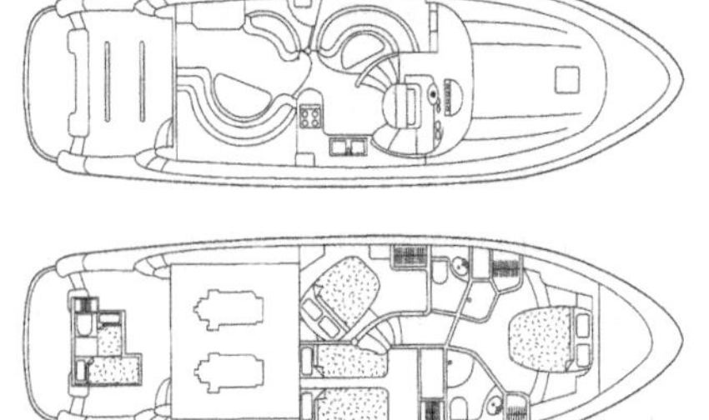

Not Enough Resale Data to Set Values

Length Overall	50'11"	Fuel	540 gals.
Beam	14'11"	Water	168 gals.
Draft	4'7"	Waste	60 gals.
Weight	44,000#	Hull Type	Deep-V
Clearance	12'6"	Deadrise Aft	21°

Selene

Quick View

- Selene trawlers are built in China by Jet-Tern Marine, an experienced manufacturer with modern, state-of-the-art facilities located just north of Hong Kong.
- The first Selene model, the Selene 43, arrived in the U.S. in 1999.
- She was soon followed by the Selene 47, and by 2003 Jet-Tern was producing a full line of Selene trawlers for dealers in the U.S., Europe, and Asia.
- Selene Trawlers are widely admired for their traditional full-displacement design, modern engineering, and quality construction.
- To date, the company has sold more than 300 boats from 37 feet to 75 feet in length.
- A Selene owner's group can be found at www.seleneowners.org.

Selene Trawlers • Guangdong Province, China • www.selenetrawlers.com

Selene 36/38 Trawler

2003–Current

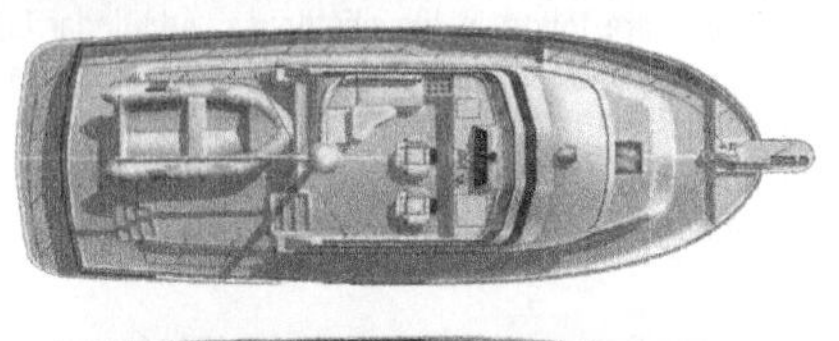

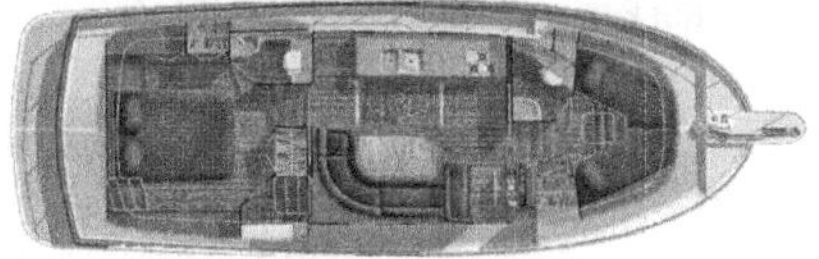

Designed for secure coastal and offshore cruising, the Selene 36 (called the Selene 38 since 2010) is a well-built small trawler with a compelling blend of comfort and value. Among her other virtues, the 36 is notable in that she's one of the smallest full-displacement yachts available on today's market. A handsome yacht with a salty profile (note the reverse-raked front windows), the interior volume of the Selene 36 is impressive for a boat this size. The galley-up accommodations include two comfortably sized staterooms, two heads, and a spacious salon with port and starboard deck doors and L-shaped sofa. There are two large hanging lockers in the master stateroom, which is arranged with separate head and shower compartments as well as an engineroom access door. Visibility from the lower helm is excellent, and the entire interior is finished with solid teak joinery and a teak-and-holly sole. Topside, the Selene's full walkaround decks and sturdy handrails make her an easy boat to get around. A windlass, bow thruster, swim platform, and bow pulpit are standard. A single 220hp Cummins diesel delivers an efficient 7–8 knot cruising speed (about 10 knots top).

Not Enough Resale Data to Set Values

Length Overall	41'9"	Clearance, Mast	21'2"
Length WL	36'6"	Fuel	500 gals.
Beam	14'6"	Water	180 gals.
Draft	4'8"	Waste	55 gals.
Weight	35,700#	Hull Type	Displacement

Selene 43/45 Pilothouse

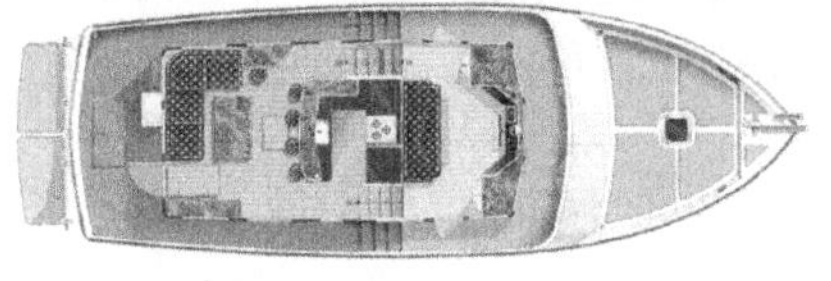

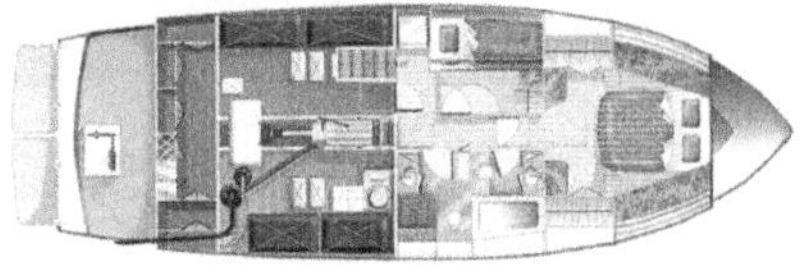

Originally marketed as the Solo 43 in 1998–2000, the Selene 43 (called the Selene 45 since 2010) is a long-range trawler whose traditional pilothouse profile conceals a practical and very innovative interior. By any standard, the 43 is a handsome yacht with a Portuguese bridge fronting the house and a salty, go-anywhere appearance. In the salon, the Selene's unusual center galley arrangement allows passage around both ends, either up to the pilothouse or down to the forward living quarters. Also unique, part of the guest cabin bulkhead folds away to create a large common area abaft the master stateroom. The Selene's salon, while not spacious compared with other 43-footers, is furnished with an L-shaped lounge aft and barstool seating at the galley. A watch berth and inside access to the flybridge are found in the pilothouse, and the entire interior is highlighted by solid teak joinery and a teak-and-holly sole. Additional features include a washer/dryer, two chain lockers at the bow, a hinged swim platform, and a huge "commissary" storage area between the engineroom and lazzarette. A single 210hp Cummins diesel will cruise efficiently at 8 knots with a range in excess of 2,000 miles.

Not Enough Resale Data to Set Values

Length Overall	48'5"	Ballast	3,000#
Length WL	43'11"	Fuel	1,000 gals.
Beam	15'8"	Water	230 gals.
Draft	5'0"	Waste	60 gals.
Weight	58,000#	Hull Type	Displacement

Selene 47 Pilothouse

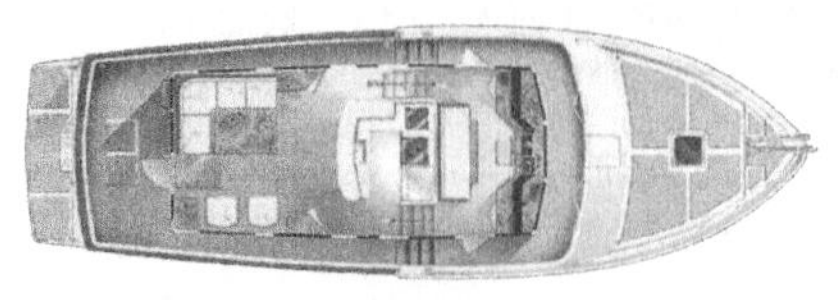

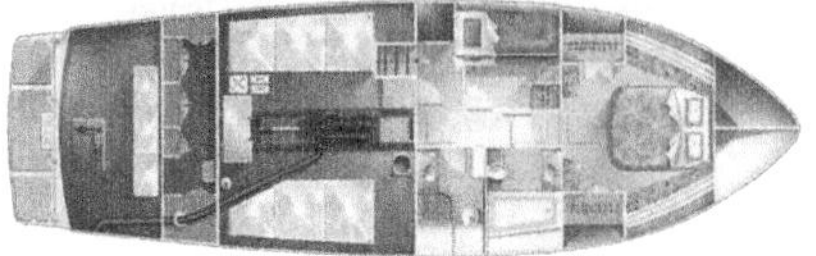

Designed for extended passages, the stately profile of the Selene 47 is more than matched by her solid construction and well-designed interior. The 47 is a stretched version of the Selene 43 with the extra length used to create a larger salon and a slightly expanded aft deck area. Built on a ballasted, full-displacement hull, the Selene's standard floorplan is as innovative as it is practical. In the salon, the Selene's unusual center galley arrangement allows passage around both ends, either up to the pilothouse or down to the forward living quarters. Also unique, part of the guest cabin bulkhead folds away to create a large common area abaft the master stateroom. The Selene's salon, while not spacious compared with other 47-footers, is furnished with an L-shaped lounge aft and barstool seating at the galley. A watch berth and inside access to the flybridge are found in the pilothouse. Additional features include a full teak interior, washer/dryer, a hinged swim platform, and a "commissary" storage area between the engineroom and lazarette. A single 330hp Cummins diesel will cruise efficiently at 8 knots with a range in excess of 2,000 miles.

Not Enough Resale Data to Set Values

Length Overall	50'1"	Ballast	4,000#
Length WL	46'1"	Fuel	1,000 gals.
Beam	15'8"	Water	210 gals.
Draft	5'1"	Waste	60 gals.
Weight	64,200#	Hull Type	Displacement

Selene 53/54 Pilothouse

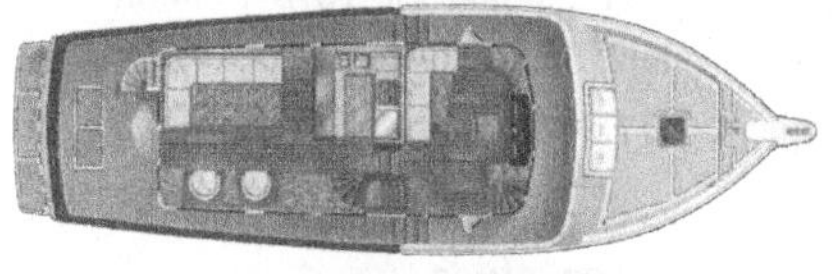

Experienced cruisers will find a lot to like in the Selene 53 (called the Selene 54 since 2010), a serious long-range passagemaker whose sturdy pilothouse profile masks a luxuriously appointed interior. Like other Selene models, the 53 rides on a full-displacement hull with a relatively sharp entry and a long, prop-protecting keel. The focal point of this yacht is her well-appointed pilothouse, fronted by a traditional Portuguese bridge, which towers high above the water for a commanding view. A big U-shaped galley is forward in the salon, and a "commissary" provides an additional storage area for cruise essentials. Below, the living quarters consist of three staterooms and two full heads. The master stateroom, which is amidships, has direct access to the Selene's standup engineroom, which can also be reached via a spiral staircase opposite the galley. Outside, the cockpit and wide side decks are sheltered from sun and spray by flybridge overhangs. A full teak interior, salon entertainment center, washer/dryer, bow and stern thrusters, and a bow pulpit are standard. A single 430hp Cummins diesel will cruise the Selene 53 at 8 knots and reach 11–12 knots wide open.

Not Enough Resale Data to Set Values

Length Overall	59'10"	Ballast	6,000#
Length WL	50'10"	Fuel	1,300 gals.
Beam	16'8"	Water	400 gals.
Draft	5'10"	Waste	120 gals.
Weight	95,000#	Hull Type	Displacement

Silverton

Quick View

- The Silverton story has its roots in depression-era New York City when Henry Luhrs began a boat-building company that eventually became known as Henry Luhrs Sea Skiffs.
- By the time Luhrs and his two sons sold out to Banger Punta in 1965, the rapidly growing firm was building over 1,000 boats a year—a large operation by the standards of the day.
- Looking for other opportunities, in 1969 Luhrs' sons John and Warren purchased a small builder in Toms River, NJ, called Silverton Sea Skiffs.
- Renamed Silverton Marine, the operation grew steadily in size during the 1970s, and in 1978 the company introduced the Silverton 34 Convertible, their all-time best-selling model.
- In 1985 Silverton moved to larger quarters in Millville, NJ.
- By 2002, Silverton had become one of the leading builders of aft-cabin family cruisers with 90 dealerships in the United States and 40 other countries.
- In February, 2012 Morgan Industries, Inc., parent company of Silverton, filed for bankruptcy. Silverton production came to an end.
- Silverton was purchased in July, 2012, by Egg Harbor Yachts.

Silverton Yachts • Egg Harbor, NJ • www.silverton.com

Silverton 271 Express

1995–97

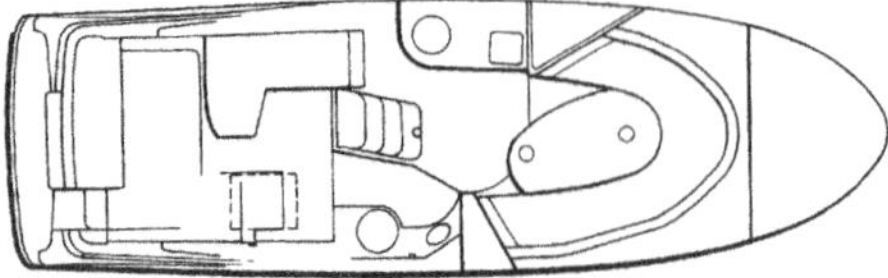

The Silverton 271 is a contemporary family cruiser with accommodations for four and the versatility of being trailerable. (Trailerable, yes, but with an over-the-road weight approaching 9,000 pounds including trailer, it'll take a 1-ton tow vehicle to do the job.) Built on a solid fiberglass hull with moderate transom deadrise, the 271 Express is a big boat on the inside thanks to her very high freeboard. The midcabin floorplan is arranged in the normal manner with double berths fore and aft, a full galley, removable dinette, and an enclosed head with shower. The high freeboard of the 271 permits plenty of cabin headroom, but there's no denying the fact that her high profile gives her a top-heavy appearance. A wraparound settee is opposite the helm, and the integrated swim platform has a hot and cold shower, swim ladder, and a handy storage locker. Lacking side decks, a walk-through windshield provides access to the foredeck. A single 250hp MerCruiser sterndrive will cruise the Silverton 271 at a rather sluggish 15 knots (mid 20s top). An optional 300hp Merc delivers a more respectable 18–19 knots at cruise and close to 30 knots wide open.

See Page 700 For Price Data

Length w/Pulpit	29'9"	Weight	7,643#
Hull Length	27'10"	Fuel	109 gals.
Beam	8'6"	Water	30 gals.
Draft, Drive Up	1'8"	Hull Type	Modified-V
Draft, Drive Down	3'1"	Deadrise Aft	14°

Silverton 31 Convertible

The 31 Convertible marketed by Silverton in 1991–95 was one of the roomier small flybridge boats of her era as well as being one of the least expensive—key factors in her ultimate sales success. Hull construction is solid fiberglass, and with an 11-foot, 8-inch beam this is a notably spacious 31-footer. Originally offered with a midcabin interior (with a claustrophobic "stateroom" off the galley extending under the salon), in 1992 Silverton offered the option of a single-stateroom "convertible" interior with a larger galley, but without the midcabin's elevated dinette. The salon, incidentally, is very spacious for a boat this size with good headroom and wraparound cabin windows. Both floorplans have an island double berth in the private forward stateroom as well as a separate stall shower in the head. With such generous interior accommodations, it comes as no surprise to find the cockpit of the Silverton 31 is quite small. A transom door was standard, and molded steps at the corners lead to the 31's notably wide side decks. Bench seating on the flybridge will seat as many as five guests. Standard 235hp gas engines cruise at a respectable 18–19 knots (mid 20s top).

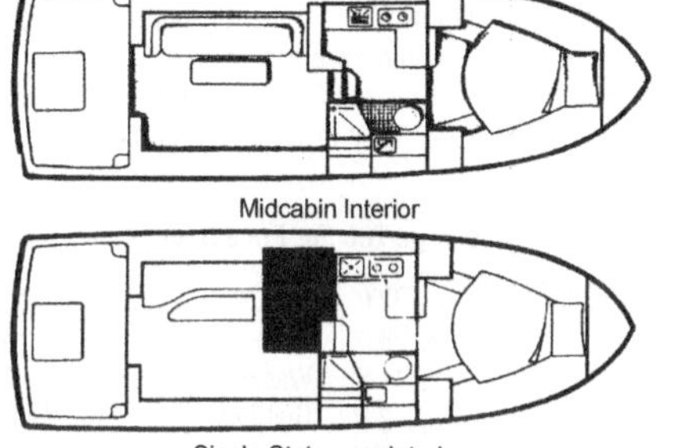
Midcabin Interior

Single-Stateroom Interior

See Page 700 For Price Data

Length	31'2"	Cockpit	48 sq. ft.
Beam	11'8"	Fuel	250 gals.
Draft	3'0"	Water	84 gals.
Weight	11,000#	Hull Type	Modified-V
Clearance	11'9"	Deadrise Aft	NA

Silverton 310 Express

A good-looking boat with her colorful hull graphics and still-modern profile, the Silverton 310 Express is a low-priced midcabin cruiser with a big interior and good overall performance. Like all Silverton boats, the 310's hull is solid fiberglass, and her 11-foot, 6-inch beam is reasonably wide for a 30-footer. Going below, the entryway steps are suspended by aluminum weldments, and the open design makes the aft cabin—tucked below the cockpit—seem unusually spacious. There are berths for six, and the opening ports and deck hatches provide excellent cabin ventilation. The cockpit is arranged with three seating areas (including a doublewide helm seat that tilts up for use as a bolster), and the cockpit table can be converted into a sun pad. Additional features include a walk-through windshield, privacy curtains for both staterooms, a foldaway transom seat, cockpit wet bar, and fender racks built into the swim platform. Standard 250hp 5.7-liter MerCruiser sterndrives cruise the 310 Express at 19–20 knots (low 30s top), and optional 300hp 7.4-liter engines deliver a 26-knot cruising speed (mid 30s top) knots.

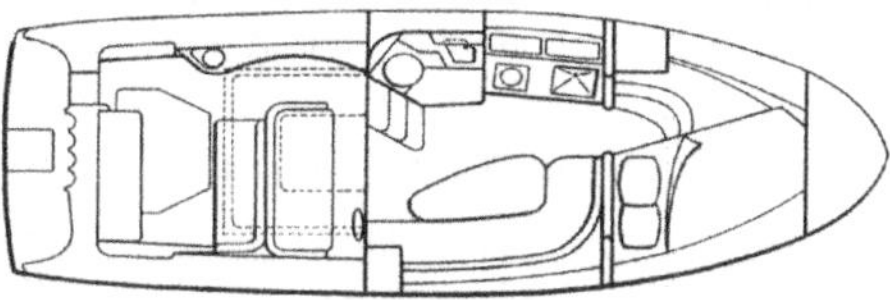

See Page 700 For Price Data

Length	32'0"	Fuel	150 gals.
Beam	11'6"	Water	54 gals.
Draft	2'2"	Waste	35 gals.
Weight	9,202#	Hull Type	Modified-V
Clearance	10'5"	Deadrise Aft	14°

Silverton 312 Sedan Cruiser

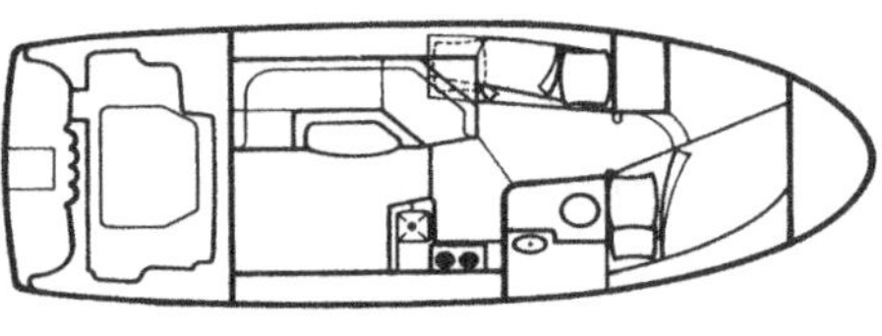

Silverton introduced the 312 Sedan in 1994 as a sporty, budget-priced family cruiser with sterndrive power—unusual in a flybridge boat. (Indeed, sterndrive-powered convertibles from U.S. builders are practically nonexistent.) Hull construction is solid fiberglass, and the rakish lines and low profile of the 312 give her a rather sporty personality. (Interestingly, the flybridge wasn't an add-on, but part of the deck mold, a cost-effective construction technique that also eliminates the possibility of leaks.) Belowdecks, the 312 sleeps six—no small feat for a 30-footer: two in the forward stateroom, two in a curtained-off open area opposite the head with upper/lower bunks, and two more when the salon dinette is converted into a double berth. A sliding glass door opens to the cockpit where a transom door is standard and a series of molded steps to port lead up to a large flybridge. Fender racks are built into the swim platform, and L-shaped lounge seating on the bridge will seat four. Among several engine options, twin 235hp MerCruisers cruise the Silverton 312 at 20 knots and reach a top speed of 30+ knots. Note that V-drive gas inboards were optional.

See Page 700 For Price Data

Length Overall	32'0"	Fuel	160 gals.
Hull Length	28'0"	Water	54 gals.
Beam	11'6"	Waste	28 gals.
Draft	2'8"	Hull Type	Modified-V
Weight	9,937#	Deadrise Aft	14°

Silverton 322 Motor Yacht

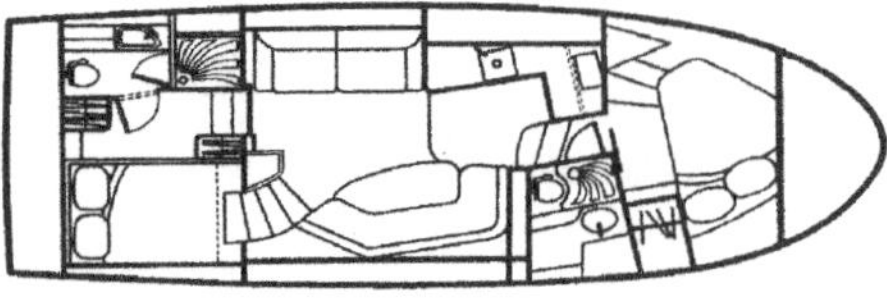

The 322 Motor Yacht expanded on Silverton's signature "Side-Walk" design—a full-beam salon configuration with twin ascending staircases instead of side decks—first seen on the Silverton 372 MY introduced two years earlier. This was a new concept in small motoryacht design, one that produced greater interior volume than many thought possible in a boat this size. Indeed, with two double staterooms, two heads, full-service galley, and a spacious, full-beam salon with convertible settee and dinette the Silverton 322 is probably the most spacious 32-footer ever built. In addition to her vast interior, the 322 features a roomy flybridge as well as a small aft deck with wet bar and hardtop. Foredeck access from the flybridge is excellent with wide, molded steps and sturdy rails, and a curved staircase provides easy boarding from the swim platform. A huge sales success for Silverton, the downside of the 322 Motor Yacht is her ungainly, top-heavy profile—a feature that can make for an uncomfortable ride in tall waves. Built on a modified-V hull with a wide 12-foot, 4-inch beam, twin 350hp MerCruiser gas engines cruise at 15–16 knots (mid 20s top).

See Page 700 For Price Data

Length Overall	37'0"	Fuel	200 gals.
Beam	12'4"	Water	72 gals.
Draft	2'11"	Waste	49 gals.
Weight	19,716#	Hull Type	Modified-V
Clearance	13'6"	Deadrise Aft	16°

Silverton 33 Convertible

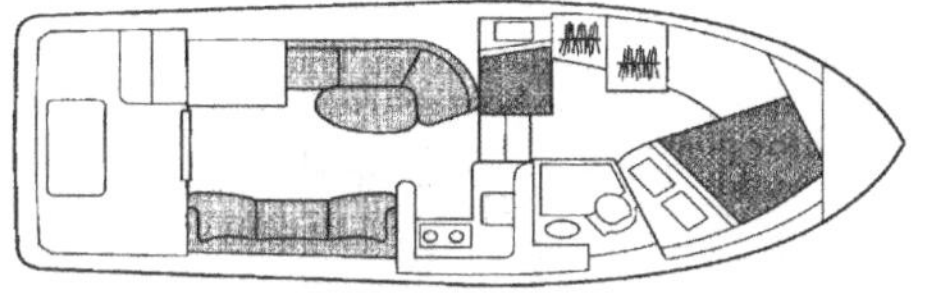

The Silverton 33 Convertible is an entry-level cruiser whose roomy interior comes as a surprise in a boat this size. Not that a two-stateroom floorplan in a 33-foot boat is unusual—there have been several such designs in the past, some more successful than others. The wide 12'8" beam of the Silverton 33, however, results in an exceptionally open layout that is enhanced by her large cabin windows. A sleeper sofa and dinette are standard in the salon, and the U-shaped galley includes a built-in microwave, single-burner stove, and an under-counter refrigerator/freezer. Sliding windows provide good cabin ventilation, and two hatches in the salon sole provide access to the engineroom. Below, the double bed in the master stateroom faces forward rather than aft, a space-saving design that might prove uncomfortable while underway. The small guest stateroom, aft and to port, has a double berth, hanging locker, and standing headroom by the doorway. The cockpit of the Silverton 33, which is small to begin with owing to the expansive salon, comes with a transom door and molded steps leading up the flybridge. Cruise at 20 knots with 375hp gas inboards (high 20s top).

See Page 700 For Price Data

Length	32'7"	Fuel	208 gals.
Beam	12'8"	Water	82 gals.
Draft	2'5"	Waste	30 gals.
Weight	16,800#	Hull Type	Modified-V
Clearance	15'6"	Deadrise Aft	14°

Silverton 330 Sport Bridge

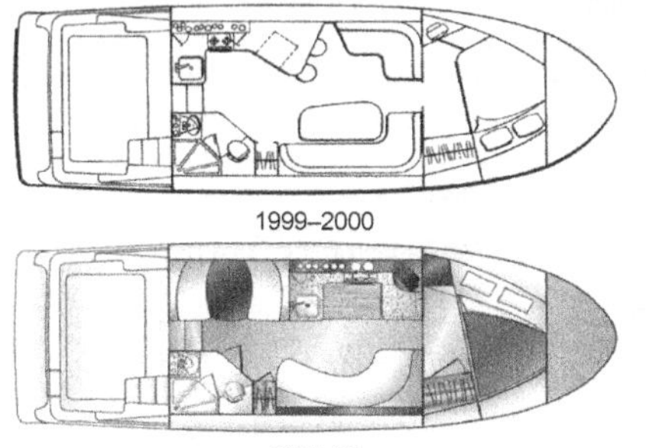
1999–2000

2001–07

Silverton has proven very adept in recent years at marketing affordably priced family yachts with mega-volume interiors and innovative design features. The 330 Sport Bridge follows in that tradition, and she's been a popular model for Silverton since her 1999 introduction. Built on a solid fiberglass hull with a wide beam, the single-stateroom floorplan of the 330 is laid out on a single level a few steps down from the cockpit. These are expansive accommodations indeed for a 33-foot boat with excellent headroom, attractive furnishings, and a full-beam salon. (Note that the floorplan was rearranged in 2001.) On deck, a stairway in the cockpit leads to an oversized flybridge with a wet bar and seating for six to seven adults, and molded steps on either side of the bridge lead down to the foredeck area. Engine access is via a gas-assist hatch in the cockpit, and a transom door and swim platform were standard. Additional features include opening salon windows, a flybridge sun pad, side exhausts, anchor locker, and bow pulpit. Twin V-drive 300hp gas inboards cruise the 330 Sport Bridge at 18 knots (25–26 knots top), and later models with 385hp engines cruise at 20 knots (about 30 knots top).

See Page 700 For Price Data

Length Overall	35'4"	Fuel	214 gals.
Beam	12'4"	Water	104 gals.
Draft	2'11"	Waste	30 gals.
Weight	15,685#	Hull Type	Modified-V
Clearance	11'0"	Deadrise Aft	16°

Silverton 34 Convertible

A restyled version of the company's previous 34-foot convertible (1989–90), the Silverton 34 Convertible offers an impressive combination of low cost, contemporary styling, and comfortable accommodations. She was built on a solid fiberglass hull with a reworked bottom and slightly more beam than her predecessor. Both single- and twin-stateroom floorplans were offered in this boat, both with an island berth in the forward stateroom, and both with the galley down from the salon level. The single-stateroom floorplan has a full-size dinette opposite the galley. In the two-stateroom version, a small cabin with upper/lower berths is available for guests, and the dinette is relocated to the salon. Either way, the salon dimensions are somewhat modest although the wraparound cabin windows, light oak cabinets and pastel fabrics add to the impression of space. Additional features include a stall shower in the head, wide side decks, side-dumping exhausts, a swim platform, and a bow pulpit. Note that in 1995 the flybridge was restyled. A good-selling boat, standard 350hp Crusader gas inboards cruise the Silverton 34 at 18 knots and reach a top speed of in the high 20s.

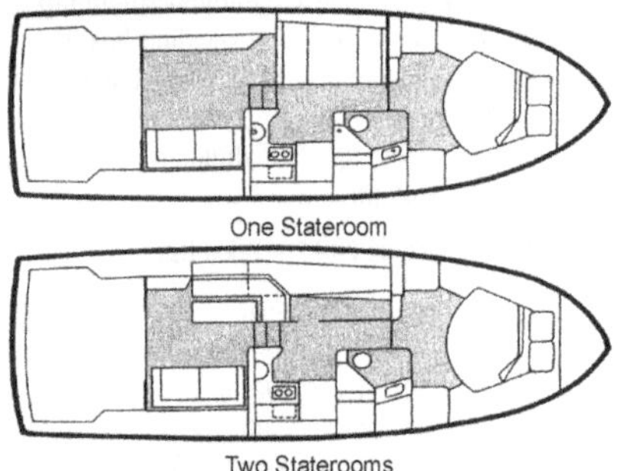
One Stateroom

Two Staterooms

See Page 700 For Price Data

Length	34'6"	Fuel	300 gals.
Beam	12'11"	Water	84 gals.
Draft	2'11"	Waste	28 gals.
Weight	18,000#	Hull Type	Modified-V
Clearance	14'11"	Deadrise Aft	17°

Silverton 34 Convertible

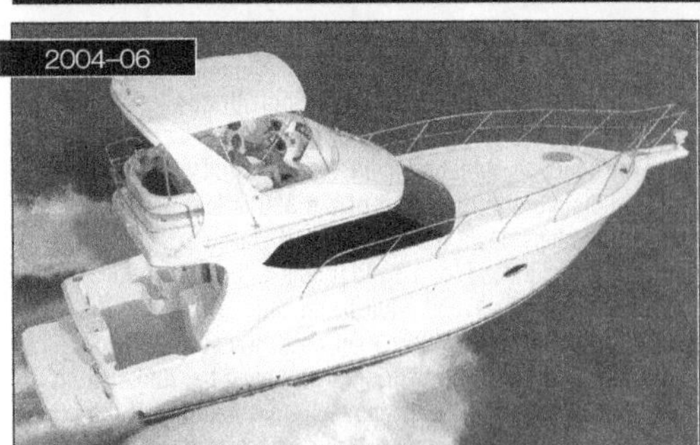

Silverton has offered a 34-foot convertible in their lineup ever since the late 1970s. This is the latest version, a stylish flybridge cruiser that might best be described as a lot of boat for the money. With nearly 14 feet of beam, this 34 is a more spacious boat than any of her predecessors. The extra volume is especially noticed in the salon where Silverton designers were able to find room for a dinette in addition to an entertainment center aft and starboardside sofa. The large galley includes an upright refrigerator as well as Corian counters and generous storage. Forward, an angled double berth is found in the master stateroom, while the small guest stateroom is fitted with over/under single berths. To save space, the head is split with the shower stall to starboard. The Silverton's interior is tastefully appointed with cherry cabinets, vinyl overheads, and earth-tone fabrics. A transom door and in-deck fish box were standard in the small cockpit, and molded access steps lead up to the flybridge. (Note that bridge overhang shades the forward part of the cockpit from the sun.) A modest performer with 330hp gas inboards, the Silverton 34 will cruise at 16 knots and top out at just over 20 knots.

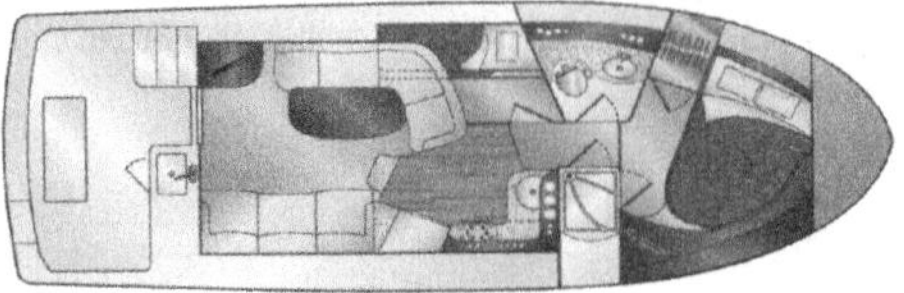

See Page 700 For Price Data

Length	37'7"	Fuel	286 gals.
Beam	13'10"	Water	94 gals.
Draft	3'3"	Waste	37 gals.
Weight	18,550#	Hull Type	Modified-V
Clearance	12'7"	Deadrise Aft	12°

Silverton 34 Motor Yacht

The Silverton 34 Motor Yacht is one of the smallest aft-cabin designs to have been built in recent years. An attractively priced but boxy-looking boat with a fairly wide beam, she somehow manages to include two reasonably sized staterooms inside along with a full-size dinette and stall showers in both head compartments—no small achievement in a 34-foot hull. The forward stateroom is surprisingly roomy and very much the equal of the aft cabin when it comes to floor space. Both head compartments come with shower stalls, and a serving counter separates the galley from the small salon. On the downside, usable storage space is in short supply. Topside, the aft deck of the Silverton 34 is really too small for anything other than a couple of folding chairs, and the flybridge is arranged with guest seating forward of the helm. Additional features include a hardtop and radar arch, light oak interior woodwork, molded steps from the aft deck to the swim platform, and a bow pulpit. A good performer with standard 320hp Crusader gas engines, the Silverton 34 MY will cruise at 17–18 knots and reach a top speed of around 28 knots.

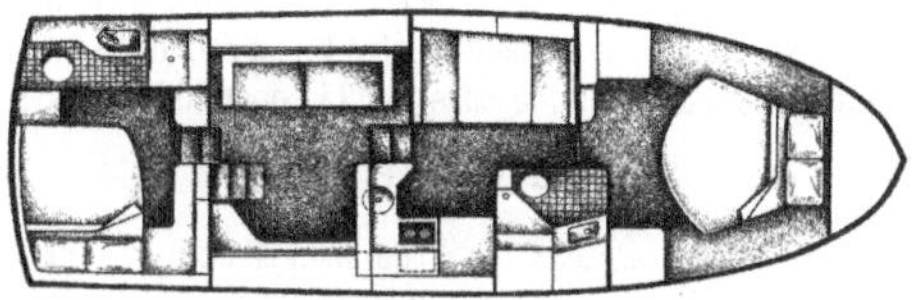

See Page 701 For Price Data

Length w/Pulpit	39'10"	Fuel	260 gals.
Hull Length	34'6"	Water	74 gals.
Beam	12'10"	Waste	45 gals.
Draft	3'0"	Hull Type	Modified-V
Weight	16,368#	Deadrise Aft	17°

Silverton 35 Motor Yacht

It's easy to find a boat with luxurious accommodations, and it's easy to find a boat with beautiful styling. In the Silverton 35 Motor Yacht, you get one of these attributes, but not both. The Silverton is a remarkably spacious motor yacht considering her modest length—and the price is certainly competitive—but her bloated, top-heavy appearance leaves a lot to be desired from the standpoint of yachting aesthetics. Built on a modified-V hull with prop pockets and a wide beam, the wide-open interior of the Silverton 34 is dominated by a lavish, full-beam salon with a convertible sofa, four-person dinette, and roomy step-down galley. Considering her expansive salon dimensions, it's hardly a surprise to find that the staterooms in the Silverton 35 are small with the berths positioned athwartships to save space. Note that the forward head is spilt with the shower stall to starboard. Topside, Silverton's trademark "BridgeWalk" allows passage from the aft deck to the bridge and foredeck without climbing a ladder. A hardtop, bow pulpit, underwater exhausts, and aft-deck wet bar were standard. Crusader 385hp gas inboards cruise the Silverton 35 MY in the low 20s and reach 26–27 knots top.

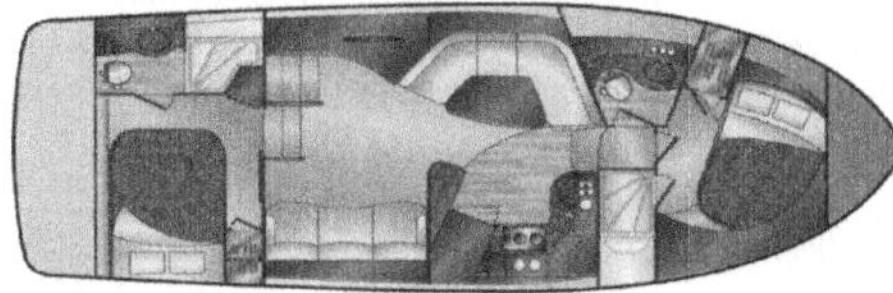

See Page 701 For Price Data

Length Overall	40'2"	Fuel	286 gals.
Beam	13'4"	Water	94 gals.
Draft	2'11"	Waste	55 gals.
Weight	22,618#	Hull Type	Modified-V
Clearance	16'0"	Deadrise Aft	12.5°

Silverton 351 Sedan

With the introduction of the 351 Sedan in 1997, Silverton engineers introduced a dramatically different approach to the design of the modern family cruiser. All manufacturers recognize the appeal of a roomy interior, but Silverton made it happen with the introduction of their "SideWalk" concept, a series of molded steps on the starboard side of the boat leading from the foredeck up to the flybridge and then down again to the cockpit. The result of this clever design is a spacious full-width salon with the floor space of a much larger boat. Built on a modified-V hull with side exhausts and prop pockets, the engines are located aft, beneath the cockpit rather than under the salon, which allows the cabin floor to sit low in the hull. Lacking side decks, the interior is huge and the apartment-sized galley will be a real crowd-pleaser, but with only a single stateroom these expansive living areas come as no great surprise. A pair of glass sliding doors open to a spacious cockpit, and the flybridge is arranged with a walkaround centerline helm and lounge seating forward. No racehorse, 320hp V-drive gas engines cruise at 14–15 knots and reach a top speed in the mid 20s. (Note that she was called the Silverton 35 Convertible in 2001.)

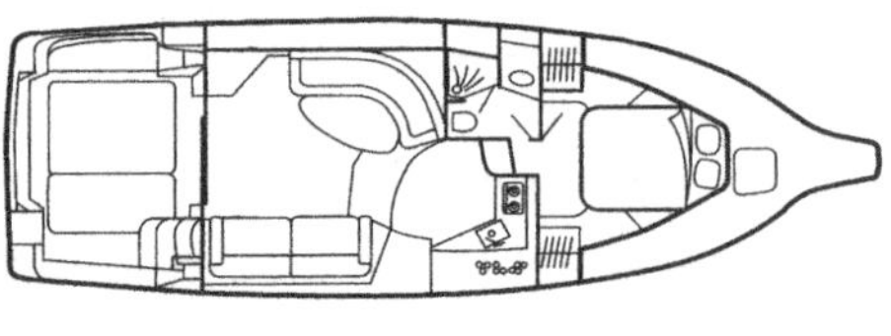

See Page 701 For Price Data

Length	38'10"	Fuel	300 gals.
Beam	13'0"	Water	94 gals.
Draft	2'5"	Waste	37 gals.
Weight	16,094#	Hull Type	Modified-V
Clearance	12'0"	Deadrise Aft	12°

Silverton 352 Motor Yacht

One of the most affordably priced yachts in her class, the Silverton 352 Motor Yacht employs the "SideWalk" deck configuration made popular in previous Silverton models. This unusual design, which replaces the side decks with a set of molded steps running down both sides of the house, gives the 352 a spacious full-beam salon at the expense of an unflattering, somewhat slab-sided profile. Built on a solid fiberglass modified-V hull, the two-stateroom floorplan is arranged with a mid-level galley and dinette and double berths in both staterooms. This is a huge interior for a 35-footer, and the salon dimensions can easily be compared to those of a much larger boat. Both heads are fitted with separate stall showers, and the mid-level galley has plenty of counter space and storage. An aft-deck wet bar was standard along with a hardtop, and there's seating for six on the flybridge. (Note that this is the same flybridge mold used for Silverton's 351 Sedan.) Additional features include a curved staircase from the swim platform to the aft deck and a spacious engineroom. A high-freeboard boat, 385hp gas engines cruise the 352 at a modest 16 knots (26–27 knots top). Optional 315hp Cummins diesels cruise at 18–19 knots.

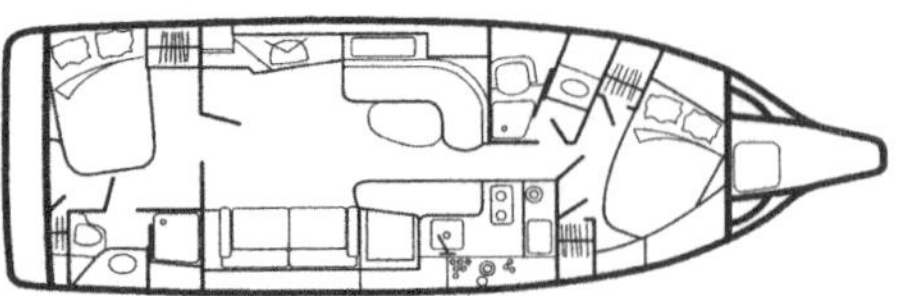

See Page 701 For Price Data

Length Overall	41'4"	Fuel	286 gals.
Beam	13'0"	Water	100 gals.
Draft	3'3"	Waste	68 gals.
Weight	20,809#	Hull Type	Modified-V
Clearance	16'2"	Deadrise Aft	16°

Silverton 360/361 Express

1995–2000

Introduced in 1995, the Silverton 361 Express (called the Silverton 360 Express in 1997–2000) combined the elements of style, comfort, and performance in a contemporary sportboat package. She was built on a solid fiberglass, low-deadrise hull with a wide beam and prop pockets to reduce draft. The midcabin floorplan of the 361 Express is arranged with double berths fore and aft, a full galley, and a circular salon dinette. There are privacy doors for both staterooms—a convenience seldom found in midcabin cruisers these days—and the interior is tastefully finished with cherrywood joinery and earth tone fabrics. There's comfortable seating in the cockpit for six, and the transom has a built-in storage and a hot-and-cold water shower. Lacking side decks, a walk-through windshield provides access to the foredeck. Note the sporty air intake vents in the hullsides. Additional features include a radar arch, swim platform, transom door, cockpit wet bar, and a foredeck sun pad. A very affordable boat by the standards of her day, twin 320hp Crusader gas inboards (with V-drives) will cruise the Silverton 360/361 Express at 18–19 knots and reach a top speed in the high 20s.

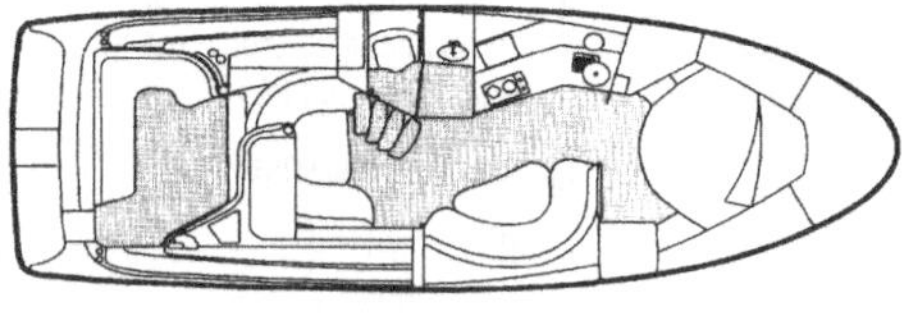

See Page 4701 For Price Data

Length	36'1"	Water	100 gals.
Beam	12'11"	Waste	40 gals.
Draft	2'6"	Clearance	9'10"
Weight	16,032#	Hull Type	Modified-V
Fuel	286 gals.	Deadrise Aft	12°

Silverton 362 Sedan

1994–98

A stylish sedan with sporty lines, the Silverton 362 is an appealing, entry-level family cruiser with a lot of living space packed into her 36-foot length. She's built on a solid fiberglass hull with a wide beam and a relatively steep 17 degrees of transom deadrise. The two-stateroom floorplan is arranged with a mid-level galley and an island berth in the forward stateroom. The guest stateroom (which extends beneath the salon settee) has two single berths that convert into a queen berth with a filler. Note the split head/shower compartments, a great idea that allows someone to take a shower without tying up the head. With her spacious interior dimensions, it's no surprise that the 362's cockpit is on the small side. Two hatches in the sole provide easy access to the engines, and molded steps lead up to the oversize flybridge with its wraparound lounge seating. Additional features include side-dumping exhausts, radar arch, transom door, and foldaway bench seating at the transom. On the downside, the uneven finish reflects her low price. Twin 320hp V-drive Crusader gas inboards cruise the 362 Sedan at 18 knots and deliver a top speed in the high 20s.

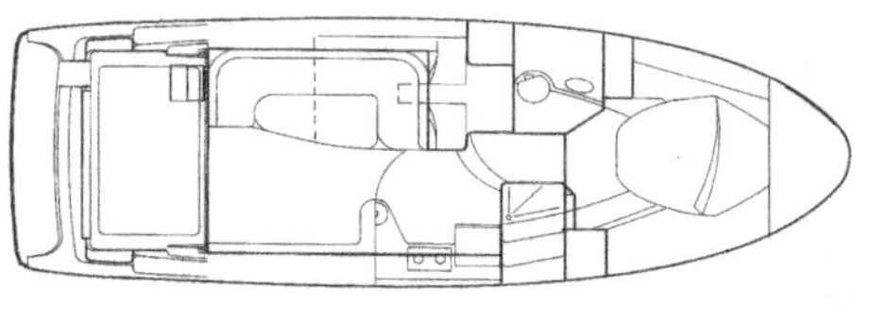

See Page 701 For Price Data

Length	36'1"	Fuel	300 gals.
Beam	12'11"	Water	100 gals.
Draft	3'0"	Waste	40 gals.
Weight	15,058#	Hull Type	Modified-V
Clearance	13'0"	Deadrise Aft	17°

Silverton 37 Convertible

With her rakish appearance, affordable price, and spacious interior, the 37 Convertible was a highly successful boat for Silverton during the 1990s. (An earlier Silverton 37 Convertible was produced from 1980–89.) Built on a solid fiberglass, modified-V hull with a wide beam and prop pockets to reduce draft, Silverton offered this model with "convertible" and "midcabin" interiors. (Note that the original floorplans were updated in 1993.) The convertible layout contains a single private stateroom forward with the galley and dinette down, while the midcabin features a small guest stateroom with over/under berths opposite the galley. A separate stall shower is found in the double-entry head, and the decor is a tasteful blend of teak or light oak trim and inexpensive fabrics. While the 37 is more family cruiser than fishboat, the cockpit is roomy enough for a couple of light-tackle anglers and features an in-deck fish box and a transom door. Additional features include wide side decks, wraparound lounge seating on the bridge, bow pulpit, a well-arranged engineroom, and side-dumping exhausts. No racehorse, standard 320hp gas engines cruise the Silverton 37 at 15–16 knots with a top speed in the mid 20s.

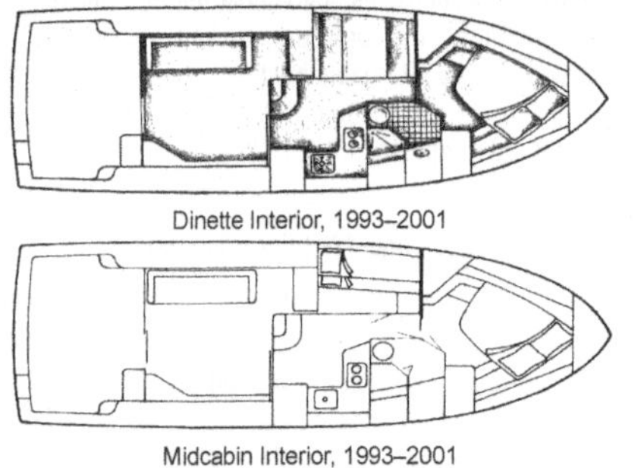
Dinette Interior, 1993–2001

Midcabin Interior, 1993–2001

See Page 701 For Price Data

Length w/Pulpit	41'3"	Fuel	375 gals.
Hull Length	37'4"	Water	100 gals.
Beam	13'11"	Waste	40 gals.
Draft	3'7"	Hull Type	Modified-V
Weight	21,852#	Deadrise Aft	17°

Silverton 372/392 Motor Yacht

A huge sales success in spite of her top-heavy appearance, those looking for an affordable, maxi-volume cruising yacht will find much to like in the Silverton 372 Motor Yacht (called the 392 MY from 1999–2001). By eliminating the side decks in favor of elevated staircases—what the company called "SideWalks"— Silverton designers were able to produce a distinctive midsize motoryacht whose salon dimensions are truly expansive for a boat this size. She rides on a high-freeboard modified-V hull with a solid fiberglass bottom and wide 14-foot, 1-inch beam. Hands down, the principal feature of the Silverton 372/392 is her enormous full-beam salon complete with cherry joinery, Ultraleather sofa, large dinette, and full-service galley. There are double berths in both staterooms (neither of which are especially roomy thanks to the huge salon), and each head contains a separate stall shower. Topside, the flybridge is arranged with bench seating fore and aft of the helm console. The afterdeck came standard with a hardtop, wet bar, and rear bench seat. Note the curved staircase descending to the swim platform. No racehorse, 320hp gas inboards cruise at a sedate 14–15 knots (20+ top)

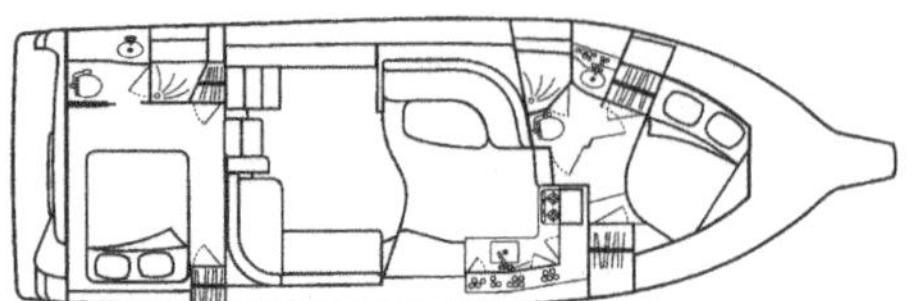

See Page 701 For Price Data

Length	43'9"	Fuel	286 gals.
Beam	14'1"	Water	100 gals.
Draft	3'3"	Waste	60 gals.
Weight	23,577#	Hull Type	Modified-V
Clearance	16'5"	Deadrise Aft	15°

Silverton 38 Convertible

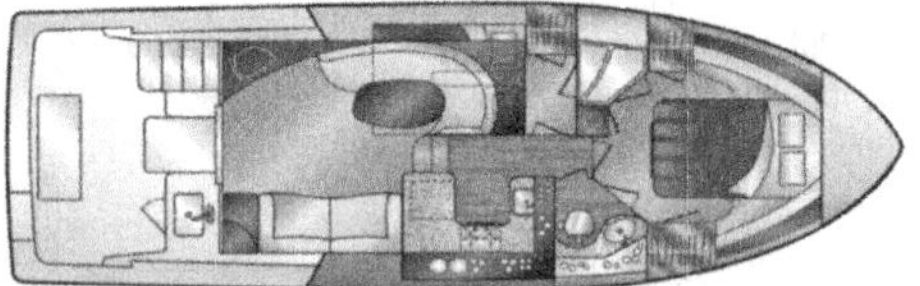

Bold styling, upscale accommodations, and a versatile personality characterize the Silverton 38 Convertible, a handsome sedan cruiser with a cockpit large enough for serious fishing. With her wide 14-foot, 3-inch beam, this is a big 38-footer with the salon space of a much larger boat. There are two staterooms in the Silverton 38, and while the pedestal berth in the master stateroom is a bit high it conceals a washer/dryer unit under the bed. The guest stateroom, which extends under the salon sole, comes with a full-size hanging locker and twin single berths, and the single head is split with the shower to port and the sink and toilet to starboard. A full-service galley, three steps down from the salon, includes generous storage as well as hardwood flooring. While not specifically designed for fishing, the cockpit has two fish boxes in the sole and a storage box in the transom. (A bait-prep center was optional.) A molded staircase makes it easy to reach the flybridge, and a cockpit hatch provides access to the engineroom. At less than 25,000 pounds, the 38 is a notably weight-efficient boat in spite of her wide beam. Standard 385hp gas inboards cruise the Silverton 38 at 18 knots and top out in the mid 20s.

See Page 701 For Price Data

Length w/Pulpit	41'1"	Fuel	360 gals.
Beam	14'3"	Water	100 gals.
Draft	3'7"	Waste	40 gals.
Weight	26,450#	Hull Type	Modified-V
Clearance	16'8"	Deadrise Aft	17°

Silverton 38 Sport Bridge

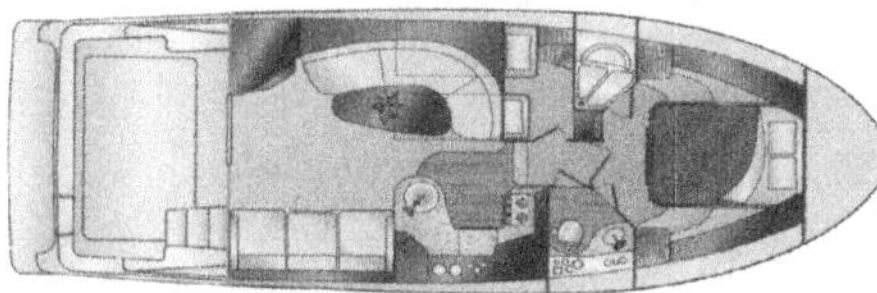

Silverton has proven adept in recent years at marketing affordably priced family yachts with maxi-volume interiors and innovative features. The 38 Sport Bridge follows in the footsteps of the company's popular 330 Sport Bridge introduced back in 1999. Built on a solid fiberglass hull with a wide beam, the spacious, full-beam interior of the 38 Sport Bridge is made possible by raising the side decks from bow to bridge on both sides of the boat. The result is a wide-open interior whose dimensions resemble those of a much larger boat. The salon is comfortable and brightly lit with windows all around and more headroom than most boats her size. The dinette is a step up from the salon floor to make room for the midcabin below, and the split head is separated with the toilet to starboard and the shower to port. Molded steps in the cockpit lead up to the 38's large flybridge with its generous lounge seating, wet bar, and forward helm position. A hatch in the cockpit sole reveals a removable storage bin, and there's additional storage in the transom for fenders and miscellaneous gear. The engineroom is a tight fit. Cruise in the low 20s with 425hp gas engines; 24–25 knots with optional 355hp Cummins diesels.

See Page 701 For Price Data

Length	39'11"	Fuel	372 gals.
Beam	14'4"	Water	110 gals.
Draft	2'11"	Waste	40 gals.
Weight	26,900#	Hull Type	Modified-V
Clearance	14'11"	Deadrise Aft	12°

Silverton 39 Motor Yacht

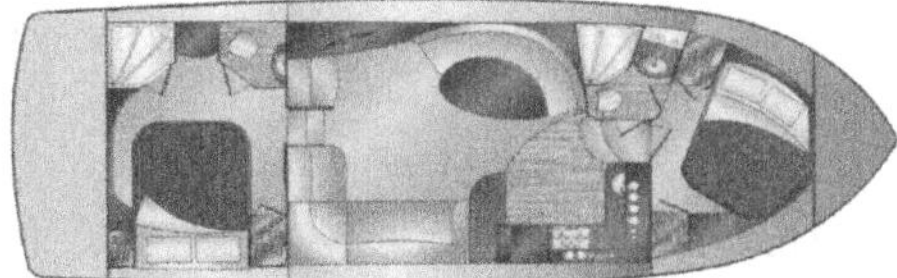

Introduced in 2002 as the replacement for Silverton's very successful 392 Motor Yacht (1996–2001), the Silverton 39 is a better looking boat than her predecessor, but not by much. Top-heavy in appearance, the appeal of this aft-cabin yacht is found in her spacious interior and civilized deck layout. The 39 employs Silverton's so-called "SideWalk" deck configuration made popular in the company's previous motor yacht designs. This layout, which replaces the side decks with a set of molded steps running down both sides of the house from the flybridge, gives the 39 MY a full-beam salon and easy foredeck access from the bridge. Both staterooms are fitted with queen beds, and both heads have separate stall showers. The salon is open and very spacious with satin-finished cherry woodwork and plenty of headroom. To provide more aft deck space, a molded bench seat slightly overhangs the integral swim platform. Topside, the helm is forward on the flybridge with a triple-wide helm seat and lounge seating for several guests. Standard 380hp gas engines cruise the Silverton 39 at a modest 16–17 knots. Optional 355hp Cat diesels cruise at 20 knots with a top speed in the mid 20s.

See Page 701 For Price Data

Length w/Pulpit	43'7"	Fuel	334 gals.
Hull Length	41'5"	Water	100 gals.
Beam	14'0"	Waste	60 gals.
Draft	3'11"	Hull Type	Modified-V
Weight	24,900#	Deadrise Aft	17°

Silverton 402/422 Motor Yacht

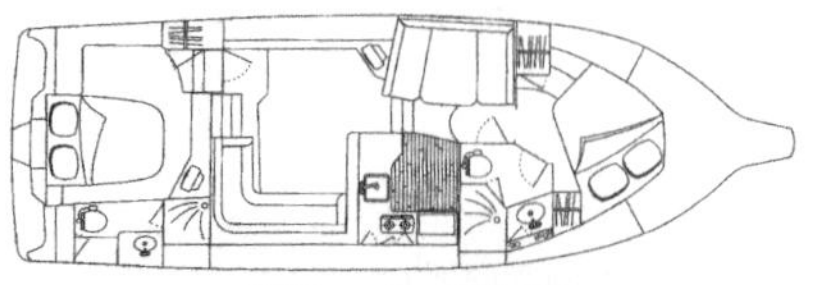
402 Floorplan, 1996–98

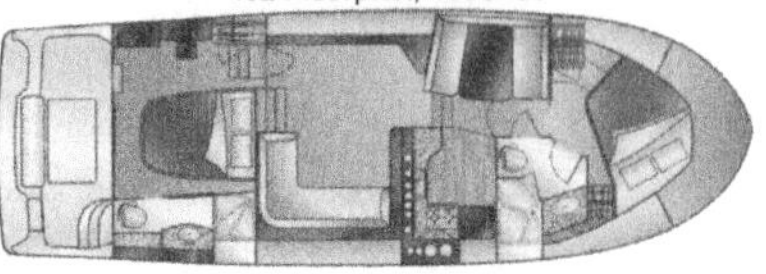
422 Floorplan, 1999–2001

The Silverton 402 Motor Yacht (called the 422 MY in 1999–2000) is a practical and affordably priced cruising yacht with conservative styling and very comfortable accommodations. Like all Silvertons, she was built on a solid fiberglass modified-V hull with generous beam and a shallow keel. Her two-stateroom, galley-down floorplan is a model of efficiency with double berths in both staterooms, a full-size dinette, a big U-shaped galley, and a roomy salon with a built-in sofa and entertainment center. A serving counter overlooks the galley, and wraparound cabin windows add to the impression of space in the salon. On the downside, the engineroom—accessed from hatches in the salon—is a tight fit, and storage space is at a premium. The aft deck came with a wet bar and hardtop, and molded steps lead from the aft deck to the swim platform where a storage locker and transom shower were standard. Additional features include a well-designed centerline flybridge helm, aft deck wet bar, radar arch, and wide side decks. A stiff ride in a chop, twin 320hp gas engines cruise the Silverton 402/422 at a leisurely 14 knots and reach a top speed in the low 20s. Several diesel options provide additional speed and range.

See Page 701 For Price Data

Length Overall	45'11	Fuel	375 gals.
Beam	14'2"	Water	132 gals.
Draft	3'6"	Waste	58 gals.
Weight	23,826#	Hull Type	Modified-V
Clearance	17'11"	Deadrise Aft	12°

Silverton 41 Aft Cabin MY

A low-cost yacht with conservative styling and an impressive list of standard equipment, the Silverton 41 Aft Cabin is a scaled-down version of the popular Silverton 46 Motor Yacht (1990–97). Like most Silvertons of her era, the 41 rides on a solid fiberglass hull with a relatively wide beam, moderate transom deadrise, and a shallow keel. While the decor is dated by today's high-glitz motor yacht standards, the two-stateroom interior is impressively large with plenty of room for entertaining. An L-shaped sofa and built-in entertainment center are found in the salon, and both staterooms are fitted with walkaround double berths. Hatches in the salon sole provide access to a large and well-arranged engineroom. Topside, the full-width aft deck of the Silverton 41 is very spacious and came with a wet bar and hardtop as standard. The flybridge, however, is rather small for a 41-foot boat with twin pedestal seats and lounge seating for four. Additional features include side-hull exhausts, a molded bow pulpit, and a radar arch. Standard 355hp gas engines cruise at a barely respectable 15–16 knots, and optional 375hp Cat diesels cruise at 20 knots and reach a top speed in the mid 20s.

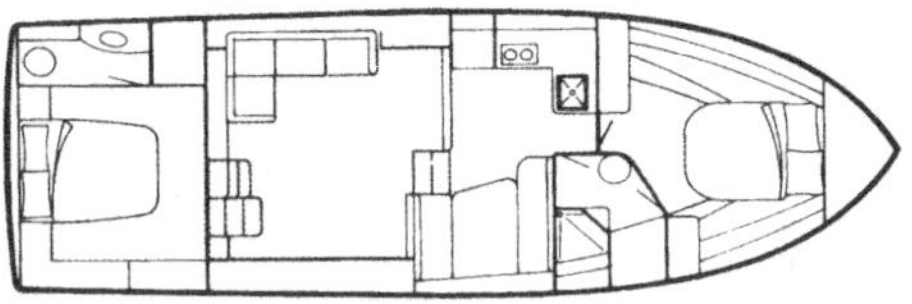

See Page 701 For Price Data

Length w/Pulpit	46'3"	Fuel	408 gals.
Hull Length	41'3"	Water	200 gals.
Beam	14'10"	Waste	68 gals.
Draft	3'7"	Hull Type	Modified-V
Weight	28,000#	Deadrise Aft	17°

Silverton 41 Convertible

The Silverton 41 Convertible is a versatile flybridge cruiser with a clean-cut profile, spacious interior, and a good turn of speed with standard big-block gas engines. With her long foredeck, step-down sheer, and rakish flybridge the 41 has the look of an offshore fishing boat although Silvertons have never been especially notable for their fishing prowess. Belowdecks, the two-stateroom interior of the Silverton 41 is arranged with the galley and dinette forward, three steps down from the salon. The Flexsteel sofa converts along with the dinette to provide extra sleeping capacity beyond the two staterooms. An island berth is located in the forward (master) stateroom, and the guest cabin is fitted with over/under berths. Buyers could choose from either oak or cherry interior woodwork. The Silverton 41's wide cockpit includes an in-sole fish box, sink, tackle storage and transom door. The flybridge—which is big for a boat this size—has lounge seating forward of the helm console. A popular model, standard 385hp gas engines cruise the Silverton 41 Convertible at 19–20 knots (high 20s top), and optional 425hp Cat diesels cruise at 24–25 knots.

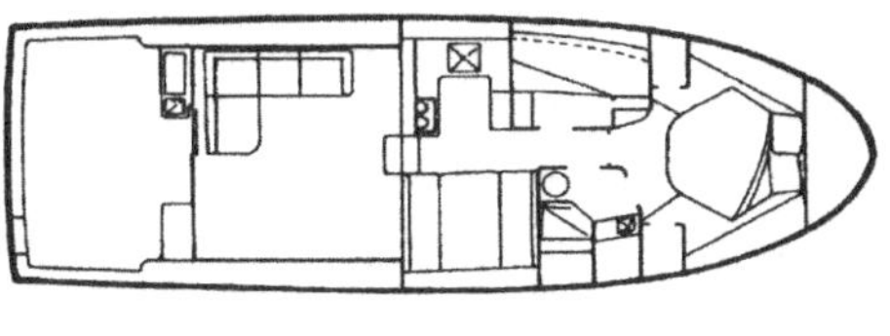

See Page 701 For Price Data

Length w/Pulpit	46'3"	Fuel	524 gals.
Hull Length	41'3"	Water	200 gals.
Beam	14'10"	Waste	60 gals.
Draft	3'7"	Hull Type	Modified-V
Weight	24,975#	Deadrise Aft	17°

Silverton 410 Sport Bridge

The apartment-size interior of the Silverton 410 Sport Bridge always appeals to boaters looking for as much living space as possible in a 40-foot boat. Indeed, the innovative interior of this boat is compelling, but traditionalists will find little to like in her slab-sided profile and top-heavy appearance. Built on a modified-V hull with a solid fiberglass bottom, the 410 uses Silverton's signature "SideWalk" design, which elevates the side decks to create a truly cavernous interior. Pushing the superstructure out to the sides of the boat to produce a huge salon gives Silverton the flexibility to create an unusual raised galley and dinette in the middle of the boat, and still leaves room for a spacious twin-cabin, twin-head layout forward. While the cockpit is on the small side, there's plenty of guest seating (and a wet bar) on the large flybridge. The descending walkways on both sides of the bridge provide safe and secure foredeck access. A transom door, radar arch and bow pulpit were standard. Twin 425hp gas inboards cruise the Silverton 410 Sport Bridge at a modest 15 knots and reach a top speed in the low-to-mid 20s. Optional 420hp Cat diesels cruise at 20 knots and reach 24–25 knots wide open.

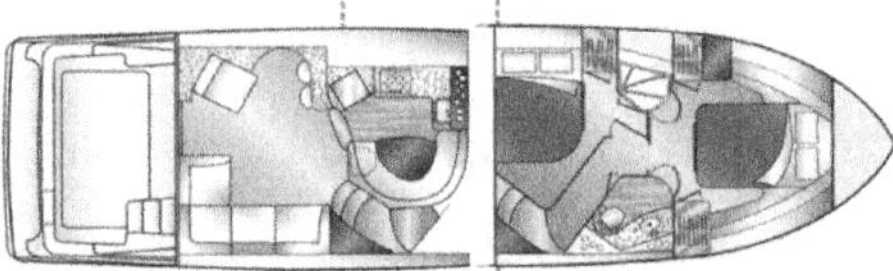

See Page 701 For Price Data

Length Overall	46'3"	Fuel	450 gals.
Beam	14'3"	Water	200 gals.
Draft	3'10"	Waste	40 gals.
Weight	28,495#	Hull Type	Modified-V
Clearance	15'4"	Deadrise Aft	16°

Silverton 42 Convertible

The Silverton 42 Convertible is a well-styled flybridge sedan whose spacious interior and large cockpit make her a good choice for family cruisers who like to do a little fishing. A distinctive design with a rakish hardtop and aggressive styling, she's built on the same proven hull used in the production of the earlier Silverton 41 Convertible. The two-stateroom interior of the Silverton 42 is a tasteful blend of cherry woodwork and earth-tone fabrics. An island double berth is located in the master stateroom, and the guest stateroom—also with a double berth—is tucked under the dinette. Note that the separate shower compartment is to port, opposite the head. On deck, the cockpit has an engineroom access door as well as a transom door and built-in tackle center. Molded steps ascend to the flybridge with its centerline helm and bench seating forward. Additional features include very wide side decks, power cabin windows (optional), an overhead rod locker in the salon, and a bow pulpit. Note that the molded hardtop was optional. A capable performer with twin 440hp Cummins diesels, the Silverton 42 Convertible will cruise at 20 knots (mid 20s top).

See Page 4701 For Price Data

Length Overall	44'6"	Fuel	524 gals.
Beam	14'11"	Water	200 gals.
Draft	3'7"	Waste	40 gals.
Weight	26,300#	Hull Type	Modified-V
Clearance	16'8"	Deadrise Aft	17°

Silverton 43 Motor Yacht

With her cavernous interior, the Silverton 43 Motor Yacht is aimed at buyers who value condo-style interior accommodations more than graceful styling. Indeed, the 43 is a big boat for her length whose vast interior is made possible by Silverton's signature "SideWalk" deck plan. Instead of traditional side decks around the salon, the 43 features a set of walkways leading forward from the flybridge along both sides of the house. This is a design Silverton has been using successfully for several years, and it makes deck access easy and very civilized. Below, the expansive salon of the 43—with its wraparound cabin windows, light cherry woodwork, and high ceilings—gives one the impression of being aboard a much bigger yacht. Both staterooms are fitted with queen berths, and both heads are split to separate the shower stalls from the toilets. A wet bar is standard on the aft deck where a curved stairway leads down to the swim platform. Topside, the helm is forward on the flybridge with guest seating aft. Built on a beamy modified-V hull, twin 480hp Volvo (or 430hp Cummins) diesels cruise the Silverton 43 at 18–19 knots with a top speed in the low 20s.

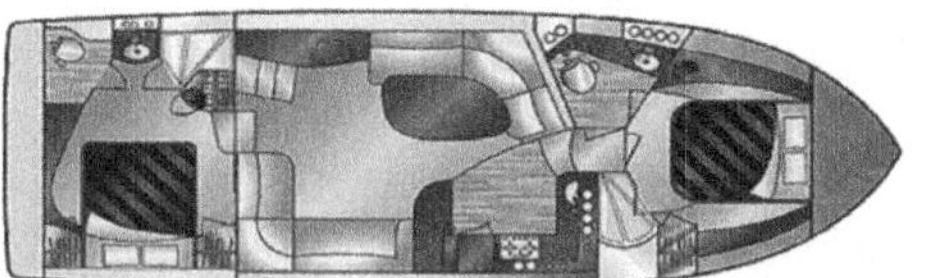

See Page 701 For Price Data

Length w/Pulpit	47'7"	Fuel	386 gals.
Beam	14'11"	Water	150 gals.
Draft	3'8"	Waste	80 gals.
Weight	29,000#	Hull Type	Modified-V
Clearance, Arch	17'0"	Deadrise Aft	17°

Silverton 43 Sport Bridge

Silverton had a reputation for rakish styling before they went out of business early in 2012, and the 43 Sport Bridge remains one of the company's more distinctive designs. With her generous beam and spacious, full-width salon, this is a big 43-footer with more interior space than most other boats in her class. (The downside, however, is a decidedly slab-sided appearance, the result of raising the side decks above the cabin windows to obtain that full-beam interior.) Her vast salon, with its cherrywood joinery, facing leather settees and sculptured overhead panels, has a large, U-shaped galley forward, opposite an elevated dinette with circular seating for five. Below, the forward master stateroom features a queen island berth, while the guest stateroom, aft and to starboard, has twin single berths. Note the divided master stateroom head and retractable salon TV. Cockpit steps lead up the 43's vast flybridge complete with wet bar, sun pad, lounge seating, and direct bow access. Twin 425hp gas engines cruise the 43 Sport Bridge at 16 knots. Volvo 480hp inboard diesels cruise at 20 knots, and Volvo 370hp diesels with IPS drives—standard after 2007—cruise efficiently at 20–22 knots (about 28 top).

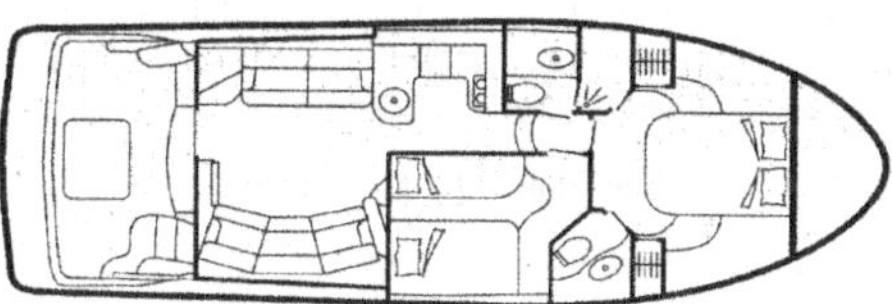

See Page 701 For Price Data

Length	43'5"	Fuel	430 gals.
Beam	14'4"	Water	118 gals.
Draft	3'10"	Waste	40 gals.
Weight	28,000#	Hull Type	Modified-V
Clearance	14'5"	Deadrise Aft	12°

Silverton 442 Cockpit MY

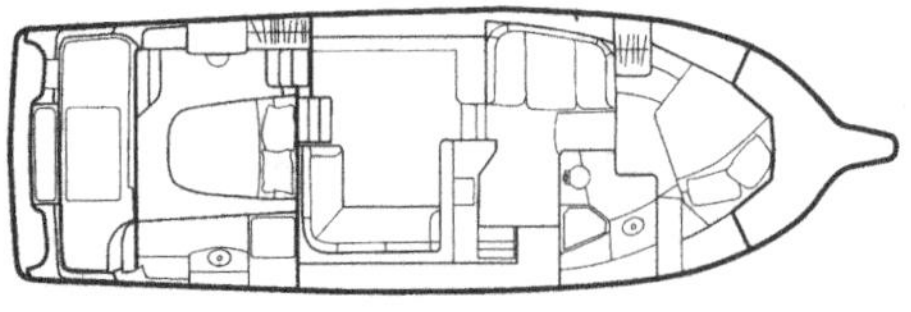

One of the more versatile yachts in her class, the Silverton 442 is a well-styled coastal cruiser with spacious accommodations, a large aft deck, and a small cockpit useful for swimming or fishing. She was built on a solid fiberglass, modified-V hull with a fully integrated swim platform—the same basic hull used in the production of the Silverton 402 Motor Yacht. Below decks, the 442's standard two-stateroom interior is arranged with the galley and dinette down. Both staterooms have double berths and both heads have separate stall showers. Note that the bed in the aft stateroom is placed against the forward bulkhead, facing aft toward a full-height sliding glass cockpit door. While this door makes cockpit access especially convenient, its vulnerability in rough, following seas makes the 442 a fair-weather vessel. Weather boards, molded seating, and a wet bar were standard on the aft deck, and a storage locker is built into the swim platform. Topside, the helm console is on the centerline, and a clear panel in the hardtop provides visibility aft. No racehorse, standard 405hp gas engines cruise at just 14–15 knots (low 20s top). Optional Cummins 355hp diesels cruise at close to 20 knots.

See Page 701 For Price Data

Length	45'11"	Fuel	375 gals.
Beam	14'3"	Water	132 gals.
Draft	3'6"	Waste	58 gals.
Weight	23,826#	Hull Type	Modified-V
Clearance	18'3"	Deadrise Aft	15°

Silverton 45 Convertible

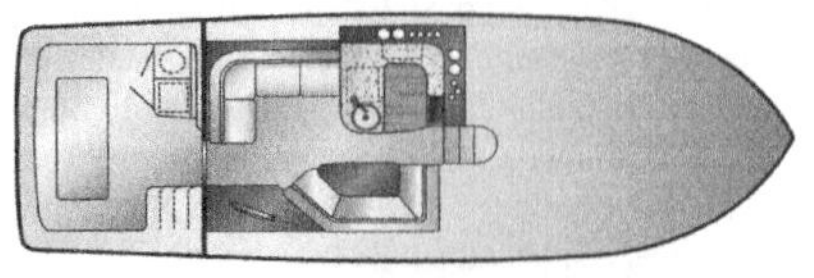

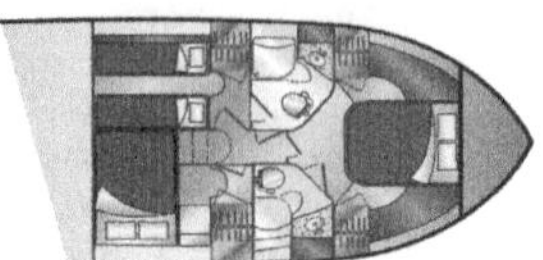

This won't come as a shock to most boaters, but there's a big difference between a Viking or Hatteras convertible and what Silverton calls a convertible. It's not just cost; convertible models are called that because they split the difference between fishing and cruising. And it's doubtful that any hardcore anglers are going to buy a Silverton 45 Convertible to fish. That said, the 45 is a fine cruising yacht, and compared with convertible models from other big-name builders the Silverton is more affordable in every way. Built on a low-deadrise hull with a wide 15'4" beam, her expansive three-stateroom interior (most 45-footers have two) can accommodate three couples in privacy and comfort. The salon, galley and dinette are on the same level—always a plus—and wraparound windows provide panoramic views of the water. Both the master stateroom and starboard guest stateroom have double beds, and a washer/dryer can be fitted in second guest cabin to port. Note that both heads have separate stall showers. The Silverton's big 80-square-foot cockpit features a wet bar with refrigerator and engineroom access door. The fiberglass hardtop was standard. Volvo 575hp diesels cruise at 22 knots (high 20s top).

See Page 701 For Price Data

Length	47'8"	Fuel	607 gals.
Beam	15'4"	Water	120 gals.
Draft	3'8"	Waste	72 gals.
Weight	42,048#	Hull Type	Modified-V
Clearance	16'10"	Deadrise Aft	13°

Silverton 453 Motor Yacht

A distinctive, heavily built yacht with a high-freeboard profile, the Silverton 453 MY will appeal to boaters more concerned with a condo-style interior than styling aesthetics. What makes this boat so boxy is the same thing that makes her so spacious; replacing the walkaround side decks of most motor yachts, the 453 has molded staircases ascending to both sides of the flybridge—what Silverton called "SideWalks." The result is a cavernous, full-beam interior whose dimensions rival those of a much larger yacht. Adding to the impression of space is a very innovative three-stateroom, two-head floorplan, a layout made possible by raising the galley and dinette forward of the salon. (An optional lower helm floorplan moved the galley into the salon.) Notably, the amidships VIP stateroom of the 453 is as big as the master stateroom aft. The entire interior is tastefully finished with rich cherrywood joinery. A wet bar is standard on the aft deck, and the flybridge has lounge seating aft of the helm. Additional features include a pilothouse deck door, large engineroom, and standard hardtop. Twin 430hp Cummins diesels cruise the Silverton 453 MY at 18 knots (low 20s top).

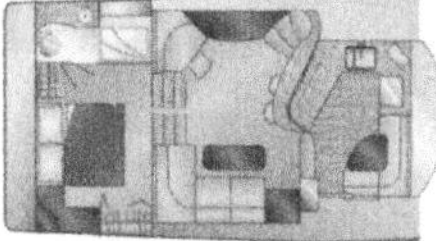
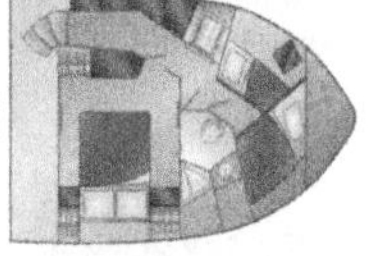

Standard Floorplan

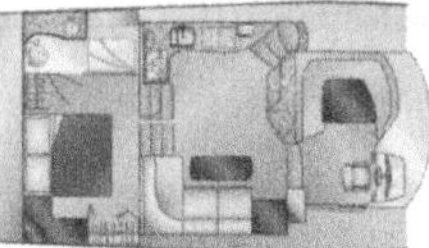
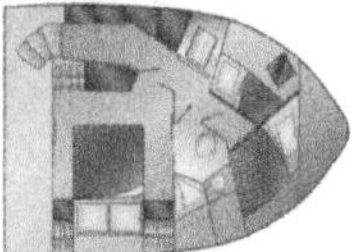

Lower Helm Floorplan

See Page 702 For Price Data

Length	47'8"	Fuel	500 gals.
Beam	15'4"	Water	190 gals.
Draft	4'0"	Waste	66 gals.
Weight	35,530#	Hull Type	Modified-V
Clearance	19'5"	Deadrise Aft	16°

Silverton 46 Aft Cabin MY

Largest boat in the Silverton fleet when she was introduced in 1990, the 46 Motor Yacht combined conservative styling and roomy accommodations in a feature-rich, low-cost package—a lot of boat for the money. Like many Silvertons of her era, the 46 rides on a solid fiberglass hull with a wide beam and a moderate 17 degrees of transom deadrise. The interior of the Silverton 46 is traditional with staterooms fore and aft and the galley and dinette down. The salon isn't large for a 46-footer, but it is quite open and includes a convertible L-shaped sofa to port. The second guest cabin has a foldaway berth that converts to a lounge. Storage is abundant throughout. (Note that the engineroom, accessed via hatches in the salon sole, is quite spacious.) Topside, the aft deck came with a hardtop, an entertainment center and wet bar, and the large flybridge is arranged with bench seating aft of the helm. Additional features include foredeck seating, radar arch, washer/dryer combo, wide side decks, bow pulpit, and a bathtub in the owner's head. Standard 485hp 6-71s cruise the Silverton 46 MY at 22 knots (mid 20s top).

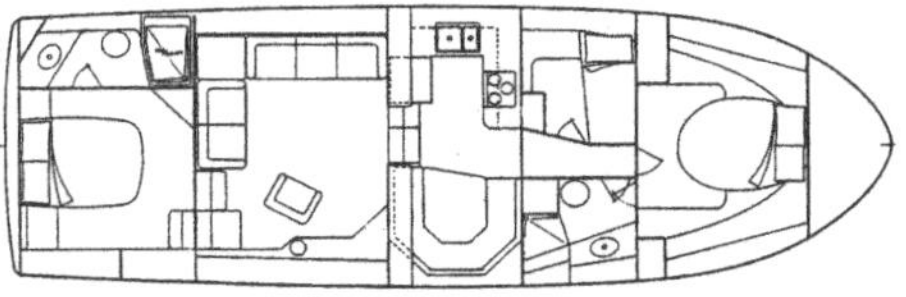

See Page 702 For Price Data

Length w/Pulpit	51'6"	Fuel	580 gals.
Hull Length	46'8"	Water	200 gals.
Beam	16'2"	Waste	56 gals.
Draft	3'9"	Hull Type	Modified-V
Weight	33,874#	Deadrise Aft	17°

Silverton 48/50 Convertible

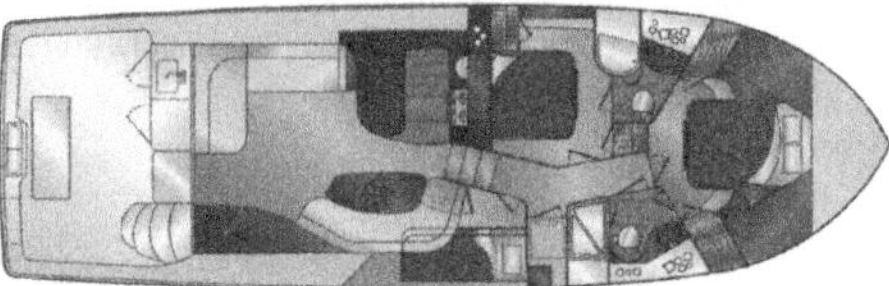

More coastal cruiser than hardcore fisherman, the Silverton 48 Convertible (called the 50 Convertible in 2007–12) is a well-styled flybridge yacht whose versatile design, spacious interior and attractive price make her a lot of boat for the money. Indeed, the 48/50 was a popular model for Silverton, probably because she offered such a good combination of sport and luxury. She's built on a modified-V hull with a wide 16-foot, 4-inch beam and prop pockets to reduce shaft angles. Below decks, the Silverton's well-appointed three-stateroom interior features a roomy main salon with Ultraleather sofa and dinette, full-service galley with under-counter refrigeration, two double staterooms, and a second guest stateroom with upper/lower bunks and washer/dryer. Front windows—unusual in most modern convertibles—provide additional natural lighting in the forward area of the salon. A hatch in the galley sole reveals a huge storage compartment. A livewell, raw water washdown, freezer, transom door, and engineroom access door are found in the cockpit. Note the molded flybridge staircase. Volvo 715hp diesels cruise the Silverton 48 in the high 20s and reach a top speed of close to 30 knots.

See Page 702 For Price Data

Length w/Pulpit	51'7"	Fuel	793 gals.
Beam	16'4"	Water	200 gals.
Draft	4'0"	Waste	80 gals.
Weight	47,600#	Hull Type	Modified-V
Clearance	17'6"	Deadrise Aft	12°

Stamas

Quick View

- Stamas began in the late 1940s when brothers Pete and Nick Stamas began building commercial and recreational boats in the West Florida fishing village of Tarpon Springs.
- Among the first to recognize the potential of the then controversial material, Stamas switched from wood to fiberglass construction in 1959.
- The 1970s and 1980s saw Stamas producing ever larger models for a growing market.
- According the the company's web site, Stamas was also the first company ever to put a head under a center console.
- Stamas boats are often noted by marine industry professionals for their conservative styling, strong owner loyalty, and durable construction.
- Stamas is the oldest continuously owned boatbuilder in the U.S., a distinction that says much about the staying power of this family builder.

Stamas Yachts • Tarpon Springs, FL • www.stamas.com

Stamas 270 Express

1997–Current

The Stamas 270 Express is a dual-purpose family boat capable of serious fishing activities as well as comfortable weekend cruising. She's built on a solid fiberglass hull with a bow pulpit and integrated transom platform, and with her wide 9-foot, 7-inch beam, the 270 provides plenty of cockpit space as well as an efficient, well-arranged cabin. Unlike similar express models from other manufacturers with their narrow side decks, the extra-wide decks of the 270 allow an angler to easily fight a fish all around the boat. Visibility from the elevated helm is excellent, and there's space in the dash for a full array of electronic equipment. The cockpit is fitted with aft-facing fish box seats, a circulating livewell, transom door, tackle storage drawers, saltwater washdown, under-gunwale rod storage and a bench seat at the transom. Belowdecks, the 270's midcabin interior is arranged with a V-berth/dinette forward, an enclosed standup head with shower, mini-galley, and generous storage. A good-riding boat, twin 200hp outboards cruise the Stamas 270 Express in the high 20s and deliver a top speed in the neighborhood of 40 knots.

Floorplan Not Available

See Page 702 For Price Data

Length w/Pulpit	28'9"	Fuel	204 gals.
Hull Length	27'1"	Water	20 gals.
Beam	9'7"	Max HP	450
Hull Draft	1'6"	Hull Type	Modified-V
Weight w/Engine	5,800#	Deadrise Aft	18°

Stamas 270 Tarpon

A scaled-down version of the popular 290 Tarpon, the Stamas 270 Tarpon is a rugged and well-finished fisherman from a company with a long-running reputation for getting things right. Indeed, Stamas historically attracts experienced boat owners or else very informed first-timers. The 270 Tarpon is built on a solid fiberglass hull with an integrated transom, and her wide 9-foot, 7-inch beam allows for a large fishing cockpit. Like most modern center consoles her size, a walk-in head compartment/storage area is concealed within the large helm console. Rod storage is abundant, and a big fish box and recirculating 19-gallon livewell are built into the transom. A large, in-deck dry storage compartment is located forward of the console, and two more storage lockers under the bow seats can handle fenders and lines. Additional features include pop-up cleats, tackle drawers, saltwater washdown, transom door, leaning post, and a bow pulpit. A good-looking boat with a clean, conservative profile, a pair of 200hp Yamaha outboards cruise the Stamas 270 Tarpon at an easy 30 knots and deliver a top speed in the neighborhood of 45 knots.

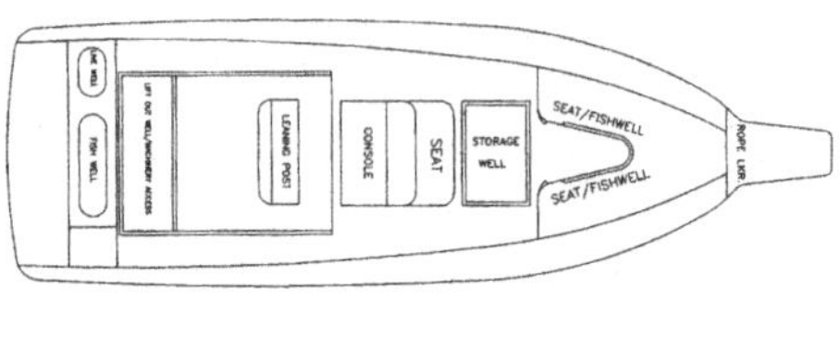

See Page 702 For Price Data

Length w/Pulpit	28'9"	Fuel	220 gals.
Hull Length	27'1"	Water	10 gals.
Beam	9'7"	Max HP	450
Hull Draft	1'8"	Hull Type	Modified-V
Weight w/Engine	5,200#	Deadrise Aft	18°

Stamas 290 Express

A good-selling boat over the years, the Stamas 290 Express combines the graceful styling, thoughtful layout, and quality construction one expects of a Stamas product. She rides on a solid fiberglass, modified-V hull with moderate beam and a substantial 18 degrees of transom deadrise. Like most modern express models, the 290 is a multipurpose boat designed to satisfy the needs of anglers who require the cabin amenities of a small family cruiser. The compact interior is arranged with a dinette/V-berth forward, enclosed head, galley with stove and refrigerator, and a midcabin berth tucked directly under the helm station—modest accommodations to be sure, but comfortable for a small family or a couple of weekend anglers. The cockpit includes a 20-gallon baitwell, transom door, insulated fish box, and three-drawer tackle box. (Note that the original double helm pod was replaced in 1998 with a separate helm and a companion seat.) Available with inboard or outboard power, twin 225hp Yamahas cruise the 290 Express in the mid 20s and reach 40+ knots top. A single 310hp gas inboard will cruise at 18 knots, and an optional 315hp Yanmar diesel inboard will cruise at 20 knots and top out in the mid 20s.

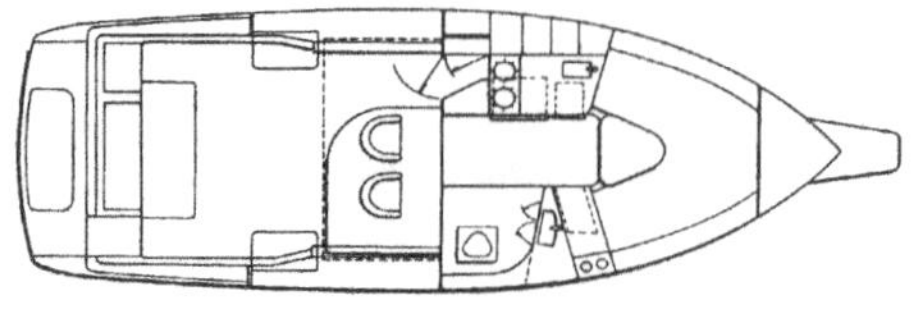

See Page 702 For Price Data

Length w/Pulpit	31'7"	Fuel	250 gals.
Hull Length	29'3"	Water	27 gals.
Beam	10'4"	Max HP	500
Hull Draft	1'5"	Hull Type	Modified-V
Weight	6,550#	Deadrise Aft	18°

Stamas 290 Tarpon

The 290 Tarpon is a long-range center console designed to appeal to serious anglers with an appreciation for the rugged durability long associated with the Stamas nameplate. Hull construction is solid fiberglass, and a sleek profile and full-height transom make her one of the best-looking rigs of her type on the market. A 300-gallon fuel capacity provides good range, even with the biggest outboards. The standard leaning post incorporates a rigging station with a freshwater sink and a large livewell. A second livewell is built into the walk-through transom, and two lockable in-deck storage boxes flank the console. There's space at the helm for flush-mounting the necessary electronics, and a private head compartment is accessed from the front of the console. Note that the deck is flush from the stern to the bow where a filler converts the U-shaped seating into a large casting platform. Available with a single inboard (gas or diesel) or twin outboards, a pair of 250hp Yamahas will deliver top speeds of 40+ knots and a cruising speed in the mid 20s. A single 320hp gas inboard cruises at 18–20 knots and tops out in the mid-to-high 20s.

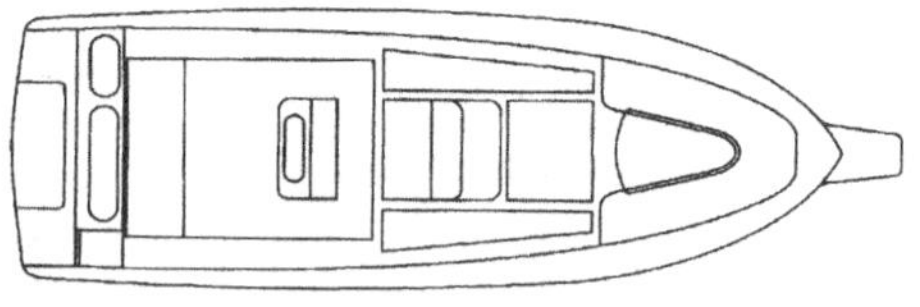

See Page 702 For Price Data

Length w/Pulpit	31'7"	Fuel	302 gals.
Hull Length	29'3"	Water	20 gals.
Beam	10'4"	Max HP	500
Hull Draft	1'5"	Hull Type	Modified-V
Weight	6,000#	Deadrise Aft	18°

Stamas 310 Express

The Stamas 310 Express is a well-built fishing boat whose rugged good looks, fine handling characteristics, and affordable price have made her a strong contender in the midsize express market since her introduction in 1993. Viewed by many as a fishing boat only, her comfortable interior is well suited to the demands of occasional family cruising. There are berths for four below with a V-berth forward and a handy mid-berth aft. Appointments include a teak-and-holly sole, compact galley, hydraulic high-low dinette, and enclosed head with shower. On deck, the cockpit comes standard with a full array of fishing features including a bait-prep station with sink, cutting board, tackle storage drawers, livewell, and transom door. (Note that the original double helm pod was replaced in 1998 with a single helm and a companion seat.) On the inboard version, three large hatches in the cockpit sole provide excellent access to the engines. Among several power options, a pair of 225hp Mercury outboards will deliver a top speed of close to 40 knots. Inboard models with twin 250hp MerCruisers cruise in the low 20 (about 30 knots top), and 170hp Yanmar diesels cruise in the low 20s and reach 26–27 knots wide open.

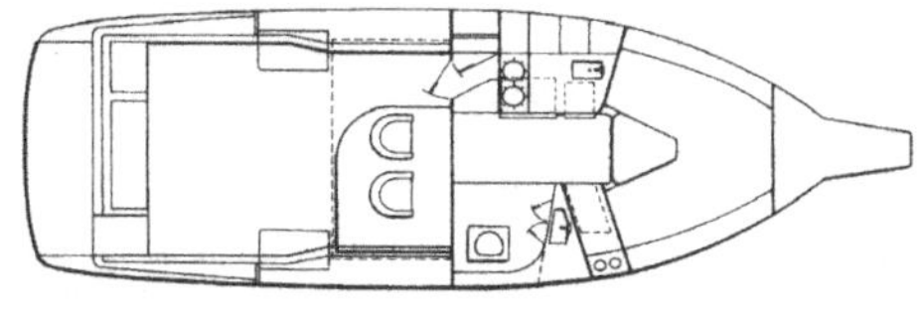

See Page 702 For Price Data

Length w/Pulpit	32'6"	Fuel	300 gals.
Hull Length	30'9"	Water	40 gals.
Beam	11'2"	Max HP	500
Hull Draft	1'8"	Hull Type	Modified-V
Weight w/OB	9,800#	Deadrise Aft	18°

Stamas 310 Tarpon

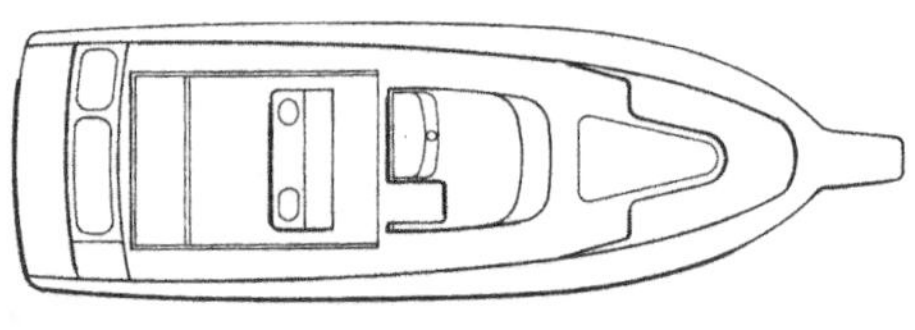

Largest of several center console models in the Stamas fleet, the 310 Tarpon is a heavily built offshore fisherman with an efficient deck layout, excellent range, and a very reasonable price. Once a rarity, 30-foot-plus center consoles have become increasingly popular in recent years among dedicated anglers. The 310 rides on a solid fiberglass hull with a relatively wide 11-foot, 2-inch beam. Like all Stamas products, she's a rugged boat with an impressive array of standard fishing features. The center console is huge and contains one of the largest head compartments—entered via a real companionway next to the helm—found on a boat of this type. The leaning post, which converts easily into a seat, incorporates a rigging station with a freshwater sink and an oval abovedeck livewell. Note that the bench seat at the transom is removable to free up cockpit space. Additional features include a U-shaped forward casting deck with cushions, three fish boxes (two forward, one aft), transom baitwell and basic foam flotation. Also offered with twin inboard power, a pair of 250hp Yamaha outboards cruise the Stamas 310 Tarpon in the mid 20s and reach a top speed of 36–38 knots.

See Page 702 For Price Data

Length w/Pulpit	32'6"	Fuel	400 gals.
Hull Length	30'9"	Water	20 gals.
Beam	11'2"	Max HP	500
Hull Draft	1'6"	Hull Type	Modified-V
Weight w/OB	9,250#	Deadrise Aft	18°

Stamas 320 Express

Floorplan Not Available

Stamas, a company with a reputation for building sturdy, no-nonsense fishing boats got it right with the 320 Express, a versatile sportfisherman with comfortable cabin accommodations and a spacious cockpit. Stamas builds boats the old-fashioned way with solid fiberglass hulls, aggressive nonskid, and deep cockpits. The wide side decks of the 320 Express make it easy to get around, and visibility from the elevated helm position is excellent. Fishing amenities include a full tackle center with sink, cockpit bolsters, insulated fish box, and transom livewell. On inboard versions, a hydraulic lift lifts the tackle center for access to the engine compartment. Below, the spacious interior of the Stamas 320 offers berths for six including a midcabin berth, convertible dinette, and V-berth forward. Just aft of the galley is a head with lots of elbow room—a rarity in a boat this size. Teak cabinets, a teak-and-holly sole, and a built-in entertainment center round out this well-appointed cabin. Note that the fuel capacity is rather modest compared with other 32-footers. Twin Yamaha 225 outboards cruise the Stamas 320 at 22–24 knots (about 35 knots top), while a pair of 320hp MerCruiser gas inboards cruise in the mid 20s (30+ top).

See Page 702 For Price Data

Length w/Pulpit	34'5"	Fuel, IB	240 gals.
Hull Length	32'3"	Fuel, OB	316 gals.
Beam	11'2"	Water	40 gals.
Draft	2'20"	Hull Type	Modified-V
Weight	13,200#	Deadrise Aft	18°

Stamas 340 Express

Like many midsize express boats, the Stamas 340 Express splits the difference between fishboat and cruiser. With a wide beam, the 340 has one of the largest fishing cockpits of any boat in her class, while her spacious interior offers the comfort and storage of a dedicated family cruiser. Built on a solid fiberglass hull with a long keel and prop pockets, her shallow 2-foot, 4-inch draft is remarkable for a boat this size. In the cockpit, the livewell and fish box are located in the transom for easy access. An aft-facing seat with cooler is to port, and a full bait-prep center is to starboard. Most of the cockpit sole lifts at the touch of a button for access to the engines. Belowdecks, the midcabin interior of the Stamas 340 provides berths for six, a large head compartment, and a compact galley. Privacy curtains separate the fore and aft sleeping areas from the main cabin, and the interior is nicely finished with teak cabinets, quality fabrics, and a teak-and-holly sole. Additional features include wide side decks, a tilt steering wheel, bow pulpit, removable transom seat, and transom door. Optional Yanmar 370hp diesels cruise the 340 Express in the mid 20s and reach a top speed of about 30 knots. An outboard version is also available.

Floorplan Not Available

See Page 702 For Price Data

Length w/Pulpit	36'2"	Clearance	7'3"
Hull Length	34'0"	Fuel	350 gals.
Beam	12'6"	Water	84 gals.
Draft	2'4"	Hull Type	Modified-V
Weight	14,000#	Deadrise Aft	18°

Stamas 360/370 Express

The Stamas 370 is a revised and updated version of the Stamas 360 Express built from 1992 through 1999. While the two boats look nearly identical, the 370 (pictured here) has a raised bridge deck (the cockpit of the 360 is flush) and full transom instead of the integrated swim platform of the original 360. These alterations result in slightly larger cockpit dimensions for the 370 as well as a cleaner, less cluttered cockpit area. Built on a solid fiberglass hull with a wide beam and prop pockets, what separates this boat from other dedicated express fishermen is the midcabin interior of the 360/370—a layout usually seen only in cruising boats with V-drives or a sterndrive. (There's additional mid-berth headroom in the 370 thanks to the raised bridge deck.) Although the 370's redesigned cockpit is quite an improvement over the 360—especially at the helm—both models have the necessary fishing amenities including a livewell, fish box, tackle storage and transom door. Engine access is excellent and the side decks are wide. Among several engine options, twin 370hp gas inboards cruise in the low 20s (30+ knots top), and a pair of 420hp Yanmar diesels cruise at 30 knots and reach a top speed in the mid 30s.

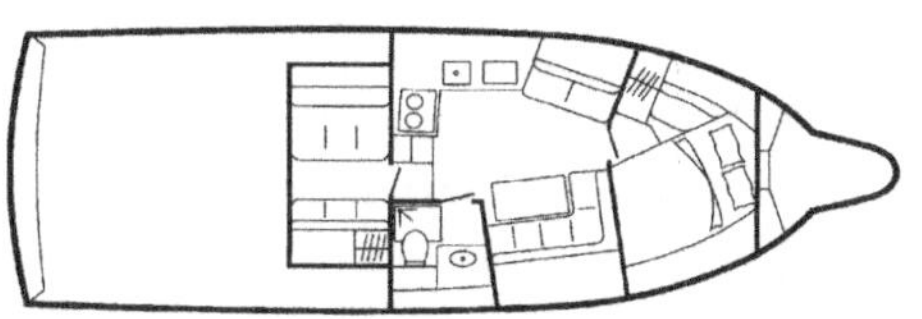

See Page 702 For Price Data

Length w/Pulpit	39'2"	Fuel	400 gals.
Hull Length	36'8"	Water	84 gals.
Beam	13'2"	Waste	25 gals.
Draft	2'4"	Hull Type	Modified-V
Weight	16,975#	Deadrise Aft	18°

Sunseeker

Quick View

- Today's Sunseeker began back in 1960 when Friars Cliff Marine was organized for the purpose of building a small plywood dinghy.
- By the late 1970s the company had grown into Poole Powerboats, a small-scale builder of runabouts and sportscruisers.
- Recognizing the need to grow its business and wanting to expand into the international market, the company hired race-boat designer Don Shead.
- As orders for custom raceboats and Med-style yachts expanded in the 1980s, Poole Powerboats evolved into Sunseeker Yachts.
- By the end of the 1980s Sunseeker had become one of Europe's most influential boat builders.
- One of the world's leading manufacturers of luxury yachts, Sunseeker operates several production facilities building a range of yachts from 40' to 155' in length.
- Until recently, about half of Sunseeker's annual production was exported to the U.S.

Sunseeker Yachts • Poole, England • www.sunseeker.com

Sunseeker 34 Superhawk

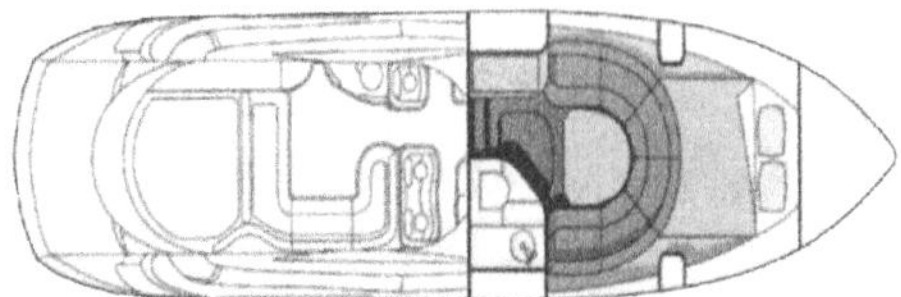

One of the most successful high-testosterone boats ever built by Sunseeker International (160 were sold, mostly in the U.K.), the slender deep-V hull of the 34 Superhawk promises the all-round performance of her racing heritage. The distinctive Superhawk lines are striking from all angles, an enormous styling compliment considering that she was introduced back in the late 1990s. Anyone considering the purchase of a 34 Superhawk does so in the knowledge that these boats are all about performance and open-air sex appeal. While the posh cockpit will accommodate eight in great comfort, the well-finished interior is short on elbow space as well as headroom. The small head is nearly worthless for showers; the galley is fine as long as you stick to sandwiches; and reaching the Superhawk's forward queen berth means climbing over the wraparound settee. On deck, there's a wet bar, swim shower, bathing platform, sunlounger, and bow bathing cushions. A power engine hatch reveals a neat-but-tight engineroom. That said, the Superhawk 34 is a terrific open-water performer that still outguns most competitors. Volvo 285hp diesel I/Os reach close to 40 knots wide open.

See Page 702 For Price Data

Length	37'2"	Clearance	NA
Beam	10'2"	Fuel	185 gals.
Draft, Drives Up	2'2"	Water	18 gals.
Draft, Drives Down	3'9"	Hull Type	Deep-V
Weight	12,800#	Deadrise Aft	21°

Sunseeker 37 Sportfisher

An English-built fishing boat is a true rarity. Fishing boats aren't popular in Europe, mostly because the fish are smaller and less challenging. The Sunseeker 37 is an attempt by this well-known U.K. builder to penetrate the American sportfish market by combining the essential elements of a good express fisherman with the performance and luxury that Sunseeker is known for. If there's a shortcoming in this versatile design, it's probably her relatively small cockpit. This is because the centerline helm console is located well aft to make room for the large curved seating arrangement forward. Swivel helm seats are a thoughtful touch, and the side-boarding ladder is an excellent safety feature designed to keep swimmers away from the props. Whatever the 37 lacks in fishability, she makes up for in her well-appointed interior with its satin-finished cherry cabinets and meticulous fit and finish. A livewell, bait-prep center, and fish boxes were standard. Built on a high-performance stepped hull, twin 310hp Volvo sterndrive diesels will reach a top speed over 35 knots, and triple 250hp Yamaha outboards will power the Sunseeker 37 to a top speed of over 40 knots. Like all Sunseeker models, the 37 is a very expensive boat.

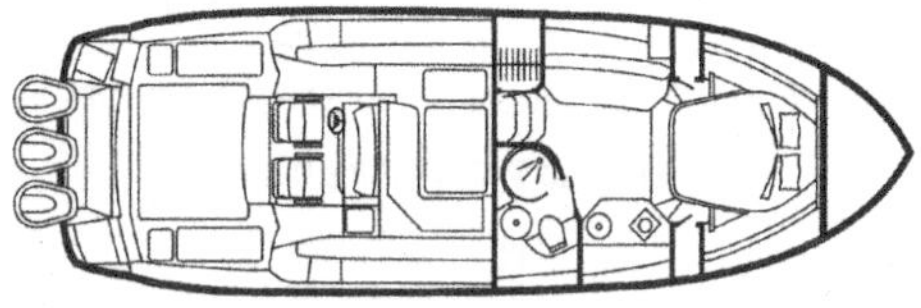

See Page 702 For Price Data

Length w/Pulpit	39'8"	Fuel	396 gals.
Hull Length	37'1"	Water	60 gals.
Beam	11'7"	Waste	10 gals.
Draft, Drives Down	3'9"	Hull Type	Deep-V
Weight	17,420#	Deadrise Aft	19°

Sunseeker 44 Camargue

One of Sunseeker's more popular models during her production years, the Camargue 44 is a well-equipped sportcruiser with a large cockpit and a very inviting interior. Like all Sunseekers, the Camargue rides on a smooth-riding deep-V hull with propeller tunnels, and the standard of fit and finish is very good for a production yacht. The Camargue's spacious cockpit is fitted with a full-size sunlounge as well as a wet bar and seating for eight around a folding dining table. Below, the luxurious midcabin interior is dominated by a stunning array of high-gloss cherry woodwork, top-quality appliances, and rich designer furnishings. With a master stateroom forward and a twin-berth aft, both with en suite facilities, the greatest amount of space has been saved for the salon amidships. Additional features include wide, secure side decks, an extended swim platform, foredeck fender storage, a drop-down helm seat, teak cockpit sole, bow thruster, and an underwater exhaust system. Note that the anchor windlass is stored inside the rode locker. A solid performer with twin 420hp Caterpillar diesels, the Camargue 44 will cruise in the mid 20s and reach a top speed in excess of 30 knots.

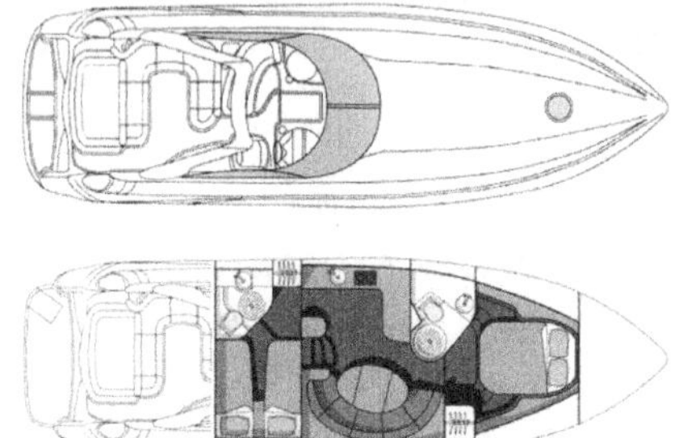

See Page 702 For Price Data

Length	44'0"	Fuel	265 gals.
Beam	13'6"	Water	80 gals.
Draft	3'5"	Headroom	6'4"
Weight	29,000#	Hull Type	Deep-V
Clearance	9'10"	Deadrise Aft	20°

Sunseeker 46 Portofino

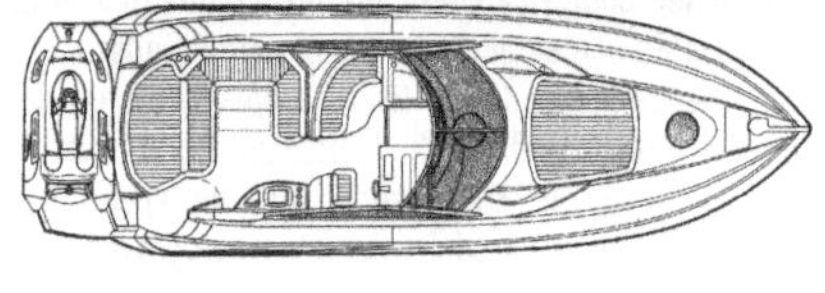

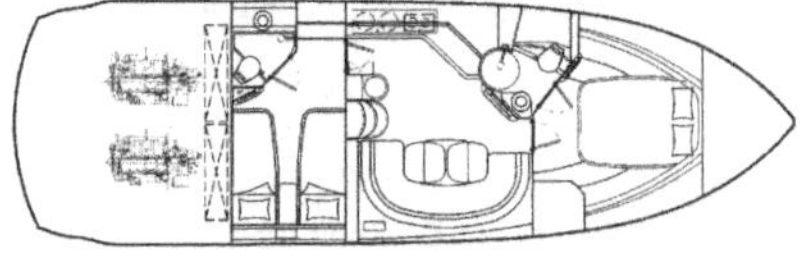

A popular boat both here and in European markets, the Sunseeker 46 Portofino combines sleek—by 2003 standards, that is—Mediterranean styling with an excellent deck layout and comfortable cabin accommodations. It's hardly necessary to wax eloquent about the meticulous fit and finish found in a Sunseeker yacht; this is a company that doesn't cut any corners in the quality department. Built on a deep-V hull with moderate beam and prop pockets to reduce shaft angles, the seductive interior of the 46 Portofino is an appealing mix of solid cherry cabinets, leather seating, hardwood flooring, and premium galley appliances. The master stateroom (with en-suite head) is forward, and a midcabin guest stateroom with twin single beds and private head is aft. Note the telescopic dining table in the salon. Topside, the Portofino's open cockpit layout features U-shaped lounge seating aft, deluxe wet bar with refrigerator, bottle storage and barbecue, and a foldaway cocktail table. Teak decks were standard, and most of these yachts were sold with a hydraulic lift swim platform. Engine access is certainly no picnic. A good performer, the 46 Portofino will cruise at 28 knots (32–33 top) with standard 480hp Volvo diesels.

See Page 702 For Price Data

Length Overall	48'5"	Headroom	6'3"
Beam	13'9"	Fuel	346 gals.
Draft	3'10"	Water	99 gals.
Weight	32,300#	Hull Type	Deep-V
Clearance	13'1"	Deadrise Aft	19°

Sunseeker 47 Camargue

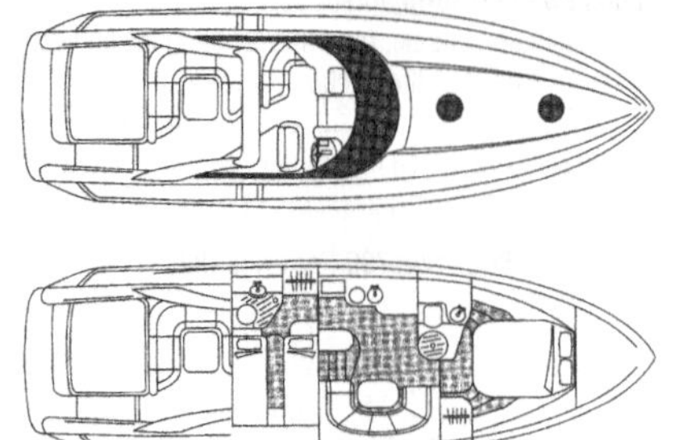

Introduced at the 1996 London Boat Show, the Sunseeker 47 Camargue is a sleek English-built sportcruiser with a huge cockpit, a lush cherrywood interior, and aggressive 1990s styling. Sunseeker has long been recognized for their exemplary production standards and the 47 is a case in point: the exterior glasswork and overall fit and finish are impressive. Like all Sunseeker sportboats, the 47 rides on a slender deep-V hull with prop pockets, a proven offshore design with excellent seakeeping qualities and a good turn of speed. The Camargue's opulent midcabin interior contains two heads, a large galley with hidden appliances, and an array of lacquered woodwork and rich upholstery. On deck, the extensive single-level cockpit is a spacious entertainment center with plenty of lounge seating, a wet bar and a foldaway table. The sun pad sits atop a transom garage for an inflatable dinghy. Additional features include a teak swim platform, hidden swim ladder, radar arch, and a stunning wraparound windshield. A good performer with 435hp inboard Cats, the Camargue will cruise at 25–26 knots (about 30 knots top), and optional 625hp Detroits cruise at 30 knots (34–35 knots top).

See Page 702 For Price Data

Length	46'9"	Fuel	365 gals.
Beam	13'5"	Water	100 gals.
Draft	3'3"	Headroom	6'5"
Weight	30,644#	Hull Type	Deep-V
Clearance	9'4"	Deadrise Aft	23°

Sunseeker 46/48 Manhattan

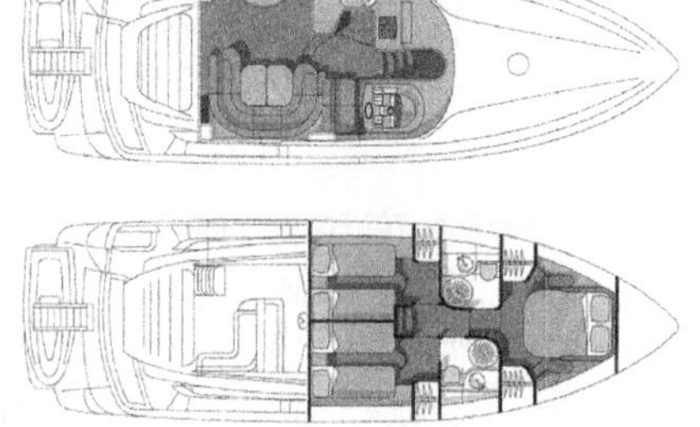

Sunseeker's Manhattan 48 (called 46 Manhattan in 1995) is a beautifully finished Mediterranean motor yacht with a streamlined profile and the kind of performance American buyers have only recently begun to demand in motor yacht designs. Like most European production yachts, she's built on a deep-V hull with moderate beam and prop pockets to reduce draft. The two-level floorplan of the Manhattan is made possible by locating the engines under the cockpit rather than fitting them under the salon where they're found in most motor yachts. The galley is down in this three-stateroom layout, and both heads are fitted with separate stall showers. While the salon dimensions are fairly modest, the leather upholstery, lacquered woodwork, and matching vinyl overheads create a rich and very appealing impression. Visibility from the elevated lower helm is excellent. Sliding glass doors open to the cockpit and swim platform (which can accommodate a PWC). Topside, there's seating for six on the flybridge plus extra sunbathing space. A teak cockpit sole, foredeck sun pad, and radar arch were standard. A good-running yacht, twin 430hp V-drive Cat diesels cruise the 48 Manhattan at 22 knots (high 20s top).

See Page 702 For Price Data

Length	48'0"	Fuel	378 gals.
Beam	14'5"	Water	115 gals.
Draft	2'11"	Headroom	6'6"
Weight	41,000#	Hull Type	Deep-V
Clearance	15'5"	Deadrise Aft	20°

Sunseeker 48 Superhawk

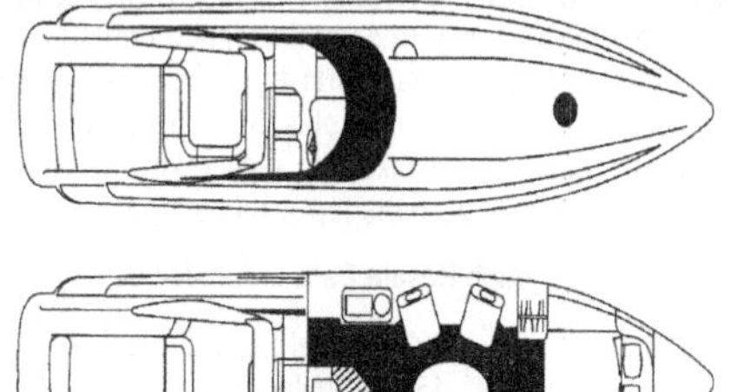

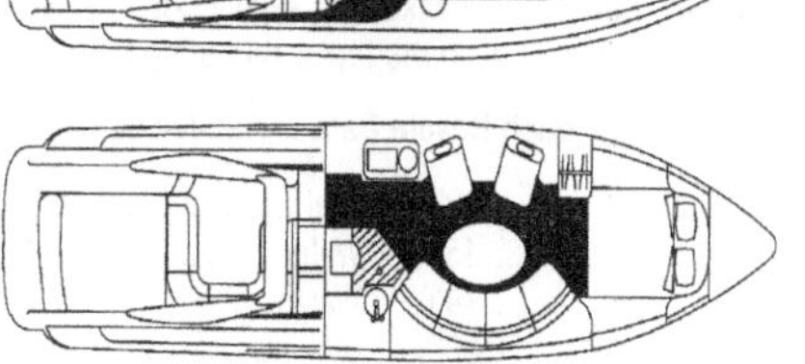

A popular model with nearly 250 sold worldwide, the Sunseeker 48 Superhawk is a powerful, triple-engine UK express that blows past most anything on the water except the fuel dock. The Superhawk is not about luxury; she's certainly well put together and the amenities are first-class, but her slender 10'8" beam means cockpit and cabin space are limited—in this case, comfort takes a back seat to performance. Built on a deep-V hull with cored hullsides and a keel pad for enhanced acceleration, the Superhawk's luxurious-but-confining interior features a private bow stateroom (with island berth) forward, head with shower aft, convertible dinette and small galley in the salon, and a built-in entertainment system. Standard topside goodies include twin racing bolsters, cockpit seating for six, sun pad, and wet bar. The engineroom hatch, beneath the aft sun pad, lifts on hydraulic struts. Inside, the three engines lie with the center motor staggered to make room for a genset and air-conditioning unit. A bow thruster and teak decks were standard. Triple 415hp MerCruiser gas engines (with surface drives) will reach a top speed of 50 knots. Triple 260hp Volvo diesel sterndrives are good for 40+ knots.

See Page 702 For Price Data

Length Overall	50'2"	Headroom	6'1"
Beam	10'8"	Fuel	280 gals.
Draft	2'6"	Water	58 gals.
Weight	22,100#	Hull Type	Deep-V
Clearance	10'4"	Deadrise Aft	22°

Sunseeker 50 Camargue

2000–03

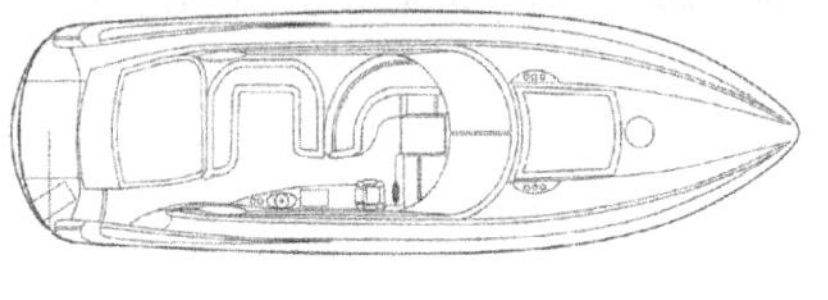

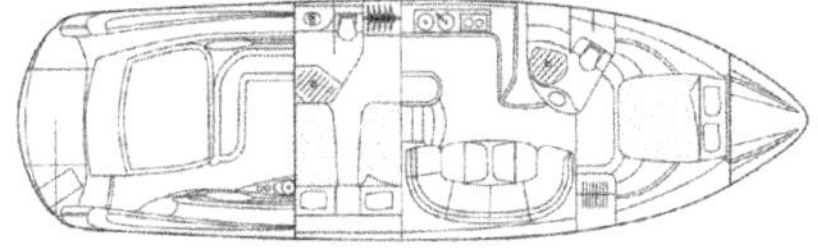

The Sunseeker 50 Camargue was one of the more popular sport-cruisers on the international market for several years thanks to her excellent build quality, aggressive styling, and luxurious cabin accommodations. Like any good Med-style cruiser, the focal point of the Camargue is her large cockpit with its wraparound lounge seating, full wet bar, and large aft sun pad. A transom garage beneath the sun pad is designed to store a hard-bottomed tender or two-person PWC, and a hatch in the teak cockpit sole provides access to the engine compartment. Below, the Camargue's elegant two-stateroom interior is accented with high-gloss cherry cabinets, recessed lighting, and rich designer fabrics. The open salon offers generous seating, a folding dining table, entertainment center, and a well-equipped galley. Hardwood doors separate the fore and aft staterooms from the salon, and both staterooms are fitted with private en suite heads with stall showers. A hardtop is a popular option. Twin 660hp inboard Cats—straight inboards, not V-drives—will cruise the 50 Camargue in the mid 20s and reach a top speed of about 30 knots.

See Page 703 For Price Data

Length	52'11"	Fuel	528 gals.
Beam	14'7"	Water	112 gals.
Draft	4'7"	Headroom	6'3"
Weight	41,400#	Hull Type	Deep-V
Clearance	12'6"	Deadrise Aft	22.5°

Sunseeker 50 Manhattan

2005–08

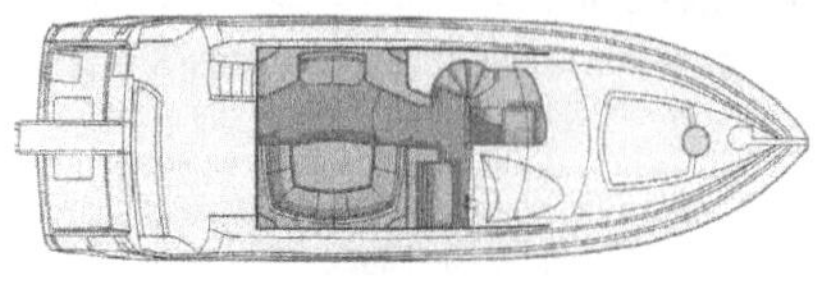

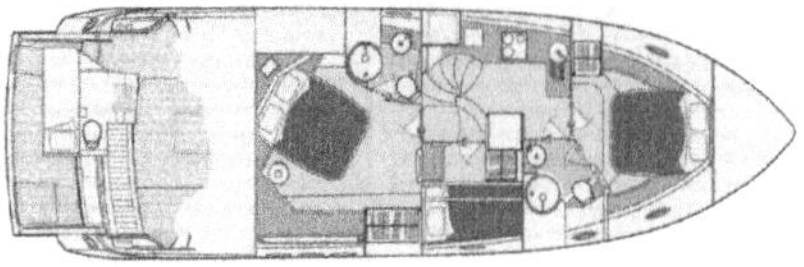

Sunseeker turned up the heat on the competition in 2005 with the introduction of the 50 Manhattan, an executive-class motoryacht with the sleek styling and world-class amenities synonymous with the Sunseeker brand. The market for 50-something yachts is one that Sunseeker knows well, having fielded several Manhattan models in that size range going back to the mid 1990s. With the 50 Manhattan, Sunseeker engineers created a completely modern, dual-helm yacht whose posh accommodations took cruising luxury to the next level. Her spacious interior, an eye-popping blend of high-gloss cherry woodwork, leather salon seating, and designer galley appliances, includes a full-beam amidships master with island berth, forward VIP stateroom with en-suite head, and a second guest stateroom with twin beds. The galley is down—"sunken," as it is in most European motoryachts—and the lower helm is two steps up from the aft salon. Huge cabin windows offer panoramic outside views, and vertical hull ports flood the master suite with lighting. The large engineroom is a plus. Built on a deep-V hull with moderate beam and prop pockets to reduce shaft angles, she'll cruise at 25–26 knots (30+ knots top) with 800hp MAN diesels.

Not Enough Resale Data to Set Values

Length Overall	52'6"	Fuel	660 gals.
Beam	15'1"	Water	132 gals.
Draft	4'0"	Waste	50 gals.
Weight	50,600#	Hull Type	Deep-V
Clearance	16'2"	Deadrise Aft	19°

Sunseeker 51 Camargue

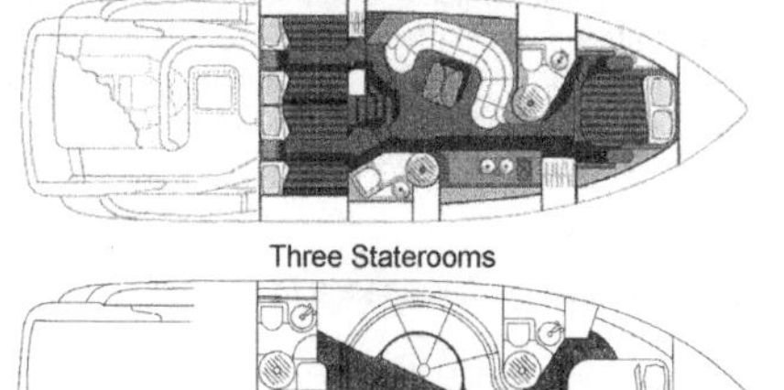

Three Staterooms

Two Staterooms

Introduced into the U.S. market in 1994, the Sunseeker 51 Camargue helped define the Sunseeker reputation in this country for sophisticated styling, meticulous workmanship, and exciting sportboat performance. Indeed, the Camargue was considered a very high-tech yacht in the mid 1990s with the sleek styling and luxury features American buyers found so attractive in European sportboats. Built on a deep-V hull with moderate beam and prop pockets, two floorplans were offered during her 5-year production run. The original interior has a single stateroom and a full head aft of the salon, while an updated arrangement has two staterooms aft with the second head in the salon. Either of these interiors is a lavish display of rich cherry woodwork and deluxe furnishings. On deck, the Camargue's elegant cockpit has seating for eight with generous storage and a huge sun lounge aft. Beneath the aft sun lounge is a garage for a tender or jet bike (with an electric winch for launch and recovery). On the downside, the engineroom—accessed from under the on-deck dinette—is a seriously tight fit. Twin 600hp Cat (or 625hp 6V92 Detroit) diesels with V-drives cruise the Sunseeker 51 Camargue in the mid 20s (30+ knots top).

Not Enough Resale Data to Set Values

Length	49'0"	Fuel	465 gals.
Beam	14'5"	Water	130 gals.
Draft	3'8"	Headroom	6'2"
Weight	42,460#	Hull Type	Deep-V
Clearance	12'9"	Deadrise Aft	19°

Sunseeker 53 Portofino

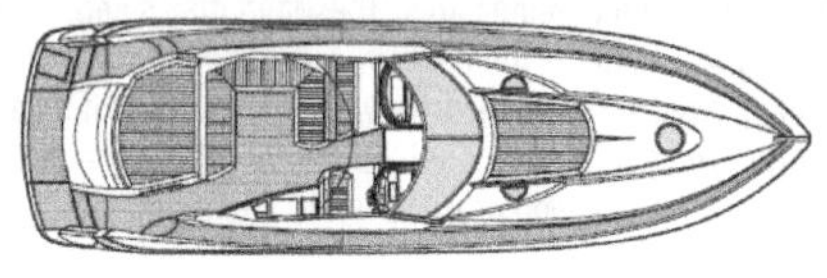

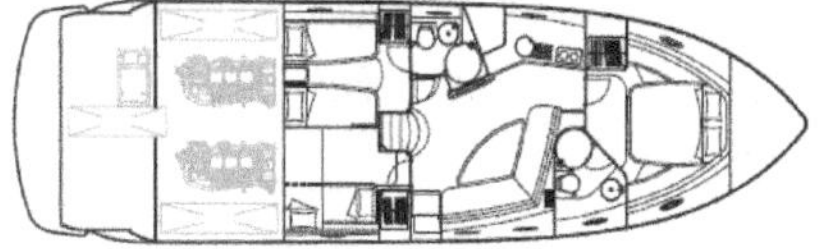

A luxurious sportyacht, the 53 Portofino incorporates the dramatic styling and spirited performance buyers have come to expect in a Sunseeker product. This is as good as it gets in a modern express cruising yacht, and for those who can afford the price the Portofino opens the door to luxury on a grand scale. With not one, but two twin-berth guest cabins as well as a spacious main salon and good-sized galley, the beautiful high-gloss cherry interior of the 53 Portofino is perfect for casual entertaining and weekend getaways. Each cabin has a flat-screen TV as standard, and both head compartments are fitted with separate shower stalls. The cockpit includes a slick foldaway table, a large U-shaped lounge and sunbathing area, and double helm and companion seats forward. The rear sun pad lifts at the push of a button to reveal a tender and storage garage, and a ladder from a hatch under the cockpit table provides access to a fairly compact engine compartment. Additional features include a cockpit wet bar, radar arch, foredeck sun pad, anchor windlass, and teak bathing platform. Built on a deep-V hull with prop pockets, 715hp Cat (or Volvo) diesels cruise the Sunseeker 53 at 27–28 knots (30+ top).

See Page 703 For Price Data

Length	56'11"	Fuel	486 gals.
Beam	15'1"	Water	88 gals.
Draft	4'0"	Waste	24 gals.
Weight	42,500#	Hull Type	Deep-V
Clearance	14'5"	Deadrise Aft	19°

Sunseeker 55 Camargue

A popular model, the Camargue 55 helped define the Sunseeker reputation in this country for aggressive styling, luxurious accommodations, and exciting open-water performance. The Camargue was an impressive yacht when she came out in 1994 with deck and cabin accommodations that could only be described as opulent. The spacious cockpit, which consumes about half of the boat's length, provides seating for three at the helm along with a mid-cockpit dinette and a huge aft sun lounge. Beneath the sun lounge is a garage for a tender or jet bike with an electric winch for launch and recovery. Belowdecks, the Camargue's three-stateroom interior was updated in 1995 when a curved galley and dinette replaced the original U-shaped galley and dinette. In both configurations, the blend of high-gloss cherry woodwork, expensive galley appliances, and plush furnishings can only be described as lush. Additional features include a teak cockpit sole, bow storage locker, radar arch, and a hot/cold transom shower. On the downside, the engine room is a tight fit. Among several diesel options, twin 760hp 8V92 Detroits cruise the 55 Camargue in the high 20s and reach 30+ knots top.

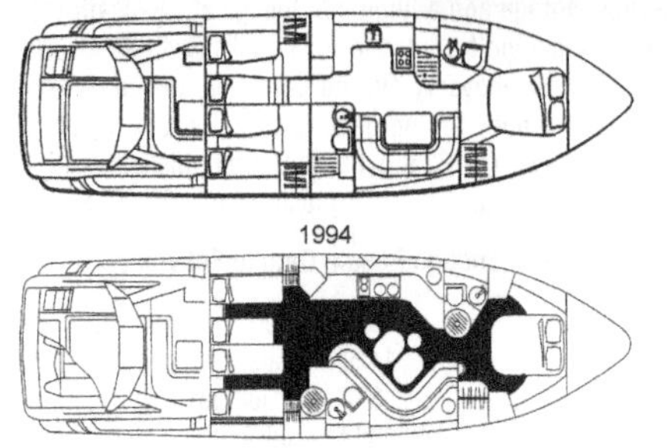

1994

1995–96

Not Enough Resale Data to Set Values

Length	55'0"	Fuel	753 gals.
Beam	14'7"	Water	150 gals.
Draft	4'1"	Headroom	6'3"
Weight	39,970#	Hull Type	Deep-V
Clearance	11'2"	Deadrise Aft	23°

Sunseeker 56 Manhattan

Sleek styling, exemplary finish, and impressive performance are the hallmarks of the Sunseeker 56 Manhattan, a sophisticated European motor yacht from a company whose name is synonymous with yachting excellence. Dramatic styling aside, the Manhattan's large cockpit and flybridge are matched by her spacious multilevel interior with its high-gloss cherry cabinets and rich designer fabrics. The elegantly appointed salon provides a separate dining area forward and facing settees aft. Adjoining the galley, several steps down from the salon level, is a small crew cabin. Forward, the master stateroom has an en suite head and shower, while a second head serves the two double guest staterooms. Each cabin features a flat-screen TV. A ladder provides direct access from the lower helm to the bridge where the seating can be converted to a panoramic lounge area. The Manhattan's engineroom is reached from a hatch in the cockpit. An extended swim platform, teak cockpit sole, and bow thruster were standard. Built on a deep-V hull with prop pockets, twin 660hp Cat diesels cruise in the mid 20s and reach a top speed of just over 30 knots.

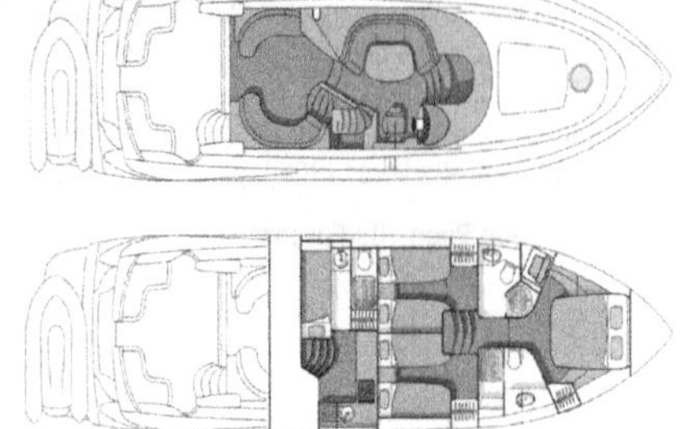

Not Enough Resale Data to Set Values

Length	61'2"	Fuel	661 gals.
Beam	15'1"	Water	198 gals.
Draft	4'3"	Headroom	6'6"
Weight	58,200#	Hull Type	Deep-V
Clearance	16'11"	Deadrise Aft	19°

Sunseeker 56 Predator

2000–04

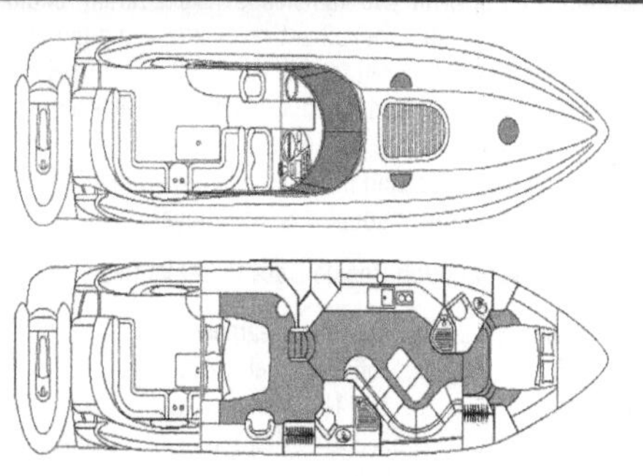

In terms of luxury, quality, and flat-out performance, the Sunseeker 56 Predator set the standards for big sportyachts during her 2000–2004 production years. The Predator boasted an array of sophisticated features including a hydraulic swim platform for launching and retrieving a tender as well as an optional hardtop with retractable sunroof. Her expansive, wide-open cockpit is still among the class leaders for comfort and amenities, and the Predator is one of the few European sportboats whose engineroom offers decent service access. Belowdecks, an elegant two-stateroom interior includes a full-width owner's stateroom aft and a large guest cabin forward. There are two heads in this layout, and while most would view the aft cabin as the master suite, it doesn't have a private head; there's a salon entrance. A washer/dryer is located in the galley, and the salon is dominated by a full-length leather settee and plenty of high-gloss cherry joinery. Additional features include a teak cockpit sole, wide side decks, cockpit engineroom access, and a telescopic passerelle. An excellent performer with 660hp Cat V-drive diesels, the 56 Predator will cruise in the mid-to-high 20s and reach a top speed of 32–33 knots.

Not Enough Resale Data to Set Values

Length	60'2"	Fuel	621 gals.
Beam	15'1"	Water	172 gals.
Draft	4'5"	Headroom	6'5"
Weight	52,030#	Hull Type	Deep-V
Clearance	12'9"	Deadrise Aft	19°

Sunseeker 58/60 Predator

1997–2002

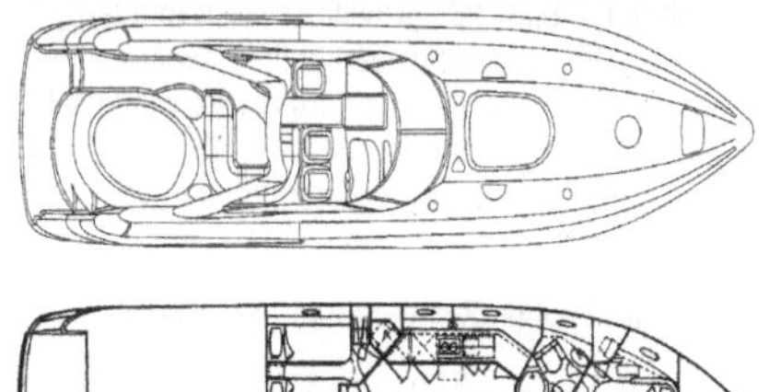

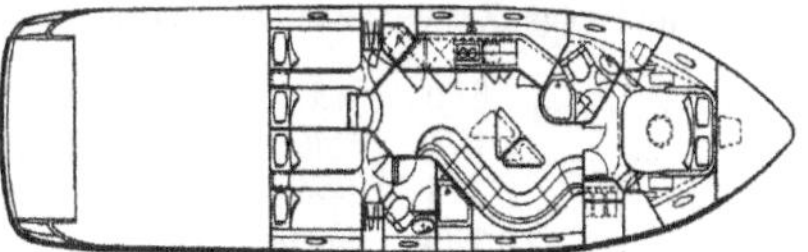

Ever since the first of Sunseeker's Predator models was launched back in 1995 these elegant yachts have set the standard for quality and performance in the 50-foot-plus luxury sportcruiser market. Long and slender, the sleek styling of the Predator 60 (called the Predator 58 in 1997–98) has aged very little since she went out of production in 2002. Below, her lush accommodations are arranged with a sweeping settee opposite the galley and a bar set along the port side. Forward is the master stateroom with its en suite bathroom, and twin guest cabins aft share an equally generous head compartment. The cockpit, which seats six at a U-shaped lounge behind the helm, is dominated by an oval sun pad that sits atop a dinghy/PWC garage with a built-in launch-and-retrieval winch. Additional features include a cockpit wet bar, wide side decks, foredeck sun pad, a teak cockpit sole, and stunning wraparound stainless-steel windshield. Note that a hardtop with sunroof was a popular option. Running on a deep-V hull with prop pockets, twin 800hp V-drive MANs (or 760hp Detroits) will cruise at 26–28 knots and top out in the mid 30s.

See Page 703 For Price Data

Length	57'11"	Fuel	753 gals.
Beam	15'1"	Water	170 gals.
Draft	4'5"	Headroom	6'8"
Weight	48,400#	Hull Type	Deep-V
Clearance	10'8"	Deadrise Aft	22.5°

Sunseeker 60 Renegade

1991–95

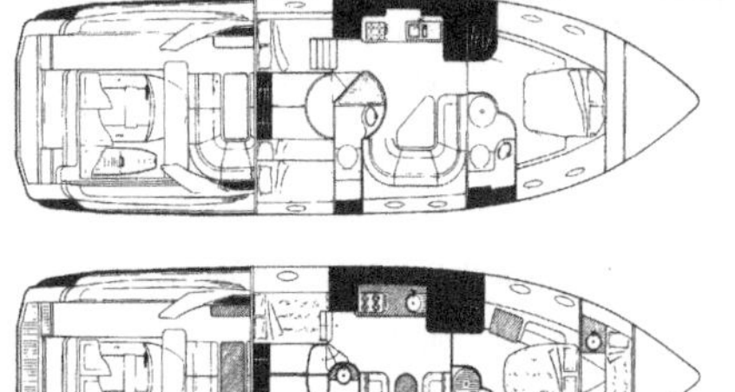

Impressive from a distance and enormous up close, the Renegade 60 stands apart from other high-performance express yachts thanks to her exotic waterjet propulsion, an Italian-made water-drive system that pumps some 32,000 gallons of water per minute at full throttle. The result is a top speed of just over 45 knots—a good deal faster than a conventional prop-driven boat this size can reach. (Surface drives, however, will attain these higher speeds as well, although they're a lot noisier.) Jet drives make boat-handling a strange sensation, and this is certainly not a yacht in which to make your first attempt at backing into a tight berth. Like all Sunseeker models, the 60 Renegade is finished to extremely high production-boat standards. Notable features include an elegant three-stateroom interior with two full heads, a beautifully engineered cockpit with a huge mid-cockpit settee/dinette and a garage under the aft sun lounge with a retractable hoist to lower the dinghy into the water. A completely impressive yacht with an exciting blend of luxury and performance, the 60 Renegade's complicated drive system—and the associated maintenance requirements—will limit her appeal among conventional U.S. boat buyers.

Not Enough Resale Data to Set Values

Length Overall	62'6"	Clearance	12'3"
Hull Length	56'1"	Fuel	940 gals.
Beam	15'11"	Water	153 gals.
Draft	3'3"	Hull Type	Deep-V
Weight	50,795#	Deadrise Aft	20°

Sunseeker 61 Predator

2002–05

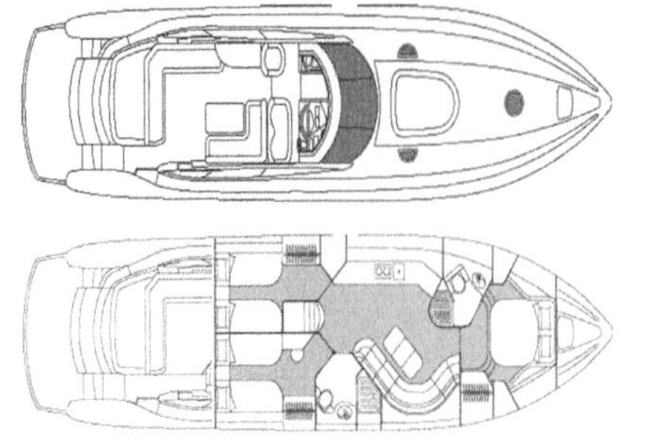

The 61 Predator is a good example of why Sunseeker continues to set the standards for high-end European sportcruisers. Aside from her aggressive styling and dazzling performance, the 61 employs the latest innovations in construction and design. Most 61s were delivered with an optional hardtop (with retractable sunroof), and the Predator's hydraulic swim platform makes launching and retrieving a tender from the aft garage simple and easy. Below, the exceptional interior finish is enhanced by high-gloss cherrywood paneling, plush leather seating, and hidden galley appliances. A fully equipped en suite master stateroom is forward, and the twin aft staterooms share a day head to starboard in the salon. The spacious cockpit of the 61 Predator has seating for eight as well as a barbecue, full wet bar, and aft sun pad. A hatch in the teak sole provides access to a fairly tight engineroom, and wide side decks lead to the foredeck where a large sun lounge is positioned just forward of the windshield. A fast ride with 1,050hp V-drive MANs, the 61 Predator can reach a top speed of over 35 knots. Note the generous fuel capacity.

Not Enough Resale Data to Set Values

Length	61'0"	Fuel	779 gals.
Beam	15'1"	Water	165 gals.
Draft	4'5"	Headroom	6'6"
Weight	57,320#	Hull Type	Deep-V
Clearance	16'1"	Deadrise Aft	19°

Sunseeker 62 Manhattan

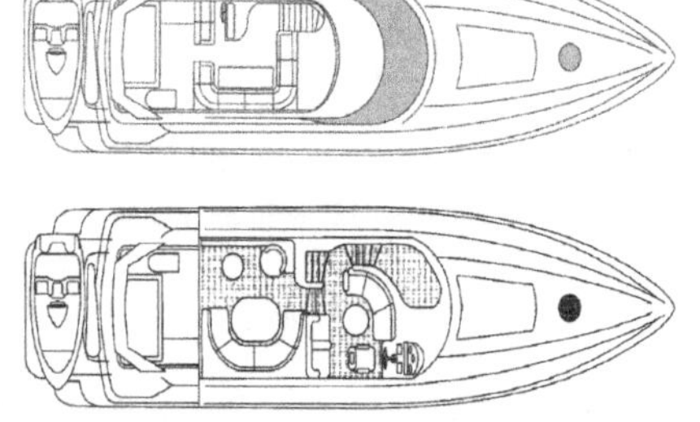

The Sunseeker 62 Manhattan (called the 58 Manhattan until an extended swim platform was added in 1997) was the largest flybridge motor yacht in the Sunseeker fleet during the late 1990s. She is, as the name implies, a floating penthouse whose lush interior is a symphony of curves, chrome and glass. The Manhattan's spacious salon is on two levels with the lower level aft providing the main dining and entertaining area, while the upper level contains a second social center grouped around the helmsman's seat. A transparent spiral staircase abaft the lower helm leads up to the flybridge, and a party of six is accommodated in a dramatic master stateroom forward and two guest staterooms. The sunken galley is huge and equipped for the preparation of comprehensive meals. (Note that a single-berth crew cabin is accessed from the galley.) Sliding glass doors open into the spacious cockpit, and the flybridge—accessible from the cockpit as well as the salon—is uniquely arranged with the helm aft and to starboard, surrounded by a huge U-shaped dinette/lounge with seating for eight. An excellent performer, 760hp Detroit (or 800hp MAN) V-drive diesels cruise at 25 knots and reach a top speed of around 30 knots.

Not Enough Resale Data to Set Values

Length	62'0"	Headroom	6'6"
Beam	15'6"	Fuel	909 gals.
Draft	4'1"	Water	172 gals.
Weight	50,600#	Hull Type	Deep-V
Clearance	14'6"	Deadrise Aft	20°

Sunseeker 64 Manhattan

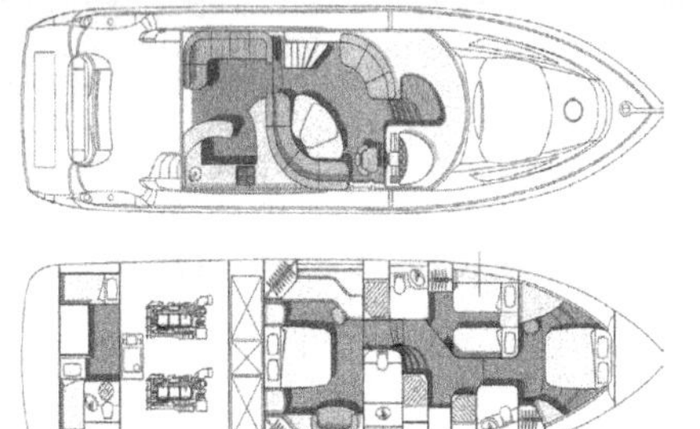

Viewing the Manhattan 64, it's difficult not to be impressed with the visual beauty of this luxurious yacht. With her triple salon windows and a sculpted form, the 64 is a study in modern yacht design. Built on a relatively lightweight deep-V hull with a wide beam and propeller tunnels, her three-stateroom interior is notable in that the large galley is aft in the salon rather than forward—an exceedingly practical design that makes the galley much more accessible from the cockpit. Forward of the salon and up a couple of steps is the lower helm, which is small, as well as a very spacious dining/conversation area with facing settees and a panoramic view of the outdoors. The interior is lavishly appointed and features an opulent full-beam master stateroom, three full heads and a comfortable VIP cabin forward. Crew quarters are aft, accessed from the cockpit, and the flybridge features a wet bar, lounge seating, and a dinette. A foredeck sun pad, bow thruster, twin transom doors, hydraulic passerelle, and lower helmdeck door were standard. Twin 800 MAN (or Cat) diesels cruise the Manhattan 64 in the mid 20s and reach a top speed of 29–30 knots—very good performance indeed for a yacht this size.

Not Enough Resale Data to Set Values

Length Overall	71'6"	Headroom	6'5"
Beam	17'1"	Fuel	878 gals.
Draft	4'9"	Water	259 gals.
Weight	65,920#	Hull Type	Deep-V
Clearance	18'1"	Deadrise Aft	19°

Sunseeker 68 Predator

2002-06

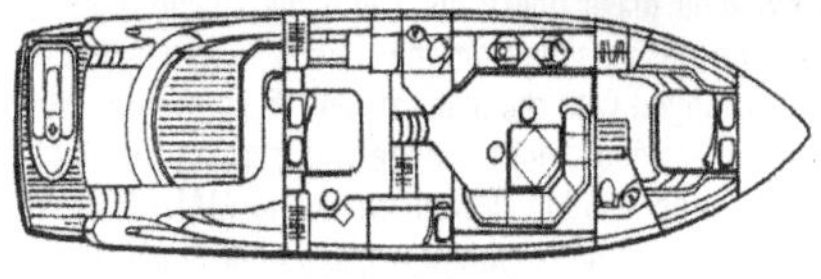

Master Suite Aft

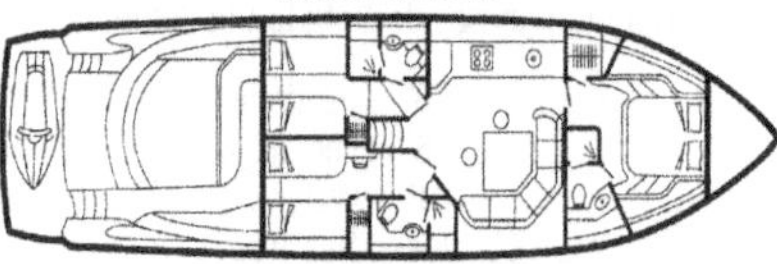

Master Suite Forward

Describing the Sunseeker 68 Predator an "express" yacht is a little like calling Windsor Castle a country residence; the words fall short of reality. In fact, the Predator is more motoryacht than express, at least when it comes to luxury. Sunseeker has years of experience building superyachts like the 68 Predator, and they continue to set the quality and performance standards for yachts in this class. Built on a deep-V hull with a wide 17'1" beam and prop pockets to reduce shaft angles, the opulent three-stateroom interior of the 68 Predator is a stunning display of satin-finished cherry woodwork, posh leather seating, and designer hardware and fabrics. A gourmet galley with copious storage is to port in the cavernous salon, opposite a massive sofa with seating for eight. Two floorplans were offered, one with the master stateroom forward, the other with a full-beam master aft. Most entertaining on the Predator will be done on the top deck where the hardtop (with massive retractable sunroof) and lounge-bar area are ideal for soaking up sun. A hydraulic swim platform and tender garage were standard, and the 68's large engineroom offers good access to the motors. A fast ride, MAN 1,300hp engines top out at 35+ knots.

Not Enough Resale Data to Set Values

Length	66'9"	Fuel	1,030 gals.
Beam	17'1"	Water	185 gals.
Draft	4'8"	Waste	60 gals.
Weight	66,140#	Hull Type	Deep-V
Clearance	11'6"	Deadrise Aft	19°

Sunseeker 74 Manhattan

1999–2005

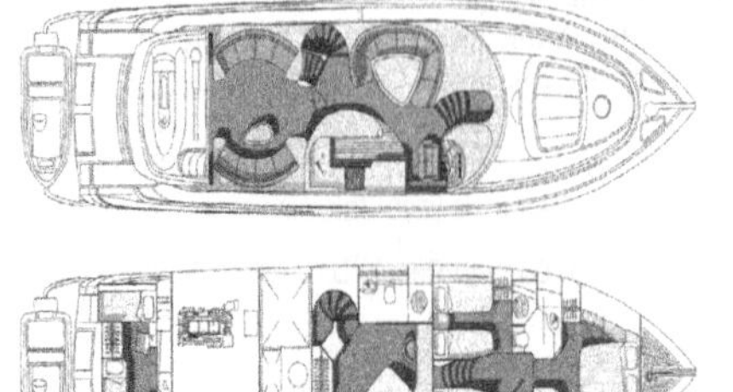

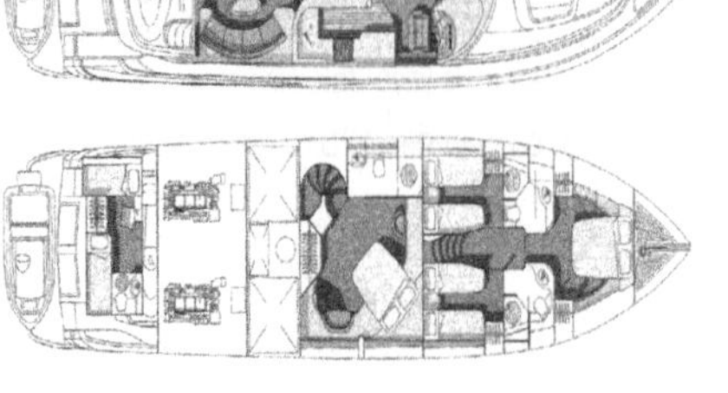

With her dramatic "new edge" styling, the Sunseeker 74 Manhattan is a sleek and powerful luxury motor yacht with a level of finish seldom encountered in a production boat. The styling is aggressive without being overdone, and the Manhattan's spacious four-stateroom interior is highlighted throughout by a sea of high-gloss cherry joinery and costly designer furnishings. The floorplan is arranged with a formal dining area forward, opposite the galley on the helmdeck level, and a circular staircase in the salon provides private access to the opulent owner's suite. Crew quarters for two are aft of the engineroom with access from the cockpit. Topside, the spacious flybridge comes with a built-in food-prep center with grill and sink, seating for eight and a sun pad. Additional features include a teak cockpit sole, a deck access door at the lower helm, a hydraulically operated transom platform (for retrieving a tender), and a spacious, full-width salon. Built on a weight-efficient deep-V hull with propeller tunnels, twin V-drive 1,300hp MANs cruise the 74 Manhattan in the mid to high 20s and reach a top speed in excess of 30 knots—impressive performance for a yacht this size.

Not Enough Resale Data to Set Values

Length Overall	74'2"	Fuel	1,321 gals.
Beam	17'10"	Water	243 gals.
Draft	4'11"	Waste	75 gals.
Weight	81,600#	Hull Type	Deep-V
Clearance	15'7"	Deadrise Aft	20°

Sunseeker 75 Predator

1999–2004

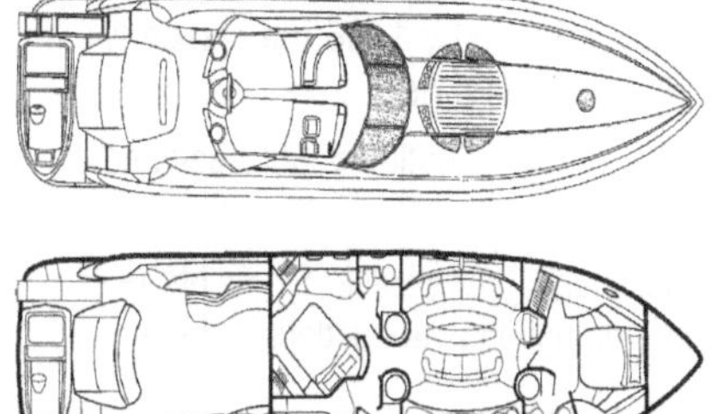

Standing next to a Predator 75 is to appreciate firsthand the sheer size and bulk of this beautifully proportioned yacht. Bold and aggressive, the Predator is among the larger express boats available and the gold standard in quality and design. Built on a beamy, fully cored deep-V hull with propeller tunnels, the Predator's layout is dominated by her fully enclosed helmdeck with five pedestal chairs at the helm, opening side windows, twin sunroofs and massive stainless-and-glass sliding doors that open to the cockpit. There are three staterooms and three heads on the lower level, and the ultra-luxurious salon—with its facing settees, high-gloss joinery, full-length galley, and lush furnishings—is quite overwhelming. A huge sun pad sits atop the transom garage aft and an optional hydraulic swim platform facilitates launching and retrieving a PWC. Additional features (among many) include a teak cockpit sole, a circular foredeck sun pad and compact crew quarters aft, under the cockpit. A superb performer for a yacht this size, twin 1300hp MAN diesels cruise the Predator 75 at a fast 28 knots and reach a top speed of around 32 knots. Note that triple diesels with surface drives were available.

Not Enough Resale Data to Set Values

Length Overall	75'0"	Fuel	1,321 gals.
Beam	17'10"	Water	300 gals.
Draft	4'11"	Waste	60 gals.
Weight	75,000#	Hull Type	Deep-V
Clearance	16'8"	Deadrise Aft	20°

Sunseeker 80 Predator

1997–2002

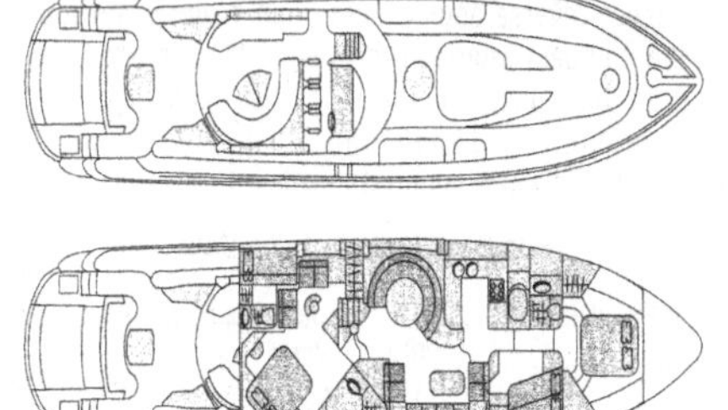

Among the largest production sport yachts of her era, the Predator 80 is a striking blend of world-class styling, lush accommodations, and best-in-class performance. She's built on a deep-V hull with a unique bottom configuration designed to ensure a clean flow of water to the central prop. While the interior can be customized to meet an owner's requirements, the standard floorplan includes three owner and guest staterooms and a small two-bunk crew cabin. Like all Sunseekers, the Predator's polished cherrywood interior is simply lavish, although the passageways and cabin doors are quite narrow. A pair of sliding glass doors separate the enclosed deckhouse (or day salon) from the aft deck, and the transom opens to reveal a huge garage for storing a personal watercraft or an inflatable. A few of her more notable features include a hydraulically operated sunroof, bow and stern thrusters, teak decks, cockpit and foredeck sun pads, and good access to the engines via port and starboard deck hatches in the cockpit. Triple 1,200hp MAN diesels linked to Arneson surface drives cruise the Predator 80 at a fast 35 knots and reach a top speed of just over 40 knots.

Not Enough Resale Data to Set Values

Length Overall	81'6"	Fuel	1,584 gals.
Beam	19'5"	Water	274 gals.
Draft	4'11"	Headroom	6'6"
Weight	100,100#	Hull Type	Deep-V
Clearance	13'2"	Deadrise Aft	20°

Tiara

Quick View

- Pursuit traces its roots back to 1955 when Leon Slikkers left his job at the Chris Craft plant in Holland, MI, and began the Slickcraft Boat Company.
- The company was sold to the AMF Corp. in 1969, and Slikkers stayed on as president until 1973 when he resigned.
- In 1974 Slikkers founded S2 Yachts and began building cruising and racing sailboats. The Pursuit series of fishing boats followed in 1977, and in 1979 the Tiara series was introduced.
- The 1980s saw S2 Yachts enter a period of steady growth; by 1986 the company employed 500 workers, and by 1990 the employee count had risen to 800.
- In 2006 Tiara introduced the Sovran 4000, the first U.S. production yacht designed specifically for Volvo's new IPS pod drives.
- One of the marine industry's most admired and successful companies, S2 Yachts remains one of the few privately-owned and operated production boat builders in the U.S.

Tiara Yachts • Holland, MI • www.tiarayachts.com

Tiara 2900 Coronet

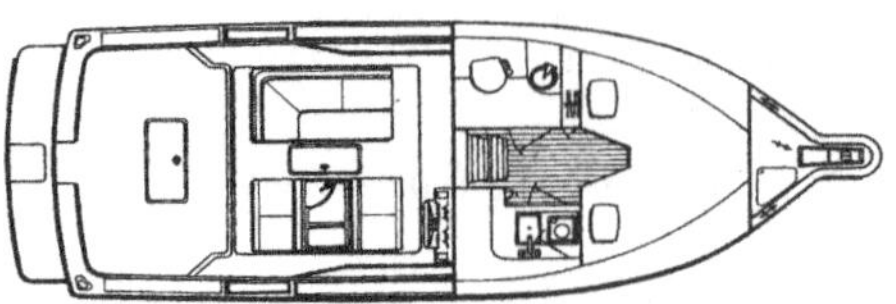

The Tiara 2900 Coronet is a stylish and extremely versatile sport-cruiser whose wide-open cockpit is among the largest to be found in a 29-foot boat. She's constructed on a modified-V hull with a wide beam and a substantial 19 degrees of transom deadrise. While the 2900 Coronet was one the smallest boats produced by Tiara in recent years she retains the superb fit and finish found in all Tiara models. By design, the Coronet's emphasis is on open-air enjoyment, and her large single-level cockpit can seat a small crowd in comfort. The engines are under the two seat boxes, and the entire forward section of the deck can be electrically raised for access to the motors. Aside from the generous seating arrangements, the cockpit is equipped with a wet bar aft of the helm seat as well as coaming bolsters and a centerline transom door. The high windshield is notable, not just for its sturdy construction but for the clever reverse-angled spray guard along the top. Below decks, the compact interior provides berths for two with an enclosed head, mini-galley, and teak-and-holly cabin sole. The Coronet will cruise at 21–22 knots with a pair of 320hp gas inboards and reach a top speed of about 31 knots.

See Page 703 For Price Data

Length w/Pulpit	31'7"	Fuel	200 gals.
Hull Length	28'2"	Water	30 gals.
Beam	11'4"	Waste	20 gals.
Draft	2'8"	Hull Type	Modified-V
Weight	10,000#	Deadrise Aft	19°

Tiara 2900 Open

With her conservative styling and quality construction, the Tiara 2900 Open has long appealed to those seeking a dual-purpose express capable of serious fishing pursuits as well as comfortable family cruising. She's built on a proven modified-V hull with cored hullsides and a relatively wide beam, and anyone who's spent much time aboard the 2900 Open will attest to her excellent finish and rugged construction. The interior is simple and efficient. An angled double berth forward and a convertible dinette will sleep four, and the galley comes with an electric stove, Corian counters and a refrigerator. While the cabin is very comfortable for a 29-footer, it's the large, unobstructed cockpit that draws the attention of serious anglers. A transom door and coaming bolsters are standard, and the nonskid is about as good as it gets in a fishing boat. Note that the entire bridge deck of the 2900 rises electrically to reveal the engine compartment (although it's a tight fit getting down there). Twin 320hp 5.7-liter gas inboards cruise the 2900 Open at 20 knots and reach a top speed of 30+ knots. Note that the interior was slightly revised in 1997. A popular boat, resale values have been very good for this model.

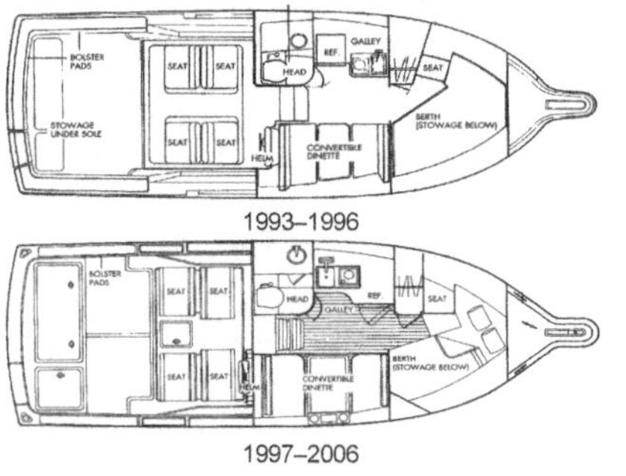
1993–1996

1997–2006

See Page 703 For Price Data

Length w/Pulpit	30'9"	Fuel	200 gals.
Hull Length	28'9"	Water	30 gals.
Beam	11'4"	Waste	20 gals.
Draft	2'8"	Hull Type	Modified-V
Weight	10,700#	Deadrise Aft	19°

Tiara 3000 Open

Tiara doesn't cut corners when it comes to quality, an opinion shared by many marine industry pros, and one on clear display with the Tiara 3000 Open. This is a boat that neatly splits the difference between luxury family cruiser and capable sportfisherman, a claim often made by boat manufacturers but seldom really attained. With her tall windshield, integrated hardtop and distinctive reverse transom, the 3000 Open strikes many as being larger than 30 feet. A wide 12'6" beam results in a big cockpit with two in-sole fish/storage boxes, foldaway transom seat, fresh and raw water washdowns, and transom bait prep station. Like most express boats of this type, the bridge deck lifts electrically for engine access. Below, the Tiara's well-appointed cabin is arranged with facing leather settees, teak/maple dinette table, offset double berth forward, and galley aft. Note the sculptured overhead lighting and handsome teak-and-holly floor. There's no shower stall in the head, but there is a wall-mounted shower fixture and curtain—very nice. The tall windshield provides better helm visibility by far than most express boats. Hardtop and windshield vents are a plus. Cruise at 22–24 knots with 385hp gas inboards (low-to-mid 30s top).

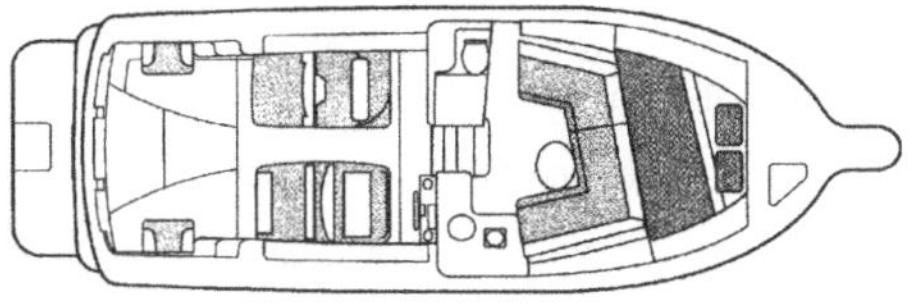

See Page 703 For Price Data

Length w/Pulpit	33'0"	Fuel	210 gals.
Hull Length	30'6"	Water	32 gals.
Beam	12'6"	Waste	20 gals.
Draft	2'8"	Hull Type	Modified-V
Weight	13,225#	Deadrise Aft	14°

Tiara 3100 Open

Introduced in 1992, the latest Tiara 3100 Open is a complete update of the original Tiara 3100 Open built from 1979–91. Her reworked hull features a sharper entry, additional transom deadrise (18 degrees vs. the 14-degree deadrise of the original 3100), greater bow flare for a drier ride, and prop pockets to reduce shaft angles. Significantly, the 3100 Open also has a new bi-level cockpit layout that allows for the installation of optional Volvo, Cat, or Cummins diesels in an enlarged engine compartment. Tiara has always been a conservative builder and it's no surprise that the new 3100 looks a lot like the original—basically a no-glitz express with quality construction, systems, and hardware. The slightly enlarged interior of the new 3100 has a little more headroom than her predecessor, and there's also a bigger U-shaped dinette. Additional updates included increased fuel, a tilt-away helm console, recessed trim tabs, and an in-deck fish box and livewell in the cockpit. Note that a transom door became standard in 1994. Early models with 350hp gas engines cruise at 20–21 knots (about 30 knots top), and later models with 330 Cummins diesels cruise efficiently in the mid 20s (30+ knots wide open).

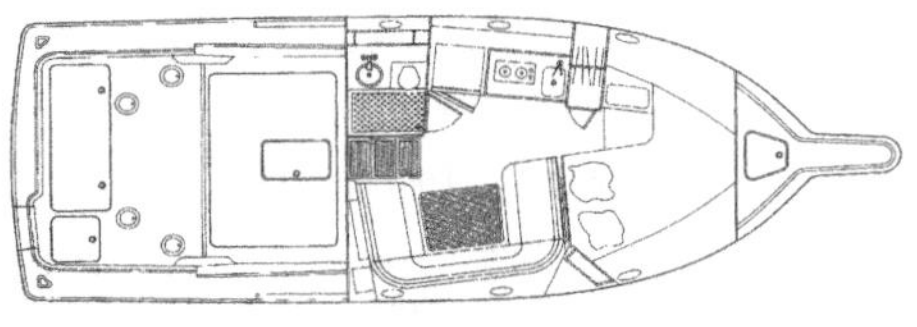

See Page 703 For Price Data

Length w/Pulpit	33'10"	Fuel	246 gals.
Hull Length	31'6"	Water	38 gals.
Beam	12'0"	Waste	20 gals.
Draft	3'0"	Hull Type	Modified-V
Weight	12,300#	Deadrise Aft	18°

Tiara 3200 Open

The Tiara 3200 Open was filling some big shoes when she replaced the popular 3100 Open in the Tiara fleet for 2004. Gracefully styled and boasting some impressive performance figures with standard gas power, the 3200 is designed to satisfy the needs of both anglers and cruisers. Her bi-level deck layout is arranged with L-shaped lounge seating to port on the helmdeck, and an aft-facing seat (or optional bait-prep station or wet bar) is positioned behind the helm seat. A livewell can be added in place of the standard fold-down transom seat in the cockpit. Below decks, the well-appointed interior of the 3200 Open is an appealing blend of solid teak joinery, Ultraleather seating, and hardwood flooring. A privacy curtain separates the forward berth from the salon, and the settee converts to a double lower berth and single upper berth. The entire helmdeck lifts on hydraulic rams for access to the engineroom. Additional features include an integral bow pulpit, wide side decks, in-deck fish boxes, swim platform, and prop pockets. A fiberglass hardtop was a popular option. Crusader 385hp gas engines cruise the 3200 Open at 22 knots (about 30 knots top), and 310hp Volvo diesels cruise at 25 knots (28–29 top).

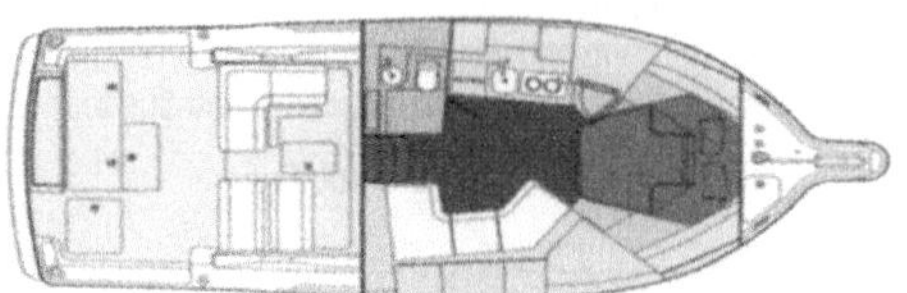

See Page 703 For Price Data

Length w/Pulpit	35'1"	Fuel	256 gals.
Hull Length	32'7"	Water	38 gals.
Beam	13'0"	Waste	20 gals.
Draft	3'0"	Hull Type	Modified-V
Weight	15,950#	Deadrise Aft	18°

Tiara 3300 Open

1988–97

Anyone who's been around the boat business for any length of time knows that Tiara "gets it" when it comes to building a quality product. A big part of the company's success over the years has come from their Open series of inboard express cruisers, dual-purpose boats that split the difference between fishing and cruising. Unlike her predecessors, however, the 3300 Open is more at home in the family cruiser role where her expansive cockpit and deluxe accommodations will be most appreciated. Below decks, her teak-trimmed interior includes berths for six in a cabin of unusual elegance and luxury. A private forward stateroom—rare in a 33-footer—contains a double berth, and the starboard lounge converts to upper and lower pipe berths. The huge cockpit of the 3300 came standard with aft-facing jump seats, cockpit bolsters, washdown, and transom door. An optional fishing package included an insulated fish box, tackle center, and sink with cutting board. The entire bridge deck lifts electrically for engine access. Note the tall, super-sturdy windshield and wide side decks. Twin 350hp inboard gas engines cruise at 22 knots (30+ knots top), and optional 315hp Cummins diesels cruise in the mid 20s.

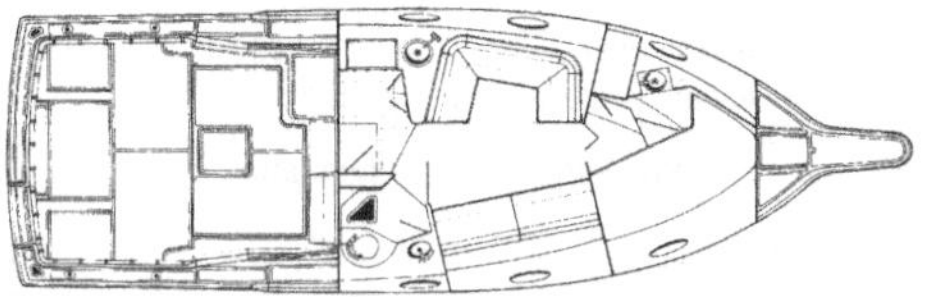

See Page 703 For Price Data

Length w/Pulpit	35'8"	Fuel	295 gals.
Hull Length	32'10"	Water	46 gals.
Beam	12'6"	Waste	20 gals.
Draft	2'3"	Hull Type	Modified-V
Weight	13,500#	Deadrise Aft	14°

Tiara 3500 Express

1995–2003

A scaled-down version of Tiara's popular 4000 Open, the 3500 Express is a high-style family cruiser with impressive accommodations and an upscale price tag. She's heavily built on a beamy modified-V hull with a shallow keel and prop pockets to reduce the draft. The interior is huge for a 35-footer thanks to her super-wide beam. The big lounge next to the cockpit steps can be converted into a private stateroom at night, and both sleeping areas have folding privacy doors instead of curtains. A removable pedestal seat allows the dinette to seat five, and a nighttime lighting system activates when you step on the top companionway step. All in all, this is easily one of the nicest interiors we've seen in any midsize express. Additional features include a teak cabin sole, a huge storage trunk built into the transom, single-level cockpit seating for eight, and an optional 4-foot swim platform for stowing an inflatable or PWC. Optional 370hp V-drive Cummins diesels cruise the Tiara 3500 at 24 knots (27–28 knots top), and 420hp Cummins (or 435hp Cat) diesels cruise in the mid 20s and reach a top speed of around 30 knots. Standard big-block gas engines cruise around 18 knots.

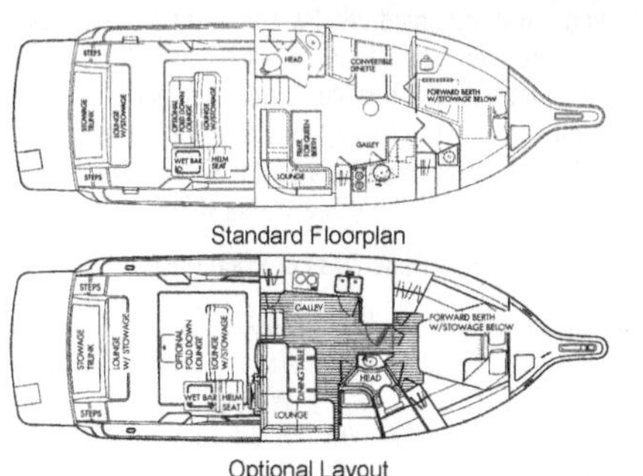

Standard Floorplan

Optional Layout

See Page 703 For Price Data

Length w/Pulpit	38'10"	Weight, Diesel	21,500#
Hull Length	35'8"	Fuel	354 gals.
Beam	13'9"	Water	124 gals.
Draft	2'10"	Hull Type	Modified-V
Weight, Gas	18,600#	Deadrise Aft	18°

Tiara 3500 Open

Few domestic builders can match Tiara's reputation for engineering and quality, and fewer still exceed the company when it comes to timeless design. The 3500 Open is a case in point: hardly revolutionary in concept, she's a beautifully crafted express cruiser whose classic styling will still look good a decade from now. She's built on a beamy modified-V hull with a well-flared bow and prop pockets to reduce draft and shaft angles. Primarily a cruising boat, the large cockpit of the 3500 Open provides an excellent platform for anglers as well. A transom door, wet bar, and in-deck fish box are standard, and the entire bridge deck rises on hydraulic rams for access to the motors. Belowdecks, the spacious single-stateroom interior of the 3500 Open can only be described as lush, with hand-crafted teak joinery, leather upholstery, and a full teak-and-holly cabin sole. Additional features include an L-shaped lounge opposite the helm, aft-facing cockpit seats, an electric windshield vent, an integral swim platform, and a bow pulpit. Standard big-block gas inboards will provide a cruising speed of 18 knots (29–30 knots top), and optional 370hp Cummins diesels cruise at 25–26 knots and reach a top speed of around 30 knots.

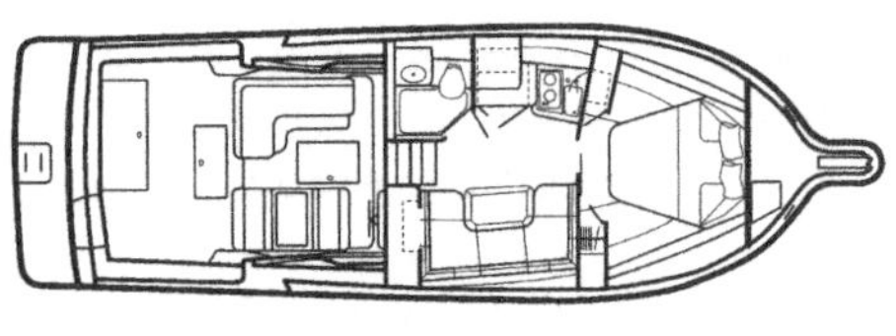

See Page 703 For Price Data

Length w/Pulpit	40'8"	Fuel	360 gals.
Hull Length	35'6"	Water	70 gals.
Beam	13'3"	Waste	30 gals.
Draft	3'3"	Hull Type	Modified-V
Weight	14,000#	Deadrise Aft	18°

Tiara 3500 Sovran

With her distinctive lines, spacious layout, and standard IPS drives the Tiara 3500 Sovran provides uncommon luxury and comfort for the cruising couple. Hardtop cruisers like the Sovran have grown in popularity in the past several years thanks to their weather-protected—often climate-controlled—helms and sociable deck layouts. With the 3500 Sovran, a wide 12-foot, 11-inch beam adds another appealing feature: space, and lots of it. Indeed, the cockpit and helm deck—with combined seating for ten—are larger and more comfortable than any boat in her class. Below, the Sovran's cabin is unusually large for a boat this size. Because pod drives require less engineroom space than conventional inboards, the interior of the 3500 has been expanded aft to include a midcabin media room complete with facing lounge seats (convertible to a berth) and a wall-mounted 26" TV. The portside head has a separate stall shower, and the interior is finished with high-gloss woodwork, premium galley appliances, and an elegant hardwood sole. The cockpit sole lifts electrically for access to the engine compartment. Hull freeboard is high for a 35-footer. Cruise at 25–26 knots (30+ top) with Volvo 300hp IPS diesels (with joystick controls).

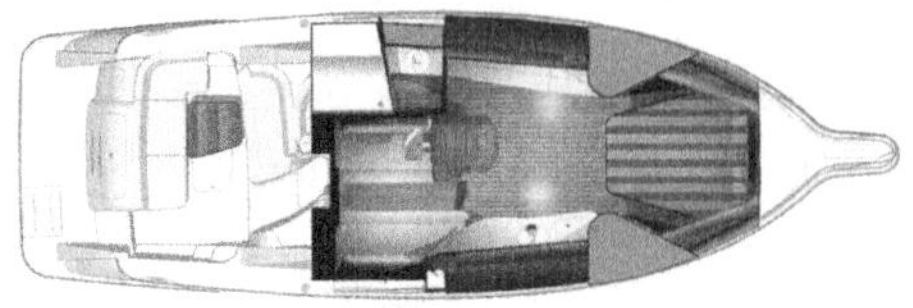

See Page 703 For Price Data

Length Overall	37'9"	Fuel	250 gals.
Beam	12'11"	Water	70 gals.
Draft	3'1"	Waste	30 gals.
Weight	17,600#	Hull Type	Modified-V
Clearance	9'8"	Deadrise Aft	15°

Tiara 3600 Convertible

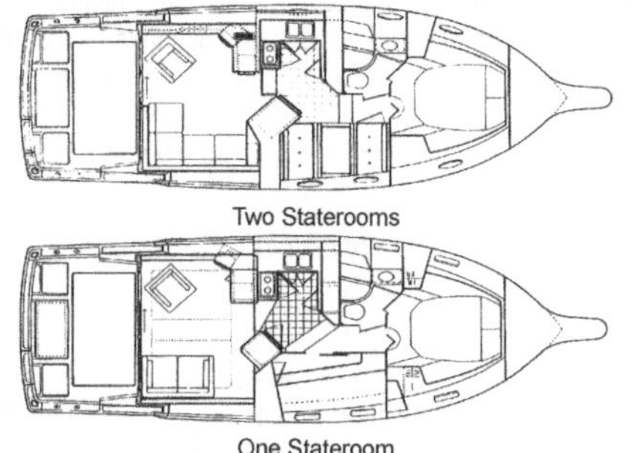
Two Staterooms

One Stateroom

The Tiara 3600 Convertible is a well-built flybridge sedan whose blend of interior comforts and open-water performance made her a popular boat with cruisers and anglers alike. She's built on the same hull used for the 3600 Open, a proven offshore design with cored hullsides and a relatively wide beam—a stable fishing platform, but a stiff ride in a chop. Fit and finish is excellent—typical of the quality you get in any Tiara product. A sliding glass door leads into a salon whose open front windshield makes the cabin seem larger than it actually is. Two floorplans were available; owners could select the original two-stateroom interior, or opt for the less popular single-stateroom layout with a dinette in place of the guest cabin. Both layouts include a mid-level galley, a double berth forward, and a separate stall shower in the head. The cockpit came with a transom door, however the modest cockpit dimensions preclude the installation of a tackle center—a matter of little consequence to cruisers, but a definite drawback for anglers. Standard 350hp inboard gas engines cruise the 3600 at 19–20 knots and reach a top speed in the high 20s. Optional Cat 375hp diesels cruise at 25 knots and post a top speed of 29–30 knots.

See Page 703 For Price Data

Length w/Pulpit	39'8"	Clearance	12'6"
Hull Length	36'8"	Fuel	396 gals.
Beam	13'9"	Water	85 gals.
Draft	3'0"	Hull Type	Modified-V
Weight	18,300#	Deadrise Aft	14°

Tiara 3600 Open

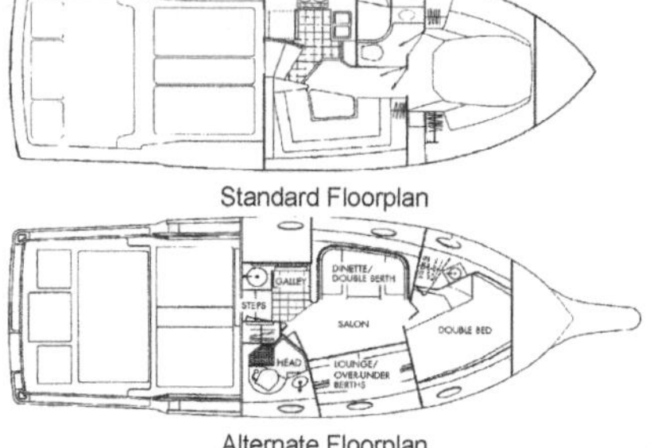
Standard Floorplan

Alternate Floorplan

An extremely popular model for Tiara with a long production run, the 3600 Open is a well built offshore express with a big fishing cockpit, comfortable cabin accommodations, and surprisingly agile performance. Indeed, the 3600 Open set the standards in her era for express boat versatility and luxury, able to serve as a great fishing platform as well as a stable family cruiser. Built on a modified-V hull with a wide 13-foot, 9-inch beam, the original 3600 Open interior slept four with an island berth forward and a separate stall shower in the head. An alternate layout introduced in 1989 sleeps six with a convertible settee opposite the dinette, and the head aft (without the stall shower). Either way, the upscale interior is an appealing blend of grain-matched teak joinery and quality hardware and furnishings—just what one expects in a Tiara product. The cockpit is large enough for a mounted chair, and the entire bridge deck lifts on hydraulic rams for engine access. Notably, the conservative styling of the Tiara 3600 has stood up well over the years. Standard 350hp gas engines cruise at 20 knots (about 28 knots top), and optional 375hp Cats cruise in the mid 20s.

See Page 703 For Price Data

Length w/Pulpit	39'8"	Headroom	6'2"
Beam	13'9"	Fuel	396 gals.
Draft	2'11"	Water	85 gals.
Weight	16,500#	Hull Type	Modified-V
Clearance	9'7"	Deadrise Aft	14°

Tiara 3600 Open

The Tiara 3600 Open (note that Tiara built an earlier 3600 Open from 1985–96) is designed to satisfy both anglers and cruisers with a functional, 70-square-foot cockpit and a comfortable, well-appointed cabin. Like most late-model Tiaras, the 3600 rides on a modified deep-V hull with a sharp entry, solid fiberglass bottom, and a relatively broad beam. Experienced anglers will appreciate the professional-grade cockpit with its aft-facing seats, overbuilt transom door, in-deck fish boxes, and fold-down transom seat. The helmdeck has a portside lounge (with insulated cooler) along with a wet bar and tilt-away dash. Below decks, the posh interior is a blend of solid-wood floors, flawless teak joinery, Ultraleather upholstery, and brushed stainless-steel hardware. The U-shaped dinette converts into a double berth, and the backrest flips up to create a Pullman berth. Note that a sliding door provides real privacy in the master stateroom. Additional features include fresh- and raw-water washdowns, excellent nonskid, reasonably wide side decks, and padded cockpit bolsters. Cummins 380hp diesels cruise at 26–28 knots. Newer models with 370hp Volvo IPS pod drives cruise efficiently at 28 knots.

See Page 703 For Price Data

Length	36'5"	Fuel	400 gals.
Beam	13'3"	Water	70 gals.
Draft	3'5"	Waste	30 gals.
Weight	19,100#	Hull Type	Modified-V
Clearance	9'10"	Deadrise Aft	18°

Tiara 3600 Sovran

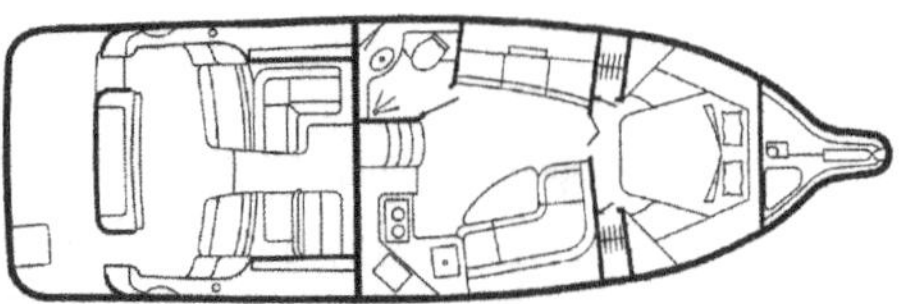

A dedicated cruising yacht from a builder with a reputation for quality, the conservative profile of the Tiara 3600 Sovran masks a yacht of enviable comfort and sophistication. While the Sovran may lack the euro-style sex appeal of other high-end sportyachts few would deny that she's a strikingly handsome and sophisticated design. Below, the interior of the Sovran is a traditional blend of teak joinery, Corian counters, and posh Ultraleather seating. The head is conveniently positioned adjacent to the entryway, and the bulkhead between the master stateroom and the salon has both a door and a panel that slides open. In the salon, both the dinette and portside settee convert to berths. The bi-level cockpit of the Sovran is arranged with an L-shaped lounge opposite the helm, aft-facing seats, foldaway rear seat, and deluxe wet bar. An electrically operated transom locker stows the fenders, and the entire helmdeck can raised at the push of a button for access to the engines. The fiberglass hardtop and extended swim platform—large enough to support a dinghy—were standard. Twin 385hp V-drive gas engines cruise 22–23 knots; 450hp Cummins diesels cruise at 25–24 knots (low 30s top).

See Page 703 For Price Data

Length w/Pulpit	41'8"	Fuel	326 gals.
Hull Length	36'4"	Water	105 gals.
Beam	13'0"	Waste	40 gals.
Draft	3'8"	Hull Type	Modified-V
Weight	18,000#	Deadrise Aft	19°

Tiara 3700 Open

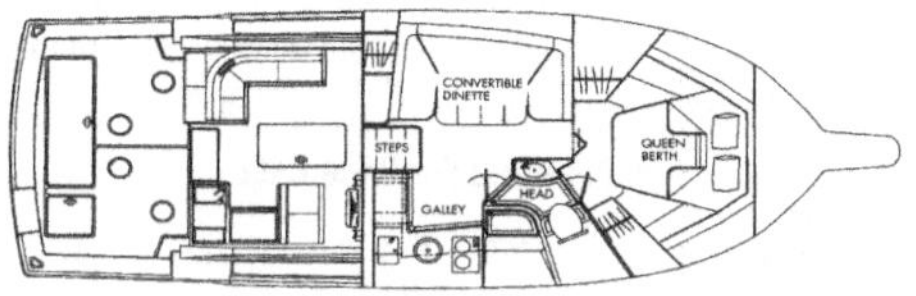

Introduced in 1995 to replace the original Tiara 3600 Open (1985–96), the Tiara 3700 Open retained the classic profile and versatile layout of her predecessor, and for good reason. Like the 3600, the 3700 is a true dual-purpose boat with the comfortable accommodations demanded by family cruisers and the cockpit dimensions of a serious sportfishing machine. She has more beam and deadrise than the 3600, and she's a measurably better rough-water performer. The luxurious teak interior of the 3700 Open is arranged with a private stateroom forward, a huge U-shaped dinette, a double-entry head, and a surprisingly roomy galley. As it is in all Tiara yachts, the cabin joinery, galley appliances, and interior furnishings are first rate. In the cockpit, an L-shaped lounge is opposite the helm, and the big 72-square-foot cockpit has a transom door and coaming bolsters. Note that the entire bridge deck can be raised electrically for access to the engines. A bow pulpit was standard, and a radar arch, cockpit shower and foldaway rear cockpit seat were popular options. Among several diesel engine choices, twin 435hp Cat 3208s cruise the 3700 Open in the mid 20s and reach a top speed of just over 30 knots.

See Page 703 For Price Data

Length w/Pulpit	39'8"	Fuel	411 gals.
Hull Length	37'1"	water	98 gals.
Beam	14'2"	Waste	40 gals.
Draft	3'9"	Hull Type	Modified-V
Weight	21,800#	Deadrise Aft	18°

Tiara 3800 Open

Tiara is one of the country's premier builders of dual-purpose express boats, combining hardcore fishing capabilities with beautifully crafted interiors. Like all of Tiara's Open models, the 3800 could be ordered as a tournament-ready fishing machine or equipped with the cruising amenities of a comfortable family express. A huge U-shaped settee to starboard, opposite the galley, dominates her elegant single-stateroom interior. There's a separate stall shower in the head, and the beautiful teak-and-holly cabin sole gives the interior of the 3800 a traditional feel found in few other boats. (Note that an alternate floorplan introduced in 2003 has a smaller head but adds a portside settee.) The cockpit, with about 70 square feet of space, can be ordered with an aft-facing jump seat or a complete tackle center. The entire helmdeck lifts mechanically for easy access to the large engineroom. Additional features include a hideaway TV in the salon, a cockpit wet bar, a fold-down transom seat, transom door and shower, side exhausts and wide side decks. Note that prop pockets are used to reduce the shaft angles and draft. Cummins 480hp diesels cruise the Tiara 3800 at 25–26 knots (about 30 knots top).

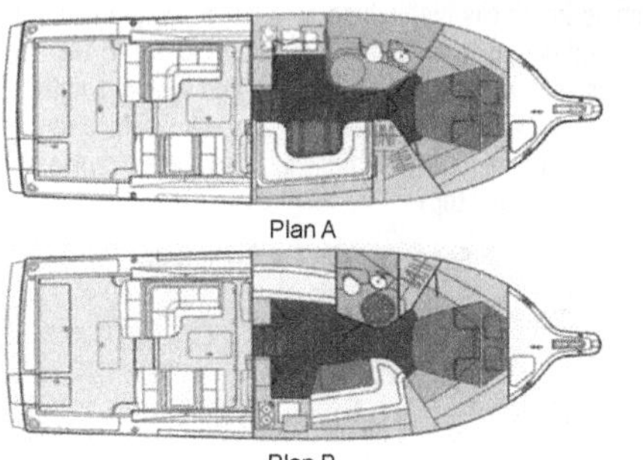
Plan A

Plan B

See Page 703 For Price Data

Length Overall	40'9"	Fuel	411 gals.
Beam	14'2"	Water	110 gals.
Draft	3'6"	Waste	40 gals.
Weight	22,600#	Hull Type	Modified-V
Clearance	9'7"	Deadrise Aft	18°

Tiara 3900 Convertible

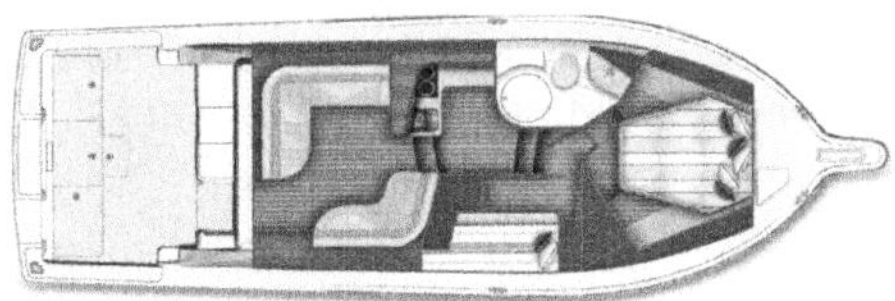

A good-looking convertible with polished lines, the Tiara 3900 strikes the right balance between capable sportfishing boat and upscale family cruiser. Tiara has never been a big player in the convertible market; the company is much better known for its long-running series of express fishing boats and luxury sport cruisers. With the 3900 Convertible, Tiara engineers attached a bit more importance to interior volume than cockpit space. The interior is large and inviting with a spacious salon/galley and two staterooms below. The salon has facing Ultraleather L-lounges; the starboard lounge has a removable teak/birds eye maple table, and the port lounge converts to a berth. A teak-and-holly sole is standard, and the built-in entertainment center above the dinette includes a flat screen TV and Bose sound system. The front salon window is a nice touch for cruising—most convertibles don't have glass windshields. Note the round shower door in the head. The 80-square-foot cockpit includes a bait prep center with cutting board and tackle drawers, large transom livewell, in-floor storage boxes, transom shower, and engineroom access door. Cummins 540hp diesels cruise in the mid 20s (30+ wide open).

See Page 703 For Price Data

Length w/Pulpit	41'7"	Fuel	470 gals.
Hull Length	39'0"	Water	110 gals.
Beam	14'5"	Waste	38 gals.
Draft	3'6"	Hull Type	Modified-V
Weight	30,125#	Deadrise Aft	14°

Tiara 3900 Open

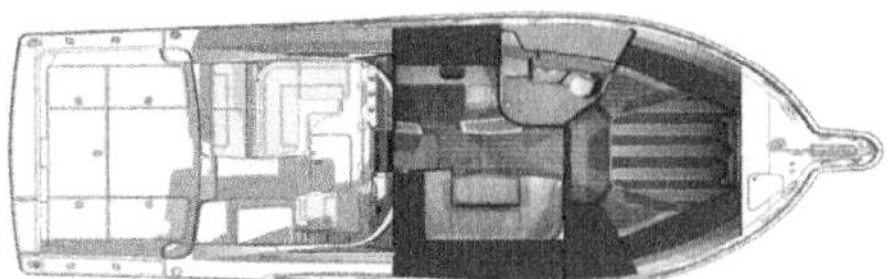

Tiara took big express-boat versatility to the next level in 2009 with the introduction of the 3900 Open. Offering the creature comforts of a luxury sportyacht or the cockpit amenities of a full-on sportfisher, the 3900 is one of the few crossover boats her size that really can have it both ways. Regardless of how she's outfitted, the 3900 is a handsome yacht whose sleek-but-conservative lines will certainly stand the test of time. Key to her multipurpose character are a large cockpit and equally spacious bridge deck, either of which can be configured for fishing or cruising with the right options. In-deck fish (or storage) boxes and a beefy transom door are standard, and the hardtop can be ordered with overhead rod storage. Note the raised, aft-facing bench overlooking the cockpit—what Tiara calls "mezzanine seating." Below, the teak-trimmed interior is highlighted by a large skylight hatch that runs nearly full-length from the master stateroom into the salon. The galley is semi-closed off by a partition that houses a flat-screen TV, and a single upper Pullman berth is concealed behind the U-shaped dinette. Cummins 600hp straight-inboard diesels cruise at close to 30 knots (low 30s top).

See Page 704 For Price Data

Length w/Pulpit	41'11"	Fuel	535 gals.
Beam	15'0"	Water	120 gals.
Draft	3'6"	Waste	38 gals.
Weight	24,500#	Hull Type	Modified-V
Clearance, Top	10'4"	Deadrise Aft	18°

Tiara 3900 Sovran

2007–Current

Leadership is a much-abused term in the boating industry (or any industry, for that matter), but Tiara Yachts can fairly claim leadership with respect to the revolution the industry is now experiencing with pod-drive propulsion systems. The 3900 Sovran followed by one year the introduction of the 4000 Sovran, both among the first boats to be designed specifically for Volvo's then-new IPS drive system. Pod drives don't just outperform conventional inboard power; they also require less engineroom space that, in turn, allows designers to increase interior volume in a meaningful way. Indeed, one feature builders were never able to do prior to IPS was to use the space below the bridge deck for living quarters. Described as a "theatre room" in the 3900 Sovran, it's furnished with a wall-mounted TV and facing leather settees. A pair of beautifully crafted pocket doors provide privacy for the forward stateroom, and an elegant teak-and-holly sole compliments the salon's cherry cabinets and Corian counter. A fiberglass hardtop shades much of the cockpit with its wraparound rear seating and deluxe wet bar. Volvo 370hp diesels cruise at 26 knots (30+ top).

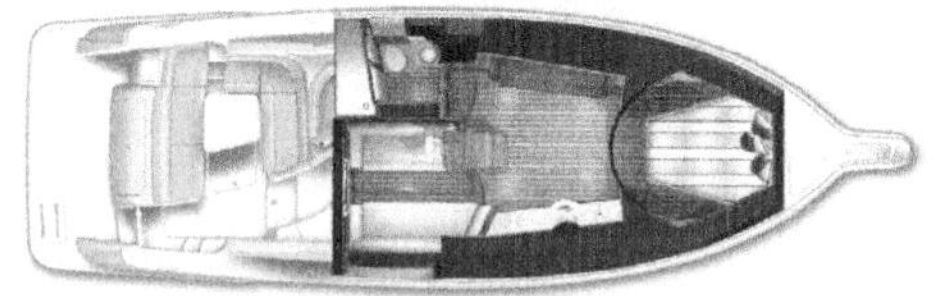

See Page 704 For Price Data

Length	39'3"	Fuel	300 gals.
Beam	13'3"	Water	102 gals.
Draft	3'5"	Waste	38 gals.
Weight	23,000#	Hull Type	Modified-V
Clearance	10'3"	Deadrise Aft	14.5°

Tiara 4000 Express

1994–2003

An innovative yacht when she was introduced in 1994, the 4000 Express was the first midcabin design ever built by Tiara. With her sleek profile, lush interior and wide-open cockpit, the 4000 became a popular model during her production years in spite of a seriously upmarket price. With her wide 14-foot, 6-inch beam, the accommodations are spacious for a 40-footer. A huge, 11-foot salon lounge will seat a small crowd around the extendable table, and the open galley includes a separate freezer and tremendous storage. Both staterooms define Tiara luxury, and the midcabin area has a full 7 feet of headroom and a small head hidden beneath a cushioned seat. (Note that an alternate floorplan introduced in 1994 has an enlarged salon but no aft cabin.) Twin transom doors lead down to the extended swim platform, and built into the transom is a large, hydraulically opened trunk for storing bikes or dive equipment. Note that a pair of hydraulic rams lift the entire center section of the cockpit sole for access to the engines. Additional features include radar arch, foredeck sun pad, electric helm seat and a cockpit wet bar. Twin 450hp Cummins (or 435hp Cat) diesels cruise the Tiara 4000 Express at 23–24 knots (high 20s top).

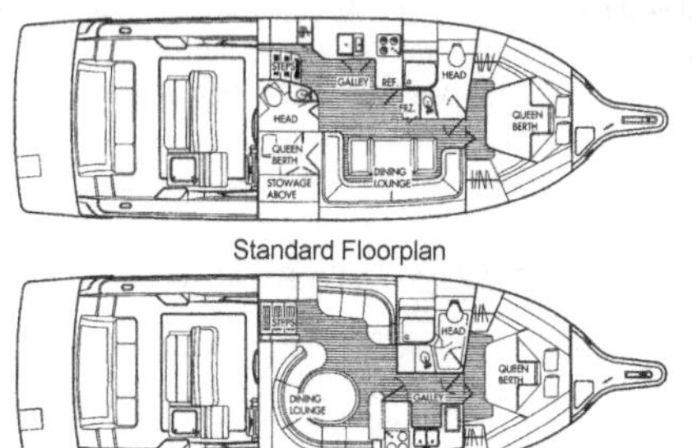
Standard Floorplan

Optional Layout

See Page 704 For Price Data

Length w/Pulpit	43'6"	Fuel	444 gals.
Hull Length	40'6"	Water	160 gals.
Beam	14'6"	Waste	57 gals.
Draft	4'0"	Hull Type	Modified-V
Weight	26,500#	Deadrise Aft	18°

Tiara 4000/4300 Sovran

2006–10

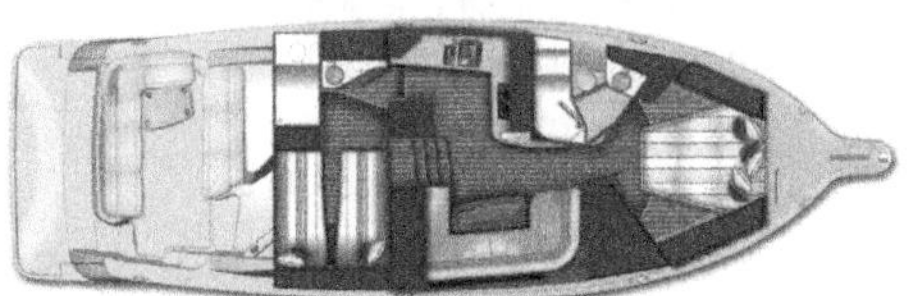

The Tiara 4300 Sovran (called the 4000 Sovran when she was introduced in 2006) was a game-changer in the boating industry, the first American boat to be designed exclusively for Volvo's then new—and soon to be revolutionary—IPS drive system. Pod drives don't just outperform conventional inboard power; they also require less engineroom space. In the 4300 Sovran, Tiara engineers were able to use this extra space by extending the midcabin bulkhead aft, beneath the bridge deck to create a full-size guest cabin complete with its own head. The Sovran's luxurious interior, an appealing blend of high-gloss cherry cabinets, Ultraleather upholstery and hardwood flooring, features an open salon with convertible settee to starboard and full-service galley to port. The forward stateroom has a queen island berth and flat screen TV. The Sovran's open cockpit features forward and rear facing lounge seating with a centerline table. A transom door leads to an extended swim platform with freshwater shower. The hardtop is fully integrated into the windshield. Volvo 370hp diesels cruise at 22–23 knots; optional 425hp Volvos cruise in the high 20s. One of Tiara's best-selling models ever, over 100 were sold.

See Page 704 For Price Data

Length w/Pulpit	45'3"	Fuel	375 gals.
Hull Length	40'2"	Water	110 gals.
Beam	14'9"	Waste	50 gals.
Draft	3'7"	Hull Type	Modified-V
Weight	26,800#	Deadrise Aft	17°

Tiara 4100 Open

1996–2002

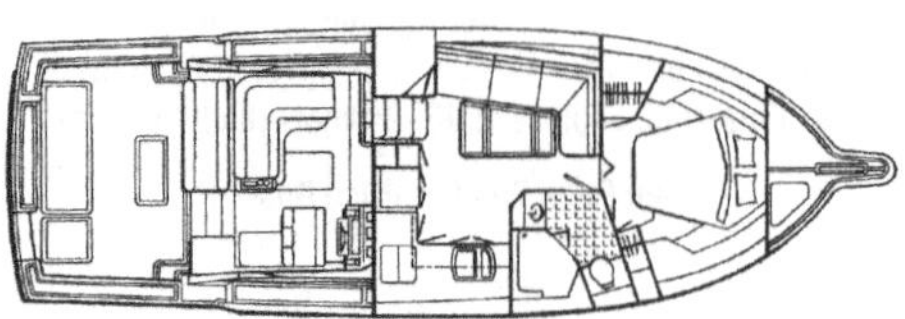

The Tiara 4100 Open is a big offshore express whose lasting appeal says much about her versatile personality. Part luxury cruiser and part hardcore fishing machine, the 4100 is a very roomy boat thanks to a wide 14-foot, 8-inch beam. Below decks, her spacious light-ash interior features a full-service galley, Ultrasuede dinette, private master stateroom, and a large head with a separate shower stall. The dinette converts to a double berth and the backrest lifts to create a single Pullman berth. A teak-and-holly cabin sole, Corian galley counter, and wine cooler were standard. Topside, a deluxe wet bar with ice maker is aft of the helm, and the cockpit—three steps down from the bridge deck—came standard with a circulating livewell, bait prep center, in-deck fish box (with macerator), freezer, and transom door. There's also a foldaway rear bench seat for evening cruises. An access hatch to the engineroom in the bridge deck sole provides quick sight checks while underway. A factory hardtop was a popular option. A heavily built boat with excellent range, Cat 435hp diesels cruise the Tiara 4100 Open at 22 knots and reach a top speed of 26–27 knots.

See Page 704 For Price Data

Length w/Pulpit	43'6"	Fuel	524 gals.
Hull Length	41'3"	Water	130 gals.
Beam	14'8"	Waste	50 gals.
Draft	3'6"	Hull Type	Modified-V
Weight	27,500#	Deadrise Aft	18°

Tiara 4200 Open

Apart from her quality construction and superb finish, the chief attribute of the Tiara 4200 Open is her ability to serve equally well as a cruising yacht or sportfishing boat. Tiara has been building practical, dual-purpose express yachts like this for years. No surprise, then, that the 4200 Open raised the bar for boats of her type when she was introduced in 2003. She's built on a steep-deadrise modified-V hull with prop pockets and a wide 14-foot, 11-inch beam. Two interior layouts were offered: Plan A, the original floorplan, has an extended portside lounge/dinette with the galley and head opposite, while Plan B adds a starboard lounge with privacy enclosure, sort of a second stateroom. In both layouts Tiara's satin-finished teak joinery and traditional teak-and-holly sole offer a pleasant contrast to the high-gloss cherry interiors found in most express yachts. The 4200's spacious 85-square-foot cockpit—with coaming bolsters, fresh and raw water washdowns, storage boxes and foldaway rear seat—could be factory-configured for fishing with an optional livewell and bait prep station. Note the fiberglass windshield frame and distinctive reverse transom. Cummins 670hp diesels cruise at 28 knots (32–33 knots top).

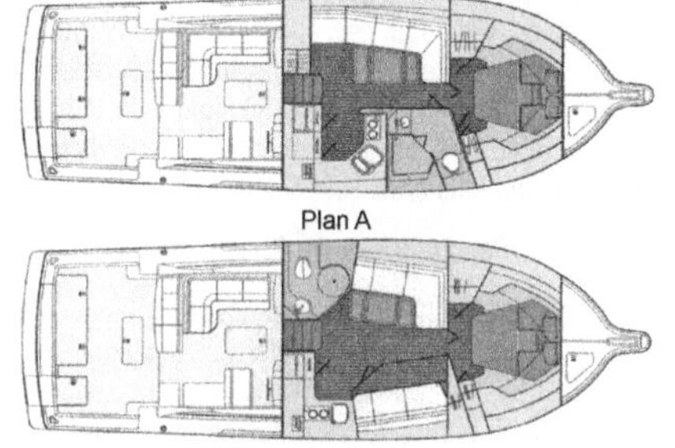
Plan A

Plan B

See Page 704 For Price Data

Length w/Pulpit	44'10"	Fuel	520 gals.
Hull Length	42'6"	Water	130 gals.
Beam	14'11"	Waste	50 gals.
Draft	4'2"	Hull Type	Modified-V
Weight	28,600#	Deadrise Aft	17.5°

Tiara 4300 Convertible

The 4300 Convertible enjoyed a long production run for Tiara thanks to her appealing styling, upscale accommodations and a large, uncluttered fishing cockpit. She's built on a beamy modified-V hull with a stepped sheer, a shallow keel and balsa-cored hullsides. Two floorplans were offered during her production years. The standard two-stateroom, two-head layout has the galley separated from the salon by a breakfast bar, and an alternate floorplan introduced in 1992 trades the guest stateroom for a large U-shaped dinette. Either way, the interior of the 4300 is luxurious, comfortable and extremely well appointed. The cockpit—large enough for several anglers and their gear—has a transom door, in-deck storage boxes, fresh- and salt-washdowns, and, beginning in 1994, direct access to the engineroom. Topside, there's plenty of space in the helm console for flush-mounting an array of electronics. Additional features include overhead rod storage in the salon, wide side decks, integral bow pulpit, and a choice of teak or oak interior woodwork. A heavily built boat, the Tiara 4300 will cruise at a respectable 24 knots with 550hp 6V92 GM diesels (28–29 knots top). More recent models with 660hp Cats cruise in the high 20s.

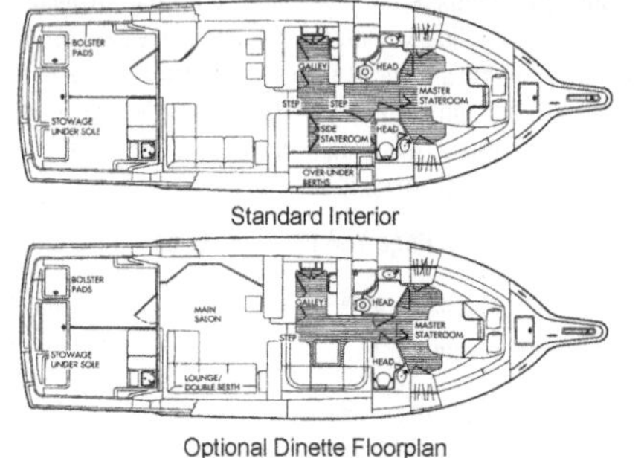
Standard Interior

Optional Dinette Floorplan

See Page 4704 For Price Data

Length w/Pulpit	46'7"	Fuel	640 gals.
Hull Length	43'2"	Water	160 gals.
Beam	15'2"	Waste	60 gals.
Draft	4'0"	Hull Type	Modified-V
Weight	31,500#	Deadrise Aft	16°

Tiara 4300 Open

1991–2002

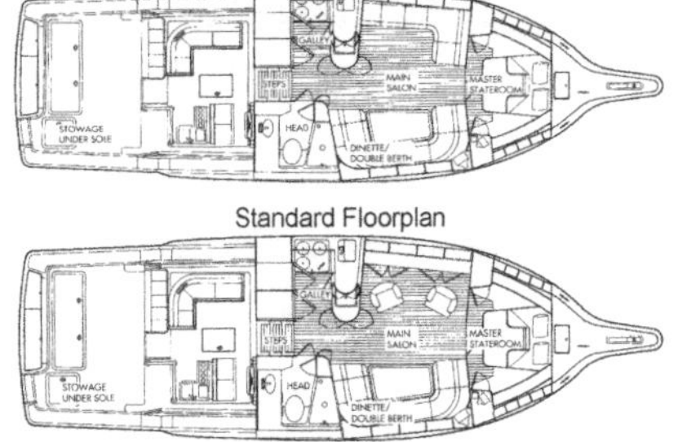
Standard Floorplan

Optional Floorplan

Heavily constructed, conservatively styled, and elegantly appointed the Tiara 4300 Open was one of the largest production sportboats available when she was introduced in 1991. Built on a beamy modified-V hull, the Open has enough built-in luxury to satisfy family cruisers and a cockpit large enough to meet the demands of hardcore anglers. The belowdecks accommodations are opulent (by the standards of her day, of course) with light ash joinery, leather upholstery, teak-and-holly sole, hydraulically operated dinette, and a spacious master stateroom with a walkaround island bed and built-in TV. Topside, the huge bi-level cockpit—reinforced for a mounted chair—comes with in-deck storage compartments, fresh and raw water washdowns, coaming bolsters, and a beefy transom door with gate. Additional features include a well-designed helm console with room for flush-mounting an array of electronics, wide side decks, excellent engineroom access, and a foldaway bench seat at the transom. Note that in 1999 the cockpit seating was rearranged. A quick boat with 550hp 6V92s, she'll cruise around 25 knots and reach 30+ knots wide open. Later models with 660hp Cats cruise at 26–27 knots.

See Page 704 For Price Data

Length w/Pulpit	46'7"	Fuel	526 gals.
Hull Length	43'2"	Water	150 gals.
Beam	15'2"	Waste	62 gals.
Draft	4'0"	Hull Type	Modified-V
Weight	29,500#	Deadrise Aft	16°

Tiara 4400/4700 Sovran

2003–08

Lots of manufacturers build quality, high-end sportcruisers but only a few reach the standards of engineering and finish consistently attained by Tiara. In the 4400 Sovran (called the 4700 Sovran in 2007–08), Tiara delivered a yacht of remarkable luxury and design sophistication. Not inexpensive, the Sovran's handsome styling is highlighted by her fully integrated hardtop, graceful sheer, and slightly reversed transom. Focusing on comfort and function, the posh, two-stateroom interior of the Sovran offers a luxurious blend of satin-finished teak woodwork, Corian counters, and Ultraleather seating. The large salon settee seats five and is served by a bird's-eye maple table. Each stateroom has an en suite head, and a washer/dryer combo is concealed in the aft stateroom. Topside, an impressive Stidd helm seat can be raised or lowered electrically. An L-lounge is opposite the helm, and fore- and aft-facing seats and a pair of hydraulically operated high/low tables are found in the cockpit. The Sovran's extended swim platform is large enough to accommodate a dinghy or PWC. On the downside, the engineroom is a tight fit. Cummins 670hp diesels cruise at 26–28 knots; 715hp Cummins cruise in the low 30s.

See Page 704 For Price Data

Length w/Pulpit	50'4"	Fuel	526 gals.
Hull Length	43'8"	Water	150 gals.
Beam	14'6"	Waste	50 gals.
Draft	4'5"	Hull Type	Modified-V
Weight	33,150#	Deadrise Aft	17°

Tiara 5000 Express

Flagship of the Tiara fleet when she was introduced in 1999, the 5000 Express is a distinctly American sportcruiser from a company whose reputation for quality is recognized throughout the industry. The 5000 may lack the sleek styling and high-performance persona of her European counterparts, but her cockpit is larger and the cabin more spacious than any sportboat import of her day. Built on a fully cored hull with prop pockets and a shallow keel, the posh interior of the 5000 Express is a blend of teak cabinets, solid-wood floors, vinyl overheads, and Ultraleather upholstery. Two floorplans were available: Plan A is a two-stateroom layout with a huge salon and the galley aft, while Plan B features three private staterooms with the galley forward in the salon. In the cockpit, electric tables rise for dining and lower for use as a cushion-covered sun pad. A 100-square-foot storage trunk is built into the transom, and the swim platform is designed to carry a dinghy or PWC. An extended fiberglass hardtop was a popular option. Twin 800hp Cat diesels cruise the 5000 Express at a respectable 25–26 knots and deliver a top speed of just over 30 knots.

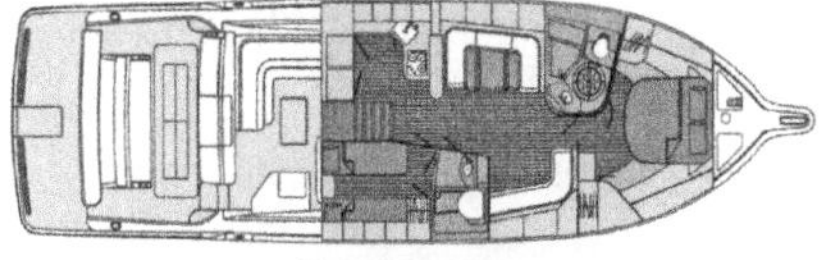
Two Staterooms

Three Staterooms

See Page 4704 For Price Data

Length w/Pulpit	55'0"	Fuel	700 gals.
Hull Length	50'9"	Water	200 gals.
Beam	15'11"	Waste	80 gals.
Draft	5'1"	Hull Type	Modified-V
Weight	38,600#	Deadrise Aft	17°

Tiara 5200 Sovran Salon

Tiara's largest boat ever, the 5200 Sorvan is a distinctly American sportcruiser from a company whose reputation for quality is recognized throughout the industry. The 5200 may lack the ultra-sleek styling and high-speed performance of high-end European sportyachts, but her fully enclosed pilothouse—with its dual reclining seats, built-in wet bar, and concealed flat-panel TV—creates a luxurious, weather-protected living space seldom found in her European counterparts. Built on a fully cored hull with a wide beam and prop pockets, the posh interior of the Sovran is a blend of teak joinery, hardwood flooring, designer fabrics, and Ultraleather upholstery. Two floorplans were available: Plan A is a two-stateroom layout with a huge salon and the galley aft, while Plan B features three private staterooms with the galley forward in the salon. In the cockpit, electric tables rise for dining and lower for use as a cushion-covered sun pad. Note the power sunroof, foredeck sun pad, and aft-facing cockpit seats. A huge storage trunk is built into the transom, and the extended swim platform is designed to carry a dinghy or PWC. Cat 865hp C-15 diesels cruise at a respectable, if not exciting, 26 knots (low 30s top).

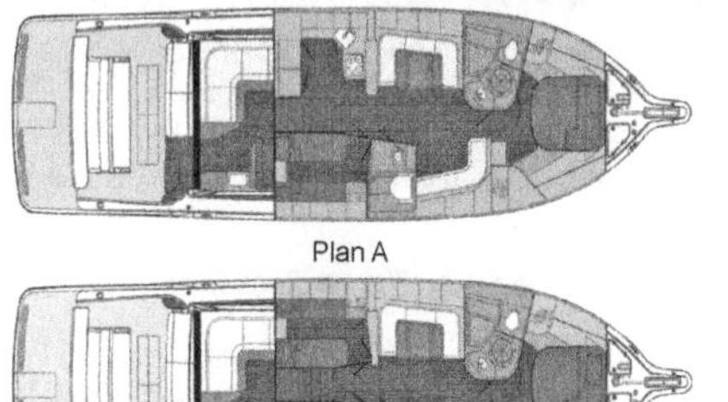
Plan A

Plan A

See Page 704 For Price Data

Length w/Pulpit	58'3"	Fuel	700 gals.
Hull Length	50'9"	Water	200 gals.
Beam	15'11"	Waste	80 gals.
Draft	5'1"	Hull Type	Modified-V
Weight	49,000#	Deadrise Aft	17°

Tollycraft

Quick View

- Founded in 1936 by R.M Tollefson, Tollycraft began as a small regional builder of wooden cruisers for the Pacific Northwest market.
- The conversion to fiberglass was made in the early 1960s, and by 1970 the Tollycraft line had grown to include a series of sedan and double cabin models from 24 to 40 feet.
- By the late 1980s Tollycraft was selling its boats nationwide as the company continued to build its reputation as a quality builder of motor yachts and sedans.
- In 1987 Tollycraft, called the "Cadillac of Yachts" by well-known naval architect Ed Monk, was sold to a group of outside investors who promptly attempted a huge expansion of both employees and plant facilities.
- By 1989 Tollycraft Yachts was in bad financial shape and a turnaround-specialist was brought in to cut costs and stabilize the company.
- In 1993 Tollycraft was forced to file bankruptcy and the company was shut down.
- Resuming operation under new management, Tollycraft production was suspended for the last time in the fall of 1996.

No longer in business.

Tollycraft 40 Sport Sedan

1987–95

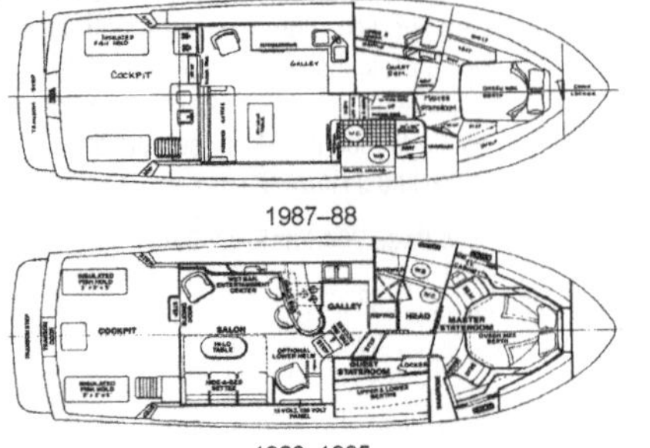

1987–88

1989–1995

An excellent sea boat, the 40 Sport Sedan is the only dedicated sportfishing design ever offered by Tollycraft. Introduced in 1987, she rides on the proven low-deadrise hull design used in several previous Tollycraft models. Originally offered with the galley in the salon and two staterooms forward, a revised interior in 1989 expanded the main deck area by moving the galley farther forward and separating it from the salon with a snack bar. Finally, in 1995—the final year of production—Tollycraft introduced an all-new, galley-down floorplan with a more open salon and a slightly smaller bow stateroom. In each of these floorplans, a lower helm was optional, and the interior was tastefully decorated with teak woodwork, designer fabrics, and quality hardware and furnishings. Topside, a transom door was standard in the large cockpit, and wide side decks make foredeck access easy and secure. The flybridge—available with the helm forward or aft—seats up to six in comfort. Note that a radar arch was a popular option. Caterpillar 375hp diesels cruise the Tollycraft 40 at 23 knots (26–27 knots top), and 485hp Detroit 6-71s cruise in the mid 20s and reach 30 knots wide open.

See Page 704 For Price Data

Length	40'2"	Fuel	500 gals.
Beam	14'8"	Water	140 gals.
Draft	3'0"	Cockpit	100 sq. ft.
Weight	26,000#	Hull Type	Modified-V
Clearance	12'4"	Deadrise Aft	10°

Tollycraft 44/45 Cockpit MY

One of Tollycraft's most popular boats, the 44 Cockpit MY is basically a Tollycraft 40 Sundeck with a cockpit extension. As it turned out, the 44 became more popular than her sibling thanks to the added versatility a cockpit brings to any yacht. Indeed, over 100 were built before Tollycraft incorporated a reverse-transom design in 1994 and reintroduced her as the 45 Cockpit MY. The two-stateroom, galley-down accommodations include a full-size dinette and a lower helm in addition to a roomy owner's stateroom, a deck access door in the salon, and plenty of storage. (Note that the 45 has an angled double berth in the bow stateroom rather than V-berths.) Topside, the full-width aft deck has room for a dinghy, and wide side decks make foredeck access easy and safe. The cockpit of either model is large enough for light-tackle fishing and makes an excellent swim or dive platform. Twin 350hp gas engines were originally standard in the Tollycraft 44 (18–19 knots cruise/27 knots top). Optional 375hp Cat diesels cruise around 23 knots (about 26 top), and the 400hp Detroit 6V53s cruise around 24 knots and reach a top speed in the mid to high 20s. Note that the fuel was increased in 1991.

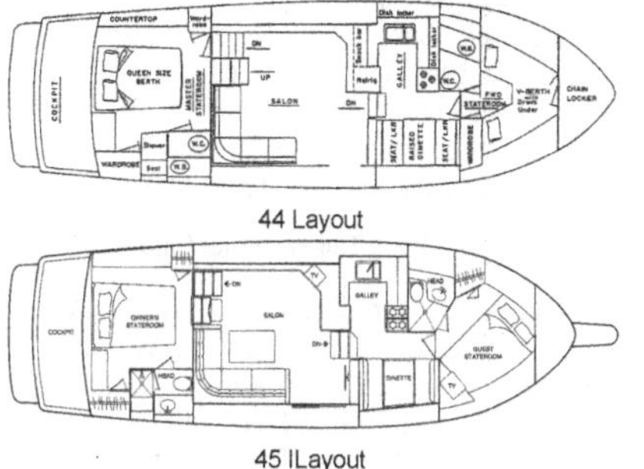
44 Layout

45 lLayout

See Page 704 For Price Data

Length, 44 CMY	44'2"	Clearance	14'9"
Length, 45 CMY	45'3"	Fuel	300/398 gals.
Beam	14'8"	Water	140 gals.
Draft	3'0"	Hull Type	Modified-V
Weight	28,000#	Deadrise Aft	10°

Tollycraft 48 Motor Yacht

Regarded by many as one of the finest West Coast cruising yachts ever produced, the Tollycraft 48 Motor Yacht (often called the 48 Cockpit MY) combines classic Tollycraft styling and quality in a yacht of exceptional elegance. Introduced in 1976, the popularity of this yacht was such that a total of 80 were built before she was retired from the fleet in 1986. Demand continued, however, and in 1991 production was resumed with another 25 produced before the last hull was delivered in 1998. Built on a solid fiberglass, semi-displacement hull with rounded chines and a long keel, the Tollycraft 48 is well known for her superb seakeeping attributes. Several two-stateroom, galley-down floorplan variations were offered over the years, all with a standard lower helm and port and starboard deck doors in the salon. Exterior features include a large cockpit with transom door, full walkaround side decks with protective bulwarks, radar mast, and swim platform. The aft cabin top is designed for dinghy storage. Early models with 210hp Cat diesels cruise efficiently at 10 knots. More recent models with 300hp Cummins (or 375hp Cats) cruise at 15–18 knots. Used Tollycraft 48s are always in demand.

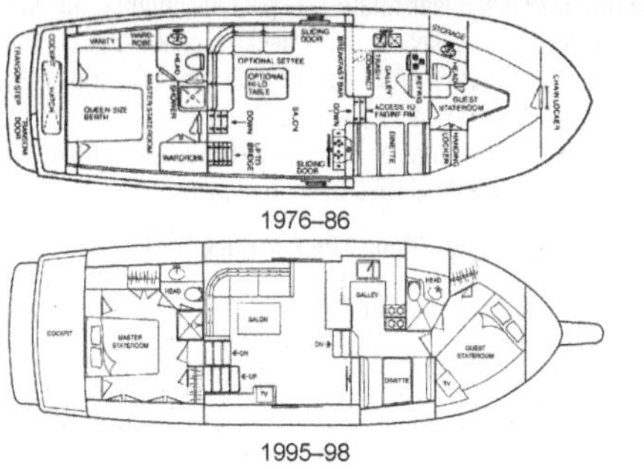
1976–86

1995–98

See Page 704 For Price Data

Length w/Pulpit	52'10"	Clearance, Mast	17'0"
Hull Length	48'2"	Fuel	600 gals.
Beam	15'2"	Water	188 gals.
Draft	3'8"	Waste	98 gals.
Weight	42,000#	Hull Type	Semi-Disp.

Tollycraft 57 Cockpit Motor Yacht

1989–96

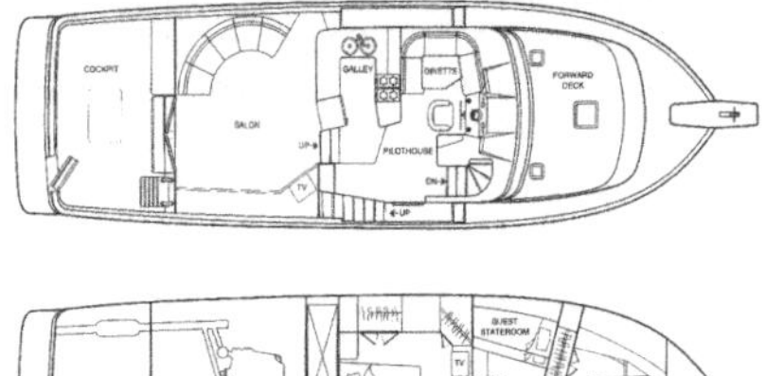

The Tollycraft 57 Motor Yacht is a stretched and modified version of the earlier Tollycraft 53 MY (1988–94) with a much larger cockpit and increased fuel capacity. In many respects the two boats quite similar, but the extra cockpit space of the 57—as well as the increased cruising range—were notable improvements from the original. She was built on an efficient semi-displacement hull with a solid fiberglass bottom and mega-wide 17-foot, 3-inch beam. The standard three-stateroom floorplan of the Tollycraft 57 is arranged with the dinette and galley forward, on the pilothouse level. The spacious, full-beam salon with entertainment center has a single portside wing door for access to the foredeck. On the lower level, the amidships master and both guest staterooms are forward of the engineroom. Accessed from the large cockpit, the engineroom has crouching headroom only but outboard access is excellent. A cockpit transom door and swim platform were standard. Note that in 1996, Tollycraft introduced the 57 Walkaround model with full side decks. Twin 735hp Detroits, 800hp Cats, or 820hp MANs cruise at a respectable 20 knots (mid 20s top). Over thirty of these quality yachts were built.

See Page 704 For Price Data

Length w/Pulpit	63'7"	Fuel	1,200 gals.
Hull Length	57'0"	Water	280 gals.
Beam	17'3"	Waste	120 gals.
Draft	3'6"	Hull Type	Modified-V
Weight	58,000#	Deadrise Aft	11°

Tollycraft 65 Pilothouse Cockpit MY

1993–98

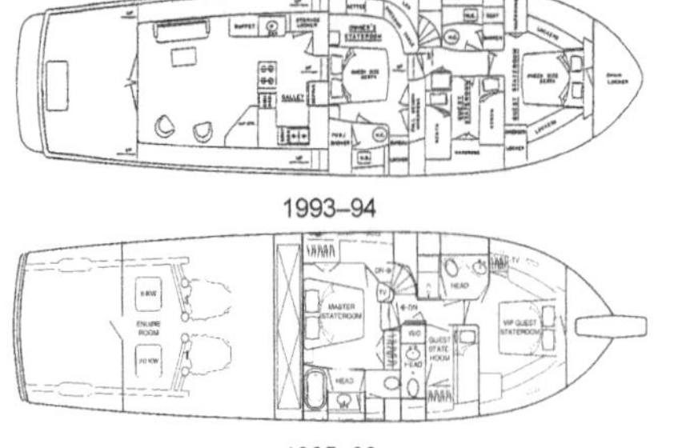

1993–94

1995–98

Like the Tollycraft 61 before her, the Tollycraft 65 Cockpit MY is a modern pilothouse cruiser with a handsome Pacific Northwest profile and best-in-class accommodations. In most regards, the 65 is a lengthened version of the Tollycraft 61 with a larger cockpit and a revised lower level floorplan. She rides on a semi-displacement hull with cored hullsides, a wide beam, and a shallow prop-protecting keel. Her luxurious pilothouse accommodations are arranged with the galley forward in the salon and three staterooms and three heads forward. A washer/dryer is standard, and the full-width master suite can only be described as opulent. There are port and starboard sliding doors in the pilothouse for easy deck access, and the 23-foot-long flybridge comes with a wet bar and a hydraulic davit. Practical features include covered side decks, a beautifully finished teak interior, a spacious engineroom with direct cockpit access, well secured side decks, and a big 175-square-foot cockpit. Twin 820hp MANs (or 800hp Cats) will cruise the Tollycraft 65 Cockpit MY at 22 knots and reach a top speed of 23–24 knots. Note that a total of 13 Tollycraft 65s were built, and used models will probably always be in demand.

See Page 704 For Price Data

Length w/Pulpit	67'10"	Fuel	1,160 gals.
Hull Length	65'2"	Water	400 gals.
Beam	17'11"	Waste	120 gals.
Draft	4'9"	Hull Type	Modified-V
Weight	68,000#	Deadrise Aft	10°

Viking

Quick View

- Viking was started by brothers Bob and Bill Healey in 1964 when they bought Peterson-Viking Builders, a small New Jersey builder of 37-foot, wooden sportfishing boats.
- In 1971 the company built its first all-fiberglass model, the Viking 33 Convertible, and the following fall the Viking 40 made its debut—a huge marketing success (over 400 were sold in the next 10 years) that established Viking as a leader in the pleasureboat industry.
- In 1987 the company moved into the large motor yacht market with the purchase of Gulfstar Yachts, a West Florida builder whose yachts were then considered among the most innovative in the industry.
- By 1990 Viking was offering a full line of high-end convertibles and motor yachts.
- The 1991-era recession, together with the ill-timed 10 percent luxury tax—whose repeal owed much to the efforts of Bob Healey—crippled Vikings production for a time.
- By 2003, Viking was back, building over 100 sportfishing yachts, 45' to 82', each year.
- Still family owned and operated, Viking has built over 4,000 yachts in the last 40 years.

Viking Yachts • New Gretna, NJ • www.vikingyachts.com

Viking 38 Convertible

1990–95

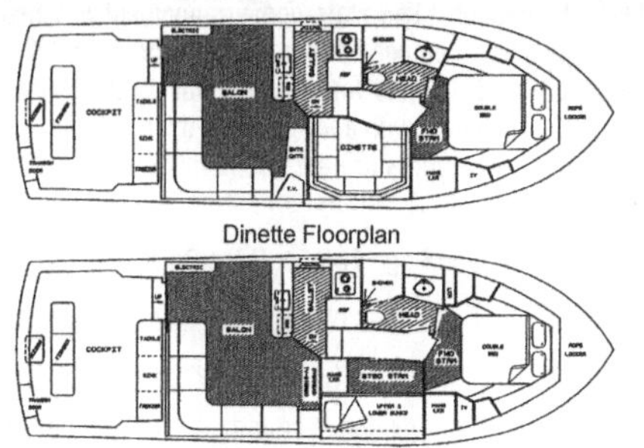

Dinette Floorplan

Two Staterooms

Still a handsome yacht in spite of the years, the Viking 38 Convertible was the smallest model in the Viking fleet during the early 1990s. She was an expensive boat with the same finish and attention to detail seen in Viking's larger yachts. The 38 was built on a modified-V hull with cored hullsides, a solid fiberglass bottom, and better than 14 feet of beam—wide indeed for a boat this size. Belowdecks, the expansive interior of the Viking 38, with its rich teak paneling and upscale fabrics, was available in two floorplan configurations. Both the dinette and two-stateroom layouts retain the convenient mid-level galley and double entry head. In the dinette arrangement, the salon dimensions seem huge for a 38-footer. The cockpit has over 100 square feet of space and comes with an in-deck fish box, transom door, and molded tackle centers. Topside, the spacious flybridge will seat a small crowd. Additional features include a bow pulpit, a well-finished engineroom, and an 8 KW genset. Big-block Crusader gas engines were standard until 1992 when they were replaced with 485hp Detroit 6-71 diesels. A great-running boat with a solid ride, the Viking 38 Convertible will cruise around 22 knots and reach 25 knots wide open.

See Page 704 For Price Data

Length	39'4"	Fuel	430 gals.
Beam	14'2"	Water	110 gals.
Draft	4'1"	Waste	40 gals.
Weight	32,890#	Hull Type	Modified-V
Clearance	11'10"	Deadrise Aft	15.5°

Viking 43 Convertible

1990–2002

The Viking 43 Convertible earned a reputation over the years as a first-rate tournament fisherman and an excellent open-water performer. She has more beam and fuel than the Viking 41 Convertible, the boat she replaced in the Viking fleet, and she offered a choice of a dinette or two-stateroom floorplan. Either way, the mid-level galley is wide open to the salon and the head compartment and master stateroom are both very spacious. The interior of the Viking 43 is comprised of rich teak cabinets and trim with quality appliances and rich designer fabrics—upscale accommodations indeed for a serious fishing boat. Topside, the flybridge (extended in 1997) is among the largest in her class and features an efficient wraparound helm console. The cockpit includes a transom door, molded tackle center, an in-deck fish box and—after 1995—direct engineroom access. Among many engine options, early models with 485hp 6-71s cruise at 22–23 knots (26 knots top), and 625hp 6V-92s cruise at 26 knots (29–30 knots top). Twin 680hp MANS (standard after 1999) will cruise at 28–29 knots and reach a top speed of 32 knots. Note that the fuel capacity was increased in 1996.

Dinette Floorplan

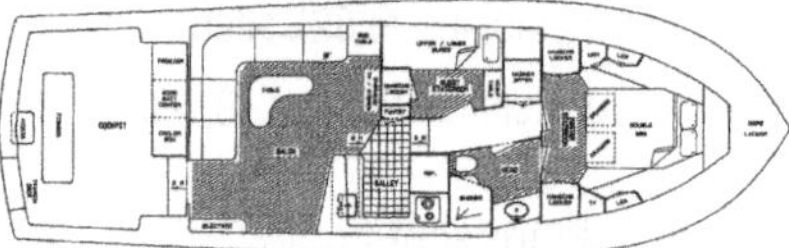
Two Staterooms

See Page 705 For Price Data

Length	43'0"	Fuel	525/600 gals.
Beam	15'3"	Water	115 gals.
Draft	4'3"	Waste	40 gals.
Weight	38,595#	Hull Type	Modified-V
Clearance	15'10"	Deadrise Aft	15.5°

Viking 43 Open

1994–2002

A big, muscular fishing boat with tremendous eye appeal, the Viking 43 Open was the best-selling express fisherman in her class during most of the 1990s. Viking offered this model in an Open Sportfish or Express configuration with the difference being the bolt-on swim platform and radar arch of the Express model. The deck plan was quite innovative when the 43 was introduced back in 1994—the helm is centered on the raised bridge deck, and the steps leading down to the cockpit are offset to starboard. This permits a full set of in-line tackle centers and a centerline access door to the engineroom. A fish box is built into the cockpit sole, and a transom door and transom livewell were standard. The standard single-stateroom floorplan has a spacious, wide-open salon with a big U-shaped settee and a roomy galley—an excellent day-boat layout, although a two-stateroom arrangement was also available. Among several engine options, a pair of 550hp 6V92s cruise in the high 20s (30+ knots top). Later models with 680hp MANs cruise at a fast 30 knots with a top speed in the neighborhood of 35 knots. Over 70 were built during her production years.

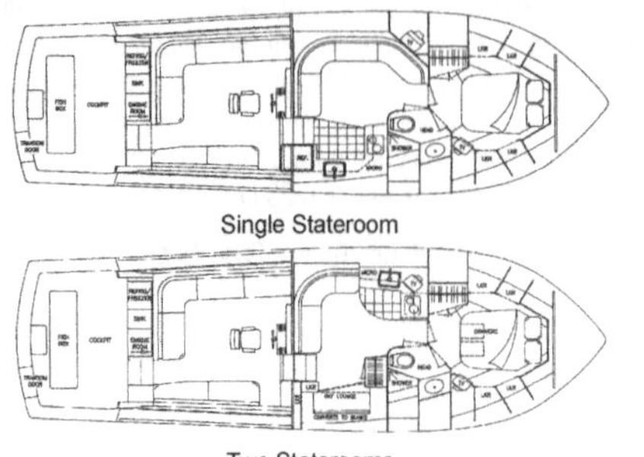
Single Stateroom

Two Staterooms

See Page 705 For Price Data

Length	43'0"	Fuel	525/600 gals.
Beam	15'3"	Water	115 gals.
Draft	4'3"	Waste	40 gals.
Weight	34,500#	Hull Type	Modified-V
Clearance, Hardtop	9'11"	Deadrise Aft	15.5°

Viking 45 Convertible

2003–09

A top-quality yacht in every respect, more than a few boating enthusiasts consider the Viking 45 to be about as good as it gets in a midsize convertible. Expecting good things in a Viking yacht comes naturally these days, and the 45 delivers an impressive mix of luxury and performance in a beautifully styled package. The interior layout is similar in many ways to Viking's larger convertibles. The galley and dinette are forward in the salon, and rods stow handily below a posh L-shaped leather sofa. Frameless windows are capped with upholstered valances, which conceal the air-conditioning ducts. Below, both staterooms are served by a private head and stall shower. Rich designer fabrics, lacquered teak cabinets, and deep pile carpeting highlight an interior notable for its elegance and attention to detail. The Viking's 119-square-foot cockpit features tackle storage, a bait freezer, and a cooler under the salon step. On the bridge, an L-shaped settee forward of the helm will seat several guests. The engineroom, reached from a cockpit hatch, offers superb service access. A fast ride, MAN 900hp diesels cruise the Viking 45 at an honest 30 knots (33–34 knots top).

See Page 705 For Price Data

Length	45'10"	Fuel	848 gals.
Beam	16'4"	Water	150 gals.
Draft	4'6"	Waste	50 gals.
Weight	49,750#	Hull Type	Modified-V
Clearance	16'4"	Deadrise Aft	15.5°

Viking 45 Open

2004–09

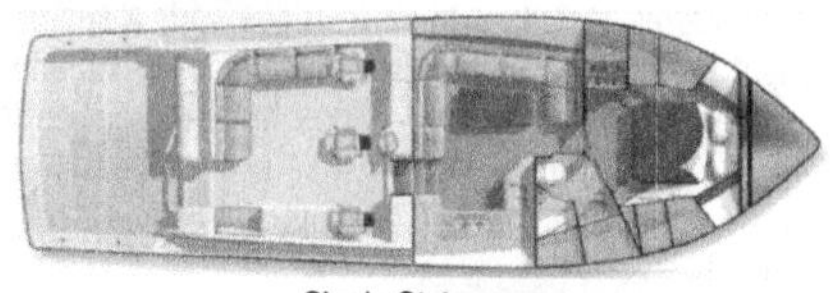

Single Stateroom

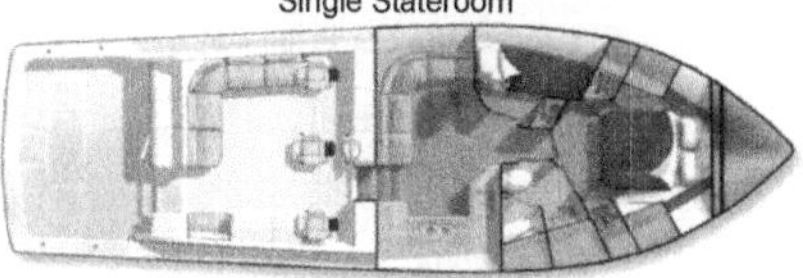

Two Staterooms

Introduced in 2004, the Viking 45 Open is a big, dual-purpose express designed to appeal as much to tournament anglers as family cruisers. Built on the same proven hull form as Viking's 45 Convertible, the spacious deck layout of the 45 Open is notable for its state-of-the-art centerline helm. There are three Murray helm chairs on the helmdeck, as well as an L-shaped lounge to port (with rod storage under) and a full wet bar. A sliding acrylic door leads to the spacious salon with its beautiful teak joinery, faux granite countertops, and posh leather seating. Available with one or two staterooms, both arrangements include a queen island berth forward and a large head with separate shower. Typical of all Viking yachts, the interior of the 45 Open is remarkable for its elegance and obvious attention to detail. The large 119-square-foot cockpit features insulated fish boxes, a rigging station, tackle storage, and direct access to a spacious, well-arranged engineroom. Additional features include wide side decks, recessed electronics box, and a transom door. A good performer with 900hp MANs, the Viking 45 Open will cruise at a fast 30 knots and reach 33–34 knots top.

See Page 705 For Price Data

Length	45'10"	Fuel	848 gals.
Beam	16'4"	Water	150 gals.
Draft	4'6"	Waste	50 gals.
Weight	49,760#	Hull Type	Modified-V
Clearance	NA	Deadrise Aft	15.5°

Viking 46 Convertible

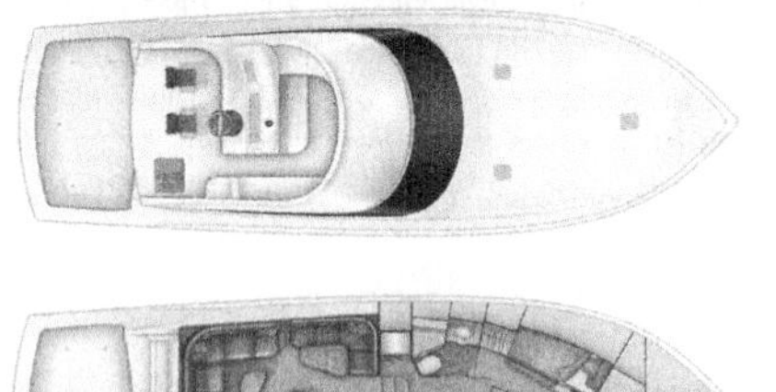

Smallest model in the Viking fleet when she was introduced, the 46 Convertible could hardly be defined as an "entry-level" boat. Bigger was nearly always better prior to the Great Recession, but by 2010 manufacturers were starting to focus on smaller, more affordable (and fuel-efficient) models to keep their order books filled. Built on a new Viking hull form with propeller pockets and 12 degrees of transom deadrise, the 46 is among a handful of boats her size to feature a cockpit mezzanine deck complete with bait freezer, seating, storage, and engineroom access. The Viking's beautifully crafted interior consists of a starboard-side galley with Corian counters, undercounter refrigerator/freezer drawers, and a small, triangular island counter with two stools. Below, a companionway laundry center is to port followed by the guest/day head and, further forward, the guest stateroom with over/under berths. The master stateroom is to starboard with a walkaround double berth and private head with an enormous forepeak shower. Additional features include a teak-and-holly galley sole, two large in-deck fish boxes, frameless salon windows, and a huge flybridge. MAN 1,100hp diesels cruise at 33–34 knots.

Not Enough Resale Data to Set Values

Length	46'11"	Fuel	870 gals.
Beam	16'6"	Water	150 gals.
Draft	4'5"	Cockpit	121 Sq. Ft.
Weight	54,120#	Hull Type	Modified-V
Clearance	NA	Deadrise Aft	12°

Viking 47 Convertible

Replacing the 45 Convertible in the Viking lineup in 1994, the Viking 47 rides on a revised hull design with a deepened forefoot for improved headsea handling and additional flare at the bow to reduce spray. The two-stateroom layout of the Viking 47 is unusual in that the salon, galley, and dinette are on a single level—rare in a modern convertible under 50 feet. The master stateroom is huge, and both head compartments have separate stall showers. Viking interiors have always been an elegant blend of grain-matched teak cabinets and designer fabrics, and the 47's accommodations are plush indeed. (Note the starboard-side, rather than centerline, salon door.) Outside, the tournament-level cockpit comes with an in-deck fish box in addition to a molded tackle center, transom door, and direct access to the spacious, well-engineered engineroom. Additional features include a huge flybridge with a superb helm console and seating for six, relatively wide side decks, and balsa coring in the hullsides. Standard 680hp MAN diesels cruise the Viking 47 at a fast 27 knots and reach 31 knots top, and optional 800hp MANs cruise at an honest 30 knots and deliver a top speed of 33–34 knots.

See Page 705 For Price Data

Length	47'2"	Fuel	700 gals.
Beam	15'6"	Water	160 gals.
Draft	4'5"	Cockpit	135 sq. ft.
Weight	46,300#	Hull Type	Modified-V
Clearance	16'10"	Deadrise Aft	15.5°

Viking 48 Convertible

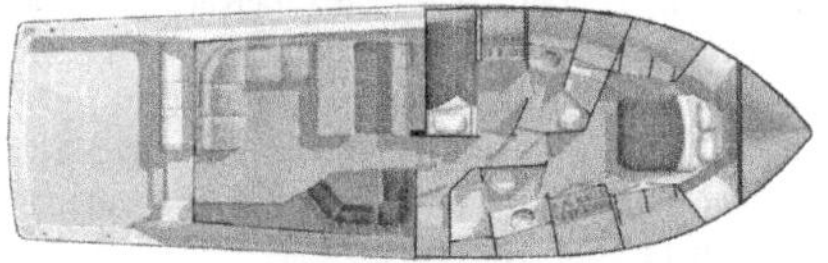
Two-Stateroom Layout

Three-Stateroom Layout

Introduced in 2002, the Viking 48 Convertible (note that Viking built an earlier 48-foot convertible during 1985–90) is yet another example of why Viking so dominates the market for premium, executive-class convertibles. It isn't just beautiful styling that sets her apart from the competition; what makes the Viking 48 special is her redundant engineering, exemplary finish, and superior open-water performance. Built on a modified-V hull with a wide beam and shallow keel, the interior is big for a 48-footer. The layout is arranged with the galley and dinette forward in the salon with a choice of two or three staterooms below. Both floorplans include two full heads as well as a standard washer/dryer adjacent to the companionway steps. Varnished teak cabinets, rich designer fabrics, and deep pile carpeting are applied throughout the interior. The spacious 130-square-foot cockpit sports a recessed fish box, bait-prep station, and direct access to the spacious engineroom. Note that the bridge ladder is positioned over the salon steps to save cockpit space. A terrific open-water performer, 1,100hp MANs (or 1,015hp Cats) will cruise the Viking 48 Convertible at an honest 30 knots (34–35 top).

See Page 705 For Price Data

Length	48'10"	Fuel	1,012 gals.
Beam	16'6"	Water	175 gals.
Draft	4'9"	Waste	50 gals.
Weight	56,450#	Hull Type	Modified-V
Clearance	NA	Deadrise Aft	15°

Viking 50 Convertible

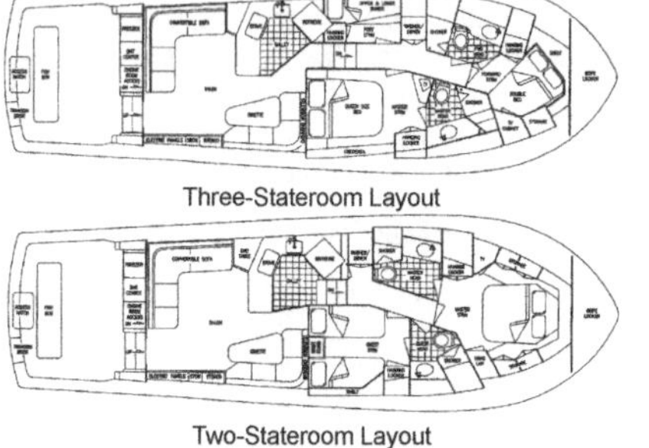
Three-Stateroom Layout

Two-Stateroom Layout

The Viking 50 is best described as a scaled-down version of the Viking 53 Convertible introduced a few years earlier. She's built on a modified-V hull with a relatively wide beam, a well-flared bow, and balsa coring in the hullsides. Her lush three-stateroom layout is similar in most respects to her predecessor, but with reduced dimensions. The master stateroom is amidships, a washer/dryer was standard, and the salon is open to the galley and dinette. Notable features of the Viking 50 include a spacious, standup engineroom, a huge in-deck fish box, direct cockpit engineroom access, and a superb bridge layout with seating for eight. Updates in 1997 included newly styled (frameless) deckhouse windows and an extended flybridge. At nearly 60,000 pounds, the Viking 50 is no lightweight. Standard power in 1991 was 730hp Detroit 8V92s (23 knots cruise/29 top), however, those engines were replaced in 1992 with 820hp MANs (26/30 knots respectively). Optional 1200hp MANs available after 1995 will cruise at a fast 32 knots with a top speed of 37–38 knots, making the Viking 50 Convertible one of the fastest boats in her class. Over 120 of these quality yachts were built during her production run.

See Page 705 For Price Data

Length	50'7"	Fuel	805 gals.
Beam	16'4"	Water	208 gals.
Draft	4'9"	Cockpit	144 sq. ft.
Weight	58,814#	Hull Type	Modified-V
Clearance	16'5"	Deadrise Aft	15.5°

Viking 50 Open

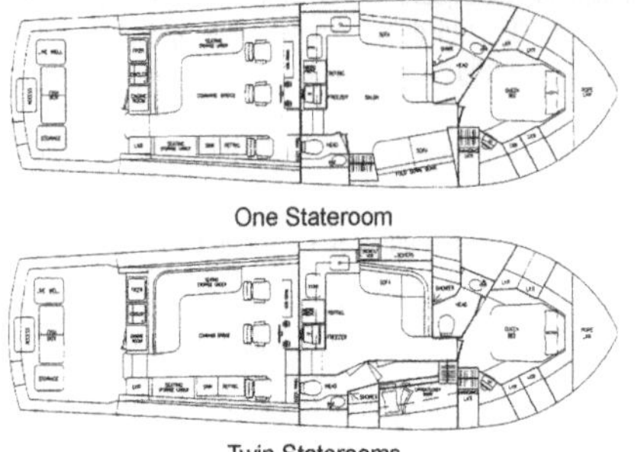
One Stateroom

Twin Staterooms

One of the largest express fishermen on the market when she was introduced in 1999, the Viking 50 Open is as beautifully styled as she is functional. She's built on the same fully hull as the Viking 50 Convertible—one of the most successful fishing boats ever—with a wide beam, cored hullsides, and a well-flared bow. The unobstructed cockpit of the 50 Open is huge, and the raised command bridge, with its centerline helm, L-shaped lounge and triple helm seats, is the focal center of the boat. Belowdecks, the lush single- or twin-stateroom interior is an appealing blend of high-gloss teak woodwork, Corian countertops, and quality hardware and appliances. (Note the convenient day head near the cabin entryway in both layouts.) Fishing features include two in-deck fish boxes, a big livewell, a custom tackle center with sink and freezer, fresh- and saltwater washdowns, and a transom door. The engine room, reached directly from the cockpit, is one of the best in the business with excellent all-around access. Standard 800hp MANs cruise the Viking 50 Open at 30 knots (33–34 knots top), and optional 1200hp MANs cruise at 35 knots and reach a top speed of close to 40 knots.

See Page 705 For Price Data

Length	50'7"	Fuel	805 gals.
Beam	16'4"	Water	208 gals.
Draft	4'9"	Cockpit	140 sq. ft.
Weight	55,700#	Hull Type	Modified-V
Clearance, Hardtop	11'5"	Deadrise Aft	15.5°

Viking 52 Convertible

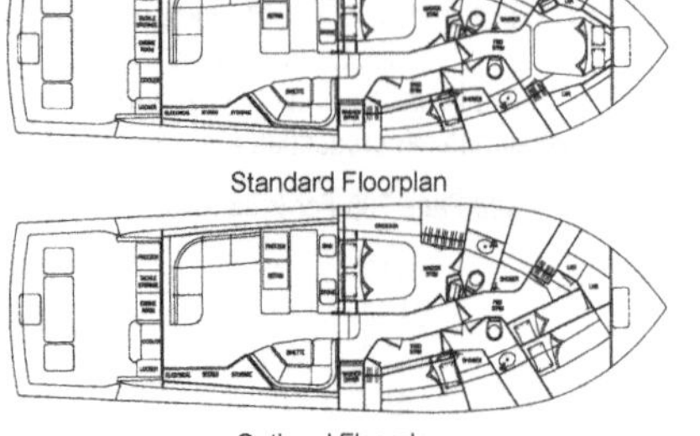
Standard Floorplan

Optional Floorplan

Introduced in 2002 as a replacement for the Viking 50 Convertible, exceptional performance and lavish accommodations made the Viking 52 Convertible a favorite with sportfishing and cruising enthusiasts alike. Built on a modified-V hull with a wide 17-foot, 5-inch beam, the luxurious three-stateroom, two-head interior of the Viking 52 features a spacious salon with L-shaped sofa to port, dinette to starboard, teak valences, and complete entertainment center. The home-size galley came standard with granite counters and Sub-Zero refrigerator and freezer. Below, the amidships master stateroom contains a walkaround queen berth, and the VIP forward stateroom was available with an island berth or stacked single berths. Note the companionway laundry closet with stacked washer/dryer. At 145 square feet, the cockpit of the 52 Convertible is one of the largest in her class. Fishing amenities include a bait prep center with sink and freezer, tackle center, washdowns, and a large transom door. The meticulous engineroom is accessed directly from the cockpit. A fast ride with standard 1,050hp MANs cruise the Viking 52 at 28–30 knots (low 30s top). Optional 1,300hp MANs cruise at 32–33 knots.

See Page 705 For Price Data

Length w/Pulpit	56'11"	Fuel	1,200 gals.
Hull Length	52'10"	Water	205 gals.
Beam	17'5"	Waste	52 gals.
Draft	5'1"	Hull Type	Modified-V
Weight	62,000#	Deadrise Aft	15.5°

Viking 52 Open

2007–Current

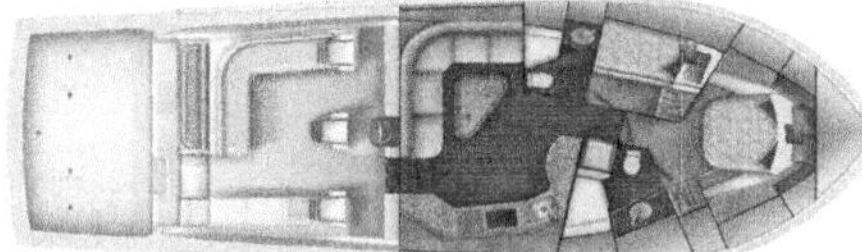

It wasn't all that many years ago that the idea of a production 50-foot express fishing boat was little more than a gleam in some designer's eye. Flash forward to 2006 when the Cabo 52 Express first appeared. A year later comes the Viking 52 Open, an equally broad-beamed sportfishing heavyweight whose luxury-class accommodations belie her fishboat pedigree. There are many similarities between the two boats—both feature huge bridgedecks with center helm positions; both have enormous enginerooms; and both offer lavish two-stateroom interiors with two heads and luxury-class amenities. Only the 52 Open, however, has mezzanine seating like the Viking convertibles. Housing a freezer and storage boxes under, mezzanines offer the extra seating many owners demand these days for cruising and entertaining. Cockpit features include a large in-sole livewell, refrigerated step box, transom fish box, and a beefy transom door with gate. The 52's meticulously detailed engineroom is simply a work of art. Built on a modified-V hull with cored hullsides and a solid glass bottom, MAN 1,360 V-12 diesels cruise at a blistering 35 knots. A hardtop version of the 52 Open is also available.

Not Enough Resale Data to Set Values

Length	52'10"	Fuel	1,200 gals.
Beam	17'3"	Water	200 gals.
Draft	5'0"	Waste	50 gals.
Weight	57,040#	Hull Type	Modified-V
Cockpit	145 sq. ft.	Deadrise Aft	15°

Viking 53 Convertible

1990–98

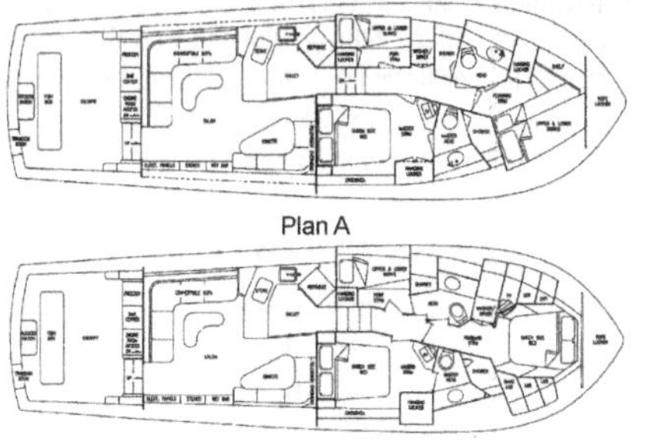

Plan A

Plan B

A strong-selling boat with over 100 delivered, Viking got it right with the 53 Convertible, a balanced blend of handsome styling, luxurious accommodations, and solid performance. She was built on a low-deadrise, modified-V hull with a wide beam and a shallow keel for directional stability. Several interior layouts were available during her production run. The original galley-up floorplan has three staterooms and two heads on the lower level with the master stateroom to starboard. In 1992 an angled double bed replaced the single berths in the forward stateroom, and the last layout—introduced in 1993—has a walkaround queen bed in the bow stateroom. The beautifully appointed interior of the Viking 53 was lavish indeed by the standards of her day, especially for a sportfishing yacht. The cockpit features a full tackle center, transom door, in-deck fish box, and access to a huge engineroom. The flybridge is equally large and features well-conceived helm console. Updates in 1997 included restyled (frameless) deckhouse windows and an extended flybridge. Standard 840hp MANs cruise at 26–27 knots (30 knots top). Twin 1,000hp MANs cruise at 30 knots (low 30s top), and 1,200hp MANs cruise at 33 knots (36–37 knots top).

See Page 705 For Price Data

Length	53'7"	Fuel	900/1,100 gals.
Beam	16'7"	Water	200 gals.
Draft	4'10"	Cockpit	150 sq. ft.
Weight	63,500#	Hull Type	Modified-V
Clearance	13'4"	Deadrise Aft	15°

Viking 54 Convertible

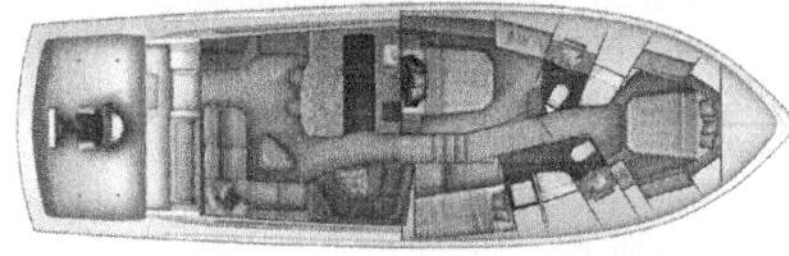

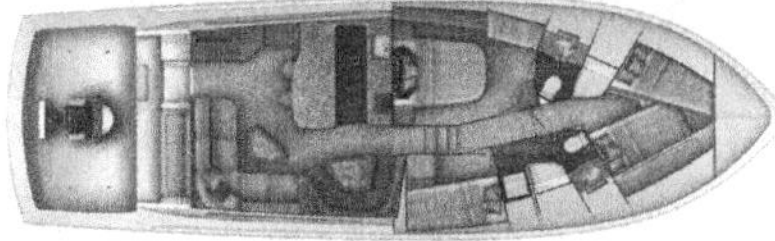

Viking Yachts sets the standards for big convertibles these days. Where once Bertram and Hatteras called the shots, today the leader in convertible design and production is clearly Viking. With convertible models ranging in size up to 82 feet (as of mid 2012, that is), the 54 is barely midsize in today's Viking convertible fleet. There is much to admire about this sophisticated yacht; powerful styling, state-of-the-art hull construction, huge 160-square-foot cockpit complete with mezzanine deck, and luxury-class accommodations with the amenities of a small motoryacht. Her spacious three-stateroom, two-head interior is an awesome blend of high-gloss teak joinery, Ultraleather upholstery, Corian counters, and high-end appliances and hardware. The L-lounge in the salon has rod storage under, and a laundry center is behind the teak companionway door. Both heads include separate stall showers. The 54's mezzanine deck features lounge seating to starboard and, to port, a hinged seat with freezer under. A meticulous engineroom, world-class helm layout, and near-flawless fit and finish are reminders of Viking's production-boat excellence. A fast ride, MAN 1,550hp V12 engines cruise at 34–35 knots (about 40 top).

Not Enough Resale Data to Set Values

Length	54'8"	Fuel	1,445 gals.
Beam	17'9"	Water	225 gals.
Draft	5'2"	Waste	100 gals.
Weight	77,900#	Hull Type	Modified-V
Cockpit	160 sq. ft.	Deadrise Aft	15°

Viking 54 Sports Yacht

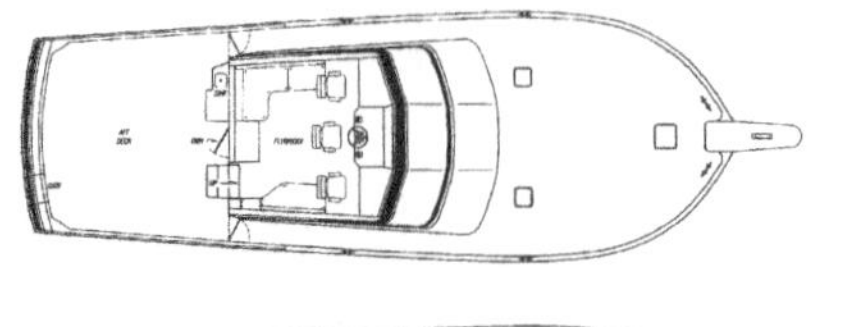

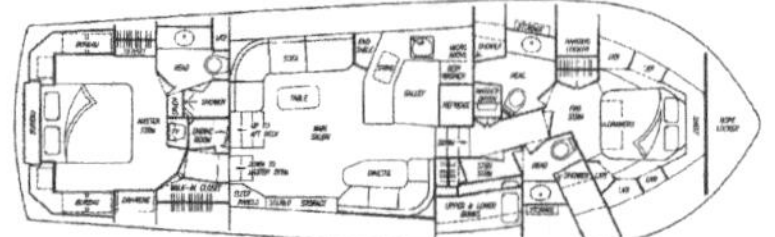

The Viking 54 Sports Yacht is a modern aft-cabin motor yacht whose aggressive styling was considered quite bold in the 1990s. Her impressive performance is due in part to the fact that she was built on a reworked version of Viking's 53 Convertible hull, a proven design with a good turn of speed. Belowdecks, the three-stateroom floorplan of the 54 Sports Yacht is dominated by a spacious and well-appointed salon with recessed halogen lighting and large, expansive windows. There's a queen bed in the bow stateroom and upper and lower berths in the guest stateroom, both of which have private heads. A stairway from the salon leads down to the palatial master suite with its king-size bed and walk-in closet. The spacious, full-width aft deck of the 54 Sports Yacht is a superb open-air entertainment platform with wing doors and room for a small crowd. Additional features include a standard washer/dryer, a huge walk-in engine room, and—after 1998—a fully enclosed flybridge. A fast boat in spite of her relatively heavy displacement, twin 820hp MAN diesels cruise at 24 knots (28 knots top), and 1,050 MANs cruise at 26 knots and reach a top speed of about 30 knots.

See Page 705 For Price Data

Length	54'1"	Fuel	900 gals.
Beam	17'5"	Water	200 gals.
Draft	4'10"	Headroom	6'6"
Weight	72,000#	Hull Type	Modified-V
Clearance	16'6"	Deadrise Aft	15.5°

Viking 55 Convertible

One of the best-selling boats her size ever produced, the Viking 55 is a world-class tournament machine with a graceful profile, elegant accommodations and remarkable performance. Indeed, there are many who believe this is about as good as it gets in a modern sportfisherman. Built on a soft-riding modified-V hull with cored hullsides, a solid fiberglass bottom and reverse chines, the lush three-stateroom, galley-up floorplan of the Viking 55 is arranged with the master suite amidships, a roomy VIP stateroom forward and two full heads—both with separate stall showers. A washer/dryer is standard in the companionway, and a dinette is located forward in the spacious 200-square-foot salon. Outside, the large cockpit is fitted with a bait-prep center, freezer, two in-deck baitwells, fish box, and direct access to the spacious engine-room. The massive flybridge, with its wraparound helm console and cockpit overhang, provides guest seating for a small crowd. Optional 1,200hp MAN diesels cruise the Viking 55 Convertible at an honest 33 knots and reach a top speed of around 37 knots—impressive performance for a 55-footer. A total of 115 were built making this one of the company's most popular models ever.

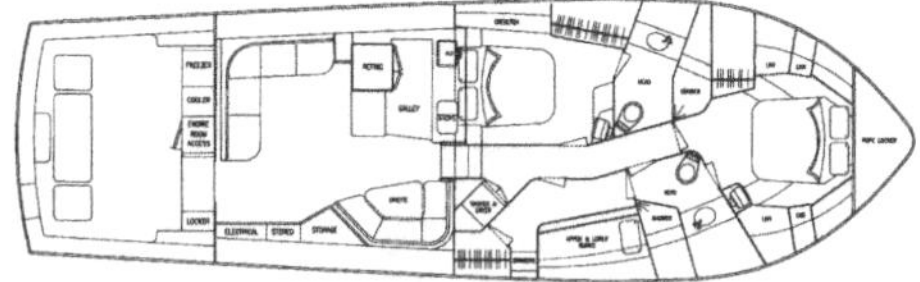

See Page 705 For Price Data

Length	55'10"	Fuel	1,250 gals.
Beam	17'4"	Water	250 gals.
Draft	4'10"	Cockpit	153 sq. ft.
Weight	68,800#	Hull Type	Modified-V
Clearance	17'1"	Deadrise Aft	15°

Viking 56 Convertible

The Viking 56 Convertible had some big shoes to fill when she replaced the highly popular 55 Convertible in Viking's fleet late in 2003. Longer and wider than her predecessor, the 56 has propeller pockets to reduce draft along with numerous equipment and mechanical upgrades. An impressive yacht with powerful lines, the lavish three-stateroom interior of the Viking 56 is an appealing blend of high-gloss teak joinery, designer fabrics, and luxury-class furnishings. The galley and dinette are forward in the salon that boasts an electric entryway door, full entertainment center and Ultraleather sofa. Granite counters and under-counter Sub-Zero refrigeration are standard in the galley. Note the companionway laundry center. The amidships master stateroom includes walkaround queen bed, flat-screen TV, and a wall of hanging lockers. The VIP forward stateroom was offered with an island queen berth or crossover berths. On deck, the vast 157-square-foot cockpit (with mezzanine seating) of the Viking 56 includes a large in-deck fish box, in-deck livewell, refrigerated step box, tackle center, and transom door with lift gate. The fastest boat in her class, MAN 1,550hp diesels cruise at 35 knots and top out at just over 40 knots.

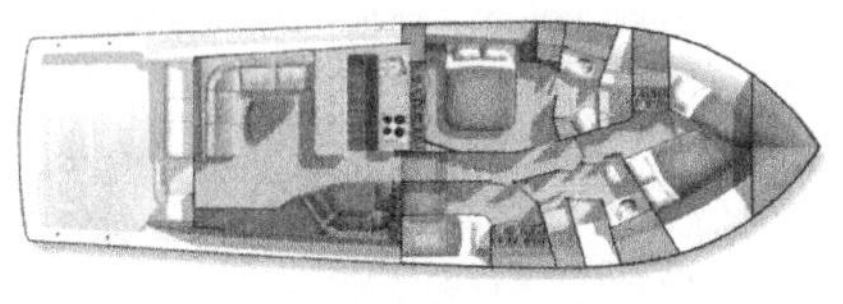

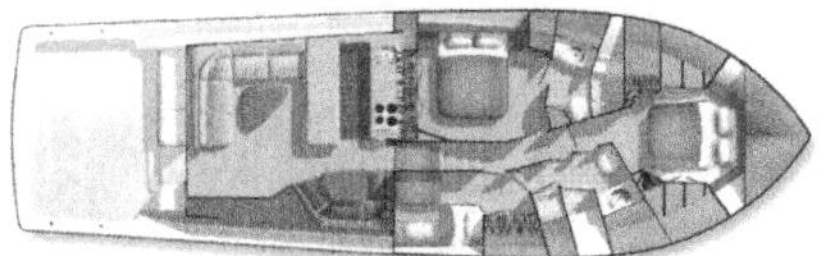

See Page 705 For Price Data

Length	57'6"	Fuel	1,500 gals.
Beam	18'2"	Water	240 gals.
Draft	4'10"	Waste	125 gals.
Weight	80,800#	Hull Type	Modified-V
Clearance	20'3"	Deadrise Aft	15°

Viking 57 Motor Yacht

1991–95

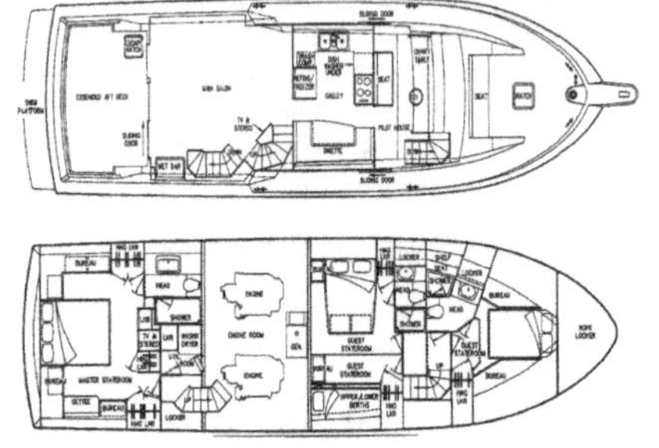

A big boat for her size even by today's standards, the Viking 57 Motor Yacht is a spin-off of the original Gulfstar/Viking 55 Motor Yacht hull with the extra length used to add space in the engineroom and—on the deckhouse level—to create a more spacious aft deck. She's built on a fully cored hull with a relatively wide beam, a shallow keel for directional stability, and moderate transom deadrise. Her galley-up, four-stateroom floorplan is arranged with the full-width salon separated from the galley and dinette. A queen berth is located in the amidships VIP guest cabin, and all three heads have stall showers. The engineroom is entered from the utility room aft of the salon. The upscale decor of the Viking 57—teak woodwork, Corian countertops, etc.—was quite impressive back in the early 1990s. Additional features include narrow service decks around the house, a bow pulpit, foredeck seating, and quiet lift-type mufflers (not the baffled exhausts of the 55 MY) in the engineroom. Twin 820hp MANs cruise the Viking 57 Motor Yacht at 19–20 knots (23 knots top), and 760hp Detroit 8V92s cruise at 18 knots (about 20 knots top).

See Page 705 For Price Data

Length	57'7"	Fuel	750 gals.
Beam	17'4"	Water	350 gals.
Draft	4'5"	Headroom	6'6"
Weight	78,000#	Hull Type	Modified-V
Clearance	21'2"	Deadrise Aft	15°

Viking 58 Convertible

1991–2000

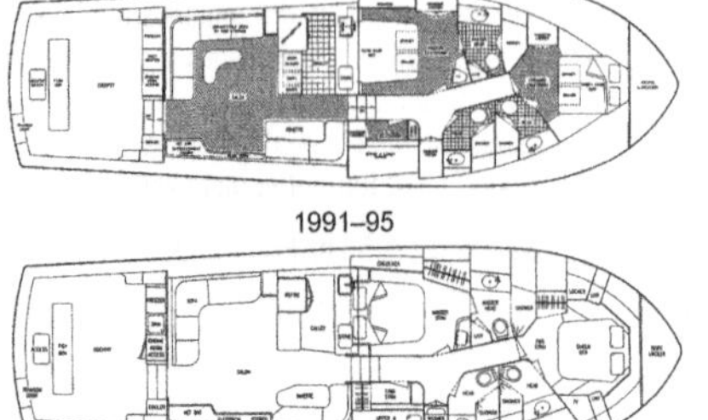

1991–95

1996–97

The Viking 58 is an updated version of the earlier Viking 57 Convertible (1989–91) with a sharper entry, additional bow flare, and a redesigned transom. Her modified-V hull retains the same wide 18-foot beam as her predecessor, which accounts for her spacious interior and cockpit dimensions. Viking employed several three-stateroom, galley-up floorplans in the 58 during her production years, all with an amidships owner's suite and three full heads. The massive cockpit includes a transom door, in-deck fish box, direct engineroom access, and a molded tackle center. The 58's meticulously arranged engineroom ranks among the best to be found in her day. An enclosed flybridge (with internal salon access) became optional in 1995, and updates in 1997 included restyled (frameless) deckhouse windows and an extended flybridge. Additional features include high-gloss teak interior joinery, home-size galley with upright refrigerator and Corian counters, and a huge flybridge with rod storage and seating for a small crowd. An extremely popular model (over 110 were built), twin 1,200hp MANs cruise at 28 knots (31–32 knots top), and 1,200hp MANs cruise at close to 30 knots (33–34 top).

See Page 705 For Price Data

Length	58'11"	Fuel	1,500 gals.
Beam	18'0"	Water	260 gals.
Draft	5'3"	Cockpit	168 sq. ft.
Weight	81,500#	Hull Type	Modified-V
Clearance	17'7"	Deadrise Aft	15.5°

Viking 60 Cockpit Sports Yacht

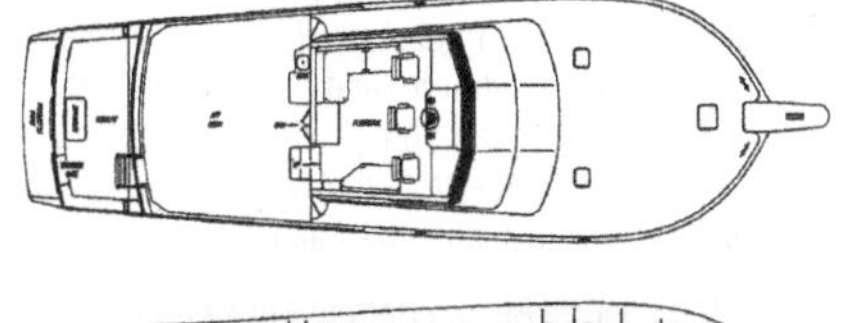

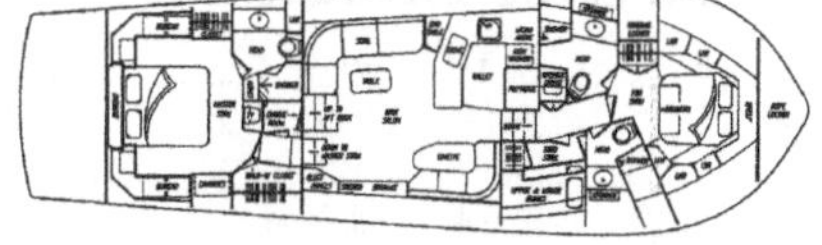

A versatile yacht combining motoryacht luxury with the performance of a modern sportfishing yacht, the Viking 60 Cockpit Sports Yacht is basically a Viking 54 Sports Yacht (1994–2001) with a cockpit extension. A cockpit adds great versatility to any motor yacht and, with some 70 square feet of space it's big enough to provide a good swimming and diving platform while also making the boarding process a whole lot easier. (Note that the extra hull length also adds a knot or so to her performance.) The Sports Yacht is built on an easily driven modified-V hull with a solid fiberglass bottom, side exhausts, and a shallow keel. Her three-stateroom teak interior includes a spacious and beautifully appointed salon wide open to the mid-level galley. The aft stateroom is huge with excellent storage and nearby access to the standup engine-room. The sprawling aft deck (almost 200 square feet) can be fully enclosed as a factory option, and the flybridge—also very spacious—could be enclosed as well. A popular model with an excellent turn of speed, twin 1,050hp MANs cruise the Viking 60 Sports Yacht at 26 knots (28–29 knots top), and optional 1,200hp MANs cruise at 28 knots (30+ top).

See Page 705 For Price Data

Length Overall	60'1"	Fuel	1,300 gals.
Beam	17'5"	Water	200 gals.
Draft	4'10"	Headroom	6'5"
Weight	78,000#	Hull Type	Modified-V
Clearance	16'6"	Deadrise Aft	15.5°

Viking 60 Convertible

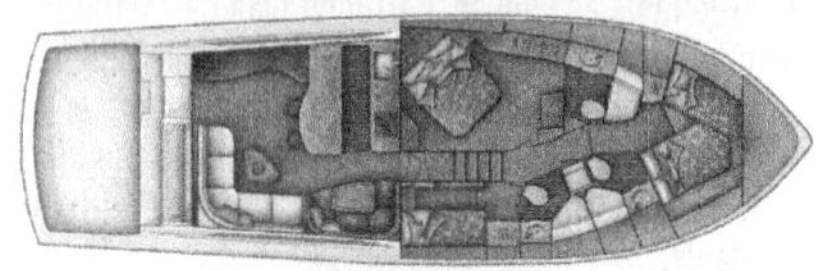

3 Staterooms

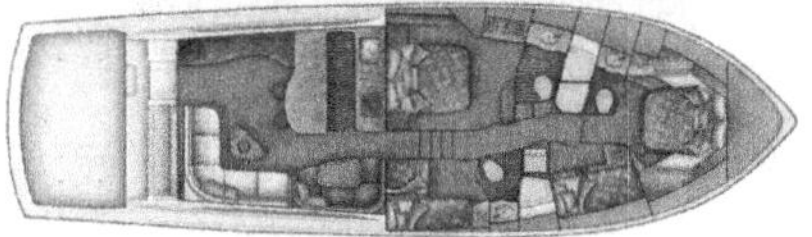
4 Staterooms

The Viking 60 is a good example of why Viking continues to dominate the high-end market for convertible sportfishing yachts. A classic blend of cutting-edge styling and world-class engineering, the Viking 60 sets the standards in her class for beauty, luxury and performance. She comes in either a three- or four-stateroom configuration, both with the master stateroom to port. The forward master and guest staterooms come with their own head with shower while the aft head doubles as a day head. The spacious salon has the dinette to starboard, U-shaped galley (with granite counters and Sub-Zero refrigeration) to port, and a huge Ultraleather settee aft. Forward, a 42-inch flat-screen TV is mounted on the bulkhead above the dinette. For many, the heart of the Viking 60 Convertible is her sprawling 170-square-foot cockpit complete with mezzanine seating (with freezer under), huge in-deck livewell, and tackle center. Topside, the flybridge boasts a state-of-the-art helm with single-lever controls, freezer, drink box, and plenty of seating. Built on a modified-V hull a wide beam and prop pockets, 1,825hp Cat C32 diesels cruise at an honest 35 knots (40 top). Note that an enclosed bridge model is also available.

Not Enough Resale Data to Set Values

Length	60'8"	Fuel	1,620 gals.
Beam	18'9"	Water	300 gals.
Draft	5'1"	Waste	135 gals.
Weight	91,300#	Hull Type	Modified-V
Cockpit	170 sq. ft.	Deadrise Aft	15°

Viking 61 Convertible

Viking got it right in 2001 with the introduction of the 61 Convertible. Lean and muscular on the outside, her lavish interior, massive cockpit and superb open-water handling set the standards in her day for sportfishing luxury and performance. Descended from the popular Viking 55 Convertible, the 61 has a sharper entry than previous Vikings for a drier ride and improved headsea performance. Like the Viking 65 Convertible and 72 Convertible before her, the hull of the Viking 61 is fully cored. The standard interior includes three staterooms with a queen-size berth in the amidships owner's cabin. A large dinette is opposite the galley, and a huge U-shaped sofa dominates the salon. Like all Viking interiors, the high-gloss woodwork and rich decor make for truly elegant accommodations. The cockpit is fitted with a full array of fishing amenities, and the flybridge is arranged with a centerline helm with a huge console and plenty of guest seating forward. The engineroom features standing headroom, and a separate pump room is forward. A fast ride, optional 1,500hp MTUs cruise the Viking 61 at 32 knots (35–36 knots top). Note that in 2003 propeller pockets were introduced to reduce shaft angles and draft.

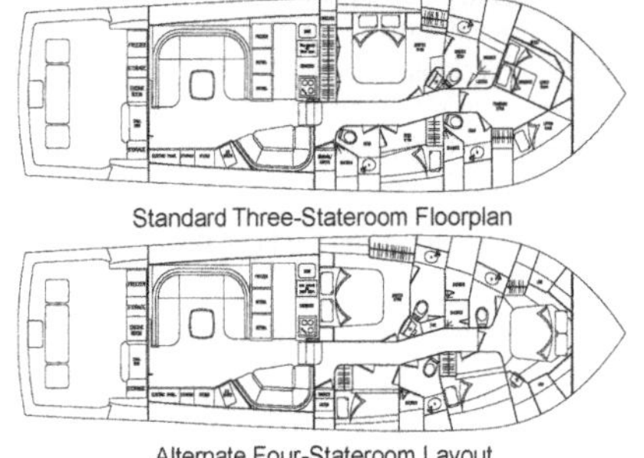
Standard Three-Stateroom Floorplan

Alternate Four-Stateroom Layout

Not Enough Resale Data to Set Values

Length w/Pulpit	65'11"	Fuel	1,850 gals.
Hull Length	61'9"	Water	310 gals.
Beam	18'2"	Waste	125 gals.
Draft	5'4"	Hull Type	Modified-V
Weight	90,000#	Deadrise Aft	15°

Viking 64 Convertible

The Viking 64 is one more example, if indeed any were required, of why Viking Yachts practically owns the market for high-end, luxury convertibles. By Viking standards, the 64 is a midsize yacht falling near the middle of a model lineup running from 42 to 82 feet in length. Introduced in 2006, the Viking 64 embodies the same world-class styling, engineering, and luxury that have made this company's products so admired over the years. A mega-wide 19-foot, 2-inch beam results in a huge cockpit with some 180 square feet of working space, including a mezzanine deck. The interior, available with three or four staterooms and three heads, is equally spacious and rivals most motoryachts for opulence. In the salon, for instance, there is a choice of either an L-shaped sofa with bar stools at the galley counter, or a posh U-shaped sofa. Both include a custom hi-lo table as well as a 40-inch plasma TV framed in teak above the dinette. An electrically operated door simplifies egress to the salon from the cockpit. The 64's massive standup engineroom is a work of art. Caterpillar 1,825hp engines cruise the Viking 64 at a fast 32 knots (mid-to-high 30s top). An enclosed bridge model is also available.

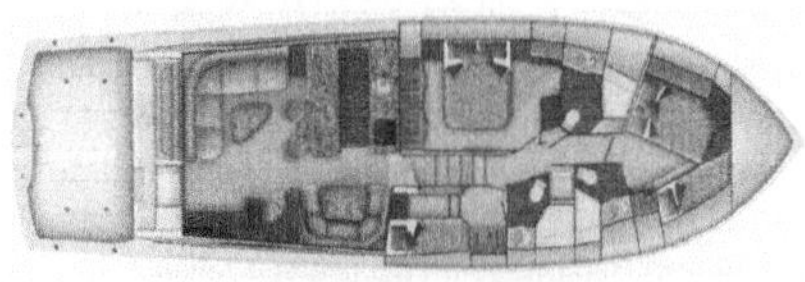
Three-Stateroom Layout

Four-Stateroom Layout

Not Enough Resale Data to Set Values

Length	63'9"	Fuel	1,930 gals.
Beam	19'2"	Water	325 gals.
Draft	5'2"	Waste	200 gals.
Weight	105,000#	Hull Type	Modified-V
Clearance	18'6"	Deadrise Aft	15°

Viking 65 Convertible

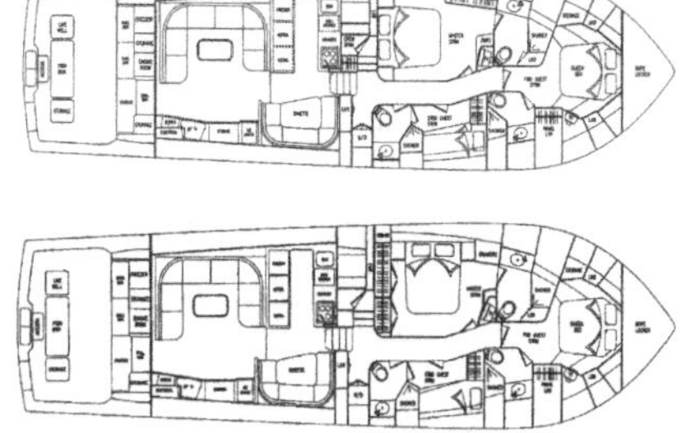

Fast and agile with muscular lines and lavish accommodations, a backlog of advance orders made the Viking 65 Convertible a sales success before the first hull was ever commissioned. She's built on a fully cored, modified-V hull with a shallow keel, wide reverse chines and a wide 18'9" beam. The standard three-stateroom layout provides an uncompromising level of comfort with an amidships master suite, VIP stateroom forward, starboard guest cabin, and step-down crew quarters aft with direct engineroom access. (An alternate three-stateroom layout trades the crew quarters for a lounge area abaft the master suite.) The massive cockpit of the Viking 65 comes with a full array of tournament-class fishing amenities. Topside, the optional enclosed bridge, reached from a spiral staircase in the salon, offers excellent all-weather visibility and entertaining, and includes an after station for docking and fishing maneuvers. Standard 1,350hp MTUs cruise the Viking 65 at 28 knots (30+ top), and optional 1,800hp Detroit (or MTU) diesels cruise at a fast 33 knots with a top speed of nearly 40 knots. Note that in 2002 Viking introduced a prop-pocket version of the 65 Convertible with slightly less draft.

Not Enough Resale Data to Set Values

Length w/Pulpit	69'10"	Fuel	2,000 gals.
Hull Length	65'10"	Water	360 gals.
Beam	18'9"	Cockpit	179 sq. ft.
Draft	6'1"	Hull Type	Modified-V
Weight	96,000#	Deadrise Aft	15.5°

Viking 65 Motor Yacht

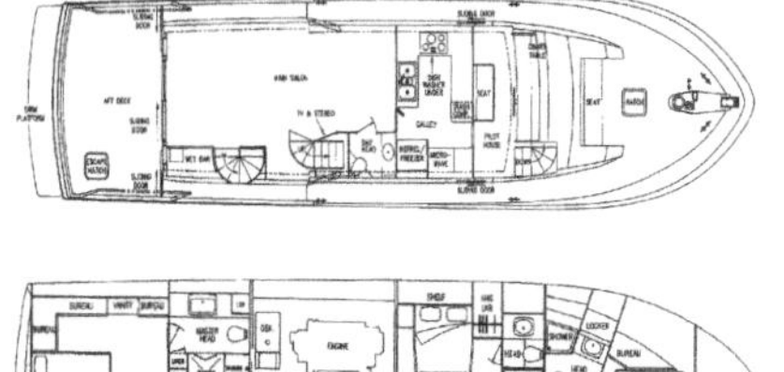

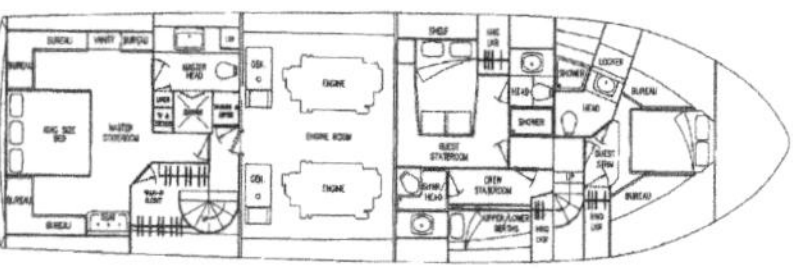

Introduced in 1991, the Viking 65 Motor Yacht combined a lavish four-stateroom interior with a spacious aft deck and a huge flybridge to create a versatile and extremely comfortable cruising yacht. The styling is clearly improved over the earlier 63 Motor Yacht (the boat she replaced in the Viking fleet) with a sweeping flybridge profile and raised wraparound bulwarks. There are many highlights in this boat—the utility room, the enclosed eat-in galley, and the convenient deckhouse day head are certainly notable—but the opulent master suite of the 65, with its walk-in wardrobe, home-size head, and floor-to-ceiling entertainment center (with refrigerator and wineglass storage, no less) simply dominates the layout. A sliding glass salon door opens to the huge aft deck whose sliding (not hinged) wing doors are unique. Topside, the extended flybridge has a wraparound helm and seating for a dozen guests. Note that the large engine room allows space for lift mufflers—much quieter than the baffled exhausts used in earlier Viking 55s and 63 MYs. A good sea boat, standard 1,000hp MANs cruise the Viking 65 MY at 20 knots (low 20s top).

See Page 705 For Price Data

Length	64'7"	Fuel	1,030 gals.
Beam	17'4"	Water	300 gals.
Draft	4'9"	Headroom	6'5"
Weight	94,000#	Hull Type	Modified-V
Clearance	20'8"	Deadrise Aft	15°

Viking 68 Convertible

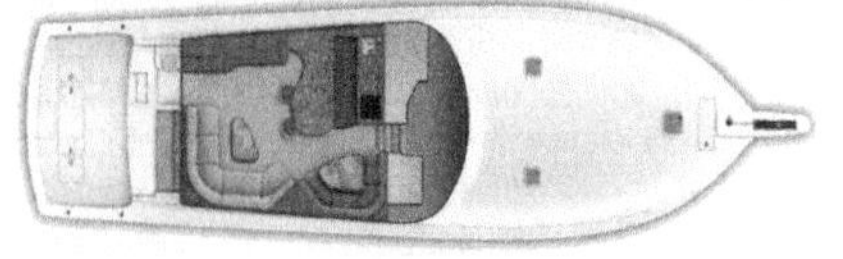

Finding the right superlatives to describe the Viking 68 Convertible is no easy task—Viking simply builds the best convertible sportfishing yachts in the business. Introduced in 2006 as the successor to the company's 65 Convertible, Viking designers gave the 68 an accommodation plan similar to the three-stateroom layout of the 65, using the extra 3 feet of length to add a fourth stateroom. Entering the salon through electrically pulsed sliding doors, the 68 is richly furnished throughout with precise teak joinery, premium designer fabrics, and expensive hardware and appliances. The entertainment center on the salon's port side contains a 42-inch plasma TV that rises silently from the counter at the touch of a button. Below, a king-size island berth is athwartships in the master stateroom; the VIP forward stateroom boasts an island queen berth; and both guest cabins sport over/under single berths. The 68's sprawling 186-square-foot cockpit is overlooked by a mezzanine deck, beneath which is a 9.9 cu. ft. freezer, tackle locker, chill box, and engineroom hatch. Note the frameless cabin windows. Offered with an open or enclosed flybridge, optional 2,400hp MTUs cruise at an honest 35 knots (38–40 knots top).

Not Enough Resale Data to Set Values

Length	68'8"	Fuel	2,060 gals.
Beam	19'4"	Water	355 gals.
Draft	5'5"	Cockpit	186 sq. ft.
Weight	115,000#	Hull Type	Modified-V
Clearance	NA	Deadrise Aft	15°

Viking Sport Cruisers

Quick View

- The Viking Sport Cruiser series is the result of a collaboration begun in 1995 between Viking Yachts and Marine Projects, the Plymouth, England builder of Princess Yachts.
- The first Viking Sport Cruisers models—production Princess models built to Viking's specifications—were imported into the U.S. for the 1996 model year.
- As the U.S. market for European production yachts expanded in the late 1990s, Viking expanded the Viking Sport Cruisers series to include 13 models from 40' to 84' in length.
- According the the Viking web site, in 2010 Viking Sport Cruisers and Princess Yachts International announced that, beginning with the 2011 model year, yachts built for North America, Central America, and the Caribbean would be branded as Princess, with Viking Sport Cruisers continuing as the distributor for these markets and providing sales and service support for customers through its dealers.

Viking Yachts • New Gretna, NJ • www.vikingyachts.com

Viking Sport Cruisers 40 Flybridge

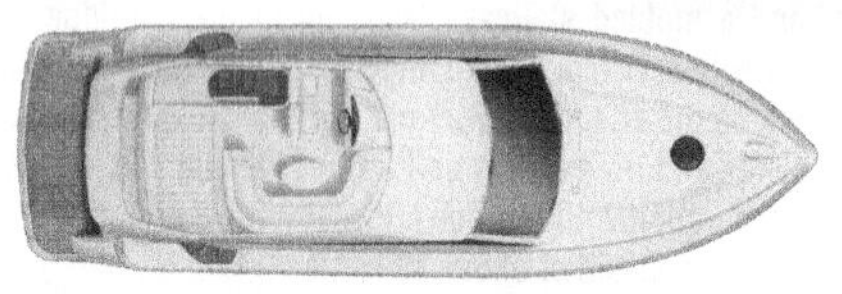

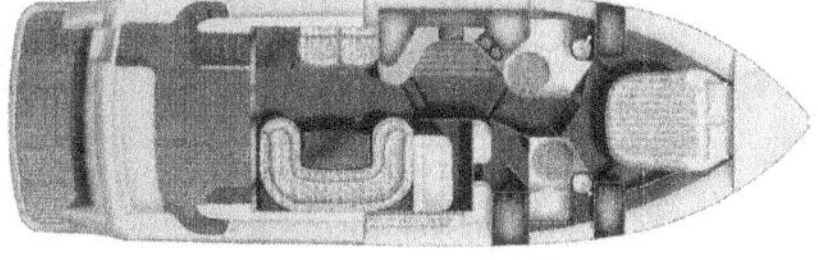

Introduced in England as the Princess 40 in 1998, the 40 Flybridge made her debut in this country in 2000 when she became the smallest of Viking's growing fleet of British-built sportcruisers. She's constructed on a good-running deep-V hull with prop pockets and an extended swim platform capable of carrying a personal watercraft. The contemporary two-stateroom interior of the Viking 40, with its high-gloss cherry woodwork and designer fabrics, is arranged with a step-down galley and a notably well-arranged lower helm position. A separate stall shower is found in the owner's head, and the guest cabin is tucked beneath the helm station above. In the cockpit, a large in-sole hatch provides easy access to a rather tight engine room. (Note that an expanded lazarette abaft the engine room houses the generator.) Molded steps ascend from the cockpit to the flybridge where a U-shaped settee and an aft sun lounge were standard. Additional features include a radar mast, transom door, wide side decks, a cockpit shower, and sliding, stainless-steel-framed salon doors. Twin 370hp Volvo (or 350hp Cat) diesels cruise the Viking 40 at 25 knots and reach a top speed of about 30 knots.

See Page 704 For Price Data

Length Overall	40'8"	Water	128 gals.
Beam	13'3"	Clearance	11'9"
Draft	3'1"	Headroom	6'3"
Weight	25,760#	Hull Type	Deep-V
Fuel	318 gals.	Deadrise Aft	19°

Viking Sport Cruisers 43 Flybridge

1995–99

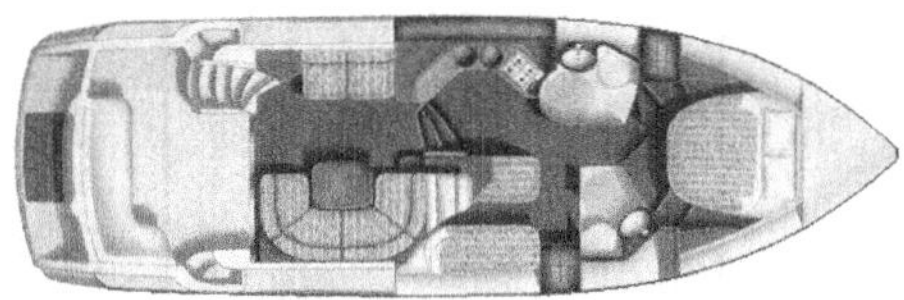

The Viking SC43 Flybridge (called the Viking SC42 until the swim platform was lengthened in 1997) is a UK-built flybridge yacht introduced into the American market at a time when European yachts were rapidly gaining favor with sophisticated buyers. She's built on a solid fiberglass hull with moderate beam, prop pockets, and a fully integrated swim platform. The interior was a big departure from most domestic boats of the late 1990s. The two-stateroom floorplan is arranged with the galley down, just across from an elevated lower helm station. Not only does this layout result in excellent helm visibility, it also provides the space for a second head. Low-level windows with mini-blinds in the salon allow outside visibility while seated—a nice touch. On the downside, neither head has a separate stall shower. The cockpit of the SC43 Flybridge is partially shaded by a flybridge overhang and includes a built-in bench seat aft, port and starboard boarding steps, and a transom door. Note that the flybridge is accessed via a curved staircase rather than the traditional cockpit ladder. A good performer, twin 420hp Cat (or 370hp Volvo) diesels cruise at 22 knots (28–29 top).

See Page 704 For Price Data

Length Overall	43'6"	Water	128 gals.
Beam	13'11"	Waste	42 gals.
Draft	3'3"	Clearance	11'6"
Weight	23,520#	Hull Type	Deep-V
Fuel	360 gals.	Deadrise Aft	19°

Viking Sport Cruisers 45 Flybridge

1999–2004

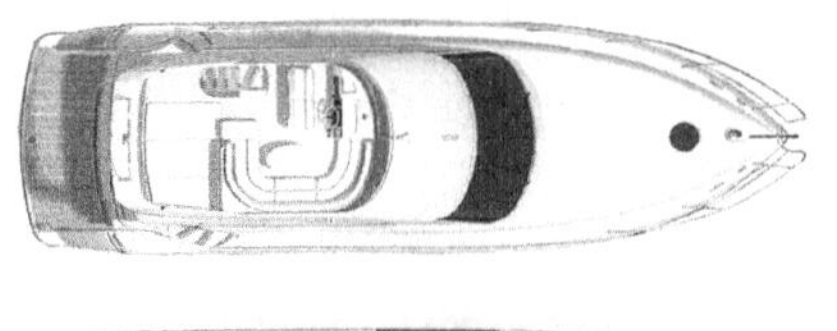

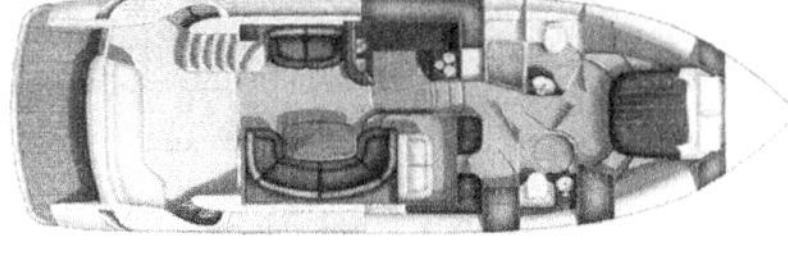

The Viking SC45 Flybridge combines the sleek styling and capable open-water performance of all of Viking's imported Sport Cruiser series, but in a smaller and more affordable package. Built on a smooth-running deep-V hull, the lean and angular profile of the 45 is aggressive without the overstyling seen in so many similar yachts. Her two-stateroom, mid-galley floorplan is arranged with a centerline double berth in the master stateroom and twin single berths in the guest cabin. A washer/dryer is off the companionway, and a separate stall shower is fitted in the owner's head compartment. (Note that a three-stateroom floorplan is optional.) High-gloss cherry cabinetry and luxurious furnishings make the salon of the SC45 among the more appealing in her class. Hatches in the teak cockpit sole provide access to the lazarette and engine room, and a molded staircase leads up to the flybridge with its U-shaped settee, cocktail table and aft sun lounge. Additional features include an extended swim platform, a cockpit transom seat, cockpit shower, bow thruster and a foredeck sun pad. A good performer with optional 480hp Volvo diesels, she'll cruise at 25 knots and reach a top speed of about 30 knots.

See Page 705 For Price Data

Length Overall	45'0"	Water	152 gals.
Beam	14'3"	Waste	42 gals.
Draft	3'7"	Clearance	13'7"
Weight	28,000#	Hull Type	Deep-V
Fuel	383 gals.	Deadrise Aft	19°

Viking Sport Cruisers 45/46 Flybridge

The Viking Sport Cruisers 46 Flybridge (called the Viking SC45 until 1998 when the swim platform was extended) combines the rakish lines and spirited performance of a modern European sportyacht with the accommodations of a much larger boat. Built in England, her solid fiberglass, deep-V hull (with prop pockets to reduce the shaft angles) is fairly light for a boat this size. The three-stateroom floorplan—rare in a boat this size—is arranged with the galley forward, a step down from the salon level. A huge wraparound settee dominates the salon where unique lower-level windows allow seated guests a panoramic view of the outdoors. Both guest staterooms have single berths, and the forward master stateroom features an island berth and private head. The cockpit, with its teak sole, L-lounge seating and transom door, is shaded by the extended flybridge. Additional features include high-gloss cherry joinery, foredeck sun pads, bow thruster, and teak swim platform. On the downside, the engineroom is a tight fit. A good performer, 370hp Volvo diesels cruise at 23 knots (25–26 knots top), and 430hp Volvos cruise at a fast 27 knots (about 30 knots top).

See Page 705 For Price Data

Length Overall	46'9"	Water	128 gals.
Beam	13'10"	Clearance	12'1"
Draft	3'4"	Headroom	6'5"
Weight	28,000#	Hull Type	Deep-V
Fuel	370 gals.	Deadrise Aft	19°

Viking Sport Cruisers 48/50 Flybridge

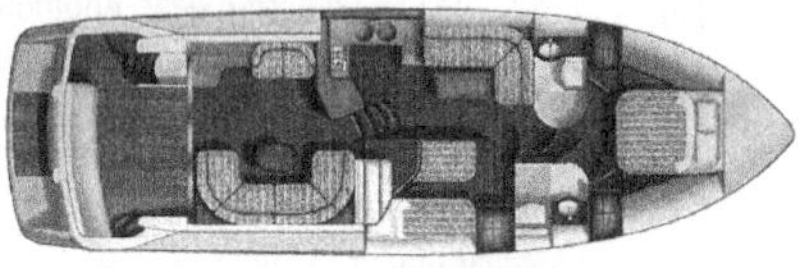

Standard Two-Stateroom Layout

Optional Three-Stateroom Layout

Introduced in 1994, the Viking Sport Cruisers 50 Flybridge (called the Viking SC48 until 1998 when the swim platform was extended) is a high-performance cruising yacht from England with a Med-style profile and true motor yacht accommodations. Like her sisterships in the Viking Sport Cruiser series, the hull is a deep-V design with moderate beam and prop pockets for reduced shaft angles and draft. The floorplan is unusual for a boat this size in that it could be configured with three staterooms forward (where there are usually only two) with the option of a fourth, low-headroom cabin under the aft deck for children or crew. The standard floorplan, however, was a two-stateroom layout with the galley and dinette down and two full heads. Outside, the spacious cockpit has a built-in bench seat at the transom, direct engineroom access, and a walk-through transom door. Note that the side decks are quite wide, and the flybridge—accessed via molded cockpit steps in the salon bulkhead—features lounge seating for six. Volvo 380hp diesels cruise the Viking SC50 Flybridge at 22 knots and deliver a top speed of 25–26 knots. Twin 435 Cats (or 430hp Volvos) will run a couple of knots faster.

See Page 705 For Price Data

Length Overall	51'0"	Water	187 gals.
Beam	14'2"	Clearance	12'6"
Draft	3'9"	Headroom	6'4"
Weight	33,600#	Hull Type	Deep-V
Fuel	428 gals.	Deadrise Aft	19°

Viking Sport Cruisers 50 Flybridge

2001–10

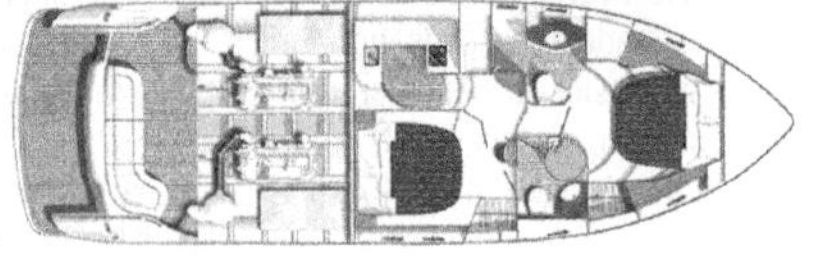

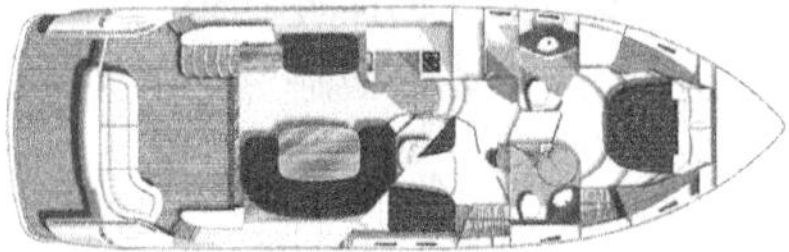

A popular model, the Viking Sport Cruisers 50 Flybridge took sportyacht styling and performance to the next level when she was introduced into the U.S. market in 2001. Indeed, with her elegant two-stateroom interior and near 30-knot performance the VSC 50 remains one of the more compelling midsize motor yachts available. Built by UK-based Marine Projects, she rides on a proven deep-V hull with moderate beam and propeller tunnels to reduce draft. Below decks, the open layout features Ultraleather salon seating, recessed galley forward, and an elevated lower helm to starboard. Both staterooms have double berths, and each head compartment includes a separate stall shower. The cockpit, shaded by the extended flybridge, comes with a teak sole as well as a full-width transom seat and an access door to the lazarette and engineroom. A curved staircase ascends to a roomy flybridge with wraparound lounge seating, wet bar, and aft sun lounger. Additional features include a washer/dryer forward of the galley, cockpit shower and icemaker, and a teak swim platform. Twin 480hp Volvos cruise the VSC50 at 22 knots (26–27 knots top), and optional 675hp Volvos cruise at a fast 28 knots (30+ top).

See Page 705 For Price Data

Length Overall	50'3"	Water	160 gals.
Beam	14'8"	Clearance	13'1"
Draft	3'8"	Headroom	6'4"
Weight	33,600#	Hull Type	Deep-V
Fuel	540 gals.	Deadrise Aft	19°

Viking Sport Cruisers V50 Express

1999–2005

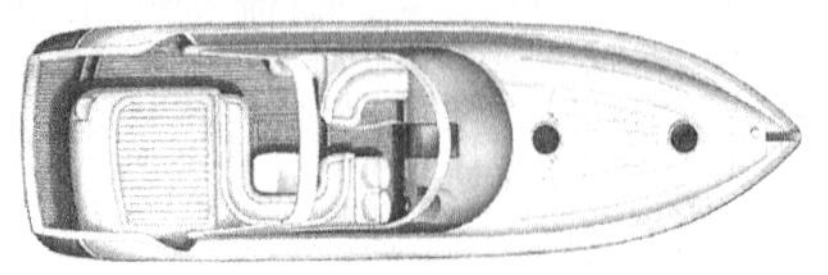

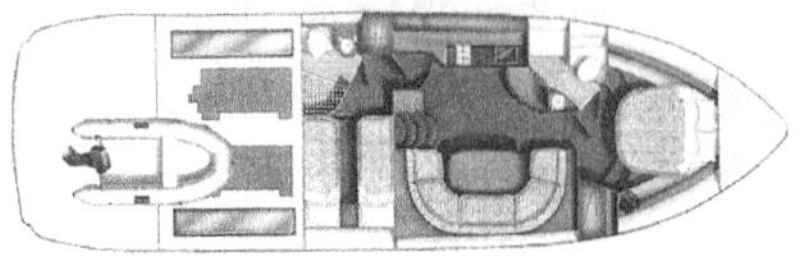

A well-styled yacht, the Viking V50 is a finely crafted, Med-style express yacht with more interior volume and elbow room than most other European sportboats her size. Like her sisterships in the Viking Sport Cruisers fleet, she rides on a solid fiberglass deep-V hull with a relatively wide beam and shallow prop pockets to reduce draft. Her elegant cherrywood interior includes two double cabins with ensuite heads, a concealed galley, and a plush U-shaped dinette in the salon. Both heads contain stall showers, and privacy doors—not curtains—separate both staterooms from the main cabin. Contoured seating topside provides seating for six in the cockpit, and a three-person sun pad aft rises at the touch of a button to reveal a tender garage below. Note that a machinery space behind the engine room houses the generator, batteries and steering gear. Additional features include a teak cockpit sole, a drop-down double helm seat, wet bar with refrigerator, radar arch, windshield washers, and a well-arranged engine room with good access to the motors. Twin 610hp Volvo diesel inboards cruise the Viking V50 Express at 28 knots and reach a top speed of 32–33 knots.

See Page 705 For Price Data

Length Overall	51'0"	Water	105 gals.
Beam	14'1"	Clearance	11'5"
Draft	3'6"	Headroom	6'3"
Weight	35,840#	Hull Type	Deep-V
Fuel	490 gals.	Deadrise Aft	21°

Viking Sport Cruisers 52 Flybridge

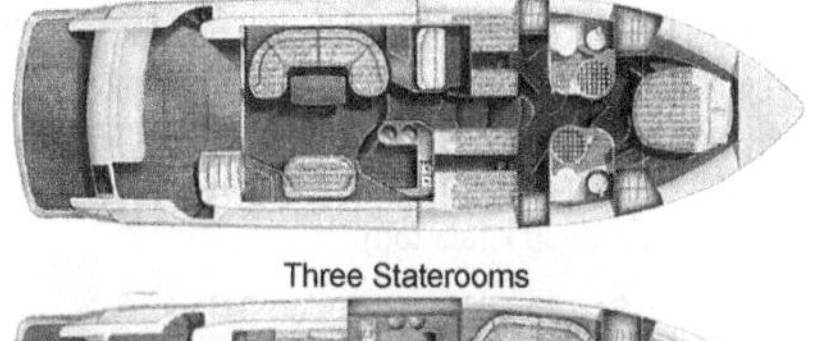

Three Staterooms

Two Staterooms

Luxury-class accommodations, graceful design, and superb open-water performance are joined in the Viking SC52 Flybridge, a yacht whose sophisticated construction and meticulous finish turned a lot of heads in the late 1990s. She's built on a high-performance deep-V hull—narrow in the beam compared with most of her mega-beam, American-built counterparts—with an extended swim platform and prop pockets. Several two- and three-stateroom floorplans were offered in the VSC52, all of which were available with crew quarters beneath the cockpit. Regardless of the layout, the high-gloss cherry joinery, designer fabrics, and tasteful furnishings of the Viking SC52 defined yachting elegance in her era. The cockpit, with its teak sole and built-in lounge seat, provides easy access to a large storage lazarette as well as the (compact) engineroom. Molded steps ascend to the flybridge with enough seating for a small crowd. Additional features include a teak swim platform, bow thruster, wide side decks, power vent windows, and a transom door. Twin 480hp Volvo diesels cruise the Viking SC52 Flybridge at 24 knots (28–29 knots top), and 610hp Volvos cruise at 27 knots with a top speed of around 32 knots.

See Page 705 For Price Data

Length Overall	51'8"	Fuel	504 gals.
Beam	15'0"	Water	187 gals.
Draft	3'8"	Headroom	6'3"
Weight	44,800#	Hull Type	Deep-V
Clearance, Arch	12'8"	Deadrise Aft	19°

Viking Sport Cruisers V55 Express

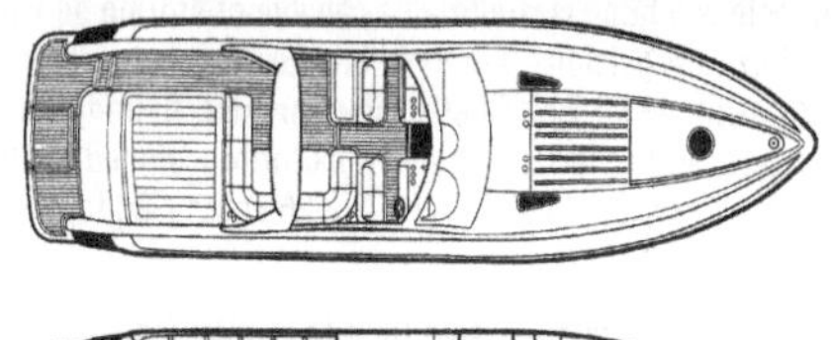

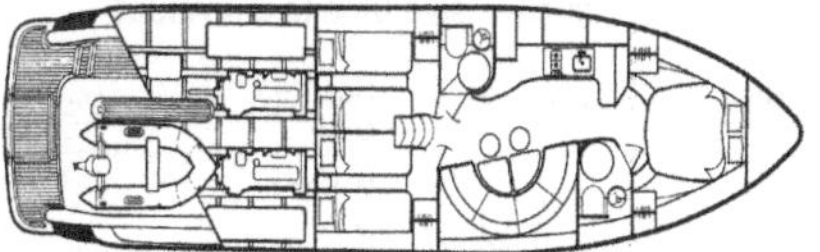

While the demand for luxury express cruisers is limited by the number of buyers who can afford such toys, there's little doubt that this is one of the most dynamic segments of the marine marketplace. The Viking V55 Express (called the Viking V52 until 1997 when the swim platform was extended) was one of the original Viking Sport Cruisers imported by Viking from UK-based Marine Products, Ltd. Still a handsome yacht a decade after her introduction, the V55 is a modern Mediterranean sportboat with an enormous cockpit and an innovative three-stateroom interior layout. While the cabin accommodations are well arranged (note the identical midcabin staterooms), more than half of the hull length is devoted to cockpit space including a huge sun pad atop a PWC garage with its own hydraulic lift system. The straight-drive engines are located below the cockpit sole where a centerline hatch provides access to the engine room. A bow thruster was standard. Built on a slender deep-V hull with prop pockets, the V55 Express is a good performer with either 610hp MAN diesels (30 knots cruise/34–35 knots top) or optional 800hp MANs (32-knots cruise/36 knots top).

Not Enough Resale Data to Set Values

Length Overall	55'0"	Fuel	540 gals.
Beam	14'4"	Water	107 gals.
Draft	3'6"	Headroom	6'3"
Weight	32,032#	Hull Type	Deep-V
Clearance	11'1"	Deadrise Aft	21°

Viking Sport Cruisers 56 Flybridge

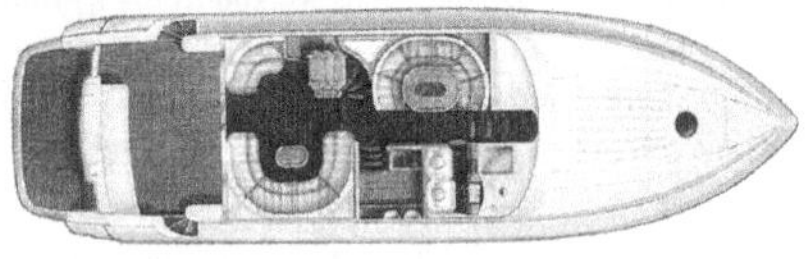

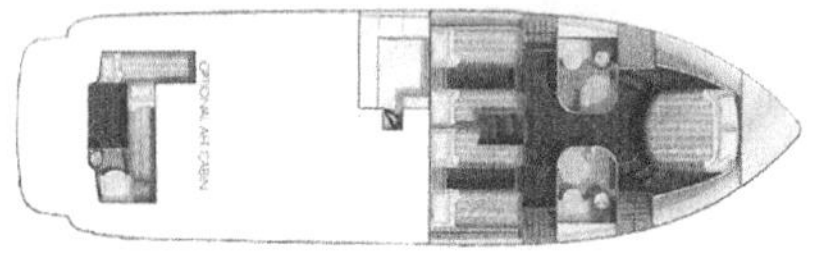

The Viking Sport Cruisers 56 Flybridge (called the Viking SC53 until 1997 when the swim platform was extended) appealed to the emerging class of mid-1990s yacht buyers seeking the sleek styling and high-end performance of a purebred European yacht. Built by Marine Projects, Ltd. in England on a deep-V hull with moderate beam, the SC56 Flybridge employs prop pockets to reduce shaft angles and draft. Below decks, two separate salon seating areas, a sunken galley (with an attached laundry room), an elevated lower helm, and inside flybridge access blend together in a graceful and notably practical layout. Three staterooms are forward of the engineroom, and twin-berth crew quarters are aft. The cockpit features a beautiful teak deck with built-in lounge seating. A hatch in the cockpit sole provides access to a large storage lazarette as well as the engineroom. Topside, there's seating for eight on the spacious flybridge with its aft sun pad, wet bar and low-profile arch. Unlike her more modern counterparts, a cockpit ladder rather than a molded staircase reaches the flybridge. A fast ride for a yacht this size, twin Volvo 610hp diesels cruise the Viking SC56 at 25 knots (28–30 knots top).

See Page 705 For Price Data

Length Overall	55'7"	Fuel	576 gals.
Beam	15'6"	Water	199 gals.
Draft	3'9"	Headroom	6'6"
Weight	47,040#	Hull Type	Deep-V
Clearance	12'10"	Deadrise Aft	19°

Viking Sport Cruisers 57 Flybridge

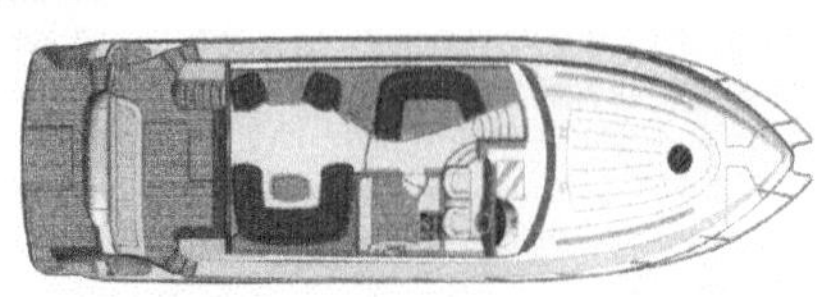

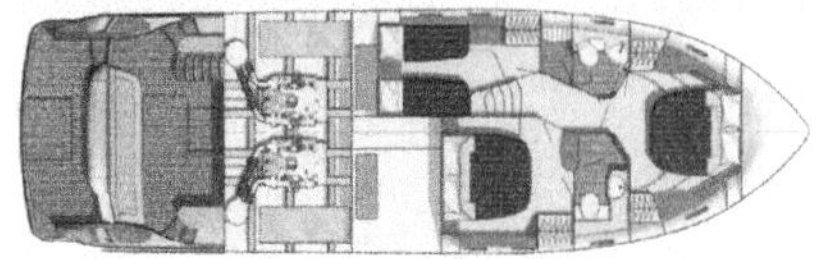

The UK-built Viking SC57 Flybridge is a top-quality motor yacht with the aggressive styling and excellent performance buyers have come to expect in a modern European luxury yacht. Her efficient deep-V hull (with prop pockers to keep the draft down) delivers high cruising speeds, and the posh three-stateroom interior of the SC57 is as beautiful as it is practical. The floorplan—similar in design to many European motor yachts her size—is arranged with a sunken galley forward of the salon and a raised lower helm position opposite the dinette. Expansive salon windows offer panoramic outside views, and a separate utility room reached from the galley accommodates a freezer and a washer/dryer. A spiral staircase in the salon provides inside access to the flybridge—a convenience not always found in a yacht under 60 feet. Under the SC57's teak cockpit sole is a huge lazarette area capable of storing all kinds of gear and extra provisions. Additional features include electric side windows at the helm and dinette, bow thruster, flybridge wet bar and sun pad, and an extended swim platform designed for tender storage. Volvo 715hp diesels cruise 25–26 knots (30 top).

Not Enough Resale Data to Set Values

Length Overall	57'6"	Headroom	6'5"
Beam	16'1"	Fuel	745 gals.
Draft	4'2"	Water	185 gals.
Weight	50,400#	Hull Type	Deep-V
Clearance	14'0"	Deadrise Aft	19°

Viking Sport Cruisers V58 Express

2003–10

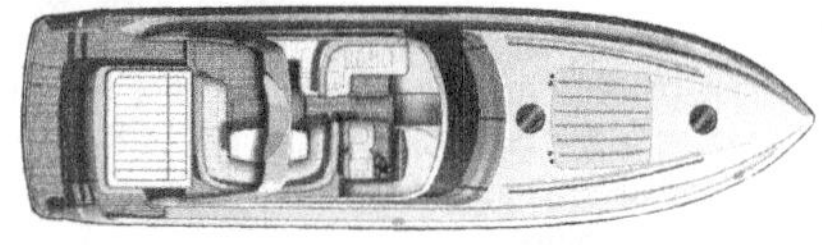

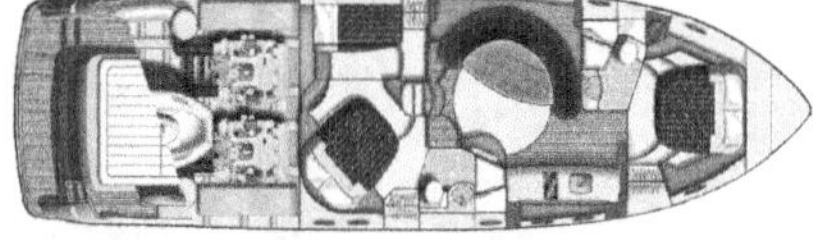

An impressive yacht with powerful lines and unsurpassed luxury, the Viking V58 is a sophisticated blend of modern engineering and state-of-the-art construction. Sleek and sporty topsides with molded spray rails and a deep-V bottom define the hull, and high-gloss cherry joinery highlights the spacious interior. While many sportcruisers are available with optional hardtops, the V58's folding sunroof offers the advantage of making the roof disappear and letting the sun shine in. The cockpit layout is centered around a huge U-shaped lounge for seating or dining. A double helm converts to a leaning post for rough-water passages, and a plush upholstered aft sun pad rises at the push of a button to reveal a large bay for a tender or PWC. The belowdecks accommodations allows six adults to sleep in three staterooms. The amidships master has a double berth and ensuite head, as does the forepeak VIP cabin. A large part of the salon is laid with a parquet-style floor. Additional features include a spacious engine room, teak cockpit sole, hidden galley appliances, and cockpit grill. An excellent performer with 860hp MANs, the V58 will cruise at an honest 30 knots and top out at close to 35 knots.

See Page 705 For Price Data

Length	58'11"	Fuel	660 gals.
Beam	15'5"	Water	125 gals.
Draft	3'6"	Waste	54 gals.
Weight	44,800#	Hull Type	Deep-V
Clearance	16'6"	Deadrise Aft	19°

Viking Sport Cruisers 60 Flybridge

1996–2001

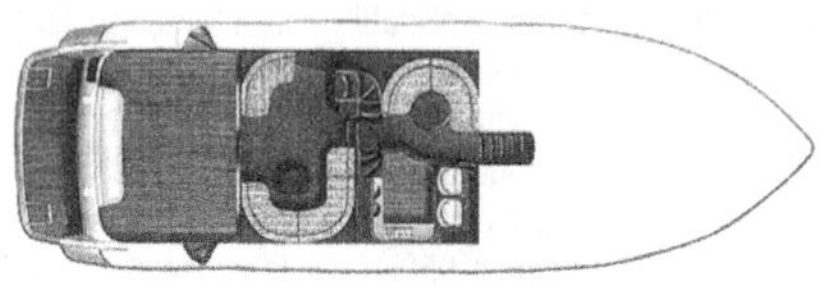

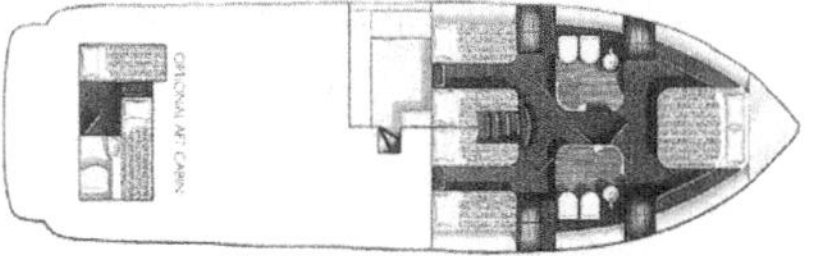

Introduced into the U.S. market in 2006, the Viking Sport Cruisers 60 Flybridge combined the rakish styling and spirited performance lacking in most American-built motor yachts of her era. Like her counterparts in the Viking Sport Cruisers fleet, she was constructed on a high-performance deep-V hull with a moderate 16-foot, 1-inch beam, reverse chines, and prop pockets. At just over 50,000 pounds, the VSC60 is a notably weight-efficient yacht. Her opulent three-stateroom interior is arranged with the dinette and lower helm forward, two steps up from the salon level. The galley is down and features a connected utility room with dishwasher, washer/dryer, freezer and storage lockers. Both guest staterooms share a common head, and an aft stateroom/crew quarters (optional) is located beneath the cockpit. The flybridge, with its centerline helm, deluxe wet bar, grill, and large sun pad, can be accessed from either the aft deck or salon. Additional features include a teak swim platform, electric aft salon window, and bow thruster. The engineroom is a tight fit. A good performer with optional 800hp MANs, she'll cruise at 28–29 knots (about 34 knots top). Standard 610hp Volvos cruise at 26 knots (29–30 knots top).

See Page 705 For Price Data

Length Overall	59'11"	Fuel	756 gals.
Beam	16'1"	Water	199 gals.
Draft	3'11"	Headroom	6'5"
Weight	50,400#	Hull Type	Deep-V
Clearance	13'7"	Deadrise Aft	19°

Viking Sport Cruisers 61 Flybridge

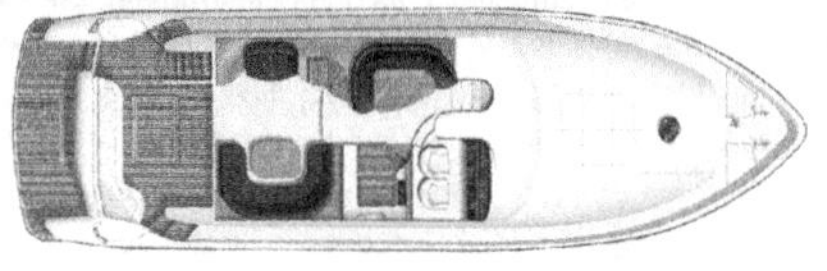

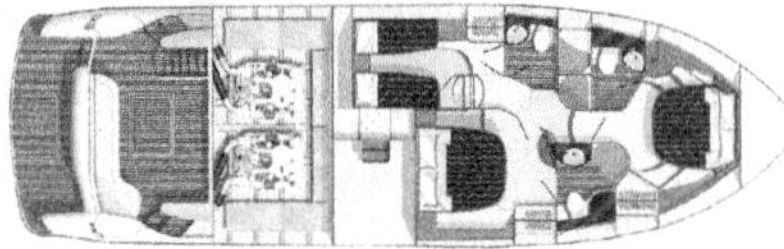

Sophisticated styling, luxury-class accommodations, and leading-edge performance combine in the Viking Sport Cruisers 61 Flybridge, a purebred European cruising yacht built in England by Princess Yachts. While the lines of the SC61 are somewhat conservative (especially compared with Azimut's shark-fin inspired styling of that era), her lavish accommodations and spirited performance are still a match for most competitors. Below decks, the beautifully appointed three-stateroom interior with high-gloss cherry joinery features a split-level salon with an enormous U-shaped leather sofa, sunken galley with dishwasher and Avonite counters, amidships owner's suite, and three full heads. The forward VIP stateroom is nearly as large as the master, and the port stateroom offers twin beds. A utility room under the galley steps houses a freezer and washer/dryer combination. Cockpit amenities include built-in bench seating, teak dining table, transom door, and access to the storage lazarette and engineroom. The huge flybridge can be accessed from either the cockpit or salon. MAN 800hp diesels cruise the Viking Sport Cruisers 61 in the mid 20s and reach a top speed of around 30 knots.

Not Enough Resale Data to Set Values

Length Overall	61'7"	Fuel	790 gals.
Beam	16'0"	Water	185 gals.
Draft	4'4"	Waste	70 gals.
Weight	58,240#	Hull Type	Deep-V
Clearance	NA	Deadrise Aft	19°

Viking Sport Cruisers 65 Motoryacht

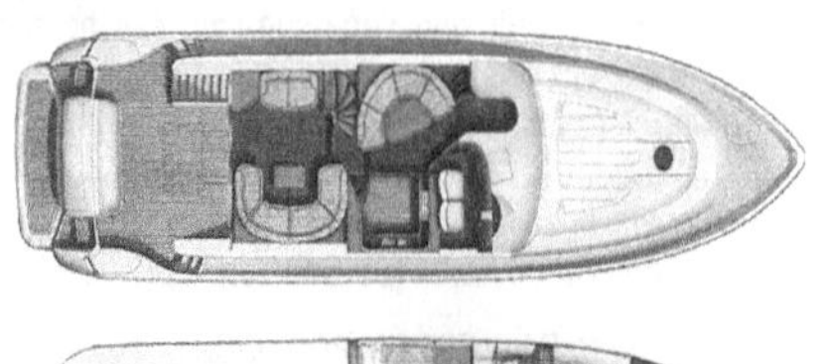

The Viking Sport Cruisers 65 Motoryacht ranks among the more impressive European cruising yachts built in recent years. Beautifully styled and boasting an opulent cherrywood interior, she was a popular model for Viking with just the right blend of luxury, comfort, and performance. Available with up to five staterooms (crew quarters aft were optional), highlights include a spacious, split-level salon with Ultraleather seating and aft electric window, circular five-person dinette with cherry table, sunken galley with dishwasher, flybridge staircase, and an elevated lower helm with two chairs and a power deck door. There are four staterooms forward including an amidships master with walkaround queen berth, spacious VIP bow stateroom, and two guest staterooms to port with single berths. (The aft guest stateroom/utility area also contains washer/dryer combo, worktable, and storage lockers.) The cockpit provides easy access to the lazarette, crew cabin, and engineroom. Topside, the flybridge features a hideaway electronics console, wet bar with refrigerator and grill, and U-shaped lounge seating. A good performer considering her size, 800hp MAN diesels cruise at 25 knots, and 1,050hp MANs cruise at 30 knots.

Not Enough Resale Data to Set Values

Length Overall	64'10"	Fuel	960 gals.
Beam	16'9"	Water	180 gals.
Draft	4'6"	Waste	100 gals.
Weight	66,774#	Hull Type	Deep-V
Clearance	13'6"	Deadrise Aft	19°

Viking Sport Cruisers V65 Express

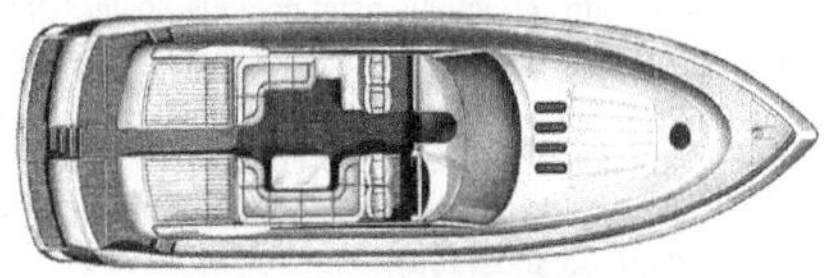

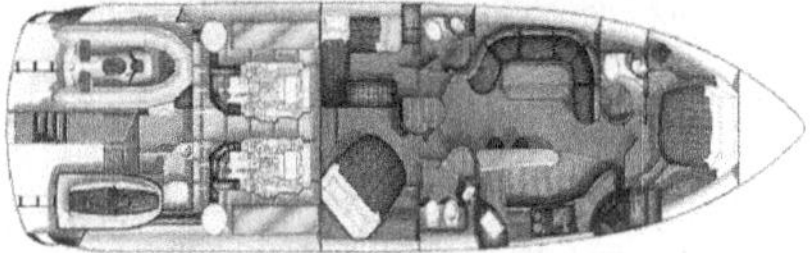

A beautifully styled yacht with a striking profile, the Viking V65 is an exciting, state-of-the-art luxury express that delivers excellent performance and truly impressive accommodations. The hardtop gives the V65 the best of both worlds, the security of a weather-protected helm and—with the sunroof retracted—the enjoyment of an open express design. Built on a relatively narrow deep-V hull with propeller tunnels, the three-stateroom interior is highlighted by lacquered cherry woodwork and an elegant designer decor. The master stateroom is amidships, and all three heads are fitted with stall showers. On deck, the cockpit contains a complete wet bar, an electric grill and plenty of seating. At the stern, beneath huge sun pads, are a pair of storage garages, one for a small tender and the other for a PWC. Additional features include a teak cockpit sole, a foredeck sun pad, bow thruster and wide side decks. On the downside, the engineroom is a tight fit. An outstanding performer, optional 1,300hp MANs cruise the Viking V65 Express at a fast 32 knots and reach a top speed of 37–38 knots.

Not Enough Resale Data to Set Values

Length Overall	65'2"	Fuel	960 gals.
Beam	16'11"	Water	180 gals.
Draft	4'5"	Headroom	6'6"
Weight	64,752#	Hull Type	Deep-V
Clearance	14'3"	Deadrise Aft	21°

Viking Sport Cruisers 67 Motoryacht

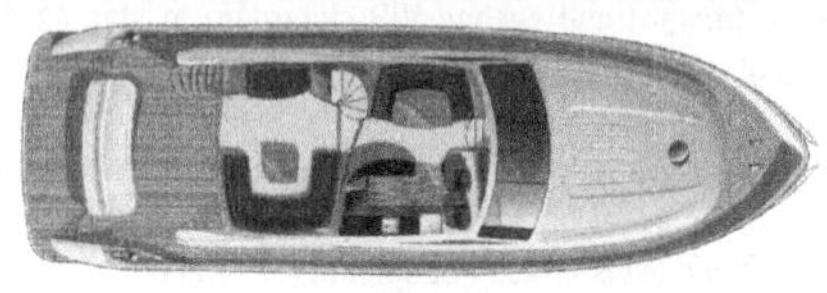

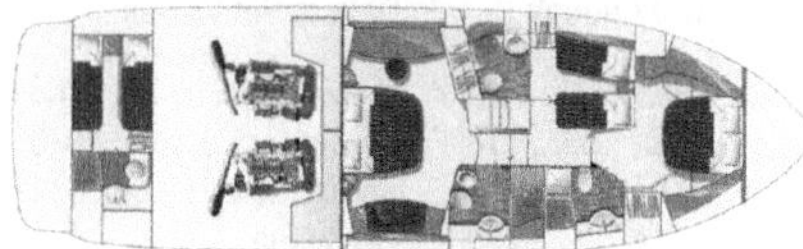

A blend of sophisticated styling and state-of-the-art construction, the Viking Sport Cruisers 67 raised the bar for yachting elegance when she was introduced in 2004. In the eyes of many experienced brokers, Princess Yachts—manufacturer of the Viking Sport Cruisers series—has been the leading builder of European luxury yachts for many years. Indeed, the immaculate finish of the 67 Motoryacht will come as no surprise to those familiar with the company's reputation for quality. Built on a deep-V hull with a solid fiberglass bottom and prop pockets, the spacious three-stateroom, three-head interior of the VSC 67 features a spacious salon with facing leather settees, wet bar, and entertainment center. The galley (with upright refrigerator and dishwasher) and dinette are on the pilothouse level, two steps up from the salon. An innovative glass galley partition turns translucent at the flip of a switch. Below, the 67 boasts an opulent full-beam master with king-size berth, vertical hull windows, and copious storage. Additional features include aft crew quarters, electric dinette window, swim platform davit, and teak decks. MAN 1,100hp diesels cruise at 25 knots (29–30 knots top).

Not Enough Resale Data to Set Values

Length	67'1"	Fuel	1,080 gals.
Beam	17'2"	Water	240 gals.
Draft	4'6"	Waste	75 gals.
Weight	78,400#	Hull Type	Deep-V
Clearance	16'11"	Deadrise Aft	19°

Viking Sport Cruisers 68 Motoryacht

1998–2003

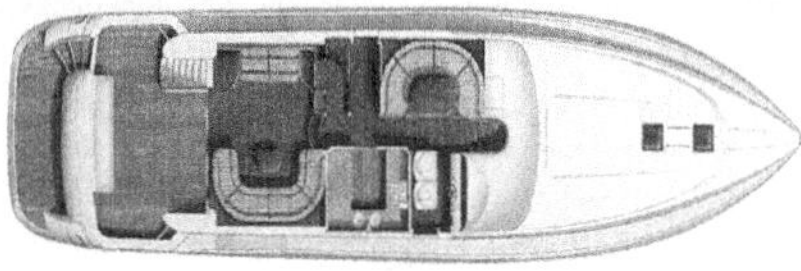

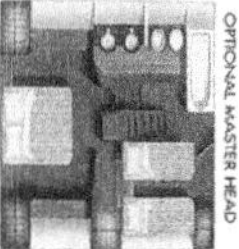

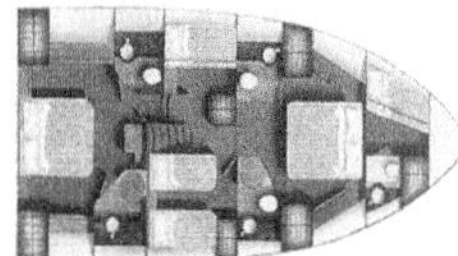

A distinctively styled yacht with a powerful, low-profile silhouette and vertical salon windows, the UK-built Viking Sport Cruisers 68 Motoryacht is constructed on a deep-V hull with a relatively wide beam and prop pockets to reduce the shaft angles. Her sumptuous four-stateroom interior is arranged with a full-beam owner's suite (with his-and-hers heads and a king-size bed), two small guest cabins with single berths, and a spacious VIP stateroom forward with a private head. The enclosed galley (with electrically operated partitions) and dinette are on the bridge deck level, two steps up from the salon, and a circular staircase opposite the galley provides inside access to the flybridge. On deck, a bridge overhang shades the cockpit with its teak sole and engineroom/lazarette hatch. Notable features include crew quarters at the bow, a spacious flybridge with retractable helm console, lower helm deck door, bow thruster, and transom storage lockers. Where most European yachts have small enginerooms, machinery access in the Viking SC68 is quite good. Twin 770hp Volvo diesels cruise at 22 knots (26–27 knots top), and optional 1,300hp MANs cruise at a fast 28 knots (about 33 knots top).

Not Enough Resale Data to Set Values

Length Overall	69'2"	Fuel	1,176 gals.
Beam	17'6"	Water	422 gals.
Draft	5'0"	Headroom	6'5"
Weight	80,640#	Hull Type	Deep-V
Clearance	16'6"	Deadrise Aft	19°

Viking Sport Cruisers 70 Motoryacht

2005–08

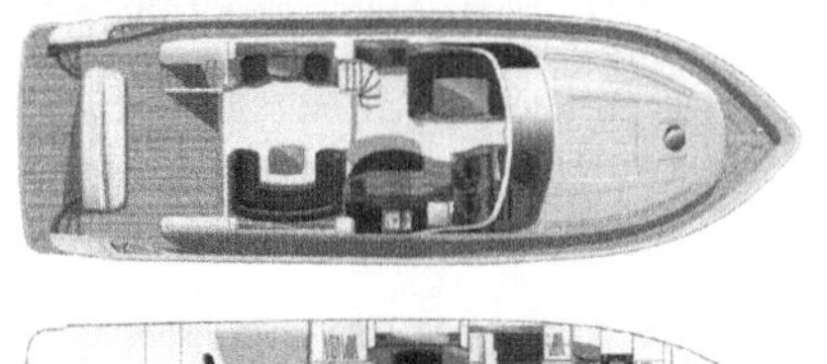

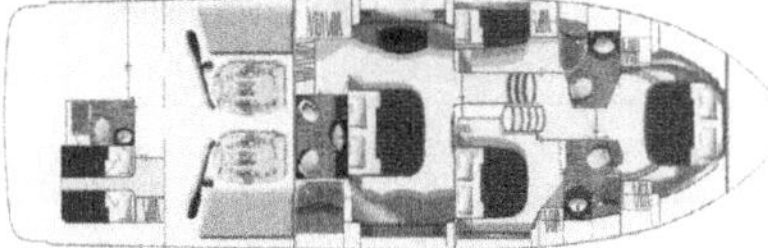

A popular model, the Viking Sport Cruisers 70 bypassed the dramatic styling elements common to her Azimut and Sunseeker contemporaries in favor of a more conservative—but still elegant—appearance. Introduced in 2005, the generous 18'4" beam creates tremendous interior volume for a yacht this size. The opulent main salon makes excellent use of this wide beam with plentiful seating for family and guests. A bar area separates the salon from the dining area, while the adjacent raised dinette forward offers panoramic views and enjoys plenty of natural lighting thanks to the large forward windshield. The prominent feature on the lower deck is the full-beam master suite with its walk through dressing area, entertainment system, and spacious en suite head. The lower lobby area houses a laundry center and storage area. Both the VIP stateroom forward and second VIP stateroom to starboard have walkaround queen berths. A two-berth crew quarter with head is aft under the cockpit deck. Note that the main deck galley can be closed off for privacy. The flybridge, accessed from the aft deck or salon, includes a wet bar with sink, electric grill, and refrigerator. MAN 1,300hp diesels cruise at 28 knots (32–33 knots top).

Not Enough Resale Data to Set Values

Length	70'0"	Fuel	1,320 gals.
Beam	18'4"	Water	335 gals.
Draft	5'2"	Waste	125 gals.
Weight	80,000#	Hull Type	Deep-V
Clearance	30'11"	Deadrise Aft	19°

Viking Sport Cruisers 72 Motoryacht

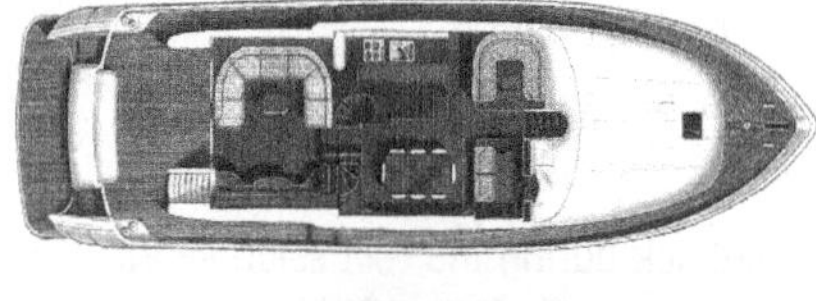

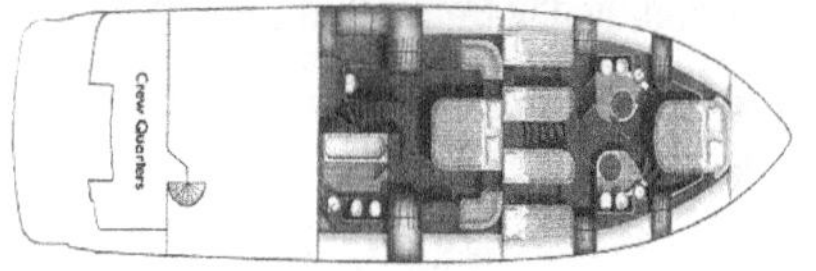

Modern styling, old-world craftsmanship, and sophisticated engineering characterize the Viking Sport Cruisers 72, an executive-class motoryacht built in England by Marine Products. A striking design (note the distinctive vertical salon windows), the Viking SC72 rides on a deep-V hull with a mega-wide 19-foot, 1-inch beam and propeller tunnels to reduce draft. Her spacious four-stateroom (plus crew quarters aft) interior boasts an opulent main salon with high-gloss cherry joinery, Ultraleather seating, liquor locker, and custom entertainment center. Forward of the salon, to starboard, is a private staircase descending to an enormous full-beam owner's suite with en-suite head and office. A formal dining area and country-kitchen galley are further forward on the pilothouse level. The VIP stateroom has a centerline queen berth and private head, and both guest staterooms share a single head and shower. Crew quarters with head and private doorway are aft, accessed from the cockpit. Additional features include teak decks, port and starboard transom doors, laundry area, pilothouse deck doors, and a foredeck sun pad. Twin 1,300hp MANs cruise the Viking Sport Cruisers 72 MY at 24 knots (high 20s top).

Not Enough Resale Data to Set Values

Length	72'4"	Fuel	1,500 gals.
Beam	19'1"	Water	315 gals.
Draft	4'9"	Waste	180 gals.
Weight	100,800#	Hull Type	Deep-V
Clearance	20'0"	Deadrise Aft	19°

Viking Sport Cruisers 75 Motoryacht

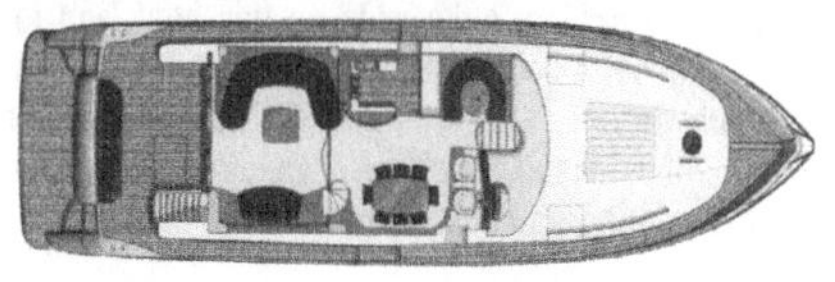

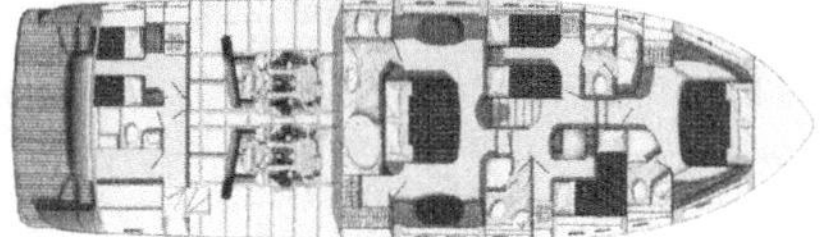

In the exclusive domain of 70-foot-plus motoryachts, the Viking Sport Cruisers 75 stands apart for her distinctive profile (note the rectangular salon windows) and impressive—make that very impressive—30-knot performance. From bow to stern the 75 is rich with the luxurious features and amenities one expects in a premium cruising yacht. Large side windows bathe the salon with natural lighting, while the U-shaped settee and loveseat opposite provide comfortable seating for family and friends. A bar area is tucked in the starboard corner to serve both the salon and aft deck. The formal dining area and galley are forward, two steps above the salon. A second, more casual dining area is opposite the lower helm. Below, the four-stateroom, four-head layout includes a full-beam master suite complete with walk-in closet, built-in entertainment system, and en suite head. The forward VIP stateroom has amenities to rival the master stateroom including a dressing table and en suite head, while the two guest staterooms also feature private en suite heads. A two-berth crew quarter with private head is accessed from the aft deck. All in all, this is opulence on a grand scale. Cat 1,675hp C-32 engines cruise at 28 knots (low 30s top).

Not Enough Resale Data to Set Values

Length Overall	74'2"	Fuel	1,540 gals.
Beam	19'0"	Water	385 gals.
Draft	5'3"	Waste	180 gals.
Weight	112,000#	Hull Type	Modified-V
Clearance	22'8"	Deadrise Aft	13°

Wellcraft

Quick View

- Wellcraft was formed in 1955 when the founders began building small wooden runabouts.
- By the mid 1960s Wellcraft had completed the transition to fiberglass by which time the Wellcraft line had grown to include a series of cuddy cabins and runabouts from 17' to 23' in length.
- The 1970s were an era of rapid grown for Wellcraft Marine, and in 1984, when the company was acquired by industry-giant Genmar Corp, Wellcraft had become one of the best known boat manufacturers in the country.
- In 1984 Wellcraft introduced their Coastal series of fishing boats.
- With the purchase of Californian Yachts in 1992, Wellcraft fielded a full line of ski boats, sportboats, high-performance Scarabs, fishing boats, sedans, express cruisers, and motor yachts.
- Like most builders, Wellcraft was dealt a severe setback during the recession years of the early 1990s, and production and quality fell dramatically from 1980's levels.
- Wellcraft ended production in 2010 when parent company Genmar Holdings declared bankruptcy.

No longer in business.

Wellcraft 2600 Coastal

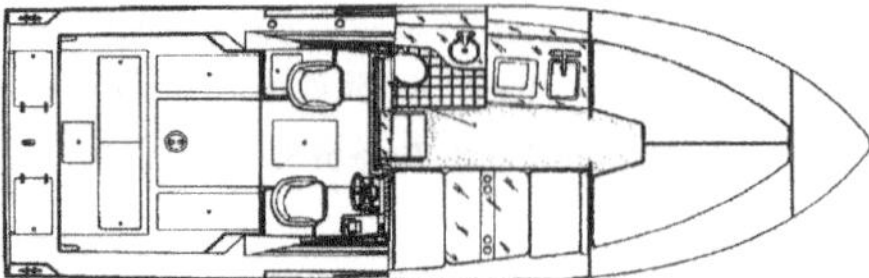

Introduced in 1990, the Wellcraft 2600 is a conventional express fisherman with conservative lines and a space-efficient layout. She's built on a solid fiberglass deep-V hull with a well-flared bow and a seriously wide 9-foot, 8-inch beam. Built in both outboard and sterndrive versions, the 2600 is a sturdy boat with a big cockpit and roomy belowdecks accommodations. The cabin will sleep four and includes a convertible dinette, compact galley, and standup head with shower. (Note that the head was slightly enlarged in 1994 at the expense of galley space.) The bi-level cockpit is arranged with elevated helm and companion seats forward with under-gunwale rod storage, tackle drawers, and a circulating livewell beneath the companion seat. An in-deck fish box is standard in outboard models, and a full-height wave gate became available in 1993. The side decks are quite wide on this boat, and foredeck access is very good. A bow pulpit was standard. Windshield vents come in handy on hot days. With twin 200hp Yamaha outboards the Wellcraft 2600 Coastal will cruise at 26–27 knots and reach top speeds in the neighborhood of 40 knots.

See Page 705 For Price Data

Length w/Pulpit	28'0"	Weight, IO	7,100#
Hull Length	26'1"	Fuel	150/200 gals.
Beam	9'8"	Water	20 gals.
Draft	3'0"	Hull Type	Modified-V
Dry Weight, OB	5,500#	Deadrise Aft	18°

Wellcraft 2600 Martinique

The original Wellcraft 2600 Martinique (an updated 2600 Martinique was introduced in 2002) began life back in 1994 as the Excel 26 SE. In 1997 she became the Wellcraft 26 SE; in 1998 she was called the 260 SE, and in 1999 she picked up the 2600 Martinique nameplate—a lot of confusing marketing hype. Whatever the name, she's been tough competition for other boats her size thanks to a very low price. There are few options—the equipment list is pretty much the same on every boat—and the result is a super inexpensive trailerable package. Hull construction is solid fiberglass, and at just 5,000 pounds the 2600 is a relatively light boat for her size. The basic midcabin floorplan is arranged with double berths fore and aft, a compact galley, and an enclosed, standup head with vanity and shower. Outside, the cockpit will seat up to eight and the bench seat opposite the helm converts into a sun lounge. Lacking side decks, a walk-through windshield provides access to the bow. Note that opening ports replaced the original cabin windows in 1998. A single 250hp sterndrive engine will cruise at 25 knots (low 30s top)—not bad for a single-engine 26-footer.

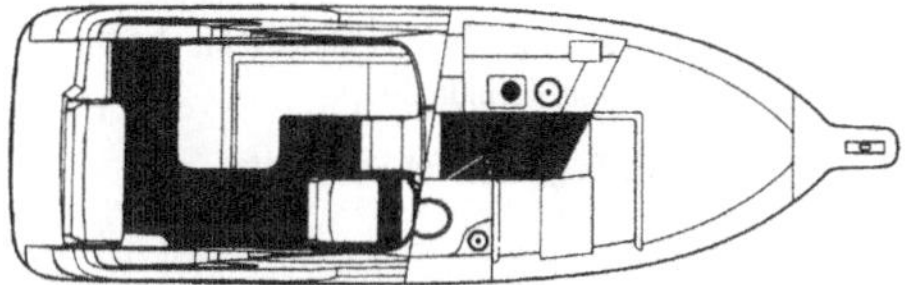

See Page 705 For Price Data

Length	27'5"	Fuel	77 gals.
Beam	8'6"	Water	22 gals.
Draft, Up	1'7	Waste	12 gals.
Draft, Down	3'4	Hull Type	Deep-V
Weight	5,000#	Deadrise Aft	20°

Wellcraft 264/270 Coastal

While the Wellcraft 264 Coastal (called the 270 Coastal in 1999–2000) closely resembles the company's earlier 26 Coastal, the two are completely different boats. Aside from the fact that the 270 has deeply recessed—if narrow—walkaround side decks, her 8-foot, 6-inch beam makes her trailerable which the 2600 Coastal is not. A stylish boat with a handsome profile, hull construction is solid fiberglass and her dry weight of 5,000 lbs. is about average for a boat of this size and type. The beauty of any walkaround cuddy design lies in her ability to provide basic overnight accommodations along with the fish-fighting capabilities of a full 360-degree platform. With both V-berths and quarter berths below, the 264 can sleep four in a surprisingly spacious cabin with a full galley, removable dinette, and a standup head and shower. Fishing features include two in-deck fish boxes, livewell, undergunwale rod racks, transom bait station, and raw-water washdown. A good-running boat and a comfortable ride in a chop, a pair of 150hp outboards cruise the Wellcraft 270 Coastal at close to 30 knots and reach a top speed of 40+ knots depending on the load.

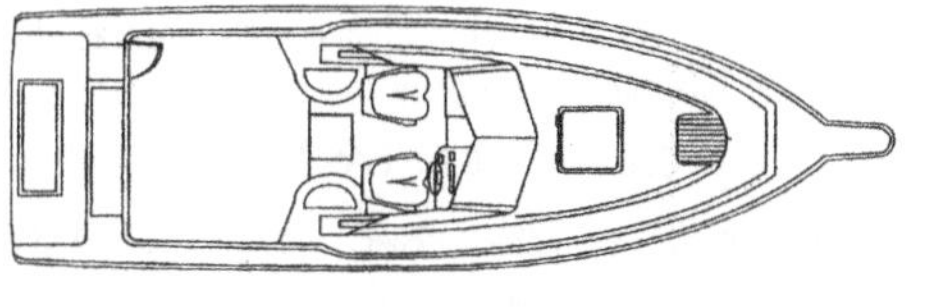

See Page 705 For Price Data

Length w/Pulpit	28'0"	Fuel	150 gals.
Beam	8'6"	Water	13 gals.
Draft, Up	1'8"	Max HP	450
Draft, Down	3'2"	Hull Type	Deep-V
Dry Weight	5,400#	Deadrise Aft	20°

Wellcraft 2700/2800 Martinique

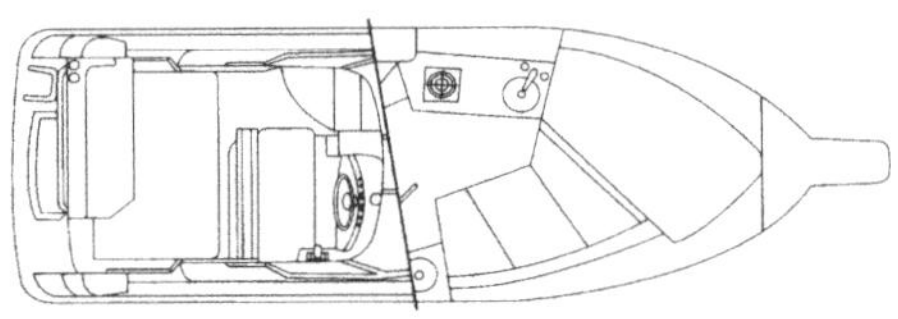

The Wellcraft 2800 Martinique (called the 2700 Martinique in 1994–96) is generic midcabin cruiser whose principal assets are a roomy interior and—during her production years—a very affordable price. Built on a solid fiberglass, modified-V hull with a wide 9-foot, 6-inch beam, the Martinique sleeps six below, two in the angled forward berth, two in the midcabin, and two more in the convertible dinette. The accommodations are basic—the cabinets and carpeting are inexpensive, and the no-frills decor is unimpressive. Storage is adequate, however, and the galley has more counter space than most cruisers her size. On deck, visibility from the elevated helm is excellent. Cockpit seating includes a triple-wide helm seat and an aft-facing companion seat forward, and an L-shaped bench seat aft. A transom door, bow pulpit, walk-through windshield, and transom shower were standard. A radar arch was a popular option. Introduced in 1994 as the 2700 Martinique, she was completely restyled on the outside in 1997 when she became the 2800 Martinique (pictured here). A single 310hp sterndrive will cruise the 2700/2800 at 20 knots (30+ knots top), and twin 190hp engines will reach the mid-to-high 30s.

See Page 706 For Price Data

Length w/Pulpit	28'4"	Fuel	100 gals.
Hull Length	26'6"	Water	22 gals.
Beam	9'6"	Waste	15 gals.
Draft	3'0"	Hull Type	Modified-V
Weight	7,100#	Deadrise Aft	17°

Wellcraft 270 Coastal

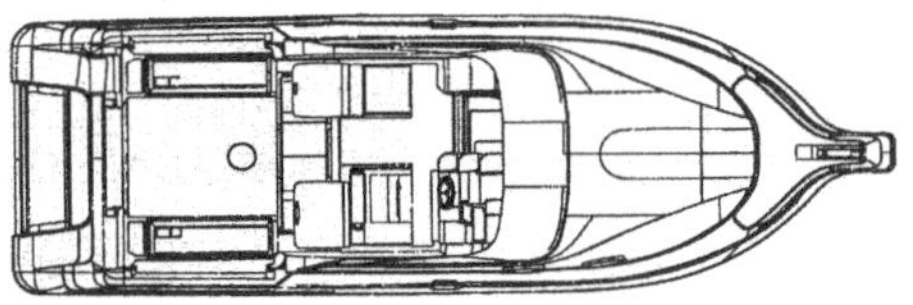

A popular boat, the Wellcraft 270 Coastal is an affordably priced express fisherman whose 9-foot, 6-inch beam is among the widest of any boat in her class. Like her sisterships in the Wellcraft Coastal series, the 270 was built on a smooth-running deep-V hull with moderate beam, a sharp entry, and a solid fiberglass bottom. Thanks to her broad beam, the Coastal's cockpit is notably spacious for a 27-footer. Storage lockers are found beneath the port and starboard helm seats, and fishing amenities include a lighted livewell, insulated in-deck fish boxes, bait-prep station, rod holders, transom door, raw water washdown, and a tackle center. Because the side decks are narrow, a walk-through panel in the curved windshield provides access to the foredeck. Below decks, the 270 Coastal sleeps four with V-berths forward and a wide mid-cabin berth aft. The enclosed standup head contains a shower and molded sink. Twin 225hp Yamaha outboards cruise the 270 Coastal at 28 knots and deliver a top speed of close to 45 knots. Also offered with sterndrive power, she'll top out at 30 knots with a single 330hp MerCruiser I/O. Out of production in 2004, she was reintroduced for the 2007–08 models years.

See Page 706 For Price Data

Length w/Pulpit	28'3"	Fuel	188 gals.
Beam	9'9"	Water	27 gals.
Draft, Up	1'10"	Max HP	500
Draft, Down	2'10"	Hull Type	Deep-V
Hull Weight	7,225#	Deadrise Aft	21°

Wellcraft 2800 Martinique

2001–02

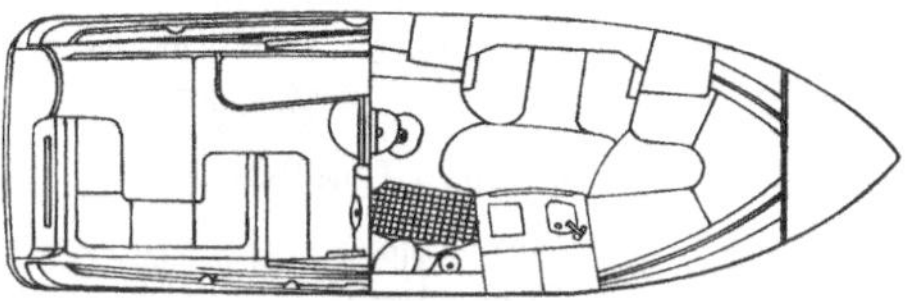

The Wellcraft 2800 Martinique (note that an earlier 2800 Martinique model ran from 1997–99) us a sporty midcabin cruiser designed to appeal to entry-level buyers with an eye for value. The market for sub-30-foot family cruisers is always competitive with entries from several manufacturers, all incorporating efficient midcabin floorplans with berths for six, enclosed head with shower, compact galley, and standing headroom in the main cabin. What set the Martinique apart from many of her competitors, however, was her clean styling; indeed, she's quite a good-looking boat even today in spite of her high freeboard. Built on a modified-V hull with moderate beam, cockpit features include a doublewide helm with storage under, wet bar, and U-shaped aft seating that converts into a sun pad. A tilt wheel was standard, and a walk-through windshield provides access to the bow. The entry light switch at the transom door is a thoughtful touch. An electric hatch provides easy access to the engine compartment. Among several single- and twin-engine options, a pair of 210hp sterndrive engines cruise the 2800 Martinique in the mid 20s (about 40 knots top). Note that production lasted only two years.

See Page 706 For Price Data

Length	27'10"	Clearance w/Arch	8'6"
Beam	9'6"	Fuel	100 gals.
Draft, Up	2'0"	Water	28 gals.
Draft, Down	3'6"	Hull Type	Modified-V
Weight	6,600#	Deadrise Aft	20°

Wellcraft 29 Scarab Sport; 29 CCF

2001–04

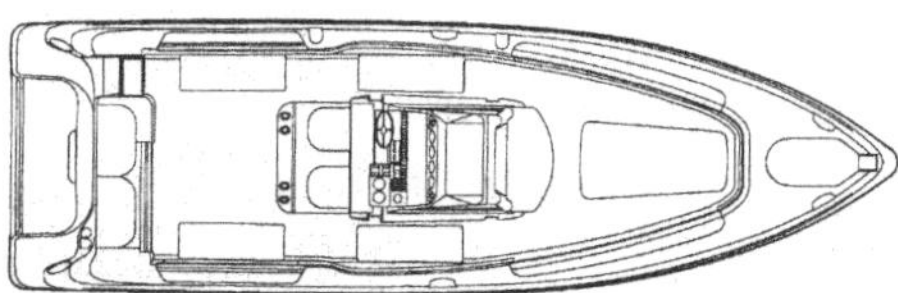

The Wellcraft 29 Scarab Sport (called the 29 CCF in 2003–04) is basically a go-fast boat that also fishes; speed is her most notable feature and she's designed to keep going fast when the going gets rough. Her deep-V hull is a variation of the traditional Scarab race boat hull with a slender beam and a keel pad for increased lift. The deck plan is fairly typical for boats of this type. A large-capacity livewell is built into the port side of the transom and a bait-prep station with sink and cutting board is to starboard. There are four insulated fish boxes with pumpouts in the 29 Sport, two in the aft deck and one on each side of the console. A standup head with sink, handheld shower, VacuFlush toilet (with 10-gallon holding tank), and two opening ports are built into the console. There's plenty of room for electronics at the helm where a standup, dropout bolster seat was standard. Experienced anglers will appreciate thick coaming pads, a toe rail in the bow, and pop-up cleats. Additional features include a swim platform and boarding ladder, anchor locker, console seat with cooler, dual washdowns, and a foldaway transom seat. Twin 225hp Mercury outboards deliver a top speed of over 45 knots.

See Page 706 For Price Data

Length	28'6"	Fuel	214 gals.
Beam	8'10"	Water	8 gals.
Draft, Up	1'9"	Max HP	500
Draft, Down	2'5"	Hull Type	Deep-V
Hull Weight	6,345#	Deadrise Aft	24°

Wellcraft 290 Coastal

The Wellcraft 290 Coastal is a well-regarded outboard-powered fisherman with a cruising-style interior and a large fishing cockpit. Dual-purpose boats like this have long been popular with active families who like to mix fishing and cruising, and with her wide 10-foot, 5-inch beam and generous cockpit, the Coastal provides an excellent platform for both activities. Built on a solid fiberglass deep-V hull, the midcabin interior of the 290 is arranged with a convertible dinette/V-berth forward, a compact galley and head, and a midcabin lounge that converts into a double berth. Note that the V-berth backrests swing up to form two pilot berths. On deck, the elevated bridge deck is fitted with a baitwell (with a Lucite window) and tackle storage as well as a doublewide helm seat and a companion seat to port. In the cockpit, a pair of insulated fish boxes are located just forward of the transom. Additional features include cockpit bolsters, transom door, wide side decks, bow pulpit, and a large in-deck storage box. Twin 225hp outboards cruise the 290 Coastal in the mid 20s and reach a top speed of 35+ knots. More than a few owners consider the 290 Coastal a lot of boat for the money.

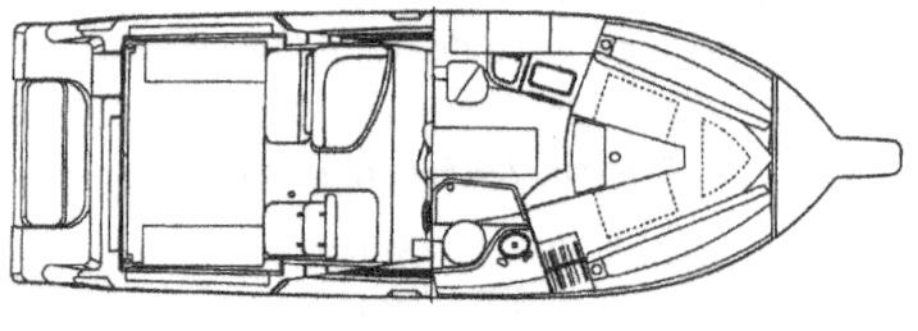

See Page 706 For Price Data

Length w/Pulpit	30'2"	Fuel	225 gals.
Hull Length	27'10"	Water	42 gals.
Beam	10'5"	Max HP	600
Draft	2'9"	Hull Type	Modified-V
Weight	8,735#	Deadrise Aft	18°

Wellcraft 30 Scarab Tournament

The 30 Scarab Tournament is a well-built center console descended from the original Wellcraft Scarabs so prominent in the offshore racing scene over 30 years ago. Wellcraft eventually matched the Scarab hull to a series of outboard-powered fishing boats that, after a slow start, went on to create an entirely new market for high-performance center consoles. That said, the 30 Scarab Tournament is not built on one of those race-bred Scarab hulls—they went out of production years ago. Like most of her modern go-fast counterparts, however, she rides on a slender deep-V hull designed for speed, agility, and superior rough-water handling. Her efficient deck layout includes large fore and aft macerated fish boxes, leaning post with lighted 21-gallon livewell, transom rigging station with sink, freshwater washdown, and 18 rod holders. At the bow are two more fish boxes under the seats, both with overboard drains. A nifty foldaway transom seat frees up cockpit space when necessary. The helm console has space for flush-mounting two big-screen video displays. A T-top with rocket launchers, flip-up bolster seats, and cockpit bolsters were standard. Yamaha 250hp outboards max out at nearly 45 knots.

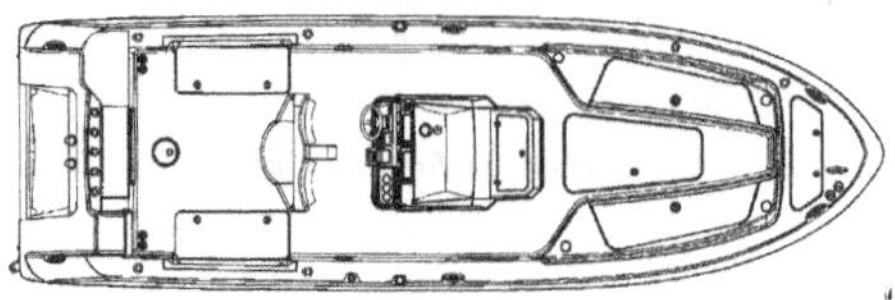

See Page 706 For Price Data

Length	30'2"	Fuel	288 gals.
Beam	9'2"	Water	13 gals.
Draft, Up	1'8"	Max HP	600
Draft, Down	2'6"	Hull Type	Deep-V
Dry Weight	6,635#	Deadrise Aft	23°

Wellcraft 3000 Martinique

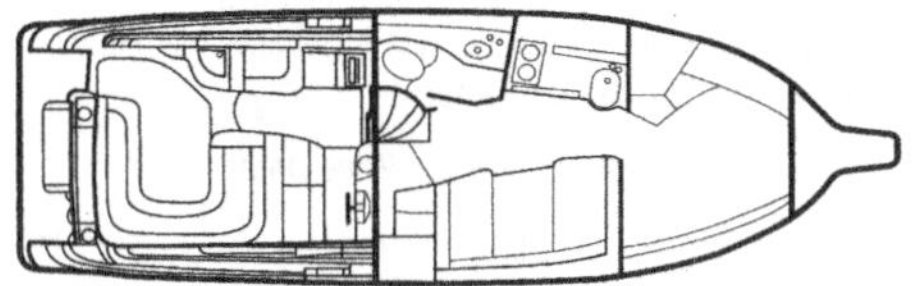

Wellcraft got it right in 1998 with the introduction of the 3000 Martinique, a good-looking family express with roomy accommodations and a good turn of speed. She's built on a solid fiberglass modified-V hull, and her generous 10-foot, 6-inch beam results in an expansive, user-friendly layout in both the cockpit and cabin. Like most express cruisers in this size range, the Martinique has a traditional midcabin floorplan designed to meet the cruising needs of four adults and two kids. Privacy curtains separate the fore and aft sleeping areas from the salon, and locating the refrigerator under the forward dinette seat increased galley storage. Topside, the driver's side of the doublewide helm flips up to form a bolster for standup driving. Cockpit amenities include a wet bar with sink and refrigerator, transom shower, and removable cockpit table. An electrically operated hatch in the cockpit sole lifts to reveal a roomy engine compartment. On the downside, the swim platform is narrow compared with newer express boats. A good performer with twin 250hp or 300hp I/Os, the 3000 Martinique will cruise in the mid 20s and hit a top speed in excess of 40 knots.

See Page 706 For Price Data

Length w/Pulpit	32'4"	Clearance	8'7"
Beam	10'6"	Fuel	160 gals.
Draft, Drives Up	2'3"	Water	41 gals.
Draft, Drives Down	3'1"	Hull Type	Modified-V
Weight	11,000#	Deadrise Aft	16°

Wellcraft 302 Scarab Sport

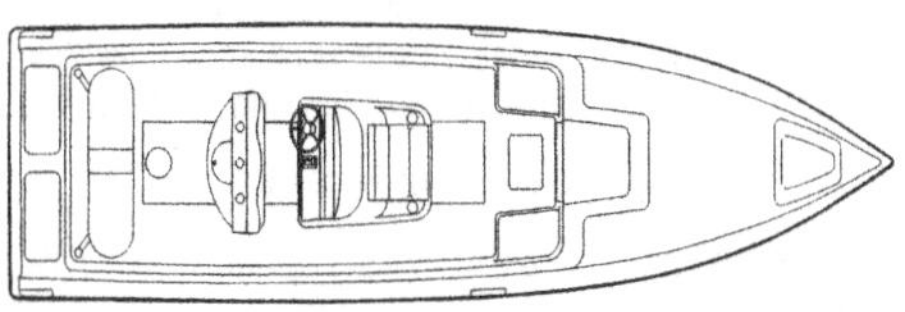

Wellcraft's 302 Scarab Sport is an updated (and much-improved) version of the original 30 Scarab Sport with a sleeker profile, a new deck and console, colorful hull graphics and a reverse arch. Like her predecessor, the 302 evolved from Wellcraft's successful offshore racing program of the early 1970s. She combines the speed and rough-water handling characteristics of her original raceboat hull with a fishing-boat cockpit in a very exciting high-performance package. The helm console is designed with lockable electronics storage and a large forward-opening storage compartment; an oval 40-gallon livewell and washdown is built into the base of the leaning post. Additional fishing features include an in-deck fish box, a transom fish box, under-gunnel rod storage, and coaming bolsters. The bow cuddy contains a V-berth, storage lockers, and space for a portable head. On the downside, the 302's narrow beam results in poor low-speed stability. Twin 150hp outboards cruise in the high 20s (about 40 knots top), and a pair of 225hp motors cruise at 30 knots and reach 50+ knots wide open. Note that the fuel capacity has increased over the years.

See Page 706 For Price Data

Length	29'6"	Fuel	238 gals.
Beam	8'0"	Water	9 gals.
Draft, Up	2'0"	Max HP	600
Draft, Down	3'0"	Hull Type	Deep-V
Dry Weight	5,000#	Deadrise Aft	24°

Wellcraft 32 Scarab Sport; 32 CCF

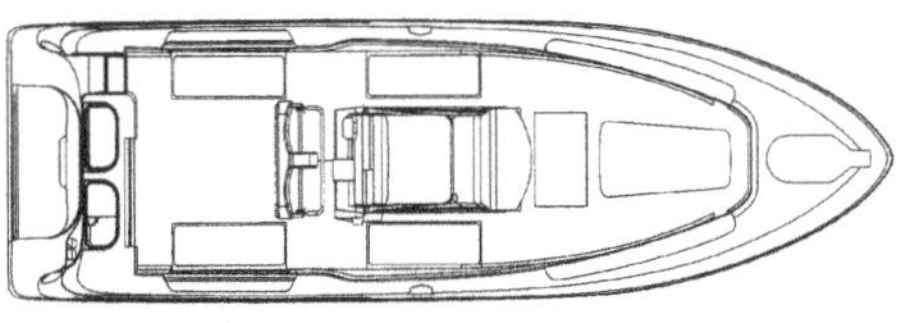

The Wellcraft 32 CCF (called the 32 Scarab Sport in 2001–03) will appeal to anglers who like to get to their favorite fishing grounds in a hurry. With her wide beam and deep cockpit, the 32 is a roomy and stable fishing platform, and her high-performance stepped hull is quick to accelerate and fast across the water. The Scarab's deck layout is similar to most boats of her type. A large-capacity livewell and a bait-prep station with sink and cutting board are built into the transom, and each of the four insulated fish boxes—two aft and one on either side of the console—are fitted with pumpouts. A standup head compartment with sink, handheld shower, marine toilet (with 10-gallon holding tank), and two opening ports is concealed within the console. There's plenty of room for electronics at the helm where a flip-up bolster seat was standard. Experienced anglers will appreciate coaming pads, a recessed toe rail in the bow, and pop-up cleats. Additional features include a swim platform and boarding ladder, anchor locker, console seat with cooler, dual washdowns, and a walk-through transom. A fast ride, twin 250hp Yamaha outboards will deliver a top speed in the neighborhood 45 knots.

See Page 706 For Price Data

Length	31'1"	Fuel	281 gals.
Beam	9'2"	Water	8 gals.
Draft, Up	1'11"	Max HP	600
Draft, Down	2'5"	Hull Type	Deep-V
Hull Weight	7,865#	Deadrise Aft	24°

Wellcraft 3200 Martinique

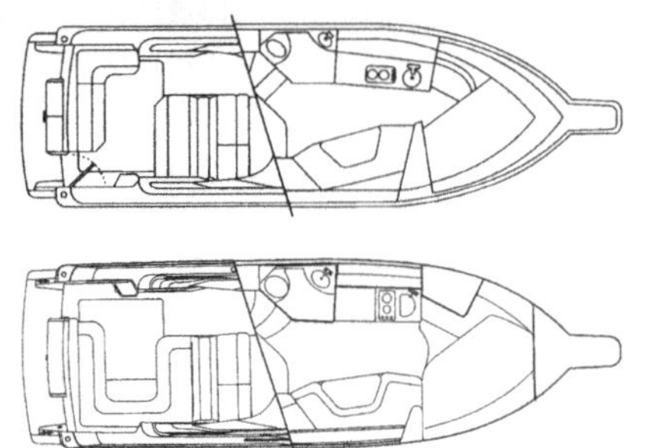

Wellcraft was a big name in the boating industry in the late 1990s, and their popular series of Martinique express boats had much to do with their success. Ranging in size from 24 to 37 feet, Martiniques were stylish, affordably priced cruisers with roomy interiors and lots of standard equipment. That pretty much describes the 3200 Martinique, a maxi-volume express with attractive lines and a generic midcabin floorplan. Built on a solid fiberglass hull, the Martinique differs from most express boats in that the companionway is to port rather than centered. The upside of such a design is a more expansive helm layout with a triple wide seat. (The downside: center companionways are usually easier to use when underway.) Below decks, the well-appointed interior sleeps six and includes a full galley with Corian counter, convertible settee, and a standup head with shower. Curtains are used for privacy in the fore and aft sleeping areas. Cockpit features include an aft-facing bench seat, L-shaped rear seating, wet bar, and transom shower. Volvo 310hp I/Os cruise at 25 knots (mid 30s top), and 320hp V-drive MerCruisers cruise at 22 knots (low 30s top). Note that the cockpit was updated in 1998 with U-shaped seating.

See Page 706 For Price Data

Length w/Pulpit	34'5"	Fuel	162 gals.
Hull Length	32'0"	Water	43 gals.
Beam	11'2"	Waste	20 gals.
Draft	3'1"	Hull Type	Modified-V
Weight	10,300#	Deadrise Aft	16°

Wellcraft 330 Coastal

1989–2009

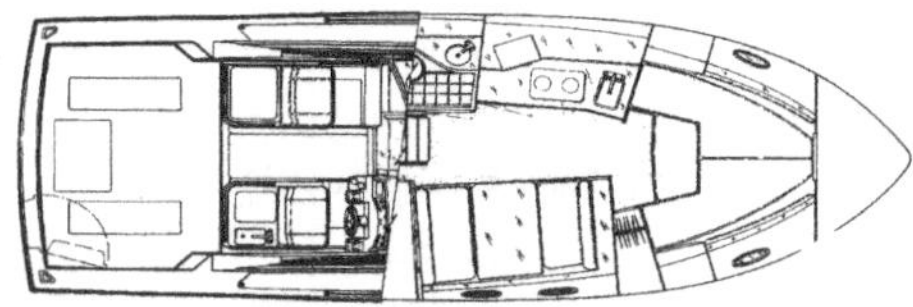

For several years the 330 Coastal was the largest model in Wellcraft's fleet of fishing boats. Introduced in 1989, she's constructed on a modified-V hull with a relatively wide beam and prop pockets (side exhausts were added in 1992). Designed as a dedicated sportfisherman, the 330 Coastal came with a good deal of standard equipment including two in-deck fish boxes, a circular livewell, tackle center, and a transom door. (A factory marlin or tuna tower was a popular option.) Both helm and companion seats are mounted on raised boxes with built-in livewell and bait-prep station that swing back for engine access. Although she's primarily a fishing boat, the cabin accommodations are suitable for weekend cruising with berths for four, a full galley, dinette and a small head compartment. Note that oval ports replaced the original cabin windows in 1998. A bow pulpit is standard, and the side decks are wide enough for secure bow access. A popular boat with a long production run, twin 310hp gas inboards cruise the 330 Coastal at 18–20 knots (high 20s top). More recent models with twin 375hp Volvo gas inboards cruise in the low 20s and hit 30 knots wide open.

See Page 706 For Price Data

Length w/Pulpit	38'5"	Fuel	288/370 gals.
Hull Length	33'3"	Water	52 gals.
Beam	12'5"	Waste	20 gals.
Draft	3'0"	Hull Type	Modified-V
Weight	16,000#	Deadrise Aft	16°

Wellcraft 3300 Martinique

2001–02

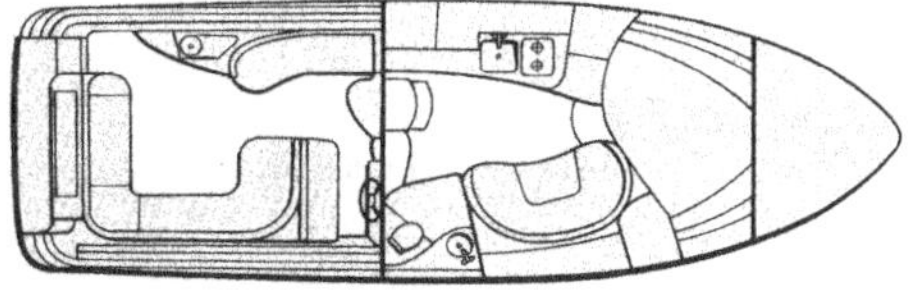

In production for only a few years before Wellcraft turned their attention to fishing boats only, the 3300 Martinique was the company's economy-class entry in the highly competitive midsize sportboat market. The Martinique's inboard power is notable—most other express boats this size come with sterndrive power. Notable, too, is her deep-V hull, which delivers an exceptional rough-water ride. The interior follows the standard midcabin approach seen in most of today's family cruisers with berths for six, a capable galley area (with lots of counter space), decent storage, and a compact head with sink and shower. Privacy curtains separate the fore and aft sleeping areas from the main cabin, and two overhead hatches and four opening ports provide adequate cabin ventilation. The cockpit is arranged with a sun lounge opposite the helm, a U-shaped settee aft, wet bar, and transom door. Service access to the engines is very good, and a walk-through windshield provides access to the bow. On the downside, the so-so finish is unimpressive. Among several engine options, twin 310hp V-drive MerCruisers cruise the 3300 Martinique at 20 knots and reach a top speed of close to 30 knots.

See Page 706 For Price Data

Length	33'2"	Fuel	226 gals.
Beam	11'7"	Water	40 gals.
Draft	2'11"	Waste	35 gals.
Weight	11,000#	Hull Type	Deep-V
Clearance, Arch	9'0"	Deadrise Aft	22°

Wellcraft 350 Coastal

Built in Australia by Riviera Marine, the Wellcraft 350 Coastal is a downsized version of the Wellcraft 400 Coastal introduced in 1999. Like her larger sibling, the rakish styling of the 350 is her most distinguishing feature. She rides on a conventional modified-V hull with a solid fiberglass bottom, a shallow keel, and a relatively wide beam. The single-stateroom interior of the Coastal is surprisingly comfortable (considering this is just a 35-foot boat) with a spacious U-shaped lounge, a full galley, a stall shower in the head, and over 6 feet of headroom. A solid door provides privacy in the stateroom, and a lower helm was standard in the salon. Notably, opening side windows allow for excellent cabin ventilation. On deck, the cockpit compares well with competitive boats her size and includes padded coaming, a large insulated fish box, portside freezer, a lighted baitwell, and a transom door (which opens in rather than out). Engine room access, via a hatch in the cockpit sole, is a tight fit. Topside, the flybridge is arranged with bench seating forward of the wraparound helm console. Among several engine options, twin 370hp Volvo diesels cruise at 25 knots (about 30 knots top).

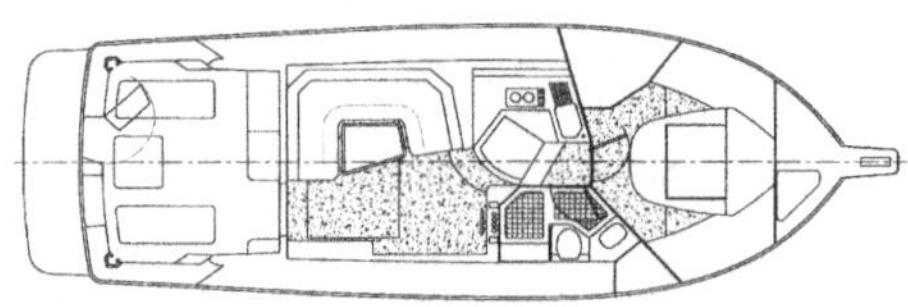

See Page 706 For Price Data

Length w/Pulpit	37'6"	Fuel	227 gals.
Hull Length	33'2"	Water	81 gals.
Beam	12'6"	Waste	20 gals.
Draft	3'4"	Hull Type	Modified-V
Weight	19,900#	Deadrise Aft	15°

Wellcraft 352 Tournament; 35 Scarab Tournament

Wellcraft's largest open-bow fishing boat during the late 2000s, the 35 Scarab Tournament (introduced as the 352 Tournament in 2006) combines versatility and performance in a world-class fishing machine. Key to her appeal is a wide 9'11" beam that offers plenty of cockpit space for fishing and baiting. Standard features include a rigging station with washdown sink and cutting board, 84-quart lighted baitwell, fiberglass T-top (with rod holders, spreader lights and electronics box), foldaway rear bench seat, forward casting platform, and an integrated swim platform. Bow storage consists of two insulated fish boxes, and the console head compartment features a vanity and pull-out shower in addition to a marine toilet. Several seating options allow anglers to design the cockpit space the way they like it, and there is plenty of room at the helm for flush-mounted big-screen electronics. On each side of the console, under the gunwales, are twin tip-out boxes for storage of tackle. An optional leaning post contains a 40-gallon livewell. Note the quality gas-assist struts on hatch lids. Triple 250hp Yamaha outboards deliver a top speed of 45+ knots.

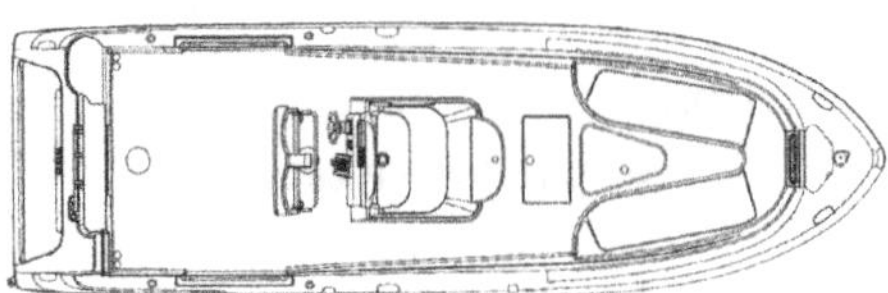

See Page 706 For Price Data

Length	35'4"	Fuel	400 gals.
Beam	9'11"	Water	13 gals.
Draft, Up	1'11"	Max HP	900
Draft, Down	3'3"	Hull Type	Deep-V
Dry Weight	8,600#	Deadrise Aft	23°

Wellcraft 35 Scarab Sport; 35 CCF

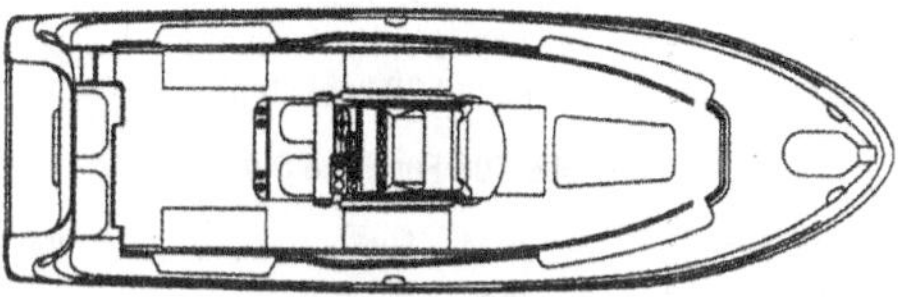

Wellcraft's 35 CCF (called the 35 Scarab Sport in 2001–04) is a high-performance center console whose principal mission in life is speed. Indeed, anglers who want to maximize their onsite fishing time will find a lot to like in the 35 Scarab. With her slender beam and offshore-proven deep-V hull, she's quick to accelerate and able to maintain speed even in a stiff chop. But the Scarab isn't just built for speed; she's a fully rigged fishboat with five insulated fish boxes with pumpouts, a 37-gallon transom livewell, and a transom bait-prep station with sink and cutting board. The console head, which includes a VacuFlush toilet with 10-gallon holding tank as well as a sink and shower, features a wide front entry door that lifts at the push of a button. There's plenty of space for electronics at the well-designed helm, and a drop-down bolster seat with tackle storage, 68-quart cooler, and rod holders were standard. A foldaway bench seat at the transom provides seating for guests. Additional features include Kiekhaefer racing tabs, cockpit bolsters, dual washdowns, anchor locker, and tilt steering. Twin 225hp outboards will deliver a top speed of over 40 knots, and triple 250hp outboards are capable of speeds of 50+ knots.

See Page 706 For Price Data

Length	34'10"	Fuel	300 gals.
Beam	9'11"	Water	29 gals.
Draft, Up	1'11"	Max HP	900
Draft, Down	2'9"	Hull Type	Deep-V
Weight w/OBs	10,000#	Deadrise Aft	23°

Wellcraft 35 Scarab Sport

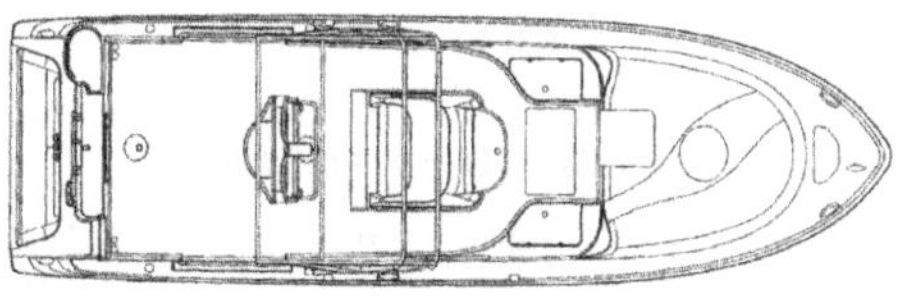

The 35 Scarab Sport is a hard-charging fishing boat descended from the original Wellcraft Scarabs prominent in the offshore racing scene some 30 years ago. Wellcraft eventually matched the Scarab hull to a series of outboard-powered fishing boats that, after a slow start, went on to create an entirely new market for high-performance center consoles. That said, the 35 Scarab Sport is not built on one of those race-bred Scarab hulls—they went out of production years ago. Instead, she rides on a solid fiberglass deep-V hull with a moderate 9'11" beam—enough beam to keep her stable in a trough, but not too wide to impede performance. Highlights include a leaning post with removable cooler, 21-gallon aft livewell, foldaway rear seat, tilt-out tackle box, cockpit bolsters, fresh and raw water washdowns, and a console head compartment with sink and shower. There's space at the helm for two big-screen video displays. Note the forward jump seats with storage under. The Scarab's cuddy with V-berths and storage sleeps two. A T-top with electronics box, rocket launchers and spreader lights was standard. Good fit and finish throughout. Twin 225hp outboards top out at 40+ knots; triple 250s reach speeds of 50+ knots.

See Page 706 For Price Data

Length	35'4"	Fuel	400 gals.
Beam	9'11"	Water	13 gals.
Draft, Up	1'11"	Max HP	900
Draft, Down	3'3"	Hull Type	Deep-V
Dry Weight	8,600#	Deadrise Aft	23°

Wellcraft 360 Coastal

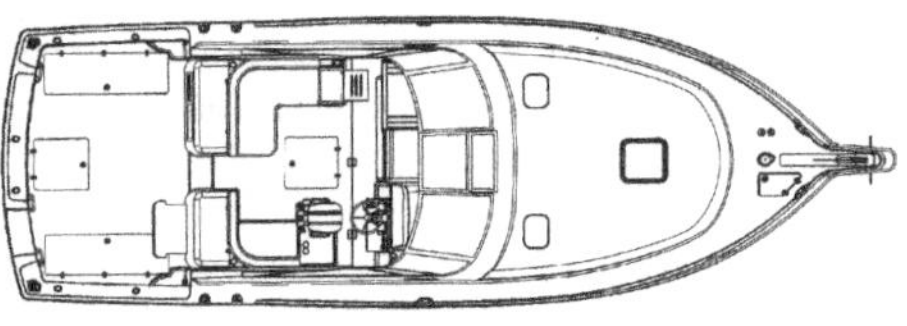

One part fishing boat and one part family cruiser, the 360 Coastal made good on Wellcraft's claim of versatility and comfort. This is a big 36-footer; her tall freeboard and a wide 13'8" beam add up to a spacious boat both inside and out. While the 360 Coastal may boast more luxury than some may expect in a fishing machine, the cockpit is still the focal center of the boat. This wide-open space provides all the room required for anglers to work without bumping elbows. The two in-deck fish boxes are completely gasketed to reduce noise, and the bait center is on the port side, just behind the bridge deck lounge. On the starboard side is a 38-gallon standup livewell. The entire bridge deck lifts on hydraulic rams for access to the engines. Note the single-level electronic controls. The fiberglass hardtop was standard. Below, the cabin of the 360 Coastal is exceptionally spacious. Cherry woodwork and quality fabrics showcase the interior's convertible dinette, full-service galley, and queen-sized island berth in the bow. Underway, the Coastal's Hunt-designed hull delivers steady open-water performance in spite of her wide beam. Volvo 370hp diesels cruise at 25 knots (about 30 knots top).

See Page 706 For Price Data

Length w/Pulpit	39'6"	Fuel	400 gals.
Hull Length	36'6"	Water	52 gals.
Beam	13'8"	Waste	18 gals.
Draft	3'4"	Hull Type	Modified-V
Weight	20,000#	Deadrise Aft	18°

Wellcraft 3600 Martinique

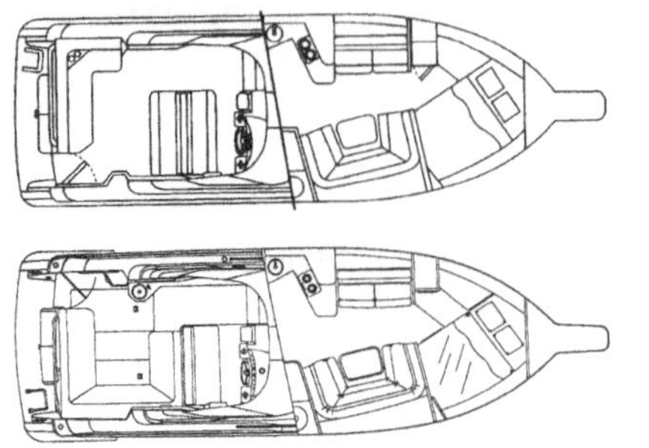

The 3600 Martinique is basically an updated version of the Wellcraft 3500 Corsair/3600 St. Tropez (1992–93) with a new floorplan and a redesigned cockpit. She's built on a conventional modified-V hull with a solid fiberglass bottom, an integral swim platform, and prop pockets to reduce the shaft angle. Inside, the Martinique was built without bulkheads to create a more open and spacious cabin. Her midcabin floorplan sleeps six—two forward, two on the converted dinette, and two more when the midcabin lounge is converted. While the L-shaped galley counter extends into the salon, it doesn't restrict traffic. (Note that the galley floor is covered with a vinyl nonskid.) On deck, the cockpit is configured with a triple wide helm seat, an aft-facing bench seat, and L-shaped lounge seating aft. (Note that in 1999 the cockpit seating was redesigned.) Lacking side decks, a windshield walk-through provides access to the bow. Additional features include a transom door, radar arch, integral bow pulpit, and a roomy engineroom. Among several engine options, twin 310hp MerCruiser gas inboards (with V-drives and side exhausts) will cruise the Martinique at 18–19 knots and top out in the high 20s.

See Page 706 For Price Data

Length w/Pulpit	38'0"	Fuel	264 gals.
Hull Length	35'6"	Water	47 gals.
Beam	12'6"	Waste	28 gals.
Draft	3'0"	Hull Type	Modified-V
Weight	15,000#	Deadrise Aft	16°

Wellcraft 3700 Martinique

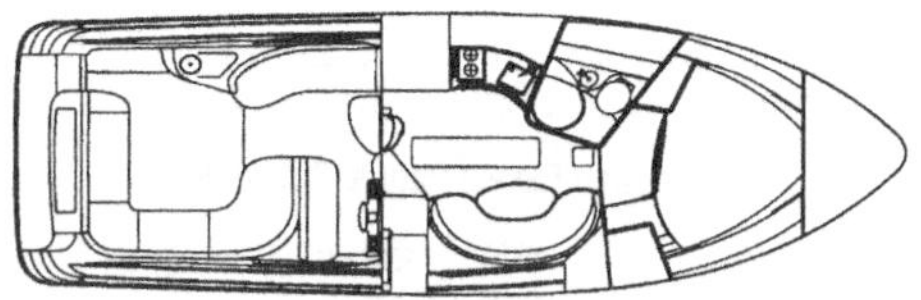

Good styling, a spacious interior, and a very affordable price made the Wellcraft 3700 Martinique a serious competitor in the big family cruiser market of the early 2000s. Built on a good-running deep-V hull with a wide beam, the Martinique sleeps six below in a midcabin floorplan that seems surprisingly open and comfortable. In a departure from so many midcabin interiors, a solid door—instead of a curtain—separates the bow stateroom from the main cabin. The galley may be a little compact, but there are more storage lockers and compartments in the Martinique than in most other boats her size. Laminated cherry woodwork is used throughout the interior, and a pair of deck hatches provide a small amount of natural lighting. Outside, the single-level cockpit can accommodate a small crowd with a sun lounge opposite the double helm seat and wraparound lounge seating aft. Additional features include a cockpit wet bar, a walk-through windshield, an electrically activated engineroom hatch, transom door, and transom shower. Twin 380hp MerCruiser gas engines (with V-drives) will cruise the 3700 Martinique at 20 knots and reach a top speed of just under 30 knots.

See Page 706 For Price Data

Length	36'11"	Fuel	288 gals.
Beam	13'0"	Water	57 gals.
Draft	3'4"	Waste	35 gals.
Weight	16,400#	Hull Type	Deep-V
Clearance	9'5"	Deadrise Aft	22°

Wellcraft 38 Excalibur

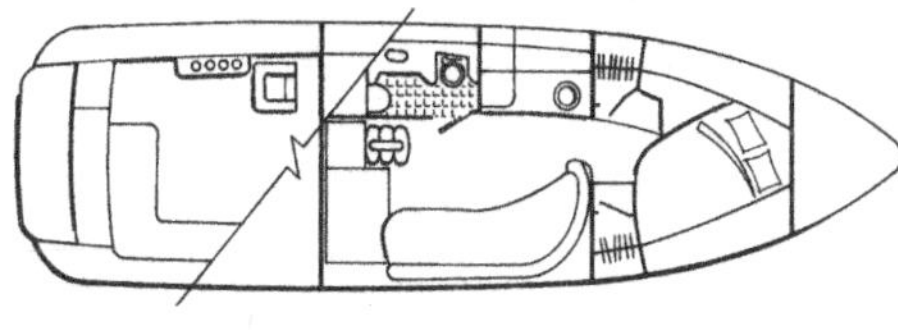

The 38 Excalibur was one of several Wellcraft models manufactured in Australia by Riviera Marine. She was built on a solid fiberglass, deep-V hull with a rounded keel and a narrow, performance-enhancing beam. With her long foredeck and sleek profile, the 38 Excalibur was considered by many to be one of the better-looking express boats of her era. Experienced boaters will be impressed with the Excalibur's level of fit and finish—the tooling and gelcoat work is quite impressive. The interior, which is small compared with most of her wider-beam competitors, is arranged with the master stateroom forward (with a curtain for privacy), posh Ultrasuede salon sofa, full-service galley, and an aft bunk suitable for a couple of kids. On deck, cockpit seating is comprised of a two-person helm with a bucket seat opposite and an L-shaped aft lounge. A wet bar (with refrigerator) is standard as is a transom door and shower. Engine access—under the aft cockpit seat—is good, but the Excalibur's side decks are narrow. Note that the helm seat can be adjusted electrically. A good performer with MerCruiser 385hp gas sterndrives, she'll cruise at 30–32 knots and reach a top speed of over 40 knots.

See Page 706 For Price Data

Length	37'11"	Clearance	7'5"
Beam	10'8"	Fuel	240 gals.
Draft, Drive Up	2'3"	Water	60 gals.
Draft, Drive Down	3'2"	Hull Type	Deep-V
Weight	13,200#	Deadrise Aft	21°

Wellcraft 390 Coastal

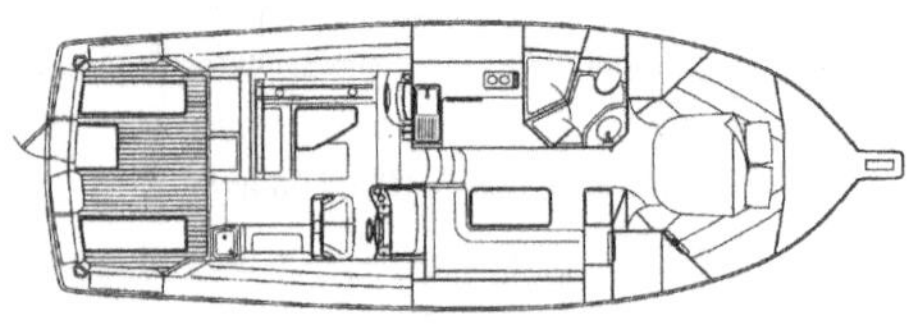

Flagship of the Wellcraft fleet in 2004, the 390 Coastal is a modern express fishing boat whose moderate price includes a lengthy list of standard equipment. Anglers will find a lot to like about the 390—the focal point of the boat is her spacious, wide open cockpit with its transom livewell, tackle center with built-in refrigerator, generous rod storage, hefty 30-inch tuna door, and cockpit coaming pads. A hardtop (with spreader lights and rocket launchers) is standard, and a backing plate under the cockpit sole makes it easy to mount a full-size fighting chair. Like most express fishermen her size, the Coastal's entire helmdeck rises on hydraulic rams for access to the engines and generator. (Note the clear tube on the aft engine compartment bulkhead that displays the fuel level.) Belowdecks, the well-appointed interior includes a full galley, private master stateroom, enclosed stall shower in the head, and a U-shaped settee whose backrest flips up to form a Pullman-style bunk. Additional standard features of the 390 Coastal include a bow pulpit, swim platform, spotlight, fresh and salt water washdowns, and cockpit shower. Cruise at 25–26 knots with 480hp Volvo diesels (around 30 top).

Not Enough Resale Data to Set Values

Length w/Pulpit	44'7"	Clearance	7'11"
Hull Length	41'4"	Fuel	394 gals.
Beam	14'8"	Water	119 gals.
Draft	3'11"	Waste	18 gals.
Weight	25,400#	Hull Type	Modified-V

Wellcraft 400 Coastal

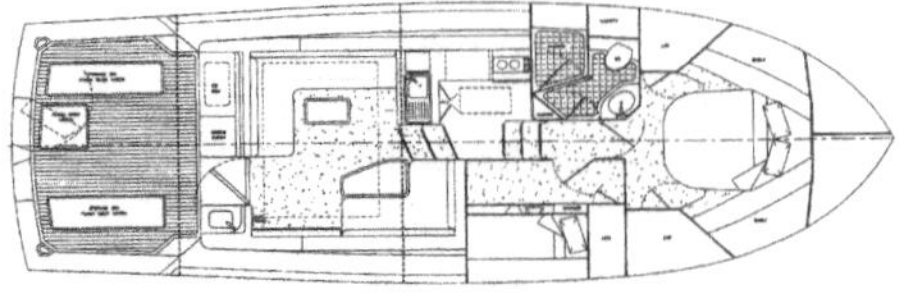

The Wellcraft 400 Coastal is a value-priced convertible sportfisherman with a practical interior layout, a large fishing cockpit, and an extremely rakish profile. Built for Wellcraft by Riviera Marine in Australia, the Coastal rides on a solid fiberglass hull with a well-flared bow, generous beam, and a moderate-deadrise running surface. The standard two-stateroom, mid-galley floorplan of the 400 Coastal is arranged with a centerline double berth in the forward stateroom and over/under berths in the small guest cabin. A leather-upholstered dinette is forward in the salon, and beechwood cabinetry and large bow and side windows make the salon seem open and very inviting. On deck, the Coastal's large cockpit is fitted with 12 rod holders, a tackle center, a see-through livewell, fish box, and a transom door. A retractable sun shade extends out from the flybridge overhang, and access to the engine room is via a hatch in the cockpit sole. Topside, the flybridge is arranged with bench seating forward of the helm console. (Note that a hardtop was standard.) Twin 480hp Volvo diesels cruise the 400 Coastal at 25 knots and reach a top speed of 28–29 knots.

See Page 706 For Price Data

Length w/Pulpit	44'7"	Cockpit	94 sq. ft.
Hull Length	39'1"	Fuel	469 gals.
Beam	14'4"	Water	121 gals
Draft	4'1"	Hull Type	Modified-V
Weight	23,400#	Deadrise Aft	15°

Wellcraft 43 Portofino

1987–97

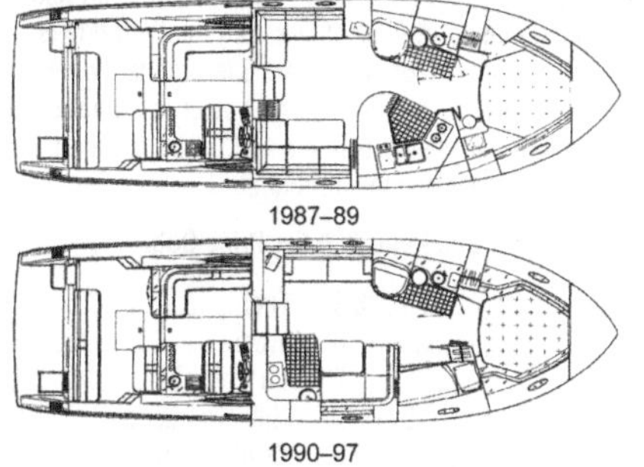

1987–89

1990–97

A good-selling boat during her decade-long production years, the 43 Portofino was one of the largest production express cruisers on the market when she came out in the late 1980s. With her bold Euro-style appearance and spacious accommodations, the Portofino conveyed an aura of comfort and luxury seldom seen in earlier express boats. She was constructed on a low-deadrise hull with a wide 14-foot, 6-inch beam, and prop pockets were used to move the engines as far aft as possible. Originally offered with a single-stateroom interior, in 1990 a two-stateroom floorplan proved more practical for cruising with friends. Either way, the head contains a separate stall shower and the sofa converts to a double berth. On deck, the Portifino's huge bi-level cockpit provides seating for a dozen guests. Note that hull graphics were reduced and the helm console upgraded in 1990. Engine access is excellent—the hatch in the bridge deck reveals a ladder that leads down between the engines. With standard 340hp gas engines, the 43 Portofino has a barely respectable cruising speed of 16 knots and a top speed of about 25 knots. Optional 375hp Cat diesels cruise at 20–22 knots and top out in the mid 20s.

See Page 706 For Price Data

Length w/Pulpit	45'7"	Fuel	436 gals.
Hull Length	42'10"	Water	100 gals.
Beam	14'6"	Waste	20 gals.
Draft	3'0"	Hull Type	Modified-V
Weight	20,000#	Deadrise Aft	14°

Wellcraft 45 Excalibur

1995–2001

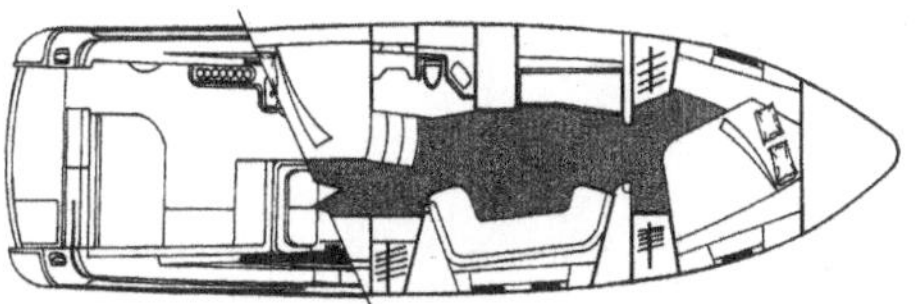

Built for Wellcraft by Australian-based Riviera Marine, the 45 Excalibur strikes a balance between a go-fast sportboat and high-end express cruiser. The Excalibur is constructed on a solid fiberglass deep-V hull, and while her slender 11-foot, 8-inch beam restricts interior volume, the payoff is a more efficient and easily driven hull capable of higher speeds than most other express designs with greater beam. The cockpit is arranged with an elevated helm position, a full wet bar to port, and a U-shaped lounge/sun pad aft. Under the sun pad is a large storage well, and the entire aft section of the cockpit floor rises electrically for access to the engines. Belowdecks, the salon of the Excalibur's midcabin interior is dominated by a richly upholstered settee opposite the portside galley. Both sleeping areas are separated from the salon with privacy doors. Additional features include a separate stall shower in the head, cockpit boarding steps, anchor windlass locker, radar arch, transom door, and a concealed swim ladder. Big-block 415hp gas sterndrive engines cruise the Wellcraft 45 Excalibur at 28 knots and reach a top speed in the low 40s.

See Page 706 For Price Data

Length	44'6"	Fuel	274 gals.
Beam	11'8"	Water	70 gals.
Draft	3'3"	Headroom	6'5"
Weight	15,000#	Hull Type	Deep-V
Clearance	8'6"	Deadrise Aft	21°

Wellcraft 46 Cockpit Motor Yacht

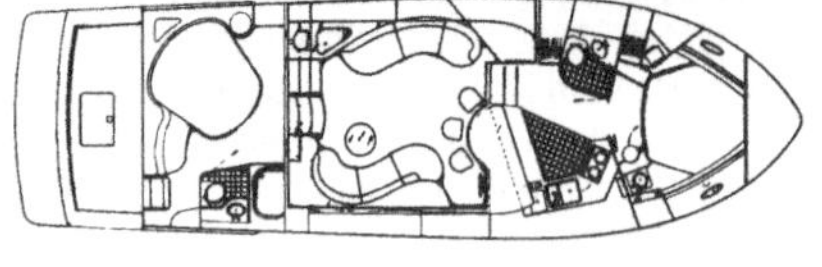

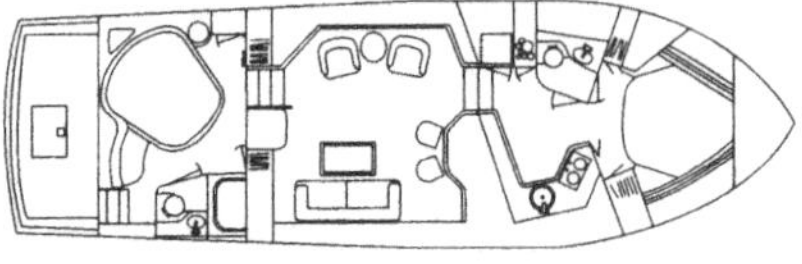

With the addition of a small cockpit, the Wellcraft 43 San Remo was transformed into the 46 Cockpit Motor Yacht—the largest model ever built by Wellcraft Marine. Cockpit yachts have become increasingly popular in recent years due to their increased versatility; boarding is made much easier, and it's also possible to do a little fishing or diving from the cockpit. (Equally important, the extra hull length makes the 46 Cockpit MY a better looking yacht than the original San Remo model.) Below decks, the two-stateroom floorplan was available with a choice of salon configurations—a glitzy Euro-style layout with facing S-shaped salon settees and lots of rounded corners, and a more contemporary arrangement with traditional salon seating. Either way, a breakfast bar separates the galley from the main salon, and both staterooms contain queen-size berths. Topside, the full-width aft deck will accommodate a couple of deck chairs, and the flybridge is arranged with guest seating aft of the helm. Gas engines were standard, but most buyers would expect diesel power in a boat of this size. Caterpillar 425hp diesels cruise the 46 Cockpit MY at 19 knots and deliver a top speed in the low to mid 20s.

See Page 706 For Price Data

Length	46'3"	Fuel	400 gals.
Beam	14'6"	Water	120 gals.
Draft	3'2"	Cockpit	46 sq. ft.
Weight	27,000#	Hull Type	Modified-V
Clearance	14'0"	Deadrise Aft	14°

World Cat

Quick View

- Founded in 1997 by marine industry veteran Forrest Mulden, World Class Catamarans are built in Tarboro, North Carolina.
- Mulden launched the company by purchasing the facilities and assets of Sea Cat, a pioneer in production fishing catamarans.
- World Class boats are built on high-performance semi-displacement hulls.
- Starting with Sea Cat's existing molds and tooling, World Class expanded rapidly in recent years offering a full line of modern catamaran designs.
- In 2009 World Cat's parent company, The PowerCat Group, grew significantly after the purchase of World Cat's main competitor, Glacier Bay.

World Cat • Tarboro, NC • www.worldcat.com

World Cat 266 SF/270 TE

1998–Current

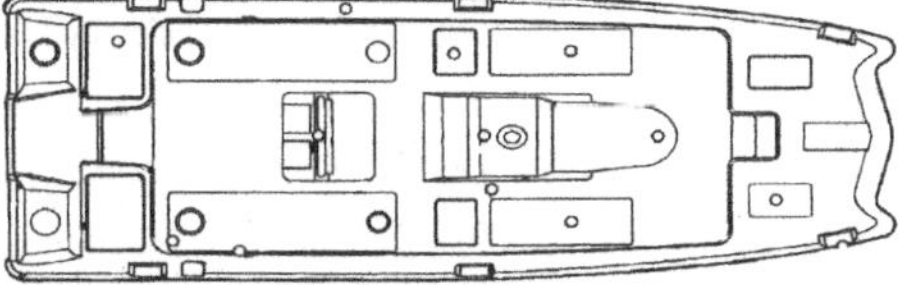

The World Cat 270 TE (called the 266 SF in 1998–2002) began life as the SeaCat 25 Center Console back in the late 1990s. World Cat acquired the molds and, after a complete redesign and many improvements, reintroduced her in 1998 as the 266 SF. The World Cat rides on a pair of soft riding, semi-displacement hulls rather than the higher-speed (but harder riding) planing hulls used by some catamaran builders. The construction materials and workmanship of the 270 are very good and the deck layout, with its generous storage capacity, is completely uncluttered. A walk-in head (or storage area) under the console is standard as is tilt steering, a wraparound windshield and a weather-protected electronics locker. Unlike a monohull, the wide foredeck of the World Cat has room for a couple of anglers to work in relative freedom. Additional features include a fish box and livewell in the transom, in-deck fish boxes flanking the console, padded cockpit bolsters, a large tackle box, a weather-protected electronics locker and full foam flotation. A good-quality boat, twin 225hp Honda outboards cruise the 270 in the high 20s and reach a top speed of just over 40 knots.

See Page 707 For Price Data

Length Overall	28'0"	Clearance	8'6"
Hull Length	26'6"	Fuel	240 gals.
Beam	8'6"	Water	20 gals.
Hull Draft	12"	Max HP	450
Hull Weight	6,600#	Hull Type	Semi-Disp.

World Cat 266/270 LC

1999–2005

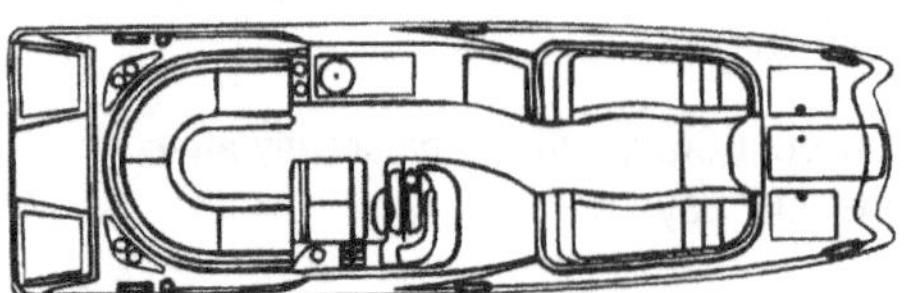

Not your traditional deckboat, the World Cat 270 LC (called the 266 LC in 1999–2002) combines a huge party platform with a stable, smooth-riding catamaran hull capable of handling offshore waters. Building a deckboat on a catamaran hull makes a lot of sense; catamarans are far more stable than monohulls, and the rectangular deckboat shape fits easily on a cat's twin hulls. The comfortable, deep cockpit of the 270 LC offers lots of room to move around and plenty of storage under each bow seat. The aft U-shaped lounge converts to a huge sun pad, but the absence of a transom door means passengers have to climb over the seat to get to the swim platform. An open-air galley is to port, opposite the helm, and the head—forward in the port console—features an innovative two-part door that admits light and fresh air. Beneath the helm is a massive storage locker for skis and wakeboards. (Note-Hull Type the low helm windshield.) While the World Cat 270 LC is more expensive than a conventional deckboat, her ability to handle rough water is far superior to any of her monohull counterparts. A quality product, twin Honda 130hp outboards will deliver a top speed of 30+ knots.

See Page 706 For Price Data

Length	26'6"	Headroom	5'10"
Beam	8'6"	Fuel	200 gals.
Hull Draft	12"	Water	30 gals.
Hull Weight	4,400#	Max HP	500
Clearance	NA	Hull Type	Semi-Disp.

World Cat 266/270 Sport Cabin

1998–2008

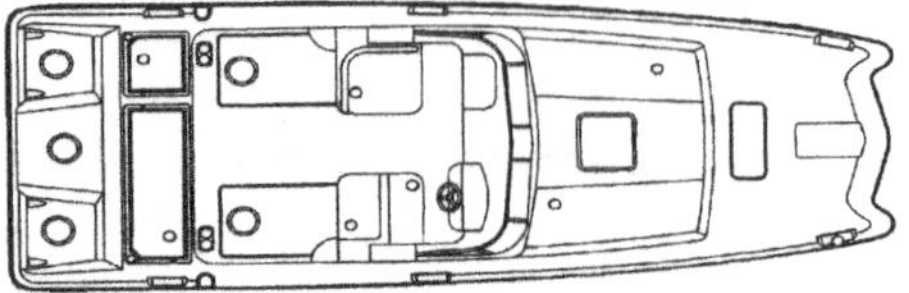

Power cats have made believers out of a good many serious anglers in recent years thanks to their combination of stability, increased foredeck space, and excellent low-speed handling. There are some drawbacks to cats, however—they don't look as good as most monohulls, the cornering is sluggish, and walkaround models suffer from limited cabin space because they don't have a deep hull to step into. Those caveats aside, the World Cat 270 SC (called the 266 SC in 1998–2002) will satisfy anglers looking for a trailerable fishing cat with basic overnight cabin accommodations and better-than-average finish. She rides on a pair of semi-displacement hulls rather than the higher-speed (but harder-riding) planing hulls used by some catamaran builders. Her uncluttered cockpit contains a transom fish box, thickly padded bolsters, a bait-rigging station behind the helm seat, and a raw-water washdown. The foredeck casting platform is very wide, and the side decks are easily negotiated. If the cabin suffers from low headroom, it's nonetheless broad and comfortable with an athwartships double berth, rod storage, and a marine head. Twin 200hp Yamaha outboards cruise at 30 knots (40+ top).

See Page 706 For Price Data

Length Overall	28'0"	Clearance	8'6"
Hull Length	26'6"	Fuel	200 gals.
Beam	8'6"	Water	32 gals.
Hull Draft	12"	Max HP	500
Hull Weight	7,000#	Hull Type	Semi-Disp.

World Cat 270 Express Cabin

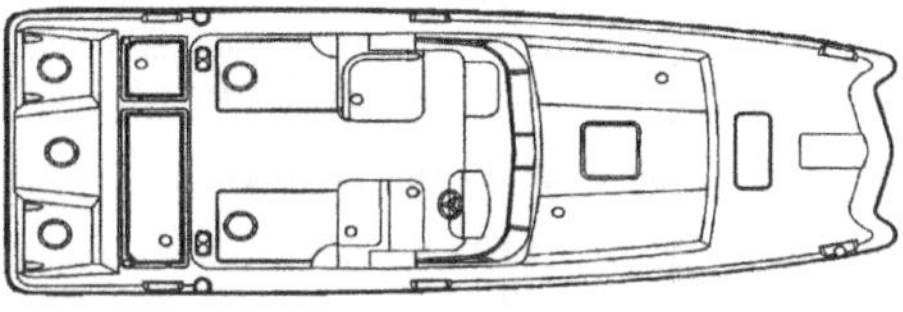

An excellent family fisherman, the World Cat 270 Express Cabin is geared to the weekend cruiser with serious fishing ambitions. There's a considerable amount of cabin space below as well as enough cockpit space for several anglers and their gear. Built on a pair of semi-displacement hulls, the focal point of the 270 EC is her well-equipped cockpit with its 300-quart centerline fish box, 27-gallon lighted livewell, tackle station with freshwater washdown, coaming pads, and removable tackle storage. A recessed toe rail on both sides of the cockpit gives anglers an added measure of security, and two ladderback helm seats are mounted atop aft-facing jump seats with built-in coolers. Belowdecks, the cabin boasts a queen-sized berth, electric pumpout porcelain head, galley package, and plenty of storage for personal gear as well as rods. Additional features include a large dash area with room for flush-mounting electronics, tilt steering, two opening cabin ports and a bow pulpit. World Class builds a top-quality boat and experienced boaters will appreciate the EC's high level of fit and finish. A pair of Yamaha 225 outboards will deliver a top speed in the neighborhood of 40 knots.

See Page 707 For Price Data

Length Overall	28'0"	Clearance	8'6"
Hull Length	26'6"	Fuel	200 gals.
Beam	8'6"	Water	32 gals.
Draft	12"	Max HP	500
Weight	6,800#	Hull Type	Semi-Disp.

World Cat 320 Express Cabin

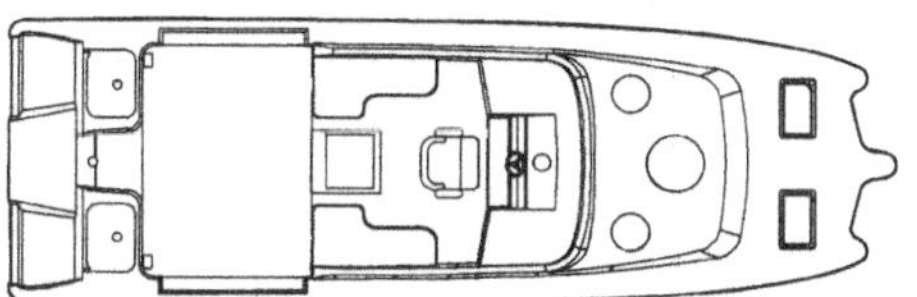

Anglers seeking a fuel-efficient alternative to traditional express fishermen might find a lot to like in the World Cat 320 Express Cabin. Cats aren't for everyone—purists will probably never come to terms with the prominent bow and broad foredeck of catamarans; others complain about their lack of cabin space. The 320 EC could be just the boat to put those complaints to rest. One of the largest express catamarans available, the 320 is a quality, cruise-ready sportfishing boat whose exceptional rough-water performance and outstanding fuel economy are better by far than any monohull her size on the water. Her versatile layout has the helm located on the centerline with port and starboard entry doors leading to the galley and standup head. Both the galley and head doors lead to the forward master stateroom with queen berth. The aft cockpit has two aft-facing jump seats and two forward jump seats that fold away. Fishing amenities include tackle storage, rod racks, 40-gallon livewell, and bait-prep station. The bridge deck has facing L-shaped lounges with cooler and storage under. Twin 250hp outboards cruise the 320 EC at 28 knots at close to 2 miles per gallon.

See Page 707 For Price Data

Length Overall	32'0"	Clearance	9'6"
Beam	10'6"	Fuel	260 gals.
Draft, Up	1'4"	Water	45 gals.
Draft, Down	2'4"	Max HP	600
Dry Weight	10,900#	Hull Type	Semi-Disp.

World Cat 330 TE

The 330 TE (Tournament Edition) was the flagship model for World Class Catamarans during her production years. She incorporates the high-tech construction common to all World Class boats with premium, hand-laid fiberglass and no encapsulated wood. As her name implies, the 330 is designed for serious anglers. She came with an impressive array of standard fishing features including two huge 45-gallon lighted livewells, two tackle centers, fresh and raw-water washdowns, and molded-in toe rail around the forward deck. Each sponson has a large insulated fish box, and there's a third insulated storage box forward of the console. Below decks, the 330's compact cabin includes an electric head, port and starboard berths, and plenty of rod storage—modest accommodations indeed for a 33-foot boat. The World Cat's high freeboard makes for a dry ride in rough water, but it's a long reach down to the water for billfishers. A transom door, cockpit bolsters, and leaning post were standard. With a 300-gallon fuel capacity, the 330 TE offers an impressive combination of speed and range. Twin 225hp Yamaha outboards cruise in the mid 20s (about 35 knots top) with a cruising range in excess of 300 miles.

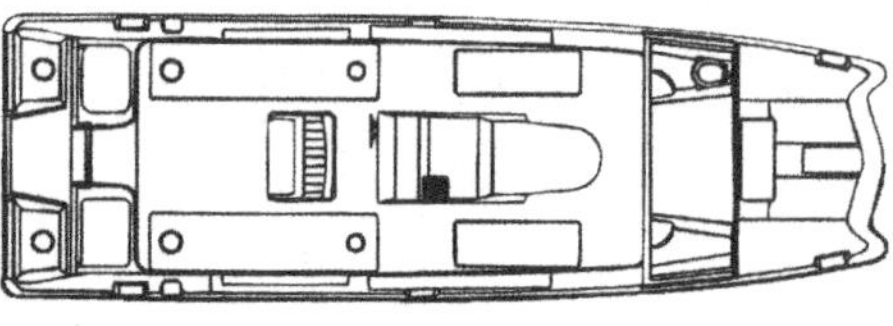

See Page 707 For Price Data

Length Overall	34'0"	Headroom	4'11"
Beam	10'6"	Fuel	300 gals.
Hull Draft	16"	Water	20 gals.
Hull Weight	10,400#	Max HP	500
Clearance	6'2"	Hull Type	Semi-Disp.

Notable Designs

The Notable Designs chapter is reserved for boats not featured in one of the previous Manufacturer chapters. In general, a chapter consists of at least three boats from a single manufacturer. There are numerous cases, however, where the editors wished to include only one or two boats from a particular builder — not enough to create a separate chapter. The Notable Designs chapter, then, is the "collection point" for those boats not featured elsewhere in this book.

Alden 50 Motor Yacht

1995–2002

Given Alden's no-compromise approach to boatbuilding, it comes as no surprise that the semicustom 50 Motor Yacht is a finely crafted and meticulously finished vessel inside and out. Don't let her traditional appearance fool you—she's built on a fully cored vacuum-bagged hull utilizing the latest in high-tech materials. Prop pockets reduce the draft, and a shallow keel protects the running gear from damage in a grounding. While the Alden 50 is a semi-production yacht and buyers can alter the layout to suit their needs, the standard three-stateroom floorplan is quite spacious and impressively executed. The galley is forward in the salon, opposite the lower helm, and both heads contain separate stall showers. (Note the cockpit access door in the aft cabin.) The Alden's aft deck is designed to accommodate a dinghy, and the flybridge has plenty of guest seating aft of the helm. Additional features include walkaround side decks with raised bulwarks, handcrafted teak interior, sliding deck access door at the lower helm, fold-down radar mast, and underwater exhausts. Cat 600hp diesels will cruise the Alden 50 at 18 knots (low 20s top).

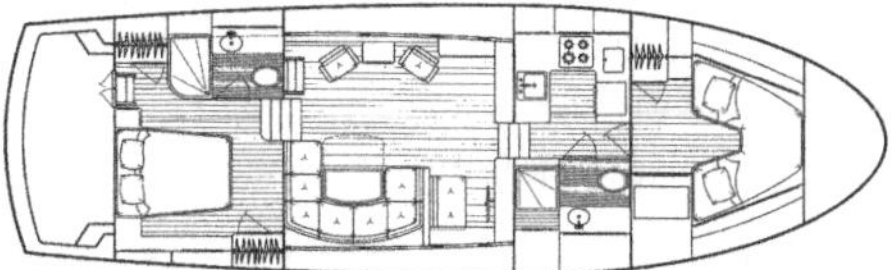

Not Enough Resale Data to Set Values

Length Overall	51'6"	Clearance	NA
Length WL	43'5"	Fuel	620 gals.
Beam	15'8"	Water	240 gals.
Draft	4'5"	Hull Type	Deep-V
Weight	48,000#	Deadrise Aft	18°

American Tug 34

Designed for economical, fuel-efficient operation, the American 34 Tug is a sturdy and well-constructed family cruiser with a roomy interior and a salty, workboat profile. The similarity of the American 34 to the Nordic 32 and 37 Tug is obvious; all share the same designer, and only the slightly reversed front windshield of the American 34 sets her apart in appearance from the Nordics. Built on a beamy semi-displacement hull with a full-length keel, the spacious teak interior of the 34 is ideal for the cruising couple. Both the stateroom and head are particularly large for a boat this size, and visibility from the raised pilothouse, with weathertight deck doors, is excellent. In the salon, a linear galley to starboard provides an abundance of counter and storage space—features quickly appreciated when it comes to daily food-prep activities. The side decks are wide with raised bulwarks all around for added security. Additional features include an Ultraleather salon settee, granite galley counter, transom storage locker, and bow thruster. The cabintop can stow a dinghy. A single 330hp Cummins diesel will cruise efficiently at 13–14 knots. At 8 knots the range can exceed 1,000 miles.

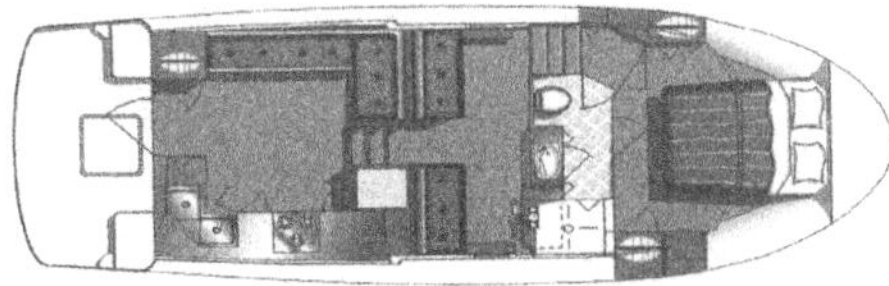

See Page 668 For Price Data

Length Overall	34'5"	Clearance	NA
Length WL	32'9"	Fuel	400 gals.
Beam	13'3"	Water	150 gals.
Draft	3'5"	Waste	45 gals.
Weight	20,000#	Hull Type	Semi-Disp.

American Tug 41/435

In the real world, few trawler owners need the heavy-weather security (and rolling) that goes with a full-displacement hull. Indeed, there's a big divide between those who hope to circumnavigate the globe and those who really do it. That's why semi-displacement trawlers like the American Tug 41 (called the 435 since 2010) are so popular; they combine the low-speed efficiency of a displacement hull with the planing-speed performance of a modified-V hull. With her broad 15'10" beam and prominent bow, the 41 is a big, muscular vessel. Below decks, her layout is dominated by a huge salon with an Ultraleather settee, U-shaped galley, high-gloss cherry joinery, and four large cabin windows. Note that her false stack creates a unique raised area in the forward salon overhead. The 41's raised pilothouse, with reverse windshield to reduce glare, has a desk to starboard and lounge to port. Both staterooms are fitted with queen berths and en suite heads with separate stall showers. A large hatch in the salon floor provides access to the spacious engineroom. A bow thruster and underwater exhaust system are standard; a flybridge is optional. Cruise at 12–14 knots with a single 540hp Cummins diesel (about 16 knots top).

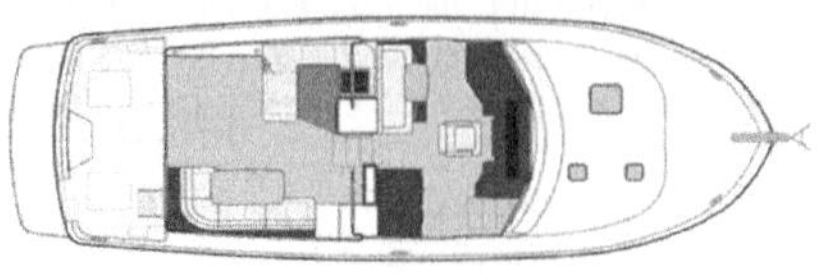

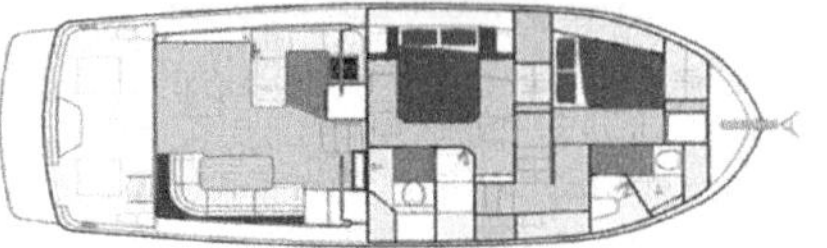

See Page 668 For Price Data

Length Overall	43'7"	Clearance	16'0"
Length WL	38'6"	Fuel	640 gals.
Beam	15'10"	Water	210 gals.
Draft	4'10"	Waste	60 gals.
Weight	35,360#	Hull Type	Semi-Disp.

Benchmark 36/38 Catamaran

1997–2002

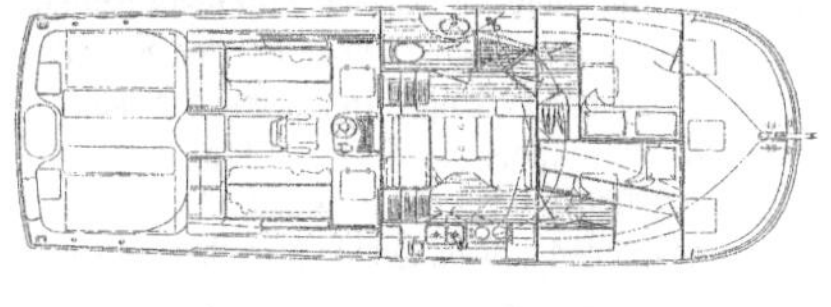

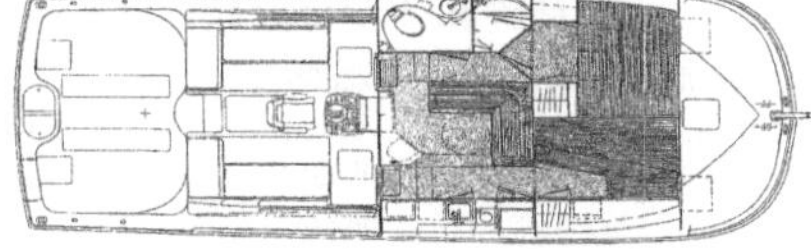

The Benchmark 38 (called the Benchmark 36 until 1999) is an upmarket catamaran fishing boat whose unique asymmetrical hulls—the inner surfaces have less deadrise than the outer surfaces—set her apart from other catamaran designs. Cats with symmetrical hulls maintain a level attitude in a turn, but the Benchmark leans into a turn similar to a monohull, a feature that tends to keep things from flying around (or off) the boat in a hard turn. Propeller pockets—also unusual in cats—reduce draft, and the entire boat is cored and vacuum bagged with no wood. With a wide 14-foot beam, the cockpit is huge and so is the full-beam foredeck. Lightweight bench seats are easily removed to clear the cockpit for fishing, and a transom door, livewell, two in-sole fish boxes and a swim platform are standard. There are two staterooms below, one with a double berth and the other with bunks. The salon could be configured with either a dinette or an L-shaped lounge. Note that the helm console is quite small. A good-running boat, 420hp Cummins diesels cruise the Benchmark at an economical 28 knots and reach a top speed of 32–33 knots.

Not Enough Resale Data to Set Values

Length	38'0"	Fuel	500 gals.
Beam	14'0"	Water	90 gals.
Draft	3'3"	Headroom	7'0"
Weight	22,500#	Cockpit	115 sq. ft.
Clearance	8'2"	Hull Type	Catamaran

Beneteau 42 Swift Trawler

2004–09

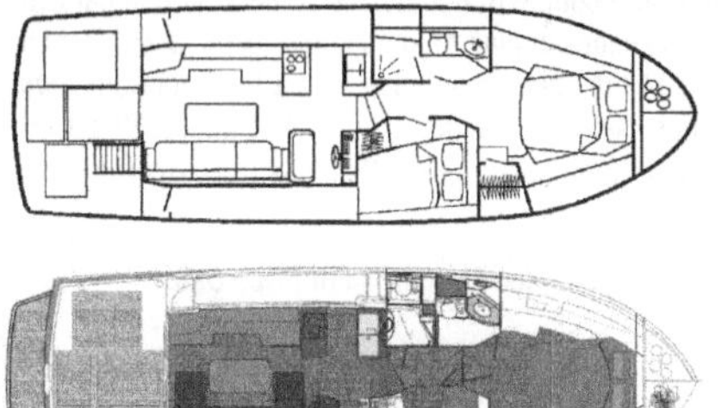

Built by one of Europe's leading manufacturers, the Beneteau 42 Swift Trawler is notable for her distinctive styling as well as her simple, no-nonsense approach to construction. She was the first of several powerboat models Beneteau has exported into the U.S. market in recent years. A trawler in appearance only, the 42 is built on a modified-V hull making her capable of cruising speeds well beyond those of traditional trawlers. Below decks, her appealing two-stateroom interior features a well-appointed salon with mahogany joinery, compact galley with deck access door, and a lower helm with doublewide seat. An island queen berth is in the master stateroom while the guest stateroom is fitted with a large double berth. Note that galley storage is inconveniently located along the port side of the salon. Topside, flybridge overhangs shade both side decks as well as the entire cockpit. Wing doors—unique in any trawler design—close off the cockpit from wind and spray. The wide side decks are a plus. Additional features include a cockpit storage lazarette, spacious engineroom, centerline transom door, and a nifty entry gate in the starboard bulwark. Cruise at 20 knots with twin Yanmar 370hp diesels (low to mid 20s top).

See Page 669 For Price Data

Length Overall	44'3"	Fuel	395 gals.
Length WL	37'5"	Water	169 gals.
Beam	13'11"	Waste	24 gals.
Draft	3'5"	Hull Type	Modified-V
Weight	33,000#	Deadrise Aft	12°

Camano 28/31

1990–2007

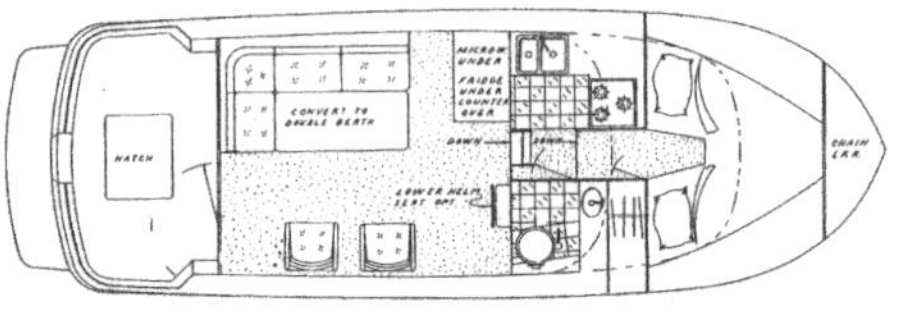

For those who enjoy a little character in their boats, check out the Camano 31 (originally called the Camano 28), a salty sedan cruiser from British Columbia with a trawler-like profile and an efficient cabin layout. She's built on a lightweight flat-bottom hull with a wide beam, cored hullsides, and an unusually wide prop-protecting keel. (Indeed, the keel cavity is big enough to contain the engine, keeping the weight down low for added stability.) The Camano's no-nonsense interior is well finished, and her trolly-style foredeck windows are almost unique in the boating world. With the galley down, the salon is big for a 28-footer and visibility from the lower helm is excellent in all directions. The cockpit, however, is small with just enough room for a couple of folding deck chairs. With her wide beam, the Camano is able to carry a relatively large flybridge without difficulty—a feat few 28-footers can claim. Updates in 2003 included a standard bow thruster as well as a fuel increase to 133 gallons. A single 150hp Volvo diesel will cruise the Camano 28 at 12 knots (16–17 knots top), and more recent models with a 200hp Volvo cruise around 14 knots. A popular, well-finished boat, used models tend to be rather expensive.

See Page 671 For Price Data

Length w/Pulpit	31'0"	Clearance	NA
Hull Length	28'0"	Fuel	100/133 gals.
Beam	10'6"	Water	77 gals.
Draft	3'3"	Waste	12 gals.
Weight	10,000#	Hull Type	Semi-Disp.

Catalina Islander 34

1993–2001

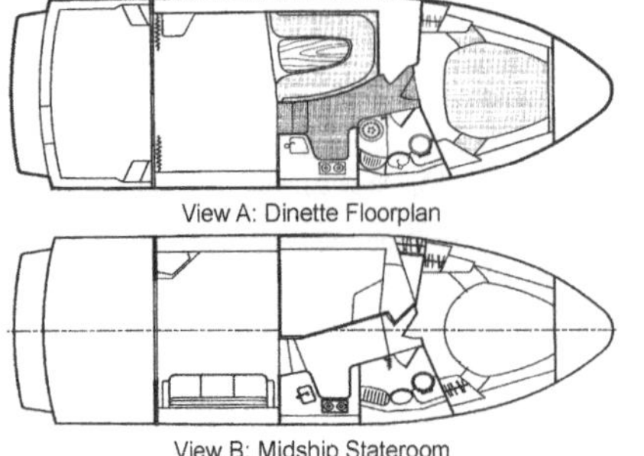

View A: Dinette Floorplan

View B: Midship Stateroom

The Islander 34 (built by sailboat-manufacturer Catalina Yachts) began life in 1989 as the Pearson 34, a good-running deep-V design aimed at the family cruiser market. Catalina obtained the tooling to this model in 1993 when Pearson went out of business and introduced her as the Islander 34—a completely reengineered boat with a revised interior favored by many for its utility and space utilization. With 6 feet, 4 inches of headroom and a light, airy salon, the Islander's two-stateroom floorplan is arranged with a midcabin berth tucked under the elevated dinette—an innovative and seldom-seen configuration capable of sleeping eight people. The forward stateroom has an island berth, and the head compartment is very spacious. On the downside, the galley is compact with little counter space. While not large, the Islander's cockpit is big enough for a couple of light-tackle anglers. Additional features include a spacious engine room, a large flybridge with bench seating forward of the helm, bow pulpit, and a transom door. Twin 250hp Cummins diesels cruise the Islander at 18 knots (22–23 knots top), and 315hp Cummins cruise at 20 knots (mid 20s top).

See Page 673 For Price Data

Length	33'9"	Fuel	300 gals.
Beam	13'0"	Water	54 gals.
Draft	3'4"	Headroom	6'3"
Weight	21,000#	Hull Type	Deep-V
Clearance	15'10"	Deadrise Aft	19°

Cherubini Independence 50

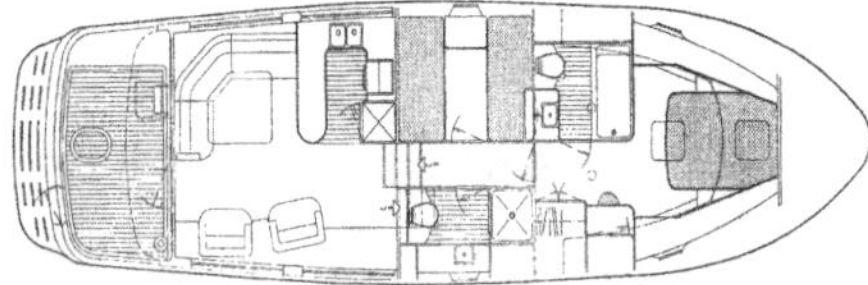

An enlarged version of the Hans Christian Independence 45, the limited-production Independence 50 retains the same sturdy profile as her predecessor with the advantages of a larger main salon and additional cockpit space. Like her sistership, the Independence 50 is built on a semi-displacement hull with moderate beam, hard aft chines to reduce roll (rather than rounded bilges common to displacement designs), and a long, prop-protecting keel. Because she's a semi-custom yacht, several floorplan arrangements are possible including both two- and three-stateroom layouts. The galley is forward in the spacious full-width salon and visibility from the raised pilothouse is excellent. There's room on the large aft deck atop the salon for dinghy storage and/or entertaining. Additional features include reverse-angle pilothouse windows, bow thruster, raised bulwarks, varnished teak interior joinery, a well-arranged engine room and commercial-grade cabin windows. (A flybridge was optional.) The Independence 50 was offered with a single engine for economical long range cruising, or with twin engines for top speeds in the 17–18 knot range.

Not Enough Resale Data to Set Values

Length Overall	54'2"	Clearance	13'6"
Length WL	46'2"	Fuel	900 gals.
Beam	14'6"	Water	300 gals.
Draft	4'9"	Headroom	6'5"
Weight	46,000#	Hull	Semi-Disp.

Conch 27

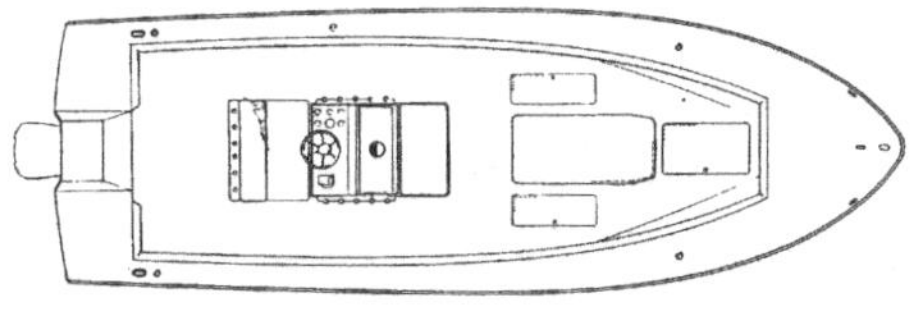

The Conch 27, designed to suit the needs of Key West fishing guides, is a fast and stable offshore center console with a superb deck plan and modern construction. Built on a Hunt-designed deep-V hull, the Conch is fully cored from the bottom up resulting in a rigid and relatively lightweight boat for her size. Her 9-foot beam provides a roomy fishing platform for anglers, and wide chine flats work to reduce roll—the bane of most deep-V hulls. The deck is flat because storage compartments are below the sole. The console allows plenty of walking space on either side, and wide gunwales can accommodate downriggers, outriggers, and rod holders. The absence of a bow rail adds to the Conch's clean look and further eliminates clutter. Features include a large 90-gallon in-sole livewell, console storage/head compartment, a big foredeck fish box, and of course a level of craftsmanship consistent with her premium price. Sold factory-direct, power options include a single or twin V-6 outboards, a single V-8 outboard, or a diesel inboard. Outboard engines can be mounted either on the transom or a bracket. While her 9-foot beam will require a permit, the Conch is easily trailered which adds to her versatility.

Not Enough Resale Data to Set Values

Length	27'0"	Fuel	225 gals.
Beam	9'0"	Water	50 gals.
Hull Draft	1'4"	Max HP	
Dry Weight	4,400#	Hull Type	Deep-V
Clearance	NA	Deadrise Aft	22.5°

Delta 36 SFX

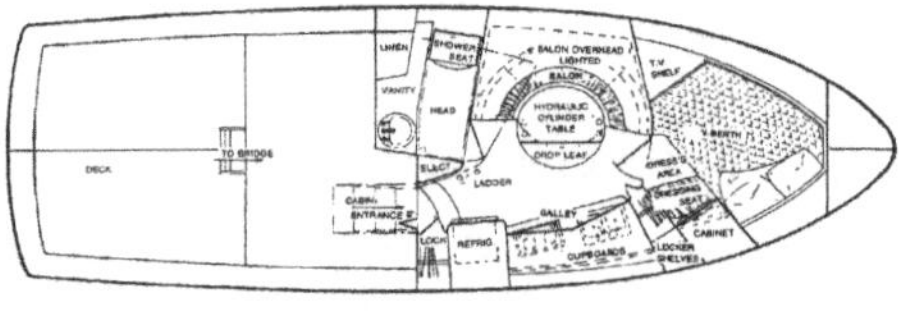

Built by Canaveral Custom Boats in Cape Canaveral, FL, Delta boats are well known in the charter boat trade for their no-nonsense approach to the basics. The hulls are generally USCG certified, and construction is rugged with the emphasis on durability. In the Delta 36 SFX, however, there's more than just a tough deep-V hull and a big—make that huge—fishing cockpit. This is truly an innovative and practical boat with very distinctive styling. What sets her apart from most other sportfish boats in the mid-range market is her unique raised command bridge—a spacious platform that splits the difference between a true flybridge and the raised bridge deck used in open express boats. Positioned about three feet above the cockpit level, this sensible concept provides a standup engineroom (virtually unheard of in a small fisherman) with direct cockpit access and extraordinary headroom below. Below decks, the compact interior is thoughtfully arranged with a circular, pit-style dinette, full galley, and private bow stateroom with offset double berth. A good sea boat, she'll cruise around 24–26 knots with 435hp Cat (or 400hp Cummins) diesels with a top speed of close to 30 knots.

Not Enough Resale Data to Set Values

Length	36'3"	Cockpit	98 sq. ft.
Beam	12'2"	Fuel	410 gals.
Draft	3'0"	Water	50 gals.
Weight	17,200#	Hull Type	Deep-V
Clearance	NA	Deadrise Aft	23°

Dyer 29

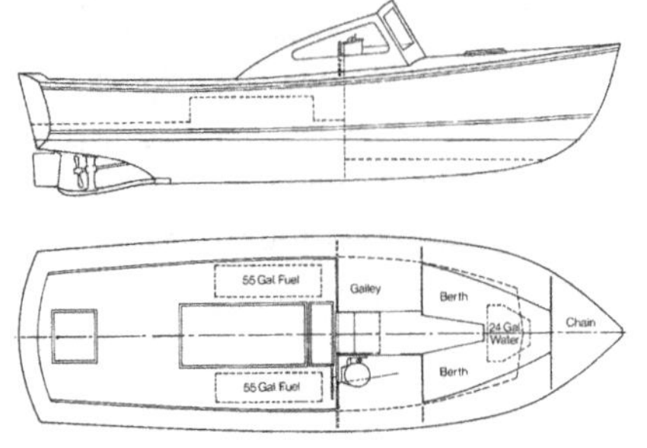

Designed for cruising, fishing, or as a general utility boat the durable Dyer 29 is an industry classic. Indeed, there are those who think she's one of the most alluring small boats ever designed. Production of the Dyer 29 began over 40 years ago making her the longest-running fiberglass model in the business. Each of the over 350 sold has been customized to some extent and no two are exactly alike. At 7,400 pounds, the Dyer 29 would be considered a light boat were it not for her narrow beam. She's built on a soft-chine hull with a long, prop-protecting keel and an uncommonly graceful sheer. The ability of the hull to tackle heavy sea conditions is legendary. Those who own these boats tolerate her tight cabin quarters and intrusive engine box while delighting in the fingertip control and positive response of this easily driven hull. In addition to the popular Trunk Cabin and Bass Boat models, the 29 has also been produced in hardtop and express versions. Note that recent models have the engine under the bridge deck which, by eliminating the engine box, results in a much more open cockpit. Among several engine options, a single 250hp diesel will cruise the Dyer 29 efficiently at 18 knots (23–24 knots top).

See Page 677 For Price Data

Length Overall	28'6"	Clearance	6'0"
Length WL	26'0"	Water	24 gals.
Beam	9'5"	Fuel	110 gals.
Draft	2'6"	Clearance	NA
Weight	7,400#	Hull Type	Semi-Disp.

Ellis 36

1998–2003

Looking for a true Downeast lobster yacht? The primary designer of the Ellis 36 was the late Ralph Ellis who, with partner Ray Bunker, developed the original wooden lobster boats back in the 1950's. The Ellis 36 is a refined version of the original Ellis full-keel hull, a well crafted small yacht built with modern materials and loaded with first-class amenities. She was available with a soft top or optional hardtop, and buyers could choose a windshield-forward version (pictured above) if increased cockpit space was a priority, or with the windshield aft configuration for those wishing to maximize cabin space. The Ellis 36 is not just easy on the eye; she's loaded with practical features. In the single-level cockpit, the side tables fold out, stern seats can be brought forward, and innovative helm/navigation seats adjust to seat a party of eight for dinner. There's a separate stall shower in the head, and the compact galley is more than adequate for producing a full-scale meal. A bow thruster, swim platform, bow pulpit, and teak dining tables were standard. A seriously expensive ride, a single 440hp Yanmar diesel will cruise the Ellis 36 at 20 knots (23–24 knots top). Note that twin waterjet propulsion was also available.

Not Enough Resale Data to Set Values

Length	35'10"	Headroom	6'3"
Beam	13'2"	Fuel	200 gals.
Draft	3'10"	Water	100 gals.
Weight	15,500#	Hull Type	Modified-V
Clearance	NA	Deadrise Aft	0°

Endeavour TrawlerCat 36

1998–2005

The Endeavour 36 TrawlerCat is a midsized catamaran trawler whose spacious interior and comfortable ride make her a compelling alternative to conventional monohull trawlers. Sold factory-direct from the company's Clearwater, FL, facilities, the TrawlerCat was more affordably priced than most of her catamaran counterparts. She rides on a pair of full-displacement hulls, and a moderate 15-foot beam insures that she'll fit into most standard marina slips without too much difficulty. Lacking a flybridge, the Endeavour's helm is in the cockpit where it's protected by a hardtop and canvas enclosure panels. There are three staterooms below, one aft in each hull and the other athwartships, forward of the salon dinette. A single head with a separate stall shower is in the starboard hull, and the galley is in the port hull with a pass-through to the dinette. The TrawlerCat's three-stateroom floorplan is great for a charter boat, however the third (forward) stateroom makes for a rather compact salon compared with most other cats her size. Twin 100hp Yanmar diesels cruise very efficiently at a steady 11–12 knots.

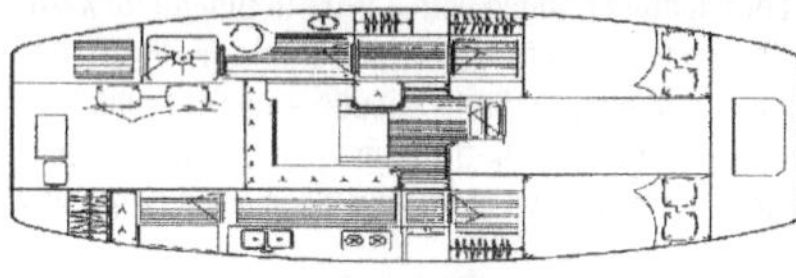

Original Layout

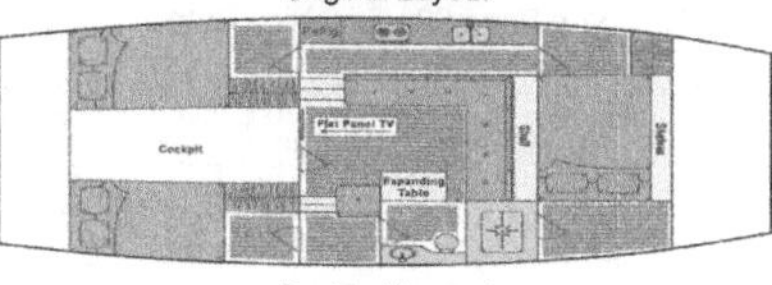

Revised Layout

See Page 678 For Price Data

Length Overall	36'0"	Clearance	14'0"
Length WL	34'6"	Fuel	300 gals.
Beam	15'0"	Water	90 gals.
Draft	2'10"	Waste	30 gals.
Weight	16,000#	Hull Type	Catamaran

Fleming 55 Pilothouse

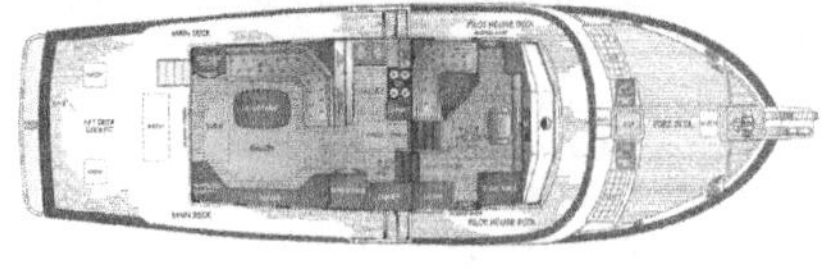

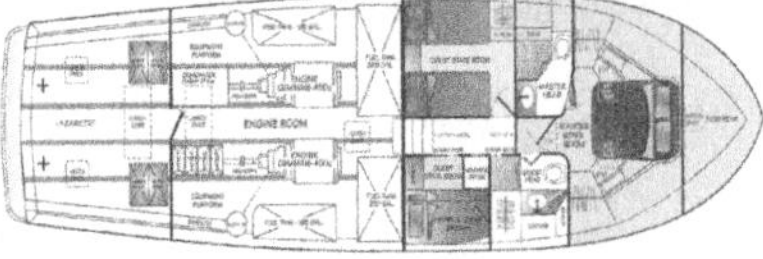

The Fleming 55 is a modern-day version of the classic Alaskan 49 built by Grand Banks in the 1960s. Introduced as a 50-footer in 1987, she was also built as a 53-footer until the current 55-foot model came out in 1991. (The three models have different cockpit dimensions.) Flemings are built on an easily driven, semi-displacement hull with a wide 16-foot beam and long, prop-protecting keel. The traditional teak interior of the Fleming 55 is highlighted by a roomy salon with an L-shaped settee, wet bar, entertainment center, and hardwood flooring. The galley, with full-size refrigerator and copious storage, is forward. There are three staterooms and two full heads below, and the master stateroom is forward rather than amidships as it is in most other pilothouse yachts. The port guest stateroom has twin berths, the starboard stateroom has upper/lower berths, and a washer/dryer is located in the companionway. The flybridge can be accessed from both the cockpit and pilothouse. Note the teak decks, large cockpit lazarette, and wide, well secured side decks. Early models with Cat 210hp diesels cruise at 10 knots. Later models with 435hp Cat (or 450hp Cummins) diesels cruise at 15–16 knots. Over 200 have been built to date.

See Page 679 For Price Data

Length Overall	55'9"	Clearance, Arch	16'0"
Length WL	50'10"	Fuel	1,000 gals.
Beam	16'0"	Water	300 gals.
Draft	5'0"	Waste	100 gals.
Weight	66,000#	Hull Type	Semi-Disp.

Glastron GS 279 Sport Cruiser

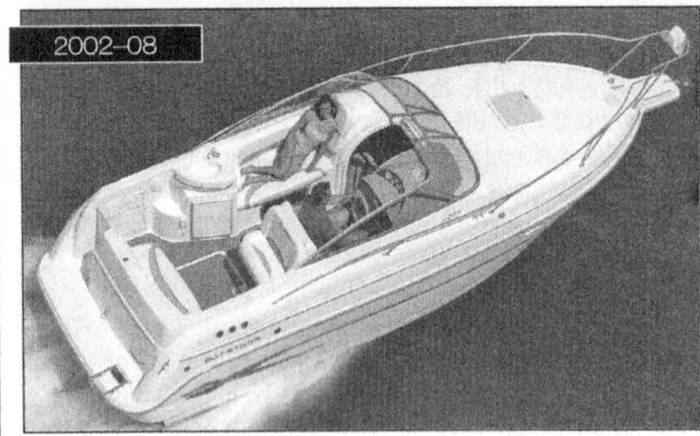

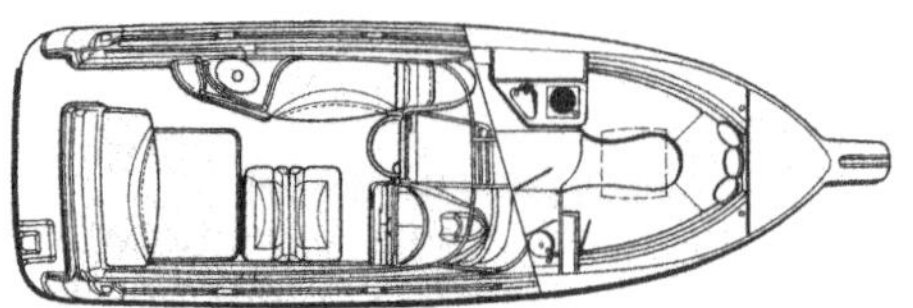

Glastron has long been known for their series of sportboats and runabouts, but their lineup has never included anything as big as the GS 279 Sport Cruiser. With her slender 8'6" beam, the 279 is one of the larger trailerable midcabin boats on the used-boat market. She's also light—only 5,375 pounds—and affordably priced, features sure to appeal to trailer-boat buyers on a budget. Glastron designed this boat with the emphasis on cockpit space in the belief that most weekend boaters prefer to spend their time in the sun rather than below. There's room for nine (according to Glastron) in the single-level cockpit, which includes a doublewide helm/aft-facing seat that converts into a sun pad. A comfortable sun lounge is opposite the helm, and there's a removable bench seat at the transom. Belowdecks, the cabin of the GS 279 is compact but efficiently arranged with a V-berth/dinette forward, a small head with shower, a mini-galley, and a mid-berth aft with sitting headroom. Additional features include a cockpit sink, an integral swim platform, and a walk-through windshield. A good handling boat, a single 315hp Volvo sterndrive engine will cruise at 20 knots (low 30s top).

See Page 681 For Price Data

Length	27'5"	Headroom	6'2"
Beam	8'6"	Fuel	72 gals.
Draft	3'4"	Water	18 gals.
Weight	5,375#	Hull Type	Deep-V
Clearance	7'0"	Deadrise Aft	20°

Grand Alaskan 53 Pilothouse

A handsome yacht, the Grand Alaskan 53 Pilothouse has the businesslike appearance of a serious long-range cruiser. Like her larger siblings in the Alaskan fleet, the 53 is a semicustom yacht. She was built in Taiwan on a semi-displacement hull with a shallow keel, moderate beam, and foam coring above the waterline. Rather than packing three staterooms and two heads in the lower deck level, the Alaskan has two large staterooms and two equally spacious heads—a more practical arrangement for many cruising couples. The galley and salon are aft on the deckhouse level, four steps down from the pilothouse with its centerline helm, expansive windows, settee and chart table. The interior is beautifully finished with grain-matched teak woodwork and cabinetry throughout. Additional features include wide, secure side decks, a spacious flybridge, large lazarette storage compartment, and a well-arranged engine room. Note the wave-breaking Portuguese bridge wrapping around the pilothouse. Standard 300hp Cat diesels cruise the Alaskan 53 at 10 knots (12–13 top), and optional 450hp Cats cruise at 14 knots and reach a top speed of around 17 knots.

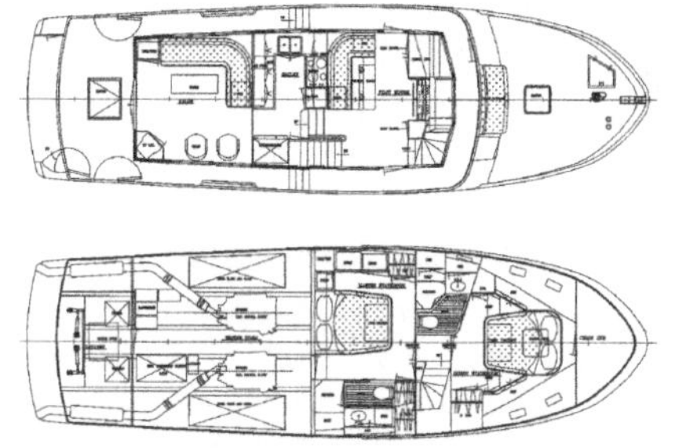

Not Enough Resale Data to Set Values

Length	53'0"	Fuel, Std.	800 gals.
Beam	15'3"	Fuel, Opt.	1,000 gals.
Draft	4'7"	Water	250 gals.
Weight	53,000#	Waste	100 gals.
Clearance	NA	Hull Type	Semi-Disp

Grand Alaskan 64 Pilothouse

The Grand Alaskan 64 bears a strong resemblance to the old DeFever Alaskan series built during the late 1960s and 1970s. Where the original Alaskans were built of wood on a full displacement, round-chined hull, the Grand Alaskans were constructed on a modern semi-displacement fiberglass hull with cored hullsides, a prop-protecting keel, hard chines, and a fully integrated swim platform. Built in Taiwan, the Grand Alaskan 64 is a semicustom yacht, and several interior layouts were available during her production years. The standard three-stateroom floorplan includes the owner's suite amidships with a private salon entrance, and while the galley location (forward in the salon) is common in pilothouse designs, the day head opposite the galley is a very practical convenience. Additional features include a spacious engineroom with near-standing headroom, stabilizers, lifting davit, bow and stern bow thrusters, cockpit storage lazarette, and protected side decks. Cat 715hp C-12 Cat engines deliver a cruising speed of 12–14 knots. Over 30 of these yachts were built. Note that the Grand Alaskan 60 is basically the same boat without the extended cockpit.

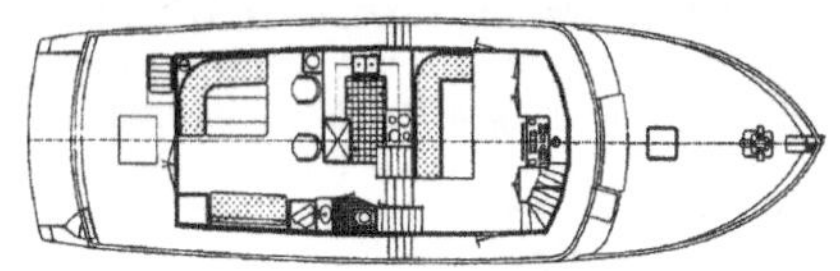

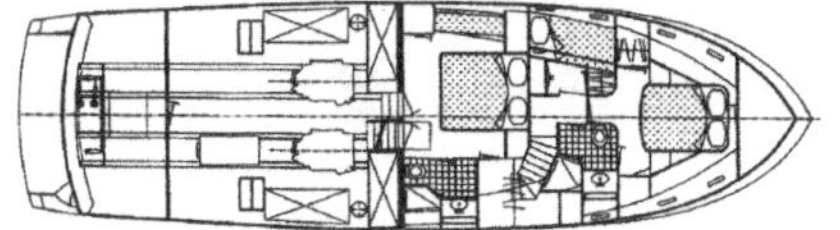

Not Enough Resale Data to Set Values

Length	64'0"	Fuel, Std.	1,300 gals.
Beam	17'2"	Water	400 gals.
Draft	4'9"	Waste	100 gals.
Weight	85,000#	Hull Type	Semi-Disp.
Clearance	NA	Deadrise Aft	NA

Great Harbour 37

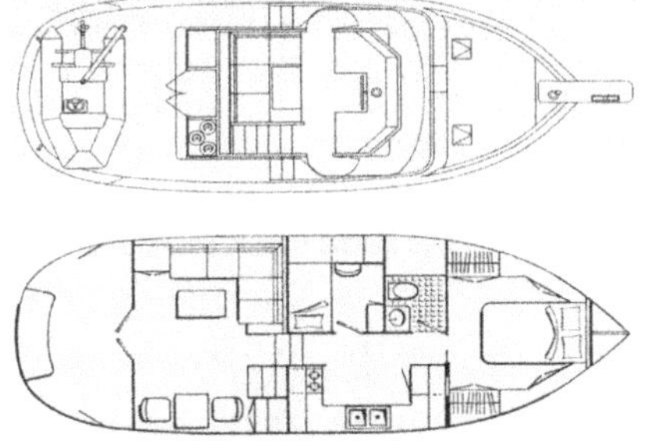

From the first look, it's apparent that the Great Harbour 37 is all about living space, and plenty of it. This maxi-volume liveaboard targets coastal cruisers seeking true condo-like accommodations. The GH37 is built on a full-displacement hull with a wide 15'10" beam, cored hullsides, and a solid fiberglass bottom. According to the builder (Mirage Manufacturing in Gainsville, FL), the cored superstructure and deck have enough buoyancy to keep the vessel afloat. Entering from the protected cockpit, the spacious full-beam salon features two seating areas, a convertible L-shaped settee to port, and two swivel chairs to starboard. There are two versions of the interior layout: In version "A" there is a guest stateroom/study to port with a desk and settee/berth. To starboard is the galley. Version "B" locates the galley to port with a pass-through to the salon. This version features a guest stateroom to starboard with its own head and shower. A washer and dryer are standard. Topside, a Portuguese bridge surrounds the pilothouse with it's convertible settee and pilot berth. Designed for near-shore and coastal cruising, the GH37 will cruise at 7–8 knots with twin 56hp Yanmar diesels.

See Page 682 For Price Data

Length Overll	36'10"	Clearance	14'8"
Length WL	36'1"	Fuel	500 gals.
Beam	15'10"	Water	300 gals.
Draft	2'10"	Waste	100 gals.
Weight	48,000#	Hull Type	Displacement

Hampton 558 Pilothouse

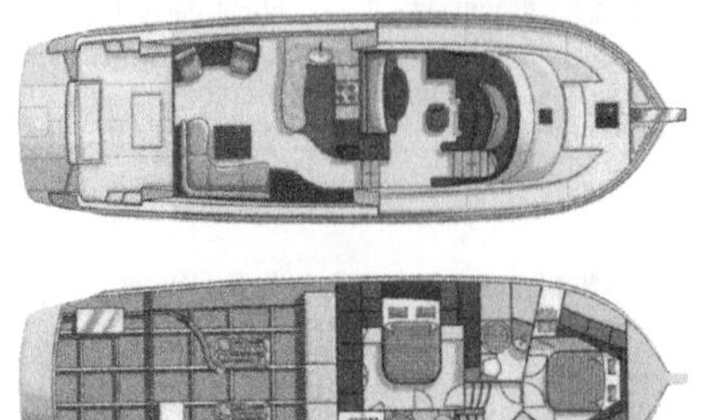

Graceful styling, spacious accommodations, and the ability to operate in poor weather conditions have made pilothouse designs extremely popular over the years with serious cruisers. The Hampton 558 embodies all of these characteristics with the added benefits of a full-width salon, a strong list of standard equipment, and a surprisingly competitive price. Built in Shanghai, China, on a semi-displacement hull with a moderate keel and underwater exhausts, the 558's standard two-stateroom interior is arranged with walkaround queen berths in both cabins, a built-in washer/dryer combo, and Corian counters in the heads and galley. A large-screen TV with electric lift is standard in the salon, and high-gloss cherry cabinets and woodwork are applied throughout the interior. Visibility from the pilothouse, four steps up from the salon level, is excellent. A flybridge overhang shades the cockpit, and an electric hatch in the cockpit sole provides easy access to the engineroom. Note that the flybridge is large enough to accommodate a dinghy and davit. Additional features include twin transom doors, integral swim platform, bow thruster, and hardtop. Cummins 540hp diesels cruise at 16–18 knots (20+ top).

Not Enough Resale Data to Set Values

Length	57'8"	Fuel	800 gals.
Beam	16'4"	Water	230 gals.
Draft	4'6	Waste	80 gals.
Weight	48,000#	Hull Type	Modified-V
Clearance	18'3"	Deadrise Aft	11°

Hampton 680 Pilothouse

2004–Current

The Hampton 680 Pilothouse is a modern luxury cruising yacht whose sleek styling and spacious accommodations offer buyers an affordable alternative to most European motor yachts. Built in China, the 680 is a comfortable and well-planned yacht. A generous 18-foot, 4-inch beam allows for three staterooms, each with an en-suite head (the master's with a whirlpool tub), built-in TV, and premium sound system. Crew quarters, accessible through the transom door or by a salon staircase, include a single berth, head, and mini-galley with washer/dryer. The social center of the 680 is likely to be the pilothouse since this is where the galley and dinette are located. A pass-through from the galley to the dinette is a thoughtful touch, and the excellent finish of the cherry woodwork found throughout the yacht is notable. The salon—with nearly 7 feet of headroom—is large enough to entertain a small crowd in comfort and elegance. Deep side decks, substantial deck hardware, and a smooth-running modified-V hull (with prop pockets) personify the 680's open-water capabilities. Delivered with an extensive inventory of standard equipment, 1,015hp Caterpillar diesels cruise the Hampton 680 at 22 knots and reach a top speed of 24–25 knots.

Not Enough Resale Data to Set Values

Length Overall	68'0"	Fuel	1,500 gals.
Hull Length	67'0"	Water	400 gals.
Beam	18'4"	Waste	120 gals.
Draft	4'10"	Hull Type	Modified-V
Weight	82,000#	Deadrise Aft	13°

Hans Christian Independence 45

1985–2000

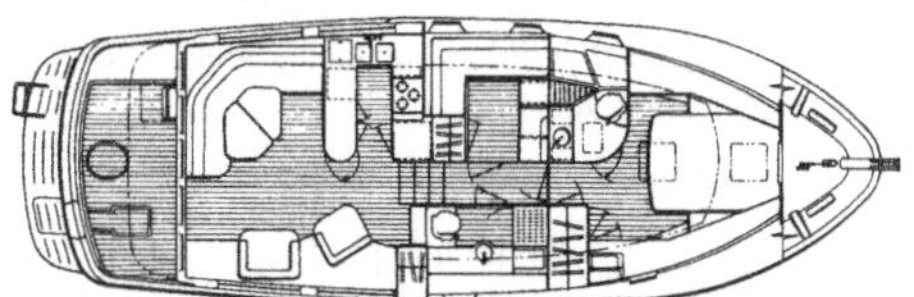

A handsome yacht with a distinctive profile, the Independence 45 is a sturdy raised pilothouse trawler intended for those who take their cruising seriously. She's built on a semi-displacement hull with moderate beam, hard aft chines to reduce roll (rather than rounded bilges common to most displacement designs), and a long, prop-protecting keel. Originally built in Taiwan and imported by Hans Christian as the Positive 42 (1983–85), she was lengthened in 1985 to 45 feet. A total of 18 Independent 45s were sold through 1995 by Hans Christian. Production shifted to the U.S. in 1996 where the well-regarded Cherubini Boat Company built hull #19 that same year. The floorplan, which has remained essentially unchanged over the years, differs from many pilothouse designs in that both staterooms are reached via a corridor from the salon. Visibility from the raised pilothouse is excellent. Lacking side decks, the full-width salon is particularly spacious with plenty of seating space and room for a large U-shaped galley. A single 135hp Lehman (or Lugger) diesel will cruise at 7–8 knots, and a single 315hp Cummins cruise at 9 knots. Optional twin 355hp Cummins cruise at 15–16 knots.

Not Enough Resale Data to Set Values

Length Overall	48'8"	Clearance	13'6"
Length WL	40'9"	Fuel	630 gals.
Beam	14'6"	Water	300 gals.
Draft	4'6"	Waste	80 gals.
Weight	38,000#	Hull	Semi-Disp.

Heritage East 36 Sundeck

1985–Current

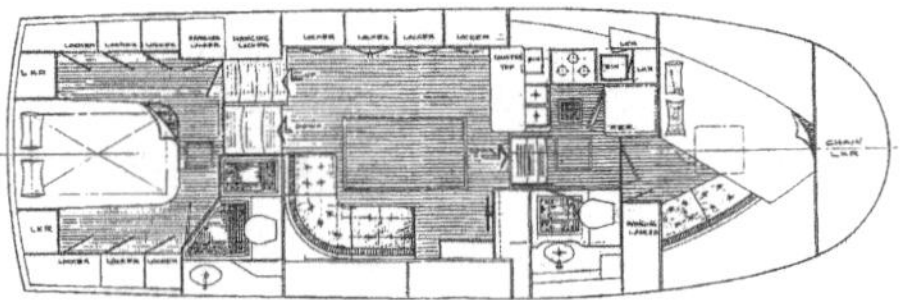

The Heritage East 36 Sundeck is an updated version of the popular Nova 36 Sundeck, one of the better-selling Taiwan imports of her type during the 1980s. Now produced in mainland China, she's built on a solid fiberglass semi-displacement hull with moderate beam, hard chines, and a full-length, prop-protecting keel. The galley-down, total-teak interior of the Heritage East 36 features a roomy salon with large windows, and two comfortable staterooms, each with a double berth. Storage is plentiful for a boat this size, and a deck door is provided next to the lower helm. The overhead grab rails in the salon are worth noting—more cruising boats should have them. The full-beam aft deck of the 36 is large enough for entertaining several guests. Topside, the flybridge will seat for four to six around the helm. Additional features include a teak-and-holly cabin sole, hinged radar arch, wide side decks, spacious engine room, and a molded transom stairway. A fiberglass hardtop is standard. A fuel-efficient ride, a single 220hp Cummins will cruise the Heritage East 36 at 8–10 knots. Over 250 are said to have been produced.

See Page 683 For Price Data

Length Overall	36'0"	Clearance	15'8"
Length WL	32'1"	Fuel	420 gals.
Beam	12'7"	Water	180 gals.
Draft	3'8"	Waste	60 gals.
Weight	23,000#	Hull Type	Semi-Disp.

Hi-Star Star 55 Pilothouse

2002-06

The Hi-Star 55 (also marketed as the Altima 55) is handsome pilothouse yacht whose combination of quality construction, spacious accommodations, and affordable price make her a serious contender in the U.S. motor yacht market. Built by Hi-Star in Shanghai, the 55's vacuum-bagged hull is cored above the waterline and features a shallow keel for directional stability. Like most modern pilothouse yachts, her three-stateroom interior is arranged with the galley and dinette forward, on the pilothouse level, creating a spacious and wide-open salon area. Note that a day head is located just inside the salon entryway—a convenience almost never seen in a yacht this size. Below, there are three staterooms on the lower level, including a lavish full-beam master, a VIP cabin forward, and a second guest stateroom with twin berths that can also be configured as an office. A cockpit hatch provides access to a spacious, standup engine room. Topside, the large flybridge includes a refrigerator and grill in addition to dinghy storage aft and a well-designed helm console. No lightweight, the Hi-Star 55 is a good heavy-weather performer. Cummins 660hp diesels cruise at a respectable 16–18 knots.

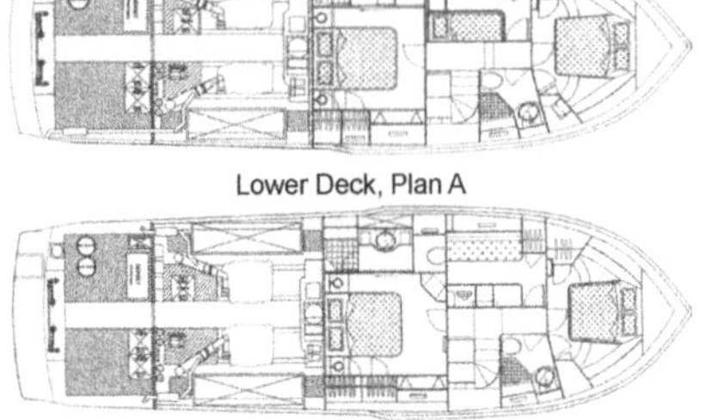

Lower Deck, Plan A

Lower Deck, Plan B

Not Enough Resale Data to Set Values

Length	57'10"	Fuel	930 gals.
Beam	17'4"	Water	300 gals.
Draft	4'4"	Waste	80 gals.
Weight	56,000#	Hull Type	Modified-V
Clearance	NA	Deadrise Aft	14°

Huckins 44 Atlantic

A highly regarded name in the boating industry with roots reaching back to 1928, Huckins is perhaps best known among marine professionals for the company's post-war Fairform Flyer wood boats made famous for their fast-riding Quadraconic hull form. The 44 Atlantic follows in that tradition, a highly finished semi-custom yacht with the classic styling of earlier Huckins designs. The hull is fully cored, and her beam is modest compared with many of today's mega-wide designs. Buyers can choose from various single-stateroom floorplans with the galley down or twin-stateroom layouts with the galley up. A choice of teak, maple or cherry woodwork is offered, and one can only describe the interior of the Atlantic as understated elegance. Visibility from the semi-enclosed helm, two steps up from the cockpit level, is excellent. Facing settees aft of the helm seats provide comfortable guest seating, and the engine room is spacious and extremely well finished. Additional features include Awlgrip exterior paint, radar mast, a teak swim platform and bow pulpit, and bridge enclosure panels. Twin 350hp Cummins or Cat diesels cruise the Atlantic 44 efficiently at 24 knots (at nearly 1 mpg!) and reach a top speed of 27–28 knots.

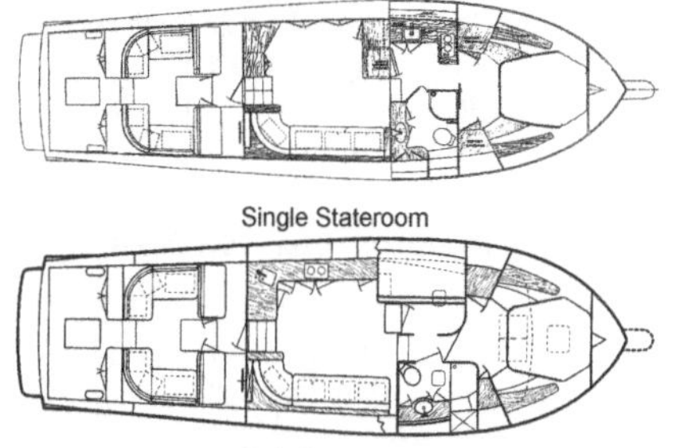

Single Stateroom

Twin Staterooms

Not Enough Resale Data to Set Values

Length	44'10"	Headroom	6'4"
Beam	13'9"	Fuel	406 gals.
Draft	3'0"	Water	115 gals.
Weight	23,500#	Hull Type	Modified-V
Clearance	13'0"	Deadrise Aft	1°

Hunt 29 Surfhunter

Traditional styling and outstanding open-water performance are the hallmarks of the Hunt 29 Surfhunter, a well-designed express whose upscale price hints at her quality construction. The Surfhunter is essentially a day boat; her spacious cockpit results in a fairly compact interior more suitable for occasional overnight stays than extended cruising. Built on a deep-V hull with cored hullsides and a solid fiberglass bottom, the Surfhunter's single-level cockpit features an L-lounge, removable transom seating, and an aft-facing bench seat atop the engine box. Going forward is easy thanks to wide side decks, good nonskid, and high rails. The interior of the Surfhunter includes a good-sized galley and head in addition to a standard V-berth and a classy teak-and-holly sole. While the overall finish is very good, the cabin headroom is a bit low for most. Back in the cockpit, the engine cover lifts to reveal a single Volvo 310hp diesel with a jackshaft connecting the engine to the drive unit. This propulsion system allows the engine weight to be located forward, thus optimizing the boat's center of gravity for a more comfortable ride. With a cruising speed in the mid 20s (about 30 top), the Surfhunter excels in rough-water conditions.

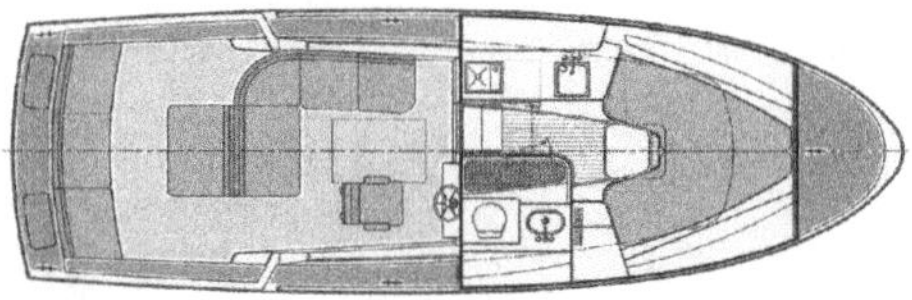

See Page 683 For Price Data

Length	29'6"	Fuel	150 gals.
Beam	10'6"	Water	28 gals.
Draft	3'0"	Waste	15 gals.
Weight	8,000#	Hull Type	Deep-V
Clearance	5'9"	Deadrise Aft	22°

Hunt 33 Express

1999–2004

The Hunt 33 is a semicustom diesel cruiser with traditional Downeast styling, elegant appointments, and modern, state-of-the-art construction. Beauty is of course a matter of personal taste, but by any standard the Hunt is a singularly graceful and handsome yacht. Built on a fully cored deep-V hull with moderate beam and a propeller tunnel to reduce draft, the Hunt 33 is available in express, hardtop express, and hardtop sedan (pictured above) versions. The cabin, with its varnished mahogany trim and teak-and-holly sole, is reminiscent of a high-quality sailboat. Headroom is limited, but the accommodations are beautifully finished and the attention to detail is obvious. For access to the engine, the entire bridgedeck raises up on hydraulic rams. Additional features include a standard bow thruster, wide side decks, an underwater exhaust system, four opening ports, and a roomy cockpit. Designed for the cruising couple, a 370hp Cummins diesel will cruise the Hunt 33 at an economical 24 knots and reach a top speed of around 30 knots—impressive numbers for a 33-footer with just a single engine. An optional 440hp Yanmar diesel will run a few knots faster.

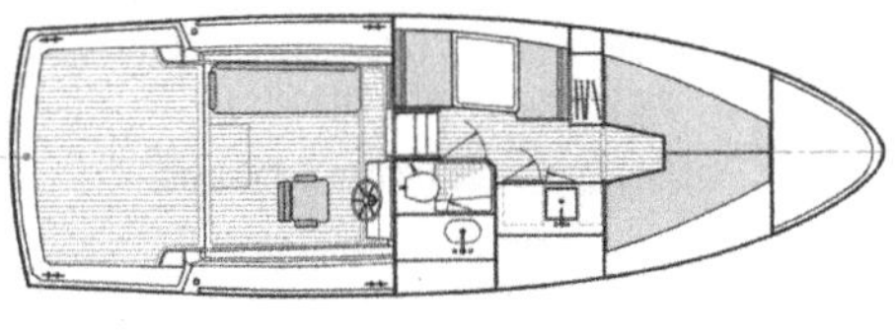

Not Enough Resale Data to Set Values

Length	32'9"	Fuel	125 gals.
Beam	10'10"	Water	30 gals.
Draft	3'0"	Headroom	6'1"
Weight	10,000#	Hull Type	Deep-V
Clearance	15'0"	Deadrise Aft	20°

Johnson 56/58 Motor Yacht

1992–2005

Euro-style motor yachts gained rapid popularity in the 1990's American market thanks to their sleek styling, excellent performance, and practical pilothouse layouts. Built in Taiwan, the Johnson 58 (also marketed as the High-Tech 56 from 1992–99) rides on a modern semi-V hull with cored hullsides and a relatively wide 16-foot beam. Her standard three-stateroom interior includes three full heads and a spacious salon dominated by a huge U-shaped sofa. A separate raised dining area with a permanent table is opposite the lower helm, and the large L-shaped galley is forward, three steps down from the salon. Her bold styling aside, one of the more attractive features of the Johnson 56 is her superb cockpit with its protective bridge overhang, waist-level enclosure panels, and beautiful teak sole. Wide side decks make bow access easy, and sun pads are located on both the flybridge and foredeck. Early models with 550hp 6V92 Detroit diesels cruise at 22 knots (about 25 knots top). Twin 735hp 8V92 Detroits cruise in the low-to-mid 20s and top out at 26–28 knots. Later models with 800hp Cats cruise in the mid 20s and deliver a top speed of about 30 knots.

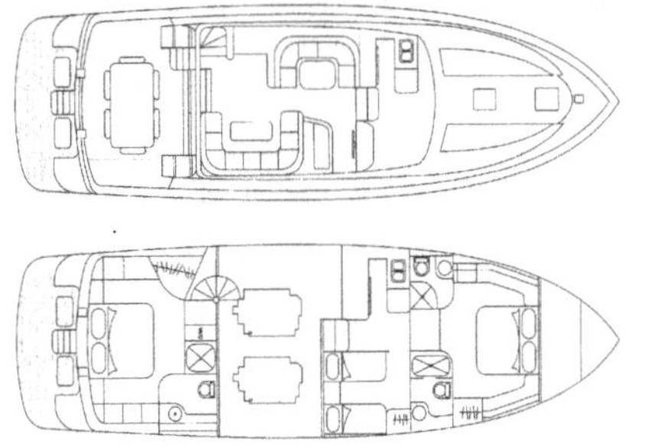

See Page 685 For Price Data

Length	58'0"	Fuel	1,000 gals.
Beam	16'0"	Water	200 gals.
Draft	4'10"	Waste	60 gals.
Weight	64,000#	Hull Type	Modified-V
Clearance	NA	Deadrise Aft	16°

Johnson 63/65 Motor Yacht

1990–2002

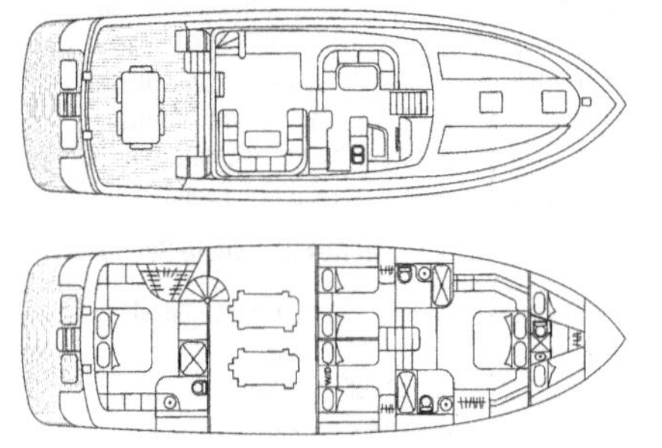

The Johnson 65 (called the Johnson 63 until 1993) is a Euro-style pilothouse yacht from Taiwan whose versatile layout, distinctive styling, and impressive inventory of standard features represented a good yachting value in the 1990s. Built on a modified-V hull with cored hullsides and a wide 19-foot beam, the accommodations of the 65 are spacious indeed. The well-appointed salon is divided into two levels with the lower aft section housing a big U-shaped lounge with a coffee table, and the forward, upper level containing a dining area to port and the galley and lower helm to starboard. Two of the Johnson's four staterooms contain queen berths, and the Med-style crew quarters at the bow are accessed from the foredeck. Additional features include a stainless-steel-and-glass salon bulkhead, very roomy aft deck with a protective bridge overhang, light ash (or teak) interior woodwork, and a spacious, low-profile flybridge. On the downside, the side decks are narrow. A popular yacht, the Johnson 65 will cruise at 17–18 knots with 735hp 8V92 diesels and reach a top speed of around 22 knots. Later models with 1,150hp MANs cruise in the mid 20s and reach close to 30 knots.

Not Enough Resale Data to Set Values

Length	63'0"/65'0"	Fuel	1,000 gals
Beam	19'0"	Water	400 gals.
Draft	4'11"	Headroom	6'5"
Weight	75,000#	Hull Type	Modified-V
Clearance	NA	Deadrise Aft	16°

Johnson 63/65 Motor Yacht

1990–2002

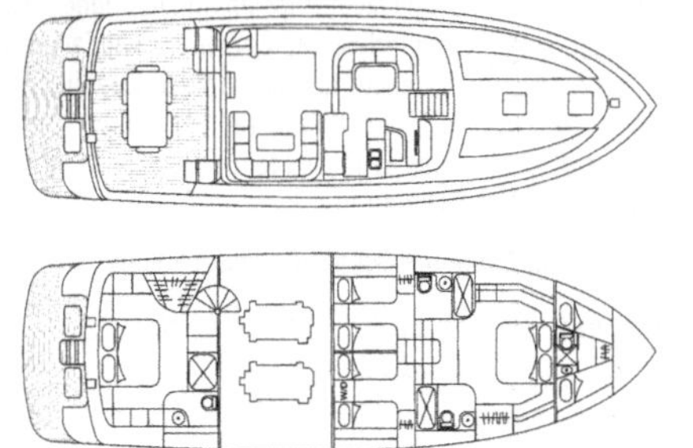

The Johnson 65 (called the Johnson 63 until 1993) is a Euro-style pilothouse yacht from Taiwan whose versatile layout, distinctive styling, and impressive inventory of standard features represented a good yachting value in the 1990s. Built on a modified-V hull with cored hullsides and a wide 19-foot beam, the accommodations of the 65 are spacious indeed. The well-appointed salon is divided into two levels with the lower aft section housing a big U-shaped lounge with a coffee table, and the forward, upper level containing a dining area to port and the galley and lower helm to starboard. Two of the Johnson's four staterooms contain queen berths, and the Med-style crew quarters at the bow are accessed from the foredeck. Additional features include a stainless-steel-and-glass salon bulkhead, very roomy aft deck with a protective bridge overhang, light ash (or teak) interior woodwork, and a spacious, low-profile flybridge. On the downside, the side decks are narrow. A popular yacht, the Johnson 65 will cruise at 17–18 knots with 735hp 8V92 diesels and reach a top speed of around 22 knots. Later models with 1,150hp MANs cruise in the mid 20s and reach close to 30 knots.

Not Enough Resale Data to Set Values

Length	63'0"/65'0"	Fuel	1,000 gals
Beam	19'0"	Water	400 gals.
Draft	4'11"	Headroom	6'5"
Weight	75,000#	Hull Type	Modified-V
Clearance	NA	Deadrise Aft	16°

Krogen Express 49

1995–2002

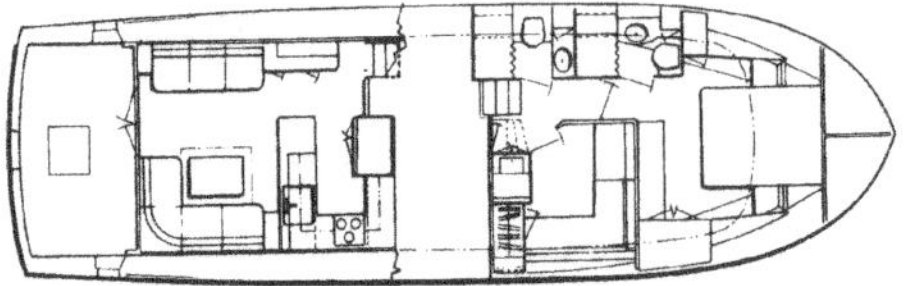

The plumb bow and traditional pilothouse profile of the Krogen Express 49 make her one of the more distinctive and appealing trawler-style designs on the market. While the beam is comparatively narrow for a boat this size, her deep forefoot, rounded bilges, and hard aft chines result in a very efficient hull capable of a good turn of speed. A long keel provides prop protection, and the plumb bow is very salty indeed. Belowdecks, the accommodations emphasize room and comfort for extended cruising. The traditional pilothouse floorplan is arranged with the deckhouse galley aft and two staterooms forward, three steps down from the pilothouse. Note that the guest stateroom can also be set up as an office or den. The helm is on the centerline in the wheelhouse, which includes a settee/watch berth, a chart table, and deck doors port and starboard. Additional features include full walkaround side decks, a spacious covered cockpit, a meticulously arranged walk-in engine room, stall showers in both heads, and dinghy storage on the flybridge. Cat 350hp diesels (16–17 knots cruise/20 knots top) were standard until 2000 when 420hp Yanmars (19 knots cruise/23 knots top) became standard. A total of 16 were built.

Not Enough Resale Data to Set Values

Length Overall	49'6"	Clearance, Mast	21'7"
Length WL	47'11"	Fuel	600 gals.
Beam	14'9"	Water	300 gals.
Draft	4'0"	Waste	75 gals.
Weight	42,000#	Hull Type	Semi-Disp.

Krogen Express 52

2003–Current

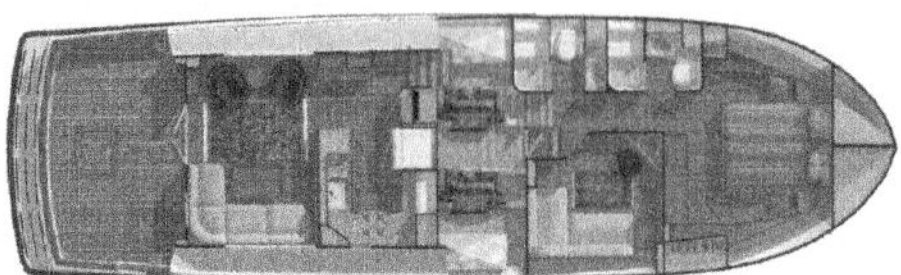

The Krogen Express 52 is a longer, wider version of the successful Krogen Express 49, of which 16 were delivered. She's built in Taiwan by Asia Marine (the same yard that builds Kady-Krogen trawlers) on a Kevlar-reinforced semi-displacement hull with moderate beam, hard aft chines, and a shallow keel for directional stability. While the interior of the 52 is very similar to the 49, the extra length can be seen in a larger cockpit, a slightly more expansive salon, and a bigger pilothouse with room for a fixed helm chair. Built to go places, the distinctive profile of the Express is matched with a beautiful cherry interior. The pilothouse, which is the focal point of this boat, offers excellent visibility and includes a dinette that converts to a double watch berth. Large windows bathe the salon and galley in light, and the cockpit, salon and galley all flow into one another on a single level. Topside, the flybridge boasts an L-shaped settee and a centerline helm position. The layout of the engine room, with its excellent access and serviceability, is very impressive. Powered with twin 440hp Yanmar diesels, the generous tankage of the Express 52 makes for impressive range—about 400 nautical miles at 18 knots.

Not Enough Resale Data to Set Values

Length Overall	57'6"	Clearance, Mast	21'8"
Length WL	51'4"	Fuel	700 gals.
Beam	15'11"	Water	370 gals.
Draft	4'0"	Waste	100 gals.
Weight	43,000#	Hull Type	Semi-Disp.

Lagoon 43

Lagoon, a company best known for its line of sailing catamarans, is a division of French sailboat manufacturer Beneteau Yachts. The Lagoon 43 is the company's first powerboat design, a very distinctive cruising yacht with wraparound cabin windows and a mega-wide 21-foot, 3-inch beam. She rides on a pair of shallow-draft, semi-displacement hulls with balsa coring above the waterline and prop-protecting keels. The Lagoon's aft-cabin layout is unique; no other power cat available in the U.S. market to date incorporates this design. Two floorplans are offered: a three-stateroom arrangement with guest cabins forward in each hull, and a two-stateroom layout with a den/office in the starboard hull. The salon isn't as spacious as one might imagine (the aft stateroom takes up a lot of space), but the panoramic view is impressive and helm visibility is excellent. Molded steps lead from the covered cockpit to the small flybridge, and a U-shaped foredeck lounge is a great place to enjoy the view. On the downside, headroom in the master stateroom is modest, and finding a marina to accommodate the Lagoon's enormous beam will be a challenge. Yanmar 250hp diesels cruise at 16–18 knots with a 400-mile-plus range.

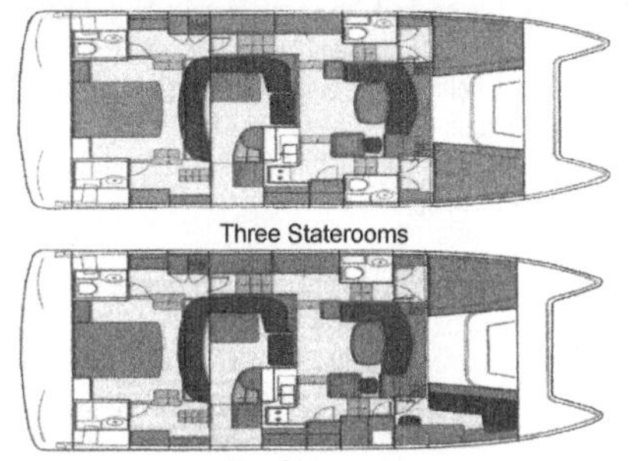
Three Staterooms

Two Staterooms

See Page 685 For Price Data

Length Overall	42'9"	Headroom	6'3"
Length WL	39'1"	Fuel	412 gals.
Beam	21'1"	Water	206 gals.
Draft	3'11"	Waste	45 gals.
Weight	24,693#	Hull Type	Catamaran

Marlin 350 Cuddy

The Marlin 350 is a semicustom center console with excellent speed and stability. Built in Miami and sold factory-direct, the Marlin rides on a rigid, lightweight, and stable deep-V hull capable of handling some very rough seas. The standard version features a V-berth and electric head in the cuddy, and a new option in 1998 has a standup head/shower inside the center console. Built for the angling purist who appreciates a well-made boat, the Marlin's finish and attention to fishing details is exceptional. Two outboard sinks and a centerline bait-prep station are built into the transom, all with pressure water. Add to that such features as an elevated 50-gallon livewell, custom tackle drawers, two large fish boxes, fresh and saltwater washdowns, and padded coamings all around, and the deck layout is among the best to be found in a boat of this type. Note the huge dash panel on the console and the wide walkaround decks. A very fuel-efficient boat thanks to her light weight, the Marlin will hit a top speed of around 45 knots with twin 250hp Mercury outboards. Single-diesel and jet-drive power were also available.

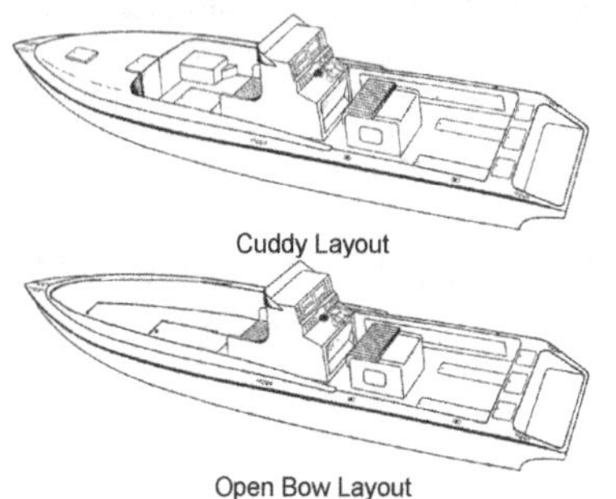
Cuddy Layout

Open Bow Layout

See Page 688 For Price Data

Length	35'6"	Fuel	250 gals.
Beam	9'4"	Water	40 gals.
Hull Draft	1'6"	Max HP	600
Weight w/Engines	9,000#	Hull Type	Deep-V
Clearance	8'0"	Deadrise Aft	24°

Mediterranean 38 Convertible

1985–2007

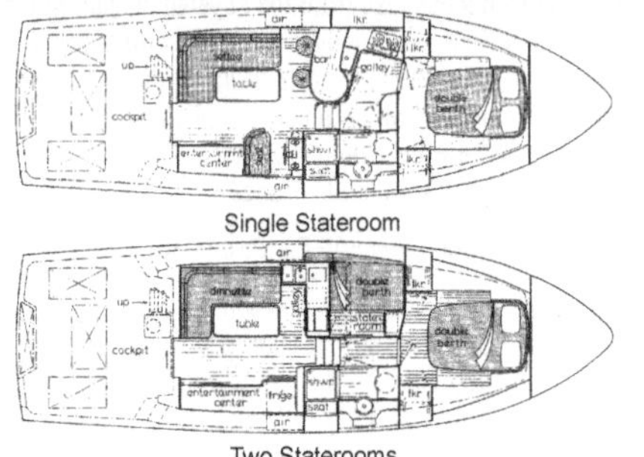

Single Stateroom

Two Staterooms

Introduced in 1985, the Mediterranean 38 is among the more popular convertibles her size ever developed. She was also one of the better values in the boating world; whatever the 38 might lack in finish and detailing was more than compensated by her sturdy construction and a low, factory-direct price. The 38 is a traditional convertible design built in California on a semi-V hull suitable for fishing, diving, or family cruising. Two floorplans are available: a single-stateroom layout with the galley down and a lower helm in the salon, and a twin-stateroom interior with the galley up and no lower helm. Both plans include a built-in entertainment center in the salon, and a breakfast bar overlooks the galley in the single-stateroom version. Because of her narrow hull and wide walkaround side decks, the Mediterranean's interior is small for a 38-footer. The cockpit, however, is quite large with plenty of space for some serious fishing. (Note that the flybridge can be ordered with the helm console forward or aft). Several gas and diesel engine options were offered over the years, most of which will cruise the Mediterranean 38 in the low-to-mid 20s. Over 200 are said to have been sold.

See Page 688 For Price Data

Length w/Pulpit	43'6"	Fuel	390 gals.
Hull Length	38'4"	Water	100 gals.
Beam	12'8"	Waste	25 gals.
Draft	3'4"	Hull Type	Modified-V
Weight	28,000#	Deadrise Aft	18°

Mediterranean 54 Convertible

1994–2007

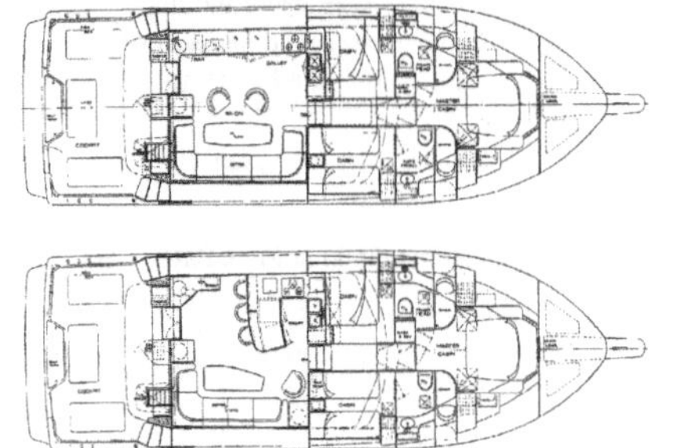

Built in California and sold factory-direct, the Mediterranean 54 is a no-frills convertible with serious sportfishing potential and a very competitive price. She's constructed on a conventional modified-V hull, and at 55,000 pounds she's a weight-efficient boat for her size. Several floorplans have been available in the 54 since her 1994 introduction, and the factory promotes its ability to custom-design the interior to an owner's requirements. Wraparound salon windows admit plenty of natural lighting, and a lower helm station is a popular option. On deck, the 54's large cockpit is arranged with molded steps at the corners, an engine room access door, two in-deck fish boxes, and a baitwell in the transom. Topside, the helm is aft on the flybridge with lounge seating and a wet bar forward. Like most West Coast designs, the Mediterranean 54's side decks are very wide and she carries more fuel than any boat in her class. Note that a Pilothouse (enclosed bridge) version is also available. Among several engine choices, twin 550hp Detroit 6V92s (small engines for a 54-footer) cruise at 20 knots (low 20s top). Optional 760hp 8V92s cruise at 25–26 knots (about 28 top).

Not Enough Resale Data to Set Values

Length w/Pulpit	56'7"	Cockpit	160 sq. ft.
Hull Length	53'7"	Fuel	1,400 gals.
Beam	16'8"	Water	365 gals.
Draft	4'6"	Hull Type	Modified-V
Weight	68,000#	Deadrise Aft	15°

Midnight Express 39 Cuddy

2000–Current

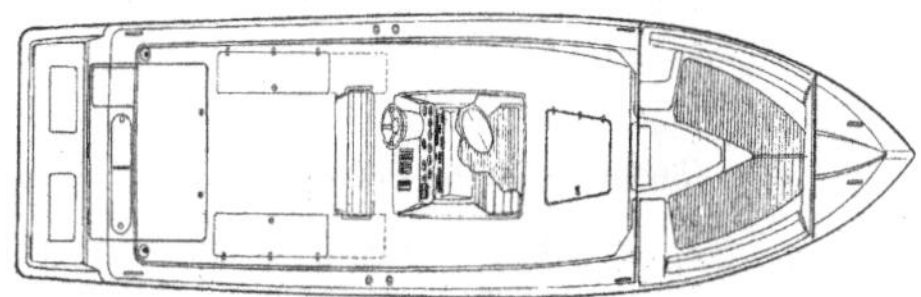

One of the largest production center console boats available when she was introduced in 2000, the Midnight Express 39 is a high-performance fish boat with a huge cockpit and a level of workmanship that should satisfy the most discerning anglers. She rides on a reworked version of the original Cigarette 36 offshore racing hull with increased freeboard, a little less transom deadrise, and the addition of an integrated swim platform/outboard bracket. While the hullsides are cored the bottom of the 39 is solid fiberglass. The deck layout is arranged with a small cuddy forward (with V-berths sitting headroom), a console head compartment, a big 50-gallon transom livewell and a pair of 7-foot in-deck fish boxes. The list of standard features is extensive and includes a radar arch with T-top, cockpit bolsters, transom door, fore and aft freshwater showers, trim tabs, and a custom leaning post with rod holders. With twin 225hp outboards, the Midnight Express 39 will cruise at 25 knots and attain a top speed in the neighborhood of 35 knots. For extra performance, triple 250hp motors will reach speeds in excess of 50 knots. Note that sterndrive power is also available.

Not Enough Resale Data to Set Values

Length	39'2"	Fuel	325 gals.
Beam	9'6"	Water	45 gals.
Hull Draft	1'10"	Max HP	900
Dry Weight	13,000#	Hull Type	Deep-V
Headroom	6'2"	Deadrise Aft	22°

MJM 34Z Downeast

2004–Current

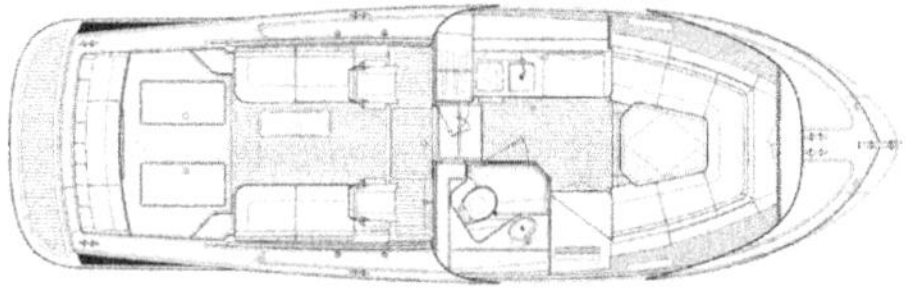

Built by Boston Boat Works for MJM Yachts in Boston, the MJM 34Z is a single-engine Downeast cruiser who's super-practical character sets her apart from just about everything else on the water. It's not just the fuel-efficient economy of the 34Z that enthusiasts find so appealing; she's big enough to entertain as many as eight on a day trip of evening cruise, and her excellent range and shallow draft provide access to remote locations. Built on a Kevlar-reinforced hull with a narrow beam, the propeller is recessed in a pocket and protected by a prop guard. Note the classic speedboat transom and aft tumblehome. More day boat than extended cruiser, the well-finished interior of the MJM 34Z includes a small galley with microwave, stove and refrigerator, enclosed head with shower, and a dinette forward that converts to a double berth. Cherry ceiling boards line the hull, and cherry cabinets and a varnished teak-and-holly sole make this an elegant living space indeed. The entire pilothouse deck rises on electric lifters for engine access. The 34Z's lightweight hull contributes to her exceptional fuel efficiency (about 2 mpg at 22 knots) with a single 440hp Yanmar diesel. Definitely not an inexpensive boat.

Not Enough Resale Data to Set Values

Length	34'0"	Fuel	148 gals.
Beam	11'0"	Water	60 gals.
Draft	2'4"	Waste	20 gals.
Weight	10,600	Hull Type	Modified-V
Clearance	9'6"	Deadrise Aft	18°

Monk 36 Trawler

1982–2007

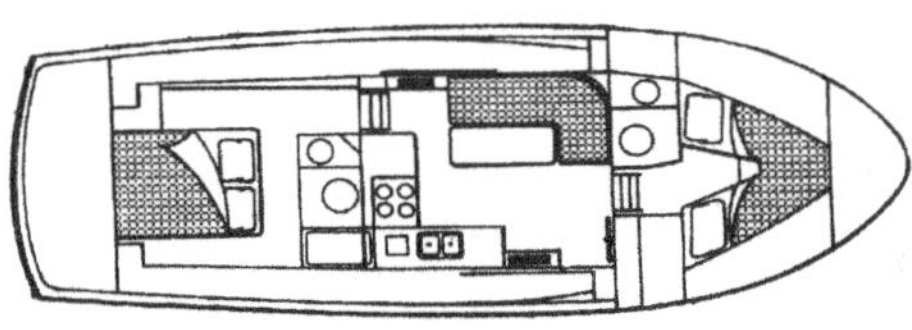

Built in Nova Scotia since 1992, the Monk 36 gained popularity in the 1980s as a durable and affordable Taiwan import with a classic trawler profile and a traditional all-teak interior. Construction is solid fiberglass, and the hull features a skeg-protected prop as well as an upswept, highly flared bow, which contributes to her dry ride. Early models came with plenty of exterior teak—decks, window frames, hatches, etc.—but in current models only the handrails are teak. The galley-up floorplan of the Monk 36 has remained essentially unchanged over the years although post-1992 models have eliminated the tub in the aft head and moved the bed away from the wall in the owner's stateroom—a big improvement. On deck, raised bulwarks and a high rail make movement around the house safe and secure. Additional features include a functional mast and boom assembly, a well-arranged flybridge, bow pulpit and swim platform. A single 120hp or 135hp Lehman diesel was standard in early models (about 7 knots at cruise). Later models with a single 220hp Cummins cruise at 9–10 knots. Always a good-selling model, over 250 Monk 36s have been built over the years.

See Page 689 For Price Data

Length Overall	36'0"	Clearance, Mast	17'11"
Length WL	33'0"	Fuel	320 gals.
Beam	13'0"	Water	120 gals.
Draft	4'0"	Waste	45 gals.
Weight	18,000#	Hull Type	Semi-Disp.

Monte Fino 65 Motor Yacht

1993–98

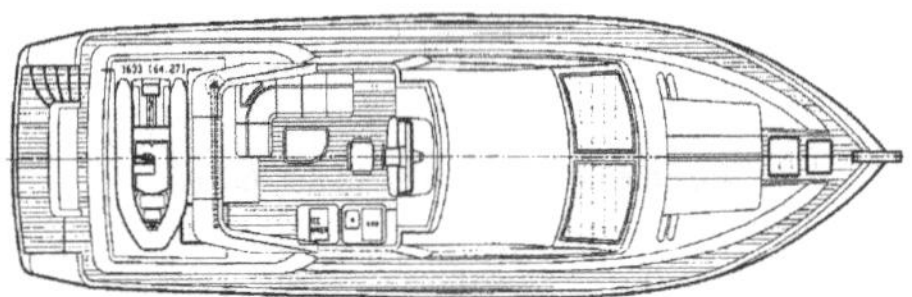

The Monte Fino 65 is an Asian-built pilothouse yacht whose lush accommodations, quality construction, and very competitive price came as a surprise to many luxury-yacht buyers in the 1990s. Offered with a high degree of customization, several interior layouts were offered for the 65 with a four-stateroom floorplan being the most popular. The spacious salon of the Monte Fino is arranged on two levels with the dining area, galley, and lower helm forward, and the formal salon aft. The lavish owner's suite is accessed via a curved staircase in the salon, and each of the three forward guest staterooms has a private head. (Note that the bow crew quarters are reached from a hatch in the foredeck.) The customizing extended to a wide variety of wood finishes which could be specified for the salon and cabin. Topside, the extended flybridge comes complete with a wet bar, tender storage, and plenty of lounge seating. Additional features include a spacious engine room (accessed from the owner's stateroom), galley deck door, a roomy aft deck, and an integral swim platform with built-in storage. Cat 800hp engines cruise at a respectable 18 knots (low 20s top).

Not Enough Resale Data to Set Values

Length Overall	64'6"	Clearance	NA
Length WL	56'6"	Fuel	1,500 gals.
Beam	16'9"	Water	300 gals.
Draft	5'6"	Hull Type	Modified-V
Weight	64,960#	Deadrise Aft	NA

Monte Fino Fino 82 Cockpit MY

The dramatic styling of the Monte Fino 82—together with her spacious accommodations and a competitive price—made this Taiwan-built luxury cruiser one of the more impressive big-boat values available in her era. She's heavily built on a semi-V hull with a wide 20-foot beam, a shallow keel, and prop pockets to reduce shaft angles. While the 82 can be highly customized to meet a buyer's requirements, a typical floorplan (shown below) would be arranged with crew quarters forward and three staterooms aft including a huge full-beam master suite. (Note that a salon staircase provides private access to the owner and guest cabins.) The elegant salon, with its facing settees and formal dining area, is separated from the galley and wheelhouse by a bulkhead. Topside, the aft engine room is entered from the cockpit via a watertight door. Additional features include port and starboard pilothouse deck doors, a day head opposite the galley, a huge flybridge, cherry interior woodwork, and twin sleeping cabins in the crew quarters. Twin 1,350hp Cat diesels cruise the Monte Fino 82 Cockpit MY at 19–20 knots (low 20s top).

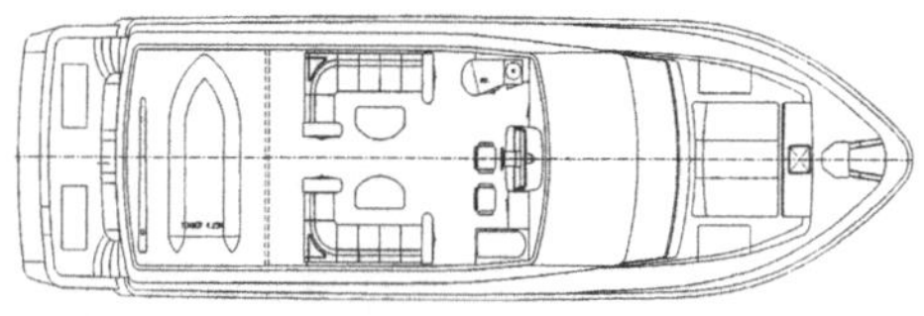

Not Enough Resale Data to Set Values

Length Overall	81'9"	Fuel	2,800 gals.
Length WL	71'5"	Water	610 gals.
Beam	20'0"	Headroom	6'6"
Draft	5'3"	Hull Type	Modified-V
Weight	124,000#	Deadrise Aft	NA

North Pacific 42/43 Pilothouse

Built in China and sold on the West Coast, the North Pacific 43 Pilothouse (originally called the North Pacific 42 Pilothouse) is a durable cruising yacht whose traditional lines and attractive price make her a serious player in this segment of the market. As 43-footers go, the North Pacific is not a "big" boat inside; indeed, her 12'7" beam is moderate compared with many other trawler-style boats her length. The raised pilothouse floorplan consists of a full-beam salon with a settee along the starboard side and convertible dinette and U-shaped galley to port. Two staterooms and a single head are forward and below, and the guest stateroom to port is available with a single or double bed or it can be finished out as an office. A bench seat sits behind the pilothouse helm seat, and molded steps ascend to the bridge deck on both sides of the boat. An upper (flybridge) helm station is standard. The North Pacific is constructed on a solid fiberglass, semi-displacement hull (complete with simulated plank lines), and her slender beam results in a hull that is easily driven and fuel-efficient. She'll cruise at 8–10 knots with a single 230hp Cummins diesel burning 4–5 gallons per hour. Twin engines are optional.

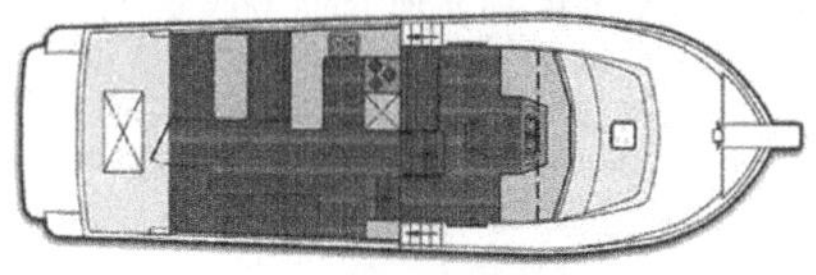

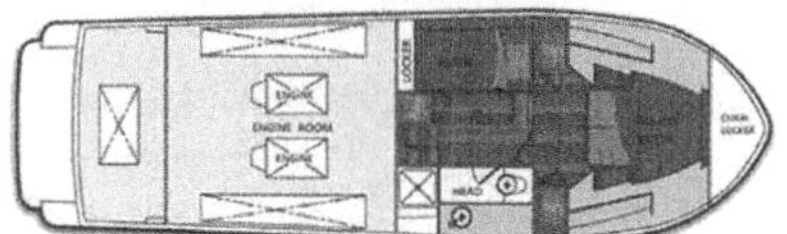

Not Enough Resale Data to Set Values

Length Overall	43'0"	Clearance	NA
Length WL	38'3"	Fuel	380 gals.
Beam	12'7"	Water	350 gals.
Draft	4'5"	Waste	50 gals.
Weight	31,000#	Hull Type	Semi-Disp.

Osprey 30

1999–2004

She may not have the most graceful lines, but the Osprey 30 gets the job done for anglers who demand exceptional heavy-weather performance and tough-as-nails construction. Designed and built for the rigors of the Pacific Northwest, the Osprey rides on a solid fiberglass deep-V hull with moderate beam, reverse chines and an integral swim platform. If the Osprey looks a little ungainly, it's mostly because of her high freeboard—a feature that results in a deep cockpit as well as a roomy cabin. As a fishing boat, the Osprey's walkaround decks, enclosed pilothouse and uncluttered cockpit will appeal to cold-weather anglers. The interior is arranged with a convertible dinette and a small galley on the upper level, and a double berth below along with an enclosed head with shower. Although the cabin accommodations are well conceived and executed, the absence of a privacy door forward is notable. Additional features include heavy-duty windows, watertight cabin door, in-deck fish box, transom door, and anchor locker. Offered with sterndrive or inboard power, twin 188hp Volvo diesel sterndrives cruise the Osprey 30 at 28 knots and reach a top speed of 32–33 knots.

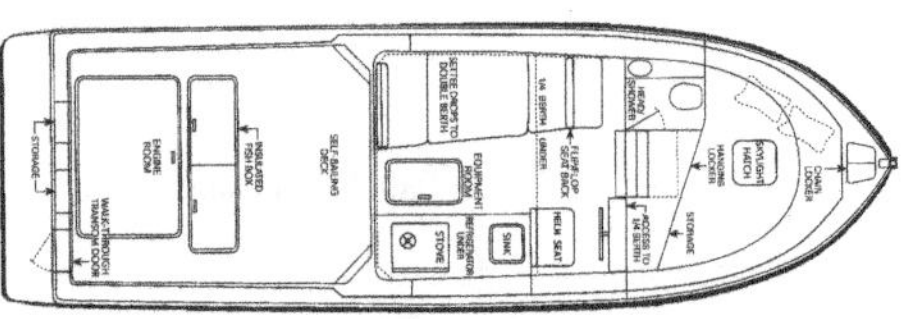

See Page 691 For Price Data

Length	30'4"	Water	36 gals.
Beam	10'0"	Waste	21 gals.
Draft	2'8"	Headroom	6'4"
Weight	11,000#	Cockpit	64 sq. ft.
Fuel	230/280 gals.	Hull Type	Deep-V

Outer Reef 65 Raised Pilothouse

2007–Current

Joining executive-class accommodations with the cruising range to reach distant destinations, the Outer Reef 65 was designed to travel the world's oceans in comfort and security. A wide 18-foot, 6-inch beam makes this Outer Reef among the more spacious pilothouse yachts in her class. Built on semi-displacement hull with a deep, prop-protecting keel, the 65 has a fully covered walkaround main deck and a Portuguese bridge forward with an opening to the foredeck. Dual staircases from her extended swim platform lead to a fully covered aft deck. Belowdecks, the elegant three-stateroom interior of the Outer Reef 65 includes a spacious salon with cherry cabinets and granite counters, full-beam master suite with king bed, three full heads, and a laundry center. A day head is located just opposite the galley, and a watertight door in the master stateroom provides access to the engineroom. Crew quarters or a forth stateroom aft are optional. Topside, the enormous full-beam flybridge of the Outer Reef 65 features Stidd helm chairs, BBQ grill, wet bar with refrigerator, and two L-shaped lounges aft. Cruise at 12 knots (14–15 top) with Cat 503hp C-9 diesels.

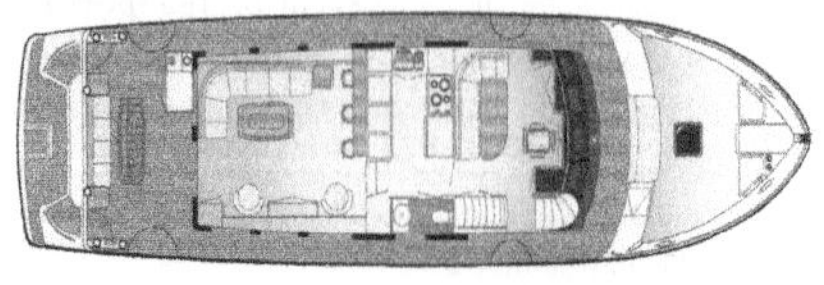

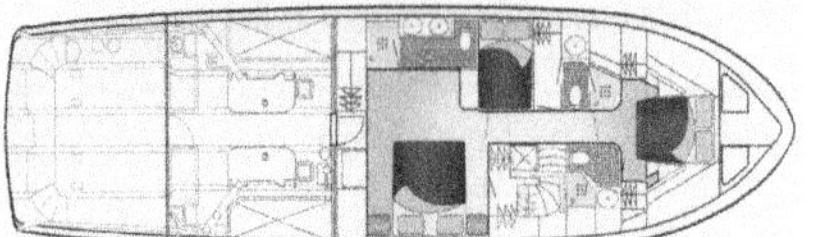

Not Enough Resale Data to Set Values

Length Overall	65'0"	Clearance	NA
Length WL	58'6"	Fuel	2,000 gals.
Beam	18'6"	Water	400 gals.
Draft	5'0"	Waste	150 gals.
Weight	93,500#	Hull Type	Semi-Disp.

Pacific Mariner 65 Motor Yacht

1998–2008

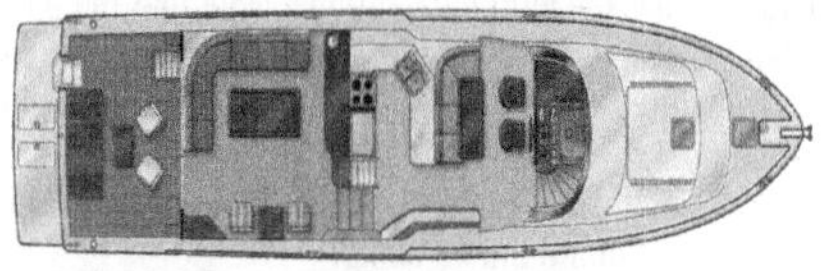

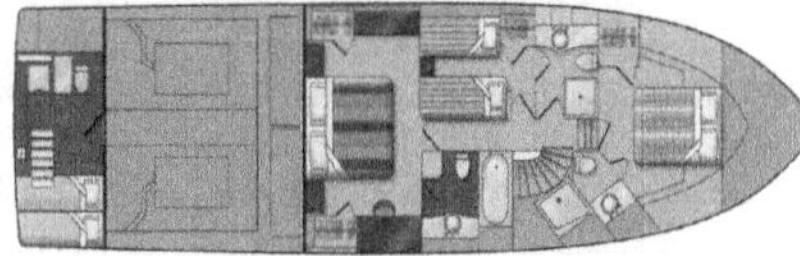

Marketed as a fully equipped, turnkey yacht with few options, the affordable price of the Pacific Mariner 65 was the result of old-fashioned production efficiency; producing the same boat over and over cuts costs. She was built in the state of Washington on a low-deadrise modified-V hull with generous beam, cored hullsides, and a solid fiberglass bottom. The Pacific Mariner isn't a flashy boat—her pilothouse profile is on the conservative side, and she lacks a eurostyle swim platform—but her three-stateroom interior is spacious and quite well appointed. The galley and dinette are forward on the pilothouse level where they're separated from the salon by a built-in entertainment center. The lavish full-beam master suite includes a king-size bed (as well as a tub in the adjoining head), and both guest staterooms have private head access. The engineroom and crew quarters are reached via a hatch in the cockpit sole. On the downside, the side decks are narrow. Note that in 2003 (beginning with hull #37), an upgraded "SE" version incorporates a series of subtle design revisions. A good performer with 800hp Cat (or 825hp MTU) diesels, the Pacific Mariner will cruise at 22 knots and reach 26–27 knots top.

See Page 691 For Price Data

Length	64'11"	Water	285 gals.
Beam	17'3"	Waste	110 gals.
Draft	4'9"	Waste	
Weight	69,000#	Hull Type	Modified-V
Fuel	1,100 gals.	Deadrise Aft	10°

Pacific Seacraft 38T Fast Trawler

1999–2002

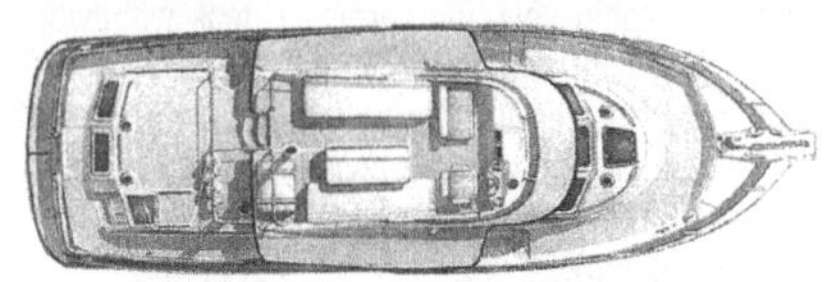

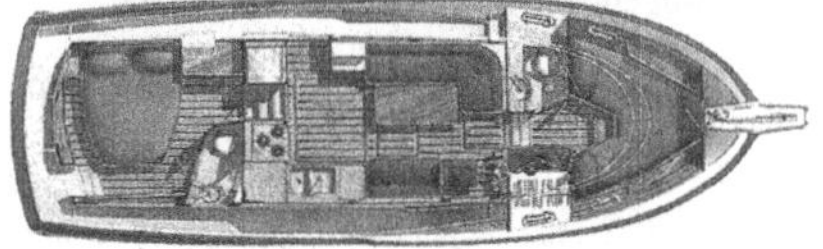

Distinctive styling, an efficient hull, and quality construction characterize the Pacific Seacraft 38T, one of the new breed of "fast trawlers" made popular in recent years by those seeking traditional trawler styling with cruising-speed performance. Pacific Seacraft has long been recognized in the marine industry for their series of sophisticated bluewater sailboats, and the 38T—designed by Bruce King—is an especially handsome and seaworthy yacht. Her luxurious two-stateroom interior is arranged with the galley aft in the salon and an athwartships double berth in the master stateroom. A lower helm is standard, and the built-in salon settee converts into a double berth for extra overnight guests. Topside, the spacious flybridge features guest seating for a small crowd. A unique feature of this yacht is that it offers protected side decks in an aft-cabin configuration. Additional features include a fold-down mast and boom, full teak interior, boarding gates in both gunwales (a thoughtful touch), dual salon deck doors, and a bow pulpit. Not an inexpensive boat during her production years, twin Cat 350hp diesels cruise the Pacific Seacraft 38T at 15–16 knots (about 20 knots top).

See Page 692 For Price Data

Length Overall	37'6"	Fuel	320 gals.
Length WL	33'6"	Water	240 gals.
Beam	13'2"	Waste	55 gals.
Draft	3'11"	Hull Type	Modified-V
Weight	27,000#	Deadrise Aft	14°

Pacific Trawler 40

2000–03

The Pacific Trawler 40 is an enlarged version of the Pacific Trawler 37 introduced in 1997. The added hull length of the 40 allows for increased fuel and water tankage as well as a larger, more expansive salon. Originally, the Pacific Trawler 40 had an open transom with stainless steel railings—an unconventional design that had the cockpit extending out to the end of the swim platform. Twelve of these open transom boats were built until the so-called Closed Transom model, introduced in 2002, replaced the cockpit railings with a conventional transom and lengthened the salon, allowing for the inclusion of a small desk area. The floorplan is somewhat unusual in that the head compartment is opposite the galley rather than forward, next to the stateroom. On deck, a flybridge overhang shelters the cockpit, and molded steps on the starboard-side deck lead to the flybridge. Note that the pilothouse is situated well forward on the deck for improved helm visibility. Additional features include cabintop dinghy storage, twin pilothouse deck doors, bow thruster, and mahogany interior joinery. A single 330hp Cummins diesel will cruise efficiently at 10 knots and reach a top speed of around 15 knots.

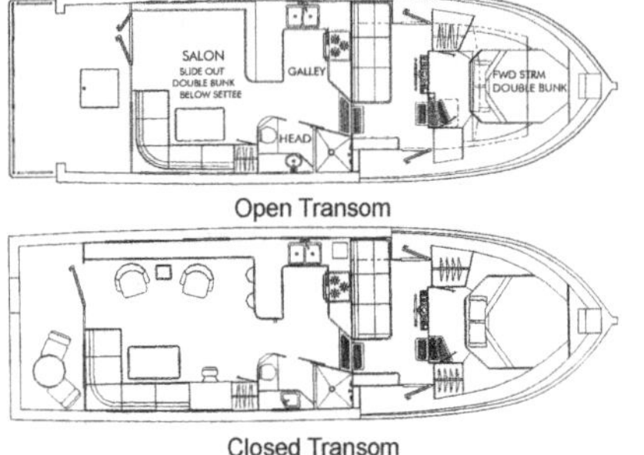

Open Transom

Closed Transom

See Page 692 For Price Data

Length Overall	39'10"	Fuel	465 gals.
Length WL	37'2"	Water	265 gals.
Beam	13'3"	Waste	50 gals.
Draft	4'2"	Clearance	12'6"
Weight	26,000#	Hull Type	Semi-Disp.

Packet Craft Craft 360 Express

2002–05

The Packet Craft 360 was built by sailboat-manufacturer Island Packet Yachts, company with a reputation for high-quality engineering and construction. The 360 Express represents a distinctive blend of classic beauty and traditional cruising elegance. Built on a modified-V hull, deep prop pockets allow the engines to lie almost flat beneath the cockpit sole. The 12-foot beam of the 360 Express—slender compared with many of today's mega-beam designs—makes for an easily driven and notably efficient hull. The bridgedeck (which lifts on hydraulic rams for access to the engines) is arranged with an L-shaped settee opposite the helm, and opening forward and side windows provide plenty of ventilation on hot days. Additional guest seating is found in the cockpit, and wide side decks make foredeck access safe and secure. Belowdecks, a teak-and-holly cabin sole and varnished teak woodwork highlight the 360's elegant single-stateroom interior. A well finished yacht, additional features include an integral swim platform and bow pulpit, eight opening ports, a transom door, and side-dumping exhausts. Twin 370hp Yanmar diesels cruise the Packet Craft in the mid 20s (30 knots top).

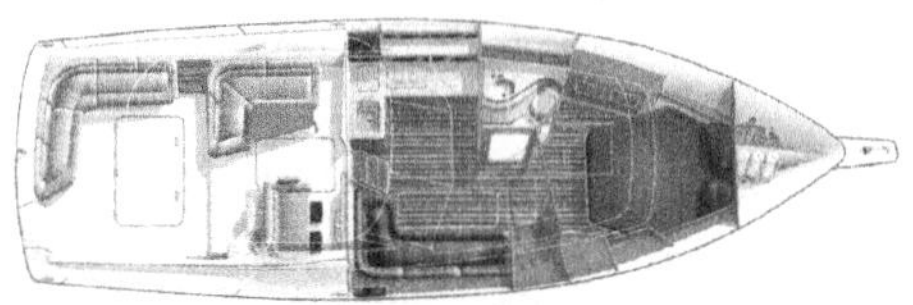

Not Enough Resale Data to Set Values

Length Overall	41'8"	Fuel	300 gals.
Hull Length	38'7"	Water	75 gals.
Beam	12'0"	Waste	30 gals.
Draft	2'8"	Hull Type	Modified-V
Weight	18,000#	Deadrise Aft	14°

PDQ 32/34 Catamaran

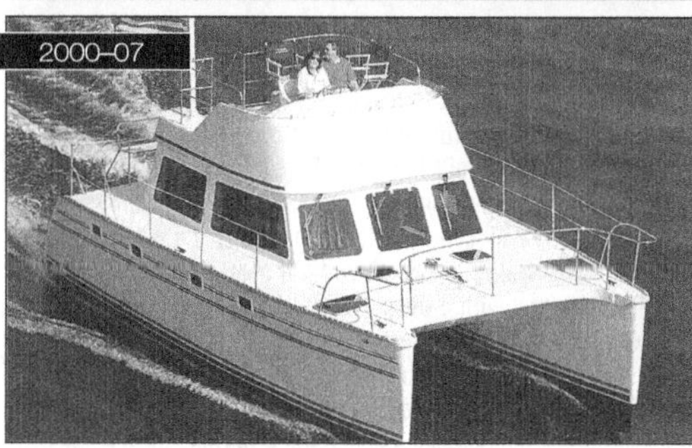

The PDQ 34 (called the PDQ 32 until the hulls were lengthened in 2003) is a very distinctive catamaran trawler whose stable ride and exceptional fuel economy made her a popular boat during her production years. Built in Canada, she's a great choice for cruising enthusiasts looking for an alternative to traditional monohull trawlers. This is a very roomy boat—indeed, there's more usable living space in the PDQ than one expects in a 34-footer. Her two-stateroom layout allows for a huge salon with a U-shaped lounge on the centerline (providing seating for six) and an elevated lower helm aft. The galley is down in the portside hull (the head is forward in the opposite hull), and both staterooms are aft, extending from the hulls under the aft deck. Note the appealing cherry joinery and large cabin windows. Additional features include broad, safe decks for lounging and line handling, a roomy flybridge, protected running gear, and an underwater exhaust system. With her thin hulls, the PDQ 34 cuts through waves without the pounding of a conventional hull. Twin 75hp Yanmar inboard diesels cruise at 13–14 knots (burning only 4 gallons per hour) with a top speed of just under 20 knots.

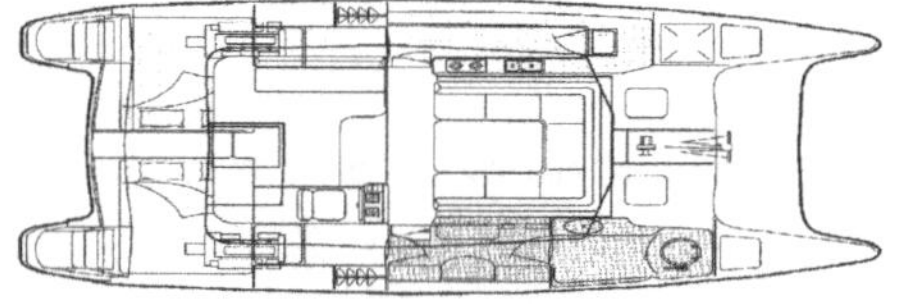

See Page 692 For Price Data

Length Overall	34'6"	Clearance	12'3"
Length WL	33'11"	Fuel	184 gals.
Beam	16'10"	Water	80 gals.
Draft	2'4"	Waste	38 gals.
Weight	12,000#	Hull Type	Catamaran

Pearson True North 33

The Pearson True North 33 is a scaled-down version of the True North 38 Pearson introduced in 2002. Possessing the same Downeast styling as her sibling, the plumb bow, sharply raked transom, and low-profile pilothouse of the True North distinguish her from just about anything else on the water. The tapered hull carries the beam well forward, and the rudder and prop are fully protected by an integral skeg. Note that the transom incorporates a pair of wide "clamshell" doors, which make it possible to lift a dinghy into the cockpit for storage—a feature experienced cruisers are sure to appreciate. The layout of the True North 33 has the galley and dinette on the pilothouse level, which is open to the cockpit, a design that affords the helmsman excellent all-around visibility. (The forward dinette seat can be converted at the touch of a button into a forward-facing bench seat.) Sleeping accommodations and a full-sized head with shower are below, and the level of finish found throughout the interior is impressive in every respect. A relatively light boat for her size, she'll cruise at 20 knots with a single 440hp Yanmar diesel.

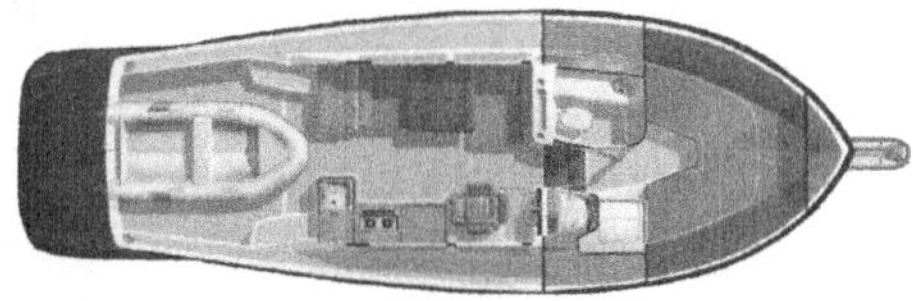

See Page 692 For Price Data

Length	36'2"	Fuel	200 gals.
Beam	12'4"	Water	80 gals.
Draft	3'4"	Waste	25 gals.
Weight	12,500#	Hull Type	Modified-V
Clearance, Mast	11'7"	Deadrise Aft	18°

Pearson True North 38

2002–08

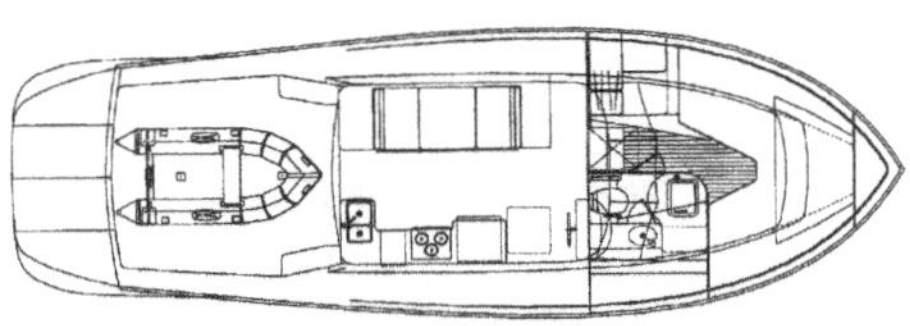

The Pearson True North 38 is one of those rare cases where beauty and practicality seem to merge in perfect harmony. Innovation is an overused term in the yachting industry, but it certainly applies to the True North. Her Downeast styling is unique, and the twin doors built into the 38's reverse transom can open wide enough to haul a dinghy into the cockpit for storage. A life raft, bikes, or kayak can lie atop the hardtop, and extra-wide side decks provide seating space along both sides of the cockpit. Built on high-tech hull with a deep forefoot and skeg-mounted rudder, the deck plan of the True North 38 includes a sliding seat arrangement at the dinette that expands seating from four to six people while also converting to a double berth at night. A "sleeping loft" for young children is located above the V-berths, and the galley is positioned aft in the semi-enclosed pilothouse where it's convenient to the cockpit. (Note that the pilothouse can be fully enclosed with an optional bulkhead and door.) A bow thruster is standard. A single 440hp Yanmar diesel will cruise the True North 38 at 20 knots and reach a top speed of 25–26 knots. Over 100 were built.

See Page 692 For Price Data

Length	38'6"	Fuel	220 gals.
Beam	13'6"	Water	100 gals.
Draft	3'6"	Waste	35 gals.
Weight	15,000#	Hull Type	Modified-V
Clearance	15'5"	Deadrise Aft	12°

Powerplay 33 Sportfish

1998–2003

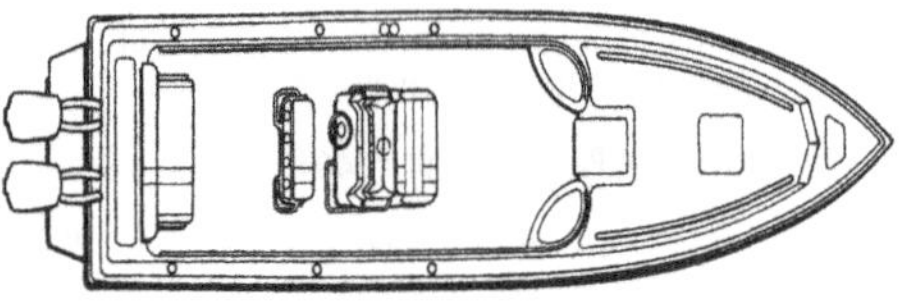

The Powerplay 33 SF is an unabashed go-fast boat rigged for fishing. She is, in fact, a sportfish version of the Powerplay 33 Sport, a championship racing machine with a proven offshore pedigree. Built to exacting standards using high-tech materials and state-of-the-art construction techniques, the 33 Sportfish rides on a slender deep-V hull, and her performance is about as much as any nonprofessional driver would care to deal with. One of the longer center consoles available, there's plenty of cockpit space fore and aft of the console in spite of the narrow 8-foot, 4-inch beam. Fishing amenities include a 40-gallon livewell, two rod lockers, and tackle storage. Side-by-side bolster seats are fitted at the helm, and a two-person bench seat is forward of the console. The utilitarian cuddy cabin has an 8-foot V-berth and a portable head. Additional features include an insulated cooler, a first-rate helm layout, anchor locker and Imron hull graphics. Not inexpensive (most were custom built), a pair of 415hp 8.2-liter MerCruiser gas sterndrives reach a top speed of around 60 knots, and twin 250hp outboards deliver a top speed in the neighborhood of 50 knots.

See Page 692 For Price Data

Length	32'7"	Clearance	5'9"
Beam	8'4"	Fuel	250 gals.
Hull Draft	1'0"	Headroom	4'7"
Dry Weight	2,980#	Hull Type	Deep-V
Weight with I/Os	7,400#	Deadrise Aft	24°

San Juan 38

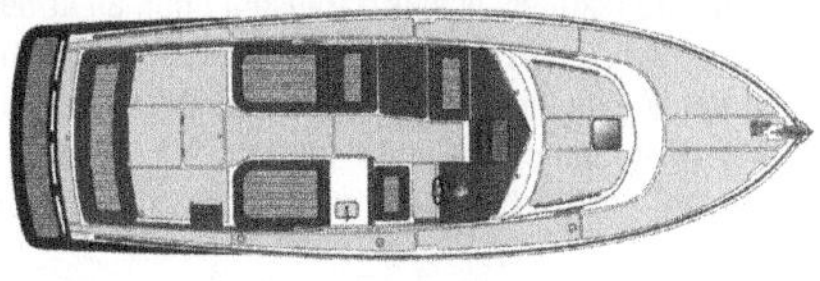

The San Juan 38 is a Downeast-inspired runabout with an impressive blend of beautiful styling, state-of-the-art hull construction, and luxurious accommodations. Her sophisticated, foam-cored hull is vacuum-bagged, and the use of Kevlar in the construction process greatly increases strength and impact resistance. The heart of the San Juan 38 is her semi-enclosed pilothouse with its 360-degree visibility, convertible dinette, and elegant teak helm station. Port and starboard sun pads, extending aft into the cockpit, lift to provide excellent service access to the engines. Belowdecks, the San Juan's traditional two-stateroom interior is richly appointed with varnished teak cabinetry, faux granite counters, and a teak-and-holly sole. The layout has a V-berth forward and a queen berth amidships, abaft the companionway stairs. The arched doorways are notable, as are the quality fabrics and hardware. Additional features include a transom seat, bow thruster, custom drop curtain, wet bar, and teak exterior trim. A lightweight boat for her size, Yanmar 350hp diesel inboards cruise the San Juan 38 in the mid 20s and reach a top speed of close to 30 knots.

Not Enough Resale Data to Set Values

Length Overall	40'7"	Fuel	300 gals.
Beam	12'2"	Waste	80 gals.
Draft	2'2"	Waste	15 gals.
Weight	15,800#	Hull Type	Modified-V
Clearance	9'11"	Deadrise Aft	14°

Seacraft 32 Center Console

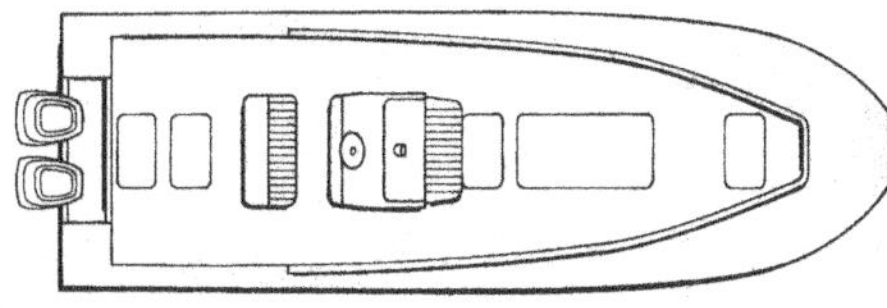

A name still revered among serious anglers for their hardcore center consoles of the 1970s and '80s, the original SeaCraft company went out of business in 1986 after a series of management changes. Revived in 1996 by the Tracker Marine conglomerate, the beautifully finished SeaCraft 32 preserves the classic, notched-transom look of her predecessors as well as the unique SeaCraft hull bottom with its longitudinal steps replacing the lifting strakes common to most deep-Vs. The 32 is a big boat with room for several anglers to fish with relative freedom. The helm console has space for a marine head inside, and there's a huge 80-gallon in-deck livewell just forward of the transom. An optional dry storage/coffin box (see picture above) includes a second live well forward and lifts on a hydraulic ram to expose a cavernous storage area belowdecks. Note that the steering wheel is on the console centerline rather than offset to one side, an unusual arrangement. Note also that there's a pump room in the lazarette forward of the livewell—very professional. Additional features include a leaning post, recessed bow rails, console electronics box, and an in-deck brine tank. Twin 250hp Mercs reach close to 40 knots wide open.

See Page 700 For Price Data

Length	32'0"	Fuel	300 gals.
Beam	9'6"	Water	30 gals.
Draft, Up	1'6"	Max HP	600
Draft, Down	2'8"	Hull Type	Modified-V
Dry Weight	7,000#	Deadrise Aft	20°

Shamrock 270 Mackinaw

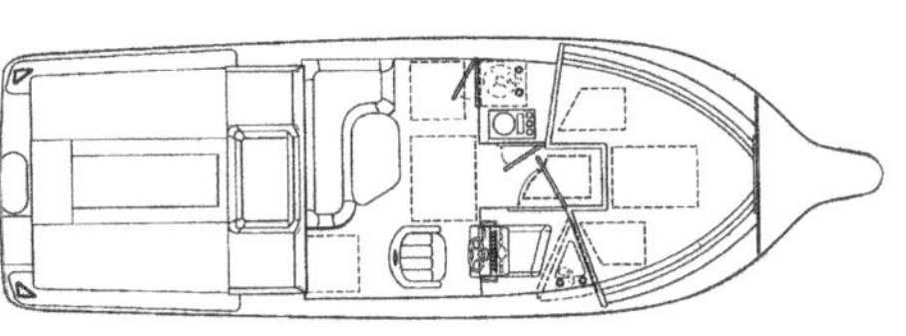

Shamrock's 270 Mackinaw is a durable, single-engine inboard cruiser with a fully enclosed pilothouse and a large fishing cockpit. This is a boat ideally suited for northern anglers and cruisers alike, and she's in a class by herself since there are no other production inboard boats of her type on the market. Unlike smaller Shamrock models, the 270 forgoes their famous "Keel Drive" for a more conventional modified-V hull bottom with a prop pocket to reduce the draft and shaft angle. With only 27 feet to work with, the Mackinaw's interior is practical but necessarily confining. The cabin contains a small galley as well as a dinette with a removable table and a fully equipped helm station to starboard. A V-berth below sleeps two comfortably, but the enclosed head is very small with only sitting headroom. The cockpit has aft-facing bench seating, and standard features include a transom door, an in-deck fish box, transom livewell, opening cabin windows and a bow pulpit. A swim platform is a popular option. Heavily built and well finished, the 270 Mackinaw will cruise at 18 knots with a standard 320hp gas engine and reach a top speed of around 30 knots. Close to 100 were built.

See Page 700 For Price Data

Length w/Pulpit	30'6"	Weight	7,525#
Hull Length	28'10"	Fuel	156 gals.
Beam	9'3"	Water	20 gals.
Draft	2'5"	Hull Type	Modified-V
Clearance	8'2"	Deadrise Aft	14°

Shamrock 290 Walkaround

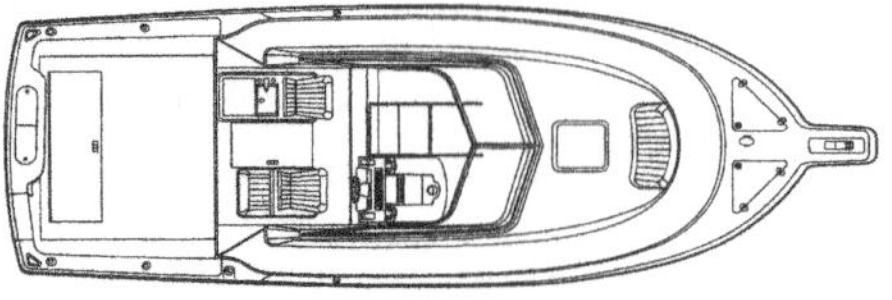

Introduced in 1999, the Shamrock 290 Walkaround is a handsome deep-V fisherman whose rugged construction and large, well-equipped cockpit will appeal to serious anglers. No lightweight, the 290 offers a solid ride in a chop, and wide side decks make her a true 360-degree fishing platform. Fishing amenities include a 38-gallon livewell, a rigging station with tackle storage behind the passenger seat, a big in-deck insulated fish box with macerator, raw- and freshwater washdowns, coaming bolsters, rod holders, under-gunwale rod storage, and a transom door—all standard. The helm station, located on the centerline, has a tilt-away console and room for flush-mounting an array of electronics. Below, the roomy interior of the Shamrock 290 comes as a real surprise considering her wide side decks. An offset double berth is forward; the settee converts into upper and lower berths; the galley is opposite the settee, and a roomy head compartment with shower is aft. For engine access, the entire bridge deck lifts on hydraulic rams. A well-finished boat, a pair of 300hp inboard gas engines cruise the 290 Walkaround in the low-to-mid 20s and reach a top speed in excess of 30 knots.

See Page 700 For Price Data

Length w/Pulpit	30'10"	Clearance, Top	10'5"
Hull Length	28'10"	Fuel	250 gals.
Beam	11'3"	Water	30 gals.
Draft	2'10"	Hull Type	Deep-V
Weight	10,500#	Deadrise Aft	19°

Shannon 36 Voyager

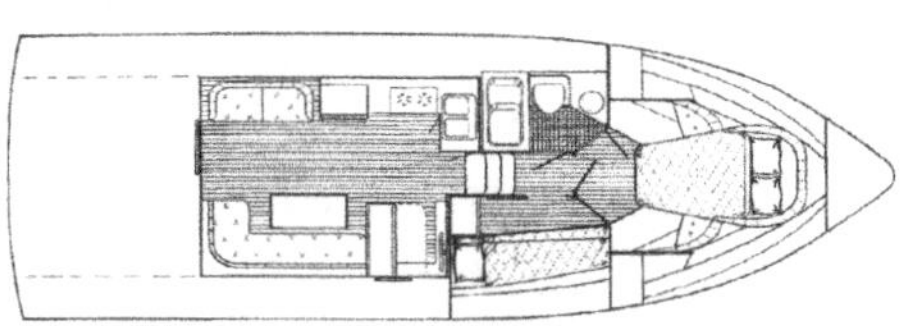

While she may look a little like a trawler, the Shannon 36 is built on a planing hull with the power to cruise efficiently at faster speeds than traditional, semi-displacement trawlers (Grand Banks, Inland Gypsy, etc.). The modified-V hull of the Shannon, which is fully cored and very light, is quick to plane, and her fine entry and well-flared bow make for a comfortable, dry ride in a chop. The two-stateroom, galley-up teak interior features a lower helm station and built-in dinette in the salon, a sit-down shower in the head, and a queen bed in the forward stateroom. A hatch in the salon sole provides access to the engines. Like all trawler-style boats, the Shannon's salon dimensions are somewhat limited thanks to her wide side decks. The cockpit is very large with room for a small crowd. Topside, the flybridge will seat siand includes a wet bar and cocktail table. Additional features include a teak parquet cabin sole, radar mast, wide side decks, and a bow pulpit. Built on a semi-custom basis, a pair of 300hp Cat 3126 diesels will provide a cruising speed of 18 knots and a top speed in the low-to-mid 20s

Not Enough Resale Data to Set Values

Length w/Pulpit	38'3"	Clearance	12'6"
Hull Length	35'7"	Fuel	350 gals.
Beam	13'3"	Water	150 gals.
Draft	3'0"	Hull Type	Modified-V
Weight	17,500#	Deadrise Aft	13°

Skipjack 262 Flybridge

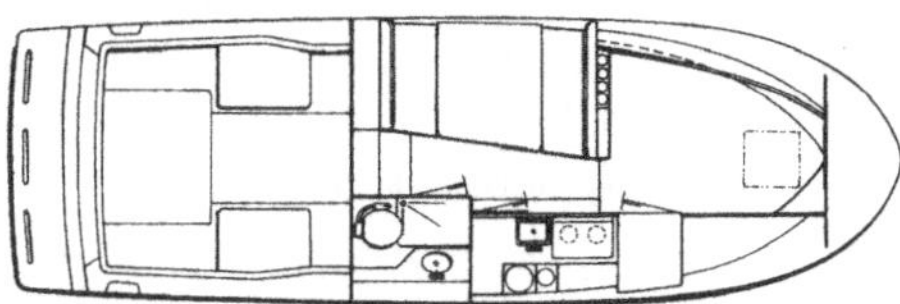

The Skipjack 26 is a sturdy, well-built West Coast fisherman designed to satisfy the needs of anglers seeking a trailerable, offshore-capable design. There are just a handful of flybridge models (from any manufacturer) in this size range; the added topside weight of a flybridge—combined with a narrow beam—often results in a very tender boat. The Skipjack avoids this problem by using a small bridge and a low-profile deckhouse to provide sufficient stability for open-water cruising. Heavily built on a solid fiberglass hull and well finished throughout, there are basic accommodations for four in the oak-trimmed cabin which includes a small galley, dinette, an enclosed head with shower, and adequate storage. The cockpit, with about 60 square feet of open space, is roomy enough for two anglers, and a large hatch in the sole provides easy access to the engine. Additional features include twin bucket seats on the bridge, a full fiberglass cabin liner, fairly wide side decks, storage lockers, and a swim platform. Among several engine options offered over the years, a single 280hp Volvo gas sterndrive will cruise at 25–26 knots and reach a top speed of close to 30 knots.

See Page 702 For Price Data

Hull Length	26'0"	Fuel	160 gals.
Length w/Pulpit	29'0"	Water	40 gals.
Beam	8'6"	Waste	15 gals.
Draft	30"	Hull Type	Modified-V
Weight	6,000#	Deadrise Aft	18°

Southport 28 Center Console

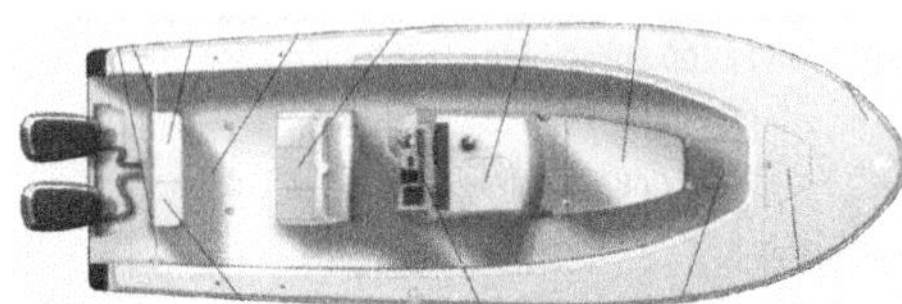

By any standard, the Southport 28 delivers the quality and performance one expects in a tournament-level center console. Introduced in 2005, she was specifically designed for the then-new heavyweight four-stroke outboards. From the mirror-like gelcoat on the outside to the state-of-the art construction materials on the inside, the 28 compares well with top-tier competitors like Pursuit, Regulator, Grady-White, and Boston Whaler. With a wide 10'6" beam, the Southport is one of the roomier 28-footers around with enough storage and high-end fishing features to satisfy the most demanding anglers. Highlights include a 157-gallon coffin box forward (which doubles as lounge seating), a 38-gallon lift-out fishbox aft, 45-gallon oval livewell, and a transom rigging station with sink and pullout shower. A leaning post, windlass, and custom T-top were standard, and gimbal-mounted rod stowage is located in the spacious head. Note that the rigging area is lighted by red LED lights for nighttime fishing. Twin Yamaha 225s top out at over 40 knots, while the larger Yamaha 250s deliver a top speed of 45+ knots. Used models aren't cheap, but it's doubtful you'll find a better built 28-footer at any price.

See Page 702 For Price Data

Length	28'6"	Fuel	250 gals.
Beam	10'6"	Water	NA
Draft, Up	1'7"	Max HP	700
Draft, Down	2'10"	Hull Type	Deep-V
Hull Weight	5,800#	Deadrise Aft	22°

Tides 27

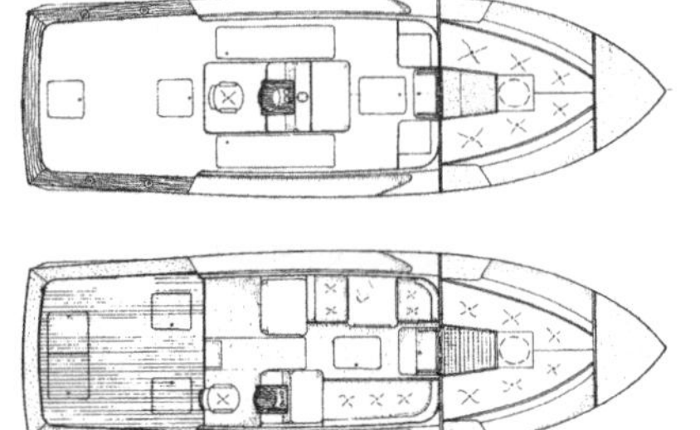

With her flared bow and stylish helm console, the Tides 27 has the appearance of a custom-built, high-dollar dayboat. She's one of a handful of inboard center consoles in this size range, and while not as fast as some outboard-powered boats her size, the reliability, range, and economy of inboard power will appeal to experienced anglers. Hull construction is solid fiberglass, and the builder promoted its ability to custom-build each boat to an owner's requirements. Offered in a center console layout, twin-engine installations can be set up with dual consoles or a raised-deck center console layout. Fishing amenities include a livewell at the transom, a built-in bait-prep station, fresh- and saltwater washdowns, and two in-deck fish boxes. The forward cabin offers a V-berth, hanging locker, rod storage, and a concealed head. Note that the Tides 27 was available in both inboard (gas or diesel) and bracket-mounted outboard versions. A single 300hp Cat (or Cummins) diesel will cruise in the mid 20s, and twin 170hp Yanmar diesels cruise at 25 knots (about 30 knots top). No longer in productiont, the Tides 27 was custom-built in later years by Tides Boatworks in Sarasota, Florida.

Not Enough Resale Data to Set Values

Length	27'6"	Water	20 gals.
Beam	9'6"	Clearance	NA
Draft	1'11"	Cockpit	70 sq. ft.
Weight	8,500#	Hull Type	Modified-V
Fuel	180 gals.	Deadrise Aft	16°

Topaz 32/33 Express

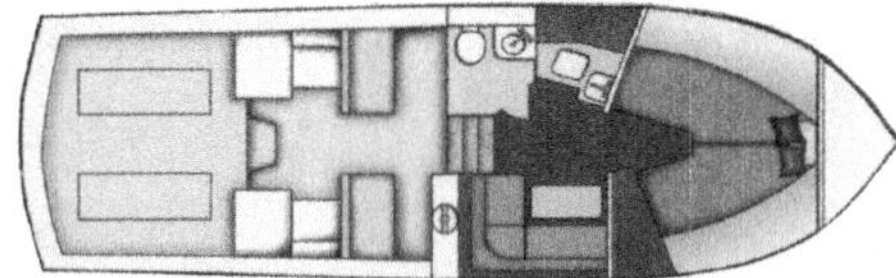

The Topaz 33 Express (called the Topaz 32 Express in 2004–06) is an updated version of the original Topaz 32 Sportfisherman built from 1986 to 1991. While the two boats share the same basic hull design, the newer model incorporates modifications to the running surface aimed at reducing the bow-high running angles that plagued her predecessor. The two boats share little in the way of appearance—the 32/33 Express has a semicustom look that blows away the old 32 SF. Too, the bridge deck sits several inches higher than in the old model. This not only makes for a larger engine compartment, it dramatically improves helm visibility as well. The cockpit includes such standard features as a raw-water washdown, large-capacity macerated fish box, three-tray tackle box, and a bait freezer/tackle station. Note the clean transom—with the fish box located in the sole and the livewell positioned forward, the entire stern is open for fishing. Below decks, the teak-trimmed cabin includes a large berth forward, a dinette that folds into a second berth, fully enclosed head, and rod storage over the main berth. No lightweight, the 32/33 Express cruise at 25–26 knots with 370hp Cummins diesels (about 30 knots top).

See Page 704 For Price Data

Length	32'8"	Headroom	6'3"
Beam	12'2"	Fuel	400 gals.
Draft	3'1"	Water	40 gals.
Weight	20,500#	Hull Type	Modified-V
Clearance	NA	Deadrise Aft	18°

Topaz 40 Express

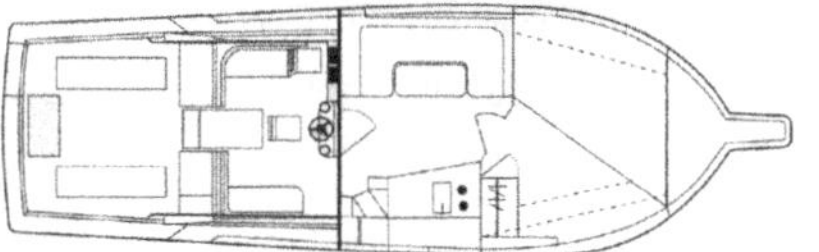

With her graceful lines and flared bow, the Topaz 40 Express ranks with the best-looking express fishing boats in her class. She was introduced in 2005, the same year Egg Harbor acquired the Topaz name and brought the brand back into production. Designed to compete in the offshore tournament wars, the 13-foot beam of the Topaz 40 is modest indeed compared with competitive express boats like the Cabo 40 (15'9" beam), Luhrs 38/40 (14'11"), or even the Ocean 40 (14'2"). That said, less beam translates into greater hull efficiency that, in turn, results in better fuel economy—no small consideration in today's era of high fuel costs. The layout of the Topaz 40 features a center helm with flanking settees on the bridge deck that, like most express boats, lifts on hydraulic rams for engine access. Standard cockpit amenities include a bait prep center with sink, two macerated fish boxes, fresh and raw water washdowns, livewell, and transom door with lift gate. Below decks, the original teak-trimmed interior has V-berths forward, a large head with separate stall shower, and a convertible dinette. Newer models have a private stateroom forward with an offset double berth. Cat 715hp C-12 engines cruise at 30 knots (mid 30s top).

See Page 704 For Price Data

Length	41'6"	Fuel	600 gals.
Beam	13'0"	Water	60 gals.
Draft	3'6"	Waste	15 gals.
Weight	30,400#	Hull Type	Modified-V
Clearance	NA	Deadrise Aft	NA

Triton 2895 Center Console

2004–07

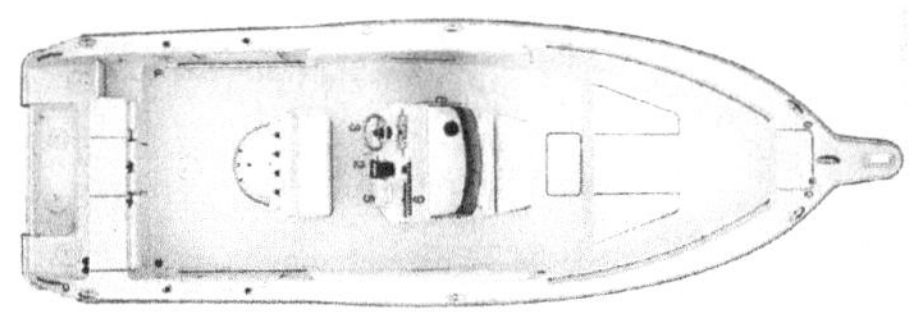

The Triton 2895 is an extremely well laid out center console whose rugged construction and impressive list of standard features are sure to appeal to both hard core anglers and fishing families alike. Triton builds a good boat: The company's fiberglass and aluminum bass boats are top sellers in the freshwater fishing world, and their series of saltwater center consoles and walkarounds are equally well regarded throughout the industry. Built on a solid fiberglass deep-hull with moderate beam and a fully integrated transom, a step in the bottom about two-thirds back from the bow provides increased lift. The roomy cockpit of the 2895 boasts plenty of storage space for tackle and boating gear. Highlights include a two-person leaning post with built-in 50-gallon livewell, 21-gallon transom livewell, forward console seat, pop-up cleats, raw water washdown, and transom door. The walk-in console features an enclosed head with holding tank and 5'8" head room, and the forward casting platform includes ample storage underneath. Recessed bow rails mean no snagged lines. An impressive rough-water performer, twin Honda 225s deliver a top speed of 45 knots.

See Page 704 For Price Data

Length w/Pulpit	29'10"	Fuel	204 gals.
Beam	9'5"	Water	18 gals.
Draft, Up	1'9"	Max HP	500
Draft, Down	3'0"	Hull Type	Deep-V
Hull Weight	5,300#	Deadrise Aft	20°

Triton 351 Center Console

2005–10

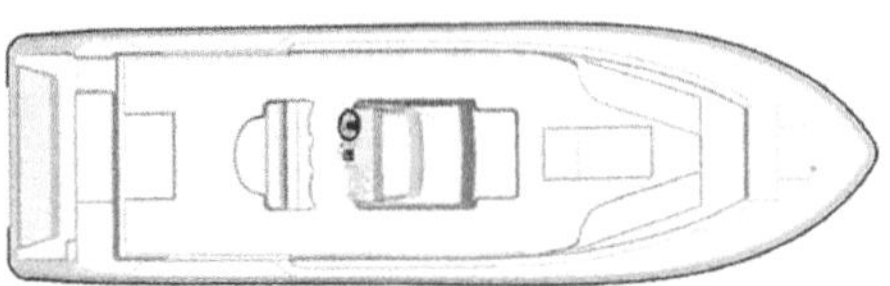

The Triton 351 is a heavily built center console built to handle the added weight and power of today's four-stroke outboards. Triton builds a good boat: Their fiberglass and aluminum bass boats are top sellers in the freshwater fishing world, and Triton's series of saltwater fishing boats is well regarded throughout the industry. Introduced in 2005, the Triton 351 rides on a solid fiberglass deep-V hull with moderate beam and an aggressive 24 degrees of transom deadrise. Triton uses no wood in the 351, relying instead on composite unibody construction with hand-laid-up hull and foam-filled stringers. A single-level deck makes it easy to get around, and the large (tilt-up) console has enough space at the helm to install two 15-inch displays. Highlights include a triple helm seat with 50-gallon livewell, 21-gallon transom livewell, transom storage box, lockable rod lockers (2), foldaway rear seat, fender storage, and a forward fish box with macerator. A cockpit hatch provides easy access to the bilge. With 355 gallons of fuel capacity, the 351 has a range of 350–350 nautical miles at cruising speed. A fast ride, triple 275hp Verados deliver a top end of close to 50 knots.

See Page 704 For Price Data

Length	34'10"	Fuel	355 gals.
Beam	10'0"	Water	20 gals.
Draft, Up	2'0"	Max HP	1,050
Draft, Down	3'0"	Hull Type	Deep-V
Hull Weight	8,352#	Deadrise Aft	24°

Trophy 2802 Walkaround

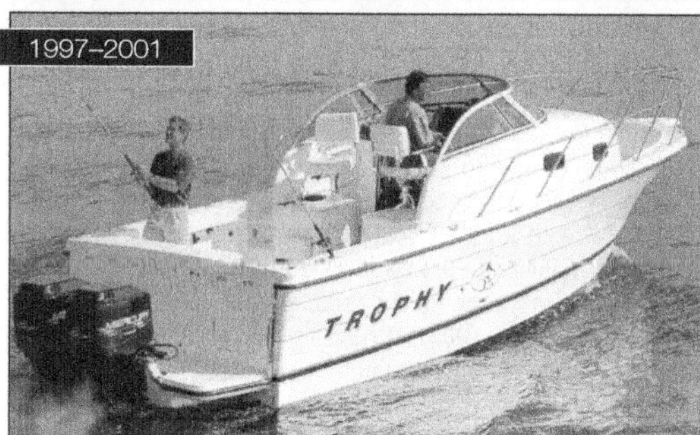

1997–2001

The Trophy 2802 is an affordably priced walkaround fisherman whose durable construction and traditional lines will appeal to budget-minded anglers seeking a capable, entry-level fishing boat. Thanks to a relatively wide 9-foot, 9-inch beam, the Trophy is a roomy boat with plenty of cockpit space as well as a comfortable cuddy cabin. Unlike many outboard-powered fishermen her size, the 2802 has a full-height transom so anglers will have no concern about flooding the cockpit when backing down hard on a fish. Note that the cockpit is quite deep—so deep, in fact, that the bolster pads on the coaming strike tall anglers at mid-thigh. A transom door was standard, and a pair of fold-down jump seats at the forward end of the cockpit are useful for watching the baits. A raised bait-prep station was also standard along with storage lockers, tackle drawers, and rod storage under the coaming. Below, the efficient cabin features an enclosed standup head, a small galley to port, and a convertible U-shaped settee forward. There's also a pilot berth aft, under the raised bridge deck. Twin 175hp outboards cruise the Trophy 2802 at 22–23 knots and deliver a top speed in the mid 30s.

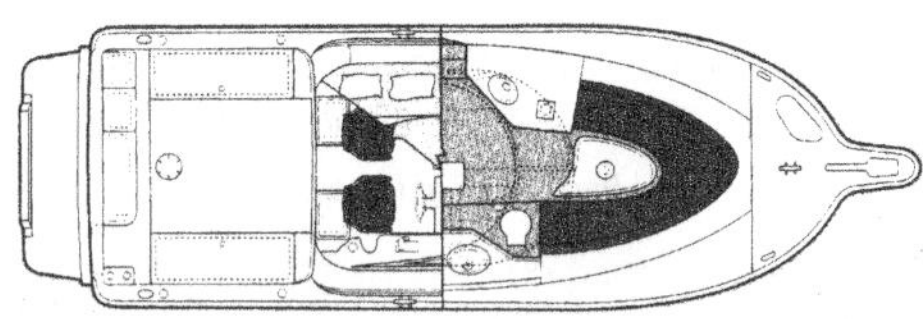

See Page 704 For Price Data

Length	31'0"	Fuel	240 gals.
Beam	9'9"	Water	30 gals.
Draft, Up	1'3"	Max HP	450
Draft, Down	2'6"	Hull Type	Modified-V
Dry Weight	7,394#	Deadrise Aft	19°

Trophy 2902 Walkaround

2003–09

Trophy's largest model, the 2902 Walkaround is a well-conceived fishing boat whose versatile layout and low cost make her an appealing choice for budget-minded anglers. The Trophy weighs in at just over 8,500 pounds which makes her a middleweight for boats her size. A full transom and bracket-mounted outboards allow the Trophy to maximize cockpit space, and deep walkways provide secure foredeck access. An overhead electronics box and a rocket launcher come with the optional hardtop, and a bimini top was standard. Below, the compact cabin offers near-standing headroom, convertible dinette/V-berth, galley with stove, sink, and icebox, and a mid-berth under the entryway steps. An enclosed head with pumpout toilet was standard. Storage for tackle and miscellaneous gear is plentiful. Back in the cockpit, visibility from the helm is excellent in all directions. Additional features include recessed trim tabs, bow pulpit, transom door, generous rod storage, Armstrong engine bracket with swim ladder, twin fish boxes, and a bait-prep station with cutting board. Twin 225hp Mercury outboards will deliver a top speed in excess of 35 knots.

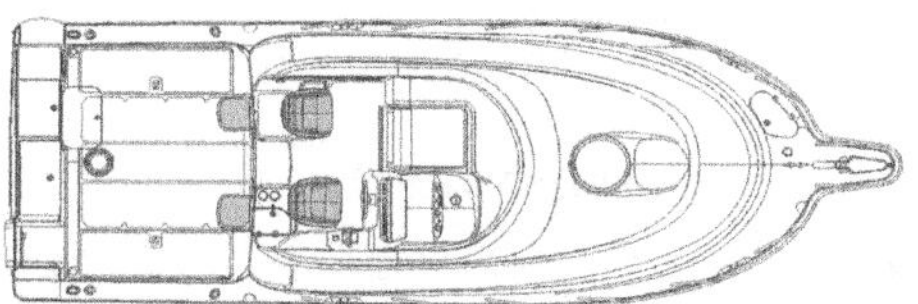

See Page 704 For Price Data

Length w/Pulpit	31'5"	Fuel	218 gals.
Beam	9'9"	Water	30 gals.
Draft, Up	2'0"	Max HP	500
Draft, Down	2'10"	Hull Type	Modified-V
Weight w/OB	8,200#	Deadrise Aft	19°

True World TE288

Originally designed for commercial tuna fishing, the True World TE288 is a single-diesel hardtop express whose sterndrive/jackshaft power system offers an economical alternative to the many outboard-powered fishing boats in this size range. The TE288 is a pure fishing boat, not a crossover design loaded with cruising amenities. Built on a solid fiberglass hull with a flared bow and moderate beam, the semi-enclosed helm and super-wide side decks of the TE288 are two of her more notable characteristics. Cockpit features include under-gunwale rod holders, two in-deck fish boxes, leaning post with rocket launchers, and a 28-gallon transom livewell. Note the transom storage compartments. Below, the no-frills cabin features a dinette/V-berth, mini-galley, and standup head with shower. On the downside, the pilothouse superstructure impairs helm visibility. The TE 288's amidships engine location lowers the boat's center of gravity for improved balance and low-speed stability. No racehorse, cruise at 22–23 knots with a Yanmar 315hp diesel (and Bravo III outdrive) burning just 6–7 gallons per hour.

Floorplan Not Available

See Page 704 For Price Data

Length w/Pulpit	29'6"	Clearance	8'8"
Hull Length	28'0"	Fuel	130 gals.
Beam	9'3"	Water	15 gals.
Draft	1'8"	Hull Type	Modified-V
Weight	6,800#	Deadrise Aft	18°

Venture 34 Open

Big center consoles like the Venture 34 are the domain of serious anglers who want a no-frills, high-performance fishing platform capable of getting well offshore and back in the least amount of time. Among the ranks of these large, deep-V center consoles, the Venture stands apart for her handsome lines and heavy, state-of-the-art construction. Her solid fiberglass hull bottom is reinforced with Kevlar; the vacuum-bagged hullsides are cored with PVC foam; and the transom is cored with a high-strength ceramic compound rather than plywood. Standard fishing amenities include a huge 55-gallon transom livewell, two insulated fish boxes forward, bait prep center with fresh and salt water washdowns, and a transom door and gate. On each side of the console are in-deck storage boxes, and a massive storage area with an overboard drain is behind the leaning post. A well-designed wraparound helm keeps the electronics and controls within easy reach. The Venture's walk-in console includes a standup head with shower and sink. (Note that a cuddy version was also available.) A fast ride, twin 250hp outboards deliver a top speed of around 45 knots.

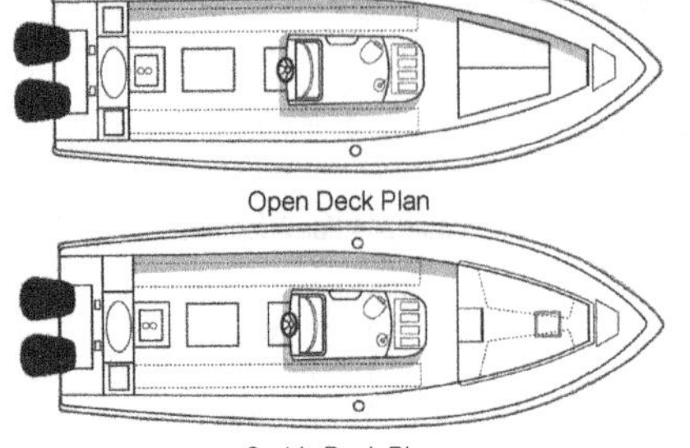

Open Deck Plan

Cuddy Deck Plan

See Page 704 For Price Data

Length	34'0'	Fuel	300 gals.
Beam	10'0"	Water	55 gals.
Draft, Up	1'9"	Max HP	600
Draft, Down	2'4"	Hull Type	Deep-V
Weight	6,400#	Deadrise Aft	24°

West Bay 58 SonShip

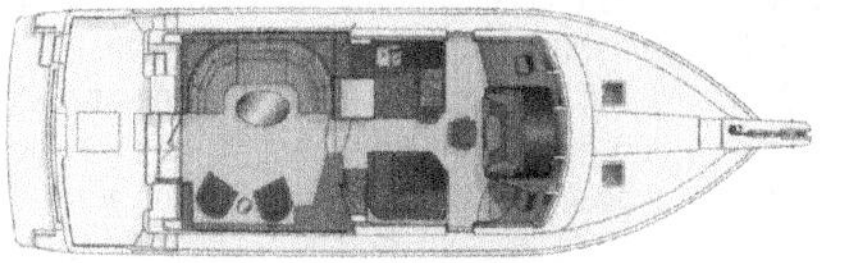

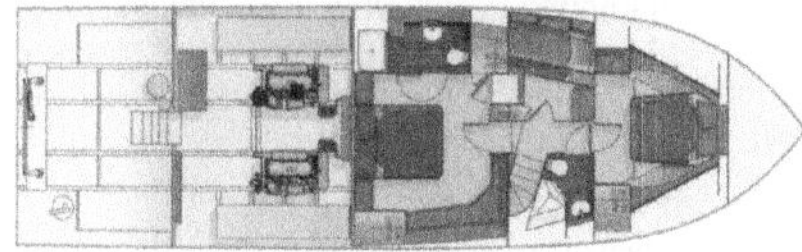

West Bay's most popular model, the 58 Sonship is a classic blend of modern pilothouse styling, luxurious accommodations, and sophisticated, world-class construction. A total of 87 (!) were delivered during her production years, and she remains among the most highly regarded yachts in her size range ever produced. Built in British Columbia on a modified-V hull with Airex coring, prop pockets, and underwater exhausts, the wide 17-foot beam of the 58 Sonship allows for an exceptionally roomy open-plan interior with accommodations for six in three staterooms. Highlights include a tastefully furnished salon with large U-shaped sofa and hidden entertainment center, extended pilothouse with full-service galley and dinette, full-beam master stateroom with walkaround queen berth, and a standup engineroom with cockpit access. Light oak, cherry, or maple interior joinery were available. Note the lazarette storage area under the cockpit sole. The Sonship's full walkaround side decks are a plus as is the spacious flybridge with its combined wet bar/grill and comfortable lounge seating. Twin 660hp Cats cruise at 18 knots (22 top), and optional 820hp MANs—or 800hp Cats—cruise at 22 knots (mid 20s top).

Not Enough Resale Data to Set Values

Length w/Pulpit	63'6"	Fuel	1,000 gals.
Hull Length	59'6"	Water	260 gals.
Beam	17'1"	Waste	95 gals.
Draft	4'10"	Clearance	14'0"
Weight	62,000#	Hull Type	Modified-V

West Bay 78 SonShip

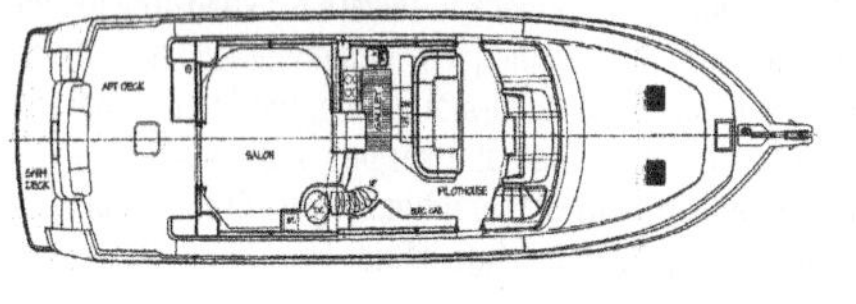

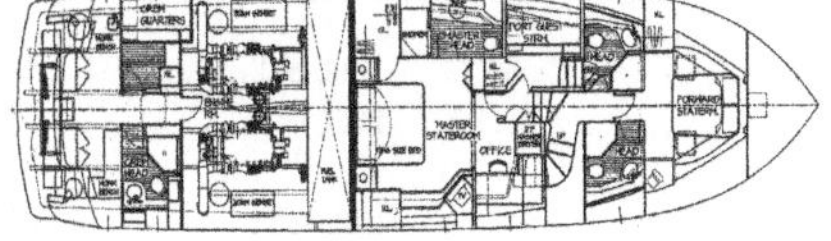

With her muscular pilothouse styling and luxury-class accommodations, the West Bay 78 SonShip exudes a sophisticated elegance seldom surpassed in the world of semicustom motoryachts. Built in the Canadian Northwest, the 78 became a popular model for West Bay following her introduction as a 75-footer in 1998. Stretched to her current length in 2000, several floorplan variations were available during her production years. The standard three-stateroom layout has the galley to port on the pilothouse level, separated from the salon by a full-height bulkhead. Forward of the galley is a raised settee with a spectacular view through the pilothouse windows. Each stateroom on the lower level is served by an en-suite head, and an office in the full-beam master can easily be configured as a fourth stateroom. Crew quarters are aft, accessed from a watertight door on the swim platform. The covered afterdeck is particularly spacious, and the flybridge comes with a barbecue, refreshment center, and an optional Jacuzzi. The engineroom contains a workbench and provides good access to the motors. Among several engine choices, 1,500hp MTUs cruise the 78 Sonship at 23 knots (mid to high 20s top).

Not Enough Resale Data to Set Values

Length w/Pulpit	81'6"	Fuel	2,750 gals.
Hull Length	78'0"	Water	600 gals.
Beam	20'0"	Waste	200 gals.
Draft	5'0"	Hull Type	Modified-V
Weight	110,000#	Deadrise Aft	16°

Willard 30/4 Trawler

1976–2002

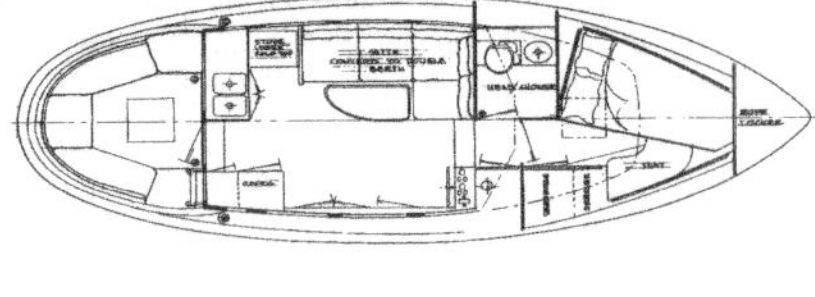

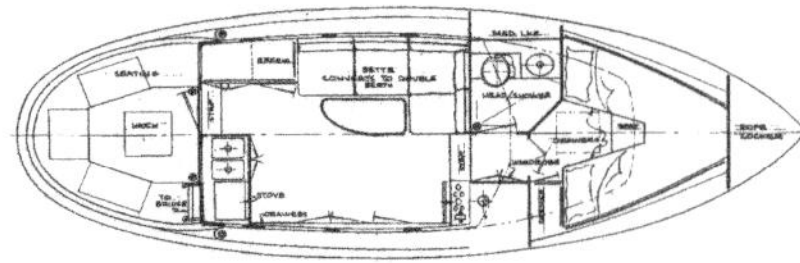

The Willard 30 is a salty-looking small trawler with a true displacement hull and a ballasted keel. A little topheavy in appearance, her classic double-ended hull and relatively heavy displacement provide a secure and comfortable ride in a variety of sea conditions. With only 30 feet, 6 inches of length overall, the Willard offers a surprising amount of interior space for her size. Several floorplans have been used over the years, the latest featuring a double berth in the stateroom. The lower helm is standard, of course, and the salon can best be described as cozy. Never a full production boat (none were built from 1982–87), the updated Willard 30 built since 1988 features a direct-drive engine (replacing the V-drive of previous models) and internal lead ballast rather than external cast iron. With a 50hp Perkins (or 56hp Yanmar) diesel, the efficiency of the Willard 30 is truly phenomenal—at 6 knots, she's actually burning less than 1 gallon per hour! With only 150 gallons of fuel, her average cruising range is still over 1,000 nautical miles. About 40 of these boats are reported to have been built during her production years

Not Enough Resale Data to Set Values

Length Overall	30'0"	Ballast	4,300#
Length WL	27'6"	Fuel	150 gals.
Beam	10'6"	Water	100 gals.
Draft	3'6"	Waste	25 gals.
Weight	17,000#	Hull Type	Displacement

Yellowfin 31

2001–07

Floorplan Not Available

There are many high-performance 30-foot-plus center consoles on the used market these days, but few combine the high-tech construction and advanced hull design of the Yellowfin 31. Built on a fully cored stepped hull with a keel pad, the Yellowfin 31 is quick to accelerate and fast across the water, even when the going gets rough. In a departure from most big center consoles, the transom bulkhead is fitted with rod holders rather than a livewell. (A huge 60-gallon in-deck livewell is standard, and a second 30-gallon abovedeck livewell was optional.) The Yellowfin's deck layout is notable for its practical design and generous storage. The T-top is ideally suited for easy control of outriggers, and there's plenty of space for flush-mounting electronics at the helm. Forward, a giant in-deck fish box measures a full five feet in length. Additional features include pop-up deck hardware for snag-free fishing, high-performance K-Plane trim tabs, coaming bolster pads from the console aft, enclosed head/storage compartment, and a transom door. A favorite of guides and serious anglers alike, the Yellowfin 31 is a notably weight-efficient boat. Twin 250hp Suzuki outboards will deliver a top speed of 50+ knots.

See Page 707 For Price Data

Length	30'11"	Fuel, Std.	225 gals.
Beam	9'6"	Fuel, Opt.	300 gals.
Draft, Up	1'6"	Max HP	600
Draft, Down	3'0"	Hull Type	Deep-V
Dry Weight	4,550#	Deadrise Aft	22°

About The Prices

Retail high/low values are provided for boats built since 1995 except in those cases where limited resale activity makes it impossible to develop a reliable estimate. The prices are estimates only and are not meant to represent precise market values. They apply from the fall of 2013 to the fall of 2014.

The "Retail High" is the estimated selling price of a clean, well-maintained boat with average equipment. The "Retail Low" is the estimated selling price of a boat showing below-average maintenance, limited equipment, and high-hour engines.

The prices quoted here apply to boats found in the Florida, East Coast, and Gulf Coast markets. Prices for boats located in other regions should be adjusted as follows:

Great Lakes .... Add 10 to 15%
California & Pacific Northwest .... Add 5 to 10%
Inland Rivers & Lakes .... Add 5 to 10%

Year	Power	Retail Low	Retail High
Albemarle 262 Center Console			
2003	320G I/O	26,000	31,000
2002	320G I/O	23,000	28,000
2001	320G I/O	21,000	26,000
2000	310G I/O	19,000	23,000
1999	310G I/O	18,000	21,000
1998	310G I/O	16,000	19,000
Albemarle 265/268 XF			
2008-2012		******	******
2007	375G I/O	65,000	75,000
2006	375G I/O	59,000	68,000
2005	375G I/O	53,000	61,000
2004	375G I/O	47,000	55,000
2003	375G I/O	43,000	50,000
2002	375G I/O	39,000	45,000
2001	310G I/O	36,000	41,000
2000	310G I/O	32,000	37,000
1999	310G I/O	29,000	34,000
1998	310G I/O	27,000	31,000
1997	310G I/O	25,000	28,000
1996	300G I/O	23,000	26,000
1995	300G I/O	21,000	24,000
Albemarle 27/280 Express (Inboard)			
2007	T280G	74,000	88,000
2007	T225D	83,000	98,000
2006	T280G	68,000	81,000
2006	T225D	76,000	90,000
2005	T280G	63,000	74,000
2005	T210D	70,000	83,000
2003	T300G	58,000	69,000
2003	T210D	65,000	77,000
2002	T300G	54,000	64,000
2002	T210D	61,000	72,000
2001	T300G	50,000	60,000
2001	T210D	56,000	67,000
2000	T300G	47,000	55,000
2000	T210D	52,000	62,000
1999	T300G	43,000	51,000
1999	T230D	49,000	57,000
1998	T300G	40,000	48,000
1998	T230D	45,000	53,000
1997	T290G	38,000	44,000
1997	T230D	42,000	50,000
1996	T275G	35,000	41,000
1996	T230D	******	******
1995	T275G	32,000	38,000
1995	T230D	******	******
Albemarle 290 XF			
2010-2012		******	******
2009	T315D	187,000	215,000
2008	T315D	172,000	198,000
Albemarle 30 Express; 305/310 XF			
2009-2012		******	******
2008	T330D	149,000	171,000
2007	T330D	135,000	156,000
2006	T330D	123,000	142,000
2005	T315D	112,000	129,000
2004	T315D	102,000	117,000
2003	T315D	93,000	107,000
2002	T300D	84,000	97,000
2001	T300D	77,000	88,000
2000	T300D	70,000	80,000
1999	T300D	63,000	73,000
1998	T300D	58,000	66,000
1997	T300D	52,000	60,000
1996	T300D	48,000	55,000
1995	T300D	43,000	50,000
Albemarle 320 Express			
2006	T350D	128,000	147,000
2005	T350D	116,000	133,000
2004	T350D	106,000	121,000
2003	T350D	96,000	110,000
2002	T350D	87,000	100,000
2001	T350D	80,000	92,000
2000	T350D	74,000	85,000
1999	T350D	68,000	78,000
1998	T350D	62,000	72,000
1997	T350D	57,000	66,000
1996	T300D	53,000	61,000
1995	T300D	48,000	56,000
Albemarle 325 Convertible			
2003	T350D	95,000	109,000
2002	T350D	87,000	100,000
2001	T350D	80,000	92,000
2000	T350D	74,000	85,000
1999	T300D	68,000	78,000
1998	T300D	62,000	72,000
1997	T300D	57,000	66,000
1996	T300D	53,000	60,000
1995	T300D	48,000	56,000
Albemarle 360 XF			
2011	T530D	******	******
2010	T530D	******	******
2009	T540D	******	******
2008	T500D	261,000	300,000
2007	T500D	237,000	273,000
2006	T500D	216,000	248,000
Albemarle 410 XF			
2009-12		******	******
2008	T725D	383,000	429,000
2007	T700D	348,000	390,000
2006	T700D	317,000	355,000
2005	T700D	288,000	323,000
2004	T700D	262,000	294,000
2003	T660D	239,000	267,000
2002	T660D	217,000	243,000
Albin 27 Family Cruiser			
1995	216D	23,000	28,000
Albin 27 Sport Cruiser			
1995	S-Diesel	22,000	26,000
Albin 28 TE			
2007	315D	72,000	83,000
2006	315D	66,000	76,000
2005	370D	60,000	69,000
2004	370D	54,000	63,000
2003	370D	49,000	57,000
2002	370D	45,000	52,000
2001	370D	41,000	47,000
2000	370D	38,000	43,000
1999	370D	34,000	40,000
1998	300D	32,000	36,000
1997	300D	29,000	34,000

Year	Power	Retail Low	Retail High
1996	300D	27,000	31,000
1995	280D	25,000	28,000

Albin 30 Family Cruiser

Year	Power	Retail Low	Retail High
2007	315D	73,000	85,000
2006	315D	67,000	78,000
2005	315D	62,000	72,000
2004	315D	57,000	66,000

Albin 31 TE

Year	Power	Retail Low	Retail High
2007	500D	125,000	143,000
2007	T370D	147,000	169,000
2006	500D	113,000	130,000
2006	T370D	134,000	154,000
2005	500D	103,000	119,000
2005	T370D	122,000	140,000
2004	450D	94,000	108,000
2004	T370D	111,000	127,000
2003	450D	85,000	98,000
2003	T350D	101,000	116,000
2002	450D	78,000	89,000
2002	T350D	92,000	105,000
2001	450D	71,000	81,000
2001	T350D	83,000	96,000
2000	450D	64,000	74,000
2000	T350D	77,000	88,000
1999	420D	59,000	68,000
1999	T350D	70,000	81,000
1998	420DD	54,000	62,000
1998	T350D	65,000	74,000
1997	300D	50,000	57,000
1996	300D	46,000	53,000
1995	300D	42,000	49,000

Albin 32+2 Command Bridge

Year	Power	Retail Low	Retail High
2003	370D	80,000	105,000
2002	370D	74,000	97,000
2001	370D	68,000	89,000
2000	370D	62,000	82,000
1999	350D	57,000	75,000
1998	300D	53,000	69,000
1997	300D	48,000	64,000
1996	300D	45,000	59,000
1995	300D	41,000	54,000

Albin 35 Command Bridge

Year	Power	Retail Low	Retail High
2007	370D	115,000	138,000
2006	370D	105,000	126,000
2005	370D	97,000	116,000
2004	370D	89,000	107,000

Albin 35 TE

Year	Power	Retail Low	Retail High
2007	T370D	169,000	195,000
2006	T370D	154,000	177,000
2005	T370D	140,000	161,000
2004	T370D	127,000	147,000
2003	T370D	116,000	133,000
2002	T370D	105,000	121,000
2001	T370D	96,000	110,000
2000	T370D	88,000	101,000
1999	T350D	81,000	93,000
1998	T350D	75,000	86,000
1997	T350D	69,000	79,000
1996	T350D	63,000	73,000
1995	T350D	58,000	67,000

Albin 36 Express Trawler

Year	Power	Retail Low	Retail High
2004	450D	112,000	129,000
2003	450D	103,000	119,000
2002	450D	95,000	109,000
2001	450D	87,000	100,000
2000	420D	80,000	92,000
1999	420D	74,000	85,000

Albin 40 North Sea Cutter

Year	Power	Retail Low	Retail High
2007	T315D	******	******
2006	T315D	155,000	178,000
2005	T315D	142,000	164,000

Albin 45 Command Bridge

Year	Power	Retail Low	Retail High
2007	T480D	******	******
2006	T480D	******	******
2005	T480D	223,000	249,000
2004	T450D	203,000	227,000
2003	T450D	184,000	206,000

American 34 Tug

Year	Power	Retail Low	Retail High
2009	380D	259,000	298,000
2008	380D	241,000	278,000
2007	380D	224,000	258,000
2006	380D	209,000	240,000
2005	380D	194,000	223,000
2004	380D	180,000	207,000
2003	380D	168,000	193,000
2002	370D	156,000	179,000
2001	370D	145,000	167,000

American 41/435 Tug

Year	Power	Retail Low	Retail High
2010-2012		******	******
2009	575D	460,000	516,000
2008	575D	428,000	479,000
2007	575D	398,000	446,000
2006	575D	370,000	415,000
2005	575D	344,000	386,000

Azimut 39 Flybridge

Year	Power	Retail Low	Retail High
2005	T350D	211,000	243,000
2004	T350D	194,000	223,000
2003	T355D	178,000	205,000
2002	T350D	164,000	189,000
2001	T350D	151,000	174,000
2000	T325D	139,000	160,000
1999	T325D	128,000	147,000

Azimut 42 Flybridge

Year	Power	Retail Low	Retail High
2005	T385D	252,000	290,000
2004	T390D	232,000	266,000
2003	T390D	213,000	245,000
2002	T375D	196,000	225,000
2001	T375D	180,000	207,000
2000	T375D	166,000	191,000
1999	T375D	152,000	175,000

Azimut 43 Flybridge

Year	Power	Retail Low	Retail High
2010-2012		******	******
2009	T480D	512,000	573,000
2008	T480D	471,000	440,000
2007	T425D	433,000	405,000

Azimut 43S

Year	Power	Retail Low	Retail High
2010-2012		******	******
2009	T435 IPS	388,000	434,000
2008	T435 IPS	353,000	395,000
2007	T370 IPS	321,000	359,000

Azimut 46 Flybridge

Year	Power	Retail Low	Retail High
2004	T505D	343,000	384,000
2003	T435D	312,000	349,000
2002	T435D	284,000	318,000
2001	T435D	258,000	289,000
2000	T435D	235,000	263,000
1999	T435D	214,000	239,000
1998	T435D	194,000	218,000
1997	T435D	177,000	198,000

Azimut 50 Flybridge

Year	Power	Retail Low	Retail High
2007-2010		******	******
2006	T715D	504,000	564,000
2005	T700D	459,000	514,000
2004	T700D	417,000	467,000

Azimut 54/58 Flybridge

Year	Power	Retail Low	Retail High
2001	T765D	398,000	446,000
2000	T765D	366,000	410,000
1999	T765D	337,000	377,000
1998	T765D	310,000	347,000
1997	T765D	288,000	323,000
1996	T765D	268,000	300,000
1995	T765D	249,000	279,000

Azimut 55 Flybridge

Year	Power	Retail Low	Retail High
2005	T710D	572,000	640,000
2004	T710D	520,000	583,000
2003	T660D	473,000	530,000
2002	T660D	431,000	483,000
2001	T660D	392,000	439,000

Azimut 62 Flybridge

Year	Power	Retail Low	Retail High
2006	T1015D	814,000	912,000
2005	T1015D	749,000	839,000
2004	T910D	689,000	772,000
2003	T910D	634,000	710,000

Azimut 62S

Year	Power	Retail Low	Retail High
2010-2012		******	******
2009	T1015D	1,067,000	1,195,000
2008	T1015D	981,000	1,099,000
2007	T1015D	903,000	1,011,000
2006	T1015D	830,000	930,000

Azimut 68S

Year	Power	Retail Low	Retail High
2010	1015D	1,503,000	1,683,000
2009	1015D	1,383,000	1,549,000
2008	1015D	1,272,000	1,425,000
2007	1015D	1,170,000	1,311,000
2006	1015D	1,077,000	1,206,000
2005	1015D	990,000	1,109,000

Back Cove 26

Year	Power	Retail Low	Retail High
2009	260D	******	******
2008	260D	79,000	93,000
2007	260D	73,000	86,000
2006	260D	68,000	80,000
2005	260D	63,000	74,000

Back Cove 29

Year	Power	Retail Low	Retail High
2009	260D	117,000	134,000
2008	260D	106,000	122,000
2007	260D	97,000	111,000
2006	260D	88,000	101,000
2005	260D	80,000	92,000
2004	260D	73,000	84,000

Back Cove 33/34

Year	Power	Retail Low	Retail High
2009-2012		******	******
2008	380D	169,000	195,000
2007	380D	156,000	179,000

Bayliner 275 SB Cruiser

Year	Power	Retail Low	Retail High
2008	250 I/O	48,000	58,000
2007	250 I/O	43,000	52,000
2006	250 I/O	39,000	47,000
2005	250 I/O	35,000	42,000

Bayliner 2855 Ciera SB

Year	Power	Retail Low	Retail High
1999	310 I/O	21,000	25,000
1998	310 I/O	19,000	23,000
1997	310 I/O	18,000	21,000
1996	300 I/O	16,000	19,000
1995	300 I/O	15,000	18,000

Bayliner 2859 Super Classic

Year	Power	Retail Low	Retail High
2002	300 I/O	26,000	31,000
2001	300 I/O	23,000	28,000

Year	Power	Retail Low	Retail High
2000	300 I/O	21,000	26,000
1999	310 I/O	19,000	23,000
1998	310 I/O	17,000	21,000
1997	310 I/O	16,000	19,000
1996	310 I/O	15,000	18,000
1995	310 I/O	13,000	16,000

Bayliner 2855 Ciera SB; 285 SB

Year	Power	Retail Low	Retail High
2012	300 I/O	******	******
2011	300 I/O	69,000	83,000
2010	300 I/O	62,000	75,000
2009	300 I/O	56,000	67,000
2008	300 I/O	50,000	61,000
2007	300 I/O	45,000	54,000
2006	300 I/O	41,000	49,000
2005	300 I/O	37,000	44,000
2004	320 I/O	33,000	40,000
2003	320 I/O	30,000	36,000
2002	320 I/O	27,000	33,000
2001	320 I/O	25,000	30,000
2000	320 I/O	22,000	27,000

Bayliner 288 Classic Cruiser

Year	Power	Retail Low	Retail High
2005	300 I/O	32,000	38,000
2004	300 I/O	29,000	35,000
2003	300 I/O	27,000	32,000
2002	300 I/O	25,000	30,000
2001	300 I/O	23,000	27,000
2000	300 I/O	21,000	25,000
1999	330 I/O	19,000	23,000
1998	330 I/O	18,000	21,000
1997	330 I/O	17,000	20,000
1996	330 I/O	15,000	19,000

Bayliner 300/315 SB Cruiser

Year	Power	Retail Low	Retail High
2011-2012		******	******
2010	T260 I/O	114,000	131,000
2009	T260 I/O	103,000	118,000
2008	T260 I/O	92,000	106,000

Bayliner 3055 SB Cruiser; 305 SB

Year	Power	Retail Low	Retail High
2007	T300G I/O	70,000	83,000
2006	T300G I/O	63,000	75,000
2005	T300G I/O	57,000	67,000
2004	T260G I/O	51,000	60,000
2003	T260G I/O	46,000	54,000
2002	T260G I/O	42,000	49,000
2001	T260G I/O	38,000	45,000
2000	T260G I/O	35,000	41,000
1999	T260G I/O	31,000	37,000

Bayliner 325 SB Cruiser

Year	Power	Retail Low	Retail High
2007	T260 I/O	77,000	89,000
2006	T260 I/O	70,000	81,000
2005	T260 I/O	64,000	73,000

Bayliner 3255 Avanti SB

Year	Power	Retail Low	Retail High
1999	T300G I/O	30,000	35,000
1998	T300G I/O	28,000	32,000
1997	T300G I/O	26,000	30,000
1996	T300G I/O	25,000	28,000
1995	T300G I/O	23,000	27,000

Bayliner 3258 Command Bridge

Year	Power	Retail Low	Retail High
2000	T310G I/O	44,000	50,000
1999	T310G I/O	40,000	46,000
1998	T310G I/O	36,000	42,000
1997	T300G I/O	33,000	38,000
1996	T300G I/O	30,000	35,000
1995	T300G I/O	27,000	31,000

Bayliner 3270/3288 MY

Year	Power	Retail Low	Retail High
1995	T150D	42,000	51,000

Bayliner 3388 Motor Yacht

Year	Power	Retail Low	Retail High
2000	T260G	64,000	76,000
2000	T250D	59,000	69,000
1999	T260G	53,000	62,000
1999	T250D	48,000	57,000
1988	T260G	44,000	52,000
1998	T250D	41,000	47,000
1997	T260G	37,000	44,000
1997	T250D	34,000	40,000
1996	T260G	31,000	37,000
1996	T210D	29,000	34,000

Bayliner 340 SB Cruiser

Year	Power	Retail Low	Retail High
2009	T260 I/O	114,000	137,000
2008	T300 I/O	103,000	99,000

Bayliner 3488 Avanti CB

Year	Power	Retail Low	Retail High
1999	T310G	50,000	58,000
1998	T310G	47,000	54,000
1997	T310G	43,000	50,000
1996	T310G	40,000	46,000

Bayliner 3488 CB

Year	Power	Retail Low	Retail High
2002	T260G	64,000	74,000
2001	T260G	59,000	68,000

Bayliner 3587 Motor Yacht

Year	Power	Retail Low	Retail High
1999	T310G	82,000	94,000
1999	T330D	75,000	86,000
1998	T310G	68,000	78,000
1998	T330D	62,000	71,000
1997	T310G	56,000	65,000
1997	T315D	52,000	59,000
1996	T310G	47,000	55,000
1996	T315D	44,000	50,000
1995	T310G	40,000	46,000
1995	T315D	37,000	42,000

Bayliner 3788 MY (1996-99)

Year	Power	Retail Low	Retail High
1999	T310G	82,000	94,000
1999	T330D	95,000	109,000
1998	T310G	75,000	86,000
1998	T330D	86,000	99,000
1997	T310G	68,000	78,000
1997	T250D	78,000	90,000
1996	T310G	62,000	71,000
1996	T250D	71,000	82,000

Bayliner 3788 MY (2001-02)

Year	Power	Retail Low	Retail High
2002	T310G	113,000	130,000
2002	T330D	128,000	147,000
2001	T310G	103,000	118,000
2001	T330D	116,000	133,000

Bayliner 3988 Motor Yacht

Year	Power	Retail Low	Retail High
2002	T320G	136,000	157,000
2002	T330D	155,000	178,000
2001	T320G	124,000	143,000
2001	T330D	141,000	162,000
2000	T320G	113,000	130,000
2000	T330D	128,000	147,000
1999	T310G	103,000	118,000
1999	T330D	116,000	134,000
1998	T310G	93,000	107,000
1998	T330D	106,000	122,000
1997	T310G	86,000	99,000
1997	T315D	97,000	112,000
1996	T310G	79,000	91,000
1996	T315D	90,000	103,000
1995	T310G	73,000	83,000
1995	T315D	82,000	95,000

Bayliner 4085 Avanti SB

Year	Power	Retail Low	Retail High
1999	T310G	81,000	95,000
1999	T330D	97,000	114,000
1998	T310G	74,000	87,000
1998	T330D	90,000	105,000
1997	T310G	68,000	80,000
1997	T-Diesel	82,000	97,000

Bayliner 4087 Cockpit MY

Year	Power	Retail Low	Retail High
2001	T320G	111,000	128,000
2001	T330D	121,000	139,000
2000	T320G	101,000	116,000
2000	T330D	110,000	126,000
1999	T310G	92,000	106,000
1999	T330D	100,000	115,000
1998	T310G	84,000	96,000
1998	T330D	91,000	105,000
1997	T310G	76,000	87,000
1997	T330D	83,000	95,000

Bayliner 4587 Cockpit MY

Year	Power	Retail Low	Retail High
1995	T300G	82,000	94,000
1995	T310D	94,000	108,000

Bayliner 4788 Pilothouse MY

Year	Power	Retail Low	Retail High
2002	T370D	222,000	251,000
2001	T370D	202,000	228,000
2000	T370D	183,000	207,000
1999	T315D	167,000	189,000
1998	T315D	153,000	174,000
1997	T315D	141,000	160,000
1996	T315D	130,000	147,000
1995	T310D	119,000	135,000

Bayliner 5288 Pilothouse MY

Year	Power	Retail Low	Retail High
2002	T610D	514,000	575,000
2001	T610D	472,000	529,000
2000	T610D	435,000	487,000
1999	T600D	400,000	448,000

Bayliner 5788 Motor Yacht

Year	Power	Retail Low	Retail High
2002	T610D	465,000	535,000
2001	T610D	433,000	498,000
2000	T610D	403,000	463,000
1999	T600D	378,000	435,000
1998	T600D	356,000	409,000
1997	T600D	334,000	384,000

Beneteau 42 Trawler

Year	Power	Retail Low	Retail High
2008-2009		******	******
2007	T370D	281,000	323,000
2006	T370D	258,000	297,000
2005	T370D	238,000	273,000
2004	T370D	219,000	251,000

Bertram 30 Moppie

Year	Power	Retail Low	Retail High
1997	T320G	47,000	54,000
1997	T300D	57,000	65,000
1996	T320G	43,000	50,000
1996	T300D	52,000	60,000
1995	T320G	40,000	46,000
1995	T300D	48,000	55,000

Bertram 36 Convertible

Year	Power	Retail Low	Retail High
1997	T420D	140,000	161,000
1996	T420D	129,000	148,000

Bertram 36 Moppie

Year	Power	Retail Low	Retail High
2000	T430D	174,000	200,000
1999	T430D	158,000	182,000
1998	T430D	144,000	166,000
1997	T330D	131,000	151,000
1996	T315D	119,000	137,000

Bertram 390 Convertible

Year	Power	Retail Low	Retail High
2006	460D	373,000	429,000
2005	480D	339,000	390,000
2004	480D	309,000	355,000
2003	480D	281,000	323,000
2002	480D	256,000	294,000

Year	Power	Retail Low	Retail High
2001	480D	233,000	268,000
2000	480D	212,000	243,000

Bertram 43 Convertible

Year	Power	Retail Low	Retail High
1996	625D	182,000	209,000
1995	600D	167,000	192,000

Bertram 450 Convertible

Year	Power	Retail Low	Retail High
2007-2009		******	******
2006	900D	639,000	715,000
2005	900D	588,000	658,000
2004	660D	541,000	605,000
2003	660D	497,000	557,000
2002	660D	457,000	512,000
2001	660D	421,000	471,000
2000	660D	387,000	434,000

Bertram 46 Convertible

Year	Power	Retail Low	Retail High
1997	760D	258,000	295,000
1996	760D	240,000	274,000
1995	735D	224,000	255,000

Bertram 46 Moppie

Year	Power	Retail Low	Retail High
1996	760D	213,000	243,000
1995	735D	198,000	226,000

Bertram 50 Convertible

Year	Power	Retail Low	Retail High
1997	820D	462,000	527,000
1996	820D	425,000	485,000
1995	735D	391,000	446,000

Bertram 510 Convertible

Year	Power	Retail Low	Retail High
2006-2010		******	******
2005	800D	764,000	863,000
2004	800D	695,000	785,000
2003	800D	632,000	715,000
2002	800D	576,000	650,000
2001	800D	524,000	592,000
2000	800D	476,000	538,000

Bertram 54 Convertible

Year	Power	Retail Low	Retail High
2003	1200D	******	******
2002	1200D	1,030,000	1,175,000
2001	1400D	958,000	1,092,000
2000	1400D	891,000	1,016,000
2000	1350D	829,000	945,000
1999	1350D	771,000	878,000
1998	1350D	717,000	817,000
1997	1350D	666,000	760,000
1996	1100D	620,000	707,000
1995	1100D	576,000	657,000

Bertram 570 Convertible

Year	Power	Retail Low	Retail High
2007-2008		******	******
2006	1300D	989,000	1,118,000
2005	1300D	939,000	1,062,000
2004	1300D	892,000	1,009,000
2003	1300D	848,000	958,000
2002	1300D	805,000	910,000

Bertram 60 Conv. (Open Bridge)

Year	Power	Retail Low	Retail High
2003-2005		******	******
2002	1400D	1,144,000	1,281,000
2001	1400D	1,041,000	1,166,000
2000	1400D	947,000	1,061,000
1999	1400D	862,000	966,000
1998	1450D	784,000	879,000
1997	1450D	714,000	799,000
1996	1400D	649,000	727,000
1995	1400D	591,000	662,000

Black Watch 26 Express

Year	Power	Retail Low	Retail High
1997	T250 I/B	29,000	34,000
1996	T250 I/B	27,000	32,000
1995	T250 I/B	25,000	30,000

Black Watch 30 Sportfisherman

Year	Power	Retail Low	Retail High
1995	T250G	35,000	43,000
1995	T300D	44,000	53,000

Blackfin 27 Sportsman

Year	Power	Retail Low	Retail High
1998	T270G	33,000	40,000
1998	T230D	42,000	51,000
1997	T270G	31,000	38,000
1997	T230D	40,000	48,000
1996	T270G	29,000	35,000
1996	T230D	37,000	45,000
1995	T270G	28,000	33,000
1995	T230D	35,000	42,000

Blackfin 29 Combi

Year	Power	Retail Low	Retail High
1998	T320G	44,000	51,000
1998	T330D	55,000	64,000
1997	T320G	40,000	47,000
1997	T330D	51,000	60,000
1996	T320G	38,000	44,000
1996	T330D	47,000	55,000
1995	T320G	35,000	41,000
1995	T330D	44,000	51,000

Blackfin 29 Flybridge

Year	Power	Retail Low	Retail High
1998	T320G	49,000	57,000
1998	T330D	60,000	71,000
1997	T320G	46,000	53,000
1997	T330D	56,000	66,000
1996	T320G	42,000	50,000
1996	T330D	52,000	61,000
1995	T320G	39,000	46,000
1995	T330D	49,000	57,000

Blackfin 31 Combi

Year	Power	Retail Low	Retail High
1997	T320G	56,000	66,000
1997	T300D	72,000	85,000
1996	T320G	52,000	61,000
1996	T300D	66,000	78,000
1995	T320G	48,000	56,000
1995	T300D	61,000	72,000

Blackfin 33 Combi

Year	Power	Retail Low	Retail High
1998	T375D	89,000	104,000
1997	T375D	83,000	98,000
1996	T375D	78,000	92,000
1995	T375D	74,000	86,000

Blackfin 33 Convertible

Year	Power	Retail Low	Retail High
1999	T435D	99,000	116,000
1998	T375D	93,000	109,000
1997	T375D	88,000	103,000
1996	T-Gas	68,000	79,000
1996	T375D	82,000	97,000
1995	T-Gas	64,000	74,000
1995	T375D	77,000	91,000

Blackfin 36/38 Combi

Year	Power	Retail Low	Retail High
1998	435D	138,000	161,000
1997	450D	130,000	152,000
1996	450D	122,000	143,000
1995	450D	116,000	135,000

Blackfin 36/38 Convertible

Year	Power	Retail Low	Retail High
1998	550D	163,000	191,000
1997	550D	153,000	179,000
1996	485D	144,000	168,000
1995	485D	135,000	158,000

Boston Whaler 26 Outrage

Year	Power	Retail Low	Retail High
2002	T200 O/B	38,000	46,000
2001	T200 O/B	35,000	42,000
2000	T200 O/B	32,000	38,000
1999	T200 O/B	29,000	35,000
1998	T200 O/B	26,000	31,000

Boston Whaler 26/275 Conquest

Year	Power	Retail Low	Retail High
2005	T225 O/B	65,000	79,000
2004	T225 O/B	60,000	72,000
2003	T225 O/B	54,000	65,000
2002	T225 O/B	49,000	59,000
2001	T225 O/B	45,000	54,000

Boston Whaler 27 Offshore

Year	Power	Retail Low	Retail High
1998	T225 O/B	30,000	36,000
1997	T225 O/B	29,000	34,000
1996	T225 O/B	27,000	33,000
1995	T225 O/B	26,000	31,000

Boston Whaler 270 Outrage

Year	Power	Retail Low	Retail High
2008	T225 O/B	86,000	103,000
2007	T225 O/B	78,000	94,000
2006	T225 O/B	71,000	85,000
2005	T225 O/B	65,000	78,000
2004	T225 O/B	59,000	71,000
2003	T225 O/B	53,000	64,000

Boston Whaler 28/295 Conquest

Year	Power	Retail Low	Retail High
2003	T225 O/B	78,000	94,000
2002	T225 O/B	71,000	85,000
2001	T225 O/B	65,000	78,000
2000	T225 O/B	59,000	71,000
1999	T225 O/B	53,000	64,000

Boston Whaler 28/290 Outrage

Year	Power	Retail Low	Retail High
2003	T225 O/B	66,000	80,000
2002	T225 O/B	62,000	74,000
2001	T225 O/B	57,000	69,000
2000	T225 O/B	53,000	64,000
1999	T225 O/B	50,000	60,000

Boston Whaler 280 Outrage

Year	Power	Retail Low	Retail High
2011-2012		******	******
2010	T225 O/B	121,000	143,000
2009	T225 O/B	111,000	131,000

Boston Whaler 285 Conquest

Year	Power	Retail Low	Retail High
2010	T225 O/B	133,000	157,000
2009	T225 O/B	121,000	143,000
2008	T225 O/B	110,000	130,000
2007	T225 O/B	100,000	119,000
2006	T225 O/B	91,000	108,000

Boston Whaler 305 Conquest

Year	Power	Retail Low	Retail High
2012	T225 O/B	******	******
2011	T225 O/B	164,000	197,000
2010	T225 O/B	150,000	180,000
2009	T225 O/B	136,000	163,000
2008	T225 O/B	124,000	149,000
2007	T225 O/B	114,000	137,000
2006	T225 O/B	105,000	126,000
2005	T225 O/B	96,000	116,000
2004	T225 O/B	89,000	106,000

Boston Whaler 320 Outrage

Year	Power	Retail Low	Retail High
2012	T250 O/B	******	******
2011	T250 O/B	159,000	190,000
2010	T250 O/B	143,000	171,000
2009	T250 O/B	128,000	154,000
2008	T250 O/B	115,000	139,000
2007	T250 O/B	105,000	126,000
2006	T250 O/B	96,000	115,000
2005	T250 O/B	87,000	104,000
2004	T250 O/B	79,000	95,000
2003	T250 O/B	72,000	86,000

Boston Whaler 320 Outrage Cuddy

Year	Power	Retail Low	Retail High
2012	T250 O/B	******	******
2011	T250 O/B	169,000	203,000
2010	T250 O/B	154,000	185,000
2009	T250 O/B	140,000	168,000

Year	Power	Retail Low	Retail High
2008	T250 O/B	127,000	153,000
2007	T250 O/B	116,000	139,000
2006	T250 O/B	105,000	127,000

Boston Whaler 34 Defiance

Year	Power	Retail Low	Retail High
2002	T355D	179,000	215,000
2001	T355D	163,000	195,000
2000	T355D	148,000	178,000
1999	T355D	135,000	162,000

Boston Whaler 345 Conquest

Year	Power	Retail Low	Retail High
2011-2012		******	******
2010	3/225 O/B	259,000	306,000
2009	3/225 O/B	236,000	279,000
2008	3/225 O/B	215,000	254,000
2007	3/225 O/B	195,000	231,000

Boston Whaler 370 Outrage

Year	Power	Retail Low	Retail High
2012	3/250 O/B	******	******
2011	3/250 O/B	330,000	379,000
2010	3/250 O/B	306,000	352,000

Cabo 31 Express

Year	Power	Retail Low	Retail High
2004	T385D	114,000	137,000
2003	T385D	104,000	124,000
2002	T385D	94,000	113,000
2001	T385D	86,000	103,000
2000	T385D	78,000	94,000
1999	T350D	72,000	86,000
1998	T350D	66,000	79,000
1997	T350D	61,000	73,000
1996	T350D	56,000	67,000
1995	T350D	51,000	62,000

Cabo 32 Express

Year	Power	Retail Low	Retail High
2009-2012		******	******
2008	T425D	203,000	240,000
2007	T425D	185,000	218,000
2006	T461D	168,000	199,000
2005	T461D	153,000	181,000

Cabo 35 Express

Year	Power	Retail Low	Retail High
2008	T425D	******	******
2007	T425D	******	******
2006	T461D	203,000	238,000
2005	T461D	185,000	216,000
2004	T450D	168,000	197,000
2003	T450D	153,000	179,000
2002	T435D	139,000	163,000
2001	T435D	128,000	150,000
2000	T435D	118,000	138,000
1999	T435D	108,000	127,000
1998	T435D	100,000	117,000
1997	T435D	92,000	107,000
1996	T435D	84,000	99,000
1995	T375D	77,000	91,000

Cabo 35 Flybridge

Year	Power	Retail Low	Retail High
2008	425D	******	******
2007	425D	233,000	273,000
2006	461D	212,000	248,000
2005	461D	193,000	226,000
2004	450D	176,000	206,000
2003	450D	160,000	187,000
2002	435D	145,000	170,000
2001	435D	134,000	157,000
2000	435D	123,000	144,000
1999	435D	113,000	132,000
1998	435D	104,000	122,000
1997	435D	96,000	112,000
1996	435D	88,000	103,000
1995	375D	81,000	95,000

Cabo 38 Express

Year	Power	Retail Low	Retail High
2010	715D	******	******
2009	715D	******	******
2008	715D	358,000	419,000

Cabo 38 Flybridge

Year	Power	Retail Low	Retail High
2009-2012		******	******
2008	715D	407,000	480,000

Cabo 40 Flybridge

Year	Power	Retail Low	Retail High
2008-2012		******	******
2007	710D	436,000	510,000
2006	710D	401,000	469,000
2005	710D	369,000	432,000
2004	700D	339,000	397,000

Cabo 40 Express

Year	Power	Retail Low	Retail High
2010-2012		******	******
2009	720D	453,000	531,000
2008	720D	417,000	488,000
2007	710D	384,000	449,000
2006	710D	353,000	413,000
2005	710D	325,000	380,000
2004	700D	299,000	350,000
2003	700D	275,000	322,000

Cabo 43 Flybridge

Year	Power	Retail Low	Retail High
2010	720D	******	******
2009	720D	******	******
2008	720D	543,000	635,000
2007	710D	499,000	584,000
2006	710D	459,000	537,000
2005	710D	422,000	494,000
2004	680D	389,000	455,000
2003	680D	358,000	418,000
2002	680D	329,000	385,000

Cabo 45 Express

Year	Power	Retail Low	Retail High
2010-2012		******	******
2009	1100D	582,000	680,000
2008	800D	535,000	626,000
2007	800D	492,000	576,000
2006	800D	453,000	530,000
2005	800D	416,000	487,000
2004	800D	383,000	448,000
2003	800D	352,000	412,000
2002	800D	324,000	379,000
2001	800D	298,000	349,000
2000	800D	274,000	321,000
1999	800D	252,000	295,000
1998	800D	232,000	272,000
1997	800D	213,000	250,000

Cabo 47/48 Flybridge

Year	Power	Retail Low	Retail High
2008	800D	******	******
2007	800D	609,000	712,000
2006	800D	560,000	655,000
2005	800D	515,000	603,000
2004	800D	474,000	554,000
2003	800D	436,000	510,000
2002	800D	401,000	469,000
2001	800D	369,000	432,000
2000	800D	339,000	397,000

Camano 28/31

Year	Power	Retail Low	Retail High
2007	S-Diesel	126,000	146,000
2006	S-Diesel	119,000	138,000
2005	S-Diesel	113,000	132,000
2004	S-Diesel	108,000	125,000
2003	S-Diesel	102,000	119,000
2002	S-Diesel	98,000	114,000
2001	S-Diesel	94,000	109,000
2000	S-Diesel	90,000	105,000
1999	S-Diesel	87,000	101,000
1998	S-Diesel	83,000	97,000
1997	S-Diesel	80,000	93,000
1996	S-Diesel	77,000	89,000
1995	S-Diesel	74,000	85,000

Camano 41

Year	Power	Retail Low	Retail High
2007	440D	******	******
2006	440D	310,000	356,000

Carolina Classic 25

Year	Power	Retail Low	Retail High
2010	385G	65,000	78,000
2009	385G	59,000	70,000
2008	385G	53,000	64,000
2007	385G	48,000	58,000
2006	385G	44,000	53,000
2005	385G	40,000	48,000
2004	375G	36,000	44,000
2003	375G	33,000	40,000
2002	375G	30,000	36,000
2001	375G	28,000	33,000
2000	375G	25,000	31,000
1999	300G	23,000	28,000
1998	300G	21,000	26,000
1997	300G	20,000	24,000
1996	300G	18,000	22,000
1995	300G	17,000	20,000

Carolina Classic 28

Year	Power	Retail Low	Retail High
2012	T375G	******	******
2012	T300D	******	******
2011	T375G	******	******
2011	T300D	******	******
2010	T375G	91,000	104,000
2010	T300D	124,000	143,000
2009	T375G	83,000	96,000
2009	T315D	114,000	131,000
2008	T375G	76,000	88,000
2008	T315D	104,000	120,000
2007	T375G	71,000	81,000
2007	T315D	97,000	112,000
2006	T375G	66,000	76,000
2006	T315D	90,000	104,000
2005	T375G	61,000	70,000
2005	T300D	84,000	96,000
2004	T375G	57,000	65,000
2004	T300D	78,000	90,000
2003	T375G	53,000	61,000
2003	T300D	72,000	83,000
2002	T375G	49,000	57,000
2002	T250D	67,000	77,000
2001	T375G	46,000	53,000
2001	T250D	63,000	72,000
2000	T300G	42,000	49,000
2000	T250D	59,000	68,000
1999	T300G	40,000	46,000
1999	T250D	55,000	64,000
1998	T300G	37,000	43,000
1998	T230D	52,000	60,000
1997	T300G	35,000	40,000
1997	T230D	49,000	56,000
1996	T300G	33,000	38,000
1996	T230D	46,000	53,000
1995	T300G	31,000	36,000
1995	T230D	43,000	50,000

Carolina Classic 32

Year	Power	Retail Low	Retail High
2009-2012		******	******
2008	T425D	211,000	247,000
2007	T425D	192,000	225,000
2006	T500D	175,000	204,000
2005	T500D	159,000	186,000
2004	T440D	145,000	169,000

Carolina Classic 35

Year	Power	Retail Low	Retail High
2009-2012		******	******

Year	Power	Retail Low	Retail High
2008	T540D	232,000	265,000
2007	T540D	218,000	249,000
2006	T500D	205,000	234,000
2005	T480D	193,000	220,000
2004	T480D	181,000	207,000
2003	T480D	170,000	194,000
2002	T480D	160,000	183,000
2001	T450D	150,000	172,000
2000	T450D	141,000	161,000
1999	T450D	133,000	152,000
1998	T450D	125,000	142,000

Carver 26 CB; 280 Sedan

Year	Power	Retail Low	Retail High
1998	T205G	24,000	28,000
1997	T205G	22,000	26,000
1996	T205G	20,000	24,000
1995	T205G	19,000	23,000

Carver 280 Mid-Cabin Express

Year	Power	Retail Low	Retail High
1998	T205G	21,000	25,000
1997	T205G	19,000	23,000
1996	T205G	18,000	21,000
1995	T205G	17,000	20,000

Carver 310 Mid-Cabin Express

Year	Power	Retail Low	Retail High
1997	T220 I/O	26,000	31,000
1996	T220 I/O	24,000	29,000
1995	T220 I/O	22,000	27,000

Carver 310 Santego

Year	Power	Retail Low	Retail High
1998	T220 I/O	35,000	43,000
1997	T220 I/O	33,000	40,000
1996	T220 I/O	31,000	37,000
1995	T220 I/O	28,000	34,000

Carver 320 Voyager

Year	Power	Retail Low	Retail High
1999	T300G	41,000	48,000
1998	T300G	38,000	45,000
1997	T260G	36,000	42,000
1996	T260G	33,000	39,000
1995	T260G	31,000	36,000

Carver 325/326 Aft Cabin

Year	Power	Retail Low	Retail High
2001	T300G	56,000	65,000
2000	T300G	52,000	61,000
1999	T300G	48,000	56,000
1998	T260G	45,000	52,000
1997	T260G	42,000	49,000
1996	T260G	39,000	45,000
1995	T260G	36,000	42,000

Carver 32/330 Mariner

Year	Power	Retail Low	Retail High
1996	T260G	40,000	47,000
1995	T260G	38,000	44,000

Carver 33/35/36 Super Sport

Year	Power	Retail Low	Retail High
2008	T375G	198,000	232,000
2007	T320G	182,000	214,000
2006	T320G	168,000	196,000
2005	T320G	154,000	181,000

Carver 350 Mariner

Year	Power	Retail Low	Retail High
2003	T300G	90,000	106,000
2002	T300G	82,000	96,000
2001	T300G	74,000	88,000
2000	T300G	67,000	80,000
1999	T260G	61,000	72,000
1998	T260G	56,000	66,000
1997	T260G	51,000	60,000

Carver 355/356 Motor Yacht

Year	Power	Retail Low	Retail High
2003	T320G	100,000	118,000
2002	T320G	91,000	107,000
2001	T320G	83,000	97,000
2000	T310G	76,000	88,000
1999	T310G	69,000	80,000
1998	T310G	63,000	74,000
1997	T310G	58,000	68,000
1996	T320G	53,000	63,000
1995	T320G	49,000	57,000

Carver 36 Mariner

Year	Power	Retail Low	Retail High
2010	T320G	******	******
2009	T320G	201,000	236,000
2008	T320G	183,000	214,000
2007	T320G	167,000	195,000
2006	T320G	152,000	177,000
2005	T320G	138,000	161,000
2004	T320G	125,000	147,000

Carver 36 Motor Yacht

Year	Power	Retail Low	Retail High
2007	T375G	203,000	238,000
2007	T315D	218,000	255,000
2006	T320G	187,000	219,000
2006	T315D	200,000	234,000
2006	T320G	172,000	201,000
2006	T315D	184,000	216,000
2005	T320G	160,000	187,000
2005	T280D	171,000	201,000
2004	T320G	149,000	174,000
2004	T280D	159,000	186,000
2003	T320G	138,000	162,000
2003	T280D	148,000	173,000
2002	T320G	128,000	150,000
2002	T280D	138,000	161,000

Carver 360 Sport Sedan

Year	Power	Retail Low	Retail High
2006	T375G	162,000	190,000
2005	T375G	151,000	177,000
2004	T375G	140,000	164,000
2003	T320G	131,000	153,000

Carver 36/370 Aft Cabin MY

Year	Power	Retail Low	Retail High
1996	T300G	72,000	84,000
1996	T300D	91,000	105,000
1995	T300G	68,000	79,000
1995	T300D	85,000	99,000

Carver 370/374 Voyager

Year	Power	Retail Low	Retail High
2002	T320G	97,000	113,000
2002	T330D	111,000	130,000
2001	T320G	89,000	104,000
2001	T330D	102,000	120,000
2000	T320G	82,000	97,000
2000	T330D	95,000	111,000
1999	T320G	77,000	90,000
1999	T315D	88,000	103,000
1998	T300G	71,000	83,000
1998	T315D	82,000	96,000
1997	T300G	66,000	78,000
1997	T315D	76,000	89,000
1996	T300G	62,000	72,000
1996	T315D	71,000	83,000
1995	T300G	57,000	67,000
1995	T315D	66,000	77,000

Carver 34/638/380 Santego

Year	Power	Retail Low	Retail High
2002	T320G	89,000	104,000
2001	T320G	82,000	97,000
2000	T310G	77,000	90,000
1999	T310G	71,000	83,000
1998	T300G	66,000	78,000
1997	T320G	62,000	72,000
1996	T320G	57,000	67,000
1995	T320G	53,000	62,000

Carver 38 Super Sport

Year	Power	Retail Low	Retail High
2009-2012		******	******
2008	T375G	227,000	266,000
2007	T375G	209,000	245,000
2006	T375G	192,000	225,000
2005	T375G	177,000	207,000

Carver 38/390 Aft Cabin

Year	Power	Retail Low	Retail High
1995	T330G	67,000	78,000
1995	T-Diesel	80,000	93,000

Carver 396/39/40 Motor Yacht

Year	Power	Retail Low	Retail High
2007	T385G	240,000	280,000
2007	T370D	276,000	322,000
2006	T385G	220,000	258,000
2006	T370D	253,000	297,000
2005	T385G	200,000	235,000
2005	T370D	231,000	270,000
2004	T385G	182,000	213,000
2004	T370D	210,000	246,000
2003	T370G	168,000	196,000
2003	T370D	193,000	226,000
2002	T370G	156,000	183,000
2002	T370D	179,000	210,000
2001	T370G	145,000	170,000
2001	T330D	167,000	195,000
2000	T380G	135,000	158,000
2000	T330D	155,000	182,000

Carver 390/400/404 Cockpit MY

Year	Power	Retail Low	Retail High
2003	T320G	116,000	136,000
2003	T370D	139,000	163,000
2002	T320G	105,000	123,000
2002	T370D	127,000	148,000
2001	T320G	96,000	112,000
2001	T370D	115,000	135,000
2000	T310G	87,000	102,000
2000	T370D	105,000	123,000
1999	T310G	79,000	93,000
1999	T370D	96,000	113,000
1998	T310G	73,000	85,000
1998	T370D	89,000	104,000
1997	T310G	67,000	79,000
1997	T370D	81,000	95,000
1996	T310G	62,000	72,000
1996	T370D	75,000	88,000
1995	T310G	57,000	66,000
1995	T315D	69,000	81,000

Carver 405/406 Aft Cabin MY

Year	Power	Retail Low	Retail High
2002	T320G	126,000	146,000
2002	T330D	138,000	160,000
2001	T320G	116,000	134,000
2001	T330D	127,000	148,000
2000	T320G	106,000	123,000
2000	T330D	117,000	136,000
1999	T310G	98,000	113,000
1999	T330D	108,000	125,000
1998	T310G	90,000	104,000
1998	T330D	99,000	115,000
1997	T310G	83,000	96,000
1997	T315D	91,000	106,000

Carver 41 Cockpit MY

Year	Power	Retail Low	Retail High
2007	T375G	189,000	219,000
2007	T370D	210,000	244,000
2006	T375G	172,000	199,000
2006	T370D	191,000	222,000
2005	T385G	156,000	181,000
2005	T370D	174,000	202,000

Carver 410 Sport Sedan

Year	Power	Retail Low	Retail High
2003	T375G	124,000	144,000
2003	T370D	140,000	163,000
2002	T375G	114,000	132,000
2002	T370D	129,000	150,000

Carver 42 Mariner

Year	Power	Retail Low	Retail High
2006	T385G	194,000	226,000
2006	T370D	227,000	263,000
2005	T385G	179,000	208,000
2005	T370D	208,000	242,000
2004	T385G	165,000	191,000
2004	T330D	192,000	222,000

Carver 42/43 Super Sport

Year	Power	Retail Low	Retail High
2008-2012		******	******
2007	T375G	******	******
2007	T370D	242,000	200,000
2006	T375G	******	******
2006	T370D	223,000	263,000

Carver 430 Cockpit MY

Year	Power	Retail Low	Retail High
1997	T380G	102,000	118,000
1997	T315D	119,000	138,000
1996	T380G	96,000	111,000
1996	T315D	111,000	129,000
1995	T380G	90,000	104,000
1995	T315D	105,000	122,000

Carver 43/47 Motor Yacht

Year	Power	Retail Low	Retail High
2009	T370D	******	******
2008	T370D	******	******
2007	T370D	281,000	329,000
2006	T370D	258,000	302,000

Carver 440/445 Aft Cabin

Year	Power	Retail Low	Retail High
1999	T450D	167,000	193,000
1998	T420D	155,000	180,000
1997	T420D	144,000	167,000
1996	T420D	134,000	155,000
1995	T420D	125,000	145,000

Carver 444 Cockpit MY

Year	Power	Retail Low	Retail High
2006	T370D	203,000	238,000
2005	T370D	189,000	221,000
2004	T330D	176,000	206,000
2003	T330D	163,000	191,000
2002	T330D	152,000	178,000
2001	T330D	141,000	165,000

Carver 450 Voyager

Year	Power	Retail Low	Retail High
2004	T370D	237,000	278,000
2003	T370D	216,000	253,000
2002	T370D	196,000	230,000
2001	T370D	179,000	209,000
2000	T315D	162,000	190,000
1999	T315D	148,000	173,000

Carver 455/456 Aft Cabin MY

Year	Power	Retail Low	Retail High
2000	T315D	208,000	244,000
1999	T315D	193,000	226,000
1998	T315D	180,000	211,000
1997	T315D	167,000	196,000
1996	T315D	156,000	182,000

Carver 460/46 Voyager

Year	Power	Retail Low	Retail High
2007-2012		******	******
2006	T370D	305,000	351,000
2005	T370D	284,000	326,000
2004	T370D	264,000	303,000
2003	T370D	245,000	282,000

Carver 466 Motor Yacht

Year	Power	Retail Low	Retail High
2007	T370D	329,000	382,000
2006	T370D	300,000	348,000
2005	T370D	273,000	316,000
2004	T370D	248,000	288,000
2003	T370D	226,000	262,000
2002	T370D	205,000	238,000
2001	T370D	187,000	217,000

Carver 500/504 Cockpit MY

Year	Power	Retail Low	Retail High
2000	T400D	205,000	238,000
1999	T400D	193,000	224,000
1998	T420D	181,000	211,000
1997	T420D	170,000	198,000
1996	T420D	160,000	186,000

Carver 506 Motor Yacht

Year	Power	Retail Low	Retail High
2004	T480D	******	******
2003	T480D	310,000	360,000
2002	T480D	285,000	331,000
2001	T480D	262,000	304,000
2000	T480D	241,000	280,000

Carver 530 Voyager PH

Year	Power	Retail Low	Retail High
2005	T480D	325,000	380,000
2004	T480D	320,000	375,000
2003	T480D	298,000	348,000
2002	T480D	280,000	328,000
2001	T480D	260,000	305,000
2000	T480D	242,000	283,000
1999	T480D	225,000	263,000
1998	T480D	209,000	245,000

Carver 564 Cockpit MY

Year	Power	Retail Low	Retail High
2006	T480D	******	******
2005	T480D	******	******
2004	T480D	363,000	414,000
2003	T480D	338,000	385,000
2002	T480D	314,000	358,000

Carver 570/56 Voyager Sedan

Year	Power	Retail Low	Retail High
2009	T500D	683,000	793,000
2008	T500D	622,000	721,000
2007	T500D	566,000	656,000
2006	T675D	515,000	597,000
2005	T675D	468,000	543,000
2004	T660D	426,000	495,000
2003	T635D	392,000	455,000
2002	T635D	361,000	418,000
2001	T635D	332,000	385,000

Catalina Islander 34

Year	Power	Retail Low	Retail High
2001	T125D	84,000	100,000
2000	T125D	78,000	93,000
1999	T210D	72,000	87,000
1998	T210D	67,000	81,000
1997	T210D	62,000	75,000
1996	T210D	58,000	70,000
1995	T210D	54,000	65,000

Century 2600 Center Console

Year	Power	Retail Low	Retail High
2009	T200 O/B	75,000	88,000
2008	T150 O/B	68,000	80,000
2007	T150 O/B	62,000	73,000
2006	T150 O/B	56,000	66,000
2005	T150 O/B	51,000	60,000
2004	T150 O/B	46,000	55,000
2003	T150 O/B	42,000	50,000
2002	T150 O/B	38,000	45,000
2001	T150 O/B	35,000	41,000
2000	T150 O/B	32,000	38,000
1999	T150 O/B	29,000	35,000
1998	T150 O/B	27,000	32,000
1997	T150 O/B	25,000	29,000
1996	T150 O/B	23,000	27,000

Century 2600 Walkaround

Year	Power	Retail Low	Retail High
2009	T150 O/B	78,000	92,000
2008	T150 O/B	71,000	84,000
2007	T150 O/B	65,000	76,000
2006	T150 O/B	59,000	69,000
2005	T150 O/B	53,000	63,000
2004	T150 O/B	48,000	57,000
2003	T150 O/B	44,000	52,000
2002	T150 O/B	40,000	47,000
2001	T150 O/B	37,000	44,000
2000	T150 O/B	34,000	40,000
1999	T150 O/B	31,000	37,000
1998	T150 O/B	29,000	34,000
1997	T150 O/B	26,000	31,000
1996	T150 O/B	24,000	29,000

Century 2900/2901 Center Console

Year	Power	Retail Low	Retail High
2008	T250 O/B	72,000	87,000
2007	T250 O/B	66,000	79,000
2006	T250 O/B	60,000	72,000
2005	T250 O/B	55,000	66,000
2004	T250 O/B	50,000	61,000
2003	T250 O/B	46,000	56,000
2002	T250 O/B	43,000	51,000
2001	T250 O/B	39,000	47,000
2000	T250 O/B	36,000	43,000

Century 3000 Center Console

Year	Power	Retail Low	Retail High
1999	T250 O/B	27,000	31,000
1998	T250 O/B	25,000	29,000
1997	T250 O/B	23,000	27,000
1996	T250 O/B	21,000	25,000
1995	T250 O/B	20,000	23,000

Century 3000 Sport Cabin

Year	Power	Retail Low	Retail High
2002	T250 O/B	32,000	37,000
2001	T250 O/B	29,000	34,000
2000	T250 O/B	27,000	31,000
1999	T250 O/B	24,000	29,000
1998	T250 O/B	22,000	26,000
1997	T250 O/B	21,000	24,000

Century 3100/3200 Center Console

Year	Power	Retail Low	Retail High
2009	T250 O/B	130,000	157,000
2008	T250 O/B	119,000	142,000
2007	T250 O/B	108,000	130,000
2006	T250 O/B	98,000	118,000
2005	T250 O/B	89,000	107,000
2004	T250 O/B	82,000	99,000
2003	T250 O/B	76,000	91,000
2002	T250 O/B	69,000	83,000
2001	T250 O/B	64,000	77,000
2000	T250 O/B	59,000	71,000
1999	T250 O/B	54,000	65,000

Century 3100/3200 Walkaround

Year	Power	Retail Low	Retail High
2007	T250 O/B	117,000	137,000
2006	T250 O/B	106,000	124,000
2005	T250 O/B	97,000	113,000
2004	T250 O/B	88,000	103,000
2003	T250 O/B	81,000	95,000
2002	T250 O/B	74,000	87,000
2001	T250 O/B	68,000	80,000
2000	T250 O/B	63,000	74,000

Chaparral Signature 260

Year	Power	Retail Low	Retail High
2005	260G I/O	33,000	39,000
2004	260G I/O	30,000	36,000
2003	250G I/O	27,000	33,000
2002	250G I/O	25,000	30,000
2001	250G I/O	23,000	28,000
2000	250G I/O	21,000	26,000
1999	250G I/O	20,000	24,000
1998	250G I/O	18,000	22,000
1997	250G I/O	16,000	20,000
1996	250G I/O	15,000	18,000

Chaparral 260 SSi

Year	Power	Retail Low	Retail High
2006	300 I/O	30,000	36,000
2005	300 I/O	27,000	33,000
2004	300 I/O	25,000	30,000

Year	Power	Retail Low	Retail High
2003	300 I/O	23,000	28,000
2002	300 I/O	21,000	25,000
2001	300 I/O	19,000	23,000

Chaparral 265 SSi

Year	Power	Retail Low	Retail High
2006	300 I/O	33,000	39,000
2005	300 I/O	30,000	36,000
2004	300 I/O	27,000	33,000
2003	300 I/O	25,000	30,000
2002	300 I/O	23,000	28,000
2001	300 I/O	21,000	26,000

Chaparral Signature 26/27/270

Year	Power	Retail Low	Retail High
2000	310 I/O	30,000	34,000
1999	310 I/O	27,000	32,000
1998	310 I/O	26,000	29,000
1997	310 I/O	24,000	27,000
1996	310 I/O	22,000	25,000
1995	310 I/O	20,000	24,000

Chaparral Signature 270

Year	Power	Retail Low	Retail High
2011	320 I/O	******	******
2010	320 I/O	65,000	79,000
2009	320 I/O	60,000	72,000
2008	300 I/O	54,000	65,000
2007	300 I/O	49,000	59,000

Chaparral 275 SSi

Year	Power	Retail Low	Retail High
2010	375 I/O	67,000	80,000
2009	375 I/O	61,000	73,000
2008	300 I/O	56,000	68,000
2007	300 I/O	52,000	62,000
2006	300 I/O	47,000	57,000

Chaparral 276 SSX

Year	Power	Retail Low	Retail High
2010	375 I/O	71,000	85,000
2009	375 I/O	65,000	78,000
2008	300 I/O	60,000	72,000
2007	300 I/O	55,000	66,000
2006	300 I/O	50,000	61,000

Chaparral Signature 270/280

Year	Power	Retail Low	Retail High
2009	T270 I/O	89,000	104,000
2008	T270 I/O	81,000	95,000
2007	T270 I/O	73,000	86,000
2006	T270 I/O	67,000	78,000
2005	T260 I/O	61,000	71,000
2004	T260 I/O	55,000	65,000
2003	T260 I/O	50,000	59,000

Chaparral 280 SSi

Year	Power	Retail Low	Retail High
2006	T260 I/O	46,000	55,000
2006	375 I/O	42,000	50,000
2005	T260 I/O	42,000	50,000
2005	375 I/O	38,000	46,000
2004	T260 I/O	38,000	46,000
2004	375 I/O	35,000	42,000
2003	T260 I/O	35,000	42,000
2003	375 I/O	32,000	39,000
2002	T260 I/O	32,000	39,000
2002	320 I/O	30,000	36,000
2001	T260 I/O	30,000	36,000
2001	320 I/O	27,000	33,000
2000	T260 I/O	27,000	33,000
2000	320 I/O	25,000	30,000
1999	T260 I/O	25,000	30,000
1999	320 I/O	23,000	28,000

Chaparral 2835 SS; 285 SSi

Year	Power	Retail Low	Retail High
2006	T260 I/O	49,000	58,000
2005	T260 I/O	45,000	54,000
2004	T260 I/O	41,000	49,000
2003	T260 I/O	38,000	45,000
2002	T260 I/O	35,000	42,000

Year	Power	Retail Low	Retail High
2001	T260 I/O	32,000	38,000
2000	T280 I/O	29,000	35,000
1999	T28 I/00	27,000	32,000

Charappal 28/29 Signature

Year	Power	Retail Low	Retail High
2000	T190 I/O	34,000	40,000
1999	T190 I/O	32,000	38,000
1998	T190 I/O	30,000	36,000
1997	T190 I/O	29,000	33,000
1996	T190 I/O	27,000	31,000
1995	T190 I/O	25,000	29,000

Chaparral 280/290 Signature

Year	Power	Retail Low	Retail High
2009	T220 I/O	101,000	120,000
2008	T220 I/O	92,000	109,000
2007	T220 I/O	84,000	99,000
2006	T220 I/O	76,000	90,000
2005	T220 I/O	70,000	83,000
2004	T220 I/O	64,000	76,000
2003	T220 I/O	59,000	70,000
2002	T190 I/O	54,000	64,000
2001	T190 I/O	50,000	59,000

Chaparral Signature 300

Year	Power	Retail Low	Retail High
2003	T260 I/O	63,000	73,000
2002	T260 I/O	58,000	67,000
2001	T260 I/O	53,000	62,000
2000	T260 I/O	49,000	57,000
1999	T260 I/O	45,000	52,000
1998	T260 I/O	41,000	48,000

Chaparral Signature 30/31

Year	Power	Retail Low	Retail High
1997	T260 I/O	25,000	29,000
1996	T260 I/O	23,000	27,000
1995	T260 I/O	22,000	26,000

Chaparral Signature 310

Year	Power	Retail Low	Retail High
2009	T300 I/O	126,000	147,000
2008	T300 I/O	116,000	135,000
2007	T300 I/O	106,000	124,000
2006	T300 I/O	98,000	114,000
2005	T300 I/O	90,000	105,000
2004	T300 I/O	83,000	97,000

Chaparral Signature 330

Year	Power	Retail Low	Retail High
2009	T300 I/O	160,000	187,000
2008	T300 I/O	147,000	172,000
2007	T300 I/O	135,000	158,000
2006	T300 I/O	124,000	145,000
2005	T300 I/O	114,000	134,000
2004	T300 I/O	105,000	123,000
2003	T300 I/O	97,000	113,000

Chaparral Signature 350

Year	Power	Retail Low	Retail High
2009	T320	204,000	235,000
2008	T320	186,000	214,000
2007	T320	169,000	194,000
2006	T320	154,000	177,000
2005	T300	140,000	161,000
2004	T300	129,000	148,000
2003	T300	118,000	136,000
2002	T300	109,000	125,000
2001	T300	100,000	115,000

Chris Craft 272/282/30 Crowne

Year	Power	Retail Low	Retail High
1997	T215 I/O	21,000	24,000
1996	T215 I/O	20,000	23,000
1995	T215 I/O	19,000	22,000

Chris Craft 28 Corsair

Year	Power	Retail Low	Retail High
2008	T280 I/O	90,000	106,000
2007	T320 I/O	82,000	97,000
2006	T320 I/O	76,000	90,000
2005	T320 I/O	70,000	82,000
2004	T375 I/O	64,000	76,000

Year	Power	Retail Low	Retail High
2003	T375 I/O	59,000	70,000

Chris Craft 28 Launch

Year	Power	Retail Low	Retail High
2009	T320 I/O	111,000	133,000
2008	T320 I/O	102,000	123,000
2007	T320 I/O	94,000	113,000
2006	T320 I/O	86,000	104,000
2005	T320 I/O	79,000	95,000
2004	T375 I/O	73,000	88,000
2003	T375 I/O	67,000	81,000

Chris Craft 300/308 Express Cruiser

Year	Power	Retail Low	Retail High
2003	T270 I/O	53,000	64,000
2002	T270 I/O	48,000	58,000
2001	T250 I/O	44,000	53,000
2000	T250 I/O	40,000	48,000
1999	T250 I/O	36,000	43,000

Chris Craft 320/328 Express Cruiser

Year	Power	Retail Low	Retail High
2003	T270 I/O	60,000	72,000
2002	T270 I/O	54,000	65,000
2001	T280 I/O	49,000	59,000
2000	T280 I/O	45,000	54,000
1999	T280 I/O	41,000	49,000
1998	T280 I/O	37,000	45,000
1997	T280 I/O	34,000	40,000

Chris Craft 33 Corsair

Year	Power	Retail Low	Retail High
2010	T420 I/O	******	******
2009	T420 I/O	******	******
2008	T420 I/O	195,000	231,000
2007	T420 I/O	180,000	212,000
2006	T420 I/O	165,000	195,000

Chris Craft 33 Crowne

Year	Power	Retail Low	Retail High
1997	T250 I/O	27,000	32,000
1996	T250 I/O	24,000	29,000
1995	T250 I/O	22,000	27,000

Chris Craft 34 Crowne

Year	Power	Retail Low	Retail High
1997	T320G I/B	31,000	36,000
1996	T320G I/B	29,000	34,000
1995	T300G I/B	27,000	32,000

Chris Craft 36 Corsair

Year	Power	Retail Low	Retail High
2008-2012		******	******
2007	T420 I/O	208,000	244,000
2006	T420 I/O	191,000	224,000
2005	T420 I/O	176,000	206,000

Chris Craft 36 Roamer

Year	Power	Retail Low	Retail High
2005	T375G	******	******
2004	T375G	111,000	133,000
2003	T375G	102,000	123,000

Chris Craft 380 Continental

Year	Power	Retail Low	Retail High
1997	T380G	58,000	69,000
1996	T330G	53,000	64,000
1995	T330G	49,000	59,000

Chris Craft 40/43 Roamer

Year	Power	Retail Low	Retail High
2008	T370D	******	******
2007	T370D	******	******
2006	T370D	268,000	308,000
2005	480D	247,000	284,000
2004	480D	227,000	261,000
2003	480D	209,000	240,000

Cobalt 262

Year	Power	Retail Low	Retail High
2007	320 I/O	49,000	58,000
2996	320 I/O	44,000	53,000
2005	320 I/O	40,000	48,000
2004	320 I/O	37,000	44,000
2003	300 I/O	33,000	40,000
2002	300 I/O	30,000	36,000
2001	300 I/O	27,000	33,000

Year	Power	Retail Low	Retail High
2001	300 I/O	25,000	30,000
Cobalt 263			
2007	320 I/O	51,000	61,000
2006	320 I/O	46,000	55,000
2005	320 I/O	42,000	50,000
2004	320 I/O	38,000	46,000
2003	320 I/O	35,000	41,000
2002	320 I/O	28,000	34,000
2001	320 I/O	26,000	31,000
Cobalt 272			
2000	300 I/O	25,000	20,000
1999	300 I/O	23,000	27,000
1998	300 I/O	21,000	25,000
1997	300 I/O	19,000	23,000
1996	300 I/O	18,000	21,000
1995	300 I/O	16,000	19,000
Cobalt 282			
2008	T260 I/O	******	******
2008	425 I/O	******	******
2007	T260 I/O	65,000	76,000
2007	425 I/O	60,000	70,000
2006	T260 I/O	59,000	70,000
2006	425 I/O	55,000	65,000
2005	T260 I/O	55,000	64,000
2005	425 I/O	50,000	59,000
2004	T260 I/O	50,000	59,000
2004	425 I/O	46,000	55,000
2003	T260 I/O	46,000	54,000
2003	425 I/O	42,000	50,000
2002	T260 I/O	43,000	50,000
2002	425 I/O	39,000	46,000
Cobalt 292			
2002	425 I/O	43,000	50,000
2002	T260 I/O	47,000	55,000
2001	425 I/O	39,000	46,000
2001	T260 I/O	43,000	51000
2000	425 I/O	36,000	42,000
2000	T260 I/O	39,000	46,000
1999	425 I/O	33,000	39,000
1999	T260 I/O	36,000	43,000
Cobalt 293			
2004	425 I/O	50,000	59,000
2004	T260 I/O	53,000	62,000
2003	425 I/O	46,000	54,000
2003	T260 I/O	48,000	57,000
2002	425 I/O	42,000	49,000
2002	T260 I/O	44,000	52,000
2001	415 I/O	39,000	45,000
2001	T260 I/O	41,000	48,000
2000	415 I/O	35,000	42,000
2000	T260 I/O	38,000	44,000
1999	415 I/O	32,000	38,000
1999	T260 I/O	34,000	41,000
1998	415 I/O	30,000	35,000
1998	T260 I/O	32,000	37,000
1997	375 I/O	27,000	32,000
1997	T260 I/O	29,000	34,000
Cobalt 323			
2008-2012		******	******
2007	T300 I/O	117,000	138,000
2006	T300 I/O	107,000	127,000
Cobalt 343			
2007	T375 I/O	118,000	139,000
2006	T375 I/O	108,000	128,000
2005	T375 I/O	100,000	117,000
2004	T375 I/O	91,000	108,000
Cobalt 360			
2005	T375	135,000	160,000
2004	T375	123,000	145,000
2003	T375	112,000	132,000
2002	T375	102,000	120,000
Cobia 250/260/270 Walkaround			
2007	T200 O/B	46,000	54,000
2006	T200 O/B	42,000	49,000
2005	T200 O/B	38,000	45,000
2004	T200 O/B	35,000	41,000
2003	T200 O/B	31,000	37,000
2002	T200 O/B	29,000	34,000
2001	T200 O/B	27,000	31,000
2000	T200 O/B	24,000	29,000
1999	T200 O/B	22,000	26,000
1998	T200 O/B	21,000	24,000
1997	T200 O/B	19,000	22,000
Cobia 254/264/274 Center Console			
2002	T200 O/B	27,000	32,000
2001	T200 O/B	25,000	29,000
2000	T200 O/B	22,000	26,000
1999	T200 O/B	20,000	24,000
1998	T200 O/B	18,000	22,000
1997	T200 O/B	17,000	20,000
Cobia 274 Center Console			
2007	T200 O/B	45,000	53,000
2006	T200 O/B	41,000	48,000
2005	T200 O/B	37,000	43,000
2004	T200 O/B	33,000	39,000
2003	T200 O/B	30,000	35,000
Cobia 312 Sport Cabin			
2007	T250 O/B	64,000	74,000
2006	T250 O/B	58,000	68,000
2005	T250 O/B	52,000	61,000
2004	T250 O/B	48,000	56,000
2003	T250 O/B	43,000	51,000
Cobia 314 Center Console			
2007	T250 O/B	61,000	72,000
2006	T250 O/B	55,000	64,000
2005	T250 O/B	50,000	58,000
2004	T250 O/B	44,000	52,000
2004	T250 O/B	40,000	47,000
2003	T250 O/B	36,000	42,000
Contender 25 Open			
2009-2012		******	******
2008	T200 O/B	72,000	86,000
2007	T200 O/B	65,000	78,000
2006	T200 O/B	59,000	71,000
2005	T200 O/B	54,000	65,000
2004	T200 O/B	49,000	59,000
2003	T200 O/B	44,000	53,000
2002	T200 O/B	40,000	49,000
2001	T200 O/B	37,000	45,000
2000	T200 O/B	34,000	41,000
1999	T200 O/B	31,000	38,000
1998	T200 O/B	29,000	35,000
1997	No. Production		
1996	T150 O/B	21,000	25,000
1995	T150 O/B	19,000	23,000
Contender 27 Open			
2004-2007		******	******
2003	T200 O/B	52,000	62,000
2002	T200 O/B	48,000	57,000
2001	T200 O/B	44,000	53,000
2000	T200 O/B	40,000	48,000
1999	T200 O/B	37,000	45,000
1998	T200 O/B	35,000	42,000
1997	T200 O/B	32,000	39,000
1996	T200 O/B	30,000	36,000
1995	T200 O/B	28,000	34,000
Contender 31 Open			
2007	T225 O/B	79,000	95,000
2006	T225 O/B	72,000	86,000
2005	T225 O/B	65,000	79,000
2004	T225 O/B	59,000	71,000
2003	T225 O/B	54,000	65,000
2002	T225 O/B	49,000	59,000
2001	T225 O/B	45,000	54,000
2000	T225 O/B	41,000	49,000
1999	T225 O/B	37,000	45,000
1998	T225 O/B	34,000	41,000
1997	T225 O/B	32,000	38,000
1996	T225 O/B	29,000	35,000
1995	T225 O/B	27,000	32,000
Contender 33 Tournament			
200-20129		******	******
2008	3/250 O/B	111,000	133,000
2007	3/250 O/B	101,000	121,000
2006	3/250 O/B	92,000	110,000
Contender 36 Open			
2007	3/250 O/B	91,000	109,000
2006	3/250 O/B	84,000	101,000
2005	3/250 O/B	78,000	94,000
2004	3/250 O/B	73,000	88,000
2003	3/250 O/B	68,000	81,000
2002	3/250 O/B	63,000	76,000
2001	3/250 O/B	58,000	70,000
Crownline 262 CR			
2004	320 I/O	34,000	40,000
2003	320 I/O	31,000	37,000
2002	320 I/O	28,000	34,000
2001	320 I/O	26,000	31,000
Crownline 268 CR			
2000	310 I/O	19,000	23,000
1999	310 I/O	17,000	21,000
1998	310 I/O	16,000	19,000
Crownline 270 CR			
2009	300 I/O	67,000	80,000
2008	300 I/O	61,000	73,000
2007	300 I/O	55,000	66,000
2006	300 I/O	50,000	60,000
2005	300 I/O	46,000	55,000
2004	300 I/O	41,000	50,000
Crownline 290 CR			
2004	T250G	42,000	48,000
2003	T250G	38,000	44,000
2002	T250G	35,000	40,000
2001	T250G	32,000	36,000
2000	T250G	29,000	33,000
1999	T250G	26,000	30,000
Crownline 330 CR			
2000	T310G	55,000	65,000
1999	T310G	51,000	60,000
1998	T310G	47,000	55,000
1997	T310G	43,000	51,000
1996	T310G	39,000	47,000
Crownline 340/350 CR			
2010-2012		******	******
2009	T300G	139,000	164,000
2008	T300G	126,000	149,000
2007	T300G	115,000	136,000

See Page 667 For Price Adjustments

Cruisers 2870 Exp; 280 CXi

Year	Power	Retail Low	Retail High
2007	T220G	49,000	58,000
2006	T220G	44,000	52,000
2005	T220G	40,000	48,000
2004	T220G	37,000	43,000
2003	T220G	33,000	39,000
2002	T220G	30,000	36,000
2001	T220G	27,000	33,000
2000	T220G	25,000	30,000
1999	T220G	23,000	27,000
1998	T220G	21,000	25,000

Cruisers 2870 Rogue

Year	Power	Retail Low	Retail High
1995	T235G	13,000	16,000

Cruisers 300 Cxi; 300/310 Express

Year	Power	Retail Low	Retail High
2010-201		******	******
2009	T225 I/O	91,000	106,000
2008	T225 I/O	82,000	97,000
2007	T225 I/O	75,000	88,000

Cruisers 300 Express

Year	Power	Retail Low	Retail High
2007	T270G	86,000	101,000
2006	T270G	78,000	91,000
2005	T270G	71,000	83,000

Cruisers 3075 Express

Year	Power	Retail Low	Retail High
2003	T260G	43,000	51,000
2002	T260G	39,000	47,000
2001	T260G	35,000	42,000
2000	T260G	32,000	39,000
1999	T260G	29,000	35,000
1998	T260G	27,000	32,000
1997	T260G	25,000	30,000

Cruisers 3020/3120 Aria

Year	Power	Retail Low	Retail High
1997	T230G	28,000	33,000
1996	T230G	26,000	30,000
1995	T230G	24,000	28,000

Cruisers 3175 Rogue

Year	Power	Retail Low	Retail High
1998	T260G	34,000	40,000
1997	T260G	31,000	36,000
1996	T260G	28,000	33,000
1995	T260G	26,000	31,000

Cruisers 320 Express

Year	Power	Retail Low	Retail High
2006	T320 I/O	74,000	87,000
2005	T320 I/O	67,000	79,000
2004	T320 I/O	61,000	72,000
2003	T320 I/O	56,000	65,000
2002	T320 I/O	51,000	59,000

Cruisers 3375 Esprit

Year	Power	Retail Low	Retail High
2000	T300G	48,000	57,000
1999	T300G	44,000	52,000
1998	T300G	40,000	48,000
1997	T300G	37,000	44,000
1996	T300G	34,000	41,000

Cruisers 330/350 Express

Year	Power	Retail Low	Retail High
2011-2012		******	******
2010	T320G VD	165,000	191,000
2010	400G I/O	159,000	184,000
2009	T320G VD	150,000	174,000
2009	400G I/O	144,000	167,000
2008	T320G VD	136,000	158,000
2008	400G I/O	131,000	152,000

Cruisers 3470/340 Express

Year	Power	Retail Low	Retail High
2007	T370G VD	125,000	145,000
2007	T375G I/O	118,000	136,000
2006	T370G VD	114,000	132,000
2006	T320G I/O	107,000	124,000
2005	T320G VD	104,000	120,000
2005	T320G I/O	97,000	113,000
2004	T320G VD	95,000	111,000
2004	T320G I/O	89,000	104,000
2003	T320G VD	88,000	102,000
2003	T320G I/O	82,000	96,000
2002	T320G VD	81,000	94,000
2002	T320G I/O	76,000	88,000
2001	T320G VD	74,000	86,000
2001	T320G I/O	70,000	81,000

Cruisers 3570/3575 Esprit; 3572 Exp.

Year	Power	Retail Low	Retail High
2002	T370G	90,000	104,000
2001	T310G	83,000	96,000
2000	T310G	76,000	88,000
1999	T310G	70,000	81,000
1998	T310G	64,000	74,000
1997	T310G	59,000	68,000
1996	T310G	54,000	63,000
1995	T310G	50,000	58,000

Cruisers 3580/3585 Flybridge

Year	Power	Retail Low	Retail High
1999	T320G	66,000	77,000
1998	T320G	60,000	70,000
1997	T320G	55,000	63,000
1996	T320G	50,000	58,000

Cruisers 360/380 Express

Year	Power	Retail Low	Retail High
2010-2012		******	******
2009	T375 VD	222,000	256,000
2008	T375 VD	204,000	235,000

Cruisers 3670/3675/3775 Esprit

Year	Power	Retail Low	Retail High
1996	T310G	57,000	66,000
1995	T310G	53,000	61,000

Cruisers 3672/3772/370 Express

Year	Power	Retail Low	Retail High
2007	T375G	162,000	186,000
2006	T375G	147,000	169,000
2005	T370G	134,000	154,000
2004	T370G	122,000	140,000
2003	T370G	111,000	128,000
2002	T370G	101,000	116,000
2001	T370G	92,000	106,000
2000	T370G	83,000	96,000

Cruisers 3650/3750 Motor Yacht; 375 MY

Year	Power	Retail Low	Retail High
2005	T370G	155,000	181,000
2005	T310D	178,000	208,000
2004	T370G	141,000	165,000
2004	T370D	162,000	190,000
2003	T370G	128,000	150,000
2003	T370D	147,000	173,000
2002	T370G	117,000	137,000
2002	T370D	134,000	157,000
2001	T310G	106,000	124,000
2001	T370D	122,000	143,000
2000	T310G	98,000	114,000
2000	T370D	112,000	131,000
1999	T310G	90,000	105,000
1999	T370D	103,000	121,000
1998	T310G	83,000	97,000
1998	T350D	95,000	111,000
1997	T310G	77,000	90,000
1997	T350D	88,000	103,000
1996	T310G	71,000	84,000
1996	T350D	82,000	96,000
1995	T310G	66,000	78,000
1995	T350D	76,000	89,000

Cruisers 3870 Express

Year	Power	Retail Low	Retail High
2003	T370G	129,000	148,000
2002	T370G	117,000	135,000
2001	T370G	106,000	122,000
2000	T370G	97,000	111,000
1999	T380G	88,000	101,000
1998	T380G	80,000	92,000
1997	T380G	73,000	84,000

Cruisers 3850/3950 Aft Cabin MY

Year	Power	Retail Low	Retail High
1997	T310G	92,000	106,000
1997	T300D	115,000	132,000
1996	T310G	84,000	97,000
1996	T300D	106,000	122,000
1995	T310G	78,000	89,000
1995	T300D	97,000	112,000

Cruisers 385/395 Motor Yacht

Year	Power	Retail Low	Retail High
2008	T375G	263,000	303,000
2008	T310D	299,000	344,000
2007	T370G	242,000	278,000
2007	T310D	275,000	316,000
2006	T370G	223,000	256,000
2006	T310D	253,000	291,000

Cruisers 390 Sports Coupe

Year	Power	Retail Low	Retail High
2011	T425G	******	******
2010	T425G	******	******
2009	T375G	249,000	287,000
2008	T375G	227,000	261,000
2007	T375G	206,000	237,000

Cruisers 3970/400/420 Express

Year	Power	Retail Low	Retail High
2010	T420G IPS	******	******
2010	T370D IPS	******	******
2009	T375G IPS	******	******
2009	T370D IPS	******	******
2008	T375G	******	******
2008	T435D	******	******
2007	T375G	215,000	247,000
2007	T435D	250,000	288,000
2006	T375G	195,000	225,000
2006	T370D	227,000	262,000
2005	T375G	178,000	205,000
2005	T370D	207,000	238,000
2004	T375G	164,000	188,000
2004	T370D	190,000	219,000
2003	T375G	150,000	173,000
2003	T370D	175,000	201,000

Cruisers 405/415 Express MY

Year	Power	Retail Low	Retail High
2008	T435D	354,000	410,000
2007	T435D	322,000	373,000
2006	T370D	293,000	340,000
2005	T370D	266,000	309,000
2004	T370D	245,000	284,000
2003	T370D	225,000	262,000

Cruisers 4270 Express

Year	Power	Retail Low	Retail High
2003	T440D	194,000	223,000
2002	T440D	177,000	203,000
2001	T420D	161,000	185,000
2000	T420D	146,000	168,000
1999	T420D	133,000	153,000
1998	T420D	121,000	139,000
1997	T420D	110,000	127,000

Cruisers 4285 Express Bridge

Year	Power	Retail Low	Retail High
1996	T375D	85,000	99,000
1995	T375D	79,000	92,000

Cruisers 4370 Express; 440 Express

Year	Power	Retail Low	Retail High
2005	T440D	244,000	281,000
2004	T440D	225,000	258,000
2003	T440D	207,000	238,000

Cruisers 4450 Express MY

Year	Power	Retail Low	Retail High
2003	T480D	248,000	285,000
2002	T480D	228,000	263,000
2001	T480D	210,000	242,000

Year	Power	Retail Low	Retail High
2000	T480D	193,000	222,000
Cruisers 447 Sport Sedan			
2009-2012		******	******
2008	T435D	357,000	400,000
2007	T440D	325,000	364,000
Cruisers 455 Express MY			
2008-2012		******	******
2007	T480D	374,000	419,000
2006	T480D	340,000	381,000
2005	T480D	310,000	347,000
2004	T480D	285,000	319,000
Cruisers 477/497 Sport Sedan			
2007	T500D	393,000	452,000
2006	T500D	362,000	405,000
Cruisers 5000 Sedan Sport			
2003	T710D	338,000	379,000
2002	T660D	308,000	345,000
2001	T660D	280,000	314,000
2000	T660D	255,000	285,000
1999	T660D	232,000	260,000
1998	T625D	211,000	236,000
Cruisers 520 Express			
2009	T715D	******	******
2008	T715D	******	******
2007	T715D	475,000	532,000
2006	T715D	432,000	484,000
Cruisers 540/560 Express			
2007-2011			
2006	T715D	535,000	620,000
2005	T715D	492,000	570,000
2004	T715D	452,000	525,000
2003	T800D	416,000	483,000
2002	T800D	383,000	444,000
2001	T800D	352,000	409,000
DeFever 44 Trawler			
2004	T-Diesel	331,000	381,000
2003	T-Diesel	308,000	354,000
2002	T-Diesel	287,000	330,000
2001	T-Diesel	266,000	306,000
2000	T135D	253,000	291,000
1999	T135D	240,000	277,000
1998	T135D	228,000	263,000
1997	T135D	217,000	250,000
1996	T135D	206,000	237,000
1995	T135D	198,000	228,000
DeFever 49 PH (1977-2004)			
2004	T135D	******	******
2003	T135D	******	******
2002	T135D	289,000	323,000
2001	T135D	271,000	304,000
2000	T135D	255,000	286,000
1999	T135D	240,000	268,000
1998	T135D	225,000	252,000
1997	T135D	214,000	240,000
1996	T135D	203,000	228,000
1995	T135D	193,000	216,000
Donzi 275 Express			
2000	310 I/O	24,000	29,000
1999	310 I/O	22,000	27,000
1998	310 I/O	20,000	24,000
1997	310 I/O	19,000	22,000
1996	300 I/O	17,000	21,000
1995	300 I/O	16,000	19,000
Donzi 28 ZF			
2001	T225 O/B	33,000	39,000
2000	T225 O/B	29,000	35,000
1999	T225 O/B	26,000	32,000
Donzi 29 ZF Open			
2009	T250 O/B	******	******
2008	T250 O/B	81,000	96,000
2007	T250 O/B	74,000	87,000
2006	T250 O/B	67,000	79,000
2005	T250 O/B	61,000	72,000
2004	T250 O/B	56,000	66,000
2003	T250 O/B	50,000	60,000
Donzi 32 ZF Open			
2007	T250 O/B	68,000	80,000
2006	T250 O/B	62,000	73,000
2005	T250 O/B	56,000	66,000
2004	T250 O/B	51,000	60,000
2003	T250 O/B	47,000	55,000
2002	T250 O/B	43,000	51,000
2001	T250 O/B	40,000	47,000
2000	T250 O/B	36,000	43,000
Donzi 3250 LXC/Express			
2000	T310 I/O	55,000	65,000
1999	T310 I/O	50,000	59,000
1998	T300 I/O	46,000	55,000
1997	T300 I/O	42,000	50,000
1996	T300 I/O	39,000	46,000
Donzi 35 ZF Open			
2008-2011		******	******
2007	T275 O/B	99,000	117,000
2006	T275 O/B	90,000	107,000
2005	T275 O/B	82,000	97,000
2004	T275 O/B	75,000	88,000
2003	T275 O/B	68,000	80,000
2002	T225 O/B	62,000	73,000
2001	T225 O/B	56,000	66,000
2000	T225 O/B	51,000	60,000
1999	T225 O/B	46,000	55,000
1998	T225 O/B	42,000	50,000
Donzi 38 ZF Cuddy			
2008-2011		******	******
2007	3/250	138,000	159,000
2006	3/250	127,000	146,000
2005	3/250	117,000	135,000
Donzi 38 ZFX Open			
2008-2012		******	******
2007	3/250	133,000	154,000
2006	3/250	123,000	143,000
Donzi 38 ZSF			
200-20128		******	******
2007	3/250	144,000	166,000
2006	3/250	132,000	152,000
2005	3/250	122,000	140,000
2004	3/250	112,000	129,000
Donzi 39 ZSC			
2007	T525G	******	******
2006	T425G	******	******
2005	T425G	******	******
2004	T425G	119,000	142,000
2003	T425G	109,000	131,000
2002	T425G	100,000	120,000
2001	T425G	92,000	111,000
Doral 270 Prestancia			
1995	T205 I/O	16,000	19,000
Doral 270 SC			
2002	260 I/O	27,000	32,000
2001	260 I/O	24,000	29,000
2000	250 I/O	22,000	27,000
1999	260 I/O	21,000	25,000
1998	260 I/O	19,000	23,000
1997	220 I/O	17,000	21,000
1996	220 I/O	16,000	19,000
Doral 28 Prestancia			
2006	T220 I/O	73,000	87,000
2005	T220 I/O	67,000	80,000
2004	T220 I/O	61,000	74,000
2003	T220 I/O	56,000	68,000
Doral 300 Prestancia			
1995	T235 I/O	18,000	21,000
Doral 300 SC			
2000	T205 I/O	33,000	39,000
1999	T205 I/O	30,000	36,000
1998	T205 I/O	27,000	33,000
1997	T205 I/O	25,000	30,000
1996	T205 I/O	23,000	28,000
Doral 32 Intrigue			
2009	T320 I/O	******	******
2008	T320 I/O	******	******
2007	T320 I/O	81,000	95,000
2006	T320 I/O	74,000	87,000
2005	T320 I/O	68,000	80,000
2004	T320 I/O	63,000	74,000
2003	T320 I/O	58,000	68,000
2002	T320 I/O	53,000	62,000
2001	T320 I/O	49,000	57,000
Doral 330 SE; 33 Elegante			
2009	T320 I/O	******	******
2008	T320 I/O	******	******
2007	T320 I/O	92,000	108,000
2006	T320 I/O	84,000	99,000
2005	T320 I/O	77,000	91,000
2004	T320 I/O	71,000	84,000
2003	T320 I/O	65,000	77,000
2002	T320 I/O	60,000	71,000
2001	T320 I/O	55,000	65,000
Doral 350 SC			
1999	T260 I/O	50,000	59,000
1998	T260 I/O	46,000	54,000
1997	T260 I/O	42,000	49,000
1996	T260 I/O	38,000	45,000
Doral 360 SC; 36 Boca Grande			
2009	T375 I/O	******	******
2008	T375 I/O	******	******
2007	T375 I/O	112,000	132,000
2006	T375 I/O	103,000	121,000
2005	T375 I/O	94,000	111,000
2004	T375 I/O	87,000	102,000
2003	T375 I/O	80,000	94,000
2002	T320 I/O	73,000	87,000
2001	T320 I/O	67,000	80,000
2000	T320 I/O	62,000	73,000
1999	T320 I/O	57,000	67,000
1998	T320 I/O	52,000	62,000
Doral 45 Alegria			
2009	435 IPS	******	******
2008	435 IPS	******	******
2007	T480D	******	******
2006	T480D	******	******
2005	T480D	295,000	354,000
2004	T480D	271,000	325,000
Dyer 29 Trunk Cabin			
2003	S-Diesel	******	******
2002	S-Diesel	******	******
2001	S-Diesel	******	******
2000	S-Diesel	******	******

Year	Power	Retail Low	Retail High
1999	S-Diesel	62,000	74,000
1998	S-Diesel	58,000	70,000
1997	S-Diesel	55,000	67,000
1996	S-Diesel	53,000	63,000
1995	S-Diesel	50,000	60,000

Eagle 40 PH Trawler

Year	Power	Retail Low	Retail High
2002	S/Diesel	******	******
2001	S/Diesel	******	******
2000	S/Diesel	170,000	204,000
1999	S/Diesel	161,000	193,000
1998	S/Diesel	153,000	184,000
1997	S/Diesel	145,000	174,000
1996	S/Diesel	138,000	166,000
1995	S/Diesel	131,000	157,000

Edgewater 260 Center Console

Year	Power	Retail Low	Retail High
2001	T150 O/B	22,000	26,000
2000	T150 O/B	20,000	24,000
1999	T150 O/B	18,000	22,000
1998	T150 O/B	16,000	20,000
1997	T150 O/B	15,000	18,000
1996	T150 O/B	13,000	16,000
1995	T150 O/B	12,000	15,000

Edgewater 265 Express

Year	Power	Retail Low	Retail High
2012	T225 O/B	******	******
2011	T225 O/B	129,000	154,000
2010	T225 O/B	117,000	140,000
2009	T225 O/B	106,000	128,000
2008	T225 O/B	97,000	116,000
2007	T225 O/B	88,000	106,000
2006	T225 O/B	80,000	96,000
2005	T225 O/B	73,000	87,000
2004	T225 O/B	66,000	79,000
2003	T225 O/B	60,000	72,000
2002	T225 O/B	55,000	66,000

Edgewater 265/268 Center Console

Year	Power	Retail Low	Retail High
2012	T225 O/B	******	******
2011	T225 O/B	110,000	132,000
2010	T225 O/B	100,000	120,000
2009	T225 O/B	91,000	109,000
2008	T225 O/B	82,000	99,000
2007	T225 O/B	75,000	90,000
2006	T225 O/B	68,000	82,000
2005	T225 O/B	62,000	74,000
2004	T225 O/B	56,000	68,000
2003	T225 O/B	51,000	62,000
2002	T225 O/B	47,000	56,000

Edgewater 318 Center Console

Year	Power	Retail Low	Retail High
2012	T250 O/B	******	******
2011	T250 O/B	155,000	186,000
2010	T250 O/B	141,000	169,000
2009	T250 O/B	128,000	154,000
2008	T250 O/B	116,000	140,000
2007	T250 O/B	106,000	127,000
2006	T250 O/B	96,000	116,000

Egg Harbor 35 Sport Yacht

Year	Power	Retail Low	Retail High
1998	T320G	81,000	94,000
1998	T350D	96,000	111,000
1997	T320G	75,000	87,000
1997	T350D	88,000	102,000

Egg Harbor 35 Predator

Year	Power	Retail Low	Retail High
2010	T450D	******	******
2009	T450D	******	******
2008	T450D	******	******
2007	T440D	******	******
2006	T440D	188,000	216,000
2005	T440D	171,000	197,000
2004	T440D	156,000	179,000
2003	T440D	142,000	163,000
2002	T440D	******	******
2001	T440D	******	******
2000	T440D	******	******

Egg Harbor 37 Sport Yacht

Year	Power	Retail Low	Retail High
2007-2012		******	******
2006	T440D	225,000	259,000
2005	T440D	205,000	236,000
2004	T440D	186,000	214,000
2003	T440D	170,000	195,000
2002	T420D	154,000	177,000
2001	T420D	140,000	161,000

Egg Harbor 38 Convertible

Year	Power	Retail Low	Retail High
1997	T420D	139,000	164,000
1996	T420D	128,000	151,000
1995	T420D	117,000	139,000

Egg Harbor 42 Sport Yacht

Year	Power	Retail Low	Retail High
2003	T660D	264,000	303,000
2002	T660D	242,000	279,000
2001	T660D	223,000	256,000

Egg Harbor 43 Sport Yacht

Year	Power	Retail Low	Retail High
2009	715D	******	******
2008	715D	******	******
2007	715D	432,000	496,000
2006	715D	397,000	457,000
2005	700D	365,000	420,000
2004	700D	336,000	386,000

Endeavour TrawlerCat 36

Year	Power	Retail Low	Retail High
2005	T125D	******	******
2004	T125D	******	******
2003	T125D	123,000	148,000
2002	T125D	119,000	143,000
2001	T100D	116,000	139,000
2000	T100D	112,000	135,000
1999	T100D	109,000	131,000
1998	T100D	106,000	127,000

Everglades 260/270/275 Ctr. Console

Year	Power	Retail Low	Retail High
2011	T250 O/B	******	******
2010	T250 O/B	99,000	118,000
2009	T250 O/B	90,000	108,000
2008	T250 O/B	81,000	98,000
2007	T250 O/B	74,000	89,000
2006	T250 O/B	67,000	81,000

Everglades 29/2950 Center Console

Year	Power	Retail Low	Retail High
2012	T250 O/B	******	******
2011	T250 O/B	******	******
2010	T250 O/B	******	******
2009	T250 O/B	103,000	124,000
2008	T250 O/B	93,000	111,000
2007	T250 O/B	83,000	100,000
2006	T250 O/B	75,000	90,000
2005	T250 O/B	68,000	81,000

Everglades 35/3550 Center Console

Year	Power	Retail Low	Retail High
2012	3/250 O/B	******	******
2011	3/250 O/B	******	******
2010	3/250 O/B	******	******
2009	3/250 O/B	168,000	194,000
2008	3/250 O/B	154,000	179,000
2007	3/250 O/B	142,000	164,000

Fairline 40 Targa

Year	Power	Retail Low	Retail High
2007	310D	243,000	272,000
2006	310D	223,000	250,000
2005	310D	205,000	230,000
2004	310D	189,000	212,000
2003	310D	174,000	195,000
2002	310D	160,000	179,000
2001	260D	147,000	165,000
2000	260D	135,000	152,000

Fairline 43 Phantom

Year	Power	Retail Low	Retail High
2004	480D	308,000	345,000
2003	480D	283,000	318,000
2002	480D	261,000	292,000
2001	480D	240,000	269,000
2000	480D	221,000	247,000

Fairline 43 Targa

Year	Power	Retail Low	Retail High
2004	480D	238,000	267,000
2003	480D	219,000	245,000
2002	480D	201,000	226,000
2001	480D	185,000	207,000
2000	480D	170,000	191,000
1999	480D	157,000	176,000
1998	480D	144,000	161,000

Fairline 46 Phantom

Year	Power	Retail Low	Retail High
2005	500D	402,000	450,000
2004	480D	370,000	414,000
2003	480D	340,000	381,000
2002	480D	313,000	350,000
2001	480D	288,000	322,000
2000	480D	265,000	296,000
1999	480D	243,000	273,000

Fairline 48 Targa

Year	Power	Retail Low	Retail High
2002	430D	240,000	268,000
2001	430D	223,000	249,000
2000	420D	207,000	232,000
1999	420D	193,000	216,000
1998	420D	179,000	201,000

Fairline 52 Squadron

Year	Power	Retail Low	Retail High
2002	T700D	357,000	400,000
2001	T600D	332,000	372,000
2000	T600D	309,000	346,000
1999	T600D	287,000	322,000
1998	T600D	267,000	299,000

Fairline 52 Targa

Year	Power	Retail Low	Retail High
2007-2012		******	******
2006	T715D	529,000	593,000
2005	T715D	487,000	546,000
2004	T715D	448,000	502,000
2003	T715D	412,000	462,000

Fairline 55 Squadron

Year	Power	Retail Low	Retail High
2004	T715D	573,000	641,000
2003	T715D	532,000	596,000
2002	T700D	495,000	555,000
2001	T660D	460,000	516,000
2000	T660D	433,000	485,000
1999	T660D	407,000	456,000
1998	T660D	382,000	428,000
1997	T660D	359,000	403,000
1996	T660D	338,000	378,000

Fairline 58 Squadron

Year	Power	Retail Low	Retail High
2008	T715D	******	******
2007	T715D	******	******
2006	T800D	777,000	870,000
2005	T800D	723,000	809,000
2004	T800D	672,000	753,000
2003	T800D	625,000	700,000
2002	T700D	581,000	651,000

Fairline 59 Squadron

Year	Power	Retail Low	Retail High
1999	T650D	393,000	440,000
1998	T650D	366,000	409,000
1997	T650D	340,000	381,000
1996	T650D	316,000	354,000

See Page 667 For Price Adjustments

Fairline 65 Squadron

Year	Power	Retail Low	Retail High
2003	T1400D	******	******
2002	T1400D	******	******
2001	T1400D	******	******
2000	T1400D	761,000	852,000
1999	T1000D	715,000	801,000
1998	T1000D	672,000	753,000
1997	T1000D	632,000	708,000
1996	T1000D	594,000	665,000
1995	T1000D	558,000	625,000

Fleming 55 Pilothouse

Year	Power	Retail Low	Retail High
2009-2012		******	******
2008	T500D	1,220,000	1,366,000
2007	T450D	1,122,000	1,257,000
2006	T450D	1,032,000	1,156,000
2005	T450D	949,000	1,063,000
2004	T450D	873,000	978,000
2003	T450D	804,000	900,000
2002	T450D	739,000	828,000
2001	T450D	680,000	762,000
2000	T435D	626,000	701,000
1999	T435D	582,000	652,000
1998	T435D	541,000	606,000
1997	T435D	503,000	564,000
1996	T435D	468,000	524,000
1995	T435D	435,000	487,000

Formula 260 Sun Sport

Year	Power	Retail Low	Retail High
2010	300 I/O	75,000	90,000
2009	300 I/O	68,000	81,000
2008	300 I/O	62,000	74,000
2007	300 I/O	56,000	67,000
2006	300 I/O	51,000	61,000
2005	300 I/O	46,000	56,000
2004	300 I/O	42,000	51,000
2003	300 I/O	38,000	46,000
2002	300 I/O	35,000	42,000
2001	300 I/O	32,000	39,000
2000	300 I/O	30,000	36,000
1999	300 I/O	27,000	33,000

Formula 27 PC

Year	Power	Retail Low	Retail High
2012	T320 I/O	******	******
2011	T320 I/O	132,000	158,000
2010	T320 I/O	120,000	144,000
2009	T320 I/O	109,000	131,000
2008	T280 I/O	99,000	119,000
2007	T280 I/O	90,000	108,000
2006	T280 I/O	82,000	98,000
2005	T280 I/O	75,000	90,000
2004	T260 I/O	69,000	83,000
2003	T260 I/O	64,000	76,000
2002	T260 I/O	59,000	70,000
2001	T260 I/O	54,000	65,000
2000	T260 I/O	49,000	59,000
1999	T260 I/O	45,000	55,000
1998	T260 I/O	42,000	50,000
1997	T250 I/O	38,000	46,000
1996	T250 I/O	35,000	42,000
1995	T250 I/O	32,000	39,000

Formula 280 Bowrider

Year	Power	Retail Low	Retail High
2008	T260 I/O	59,000	71,000
2008	375 I/O	55,000	66,000
2007	T260 I/O	54,000	65,000
2007	375 I/O	50,000	60,000
2006	T260 I/O	49,000	59,000
2006	375 I/O	45,000	54,000
2005	T260 I/O	45,000	54,000
2005	375 I/O	41,000	49,000
2004	T260 I/O	41,000	49,000
2004	375 I/O	37,000	45,000
2003	T260 I/O	37,000	44,000
2003	375 I/O	34,000	41,000
2002	T260 I/O	34,000	41,000
2002	375 I/O	31,000	37,000
2001	T260 I/O	31,000	38,000
2001	375 I/O	29,000	34,000
2000	T260 I/O	29,000	34,000
2000	375 I/O	26,000	32,000
1999	T260 I/O	26,000	32,000
1999	375 I/O	24,000	29,000
1998	T260 I/O	24,000	29,000
1998	375 I/O	22,000	27,000

Formula 280 Sun Sport

Year	Power	Retail Low	Retail High
2008	T260 I/O	62,000	74,000
2007	T260 I/O	56,000	67,000
2006	T260 I/O	51,000	61,000
2005	T260 I/O	46,000	56,000
2004	T260 I/O	42,000	51,000
2003	T260 I/O	38,000	46,000
2002	T260 I/O	35,000	42,000
2001	T260 I/O	32,000	38,000
2000	T260 I/O	29,000	35,000
1999	T260 I/O	27,000	32,000
1998	T260 I/O	25,000	30,000
1997	T250 I/O	23,000	27,000
1996	T250 I/O	21,000	25,000
1995	T250 I/O	19,000	23,000

Formula 31 PC

Year	Power	Retail Low	Retail High
2012	T320 I/O	******	******
2011	T320 I/O	******	******
2010	T320 I/O	******	******
2009	T320 I/O	140,000	168,000
2008	T320 I/O	127,000	152,000
2007	T320 I/O	115,000	139,000
2006	T320 I/O	105,000	126,000
2005	T320 I/O	96,000	115,000
2004	T320 I/O	87,000	104,000
2003	T320 I/O	79,000	95,000
2002	T320 I/O	72,000	86,000
2001	T320 I/O	65,000	79,000
2000	T320 I/O	60,000	72,000
1999	T310 I/O	55,000	66,000
1998	T310 I/O	51,000	61,000
1997	T310 I/O	47,000	56,000
1996	T330 I/O	43,000	52,000
1995	T330 I/O	39,000	47,000

Formula 310 Sun Sport

Year	Power	Retail Low	Retail High
2012	T320 I/O	******	******
2011	T320 I/O	145,000	174,000
2010	T320 I/O	133,000	160,000
2009	T320 I/O	122,000	147,000
2008	T320 I/O	112,000	135,000
2007	T320 I/O	103,000	124,000

Formula 310 Bowrider

Year	Power	Retail Low	Retail High
2012	T320 I/O	******	******
2011	T320 I/O	140,000	168,000
2010	T320 I/O	128,000	154,000
2009	T320 I/O	118,000	142,000
2008	T320 I/O	109,000	130,000
2007	T320 I/O	100,000	120,000

Formula 330 Sun Sport

Year	Power	Retail Low	Retail High
2006	T320 I/O	77,000	92,000
2005	T320 I/O	70,000	84,000
2004	T320 I/O	63,000	76,000
2004	T320 I/O	58,000	69,000
2002	T320 I/O	52,000	63,000
2001	T320 I/O	48,000	57,000
2000	T320 I/O	43,000	52,000
1999	T310 I/O	40,000	48,000
1998	T310 I/O	37,000	44,000
1997	T310 I/O	34,000	40,000
1996	T310 I/O	31,000	37,000

Formula 34 PC (1991-2002)

Year	Power	Retail Low	Retail High
2002	T375 I/O	72,000	69,000
2001	T375 I/O	65,000	62,000
2000	T375 I/O	59,000	57,000
1999	T375 I/O	54,000	52,000
1998	T310 I/O	49,000	47,000
1997	T300 I/O	45,000	43,000
1996	T300 I/O	41,000	40,000
1995	T300 I/O	38,000	36,000

Formula 34 PC (2004-Current)

Year	Power	Retail Low	Retail High
2012	T375 I/O	******	******
2011	T375 I/O	******	******
2010	T375 I/O	******	******
2009	T375 I/O	225,000	270,000
2008	T375 I/O	204,000	245,000
2007	T375 I/O	186,000	223,000
2006	T375 I/O	169,000	203,000
2005	T370 I/O	154,000	185,000
2004	T370 I/O	140,000	168,000

Formula 350 Sun Sport

Year	Power	Retail Low	Retail High
2012	T320 I/O	******	******
2011	T320 I/O	******	******
2010	T320 I/O	175,000	210,000
2009	T320 I/O	159,000	191,000
2008	T320 I/O	144,000	173,000

Formula 36 PC

Year	Power	Retail Low	Retail High
1995	T300G	45,000	55,000

Formula 37 PC

Year	Power	Retail Low	Retail High
2011	T380G I/O	******	******
2011	T400G INBD	******	******
2010	T380G I/O	******	******
2010	T400G INBD	******	******
2009	T375G I/O	257,000	301,000
2009	T400G INBD	280,000	328,000
2008	T375G I/O	231,000	271,000
2008	T420G INBD	252,000	295,000
2007	T375G I/O	208,000	243,000
2007	T420G INBD	227,000	265,000
2006	T375G I/O	187,000	219,000
2006	T420G INBD	204,000	239,000
2005	T375G I/O	170,000	199,000
2005	T420G INBD	184,000	215,000
2004	T375G I/O	153,000	179,000
2004	T420G INBD	167,000	195,000
2003	T375G I/O	139,000	163,000
2003	T420G INBD	152,000	178,000
2002	T375G I/O	127,000	148,000
2002	T420G INBD	138,000	162,000
2001	T375G I/O	115,000	135,000
2001	T420G INBD	126,000	147,000
2000	T375G I/O	105,000	123,000
2000	T420G INBD	114,000	134,000

Formula 370 Super Sport

Year	Power	Retail Low	Retail High
2011	T430G I/O	******	******
2010	T430G I/O	******	******
2009	T425G I/O	******	******
2008	T425G I/O	198,000	231,000
2007	T425G I/O	180,000	210,000
2006	T425G I/O	163,000	191,000
2005	T425G I/O	149,000	174,000
2004	T425G I/O	135,000	158,000
2003	T425G I/O	123,000	144,000
2002	T425G I/O	112,000	131,000
2001	T425G I/O	102,000	119,000

Formula 40 PC

Year	Power	Retail Low	Retail High
2011	T400G	******	******
2011	T370D	******	******
2010	T400G	******	******
2010	T370D	******	******
2009	T400G	******	******
2009	T370D	******	******
2008	T425G	234,000	280,000
2008	T370D	215,000	258,000
2007	T425G	198,000	237,000
2007	T440D	182,000	218,000
2006	T425G	167,000	201,000
2006	T440D	154,000	185,000
2005	T425G	141,000	170,000
2005	T440D	130,000	156,000
2004	T420G	120,000	144,000
2004	T440D	110,000	132,000
2003	T420G	101,000	121,000
2003	T440D	93,000	112,000
2002	T420G	86,000	103,000
2002	T440D	79,000	94,000

Formula 400 Super Sport

Year	Power	Retail Low	Retail High
2011	T430G	******	******
2011	T300D	******	******
2010	T430G	******	******
2010	T300D	******	******
2009	T425G	******	******
2009	T370D	******	******
2008	T425G	******	******
2008	T370D	******	******
2007	T425G	204,000	238,000
2007	T350D	231,000	271,000
2006	T425G	185,000	217,000
2006	T350D	210,000	246,000
2005	T425G	169,000	197,000
2005	T350D	191,000	224,000
2004	T425G	153,000	180,000
2004	T350D	174,000	204,000
2003	T425G	140,000	163,000
2003	T350D	158,000	185,000
2002	T425G	127,000	149,000
2002	T350D	144,000	169,000
2001	T425G	117,000	137,000
2001	T470D	133,000	155,000
2000	T415G	107,000	126,000
2000	T470D	122,000	143,000
1999	T415G	99,000	116,000
1999	T470D	112,000	131,000

Formula 41 PC

Year	Power	Retail Low	Retail High
2004	T480D	******	******
2003	T480D	******	******
2002	T480D	178,000	204,000
2001	T450D	162,000	186,000
2000	T450D	149,000	171,000
1999	T450D	137,000	157,000
1998	T420D	126,000	145,000
1997	T420D	116,000	133,000
1996	T420D	106,000	122,000

Formula 45 Yacht

Year	Power	Retail Low	Retail High
2011	T435D	******	******
2010	T435D	******	******
2009	T435D	******	******
2008	T435D	413,000	475,000
2007	T435D	376,000	432,000

Formula 48 Yacht

Year	Power	Retail Low	Retail High
2007	T660D	483,000	545,000
2006	T660D	439,000	496,000
2005	T660D	399,000	451,000
2004	T660D	363,000	411,000

Four Winns 268 Vista

Year	Power	Retail Low	Retail High
2005	280 I/O	33,000	39,000
2004	280 I/O	30,000	36,000
2003	280 I/O	27,000	33,000
2002	280 I/O	25,000	30,000
2001	280 I/O	22,000	27,000
2000	280 I/O	20,000	24,000
1999	280 I/O	18,000	22,000

Four Winns 278 Vista (1994-98)

Year	Power	Retail Low	Retail High
1998	T205 I/O	17,000	20,000
1997	T205 I/O	15,000	19,000
1996	T205 I/O	14,000	17,000
1995	T190 I/O	13,000	16,000

Four Winns 278 Vista; V285

Year	Power	Retail Low	Retail High
2012	320 I/O	******	******
2011	320 I/O	******	******
2010	320 I/O	80,000	96,000
2009	300 I/O	73,000	88,000
2008	300 I/O	66,000	80,000
2007	300 I/O	60,000	73,000
2006	280 I/O	55,000	66,000

Four Winns 280 Horizon

Year	Power	Retail Low	Retail High
2005	T270 I/O	32,000	38,000
2005	375 I/O	29,000	34,000
2004	T270 I/O	29,000	35,000
2004	375 I/O	26,000	32,000
2003	T270 I/O	27,000	32,000
2003	375 I/O	24,000	29,000
2002	T270 I/O	24,000	29,000
2002	375 I/O	22,000	27,000
2001	T270 I/O	22,000	27,000
2001	375 I/O	20,000	24,000
2000	T270 I/O	21,000	25,000
2000	375 I/O	19,000	22,000

Four Winns 288 Vista

Year	Power	Retail Low	Retail High
2009	T270G	92,000	111,000
2008	T270G	84,000	101,000
2007	T270G	76,000	91,000
2006	T270G	69,000	83,000
2005	T270G	64,000	77,000
2004	T270G	59,000	70,000

Four Winns 298 Vista

Year	Power	Retail Low	Retail High
2005	T280G	66,000	79,000
2004	T280G	60,000	72,000
2003	T280G	54,000	65,000
2002	T280G	49,000	59,000
2001	T280G	45,000	54,000
2000	T280G	41,000	49,000
1999	T280G	37,000	45,000

Four Winns 310 Horizon

Year	Power	Retail Low	Retail High
2009	T270G	80,000	96,000
2008	T270G	73,000	88,000
2007	T270G	67,000	81,000

Four Winns 318 Vista; V335

Year	Power	Retail Low	Retail High
2012	T300 I/O	******	******
2011	T300 I/O	******	******
2010	T300 I/O	102,000	123,000
2009	T270 I/O	92,000	110,000
2008	T270 I/O	83,000	99,000
2007	T270 I/O	74,000	89,000
2006	T270 I/O	68,000	81,000

Four Winns 328 Vista

Year	Power	Retail Low	Retail High
2006	T280G	95,000	111,000
2005	T280G	86,000	101,000
2004	T280G	78,000	92,000
2003	T280G	71,000	83,000
2002	T280G	65,000	76,000
2001	T280G	59,000	69,000
2000	T280G	53,000	63,000
1999	T280G	49,000	57,000

Four Winns 338/348 Vista

Year	Power	Retail Low	Retail High
2004	T320 I/B	97,000	114,000
2003	T320 I/B	89,000	104,000
2002	T320 I/B	81,000	94,000
2001	T320 I/B	73,000	86,000

Four Winns V338 Vista; V355

Year	Power	Retail Low	Retail High
2011	T300 I/O	******	******
2010	T300 I/O	******	******
2009	T300 I/O	144,000	173,000
2008	T320 I/O	131,000	157,000
2007	T320 I/O	119,000	143,000

Four Winns 348 Vista; V358

Year	Power	Retail Low	Retail High
2009	T320 I/B	******	******
2009	T320 I/O	******	******
2008	T320 I/B	152,000	178,000
2008	T320 I/O	145,000	170,000
2007	T320 I/B	138,000	162,000
2007	T320 I/O	132,000	155,000
2006	T320 I/B	126,000	147,000
2006	T320 I/O	120,000	141,000
2005	T320 I/B	114,000	134,000
2005	T320 I/O	109,000	128,000

Four Winns 378 Vista

Year	Power	Retail Low	Retail High
2009	T400G IPS	******	******
2008	T375G	212,000	249,000
2007	T375G	193,000	226,000
2006	T370G	176,000	206,000
2005	T420G	160,000	187,000
2004	T420G	147,000	172,000
2003	T420G	135,000	158,000
2002	T420G	124,000	146,000

Four Winns V458/V475

Year	Power	Retail Low	Retail High
2012	T418D IPS	******	******
2011	T418D IPS	******	******
2010	T418D IPS	******	******
2009	T435D IPS	410,000	492,000
2008	T435D IPS	377,000	452,000

Glacier Bay 260/2665 Canyon Runner

Year	Power	Retail Low	Retail High
2008	T150 O/B	49,000	59,000
2007	T150 O/B	44,000	53,000
2006	T150 O/B	40,000	49,000
2005	T150 O/B	37,000	44,000
2004	T150 O/B	33,000	40,000
2003	T150 O/B	30,000	36,000
2002	T150 O/B	28,000	34,000
2001	T150 O/B	26,000	31,000
2000	T150 O/B	24,000	28,000
1999	T150 O/B	22,000	26,000
1998	T150 O/B	20,000	24,000
1997	T150 O/B	18,000	22,000
1996	T150 O/B	17,000	20,000

Glacier Bay 2670 Island Runner

Year	Power	Retail Low	Retail High
2008	T150 O/B	61,000	74,000
2007	T150 O/B	56,000	67,000
2006	T150 O/B	51,000	61,000
2005	T150 O/B	46,000	55,000
2004	T150 O/B	42,000	50,000
2003	T150 O/B	38,000	46,000
2002	T150 O/B	35,000	42,000
2001	T150 O/B	32,000	38,000
2000	T150 O/B	29,000	35,000
1999	T150 O/B	27,000	32,000
1998	T150 O/B	25,000	30,000

Glacier Bay 2680 Coastal Runner

Year	Power	Retail Low	Retail High
2008	T150 O/B	64,000	77,000
2007	T150 O/B	58,000	70,000
2006	T150 O/B	53,000	64,000
2005	T150 O/B	48,000	58,000
2004	T150 O/B	44,000	53,000
2003	T150 O/B	40,000	48,000
2002	T150 O/B	36,000	44,000
2001	T150 O/B	33,000	40,000
2000	T150 O/B	31,000	37,000
1999	T150 O/B	28,000	34,000

Glacier Bay 2690 Coastal Runner

Year	Power	Retail Low	Retail High
2008	T150 O/B	69,000	83,000
2007	T150 O/B	63,000	75,000
2006	T150 O/B	57,000	68,000
2005	T150 O/B	52,000	62,000
2004	T150 O/B	47,000	57,000
2003	T150 O/B	43,000	51,000
2002	T150 O/B	39,000	47,000
2001	T150 O/B	36,000	43,000
2000	T150 O/B	33,000	39,000

Glacier Bay 3470 Ocean Runner

Year	Power	Retail Low	Retail High
2008	T250 O/B	******	******
2007	T250 O/B	******	******
2006	T250 O/B	153,000	180,000
2005	T250 O/B	139,000	164,000

Glacier Bay 3480 Ocean Runner

Year	Power	Retail Low	Retail High
2008	T250 O/B	******	******
2007	T250 O/B	190,000	224,000
2006	T250 O/B	172,000	204,000
2005	T250 O/B	157,000	185,000

Glastron GS 279 Sport Cruiser

Year	Power	Retail Low	Retail High
2007	280 I/O	36,000	43,000
2006	280 I/O	32,000	39,000
2005	280 I/O	29,000	35,000
2004	280 I/O	27,000	32,000
2003	280 I/O	24,000	29,000
2002	280 I/O	22,000	26,000

Grady-White 265 Express

Year	Power	Retail Low	Retail High
2005	T225 O/B	63,000	76,000
2004	T225 O/B	57,000	69,000
2003	T225 O/B	52,000	62,000
2002	T225 O/B	47,000	57,000
2001	T225 O/B	43,000	52,000
2000	T225 O/B	39,000	47,000

Grady-White 268 Islander

Year	Power	Retail Low	Retail High
2002	T225 O/B	46,000	55,000
2001	T225 O/B	41,000	50,000
2000	T225 O/B	38,000	45,000
1999	T225 O/B	34,000	41,000
1998	T225 O/B	31,000	37,000
1997	T225 O/B	28,000	34,000
1996	T225 O/B	26,000	31,000
1995	T225 O/B	23,000	28,000

Grady-White 263/273 Chase

Year	Power	Retail Low	Retail High
2011	T225 O/B	******	******
2010	T225 O/B	97,000	117,000
2009	T225 O/B	88,000	105,000
2008	T225 O/B	79,000	95,000
2007	T225 O/B	71,000	85,000
2006	T225 O/B	64,000	77,000
2005	T225 O/B	57,000	69,000
2004	T225 O/B	52,000	63,000
2003	T225 O/B	47,000	57,000
2002	T225 O/B	43,000	52,000
2001	T225 O/B	39,000	47,000
2000	T225 O/B	36,000	43,000
1999	T225 O/B	32,000	39,000
1998	T225 O/B	29,000	35,000
1997	T225 O/B	27,000	32,000
1996	T225 O/B	24,000	29,000
1995	T225 O/B	22,000	27,000

Grady-White 270 Islander

Year	Power	Retail Low	Retail High
2005	T225 O/B	47,000	57,000
2004	T225 O/B	43,000	52,000
2003	T225 O/B	40,000	48,000
2002	T225 O/B	36,000	44,000

Grady-White 272 Sailfish

Year	Power	Retail Low	Retail High
2000	T225 O/B	40,000	49,000
1999	T225 O/B	37,000	44,000
1998	T225 O/B	33,000	40,000
1997	T225 O/B	30,000	36,000
1996	T225 O/B	28,000	33,000
1995	T225 O/B	25,000	30,000

Grady-White 282 Sailfish

Year	Power	Retail Low	Retail High
2008	T225 O/B	96,000	114,000
2007	T225 O/B	88,000	104,000
2006	T225 O/B	80,000	94,000
2005	T225 O/B	73,000	86,000
2004	T225 O/B	66,000	78,000
2003	T225 O/B	60,000	71,000
2002	T225 O/B	55,000	64,000
2001	T225 O/B	50,000	59,000

Grady-White 283 Release

Year	Power	Retail Low	Retail High
2012	T225 O/B	******	******
2011	T225 O/B	99,000	118,000
2010	T225 O/B	90,000	108,000
2009	T225 O/B	81,000	98,000
2008	T225 O/B	74,000	89,000
2007	T225 O/B	67,000	81,000
2006	T225 O/B	61,000	74,000
2005	T225 O/B	56,000	67,000
2004	T225 O/B	51,000	61,000
2003	T225 O/B	46,000	55,000
2002	T225 O/B	42,000	50,000

Grady White 300 Marlin

Year	Power	Retail Low	Retail High
2011	T225 O/B	******	******
2010	T225 O/B	131,000	157,000
2009	T225 O/B	119,000	143,000
2008	T225 O/B	108,000	130,000
2007	T225 O/B	98,000	118,000
2006	T225 O/B	89,000	107,000
2005	T225 O/B	81,000	98,000
2004	T225 O/B	74,000	89,000
2003	T225 O/B	67,000	81,000
2002	T225 O/B	61,000	73,000
2001	T225 O/B	56,000	67,000
2000	T225 O/B	51,000	61,000
1999	T225 O/B	47,000	56,000
1998	T225 O/B	43,000	52,000
1997	T225 O/B	40,000	48,000
1996	T225 O/B	36,000	44,000
1995	T225 O/B	33,000	40,000

Grady-White 305 Express

Year	Power	Retail Low	Retail High
2012	T250 O/B	******	******
2011	T250 O/B	******	******
2010	T250 O/B	139,000	162,000
2009	T250 O/B	126,000	148,000
2008	T250 O/B	115,000	134,000
2007	T250 O/B	104,000	122,000

Grady-White 306 Bimini

Year	Power	Retail Low	Retail High
2012	T250 I/O	******	******
2011	T250 I/O	******	******
2010	T250 I/O	132,000	155,000
2009	T250 I/O	120,000	141,000
2008	T250 I/O	109,000	128,000
2007	T250 I/O	99,000	116,000
2006	T250 I/O	90,000	106,000
2005	T250 I/O	83,000	97,000
2004	T250 I/O	76,000	89,000
2003	T250 I/O	70,000	82,000
2002	T250 I/O	65,000	76,000
2001	T250 I/O	59,000	70,000
2000	T250 I/O	55,000	64,000
1999	T250 I/O	50,000	59,000
1998	T250 I/O	46,000	54,000

Grady-White 330 Express

Year	Power	Retail Low	Retail High
2012	T250 O/B	******	******
2011	T250 O/B	******	******
2010	T250 O/B	202,000	234,000
2009	T250 O/B	184,000	213,000
2008	T250 O/B	167,000	194,000
2007	T250 O/B	152,000	177,000
2006	T250 O/B	138,000	161,000
2005	T250 O/B	127,000	148,000
2004	T250 O/B	117,000	136,000
2003	T250 O/B	108,000	125,000
2002	T250 O/B	99,000	115,000
2001	T250 O/B	91,000	106,000

Grady-White 336 Canyon

Year	Power	Retail Low	Retail High
2012	T250 O/B	******	******
2011	T250 O/B	******	******
2010	T250 O/B	******	******
2009	T250 O/B	144,000	167,000
2008	T250 O/B	131,000	152,000

Grady-White 360 Express

Year	Power	Retail Low	Retail High
2012	3/250 O/B	******	******
2011	3/250 O/B	******	******
2010	3/250 O/B	266,000	306,000
2009	3/250 O/B	242,000	279,000
2008	3/250 O/B	223,000	256,000
2007	3/250 O/B	205,000	236,000
2006	3/250 O/B	189,000	217,000
2005	3/250 O/B	173,000	200,000

Grand Alaskan 64 PH

Year	Power	Retail Low	Retail High
2006	T715D	854,000	1,025,000
2005	T715D	803,000	963,000
2004	T715D	754,000	905,000
2003	T715D	709,000	851,000
2002	T450D	667,000	800,000
2001	T435D	633,000	760,000
2000	T435D	602,000	722,000
1999	T435D	571,000	686,000
1998	T435D	543,000	652,000

Grand Banks 32 Sedan

Year	Power	Retail Low	Retail High
1995	135D	80,000	93,000

Grand Banks 36 Classic

Year	Power	Retail Low	Retail High
2000-2012		******	******
1999	No Prod	******	******
1998	No Prod	******	******
1997	No Prod	******	******
1996	210D	124,000	149,000
1996	T210D	138,000	165,000
1995	210D	118,000	142,000
1995	T210D	131,000	157,000

Grand Banks 36 Europa

Year	Power	Retail Low	Retail High
1998	210D	******	******
1997	210D	******	******
1996	210D	124,000	149,000
1996	T210D	138,000	165,000
1995	210D	118,000	142,000

See Page 667 For Price Adjustments

Year	Power	Retail Low	Retail High
1995	T210D	131,000	157,000

Grand Banks 38 Eastbay Express

Year	Power	Retail Low	Retail High
2004	T420D	******	******
2003	T350D	******	******
2002	T375D	******	******
2001	T375D	177,000	207,000
2000	T375D	163,000	191,000
1999	T375D	150,000	175,000
1998	T375D	138,000	161,000
1997	T375D	127,000	148,000
1996	T375D	118,000	138,000
1995	T375D	110,000	128,000

Grand Banks Eastbay 39 SX

Year	Power	Retail Low	Retail High
2008-2012		******	******
2007	T445D	364,000	419,000
2006	T480D	335,000	385,000

Grand Banks 41 Heritage EU

Year	Power	Retail Low	Retail High
2012	T425D Zeus	******	******
2011	T425D Zeus	******	******
2010	T425D Zeus	672,000	752,000
2009	T425D Zeus	618,000	692,000

Grand Banks 42 Classic

Year	Power	Retail Low	Retail High
2004	T450D	336,000	386,000
2003	T450D	312,000	359,000
2002	T450D	290,000	334,000
2001	T450D	270,000	310,000
2000	T375D	251,000	289,000
1999	T350D	233,000	268,000
1998	T350D	217,000	249,000
1997	T375D	202,000	232,000
1996	T375D	188,000	216,000
1995	T375D	174,000	201,000

Grand Banks 42 Europa

Year	Power	Retail Low	Retail High
2004	T450D	355,000	408,000
2003	T450D	330,000	379,000
2002	T450D	307,000	353,000
2001	T450D	285,000	328,000
2000	T375D	265,000	305,000
1999	T350D	247,000	284,000
1998	T350D	229,000	264,000
1997	T375D	213,000	245,000
1996	T375D	198,000	228,000
1991-95	No Prod.	******	******

Grand Banks 42 Motor Yacht

Year	Power	Retail Low	Retail High
2004	T450D	345,000	397,000
2003	T450D	321,000	369,000
2002	T450D	298,000	343,000
2001	T450D	277,000	319,000
2000	T375D	258,000	297,000
1999	T350D	240,000	276,000
1998	T350D	223,000	257,000
1997	T375D	207,000	239,000
1996	T375D	193,000	222,000
1995	T375D	179,000	206,000

Grand Banks 43 Eastbay Flybridge

Year	Power	Retail Low	Retail High
2004	T420D	292,000	345,000
2003	T420D	278,000	328,000
2002	T420D	264,000	311,000
2001	T420D	251,000	296,000
2000	T420D	238,000	281,000
1999	T420D	228,000	270,000
1998	T420D	219,000	259,000

Grand Banks 43 Eastbay Express

Year	Power	Retail Low	Retail High
2004	T420D	278,000	328,000
2003	T420D	264,000	312,000
2002	T420D	251,000	296,000
2001	T420D	238,000	281,000
2000	T420D	226,000	267,000

Grand Banks 43 Eastbay HX

Year	Power	Retail Low	Retail High
2007	T455D	336,000	396,000
2006	T455D	315,000	372,000
2005	T440D	296,000	350,000
2004	T440D	279,000	329,000
2003	T440D	262,000	309,000
2002	T440D	246,000	290,000

Grand Banks 43 Eastbay SX

Year	Power	Retail Low	Retail High
2007	T455D	355,000	419,000
2006	T455D	333,000	393,000
2005	T440D	313,000	370,000
2004	T440D	295,000	348,000
2003	T440D	277,000	327,000
2002	T440D	260,000	307,000

Grand Banks 46 Classic

Year	Power	Retail Low	Retail High
2007	T455D	******	******
2006	T455D	427,000	499,000
2005	T465D	405,000	474,000
2004	T465D	385,000	451,000
2003	T420D	366,000	428,000
2002	T420D	351,000	411,000
2001	T420D	337,000	394,000
2000	T375D	324,000	379,000
1999	T375D	311,000	363,000
1998	T375D	298,000	349,000
1997	T375D	286,000	335,000
1996	T375D	275,000	322,000
1995	T375D	264,000	309,000

Grand Banks 46 Europa

Year	Power	Retail Low	Retail High
2008	T500D	******	******
2007	T500D	******	******
2006	T500D	409,000	475,000
2005	T500D	385,000	446,000
2004	T450D	362,000	420,000
2003	T420D	344,000	399,000
2002	T420D	326,000	379,000
2001	T420D	310,000	360,000
2000	T375D	295,000	342,000
1999	T375D	280,000	325,000
1998	T375D	266,000	308,000
1997	T375D	252,000	293,000
1996	T375D	242,000	281,000
1995	T375D	233,000	270,000

Grand Banks 47 Eastbay FB

Year	Power	Retail Low	Retail High
200-20127		******	******
2006	T720D	528,000	617,000
2005	T720D	501,000	586,000

Grand Banks 47 Heritage CL

Year	Power	Retail Low	Retail High
2009-2012		******	******
2008	T567D	508,000	595,000
2007	T567D	483,000	565,000

Grand Banks 47 Heritage EU

Year	Power	Retail Low	Retail High
2009-2012		******	******
2008	T567D	499,000	584,000
2007	T567D	474,000	554,000

Grand Banks 49 Classic

Year	Power	Retail Low	Retail High
1997	T375D	******	******
1996	T375D	******	******
1995	T375D	384,000	449,000

Grand Banks 49 Eastbay SX

Year	Power	Retail Low	Retail High
2008	T705D	******	******
2007	T705D	576,000	673,000
2006	T705D	541,000	633,000
2005	T700D	508,000	595,000
2004	T700D	478,000	559,000
2003	T700D	454,000	531,000
2002	T700D	431,000	505,000
2001	T700D	410,000	479,000
2000	T670D	389,000	455,000
1999	T670D	370,000	433,000

Grand Banks 49 Motor Yacht

Year	Power	Retail Low	Retail High
1999	T375D	408,000	478,000
1998	T375D	388,000	454,000
1997	T375D	369,000	431,000
1996	T375D	350,000	410,000
1995	T375D	333,000	389,000

Grand Banks 52 Europa

Year	Power	Retail Low	Retail High
2008	T660D	******	******
2007	T660D	******	******
2006	T660D	840,000	983,000
2005	T660D	798,000	934,000
2004	T660D	758,000	887,000
2003	T375D	720,000	843,000
2002	T375D	684,000	800,000
2001	T375D	650,000	760,000
2000	T375D	624,000	730,000
1999	T375D	599,000	701,000
1998	T375D	575,000	673,000

Grand Banks 54 Eastbay SX

Year	Power	Retail Low	Retail High
2007	T1000D	******	******
2006	T1000D	595,000	696,000
2005	T1000D	565,000	661,000
2004	T800D	537,000	628,000
2003	T800D	510,000	597,000

Great Harbor 37

Year	Power	Retail Low	Retail High
2001-2012		******	*******
2000	T/56D	270,000	313,000
1999	T/56D	259,000	300,000
1998	T/56D	248,000	288,000
1997	T/56D	238,000	277,000
1996	T/56D	229,000	266,000

Hatteras 39 Convertible

Year	Power	Retail Low	Retail High
1998	485D	150,000	178,000
1997	485D	138,000	163,000
1996	485D	127,000	150,000
1995	485D	117,000	138,000

Hatteras 39 Sport Express

Year	Power	Retail Low	Retail High
1998	485D	134,000	159,000
1997	485D	124,000	146,000
1996	485D	114,000	134,000
1995	485D	104,000	123,000

Hatteras 40 Motor Yacht

Year	Power	Retail Low	Retail High
1997	T340D	142,000	171,000
1996	T340D	132,000	159,000
1995	T340D	123,000	147,000

Hatteras 42 Cockpit MY

Year	Power	Retail Low	Retail High
1997	T364D	160,000	189,000
1996	T364D	149,000	176,000
1995	T340D	138,000	163,000

Hatteras 43 Convertible

Year	Power	Retail Low	Retail High
1998	T625D	215,000	254,000
1997	T625D	198,000	233,000
1996	T535D	182,000	215,000
1995	T535D	167,000	197,000

Hatteras 43 Sport Express

Year	Power	Retail Low	Retail High
1998	T625D	197,000	233,000
1997	T600D	181,000	214,000
1996	T600D	167,000	197,000

Hatteras 46 Conv. (1992-95)

Year	Power	Retail Low	Retail High
1995	720D	237,000	277,000

See Page 667 For Price Adjustments

Hatteras 48 Cockpit MY

Year	Power	Retail Low	Retail High
1996	T535D	236,000	276,000
1995	T535D	227,000	265,000

Hatteras 48 MY (1990-96)

Year	Power	Retail Low	Retail High
1996	T720D	256,000	294,000
1995	T720D	235,000	271,000

Hatteras 50 Convertible

Year	Power	Retail Low	Retail High
2006	1000D	******	******
2005	1000D	712,000	826,000
2004	1000D	655,000	760,000
2003	1000D	603,000	699,000
2002	800D	554,000	643,000
2001	800D	510,000	592,000
2000	800D	469,000	544,000
1999	800D	432,000	501,000
1998	900D	397,000	461,000
1997	870D	365,000	424,000
1996	870D	336,000	390,000
1995	870D	309,000	359,000

Hatteras 50 Sport Deck MY

Year	Power	Retail Low	Retail High
1998	T565D	323,000	377,000
1997	T545D	300,000	351,000
1996	T545D	279,000	326,000

Hatteras 52 Cockpit MY

Year	Power	Retail Low	Retail High
1999	800D	380,000	444,000
1998	760D	349,000	409,000
1997	735D	321,000	376,000
1996	720D	295,000	346,000
1995	720D	272,000	318,000

Hatteras 52 Motor Yacht

Year	Power	Retail Low	Retail High
1996	720D	298,000	349,000
1995	720D	283,000	332,000

Hatteras 54 Conv. (1991-98)

Year	Power	Retail Low	Retail High
1998	1100D	427,000	500,000
1997	1075D	397,000	465,000
1996	1040D	369,000	432,000
1995	1040D	343,000	402,000

Hatteras 54 Conv. (2008-12)

Year	Power	Retail Low	Retail High
2008-2012		******	******
2007	1400D	1,045,000	1,212,000
2006	1400D	950,000	1,103,000
2005	1400D	865,000	1,003,000
2004	1400D	787,000	913,000
2003	1400D	716,000	831,000
2002	1400D	652,000	756,000

Hatteras 55 Convertible

Year	Power	Retail Low	Retail High
2002	1450D	669,000	790,000
2001	1450D	609,000	719,000
2000	1450D	554,000	654,000
1999	1450D	504,000	595,000

Hatteras 60 Convertible

Year	Power	Retail Low	Retail High
2006	1800D	******	******
2005	1650D	950,000	1,092,000
2004	1650D	874,000	1,005,000
2003	1400D	804,000	924,000
2002	1400D	739,000	850,000
2001	1400D	680,000	782,000
2000	1400D	626,000	720,000
1999	1400D	576,000	662,000
1998	1350D	529,000	609,000

Hatteras 6300 Raised PH

Year	Power	Retail Low	Retail High
2003	1500D	855,000	1,000,000
2002	1400D	786,000	920,000
2001	1400D	723,000	846,000
2000	1400D	665,000	778,000

Hatteras 65 Convertible

Year	Power	Retail Low	Retail High
2003	1400D	1,035,000	1,211,000
2002	1400D	952,000	1,114,000
2001	1400D	876,000	1,025,000
2000	1400D	806,000	943,000
1999	1400D	741,000	867,000
1998	1450D	682,000	798,000
1997	1400D	627,000	734,000
1996	1350D	577,000	675,000
1995	1350D	531,000	621,000

Hatteras 65 Motor Yacht

Year	Power	Retail Low	Retail High
1996	870D	646,000	755,000
1995	870D	601,000	700,000

Heritage East 36 Sundeck

Year	Power	Retail Low	Retail High
2004-2012		******	******
2003	230D	121,000	145,000
2002	230D	115,000	138,000
2001	230D	109,000	131,000
2000	230D	104,000	125,000
1999	230D	99,000	118,000
1998	230D	94,000	112,000
1997	230D	89,000	107,000
1996	135D	84,000	101,000
1995	135D	80,000	96,000

Hinckley Tararia T29R

Year	Power	Retail Low	Retail High
2009-2012		******	******
2008	S370D	192,000	228,000
2007	S370D	178,000	212,000
2006	S440D	166,000	197,000
2005	S440D	154,000	184,000
2004	S440D	143,000	171,000
2003	S440D	133,000	159,000

Hinckley 36 Picnic Boat

Year	Power	Retail Low	Retail High
2007	S440 Jet	345,000	401,000
2006	S440 Jet	321,000	373,000
2005	S440 Jet	298,000	347,000
2004	S440 Jet	277,000	323,000
2003	S440 Jet	258,000	300,000
2002	S350 Jet	240,000	279,000
2001	S350 Jet	223,000	259,000
2000	S350 Jet	207,000	241,000
1999	S350 Jet	195,000	227,000
1998	S350 Jet	183,000	213,000
1997	S350 Jet	172,000	200,000
1996	S350 Jet	162,000	188,000
1995	S350 Jet	152,000	177,000

Hinckley Talaria 40

Year	Power	Retail Low	Retail High
2011	T440D	******	******
2010	T440D	******	******
2009	T440D	******	******
2008	T440D	489,000	568,000
2007	T440D	465,000	563,000
2006	T440D	441,000	535,000
2005	T440D	424,000	514,000
2004	T440D	407,000	493,000
2003	T440D	390,000	474,000
2002	T440D	375,000	455,000

Hunt 29 Surfhunter

Year	Power	Retail Low	Retail High
2011	315D	******	******
2010	315D	******	******
2009	315D	******	******
2008	315D	172,000	209,000
2007	315D	157,000	190,000
2006	315D	143,000	173,000
2005	315D	130,000	157,000
2004	310D	118,000	143,000

Hydra-Sports 2596 Center Console

Year	Power	Retail Low	Retail High
2002	T225 O/B	24,000	29,000
2001	T225 O/B	22,000	26,000
2002	T225 O/B	20,000	24,000

Hydra-Sports 2796/2800 Vector

Year	Power	Retail Low	Retail High
2005	T225/OB	47,000	57,000
2004	T225/OB	42,000	51,000
2003	T225/OB	38,000	46,000
2002	T225/OB	34,000	42,000
2001	T225/OB	31,000	38,000
2000	T225/OB	28,000	35,000

Hydra-Sports 2800 Walkaround

Year	Power	Retail Low	Retail High
2005	T225/OB	52,000	64,000
2004	T225/OB	48,000	58,000
2003	T225/OB	43,000	54,000
2002	T225/OB	39,000	48,000
2001	T225/OB	36,000	44,000

Hydra-Sports 2800/3100 SF

Year	Power	Retail Low	Retail High
1998	T225 O/B	31,000	38,000
1997	T225 O/B	29,000	34,000
1996	T225 O/B	26,000	31,000
1995	T225 O/B	24,000	29,000

Hydra-Sports Vector 2900 CC

Year	Power	Retail Low	Retail High
2012	T250 O/B	******	******
2011	T250 O/B	******	******
2010	T250 O/B	******	******
2009	T250 O/B	105,000	128,000
2008	T250 O/B	96,000	116,000
2007	T250 O/B	87,000	106,000
2006	T250 O/B	79,000	96,000

Hydra-Sports 2900 VX Express

Year	Power	Retail Low	Retail High
2010	T250 O/B	******	******
2009	T250 O/B	100,000	122,000
2008	T250 O/B	91,000	111,000
2007	T250 O/B	83,000	101,000
2006	T250 O/B	76,000	92,000

Hydra-Sports Vector 3000 CC

Year	Power	Retail Low	Retail High
2000	T225/OB	33,000	40,000
1999	T225/OB	30,000	36,000
1998	T225/OB	27,000	32,000
1997	T225/OB	24,000	29,000

Hydra-Sports Vector 3300 CC

Year	Power	Retail Low	Retail High
2010	3/250 O/B	******	******
2009	3/250 O/B	******	******
2008	3/250 O/B	115,000	138,000
2007	3/250 O/B	104,000	124,000
2006	3/250 O/B	93,000	111,000
2005	3/250 O/B	85,000	101,000
2004	3/250 O/B	77,000	92,000
2003	3/250 O/B	70,000	84,000

Hydra-Sports 3300 VX Express

Year	Power	Retail Low	Retail High
2007	3/250 O/B	126,000	150,000
2006	3/250 O/B	115,000	137,000
2005	3/250 O/B	104,000	125,000
2004	3/250 O/B	95,000	113,000

Intrepid 26 Center Console

Year	Power	Retail Low	Retail High
1996	T200 O/B	15,000	18,000
1995	T200 O/B	14,000	17,000

Intrepid 262 Center Console

Year	Power	Retail Low	Retail High
2000	T200 O/B	23,000	27,000
1999	T200 O/B	21,000	25,000
1998	T200 O/B	19,000	23,000
1997	T200 O/B	17,000	21,000

Intrepid 289 Center Console

Year	Power	Retail Low	Retail High
2003	T225 O/B	37,000	44,000

Year	Power	Retail Low	Retail High
2002	T225 O/B	34,000	40,000
2001	T225 O/B	31,000	37,000
2000	T225 O/B	28,000	34,000
1999	T225 O/B	26,000	31,000
1998	T225 O/B	24,000	29,000
1997	T225 O/B	22,000	26,000
1996	T225 O/B	20,000	24,000
1995	T225 O/B	19,000	22,000
Intrepid 289 Walkaround			
2003	T225 O/B	41,000	50,000
2002	T225 O/B	38,000	45,000
2001	T225 O/B	34,000	41,000
2000	T225 O/B	32,000	38,000
1999	T225 O/B	29,000	35,000
1998	T225 O/B	27,000	32,000
1997	T225 O/B	25,000	30,000
Intrepid 300 Center Console			
2011	T250 I/O	******	*******
2010	T250 O/B	******	******
2009	T250 O/B	******	******
2008	T250 O/B	107,000	128,000
2007	T250 O/B	97,000	117,000
2006	T250 O/B	89,000	106,000
2005	T250 O/B	80,000	97,000
2004	T250 O/B	73,000	88,000
Intrepid 310 Walkaround			
2009-2012		******	******
2008	T250 O/B	112,000	134,000
2007	T250 O/B	102,000	122,000
2006	T250 O/B	92,000	111,000
2005	T250 O/B	84,000	101,000
2004	T250 O/B	76,000	92,000
Intrepid 322 Console Cuddy			
2003	T250 O/B	55,000	66,000
2002	T250 O/B	50,000	60,000
2001	T250 O/B	46,000	55,000
2000	T250 O/B	42,000	51,000
1999	T250 O/B	39,000	47,000
1998	T250 O/B	36,000	43,000
1997	T250 O/B	33,000	40,000
1996	T250 O/B	30,000	36,000
Intrepid 323 Cuddy			
2009	T250 O/B	******	******
2008	T250 O/B	119,000	143,000
2007	T250 O/B	108,000	130,000
2006	T250 O/B	99,000	118,000
2005	T250 O/B	90,000	108,000
Intrepid 33 Cuddy			
1995	T250 O/B	28,000	33,000
Intrepid 339 Center Console			
2002	T250 O/B	49,000	59,000
2001	T250 O/B	44,000	53,000
2000	T250 O/B	40,000	49,000
1999	T250 O/B	37,000	44,000
1998	T250 O/B	34,000	41,000
1997	T250 O/B	31,000	37,000
1996	T250 O/B	28,000	34,000
Intrepid 339 Walkaround			
2002	T250 O/B	53,000	63,000
2001	T250 O/B	48,000	58,000
2000	T250 O/B	44,000	52,000
1999	T250 O/B	40,000	48,000
1998	T250 O/B	37,000	44,000
1997	T250 O/B	34,000	41,000
1996	T250 O/B	31,000	37,000
1995	T250 O/B	29,000	34,000

Year	Power	Retail Low	Retail High
Intrepid 348 Walkaround			
2004	T250 O/B	80,000	96,000
2003	T250 O/B	72,000	87,000
2002	T250 O/B	65,000	78,000
Intrepid 350 Walkaround			
2011	T250 O/B	******	******
2010	T250 O/B	******	******
2009	T250 O/B	190,000	224,000
2008	T250 O/B	172,000	204,000
2007	T250 O/B	157,000	185,000
2006	T250 O/B	143,000	168,000
2005	T250 O/B	130,000	153,000
Intrepid 356 Cuddy			
2001	T250 O/B	61,000	74,000
2000	T250 O/B	56,000	68,000
1999	T250 O/B	52,000	62,000
1998	T250 O/B	48,000	57,000
1997	T250 O/B	44,000	53,000
1996	T250 O/B	40,000	48,000
1995	T250 O/B	37,000	44,000
Intrepid 366 Cuddy			
2003	3/225 O/B	76,000	91,000
2002	3/225 O/B	69,000	82,000
2001	3/225 O/B	62,000	75,000
2000	3/225 O/B	57,000	68,000
1999	3/225 O/B	52,000	62,000
Intrepid 370 Cuddy			
2011	2/300 O/B	******	******
2010	2/300 O/B	******	******
2009	3/275 O/B	242,000	285,000
2008	3/275 O/B	218,000	257,000
2007	3/275 O/B	196,000	231,000
2006	3/250 O/B	176,000	208,000
2005	3/250 O/B	160,000	189,000
2004	3/250 O/B	146,000	172,000
2003	3/250 O/B	133,000	157,000
Intrepid 377 Walkaround			
2008	3/250 O/B	******	******
2007	3/250 O/B	199,000	239,000
2006	3/250 O/B	179,000	215,000
2005	3/250 O/B	161,000	193,000
2004	3/250 O/B	147,000	176,000
2003	3/250 O/B	133,000	160,000
2002	3/250 O/B	121,000	146,000
2001	3/250 O/B	110,000	132,000
2000	3/250 O/B	100,000	121,000
Intrepid 390 Sport Yacht			
2009-2012		******	******
2008	3/300 O/B	285,000	336,000
2007	3/300 O/B	262,000	309,000
Island Gypsy 32 Europa			
2003	220D	124,000	149,000
2002	220D	112,000	135,000
2001	220D	105,000	126,000
2000	220D	99,000	119,000
1999	220D	93,000	112,000
1998	220D	87,000	105,000
1997	220D	82,000	99,000
1996	210D	77,000	93,000
1995	210D	72,000	87,000
Island Gypsy 32 Sedan			
1997-2001		******	******
1996	220D	73,000	88,000
1995	220D	71,000	86,000
Island Gypsy 36 Classic			
2001	220D	******	******

Year	Power	Retail Low	Retail High
2000	220D	******	******
1999	220D	******	******
1998	220D	110,000	132,000
1997	210D	105,000	126,000
1996	210D	101,000	121,000
1995	210D	97,000	116,000
Island Gypsy 36 Europa			
1998	210D	113,000	135,000
1997	210D	109,000	131,000
1996	210D	106,000	127,000
1995	210D	103,000	123,000
Island Gypsy 44 Flush Aft Deck			
1996	T300D	138,000	165,000
1995	T300D	129,000	155,000
Island Gypsy 44 Motor Cruiser			
1996	T135D	133,000	159,000
1995	T135D	126,000	151,000
Jefferson 35 Marlago Cuddy			
2010	T250 O/B	******	******
2009	T250 O/B	******	******
2008	T250 O/B	******	******
2007	T250 O/B	76,000	92,000
2006	T250 O/B	69,000	84,000
2005	T250 O/B	62,000	76,000
2004	T250 O/B	57,000	69,000
2003	T250 O/B	52,000	63,000
2002	T250 O/B	47,000	57,000
2001	T250 O/B	43,000	52,000
2000	T250 O/B	39,000	47,000
1999	T250 O/B	36,000	44,000
1998	T250 O/B	33,000	40,000
1997	T250 O/B	30,000	37,000
1996	T250 O/B	28,000	34,000
1995	T250 O/B	25,000	31,000
Jefferson 50 Rivanna SE			
2010	500D	******	******
2009	500D	******	******
2008	500D	******	******
2007	500D	315,000	369,000
2006	500D	287,000	336,000
2005	480D	261,000	305,000
2004	480D	237,000	278,000
Jefferson 52 Marquessa			
2001	T600D	291,000	341,000
2000	T600D	268,000	314,000
1999	T550D	247,000	289,000
1998	T550D	227,000	266,000
1997	T550D	209,000	244,000
1996	T550D	192,000	225,000
1995	T550D	177,000	207,000
Jefferson 52 Rivanna CMY			
1999	T450D	207,000	249,000
1998	T450D	191,000	229,000
1997	T450D	175,000	211,000
1996	T450D	161,000	194,000
1995	T435D	148,000	178,000
Jefferson 56 Marquessa CMY			
1998-2001		******	******
1997	T550D	225,000	265,000
1996	T550D	211,000	249,000
1995	T550D	198,000	234,000
Jefferson 56 Rivanna CMY			
200-20095		******	******
2004	T635D	369,000	435,000
2003	T635D	346,000	409,000
2002	T635D	326,000	384,000

Year	Power	Retail Low	Retail High
2001	T635D	306,000	361,000
2000	T600D	288,000	339,000
1999	T600D	273,000	322,000
1998	T600D	260,000	306,000
1997	T550D	247,000	291,000
1996	T550D	234,000	276,000
1995	T550D	222,000	263,000

Johnson 56/58 Motor Yacht

Year	Power	Retail Low	Retail High
2005	800D	475,000	560,000
2004	800D	441,000	521,000
2003	000D	410,000	484,000
2002	800D	382,000	450,000
2001	800D	355,000	419,000
2000	800D	330,000	389,000
1999	800D	310,000	366,000
1998	735D	291,000	344,000
1997	735D	274,000	323,000
1996	735D	258,000	304,000
1995	735D	242,000	286,000

Jupiter 27 Open

Year	Power	Retail Low	Retail High
2006	T225 O/B	74,000	88,000
2005	T225 O/B	66,000	80,000
2004	T225 O/B	60,000	72,000
2003	T225 O/B	54,000	64,000
2002	T225 O/B	48,000	58,000
2001	T225 O/B	43,000	52,000
2000	T225 O/B	39,000	47,000
1999	T225 O/B	35,000	42,000
1998	T225 O/B	31,000	38,000

Jupiter 29 Forward Seating

Year	Power	Retail Low	Retail High
2010-2012		******	******
2009	T250 O/B	108,000	129,000
2008	T250 O/B	98,000	118,000
2007	T250 O/B	89,000	107,000
2006	T250 O/B	81,000	97,000

Jupiter 31 Open

Year	Power	Retail Low	Retail High
2010-2012		******	******
2009	T250 O/B	125,000	150,000
2008	T250 O/B	112,000	135,000
2007	T250 O/B	101,000	121,000
2006	T250 O/B	91,000	109,000
2005	T250 O/B	82,000	98,000
2004	T250 O/B	74,000	88,000
2003	T250 O/B	66,000	79,000
2002	T250 O/B	59,000	71,000
2001	T250 O/B	54,000	65,000
2000	T250 O/B	49,000	59,000
1999	T250 O/B	45,000	54,000
1998	T250 O/B	41,000	49,000
1997	T250 O/B	37,000	44,000
1996	T250 O/B	34,000	40,000
1995	T225 O/B	30,000	37,000

Jupiter 34 Forward Seating

Year	Power	Retail Low	Retail High
2010-2012		******	******
2009	T350 O/B	152,000	182,000
2008	T350 O/B	136,000	164,000

Jupiter 38 Forward Seating

Year	Power	Retail Low	Retail High
2009-2012		******	******
2008	3/300 O/B	161,000	193,000
2007	3/300 O/B	146,000	176,000
2006	3/300 O/B	133,000	160,000
2005	T300 O/B	121,000	146,000

Krogen 39 Trawler

Year	Power	Retail Low	Retail High
2006-2012		******	******
2005	120D	342,000	410,000
2004	115D	324,000	389,000
2003	115D	308,000	370,000
2002	115D	293,000	351,000
2001	80D	278,000	334,000
2000	80D	264,000	317,000
1999	80D	251,000	301,000
1998	80D	238,000	286,000

Krogen 42 Trawler

Year	Power	Retail Low	Retail High
1997	135D	261,000	313,000
1996	135D	250,000	300,000
1995	135D	240,000	288,000

Krogen 44 Trawler

Year	Power	Retail Low	Retail High
2009-2012		******	******
2008	156D	570,000	684,000
2007	156D	541,000	649,000
2006	156D	514,000	617,000
2005	156D	488,000	586,000
2004	156D	464,000	557,000

Krogen 48 North Sea Trawler

Year	Power	Retail Low	Retail High
2008	201D	******	******
2007	201D	688,000	826,000
2006	201D	647,000	776,000
2005	201D	608,000	730,000
2004	201D	572,000	686,000
2003	201D	543,000	652,000
2002	201D	516,000	619,000
2001	201D	490,000	588,000
2000	201D	465,000	559,000
1999	201D	447,000	536,000
1998	201D	429,000	515,000
1997	201D	412,000	494,000
1996	201D	395,000	474,000

Krogen 48 Whaleback

Year	Power	Retail Low	Retail High
2003	210D	******	******
2002	210D	522,000	627,000
2001	210D	496,000	595,000
2000	210D	471,000	565,000
1999	210D	447,000	537,000
1998	210D	425,000	510,000
1997	210D	404,000	485,000
1996	210D	384,000	460,000
1995	210D	364,000	437,000

Krogen 58 Trawler

Year	Power	Retail Low	Retail High
2006-2012		******	******
2005	154D	1,045,000	1,233,000
2004	154D	992,000	1,171,000
2003	154D	943,000	1,112,000
2002	154D	895,000	1,057,000
2001	154D	851,000	1,004,000

Lagoon 43

Year	Power	Retail Low	Retail High
2005	T250D	285,000	342,000
2004	T250D	265,000	318,000
2003	T250D	246,000	295,000
2002	T250D	229,000	275,000
2001	T250D	213,000	255,000

Larson 270 Cabrio

Year	Power	Retail Low	Retail High
2001	320 I/O	22,000	26,000
2000	310 I/O	20,000	24,000
1999	310 I/O	18,000	22,000
1998	310 I/O	17,000	20,000
1997	310 I/O	15,000	18,000
1996	310 I/O	14,000	17,000

Larson 274 Cabrio

Year	Power	Retail Low	Retail High
2009	300 I/O	47,000	57,000
2008	300 I/O	43,000	51,000
2007	300 I/O	39,000	47,000
2006	300 I/O	35,000	42,000
2005	300 I/O	32,000	39,000
2004	300 I/O	29,000	35,000
2003	300 I/O	26,000	32,000
2002	300 I/O	24,000	29,000

Larson 280/290 Cabrio

Year	Power	Retail Low	Retail High
2001	T260 I/O	33,000	39,000
2001	320 I/O	29,000	35,000
2000	T260 I/O	30,000	36,000
2000	320 I/O	27,000	32,000
1999	T260 I/O	28,000	33,000
1999	320 I/O	24,000	29,000
1998	T260 I/O	25,000	31,000
1998	320 I/O	22,000	27,000
1997	T260 I/O	23,000	28,000
1997	310 I/O	21,000	25,000
1996	T250 I/O	21,000	26,000
1996	300 I/O	19,000	23,000
1995	T250 I/O	20,000	24,000
1995	300 I/O	17,000	21,000

Larson 300/310 Cabrio

Year	Power	Retail Low	Retail High
1998	T250 I/O	30,000	36,000
1997	T250 I/O	27,000	33,000
1996	T250 I/O	25,000	30,000
1995	T250 I/O	23,000	28,000

Larson 310 Cabrio

Year	Power	Retail Low	Retail High
2008	T260 I/O	118,000	142,000
2007	T260 I/O	108,000	129,000
2006	T260 I/O	98,000	118,000
2005	T280 I/O	89,000	107,000
2004	T280 I/O	81,000	97,000
2003	T280 I/O	74,000	88,000

Larson 330 Cabrio

Year	Power	Retail Low	Retail High
2009	T260 I/O	******	******
2008	T260 I/O	123,000	148,000
2007	T260 I/O	112,000	134,000
2006	T260 I/O	102,000	122,000
2005	T280 I/O	93,000	111,000
2004	T280 I/O	84,000	101,000
2003	T280 I/O	77,000	92,000
2002	T280 I/O	70,000	84,000
2001	T280 I/O	64,000	77,000
2000	T280 I/O	59,000	71,000
1999	T280 I/O	54,000	65,000

Larson 350 Cabrio

Year	Power	Retail Low	Retail High
2009	T300 I/O	******	******
2008	T300 I/O	153,000	184,000
2007	T300 I/O	140,000	168,000
2006	T300 I/O	127,000	152,000

Larson 370 Cabrio

Year	Power	Retail Low	Retail High
2009	T370G I/O	175,000	210,000
2008	T370G I/O	159,000	191,000
2007	T370G I/O	145,000	174,000
2006	T370G I/O	132,000	158,000
2005	T370G I/O	120,000	144,000
2004	T370G I/O	109,000	131,000

Legacy 28 Express

Year	Power	Retail Low	Retail High
2006	250D	90,000	108,000
2005	250D	83,000	100,000
2004	250D	78,000	93,000
2003	250D	72,000	87,000
2002	250D	67,000	81,000
2001	250D	62,000	75,000
2000	250D	58,000	70,000
1999	250D	54,000	65,000

Legacy 34 Express

Year	Power	Retail Low	Retail High
2006	T380D	******	******
2005	T380D	171,000	205,000
2004	T380D	155,000	186,000
2003	T300D	141,000	169,000

Year	Power	Retail Low	Retail High
2002	T300D	128,000	154,000
2001	T330D	117,000	140,000
2000	T330D	106,000	128,000
1999	T270D	97,000	116,000
1998	T270D	88,000	106,000
1997	T270D	80,000	96,000
1996	T270D	73,000	87,000

Luhrs 250 Center Console

Year	Power	Retail Low	Retail High
1996	T280G	23,000	28,000
1995	T280G	21,000	26,000

Luhrs 250 Open

Year	Power	Retail Low	Retail High
1996	T280G	26,000	32,000
1995	T280G	23,000	29,000

Luhrs 28 Open

Year	Power	Retail Low	Retail High
2009	T330G	152,000	182,000
2009	T260D	136,000	164,000
2008	T330G	123,000	147,000
2008	T260D	110,000	132,000
2007	T320G	99,000	119,000
2007	T260D	89,000	107,000
2006	T320G	80,000	96,000
2006	T240D	72,000	87,000
2005	T320G	65,000	78,000
2005	T240D	58,000	70,000

Luhrs 290 Open

Year	Power	Retail Low	Retail High
2002	T325G	55,000	66,000
2001	T325G	50,000	60,000
2000	T325G	45,000	54,000
1999	T320G	41,000	50,000
1998	T320G	38,000	46,000
1997	T270G	35,000	42,000
1996	T270G	32,000	38,000
1995	T270G	29,000	35,000

Luhrs 300 Tournament

Year	Power	Retail Low	Retail High
1996	T270G	28,000	34,000
1995	T270G	26,000	32,000

Luhrs 30/31 Open

Year	Power	Retail Low	Retail High
2009	T260D IPS	******	******
2008	T260D IPS	******	******
2007	T320G	114,000	136,000
2007	T315D	131,000	157,000
2006	T320G	103,000	124,000
2006	T315D	119,000	143,000
2005	T320G	94,000	113,000
2005	T315D	108,000	130,000
2004	T320G	85,000	103,000
2004	T315D	98,000	118,000

Luhrs 320 Convertible

Year	Power	Retail Low	Retail High
1999	T320G	52,000	62,000
1999	T300D	68,000	82,000
1998	T320G	48,000	57,000
1998	T300D	62,000	75,000
1997	T340G	44,000	53,000
1997	T300D	57,000	69,000
1996	T340G	40,000	48,000
1996	T300D	53,000	63,000
1995	T340G	37,000	44,000
1995	T300D	49,000	58,000

Luhrs 320 Open

Year	Power	Retail Low	Retail High
2008	T375G	171,000	206,000
2008	T315D	199,000	239,000
2007	T375G	154,000	185,000
2007	T315D	179,000	215,000
2006	T375G	139,000	167,000
2006	T315D	161,000	193,000
2005	T320G	125,000	150,000
2005	T315D	145,000	174,000
2004	T320G	112,000	135,000
2004	T315D	130,000	157,000
2003	T320G	101,000	121,000
2003	T315D	117,000	141,000
2002	T320G	92,000	110,000
2002	T315D	107,000	128,000
2001	T320G	84,000	100,000
2001	T300D	97,000	117,000
2000	T320G	76,000	91,000
2000	T300D	88,000	106,000
1999	T320G	69,000	83,000
1999	T300D	80,000	96,000
1998	T320G	63,000	76,000
1998	T300D	73,000	88,000
1997	T340G	57,000	69,000
1997	T300D	66,000	80,000
1996	T340G	52,000	62,000
1996	T300D	60,000	73,000
1995	T340G	47,000	57,000
1995	T300D	55,000	66,000

Luhrs 34 Convertible

Year	Power	Retail Low	Retail High
2003	T320G	114,000	136,000
2003	T315D	138,000	165,000
2002	T375G	103,000	124,000
2002	T300D	125,000	150,000
2001	T310G	94,000	113,000
2001	T300D	114,000	137,000
2000	T310G	85,000	103,000
2000	T300D	104,000	125,000

Luhrs 35 Convertible

Year	Power	Retail Low	Retail High
2009	T480D	302,000	362,000
2008	T380D	278,000	333,000

Luhrs 350 Convertible

Year	Power	Retail Low	Retail High
1996	T370G	67,000	81,000
1996	T300D	82,000	99,000
1995	T370G	62,000	74,000
1995	T300D	76,000	91,000

Luhrs 36 Convertible

Year	Power	Retail Low	Retail High
2007	T425G	207,000	249,000
2007	T440D	245,000	294,000
2006	T420G	188,000	226,000
2006	T440D	223,000	268,000
2005	T420G	171,000	206,000
2005	T440D	203,000	244,000
2004	T-Gas	156,000	187,000
2004	T420D	185,000	222,000
2003	T-Gas	142,000	170,000
2003	T420D	168,000	202,000
2002	T-Gas	129,000	155,000
2002	T420D	153,000	184,000
2001	T-Gas	119,000	142,000
2001	T420D	141,000	169,000
2000	T-Gas	109,000	131,000
2000	T420D	129,000	155,000
1999	T-Gas	100,000	121,000
1999	T420D	119,000	143,000
1998	T-Gas	92,000	111,000
1998	T420D	109,000	131,000

Luhrs 36 Open; 36 SX

Year	Power	Retail Low	Retail High
2007	T425G	196,000	236,000
2007	T440D	234,000	281,000
2006	T425G	178,000	214,000
2006	T440D	213,000	256,000
2005	T420G	162,000	195,000
2005	T420D	194,000	233,000
2004	T420G	148,000	177,000
2004	T420D	176,000	212,000
2003	T420G	134,000	161,000
2003	T420D	160,000	193,000
2002	T420G	122,000	147,000
2002	T420D	146,000	175,000
2001	T420G	112,000	135,000
2001	T420D	134,000	161,000
2000	T420G	103,000	124,000
2000	T420D	123,000	148,000
1999	T420G	95,000	114,000
1999	T420D	113,000	136,000
1998	T340G	87,000	105,000
1998	T420D	104,000	125,000
1997	T340G	80,000	97,000
1997	T420D	96,000	115,000

Luhrs 380/40/38 Convertible

Year	Power	Retail Low	Retail High
2007	T440D	282,000	338,000
2006	T440D	256,000	308,000
2005	T440D	233,000	280,000
2004	T420D	212,000	255,000
2003	T420D	193,000	232,000
2002	T420D	176,000	211,000
2001	T420D	160,000	192,000
2000	T420D	147,000	176,000
1999	T420D	135,000	162,000
1998	T420D	124,000	149,000
1997	T420D	114,000	137,000
1996	T420D	105,000	126,000
1995	T420D	97,000	116,000

Luhrs 380/40/38 Open

Year	Power	Retail Low	Retail High
2007	T440D	256,000	307,000
2006	T440D	233,000	280,000
2005	T440D	212,000	254,000
2004	T420D	193,000	231,000
2003	T420D	175,000	211,000
2002	T420D	160,000	192,000
2001	T420D	145,000	174,000
2000	T420D	134,000	160,000
1999	T420D	123,000	147,000
1998	T420D	113,000	136,000
1997	T420D	104,000	125,000
1996	T420D	96,000	115,000
1995	T420D	88,000	105,000

Luhrs 41 Convertible

Year	Power	Retail Low	Retail High
2009	T665D	******	******
2008	T540D	******	******
2007	T540D	301,000	349,000
2006	T540D	274,000	318,000
2005	T535D	249,000	289,000
2004	T535D	227,000	263,000

Luhrs 41 Open

Year	Power	Retail Low	Retail High
2009	T665D	******	******
2008	T540D	******	******
2007	T540D	299,000	353,000
2006	T540D	272,000	321,000

Luhrs 44 Convertible

Year	Power	Retail Low	Retail High
2005	T635D	******	******
2004	T500D	******	******
2003	T500D	175,000	210,000

Luhrs 50 Convertible

Year	Power	Retail Low	Retail High
2003	T900D	******	******
2002	T900D	******	******
2001	T900D	******	******
2000	T800D	427,000	513,000
1999	T800D	393,000	471,000

Mainship 30 Pilot

Year	Power	Retail Low	Retail High
2007	S315D	80,000	96,000
2006	S315D	73,000	88,000
2005	S315D	66,000	80,000

Year	Power	Retail Low	Retail High
2004	S315D	60,000	73,000
2003	S315D	55,000	67,000
2002	S230D	51,000	61,000
2001	S230D	47,000	56,000
2000	S230D	44,000	52,000
1999	S230D	40,000	49,000
1998	S230D	38,000	45,000

Mainship 30 Pilot Sedan

Year	Power	Retail Low	Retail High
2007	S315D	88,000	106,000
2006	S315D	80,000	96,000
2005	S315D	73,000	88,000
2004	S315D	66,000	80,000
2003	S315D	61,000	73,000
2002	S230D	56,000	67,000
2001	S230D	52,000	62,000
2000	S230D	47,000	57,000

Mainship 31 Pilot

Year	Power	Retail Low	Retail High
2011	S380D	******	******
2010	S380D	******	******
2009	S380D	161,000	193,000
2008	S315D	148,000	178,000

Mainship 31 Sedan Bridge

Year	Power	Retail Low	Retail High
1999	T290G	45,000	54,000
1998	T290G	41,000	50,000
1997	T270G	38,000	46,000
1996	T270G	35,000	42,000
1995	T270G	32,000	39,000

Mainship 34 Motor Yacht

Year	Power	Retail Low	Retail High
1998	T320G	58,000	70,000
1997	T340G	54,000	65,000
1996	T340G	49,000	59,000

Mainship 34 Pilot

Year	Power	Retail Low	Retail High
2008	370D	133,000	159,000
2007	370D	121,000	145,000
2006	370D	110,000	132,000
2005	370D	100,000	120,000
2004	370D	91,000	109,000
2003	330D	83,000	100,000
2002	330D	77,000	92,000
2001	300D	71,000	85,000
2000	300D	65,000	78,000
1999	300D	60,000	72,000

Mainship 34 Pilot Sedan

Year	Power	Retail Low	Retail High
2009	370D	******	******
2008	370D	144,000	173,000
2007	370D	131,000	157,000
2006	370D	119,000	143,000
2005	370D	108,000	130,000
2004	370D	99,000	118,000
2003	330D	90,000	108,000
2002	330D	82,000	98,000
2001	300D	74,000	89,000

Mainship 34 Trawler

Year	Power	Retail Low	Retail High
2009	380D	180,000	216,000
2008	380D	166,000	199,000
2007	240D	152,000	183,000
2006	240D	140,000	168,000
2005	240D	129,000	155,000

Mainship 350/390 Trawler

Year	Power	Retail Low	Retail High
2005	370D	123,000	148,000
2005	T240D	150,000	180,000
2004	370D	112,000	135,000
2004	T370D	136,000	163,000
2003	370D	102,000	123,000
2003	T240D	124,000	149,000
2002	300D	94,000	113,000
2002	T240D	114,000	137,000

Year	Power	Retail Low	Retail High
2001	300D	86,000	104,000
2001	T230D	105,000	126,000
2000	S-Diesel	79,000	95,000
2000	T230D	96,000	116,000
1999	S-Diesel	73,000	88,000
1999	T200D	89,000	106,000
1998	S-Diesel	67,000	81,000
1998	T-Diesel	81,000	98,000
1997	S-Diesel	62,000	74,000
1997	T-Diesel	75,000	90,000
1996	S-Diesel	57,000	68,000
1996	T-Diesel	69,000	83,000

Mainship 37 Motor Yacht

Year	Power	Retail Low	Retail High
1998	T320G	85,000	102,000
1997	T320G	78,000	94,000
1996	T340G	72,000	86,000
1995	T340G	66,000	79,000

Mainship 395 Trawler

Year	Power	Retail Low	Retail High
2011	380D	******	******
2011	T220D	******	******
2012	380D	228,000	278,000
2012	T220D	264,000	322,000

Mainship 40 Sedan Bridge

Year	Power	Retail Low	Retail High
1999	T320G	80,000	96,000
1998	T320G	74,000	89,000
1997	T320G	68,000	82,000
1996	T320G	62,000	75,000
1995	T320G	57,000	69,000

Mainship 400 Trawler; 414 Trawler

Year	Power	Retail Low	Retail High
2011	380D	******	******
2011	T220D	******	******
2010	380D	******	******
2010	T220D	******	******
2009	370D	256,000	302,000
2009	T220D	294,000	347,000
2008	370D	238,000	281,000
2008	T260D	238,000	281,000
2007	370D	273,000	323,000
2007	T240D	221,000	261,000
2006	370D	221,000	261,000
2006	T240D	254,000	300,000
2005	370D	206,000	243,000
2005	T240D	206,000	243,000
2004	370D	236,000	279,000
2004	T240D	191,000	226,000
2003	315D	191,000	226,000
2003	T240D	220,000	259,000

Mainship 430 Aft Cabin Trawler

Year	Power	Retail Low	Retail High
2006	T370D	275,000	325,000
2005	T370D	250,000	295,000
2004	T370D	228,000	269,000
2003	T315D	207,000	244,000
2002	T315D	188,000	222,000
2001	T300D	173,000	205,000
2000	T300D	159,000	188,000
1999	T300D	147,000	173,000

Mainship 43/4/479 Trawler

Year	Power	Retail Low	Retail High
2009-2012		******	******
2008	T440D	357,000	428,000
2007	T440D	332,000	398,000
2006	T440D	308,000	370,000

Mainship 47 Motor Yacht

Year	Power	Retail Low	Retail High
1999	T485D	133,000	159,000
1998	T485D	122,000	146,000
1997	T485D	112,000	135,000
1996	T485D	103,000	124,000
1995	T485D	95,000	114,000

Mako 261 Center Console

Year	Power	Retail Low	Retail High
1995	T150 O/B	14,000	17,000

Mako 282 Center Console

Year	Power	Retail Low	Retail High
2003	T225 O/B	29,000	35,000
2002	T225 O/B	26,000	31,000
2001	T225 O/B	23,000	28,000
2000	T225 O/B	21,000	25,000
1999	T225 O/B	19,000	23,000
1998	T225 O/B	17,000	20,000

Mako 284 Center Console

Year	Power	Retail Low	Retail High
200-20129		******	******
2008	T250 O/B	55,000	66,000
2007	T250 O/B	50,000	60,000
2006	T250 O/B	45,000	54,000
2005	T250 O/B	40,000	48,000

Mako 293 Walkaround

Year	Power	Retail Low	Retail High
2003	T250 O/B	34,000	41,000
2002	T250 O/B	31,000	37,000
2001	T250 O/B	28,000	33,000
2000	T250 O/B	25,000	30,000
1999	T250 O/B	23,000	28,000
1998	T250 O/B	21,000	25,000
1997	T250 O/B	19,000	23,000
1996	T250 O/B	17,000	21,000
1995	T250 O/B	16,000	19,000

Make 314 Cuddy

Year	Power	Retail Low	Retail High
2006	T250 O/B	72,000	86,000
2005	T250 O/B	65,000	78.000
2004	T250 O/B	59,000	71,000
2003	T250 O/B	54,000	65,000
2002	T250 O/B	49,000	59,000

Mako 333 Attack

Year	Power	Retail Low	Retail High
2000	T250 O/B	44,000	53,000
1999	T250 O/B	40,000	48,000
1998	T250 O/B	36,000	44,000
1997	T250 O/B	33,000	40,000

Marine Trader 34 DC

Year	Power	Retail Low	Retail High
2001	135D	74,000	88,000
2000	135D	69,000	83,000
1999	135D	65,000	78,000
1998	135D	61,000	73,000
1997	135D	57,000	69,000
1996	135D	54,000	65,000
1995	135D	51,000	61,000

Marine Trader 34 Sedan

Year	Power	Retail Low	Retail High
2001	135D	76,000	91,000
2000	135D	72,000	86,000
1999	135D	68,000	82,000
1998	135D	65,000	78,000
1997	135D	61,000	74,000
1996	135D	58,000	70,000
1995	135D	55,000	67,000

Marine Trader 38 Double Cabin

Year	Power	Retail Low	Retail High
2000	T135D	******	******
1999	T135D	******	******
1998	T135D	******	******
1997	T135D	95,000	114,000
1996	T135D	90,000	108,000
1995	T135D	85,000	102,000

Marine Trader 40 Sundeck

Year	Power	Retail Low	Retail High
2000	T135D	114,000	136,000
1999	T135D	106,000	127,000
1998	T135D	98,000	118,000
1997	T135D	92,000	111,000
1996	T135D	87,000	104,000
1995	T135D	81,000	98,000

Year	Power	Retail Low	Retail High
Marlin 350 Cuddy			
2002	T250 O/B	50,000	60,000
2001	T250 O/B	46,000	55,000
2000	T250 O/B	42,000	51,000
1999	T250 O/B	39,000	46,000
1998	T250 O/B	35,000	43,000
1997	T250 O/B	33,000	39,000
1996	T250 O/B	30,000	36,000
1995	T250 O/B	28,000	33,000
Marquis 40/420 Sport Coupe			
2010	T435 IPS	******	******
2009	T435 IPS	******	******
2008	T435 IPS	378,000	453,000
Marquis 55 LS; 560			
2009-2012		******	******
2008	T715D	655,000	753,000
2007	T715D	603,000	693,000
Marquis 59/600 PH			
2010	715D	******	******
2009	715D	******	******
2008	715D	783,000	940,000
2007	825D	728,000	874,000
2006	825D	677,000	813,000
2005	825D	630,000	756,000
2004	825D	586,000	703,000
2003	825D	545,000	654,000
Marquis 65 PH			
2010	T1360D	******	******
2009	T1360D	******	******
2008	T1360D	1,235,000	1,457,000
2007	T1360D	1,148,000	1,355,000
2006	T1360D	1,068,000	1,260,000
2005	T1360D	993,000	1,172,000
Maxum 2600/2700 SE			
2009	300 I/O	45,000	54,000
2008	320 I/O	41,000	49,000
2007	320 I/O	37,000	45,000
2006	320 I/O	34,000	41,000
Maxum 2700 SCR			
1996	T190 I/O	15,000	19,000
1995	T190 I/O	15,000	18,000
Maxum 2700 SE			
2007	320 I/O	39,000	47,000
2006	320 I/O	36,000	43,000
2005	320 I/O	33,000	39,000
2004	320 I/O	30,000	36,000
2003	320 I/O	27,000	33,000
2002	320 I/O	25,000	30,000
2001	320 I/O	23,000	28,000
Maxum 2800/2900 SCR; 2900 SE			
2006	320 I/O	44,000	53,000
2006	T190 I/O	46,000	55,000
2005	320 I/O	40,000	48,000
2005	T190 I/O	42,000	50,000
2004	320 I/O	36,000	44,000
2004	T190 I/O	38,000	46,000
2003	320 I/O	33,000	40,000
2003	T190 I/O	34,000	41,000
2002	320 I/O	30,000	36,000
2002	T190 I/O	31,000	38,000
2001	310 I/O	28,000	33,000
2001	T190 I/O	29,000	35,000
2000	310 I/O	25,000	31,000
2000	T190 I/O	26,000	32,000
1999	310 I/O	23,000	28,000
1999	T190 I/O	24,000	29,000
1998	310 I/O	22,000	26,000
1998	T190 I/O	23,000	27,000
1997	310 I/O	20,000	24,000
1997	T190 I/O	21,000	25,000
1996	310 I/O	19,000	22,000
1996	T190 I/O	19,000	23,000
1995	300 I/O	17,000	21,000
1995	T180 I/O	18,000	22,000
Maxum 2900 SE			
2009	T260 Axius I/O	85,000	102,000
2008	T260 I/O	78,000	94,000
Maxum 3000 SCR			
2001	T260 I/O	32,000	38,000
2000	T260 I/O	29,000	35,000
1999	T260 I/O	26,000	32,000
1998	T260 I/O	24,000	29,000
1997	T260 I/O	22,000	26,000
Maxum 3100 SE			
2008	T260 I/O	92,000	110,000
2007	T260 I/O	84,000	100,000
2006	T260 I/O	76,000	91,000
2005	T260 I/O	69,000	83,000
2004	T260 I/O	63,000	75,000
2003	T260 I/O	57,000	69,000
2002	T260 I/O	52,000	62,000
Maxum 3200 SCR			
1998	T260 I/O	31,000	37,000
1997	T260 I/O	29,000	34,000
1996	T260 I/O	26,000	32,000
1995	T260 I/O	24,000	29,000
Maxum 3300 SCR/SE			
2007	T320 I/O	97,000	116,000
2006	T320 I/O	90,000	108,000
2005	T320 I/O	82,000	98,000
2004	T320 I/O	74,000	89,000
2003	T320 I/O	68,000	81,000
2002	T320 I/O	61,000	74,000
2001	T320 I/O	56,000	67,000
2000	T310 I/O	51,000	62,000
1999	T310 I/O	47,000	57,000
Maxum 3500 SCR; 3500 SY			
2008	T370G	129,000	155,000
2007	T370G	117,000	141,000
2006	T370G	107,000	128,000
2005	T370G	97,000	117,000
2004	T370G	89,000	107,000
2003	T370G	82,000	99,000
2002	T380G	76,000	91,000
2001	T380G	69,000	83,000
Maxum 3700 SCR			
2001	T400G	89,000	107,000
2000	T380G	81,000	98,000
1999	T380G	74,000	89,000
1998	T380G	71,000	85,000
Maxum 3700 SY			
2009	T370G	156,000	188,000
2008	T370G	144,000	173,000
2007	T370G	132,000	159,000
2005	T370G	122,000	146,000
2004	T370G	112,000	134,000
2003	T370G	103,000	123,000
Maxum 3900/4100 SCR			
1999	T400G	77,000	93,000
1999	T370D	87,000	105,000
1998	T400G	71,000	86,000
1998	T370D	80,000	97,000
1997	T310G	65,000	79,000
1997	T315D	74,000	89,000
1996	T310G	60,000	72,000
1996	T315D	68,000	82,000
Maxum 4100 SCA			
2001	T400G	99,000	119,000
2001	T330D	127,000	153,000
2000	T400G	90,000	108,000
2000	T330D	116,000	139,000
1999	T400G	82,000	98,000
1999	T330D	105,000	126,000
1998	T400G	75,000	90,000
1998	T330D	97,000	116,000
1997	T400G	69,000	83,000
1997	T330D	89,000	107,000
Maxum 4100 SCB			
2001	T-Gas	95,000	114,000
2001	T330D	123,000	148,000
2000	T-Gas	86,000	104,000
2000	T330D	112,000	134,000
1999	T-Gas	78,000	94,000
1999	T330D	102,000	122,000
1998	T-Gas	72,000	87,000
1998	T330D	94,000	112,000
1997	T-Gas	66,000	80,000
1997	T330D	86,000	103,000
Maxum 4200 SY			
2008	T425D	295,000	354,000
2007	T425D	268,000	322,000
2006	T450D	244,000	293,000
2005	T450D	222,000	267,000
2004	T450D	202,000	243,000
2003	T450D	184,000	221,000
2002	T450D	167,000	201,000
Maxum 4600 SCB			
2001	T450D	164,000	197,000
2000	T370D	151,000	181,000
1999	T370D	139,000	166,000
1998	T370D	128,000	153,000
1997	T370D	117,000	141,000
McKinna 47/481 Sedan			
2006	T370D	******	******
2005	T370D	285,000	342,000
2004	T370D	259,000	311,000
2003	T370D	236,000	283,000
2002	T370D	214,000	257,000
2001	T370D	197,000	237,000
2000	T330D	181,000	218,000
1999	T330D	167,000	200,000
McKinna 57 Pilothouse			
2002-2006		******	******
2001	T450D	347,000	410,000
2000	T450D	323,000	381,000
1999	T450D	300,000	354,000
1998	T450D	279,000	329,000
1997	T450D	259,000	306,000
Mediterranean 38 Convertible			
2007	T330D	******	******
2006	T330D	******	******
2005	T330D	******	******
2004	T330D	******	******
2003	T330D	******	******
2002	T330D	106,000	128,000
2001	T330D	97,000	116,000
2000	T330D	89,000	107,000
1999	T330D	82,000	98,000
1998	T-Diesel	75,000	90,000

Year	Power	Retail Low	Retail High
1997	T-Diesel	69,000	83,000
1996	T-Diesel	64,000	76,000
1995	T-Diesel	59,000	70,000

Mediterranean 38 Express

Year	Power	Retail Low	Retail High
2007	T330D	******	******
2006	T330D	******	******
2005	T330D	103,000	123,000
2004	T330D	93,000	112,000
2003	T330D	85,000	102,000
2002	T330D	77,000	93,000
2001	T330D	70,000	84,000
2000	T315D	64,000	77,000
1999	T315D	58,000	70,000

Meridian 341 Sedan

Year	Power	Retail Low	Retail High
2010-2012		******	******
2009	T320G	183,000	219,000
2009	T330D	210,000	252,000
2008	T320G	155,000	186,000
2008	T330D	181,000	217,000
2007	T320G	141,000	169,000
2007	T330D	165,000	198,000
2006	T320G	128,000	154,000
2006	T250D	150,000	180,000
2005	T320G	116,000	140,000
2005	T250D	136,000	164,000
2004	T260G	106,000	127,000
2004	T250D	124,000	149,000
2003	T260G	96,000	116,000
2003	T250D	113,000	135,000

Meridian 368 Motor Yacht

Year	Power	Retail Low	Retail High
2008	T370G	184,000	221,000
2008	T370D	218,000	262,000
2007	T370G	168,000	201,000
2007	T330D	198,000	238,000
2006	T370G	153,000	183,000
2006	T330D	181,000	217,000
2005	T370G	139,000	167,000
2005	T330D	164,000	197,000

Meridian 381 Sedan

Year	Power	Retail Low	Retail High
2005	T320G	133,000	159,000
2005	T330D	148,000	177,000
2004	T320G	121,000	145,000
2004	T270D	134,000	161,000
2003	T320G	110,000	132,000
2003	T270D	122,000	147,000

Meridian 391 Sedan

Year	Power	Retail Low	Retail High
2010-2012		******	******
2009	T370G	159,000	191,000
2009	T370D	185,000	222,000
2008	T370G	145,000	174,000
2008	T370D	168,000	202,000
2007	T370G	132,000	158,000
2007	T330D	153,000	184,000
2006	T370G	120,000	144,000
2006	T330D	139,000	167,000

Meridian 408 Motor Yacht

Year	Power	Retail Low	Retail High
2008	T380D	299,000	353,000
2007	T380D	275,000	324,000
2006	T380D	253,000	298,000
2005	T370D	233,000	274,000
2004	T370D	214,000	252,000
2003	T370D	197,000	232,000

Meridian 411 Sedan

Year	Power	Retail Low	Retail High
2007	T380D	261,000	308,000
2006	T380D	240,000	283,000
2005	T370D	221,000	261,000
2004	T370D	203,000	240,000
2003	T370D	187,000	220,000

Meridian 441 Sedan

Year	Power	Retail Low	Retail High
201-20120		******	******
2009	T425D	351,000	414,000
2008	T425D	323,000	381,000

Meridian 459 Cockpit MY

Year	Power	Retail Low	Retail High
2008	T330D	366,000	432,000
2007	T330D	337,000	398,000
2006	T330D	310,000	366,000
2005	T370D	285,000	336,000
2004	T370D	262,000	309,000
2003	T370D	241,000	285,000

Meridian 490 Pilothouse

Year	Power	Retail Low	Retail High
2008	T330D	385,000	455,000
2007	T330D	354,000	418,000
2006	T330D	326,000	385,000
2005	T330D	300,000	354,000
2004	T330D	276,000	326,000

Meridian 540 Pilothouse

Year	Power	Retail Low	Retail High
2006	T635D	******	******
2005	T635D	******	******
2004	T635D	389,000	459,000
2003	T635D	362,000	427,000

Meridian 580 Pilothouse

Year	Power	Retail Low	Retail High
2009	T715D	******	******
2008	T715D	627,000	733,000
2007	T635D	583,000	682,000
2006	T635D	542,000	634,000
2005	T635D	504,000	590,000
2004	T635D	469,000	548,000
2003	T635D	436,000	510,000

Midnight Express 37 Cuddy

Year	Power	Retail Low	Retail High
2010-2012		******	******
2009	3/275 O/B	228,000	273,000
2008	3/275 O/B	207,000	248,000
2007	3/275 O/B	188,000	226,000
2006	3/275 O/B	171,000	206,000

Mikelson 43 Sportfisher

Year	Power	Retail Low	Retail High
2006-2012		******	******
2005	T450D	351,000	414,000
2004	T450D	319,000	377,000
2003	T450D	291,000	343,000
2002	T430D	267,000	315,000
2001	T430D	246,000	290,000
2000	T420D	226,000	267,000
1999	T420D	208,000	246,000
1998	T420D	191,000	226,000
1997	T420D	176,000	208,000

Mikelson 50 Sportfisher

Year	Power	Retail Low	Retail High
2009	T600D	******	******
2008	T600D	******	******
2007	T540D	******	******
2006	T450D	522,000	627,000
2005	T450D	485,000	583,000
2004	T450D	451,000	542,000
2003	T450D	420,000	504,000
2002	T450D	390,000	469,000
2001	T435D	363,000	436,000
2000	T435D	338,000	405,000
1999	T435D	314,000	377,000
1998	T435D	292,000	350,000
1997	T435D	271,000	326,000
1996	T435D	252,000	303,000
1995	T435D	235,000	282,000

Mikelson 60 Sportfisher

Year	Power	Retail Low	Retail High
1999	T735D	******	******
1998	T735D	******	******
1997	T735D	342,000	404,000
1996	T735D	318,000	376,000
1995	T735D	296,000	349,000

Mikelson 64 Sportfisher

Year	Power	Retail Low	Retail High
2001	T1400D	724,000	869,000
2000	T800D	666,000	800,000
1999	T800D	613,000	736,000
1998	T800D	564,000	677,000
1997	T800D	519,000	623,000

Monk 36 Trawler

Year	Power	Retail Low	Retail High
2007	230D	170,000	204,000
2006	230D	161,000	193,000
2005	220D	153,000	184,000
2004	220D	145,000	174,000
2003	220D	138,000	166,000
2002	220D	131,000	157,000
2001	220D	126,000	151,000
2000	220D	121,000	145,000
1999	220D	116,000	139,000
1998	220D	111,000	134,000
1997	220D	107,000	128,000
1996	220D	102,000	123,000
1995	220D	98,000	118,000

Monterey 262 Cruiser

Year	Power	Retail Low	Retail High
2002	250 I/O	24,000	28,000
2001	250 I/O	22,000	26,000
2000	260 I/O	19,000	23,000
1999	260 I/O	18,000	21,000
1998	260 I/O	16,000	19,000
1997	260 I/O	15,000	17,000

Monterey 265/276 Cruiser

Year	Power	Retail Low	Retail High
1999	310 I/O	20,000	25,000
1998	310 I/O	19,000	23,000
1997	310 I/O	18,000	21,000
1996	310 I/O	16,000	20,000
1995	310 I/O	15,000	18,000

Monterey 270 Cruiser

Year	Power	Retail Low	Retail High
2008	300 I/O	54,000	64,000
2007	300 I/O	49,000	59,000
2006	320 I/O	44,000	53,000

Monterey 282 Cruiser

Year	Power	Retail Low	Retail High
2006	T220 I/O	52,000	62,000
2005	T220 I/O	47,000	57,000
2004	T220 I/O	43,000	51,000
2003	T220 I/O	39,000	47,000
2002	T220 I/O	35,000	42,000
2001	T190 I/O	32,000	39,000

Monterey 290 CR; 300 SCR

Year	Power	Retail Low	Retail High
2012	T260 I/O	******	******
2011	T260 I/O	******	******
2010	T260 I/O	136,000	164,000
2009	T260 I/O	124,000	149,000
2008	T260 I/O	113,000	135,000
2007	T260 I/O	103,000	123,000
2006	T260 I/O	93,000	112,000

Monterey 286/296 Cruiser

Year	Power	Retail Low	Retail High
2000	T250 I/O	29,000	35,000
1999	T250 I/O	27,000	32,000
1998	T250 I/O	24,000	29,000
1997	T250 I/O	22,000	27,000
1996	T250 I/O	21,000	25,000
1995	T250 I/O	19,000	23,000

Monterey 298 Sport Cruiser

Year	Power	Retail Low	Retail High
2007	T260 I/O	52,000	62,000
2006	T260 I/O	47,000	57,000

Year	Power	Retail Low	Retail High
2005	T260 I/O	44,000	52,000
2004	T260 I/O	40,000	48,000
2003	T260 I/O	37,000	44,000
Monterey 298 Super Sport			
2007	T260 I/O	49,000	58,000
2006	T260 I/O	45,000	54,000
2005	T260 I/O	41,000	49,000
2004	T260 I/O	38,000	45,000
2003	T260 I/O	35,000	42,000
2002	T260 I/O	32,000	38,000
2001	T260 I/O	29,000	35,000
Monterey 302 Cruiser			
2006	T320 I/O	58,000	70,000
2005	T320 I/O	53,000	64,000
2004	T320 I/O	48,000	58,000
2003	T320 I/O	44,000	53,000
2002	T320 I/O	40,000	48,000
2001	T320 I/O	36,000	44,000
2000	T320 I/O	33,000	40,000
Monterey 322 Cruiser			
2007	T300 I/O	104,000	125,000
2006	T300 I/O	95,000	114,000
2005	T300 I/O	86,000	103,000
2004	T300 I/O	78,000	94,000
2003	T320 I/O	71,000	85,000
2002	T320 I/O	65,000	78,000
2001	T320 I/O	59,000	71,000
2000	T310 I/O	55,000	66,000
1999	T310 I/O	50,000	60,000
1998	T310 I/O	46,000	56,000
Monterey 330/340 Sport Yacht			
2011	T320 I/O	******	******
2010	T300 I/O	******	******
2009	T300 I/O	170,000	204,000
2008	T320 I/O	154,000	185,000
2007	T300 I/O	140,000	168,000
Monterey 350/360 Sport Yacht			
200-2012		******	******
2007	T375G	142,000	171,000
2006	T375G	131,000	157,000
2005	T375G	120,000	144,000
Navigator 44 Classic			
2007	T318D	247,000	296,000
2006	T318D	227,000	272,000
2005	T318D	209,000	250,000
2004	T318D	192,000	230,000
2003	T318D	176,000	212,000
2002	T318D	162,000	195,000
Navigator 48 Classic			
2007	T318D	******	******
2006	T318D	******	******
2005	T318D	270,000	324,000
2004	T318D	249,000	298,000
2003	T318D	229,000	274,000
2002	T318D	210,000	252,000
2001	T318D	193,000	232,000
2000	T318D	180,000	216,000
1999	T318D	167,000	201,000
1998	T318D	156,000	187,000
1997	T318D	145,000	174,000
Navigator 50 Classic			
2000	T370D	199,000	239,000
1999	T370D	183,000	220,000
1998	T370D	168,000	202,000
1997	T370D	155,000	186,000
1996	T370D	144,000	173,000
1995	T370D	134,000	161,000

Year	Power	Retail Low	Retail High
Navigator 53 Classic			
2006	T370D	******	******
2005	T370D	******	******
2004	T370D	304,000	364,000
2003	T370D	279,000	335,000
2002	T370D	257,000	308,000
2001	T370D	236,000	284,000
2000	T370D	217,000	261,000
1999	T370D	202,000	243,000
1998	T370D	188,000	226,000
1997	T370D	175,000	210,000
1996	T370D	162,000	195,000
1995	T370D	151,000	181,000
Navigator 56 Classic			
2005	T370D	418,000	501,000
2004	T370D	384,000	461,000
2003	T370D	353,000	424,000
2002	T370D	325,000	390,000
2001	T370D	302,000	363,000
2000	T370D	281,000	337,000
Navigator 5600 Pilothouse			
1999	T430D	261,000	314,000
1998	T430D	243,000	292,000
1997	T430D	226,000	271,000
1996	T430D	210,000	252,000
1995	T430D	195,000	235,000
Navigator 5800 Pilothouse			
2001	T485D	******	******
2000	T485D	******	******
1999	T485D	332,000	392,000
Navigator 6100 Pilothouse			
2002	T700D	484,000	571,000
2001	T700D	445,000	525,000
2000	T700D	410,000	483,000
1999	T700D	377,000	445,000
Nordhavn 35 Coastal Pilot			
2005	370D	240,000	288,000
2004	370D	232,000	279,000
2003	370D	225,000	271,000
2002	370D	219,000	262,000
2001	370D	212,000	255,000
Nordhavn 40			
2008-2012		******	******
2007	105D	401,000	470,000
2006	105D	381,000	446,000
2005	105D	362,000	424,000
2004	105D	344,000	403,000
2003	105D	327,000	382,000
2002	105D	314,000	367,000
2001	105D	301,000	352,000
2000	105D	289,000	338,000
1999	105D	277,000	325,000
Nordhavn 46			
2005	140D	******	******
2004	140D	******	******
2003	140D	******	******
2002	140D	401,000	470,000
2001	140D	385,000	451,000
2000	140D	370,000	433,000
1999	140D	355,000	415,000
1998	140D	341,000	399,000
1997	140D	327,000	383,000
1996	140D	314,000	367,000
1995	140D	301,000	353,000
Nordhavn 47			
2007-2012		******	******

Year	Power	Retail Low	Retail High
2006	173D	749,000	884,000
2005	173D	712,000	840,000
2004	173D	676,000	798,000
2003	173D	642,000	758,000
Nordic 26 Tug			
2012	110D	******	******
2011	110D	125,000	150,000
2010	110D	118,000	142,000
2009	S/Diesel	112,000	135,000
1998-2008		No Prod.	
1997	S/Diesel	72,000	86,000
1996	S/Diesel	66,000	80,000
1995	S/Diesel	62,000	74,000
Nordic 32 Tug			
2010	280D	******	******
2009	280D	199,000	239,000
2008	280D	187,000	225,000
2007	280D	176,000	211,000
2006	270D	165,000	198,000
2005	270D	155,000	186,000
2004	270D	146,000	175,000
2003	270D	137,000	165,000
2002	220D	129,000	155,000
2001	220D	122,000	147,000
2000	220D	116,000	140,000
1999	220D	110,000	133,000
1998	220D	105,000	126,000
1997	210D	100,000	120,000
1996	210D	95,000	114,000
1995	210D	90,000	108,000
Nordic 37 Tug			
2011	380D	******	******
2010	380D	******	******
2009	380D	368,000	434,000
2008	380D	346,000	408,000
2007	380D	325,000	384,000
2006	380D	306,000	361,000
2005	330D	287,000	339,000
2004	330D	270,000	319,000
2003	330D	254,000	300,000
2002	330D	239,000	282,000
2001	330D	227,000	267,000
2000	330D	215,000	254,000
1999	330D	204,000	241,000
1998	330D	194,000	229,000
Nordic 42 Tug			
2009-2012		******	******
2008	540D	446,000	522,000
2007	540D	419,000	491,000
2006	540D	394,000	461,000
2005	450D	370,000	433,000
2004	450D	348,000	407,000
2003	450D	331,000	387,000
2002	450D	314,000	368,000
2001	330D	298,000	349,000
2000	330D	283,000	332,000
1999	330D	269,000	315,000
1998	330D	256,000	299,000
1997	330D	243,000	284,000
1996	330D	231,000	270,000
Ocean Alexander 390 Sundeck			
1999	T220D	117,000	140,000
1998	T220D	107,000	129,000
1997	T220D	99,000	118,000
1996	T220D	91,000	109,000
1995	T220D	84,000	101,000
Ocean Alexander 420/440 Sundeck			
1999	T220D	132,000	180,000

Year	Power	Retail Low	Retail High
1998	T220D	122,000	165,000
1997	T220D	112,000	152,000
1996	T250D	103,000	140,000
1995	T250D	95,000	128,000

Ocean Alexander 420/422 Sport Sedan

Year	Power	Retail Low	Retail High
2001	T420D	193,000	278,000
2000	T420D	177,000	256,000
1999	T420D	163,000	235,000
1998	T420D	150,000	217,000
1997	T375D	138,000	199,000
1996	T375D	128,000	185,000
1995	T375D	119,000	172,000

Ocean Alexander 423 Classico

Year	Power	Retail Low	Retail High
2002	T220D	203,000	293,000
2001	T220D	186,000	269,000
2000	T220D	171,000	248,000
1999	T220D	158,000	228,000
1998	T220D	145,000	210,000
1997	T220D	133,000	193,000
1996	T220D	123,000	177,000
1995	T220D	114,000	165,000

Ocean Alexander 426 Classico

Year	Power	Retail Low	Retail High
1999	T220D	162,000	194,000
1998	T220D	151,000	181,000
1997	T220D	140,000	168,000
1996	T220D	130,000	156,000
1995	T220D	121,000	145,000

Ocean Alexander 430/460 Classico MKI

Year	Power	Retail Low	Retail High
2006	T220D	******	******
2005	T220D	******	******
2004	T220D	******	******
2003	T220D	205,000	379,000
2002	T220D	189,000	348,000
2001	T220D	174,000	320,000
2000	T220D	160,000	295,000

Ocean Alexander 456 Classico

Year	Power	Retail Low	Retail High
2002	T375D	235,000	275,000
2001	T375D	216,000	253,000
2000	T375D	199,000	233,000
1999	T375D	183,000	214,000
1998	T375D	168,000	197,000
1997	T375D	155,000	181,000
1996	T375D	144,000	169,000
1995	T375D	134,000	157,000

Ocean Alexander 480 Sport Sedan

Year	Power	Retail Low	Retail High
2003	T420D	******	******
2002	T420D	******	******
2001	T420D	226,000	264,000
2000	T420D	208,000	243,000
1999	T420D	191,000	223,000
1998	T420D	176,000	206,000
1997	T420D	162,000	189,000
1996	T375D	149,000	174,000

Ocean Master 27 Center Console

Year	Power	Retail Low	Retail High
2003-2012		******	******
2002	T200 O/B	50,000	61,000
2001	T200 O/B	45,000	55,000
2000	T200 O/B	41,000	50,000
1999	T200 O/B	37,000	45,000
1998	T200 O/B	34,000	41,000
1997	T200 O/B	31,000	37,000
1996	T200 O/B	28,000	34,000

Ocean 37 Billfish

Year	Power	Retail Low	Retail High
2012	T480D	******	******
2011	T480D	******	******
2010	T480D	******	******
2009	T480D	294,000	353,000
2008	T480D	270,000	325,000

Ocean 38 Super Sport

Year	Power	Retail Low	Retail High
1995	T420D	110,000	132,000

Ocean 40 Sport Fish

Year	Power	Retail Low	Retail High
2005	T420D	194,000	229,000
2004	T420D	177,000	209,000
2003	T420D	161,000	190,000
2002	T420D	146,000	173,000
2001	T420D	133,000	157,000
2000	T420D	122,000	144,000
1999	T420D	113,000	133,000

Ocean 40 Super Sport

Year	Power	Retail Low	Retail High
2005	T420D	212,000	250,000
2004	T420D	193,000	228,000
2003	T420D	176,000	207,000
2002	T420D	160,000	189,000
2001	T420D	145,000	171,000
2000	T420D	132,000	156,000
1999	T420D	120,000	142,000
1998	T420D	109,000	129,000
1997	T420D	99,000	117,000

Ocean 42 SS (1991-95)

Year	Power	Retail Low	Retail High
1995	T485D	118,000	140,000

Ocean 42 SS (Current)

Year	Power	Retail Low	Retail High
2008-2012		******	******
2007	T510D	313,000	369,000
2006	T510D	288,000	340,000

Ocean 43 Super Sport

Year	Power	Retail Low	Retail High
2005	T480D	232,000	274,000
2004	T480D	211,000	249,000
2003	T480D	192,000	227,000
2002	T480D	175,000	206,000
2001	T480D	159,000	188,000
2000	T480D	145,000	171,000

Ocean 44 Motor Yacht

Year	Power	Retail Low	Retail High
1999	T485D	186,000	220,000
1998	T485D	171,000	202,000
1997	T485D	158,000	186,000
1996	T485D	145,000	171,000
1995	T485D	133,000	157,000

Ocean 45 Super Sport

Year	Power	Retail Low	Retail High
1999	T485D	188,000	222,000
1998	T485D	173,000	204,000
1997	T485D	159,000	188,000
1996	T485D	147,000	173,000

Ocean 46 Super Sport

Year	Power	Retail Low	Retail High
2009	T715D	******	******
2008	T715D	469,000	548,000
2007	T715D	431,000	505,000
2006	T710D	397,000	464,000
2005	T710D	365,000	427,000

Ocean 48 Cockpit MY

Year	Power	Retail Low	Retail High
1999	T485D	193,000	226,000
1998	T485D	177,000	207,000
1997	T485D	163,000	191,000
1996	T485D	150,000	176,000
1995	T485D	138,000	161,000

Ocean 48 Super Sport

Year	Power	Retail Low	Retail High
2003	T660D	311,000	364,000
2002	T660D	286,000	334,000
2001	T660D	263,000	308,000
2000	T660D	242,000	283,000
1999	T660D	222,000	260,000
1998	T625D	205,000	239,000
1997	T625D	188,000	220,000
1996	T625D	173,000	203,000
1995	T625D	161,000	188,000

Ocean 50 Super Sport

Year	Power	Retail Low	Retail High
200-20128		******	******
2007	T825D	483,000	565,000
2006	T800D	444,000	519,000
2005	T800D	408,000	478,000
2004	T800D	376,000	440,000

Ocean 52 Super Sport

Year	Power	Retail Low	Retail High
2006	T800D	503,000	589,000
2005	T800D	463,000	542,000
2004	T800D	426,000	498,000
2003	T800D	392,000	458,000
2002	T800D	360,000	422,000
2001	T800D	331,000	388,000

Ocean 53 Super Sport

Year	Power	Retail Low	Retail High
1999	T820D	247,000	288,000
1998	T820D	227,000	265,000
1997	T820D	209,000	244,000
1996	T820D	192,000	225,000
1995	T820D	176,000	207,000

Ocean 54 Super Sport

Year	Power	Retail Low	Retail High
2009-2012		******	******
2008	1050D	712,000	833,000
2007	1050D	655,000	766,000

Ocean 60 Super Sport

Year	Power	Retail Low	Retail High
2001	1350D	******	******
2000	1350D	******	******
1999	1350D	494,000	573,000
1998	1350D	454,000	527,000
1997	1350D	418,000	485,000
1996	1350D	384,000	446,000

Ocean 66 Super Sport

Year	Power	Retail Low	Retail High
1999	1350D	494,000	573,000
1998	1350D	454,000	527,000
1997	1350D	418,000	485,000
1996	1350D	384,000	446,000
1995	1150D	353,000	410,000

Offshore 48 Pilothouse

Year	Power	Retail Low	Retail High
2001	T435D	346,000	409,000
2000	T420D	322,000	380,000
1999	T420D	299,000	353,000

Offshore 48 Sedan

Year	Power	Retail Low	Retail High
2001	T435D	351,000	414,000
2000	T435D	326,000	385,000
1999	T435D	304,000	358,000
1998	T435D	282,000	333,000
1997	T435D	262,000	310,000
1996	T435D	244,000	288,000
1995	T375D	227,000	268,000

Offshore 48 Yachtfish

Year	Power	Retail Low	Retail High
1999	T435D	266,000	313,000
1998	T435D	247,000	291,000
1997	T435D	230,000	271,000
1996	T435D	213,000	252,000
1995	T375D	198,000	234,000

Osprey 30

Year	Power	Retail Low	Retail High
2004	T188D I/O	******	******
2003	T188D I/O	82,000	99,000
2002	T188D I/O	76,000	91,000
2001	T188D I/O	69,000	83,000
2000	T188D I/O	64,000	77,000
1999	T188D I/O	59,000	71,000

Pacific Mariner 65 Motor Yacht

Year	Power	Retail Low	Retail High
2008	T825D	******	******

Year	Power	Retail Low	Retail High
2007	T825D	******	******
2006	T825D	1,040,000	1,227,000
2005	T825D	956,000	1,129,000
2004	T825D	880,000	1,038,000
2003	T825D	809,000	955,000
2002	T800D	745,000	879,000
2001	T800D	692,000	817,000
2000	T800D	644,000	760,000
1999	T800D	599,000	707,000
1998	T800D	557,000	657,000

Pacific Seacraft 38T Fast Trawler

Year	Power	Retail Low	Retail High
2002	350D	******	******
2001	350D	******	******
2000	350D	199,000	239,000
1999	350D	187,000	225,000

Pacific Trawler 40

Year	Power	Retail Low	Retail High
2003	220D	******	******
2002	220D	180,000	216,000
2001	220D	169,000	203,000
2000	220D	159,000	191,000

PDQ 32/34 Catamaran

Year	Power	Retail Low	Retail High
2007	T100D	209,000	250,000
2006	T100D	198,000	238,000
2005	T100D	188,000	226,000
2004	T100D	179,000	215,000
2003	T100D	172,000	206,000
2002	T75D	165,000	198,000
2001	T75D	158,000	190,000
2000	T75D	152,000	182,000

Pearson True North 33

Year	Power	Retail Low	Retail High
2008	440D	******	******
2007	440D	******	******
2006	440D	137,000	165,000
2005	440D	126,000	152,000
2004	440D	116,000	140,000

Pearson True North 38

Year	Power	Retail Low	Retail High
2008	440D	******	******
2007	440D	256,000	302,000
2006	440D	238,000	281,000
2005	440D	221,000	261,000
2004	440D	206,000	243,000
2003	440D	191,000	226,000
2002	440D	178,000	210,000

Phoenix 27 Tournament

Year	Power	Retail Low	Retail High
1999	T260G	36,000	43,000
1998	T260G	33,000	40,000
1997	T260G	30,000	37,000
1996	T260G	28,000	34,000
1995	T260G	26,000	31,000

Phoenix 29 SFX Convertible

Year	Power	Retail Low	Retail High
1999	T310G	41,000	50,000
1999	T240D	52,000	62,000
1998	T310G	38,000	46,000
1998	T240D	48,000	58,000
1997	T310G	36,000	43,000
1997	T240D	45,000	54,000
1996	T310G	33,000	40,000
1996	T240D	42,000	50,000
1995	T310G	31,000	37,000
1995	T240D	39,000	46,000

Phoenix 32 Tournament

Year	Power	Retail Low	Retail High
1999	T350D	49,000	59,000
1998	T350D	44,000	53,000
1997	T350D	40,000	49,000

Phoenix 33/34 SFX Convertible

Year	Power	Retail Low	Retail High
1999	T310G	69,000	83,000
1999	T385D	85,000	102,000
1998	T310G	64,000	77,000
1998	T375D	78,000	94,000
1997	T310G	59,000	70,000
1997	T375D	72,000	86,000
1996	T310G	54,000	65,000
1996	T375D	66,000	79,000
1995	T310G	50,000	60,000
1995	T350D	61,000	73,000

Phoenix 37/38 SFX Convertible

Year	Power	Retail Low	Retail High
1999	480D	129,000	154,000
1998	485D	119,000	143,000
1997	485D	111,000	133,000
1996	485D	103,000	124,000
1995	485D	96,000	115,000

Post 42 Sport Fisherman

Year	Power	Retail Low	Retail High
2009	T510D	******	******
2008	T510D	******	******
2007	T510D	361,000	422,000
2006	T510D	328,000	384,000
2005	T480D	298,000	349,000
2004	T480D	272,000	318,000
2003	T480D	247,000	289,000
2002	T480D	225,000	263,000
2001	T430D	207,000	242,000
2000	T430D	190,000	223,000
1999	T430D	175,000	205,000
1998	T430D	161,000	188,000
1997	T430D	148,000	173,000

Post 43 Sport Fisherman

Year	Power	Retail Low	Retail High
1996	T550D	145,000	170,000
1995	T550D	138,000	161,000

Post 46 Sport Fisherman

Year	Power	Retail Low	Retail High
1996	T550D	194,000	233,000
1995	T550D	179,000	215,000

Post 47 Sport Fisherman

Year	Power	Retail Low	Retail High
2002-2009		******	******
2001	T680D	294,000	353,000
2000	T680D	267,000	321,000
1999	T680D	243,000	292,000
1998	T680D	221,000	266,000
1997	T550D	201,000	242,000

Post 50 Convertible

Year	Power	Retail Low	Retail High
2004-2009		******	******
2003	T860D	484,000	571,000
2002	T820D	440,000	520,000
2001	T820D	401,000	473,000
2000	T820D	365,000	430,000
1999	T820D	332,000	392,000
1998	T820D	302,000	356,000
1997	T735D	275,000	324,000
1996	T735D	250,000	295,000
1995	T735D	227,000	268,000

Post 53 Convertible

Year	Power	Retail Low	Retail High
2007-2009		******	******
2006	T1100D	636,000	751,000
2005	T1100D	591,000	698,000

Post 56 Convertible

Year	Power	Retail Low	Retail High
200-2009		******	******
2004	T1300D	665,000	778,000
2003	T1300D	618,000	723,000
2002	T1300D	575,000	672,000

Powerplay 33 Sportfish

Year	Power	Retail Low	Retail High
2003	T250 O/B	40,000	48,000
2002	T250 O/B	36,000	43,000
2001	T250 O/B	32,000	38,000
2000	T250 O/B	29,000	34,000
1999	T250 O/B	26,000	31,000
1998	T250 O/B	23,000	28,000

Pro-Line 26 Sport

Year	Power	Retail Low	Retail High
2004	T150 O/B	27,000	32,000
2003	T150 O/B	24,000	29,000
2002	T150 O/B	22,000	26,000
2001	T150 O/B	20,000	24,000
2000	T150 O/B	18,000	22,000

Pro-Line 26 Super Sport

Year	Power	Retail Low	Retail High
2012	T150 O/B	******	******
2011	T150 O/B	******	******
2010	T150 O/B	50,000	60,000
2009	T150 O/B	45,000	54,000
2008	T150 O/B	40,000	48,000
2007	T150 O/B	36,000	43,000
2006	T150 O/B	32,000	39,000

Pro-Line 2610 Walkaround

Year	Power	Retail Low	Retail High
2004	T150 O/B	30,000	36,000
2003	T150 O/B	27,000	32,000
2002	T150 O/B	24,000	29,000
2001	T150 O/B	22,000	27,000
2000	T150 O/B	20,000	24,000
1999	T150 O/B	18,000	22,000
1998	T150 O/B	17,000	20,000

Pro-Line 27/29 Express

Year	Power	Retail Low	Retail High
2005	T200 O/B	49,000	58,000
2004	T200 O/B	44,000	53,000
2003	T200 O/B	40,000	48,000
2002	T200 O/B	37,000	44,000
2001	T200 O/B	33,000	40,000

Pro-Line 2610 WA; 27 Walk

Year	Power	Retail Low	Retail High
2004	T200 O/B	41,000	49,000
2003	T200 O/B	37,000	44,000
2002	T200 O/B	33,000	40,000
2001	T200 O/B	30,000	37,000
2000	T200 O/B	28,000	33,000
1999	T200 O/B	25,000	30,000
1998	T200 O/B	23,000	27,000

Pro-Line 27/29 Sport

Year	Power	Retail Low	Retail High
2006	T200 O/B	44,000	53,000
2005	T200 O/B	40,000	48,000
2004	T200 O/B	36,000	44,000
2003	T200 O/B	33,000	40,000
2001	T200 O/B	30,000	36,000
2000	T200 O/B	27,000	33,000

Pro-Line 2700 Sportsman

Year	Power	Retail Low	Retail High
1999	T200 O/B	24,000	28,000
1998	T200 O/B	22,000	26,000
1997	T200 O/B	20,000	24,000
1996	T200 O/B	18,000	22,000
1995	T200 O/B	17,000	20,000

Pro-Line 2810 Walkaround

Year	Power	Retail Low	Retail High
2000	T225 O/B	28,000	34,000
1999	T225 O/B	25,000	30,000
1998	T225 O/B	23,000	27,000
1997	T225 O/B	20,000	24,000

Pro-Line 29 Grand Sport

Year	Power	Retail Low	Retail High
2009-2012		******	******
2008	T225 O/B	62,000	74,000
2007	T225 O/B	56,000	67,000

Pro-Line 29 Super Sport

Year	Power	Retail Low	Retail High
2009	T225 O/B	******	******
2008	T225 O/B	******	******
2007	T225 O/B	54,000	65,000

Year	Power	Retail Low	Retail High
2006	T225 O/B	48,000	58,000
2005	T225 O/B	43,000	52,000

Pro-Line 2950 Mid Cabin

Year	Power	Retail Low	Retail High
2000	T225 O/B	28,000	34,000
1999	T250 I/O	26,000	31,000
1998	T225 O/B	23,000	28,000
1998	T250 I/O	21,000	26,000
1997	T225 O/B	19,000	23,000
1997	T250 I/O	17,000	21,000
1996	T225 O/B	16,000	19,000
1996	T250 I/O	15,000	18,000
1995	T225 O/B	14,000	16,000
1995	T250 I/O	12,000	15,000

Pro-Line 30 Walkaround

Year	Power	Retail Low	Retail High
2004	T225 O/B	49,000	59,000
2003	T225 O/B	44,000	53,000
2002	T225 O/B	40,000	49,000
2001	T225 O/B	37,000	44,000
2000	T225 O/B	33,000	40,000

Pro-Line 30 Express

Year	Power	Retail Low	Retail High
2005	T225 O/B	53,000	63,000
2004	T225 O/B	48,000	58,000
2003	T225 O/B	44,000	52,000
2002	T225 O/B	40,000	48,000
2001	T225 O/B	36,000	43,000
2000	T225 O/B	33,000	39,000

Pro-Line 30/31 Sport

Year	Power	Retail Low	Retail High
2006	T225 O/B	57,000	68,000
2005	T225 O/B	51,000	62,000
2004	T225 O/B	47,000	56,000
2003	T225 O/B	42,000	51,000
2002	T225 O/B	39,000	46,000
2001	T225 O/B	35,000	42,000
2000	T225 O/B	32,000	38,000

Pro-Line 3250/32 Express

Year	Power	Retail Low	Retail High
2002	T320G	58,000	70,000
2001	T320G	53,000	64,000
2000	T310G	48,000	58,000
1999	T310G	44,000	53,000
1998	T310G	40,000	48,000
1997	T310G	36,000	44,000

Pro-Line 32 Express

Year	Power	Retail Low	Retail High
2011	T250 O/B	******	******
2010	T250 O/B	******	******
2009	T250 O/B	115,000	139,000
2008	T250 O/B	105,000	126,000
2007	T250 O/B	95,000	115,000
2006	T250 O/B	87,000	104,000
2005	T250 O/B	79,000	95,000

Pro-Line 33 Express

Year	Power	Retail Low	Retail High
2006	T370G I/B	******	******
2006	T315D I/B	142,000	171,000
2005	T370G I/B	******	******
2005	T315D I/B	129,000	155,000
2004	T370G I/B	104,000	125,000
2004	T315D I/B	118,000	141,000
2003	T370G I/B	95,000	114,000
2003	T315D I/B	107,000	128,000
2002	T370G I/B	86,000	103,000
2002	T315D I/B	97,000	117,000
2001	T310G I/B	78,000	94,000
2001	T350D I/B	88,000	106,000
2000	T310G I/B	71,000	85,000
2000	T350D I/B	80,000	97,000
1999	T310G I/B	65,000	78,000
1999	T350D I/B	73,000	88,000

Pro-Line 33 Walkaround

Year	Power	Retail Low	Retail High
2005	T250 O/B	76,000	91,000
2004	T250 O/B	69,000	82,000
2003	T250 O/B	62,000	75,000

Pro-Line 3400 SS Cuddy

Year	Power	Retail Low	Retail High
2001	T250 O/B	52,000	62,000
2000	T250 O/B	47,000	56,000
1999	T250 O/B	42,000	50,000
1998	T250 O/B	38,000	45,000

Pro-Line 35 Express

Year	Power	Retail Low	Retail High
2009-2012		******	******
2008	3/225 O/B	127,000	152,000
2007	3/225 O/B	115,000	138,000
2006	3/225 O/B	105,000	126,000

Pursuit 2670 Cuddy Console

Year	Power	Retail Low	Retail High
2005	T225 O/B	47,000	56,000
2004	T225 O/B	42,000	51,000
2003	T225 O/B	38,000	46,000
2002	T225 O/B	35,000	42,000

Pursuit 2670 CC; C 260

Year	Power	Retail Low	Retail High
2007	T200 O/B	56,000	67,000
2006	T200 O/B	50,000	61,000
2005	T200 O/B	46,000	55,000

Pursuit 2670 Denali; LS 265

Year	Power	Retail Low	Retail High
2007	T225 O/B	61,000	72,000
2006	T225 O/B	55,000	66,000
2005	T225 O/B	50,000	60,000
2004	T225 O/B	46,000	54,000
2003	T200 O/B	42,000	50,000

Pursuit 2855 Express Fish

Year	Power	Retail Low	Retail High
1995	T200 O/B	21,000	25,000

Pursuit 2860/2865 Denali

Year	Power	Retail Low	Retail High
2004	375G I/O	42,000	50,000
2003	375G I/O	38,000	46,000
2002	375G I/O	35,000	42,000
2001	310G I/O	32,000	39,000
2000	310G I/O	30,000	36,000
1999	310G I/O	27,000	33,000
1998	310G I/O	25,000	30,000
1997	310G I/O	23,000	28,000

Pursuit 2870 CC; C280

Year	Power	Retail Low	Retail High
2008	T225 O/B	85,000	101,000
2007	T225 O/B	76,000	91,000
2006	T225 O/B	69,000	82,000
2005	T225 O/B	62,000	73,000
2004	T225 O/B	56,000	67,000
2003	T225 O/B	51,000	61,000
2002	T225 O/B	46,000	55,000
2001	T225 O/B	42,000	50,000
2000	T225 O/B	38,000	46,000
1999	T225 O/B	35,000	42,000
1998	T225 O/B	32,000	38,000
1997	T225 O/B	29,000	34,000

Pursuit 2870 Offshore CC

Year	Power	Retail Low	Retail High
2002	T225 O/B	45,000	53,000
2001	T225 O/B	41,000	48,000
2000	T225 O/B	37,000	44,000
1999	T225 O/B	34,000	40,000
1998	T225 O/B	30,000	36,000
1997	T225 O/B	28,000	33,000
1996	T225 O/B	25,000	30,000

Pursuit 2870 Walkaround

Year	Power	Retail Low	Retail High
2006	T225 O/B	71,000	84,000
2005	T225 O/B	64,000	76,000
2004	T225 O/B	58,000	69,000
2003	T225 O/B	53,000	63,000
2002	T225 O/B	48,000	57,000
2001	T225 O/B	44,000	52,000
2000	T225 O/B	40,000	48,000
1999	T225 O/B	37,000	44,000
1998	T225 O/B	34,000	40,000
1997	T225 O/B	31,000	37,000
1996	T225 O/B	29,000	34,000

Pursuit C 280

Year	Power	Retail Low	Retail High
2012	T250 O/B	******	******
2011	T250 O/B	******	******
2010	T250 O/B	124,000	149,000
2009	T250 O/B	112,000	134,000

Pursuit OS 285

Year	Power	Retail Low	Retail High
2012	T250 O/B	******	******
2011	T250 O/B	******	******
2010	T250 O/B	******	******
2009	T250 O/B	119,000	143,000
2008	T250 O/B	108,000	130,000

Pursuit 3000 Express

Year	Power	Retail Low	Retail High
2003	T320G	67,000	81,000
2003	T250D	80,000	96,000
2002	T320G	61,000	73,000
2002	T250D	73,000	87,000
2001	T320G	55,000	67,000
2001	T250D	66,000	80,000
2000	T320G	50,000	61,000
2000	T250D	60,000	72,000
1999	T320G	46,000	55,000
1999	T250D	55,000	66,000
1998	T320G	42,000	50,000
1998	T225D	50,000	60,000

Pursuit 3000 Offshore

Year	Power	Retail Low	Retail High
2004	T375G	79,000	94,000
2004	T285D	98,000	117,000
2003	T375G	71,000	86,000
2003	T285D	89,000	107,000
2002	T375G	65,000	78,000
2002	T260D	81,000	97,000
2001	T320G	59,000	71,000
2001	T260D	73,000	88,000
2000	T320G	54,000	65,000
2000	T260D	68,000	81,000
1999	T320G	50,000	60,000
1999	T260D	62,000	75,000
1998	T320G	46,000	55,000
1998	T260D	57,000	69,000
1997	T320G	42,000	51,000
1997	T260D	53,000	63,000
1996	T320G	39,000	47,000
1996	T260D	48,000	58,000
1995	T320G	36,000	43,000
1995	T260D	44,000	53,000

Pursuit 3070 Center Console

Year	Power	Retail Low	Retail High
2007	T250 O/B	95,000	114,000
2006	T250 O/B	85,000	102,000
2005	T250 O/B	76,000	92,000
2004	T250 O/B	69,000	83,000
2003	T250 O/B	62,000	74,000
2002	T250 O/B	56,000	68,000
2001	T250 O/B	51,000	61,000

Pursuit 3070 Offshore CC

Year	Power	Retail Low	Retail High
2006	T250 O/B	103,000	124,000
2005	T250 O/B	94,000	113,000
2004	T250 O/B	85,000	102,000
2003	T250 O/B	78,000	93,000
2002	T250 O/B	71,000	85,000
2001	T250 O/B	64,000	77,000

Year	Power	Retail Low	Retail High
2000	T250 O/B	58,000	70,000
1999	T250 O/B	53,000	64,000

Pursuit 3070 Offshore Express

Year	Power	Retail Low	Retail High
2007	T250 O/B	108,000	130,000
2006	T250 O/B	98,000	118,000
2005	T250 O/B	89,000	107,000
2004	T250 O/B	81,000	98,000
2003	T250 O/B	74,000	89,000
2002	T250 O/B	67,000	81,000

Pursuit 3100 Express

Year	Power	Retail Low	Retail High
1997	T300G	44,000	53,000
1996	T300G	40,000	48,000
1995	T300G	37,000	44,000

Pursuit C 310 Center Console

Year	Power	Retail Low	Retail High
2012	T250 O/B	******	******
2011	T250 O/B	******	******
2010	T250 O/B	******	******
2009	T250 O/B	119,000	143,000
2008	T250 O/B	107,000	129,000
2007	T250 O/B	96,000	116,000

Pursuit OS 315 Offshore

Year	Power	Retail Low	Retail High
2012	T250 O/B	******	******
2011	T250 O/B	******	******
2010	T250 O/B	******	******
2009	T250 O/B	152,000	182,000
2008	T250 O/B	138,000	165,000

Pursuit 3100 Offshore

Year	Power	Retail Low	Retail High
2005	T330G	104,000	125,000
2005	T315D	120,000	144,000
2004	T330G	95,000	114,000
2004	T315D	109,000	131,000

Pursuit 3370 Offshore; OS 335

Year	Power	Retail Low	Retail High
2008	T250 O/B	152,000	182,000
2007	T250 O/B	138,000	165,000
2006	T250 O/B	125,000	151,000
2005	T250 O/B	114,000	137,000
2004	T250 O/B	104,000	125,000

Pursuit 3400 Express

Year	Power	Retail Low	Retail High
2003	T375G	104,000	125,000
2003	T370D	134,000	161,000
2002	T375G	95,000	114,000
2002	T370D	122,000	147,000
2001	T370G	86,000	103,000
2001	T370D	111,000	134,000
2000	T370G	78,000	94,000
2000	T370D	101,000	121,000
1999	T320G	71,000	85,000
1999	T370D	92,000	111,000
1998	T320G	65,000	78,000
1998	T370D	84,000	101,000
1997	T320G	59,000	71,000
1997	T370D	76,000	91,000

Pursuit 3480 CC; C 340

Year	Power	Retail Low	Retail High
2010	T250 O/B	******	******
2009	T250 O/B	128,000	153,000
2008	T250 O/B	115,000	138,000
2007	T250 O/B	103,000	124,000
2006	T250 O/B	93,000	112,000
2005	T250 O/B	84,000	100,000

Pursuit LS 345 Drummond Runner

Year	Power	Retail Low	Retail High
2008	T250 O/B	132,000	159,000
2007	T250 O/B	122,000	146,000
2006	T250 O/B	113,000	136,000

Pursuit OS 375; 385 Offshore

Year	Power	Retail Low	Retail High
2012	3/350 O/B	******	******
2011	3/350 O/B	******	******
2010	3/350 O/B	******	******
2009	3/350 O/B	337,000	394,000
2008	3/350 O/B	310,000	363,000

Pursuit 3800 Express

Year	Power	Retail Low	Retail High
2004	T480D	211,000	243,000
2003	T480D	192,000	221,000
2002	T480D	175,000	201,000

Rampage 30 Express

Year	Power	Retail Low	Retail High
2009	T375G	******	******
2009	T315D	******	******
2008	T375G	118,000	142,000
2008	T315D	144,000	173,000
2007	T375G	108,000	129,000
2007	T315D	131,000	157,000
2006	T375G	98,000	118,000
2006	T315D	119,000	143,000
2005	T300G	89,000	107,000
2005	T315D	108,000	130,000
2004	T300G	81,000	97,000
2004	T315D	99,000	118,000
2003	T300G	74,000	88,000
2003	T315D	90,000	108,000
2002	T300G	67,000	80,000
2002	T315D	82,000	98,000
2001	T300G	62,000	74,000
2001	T315D	75,000	90,000
2000	T300G	57,000	68,000
2000	T315D	69,000	83,000
1999	T300G	52,000	63,000
1999	T300D	63,000	76,000

Rampage 30 Open/Offshore

Year	Power	Retail Low	Retail High
2006	T375G	86,000	104,000
2006	T315D	103,000	123,000
2005	T375G	79,000	94,000
2005	T315D	93,000	112,000
2004	T300G	71,000	86,000
2004	T315D	85,000	102,000
2003	T300G	65,000	78,000
2003	T315D	77,000	93,000
2002	T300G	59,000	71,000
2002	T315D	70,000	84,000

Rampage 33 Express

Year	Power	Retail Low	Retail High
2008	T425G	157,000	189,000
2008	T460D	201,000	241,000
2007	T425G	143,000	172,000
2007	T460D	183,000	219,000
2006	T370G	130,000	156,000
2006	T425D	166,000	200,000
2005	T370G	118,000	142,000
2005	T425D	151,000	182,000

Rampage 38 Express

Year	Power	Retail Low	Retail High
2008	T575D	237,000	280,000
2007	T575D	216,000	255,000
2006	T480D	196,000	232,000
2005	T480D	178,000	211,000
2004	T480D	162,000	192,000
2003	T480D	148,000	174,000
2002	T480D	134,000	159,000
2001	T480D	124,000	146,000
2000	T450D	114,000	134,000
1999	T450D	105,000	123,000

Rampage 45 Convertible

Year	Power	Retail Low	Retail High
2009-2012		******	******
2008	T865D	403,000	476,000
2007	T865D	367,000	433,000
2006	T865D	334,000	394,000
2005	T800D	304,000	359,000
2004	T800D	279,000	330,000
2003	T800D	257,000	303,000
2002	T800D	236,000	279,000

Regal 2665 Commodore

Year	Power	Retail Low	Retail High
2009	320 I/O	53,000	63,000
2008	320 I/O	48,000	58,000
2007	320 I/O	44,000	52,000
2006	320 I/O	40,000	48,000
2005	320 I/O	36,000	43,000
2004	320 I/O	33,000	39,000
2003	320 I/O	30,000	36,000
2002	320 I/O	28,000	33,000

Regal 260 Valenti; 272 Commodore

Year	Power	Retail Low	Retail High
1996	S300 I/O	14,000	17,000
1996	T190 I/O	16,000	19,000
1995	S300 I/O	13,000	16,000
1995	T190 I/O	15,000	18,000

Regal 2660/2765 Commodore

Year	Power	Retail Low	Retail High
2005	375 I/O	43,000	52,000
2005	T220 I/O	46,000	55,000
2004	375 I/O	39,000	47,000
2004	T220 I/O	42,000	50,000
2003	375 I/O	36,000	43,000
2003	T220 I/O	38,000	46,000
2002	320 I/O	32,000	39,000
2002	T190 I/O	35,000	42,000
2001	310 I/O	30,000	36,000
2001	T190 I/O	32,000	38,000
2000	310 I/O	27,000	33,000
2000	T190 I/O	29,000	35,000
1999	310 I/O	25,000	30,000
1999	T190 I/O	27,000	32,000

Regal 2760/2860 Commodore

Year	Power	Retail Low	Retail High
2005	T225 I/O	53,000	63,000
2004	T220 I/O	48,000	58,000
2003	T220 I/O	44,000	52,000
2002	T220 I/O	40,000	48,000
2001	T210 I/O	36,000	43,000
2000	T210 I/O	33,000	40,000
1999	T210 I/O	30,000	37,000
1998	T210 I/O	28,000	34,000

Regal 2860 Windows Express

Year	Power	Retail Low	Retail High
2011	T220 I/O	******	******
2010	T220 I/O	68,000	82,000
2009	T220 I/O	62,000	74,000
2008	T220 I/O	56,000	67,000
2007	T220 I/O	51,000	61,000
2006	T220 I/O	46,000	56,000

Regal 292/2960/3060 Commodore

Year	Power	Retail Low	Retail High
2003	T260 I/O	47,000	57,000
2002	T260 I/O	43,000	52,000
2001	T260 I/O	40,000	48,000
2000	T260 I/O	36,000	44,000
1999	T260 I/O	34,000	40,000
1998	T260 I/O	31,000	37,000
1997	T260 I/O	28,000	34,000
1996	T260 I/O	26,000	31,000
1995	T260 I/O	24,000	29,000

Regal 3060 Window Express

Year	Power	Retail Low	Retail High
2012	T260 I/O	******	******
2011	T260 I/O	******	******
2010	T260 I/O	******	******
2009	T260 I/O	87,000	104,000
2008	T260 I/O	78,000	94,000
2007	T260 I/O	70,000	84,000
2006	T260 I/O	64,000	77,000
2005	T260 I/O	58,000	70,000

Year	Power	Retail Low	Retail High
2004	T260 I/O	53,000	64,000

Regal Ventura 9.8; 322/3260 Commodore

Year	Power	Retail Low	Retail High
2004	T320 I/B	72,000	86,000
2004	T300 I/O	62,000	75,000
2003	T320 I/B	65,000	78,000
2003	T300 I/O	57,000	68,000
2002	T320 I/B	60,000	72,000
2002	T300 I/O	52,000	62,000
2001	T310 I/B	55,000	66,000
2001	T310 I/O	48,000	57,000
2000	T310 I/B	51,000	61,000
2000	T310 I/O	44,000	53,000
1999	T310 I/B	47,000	57,000
1999	T310 I/O	41,000	49,000
1998	T310 I/B	44,000	53,000
1998	T310 I/O	38,000	46,000
1997	T310 I/B	41,000	49,000
1997	T310 I/O	35,000	42,000
1996	T310 I/B	38,000	45,000
1996	T310 I/O	33,000	39,000
1995	T310 I/B	35,000	42,000
1995	T310 I/O	30,000	37,000

Regal 3350 Sport Cruiser

Year	Power	Retail Low	Retail High
2007	T300 I/O	78,000	93,000
2006	T300 I/O	71,000	85,000
2005	T300 I/O	64,000	77,000

Regal 3360 Window Express

Year	Power	Retail Low	Retail High
2012	T300 I/O	******	******
2011	T300 I/O	******	******
2010	T300 I/O	******	******
2009	T300 I/O	122,000	147,000
2008	T300 I/O	110,000	132,000
2007	T320 I/O	99,000	119,000
2006	T320 I/O	89,000	107,000

Regal 3560/3760 Commodore

Year	Power	Retail Low	Retail High
2010	T420 VD	******	******
2010	T370 I/O	******	******
2009	T420 V/D	******	******
2009	T375 I/O	******	******
2008	T370 V/D	142,000	171,000
2008	T320 I/O	135,000	163,000
2007	T370 V/D	129,000	155,000
2007	T320 I/O	123,000	148,000
2006	T320 V/D	118,000	141,000
2006	T320 I/O	112,000	134,000
2005	T320 V/D	107,000	128,000
2005	T320 I/O	102,000	122,000
2004	T320 V/D	97,000	117,000
2004	T375 I/O	93,000	111,000
2003	T320 V/D	88,000	106,000
2003	T375 I/O	84,000	101,000

Regal 3860/4060 Commodore

Year	Power	Retail Low	Retail High
2010	T375G IPS	******	******
2010	T370D IPS	******	******
2009	T375G IPS	******	******
2009	T300D IPS	******	******
2008	T420G	182,000	218,000
2008	T370D	220,000	264,000
2007	T420G	167,000	201,000
2007	T370D	202,000	243,000
2006	T420G	154,000	185,000
2006	T370D	186,000	223,000
2005	T420G	142,000	170,000
2005	T370D	171,000	205,000
2004	T420G	132,000	158,000
2004	T370D	159,000	191,000
2003	T3420G	122,000	147,000
2003	T370D	148,000	178,000
2002	T3420G	114,000	137,000
2002	T370D	138,000	165,000

Regal 3780/3880/4080 Commodore

Year	Power	Retail Low	Retail High
2010	T375G IPS	******	******
2010	T370D IPS	******	******
2009	T420G	******	******
2009	T370D	******	******
2008	T420G	******	******
2008	T370D	******	******
2007	T420G	204,000	245,000
2007	T370D	236,000	284,000
2006	T420G	186,000	223,000
2006	T370D	215,000	258,000
2005	T420G	169,000	203,000
2005	T370D	196,000	235,000
2004	T420G	155,000	186,000
2004	T370D	180,000	216,000
2003	T420G	143,000	171,000
2003	T370D	165,000	199,000
2002	T420G	131,000	158,000
2002	T370D	152,000	183,000
2001	T420G	121,000	145,000
2001	T330D	140,000	168,000

Regal 380/400/402 Commodore

Year	Power	Retail Low	Retail High
1999	T310G	81,000	97,000
1998	T310G	74,000	89,000
1997	T310G	68,000	82,000
1996	T310G	63,000	75,000
1995	T310G	58,000	69,000

Regal 4160/4260/4460 Commodore

Year	Power	Retail Low	Retail High
2009	T435D	******	******
2009	T420G	******	******
2008	T480D	******	******
2008	T420G	******	******
2007	T480D	283,000	337,000
2007	T420G	250,000	298,000
2006	T480D	258,000	307,000
2006	T420G	228,000	271,000
2005	T450D	237,000	282,000
2005	T420G	209,000	249,000
2004	T450D	218,000	259,000
2004	T420G	193,000	229,000
2003	T450D	200,000	239,000
2003	T420G	177,000	211,000
2002	T370D	184,000	219,000
2002	T420G	163,000	194,000
2001	T370D	170,000	202,000
2001	T380G	150,000	179,000
2000	T370D	156,000	186,000
2000	T380G	138,000	164,000

Regal 52 Sport Coupe

Year	Power	Retail Low	Retail High
2012	T435D IPS	******	******
2011	T435D IPS	******	******
2010	T435D IPS	******	******
2009	T435D IPS	475,000	560,000
2008	T435D IPS	427,000	504,000

Regulator 26 Center Console

Year	Power	Retail Low	Retail High
2009-2012		******	******
2008	T225 O/B	68,000	82,000
2007	T225 O/B	62,000	74,000
2006	T225 O/B	56,000	67,000
2005	T225 O/B	51,000	61,000
2004	T225 O/B	46,000	56,000
2003	T225 O/B	42,000	51,000
2002	T225 O/B	38,000	46,000
2001	T225 O/B	35,000	42,000
2000	T225 O/B	32,000	38,000
1999	T225 O/B	29,000	35,000
1998	T225 O/B	26,000	32,000
1997	T225 O/B	24,000	29,000
1996	T225 O/B	22,000	27,000
1995	T225 O/B	20,000	25,000

Regulator 26 Express

Year	Power	Retail Low	Retail High
1998	T200 O/B	27,000	32,000
1997	T200 O/B	24,000	29,000
1996	T200 O/B	22,000	27,000
1995	T200 O/B	21,000	25,000

Regulator 29 FS

Year	Power	Retail Low	Retail High
2012	T250 O/B	******	******
2011	T250 O/B	******	******
2010	T250 O/B	118,000	142,000
2009	T250 O/B	108,000	129,000
2008	T250 O/B	98,000	118,000
2007	T250 O/B	89,000	107,000
2006	T250 O/B	81,000	97,000

Regulator 32 FS

Year	Power	Retail Low	Retail High
2012	T250 O/B	******	******
2011	T250 O/B	******	******
2010	T250 O/B	******	******
2009	T250 O/B	129,000	155,000
2008	T250 O/B	117,000	141,000
2007	T250 O/B	106,000	128,000
2006	T250 O/B	97,000	116,000
2005	T250 O/B	88,000	106,000
2004	T250 O/B	81,000	97,000
2003	T250 O/B	74,000	89,000
2002	T250 O/B	68,000	82,000
2001	T250 O/B	63,000	76,000
2000	T250 O/B	58,000	70,000
1999	T250 O/B	53,000	64,000

Regulator 34 SS

Year	Power	Retail Low	Retail High
2012	T350 O/B	******	******
2011	T350 O/B	******	******
2010	T350 O/B	******	******
2009	T350 O/B	161,000	193,000

Rinker 260/265 Fiesta Vee

Year	Power	Retail Low	Retail High
1996	250 I/O	12,000	14,000
1995	250 I/O	11,000	13,000

Rinker 266 Fiesta Vee

Year	Power	Retail Low	Retail High
1999	250 I/O	14,000	17,000
1998	250 I/O	13,000	15,000
1997	250 I/O	12,000	14,000
1996	250 I/O	11,000	13,000

Rinker 270 Fiesta Vee

Year	Power	Retail Low	Retail High
2006	300 I/O	36,000	43,000
2005	300 I/O	33,000	40,000
2004	250 I/O	31,000	37,000
2003	250 I/O	29,000	34,000
2002	250 I/O	27,000	32,000
2001	250 I/O	25,000	30,000
2000	250 I/O	23,000	28,000
1999	250 I/O	21,000	26,000

Rinker 280 Fiesta Vee

Year	Power	Retail Low	Retail High
1999	T190 I/O	21,000	26,000
1998	T190 I/O	20,000	24,000
1997	T190 I/O	18,000	22,000
1996	T180 I/O	17,000	21,000
1995	T180 I/O	16,000	19,000

Rinker 280/290 Express Cruiser

Year	Power	Retail Low	Retail High
2012	280 I/O	******	******
2011	280 I/O	******	******
2010	280 I/O	88,000	106,000
2009	300 I/O	59,000	71,000
2008	300 I/O	53,000	64,000

Year	Power	Retail Low	Retail High
Rinker 290 Fiesta; 300 Express			
2009	T260 I/O	90,000	108,000
2008	T260 I/O	82,000	98,000
2007	T260 I/O	74,000	89,000
2006	T260 I/O	68,000	82,000
2005	T260 I/O	63,000	75,000
2004	T260 I/O	58,000	69,000
2003	T260 I/O	53,000	64,000
Rinker 300 Fiesta Vee			
1997	T250 I/O	20,000	25,000
1996	T250 I/O	19,000	23,000
1995	T250 I/O	18,000	22,000
Rinker 310/312 Fiesta; 320 Express			
2009	T260 I/O	115,000	139,000
2008	T260 I/O	105,000	126,000
2007	T260 I/O	95,000	115,000
2006	T260 I/O	87,000	104,000
2005	T260 I/O	80,000	96,000
2004	T260 I/O	73,000	88,000
2003	T260 I/O	68,000	81,000
2002	T260 I/O	62,000	75,000
2001	T240 I/O	57,000	69,000
2000	T240 I/O	52,000	63,000
Rinker 330/340 Express Cruiser			
2012	T300 I/O	******	******
2011	T300 I/O	******	******
2010	T300 I/O	151,000	181,000
2009	T300 I/O	135,000	163,000
2008	T300 I/O	122,000	146,000
Rinker 330/340/342 Fiesta Vee			
2006	T300 I/O	114,000	136,000
2005	T300 I/O	104,000	125,000
2004	T300 I/O	96,000	115,000
2003	T300 I/O	88,000	106,000
2002	T300 I/O	81,000	98,000
2001	T260 I/O	75,000	91,000
2000	T260 I/O	70,000	84,000
1999	T260 I/O	65,000	78,000
1998	T260 I/O	61,000	73,000
Rinker 350/360 Express Cruiser			
2012	T300 I/O	******	******
2011	T300 I/O	******	******
2010	T300 I/O	******	******
2009	T300 I/O	158,000	190,000
2008	T300 I/O	144,000	173,000
Rinker 360/370/380 Express Cruiser			
2009	T320 I/O	190,000	228,000
2008	T320 I/O	172,000	207,000
2007	T320 I/O	157,000	188,000
2006	T320 I/O	143,000	171,000
2005	T320 I/O	130,000	156,000
Rinker 390/400 Express Cruiser			
2009-2012		******	******
2008	T375G I/O	209,000	250,000
2007	T375G I/O	192,000	230,000
2006	T375G I/O	176,000	212,000
Rinker 390/410/420 Express Cruiser			
2007	T420G	237,000	285,000
2006	T420G	218,000	262,000
2005	T420G	201,000	241,000
2004	T420G	184,000	221,000
Riviera 33 Conv. (1992-97)			
1997	T210D	95,000	114,000
1996	T210D	88,000	106,000
1995	T210D	82,000	98,000
Riviera 33 Convertible (2005-08)			
2008	T370D	******	******
2007	T370D	180,000	216,000
2006	T310D	167,000	201,000
2005	T310D	156,000	187,000
Riviera 34 Convertible			
2002	T370D	118,000	177,000
2001	T370D	107,000	129,000
2000	T350D	98,000	117,000
1999	T330D	90,000	108,000
1998	T315D	83,000	99,000
1997	T315D	76,000	91,000
Riviera 36 Convertible			
2002	T370D	129,000	155,000
2001	T370D	118,000	141,000
2000	T350D	108,000	130,000
1999	T330D	100,000	120,000
1998	T315D	92,000	110,000
1997	T315D	84,000	101,000
1996	T315D	77,000	93,000
1995	T315D	71,000	86,000
Riviera 3600 Sport Yacht			
2011	T301D IPS	******	******
2010	T301D IPS	******	******
2009	T370D	228,000	273,000
2008	T370D	209,000	251,000
2007	T370D	192,000	231,000
Riviera 37 Convertible			
2008	T370D	304,000	358,000
2007	T330D	279,000	330,000
2006	T330D	257,000	303,000
2005	T330D	236,000	279,000
2004	T330D	217,000	256,000
2003	T330D	200,000	236,000
2002	T330D	184,000	217,000
2001	T315D	169,000	200,000
Riviera 40 Convertible			
2006	T460D	272,000	321,000
2005	T455D	247,000	292,000
2004	T430D	225,000	266,000
2003	T430D	205,000	242,000
2002	T470D	186,000	220,000
2001	T470D	169,000	200,000
Riviera 4000 Offshore			
2003	T450D	168,000	198,000
2002	T450D	153,000	180,000
2001	T450D	139,000	164,000
2000	T450D	126,000	149,000
1999	T450D	115,000	136,000
1998	T435D	105,000	123,000
Riviera 42 Convertible			
2006	T480D	******	******
2005	T480D	323,000	381,000
2004	T480D	293,000	346,000
Riviera 43 Convertible			
2003	T430D	308,000	364,000
2002	T430D	280,000	331,000
2001	T430D	255,000	301,000
2000	T450D	232,000	274,000
1999	T450D	214,000	252,000
1998	T420D	196,000	232,000
1997	T420D	181,000	213,000
1996	T420D	166,000	196,000
Riviera 47 Convertible			
2007	T660D	495,000	584,000
2006	T700D	455,000	537,000
2005	T700D	419,000	494,000
2004	T700D	385,000	455,000
2003	T660D	355,000	418,000
Robalo 260 Center Console			
2012	T225 O/B	******	******
2011	T225 O/B	******	******
2010	T225 O/B	76,000	91,000
2009	T225 O/B	69,000	82,000
2008	T225 O/B	62,000	75,000
2007	T225 O/B	57,000	68,000
2006	T225 O/B	52,000	62,000
2005	T225 O/B	47,000	56,000
2004	T225 O/B	43,000	51,000
Robalo 2620 Center Console			
2001	T200 O/B	21,000	25,000
2000	T200 O/B	19,000	23,000
1999	T200 O/B	17,000	21,000
1998	T200 O/B	16,000	19,000
Robalo 2640 Walkaround			
2002	T200 O/B	******	******
2001	T200 O/B	23,000	27,000
2000	T200 O/B	21,000	25,000
1999	T200 O/B	19,000	23,000
1998	T200 O/B	17,000	21,000
Robalo 2660 Cuddy Cabin			
1995	T200 O/B	14,000	18,000
Robalo 265 Walkaround			
2012	T225 O/B	******	******
2011	T225 O/B	******	******
2010	T225 O/B	81,000	97,000
2009	T225 O/B	73,000	88,000
2008	T225 O/B	67,000	80,000
2007	T225 O/B	61,000	73,000
2006	T225 O/B	55,000	66,000
2005	T225 O/B	50,000	60,000
2004	T225 O/B	45,000	55,000
2003	T225 O/B	41,000	50,000
Robalo 300 Center Console			
2012	T250 O/B	******	******
2011	T250 O/B	******	******
2010	T250 O/B	121,000	145,000
2009	T250 O/B	110,000	132,000
2008	T250 O/B	100,000	120,000
2007	T250 O/B	91,000	109,000
Robalo 305 Walkaround			
2012	T250 O/B	******	******
2011	T250 O/B	******	******
2010	T250 O/B	130,000	156,000
2009	T250 O/B	118,000	141,000
2008	T250 O/B	107,000	129,000
2007	T250 O/B	97,000	117,000
Sabreline 34 Sedan			
2002	T220D	145,000	174,000
2001	T220D	135,000	162,000
2000	T220D	125,000	150,000
1999	T220D	117,000	140,000
1998	T220D	108,000	130,000
1997	T220D	101,000	121,000
1996	T210D	94,000	112,000
1995	T210D	88,000	106,000
Sabreline 34 Hardtop Express			
2010	T310D	******	******
2009	T310D	******	******
2008	T315D	247,000	296,000
2007	T315D	229,000	275,000
2006	T315D	213,000	256,000

Sabre 36 Aft Cabin

Year	Power	Retail Low	Retail High
1998	T300D	85,000	102,000
1997	T300D	79,000	95,000
1996	T300D	73,000	88,000
1995	T255D	68,000	82,000

Sabrlinee 36 Express

Year	Power	Retail Low	Retail High
2003	T315D	133,000	159,000
2002	T315D	122,000	146,000
2001	T315D	112,000	135,000
2000	T315D	103,000	124,000
1999	T300D	90,000	115,000
1998	T300D	89,000	107,000
1997	T300D	83,000	99,000
1996	T300D	77,000	92,000

Sabreline 36 Sedan

Year	Power	Retail Low	Retail High
2007	T315D	212,000	255,000
2006	T315D	195,000	234,000
2005	T315D	180,000	216,000
2004	T315D	165,000	198,000
2003	T315D	152,000	182,000
2002	T315D	140,000	168,000

Sabre 38 Express

Year	Power	Retail Low	Retail High
2010	T380D	******	******
2009	T380D	******	******
2008	T370D	275,000	330,000
2007	T370D	258,000	310,000
2006	T370D	243,000	292,000
2005	T370D	228,000	274,000

Sabre 42 Hardtop Express

Year	Power	Retail Low	Retail High
2011	T440D Zeus	******	******
2010	T440D Zeus	******	******
2009	T440D Zeus	******	******
2008	T440D	351,000	414,000
2007	T440D	326,000	385,000
2006	T440D	304,000	358,000
2005	T440D	282,000	333,000
2004	T440D	262,000	310,000

Sabre 42 Sedan

Year	Power	Retail Low	Retail High
2008	T440D	380,000	448,000
2007	T440D	353,000	417,000
2006	T440D	328,000	387,000
2005	T440D	305,000	360,000
2004	T440D	287,000	339,000
2003	T440D	270,000	318,000
2002	T420D	253,000	299,000
2001	T420D	238,000	281,000

Sabreline 43 Aft Cabin

Year	Power	Retail Low	Retail High
2005	T370D	******	******
2004	T370D	******	******
2003	T370D	******	******
2002	T370D	******	******
2001	T370D	307,000	363,000
2000	T350D	286,000	337,000
1999	T350D	269,000	317,000
1998	T350D	253,000	298,000
1997	T350D	237,000	280,000
1996	T350D	223,000	263,000

Sabreline 47 Aft Cabin

Year	Power	Retail Low	Retail High
2007	T465D	******	******
2006	T465D	******	******
2005	T465D	******	******
2004	T465D	342,000	400,000
2003	T465D	318,000	372,000
2002	T420D	295,000	346,000
2001	T420D	275,000	321,000
2000	T420D	255,000	299,000
1999	T420D	240,000	281,000
1998	T420D	226,000	264,000
1997	T350D	212,000	248,000

Scout 260/262 Sportfish

Year	Power	Retail Low	Retail High
2011	T200 0/B	******	******
2010	T200 0/B	70,000	84,000
2009	T200 0/B	64,000	77,000
2008	T200 0/B	59,000	70,000
2007	T200 0/B	53,000	64,000
2006	T200 0/B	48,000	58,000

Scout 280 Abaco

Year	Power	Retail Low	Retail High
2005	T200 0/B	54,000	64,000
2004	T200 0/B	49,000	59,000
2003	T200 0/B	44,000	53,000
2002	T200 0/B	40,000	48,000
2001	T200 0/B	37,000	44,000
2000	T200 0/B	33,000	40,000

Scout 280 Sportfish

Year	Power	Retail Low	Retail High
2006	T200 0/B	51,000	61,000
2005	T200 0/B	46,000	55,000
2004	T200 0/B	41,000	49,000
2003	T200 0/B	37,000	44,000
2002	T200 0/B	33,000	40,000
2001	T200 0/B	30,000	36,000

Scout 282 SF

Year	Power	Retail Low	Retail High
2012	T250 0/B	******	******
2011	T250 0/B	******	******
2010	T250 0/B	******	******
2009	T250 0/B	82,000	98,000
2008	T250 0/B	74,000	88,000
2007	T250 0/B	66,000	79,000
2006	T250 0/B	61,000	73,000

Sea Ray 260 Bowrider

Year	Power	Retail Low	Retail High
2001	320 I/O	17,000	20,000
2000	320 I/O	15,000	19,000
1999	310 I/O	14,000	17,000
1998	310 I/O	13,000	16,000
1997	310 I/O	12,000	15,000
1996	310 I/O	12,000	14,000

Sea Ray 260 Bowrider Select

Year	Power	Retail Low	Retail High
2001	320 I/O	19,000	23,000
2000	320 I/O	17,000	21,000
1999	310 I/O	16,000	19,000
1998	310 I/O	15,000	18,000

Sea Ray 260 Overnighter

Year	Power	Retail Low	Retail High
2001	310 I/O	19,000	23,000
2000	310 I/O	17,000	21,000
1999	310 I/O	16,000	19,000

Sea Ray 260 Sundeck

Year	Power	Retail Low	Retail High
2012	300 I/O	60,000	72,000
2011	300 I/O	54,000	65,000
2010	300 I/O	49,000	59,000
2009	300 I/O	45,000	54,000
2008	300 I/O	41,000	49,000
2007	300 I/O	37,000	44,000

Sea Ray 260 Sundancer

Year	Power	Retail Low	Retail High
2008	300 I/O	48,000	58,000
2007	300 I/O	44,000	52,000
2006	300 I/O	40,000	48,000
2005	300 I/O	36,000	43,000
2004	260 I/O	33,000	40,000
2003	260 I/O	30,000	37,000
2002	260 I/O	28,000	34,000
2001	260 I/O	26,000	31,000
2000	260 I/O	24,000	28,000
1999	260 I/O	22,000	26,000

Sea Ray 250/260 Sundancer

Year	Power	Retail Low	Retail High
2012	300 I/O	******	******
2011	300 I/O	63,000	75,000
2010	300 I/O	57,000	68,000
2009	300 I/O	52,000	62,000

Sea Ray 270 Select EX

Year	Power	Retail Low	Retail High
2012	300 I/O	******	******
2011	300 I/O	66,000	63,000
2010	300 I/O	60,000	57,000
2009	320 I/O	55,000	52,000
2008	320 I/O	50,000	48,000
2007	320 I/O	46,000	44,000
2006	320 I/O	43,000	40,000
2005	320 I/O	39,000	37,000

Sea Ray 270 Amberjack (2005-09)

Year	Power	Retail Low	Retail High
2009	320 I/O	54,000	52,000
2008	320 I/O	49,000	47,000
2007	320 I/O	45,000	43,000
2006	320 I/O	41,000	39,000
2005	320 I/O	37,000	35,000

Sea Ray 270 Sundancer (8'6 Beam)

Year	Power	Retail Low	Retail High
1999	310 I/O	15,000	18,000
1998	No Prod.	******	******
1997	310 I/O	13,000	15,000
1996	310 I/O	12,000	14,000
1995	310 I/O	11,000	13,000

Sea Ray 270 Sundancer (9'2 Beam)

Year	Power	Retail Low	Retail High
2001	310 I/O	25,000	30,000
2001	T190 I/O	28,000	33,000
2000	310 I/O	23,000	27,000
2000	T190 I/O	26,000	31,000
1999	300 I/O	21,000	25,000
1999	T190 I/O	24,000	29,000
1998	300 I/O	20,000	24,000
1998	T190 I/O	22,000	27,000

Sea Ray 270 Sundeck

Year	Power	Retail Low	Retail High
2007	320 I/O	38,000	45,000
2006	320 I/O	34,000	41,000
2005	320 I/O	31,000	37,000
2004	320 I/O	28,000	34,000
2003	320 I/O	26,000	31,000
2002	320 I/O	23,000	28,000

Sea Ray 280 Bowrider

Year	Power	Retail Low	Retail High
2001	T260 I/O	30,000	35,000
2000	T260 I/O	27,000	32,000
1999	T260 I/O	25,000	29,000
1998	T260 I/O	23,000	27,000
1997	T260 I/O	21,000	25,000
1996	T250 I/O	19,000	23,000

Sea Ray 280 Sun Sport

Year	Power	Retail Low	Retail High
2001	320 I/O	24,000	29,000
2001	T260 I/O	29,000	35,000
2000	320 I/O	22,000	27,000
2000	T260 I/O	27,000	32,000
1999	310 I/O	21,000	25,000
1999	T260 I/O	25,000	30,000
1998	310 I/O	19,000	23,000
1998	T260 I/O	23,000	28,000
1997	300 I/O	18,000	22,000
1997	T250 I/O	22,000	26,000
1996	300 I/O	17,000	21,000
1996	T250 I/O	20,000	25,000

Sea Ray 280 Sundancer (Current)

Year	Power	Retail Low	Retail High
2012	300 I/O	******	******
2011	300 I/O	90,000	108,000
2010	300 I/O	81,000	98,000

See Page 667 For Price Adjustments

Sea Ray 280 Sundancer (2001-09)

Year	Power	Retail Low	Retail High
2009	T260 I/O	95,000	114,000
2008	T260 I/O	86,000	103,000
2007	T260 I/O	78,000	94,000
2006	T260 I/O	71,000	85,000
2005	T260 I/O	65,000	79,000
2004	T260 I/O	60,000	72,000
2003	T260 I/O	55,000	66,000
2002	T260 I/O	51,000	61,000
2001	T260 I/O	47,000	56,000

Sea Ray 290 Amberjack

Year	Power	Retail Low	Retail High
2009	T260 I/O	112,000	131,000
2008	T260 I/O	100,000	118,000
2007	T260 I/O	90,000	106,000
2006	T260 I/O	81,000	95,000
2005	T260 I/O	73,000	86,000
2004	T260 I/O	66,000	78,000
2003	T260 I/O	60,000	71,000
2002	T240 I/O	55,000	64,000
2001	T240 I/O	50,000	59,000
2000	T240 I/O	46,000	54,000

Sea Ray 290 Bowrider

Year	Power	Retail Low	Retail High
2004	T260 I/O	39,000	47,000
2003	T260 I/O	37,000	44,000
2002	T260 I/O	34,000	41,000
2001	T260 I/O	32,000	38,000

Sea Ray 290 Select EX

Year	Power	Retail Low	Retail High
2008	T260 I/O	60,000	72,000
2007	T260 I/O	55,000	66,000
2006	T260 I/O	50,000	60,000
2005	T260 I/O	45,000	54,000

Sea Ray 290 Sun Sport

Year	Power	Retail Low	Retail High
2009	T260 I/O	85,000	102,000
2008	T260 I/O	78,000	94,000
2007	T260 I/O	72,000	86,000
2006	T260 I/O	66,000	79,000
2005	T260 I/O	61,000	74,000
2004	T260 I/O	57,000	69,000
2003	T260 I/O	53,000	64,000
2002	T260 I/O	49,000	59,000

Sea Ray 290 Sundancer (1994-2001)

Year	Power	Retail Low	Retail High
2001	T260 I/O	32,000	38,000
2000	T260 I/O	29,000	35,000
1999	T260 I/O	27,000	32,000
1998	T260 I/O	25,000	30,000
1997	T190 I/O	23,000	27,000
1996	T190 I/O	21,000	25,000
1995	T190 I/O	19,000	23,000

Sea Ray 290 Sundancer (2006-08)

Year	Power	Retail Low	Retail High
2008	T220 I/O	68,000	82,000
2007	T220 I/O	62,000	75,000
2006	T220 I/O	57,000	69,000

Sea Ray 290/300 Sundeck

Year	Power	Retail Low	Retail High
2012	300 I/O	******	******
2011	300 I/O	62,000	74,000
2010	300 I/O	57,000	68,000
2009	300 I/O	52,000	62,000

Sea Ray 300 Select EX; SLX

Year	Power	Retail Low	Retail High
2012	375 I/O	100,000	120,000
2011	375 I/O	92,000	110,000
2010	375 I/O	84,000	101,000
2009	375 I/O	77,000	93,000

Sea Ray 300 Sundancer (1994-97)

Year	Power	Retail Low	Retail High
1997	T290 VD	23,000	28,000
1997	T210 I/O	22,000	26,000
1996	T250 VD	20,000	24,000
1996	T250 I/O	19,000	22,000
1995	T250 VD	17,000	21,000
1995	T250 I/O	16,000	19,000

Sea Ray 300 Sundancer (2002-07)

Year	Power	Retail Low	Retail High
2007	T260 I/O	68,000	82,000
2006	T260 I/O	62,000	74,000
2005	T260 I/O	56,000	67,000
2004	T260 I/O	51,000	61,000
2003	T260 I/O	47,000	56,000
2002	T260 I/O	43,000	52,000

Sea Ray 310 Sundancer (1998-2002)

Year	Power	Retail Low	Retail High
2002	T260 I/O	49,000	59,000
2001	T260 I/O	45,000	54,000
2000	T260 I/O	41,000	50,000
1999	T260 I/O	38,000	46,000
1998	T260 I/O	35,000	42,000

Sea Ray 310 Sundancer (Current)

Year	Power	Retail Low	Retail High
2012	T260 I/O	******	******
2011	T260 I/O	116,000	139,000
2010	T260 I/O	106,000	128,000

Sea Ray 310/330 EC (1990-95)

Year	Power	Retail Low	Retail High
1995	T300 I/O	22,000	26,000
1995	T310 I/B	28,000	33,000

Sea Ray 310/330 Sundancer

Year	Power	Retail Low	Retail High
2012	T300 I/O	******	******
2011	T300 I/O	160,000	192,000
2010	T260 I/O	147,000	176,000
2009	T260 I/O	135,000	162,000
2008	T260 I/O	124,000	149,000
2007	T260 I/O	114,000	137,000

Sea Ray 320 Sundancer

Year	Power	Retail Low	Retail High
2007	T300 VD	107,000	128,000
2007	T300 I/O	100,000	120,000
2006	T320 VD	98,000	118,000
2006	T260 I/O	92,000	111,000
2005	T320 VD	90,000	109,000
2005	T260 I/O	85,000	102,000
2004	T300 VD	83,000	100,000
2004	T260 I/O	78,000	94,000
2003	T300 VD	76,000	92,000
2003	T260 I/O	72,000	86,000

Sea Ray 330 Express Cruiser

Year	Power	Retail Low	Retail High
2000	T310G	57,000	68,000
1999	T310G	52,000	62,000
1998	T310G	48,000	57,000
1997	T310G	44,000	53,000

Sea Ray 330 Sundancer (95-99)

Year	Power	Retail Low	Retail High
1999	T300 I/O	43,000	52,000
1999	T310 VD	47,000	57,000
1998	T300 I/O	40,000	48,000
1998	T310 VD	44,000	53,000
1997	T300 I/O	37,000	45,000
1997	T310 VD	41,000	49,000
1996	T300 I/O	35,000	42,000
1996	T310 VD	38,000	45,000
1995	T300 I/O	32,000	39,000
1995	T310 VD	35,000	42,000

Sea Ray 330/350 Sundancer

Year	Power	Retail Low	Retail High
2012	T320 I/O	******	******
2012	T375 VD	******	******
2011	T320 I/O	212,000	254,000
2011	T375 VD	225,000	270,000
2010	T320G I/O	195,000	234,000
2010	T3700G VD	207,000	248,000
2009	T320G I/O	179,000	215,000
2009	T3700G VD	190,000	228,000
2008	T320G I/O	165,000	198,000
2008	T370G VD	175,000	210,000

Sea Ray 340 Amberjack

Year	Power	Retail Low	Retail High
2003	T370G	84,000	101,000
2002	T370G	77,000	93,000
2001	T370G	71,000	85,000

Sea Ray 340 Sundancer (2003-08)

Year	Power	Retail Low	Retail High
2008	T375 I/O	121,000	145,000
2008	T375 VD	132,000	158,000
2007	T375 I/O	110,000	132,000
2007	T370 VD	120,000	144,000
2006	T320 I/O	100,000	120,000
2006	T320 VD	109,000	131,000
2005	T320 I/O	91,000	109,000
2005	T320 VD	99,000	119,000
2004	T320 I/O	83,000	100,000
2004	T320 VD	90,000	108,000
2003	T320 I/O	75,000	91,000
2003	T320 VD	82,000	98,000

Sea Ray 340 Sundancer (1999-02)

Year	Power	Retail Low	Retail High
2002	T260 I/O	54,000	64,000
2002	T320 VD	72,000	86,000
2001	T260 I/O	49,000	59,000
2001	T320 VD	66,000	79,000
2000	T260 I/O	45,000	54,000
2000	T320 VD	61,000	73,000
1999	T260 I/O	42,000	50,000
1999	T320 VD	56,000	67,000

Sea Ray 350/370 EC (1990-95)

Year	Power	Retail Low	Retail High
1995	T310G	43,000	52,000

Sea Ray 350/370 Sundancer

Year	Power	Retail Low	Retail High
2012	T370G VD	******	******
2012	T375G I/O	******	******
2011	T375G I/O	******	******
2011	T370G VD	******	******
2010	T375G I/O	247,000	296,000
2010	T370G VD	251,000	302,000
2009	T375G I/O	222,000	266,000
2009	T370G VD	226,000	271,000
2008	T375G I/O	200,000	240,000
2008	T370G VD	203,000	244,000

Sea Ray 36 Sedan Bridge

Year	Power	Retail Low	Retail High
2009	T370G	******	******
2009	T370D	******	******
2008	T370G	185,000	212,000
2008	T370D	217,000	249,000
2007	T370G	170,000	195,000
2007	T380D	199,000	229,000

Sea Ray 360 Sundancer

Year	Power	Retail Low	Retail High
2006	T370 VD	141,000	164,000
2005	T370 VD	128,000	153,000
2004	T370 VD	116,000	140,000
2003	T370 VD	106,000	127,000
2002	T370 VD	96,000	116,000

Sea Ray 370 Express Cruiser

Year	Power	Retail Low	Retail High
2000	T380G	86,000	102,000
2000	T340D	103,000	122,000
1999	T380G	79,000	93,000
1999	T340D	95,000	112,000
1998	T380G	73,000	86,000
1998	T340D	87,000	103,000
1997	T380G	67,000	79,000
1997	T340D	80,000	95,000

Sea Ray 370 Sedan Bridge

Year	Power	Retail Low	Retail High
1997	T340G	59,000	71,000
1996	T340G	55,000	66,000

Year	Power	Retail Low	Retail High
1995	T310G	52,000	62,000

Sea Ray 370 Sundancer (1995-99)

Year	Power	Retail Low	Retail High
1999	T310G	92,000	110,000
1999	T292D	109,000	131,000
1998	T310G	84,000	101,000
1998	T292D	101,000	121,000
1997	T310G	78,000	94,000
1997	T292D	94,000	112,000
1996	T310G	73,000	87,000
1996	T292D	87,000	105,000
1995	T310G	68,000	81,000
1995	T292D	81,000	97,000

Sea Ray 370/380 Aft Cabin

Year	Power	Retail Low	Retail High
2001	T380G	105,000	126,000
2001	T340D	124,000	148,000
2000	T380G	96,000	116,000
2000	T340D	114,000	136,000
1999	T380G	89,000	106,000
1999	T340D	105,000	126,000
1998	T-Gas	81,000	98,000
1998	T340D	96,000	115,000
1997	T-Gas	75,000	90,000
1997	T340D	88,000	106,000

Sea Ray 380 Sundancer

Year	Power	Retail Low	Retail High
2003	T370G	130,000	156,000
2003	T340D	118,000	142,000
2002	T370G	108,000	129,000
2002	T340D	98,000	118,000
2001	T370G	90,000	108,000
2001	T340D	83,000	100,000
2000	T310G	76,000	92,000
2000	T340D	70,000	84,000
1999	T310G	64,000	77,000
1999	T340D	59,000	71,000

Sea Ray 38/390 Sundancer

Year	Power	Retail Low	Retail High
2011	T425G	******	******
2011	T301D	******	******
2010	T4200G	296,000	340,000
2010	T301D	314,000	362,000
2009	T375G	269,000	309,000
2009	T306D	286,000	329,000
2008	T420G	245,000	281,000
2008	T306D	260,000	299,000
2007	T420G	223,000	256,000
2007	T306D	237,000	272,000
2006	T420G	203,000	233,000
2006	T306D	215,000	248,000

Sea Ray 390 MY; 40 MY

Year	Power	Retail Low	Retail High
2007	T370G	213,000	252,000
2007	T407D	249,000	294,000
2006	T370G	194,000	229,000
2006	T446D	226,000	267,000
2005	T370G	177,000	209,000
2005	T446D	206,000	243,000
2004	T370G	161,000	190,000
2004	T446D	187,000	221,000
2003	T370G	146,000	173,000
2003	T446D	170,000	201,000

Sea Ray 390/40 Sundancer

Year	Power	Retail Low	Retail High
2009	T420G	279,000	329,000
2009	T407D	325,000	384,000
2008	T420G	253,000	299,000
2008	T407D	296,000	349,000
2007	T420G	231,000	272,000
2007	T407D	269,000	318,000
2006	T420G	210,000	248,000
2006	T364D	245,000	289,000
2005	T370G	193,000	228,000
2005	T340D	225,000	266,000
2004	T370G	177,000	209,000
2004	T340D	207,000	244,000

Sea Ray 400 Express Cruiser

Year	Power	Retail Low	Retail High
1999	T380G	88,000	104,000
1999	T340D	98,000	116,000
1998	T380G	81,000	95,000
1998	T340D	90,000	107,000
1997	T340G	74,000	88,000
1997	T340D	83,000	98,000
1996	T340G	68,000	81,000
1996	T292D	76,000	90,000
1995	T340G	63,000	74,000
1995	T292D	70,000	83,000

Sea Ray 400 Sedan Bridge

Year	Power	Retail Low	Retail High
2003	T370G	132,000	156,000
2003	T417D	151,000	179,000
2002	T370G	122,000	144,000
2002	T417D	139,000	164,000
2001	T380G	113,000	134,000
2001	T340D	129,000	153,000
2000	T380G	105,000	124,000
2000	T340D	120,000	142,000
1999	T380G	98,000	116,000
1999	T340D	112,000	132,000
1998	T380G	91,000	107,000
1998	T340D	104,000	123,000
1997	T380G	86,000	101,000
1997	T340D	98,000	115,000
1996	T380G	80,000	95,000
1996	T340D	92,000	108,000

Sea Ray 400 Sundancer

Year	Power	Retail Low	Retail High
1999	T380G	111,000	131,000
1999	T340D	129,000	152,000
1998	T380G	102,000	121,000
1998	T340D	118,000	140,000
1997	T340G	94,000	111,000
1997	T340D	109,000	129,000

Sea Ray 410 Express Cruiser

Year	Power	Retail Low	Retail High
2003	T370G	120,000	145,000
2003	T417D	141,000	169,000
2002	T370G	111,000	133,000
2002	T417D	130,000	156,000
2001	T380G	102,000	122,000
2001	T340D	119,000	143,000
2000	T380G	94,000	112,000
2000	T340D	110,000	132,000

Sea Ray 410 Sundancer

Year	Power	Retail Low	Retail High
2003	T370G	158,000	189,000
2003	T340D	176,000	211,000
2002	T370G	145,000	174,000
2002	T340D	161,000	194,000
2001	T380G	133,000	160,000
2001	T340D	148,000	178,000
2000	T380G	123,000	147,000
2000	T340D	137,000	164,000

Sea Ray 420 Aft Cabin

Year	Power	Retail Low	Retail High
2002	T370G	151,000	178,000
2002	T417D	167,000	197,000
2001	T370G	139,000	164,000
2001	T417D	154,000	181,000
2000	T380G	128,000	151,000
2000	T407D	141,000	167,000
1999	T380G	118,000	139,000
1999	T407D	130,000	153,000
1998	T380G	108,000	128,000
1998	T407D	119,000	141,000
1997	T380G	99,000	117,000
1997	T407D	110,000	130,000
1996	T380G	91,000	108,000
1996	T407D	101,000	119,000

Sea Ray 420/44 Sedan Bridge

Year	Power	Retail Low	Retail High
2009	T478D	******	******
2008	T478D	325,000	374,000
2007	T478D	299,000	344,000
2006	T478D	275,000	316,000
2005	T417D	253,000	291,000
2004	T417D	235,000	271,000

Sea Ray 420/44 Sundancer

Year	Power	Retail Low	Retail High
2008	T420G	255,000	301,000
2008	T478D	297,000	351,000
2007	T420G	232,000	274,000
2007	T478D	270,000	319,000
2006	T370G	211,000	249,000
2006	T417D	246,000	290,000
2005	T370G	192,000	227,000
2005	T417D	224,000	264,000
2004	T370G	177,000	209,000
2004	T417D	206,000	243,000
2003	T370G	163,000	192,000
2003	T417D	189,000	223,000

Sea Ray 420/440 Sundancer

Year	Power	Retail Low	Retail High
1995	T330G	70,000	84,000
1995	T292D	94,000	113,000

Sea Ray 43/470 Sundancer

Year	Power	Retail Low	Retail High
2012	T425 Zeus	******	******
2011	T425 Zeus	******	******
2010	T425 Zeus	******	******
2009	T425 Zeus	475,000	570,000

Sea Ray 440 Express Bridge

Year	Power	Retail Low	Retail High
1998	T340D	150,000	180,000
1997	T340D	141,000	169,000
1996	T340D	132,000	159,000
1995	T350D	124,000	149,000

Sea Ray 450 Express Bridge

Year	Power	Retail Low	Retail High
2004	T460D	261,000	308,000
2003	T450D	240,000	283,000
2002	T430D	221,000	260,000
2001	T430D	203,000	240,000
2000	T430D	187,000	220,000
1999	T420D	174,000	205,000
1998	T420D	161,000	191,000

Sea Ray 450 Sundancer (1995-99)

Year	Power	Retail Low	Retail High
1999	T340D	158,000	187,000
1998	T340D	145,000	172,000
1997	T340D	134,000	158,000
1996	T375D	123,000	145,000
1995	T375D	113,000	134,000

Sea Ray 460 Sundancer

Year	Power	Retail Low	Retail High
2005	T446D	******	******
2004	T446D	******	******
2003	T446D	251,000	297,000
2002	T446D	231,000	273,000
2001	T430D	213,000	251,000
2000	T430D	196,000	231,000
1999	T430D	180,000	212,000

Sea Ray 47 Sedan Bridge

Year	Power	Retail Low	Retail High
2009	T574D	******	******
2008	T574D	408,000	490,000

Sea Ray 48 Sundancer

Year	Power	Retail Low	Retail High
2009	T526D	******	******
2008	T517D	******	******
2007	T517D	436,000	523,000

Year	Power	Retail Low	Retail High
2006	T517D	397,000	476,000
2005	T446D	361,000	433,000

Sea Ray 480 Motor Yacht

Year	Power	Retail Low	Retail High
2005	T660D	323,000	377,000
2004	T640D	297,000	347,000
2003	T640D	273,000	319,000
2002	T640D	251,000	294,000

Sea Ray 480 Sedan Bridge

Year	Power	Retail Low	Retail High
2004	T640D	343,000	412,000
2003	T640D	312,000	375,000
2002	T640D	284,000	341,000
2001	T640D	258,000	310,000
2000	T640D	238,000	285,000
1999	T640D	219,000	262,000
1998	T640D	201,000	241,000

Sea Ray 480/500 Sundancer

Year	Power	Retail Low	Retail High
1999	T535D	232,000	272,000
1998	T535D	216,000	253,000
1997	T535D	201,000	235,000
1996	T535D	187,000	219,000
1995	T535D	174,000	203,000

Sea Ray 500/52 Sundancer

Year	Power	Retail Low	Retail High
2009	T765D	******	******
2008	T765D	551,000	617,000
2007	T640D	506,000	582,000
2006	T640D	466,000	536,000
2005	T640D	429,000	493,000
2004	T640D	394,000	453,000
2003	T640D	363,000	417,000

Sea Ray 510 Sundancer

Year	Power	Retail Low	Retail High
2003	T616D	332,000	392,000
2002	T640D	305,000	360,000
2001	T640D	281,000	332,000
2000	T640D	258,000	305,000

Sea Ray 500/52/520 Sedan Bridge

Year	Power	Retail Low	Retail High
2012	T640D	******	******
2011	T640D	******	******
2010	T640D	******	******
2009	T640D	736,000	831,000
2008	T640D	684,000	773,000
2007	T640D	636,000	719,000
2006	T640D	592,000	669,000
2005	T640D	550,000	622,000

Sea Ray 540 Sundancer (1998-01)

Year	Power	Retail Low	Retail High
2001	T640D	318,000	375,000
2000	T640D	295,000	349,000
1999	T640D	275,000	324,000
1998	T640D	255,000	302,000

Sea Ray 550 Sedan Bridge

Year	Power	Retail Low	Retail High
1998	T776D	242,000	278,000
1997	T735D	227,000	261,000
1996	T635D	214,000	246,000
1995	T635D	203,000	233,000
1994	T635D	193,000	222,000
1993	T650D	183,000	211,000
1992	T650D	174,000	200,000

Sea Ray 550 Sundancer

Year	Power	Retail Low	Retail High
2004	T765D	407,000	481,000
2003	T765D	379,000	447,000
2002	T765D	352,000	416,000

Sea Ray 55/580 Sundancer

Year	Power	Retail Low	Retail High
2011	T768D	******	******
2010	T768D	******	******
2009	T768D	******	******
2008	T768D	760,000	874,000

Sea Ray 560 Sedan Bridge

Year	Power	Retail Low	Retail High
2004	T1000D	489,000	547,000
2003	T1000D	455,000	546,000
2002	T776D	423,000	507,000
2001	T776D	393,000	472,000
2000	T776D	369,000	443,000
1999	T776D	344,000	412,000
1998	T776D	319,000	383,000

Sea Ray 58/580 Sedan Bridge

Year	Power	Retail Low	Retail High
2012	T900D	******	******
2011	T900D	******	******
2010	T900D	******	******
2009	T900D	793,000	896,000
2008	T900D	737,000	833,000
2007	T900D	686,000	775,000
2006	T900D	638,000	721,000

Sea Ray 580 Super Sun Sport

Year	Power	Retail Low	Retail High
2002	T776D	******	******
2001	T776D	******	******
2000	T776D	******	******
1999	T776D	299,000	359,000
1998	T776D	278,000	333,000
1997	T776D	258,000	310,000

Sea Ray 60/610 Sundancer

Year	Power	Retail Low	Retail High
2011	T1051D	******	******
2010	T1051D	******	******
2009	T1051D	******	******
2008	T1051D	******	******
2007	T1051D	788,000	883,000
2006	T1051D	733,000	821,000

Sea Ray 630 Sundancer

Year	Power	Retail Low	Retail High
2000	T1040D	******	******
1999	T1040D	******	******
1998	T1040D	******	******
1997	T1040D	******	******
1996	T1040D	399,000	450,000
1995	T1040D	363,000	410,000

Sea Ray 630 Sun Sport

Year	Power	Retail Low	Retail High
2000	T1300D	******	******
1999	T1300D	******	******
1998	T1300D	******	******
1997	T1040D	******	******
1996	T1040D	304,000	343,000
1995	T1040D	285,000	322,000
1994	T1040D	268,000	303,000
1993	T1040D	252,000	285,000
1992	T1040D	237,000	268,000
1991	T1040D	223,000	252,000

Seacraft 32 Center Console

Year	Power	Retail Low	Retail High
2007	T250 O/B	71,000	85,000
2006	T250 O/B	64,000	77,000
2005	T250 O/B	58,000	69,000
2004	T250 O/B	52,000	62,000
2003	T250 O/B	46,000	56,000
2002	T250 O/B	42,000	51,000
2001	T250 O/B	38,000	46,000
2000	T250 O/B	35,000	42,000

Shamrock 270 Mackinaw

Year	Power	Retail Low	Retail High
2009	315D	******	******
2008	315D	******	******
2007	315D	69,000	83,000
2006	315D	64,000	77,000
2005	315D	59,000	70,000
2004	315D	54,000	65,000
2003	315D	49,000	59,000
2002	315D	46,000	55,000
2001	230D	43,000	51,000
2000	230D	40,000	48,000

Shamrock 270 Open

Year	Power	Retail Low	Retail High
2009	315D	******	******
2008	315D	******	******
2007	315D	60,000	72,000
2006	315D	55,000	66,000
2005	315D	50,000	60,000
2004	315D	45,000	54,000
2003	315D	41,000	49,000
2002	315D	38,000	45,000
2001	230D	35,000	42,000
2000	230D	32,000	38,000

Shamrock 290 Walkaround

Year	Power	Retail Low	Retail High
2003	T330G	48,000	58,000
2002	T300G	44,000	52,000
2001	T300G	40,000	48,000
2000	T300G	36,000	43,000
1999	T300G	33,000	39,000

Silverton 271 Express

Year	Power	Retail Low	Retail High
1997	250 I/O	16,000	20,000
1996	250 I/O	15,000	18,000
1995	250 I/O	14,000	17,000

Silverton 31 Convertible

Year	Power	Retail Low	Retail High
1995	T235G	28,000	33,000

Silverton 310 Express

Year	Power	Retail Low	Retail High
2000	T250 I/O	41,000	49,000
1999	T250 I/O	38,000	45,000
1998	T250 I/O	35,000	42,000
1997	T250 I/O	32,000	38,000
1996	T235 I/O	29,000	35,000
1995	T235 I/O	27,000	32,000

Silverton 312 Sedan Cruiser

Year	Power	Retail Low	Retail High
1999	T250 I/O	30,000	36,000
1998	T260 I/O	27,000	33,000
1997	T260 I/O	25,000	30,000
1996	T235 I/O	23,000	28,000
1995	T235 I/O	21,000	25,000

Silverton 322 Motor Yacht

Year	Power	Retail Low	Retail High
2001	T300G	65,000	78,000
2000	T300G	59,000	71,000
1999	T320G	54,000	65,000
1998	T320G	49,000	59,000
1997	T320G	45,000	54,000
1996	T320G	41,000	50,000
1995	T320G	38,000	46,000

Silverton 33 Convertible

Year	Power	Retail Low	Retail High
2011	T275G	******	******
2010	T275G	******	******
2009	T275G	140,000	168,000
2008	T275G	127,000	152,000
2007	T275G	115,000	139,000

Silverton 330 Sport Bridge

Year	Power	Retail Low	Retail High
2007	T330G	293,000	351,000
2006	T330G	266,000	320,000
2005	T330G	242,000	291,000
2004	T320G	221,000	265,000
2003	T320G	201,000	241,000
2002	T320G	183,000	219,000
2001	T320G	168,000	202,000
2000	T320G	154,000	185,000
1999	T320G	142,000	171,000

Silverton 34 Conv. (1991-95)

Year	Power	Retail Low	Retail High
1995	T300G	44,000	52,000

Silverton 34 Conv. (2004-06)

Year	Power	Retail Low	Retail High
2006	T330G	134,000	161,000

See Page 667 For Price Adjustments

Year	Power	Retail Low	Retail High
2005	T330G	122,000	146,000
2004	T320G	111,000	133,000

Silverton 34 Motor Yacht

Year	Power	Retail Low	Retail High
1996	T320G	47,000	56,000
1995	T300G	43,000	52,000

Silverton 35 Motor Yacht

Year	Power	Retail Low	Retail High
2011	T385G	******	******
2011	T315D	******	******
2010	T385G	******	******
2010	T315D	******	******
2009	T385G	******	******
2009	T315D	******	******
2008	T385G	169,000	203,000
2008	T315D	197,000	236,000
2007	T385G	153,000	184,000
2007	T315D	179,000	215,000
2006	T385G	140,000	168,000
2006	T315D	163,000	196,000
2005	T385G	127,000	153,000
2005	T315D	148,000	178,000
2004	T385G	116,000	139,000
2004	T315D	135,000	162,000
2003	T385G	105,000	126,000
2003	T315D	123,000	147,000

Silverton 351 Sedan

Year	Power	Retail Low	Retail High
2000	T320G	62,000	74,000
1999	T320G	57,000	68,000
1998	T300G	52,000	63,000
1997	T300G	48,000	57,000

Silverton 352 Motor Yacht

Year	Power	Retail Low	Retail High
2002	T370G	85,000	103,000
2002	T250D	100,000	121,000
2001	T320G	78,000	93,000
2001	T250D	91,000	110,000
2000	T320G	71,000	85,000
2000	T250D	83,000	100,000
1999	T320G	64,000	77,000
1999	T300D	76,000	91,000
1998	T320G	58,000	70,000
1998	T300D	69,000	82,000
1997	T320G	53,000	64,000
1997	T300D	62,000	75,000

Silverton 360/361 Express

Year	Power	Retail Low	Retail High
2000	T320G	57,000	69,000
1999	T320G	53,000	63,000
1998	T320G	48,000	58,000
1997	T320G	44,000	53,000
1996	T320G	41,000	49,000
1995	T300G	37,000	45,000

Silverton 362 Sedan

Year	Power	Retail Low	Retail High
1998	T320G	59,000	71,000
1997	T320G	54,000	65,000
1996	T320G	50,000	60,000
1995	T320G	46,000	55,000

Silverton 37 Convertible

Year	Power	Retail Low	Retail High
2000	T320G	83,000	100,000
2000	T350D	100,000	120,000
1999	T320G	76,000	92,000
1999	T350D	92,000	110,000
1998	T320G	70,000	84,000
1998	T350D	84,000	101,000
1997	T320G	65,000	78,000
1997	T350D	78,000	93,000
1996	T320G	59,000	71,000
1996	T350D	71,000	86,000
1995	T320G	55,000	66,000
1995	T350D	66,000	79,000

Silverton 372/392 Motor Yacht

Year	Power	Retail Low	Retail High
2001	T385G	105,000	126,000
2001	T350D	125,000	150,000
2000	T385G	95,000	114,000
2000	T350D	114,000	137,000
1999	T385G	87,000	104,000
1999	T350D	104,000	124,000
1998	T320G	80,000	96,000
1998	T350D	95,000	114,000
1997	T320G	73,000	88,000
1997	T350D	88,000	105,000
1996	T320G	67,000	81,000
1996	T350D	81,000	97,000

Silverton 38 Convertible

Year	Power	Retail Low	Retail High
2009	T385G	239,000	287,000
2009	T370D	266,000	319,000
2008	T385G	218,000	261,000
2008	T370D	242,000	290,000
2007	T385G	198,000	238,000
2007	T370D	220,000	264,000
2006	T385G	180,000	216,000
2006	T370D	200,000	240,000
2005	T385G	164,000	197,000
2005	T370D	182,000	218,000
2004	T385G	149,000	179,000
2004	T370D	166,000	199,000
2003	T385G	136,000	163,000
2003	T370D	151,000	181,000

Silverton 38 Sport Bridge

Year	Power	Retail Low	Retail High
2011	T385G	******	******
2011	T380D	******	******
2010	T385G	******	******
2010	T380D	******	******
2009	T385G	******	******
2009	T380D	******	******
2008	T385G	226,000	271,000
2008	T380D	270,000	324,000
2007	T385G	206,000	247,000
2007	T380D	246,000	295,000
2006	T385G	187,000	225,000
2006	T380D	224,000	268,000
2005	T385G	170,000	204,000
2005	T355D	203,000	244,000

Silverton 39 Motor Yacht

Year	Power	Retail Low	Retail High
2011	T385G	******	******
2011	T380D	******	******
2010	T385G	******	******
2010	T380D	******	******
2009	T385G	******	******
2009	T380D	******	******
2008	T385G	230,000	276,000
2008	T380D	265,000	319,000
2007	T385G	209,000	251,000
2007	T380D	242,000	290,000
2006	T385G	190,000	228,000
2006	T380D	220,000	264,000
2005	T385G	173,000	208,000
2005	T380D	200,000	240,000
2004	T385G	159,000	191,000
2004	T380D	184,000	221,000
2003	T385G	146,000	176,000
2003	T380D	169,000	203,000
2002	T385G	135,000	162,000
2002	T355D	156,000	187,000

Silverton 402/422 Motor Yacht

Year	Power	Retail Low	Retail High
2000	T380G	109,000	131,000
2000	T325D	126,000	151,000
1999	T380G	101,000	121,000
1999	T370D	116,000	139,000
1998	T380G	92,000	111,000
1998	T370D	106,000	128,000
1997	T380G	85,000	102,000
1997	T370D	98,000	117,000
1996	T380G	78,000	94,000
1996	T370D	90,000	108,000

Silverton 41 Convertible

Year	Power	Retail Low	Retail High
1999	T380G	114,000	137,000
1998	T380G	105,000	126,000
1997	T380G	96,000	116,000
1996	T380G	89,000	106,000
1995	T320G	81,000	98,000

Silverton 41 Aft Cabin MY

Year	Power	Retail Low	Retail High
1995	T355G	82,000	99,000
1995	T375D	104,000	125,000

Silverton 410 Sport Bridge

Year	Power	Retail Low	Retail High
2004	T425G	178,000	214,000
2004	T350D	203,000	244,000
2003	T425G	164,000	197,000
2003	T350D	187,000	225,000
2002	T425G	151,000	181,000
2002	T350D	172,000	207,000
2001	T385G	139,000	167,000
2001	T350D	158,000	190,000

Silverton 42 Convertible

Year	Power	Retail Low	Retail High
2011	T440D	******	******
2010	T440D	******	******
2009	T425G	******	******
2009	T440D	******	******
2008	T440D	291,000	349,000
2007	T440D	265,000	318,000
2006	T380D	241,000	289,000
2005	T380D	219,000	263,000
2004	T380D	199,000	239,000
2003	T380D	181,000	218,000
2002	T350D	167,000	200,000
2001	T350D	153,000	184,000
2000	T350D	141,000	169,000

Silverton 43 Motor Yacht

Year	Power	Retail Low	Retail High
2007	T440D	296,000	355,000
2006	T440D	269,000	323,000
2005	T380D	245,000	294,000
2004	T380D	223,000	267,000
2003	T380D	203,000	243,000
2002	T380D	184,000	221,000
2001	T355D	168,000	201,000

Silverton 43 Sport Bridge

Year	Power	Retail Low	Retail High
2011	T370D IPS	******	******
2010	T370D IPS	******	******
2009	T370D IPS	******	******
2008	T435D IPS	******	******
2007	T380D	258,000	310,000
2006	T380D	237,000	285,000

Silverton 442 Cockpit MY

Year	Power	Retail Low	Retail High
2001	T355D	145,000	174,000
2000	T355D	133,000	160,000
1999	T350D	122,000	147,000
1998	T350D	112,000	135,000
1997	T350D	103,000	124,000
1996	T350D	95,000	114,000

Silverton 45 Convertible

Year	Power	Retail Low	Retail High
2011	T715D	******	******
2010	T715D	******	******
2010	T715D	******	******
2009	T715D	441,000	521,000
2008	T500D	406,000	479,000
2007	T575D	373,000	441,000

Year	Power	Retail Low	Retail High
2006	T540D	344,000	405,000

Silverton 453 Motor Yacht

Year	Power	Retail Low	Retail High
2003	T430D	211,000	249,000
2002	T350D	194,000	229,000
2001	T350D	179,000	211,000
2000	T355D	164,000	194,000
1999	T350D	151,000	178,000

Silverton 46 Aft Cabin

Year	Power	Retail Low	Retail High
1997	T485D	161,000	190,000
1996	T485D	150,000	177,000
1995	T485D	139,000	164,000

Silverton 48/50 Convertible

Year	Power	Retail Low	Retail High
2011	T715D	******	******
2010	T715D	******	******
2009	T715D	******	******
2008	T715D	498,000	582,000
2007	T715D	453,000	530,000
2006	T715D	412,000	482,000
2005	T715D	375,000	439,000
2004	T715D	341,000	399,000

Skipjack 262 FB

Year	Power	Retail Low	Retail High
2008	280 I/O	******	******
2007	280 I/O	******	******
2006	280 I/O	******	******
2005	280 I/O	******	******
2004	280 I/O	******	******
2003	280 I/O	******	******
2002	280 I/O	42,000	50,000
2001	280 I/O	38,000	46,000
2000	280 I/O	35,000	42,000
1999	280 I/O	32,000	39,000
1998	280 I/O	30,000	36,000
1997	280 I/O	27,000	33,000
1996	280 I/O	25,000	30,000
1995	280 I/O	23,000	28,000

Southport 28 Center Console

Year	Power	Retail Low	Retail High
2009	T225 O/B	84,000	101,000
2008	T225 O/B	76,000	92,000
2007	T225 O/B	70,000	84,000
2006	T225 O/B	63,000	76,000
2005	T225 O/B	58,000	69,000

Stamas 270 Express

Year	Power	Retail Low	Retail High
2009-2012		******	******
2008	T225 O/B	74,000	89,000
2007	T225 O/B	68,000	82,000
2006	T225 O/B	61,000	74,000
2005	T225 O/B	55,000	66,000
2004	T225 O/B	50,000	60,000
2003	T225 O/B	45,000	54,000
2002	T225 O/B	40,000	48,000
2001	T225 O/B	37,000	44,000
2000	T225 O/B	34,000	41,000
1999	T225 O/B	31,000	37,000
1998	T225 O/B	29,000	34,000
1997	T225 O/B	26,000	32,000

Stamas 270 Tarpon

Year	Power	Retail Low	Retail High
200-2012		******	******
2008	T225 O/B	70,000	84,000
2007	T225 O/B	63,000	75,000
2006	T225 O/B	56,000	68,000
2005	T225 O/B	51,000	61,000
2004	T225 O/B	46,000	55,000
2003	T225 O/B	41,000	49,000
2002	T225 O/B	38,000	45,000
2001	T225 O/B	35,000	42,000
2000	T225 O/B	32,000	38,000
1999	T225 O/B	29,000	35,000
1998	T225 O/B	27,000	32,000
1997	T225 O/B	72,000	87,000

Stamas 290 Express

Year	Power	Retail Low	Retail High
2007-2012		******	******
2006	T225 O/B	70,000	84,000
2005	T225 O/B	64,000	76,000
2004	T225 O/B	58,000	70,000
2003	T225 O/B	53,000	63,000
2002	T225 O/B	48,000	58,000
2001	T225 O/B	43,000	52,000
2000	T225 O/B	40,000	48,000
1999	T225 O/B	37,000	44,000
1998	T225 O/B	34,000	41,000
1997	T225 O/B	31,000	37,000
1996	T225 O/B	28,000	34,000
1995	T225 O/B	26,000	32,000

Stamas 290 Tarpon

Year	Power	Retail Low	Retail High
2007-2012		******	******
2006	T225 O/B	65,000	78,000
2005	T225 O/B	59,000	71,000
2004	T225 O/B	53,000	63,000
2003	T225 O/B	47,000	57,000
2002	T225 O/B	43,000	51,000
2001	T225 O/B	39,000	47,000
2000	T225 O/B	35,000	42,000
1999	T225 O/B	32,000	39,000
1998	T225 O/B	29,000	35,000
1997	T225 O/B	26,000	32,000
1996	T225 O/B	24,000	29,000
1995	T225 O/B	22,000	26,000

Stamas 310 Express

Year	Power	Retail Low	Retail High
2007-2012		******	******
2006	T225 O/B	80,000	97,000
2005	T225 O/B	73,000	88,000
2004	T225 O/B	66,000	80,000
2002	T225 O/B	60,000	73,000
2002	T225 O/B	55,000	66,000
2001	T225 O/B	50,000	60,000
2000	T225 O/B	46,000	55,000
1999	T225 O/B	42,000	51,000
1998	T225 O/B	39,000	47,000
1997	T225 O/B	36,000	43,000
1996	T225 O/B	33,000	39,000
1995	T225 O/B	30,000	36,000

Stamas 310 Tarpon

Year	Power	Retail Low	Retail High
2007-2012		******	******
2006	T225 O/B	72,000	86,000
2005	T225 O/B	65,000	78,000
2004	T225 O/B	58,000	70,000
2003	T225 O/B	52,000	63,000
2002	T225 O/B	47,000	56,000
2001	T225 O/B	42,000	51,000
2000	T225 O/B	38,000	46,000
1999	T225 O/B	34,000	41,000

Stamas 320 Express

Year	Power	Retail Low	Retail High
200-20127		******	******
2006	T320 I/B	83,000	99,000
2006	T250 O/B	80,000	96,000
2005	T320 I/B	76,000	91,000
2005	T250 O/B	73,000	88,000
2004	T320 I/B	70,000	84,000
2004	T250 O/B	67,000	81,000

Stamas 340 Express

Year	Power	Retail Low	Retail High
2007-2012		******	******
2006	T370G	104,000	124,000
2006	T370D	135,000	162,000
2005	T370G	95,000	114,000
2005	T370D	124,000	149,000
2004	T370G	88,000	105,000
2004	T370D	114,000	137,000
2003	T370G	80,000	97,000
2003	T370D	105,000	126,000

Stamas 360/370 Express

Year	Power	Retail Low	Retail High
2007-2012		******	******
2006	T370G	141,000	169,000
2006	T440D	172,000	207,000
2005	T370G	128,000	153,000
2005	T440D	157,000	188,000
2004	T370G	116,000	140,000
2004	T440D	143,000	171,000
2003	T370G	106,000	127,000
2003	T440D	130,000	156,000
2002	T370G	96,000	116,000
2002	T440D	118,000	142,000
2001	T370G	87,000	105,000
2001	T440D	107,000	129,000
2000	T370G	80,000	96,000
2000	T440D	98,000	117,000
1999	T310G	72,000	87,000
1999	T300D	89,000	107,000
1998	T310G	66,000	79,000
1998	T300D	81,000	97,000
1997	T310G	60,000	72,000
1997	T300D	74,000	88,000
1996	T310G	54,000	65,000
1996	T300D	67,000	80,000
1995	T310G	49,000	59,000
1995	T300D	61,000	73,000

Sunseeker 34 Superhawk

Year	Power	Retail Low	Retail High
2003	T285D	131,000	158,000
2002	T285D	122,000	146,000
2001	T285D	113,000	136,000
2000	T230D	105,000	127,000
1999	T230D	98,000	118,000
1998	T230D	91,000	109,000

Sunseeker 37 Sportfisher

Year	Power	Retail Low	Retail High
2007	3/250 O/B	******	******
2006	3/250 O/B	153,000	184,000
2005	3/250 O/B	141,000	169,000
2004	3/250 O/B	130,000	156,000

Sunseeker 44 Camargue

Year	Power	Retail Low	Retail High
2002	T480D	187,000	224,000
2001	T480D	172,000	206,000
2000	T435D	158,000	190,000
1999	T435D	145,000	174,000
1998	T435D	134,000	160,000

Sunseeker 46 Portifino

Year	Power	Retail Low	Retail High
2005	T460D	312,000	374,000
2004	T480D	287,000	344,000
2003	T480D	264,000	316,000

Sunseeker 47 Camargue

Year	Power	Retail Low	Retail High
1999	T435D	168,000	201,000
1998	T435D	156,000	187,000
1997	T435D	145,000	174,000
1996	T435D	135,000	162,000

Sunseeker 46/48 Manhattan

Year	Power	Retail Low	Retail High
1999	T435D	268,000	322,000
1998	T435D	249,000	299,000
1997	T435D	232,000	278,000
1996	T435D	216,000	259,000
1995	T435D	201,000	241,000

Sunseeker 48 Superhawk

Year	Power	Retail Low	Retail High
2005	3/300 I/O	230,000	276,000
2004	3/300 I/O	211,000	254,000
2003	3/300 I/O	195,000	234,000

See Page 667 For Price Adjustments

Year	Power	Retail Low	Retail High
2002	3/260 I/O	179,000	215,000
2001	3/260 I/O	166,000	200,000
2000	3/260 I/O	155,000	186,000
1999	3/260 I/O	144,000	173,000
1998	3/260 I/O	134,000	161,000
1997	3/260 I/O	124,000	149,000
1996	3/260 I/O	116,000	139,000

Sunseeker 50 Camargue

Year	Power	Retail Low	Retail High
2003	T660D	321,000	385,000
2002	T660D	295,000	355,000
2001	T660D	272,000	326,000
2000	T660D	250,000	300,000

Sunseeker 53 Portofino

Year	Power	Retail Low	Retail High
2009	T800D	******	******
2008	T800D	******	******
2007	T800D	******	******
2006	T705D	480,000	576,000
2005	T705D	446,000	535,000
2004	T705D	415,000	498,000

Sunseeker 58/60 Predator

Year	Power	Retail Low	Retail High
2002	T800D	******	******
2001	T800D	******	******
2000	T800D	******	******
1999	T800D	374,000	449,000
1998	T800D	348,000	417,000
1997	T800D	323,000	388,000

Tiara 2900 Coronet

Year	Power	Retail Low	Retail High
2007	T330G	68,000	82,000
2006	T330G	62,000	74,000
2005	T330G	56,000	68,000
2004	T320G	51,000	62,000
2003	T320G	47,000	57,000
2002	T320G	43,000	52,000
2001	T320G	40,000	48,000
2000	T320G	37,000	44,000
1999	T320G	34,000	40,000
1998	T320G	31,000	37,000
1997	T320G	28,000	34,000

Tiara 2900 Open

Year	Power	Retail Low	Retail High
2006	T330G	75,000	90,000
2005	T330G	68,000	82,000
2004	T330G	62,000	74,000
2003	T330G	56,000	67,000
2002	T320G	52,000	62,000
2001	T320G	47,000	57,000
2000	T320G	44,000	52,000
1999	T320G	40,000	48,000
1998	T320G	37,000	44,000
1997	T320G	34,000	41,000
1996	T320G	31,000	37,000
1995	T260G	29,000	35,000

Tiara 3000 Open

Year	Power	Retail Low	Retail High
2010-2012		******	******
2009	T385G	157,000	188,000
2009	T330D	188,000	226,000
2008	T385G	142,000	171,000
2008	T330D	171,000	205,000
2007	T385G	131,000	157,000
2007	T330D	157,000	189,000

Tiara 3100 Open

Year	Power	Retail Low	Retail High
2004	T385G	84,000	101,000
2004	T330D	106,000	128,000
2003	T385G	77,000	92,000
2003	T330D	97,000	116,000
2002	T320G	70,000	84,000
2002	T330D	88,000	106,000
2001	T320G	64,000	77,000
2001	T330D	81,000	97,000
2000	T320G	59,000	71,000
2000	T230D	74,000	89,000
1999	T320G	54,000	65,000
1999	T230D	68,000	82,000
1998	T320G	50,000	60,000
1998	T230D	63,000	76,000
1997	T320G	46,000	55,000
1997	T230D	58,000	70,000
1996	T320G	42,000	51,000
1996	T230D	53,000	64,000
1995	T320G	39,000	47,000
1995	T230D	49,000	59,000

Tiara 3200 Open

Year	Power	Retail Low	Retail High
2011	T385G	******	******
2011	T300D	******	******
2010	T385G	******	******
2010	T355D	******	******
2009	T385G	171,000	205,000
2009	T355D	214,000	257,000
2008	T385G	156,000	187,000
2008	T355D	195,000	234,000
2007	T385G	141,000	170,000
2007	T355D	177,000	213,000
2006	T330G	130,000	156,000
2006	T310D	163,000	196,000
2005	T385G	120,000	144,000
2005	T310D	150,000	180,000
2004	T385G	110,000	132,000
2004	T310D	138,000	166,000

Tiara 3300 Open

Year	Power	Retail Low	Retail High
1997	T380G	50,000	61,000
1997	T315D	66,000	80,000
1996	T380G	46,000	56,000
1996	T315D	61,000	73,000
1995	T300G	43,000	51,000
1995	T300D	57,000	68,000

Tiara 3500 Express

Year	Power	Retail Low	Retail High
2003	T385G	97,000	117,000
2003	T450D	128,000	154,000
2002	T385G	88,000	106,000
2002	T435D	116,000	140,000
2001	T385G	80,000	97,000
2001	T435D	106,000	127,000
2000	T385G	74,000	89,000
2000	T435D	97,000	117,000
1999	T320G	68,000	82,000
1999	T435D	89,000	107,000
1998	T380G	63,000	75,000
1998	T435D	82,000	99,000
1997	T380G	57,000	69,000
1997	T435D	76,000	91,000
1996	T380G	53,000	63,000
1996	T435D	70,000	84,000
1995	T380G	49,000	58,000
1995	T435D	64,000	77,000

Tiara 3500 Open

Year	Power	Retail Low	Retail High
2004	T385G	97,000	117,000
2004	T370D	121,000	145,000
2003	T385G	89,000	106,000
2003	T370D	110,000	132,000
2002	T385G	81,000	97,000
2002	T370D	100,000	120,000
2001	T320G	73,000	88,000
2001	T370D	91,000	109,000
2000	T320G	67,000	80,000
2000	T370D	83,000	100,000
1999	T320G	61,000	73,000
1999	T370D	75,000	91,000
1998	T320G	55,000	66,000
1998	T370D	69,000	82,000

Tiara 3500 Sovran

Year	Power	Retail Low	Retail High
2011	T375G IPS	******	******
2011	T300D IPS	******	******
2010	T375G IPS	******	******
2010	T300D IPS	******	******
2009	T375G IPS	227,000	273,000
2009	T300D IPS	256,000	307,000
2008	T375G IPS	207,000	248,000
2008	T300D IPS	233,000	279,000

Tiara 3600 Convertible

Year	Power	Retail Low	Retail High
1995	T355G	71,000	85,000
1995	T375D	91,000	109,000

Tiara 3600 Open (1987-96)

Year	Power	Retail Low	Retail High
1996	T355G	73,000	88,000
1996	T375D	88,000	105,000
1995	T355G	67,000	81,000
1995	T375D	81,000	97,000

Tiara 3600 Open (Current)

Year	Power	Retail Low	Retail High
2011	T385G IPS	******	******
2011	T300D IPS	******	******
2010	T385G IPS	******	******
2010	T300D IPS	******	******
2009	T385G	204,000	241,000
2009	T380D	237,000	280,000
2008	T385G	185,000	219,000
2008	T380D	216,000	255,000
2007	T385G	169,000	199,000
2007	T380D	196,000	232,000
2006	T385G	153,000	181,000
2006	T380D	178,000	211,000
2005	T385G	140,000	165,000
2005	T380D	162,000	192,000

Tiara 3600 Sovran

Year	Power	Retail Low	Retail High
2006	T385G	136,000	164,000
2006	T480D	180,000	216,000
2005	T385G	124,000	149,000
2005	T480D	164,000	197,000
2004	T385G	113,000	135,000
2004	T380D	149,000	179,000

Tiara 3700 Open

Year	Power	Retail Low	Retail High
2000	T385G	114,000	137,000
2000	T435D	129,000	155,000
1999	T435D	105,000	126,000
1998	T435D	119,000	143,000
1997	T435D	96,000	116,000
1996	T435D	109,000	131,000
1995	T435D	89,000	107,000

Tiara 3800 Open

Year	Power	Retail Low	Retail High
2008	T490D	******	******
2007	T490D	256,000	307,000
2006	T490D	233,000	280,000
2005	T490D	212,000	254,000
2004	T480D	193,000	231,000
2003	T480D	177,000	213,000
2002	T480D	163,000	196,000
2001	T480D	150,000	180,000

Tiara 3900 Convertible

Year	Power	Retail Low	Retail High
2012	T550D	******	******
2011	T550D	******	******
2010	T550D	******	******
2009	T550D	399,000	478,000
2008	T540D	363,000	435,000
2007	T540D	330,000	396,000
2006	T540D	300,000	360,000

See Page 667 For Price Adjustments

Tiara 3900 Open

Year	Power	Retail Low	Retail High
2012	T550D	******	******
2011	T550D	******	******
2010	T550D	******	******
2009	T550D	399,000	470,000

Tiara 3900 Sovran

Year	Power	Retail Low	Retail High
2012	T370D IPS	******	******
2011	T370D IPS	******	******
2010	T370D IPS	******	******
2009	T370D IPS	351,000	421,000
2008	T370D IPS	319,000	383,000
2007	T370D IPS	291,000	349,000

Tiara 4000 Express

Year	Power	Retail Low	Retail High
2003	T450D	199,000	239,000
2002	T450D	183,000	219,000
2001	T450D	183,000	219,000
2000	T435D	168,000	202,000
1999	T435D	168,000	202,000
1998	T435D	155,000	186,000
1997	T435D	155,000	186,000
1996	T435D	144,000	173,000
1995	T435D	144,000	173,000

Tiara 4000/4300 Sovran

Year	Power	Retail Low	Retail High
2010	T435D IPS	******	******
2009	T435D IPS	******	******
2008	T435D IPS	378,000	453,000
2007	T435D IPS	347,000	417,000
2006	T435D IPS	320,000	384,000

Tiara 4100 Open

Year	Power	Retail Low	Retail High
2002	T450D	178,000	214,000
2001	T450D	164,000	197,000
2000	T435D	151,000	181,000
1999	T435D	139,000	166,000
1998	T435D	127,000	153,000
1997	T435D	117,000	141,000
1996	T435D	108,000	129,000

Tiara 4200 Open

Year	Power	Retail Low	Retail High
2009	T670D	******	******
2008	T670D	380,000	456,000
2007	T670D	346,000	415,000
2006	T670D	314,000	377,000
2005	T670D	286,000	343,000
2004	T660D	260,000	312,000
2003	T660D	237,000	284,000

Tiara 4300 Convertible

Year	Power	Retail Low	Retail High
2002	T660D	285,000	342,000
2001	T660D	262,000	314,000
2000	T660D	241,000	289,000
1999	T570D	222,000	266,000
1998	T550D	204,000	245,000
1997	T550D	188,000	225,000
1996	T550D	172,000	207,000
1995	T550D	160,000	193,000

Tiara 4300 Open

Year	Power	Retail Low	Retail High
2002	T660D	250,000	301,000
2001	T660D	230,000	276,000
2000	T660D	212,000	254,000
1999	T550D	195,000	234,000
1998	T550D	179,000	215,000
1997	T550D	165,000	198,000
1996	T550D	152,000	182,000
1995	T550D	141,000	169,000

Tiara 4400/4700 Sovran

Year	Power	Retail Low	Retail High
2008	T670D	******	******
2007	T670D	425,000	511,000
2006	T670D	391,000	470,000
2005	T670D	360,000	432,000
2004	T660D	331,000	398,000
2003	T660D	305,000	366,000

Tiara 5000 Express

Year	Power	Retail Low	Retail High
2003	T800D	******	******
2002	T800D	******	******
2001	T800D	380,000	456,000
2000	T800D	349,000	419,000
1999	T800D	321,000	385,000

Tiara 5200 Sovran Salon

Year	Power	Retail Low	Retail High
2006	T800D	******	******
2005	T800D	******	******
2004	T800D	475,000	570,000
2003	T800D	437,000	524,000

Tollycraft 40 Sport Sedan

Year	Power	Retail Low	Retail High
1995	T-Gas	103,000	124,000
1995	T400D	119,000	143,000

Tollycraft 44/45 Cockpit MY

Year	Power	Retail Low	Retail High
1996	T400D	142,000	171,000
1995	T400D	132,000	159,000

Tollycraft 48 Motor Yacht

Year	Power	Retail Low	Retail High
1998	T435D	189,000	227,000
1997	T435D	176,000	211,000
1996	T435D	163,000	196,000
1995	T435D	152,000	182,000

Tollycraft 57 Motor Yacht

Year	Power	Retail Low	Retail High
1996	T735D	427,000	512,000
1995	T735D	397,000	477,000

Tollycraft 65 Cockpit MY

Year	Power	Retail Low	Retail High
1998	T760D	584,000	701,000
1997	T760D	543,000	652,000
1996	T665D	505,000	606,000
1995	T665D	470,000	564,000

Topaz 32/33 Express

Year	Power	Retail Low	Retail High
2010	T440D	******	******
2009	T440D	******	******
2008	T440D	******	******
2007	T440D	150,000	180,000
2006	T440D	136,000	163,000
2005	T370D	124,000	149,000
2004	T370D	113,000	135,000

Topaz 40 Express

Year	Power	Retail Low	Retail High
2008-2011		******	******
2007	T715D	345,000	414,000
2006	T715D	313,000	376,000
2005	T715D	285,000	342,000

Triton 2895 Center Console

Year	Power	Retail Low	Retail High
2007	T225 O/B	59,000	71,000
2006	T225 O/B	54,000	65,000
2005	T225 O/B	49,000	59,000
2004	T225 O/B	44,000	53,000

Triton 351 Center Console

Year	Power	Retail Low	Retail High
2010	T250 O/B	******	******
2009	T250 O/B	******	******
2008	T250 O/B	103,000	124,000
2007	T250 O/B	93,000	111,000
2006	T250 O/B	78,000	94,000
2005	T250 O/B	70,000	85,000

Trojan 350/360 Express

Year	Power	Retail Low	Retail High
2001	T320G	71,000	85,000
2000	T320G	64,000	77,000
1999	T310G	59,000	70,000
1997	T310G	53,000	64,000
1996	T310G	48,000	58,000
1995	T310G	44,000	53,000

Trojan 370/390/400 Express

Year	Power	Retail Low	Retail High
2002	T320G	98,000	118,000
2001	T320G	89,000	107,000
2000	T320G	81,000	97,000
1999	T320G	74,000	89,000
1998	T320G	67,000	81,000
1997	T320G	61,000	73,000
1996	T320G	55,000	67,000
1995	T350G	51,000	61,000

Trojan 440 Express

Year	Power	Retail Low	Retail High
2002	T450D	213,000	256,000
2001	T450D	194,000	233,000
2000	T450D	177,000	212,000
1999	T450D	161,000	193,000
1998	T450D	146,000	175,000
1997	T450D	134,000	161,000
1996	T420D	124,000	148,000
1995	T420D	114,000	136,000

Trophy 2802 Walkaround

Year	Power	Retail Low	Retail High
2001	T225/OB	34,000	41,000
2000	T225/OB	31,000	37,000
1999	T225/OB	28,000	34,000
1998	T225/OB	25,000	31,000
1997	T225/OB	23,000	28,000

Trophy 2902 Walkaround

Year	Power	Retail Low	Retail High
2009	T225 O/B	74,000	89,000
2008	T225 O/B	68,000	81,000
2007	T225 O/B	62,000	74,000
2006	T225 O/B	56,000	67,000
2005	T225 O/B	51,000	61,000
2004	T225 O/B	46,000	56,000
2003	T225 O/B	42,000	51,000

True World TE288

Year	Power	Retail Low	Retail High
2007	315D	70,000	84,000
2006	315D	64,000	77,000
2005	315D	59,000	71,000
2004	315D	55,000	66,000
2003	315D	51,000	61,000
2002	315D	47,000	57,000

Venture 34 Open

Year	Power	Retail Low	Retail High
2008	T250 O/B	109,000	130,000
2007	T250 O/B	98,000	117,000
2006	T250 O/B	88,000	106,000
2005	T250 O/B	79,000	95,000
2004	T250 O/B	71,000	85,000
2003	T250 O/B	64,000	77,000
2002	T250 O/B	58,000	70,000
2001	T250 O/B	53,000	64,000
2000	T250 O/B	48,000	58,000
1999	T250 O/B	44,000	53,000
1998	T250 O/B	40,000	48,000
1997	T250 O/B	37,000	44,000

Viking 38 Convertible

Year	Power	Retail Low	Retail High
1995	T485D	111,000	133,000

Viking Sport Cruisers 40 FB

Year	Power	Retail Low	Retail High
2002	T370D	195,000	230,000
2001	T370D	181,000	213,000
2000	T370D	168,000	199,000

Viking Sport Cruisers 43 FB

Year	Power	Retail Low	Retail High
1999	T420D	186,000	264,000
1998	T420D	173,000	246,000
1997	T420D	161,000	228,000
1996	T420D	149,000	212,000
1995	T420D	139,000	197,000

Viking 43 Convertible

Year	Power	Retail Low	Retail High
2002	T680D	297,000	348,000
2001	T680D	270,000	316,000
2000	T680D	246,000	288,000
1999	T680D	224,000	262,000
1998	T680D	206,000	241,000
1997	T680D	189,000	222,000
1996	T600D	174,000	204,000
1995	T600D	160,000	187,000

Viking 43 Open

Year	Power	Retail Low	Retail High
2002	T680D	270,000	371,000
2001	T680D	256,000	342,000
2000	T680D	235,000	314,000
1999	T680D	216,000	289,000
1998	T680D	199,000	266,000
1997	T680D	183,000	245,000
1996	T600D	168,000	225,000
1995	T600D	155,000	207,000

Viking 45 Convertible

Year	Power	Retail Low	Retail High
2009	T900D	******	******
2008	T900D	******	******
2007	T900D	576,000	662,000
2006	T900D	529,000	609,000
2005	T900D	487,000	560,000
2004	T800D	448,000	515,000
2003	T800D	412,000	474,000

Viking 45 Open

Year	Power	Retail Low	Retail High
2009	T900D	******	******
2008	T900D	******	******
2007	T900D	552,000	634,000
2006	T900D	507,000	584,000
2005	T900D	467,000	537,000
2004	T800D	429,000	494,000

Viking Sport Cruisers 45 FB

Year	Power	Retail Low	Retail High
2004	T480D	365,000	420,000
2003	T480D	336,000	386,000
2002	T480D	309,000	355,000
2001	T480D	284,000	327,000
2000	T370D	261,000	300,000
1999	T370D	240,000	276,000

Viking Sport Cruisers 45/46 FB

Year	Power	Retail Low	Retail High
2000	T430D	213,000	250,000
1999	T430D	196,000	230,000
1998	T430D	181,000	211,000
1997	T430D	166,000	194,000
1996	T430D	153,000	179,000
1995	T430D	140,000	164,000

Viking 47 Convertible

Year	Power	Retail Low	Retail High
2002	T800D	353,000	413,000
2001	T680D	325,000	380,000
2000	T680D	299,000	349,000
1999	T680D	275,000	321,000
1998	T680D	253,000	296,000
1997	T680D	232,000	272,000
1996	T680D	214,000	250,000
1995	T680D	197,000	230,000

Viking 48 Conv. (2002-09)

Year	Power	Retail Low	Retail High
2009	T1100D	******	******
2008	T1100D	******	******
2007	T1100D	760,000	889,000
2006	T1100D	699,000	818,000
2005	T1050D	643,000	752,000
2004	T1050D	591,000	692,000
2003	T860D	544,000	637,000
2002	T860D	500,000	586,000

Viking Sport Cruisers 48/50 FB

Year	Power	Retail Low	Retail High
1999	T435D	252,000	295,000
1998	T435D	235,000	275,000
1997	T435D	218,000	255,000
1996	T435D	203,000	238,000
1995	T435D	191,000	223,000

Viking 50 Convertible

Year	Power	Retail Low	Retail High
2001	1050D	321,000	376,000
2000	1050D	296,000	346,000
1999	1050D	272,000	318,000
1998	1200D	250,000	293,000
1997	1200D	230,000	269,000
1995	820D	212,000	248,000

Viking 50 Open

Year	Power	Retail Low	Retail High
2003	T820D	507,000	593,000
2002	T800D	466,000	546,000
2001	T800D	429,000	502,000
2000	T800D	395,000	462,000
1999	T800D	363,000	425,000

Viking Sport Cruisers 50 FB

Year	Power	Retail Low	Retail High
2009	T660D	******	******
2008	T660D	******	******
2007	T660D	******	******
2007	T675D	******	******
2005	T675D	607,000	698,000
2004	T700D	558,000	642,000
2003	T700D	513,000	590,000
2002	T700D	472,000	543,000
2001	T700D	434,000	500,000

Viking Sport Cruisers V50 Express

Year	Power	Retail Low	Retail High
2005	T715D	655,000	753,000
2004	T715D	603,000	693,000
2003	T700D	554,000	638,000
2002	T700D	510,000	586,000
2001	T700D	469,000	540,000
2000	T700D	432,000	496,000
1999	T700D	397,000	457,000

Viking 52 Convertible

Year	Power	Retail Low	Retail High
2009	T1360D	******	******
2008	T1360D	******	******
2007	T1360D	******	******
2006	T1300D	783,000	885,000
2005	T1300D	721,000	814,000
2004	T1300D	663,000	749,000
2003	T1050D	610,000	689,000
2002	T1050D	561,000	634,000

Viking Sport Cruisers 52 FB

Year	Power	Retail Low	Retail High
2002	T615D	495,000	570,000
2001	T615D	456,000	524,000
2000	T610D	419,000	482,000
1999	T610D	386,000	444,000
1998	T610D	355,000	408,000
1997	T610D	326,000	375,000

Viking 53 Convertible

Year	Power	Retail Low	Retail High
1998	T820D	292,000	336,000
1997	T820D	272,000	312,000
1996	T820D	252,000	290,000
1995	T820D	235,000	270,000

Viking 54 Sports Yacht

Year	Power	Retail Low	Retail High
2001	T820D	428,000	492,000
2000	T820D	394,000	453,000
1999	T820D	362,000	416,000
1998	T820D	333,000	383,000
1997	T820D	306,000	352,000
1996	T820D	282,000	324,000
1995	T820D	259,000	298,000

Viking 55 Convertible

Year	Power	Retail Low	Retail High
2002	T1300D	756,000	869,000
2001	T1050D	695,000	799,000
2000	T1050D	639,000	735,000
1999	T1050D	588,000	676,000
1998	T1050D	541,000	622,000

Viking 56 Convertible

Year	Power	Retail Low	Retail High
2010	T1550D	******	******
2009	T1550D	******	******
2008	T1550D	******	******
2007	T1550D	1,350,000	1,552,000
2006	T1550D	1,255,000	1,443,000
2005	T1520D	1,167,000	1,342,000
2004	T1480D	1,085,000	1,248,000

Viking Sport Cruisers 56 FB

Year	Power	Retail Low	Retail High
2002	T700D	******	******
2001	T700D	515,000	592,000
2000	T700D	479,000	551,000
1999	T700D	445,000	512,000
1998	T700D	414,000	476,000
1997	T610D	385,000	443,000

Viking 57 Motor Yacht

Year	Power	Retail Low	Retail High
1995	T760D	331,000	380,000

Viking 58 Convertible

Year	Power	Retail Low	Retail High
2000	T1200D	544,000	626,000
1999	T1200D	501,000	576,000
1998	T1150D	461,000	530,000
1997	T1200D	424,000	487,000
1996	T1200D	390,000	448,000
1995	T1200D	359,000	412,000

Viking Sport Cruisers V58 Express

Year	Power	Retail Low	Retail High
2006-2010		******	******
2005	T900D	922,000	1,042,000
2004	T860D	858,000	969,000
2003	T860D	797,000	901,000

Viking 60 Cockpit Sport Yacht

Year	Power	Retail Low	Retail High
2001	T820D	576,000	651,000
2000	T820D	530,000	599,000
1999	T820D	488,000	551,000
1998	T820D	449,000	507,000
1997	T820D	413,000	466,000
1996	T820D	384,000	434,000
1995	T820D	357,000	403,000

Viking Sports Cruisers 60 FB

Year	Power	Retail Low	Retail High
2001	T800D	538,000	624,000
2000	T800D	495,000	574,000
1999	T800D	455,000	528,000
1998	T800D	419,000	486,000
1997	T800D	385,000	447,000
1996	T800D	355,000	411,000

Viking 65 Motor Yacht

Year	Power	Retail Low	Retail High
1995	T1000D	441,000	516,000

Wellcraft 2600 Coastal

Year	Power	Retail Low	Retail High
1995	T200 O/B	14,000	16,000

Wellcraft 2600 Martinique

Year	Power	Retail Low	Retail High
2002	250 I/O	17,000	20,000
2001	250 I/O	15,000	18,000
2000	250 I/O	14,000	17,000
1999	250 I/O	13,000	15,000
1998	250 I/O	12,000	14,000

Wellcraft 264/270 Coastal

Year	Power	Retail Low	Retail High
2000	T150 O/B	23,000	28,000
1999	T150 O/B	21,000	26,000
1998	T150 O/B	20,000	24,000
1997	T150 O/B	18,000	22,000

See Page 667 For Price Adjustments

Year	Power	Retail Low	Retail High
1996	T150 O/B	17,000	20,000
1995	T150 O/B	15,000	18,000
Wellcraft 270 Coastal			
2008	T225 O/B	83,000	104,000
2007	T225 O/B	75,000	95,000
2006	No Production	******	******
2005	No Producton	******	******
2004	T225 O/B	56,000	70,000
2004	S375 I/O	61,000	77,000
2003	T225 O/B	51,000	64,000
2003	S375 I/O	56,000	70,000
2002	T225 O/B	46,000	58,000
2002	S330 I/O	51,000	63,000
2001	T225 O/B	42,000	53,000
2001	S330 I/O	46,000	58,000
Wellcraft 2800 Martinique (2001-02)			
2002	T190 I/O	32,000	38,000
2002	S310 I/O	30,000	36,000
2001	T190 I/O	29,000	35,000
2001	T190 I/O	27,000	33,000
Wellcraft 2700/2800 Martinique			
1999	T190 I/O	23,000	28,000
1999	330 I/O	22,000	26,000
1998	T190 I/O	21,000	26,000
1998	330 I/O	20,000	24,000
1997	T190 I/O	20,000	24,000
1997	330 I/O	18,000	22,000
1996	T190 I/O	18,000	22,000
1996	330 I/O	17,000	20,000
1995	T190 I/O	17,000	20,000
1995	330 I/O	16,000	19,000
Wellcraft 290 Coastal			
2009	T225 O/B	107,000	128,000
2008	T225 O/B	97,000	117,000
2007	T225 O/B	88,000	106,000
2006	T225 O/B	80,000	97,000
2005	T225 O/B	73,000	88,000
2004	T225 O/B	67,000	81,000
2003	T225 O/B	62,000	74,000
2002	T225 O/B	57,000	68,000
2001	T225 O/B	52,000	63,000
2000	T225 O/B	48,000	58,000
1999	T225 O/B	44,000	53,000
Wellcraft 29 Scarab Sport; 29 CCF			
2004	T225 O/B	48,000	57,000
2003	T225 O/B	43,000	51,000
2002	T225 O/B	38,000	46,000
2001	T225 O/B	35,000	42,000
Wellcraft 30 Scarab Tournament			
2009	T250 O/B	******	******
2008	T250 O/B	82,000	98,000
2007	T250 O/B	73,000	88,000
Wellcraft 3000 Martinique			
2002	T260 I/O	45,000	54,000
2001	T260 I/O	41,000	50,000
2000	T260 I/O	38,000	46,000
1999	T260 I/O	35,000	42,000
1998	T260 I/O	32,000	39,000
Wellcraft 302 Scarab Sport			
2000	T250 O/B	33,000	39,000
1999	T250 O/B	30,000	36,000
1998	T250 O/B	27,000	33,000
1997	T250 O/B	25,000	30,000
1996	T250 O/B	22,000	27,000
1995	T250 O/B	20,000	24,000

Year	Power	Retail Low	Retail High
Wellcraft 32 Scarab Sport; 32 CCF			
2006	T250 O/B	65,000	78,000
2005	T250 O/B	59,000	70,000
2004	T250 O/B	53,000	63,000
2003	T250 O/B	47,000	57,000
2002	T250 O/B	43,000	51,000
2001	T250 O/B	38,000	46,000
Wellcraft 3200 Martinique			
2000	T310 I/O	40,000	49,000
1999	T310 I/O	37,000	45,000
1998	T310 I/O	34,000	41,000
1997	T310 I/O	31,000	38,000
1996	T300 I/O	29,000	35,000
1995	T300 I/O	27,000	32,000
Wellcraft 330 Coastal			
2009	T370D	******	******
2008	T370D	******	******
2007	T370D	150,000	180,000
2006	T370D	136,000	164,000
2005	T360D	124,000	149,000
2004	T360D	113,000	135,000
2003	T360D	103,000	123,000
2002	T360D	93,000	112,000
2001	T350D	85,000	102,000
2000	T350D	78,000	94,000
1999	T350D	72,000	86,000
1998	T350D	66,000	79,000
1997	T300D	61,000	73,000
1996	T300D	56,000	67,000
1995	T300D	51,000	62,000
Wellcraft 3300 Martinique			
2002	T310G	55,000	66,000
2001	T310G	50,000	60,000
Wellcraft 35 Scarab Sport			
2009	3/250 O/B	******	******
2008	3/250 O/B	100,000	120,000
2007	3/250 O/B	90,000	108,000
Wellcraft 35 Scarab Sport; 35 CCF			
2005	T250 O/B	61,000	73,000
2004	T250 O/B	55,000	66,000
2003	T250 O/B	49,000	59,000
2002	T250 O/B	44,000	53,000
2001	T250 O/B	40,000	48,000
Wellcraft 352 Tourn.; 35 Scarab Tourn.			
2011-2012		******	******
2010	3/250 O/B	137,000	163,000
2010	T250 O/B	115,000	136,000
2009	3/250 O/B	124,000	148,000
2009	T250 O/B	104,000	124,000
2008	3/250 O/B	113,000	135,000
2008	T250 O/B	95,000	113,000
2007	3/250 O/B	103,000	122,000
2007	T250 O/B	86,000	103,000
2006	3/250 O/B	93,000	111,000
2006	T250 O/B	78,000	93,000
Wellcraft 350 Coastal			
2003	T375G	137,000	165,000
2003	T360D	164,000	197,000
2002	T375G	126,000	152,000
2002	T360D	151,000	181,000
2001	T375G	116,000	140,000
2001	T360D	139,000	166,000
2000	T375G	107,000	128,000
2000	T370D	128,000	153,000
Wellcraft 360 Coastal			
2009	T370D	******	******

Year	Power	Retail Low	Retail High
2008	T370D	******	******
2007	T370D	220,000	264,000
2006	T370D	198,000	238,000
Wellcraft 3600 Martinique			
2000	T385G	56,000	67,000
1999	T385G	51,000	62,000
1998	T380G	47,000	57,000
1997	T330G	43,000	52,000
1996	T330G	40,000	48,000
1995	T330G	37,000	45,000
Wellcraft 3700 Martinique			
2002	T370G	92,000	111,000
2001	T370G	86,000	103,000
Wellcraft 38 Excalibur			
2002	T425 I/O	131,000	158,000
2001	T425 I/O	121,000	145,000
2000	T385 I/O	111,000	134,000
1999	T385 I/O	102,000	123,000
1998	T385 I/O	94,000	113,000
1997	T385 I/O	87,000	105,000
1996	T385 I/O	81,000	98,000
Wellcraft 400 Coastal			
2003	T480D	229,000	275,000
2002	T480D	211,000	253,000
2001	T430D	194,000	233,000
2000	T430D	179,000	214,000
1999	T430D	164,000	197,000
Wellcraft 43 Portifino			
1997	T-Gas	94,000	113,000
1997	T420D	114,000	137,000
1996	T-Gas	87,000	104,000
1996	T420D	105,000	126,000
1995	T-Gas	80,000	96,000
1995	T350D	96,000	116,000
Wellcraft 45 Excalibur			
2001	T415G	124,000	149,000
2000	T415G	115,000	138,000
1999	T415G	107,000	129,000
1998	T415G	100,000	120,000
1997	T415G	93,000	111,000
1996	T415G	86,000	103,000
1995	T415G	80,000	96,000
Wellcraft 46 Cockpit MY			
1995	T435D	129,000	155,000
World Cat 266/270 LC			
2005	T200 O/B	76,000	91,000
2004	T200 O/B	69,000	82,000
2003	T200 O/B	62,000	75,000
2002	T200 O/B	57,000	69,000
2001	T200 O/B	53,000	63,000
2000	T200 O/B	49,000	58,000
1999	T200 O/B	45,000	54,000
World Cat 266/270 Sport Cabin			
2009	T225 O/B	77,000	93,000
2008	T225 O/B	70,000	85,000
2007	T225 O/B	64,000	77,000
2006	T225 O/B	58,000	70,000
2005	T225 O/B	53,000	64,000
2004	T225 O/B	48,000	58,000
2003	T225 O/B	44,000	53,000
2002	T225 O/B	40,000	48,000
2001	T225 O/B	37,000	44,000
2000	T225 O/B	33,000	40,000
1999	T225 O/B	30,000	36,000
1998	T225 O/B	27,000	33,000

See Page 667 For Price Adjustments

Year	Power	Retail Low	Retail High
World Cat 266 SF/270 TE			
2011	T225 O/B	******	******
2010	T225 O/B	******	******
2009	T225 O/B	******	******
2008	T225 O/B	81,000	98,000
2007	T225 O/B	74,000	89,000
2006	T225 O/B	67,000	81,000
2005	T225 O/B	61,000	73,000
2004	T225 O/B	56,000	67,000
2003	T225 O/B	50,000	61,000
2002	T225 O/B	46,000	56,000
2001	T225 O/B	43,000	51,000
2000	T225 O/B	39,000	47,000
1999	T225 O/B	36,000	43,000
1998	T225 O/B	33,000	40,000
World Cat 270 Express Cabin			
2008	T225 O/B	81,000	98,000
2007	T225 O/B	74,000	89,000
2006	T225 O/B	67,000	81,000
2005	T225 O/B	61,000	73,000
2004	T225 O/B	56,000	67,000
2003	T225 O/B	50,000	61,000
World Cat 320 Express Cabin			
2010-2012		******	******
2009	T250 O/B	168,000	194,000
2008	T250 O/B	152,000	177,000
2007	T250 O/B	139,000	161,000
2006	T250 O/B	126,000	146,000
World Cat 330 TE			
2008	T250 O/B	******	******
2007	T250 O/B	105,000	126,000
2006	T250 O/B	95,000	114,000
2005	T250 O/B	86,000	104,000
2004	T250 O/B	79,000	94,000
2003	T250 O/B	72,000	86,000
Yellowfin 31			
2007	T225 O/B	******	******
2006	T225 O/B	******	******
2005	T225 O/B	86,000	103,000
2004	T225 O/B	77,000	92,000
2003	T225 O/B	69,000	83,000
2002	T225 O/B	62,000	75,000
2001	T225 O/B	56,000	67,000

CPSIA information can be obtained at www.ICGtesting.com
Printed in the USA
LVOW03s2015051014

407345LV00015B/405/P

9 781491 071731